Access regular text updates, online study materials, and a collection of Internet resources at:

Online Learning Center

McGraw Hill

Student Center
Instructor Center
Information Center

- preferences
- feedback
- help center

International Business, 4/e
Charles W.L. Hill

Welcome to the home page of Hill's: International Business, 4e

Market-defining since it was first introduced, International Business, 4e by Charles W. L. Hill, continues to set the standard for international business textbooks. The author's passion and enthusiasm for the international business arena is apparent on every page as he strives to make important theories interesting, informative, and accessible to all students.

This Online Learning Center is another interesting, informative and accessible tool. Both the student and instructor will find resources to enhance the learning experience. To learn more about this text or its supplements, please click on the "information center" bar.

© 2001 McGraw-Hill Online Learning Center
Powered by Novell
Any use is subject to the Terms of Use and Privacy Policy
McGraw-Hill Higher Education is one of the many fine businesses of The McGraw-Hill Companies

www.mhhe.com/hill

- **Online Learning Center** Review and apply text concepts with interactive practice quizzes, PowerPoint® slides, Internet exercises, and more.

- **This Week in Global News** Check out news briefs recapping the latest international business news stories.

- **International Business Web Directory** Jump to a number of other websites of interest to students of international business.

- **Newsroom** Research current events by linking to national and international news sources on the Internet.

- **Much more!**

A password-protected portion of the site is also available to instructors, offering updates related to cases in the text, downloadable supplements, an international business bulletin board service, and a complete selection of online teaching resources.

International Business

Competing in the Global Marketplace

Competing in the Global Marketplace
Fourth Edition

International Business

Charles W. L. Hill
University of Washington

McGraw-Hill
Irwin

Boston   Burr Ridge, IL   Dubuque, IA   Madison, WI   New York   San Francisco   St. Louis
Bangkok   Bogotá   Caracas   Kuala Lumpur   Lisbon   London   Madrid   Mexico City
Milan   Montreal   New Delhi   Santiago   Seoul   Singapore   Sydney   Taipei   Toronto

McGraw-Hill Higher Education 𝒳

*A Division of The **McGraw-Hill** Companies*

This book is printed on acid-free paper.

domestic   1 2 3 4 5 6 7 8 9 0 WCK/WCK 0 9 8 7 6 5 4 3 2
international   1 2 3 4 5 6 7 8 9 0 WCK/WCK 0 9 8 7 6 5 4 3 2

ISBN 0-07-247053-4

Publisher: *John E. Biernat*
Sponsoring editor: *Marianne C. P. Rutter*
Managing developmental editor: *Laura Hurst Spell*
Marketing manager: *Lisa Nicks*
Project manager: *Laura Griffin*
Production supervisor: *Debra R. Sylvester*
Senior designer: *Jennifer McQueen*
Media producer: *Craig Atkins*
Lead supplement producer: *Becky Szura*
Photo research coordinator: *David A. Tietz*
Cover image: *©Photodisc, Inc. All rights reserved.*
Typeface: *10.5/12 Goudy*
Compositor: *Carlisle Communications, Ltd.*
Printer: *Quebecor World Versailles Inc.*

Library of Congress Cataloging-in-Publication Data
Hill, Charles W. L.
    International business: competing in the global marketplace / Charles W. L. Hill. — 4th ed.
       p. cm.
    Includes bibliographical references and index.
    ISBN 0-07-247053-4 (alk. paper)
    1. International business enterprises—Management. 2. Competition, International. I.
  Title.
    HD62.4. H55 2003
658'.049—dc21   2001056207

International Edition ISBN 0-07-115116-8

www.mhhe.com

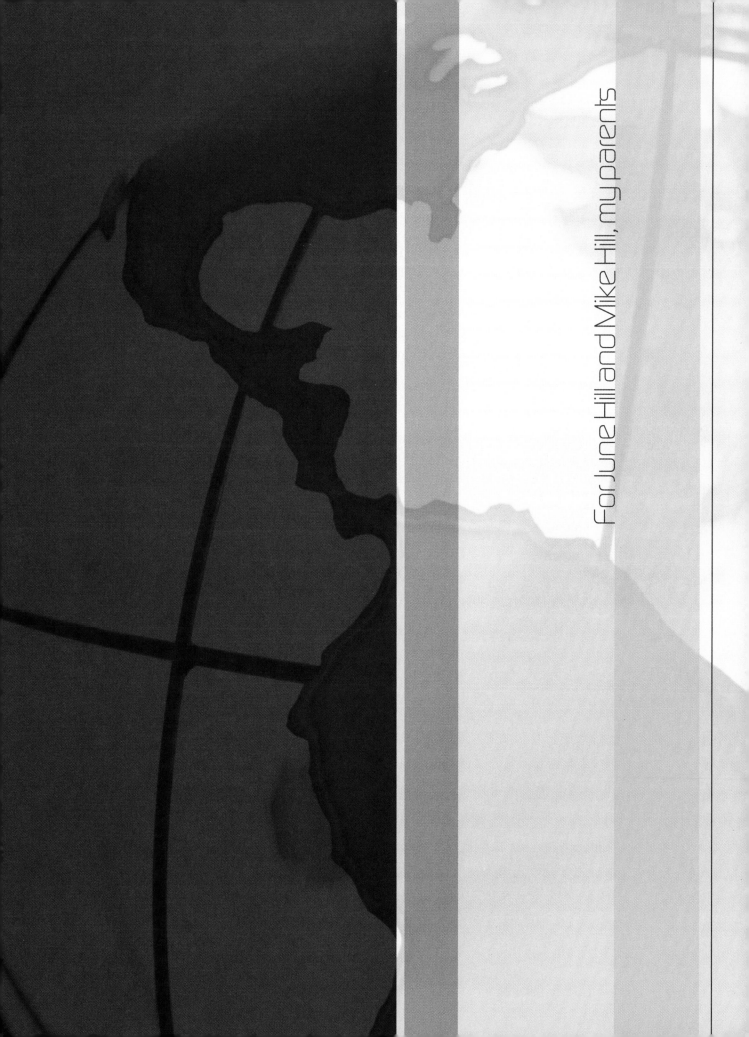

For June Hill and Mike Hill, my parents

About the Author

Charles W. L. Hill is the Hughes M. Blake Professor of International Business at the School of Business, University of Washington. Professor Hill received his Ph.D. from the University of Manchester's Institute of Science and Technology (UMIST) in Britain. In addition to the University of Washington, he has served on the faculties of UMIST, Texas A&M University, and Michigan State University.

Professor Hill has published over 40 articles in peer reviewed academic journals, including the *Academy of Management Journal, Academy of Management Review, Strategic Management Journal,* and *Organization Science.* He has also published two college texts: one on strategic management and the other on international business. Professor Hill has served on the editorial boards of several academic journals, including the *Strategic Management Journal* and *Organization Science.* Between 1993 and 1996 he was consulting editor at the *Academy of Management Review.*

Professor Hill teaches in the MBA, Executive MBA, Management, and Ph.D. programs at the University of Washington. He has received awards for teaching excellence in the MBA, Executive MBA, and Management programs. He has also taught customized executive programs.

Professor Hill works on a consulting basis with a number of organizations. His clients have included ATL, Boeing, BF Goodrich, Hexcel, House of Fraser, Microsoft, Seattle City Light, Tacoma City Light, Thompson Financial Services, and Wizards of the Coast. On occasion, Professor Hill serves as a guest commentator on National Public Radio.

Brief Contents

Contents

Part 3
The Global Trade and Investment Environment

Chapter 4
International Trade Theory 136

Chapter 5
The Political Economy of International Trade 170

Part 5
The Strategy and Structure of
International Business

List of Maps

Preface

International Business: Competing in the Global Market-place is intended for the first international business course at either the undergraduate or the MBA level. My goal in writing this book has been to set a new standard for international business textbooks: I have attempted to write a book that (1) is comprehensive and up-to-date, (2) goes beyond an uncritical presentation and shallow explanation of the body of knowledge, (3) maintains a tight, integrated flow between chapters, (4) focuses managerial implications, and (5) makes important theories accessible and interesting to students.

Comprehensive and Up-to-Date

To be comprehensive, an international business textbook must:

- Explain how and why the world's countries differ.
- Present a thorough review of the economics and politics of international trade and investment.
- Explain the functions and form of the global monetary system.
- Examine the strategies and structures of international businesses.
- Assess the special roles of an international business's various functions.

This textbook does all these things. Too many other textbooks pay scant attention to the strategies and structures of international businesses and to the implications of international business for firms' various functions. This omission is a serious deficiency, because the students in these international business courses will soon be international managers, and they will be expected to understand the implications of international business for their organization's strategy, structure, and functions. This book pays close attention to these issues.

Comprehensiveness and relevance also require coverage of the major theories. Although many international business textbooks do a reasonable job of reviewing long-established theories (e.g., the theory of comparative advantage and Vernon's product life-cycle theory) they tend to ignore such important newer work as:

- The new trade theory and strategic trade policy.
- The work of Nobel Prize–winning economist Amartya Sen on economic development.
- Samuel Huntington's influential thesis on the "clash of civilizations."

- The new growth theory of economic development championed by Paul Romer and Gene Grossman.
- Recent empirical work by Jeffery Sachs and others on the relationship between international trade and economic growth.
- Michael Porter's theory of the competitive advantage of nations.
- Robert Reich's work on national competitive advantage.
- The work of Douglass North and others on national institutional structures and the protection of property rights.
- The market imperfections approach to foreign direct investment that has grown out of Ronald Coase and Oliver Williamson's work on transaction cost economics.
- Bartlett and Ghoshal's research on the transnational corporation.
- The writings of C. K. Prahalad and Gary Hamel on core competencies, global competition, and global strategic alliances.

The failure of many books to discuss such work is a serious deficiency considering how influential these theories have become, not just in academic circles, but also in the world at large. A major proponent of strategic trade policy, Laura Tyson served for a time as chairperson of President Clinton's Council of Economic Advisors. Robert Reich served as secretary of labor in the Clinton administration. Ronald Coase won the 1992 Nobel Prize in economics, giving the market imperfections approach new respectability. Two years later, Douglass North won the Nobel Prize in economics for his work showing how a nation's economic history influences its contemporary institutions and property rights regime. More recently still, Amartya Sen won the Nobel Prize for his work on economic development. The work of Bartlett, Ghoshal, Hamel, and Prahalad is having an important impact on business practices.

I have incorporated all relevant state-of-the-art work at the appropriate points in this book. For example, in Chapter 2, "Country Differences in Political Economy," reference is made to the new growth theory, to the work of North and others on national institutional structures and property rights, and to the work of Sen. In Chapter 4, "International Trade Theory," in addition to such standard theories as the theory of comparative advantage and the Heckscher-Ohlin theory, there is detailed discussion of the new trade theory and Porter's theory of national competitive advantage. The empirical work on the relationship between trade and economic growth is also examined in this chapter. In Chapter 5, "The Political Economy of International Trade," the pros and cons of strategic trade policy are discussed. In Chapter 6, "Foreign Direct Investment," the market imperfections approach is reviewed. Chapters 12, 13, and 14, which deal with the strategy and structure of international business, draw extensively on the work of Bartlett, Ghoshal, Hamel, and Prahalad.

In addition to including leading-edge theory, in light of the fast-changing nature of the international business environment, every effort is being made to ensure that the book is as up-to-date as possible when it goes to press. A significant amount has happened in the world since the first edition of this book was published in 1993. The Uruguay Round of GATT negotiations was successfully concluded and the World Trade Organization was established. The European Union moved forward with its post-1992 agenda to achieve a closer economic and monetary union, including the establishment of a common currency in January 1999. The North American Free Trade Agreement passed into law, and Chile indicated its desire to become the next member of the free trade area. The Asian Pacific Economic Cooperation forum (APEC) emerged as the kernel of a possible future Asia Pacific free trade area. The former Communist states of Eastern Europe and Asia continued on the road to economic and political reform. As they did, the euphoric mood that followed the collapse of communism in 1989 was slowly replaced with a growing sense of realism about the hard path ahead for many of these countries. The global money market continued its meteoric growth. By 2000 over $1.5 trillion per day was flowing across national borders. The size of such flows fueled concern about the ability of short-term speculative shifts in global capital markets to destabilize the world economy. These fears were fanned by the well-publicized financial problems of a number of organizations that traded derivatives through the global money market, such as Barings Bank. The World Wide Web emerged from nowhere to become the backbone of an emerging global network for electronic commerce. The world continued to become more global. Several Asian Pacific economies, including most notably China, continued to grow their economies at a rapid rate. New multinationals continued to emerge from developing nations in addition to the world's established industrial powers. And increasingly, the globalization of the world economy affected a wide range of firms of all sizes, from the very large to the very small.

Reflecting this rapid pace change, in this edition of the book I have tried to ensure that all material and statistics are as up-to-date as possible as of 2001. However, being absolutely up-to-date is impossible since change is always with us. What is current today may be outdated tomorrow. Accordingly, I have established a home page for this book on the World Wide Web at www.mhhe.com/hill. From this home page the reader can access regular updates of chapter material and reports on topical developments that are relevant to students of international business. I hope readers find this a useful addition to the support material for this book.

Beyond Uncritical Presentation and Shallow Explanation

Many issues in international business are complex and thus necessitate considerations of pros and cons. To demonstrate this to students, I have adopted a critical approach that presents the arguments for and against economic theories, government policies, business strategies, organizational structures, and so on.

Related to this, I have attempted to explain the complexities of the many theories and phenomena unique to international business so the student might fully comprehend the statements of a theory or the reasons a phenomenon is the way it is. These theories and phenomena are typically explained in more depth in this book than they are in competing textbooks, the rationale being that a shallow explanation is little better than no explanation. In international business, a little knowledge is indeed a dangerous thing.

Integrated Progression of Topics

Many textbooks lack a tight, integrated flow of topics from chapter to chapter. In this book students are told in Chapter 1 how the book's topics are related to each other. Integration has been achieved by organizing the material so that each chapter builds on the material of the previous ones in a logical fashion.

Part One

Chapter 1 provides an overview of the key issues to be addressed and explains the plan of the book.

Part Two

Chapters 2 and 3 focus on national differences in political economy and culture. Most international business textbooks place this material at a later point, but I believe it is vital to discuss national differences first. After all, many of the central issues in international trade and investment, the global monetary system, international business strategy and structure, and international business operations arise out of national differences in political economy and culture. To fully understand these issues, students must first appreciate the differences in countries and cultures.

Part Three

Chapters 4 through 8 investigate the political economy of international trade and investment. The purpose of this part is to describe and explain the trade and investment environment in which international business occurs.

Part Four

Chapters 9 through 11 describe and explain the global monetary system, laying out in detail the monetary framework in which international business transactions are conducted.

Part Five

In Chapters 12 through 14 attention shifts from the environment to the firm. Here the book examines the strategies and structures that firms adopt to compete effectively in the international business environment.

Part Six

In Chapters 15 through 20 the focus narrows further to investigate business operations. These chapters explain how firms can perform their key functions—manufacturing, marketing, R&D, human resource management, accounting, and finance—in order to compete and succeed in the international business environment.

Throughout the book, the relationship of new material to topics discussed in earlier chapters is pointed out to the students to reinforce their understanding of how the material comprises an integrated whole.

Focus on Managerial Implications

Many international business textbooks fail to discuss the implications of the various topics for the actual practice of international business. This does not serve the needs of business school students who will soon be practicing managers. Accordingly, the usefulness of this book's material in the practice of international business is discussed explicitly. In particular, at the end of each chapter in Parts Two, Three, and Four—where the focus is on the environment of international business, as opposed to particular firms—there is a section titled "Implications for Business." In this section, the managerial implications of the material discussed in the chapter are clearly explained. For example, Chapter 4, "International Trade Theory," ends with a detailed discussion of the various trade theories' implications for international business management.

In addition, each chapter begins with a case that illustrates the relevance of chapter material for the practice of international business. Chapter 2, "Country Differences in Political Economy," for example, opens with a case that describes how changes in the political and economic institutions of India are making it a more attractive location for international businesses to operate.

I have also added a closing case to each chapter. These cases are also designed to illustrate the relevance of chapter material for the practice of international business. The closing case to Chapter 2, for example, looks at Microsoft's battle against software piracy in China. This case helps to illustrate the important role that national differences in the protection of intellectual property rights can play in international business.

Another tool that I have used to focus on managerial implications are Management Focus boxes. There is at least one Management Focus in each chapter. Like the opening case, the purpose of these boxes is to illustrate the relevance of chapter material for the practice of international business. The Management Focus in Chapter 2, for example, looks at how the South African government has adopted laws that allow the sale of cheap generic versions of patented medicines, including powerful new drugs for treating AIDS, without permission from the patent owner, which in this case are large multinational pharmaceutical firms.

Accessible and Interesting

The international business arena is fascinating and exciting, and I have tried to communicate my enthusiasm for it to the student. Learning is easier and better if the subject matter is communicated in an interesting, informative, and accessible manner. One technique I have used to achieve this is weaving interesting anecdotes into the narrative of the text—stories that illustrate theory. The opening cases and focus boxes are also used to make the theory being discussed in the text both accessible and interesting.

Each chapter has two kinds of focus boxes—a Management Focus box (described above) and a Country Focus box. Country Focus boxes provide background on the political, economic, social, or cultural aspects of countries grappling with an international business issue. In Chapter 2, for example, one Country Focus discusses how an endemic level of corruption among public officials in Nigeria has had a detrimental effect on economic development in that nation.

Just how accessible and interesting this book actually is will be revealed by time and student feedback. I am confident, however, that this book is far more accessible to students than its competitors. For those of you who view such a bold claim with skepticism, I urge you to read the sections in Chapter 1 on the globalization of the world economy, the changing nature of international business, and how international business is different.

What's New in the 4th Edition

The success of the first three editions of *International Business* was based in part upon the incorporation of leading-edge research into the text, the use of the up-to-date examples and statistics to illustrate global trends and enterprise strategy, and the discussion of current events within the context of the appropriate theory. Building on these strengths, my goals for the fourth revision have been threefold:

1. Incorporate new insights from recent scholarly research wherever appropriate.
2. Make sure the content of the text covers all appropriate issues.
3. Make sure the text is as up-to-date as possible with regard to current events, statistics, and examples.

As part of the revision process, *changes have been made to every chapter in the book*. The following are *examples* of the kinds of changes that have been made in the text.

Chapter 1: Globalization. All the statistics pertaining to globalization (such as the growth of world trade, output, and foreign direct investment) have been updated to incorporate the most recently available data. The chapter has been revised to include new material on the growing wave of protests against globalization, which began at the World Trade Organization meeting in Seattle in December 1999 and have continued at a steady pace since. The section dealing with the debate between scholars on the merits and drawbacks of globalization has been expanded. This debate is concerned with the impact of globalization on job security, income levels, labor policies, economic growth, the environment, and national sovereignty.

Chapter 2: Differences in Political Economy. The section on economic development has been expanded to include a review of the work of Amartya Sen, who recently won the Nobel Prize in economics. Sen has argued that development should be assessed less by material output measures such as GNP per capita and more by the capabilities and opportunities that people enjoy. The discussion of differences in legal systems has been rewritten to give greater emphasis to the negative impact of corruption in a country on its economic development. There is also an expanded discussion dealing with the protection of intellectual property rights, which takes into account some recent developments, such as the decision by some governments to allow the sale of cheap generic versions of patented medicines—including powerful new drugs for treating AIDS—without permission from the patent owner

Chapter 3: Differences in Culture. The "Implications for Business" section of this chapter has been expanded to incorporate a more detailed discussion of the implications of difference in culture for business ethics. Although many ethical principles are universal, some are culturally bounded. When this is the case, international businesses may be confronted with some difficult ethical dilemmas.

Chapter 4: International Trade Theory. Over the last few years, a number of empirical studies have been published that look at the relationship between a country's "openness" to international trade and its economic growth. This work is now discussed in this chapter. The work gives empirical support to the theory of comparative advantage.

Chapter 5: The Political Economy of International Trade. The chapter has been significantly updated to reflect the recent activities of the World Trade Organization (WTO). This includes an assessment of the record of the WTO in resolving trade disputes between nations. There is also a review of recent multinational agreements, brokered by the WTO, to liberalize cross-border trade and investment in financial services and telecommunications. There is a discussion of the decision to allow China to enter the WTO. Finally, the revised chapter contains a discussion of the future of the WTO in the aftermath of the Seattle protests against globalization.

Chapter 6: Foreign Direct Investment. The chapter has been updated to include all recent statistics of trends in foreign direct investment. Recent data emphasize the important fact that the majority of cross-border investments in recent years have taken the form of mergers and acquisitions, rather than green-field investments. The reasons for this empirical phenomenon are discussed in the chapter.

Chapter 8: Regional Economic Integration. In January 1999, 11 member states of the European Union officially adopted a common currency unit, the euro. This chapter has been revised to include an expanded discussion of the merits and drawbacks of the euro and a review and assessment of the early history of the euro. The chapter also includes a new discussion of the competition policy of the European Commission. This has become increasingly important to international businesses in recent years. For example, in 2001 the European Commission ruled against a proposed merger between two U.S. companies, General Electric and Honeywell, on the grounds that it would reduce competition in the European Union.

Chapter 12: The Strategy of International Business. An emerging theme in the strategy literature has been the extent to which multinational companies can leverage the skills and competencies of their foreign subsidiaries, using them to benefit the entire corporation. A new section has been added to Chapter 12 to discuss this important benefit of international expansion.

Chapter 13: The Organization of International Business. This chapter has been extensively rewritten around the concept of organization architecture. Organizational architecture refers to the totality of a firm's organization, including formal organizational structure, control systems and incentives, organizational culture, processes, and people. It is the way in which these different elements of architecture complement each other that determines whether an international business can effectively execute its strategy.

Chapter 14: Entry Strategy and Strategic Alliances. A new section in this chapter looks at the choice between acquisitions and green-field ventures as alterative strategies for entering foreign markets and establishing a wholly owned subsidiary. The pros and cons associated with each alternative are now discussed in depth in the chapter.

Chapter 16: Global Manufacturing and Materials Management. Web-based information systems now play a crucial role in materials management in the international business. By tracking component parts as they make their way across the globe toward an assembly plant, Web-based information systems enable a firm to optimize its production scheduling according to when components are expected to arrive. A new section has been added to this chapter to discuss this trend.

Instructor Support Material

Instructor's Manual

The Instructor's Manual, prepared by Glenn Johns of Cedar Crest College, contains Course Outlines; Chapter Overviews, and Teaching Suggestions, including a chapter outline, chapter objectives, teaching suggestions for opening cases, lecture outlines, answers to critical discussion questions, teaching suggestions for closing case, and two student activities (some with Internet components); Case Notes (for the part ending cases); and expanded Video Notes with discussion questions for each video.

Test Bank

The Test Bank is prepared by Bruce R. Barringer of the University of Central Florida and contains approximately 100 true-false, multiple-choice, and essay questions per chapter.

Computest

A computerized version of the test bank is available, allowing the instructor to generate random tests and to add his or her own questions.

PowerPoint®

Prepared by Richard Hall of Rockhurst University, the PowerPoint program consists of approximately 500 slides featuring original materials not found in the text in addition to reproductions of key text figures, tables, and maps.

Videos

The updated video lineup consists of PBS and NBC News footage and original business documentaries, which provide further illustration of topics, examples, and cases in the text. Some of the new video titles include "Merger Between Chrysler and Mercedes-Benz," "Cannondale Japan Bicycles and the Japanese Market," "Levi Strauss Lays Off U.S. Workers and American Companies Invest in South Africa's Economy," "MTV/Viacom China Manager Discusses the Changing Culture and Attitude in China," and "World Trade Organization Summit Ends After Days of Protest."

Presentation CD-ROM

Much of the instructor's manual, the PowerPoint slides, video clips, and more are compiled in electronic format on a CD for your convenience in customizing lecture presentations.

Website: www.mhhe.com/hill

A password-protected portion of the book's website will be available to adopters of *International Business*, featuring a Weekly Case Update Service that provides coverage of the latest in online news and links relating to the companies, countries, and situations referenced in the text. Other online and downloadable teaching resources will be available for the instructor as well.

Student Supplements

Global Business Plan Project and Interactive Atlas CD

Each new copy of the book is packaged with a free Global Business Plan Project and Interactive Atlas CD. Designed by Les Dlabay of Lake Forest College for use in his own international business class, the global business plan project helps students create their own plan to launch a new business venture. As students work through the activities in each module, they can link to glossary terms from the book, view related video clips, or launch to the book website and Internet. New to this edition, the interactive "Business Around the World" atlas allows students to research information about doing business in various countries by clicking on areas on the map to access business news and analysis, general facts, and business guidelines.

PowerWeb

With each new book, students also receive access to the International Business PowerWeb site, which offers current articles, curriculum-based materials, weekly updates, informative and timely world news, referred Web links, research tools, student study tools, interactive exercises, and much more.

Website: www.mhhe.com/hill

From the book website students can access weekly updates of chapter material and commentary on topical issues. Also available are chapter review materials, self-tests, key-term flashcards, Internet exercises, and an online Web directory containing links to websites of international organizations, news agencies, companies, and countries.

Acknowledgments

Numerous people deserve to be thanked for their assistance in preparing this book. First, thank you to all the people at McGraw-Hill/Irwin who have worked with me on this project:

John E. Biernat, Publisher

Marianne C. P. Rutter, Sponsoring Editor

Laura Hurst Spell, Managing Development Editor

Lisa Nicks, Marketing Manager

Laura Griffin, Project Manager

Debra R. Sylvester, Production Supervisor

Jennifer McQueen, Designer

David A. Tietz, Photo Research Coordinator

Second, my thanks go to the reviewers, who provided good feedback that helped shape this book.

V. N. Balasubramanyam, Lancaster University

Larry Bridwell, Pace University

William F. Donnelly, S. J., Santa Clara University

Peter Enderwick, The University of Waikato

M. Anaam Hashmi, Minnesota State University

Roderick J. Matthews, University of Wisconsin

Marco J. Menichetti, University of Applied Sciences at Liechtenstein

L. W. (Bill) Murray, University of San Francisco

Behnam Nakhai, Millersville University

Sam Okoroafo, University of Toledo

Mike W. Peng, Ohio State University

Angelo Tarallo, Ramapo College of New Jersey

Arieh A. Ullmann, Binghamton University

Andrew Yap, Florida International University

The opening cases and focus boxes throughout this book make the theory discussed in the text both accessible and interesting as well as illustrating how theory relates to the international business practice.

Food retailers are going global. The leaders in this trend include Wal-Mart of the United States, Carrefour of France, Ahold of Holland, and Tesco from the United Kingdom. Carrefour, the world's second largest retailer, is perhaps the most global of the lot. The pioneer of the hypermarket concept now operates in 26 countries and generates more than 50 percent of its sales outside France. In comparison, Wal-Mart, the world's biggest retailer, still depends on the United States for 85 percent of its sales, but this is down from 100 percent in 1990. By 2001, Wal-Mart had 1,045 stores outside the United States and was opening foreign locations at a rapid clip. Much of this expansion is being driven by acquisitions. After starting its foreign expansion in Mexico by building new stores, Wal-Mart entered Germany through acquisitions and then Britain by acquiring Asda, a nationwide discount food retailer. Holland's Ahold has also made multiple acquisitions, including many in the United States such as the 1998 acquisition of Giant Food, Inc., which helped build Ahold's network of 1,063 supermarkets in the United States and boosted its sales outside Holland to over 70 percent of its total sales. Carrefour does not yet have a U.S. presence, but is said to be looking at potential acquisitions in the United States, including Kmart and Target. Britain's Tesco, a latecomer to the global game, is now expanding rapidly, particularly in Southeast Asia and Eastern Europe, where a combination of acquisitions and expansions have helped Tesco to pass Carrefour and become the largest foreign retailer in Thailand and Poland.

Despite this frenetic activity, the global retailing market is still very fragmented. The top 25 retailers controlled just 16 percent of worldwide retail sales in 2000. However, forecasts suggest the figure could reach 40 percent by 2009, with Latin America, Southeast Asia, and Eastern Europe being the main battlegrounds. A number of factors are driving this development. First, as barriers to cross-border investment fell during the 1990s, it became possible for retailers to enter foreign nations on a significant scale. Second, many of these retailers faced market saturation and slow growth in their domestic markets. Expanding internationally seemed an obvious way to boost sales growth, particularly by entering developing nations in Southeast Asia and Latin America where rapid economic growth was raising living standards and making

these markets more attractive to retailers. Third, once Carrefour started to blaze the trail, other large retailers such as Tesco and Wal-Mart began to follow suit lest they arrive too late and find a country already dominated by other foreign retailers.

Fourth, these retailers believed that by expanding internationally, they could reap significant economies of scale from their global buying power. Many of their key suppliers had long been international companies; for example, Unilever, Procter & Gamble, and Kellogg all sold products globally. If the retailers also built global reach, they could use their size to demand deeper discounts from their suppliers, which would increase the retailers' profit margins.

Fifth, all these retailers held a strong position in their domestic markets, primarily because they were very efficient operations. Carrefour's chief executive officer, for example, believes his company's greatest advantage is its sophisticated understanding of supply chains, beginning with electronic links that tie sales rung up at a checkout register to inventory in the store to production schedules at suppliers. By keeping inventory to a minimum, Carrefour can devote more of a store's floor space to selling products, increasing sales per square foot. Retailers such as Carrefour believe they can gain market share and create significant value by transferring the operating skills they developed in their home markets to nations where indigenous retailers lack the same level of sophistication. Wal-Mart believes it can gain share in markets ranging from Mexico and Brazil to Britain and Germany by applying its skills in supply chain management, information systems, and employee management—skills that propelled Wal-Mart to U.S. dominance. If Wal-Mart, Carrefour, and others execute, they may come to dominate global retailing.

However, these grand strategic designs have run headlong into difficult realities. National differences in tastes and preferences may mean that what sells in Britain may not sell in Brazil. This reduces retailers' ability to centralize their purchasing, buying the same product from the same global suppliers and selling that product worldwide. In a concession to local tastes, the aisles in Tesco's Thai stores carry many different food products than the aisles in British stores. Wal-Mart tried to sell cheap Colombian coffee in Brazil, only to find that Brazilians insisted on

Globalization

Opening Case

Each chapter begins with a case that illustrates the relevance of chapter material for the practice of international business.

Islamic Banking in Pakistan

The Koran clearly condemns interest, which is called *riba* in Arabic, as exploitative and unjust. For many years, banks operating in Islamic countries conveniently ignored this condemnation, but starting about 25 years ago with the establishment of an Islamic bank in Egypt, Islamic banks started to open in predominantly Muslim countries. There are now some 170 Islamic financial institutions worldwide managing over $150 billion in assets and making an average return on capital of over 16 percent. Even conventional banks are entering the market—both Citigroup and HSBC, two of the world's largest financial institutions, now offer Islamic financial services. Until mid-2001, only Iran and the Sudan enforced Islamic banking conventions, but in many other countries, customers could choose between conventional banks and Islamic banks.

In July 2001, Pakistan became the third country to require its banks to adopt Islamic methods. The transition to Islamic banking in Pakistan may determine th fat f I mic ank e wt ir e rld

agreed-on ratio. Some Muslims claim this is a more efficient system than the Western banking system, since it encourages both long-term savings and long-term investment. However, there is no hard evidence of this, and many believe that a *mudarabah* system is less efficient than a conventional Western banking system.

The second Islamic banking method, the *murabaha* contract, is the most widely used among the world's Islamic banks. It seems set to become the most popular method in Pakistan, primarily because it is the easiest to implement. In a *murabaha* contract, say a firm wishes to purchase something using a loan—let's say a piece of equipment that costs $1,000—the firm tells the bank after having negotiated the price with the equipment manufacturer. The bank then buys the equipment for $1,000, and the borrower buys it back from the bank at some later date for, say, $1,100, a price that includes a $100 markup for the bank. A cynic might point out that such a markup is functionally
e va tt r es vn t t t he ila

Country Focus

Each **Country Focus** example provides background on the political, economic, social or cultural aspects of countries grappling with an international business issue.

Free Trade and REI

Recreational Equipment Inc. (REI) is a buyer's cooperative that has grown into one of the major suppliers of outdoor equipment in the United States and has a rapidly growing international business. Started in Seattle in 1938 by Lloyd Anderson, the company provided high-quality climbing gear at a low price to members of the cooperative. For its first 37 years, REI operated a single store in Seattle, but in 1975 the cooperative started opening stores in other cities. Today REI has become a $621 million a year business with 60 stores worldwide, 6,600 employees, revenue growth of 8 to 10 percent annually, and a goal of opening up three to five retail outlets per year. Despite the growth, REI is still organized as a cooperative with 1.7 million active members. All members receive a dividend check at the end of each year that amounts to about 10 percent of the value of their purchases during the year (one does not have to be a member to shop at REI). REI al ha one f th fast st g win anc mos prof

a day, compared to $8 to $10 an hour at Thaw's operation. For a labor-intensive operation such as garment production, these wage differentials are significant.

Given these economics, in mid-2000 REI announced it would be closing its Thaw subsidiary and sourcing its fleece products from Mexico. By shifting its production to Mexico, REI expects to reduce the cost of its fleece items by 20 percent. That means lower prices for REI's members and other customers and bigger profits for REI, which translates into larger dividend checks for REI's members. It also means that its employees at Thaw will be out of a job. To assist its former employees at Thaw, REI has added funds to federal money to assist with job retraining, unemployment benefits, and health insurance.

The events at Thaw are being repeated across the country. Since 1993, about 450,000 jobs have been lost in the U.S. garment industry as production has r vec to lc wa a cc ntrie suc as exic Fo

Management Focus

Management Focus examples further illustrate the relevance of chapter material for the practice of international business.

1. U. firm in ce e r of u Au alia im port nis ally isir pric in this manner by buying out the Australian firm. If the U.S. firm can buy the Australian firm, or its bauxite mine, it need no longer fear that bauxite prices will be increased after it has invested in the refinery. In other words, it would make economic sense for the U.S. firm to engage in vertical FDI. In practice, these kinds of considerations have driven aluminum firms to pursue vertical FDI to such a degree that in 1976, 91 percent of the total volume of bauxite was transferred within vertically integrated firms.[26]

Implications for Business

The implications of the theories of horizontal and vertical FDI for business practice are relatively straightforward. First, the location-specific advantages argument associated with John Dunning helps explain the direction of FDI, both with regard to horizontal and vertical FDI. However, the argument does not explain why firms prefer FDI to licensing or to exporting. In this regard, from both an explanatory and a business perspective, perhaps the most useful theory is the market imperfections approach. With regard to horizontal FDI, this approach identifies with some precision how the relative rates of return associated with horizontal FDI, exporting, and licensing vary with circumstances. The theory suggests that exporting is preferable to licensing and horizontal FDI as long as transport costs are minor and tariff barriers are trivial. As transport costs and/or tariff barriers increase, exporting becomes unprofitable, and the choice is between horizontal FDI and licensing. Since horizontal FDI is more costly and more risky than licensing, other things being equal, the theory argues that licensing is preferable to horizontal FDI. Other things are seldom equal, however. Although licensing may work, it is not an attractive option when one or more of the following conditions exist: (a) the firm has valuable know-how that cannot be adequately protected by a licensing contract, (b) the firm needs tight

Implications for Business

At the end of each chapter in Parts Two, Three, and Four—where the focus is on the environment of international business, as opposed to particular firms—sections titled Implications for Business clearly explain the managerial implications of the material discussed in the chapter.

rit ly ed ar nte ion ngh tions such as Amnesty International and Freedom Watch for major human rights violations, includ-

Ir y ol at As he ou risks of doing business in each of these nations. Which investment would you favor and why?

Microsoft's Troubles in China

Microsoft, the world's biggest personal computer software company, developed MS-DOS and then Windows, the operating system and graphical user interface that now reside on more than 90 percent of the world's personal computers. In addition, Microsoft has a slew of best-selling applications software, including its word processing program (Microsoft Word), spreadsheet program (Excel), and presentation program (PowerPoint). An integral part of Microsoft's international strategy has been expansion into mainland China, which was projected to become the third largest PC market in the world in 2001. With a population of 1.273 billion, China represents a potentially huge market for Microsoft. Microsoft's initial goal was to build up Chinese sales from nothing in 1994 to $100 million by 2000, a goal that it appears to have met. However, sales could have been very much higher were it not for a number of problems that Microsoft encountered in China.

The most obvious and serious obstacle to Microsoft's success in China has been the rampant level of software piracy. Some 90 to 95 percent of the software used in China is pirated, according to figures from the Business Software Alliance. Microsoft is a prime target of this activity. Most Microsoft i prir tar of t s act rv. Most M osoft

cracy to find cheap software solutions. Thus, Microsoft claims, much of the government ends up using pirated software. To make matters worse, China is an exporter of counterfeit software. Microsoft executives don't have to go far to see the problem. Just a few blocks from the company's Hong Kong office is a tiny shop that offers CD-ROMs, each crammed with dozens of computer programs that collectively are worth about $20,000. The asking price is about 500 Hong Kong dollars, or $52!

Microsoft officials are quick to point out the problem arises because Chinese judicial authorities do not enforce their own laws. Microsoft found this out when it first tried to use China's judicial system to sue software pirates. Microsoft pressed officials in China's southern province of Guangdong to raid a manufacturer that was producing counterfeit software that Microsoft used to authenticate its software manuals. The Chinese authorities prosecuted the manufacturer, acknowledged that a copyright violation had occurred, but awarded Microsoft only $2,600 and fined the pirate company $3,000! Undeterred by this limited victory, Microsoft continued its attempts to use the legal system in China to limit copyright violations. However, in late 1999 the tactic backfir wher Micro f sue sma Chin firm he Y

Closing Case

Each chapter concludes with a Closing Case demonstrating the relevance of the chapter material to the practice of international business.

Instructor's Manual and Video Guide

A comprehensive teaching guide includes course outlines, chapter overviews and teaching suggestions, ideas for student exercises and projects, teaching notes for all cases in the book, and video notes.

Videos

The new video collection features PBS and NBC News footage and original business documentaries that tie back to examples and cases in the text. Titles include *"How India Opened Its Economy to Foreign Markets," "Trade Agreement Allows Countries to Ban Import of Genetically Modified Food," "Merger Between Chrysler and Mercedes Benz," "Cannondale Japan Bicycles and the Japanese Market,"* and *"World Trade Organization Summit Ends After Days of Protest,"* to name just a few.

Test Bank

This timesaving resource contains about 100 questions per chapter, each tagged with the level of difficulty, correct answer, and page reference to the text.

Instructor's Presentation CD

This CD contains everything you need for a multimedia lecture or to customize your own. You can pull resources from the CD—like the Instructor's manual, Test Bank, PowerPoint, and digitized video—or add PowerPoint slides and Web screenshots from your own collection.

PowerPoint

An extensive collection of PowerPoint slides features key tables, figures, and maps from the text, as well as original materials.

Part 1

Introduction and
Overview

Chapter 1
Globalization

Globalization

Food retailers are going global. The leaders in this trend include Wal-Mart of the United States, Carrefour of France, Ahold of Holland, and Tesco from the United Kingdom. Carrefour, the world's second largest retailer, is perhaps the most global of the lot. The pioneer of the hypermarket concept now operates in 26 countries and generates more than 50 percent of its sales outside France. In comparison, Wal-Mart, the world's biggest retailer, still depends on the United States for 85 percent of its sales, but this is down from 100 percent in 1990. By 2001, Wal-Mart had 1,045 stores outside the United States and was opening foreign locations at a rapid clip. Much of this expansion is being driven by acquisitions. After starting its foreign expansion in Mexico by building new stores, Wal-Mart entered Germany through acquisitions and then Britain by acquiring Asda, a nationwide discount food retailer. Holland's Ahold has also made multiple acquisitions, including many in the United States such as the 1998 acquisition of Giant Food, Inc., which helped build Ahold's network of 1,063 supermarkets in the United States and boosted its sales outside Holland to over 70 percent of its total sales. Carrefour does not yet have a U.S. presence, but is said to be looking at potential acquisitions in the United States, including Kmart and Target. Britain's Tesco, a latecomer to the global game, is now expanding rapidly, particularly in Southeast Asia and Eastern Europe, where a combination of acquisitions and expansions have helped Tesco to pass Carrefour and become the largest foreign retailer in Thailand and Poland.

Despite this frenetic activity, the global retailing market is still very fragmented. The top 25 retailers controlled just 16 percent of worldwide retail sales in 2000. However, forecasts suggest the figure could reach 40 percent by 2009, with Latin America, Southeast Asia, and Eastern Europe being the main battlegrounds. A number of factors are driving this development. First, as barriers to cross-border investment fell during the 1990s, it became possible for retailers to enter foreign nations on a significant scale. Second, many of these retailers faced market saturation and slow growth in their domestic markets. Expanding internationally seemed an obvious way to boost sales growth, particularly by entering developing nations in Southeast Asia and Latin America where rapid economic growth was raising living standards and making

these markets more attractive to retailers. Third, once Carrefour started to blaze the trail, other large retailers such as Tesco and Wal-Mart began to follow suit lest they arrive too late and find a country already dominated by other foreign retailers.

Fourth, these retailers believed that by expanding internationally, they could reap significant economies of scale from their global buying power. Many of their key suppliers had long been international companies; for example, Unilever, Procter & Gamble, and Kellogg all sold products globally. If the retailers also built global reach, they could use their size to demand deeper discounts from their suppliers, which would increase the retailers' profit margins.

Fifth, all these retailers held a strong position in their domestic markets, primarily because they were very efficient operations. Carrefour's chief executive officer, for example, believes his company's greatest advantage is its sophisticated understanding of supply chains, beginning with electronic links that tie sales rung up at a checkout register to inventory in the store to production schedules at suppliers. By keeping inventory to a minimum, Carrefour can devote more of a store's floor space to selling products, increasing sales per square foot. Retailers such as Carrefour believe they can gain market share and create significant value by transferring the operating skills they developed in their home markets to nations where indigenous retailers lack the same level of sophistication. Wal-Mart believes it can gain share in markets ranging from Mexico and Brazil to Britain and Germany by applying its skills in supply chain management, information systems, and employee management—skills that propelled Wal-Mart to U.S. dominance. If Wal-Mart, Carrefour, and others execute, they may come to dominate global retailing.

However, these grand strategic designs have run headlong into difficult realities. National differences in tastes and preferences may mean that what sells in Britain may not sell in Brazil. This reduces retailers' ability to centralize their purchasing, buying the same product from the same global suppliers and selling that product worldwide. In a concession to local tastes, the aisles in Tesco's Thai stores carry many different food products than the aisles in British stores. Wal-Mart tried to sell cheap Colombian coffee in Brazil, only to find that Brazilians insisted on drinking their own, more expensive brands. If retailers cannot sell the same products worldwide, they cannot realize the economies of scale that they sought. Local tastes crucially affect the way retailers sell their goods too. In 1996 Wal-Mart set up efficient, clean superstores in Indonesia, only to find that Indonesians preferred Matahari, a chain of shabbier local stores that reminded shoppers of traditional street markets where they can haggle and buy the freshest fruit and vegetables. Two years later, Wal-Mart pulled out of Indonesia.

Retailing models aren't always easy to transfer from one location to another. Differences in labor costs, the supply of desirable locations, and the sophistication of the local supply base may make it difficult to transfer a retailing model across borders. In developing nations, Carrefour has found it difficult to implement the sophisticated supply chain management system it uses in France. Suppliers in developing nations lack the required computer-based infrastructure and are hesitant to invest in it. It took Wal-Mart a decade to introduce its electronic supply chain management system into Mexico, primarily because of resistance from local suppliers and confusion on the part of local employees.

Despite these difficulties, most retailers are pushing ahead in their attempts to build a global brand. In this vision of the future, Wal-Mart, Carrefour, and Tesco stores one day will blanket the world. In contrast, Holland's Ahold has adopted a different strategy for going global. Believing that brand loyalty is local and consumer tastes, preferences, and shopping habits all vary from nation to nation, Ahold varies its retailing formula and brand name from nation to nation. In the United States, it still operates under the names of acquired companies, such as Giant and Stop & Shop, because these names and their associated retailing models resonate with locals. Ahold adds value by improving the operating efficiency of the retailers it acquires and transferring valuable skills and practices between countries. In the long run, there may be room for both Ahold's "going global with a local face" strategy and Wal-Mart's "global retail brand" strategy. Despite the impediments, the globalization of retailing likely will continue— the potential payoffs are too great for this not to occur.

Sources: M. N. Hamilton, "Global Food Fight," *Washington Post,* November 19, 2000, p. H1; A. Stewart, "Easier Access to World Markets," *Financial Times,* December 3, 1997, p. 8; "Global Strategy— Why Tesco Will Beat Carrefour," *Retail Week,* April 6, 2001, p. 14; "Shopping All over the World," *The Economist,* June 19, 1999, pp. 59–61; and M. Flagg, "In Asia, Going to the Grocery Increasingly Means Heading for a European Retail Chain," *Wall Street Journal,* April 24, 2001, p. A21.

Introduction

A fundamental shift is occurring in the world economy. We are moving rapidly away from a world in which national economies were relatively self-contained entities, isolated from each other by barriers to cross-border trade and investment; by distance, time zones, and language; and by national differences in government regulation, culture, and business systems. And we are moving toward a world in which barriers to cross-border trade and investment are tumbling; perceived distance is shrinking due to advances in transportation and telecommunications technology; material culture is starting to look similar the world over; and national economies are merging into an interdependent global economic system. The process by which this is occurring is commonly referred to as **globalization.**

In this interdependent global economy, an American might drive to work in a car designed in Germany that was assembled in Mexico by DaimlerChrysler from components made in the United States and Japan that were fabricated from Korean steel and Malaysian rubber. She may have filled the car with gasoline at a service station owned by a British multinational company that changed its name from British Petroleum to BP to hide its national origins. The gasoline could have been made from oil pumped out of a well off the coast of Africa by a French oil company that transported it to the United States in a ship owned by a Greek shipping line. While driving to work, the American might talk to her stockbroker on a Nokia cell phone that was designed in Finland and assembled in Texas using chip sets produced in Taiwan that were designed by Indian engineers working at a firm in San Diego, California, called Qualcomm. She could tell the stockbroker to purchase shares in Deutsche Telekom, a German telecommunications firm transformed from a former state-owned monopoly into a global company by an energetic Israeli CEO. She may turn on the car radio, which was made in Malaysia by a Japanese firm, to hear a popular hip-hop song composed by a Swede and sung by a group of Danes in English who signed a record contract with a French music company to promote their record in America. The driver might pull into a drive-through coffee stall run by a Korean immigrant and order "single-tall-non-fat latte" and chocolate-covered biscotti. The coffee beans come from Brazil and the chocolate from Peru, while the biscotti was made locally using an old Italian recipe. After the song ends, a news announcer might inform the American listener that anti-globalization protests at a meeting of heads of state in Genoa, Italy, have turned violent. One protester has been killed. The announcer then turns to the next item, a story about how an economic slowdown in America has sent Japan's Nikkei stock market index to 16-year lows.

This is the world we live in. It is a world where the volume of goods, services, and investment crossing national borders has expanded faster than world output every year for the past two decades. It is a world where more than $1.2 billion in foreign exchange transactions are made every day. It is a world in which international institutions such as the World Trade Organization and gatherings of leaders from the world's most powerful economies have called for even lower barriers to cross-border trade and investment. It is a world where the symbols of material and popular culture are increasingly global: from Coca-Cola and McDonald's to Sony PlayStations, Nokia cell phones, MTV shows, and Disney films. It is a world in which products are made from inputs that come from all over the world. It is a world in which an economic crisis in Asia can cause a recession in the United States, and a slowdown in the United States really did help drive Japan's Nikkei index in 2001 to lows not seen since 1985. It is also a world in which a vigorous and vocal minority is protesting against globalization, which they blame for a list of ills, from unemployment in developed nations to environmental degradation and the Americanization of popular culture. And yes, these protests really have turned violent.

For businesses, this is in many ways the best of times. Globalization has increased the opportunities for a firm to expand its revenues by selling around the world and reduce its costs by producing in nations where key inputs are cheap. Since the collapse of communism at the end of the 1980s, the pendulum of public policy in nation after nation has swung toward the free market end of the economic spectrum. Regulatory and administrative barriers to doing business in foreign nations have come down, while those nations have often transformed their economies, privatizing state-owned enterprises, deregulating markets, increasing competition, and welcoming investment by foreign businesses. This has allowed businesses both large and small, from both advanced nations and developed nations, to expand internationally.

The global retailing industry, profiled in the opening case, is something of a late mover in this development. Some industries, such as commercial jet aircraft, automobiles, petroleum, semi-conductor chips, and computers, have been global for decades. Retailing has been primarily local in orientation, but in a testament to the scope and pace of globalization, this too is now changing. Falling barriers to cross-border investment have made this possible. Rapid economic growth in developing nations and market saturation at home has made globalization a strategic imperative for established retailers seeking to grow their business. Many, such as Wal-Mart and Tesco, feel that they must move aggressively now lest they lose the initiative to early movers like Carrefour. They see their strategic advantage in terms of building a global brand, realizing economies of scale, and leveraging skills across national borders. In this, they are no different from companies in other industries that have already gone global.

At the same time, going global is not without problems. This too was evident in the opening case. The grand strategic vision of retailers such as Wal-Mart and Carrefour has often run up against the hard reality that for all the superficial similarities in material and popular culture and in business systems, doing business in foreign nations still has unique challenges. Because of different tastes and preferences, what sells in Britain may not sell in Thailand, operating systems that give a retailer a competitive advantage in America may be difficult to implement in Mexico, and a brand that means something in Kansas may mean little in Indonesia.

The tension evident in the opening case between the economic opportunities associated with going global and the unique challenges associated with doing business across borders is an important one in international business. We shall return to consider this tension repeatedly in this book. To begin with, however, we need to take a closer look at the process of globalization. We need to understand what is driving this process, appreciate how it is changing the face of international businesses, and better comprehend why globalization has become a flash point for debate, demonstration, and conflict over the future direction of our civilization.

What Is Globalization?

As used in this book, **globalization** refers to the shift toward a more integrated and interdependent world economy. Globalization has two main components: the globalization of markets and the globalization of production.

The Globalization of Markets

The globalization of markets refers to the merging of historically distinct and separate national markets into one huge global marketplace. Falling barriers to cross-border trade have made it easier to sell internationally. It has been argued for some time that the tastes and preferences of consumers in different nations are beginning to converge on some global norm, thereby helping to create a global market.[1] Consumer products such as Citicorp credit cards, Coca-Cola soft drinks, Sony PlayStation, and McDonald's hamburgers are frequently held up as prototypical examples of this trend. Firms such as Citicorp, Coca-Cola, McDonald's, and Sony are more than just benefactors of this trend; they are also facilitators of it. By offering a standardized product worldwide, they help to create a global market.

A company does not have to be the size of these multinational giants to facilitate, and benefit from, the globalization of markets. In the United States, more than 200,000 small businesses with fewer than 100 employees registered foreign sales in 2000. Typical of these is Hytech, a New York-based manufacturer of solar panels that generates 40 percent of its $3 million in annual sales from exports to five countries, or B&S Aircraft Alloys, another New York company whose exports account for 40 percent of its $8 million annual revenues.[2]

Despite the global prevalence of Citicorp credit cards and McDonald's hamburgers, it is important not to push too far the view that national markets are giving way to the global market. As we shall see in later chapters, very significant differences still exist between national markets along many relevant dimensions, including consumer tastes and preferences, distribution channels, culturally embedded value systems, and the like. These differences frequently require that marketing strategies, product features, and operating practices be customized to best match conditions in a country. For example, automobile companies will promote different car models depending on a range of factors such as local fuel costs, income levels, traffic congestion, and cultural values. Similarly, as we saw in the opening case, global retailers may still need to vary their product mix from country to country depending on local tastes and preferences.

The most global markets currently are not markets for consumer products—where national differences in tastes and preferences are still often important enough to act as a brake on globalization—but markets for industrial goods and materials that serve a universal need the world over. These include the markets for commodities such as aluminum, oil, and wheat; the markets for industrial products such as microprocessors, DRAMs (computer memory chips), and commercial jet aircraft; the markets for computer software; and the markets for financial assets from U.S. Treasury bills to eurobonds and futures on the Nikkei index or the Mexican peso.

In many global markets, the same firms frequently confront each other as competitors in nation after nation. Coca-Cola's rivalry with Pepsi is a global one, as are the rivalries between Ford and Toyota, Boeing and Airbus, Caterpillar and Komatsu, and Nintendo and Sega. If one firm moves into a nation that is not currently served by its rivals, those rivals are sure to follow to prevent their competitor from gaining an advantage.[3] The opening case revealed that retailers such as Wal-Mart, Carrefour, and Tesco are starting to engage in a global rivalry. As firms follow each other around the world, they bring with them many of the assets that served them well in other national markets—including their products, operating strategies, marketing strategies, and brand names—creating some homogeneity across markets. Thus, greater uniformity replaces diversity. Due to such developments, in an increasing number of industries it is no longer meaningful to talk about "the German market," "the American market," "the Brazilian market," or "the Japanese market"; for many firms there is only the global market.

The Globalization of Production

The globalization of production refers to the sourcing of goods and services from locations around the globe to take advantage of national differences in the cost and quality of factors of production (such as labor, energy, land, and capital). By doing this, companies hope to lower their overall cost structure and/or improve the quality or functionality of their product offering, thereby allowing them to compete more effectively. Consider the Boeing Company's latest commercial jet airliner, the 777. The 777 contains 132,500 major component parts that are produced around the world by 545 suppliers. Eight Japanese suppliers make parts for the fuselage, doors, and wings; a supplier in Singapore makes the doors for the nose landing gear; three suppliers in Italy manufacture wing flaps; and so on.[4] Part of Boeing's rationale for outsourcing so much production to foreign suppliers is that these suppliers are the best in the world at performing their particular activity. A global web of suppliers yields a better final product, which enhances the chances of Boeing winning a greater share of total orders for aircraft than its global rival, Airbus Industrie. Boeing also outsources some production to foreign countries to increase the chance that it will win significant orders from airliners based in that country.

The global dispersal of productive activities is not limited to giants such as Boeing. Many much smaller firms are also getting into the act. Consider Swan Optical, a U.S.-based manufacturer and distributor of eyewear. With annual sales revenues of $20 million to $30 million, Swan is hardly a giant, yet Swan manufactures its eyewear in low-cost factories in Hong Kong and China that it jointly owns with a Hong Kong–based partner. Swan also has a minority stake in eyewear design houses in Japan, France, and Italy. The company has dispersed its manufacturing and design processes to different locations around the world to take advantage of favorable skill bases and cost structures. Foreign investments in Hong Kong and then China have helped Swan lower its cost structure, while investments in Japan, France, and Italy have helped it produce designer eyewear for which it can charge a premium price. By dispersing its manufacturing and design activities, Swan established a competitive advantage for itself in the global marketplace for eyewear, just as Boeing has tried to do by dispersing some of its activities to other countries.[5]

Robert Reich, the former secretary of labor in the Clinton administration, has argued that as a consequence of the trend exemplified by Boeing and Swan Optical, in many industries it is becoming irrelevant to talk about American products, Japanese products, German products, or Korean products. Increasingly, according to Reich, the outsourcing of productive activities to different suppliers results in the creation of products that are global in nature; that is, "global products."[6] But as with the globalization of markets, one must be careful not to push the globalization of production too far. As we will see in later chapters, substantial impediments still make it difficult for firms to achieve the optimal dispersion of their productive activities to locations around the globe. These impediments include formal and informal barriers to trade between countries, barriers to foreign direct investment, transportation costs, and issues associated with economic and political risk.

Nevertheless, we are traveling down the road toward a future characterized by the increased globalization of markets and production. Modern firms are important actors in this drama, by their very actions fostering increased globalization. These firms, however, are merely responding in an efficient manner to changing conditions in their operating environment—as well they should. In the next section, we look at the main drivers of globalization.

Drivers of Globalization

Two macro factors seem to underlie the trend toward greater globalization.[7] The first is the decline in barriers to the free flow of goods, services, and capital that has occurred since the end of World War II. The second factor is technological change, particularly the dramatic developments in recent years in communication, information processing, and transportation technologies.

Declining Trade and Investment Barriers

During the 1920s and 30s, many of the nation-states of the world erected formidable barriers to international trade and foreign direct investment. **International trade** occurs when a firm exports goods or services to consumers in another country. **Foreign direct investment** occurs when a firm invests resources in business activities outside its home country. Many of the barriers to international trade took the form of high tariffs on imports of manufactured goods. The typical aim of such tariffs was to protect domestic industries from foreign competition. One consequence, however, was "beggar thy neighbor" retaliatory trade policies with countries progressively raising trade barriers against each other. Ultimately, this depressed world demand and contributed to the Great Depression of the 1930s.

Having learned from this experience, the advanced industrial nations of the West committed themselves after World War II to removing barriers to the free flow of goods, services, and capital between nations.[8] This goal was enshrined in the treaty known as the General Agreement on Tariffs and Trade (GATT). Under the umbrella of GATT, eight rounds of negotiations among member states, which now number more than 140, have worked to lower barriers to the free flow of goods and services. The most recent round of negotiations, known as the Uruguay Round, was completed in December 1993. The Uruguay Round further reduced trade barriers; extended GATT to cover services as well as manufactured goods; provided enhanced protection for patents, trademarks, and copyrights; and established the World Trade Organization (WTO) to police the international trading system.[9] Table 1.1 summarizes the impact of GATT agreements on average tariff rates for manufactured goods. As can be seen, average tariff rates have fallen significantly since 1950 and now stand at 3.9 percent. Discussions aimed at launching a new round of cuts in barriers to cross-border trade and investment were scheduled to begin in LATE 2001. If and when the round begins, the likely focus will be services and agricultural products, where tariffs still remain high. The average agricultural tariff rates are still around 40 percent, and rich nations spend some $300 billion a year in subsidies to support their farm sectors.[10]

	1913	**1950**	**1990**	**2000**
France	21%	18%	5.9%	3.9%
Germany	20	26	5.9	3.9
Italy	18	25	5.9	3.9
Japan	30	—	5.3	3.9
Holland	5	11	5.9	3.9
Sweden	20	9	4.4	3.9
Britain	—	23	5.9	3.9
United States	44	14	4.8	3.9

Table 1.1

Average Tariff Rates on Manufactured Products as Percent of Value

Source: 1913–1990 data from "Who Wants to Be a Giant?" *The Economist: A Survey of the Multinationals*, June 24, 1995, pp. 3–4.

In addition to reducing trade barriers, many countries have also been progressively removing restrictions to foreign direct investment (FDI). Between 1991 and 2000, of the 1,121 changes worldwide in the laws governing foreign direct investment, 95 percent created a more favorable environment for FDI, according to the United Nations. During 2000 alone, 69 countries made 150 changes to regulations governing foreign direct investment, of which 147 (or 98 percent) were more favorable to foreign investors.[11] A dramatic increase in the number of bilateral investment treaties designed to protect and promote investment between two countries also reflects governments' desire to facilitate FDI. As of 2000, there were 1,856 such treaties in the world involving over 160 countries, a 10-fold increase from the 181 treaties that existed in 1980.[12]

Such trends facilitate both the globalization of markets and the globalization of production. The lowering of barriers to international trade enables firms to view the world, rather than a single country, as their market. The lowering of trade and investment barriers also allows firms to base production at the optimal location for that activity, serving the world market from that location. Thus, a firm might design a product in one country, produce component parts in two other countries, assemble the product in yet another country, and then export the finished product around the world.

The lowering of trade barriers has facilitated the globalization of production. According to data from the World Trade Organization, the volume of world trade has grown consistently faster than the volume of world output since 1950.[13] From 1950 to 2000, world trade expanded almost 20-fold, far outstripping world output, which grew by six and a half times. As suggested by Figure 1.1, the growth in world trade seems to have accelerated in recent years. In 2000, the last year for which full data are available, it increased by a strong 12.5 percent.[14] The global economic slowdown that occurred in 2001, along with the economic aftermath of the September 11th terrorist attacks on the United States, indicate that 2001 may be the first year in almost two decades during which the volume of world trade contracted. If history is any guide, however, any such contraction will be modest and short lived.

The data summarized in Figure 1.1 imply two things. First, more firms are doing what Boeing does with the 777: dispersing parts of their overall production process to different locations around the globe to drive down production costs and increase product quality. Second, the economies of the world's nation-states are becoming more intertwined. As trade expands, nations are becoming increasingly dependent on each other for important goods and services.

The evidence also suggests that foreign direct investment is playing an increasing role in the global economy as firms ranging in size from Boeing to Swan Optical increase their cross-border investments. The average yearly outflow of FDI increased from about $25 billion in 1975 to a record $1.3 trillion in 2000.[15] The flow of FDI not only accelerated over the last quarter century, but it also has accelerated faster than

Figure 1.1

The Growth of World
Trade and World Output

Source: Data compiled from World
Trade Organization, International
Trade Trends and Statistics.

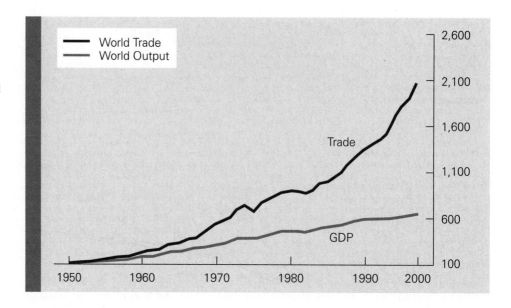

the growth in world trade. For example, between 1990 and 2000, the total flow of FDI
from all countries increased about fivefold, while world trade grew by some 82 percent
and world output by 23 percent.[16] As a result of the strong FDI flow, by 2000 the global
stock of FDI exceeded $6 trillion. In total, by 2000, 60,000 parent companies had
820,000 affiliates in foreign markets that collectively produced an estimated $14 tril-
lion in global sales, nearly twice as high as the value of global exports.[17]

The globalization of markets and production and the resulting growth of world
trade, foreign direct investment, and imports all imply that firms are finding their
home markets under attack from foreign competitors. This is true in Japan, where
U.S. companies such as Kodak, Procter & Gamble, and Merrill Lynch are expanding
their presence. It is true in the United States, where Japanese automobile firms have
taken market share away from General Motors and Ford. And it is true in Europe,
where the once-dominant Dutch company Philips has seen its market share in the
consumer electronics industry taken by Japan's JVC, Matsushita, and Sony. The bottom line is that the growing integration of the world economy into a single, huge
marketplace is increasing the intensity of competition in a range of manufacturing
and service industries.

Having said all this, declining trade barriers can't be taken for granted. As we shall
see in the following chapters, demands for "protection" from foreign competitors are
still often heard in countries around the world, including the United States. Although a return to the restrictive trade policies of the 1920s and 30s is unlikely, it is
not clear whether the political majority in the industrialized world favors further reductions in trade barriers. If trade barriers decline no further, at least for the time being, a temporary limit may have been reached in the globalization of both markets
and production.

The Role of Technological Change

The lowering of trade barriers made globalization of markets and production a theoretical possibility. Technological change has made it a tangible reality. Since the end
of World War II, the world has seen major advances in communication, information
processing, and transportation technology, including the explosive emergence of the
Internet and World Wide Web. In the words of Renato Ruggiero, director general of
the World Trade Organization,

Telecommunications is creating a global audience. Transport is creating a global village. From Buenos Aires to Boston to Beijing, ordinary people are watching MTV, they're wearing Levi's jeans, and they're listening to Sony Walkmans as they commute to work.[18]

Microprocessors and Telecommunications

Perhaps the single most important innovation has been development of the microprocessor, which enabled the explosive growth of high-power, low-cost computing, vastly increasing the amount of information that can be processed by individuals and firms. The microprocessor also underlies many recent advances in telecommunications technology. Over the past 30 years, global communications have been revolutionized by developments in satellite, optical fiber, and wireless technologies, and now the Internet and the World Wide Web. These technologies rely on the microprocessor to encode, transmit, and decode the vast amount of information that flows along these electronic highways. The cost of microprocessors continues to fall, while their power increases (a phenomenon known as Moore's Law, which predicts that the power of microprocessor technology doubles and its cost of production falls in half every 18 months).[19] As this happens, the costs of global communications are plummeting, which lowers the costs of coordinating and controlling a global organization. Thus, between 1930 and 1990, the cost of a three-minute phone call between New York and London fell from $244.65 to $3.32.[20]

The Internet and World Wide Web

The phenomenal recent growth of the Internet and the associated World Wide Web (which utilizes the Internet to communicate between World Wide Web sites) is the latest expression of this development. In 1990, fewer than 1 million users were connected to the Internet. By 1995 the figure had risen to 50 million. In 2001 it grew to 490 million. By the year 2005, forecasts suggest that the Internet may have over 1.12 billion users, or about 18 percent of the world's population.[21] In July 1993, some 1.8 million host computers were connected to the Internet (host computers host the Web pages of local users). By January 2001, the number of host computers had increased to 109 million, and the number is still growing rapidly.[22] In the United States, where Internet usage is most advanced, 58 percent of the population had Internet access at home by July 2001.[23] The rate of growth in Internet adoption is now slowing markedly in the United States as the market becomes more saturated. The increase in total Internet usage is also slowing. However, most observers believe that this is due to the dominance of slow connections to the Internet (telephone lines) and they believe that once high-speed connections become more widely available (such as cable modems that can transmit data 1,000 times faster than a slow telephone line with a conventional modem), we will see a sharp upswing in the volume of traffic on the Web.

The Internet and World Wide Web (WWW) promise to develop into the information backbone of tomorrow's global economy. According to Forrester Research, the value of Web-based transactions hit $657 billion in 2000, from virtually nothing in 1994, and could grow to $6.8 trillion by 2004, with the United States accounting for 47 percent of all Web-based transactions (see Figure 1.2).[24] Many of these transactions are not business-to-consumer transactions (e-commerce), but business-to-business (or e-business) transactions. The greatest current potential of the Web seems to be in the business-to-business arena.

Included in the expanding volume of Web-based traffic is a growing percentage of cross-border trade. Viewed globally, the Web is emerging as an equalizer. It rolls back some of the constraints of location, scale, and time zones.[25] The Web allows businesses, both small and large, to expand their global presence at a lower cost than ever before. One example is a small California-based start-up, Cardiac Science, which makes defibrillators and heart monitors. In 1996, Cardiac Science was itching to break into international markets but had little idea of how to establish an international presence. By

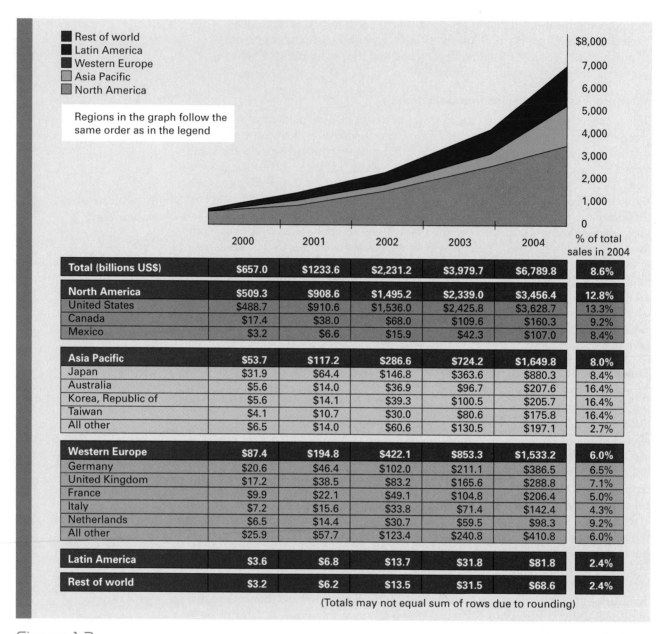

	2000	2001	2002	2003	2004	% of total sales in 2004
Total (billions US$)	$657.0	$1233.6	$2,231.2	$3,979.7	$6,789.8	8.6%
North America	$509.3	$908.6	$1,495.2	$2,339.0	$3,456.4	12.8%
United States	$488.7	$910.6	$1,536.0	$2,425.8	$3,628.7	13.3%
Canada	$17.4	$38.0	$68.0	$109.6	$160.3	9.2%
Mexico	$3.2	$6.6	$15.9	$42.3	$107.0	8.4%
Asia Pacific	$53.7	$117.2	$286.6	$724.2	$1,649.8	8.0%
Japan	$31.9	$64.4	$146.8	$363.6	$880.3	8.4%
Australia	$5.6	$14.0	$36.9	$96.7	$207.6	16.4%
Korea, Republic of	$5.6	$14.1	$39.3	$100.5	$205.7	16.4%
Taiwan	$4.1	$10.7	$30.0	$80.6	$175.8	16.4%
All other	$6.5	$14.0	$60.6	$130.5	$197.1	2.7%
Western Europe	$87.4	$194.8	$422.1	$853.3	$1,533.2	6.0%
Germany	$20.6	$46.4	$102.0	$211.1	$386.5	6.5%
United Kingdom	$17.2	$38.5	$83.2	$165.6	$288.8	7.1%
France	$9.9	$22.1	$49.1	$104.8	$206.4	5.0%
Italy	$7.2	$15.6	$33.8	$71.4	$142.4	4.3%
Netherlands	$6.5	$14.4	$30.7	$59.5	$98.3	9.2%
All other	$25.9	$57.7	$123.4	$240.8	$410.8	6.0%
Latin America	$3.6	$6.8	$13.7	$31.8	$81.8	2.4%
Rest of world	$3.2	$6.2	$13.5	$31.5	$68.6	2.4%

(Totals may not equal sum of rows due to rounding)

Figure 1.2

Worldwide E-Commerce Growth Forecast

Source: Adapted from Forrester Research, Inc., http://www.forrester.com/ER/Press/ForrFind/0,1768,0,00.html, 2001 and Forrester Report, November 2001.

1998, the company was selling to customers in 46 countries and foreign sales accounted for 85 percent of its $1.2 million revenues. Although some of this business was developed through conventional export channels, a growing percentage of it came from "hits" to the company's website, which, according to the company's CEO, "attracts international business people like bees to honey."[26] Similarly, 10 years ago no one would have thought that a small British company based in Stafford would have been able to build a global market for its products by utilizing the Internet, but that is exactly what Bridgewater Pottery has done.[27] Bridgewater has traditionally sold premium pottery through exclusive distribution channels, but the company found it difficult and laborious to identify new retail outlets. Since establishing an Internet presence in 1997, Bridgewater has conducted a significant amount of business with consumers in other countries who could not be reached through existing channels of distribution or could

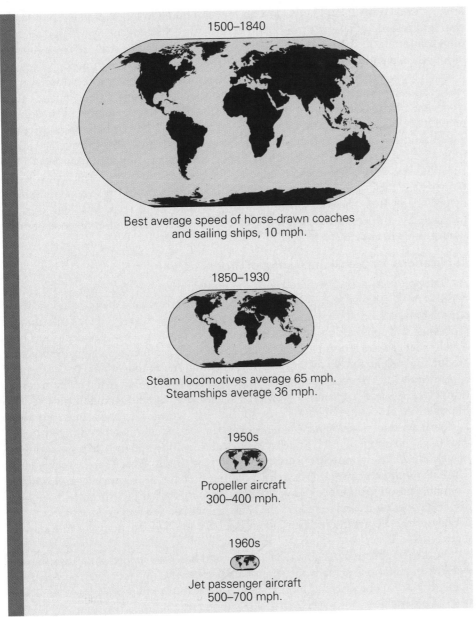

Figure 1.3

The Shrinking Globe

Source: P. Dicken, *Global Shift* (New York: Guilford Press, 1992), p. 104.

1500–1840

Best average speed of horse-drawn coaches and sailing ships, 10 mph.

1850–1930

Steam locomotives average 65 mph.
Steamships average 36 mph.

1950s

Propeller aircraft
300–400 mph.

1960s

Jet passenger aircraft
500–700 mph.

not be reached cost effectively. The Web makes it much easier for buyers and sellers to find each other, wherever they may be located and whatever their size.

Transportation Technology

In addition to developments in communication technology, several major innovations in transportation technology have occurred since World War II. In economic terms, the most important are probably the development of commercial jet aircraft and superfreighters and the introduction of containerization, which simplifies transshipment from one mode of transport to another. The advent of commercial jet travel, by reducing the time needed to get from one location to another, has effectively shrunk the globe (see Figure 1.3). In terms of travel time, New York is now "closer" to Tokyo than it was to Philadelphia in the Colonial days.

Containerization has revolutionized the transportation business, significantly lowering the costs of shipping goods over long distances. Before the advent of containerization, moving goods from one mode of transport to another was very labor intensive, lengthy, and costly. It could take days and several hundred longshoremen to unload a ship and reload goods onto trucks and trains. With the advent of widespread containerization in the 1970s and 1980s, the whole process can be executed by a handful of longshoremen in a couple of days. Since 1980, the world's containership fleet has more than quadrupled, reflecting in part the growing volume of international trade and in part the switch to this mode of transportation. As a result of the efficiency gains associated with containerization, transportation costs have plummeted, making it much more economical to ship goods around the globe, thereby helping to drive the globalization of markets and production. Between 1920 and 1990 the average ocean freight and port charges per ton of U.S. export and import cargo fell from $95 to $29 (in 1990 dollars).[28] The cost of shipping freight per ton-mile on railroads in the United States fell from 3.04 cents in 1985 to 2.3 cents in 2000, largely as a result of efficiency gains from the widespread use of containers.[29] An increased share of cargo now goes by air. Between 1930 and 1990, average air transportation revenue per passenger mile fell from $0.68 to $0.11.[30]

Implications for the Globalization of Production

As transportation costs associated with the globalization of production declined, dispersal of production to geographically dispersed locations became more economical. As a result of the technological innovations discussed above, the real costs of information processing and communication have fallen dramatically in the past two decades. These developments make it possible for a firm to create and then manage a globally dispersed production system, further facilitating the globalization of production.

A worldwide communications network has become essential for many international businesses. For example, Hewlett-Packard uses satellite communications and information processing technologies to link its worldwide operations. Hewlett-Packard's product development teams consist of individuals based in different countries (e.g., Japan, the United States, Great Britain, and Germany). When developing new products, these individuals use videoconferencing to "meet" on a weekly basis. They also communicate with each other daily via telephone, electronic mail, and fax. Communication technologies have enabled Hewlett-Packard to integrate its globally dispersed operations and to reduce the time needed for developing new products (for details see the Management Focus about Radha Basu, a global manager in the information age).[31]

The development of commercial jet aircraft has also helped knit together the worldwide operations of many international businesses. Using jet travel, an American manager need spend a day at most traveling to her firm's European or Asian operations. This enables her to oversee a globally dispersed production system.

Implications for the Globalization of Markets

In addition to the globalization of production, technological innovations have also facilitated the globalization of markets. As noted above, low-cost transportation has made it more economical to ship products around the world, thereby helping to create global markets. Low-cost global communications networks such as the World Wide Web are helping to create electronic global marketplaces. In addition, low-cost jet travel has resulted in the mass movement of people between countries. This has reduced the cultural distance between countries and is bringing about some convergence of consumer tastes and preferences. At the same time, global communication networks and global media are creating a worldwide culture. U.S. television networks such as CNN, MTV, and HBO are now received in many countries, and Hollywood films are shown the world over. In any society, the media are primary conveyors of culture; as global media develop, we must expect the evolution of something akin to a global culture. A logical result of this evolution is the emergence of global markets for consumer products. The first signs of this are already apparent. It is now as easy to find a McDonald's restaurant in Tokyo as it is in New York, to buy a Sony Walkman in Rio as it

Radha Basu—A Global Manager in the Information Age

In the era of globalization, corporations increasingly hire the best talent they can find, no matter what the nationality or gender. Radha Basu is a good example of the emerging class of internationally mobile global managers who are equally at home in different cultures and have to manage across borders on a day-to-day basis, aided by modern communications and transportation technology. Radha was born in Madra in southern India in 1953. Raised as a Hindu, she was nevertheless educated by Irish nuns in a Catholic school. Radha was a strong math student and gained entry to an Indian university to study engineering. She graduated with honors and won admission to the University of Southern California to do graduate work in computer science. Later she went to work for Hewlett-Packard where she gained her first international experience as a manager in Germany. That was followed by a stint in India, but she is now back in the United States working for Hewlett-Packard and is a naturalized American citizen.

Radha's job spans the world. She manages teams of software engineers spread across 15 time zones in California, Colorado, England, Germany, Switzerland, India, Japan, and Australia. These teams must work together on collaborative efforts, presenting Radha with a daunting management challenge. A generation ago, such a task would have been nearly impossible, but thanks to advances in communications, computing, and air travel, collaboration between such far-flung co-workers is intense and intimate. Radha logs more than 100,000 air miles a year keeping projects on track, and she communicates regularly with colleagues at distant locations using videoconferencing and teleconferencing. She exchanges scores of e-mails a day and sends simultaneous voice-mail messages to many of the 1,000 people in her division.

Impromptu conversations are the staple of her life. She may be awakened at 6 A.M. by a phone call from her Swiss team, which needs approval to sign a contract to sell software to a major customer, and spend the next hour refining her team's promises to the customer while eating breakfast and driving to work. Like all of her meetings, this one will be held in English, the language of international business. The widespread use of English is a definite plus, but it can cause confusion too, masking differences in style, practices, and interpretations. The same words in the same language don't necessarily mean the same things to people of different nationalities. Radha says she once told some German engineers that they should do something and was puzzled when they didn't. She discovered that to a German, *should* means that he has the option of not doing it, and the Germans elected to take this option. Now when Radha wants something done, she uses the word *must,* a word that conveys the imperative to her German colleagues.

Source: Adapted from G. Pascal Zachary, "The Global Me," *Public Affairs,* 2000, pp. 51–55.

is in Berlin, and to buy Levi's jeans in Paris as it is in San Francisco. The accompanying Management Focus, "Homer Simpson—A Global Brand," illustrates the power of the media to create global market opportunities.

Despite these trends, we must be careful not to overemphasize their importance. While modern communication and transportation technologies are ushering in the "global village," very significant national differences remain in culture, consumer preferences, and business practices. A firm that ignores differences between countries does so at its peril. We shall stress this point repeatedly throughout this book and elaborate on it in later chapters.

The Changing Demographics of the Global Economy

Hand in hand with the trend toward globalization has been a fairly dramatic change in the demographics of the global economy over the past 30 years. As late as the 1960s, four stylized facts described the demographics of the global economy. The first was U.S. dominance in the world economy and world trade picture. The second was U.S.

Homer Simpson—A Global Brand!

If a poll were held to identify the world's favorite dysfunctional family, the Simpsons would probably win hands down. The Fox Broadcasting Company production that documents the life and times of Homer and his irreverent clan is the most decorated and longest running animated TV show in history. Some 60 million viewers in more than 70 countries tune in to watch the weekly antics of the Simpsons. The show seems to have universal appeal, with the audience split 50/50 between adults and children, and with audience ratings running high in countries as diverse as Spain and Japan. *Time* magazine named "The Simpsons" the 20th century's best TV show, and the chair of the philosophy department at the University of Manitoba wrote an article claiming "The Simpsons" is the deepest show on television.

Whatever the sources of the show's appeal, there is no question that Homer and his family have become a powerful global brand. Not only do Fox and its parent News Corporation benefit from the huge syndication rights of the show, but they also have made a significant sum from licensing the characters. Since the inception of the show in 1990, "The Simpsons" has generated more than $1 billion in retail sales from tie-in merchandise, much of it outside the United States. In 2000, about 50 large brand and marketing partners around the world used the Simpsons to sell everything from toilet paper in Germany, Kit Kat bars and potato chips in the United Kingdom, El Cortes Bart Simpson dolls in Spain, and Intel microprocessors in the United States. Clinton Cards, a British greeting card retailer, used Father's Day in 2000 as the perfect opportunity to find the British father whose behavior most resembles that of Homer Simpson. The competition was rolled out across all of the company's 692 stores and supported by TV advertising.

So what's next for the Simpsons? Fox has been careful to manage the licensing deals so that Homer and clan don't suffer from overexposure or aren't used in inappropriate ways. According to Matt Groening, the show's creator, " 'The Simpsons' is a commercial enterprise and we embrace the capitalistic nature of this project. What we try to do with 'The Simpsons' is not do a label slap—that is, we don't just slap their drawings on the side of a product. We try to make each item witty, and sometimes we comment on the absurdity of the item itself." In short, Fox tries to make sure that "The Simpsons" characters are used in a way that is consistent with the irreverent nature of the show itself. "If we didn't do this," notes a Fox spokesman, "we would lose credibility with the fans, and we have to make sure that doesn't happen."

Source: D. Finnigan, "Homer Improvement," *Brandweek*, November 27, 2000, pp. 22–25; and "The Simpsons—Picking a Winner," *Marketing*, June 29, 2000, pp. 28–29.

dominance in world foreign direct investment. Related to this, the third fact was the dominance of large, multinational U.S. firms on the international business scene. The fourth was that roughly half the globe—the centrally planned economies of the Communist world—was off-limits to Western international businesses. As will be explained below, all four of these qualities either have changed or are now changing rapidly.

The Changing World Output and World Trade Picture

In the early 1960s, the United States was still by far the world's dominant industrial power. In 1963, for example, the United States accounted for 40.3 percent of world output. By 2000, the United States accounted for 27 percent of world output, still by far the world's largest industrial power but down significantly in relative size since the 1960s (see Table 1.2). Nor was the United States the only developed nation to see its relative standing slip. The same occurred to Germany, France, and the United Kingdom, all nations that were among the first to industrialize. This decline in the U.S. position was not an absolute decline, since the U.S. economy grew at a robust average annual rate of over 3 percent from 1963 to 2000 (the economies of Germany, France, and the United Kingdom also grew over this time period). Rather, it was a relative decline, reflecting the faster economic growth of several other economies, particularly in Asia. For example, as can be seen from Table 1.2, from 1963 to 2000, Japan's share of world output increased from 5.5 percent to 14.2 percent. Other countries that

Country	Share of World Output, 1963[†]	Share of World Output, 2000	Share of World Exports, 2000
United States	40.3%	27.0%	12.3 %
Japan	5.5	14.2	7.54
Germany[*]	9.7	7.3	8.7
France	6.3	5.2	4.7
United Kingdom	6.5	4.1	4.4
Italy	3.4	4.1	3.7
Canada	3.0	2.0	4.4
China	NA	3.2	3.92
South Korea	NA	1.4	2.7

Table 1.2

The Changing Pattern of World Output and Trade

[*]1963 figure for Germany refers to the former West Germany.

[†]Output is measured by gross national product.

Sources: Export data from World Trade Organization, *International Trade Trends and Statistics, 2000*; world output data from CIA *Factbook, 2001*.

markedly increased their share of world output included China, Thailand, Malaysia, Taiwan, and South Korea. By virtue of its huge population and rapid industrialization, China is emerging as a potential economic colossus.

By the end of the 1980s, the U.S. position as the world's leading exporter was threatened. Over the past 30 years, U.S. dominance in export markets has waned as Japan, Germany, and a number of newly industrialized countries such as South Korea and China have taken a larger share of world exports. During the 1960s, the United States routinely accounted for 20 percent of world exports of manufactured goods. But as Table 1.2 shows, the U.S. share of world exports of manufactured goods had slipped to 12.3 percent by 2000. Despite the fall, the United States still remained the world's largest exporter, ahead of Germany and Japan.

In 1997 and 1998 the dynamic economies of the Asian Pacific region were hit by a serious financial crisis that threatened to slow their economic growth rates for several years. Despite this, their powerful growth may continue over the long run, as will that of several other important emerging economies in Latin America (e.g., Brazil) and Eastern Europe (e.g., Poland). Thus, a further relative decline in the share of world output and world exports accounted for by the United States and other long-established developed nations seems likely. By itself, this is not a bad thing. The relative decline of the United States reflects the growing economic development and industrialization of the world economy, as opposed to any absolute decline in the health of the U.S. economy, which entered the new millennium stronger than ever.

If we look 20 years into the future, most forecasts now predict a rapid rise in the share of world output accounted for by developing nations such as China, India, Indonesia, Thailand, South Korea, and Brazil, and a commensurate decline in the share enjoyed by rich industrialized countries such as Great Britain, Germany, Japan, and the United States. The World Bank, for example, has estimated that if current trends continue, by 2020 the Chinese economy could be larger than that of the United States, while the economy of India will approach that of Germany. The World Bank also estimates that today's developing nations may account for over 60 percent of world economic activity by 2020, while today's rich nations, which currently account for over 55 percent of world economic activity, may account for only about 38 percent by 2020.[32] Forecasts are not always correct, but these suggest that a shift in the economic geography of the world is now under way, although the magnitude of that shift is still not totally evident. For international businesses, the implications of this changing economic geography are clear: many of tomorrow's economic opportunities may be found in the developing nations of the world, and many of tomorrow's most capable competitors will probably also emerge from these regions.

Figure 1.4

Percentage Share of Total FDI Stock, 1980–2000

Source: Data taken from the United Nations, *World Investment Report, 2001* (New York: United Nations, 2001).

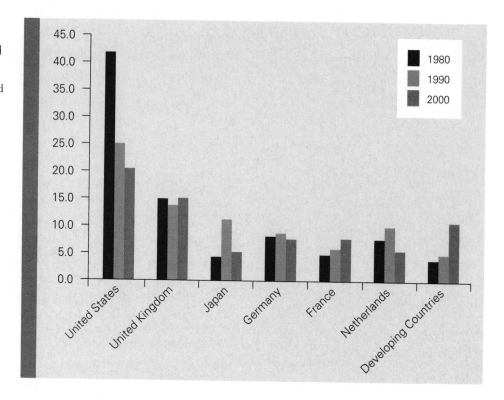

The Changing Foreign Direct Investment Picture

Reflecting the dominance of the United States in the global economy, U.S. firms accounted for 66.3 percent of worldwide foreign direct investment flows in the 1960s. British firms were second, accounting for 10.5 percent, while Japanese firms were a distant eighth, with only 2 percent. The dominance of U.S. firms was so great that books were written about the economic threat posed to Europe by U.S. corporations.[33] Several European governments, most notably that of France, talked of limiting inward investment by U.S. firms.

However, as the barriers to the free flow of goods, services, and capital fell, and as other countries increased their shares of world output, non-U.S. firms increasingly began to invest across national borders. The motivation for much of this foreign direct investment by non-U.S. firms was the desire to disperse production activities to optimal locations and to build a direct presence in major foreign markets. Thus, beginning in the 1970s, European and Japanese firms began to shift labor-intensive manufacturing operations from their home markets to developing nations where labor costs were lower. In addition, many Japanese firms invested in North America and Europe—often as a hedge against unfavorable currency movements and the possible imposition of trade barriers. For example, Toyota, the Japanese automobile company, rapidly increased its investment in automobile production facilities in the United States and Great Britain during the late 1980s and early 1990s. Toyota executives believed that an increasingly strong Japanese yen would price Japanese automobile exports out of foreign markets; therefore, production in the most important foreign markets, as opposed to exports from Japan, made sense. Toyota also undertook these investments to head off growing political pressures in the United States and Europe to restrict Japanese automobile exports into those markets.

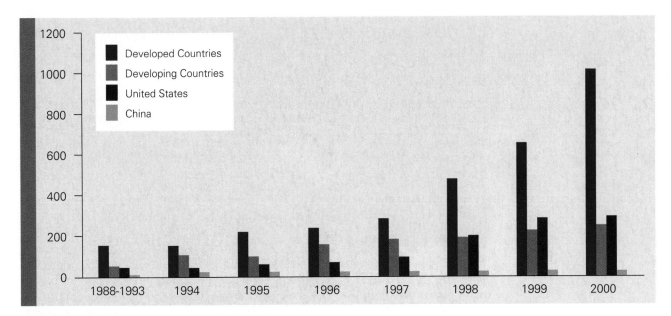

Figure 1.5

FDI Inflows, 1988–2000 (in $ billions)

Source: Data from the United Nations, *World Investment Report, 2001* (New York: United Nations, 2001).

One consequence of these developments is illustrated in Figure 1.4, which shows how the stock of foreign direct investment by the world's six most important national sources—the United States, United Kingdom, Japan, Germany, France, and the Netherlands—changed between 1980 and 1999. (The stock of foreign direct investment refers to the total cumulative value of foreign investments.) Figure 1.4 also shows the stock accounted for by firms from developing economies. The share of the total stock accounted for by U.S. firms declined substantially from about 42 percent in 1980 to 24 percent in 1999. Meanwhile, the shares accounted for by Japan, France, other developed nations, and the world's developing nations increased markedly. The rise in the share for developing nations reflects a growing trend for firms from these countries, such as South Korea, to invest outside their borders. In 1999 firms based in developing nations accounted for 9.9 percent of the stock of foreign direct investment, up from only 3.1 percent in 1980.

Figure 1.5 illustrates two other important trends—the continued rapid growth in cross-border flows of foreign direct investment and the emerging importance of developing nations as the destination of foreign direct investment. Throughout the 1990s, the amount of investment directed at both developed and developing nations increased dramatically, a trend that reflects the increasing internationalization of business corporations. Until 1998, developing nations were taking an increasingly large percentage share of this flow. This trend changed between 1998 and 2000, primarily due to the lingering effects of the 1997 Asian economic crisis and the resulting slump in economic activity in the region. Despite this slump, China retained its importance as the leading destination for foreign direct investment among developing economies, with about $40 billion in foreign investment flowing into this economy every year since the mid-1990s. In the long run, the flow of money into the developing world will probably reaccelerate, reflecting the economic opportunities in many of these nations.

❙ The Changing Nature of the Multinational Enterprise

A multinational enterprise is any business that has productive activities in two or more countries. Since the 1960s, there have been two notable trends in the demographics

Table 1.3

The National Composition
of the Largest
Multinationals

Sources: Figures for 1973 from Neil
Hood and John Young, *The
Economics of the Multinational
Enterprise* (New York: Longman,
1979). Figures for 1990 to 2000 from
United Nations, *World Investment
Report, 2001* (New York: United
Nations, 2001).

	1973	1990	1997	2000
United States	48.5%	31.5%	32.4%	26%
Japan	3.5	12	15.7	17
United Kingdom	18.8	16.8	6.6	8
France	7.3	10.4	9.8	13
Germany	8.1	8.9	12.7	12

of the multinational enterprise: (1) the rise of non-U.S. multinationals, particularly Japanese multinationals, and (2) the growth of mini-multinationals.

Non-U.S. Multinationals

In the 1960s, global business activity was dominated by large U.S. multinational corporations. With U.S. firms accounting for about two-thirds of foreign direct investment during the 1960s, one would expect most multinationals to be U.S. enterprises. According to the data summarized in Table 1.3, in 1973, 48.5 percent of the world's 260 largest multinationals were U.S. firms. The second largest source country was the United Kingdom, with 18.8 percent of the largest multinationals. Japan accounted for only 3.5 percent of the world's largest multinationals at the time. The large number of U.S. multinationals reflected U.S. economic dominance in the three decades after World War II, while the large number of British multinationals reflected that country's industrial dominance in the early decades of the 20th century.

By 1999, however, things had shifted significantly. U.S. firms accounted for 26 percent of the world's 100 largest multinationals, followed by Japan with 17 percent. France was third with 13 percent.[34] Although the 1973 data summarized in Table 1.3 are not strictly comparable with the data for the 1990s, they illustrate the trend. (The 1973 figures are based on the largest 260 firms, whereas the figures for the 1990s are based on the largest 100 multinationals.) The globalization of the world economy together with Japan's rise to the top rank of economic powers has resulted in a relative decline in the dominance of U.S. (and, to a lesser extent, British) firms in the global marketplace.

According to United Nations data, the ranks of the world's largest 100 multinationals are still dominated by firms from developed economies.[35] However, for the first time three firms from developing economies entered the UN's list of the 100 largest multinationals. They were Hutchison Whampoa of Hong Kong, China, which ranked 48 in terms of foreign assets, Petroleos de Venezuela of Venezuela, which ranked 84, and Cemex of Mexico, which came in at 100.[36] However, if we look at smaller firms, it is evident that there has been growth in the number of multinationals from developed economies. At the end of the 1990s, the largest 50 multinationals from developing economies had foreign sales of $103 billion out of total sales of $453 billion and employed 483,129 people outside of their home country. Some 22 percent of these companies came from Hong Kong, 16.7 percent from Korea, 8.8 percent from China, and 7.6 percent from Brazil. Looking to the future, we can reasonably expect growth of new multinational enterprises from the world's developing nations.

The Rise of Mini-Multinationals

Another trend in international business has been the growth of medium-sized and small multinationals (mini-multinationals). When people think of international businesses, they tend to think of firms such as Exxon, General Motors, Ford, Fuji, Kodak, Matsushita, Procter & Gamble, Sony, and Unilever—large, complex multinational corporations with operations that span the globe. Although it is certainly true that most international trade and investment is still conducted by large firms, it is also true that many medium-sized and small businesses are becoming increasingly involved in international trade and investment. We have already discussed several examples in this chapter—Swan Optical, Bridgewater Pottery, and Cardiac Science—and we have noted how the rise of the Internet is lowering the barriers that small firms face in building international sales.

For another example, consider Lubricating Systems, Inc., of Kent, Washington. Lubricating Systems, which manufactures lubricating fluids for machine tools, employs 25 people and generates sales of $6.5 million. It's hardly a large, complex multinational, yet more than $2 million of the company's sales are generated by exports to a score of countries from Japan to Israel and the United Arab Emirates. Lubricating Systems also has set up a joint venture with a German company to serve the European market.[37] Consider also Lixi, Inc., a small U.S. manufacturer of industrial X-ray equipment; 70 percent of Lixi's $4.5 million in revenues comes from exports to Japan.[38] Or take G. W. Barth, a manufacturer of cocoa-bean roasting machinery based in Ludwigsburg, Germany. Employing just 65 people, this small company has captured 70 percent of the global market for cocoa-bean roasting machines.[39] International business is conducted not just by large firms but also by medium-sized and small enterprises.

▌The Changing World Order

Between 1989 and 1991 a series of remarkable democratic revolutions swept the Communist world. For reasons that are explored in more detail in Chapter 2, in country after country throughout Eastern Europe and eventually in the Soviet Union itself, Communist governments collapsed like the shells of rotten eggs. The Soviet Union is now history, having been replaced by 15 independent republics. Czechoslovakia has divided itself into two states, while Yugoslavia has dissolved into a bloody civil war among its five successor states.

Many of the former Communist nations of Europe and Asia seem to share a commitment to democratic politics and free market economics. If this continues, the opportunities for international businesses may be enormous. For the best part of half a century, these countries were essentially closed to Western international businesses. Now they present a host of export and investment opportunities. Just how this will play out over the next 10 to 20 years is difficult to say. The economies of most of the former Communist states are in very poor condition, and their continued commitment to democracy and free market economics cannot be taken for granted. Disturbing signs of growing unrest and totalitarian tendencies continue to be seen in many Eastern European states. Thus, the risks involved in doing business in such countries are very high, but then, so may be the returns.

In addition to these changes, more quiet revolutions have been occurring in China and Latin America. Their implications for international businesses may be just as profound as the collapse of communism in Eastern Europe. China suppressed its own prodemocracy movement in the bloody Tiananmen Square massacre of 1989. Despite this, China continues to move progressively toward greater free market reforms. If what is occurring in China continues for two more decades, China may move from Third World to industrial superpower status even more rapidly than Japan did. If China's gross domestic product (GDP) per capita grows by an average of 6 percent to 7 percent, which is slower than the 8 percent growth rate achieved during the last decade, then by 2020 this nation of 1.273 billion people could boast an average income per capita of about $13,000, roughly equivalent to that of Spain's today.

The potential consequences for Western international business are enormous. On the one hand, with 1.2 billion people, China represents a huge and largely untapped market. Reflecting this, between 1983 and 2000, annual foreign direct investment in China increased from less than $2 billion to $40 billion. On the other hand, China's new firms are proving to be very capable competitors, and they could take global market share away from Western and Japanese enterprises. Thus, the changes in China are creating both opportunities and threats for established international businesses.

As for Latin America, both democracy and free market reforms also seem to have taken hold. For decades, most Latin American countries were ruled by dictators, many of whom seemed to view Western international businesses as instruments of imperialist domination. Accordingly, they restricted direct investment by foreign firms. In addition, the poorly managed economies of Latin America were characterized by low growth, high debt, and hyperinflation—all of which discouraged investment by international businesses. Now much of this seems to be changing. Throughout most of Latin America, debt and inflation are down, governments are selling state-owned enterprises to private investors, foreign investment is welcomed, and the region's economies are growing rapidly. These changes have increased the attractiveness of Latin America, both as a market for exports and as a site for foreign direct investment. At the same time, given the long history of economic mismanagement in Latin America, there is no guarantee that these favorable trends will continue. As in the case of Eastern Europe, substantial opportunities are accompanied by substantial risks.

The Global Economy of the 21st Century

The last quarter of century has seen rapid changes in the global economy. Barriers to the free flow of goods, services, and capital have been coming down. The volume of cross-border trade and investment has been growing more rapidly than global output, indicating that national economies are becoming more closely integrated into a single, interdependent, global economic system. As their economies advance, more nations are joining the ranks of the developed world. A generation ago, South Korea and Taiwan were viewed as second-tier developing nations. Now they boast large economies, and their firms are major players in many global industries from shipbuilding and steel to electronics and chemicals. The move toward a global economy has been further strengthened by the widespread adoption of liberal economic policies by countries that for two generations or more were firmly opposed to them. Thus, following the normative prescriptions of liberal economic ideology, in country after country we are seeing state-owned businesses privatized, widespread deregulation, markets being opened to more competition, and increased commitment to removing barriers to cross-border trade and investment. This suggests that over the next few decades, countries such as the Czech Republic, Poland, Brazil, China, and South Africa may build powerful market-oriented economies. In short, current trends indicate that the world is moving rapidly toward an economic system that is more favorable for the practice of international business.

On the other hand, it is always hazardous to take established trends and use them to predict the future. The world may be moving toward a more global economic system, but globalization is not inevitable. Countries may pull back from the recent commitment to liberal economic ideology if their experiences do not match their expectations. There are signs, for example, of a retreat from liberal economic ideology in Russia. Russia has experienced considerable economic pain as it tries to shift from a centrally planned economy to a market economy. If Russia's hesitation were to become more permanent and widespread, the liberal vision of a more prosperous global economy based on free market principles might not come to pass as quickly as many hope. Clearly, this would be a tougher world for international businesses to compete in.

Moreover, greater globalization brings with it risks of its own. This was starkly demonstrated in 1997 and 1998 when a financial crisis in Thailand spread first to other East Asian nations and then in 1998 to Russia and Brazil. Ultimately the crisis threatened to plunge the economies of the developed world, including the United States, into a recession. We explore the causes and consequences of this and other similar global financial crises in Chapters 10 and 11. For now it is simply worth noting that even from a purely economic perspective, globalization is not all good. The opportunities for doing business in a global economy may be significantly enhanced, but as we saw in 1997–98, the risks associated with global financial contagion are also greater. Still, as explained later in this book, there are ways for firms to exploit the opportunities associated with globalization, while at the same time reducing the risks through appropriate hedging strategies.

The Globalization Debate ▮

Is the shift toward a more integrated and interdependent global economy a good thing? Many influential economists, politicians, and business leaders seem to think so. They argue that falling barriers to international trade and investment are the twin engines driving the global economy toward greater prosperity. They say increased international trade and cross-border investment will result in lower prices for goods and services. They believe that globalization stimulates economic growth, raises the incomes of consumers, and helps to create jobs in all countries that participate in the global trading system.

The arguments of those who support globalization are covered in detail in Chapters 4, 5, 6, and 8. As we shall see, there are good theoretical reasons for believing that declining barriers to international trade and investment do stimulate economic growth, create jobs, and raise income levels. As described in Chapters 5 to 7, empirical evidence lends support to the predictions of this theory. However, despite the existence of a compelling body of theory and evidence, globalization has its critics.[40] Some of these critics have become increasingly vocal and active, taking to the streets to demonstrate their opposition to globalization. Here we look at the rising tide of protests against globalization and briefly review the main themes of the debate concerning the merits of globalization. In later chapters we elaborate on many of the points mentioned below.

▮Antiglobalization Protests

Street demonstrations against globalization date to December 1999, when over 40,000 protesters blocked the streets of Seattle in an attempt to shut down a World Trade Organization meeting being held in the city. The demonstrators were protesting against a wide range of issues, including job losses in industries under attack from foreign competitors, downward pressure on the wage rates of unskilled workers, environmental degradation, and the cultural imperialism of global media and multinational enterprises, which was seen as being dominated by what some protesters called the "culturally impoverished" interests and values of the United States. All of these ills, the demonstrators claimed, could be laid at the feet of globalization. The World Trade Organization was meeting to try to launch a new round of talks to cut barriers to cross-border trade and investment. As such, it was seen as a promoter of globalization and a legitimate target for the antiglobalization protesters. The protests turned violent, transforming the normally placid streets of Seattle into a running battle between "anarchists" and Seattle's bemused and poorly prepared police department. Pictures of brick-throwing protesters and armored police wielding their batons were duly recorded by the global media, which then circulated the images around the world. Meanwhile, the World Trade Organization meeting failed to reach agreement, and although the protests outside the meetings halls had little to do with that failure, the impression took hold that the demonstrators had succeeded in derailing the meetings.

Emboldened by the experience in Seattle, antiglobalization protesters have turned up at almost every major meeting of a global institution. In February 2000, they demonstrated at the World Economic Forum meetings in Davos, Switzerland, and vented their frustrations against global capitalism by trashing that hated symbol of

U.S. imperialism, a McDonald's restaurant. In April 2000, demonstrators disrupted talks being held at the World Bank and International Monetary Fund, and in September 2000, 12,000 demonstrated at the annual meeting of the World Bank and IMF in Prague. In April 2001, demonstrations and police firing tear gas and water cannons overshadowed the "Summit of the Americas" meeting in Quebec City, Canada. In June 2001, 40,000 protesters marched against globalization at the European Union summit in Göteborg, Sweden. The march was peaceful until a core of masked anarchists wielding cobblestones created bloody mayhem. In July 2001, antiglobalization protests in Genoa, Italy, where the heads of the eight largest economies were meeting (the so-called G8 meetings), turned violent, and in the now familiar ritual of running battles between protesters and police, a protester was killed, giving the antiglobalization movement its first martyr. Smaller scale protests have occurred in several countries, such as France, where antiglobalization protesters destroyed a McDonald's restaurant in August 1999 to protest the impoverishment of French culture by American imperialism (see the accompanying Country Focus for details).

While violent protests may give the antiglobalization effort a bad name, it is clear from the scale of the demonstrations that support for the cause goes beyond a core of anarchists. Large sections of the population in many countries believe that globalization has detrimental effects on living standards and the environment. Both theory and evidence suggest these fears are exaggerated, but this may not have been communicated clearly enough, and both politicians and businesspeople need to do more to counter these fears. Many protests against globalization are tapping into a general sense of loss at the passing of a world in which barriers of time and distance, and vast differences in economic institutions, political institutions, and the level of development of different nations, produced a world rich in the diversity of human cultures. This world is now passing into history. However, while the rich citizens of the developed world may have the luxury of mourning the fact that they can now see McDonald's restaurants and Starbucks coffeehouses on their vacations to exotic locations such as Thailand, few complaints are heard from the citizens of those countries, who welcome the higher living standards that progress brings.

Globalization, Jobs, and Income

One concern frequently voiced by opponents of globalization is that falling barriers to international trade destroy manufacturing jobs in wealthy advanced economies such as the United States and the United Kingdom. The critics argue that falling trade barriers allow firms to move their manufacturing activities to countries where wage rates are much lower.[41] D. L. Bartlett and J. B. Steele, two journalists for the *Philadelphia Inquirer* who have gained notoriety for their attacks on free trade, cite the case of Harwood Industries, a U.S. clothing manufacturer that closed its U.S. operations, where it paid workers $9 per hour, and shifted manufacturing to Honduras, where textile workers receive 48 cents per hour.[42] Because of moves like this, argue Bartlett and Steele, the wage rates of poorer Americans have fallen significantly over the last quarter of a century.

Supporters of globalization reply that critics such as Bartlett and Steele miss the essential point about free trade—the benefits outweigh the costs.[43] They argue that free trade will result in countries specializing in the production of those goods and services that they can produce most efficiently, while importing goods that they cannot produce as efficiently. When a country embraces free trade, there is always some dislocation—lost textile jobs at Harwood Industries, for example—but the whole economy is better off as a result. According to this view, it makes little sense for the United States to produce textiles at home when they can be produced at a lower cost in Honduras or China (which, unlike Honduras, is a major source of U.S. textile imports). Importing textiles from China leads to lower prices for clothes in the United States, which enables consumers to spend more of their money on other items. At the same time, the

Country Focus

Antiglobalization Protests in France

One night in August 1999, 10 men under the leadership of local sheep farmer and rural activist Jose Bove crept into the town of Millau in central France and vandalized a McDonald's restaurant under construction, causing an estimated $150,000 worth of damage. These were no ordinary vandals, however, at least according to their supporters, for the "symbolic dismantling" of the McDonald's outlet had noble aims, or so it was claimed. The attack was initially presented as a protest against unfair American trade policies. The European Union had banned imports of hormone-treated beef from the United States, primarily because of fears that hormone-treated beef might lead to health problems (although EU scientists had concluded there was no evidence of this). After a careful review, the World Trade Organization stated the EU ban was not allowed under trading rules that the EU and United States were party to, and that the EU would have to lift it or face retaliation. The EU refused to comply, so the U.S. government imposed a 100 percent tariff on imports of certain EU products, including French staples such as foie gras, mustard, and Roquefort cheese. On farms near Millau, Bove and others raised sheep whose milk was used to make Roquefort. They felt incensed by the American tariff and decided to vent their frustrations on McDonald's.

Bove and his compatriots were arrested and charged. They quickly became a focus of the emerging antiglobalization movement in France that was protesting everything from a loss of national sovereignty and "unfair" trade policies that were trying to force hormone-treated beef on French consumers, to the invasion of French culture by alien American values, so aptly symbolized by McDonald's. Lionel Jospin, France's prime Minister, called the cause of Jose Bove "just." Allowed to remain free pending his trial, Bove traveled to Seattle in December to protest against the World Trade Organization, where he was feted as a hero of the antiglobalization movement. Back in France, Bove's July 2000 trial drew some 40,000 supporters to the small town of Millau, where they camped outside the courthouse and waited for the verdict. Bove was found guilty and sentenced to three months in jail, far less than the maximum possible sentence of five years. His supporters wore T-shirts claiming, "The world is not merchandise, and neither am I."

About the same time in the Languedoc region of France, California winemaker Robert Mondavi had reached agreement with the mayor and council of the village of Aniane and regional authorities to turn 125 acres of wooded hillside belonging to the village into a vineyard. Mondavi planned to invest $7 million in the project and hoped to produce top quality wine that would sell in Europe and the United States for $60 a bottle. However, local environmentalists objected to the plan, which they claimed would destroy the area's unique ecological heritage. Jose Bove, basking in sudden fame, offered his support to the opponents, and the protests started. In May 2001, the Socialist mayor who had approved the project was defeated in local elections in which the Mondavi project had become the major issue. He was replaced by a Communist, Manuel Diaz, who denounced the project as a capitalist plot designed to enrich wealthy U.S. shareholders at the cost of his villagers and the environment. Following Diaz's victory, Mondavi announced he would pull out of the project. A spokesman noted, "It's a huge waste, but there are clearly personal and political interests at play here that go way beyond us."

So are the French opposed to foreign investment? The experience of McDonald's and Mondavi seems to suggest so, as does the associated news coverage, but look closer and a different reality seems to emerge. McDonald's has over 800 restaurants in France and continues to do well there. The level of foreign investment in France reached record levels in the late 1990s and 2000. In 2000, France recorded 563 major inward investment deals, a record, and American companies accounted for the largest number, some 178. French enterprises are also investing across borders at record levels. Given all of the talk about American cultural imperialism, it is striking that a French company, Vivendi, now owns two of the propagators of American cultural values: Universal Pictures and publisher Houghton Mifflin. And for all of their bluster, French politicians seem set on removing domestic barriers that make it difficult for French companies to compete effectively in the global economy.

Sources: "Behind the Bluster," *The Economist,* May 26, 2001; "The French Farmers' Anti-global Hero," *The Economist,* July 8, 2000; C. Trueheart, "France's Golden Arch Enemy?" *Toronto Star,* July 1, 2000; and J. Henley, "Grapes of Wrath Scare off U.S. Firm," *The Economist,* May 18, 2001, p. 11.

increased income generated in China from textile exports increases income levels in that country, which helps the Chinese to purchase more products produced in the United States, such as Boeing jets, Intel-based computers, Microsoft software, and Motorola cellular telephones. In this manner, supporters of globalization argue that free trade benefits all countries that adhere to a free trade regime.

Supporters of globalization do concede that the wage rate enjoyed by unskilled workers in many advanced economies may have declined in recent years.[44] For example, data for the Organization for Economic Cooperation and Development suggest that since 1980 the lowest 10 percent of American workers have seen a drop in their real wages (adjusted for inflation) of about 20 percent, while the top 10 percent have enjoyed a real pay increase of around 10 percent.[45] In the same vein, a Federal Reserve study found that in the seven years preceding 1996, the earnings of the best paid 10 percent of U.S. workers rose in real terms by 0.6 percent annually while the earnings of the 10 percent at the bottom of the heap fell by 8 percent. In some areas, the fall was much greater.[46] Similar trends can be seen in many other countries.

However, while globalization critics argue that the decline in unskilled wage rates is due to the migration of low-wage manufacturing jobs offshore and a corresponding reduction in demand for unskilled workers, supporters of globalization see a more complex picture. They maintain that the declining real wage rates of unskilled workers owes far more to a technology-induced shift within advanced economies away from jobs where the only qualification was a willingness to turn up for work every day and toward jobs that require significant education and skills. They point out that many advanced economies report a shortage of highly skilled workers and an excess supply of unskilled workers. Thus, growing income inequality is a result of the wages for skilled workers being bid up by the labor market, and the wages for unskilled workers being discounted. If one agrees with this logic, a solution to the problem of declining incomes is to be found not in limiting free trade and globalization, but in increasing society's investment in education to reduce the supply of unskilled workers.[47]

Research also suggests that the evidence of growing income inequality may be suspect. Robert Lerman of the Urban Institute believes that the finding of inequality is based on inappropriate calculations of wage rates. Reviewing the data using a different methodology, Lerman has found that far from income inequality increasing, an index of wage rate inequality for all workers actually fell by 5.5 percent between 1987 and 1994.[48] If future research supports this finding, the argument that globalization leads to growing income inequality may lose much of its punch. During the last few years of the 1990s, the income of the worst paid 10 percent of the population actually rose twice as fast as that of the average worker, suggesting that the high employment levels of these years have triggered a rise in the income of the lowest paid.[49]

Globalization, Labor Policies, and the Environment

A second source of concern is that free trade encourages firms from advanced nations to move manufacturing facilities to less developed countries that lack adequate regulations to protect labor and the environment from abuse by the unscrupulous.[50] Globalization critics often argue that adhering to labor and environmental regulations significantly increases the costs of manufacturing enterprises and puts them at a competitive disadvantage in the global marketplace vis-à-vis firms based in developing nations that do not have to comply with such regulations. Firms deal with this cost disadvantage, the theory goes, by moving their production facilities to nations that do not have such burdensome regulations or that fail to enforce the regulations they have.

If this is the case, one might expect free trade to lead to an increase in pollution and result in firms from advanced nations exploiting the labor of less developed nations.[51] This argument was used repeatedly by those who opposed the 1994 formation of the North American Free Trade Agreement (NAFTA) between Canada,

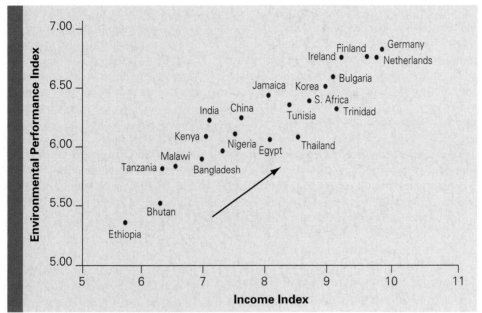

Figure 1.6

Environmental
Performance and Income

Source: *Environmental Performance
and Income* (Paris: 2000 OECD).

Mexico, and the United States. They painted a picture of U.S. manufacturing firms moving to Mexico in droves so that they would be free to pollute the environment, employ child labor, and ignore workplace safety and health issues, all in the name of higher profits.[52]

Supporters of free trade and greater globalization express serious doubts about this scenario. They point out that tougher environmental regulations and stricter labor standards go hand in hand with economic progress.[53] In general, as countries get richer, they enact tougher environmental and labor regulations.[54] Because free trade enables developing countries to increase their economic growth rates and become richer, this should lead to tougher environmental and labor laws. In this view, the critics of free trade have got it backward—free trade does not lead to more pollution and labor exploitation, it leads to less. By creating wealth and incentives for enterprises to produce technological innovations, the free market system and free trade could make it easier for the world to cope with problems of pollution and population growth. Indeed, while pollution levels are rising in the world's poorer countries, they have been falling in developed nations. In the United States, for example, the concentration of carbon monoxide and sulphur dioxide pollutants in the atmosphere decreased by 60 percent between 1978 and 1997, while lead concentrations decreased by 98 percent—and these reductions have occurred against a background of sustained economic expansion.[55] Drawn from a study undertaken for the Organization for Economic Cooperation and Development, Figure 1.6 shows there is a clear positive relationship between the income levels in a country and the environmental performance of that country as measured by various indicators.

Supporters of free trade also point out that it is possible to tie free trade agreements to the implementation of tougher environmental and labor laws in less developed countries. NAFTA, for example, was passed only after side agreements had been negotiated that committed Mexico to tougher enforcement of environmental protection regulations. Thus, supporters of free trade argue that factories based in Mexico are now cleaner than they would have been without the passage of NAFTA.[56]

They also argue that business firms are not the amoral organizations that critics suggest. While there may be a few rotten apples, most business enterprises are staffed by managers who are committed to behave in an ethical manner and would be unlikely to move production offshore just so they could pump more pollution into the atmosphere or exploit labor. Furthermore, the relationship between pollution, labor exploitation, and production costs may not be that suggested by critics. In general, a well-treated labor force is productive, and it is productivity rather than base wage rates that often has the greatest influence on costs. The vision of greedy managers who shift production to low-wage countries to exploit their labor force may be misplaced.

Globalization and National Sovereignty

Another concern voiced by critics of globalization is that today's increasingly interdependent global economy shifts economic power away from national governments and toward supranational organizations such as the World Trade Organization, the European Union, and the United Nations. As perceived by critics, unelected bureaucrats now impose policies on the democratically elected governments of nation-states, thereby undermining the sovereignty of those states and limiting the nation-state's ability to control its own destiny.[57]

The World Trade Organization (WTO) is a favorite target of those who attack the headlong rush toward a global economy. The WTO was founded in 1994 to police the world trading system established by the General Agreement on Tariffs and Trade. The WTO arbitrates trade disputes between the 140 or so states that are signatories to the GATT. The arbitration panel can issue a ruling instructing a member state to change trade policies that violate GATT regulations. If the violator refuses to comply with the ruling, the WTO allows other states to impose appropriate trade sanctions on the transgressor. As a result, according to one prominent critic, U.S. environmentalist and consumer rights advocate Ralph Nader:

> Under the new system, many decisions that affect billions of people are no longer made by local or national governments but instead, if challenged by any WTO member nation, would be deferred to a group of unelected bureaucrats sitting behind closed doors in Geneva (which is where the headquarters of the WTO are located). The bureaucrats can decide whether or not people in California can prevent the destruction of the last virgin forests or determine if carcinogenic pesticides can be banned from their foods; or whether European countries have the right to ban dangerous biotech hormones in meat . . . At risk is the very basis of democracy and accountable decision making.[58]

In contrast to Nader's rhetoric, many economists and politicians maintain that the power of supranational organizations such as the WTO is limited to that which nation-states collectively agree to grant. They argue that bodies such as the United Nations and the WTO exist to serve the collective interests of member states, not to subvert those interests. Supporters of supranational organizations point out that the power of these bodies rests largely on their ability to persuade member states to follow a certain action. If these bodies fail to serve the collective interests of member states, those states will withdraw their support and the supranational organization will quickly collapse. In this view, real power still resides with individual nation-states, not supranational organizations.

Globalization and the World's Poor

Critics of globalization argue that despite the supposed benefits associated with free trade and investment, over the last hundred years or so the gap between the rich and poor nations of the world has gotten wider. In 1870 the average income per capita in the world's 17 richest nations was 2.4 times that of all other countries. In 1990 the same group was 4.5 times as rich as the rest.[59] While recent history has shown that some of the world's poorer nations are capable of rapid periods of economic growth—witness the transformation that has occurred in some Southeast Asian nations such as

South Korea, Thailand, and Malaysia—there appear to be strong forces for stagnation among the world's poorest nations. A quarter of the countries with a GDP per capita of less than $1,000 in 1960 had growth rates of less than zero from 1960 to 1995, and a third had growth rates of less than 0.05 percent.[60] Critics argue that if globalization is such a positive development, this divergence between the rich and poor should not have occurred.

Although the reasons for economic stagnation vary, several factors stand out, none of which have anything to do with free trade or globalization. Many of the world's poorest countries have suffered from totalitarian governments, economic policies that destroyed wealth rather than facilitated its creation, scant protection for property rights, and war. Such factors help explain why countries such as Afghanistan, Cambodia, Cuba, Haiti, Iraq, Libya, Nigeria, Sudan, Vietnam, and Zaire have failed to improve the economic lot of their citizens during recent decades. A complicating factor is the rapidly expanding populations in many of these countries. Without a major change in government, population growth may exacerbate their problems. Promoters of free trade argue that the best way for these countries to improve their lot is to lower their barriers to free trade and investment and to implement economic policies based on free market economics.[61]

Managing in the Global Marketplace

Much of this book is concerned with the challenges of managing in an international business. An **international business** is any firm that engages in international trade or investment. A firm does not have to become a multinational enterprise, investing directly in operations in other countries, to engage in international business, although multinational enterprises are international businesses. All a firm has to do is export or import products from other countries. As the world shifts toward a truly integrated global economy, more firms, both large and small, are becoming international businesses. What does this shift toward a global economy mean for managers within an international business?

As their organizations increasingly engage in cross-border trade and investment, it means managers need to recognize that the task of managing an international business differs from that of managing a purely domestic business in many ways. At the most fundamental level, the differences arise from the simple fact that countries are different. Countries differ in their cultures, political systems, economic systems, legal systems, and levels of economic development. Despite all the talk about the emerging global village, and despite the trend toward globalization of markets and production, as we shall see in this book, many of these differences are very profound and enduring.

Differences between countries require that an international business vary its practices country by country. Marketing a product in Brazil may require a different approach than marketing the product in Germany; managing U.S. workers might require different skills than managing Japanese workers; maintaining close relations with a particular level of government may be very important in Mexico and irrelevant in Great Britain; the business strategy pursued in Canada might not work in South Korea; and so on. Managers in an international business must not only be sensitive to these differences, but they must also adopt the appropriate policies and strategies for coping with them. Much of this book is devoted to explaining the sources of these differences and the methods for coping with them successfully.

A further way in which international business differs from domestic business is the greater complexity of managing an international business. In addition to the problems that arise from the differences between countries, a manager in an international business is confronted with a range of other issues that the manager in a domestic business never confronts. An international business must decide where in the world to site its production activities to minimize costs and to maximize value added. Then it must decide how best to coordinate and control its globally dispersed production activities (which, as we shall see later in the book, is not a trivial problem). An international business also must decide which foreign markets to enter and which to avoid. It also must choose the appropriate mode for entering a particular foreign country. Is it best to export its product to the foreign country? Should the firm allow a local company to produce its product under license in that country? Should the firm enter into a joint venture with a local firm to produce its product in that country? Or should the firm set up a wholly owned subsidiary to serve the market in that country? As we shall see, the choice of entry mode is critical because it has major implications for the long-term health of the firm.

Conducting business transactions across national borders requires understanding the rules governing the international trading and investment system. Managers in an international business must also deal with government restrictions on international trade and investment. They must find ways to work within the limits imposed by specific governmental interventions. As this book explains, even though many governments are nominally committed to free trade, they often intervene to regulate cross-border trade and investment. Managers within international businesses must develop strategies and policies for dealing with such interventions.

Cross-border transactions also require that money be converted from the firm's home currency into a foreign currency and vice versa. Since currency exchange rates vary in response to changing economic conditions, an international business must develop policies for dealing with exchange rate movements. A firm that adopts a wrong policy can lose large amounts of money, while a firm that adopts the right policy can increase the profitability of its international transactions.

In sum, managing an international business is different from managing a purely domestic business for at least four reasons: (1) countries are different, (2) the range of problems confronted by a manager in an international business is wider, and the problems themselves more complex than those confronted by a manager in a domestic business, (3) an international business must find ways to work within the limits imposed by government intervention in the international trade and investment system, and (4) international transactions involve converting money into different currencies.

In this book we examine all these issues in depth, paying close attention to the different strategies and policies that managers pursue to deal with the various challenges created when a firm becomes an international business. Chapters 2 and 3 explore how countries differ from each other with regard to their political, economic, legal, and cultural institutions. Chapters 4 to 8 look at the international trade and investment environment within which international businesses must operate. Chapters 9 through 11 review the international monetary system. These chapters focus on the nature of the foreign exchange market and the emerging global monetary system. Chapters 12 to 14 explore the strategies and structures of international businesses. Then Chapters 15 to 20 look at the management of various functional operations within an international business, including production, marketing, human relations, finance, and accounting. By the time you complete this book, you should have a good grasp of the issues that managers working within international business have to grapple with on a daily basis, and you should be familiar with the range of strategies and operating policies available to compete more effectively in today's rapidly emerging global economy.

Chapter Summary

This chapter sets the scene for the rest of the book. We have seen how the world economy is becoming more global, and we have reviewed the main drivers of globalization and argued that they seem to be thrusting nation-states toward a more tightly integrated global economy. We have looked at how the nature of international business is changing in response to the changing global economy; we have discussed some concerns raised by rapid globalization; and we have reviewed implications of rapid globalization for individual managers. These major points were made in the chapter:

1. Over the past two decades, we have witnessed the globalization of markets and production.

2. The globalization of markets implies that national markets are merging into one huge marketplace. However, it is important not to push this view too far.

3. The globalization of production implies that firms are basing individual productive activities at the optimal world locations for the particular activities. As a consequence, it is increasingly irrelevant to talk about American products, Japanese products, or German products, since these are being replaced by "global" products.

4. Two factors seem to underlie the trend toward globalization: declining trade barriers and changes in communication, information, and transportation technologies.

5. Since the end of World War II, there has been a significant lowering of barriers to the free flow of goods, services, and capital. More than anything else, this has facilitated the trend toward the globalization of production and has enabled firms to view the world as a single market.

6. As a consequence of the globalization of production and markets, in the last decade world trade has grown faster than world output, foreign direct investment has surged, imports have penetrated more deeply into the world's industrial nations, and competitive pressures have increased in industry after industry.

7. The development of the microprocessor and related developments in communication and information processing technology have helped firms link their worldwide operations into sophisticated information networks. Jet air travel, by shrinking travel time, has also helped to link the worldwide operations of international businesses. These changes have enabled firms to achieve tight coordination of their worldwide operations and to view the world as a single market.

8. In the 1960s, the U.S. economy was dominant in the world, U.S. firms accounted for most of the foreign direct investment in the world economy, U.S. firms dominated the list of large multinationals, and roughly half the world—the centrally planned economies of the Communist world—was closed to Western businesses.

9. By the mid-1990s, the U.S. share of world output had been cut in half, with major shares now being accounted for by Western European and Southeast Asian economies. The U.S. share of worldwide foreign direct investment had also fallen, by about two-thirds. U.S. multinationals were now facing competition from a large number of Japanese and European multinationals. In addition, the emergence of mini-multinationals was noted.

10. The most dramatic environmental trend has been the collapse of Communist power in Eastern Europe, which has created enormous long-run opportunities for international businesses. In addition, the move toward free market economies in China and Latin America is creating opportunities (and threats) for Western international businesses.

11. The benefits and costs of the emerging global economy are being hotly debated among businesspeople, economists, and politicians. The debate focuses on the impact of globalization on jobs, wages, the environment, working conditions, and national sovereignty.

12. Managing an international business is different from managing a domestic business for at least four reasons: (*i*) countries are different, (*ii*) the range of problems confronted by a manager in an international business is wider and the problems themselves more complex than those confronted by a manager in a domestic business, (*iii*) managers in an international business must find ways to work within the limits imposed by governments' intervention in the international trade and investment system, and (*iv*) international transactions involve converting money into different currencies.

Critical Discussion Questions

1. Describe the shifts in the world economy over the past 30 years. What are the implications of these shifts for international businesses based in Great Britain? North America? Hong Kong?

2. "The study of international business is fine if you are going to work in a large multinational enterprise, but it has no relevance for individuals who are going to work in small firms." Evaluate this statement.

3. How have changes in technology contributed to the globalization of markets and production? Would the globalization of production and markets have been possible without these technological changes?

4. "Ultimately, the study of international business is no different from the study of domestic business. Thus, there is no point in having a separate course on international business." Evaluate this statement.

5. How might the Internet and the associated World Wide Web affect international business activity and the globalization of the world economy?

6. If current trends continue, China may be the world's largest economy by 2050. Discuss the possible implications for such a development for
   a. The world trading system.
   b. The world monetary system.
   c. The business strategy of today's European and U.S.-based global corporations.

Closing Case

Dixon Ticonderoga—Victim of Globalization?

Dixon Ticonderoga is one of the oldest public companies in the United States. The company's flagship product is the ubiquitous No. 2 yellow pencil, introduced in 1913, which is known to almost anyone who went to school or took standardized tests in the United States. With annual revenues of a little over $100 million, Dixon is the second largest pencil manufacturer in the country. For most of its history, Dixon has been a prosperous company, but the 1990s proved to be a very difficult decade. It's not that people are no longer buying pencils—in fact, demand for pencils in the United States has soared. Americans bought an estimated 4.2 billion pencils in 1999, a 53 percent jump from 1991. But an increasing proportion of these pencils have been from China.

The problem began in the early 1990s when Chinese manufacturers entered the market with low-priced pencils. The pencil industry fought back, arguing that the Chinese were dumping pencils on the U.S. market at below cost and lobbying Washington for protection. In 1994, when foreign pencil imports accounted for 16 percent of the market, the United States enacted heavy antidumping duties on Chinese pencils, effectively raising their price. Imports fell dramatically, but the Chinese kept making better, cheaper pencils, and after a couple of years imports returned to the levels attained before the imposition of duties. Nor did it stop there. In 1999, U.S. manufacturers shipped some 2.2 billion pencils domestically, down from 2.4 billion in 1991. During that time, imports jumped from 16 percent to over 50 percent of the market, with China leading the importers. The pencil industry continued to lobby for protection, and in mid-2000, the United States renewed duties on pencil imports from China, imposing import tariffs as high as 53 percent on some brands.

In the meantime, Dixon was not standing still. To try to meet the foreign competition on price, Dixon experimented with cheaper ways to make pencils. The com-

pany tried to make pencils out of recycled paper cases, but quickly backed away after the product jammed pencil sharpeners. Then the company looked at the wood used to make pencils—traditionally California incense cedar—and decided it was too expensive for all but the company's premium brand. Now the company uses lower priced Indonesian jelutong wood. As an additional cost reduction measure instituted in the late 1990s, Dixon started to buy the erasers for its pencils from a Korean supplier, rather than its traditional U.S. supplier.

Despite these steps, the company continued to lose share to imports, and by 1999 it was beginning to lose money, too. Realizing that it could bring in finished pencils cheaper than it could manufacture them in the United States, Dixon established a manufacturing operation in Mexico. The original idea behind the Mexican operation was to supplement its U.S. manufacturing, but in late 2000 the company realized it needed to be more aggressive and switched many of its processes from the United States to Mexico, cutting some 40 jobs at its U.S. facility. In another strategic move, in 2000 Dixon created a wholly-owned subsidiary in China. This subsidiary manufactures wooden slats for pencil manufacturing. The slats are then sent to Mexico, where they are turned into pencils. The lead for the pencils (carbon) is still made in the United States by Dixon, while the erasers are shipped from Korea. The Chinese subsidiary is also responsible for the production and distribution of certain products that are sold internationally.

Case Discussion Questions

1. Why do you think that the Chinese apparently have a cost advantage in the production of pencils?

2. Do you think that lobbying the U.S. government to impose antidumping duties on imports of pencils from China is a good way to protect American jobs? Who benefits most from such duties, who

loses? What alternative policy stance might the government take?

3. Dixon is now a multinational company. Why has Dixon become a multinational? What are the economic benefits to Dixon of becoming an international business?

4. Now that Dixon has a production operation in China, why does it not simply import finished pencils from China to the United States, instead of making those pencils in Mexico?

Notes

1. T. Levitt, "The Globalization of Markets," *Harvard Business Review*, May–June 1983, pp. 92–102.
2. C. M. Draffen, "Going Global: Export Market Proves Profitable for Region's Small Businesses," *Newsday*, March 19, 2001, p. C18.
3. See F. T. Knickerbocker, *Oligopolistic Reaction and Multinational Enterprise* (Boston: Harvard Business School Press, 1973), and R. E. Caves, "Japanese Investment in the US: Lessons for the Economic Analysis of Foreign Investment," *The World Economy* 16 (1993), pp. 279–300.
4. I. Metthee, "Playing a Large Part," *Seattle Post-Intelligencer*, April 9, 1994, p. 13.
5. C. S. Tranger, "Enter the Mini-Multinational," *Northeast International Business*, March 1989, pp. 13–14.
6. R. B. Reich, *The Work of Nations* (New York: A. A. Knopf, 1991).
7. J. A. Frankel, "Globalization of the Economy," National Bureau of Economic Research, Working Paper No. 7858, 2000.
8. J. Bhagwati, *Protectionism* (Cambridge, MA: MIT Press, 1989).
9. F. Williams, "Trade Round Like This May Never Be Seen Again," *Financial Times*, April 15, 1994, p. 8.
10. "Playing Games with Prosperity," *The Economist*, July 28, 2001, pp. 25–27.
11. Source: United Nations. World Investment Report, 2001. United Nations (New York and Geneva, 2001).
12. United Nations, *World Investment Report, 2001* (New York and Geneva: United Nations, 2001).
13. World Trade Organization, *International Trade Trends and Statistics, 2000*.
14. World Trade Organization, *Annual Report 2001* (Geneva: WTO, 2001).
15. United Nations, *World Investment Report, 2001* (New York and Geneva: United Nations, 2001). UN press release, "World FDI Flows Exceed US $1.1 Trillion in 2000," December 7, 2000.
16. World Trade Organization, *Annual Report 2000* (Geneva: WTO, 2000), and United Nations, *World Investment Report, 2001* (New York and Geneva: United Nations, 2001).
17. United Nations, *World Investment Report*, 2001.
18. World Trade Organization, "Beyond Borders: Managing a World of Free Trade and Deep Interdependence," press release 55, September 10, 1996.
19. Moore's Law is named after Intel founder Gorden Moore.
20. Frankel, "Globalization of the Economy."
21. Data compiled from various sources and listed at http://www.euromktg.com/globstats.
22. Data on the number of host computers can be found at http://www.nw.com/zone/WWW/report.html.
23. A. Cantrell, "Growth of the Internet," *The Industry Standard.com*, August 14, 2001.
24. Http://www.forrester.com/ER/Press/ForrFind/0,1768,0,00.html
25. For a counterpoint, see "Geography and the Net: Putting It in Its Place," *The Economist*, August 11, 2001, pp. 18–20.
26. M. Dickerson, "All Those Inflated Expectations Aside, Many Firms Are Finding the Internet Invaluable in Pursuing International Trade," *Los Angeles Times*, October 14, 1998, p. 10. The company's website is http://www.cardiacscience.com.
27. A. Stewart, "Easier Access to World Markets," *Financial Times*, December 3, 1997, p. 8.
28. Frankel, "Globalization of the Economy."
29. Data from Bureau of Transportation Statistics, 2001.
30. Frankel, "Globalization of the Economy."
31. Interviews with Hewlett-Packard personnel by the author.
32. "War of the Worlds," *The Economist: A Survey of the Global Economy*, October 1, 1994, pp. 3–4.

33. One of the classics being J. J. Servan-Schreiber, *The American Challenge* (New York: Atheneum, 1968).

34. United Nations, *World Investment Report, 2001* (New York and Geneva: United Nations, 2001).

35. Ibid.

36. World Investment Report 2001.

37. R. A. Mosbacher, "Opening Up Export Doors for Smaller Firms," *Seattle Times*, July 24, 1991, p. A7.

38. "Small Companies Learn How to Sell to the Japanese," *Seattle Times*, March 19, 1992.

39. W. J. Holstein, "Why Johann Can Export but Johnny Can't," *Business Week*, November 4, 1991, pp. 64–65.

40. See, for example, Ravi Batra, *The Myth of Free Trade* (New York: Touchstone Books, 1993); William Greider, *One World, Ready or Not: The Manic Logic of Global Capitalism* (New York: Simon and Schuster, 1997); and D. Radrik, *Has Globalization Gone Too Far?* (Washington, DC: Institution for International Economics, 1997).

41. James Goldsmith, "The Winners and the Losers," in *The Case Against the Global Economy*, ed. J. Mander and E. Goldsmith (San Francisco: The Sierra Book Club, 1996).

42. D. L. Bartlett and J. B. Steele, "America: Who Stole the Dream," *Philadelphia Inquirer*, September 9, 1996.

43. For example, see Paul Krugman, *Pop Internationalism* (Cambridge, MA: MIT Press, 1996).

44. Peter Gottschalk and Timothy M. Smeeding, "Cross-National Comparisons of Earnings and Income Inequality," *Journal of Economic Literature* 35 (June 1997), pp. 633–87, and Susan M. Collins, *Exports, Imports, and the American Worker* (Washington, DC: Brookings Institution, 1998).

45. Organization for Economic Cooperation and Development, "Income Distribution in OECD Countries," OECD Policy Studies, no. 18 (October 1995).

46. "A Survey of Pay. Winner and Losers," *The Economist*, May 8, 1999, pp. 5–8.

47. See, Krugman, *Pop Internationalism* and D. Belman and T. M. Lee, "International Trade and the Performance of US Labor Markets," in *U.S. Trade Policy and Global Growth*, ed. R. A. Blecker (New York: Economic Policy Institute, 1996).

48. See, Robert Lerman, Is Earnings Inequality Really Increasing? Economic Restructuring and the Job Market, Brief No. 1 (Washington DC: Urban Institute, March 1997).

49. "A Survey of Pay. Winner and Losers."

50. E. Goldsmith, "Global Trade and the Environment."

51. Batra, *The Myth of Free Trade*.

52. P. Choate, *Jobs at Risk: Vulnerable U.S. Industries and Jobs under NAFTA* (Washington, DC: Manufacturing Policy Project, 1993).

53. B. Lomborg, *The Skeptical Environmentalist* (Cambridge; Cambridge University Press, 2001).

54. H. Nordstrom and S. Vaughan, *Trade and the Environment*, World Trade Organization Special Studies No. 4 (Geneva: WTO, 1999).

55. These figures are from "Freedom's Journey: A Survey of the 20th Century. Our Durable Planet," *The Economist*, September 11, 1999, p. 30.

56. Krugman, *Pop Internationalism*.

57. R. Kuttner, "Managed Trade and Economic Sovereignty," in *U.S. Trade Policy and Global Growth*, ed. R. A. Blecker (New York: Economic Policy Institute, 1996).

58. Ralph Nader and Lori Wallach, "GATT, NAFTA, and the Subversion of the Democratic Process," in *US Trade Policy and Global Growth*, ed. R. A. Blecker (New York: Economic Policy Institute, 1996), pp. 93–94.

59. Lant Pritchett, "Divergence, Big Time," *Journal of Economic Perspectives*, 11, no. 3 (Summer 1997), pp. 3–18.

60. Ibid.

61. See D. Ben-David, H. Nordstrom, and L. A. Winters, *Trade, Income Disparity and Poverty. World Trade Organization Special Studies No 5.* (Geneva: WTO, 1999).

Part 2

Country Factors

National Differences in Political Economy

The Changing Political Economy of India

After gaining independence from Britain in 1947, India adopted a democratic system of government. However, the economic system that developed in India was a mixed economy characterized by a heavy dose of state-owned enterprise, centralized planning, and subsidies. This system constrained the growth of the private sector. Private companies could expand only with government permission. Under this system, dubbed the "License Raj," private companies often had to wait months for government approval of routine business activities, such as expanding production or hiring a new director. It could take years to get permission to diversify into a new product. Much of heavy industry, such as auto, chemical, and steel production, was reserved for state-owned enterprises. Production quotas and high tariffs on imports also stunted the development of a healthy private sector, as did restrictive labor laws that made it difficult to fire employees. Access to foreign exchange was limited, investment by foreign firms was severely restricted, land use was strictly controlled, and the government routinely managed prices as opposed to letting them be set by market forces.

By the early 1990s, it was clear that after 40 years of near stagnation, this system was incapable of delivering the kind of economic progress that many Southeastern Asian nations had started to enjoy. In 1994, India's economy was still smaller than Belgium's, despite having a population of 950 million. Its GDP per capita was a paltry $310; less than half the population could read; only 6 million had access to telephones; only 14 percent had access to clean sanitation; the World Bank estimated that some 40 percent of the world's desperately poor lived in India; and only 2.3 percent of the population had a household income in excess of $2,484.

In 1991, the lack of progress led the government of Prime Minister P. V. Narasimha Rao, a member of the Congress Party, to embark on an ambitious economic reform program. Much of the industrial licensing system was dismantled, and several areas once closed to the private sector were opened, including electricity generation, parts of the oil industry, steelmaking, air transport, and some areas of the telecommunications industry. Foreign invest-

ment, formerly allowed only grudgingly and subject to arbitrary ceilings, was suddenly welcomed. Approval was made automatic for foreign equity stakes of up to 51 percent in an Indian enterprise, and 100 percent foreign ownership was allowed under certain circumstances. The government announced plans to privatize many of India's state-owned businesses. Raw materials and many industrial goods could be freely imported, and the maximum tariff that could be levied on imports was reduced from 400 percent to 65 percent. The top income tax rate was also reduced, and corporate tax fell from 57.5 percent to 46 percent in 1994, and then to 35 percent in 1997.

Judged by some measures, the response to these economic reforms was impressive. The economy expanded at an annual rate of about 6.1 percent throughout the 1990s, exports began to grow at a respectable pace, and corporate profits jumped. Foreign investment, which is a good indicator of foreign companies' perceptions about the health of the Indian economy, surged from $150 million in 1991 to an estimated $3.5 billion in 1997.

However, by the late 1990s, economic reform had stalled. While economic growth remained reasonably strong, driven in part by a boom in certain sectors such as India's computer software industry, the Indian government was running a budget deficit equivalent to 9.6 percent of GDP. Subsidies still amounted to 15 percent of GDP, and the cost of financing these left the government with little cash to invest in basic infrastructure or education. Money could be raised through privatization, but political infighting and opposition from employees who feared they would lose their jobs after privatization had slowed the pace of privatization to a crawl. Between 1991 and 1997 the government sold equity stakes in about 40 companies to private investors, including state-owned telecommunications, steel, and electronics enterprises. However, in 1999 India still had about 240 state-owned companies engaged in activities ranging from banking and baking bread to making railway carriages.

Attempts to further reduce import tariffs were stalled by political opposition from employers, employees, and politicians, who feared that if barriers came down, a flood of inexpensive Chinese products would enter India. They were particularly concerned about the health of India's large textile sector, which employed one out of six manufacturing employees. There was also strong resistance to reforming many of India's laws that made it difficult for private business to operate efficiently. For example, labor laws made it almost impossible for firms with more than 100 employees to fire workers once they had been hired. Textile manufacturers were required to produce 10 percent of their output from hand looms—a throwback to Mahatma Gandhi's notions of Indian self-sufficiency. Laws mandate that certain products can be manufactured only by small companies, effectively making it impossible for companies in these industries to attain the scale required to compete internationally.

Reflecting the slowing pace of economic reform, foreign investment fell from its peak in 1997 to about $2 billion in 2000, as foreign firms reassessed their perceptions of India's economy and redirected their attention to other countries, such as China, where foreign investment surged to over $40 billion a year.

A decade of reform had done little to solve India's crippling poverty problem. While the Indian middle class had grown richer during the 1990s, by 2000 some 40 percent of India's nearly 1 billion people still lived in abject poverty, earning less than $1 a day, a figure that was little changed from 1990. At the start of the new millennium, the gross domestic product per capita of India was still only $440, which ranked India at 161 among the world's nations, 44 percent of the adult population was illiterate, 19 percent had no access to safe water supplies, 25 percent had no access to health services, 71 percent had no access to sanitation, and 16 percent of the population was not expected to survive to age 40!

Against this background, in October 1999 the nationalist BJP party was elected to power in India. There were fears that the BJP would withdraw from economic reform. The BJP has close ties to Hindu nationalist organizations that emphasize economic self-sufficiency, protectionism, and "Hindu first" policies, which are potentially socially divisive in a country with a large Muslim minority. So far, these fears have proved groundless. Far from pulling back from economic reform, the BJP prime minister, Atal Behari Vajpayee, has initiated a second wave of reforms aimed at further privatization, reducing subsidies and import barriers, and dismantling the bureaucratic mishmash of laws that hamstring private business. In March 2001, the BJP announced it planned to raise $25 billion from privatizing state-owned business, to replace subsidies for water and electricity with market rate charges, to reduce the peak duty in imports of most items from 38.5 percent to 20 percent within three years, and to remove or amend laws that limit private business practice. Thus, the BJP has proposed to raise the size threshold to which the "the no firing law" applies from firms with 100 employees to those with 1,000 employees. The jury is still out, however, as to whether the BJP will be able to deliver on these goals. The World Bank forecasts that India will have to grow its economy by 6 to 8 percent a year for the rest of the decade if it is to alleviate the crushing poverty that afflicts so much of its population. If poverty is not alleviated, a backlash against reform is likely.

Sources: "A Survey of India: The Tiger Steps Out," *The Economist*, January 21, 1995; "Tarnished Silver," *The Economist*, September 6, 1997, pp. 64–65; P. Moore, "Three Steps Forward," *Euromoney*, September 1997, pp. 190–95; "India's Breakthrough Budget?" *The Economist*, March 3, 2001; Shankar Aiyar, "Reforms: Time to Just Do It," *India Today*, January 24, 2000, p. 47; and United Nations Development Program, *Human Development Report 2000* (New York: Oxford University Press, 2000).

◼ Introduction

As noted in Chapter 1, international business is much more complicated than domestic business because countries differ in many ways. Countries have different political, economic, and legal systems. Cultural practices can vary dramatically from country to country, as can the education and skill level of the population, and countries are at different stages of economic development. All these differences can and do have major implications for the practice of international business. They have a profound impact on the benefits, costs, and risks associated with doing business in different countries; the way in which operations in different countries should be managed; and the strategy international firms should pursue in different countries. A main function of this chapter and the next is to develop an awareness of and appreciation for the significance of country differences in political systems, economic systems, legal systems, and national culture. Another function of this chapter and the next is to describe how the political, economic, legal, and cultural systems of many of the world's nation-states are evolving and to draw out the implications of these changes for the practice of international business.

The opening case illustrates the changes occurring in the political and economic systems of one nation, India. As in many other countries, since the early 1990s political and economic ideology in India has shifted away from state planning and toward a free market orientation. One consequence of this shift in ideology has been adoption of an economic reform program that includes as its main elements the privatization of state-owned enterprises, the removal of subsidies, the repeal of laws that hamstring private business practice, and the removal of barriers to foreign investment and trade. This program has made India a more attractive location in which international businesses can operate, thus increasing foreign investment in India during the 1990s.

However, as the opening case makes clear, while the Indian program has had some success, it has also run into significant roadblocks and it has yet to alleviate the poverty that afflicts so much of the nation's population. Advocates of economic reform will claim that India's economic reform program achieved only partial success because political opposition has significantly slowed the pace of reform. There is probably much truth to this claim. At the same time, the combination of political and cultural legacies and current realities in India is such that rapid reform would be difficult even under the most well-intentioned government. This is not unique to India. The pace of reform in many countries is determined by the interplay between the economic goals of the reformers and the political and cultural realities of the country. For example, in Russia, political opposition and a cultural legacy derived from 75 years of Communist rule that is antagonistic to free enterprise have combined to slow the pace of economic reform there.

Such examples suggest that the economic, political, legal, and cultural systems of a country are not independent of each other. After all, it is politicians who write the laws that help to shape economic activity in a nation-state, and politicians, like all of us, are influenced by the prevailing culture or cultures of their nation. To understand the economic prospects of a nation such as India and to appreciate its importance to international business, we must also understand the interplay between the political, economic, legal, and cultural systems prevailing in that country.

This chapter focuses on how the political, economic, and legal systems of countries differ. Collectively we refer to these systems as constituting the **political economy** of a country. We use the term *political economy* to stress that the political, economic, and legal systems of a country are not independent of each other. They interact and influence each other, and in doing so they affect the level of economic well-being in a country. In addition to reviewing these systems, we also explore how differences in political economy influence the benefits, costs, and risks associated with doing business in different countries, and how they affect management practice and strategy. In the next chapter we will look at how differences in culture influence the practice of international business. The political economy and culture of a nation are *not* independent of each other. As will become apparent in Chapter 3, culture can exert an impact on political economy—on political, economic, and legal systems in a nation—and the converse can also hold true.

Political Systems

The economic and legal systems of a country are shaped by its political system.[1] As such, it is important that we understand the nature of different political systems before discussing economic and legal systems. By **political system** we mean the system of government in a nation. Political systems can be assessed according to two related dimensions. The first is the degree to which they emphasize collectivism as opposed to individualism. The second dimension is the degree to which they are democratic or totalitarian. These dimensions are interrelated; systems that emphasize collectivism tend to be totalitarian, while systems that place a high value on individualism tend to be democratic. However, a gray area exists in the middle. It is possible to have democratic societies that emphasize a mix of collectivism and individualism. Similarly, it is possible to have totalitarian societies that are not collectivist.

Collectivism and Individualism

The term **collectivism** refers to a political system that stresses the primacy of collective goals over individual goals.[2] When collectivism is emphasized, the needs of society as a whole are generally viewed as being more important than individual freedoms. In such circumstances, an individual's right to do something may be restricted on the grounds that it runs counter to "the good of society" or to "the common good." Advocacy of collectivism can be traced to the ancient Greek philosopher Plato (427–347 B.C.), who in the *Republic* argued that individual rights should be sacrificed for the good of the majority and that property should be owned in common. In modern times the collectivist mantle has been picked up by socialists.

Socialism

Socialists trace their intellectual roots to Karl Marx (1818–1883). Marx argued that the few benefit at the expense of the many in a capitalist society where individual freedoms are not restricted. While successful capitalists accumulate considerable wealth, Marx postulated that the wages earned by the majority of workers in a capitalist society would be forced down to subsistence levels. Marx argued that capitalists expropriate for their own use the value created by workers, while paying workers only subsistence wages in return. Put another way, according to Marx, the pay of workers does not reflect the full value of their labor. To correct this perceived wrong, Marx advocated state ownership of the basic means of production, distribution, and exchange (i.e., businesses). His logic was that if the state owned the means of production, the state could ensure that workers were fully compensated for their labor. Thus, the idea is to manage state-owned enterprise to benefit society as a whole, rather than individual capitalists.[3]

In the early 20th century, the socialist ideology split into two broad camps. The **communists** believed that socialism could be achieved only through violent revolution and totalitarian dictatorship, while the **social democrats** committed themselves to achieving socialism by democratic means and turned their backs on violent revolution and dictatorship. Both versions of socialism have waxed and waned during the 20th century.

The communist version of socialism reached its high point in the late 1970s, when the majority of the world's population lived in communist states. The countries under Communist rule at that time included the former Soviet Union; its Eastern European client nations (e.g., Poland, Czechoslovakia, Hungary); China; the Southeast Asian nations of Cambodia, Laos, and Vietnam; various African nations (e.g., Angola, Mozambique); and the Latin American nations of Cuba and Nicaragua. By the mid-1990s, however, communism was in retreat worldwide. The Soviet Union had collapsed and had been replaced by a collection of 15 republics, most of which were at least nominally structured as democracies. Communism was swept out of Eastern Europe by the largely bloodless revolutions of 1989. Many believe it is now only a matter of time before communism collapses in China, the last major Communist power left. Although China is still nominally a communist state with substantial limits to individual political freedom, in the economic sphere the country has recently moved away from strict adherence to communist ideology.[4] Apart from China, communism hangs on only in some small states, such as North Korea and Cuba.

Social democracy also seems to have passed its high-water mark, although the ideology may prove to be more enduring than communism. Social democracy has had perhaps its greatest influence in a number of democratic Western nations including Australia, Great Britain, France, Germany, Norway, Spain, and Sweden, where social democratic parties have from time to time held political power. Other countries where social democracy has had an important influence include India and Brazil. Consistent with their Marxists roots, many social democratic governments nationalized private companies in certain industries, transforming them into state-owned enterprises to be run for the "public good rather than private profit." In Great Britain, for example, by the end of the 1970s, state-owned companies had a monopoly in the telecommunications, electricity, gas, coal, railway, and shipbuilding industries, as well as substantial interests in the oil, airline, auto, and steel industries.

However, experience has demonstrated that state ownership of the means of production often runs counter to the public interest. In many countries, state-owned companies have performed poorly. Protected from significant competition by their monopoly position and guaranteed government financial support, many state-owned companies became increasingly inefficient. In the end, individuals found themselves paying for the luxury of state ownership through higher prices and higher taxes. As a consequence, a number of Western democracies voted many social democratic parties out of office in the late 1970s and early 1980s. They were succeeded by political parties, such as Britain's Conservative Party and Germany's Christian Democratic Party, that were more committed to free market economics. These parties devoted considerable effort to selling state-owned enterprises to private investors (a process referred to as privatization). Thus, in Great Britain the Conservative Party government sold the state's interests in telecommunications, electricity, gas, shipbuilding, oil, airlines, autos, and steel to private investors. Even when social democratic parties have regained the levers of power, as in Great Britain in 1997 when the left-leaning Labor Party won control of the government, they now seem to be committed to greater private ownership.

Individualism

Individualism is the opposite of collectivism. In a political sense, individualism refers to a philosophy that an individual should have freedom in his or her economic and political pursuits. In contrast to collectivism, individualism stresses that the interests of the individual should take precedence over the interests of the state. Like collectivism, however, individualism can be traced to an ancient Greek philosopher, in this case Plato's disciple Aristotle (384–322 B.C.). In contrast to Plato, Aristotle argued that individual diversity and private ownership are desirable. In a passage that might have been taken from a speech by contemporary politicians who adhere to a free market ideology, he argued that private property is more highly productive than communal property and will thus stimulate progress. According to Aristotle, communal property receives little care, whereas property that is owned by an individual will receive the greatest care and therefore be most productive.

After sinking into oblivion for the best part of two millennia, individualism was reborn as an influential political philosophy in the Protestant trading nations of England and the Netherlands during the 16th century. The philosophy was refined in the work of a number of British philosophers including David Hume (1711–1776), Adam Smith (1723–1790), and John Stuart Mill (1806–1873). The philosophy of individualism exercised a profound influence on those in the American colonies who sought independence from Great Britain. Individualism underlies the ideas expressed in the Declaration of Independence. In more recent years, the philosophy has been championed by several Nobel prize-winning economists, including Milton Friedman, Friedrich von Hayek, and James Buchanan.

Individualism is built on two central tenets. The first is an emphasis on the importance of guaranteeing individual freedom and self-expression. As John Stuart Mill put it,

> The sole end for which mankind are warranted, individually or collectively, in interfering with the liberty of action of any of their number is self-protection . . . The only purpose for which power can be rightfully exercised over any

member of a civilized community, against his will, is to prevent harm to others. His own good, either physical or moral, is not a sufficient warrant . . . The only part of the conduct of any one, for which he is amenable to society, is that which concerns others. In the part which merely concerns himself, his independence is, of right, absolute. Over himself, over his own body and mind, the individual is sovereign.[5]

The second tenet of individualism is that the welfare of society is best served by letting people pursue their own economic self-interest, as opposed to some collective body (such as government) dictating what is in society's best interest. Or as Adam Smith put it in a famous passage from *The Wealth of Nations*, an individual who intends his own gain is

led by an invisible hand to promote an end which was no part of his intention. Nor is it always worse for the society that it was no part of it. By pursuing his own interest he frequently promotes that of the society more effectually than when he really intends to promote it. I have never known much good done by those who effect to trade for the public good.[6]

The central message of individualism, therefore, is that individual economic and political freedoms are the ground rules on which a society should be based. This puts individualism in conflict with collectivism. Collectivism asserts the primacy of the collective over the individual, while individualism asserts just the opposite. This underlying ideological conflict has shaped much of the recent history of the world. The Cold War, for example, was essentially a war between collectivism, championed by the now-defunct Soviet Union, and individualism, championed by the United States.

In practical terms, individualism translates into an advocacy for democratic political systems and free market economics. Viewed this way, we can see that since the late 1980s the waning of collectivism has been matched by the ascendancy of individualism. A wave of democratic ideals and free market economics is sweeping away socialism and communism worldwide. The changes of the past few years go beyond the revolutions in Eastern Europe and the former Soviet Union to include a move toward greater individualism in Latin America and in some of the social democratic states of the West (e.g., Great Britain and Sweden). This is not to claim that individualism has finally won a long battle with collectivism. It has not. But as a guiding political philosophy, individualism is on the ascendancy. This represents good news for international business, since in direct contrast to collectivism, the pro-business and pro-free trade values of individualism create a favorable environment within which international business can thrive.

Democracy and Totalitarianism

Democracy and totalitarianism are at different ends of a political dimension. **Democracy** refers to a political system in which government is by the people, exercised either directly or through elected representatives. **Totalitarianism** is a form of government in which one person or political party exercises absolute control over all spheres of human life and opposing political parties are prohibited. The democratic–totalitarian dimension is not independent of the collectivism–individualism dimension. Democracy and individualism go hand in hand, as do the communist version of collectivism and totalitarianism. However, gray areas exist; it is possible to have a democratic state where collective values predominate, and it is possible to have a totalitarian state that is hostile to collectivism and in which some degree of individualism—particularly in the economic sphere—is encouraged. For example, Chile in the 1980s was ruled by a totalitarian military dictatorship that encouraged economic freedom but not political freedom. China also has seen a move toward greater individual freedom in the economic sphere, but the country is still ruled by a totalitarian dictatorship.

Democracy

The pure form of democracy, as originally practiced by several city-states in ancient Greece, is based on a belief that citizens should be directly involved in decision making. In complex, advanced societies with populations in the tens or hundreds of millions this is impractical. Most modern democratic states practice what is commonly referred to as **representative democracy.** In a representative democracy, citizens periodically elect individuals to represent them. These elected representatives then form a government, whose function is to make decisions on behalf of the electorate. A representative democracy rests on the assumption that if elected representatives fail to perform this job adequately, they will be voted down at the next election.

To guarantee that elected representatives can be held accountable for their actions by the electorate, an ideal representative democracy has a number of safeguards that are typically enshrined in constitutional law. These include (1) an individual's right to freedom of expression, opinion, and organization; (2) a free media; (3) regular elections in which all eligible citizens are allowed to vote; (4) universal adult suffrage; (5) limited terms for elected representatives; (6) a fair court system that is independent from the political system; (7) a nonpolitical state bureaucracy; (8) a nonpolitical police force and armed service; and (9) relatively free access to state information.[7]

Totalitarianism

In a totalitarian country, all the constitutional guarantees on which representative democracies are built—such as an individual's right to freedom of expression and organization, a free media, and regular elections—are denied to the citizens. In most totalitarian states, political repression is widespread and those who question the right of the rulers to rule find themselves imprisoned, or worse.

Four major forms of totalitarianism exist in the world today. Until recently the most widespread was **communist totalitarianism.** As discussed earlier, communism is a version of collectivism that advocates that socialism can be achieved only through totalitarian dictatorship. Communism, however, is in decline worldwide and many of the old Communist dictatorships have collapsed since 1989. The major exceptions to this trend (so far) are China, Vietnam, Laos, North Korea, and Cuba, although all of these states exhibit clear signs that the Communist Party's monopoly on political power is under attack.

A second form of totalitarianism might be labeled **theocratic totalitarianism.** Theocratic totalitarianism is found in states where political power is monopolized by a party, group, or individual that governs according to religious principles. The most common form of theocratic totalitarianism is based on Islam and is exemplified by states such as Iran and Saudi Arabia. These states restrict not only freedom of political expression but also freedom of religious expression, while the laws of the state are based on Islamic principles.

A third form of totalitarianism might be referred to as **tribal totalitarianism.** Tribal totalitarianism is found principally in African countries such as Zimbabwe, Tanzania, Uganda, and Kenya. The borders of most African states reflect the administrative boundaries drawn by the old European colonial powers, rather than tribal realities. Consequently, the typical African country contains a number of different tribes. Tribal totalitarianism occurs when a political party that represents the interests of a particular tribe (and not always the majority tribe) monopolizes power. Such one-party states still exist in Africa.

A fourth major form of totalitarianism might be described as **right-wing totalitarianism.** Right-wing totalitarianism generally permits individual economic freedom but restricts individual political freedom on the grounds that it would lead to the rise of communism. One common feature of most right-wing dictatorships is an overt hostility to socialist or communist ideas. Many right-wing totalitarian governments are backed by the military, and in some cases the government may be made up of military officers. Until the early 1980s, right-wing dictatorships, many of which were military dictatorships, were common throughout Latin America. They were also found in several Asian countries, particularly South Korea, Taiwan, Singapore, Indonesia, and the Philippines. Since the early 1980s, however, this form of government has been in retreat. The majority of Latin American countries are now genuine multiparty democracies. Similarly, significant political freedoms have been granted to the political opposition in countries such as South Korea, Taiwan, and the Philippines, all of which have become functioning democracies.

Economic Systems

It should be clear from the previous section that there is a connection between political ideology and economic systems. In countries where individual goals are given primacy over collective goals, we are more likely to find free market economic systems. In contrast, in countries where collective goals are given preeminence, the state may have taken control over many enterprises, while markets in such countries are likely to be restricted rather than free. We can identify four broad types of economic systems—a market economy, a command economy, a mixed economy, and a state-directed economy.

Market Economy

In a pure market economy all productive activities are privately owned, as opposed to being owned by the state. The goods and services that a country produces, and the quantity in which they are produced, are not planned by anyone. Rather, production is determined by the interaction of supply and demand and signaled to producers through the price system. If demand for a product exceeds supply, prices will rise, signaling producers to produce more. If supply exceeds demand, prices will fall, signaling producers to produce less. In this system consumers are sovereign. The purchasing patterns of consumers, as signaled to producers through the mechanism of the price system, determine what is produced and in what quantity.

For a market to work in this manner there must be no restrictions on supply. A restriction on supply occurs when a market is monopolized by a single firm. In such circumstances, rather than increase output in response to increased demand, a monopolist might restrict output and let prices rise. This allows the monopolist to take a greater profit margin on each unit it sells. Although this is good for the monopolist, it is bad for the consumer, who has to pay higher prices. It also is probably bad for the welfare of society. Since a monopolist has no competitors, it has no incentive to search for ways to lower production costs. Rather, it can simply pass on cost increases to consumers in the form of higher prices. The net result is that the monopolist is likely to become increasingly inefficient, producing high-priced, low-quality goods, while society suffers as a consequence.

Given the dangers inherent in monopoly, the role of government in a market economy is to encourage vigorous competition between private producers. Governments do this by outlawing monopolies and restrictive business practices designed to monopolize a market (antitrust laws serve this function in the United States). Private ownership also encourages vigorous competition and economic efficiency. Private ownership ensures that entrepreneurs have a right to the profits generated by their own efforts. This gives entrepreneurs an incentive to search for better ways of serving consumer needs. That may be through introducing new products, by developing more efficient production processes, by better marketing and after-sale service, or simply through managing their businesses more efficiently than their competitors. In turn, the constant improvement in product and process that results from such an incentive has been argued to have a major positive impact on economic growth and development.[8]

Command Economy

In a pure **command economy,** the goods and services that a country produces, the quantity in which they are produced, and the prices at which they are sold are all planned by the government. Consistent with the collectivist ideology, the objective of a command economy is for government to allocate resources for "the good of society." In addition, in a pure command economy, all businesses are state owned, the rationale being that the government can then direct them to make investments that are in the best interests of the nation as a whole, rather than in the interests of private individuals. Historically, command economies were found in communist countries where collectivist goals were given priority over individual goals. Since the demise of communism in the late 1980s, the number of command economies has fallen dramatically. Some elements of a command economy were also evident in a number of democratic nations led by socialist-inclined governments. France and India both experimented with extensive government planning and state ownership, although government planning has fallen into disfavor in both countries.

While the objective of a command economy is to mobilize economic resources for the public good, the opposite seems to have occurred. In a command economy, state-owned enterprises have little incentive to control costs and be efficient, because they cannot go out of business. Also, the abolition of private ownership means there is no incentive for individuals to look for better ways to serve consumer needs; hence, dynamism and innovation are absent from command economies. Instead of growing and becoming more prosperous, such economies tend to be characterized by stagnation.

Mixed Economy

Between market economies and command economies can be found mixed economies. In a **mixed economy,** certain sectors of the economy are left to private ownership and free market mechanisms while other sectors have significant state ownership and government planning. India, which was profiled in the opening case, has a mixed economy. Mixed economies were once relatively common throughout much of the world, although they are becoming much less so. There was a time not too long ago when Great Britain, France, and Sweden were mixed economies, but extensive privatization has reduced state ownership of businesses in all three. As we saw in the opening case, a similar trend can be observed in India and in many other countries where there was once a large state sector, such as Brazil and Italy.

In mixed economies, governments also tend to take into state ownership troubled firms whose continued operation is thought to be vital to national interests. The French automobile company Renault was state owned until recently. The government took over the company when it ran into serious financial problems. The French government reasoned that the social costs of the unemployment that might result if Renault collapsed were unacceptable, so it nationalized the company to save it from bankruptcy. Renault's competitors weren't thrilled by this move, since they had to compete with a company whose costs were subsidized by the state.

State-Directed Economy

A **state-directed economy** is one in which the state plays a significant role in directing the investment activities of private enterprise through "industrial policy" and in otherwise regulating business activity in accordance with national goals. Japan and South Korea are frequently cited as examples of state-directed economies. A state-directed economy differs from a mixed economy in so far as the state does not routinely take private enterprises into public ownership. Instead, it nurtures private enterprise but proactively directs investments made by private firms in accordance with the goals of its industrial policy.

For example, in the early 1970s, the Japanese Ministry of International Trade and Industry (MITI) targeted the semiconductor industry as one in which it would like to see Japanese firms have a major presence.[9] Industrial policy often takes the form of state subsidies to private enterprises to encourage them to build significant sales in industries deemed to be of strategic value for the nation's economic development. Thus, the Japanese government subsidized research and development (R&D) investments made by Japanese semiconductor companies. It also used direct administrative pressure to persuade several companies to enter the industry. To help targeted industries develop, the state may also protect them from foreign competition by erecting barriers to imports and foreign direct investment. Accordingly, Japanese semiconductor companies were protected from foreign competition by barriers to imports and restrictions on the ability of foreigners to establish operations in Japan.

The intellectual foundation for a state-directed economy is based on the so-called infant industry argument (which we shall review in greater depth in Chapter 5). This argument suggests that in some industries, economies of scale are so large and incumbent firms from developed nations have such an advantage that it is difficult for new firms from developing nations to establish themselves. Industrial policy is seen as a way to overcome this economic disadvantage. It also is argued that state-directed industrial policy may allow a country to establish a leading position in an emerging industry where scale economies will ultimately be of great importance. (This argument is at the core of the new trade theory, which we review in Chapter 4.)

One criticism of state-directed economies is that government bureaucrats don't necessarily make better decisions about the allocation of investment capital than the market mechanism would. For a long time, the economic success of countries such as Japan and South Korea allowed advocates of state involvement to dismiss such criticisms.[10] However, a decade of stagnant growth in Japan coupled with the 1997 implosion of the South Korean economy has added legitimacy to these criticisms. The South Korean collapse has been widely attributed to uneconomic investments by Korean companies in industries that the government deemed to be of national importance, such as semiconductors.

Legal Systems

The **legal system** of a country refers to the rules, or laws, that regulate behavior along with the processes by which the laws are enforced and through which redress for grievances is obtained. The legal system of a country is of immense importance to international business. A country's laws regulate business practice, define the manner in which business transactions are to be executed, and set down the rights and obligations of those involved in business transactions. The legal environments of countries differ in significant ways. As we shall see, differences in legal systems can affect the attractiveness of a country as an investment site and/or market.

Like the economic system of a country, the legal system is influenced by the prevailing political system. The government of a country defines the legal framework within which firms do business—and often the laws that regulate business reflect the rulers' dominant political ideology. For example, collectivist-inclined totalitarian states tend to enact laws that severely restrict private enterprise, while the laws enacted by governments in democratic states where individualism is the dominant political philosophy tend to be pro-private enterprise and pro-consumer.

The variances in the structure of law among countries is a massive topic that warrants its own textbook. We do not attempt to give a full description of the variations; rather, we will focus on three issues that illustrate how legal systems can vary—and how such variations can affect international business. First, we look at the laws governing property rights with particular reference to patents, copyrights, and trademarks.

Second, we look at laws covering product safety and product liability. Third, we look at country differences in contract law.

Property Rights

In a legal sense the term *property* refers to a resource over which an individual or business holds a legal title; that is, a resource that they own. **Property rights** refer to the bundle of legal rights over the use to which a resource is put and over the use made of any income that may be derived from that resource.[11] Countries differ significantly in the extent to which their legal system protects property rights. Although almost all countries have laws on their books that protect property rights, the reality is that in many countries these laws are not well enforced by the authorities and property rights are routinely violated. Property rights can be violated in two ways—through private action and through public action.

Private Action

Private action refers to theft, piracy, blackmail, and the like by private individuals or groups. While theft occurs in all countries, a weak legal system allows for a much higher level of criminal action in some than in others. An example is Russia, where the chaotic legal system of the post-Communist era, coupled with a weak police force and judicial system, offers both domestic and foreign businesses scant protection from blackmail by the "Russian Mafia." Often successful business owners in Russia must pay "protection money" to the Mafia or face violent retribution, including bombings and assassinations (about 500 contract killings of businessmen occurred in 1995 and again in 1996).[12] In one example, Ivan Kivelidi, a banker and founder of the Russian Business Roundtable, was murdered by poison applied to the rim of his coffee cup. In another, Vladislav Listiev, the head of Channel 1, Russia's largest nationwide TV network, announced in 1996 that he was going to remove unsavory elements (i.e., Mafia) from the network. Soon afterward he was gunned down by professional assassins outside his apartment building.[13] And in perhaps the most disturbing case, American businessman Paul Tatum was assassinated in late 1996 after a Moscow hotel joint venture in which he was involved turned sour.[14]

Of course, Russia is not alone in having Mafia problems. The Mafia has a long history in the United States. In Japan, the local version of the Mafia, known as the *yakuza*, runs protection rackets, particularly in the food and entertainment industries.[15] However, there is an enormous difference between the magnitude of such activity in Russia and its limited impact in Japan and the United States. This difference arises because the legal enforcement apparatus, such as the police and court system, is so weak in Russia. Many other countries have problems similar to or even greater than those currently being experienced by Russia. In Somalia from 1993 to 1994, for example, the breakdown of law and order was so complete that even UN food relief convoys proceeding to famine areas under armed guard were held up by bandits.

Public Action and Corruption

Public action to violate property rights occurs when public officials, such as politicians and government bureaucrats, extort income or resources from property holders. This can be done through a number of legal mechanisms such as levying excessive taxation, requiring expensive licenses or permits from property holders, or taking assets into state ownership without compensating the owners (as occurred to the assets of numerous U.S. firms in Iran after the 1979 Iranian revolution). It can also be done by illegal means, or corruption, by demanding bribes from businesses in return for the rights to operate in a country, industry, or location.[16] For example, the government of the late Ferdinand Marcos in the Philippines was famous for demanding bribes from foreign businesses wishing to set up operations in that country.[17] The same was true of government officials in Indonesia under the rule of ex-President Suharto.

Figure 2.1

Country Rankings of
Corruption in 2000

Source: Transparency International
(http://www.transparency.de/).

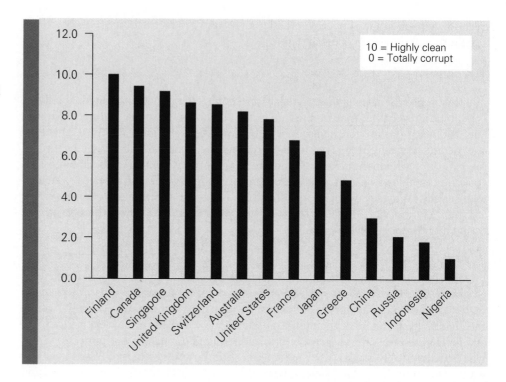

A example of how corruption often works surfaced in 1994 when the British news-paper *The Sunday Times* ran an article that alleged a 1 billion sterling ($750 million) sale of defense equipment by British companies to Malaysia was secured only after bribes had been paid to Malaysian government officials and after the British Overseas Development Administration (ODA) had agreed to approve a 234 million sterling grant to the Malaysian government for a hydroelectric dam of (according to *The Sunday Times*) dubious economic value. The clear implication was that U.K. officials, in their enthusiasm to see British companies win a large defense contract, had yielded to pressures from "corrupt" Malaysian officials for bribes—both personal and in the form of the development grant.[18]

Corruption has been well documented in every society, from the banks of the Congo River to the palace of the Dutch royal family, from Japanese politicians to Brazilian bankers, and from Indonesian government officials to the New York City Police Department. No society is immune to corruption. However, there are systematic differences in the extent of corruption across countries. In some countries, the rule of law is such that corruption is kept to a minimum. Corruption is seen and treated as illegal and, when discovered, violators are punished by the full force of the law. Unfortunately, in other countries the rule of law is weak and corruption by bureaucrats and politicians is rife. Corruption is so endemic in some countries that politicians and bureaucrats regard it as a perk of office and openly flout laws against corruption. Transparency International, an independent nonprofit organization dedicated to exposing and fighting corruption, has measured the level of corruption among public officials in different countries.[19] As can be seen in Figure 2.1, the organization rated countries such as Finland and Canada as "very clean," while countries such as China, Russia, Indonesia, and Nigeria are seen as corrupt. Nigeria ranked last out of all 90 countries in the survey, while Finland ranked first.

Economic evidence suggests that high levels of corruption significantly reduce the economic growth rate in a country.[20] By siphoning off profits, corrupt politicians and bureaucrats reduce the returns to business investment and, hence, reduce the incen-

40 Years of Corruption in Nigeria

Country Focus

When Nigeria gained independence from Great Britain in 1960, there were hopes that the country might emerge as an economic heavyweight in Africa. Not only was Nigeria Africa's most populous country, but it was also blessed with abundant natural resources, particularly oil, which rose sharply in value in the 1970s following two rounds of increases in oil prices engineered by the Organization of Petroleum Exporting Countries (OPEC). Between 1970 and 2000, Nigeria earned more than $300 billion from the sale of oil, but at the end of this period it remained one of the poorest countries in the world. In 2000, gross national product per capita was just $300, 40 percent of the adult population was illiterate, life expectancy at birth was only 50 years, and the country was begging for relief on $30 billion in debt. The Human Development Index compiled by the United Nations ranked Nigeria 151 out of 174 countries covered.

What went wrong? Although there is no simple answer, a number of factors seem to have conspired to damage economic activity in Nigeria. The country is composed of several competing ethnic, trial, and religious groups, and the conflict between them has limited political stability and led to political strife, including a brutal civil war in the 1970s. With the legitimacy of the government always in question, political leaders often purchased support by legitimizing bribes and by raiding the national treasury to reward allies. Civilian rule after independence was followed by a series of military dictatorships, each of which seemed more corrupt and inept than the last (the country returned to civilian rule in 1999).

The most recent military dictator, Sani Abacha, openly and systematically plundered the state treasury for his own personal gain. His most blatant scam was the Petroleum Trust Fund, which he set up in the mid-1990s ostensibly to channel extra revenue from an increase in fuel prices into much-needed infrastructure projects and other investments. The fund was not independently audited and almost none of the money that passed through it was properly accounted for. It was, in fact, a vehicle for Abacha and his supporters to spend at will a sum that in 1996 was equivalent to some 25 percent of the total federal budget. Abacha, aware of his position as an unpopular and unelected leader, lavished money on personal security and handed out bribes to those whose support he coveted. With examples like this at the very top of the government, it is not surprising that corruption could be found throughout the political and bureaucratic apparatus.

Some of the excesses were simply astounding. In the 1980s an aluminum smelter was built on the orders of the government, which wanted to industrialize Nigeria. The cost of the smelter was $2.4 billion, some 60 to 100 percent higher than the cost of comparable plants elsewhere in the developed world. This high cost was widely interpreted to reflect the bribes that had to be paid to local politicians by the international contractors that built the plant. The smelter has never operated at more than a fraction of its intended capacity. Another example of corruption in Nigeria was the cement scandal of the early 1980s. At that time, the president announced a grand public housing project. Public officials promptly ordered vast quantities of cement from foreign contractors, taking a percentage of each contract in the form of a kickback. They ordered far more cement than was needed and more than Nigerian ports could cope with. Soon ships loaded with cement formed a line that stretched for several miles outside of Lagos harbor and that took months to unload. Meanwhile, the officials responsible were making a fortune from selling cement import licenses.

Sources: "A Tale of Two Giants," *The Economist, Nigeria: a Survey,* January 15, 2000, p. 5; J. Coolidge and S. Rose Ackerman, "High Level Rent Seeking and Corruption in African Regimes," *World Bank Policy Research Working Paper # 1780,* June 1997; and D. L. Bevan, P. Collier, and J. W. Gunning, *Nigeria and Indonesia: The Political Economy of Poverty, Equity and Growth* (Oxford: Oxford University Press, 1999).

tive that both domestic and foreign businesses have to invest in that country. The lower level of investment that results has a negative impact on economic growth. Thus, we would expect countries such as Nigeria and Indonesia to have a much lower rate of economic growth than might otherwise have been the case. A detailed example of the negative effect that corruption can have on economic progress is given in

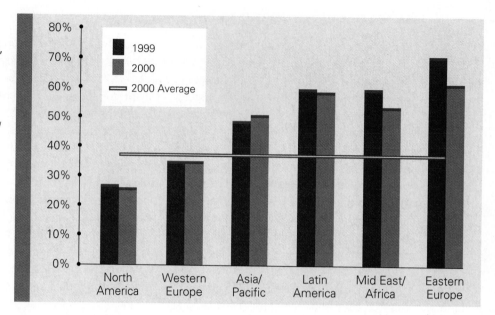

Figure 2.2

Software Piracy by Region,
(1999 and 2000)

Source: Business Software Alliance,
Sixth Annual BSA Global Software
Piracy Study, May 2001. Available
from http://www.bsa.org/usa/globallib/
piracy/piracystats99.phtml.

the accompanying Country Focus, which looks at the impact of corruption on economic growth in Nigeria.

The Protection of Intellectual Property

Intellectual property refers to property that is the product of intellectual activity, such as computer software, a screenplay, a music score, or the chemical formula for a new drug. Ownership rights over intellectual property are established through patents, copyrights, and trademarks. A **patent** grants the inventor of a new product or process exclusive rights for a defined period to the manufacture, use, or sale of that invention. **Copyrights** are the exclusive legal rights of authors, composers, playwrights, artists, and publishers to publish and disperse their work as they see fit. **Trademarks** are designs and names, often officially registered, by which merchants or manufacturers designate and differentiate their products (e.g., Christian Dior clothes). In the high-technology "knowledge" economy of the 21st century, intellectual property has become an increasingly important source of economic value for businesses. Protecting intellectual property has also become increasingly problematic, given that so much of it can be rendered in a digital form and then copied and distributed at very low cost via the Internet (e.g., computer software, music and video recordings).[21]

The philosophy behind intellectual property laws is to reward the originator of a new invention, book, musical record, clothes design, restaurant chain, and the like, for his or her idea and effort. Such laws are a very important stimulus to innovation and creative work. They provide an incentive for people to search for novel ways of doing things, and they reward creativity. For example, consider innovation in the pharmaceutical industry. A patent will grant the inventor of a new drug a 20-year monopoly in production of that drug. This gives pharmaceutical firms an incentive to undertake the expensive, difficult, and time-consuming basic research required to generate new drugs (it can cost $500 million in R&D and take 12 years to get a new drug on the market). Without the guarantees provided by patents, it is unlikely that companies would commit themselves to extensive basic research.[22]

The protection of intellectual property rights differs greatly from country to country. While many countries have stringent intellectual property regulations on their

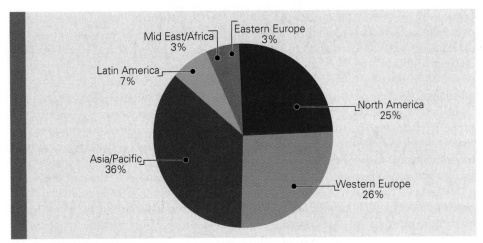

Figure 2.3

Software Piracy Dollar
Losses by Region, 2000

Source: Business Software Alliance,
Sixth Annual BSA Global Software
Piracy Study, May 2001. Available
from http://www.bsa.org/usa/
globallib/piracy/piracystats99.phtml.

books, the enforcement of these regulations has often been lax. This has been the case even among some of the 96 countries that have signed the **Paris Convention for the Protection of Industrial Property,** an important international agreement to protect intellectual property. Weak enforcement encourages the piracy of intellectual property. China and Thailand have recently been among the worst offenders in Asia. Local bookstores in China commonly maintain a section that is off-limits to foreigners; it ostensibly is reserved for sensitive political literature, but it more often displays illegally copied textbooks. Pirated computer software is also widely available in China. Similarly, the streets of Bangkok, the capital of Thailand, are lined with stands selling pirated copies of Rolex watches, Levi blue jeans, videotapes, and computer software.

Piracy in music recordings is rampant. According to one estimate, nearly 200 million illegal compact disks are stamped each year, almost 60 percent of them in China. The International Federation of the Phonographic Industry claims that its members lose $2.2 billion annually to pirates.[23] The computer software industry also suffers from lax enforcement of intellectual property rights. Estimates suggest that violations of intellectual property rights cost computer software companies revenues equal to $11.75 billion in 2000.[24] According to the Business Software Alliance, a software industry association, in 2000 some 37 percent of all software applications used in the world were pirated. The worst region was Eastern Europe, where the piracy rate was 63 percent. This was followed by piracy rates of 57 percent in the Middle East and Latin America, 51 percent in Asia, 34 percent in Western Europe, and 25 percent in North America. (See Figure 2.2 for a summary of regional differences in piracy rates for software.) One of the worst countries was China, where the piracy rate in 2000 ran 94 percent and cost the industry $1.12 billion in lost sales, up from $444 million in 1995. Although the piracy rate was much lower in the United States, the value of sales lost was more significant because of the size of the market, reaching an estimated $2.6 billion in 2000[25] (see Figure 2.3).

International businesses have a number of possible responses to violations of their intellectual property. Firms can lobby their respective governments to push for international agreements to ensure that intellectual property rights are protected and that the law is enforced. Partly as a result of such actions, international laws are being strengthened. As we shall see in Chapter 5, the most recent world trade agreement, which was signed in 1994 by 117 countries, for the first time extends the scope of the General Agreement on Tariffs and Trade (GATT) to cover intellectual property.

Under the new agreement, as of 1995 a council of the World Trade Organization is overseeing enforcement of much stricter intellectual property regulations. These regulations oblige WTO members to grant and enforce patents lasting at least 20 years and copyrights lasting 50 years. Rich countries had to comply with the rules within a year. Poor countries, in which such protection generally was much weaker, had 5 years' grace, and the very poorest have 10 years.[26] (For further details, see Chapter 5.)

In recent years, the growing global recognition of the importance of intellectual property rights has led to some progress in protecting these rights. For example, following pressure from the U.S. government, which included the threat of substantial trade sanctions, in 1996 the Chinese government agreed to enforce its existing intellectual property rights regulations (in China, as in many countries, the problem is not a lack of laws; the problem is that existing laws are not enforced). During 1996, Chinese officials closed 19 counterfeit CD-ROM factories with a capacity of 30 million to 50 million units a year. Due to stronger enforcement, the level of software piracy, although still very high, has been on the decline worldwide since the early 1990s (see Figure 2.2). The global piracy rate dropped from 52 percent of all software applications to 37 percent between 1994 and 2001.

While most governments are increasingly enforcing intellectual property rights and abiding by international agreements such as that brokered by the WTO, some have recently taken a counter position and seem to support the selective violation of intellectual property rights within their borders. In the late 1990s, the government of South Africa passed a law that allowed the country to import cheap generic versions of patented medicines, including powerful new drugs for treating AIDS, without permission from the patent owner. In 2001, this law became the focus of a legal battle between multinational drug companies seeking to protect their intellectual property rights, AIDS activists demanding access to inexpensive treatments for the poor, and the government of South Africa. The details of this case are discussed in the accompanying Management Focus. The case illustrates the difficult issues that international businesses can confront in nations that have different ideas about the value of intellectual property.

In addition to lobbying governments, firms may want to file lawsuits on their own behalf, as the drug companies are doing in South Africa (see the Management Focus). They may also choose to stay out of countries where intellectual property laws are lax, rather than risk having their ideas stolen by local entrepreneurs (such reasoning partly underlay decisions by Coca-Cola Co. and IBM to pull out of India in the early 1970s). Firms also need to be on the alert to ensure that pirated copies of their products produced in countries where intellectual property laws are lax do not turn up in their home market or in third countries. U.S. computer software giant Microsoft, for example, discovered that pirated Microsoft software, produced illegally in Thailand, was being sold worldwide as the real thing (including in the United States). In addition, Microsoft has encountered significant problems with pirated software in China.

Product Safety and Product Liability

Product safety laws set certain safety standards to which a product must adhere. **Product liability** involves holding a firm and its officers responsible when a product causes injury, death, or damage. Product liability can be much greater if a product does not conform to required safety standards. There are both civil and criminal product liability laws. Civil laws call for payment and monetary damages. Criminal liability laws result in fines or imprisonment. Both civil and criminal liability laws are probably more extensive in the United States than in any other country, although many other Western nations also have comprehensive liability laws. Liability laws are typically least extensive in less developed nations. A boom in product liability suits and awards in the United States resulted in a dramatic increase in the cost of liability insurance. Many business executives argue that the high costs of liability insurance make American businesses less competitive in the global marketplace.

ManagementFocus

Drug Patents and the AIDS Epidemic in South Africa

In December 1997, the government of South Africa passed a law that authorized two controversial practices. One, called parallel importing, allowed importers in South Africa to purchase drugs from the cheapest source available, regardless of whether the patent holders had given their approval or not. The other practice, called compulsory licensing, permitted the South African government to license local companies to produce cheaper versions of drugs whose patents are held by foreign companies. The law seems to be in violation of international agreements to protect property rights, including World Trade Organization agreements. South Africa, however, insisted that the law was necessary given its own health crisis and the high cost of patented medicines. South Africa is wrestling with an AIDS crisis of enormous proportions. Nearly 4.2 million of South Africa's 45 million people are infected with the HIV virus, more than in any other country.

Foreign drug manufacturers saw the law as an unbridled attempt to expropriate their intellectual property rights, and 39 foreign companies quickly filed a lawsuit in the country to try to block implementation of the law. Foreign pharmaceutical companies fear that South Africa is the thin end of the wedge, and if the law is allowed to stand, other countries will follow suit. Many U.S. companies also fear that if poor countries such as South Africa are allowed to buy low-priced drugs in violation of intellectual property laws, American and European consumers will soon demand the same. Drug companies argue that because drug development is a very expensive, time-consuming, and risky process, they need the protection of intellectual property laws to maintain the incentive to innovate. It can take $500 million and 12 years to develop a drug and bring it to market. Only one in five compounds that enter clinical trials actually become marketed drugs—the rest fail in trials due to poor efficacy or unfavorable side effects—and of those that make it to market, only 3 out of 10 earn profits that exceed their costs of capital. If drug companies could not count on high prices for their few successful products, the drug development process would dry up.

However, the drug companies do recognize that countries such as South Africa face special health challenges and lack the money to pay developed world prices. Accordingly, there is a long history in the industry of pricing drugs low in the developing world or giving them away. For example, AIDS drugs are sold to developing nations at an 80 to 90 percent discount over their prices in the United States. The South African government apparently thought this was not good enough. The government has been supported by various human rights and AIDS organizations, which have cast the case as an attempt by the prosperous multinational drug companies of the West to maintain their intellectual property rights in the face of desperate attempts by an impoverished government to stem a deadly crisis. For their part, the drug companies have stated that the case has little to do with AIDS and is really about the right of South Africa to break international law.

While the drug companies may have international law on their side, the tie-in with the AIDS epidemic has clearly put them on the public relations defensive. It has also limited the amount of public support that the U.S. government has been willing to give to U.S. drug companies involved in the case. The Clinton administration initially took the side of the drug companies and lobbied South Africa to repeal the law (to little effect). However, after protests from AIDS activists in the United States, the government switched its position and stated that it would consider supporting extension of the South African policy to all poor countries. The drug companies hoped that the Bush administration, which took office in 2001, would be more supportive of their position. But this administration also issued a statement in March 2001 saying officials were not contemplating a change in the current flexible policy stance. Roughly translated, that meant the Bush administration had no desire to become involved in a politically volatile issue, leaving the drug companies to fight it out in South African courts. The case began in 2001, although with appeals likely whatever the outcome, it may be several years before it is resolved.

Sources: H. Cooper, R. Zimmerman, and L. McGinley. "Patents Pending—AIDS Epidemic Traps Drug Firms in a Vise," *Wall Street Journal,* March 2, 2001, p. A1; R. Block, "Big Drug Firms Defend Right to Patent on AIDS Drugs in South African Courts," *Wall Street Journal,* March 6, 2001, p. A3; and J. Jeter, "Trial Opens in South Africa AIDS Drug Suit," *Washington Post,* March 6, 2001, p. A1.

In addition to the competitiveness issue, country differences in product safety and liability laws raise an important ethical issue for firms doing business abroad. When product safety laws are tougher in a firm's home country than in a foreign country and/or when liability laws are more lax, should a firm doing business in that foreign country follow the more relaxed local standards or should it adhere to the standards of its home country? While the ethical thing to do is undoubtedly to adhere to home-country standards, firms have been known to take advantage of lax safety and liability laws to do business in a manner that would not be allowed back home.

Contract Law

A contract is a document that specifies the conditions under which an exchange is to occur and details the rights and obligations of the parties involved. Many business transactions are regulated by some form of contract. Contract law is the body of law that governs contract enforcement. The parties to an agreement normally resort to contract law when one party feels the other has violated either the letter or the spirit of an agreement.

Contract law can differ significantly across countries, and as such it affects the kind of contracts an international business will want to use to safeguard its position should a contract dispute arise. The main differences can be traced to legal traditions. Two main legal traditions are found in the world today—the common law system and the civil law system. The common law system evolved in England over hundreds of years. It is now found in most of Great Britain's former colonies, including the United States. Common law is based on tradition, precedent, and custom. When law courts interpret common law, they do so with regard to these characteristics. Civil law is based on a very detailed set of laws organized into codes. Among other things, these codes define the laws that govern business transactions. When law courts interpret civil law, they do so with regard to these codes. Over 80 countries, including Germany, France, Japan, and Russia, operate with a civil law system. Since common law tends to be relatively ill specified, contracts drafted under a common law framework tend to be very detailed with all contingencies spelled out. In civil law systems, however, contracts tend to be much shorter and less specific because many of the issues typically covered in a common law contract are already covered in a civil code.

The Determinants of Economic Development

The political, economic, and legal systems of a country can have a profound impact on the level of economic development and hence on the attractiveness of a country as a possible market and/or production location for a firm. Here we look first at how countries differ in their level of development. Then we look at how political economy affects economic progress.

Differences in Economic Development

Different countries have dramatically different levels of economic development. One common measure of economic development is a country's gross national product per head of population. GNP is often regarded as a yardstick for the economic activity of a country; it measures the total value of the goods and services produced annually. Map 2.1 summarizes the GNP per capita of the world's nations in 2000. As can be seen, countries such as Japan, Sweden, Switzerland, and the United States are among the richest on this measure, while the large countries of China and India are among the poorest. Japan, for example, had a 2000 GNP per head of $34,210, whereas China achieved only $840 and India, $400. One of the world's poorest countries, Mozambique, had a GNP per head of only $210, while one of the world's richest, Switzerland, came in at $38,120.[27]

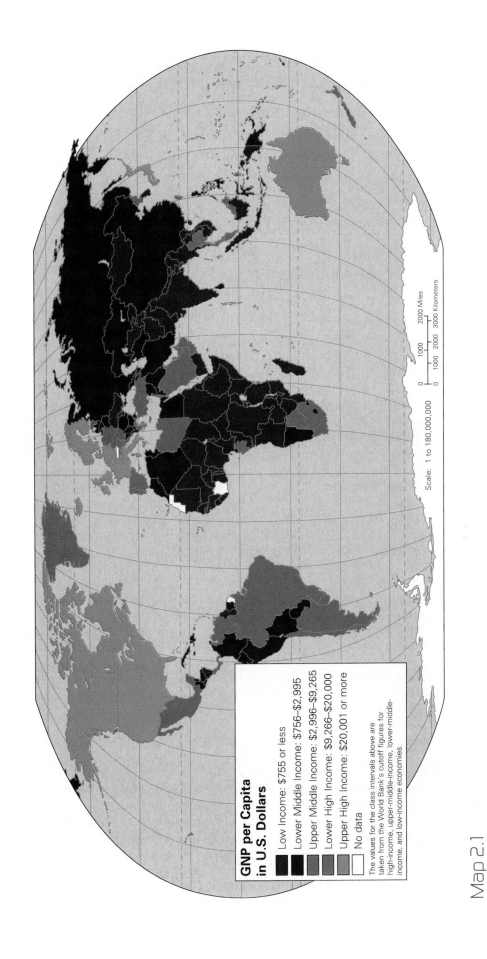

**GNP per Capita
in U.S. Dollars**

Low Income: $755 or less
Lower Middle Income: $756–$2,995
Upper Middle Income: $2,996–$9,265
Lower High Income: $9,266–$20,000
Upper High Income: $20,001 or more
No data

The values for the class intervals above are
taken from the World Bank's cutoff figures for
high-income, upper-middle-income, lower-middle-
income, and low-income economies.

Scale: 1 to 180,000,000

0   1000   2000 Miles
0   1000   2000   3000 Kilometers

Map 2.1

Gross National Product per Capita, 2000

Source: Copyright 2001 by World Bank Indicators, 2001. Reproduced with permission of World Bank (Washington, D.C.) in textbook format via Copyright Clearance Center.

Table 2.1

PPP Index and GNP Data
for Selected Countries,
2000
Source: World Bank, *World
Development Indicators, 2001*.
Copyright 2001 by World Bank
Indicators 2001. Reproduced with
permission of World Bank
(Washington, D.C.) in textbook
format via Copyright Clearance
Center.

Country	GNP per Capita	PPP per Capita	GNP Growth Rate (%) 1990–1999
Brazil	$ 3,570	$ 7,320	3.0
China	840	3,940	10.7
Germany	25,050	25,101	1.3
India	460	2,390	6.0
Japan	34,210	26,460	1.3
Nigeria	260	790	2.4
Poland	4,200	9,030	4.5
Russia	1,660	8,030	−6.1
Switzerland	38,120	24,970	0.6
United Kingdom	24,500	23,550	2.5
United States	34,260	34,260	3.3

However, GNP per head figures can be misleading because they don't consider differences in the cost of living. For example, although the 2000 GNP per capita of Switzerland, at $38,120, exceeded that of the United States, which was $34,260, the higher cost of living in Switzerland meant that American citizens could actually afford more goods and services than Swiss citizens. To account for differences in the cost of living, one can adjust GNP per capita by purchasing power. Referred to as a purchasing power parity (PPP) adjustment, it allows for a more direct comparison of living standards in different countries. The base for the adjustment is the cost of living in the United States. Table 2.1 gives the GNP per capita measured at PPP in 2000 for a selection of countries, along with their GNP per capita and their growth rate in GNP from 1990 to 1999. Map 2.2 summarizes the PPP per capita in 2000 for the nations of the world.

As can be seen, there are striking differences in the standard of living. Table 2.1 suggests that the average Indian citizen can afford to consume only 7 percent of the goods and services consumed by the average U.S. citizen. Given this, one might conclude that, despite having a population of 1 billion, India is unlikely to be a very lucrative market for the consumer products produced by many Western international businesses. However, this is not quite the correct conclusion to draw, because India has a fairly wealthy middle class, despite its large number of very poor people.

Unfortunately, the GNP and PPP data give a static picture of development. They tell us, for example, that China is much poorer than the United States, but they do not tell us if China is closing the gap. To assess this, we have to look at the economic growth rates achieved by countries. Table 2.1 gives the rate of growth in GNP achieved by a number of countries between 1990 and 1999. Map 2.3 summarizes the growth rate in GNP from 1990 to 1999. Although countries such as China and India are currently very poor, their economies are growing more rapidly than those of many advanced nations. Thus, in time they may become advanced nations and be huge markets for the products of international businesses. Given their potential, international businesses might want to get a foothold in these markets now. Even though their current contributions to an international firm's revenues might be small, their future contributions could be much larger. One might also note, however, that Table 2.1 indicates that Russia's economy shrank substantially between 1990 and 1999.

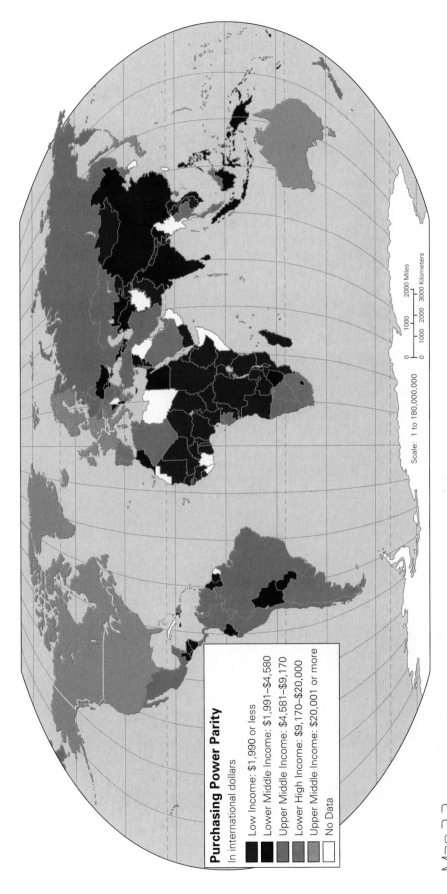

Map 2.2

Purchasing Power Parity in 2000

Purchasing Power Parity

In international dollars

Low Income: $1,990 or less
Lower Middle Income: $1,991–$4,580
Upper Middle Income: $4,581–$9,170
Lower High Income: $9,170–$20,000
Upper Middle Income: $20,001 or more
No Data

Scale: 1 to 180,000,000

0   1000   2000 Miles

0   1000   2000   3000 Kilometers

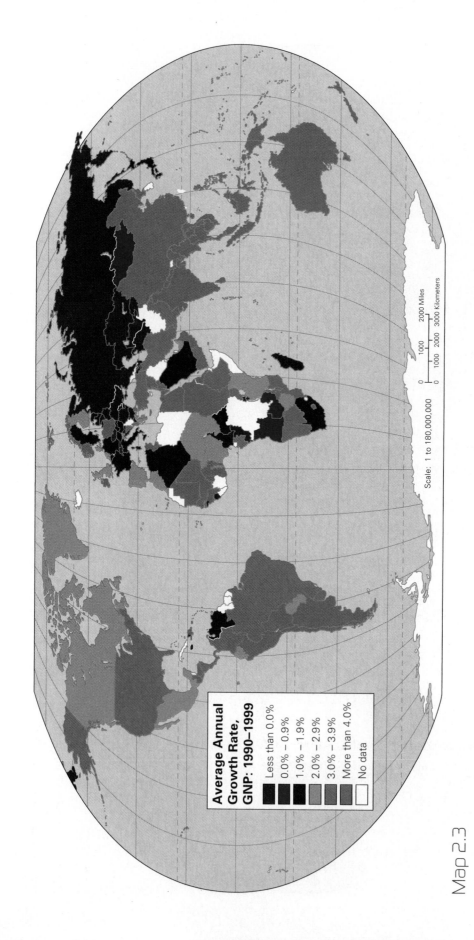

Map 2.3

Growth in Gross National Product, 1990–1999

Average Annual
Growth Rate,
GNP: 1990–1999

Less than 0.0%
0.0% – 0.9%
1.0% – 1.9%
2.0% – 2.9%
3.0% – 3.9%
More than 4.0%
No data

Scale: 1 to 180,000,000

2000 Miles

1000   2000 Miles
1000 2000 3000 Kilometers

Source: Copyright 2001 by World Bank Indicators, 2001. Reproduced with permission of the World Bank (Washington, D.C.) in textbook format via Copyright Clearance Center.

Broader Conceptions of Development: Amartya Sen

The Nobel prize-winning economist Amartya Sen has argued that development should be assessed less by material output measures such as GNP per capita and more by the capabilities and opportunities that people enjoy.[28] According to Sen, development should be seen as a process of expanding the real freedoms that people experience. Hence, development requires the removal of major impediments to freedom: poverty as well as tyranny, poor economic opportunities as well as systematic social deprivation, neglect of public facilities as well as the intolerance of repressive states. In Sen's view, development is not just an economic process, but it is a political one too, and to succeed requires the "democratization" of political communities to give citizens a voice in the important decisions made for the community. This perspective leads Sen to emphasize basic health care, especially for children, and basic education, especially for women. Not only are these factors desirable for their instrumental value in helping to achieve higher income levels, but they are also beneficial in their own right. People cannot develop their capabilities if they are chronically ill or woefully ignorant.

Sen's influential thesis has been picked up by the United Nations, which has developed the **Human Development Index** (HDI) to measure the quality of human life in different nations. The HDI is based on three measures: life expectancy at birth (which is a function of health care), educational attainment (which is measured by a combination of the adult literacy rate and enrollment in primary, secondary, and tertiary education), and whether average incomes, based on PPP estimates, are sufficient to meet the basic needs of life in a country (adequate food, shelter, and health care). As such, the HDI comes much closer to Sen's conception of how development should be measured than narrow economic measures such as GNP per capita—although Sen's thesis suggests that political freedoms should also be included in the index, and they are not. The Human Development Index is scaled from 0 to 1. Countries scoring less than 0.5 are classified as having low human development (the quality of life is poor), those scoring from 0.5 to 0.8 are classified as having medium human development, while those countries that score above 0.8 are classified as having high human development. Map 2.4 summarizes the Human Development Index scores for 1999, the most recent year for which data are available.

Political Economy and Economic Progress

It is often argued that a country's economic development is a function of its economic and political systems. What then is the nature of the relationship between political economy and economic progress? This question has been the subject of vigorous debate among academics and policymakers for some time. Despite the long debate, this remains a question for which it is not possible to give an unambiguous answer. However, it is possible to untangle the main threads of the academic arguments and make a few broad generalizations as to the nature of the relationship between political economy and economic progress.

Innovation and Entrepreneurship Are the Engines of Growth

There is wide agreement that innovation and entrepreneurial activity are the engines of long-run economic growth.[29] Those who make this argument define **innovation** broadly to include not just new products, but also new processes, new organizations, new management practices, and new strategies. Thus, Toys "Я" Us's strategy of establishing large warehouse-style toy stores and then engaging in heavy advertising and price discounting to sell the merchandise can be classified as an innovation because Toys "Я" Us was the first company to pursue this strategy. It also sees innovation as the product of entrepreneurial activity. Often, entrepreneurs first commercialize innovative new products and processes, and entrepreneurial activity provides much of the dynamism in an economy. For example, the economy of the United States has

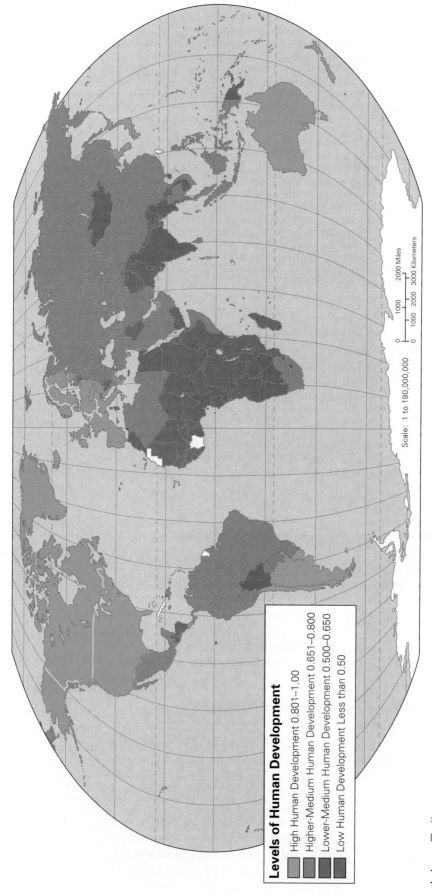

Map 2.4

The Human Development Index, 1999

Levels of Human Development

High Human Development 0.801–1.00
Higher-Medium Human Development 0.651–0.800
Lower-Medium Human Development 0.500–0.650
Low Human Development Less than 0.50

Scale: 1 to 180,000,000

0   1000   2000 Miles
0   1000   2000   3000 Kilometers

Source: United Nations, Human Development Report, 2001, Human Development Index.

benefited greatly from a high level of entrepreneurial activity, which has resulted in rapid innovation in products and process. Firms such as Cisco Systems, Dell Computer Corporation, Microsoft, and Oracle were all founded by entrepreneurial individuals to exploit advances in technology, and all these firms created significant economic value by helping to commercialize innovations in products and processes. Thus, one can conclude that if a country's economy is to sustain long-run economic growth, the business environment must be conducive to the production of product and process innovations and to entrepreneurial activity.

Innovation and Entrepreneurship Require a Market Economy

This leads logically to a further question—What is required for the business environment of a country to be conducive to innovation and entrepreneurial activity? Those who have considered this issue highlight the advantages of a market economy.[30] It has been argued that the economic freedom associated with a market economy creates greater incentives for innovation and entrepreneurship than either a planned or a mixed economy. In a market economy, any individual who has an innovative idea is free to try to make money out of that idea by starting a business (by engaging in entrepreneurial activity). Similarly, existing businesses are free to improve their operations through innovation. To the extent that they are successful, both individual entrepreneurs and established businesses can reap rewards in the form of high profits. Thus, market economies contain enormous incentives to develop innovations.

In a planned economy, the state owns all means of production. Consequently, entrepreneurial individuals have no incentives to develop valuable new innovations, since it is the state, rather than the individual, that captures all the gains. The lack of economic freedom and incentives for innovation was probably a main factor in the economic stagnation of so many former Communist states and led ultimately to their collapse at the end of the 1980s. Similar stagnation occurred in many mixed economies in those sectors where the state had a monopoly (such as health care and telecommunications in Great Britain). This stagnation provided the impetus for the widespread privatization of state-owned enterprises that we witnessed in many mixed economies during the mid-1980s and is still going on today (privatization refers to the process of selling state-owned enterprises to private investors).

A study of 102 countries over a 20-year period provided compelling evidence of a strong relationship between economic freedom (as provided by a market economy) and economic growth.[31] The study found that the more economic freedom a country had between 1975 and 1995, the more economic growth it achieved and the richer its citizens became. The six countries that had persistently high ratings of economic freedom from 1975 to 1995 (Hong Kong, Switzerland, Singapore, the United States, Canada, and Germany) were also all in the top 10 in terms of economic growth rates. In contrast, no country with persistently low economic freedom achieved a respectable growth rate. For the 16 countries for which the index of economic freedom declined the most during the 1975–95 period, gross domestic product fell at an annual rate of 0.6 percent.

Innovation and Entrepreneurship Require Strong Property Rights

Strong legal protection of property rights is another requirement for a business environment to be conducive to innovation, entrepreneurial activity, and hence economic growth.[32] Both individuals and businesses must be given the opportunity to profit from innovative ideas. Without strong property rights protection, businesses and individuals run the risk that the profits from their innovative efforts will be expropriated, either by criminal elements or by the state. The state can expropriate the profits from innovation through legal means, such as excessive taxation, or through illegal means, such as demands from state bureaucrats for kickbacks in return for granting an individual or firm a license to do business in a certain area (i.e., corruption). According to the Nobel prize-winning economist Douglass North, throughout history many governments have displayed a tendency to engage in such behavior. Inadequately enforced property rights reduce the incentives for innovation and entrepreneurial activity—since the profits from such activity are "stolen"—and hence reduce the rate of economic growth.

The Required Political System

There is a great deal of debate as to the kind of political system that best achieves a functioning market economy with strong protection for property rights.[33] We in the West tend to associate a representative democracy with a market economic system, strong property rights protection, and economic progress. Building on this, we tend to argue that democracy is good for growth.[34] However, some totalitarian regimes have fostered a market economy and strong property rights protection and have experienced rapid economic growth. Four of the fastest-growing economies of the past 30 years—South Korea, Taiwan, Singapore, and Hong Kong—had one thing in common at the start of their economic growth: undemocratic governments! At the same time, countries with stable democratic governments, such as India, experienced sluggish economic growth for long periods. In 1992, Lee Kuan Yew, Singapore's leader for many years, told an audience, "I do not believe that democracy necessarily leads to development. I believe that a country needs to develop discipline more than democracy. The exuberance of democracy leads to undisciplined and disorderly conduct which is inimical to development."[35] Others have argued that many of the current problems in Eastern Europe and the states of the former Soviet Union arose because democracy arrived before economic reform, making it more difficult for elected governments to introduce the policies that, while painful in the short run, were needed to promote rapid economic growth. China, which maintains a totalitarian government, has moved rapidly toward a market economy.

However, those who argue for the value of a totalitarian regime miss an important point: if dictators made countries rich, then much of Africa, Asia, and Latin America should have been growing rapidly for the past 40 years, and this has not been the case. Only a certain kind of totalitarian regime is capable of promoting economic growth. It must be a dictatorship that is committed to a free market system and strong protection of property rights. Also, there is no guarantee that a dictatorship will continue to pursue such progressive policies. Dictators are rarely so benevolent. Many are tempted to use the apparatus of the state to further their own private ends, violating property rights and stalling economic growth. Given this, it seems likely democratic regimes are far more conducive to long-term economic growth than are dictatorships, even benevolent ones. Only in a well-functioning, mature democracy are property rights truly secure.[36] We should not forget Amartya Sen's arguments that we reviewed earlier. Totalitarian states, by limiting human freedom, also suppress human development and therefore are detrimental to progress.

Economic Progress Begets Democracy

While it is possible to argue that democracy is not a necessary precondition for a free market economy in which property rights are protected, subsequent economic growth often leads to establishment of a democratic regime. Several of the fastest-growing Asian economies have recently adopted more democratic governments, including South Korea and Taiwan. Thus, while democracy may not always be the cause of initial economic progress, it seems to be one consequence of that progress.

A strong belief that economic progress leads to adoption of a democratic regime underlies the fairly permissive attitude that many Western governments have adopted toward human rights violations in China. Although China has a totalitarian government in which human rights are abused, many Western countries have been hesitant to criticize the country too much for fear that this might hamper the country's march toward a free market system. The belief is that once China has a free market system, democracy will follow. Whether this optimistic vision comes to pass remains to be seen.

Geography, Education, and Economic Development

While a country's political and economic system is probably the big locomotive driving its rate of economic development, other factors are also important. One that has received attention recently is geography.[37] But the belief that geography can influence economic policy, and hence economic growth rates, goes back to Adam Smith. The influential Harvard University economist Jeffrey Sachs argues

> that throughout history, coastal states, with their long engagements in international trade, have been more supportive of market institutions than landlocked states, which have tended to organize themselves as hierarchical (and often military) societies. Mountainous states, as a result of physical isolation, have often neglected market-based trade. Temperate climes have generally supported higher densities of population and thus a more extensive division of labor than tropical regions.[38]

Sachs's point is that by virtue of favorable geography, certain societies were more likely to engage in trade than others and were thus more likely to be open to and develop market-based economic systems, which in turn would promote faster economic growth. He also argues that, irrespective of the economic and political institutions a country adopts, adverse geographical conditions, such as the high rate of disease, poor soils, and hostile climate that afflict many tropical countries, can have a negative impact on development. Together with colleagues at Harvard's Institute for International Development, Sachs tested for the impact of geography on a country's economic growth rate between 1965 and 1990. He found that landlocked countries grew more slowly than coastal economies and that being entirely landlocked reduced a country's growth rate by roughly 0.7 percent per year. He also found that tropical countries grew 1.3 percent more slowly each year than countries in the temperate zone.

Education emerges as another important determinant of economic development (a point that Amartya Sen emphasizes). The general assertion is that nations that invest more in education will have higher growth rates because an educated population is a more productive population. Some rather striking anecdotal evidence suggests this is true. In 1960 Pakistanis and South Koreans were on equal footing economically. However, just 30 percent of Pakistani children were enrolled in primary schools, while 94 percent of South Koreans were. By the mid-1980s, South Korea's GNP per person was three times that of Pakistan's.[39] A survey of 14 statistical studies that looked at the relationship between a country's investment in education and its subsequent growth rates concluded investment in education did have a positive and statistically significant impact on a country's rate of economic growth.[40] Similarly, the work by Sachs discussed above suggests that investments in education help explain why some countries in Southeast Asia, such as Indonesia, Malaysia, and Singapore, have been able to overcome the disadvantages associated with their tropical geography and grow far more rapidly than tropical nations in Africa and Latin America.

States in Transition

The political economy of many of the world's nation-states has changed radically since the late 1980s. Two trends have been evident. First, during the late 1980s and early 1990s, a wave of democratic revolutions swept the world. Totalitarian governments collapsed and were replaced by democratically elected governments that were typically more committed to free market capitalism than their predecessors had been. The change was most dramatic in Eastern Europe, where the collapse of communism bought an end to the Cold War and led to the breakup of the Soviet Union, but similar changes were occurring throughout the world during the same period. Across much of Asia, Latin America, and Africa there was a marked shift toward greater democracy. Second, there has been a strong move away from centrally planned and mixed economies and toward a more free market economic model. We shall look first at the spread of democracy and then turn our attention to the spread of free market economics.

❚The Spread of Democracy

One notable development of the past 15 years has been the spread of democracy (and by extension, the decline of totalitarianism). Map 2.5 reports on the extent of totalitarianism in the world as determined by Freedom House.[41] This map charts political freedom in 2000, on a scale from 1 for the highest degree of political freedom to 7 for the lowest. Among the criteria that Freedom House uses to determine ratings for political freedom are the following:

- Free and fair elections of the head of state and legislative representatives.
- Fair electoral laws, equal campaigning opportunities, and fair polling.
- The right to organize into different political parties.
- A parliament with effective power.
- A significant opposition that has a realistic chance of gaining power.
- Freedom from domination by the military, foreign powers, totalitarian parties, religious hierarchies, or any other powerful group.
- A reasonable amount of self-determination for cultural, ethnic, and religious minorities.

Factors contributing to a low rating (i.e., to totalitarianism) include military or foreign control, the denial of self-determination to major population groups, a lack of decentralized political power, and an absence of democratic elections.

As of early 2001, Freedom House classified some 86 countries as "free" accounting for some 40.7 percent of the world's population. In these countries a broad range of political rights is respected. Another 59 countries accounting for 23.8 percent of the world's population were classified as "partly free," while 47 countries representing some 35.5 percent of the world's population were classified as "not free." The number of democracies in the world has increased from 69 nations in 1987 to 120, the highest total in history. (Not all democracies are "free," according to Freedom House, because some democracies still restrict certain political and civil liberties.) Almost 55 percent of the world's population now lives under democratic rule. Many of these new democracies are to be found in Eastern Europe and Latin America, although there have also been some notable gains in Africa during this time, such as in South Africa. Notable entrants into the ranks of the world's democracies include Mexico, which held its first fully free and fair presidential election in 2000 after free and fair parliamentary and state elections in 1997 and 1998; Senegal, where free and fair presidential elections led to a peaceful transfer of power; and Yugoslavia, where a democratic election took place despite attempted fraud by the incumbent.

Three main reasons account for the spread of democracy.[42] First, many totalitarian regimes failed to deliver economic progress to the vast bulk of their populations. The collapse of communism in Eastern Europe, for example, was precipitated by the growing gulf between the vibrant and wealthy economies of the West and the stagnant economies of the Communist East. In looking for alternatives to the socialist model, the populations of these countries could not have failed to notice that most of the world's strongest economies were governed by representative democracies. Today, the economic success of many of the newer democracies, such as Poland and the Czech Republic in the former Communist bloc, the Philippines and Taiwan in Asia, and Chile in Latin America, has strengthened the case for democracy as a key component of successful economic advancement.

Second, new information and communication technologies, including shortwave radio, satellite television, fax machines, desktop publishing, and now the Internet,

Map 2.5

Political Freedom in 2000

Source: Map data from Freedom House, Survey of Freedom, 2000–2001.

POLITICAL FREEDOM
1997

Most free

Least free

AMERICAN SAMOA	CAYMAN ISLANDS
ANDORRA	COMOROS ISLANDS
ANTIGUA AND BARBUDA	DOMINICA
BAHAMAS	FIJI
BAHRAIN	FRENCH POLYNESIA
BARBADOS	GRENADA
BERMUDA	GUADELOUPE
CAPE VERDE ISLANDS	GUAM

HONG KONG	MONACO
KIRIBATI	NAURU
LIECHTENSTEIN	NETHERLANDS ANTILLES
MACAO	NEW CALEDONIA
MALDIVES	REUNION
MALTA	ST. KITTS AND NEVIS
MARTINIQUE	ST. LUCIA
MAURITIUS	ST. VINCENT

SAN MARINO	UK VIRGIN ISLANDS
SAO TOME AND PRINCIPE	US VIRGIN ISLANDS
SEYCHELLES	VANUATU
SINGAPORE	WESTERN SAMOA
SOLOMON ISLANDS	
TONGA	
TRINIDAD AND TOBAGO	
TUVALU	

have broken down the ability of the state to control access to uncensored information. These technologies have created new conduits for the spread of democratic ideals and information from free societies. The 1989 collapse of East Germany's Communist government was in part due to unrest among a population who for years had been exposed via TV to the affluent lifestyles of West Germans. Today the Internet is allowing democratic ideals to penetrate closed societies as never before. In response, some governments have tried to restrict citizens' access to the Internet; for example, China limits access to government employees and those affiliated with universities.[43]

Third, in many countries the economic advances of the last quarter century have led to the emergence of increasingly prosperous middle and working classes who have pushed for democratic reforms. This was certainly a factor in the democratic transformation of South Korea. Entrepreneurs and other business leaders, eager to protect their property rights and ensure the dispassionate enforcement of contracts, are another force pressing for more accountable and open government.

Having said this, it would be naive to conclude that the global spread of democracy will continue unchallenged. There have been several reversals. In the former Soviet republic of Belarus, for example, President Alexander Lukashenko dissolved a democratically elected parliament and harassed the press. In the African nation of Niger, a military coup deposed a democratically elected government. In Asia, China's Marxist–Leninist leaders continue to advocate the virtues of authoritarian paths to democracy and to denounce Western democracies as an unacceptable model.

Also, democracy is still rare in large parts of the world. In Africa, just 18 nations, one-third of those on the continent, are electoral democracies. Among the 12 countries that are full or associated members of the Commonwealth of Independent States (i.e., the republics of the former Soviet Union minus the Baltic states) only four are electoral democracies. And there are no democracies in the Arab world.

❙The New World Order?

The end of the Cold War and the "new world order" that followed the collapse of communism in Eastern Europe and the former Soviet Union, taken together with the collapse of many authoritarian regimes in Latin America, have given rise to intense speculation about the future shape of global geopolitics. Author Francis Fukuyama has argued that "we may be witnessing . . . the end of history as such: that is, the end point of mankind's ideological evolution and the universalization of Western liberal democracy as the final form of human government."[44] Fukuyama goes on to say that the war of ideas may be at an end and that liberal democracy has triumphed.

Others have questioned Fukuyama's vision of a more harmonious world dominated by a universal civilization characterized by democratic regimes and free market capitalism. In a controversial book, the influential political scientist Samuel Huntington argues that there is no "universal" civilization based on widespread acceptance of Western liberal democratic ideals.[45] Huntington maintains that while many societies may be modernizing—they are adopting the material paraphernalia of the modern world, from automobiles to Coca-Cola and MTV—they are not becoming more Western. On the contrary, Huntington theorizes that modernization in non-Western societies can result in a retreat toward the traditional, such as the resurgence of Islam in many traditionally Muslim societies:

> The Islamic resurgence is both a product of and an effort to come to grips with
> modernization. Its underlying causes are those generally responsible for
> indigenization trends in non-Western societies: urbanization, social
> mobilization, higher levels of literacy and education, intensified
> communication and media consumption, and expanded interaction with
> Western and other cultures. These developments undermine traditional village
> and clan ties and create alienation and an identity crisis. Islamist symbols,
> commitments, and beliefs meet these psychological needs, and Islamist welfare

organizations, the social, cultural and economic needs of Muslims caught in the process of modernization. Muslims feel a need to return to Islamic ideas, practices, and institutions to provide the compass and the motor of modernization.[46]

Thus, the rise of Islamic fundamentalism is portrayed as a response to the alienation produced by modernization.

In contrast to Fukuyama, Huntington sees a world that is split into different civilizations, each of which has its own value systems and ideology. In addition to Western civilization, Huntington predicts the emergence of strong Islamic and Sinic (Chinese) civilizations, as well as civilizations based on Japan, Africa, Latin America, Eastern Orthodox Christianity (Russian), and Hinduism (Indian). Huntington also sees the civilizations as headed for conflict, particularly along the "fault lines" that separate them, such as Bosnia (where Muslims and Orthodox Christians have clashed), Kashmir (where Muslims and Hindus clash), and the Sudan (where a bloody war between Christians and Muslims has persisted for decades). Huntington predicts conflict between the West and Islam and between the West and China. He bases his predictions on an analysis of the different value systems and ideology of these civilizations, which in his view tend to bring them into conflict with each other. While some commentators originally dismissed Huntington's thesis, in the aftermath of the terrorist attacks on the United States on September 11, 2001, Huntington's thesis received new attention.

If Huntington's views are even partly correct, they have important implications for international business. They suggest many countries may be increasingly difficult places in which to do business, either because they are shot through with violent conflicts or because they are part of a civilization that is in conflict with an enterprise's home country. Huntington's views are speculative and controversial. It is not clear that his predictions will come to pass. More likely is the evolution of a global political system that is positioned somewhere between Fukuyama's universal global civilization based on liberal democratic ideals and Huntington's vision of a fractured world. That would still be a world, however, in which geopolitical forces periodically limit the ability of business enterprises to operate in certain foreign countries.

The Spread of Market-Based Systems

Paralleling the spread of democracy since the 1980s has been the transformation from centrally planned command economies to market-based economies. More than 30 countries that were in the former Soviet Union or the Eastern European Communist bloc are now changing their economic systems. A complete list of countries would also include Asian states such as China and Vietnam, as well as African countries such as Angola, Ethiopia, and Mozambique.[47] There has been a similar shift away from a mixed economy. Many states in Asia, Latin America, and Western Europe have sold state-owned businesses to private investors (privatization) and deregulated their economies to promote greater competition.

The underlying rationale for economic transformation has been the same the world over. In general, command and mixed economies failed to deliver the kind of sustained economic performance that was achieved by countries adopting market-based systems, such as the United States, Switzerland, Hong Kong, and Taiwan. As a consequence, even more states have gravitated toward the market-based model. Map 2.6, based on data from the Heritage Foundation, a conservative U.S. research foundation, gives some idea of the degree to which the world has shifted toward market-based economic systems. The Heritage Foundation's index of economic freedom is based on 10 indicators, such as the extent to which the government intervenes in the economy, trade policy, the degree to which property rights are protected, foreign investment regulations, and taxation rules. A country can score between 1 (most free) and 5 (least free) on each of these indicators. The lower a country's average score across all 10 indicators, the more closely its economy represents the pure market model. According to the

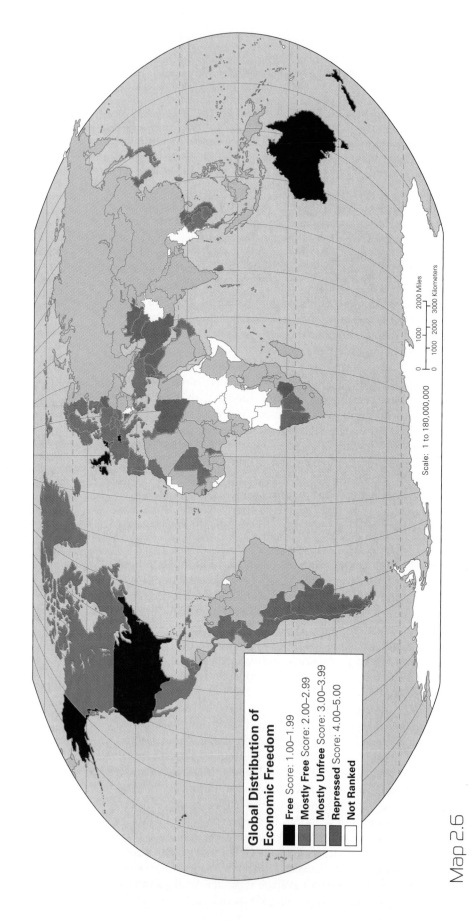

Map 2.6

Global Distribution of Economic Freedom, 2001

Global Distribution of Economic Freedom

- Free Score: 1.00–1.99
- Mostly Free Score: 2.00–2.99
- Mostly Unfree Score: 3.00–3.99
- Repressed Score: 4.00–5.00
- Not Ranked

Scale: 1 to 180,000,000

0   1000   2000 Miles
0   1000   2000   3000 Kilometers

Source: Heritage Foundation, 2001 *Index of Economic Freedom*. http://www.heritage.org:so/index/countries/maps&charts/list1.gif.

2001 index, which is summarized in Map 2.6, the world's freest economies are (in rank order) Hong Kong, Singapore, Ireland, New Zealand, Luxembourg, the United States, and the United Kingdom. Japan is ranked at 14; France at 39; Poland, 54; Turkey, 63; Mexico, 68; Brazil, 93; China, 114; Russia, 127; while the command economies of Cuba, Laos, and North Korea are to be found at the bottom of the rankings.[48]

Economic freedom does not necessarily equate with political freedom, as detailed in Map 2.6. For example, 3 of the top 10 countries in the Heritage Foundation index, Hong Kong, Singapore, and Bahrain, cannot be classified as politically free. Hong Kong was reabsorbed into Communist China in 1997, and the first thing Beijing did was shut down Hong Kong's freely elected legislature. Singapore is ranked as only "partly free" on Freedom House's index of political freedom due to practices such as widespread press censorship, while Bahrain is classified as "least free" due to the monopolization of political power by a hereditary monarchy.

The Nature of Economic Transformation

The shift toward a market-based economic system typically entails a number of steps: deregulation, privatization, and creation of a legal system to safeguard property rights.[49] We shall review each before looking at the track record of states engaged in economic transformation.

Deregulation

Deregulation involves removing legal restrictions to the free play of markets, the establishment of private enterprises, and the manner in which private enterprises operate. Before the collapse of communism, the governments in most command economies exercised tight control over prices and output, setting both through detailed state planning. They also prohibited private enterprises from operating in most sectors of the economy, severely restricted direct investment by foreign enterprises, and limited international trade. Deregulation in these cases involved removing price controls, thereby allowing prices to be set by the interplay between demand and supply; abolishing laws regulating the establishment and operation of private enterprises, and relaxing or removing restrictions on direct investment by foreign enterprises and international trade.

In mixed economies, the role of the state was more limited, but here too, in certain sectors the state set prices, owned businesses, limited private enterprise, restricted investment by foreigners, and restricted international trade. For these countries, deregulation has involved the same kind of initiatives that we have seen in former command economies, although the transformation has been easier because there was always a vibrant private sector in these countries. India is a good example of a mixed economy that is currently deregulating large areas of its economy. Deregulation has involved reforming the industrial licensing system that made it difficult to establish private enterprises and opening areas that were once closed to the private sector (including electricity generation, parts of the oil industry, steelmaking, air transport, and some areas of the telecommunications industry). It has also involved the removal of limits on foreign ownership of Indian assets and the lowering of barriers to international trade.

Another example of deregulation concerns Japan. The Japanese government is trying to abolish some of the 11,000 regulations and 10,000 administrative guidelines that regulate and constrain private enterprise in that economy. Some of these regulations are very restrictive. For example, if a private enterprise wants to open a retail store with floor space of more than 1,000 square meters, it must first gain the consent of a government advisory panel charged with limiting the influence on the local shops against which the new retail store wants to compete! In addition, the average large retailer must file more than 150 documents to gain permission to sell everyday items such as meat, tofu, and electronic appliances. In an effort to unravel such restrictions, the Japanese government plans to deregulate a diverse range of industries including power generation, gasoline retailing, financial services, retail, telecommunications, and transportation. How quickly this can be achieved, however, depends on the ability of a weak government to impose its wishes on Japan's traditionally powerful civil service bureaucracies, which are likely to resist any attempt to diminish their influence on the economy.

Privatization

Hand in hand with deregulation has come a sharp increase in privatization. Privatization transfers the ownership of state property into the hands of private individuals, frequently by the sale of state assets through an auction.[50] Privatization is seen as a way to unlock gains in economic efficiency by giving new private owners a powerful incentive—the reward of greater profits—to search for increases in productivity, to enter new markets, and to exit losing ones.[51]

The privatization movement started in Great Britain in the early 1980s when then Prime Minister Margaret Thatcher started to sell state-owned assets such as the British telephone company, British Telecom (BT). In a pattern that has been repeated around the world, this sale was linked with the deregulation of the British telecommunications industry. By allowing other firms to compete head to head with BT, deregulation ensured that privatization did not simply replace a state-owned monopoly with a private monopoly. The accompanying Country Focus looks at privatization in Brazil, and the opening case discussed privatization in India. As these two examples suggest, privatization has become a worldwide movement. In Africa, for example, Mozambique and Zambia are leading the way with very ambitious privatization plans. Zambia put over 145 state-owned companies up for sale, while Mozambique has already sold scores of enterprises, ranging from tea plantations to a chocolate factory. The most dramatic privatization programs, however, have occurred in the economies of the former Soviet Union and its Eastern European satellite states. In the Czech Republic, three-quarters of all state-owned enterprises were privatized between 1989 and 1996, helping to push the share of gross domestic product accounted for by the private sector up from 11 percent in 1989 to 60 percent in 1995. In Russia, where the private sector had been almost completely repressed before 1989, 50 percent of GDP was in private hands by 1995, again much as a result of privatization. And in Poland the private sector accounted for 59 percent of GDP in 1995, up from 20 percent in 1989.[52] However, Poland also illustrates how far some of these countries still have to travel. Despite an aggressive privatization program, Poland still had 4,000 state-owned enterprises that dominate the heavy industry, mining, and transportation sectors.

As privatization has proceeded around the world, it has become increasingly clear that simply selling state-owned assets to private investors is not enough to guarantee economic growth. Studies of privatization in central Europe have shown that the process often fails to deliver predicted benefits if the newly privatized firms continue to receive subsidies from the state and if they are protected from foreign competition by barriers to international trade and foreign direct investment.[53] In such cases, the newly privatized firms are sheltered from competition and continue acting like state monopolies. When these circumstances prevail, the newly privatized entities often have little incentive to restructure their operations to become more efficient. For privatization to work, it must also be accompanied by a more general deregulation and opening of the economy. Thus, when Brazil decided to privatize the state-owned telephone monopoly, Telebras Brazil, the government also split the company into four independent units that were to compete with each other and removed barriers to foreign direct investment in telecommunications services. This action ensured that the newly privatized entities would face significant competition and thus would have to improve their operating efficiency to survive (see the Country Focus).

The ownership structure of newly privatized firms also is important.[54] Many former command economies, for example, lack the legal regulations regarding corporate governance that are found in advanced Western economies. In advanced market economies, boards of directors are appointed by shareholders to make sure managers consider the interests of shareholders when making decisions and try to manage the firm in a manner that is consistent with maximizing the wealth of shareholders. However, some former Communist states lack laws requiring corporations to establish effective boards. In such cases, managers with a small ownership stake can often gain control over the newly privatized entity and run it for their own benefit, while ignoring the interests of other shareholders. Sometimes these managers are the same Communist bureaucrats who ran the enterprise before privatization. Because they have been schooled in the old ways of doing things, they often hesitate to take drastic action to increase the efficiency of the enterprise. Instead, they continue to run the firm as a private fiefdom, seeking to extract whatever economic value they can for their own betterment (in the form of perks that are not reported) while doing little to increase the economic efficiency of the enterprise so that shareholders benefit. Such developments seem less likely to occur, however, if a foreign investor takes a stake in the newly privatized entity. The foreign investor, who usually is a major provider of capital, is often able to use control over a critical resource (money) to push through needed change.

Legal Systems

As noted earlier in this chapter, laws protecting private property rights and providing mechanisms for contract enforcement are required for a well-functioning market economy. Without a legal system that protects property rights, and without the machinery to enforce that system, the incentive to engage in economic activity can be reduced substantially by private and public entities, including organized crime, that expropriate the profits generated by the efforts of private-sector entrepreneurs. As noted earlier, this has become a problem in many former Communist states, such as Russia, where organized crime has penetrated deeply into the fabric of many business enterprises. When communism collapsed, many of these countries lacked the legal structure required to protect property rights, all property having been held by the state. Although many states have made big strides toward instituting the required system, it will be many more years before the legal system is functioning as smoothly as it does in the West. For example, in most Eastern European nations, the title to urban and agricultural property is often uncertain because of incomplete and inaccurate records, multiple pledges on the same property, and unsettled claims resulting from demands for restitution from owners in the pre-Communist era. Also, while most countries have improved their commercial codes, institutional weaknesses still undermine contract enforcement. Court capacity is often inadequate, and procedures for resolving contract disputes out of court are often inadequate or poorly developed.[55]

The Rocky Road

In practice, the road that must be traveled to reach a market-based economic system has often turned out to be rocky.[56] This has been particularly true for the states of Eastern Europe in the post-Communist era. In this region, the move toward greater political and economic freedom has sometimes been accompanied by economic and political chaos.[57] Most Eastern European states began to liberalize their economies in the heady days of the early 1990s. They dismantled decades of price controls, allowed widespread private ownership of businesses, and permitted much greater competition. Most also planned to sell state-owned enterprises to private investors. However, given the vast number of such enterprises and how inefficient many were, making them unappealing to private investors, most privatization efforts moved forward slowly. In this new environment, many inefficient state-owned enterprises found that they could not survive without a guaranteed market. The newly democratic governments often continued to support these money-losing enterprises to stave off massive unemployment. The resulting subsidies to state-owned enterprises led to ballooning budget deficits

Country Focus

Privatization in Brazil

In the middle years of the 20th century, many Latin American governments took a large number of private companies into state ownership. This wave of nationalizations reflected a populist ideology that was interlaced with socialist, nationalist, and, on occasion, fascist rhetoric. Supported by strong trade unions, particularly in Argentina and to some extent Brazil, many politicians advocated taking private enterprises into public ownership so they could be run "for the benefit of the state and its citizens, rather than the enrichment of a small capitalist elite."

However, by the early 1990s, inefficient management, political manipulation, and corruption had turned many state-owned enterprises into national liabilities. An example was Brazil's Embraer, the only manufacturer of jet aircraft in Latin America. Founded by a military regime in 1969, Embraer developed a reputation for solid engineering. Unfortunately, protected by public ownership from the need to account for its performance to private investors, no one at Embraer seemed to care about costs or customers. As a result, in 1994 Embraer lost $310 million on sales of only $253 million.

At the same time, the winds of change were also blowing through many other economies. Communism was collapsing in Eastern Europe, socialism was in retreat throughout much of the rest of the world, and free market economics was clearly on the ascendancy. Against this background was a sharp move among the Latin American political establishment toward free market economics in the early 1990s. This shift in political and economic ideology expressed itself through adoption of programs and plans to privatize many state-owned enterprises.

In Brazil, the privatization program began slowly and quietly but accelerated throughout the 1990s. About 70 state-owned enterprises were sold to private investors between 1990 and 1996 for a total take of $14.9 billion. In 1997, Brazil sold more than $20 billion in state-owned assets, including Companhia Vale do Rio Doce (CVRD), the world's largest iron ore producer. Another $30 billion worth of state assets were sold in 1998, including Telebras, Brazil's state-owned telecommunication company, which was divided into four companies.

Evidence suggests these privatizations are having the desired effects on the companies involved. Following its privatization in December 1994, Embraer reduced its payroll from 12,700 to 3,600 in 1996 as the new management team struggled to turn the company around. Today new orders are flowing in for the company's 50-seat regional jets; production,

sales, and profits are all projected to increase. In 2000, Embraer claimed 201 orders for regional jets, ahead of its main global competitor Bombardier with 175. Another example concerns Brazil's formerly state-owned steel industry, which between 1991 and 1993 was sold as six separate companies for a total of $8.2 billion. In 1990, the state-owned monopoly employed 115,000 people and produced 22.6 million tons of steel, or 196 tons per employee. In 1996, the six successor private companies produced 25.2 million tons of steel with only 65,000 employees, or 388 tons per employee, a striking increase in employee productivity. Along similar lines, the new private owners of CVRD think they can cut operating costs by at least 20 percent in a few years.

Dramatic improvements are also evident in the telecommunication sector. In 1997, consumers still had to pay as much as $4,000 or wait several years to obtain a fixed telephone line in the state-controlled sector. Today, private telephone operators bend over backward to offer consumers fixed and mobile lines for immediate use at a fraction of their former cost. Thirty-four fixed-line and 20 wireless operators, domestic and foreign, have set up operations in Brazil in recent years, investing an estimated $30 billion. Following the end of the state monopoly and the privatization of Telebras in 1998, Brazil is now entering the final phase of liberalization toward free competition. The opening of the telecommunication sector has been one of the driving forces behind economic growth. In the five years before 1999, mobile telephony grew by an average annual rate of 89 percent, while fixed-line telephony grew by 16 percent. By comparison, GDP on average grew by only 2.28 percent.

As of late 2000, Brazil's privatization program was a significant way toward completion. Still remaining, however, were the San Paulo state-owned bank Banespa; a state-owned insurance company, IRB; and the state-owned oil company, Petrobras. Although Petrobras was not officially part of the privatization program, the state indicated in 2000 that it would sell a 28 percent minority share in the company to private investors for an estimated $4 billion, a move that many see as a prelude to the privatization of this company.

Sources: "Let the Party Begin," *The Economist,* April 26, 1997, pp. 57–58; "A Very Big Deal. A Survey of Business in Latin America," *The Economist,* December 6, 1997, pp. S9–S12; R. Colitt, "Brazil: Finance and Investment—Liberalization Drives Growth," *Financial Times,* December 20, 2000, p. 3; and V. Herror, "Region's 2000 Privatizations Disappoint," *IFR Latin America,* August 7, 2000, p. 14.

that were typically financed by printing money. Printing money, along with the lack of price controls, often led to hyperinflation. In 1993 the inflation rate was 21 percent in Hungary, 38 percent in Poland, 841 percent in Russia, and a staggering 10,000 percent in the Ukraine. Since then, however, many governments have instituted tight monetary policies and brought down their inflation rates.

Another consequence of the shift toward a market economy was collapsing output as inefficient state-owned enterprises failed to find buyers for their goods. Real gross domestic product fell dramatically in many post-Communist states between 1990 and 1994. However, the corner has been turned in several countries. Poland, the Czech Republic, and Hungary now all boast growing economies and relatively low inflation. But some countries, such as Russia and the Ukraine, still find themselves grappling with major economic problems.

A study by the World Bank suggests that the post-Communist states that have been most successful at transforming their economies were those that followed an economic policy best described as "shock therapy." In these countries—which include the Czech Republic, Hungary, and Poland—prices and trade were liberated quickly, inflation was held in check by tight monetary policy, and the privatization of state-owned industries was implemented rapidly. Among the 26 economies of Eastern Europe and the former Soviet Union, the World Bank found a strong positive correlation between the imposition of such shock therapy and subsequent economic growth. Speedy reformers suffered smaller falls in output and returned to growth more quickly than those such as Russia and the Ukraine that moved more slowly.[58]

Despite variations within the group, in general, the transformation of former command economies has progressed significantly. Figure 2.4 shows the degree to which economic liberalization has proceeded for a group of transition economies between 1989, when the process began for many, and 1997. The liberalization index used in Figure 2.4 is based on three separate indicators—the extent of domestic market liberalization, foreign trade liberalization, and enterprise privatization and banking reforms. The boundaries of the index are from 0 to 1, with 1 signifying the conditions found in advanced market economies such as the United States. As can be seen, the transition from a command economy to a functioning market economy was close to completion by 1997 for several countries. The index for the Czech Republic and Hungary was 0.93 at this point, that for Poland and Slovenia was 0.89, and for Russia it was 0.83. In contrast, the index for China and the Ukraine was only 0.66 and 0.65, respectively, indicating that both countries still had a significant way to go.[59] Other data show that for Hungary, Poland, and the Czech Republic, private-sector output as a percentage of GDP rose from 10 percent in 1987, to between 60 and 70 percent by 1997, a figure that is comparable to that found in some Western democracies.[60] Several studies have shown that countries such as Poland and the Czech Republic, which undertook a very rapid economic transformation, have on average outperformed laggards such as the Ukraine.[61] Rapid transformation may cause considerable dislocation for a number of years, but in the long run it seems to yield the greatest gains.

Implications

The global changes in political and economic systems discussed above have several implications for international business. The ideological conflict between collectivism and individualism that so defined the 20th century is winding down. The free market ideology of the West has won the Cold War and has never been more widespread than it was at the beginning of the millennium. Although command economies still remain and totalitarian dictatorships can still be found around the world, the tide is running in favor of free markets and democracy.

The implications for business are enormous. For the best part of 50 years, half of the world was off-limits to Western businesses. Now all that is changing. Many of the national markets of Eastern Europe, Latin America, Africa, and Asia may still be

Figure 2.4

Liberalization Index,
1989–1997

Source: International Monetary
Fund, *World Economic Outlook:
Focus on Transition Economies* (Geneva:
IMF, October 2000), Table 3.10.

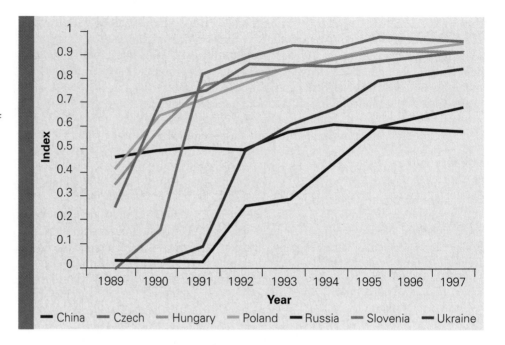

undeveloped and impoverished, but they are potentially enormous. With a population of 1.2 billion, the Chinese market alone is potentially bigger than that of the United States, the European Union, and Japan combined! Similarly India, with its one billion people, is a potentially huge future market. Latin America has another 400 million potential consumers. It is unlikely that China, Russia, Poland, or any of the other states now moving toward a free market system will attain the living standards of the West anytime soon. Nevertheless, the upside potential is so large that companies need to consider making inroads now.

However, just as the potential gains are large, so are the risks. There is no guarantee that democracy will thrive in the newly democratic states of Eastern Europe, particularly if these states have to grapple with severe economic setbacks. Totalitarian dictatorships could return, although they are unlikely to be of the communist variety. Although the bipolar world of the Cold War era has vanished, it may be replaced by a multipolar world dominated by a number of civilizations. In such a world, much of the economic promise inherent in the global shift toward market-based economic systems may evaporate in the face of conflicts between civilizations. While the long-term potential for economic gain from investment in the world's new market economies is large, the risks associated with any such investment are also substantial. It would be foolish to ignore these.

Implications for Business

The implications for international business of the material discussed in this chapter fall into two broad categories. First, the political, economic, and legal environment of a country clearly influences the attractiveness of that country as a market and/or investment site. The benefits, costs, and risks associated with doing business in a country are a function of that country's political, economic, and legal systems. Second, the political, economic, and legal systems of a country can raise important ethical issues that have implications for the practice of international business. Here we consider each of these issues.

Attractiveness

The overall attractiveness of a country as a market and/or investment site depends on balancing the likely long-term benefits of doing business in that country against the likely costs and risks. Below we consider the determinants of benefits, costs, and risks.

Benefits In the most general sense, the long-run monetary benefits of doing business in a country are a function of the size of the market, the present wealth (purchasing power) of consumers in that market, and the likely future wealth of consumers. While some markets are very large when measured by number of consumers (e.g., China and India), low living standards may imply limited purchasing power and, therefore, a relatively small market when measured in economic terms. While international businesses need to be aware of this distinction, they also need to keep in mind the likely future prospects of a country. In 1960, for example, South Korea was viewed as just another impoverished Third World nation. By 2000 it was the world's 12th largest economy, measured in terms of GDP. International firms that recognized South Korea's potential in 1960 and began to do business in that country may have reaped greater benefits than those that wrote off South Korea.

By identifying and investing early in a potential future economic star, international firms may build brand loyalty and gain experience in that country's business practices. These will pay back substantial dividends if that country achieves sustained high economic growth rates. In contrast, late entrants may find that they lack the brand loyalty and experience necessary to achieve a significant presence in the market. In the language of business strategy, early entrants into potential future economic stars may be able to reap substantial **first-mover advantages,** while late entrants may fall victim to **late-mover disadvantages.**[62] (First-mover advantages are the advantages that accrue to early entrants into a market. Late-mover disadvantages are the handicap that late entrants might suffer from.)

A country's economic system and property rights regime are reasonably good predictors of economic prospects. Countries with free market economies in which property rights are well protected tend to achieve greater economic growth rates than command economies and/or economies where property rights are poorly protected. It follows that a country's economic system and property rights regime, when taken together with market size (in terms of population), probably constitute reasonably good indicators of the potential long-run benefits of doing business in a country.

Costs A number of political, economic, and legal factors determine the costs of doing business in a country. With regard to political factors, the costs of doing business in a country can be increased by a need to pay off the politically powerful to be allowed by the government to do business. The need to pay what are essentially bribes is greater in closed totalitarian states than in open democratic societies where politicians are held accountable by the electorate (although this is not a hard-and-fast distinction). Whether a company should actually pay bribes in return for market access should be determined on the basis of the legal and ethical implications of such action. We discuss this consideration below.

With regard to economic factors, one of the most important variables is the sophistication of a country's economy. It may be more costly to do business in relatively primitive or undeveloped economies because of the lack of infrastructure and supporting businesses. At the extreme, an international firm may have to provide its own infrastructure and supporting business, which obviously raises costs. When McDonald's decided to open its first restaurant in Moscow, it found that to serve food and drink indistinguishable from that served in McDonald's restaurants elsewhere, it had to vertically integrate backward to supply its own needs. The quality of Russian-grown potatoes and meat was too poor. Thus, to protect the quality of its product, McDonald's set up its own dairy farms, cattle ranches, vegetable plots, and food processing plants within Russia. This raised the cost of doing business in Russia, relative to the cost in more sophisticated economies where high-quality inputs could be purchased on the open market.

As for legal factors, it can be more costly to do business in a country where local laws and regulations set strict standards with regard to product safety, safety in the workplace, environmental pollution, and the like (since adhering to such regulations is costly). It can also be more costly to do business in a country like the United States, where the absence of a cap on damage awards has meant spiraling liability insurance rates. It can be more costly to do business in a country that lacks well-established laws for regulating business practice (as is the case in many of the former Communist nations). In the absence of a well-developed body of business contract law, international firms may find no satisfactory way to resolve contract disputes and, consequently, routinely face large losses from contract violations. Similarly, local laws that fail to adequately protect intellectual property can lead to the "theft" of an international business's intellectual property, and lost income.

Risks As with costs, the risks of doing business in a country are determined by a number of political, economic, and legal factors. **Political risk** has been defined as the likelihood that political forces will cause drastic changes in a country's business environment that adversely affect the profit and other goals of a particular business enterprise.[63] So defined, political risk tends to be greater in countries experiencing social unrest and disorder or in countries where the underlying nature of a society increases the likelihood of social unrest. Social unrest typically finds expression in strikes, demonstrations, terrorism, and violent conflict. Such unrest is more likely to be found in countries that contain more than one ethnic nationality, in countries where competing ideologies are battling for political control, in countries where economic mismanagement has created high inflation and falling living standards, or in countries that straddle the "fault lines" between civilizations, such as Bosnia.

Social unrest can result in abrupt changes in government and government policy or, in some cases, in protracted civil strife. Such strife tends to have negative economic implications for the profit goals of business enterprises. For example, in the aftermath of the 1979 Islamic revolution in Iran, the Iranian assets of numerous U.S. companies were seized by the new Iranian government without compensation. Similarly, the violent disintegration of the Yugoslavian federation into warring states, including Bosnia, Croatia, and Serbia, precipitated a collapse in the local economies and in the profitability of investments in those countries.

On the economic front, economic risks arise from economic mismanagement by the government of a country. **Economic risks** can be defined as the likelihood that economic mismanagement will cause drastic changes in a country's business environment that adversely affect the profit and other goals of a particular business enterprise. Economic risks are not independent of political risk. Economic mismanagement may give rise to significant social unrest and hence political risk. Nevertheless, economic risks are worth emphasizing as a separate category because there is not always a one-to-one relationship between economic mismanagement and social unrest. One visible indicator of economic mismanagement tends to be a country's inflation rate. Another tends to be the level of business and government debt in the country.

In Asian states such as Indonesia, Thailand, and South Korea, businesses increased their debt rapidly during the 1990s, often at the bequest of the government, which was encouraging them to invest in industries deemed to be of "strategic importance" to the country. The result was overinvestment, with more industrial (factories) and commercial capacity (office space) being built than could be justified by demand conditions. Many of these investments turned out to be uneconomic. The borrowers failed to generate the profits required to meet their debt payment obligations. In turn, the banks that had lent money to these businesses suddenly found that they had rapid increases in nonperforming loans on their books. Foreign investors, believing that many local companies and banks might go bankrupt, pulled their money out of these countries, selling local stock bonds, and currency. This action precipitated the 1997–1998 financial crisis in Southeast Asia. The crisis included a precipitous decline in the value of Asian stock markets, which in some cases exceeded 70 percent; a similar collapse in the value of many Asian currencies against the U.S. dollar; an implosion of local demand; and a severe economic recession that will affect many Asian countries for years to come. In short, economic risks were rising throughout Southeast Asia during the 1990s. Astute foreign businesses and investors, seeing this situation, limited their exposure in this part of the world. More naive businesses and investors lost their shirts!

On the legal front, risks arise when a country's legal system fails to provide adequate safeguards in the case of contract violations or to protect property rights. When legal safeguards are weak, firms are more likely to break contracts and/or steal intellectual property if they perceive it as being in their interests to do so. Thus, **legal risks** might be defined as the likelihood that a trading partner will opportunistically break a contract or expropriate property rights. When legal risks in a country are high, an international business might hesitate entering into a long-term contract or joint-venture agreement with a firm in that country. For example, in the 1970s when the Indian government passed a law requiring all foreign investors to enter into joint ventures with Indian companies, U.S. companies such as IBM and Coca-Cola closed their investments in India. They believed that the Indian legal system did not provide for adequate protection of intellectual property rights, creating the very real danger that their Indian partners might expropriate the intellectual property of the American companies—which for IBM and Coca-Cola amounted to the core of their competitive advantage.

Overall Attractiveness The overall attractiveness of a country as a potential market and/or investment site for an international business depends on balancing the benefits, costs, and risks associated with doing business in that country. Generally, the costs and risks associated with doing business in a foreign country are typically lower in economically advanced and politically stable democratic nations and greater in less developed and politically unstable nations. The calculus is complicated, however, by the fact that the potential long-run benefits are not only dependent upon a nation's current stage of economic development or political stability. Rather, the benefits depend on likely future economic growth rates. Economic growth appears to be a function of a free market system and a country's capacity for growth (which may be greater in less developed nations). This leads one to conclude that, other things being equal, the benefit–cost–risk trade-off is likely to be most favorable in politically stable developed and developing nations that have free market systems and no dramatic upsurge in either inflation rates or private-sector debt. It is likely to be least favorable in politically unstable developing nations that operate with a mixed or command economy or in developing nations where speculative financial bubbles have led to excess borrowing.

Ethics and Regulations

Country differences give rise to some important and contentious ethical issues. Three important issues that have been the focus of much debate in recent years are (1) the ethics of doing business in nations that violate human rights, (2) the ethics of doing business in countries with very lax labor and environmental regulations, and (3) the ethics of corruption.

Ethics and Human Rights   One major ethical dilemma facing firms from democratic nations is whether they should do business in totalitarian countries, such as China, that routinely violate the human rights of their citizens. There are two sides to this issue. Some argue that investing in totalitarian countries provides comfort to dictators and can help prop up repressive regimes that abuse basic human rights. For instance, Human Rights Watch, an organization that promotes the protection of basic human rights around the world, has argued that the progressive trade policies adopted by Western nations toward China has done little to deter human rights abuses.[64] According to Human Rights Watch, the Chinese government stepped up its repression of political dissidents in 1996 after the Clinton administration removed human rights as a factor in determining China's trade status with the United States. Without investment by Western firms and the support of Western governments, many repressive regimes would collapse and be replaced by more democratically inclined governments, critics such as Human Rights Watch argue. Firms that have invested in Chile, China, Iraq, and South Africa have all been the direct targets of such criticisms. The 1994 dismantling of the apartheid system in South Africa has been credited to economic sanctions by Western nations, including a lack of investment by Western firms. This, say those who argue against investment in totalitarian countries, is proof that investment boycotts can work (although decades of U.S.-led investment boycotts against Cuba and Iran, among other countries, have failed to have a similar impact).

In contrast, some argue that Western investment, by raising the level of economic development of a totalitarian country, can help change it from within. They note that economic well-being and political freedoms often go hand in hand. Thus, when arguing against attempts to apply trade sanctions to China in the wake of the violent 1989 government crackdown on pro-democracy demonstrators, the U.S. government claimed that U.S. firms should continue to be allowed to invest in mainland China because greater political freedoms would follow the resulting economic growth. The Clinton administration used similar logic as the basis for its 1996 decision decoupling human rights issues from trade policy considerations.

Since both positions have some merit, it is difficult to arrive at a general statement of what firms should do. Unless mandated by government (as in the case of investment in South Africa) each firm must make its own judgments about the ethical implications of investing in totalitarian states on a case-by-case basis. The more repressive the regime, however, and the less amenable it seems to be to change, the greater the case for not investing.

Ethics and Regulations   A second important ethical issue is whether an international firm should adhere to the same standards of product safety, work safety, and environmental protection that are required in its home country. This is of particular concern to many firms based in Western nations, where product safety, worker safety, and environmental protection laws are among the toughest in the world. Should Western firms investing in less developed countries adhere to tough Western standards, even though local regulations don't require them to do so? This issue has taken on added importance in recent years following revelations that Western enterprises have been using child labor or very poorly paid "sweatshop" labor in developing nations. Companies criticized for using sweatshop labor include the Gap, Disney, Wal-Mart, and Nike.[65]

Again there is no easy answer. While on the face of it the argument for adhering to Western standards might seem strong, on closer examination the issue becomes more complicated. What if adhering to Western standards would make the foreign investment unprofitable, thereby denying the foreign country much-needed jobs? What is the ethical thing to do? To adhere to Western standards and not invest, thereby denying people jobs, or to adhere to local standards and invest, thereby providing jobs and income? As with many ethical dilemmas, there is no easy answer. Each case needs to be assessed on its own merits.

Ethics and Corruption A final ethical issue concerns bribes and corruption. Should an international business pay bribes to corrupt government officials to gain market access to a foreign country? To most Westerners, bribery seems to be a corrupt and morally repugnant way of doing business, so the answer might initially be no. Some countries have laws on their books that prohibit their citizens from paying bribes to foreign government officials in return for economic favors. In the United States, for example, the **Foreign Corrupt Practices Act** of 1977 prohibits U.S. companies from making "corrupt" payments to foreign officials to obtain or retain business, although many other developed nations lack similar laws. Trade and finance ministers from the member states of the Organization for Economic Cooperation and Development (OECD), an association of the world's 20 or so most powerful economies, are working on a convention that would oblige member states to make the bribery of foreign public officials a criminal offense.

However, in many parts of the world, payoffs to government officials are a part of life. One can argue that not investing ignores the fact that such investment can bring substantial benefits to the local populace in terms of income and jobs. From a pragmatic standpoint, the practice of giving bribes, although a little evil, might be the price that must be paid to do a greater good (assuming the investment creates jobs where none existed before and assuming the practice is not illegal). Several economists advocate this reasoning, suggesting that in the context of pervasive and cumbersome regulations in developing countries, corruption may actually improve efficiency and help growth! These economists theorize that in a country where preexisting political structures distort or limit the workings of the market mechanism, corruption in the form of black-marketeering, smuggling, and side payments to government bureaucrats to "speed up" approval for business investments may actually enhance welfare.[66]

However, other economists have argued that corruption reduces the returns on business investment.[67] In a country where corruption is common, the profits from a business activity may be siphoned off by unproductive bureaucrats who demand side payments for granting the enterprise permission to operate. This reduces the incentive that businesses have to invest and may hurt a country's economic growth rate. One economist's study of the connection between corruption and growth in 70 countries found that corruption had a significant negative impact on a country's economic growth rate.[68] Given the debate and the complexity of this issue, one again might conclude that generalization is difficult. Yes, corruption is bad, and yes, it may harm a country's economic development, but yes, there are also cases where side payments to government officials can remove the bureaucratic barriers to investments that create jobs. This pragmatic stance ignores, however, that corruption tends to "corrupt" both the bribe giver and the bribe taker. Corruption feeds on itself, and once an individual has started to walk down the road of corruption, pulling back may be difficult if not impossible. This strengthens the moral case for never engaging in corruption, no matter how compelling the benefits might seem.

Chapter Summary

This chapter has reviewed how the political, economic, and legal systems of different countries vary. The potential benefits, costs, and risks of doing business in a country are a function of its political, economic, and legal systems. More specifically:

1. Political systems can be assessed according to two dimensions: the degree to which they emphasize collectivism as opposed to individualism, and the degree to which they are democratic or totalitarian.

2. Collectivism is an ideology that views the needs of society as being more important than the needs of the individual. Collectivism translates into an advocacy for state intervention in economic activity and, in the case of communism, a totalitarian dictatorship.

3. Individualism is an ideology that is built on an emphasis of the primacy of individual's freedoms in the political, economic, and cultural realms. Individualism translates into an advocacy for democratic ideals and free market economics.

4. Democracy and totalitarianism are at different ends of the political spectrum. In a representative democracy, citizens periodically elect individuals to represent them and political freedoms are guaranteed by a constitution. In a totalitarian state, political power is monopolized by a party, group, or individual, and basic political freedoms are denied to citizens of the state.

5. There are four broad types of economic systems: a market economy, a command economy, a mixed economy, and a state-directed economy. In a market economy, prices are free of controls and private ownership is predominant. In a command economy, prices are set by central planners, productive assets are owned by the state, and private ownership is forbidden. A mixed economy has elements of both a market economy and a command economy. A state-directed economy is one in which the state plays a significant role in directing the investment activities of private enterprise through "industrial policy" and in otherwise regulating business activity in accordance with national goals.

6. Differences in the structure of law between countries can have important implications for the practice of international business. The degree to which property rights are protected can vary dramatically from country to country, as can product safety and product liability legislation and the nature of contract law.

7. The rate of economic progress in a country seems to depend on the extent to which that country has a well-functioning market economy in which property rights are protected.

8. Many countries are now in a state of transition. There is a marked shift away from totalitarian governments and command or mixed economic systems and toward democratic political institutions and free market economic systems.

9. The attractiveness of a country as a market and/or investment site depends on balancing the likely long-run benefits of doing business in that country against the likely costs and risks.

10. The benefits of doing business in a country are a function of the size of the market (population), its present wealth (purchasing power), and its future growth prospects. By investing early in countries that are currently poor but are nevertheless growing rapidly, firms can gain first-mover advantages that will pay back substantial dividends in the future.

11. The costs of doing business in a country tend to be greater where political payoffs are required to gain market access, where supporting infrastructure is lacking or underdeveloped, and where adhering to local laws and regulations is costly.

12. The risks of doing business in a country tend to be greater in countries that are (1) politically unstable, (2) subject to economic mismanagement, and (3) lacking a legal system to provide adequate safeguards in the case of contract or property rights violations.

13. Country differences give rise to several ethical dilemmas, including (a) should a firm do business in a repressive totalitarian state, (b) should a firm conform to its home product, workplace, and environmental standards when they are not required by the host country, and (c) should a firm pay bribes to government officials to gain market access?

Critical Discussion Questions

1. Free market economies stimulate greater economic growth, whereas state-directed economies stifle growth! Discuss.

2. A democratic political system is an essential condition for sustained economic progress. Discuss.

3. What is the relationship between corruption in a country (i.e., bribe taking by government officials) and economic growth? Is corruption always bad?

4. The Nobel prize-winning economist Amartya Sen argues that the concept of development should be broadened to include more than just economic development. What other factors does Sen think should be included in an assessment of development? How might adoption of Sen's views influence government policy? Do you think Sen is correct that development is about more than just economic development? Explain.

5. During the late 1980s and early 1990s, China was routinely cited by various international organizations such as Amnesty International and Freedom Watch for major human rights violations, includ-ing torture, beatings, imprisonment, and executions of political dissidents. Despite this, in the late 1990s China received record levels of foreign direct investment, mainly from firms based in democratic societies such as the United States, Japan, and Germany. Evaluate this trend from an ethical perspective. If you were the CEO of a firm that had the option of making a potentially very profitable investment in China, what would you do?

6. You are the CEO of a company that has to choose between making a $100 million investment in Russia or the Czech Republic. Both investments promise the same long-run return, so your choice is driven by risk considerations. Assess the various risks of doing business in each of these nations. Which investment would you favor and why?

Closing Case

Microsoft's Troubles in China

Microsoft, the world's biggest personal computer software company, developed MS-DOS and then Windows, the operating system and graphical user interface that now reside on more than 90 percent of the world's personal computers. In addition, Microsoft has a slew of best-selling applications software, including its word processing program (Microsoft Word), spreadsheet program (Excel), and presentation program (PowerPoint). An integral part of Microsoft's international strategy has been expansion into mainland China, which was projected to become the third largest PC market in the world in 2001. With a population of 1.273 billion, China represents a potentially huge market for Microsoft. Microsoft's initial goal was to build up Chinese sales from nothing in 1994 to $100 million by 2000, a goal that it appears to have met. However, sales could have been very much higher were it not for a number of problems that Microsoft encountered in China.

The most obvious and serious obstacle to Microsoft's success in China has been the rampant level of software piracy. Some 90 to 95 percent of the software used in China is pirated, according to figures from the Business Software Alliance. Microsoft is a prime target of this activity. Most Microsoft products used in China are illegal copies. China's government is believed to be one of the worst offenders. Microsoft's lawyers complain that Beijing doesn't budget for software purchases, forcing its cash-strapped bureau-cracy to find cheap software solutions. Thus, Microsoft claims, much of the government ends up using pirated software. To make matters worse, China is an exporter of counterfeit software. Microsoft executives don't have to go far to see the problem. Just a few blocks from the company's Hong Kong office is a tiny shop that offers CD-ROMs, each crammed with dozens of computer programs that collectively are worth about $20,000. The asking price is about 500 Hong Kong dollars, or $52!

Microsoft officials are quick to point out the problem arises because Chinese judicial authorities do not enforce their own laws. Microsoft found this out when it first tried to use China's judicial system to sue software pirates. Microsoft pressed officials in China's southern province of Guangdong to raid a manufacturer that was producing counterfeit holograms that Microsoft used to authenticate its software manuals. The Chinese authorities prosecuted the manufacturer, acknowledged that a copyright violation had occurred, but awarded Microsoft only $2,600 and fined the pirate company $3,000! Unde-terred by this limited victory, Microsoft continued in its attempts to use the legal system in China to limit copyright violations. However, in late 1999 the tactic backfired when Microsoft sued a small Chinese firm, the Yadu Group, for $200,000, claiming it was using pirated Microsoft products. The Chinese Press portrayed Microsoft as an American bully going after struggling Chinese start-ups. When the case came to court, the judge threw it out, claiming the engineers who actually admitted to using the pirated software were not employed by Yadu Group, but by an affiliate firm. According to the judge, Microsoft was suing the wrong firm!

Another Microsoft response to the piracy problem has been to reduce the price on its software to compete with pirated versions. In October 1994, Microsoft reduced the price on its Chinese software by as much as 200 percent and it has kept prices low ever since. However, this action may have little impact, for the programs are still priced at $100 to $200, compared to $5 to $20 for an illegal copy of the same software. Even at lower prices, the cost of Microsoft's software can amount to several months' salary for a white-collar worker.

Yet another tactic adopted by the company has been to lobby the U.S. government to pressure Chinese authorities to start enforcing their own laws. As part of its lobbying effort, Microsoft has engaged in its own version of "guerrilla warfare," digging through trash bins, paying locals to spy, even posing as money-grubbing businessmen to collect evidence of piracy, which they have then passed on to U.S. trade officials. Initially it looked as if the tactic might work, because the U.S. government had some leverage over China. China wished to join the World Trade Organization and viewed U.S. support as crucial. The United States said it would not support Chinese membership unless China started enforcing its intellectual property laws. This demand was backed up by a threat to impose tariffs of $1.08 billion on Chinese exports unless China agreed to stricter enforcement. After a tense period, the Chinese backed down and acquiesced to U.S. demands in February 1995. The Chinese government agreed to start enforcing its intellectual property rights laws, to crack down on factories that the United States identified as pirating U.S. goods, to respect U.S. trademarks including Microsoft's, and to instruct Chinese government ministries to stop using pirated software. However, by 2000 the level of software piracy in China was still running at 95 percent, suggesting that little progress had been made. The United States signed off on China's entry into the World Trade Organization in September 2000, thereby losing leverage over China on this issue. Although WTO rules prohibit the piracy of intellectual property, such as software, few observers expect the WTO to be able to solve this particular problem. It seems to be endemic worldwide.

As if piracy was not giving Microsoft enough headaches in China, in early 2000 another potentially serious problem appeared on the horizon. The Chinese government declared it was concerned about security issues related to Microsoft software. Government spokesmen started to liken China's dependence on Microsoft software as leaving the keys to the country's increasingly computerized economy in the hands of a potential enemy. Some warned that holes in Microsoft's computer code might allow the United States access to Chinese networks or even enable it, in times of war, to shut those networks down. "Without information security, there is no national security in politics, economics, and military affairs," declared an editorial in the *People's Liberation Army Daily* in early 2000.

With these fears in mind, in 2000 the Chinese government started to promote a Chinese-language version of the Linux operating system as an alternative to the Chinese-language version of Windows 2000. A Finnish university student first created Linux in 1991. The source code underlying Linux is now distributed free to anyone who wishes to use it with the stipulation that anybody can improve upon it so long as any modifications are shared with the rest of the world. In the Chinese view, the fact that the Linux code is not privately held assures that any security it wants to build into its computer systems will not have undetectable vulnerabilities.

Sources: S. Bilello, "U.S. Wages War on China's Pirates," *Newsday*, February 7, 1995, p. A41; C. S. Smith, "Microsoft May Get Help in China from its Uncle Sam," *Wall Street Journal*, November 21, 1994, p. B4; "Making War on China's Pirates," *The Economist*, February 11, 1995, pp. 33–34; interviews with Microsoft officials; M. O'Neill, "Microsoft Chairman Says China Has Key Future Role," *South China Morning Post*, December 12, 1997, p. 1; "Intellectual Property: Bazaar Software," *The Economist*, March 8, 1997, pp. 77–78; L. Chang, "In China's Software Market, a Hundred Microsoft Bashers Bloom," *Wall Street Journal*, December 31, 1999, pp. B1, 2; C.S. Smith, "China Moves to Cut Power of Microsoft," *New York Times*, July 8, 2000, p. A1; and Business Software Alliance, *1999 Global Software Piracy Report*. Available from http://www.bsa.org.

Case Discussion Questions

1. How important is China to Microsoft's long-term future?

2. What are the legal impediments to Microsoft growing its sales in China? What are the political impediments?

3. Why do you think it is so difficult to reduce software piracy in China? What strategies might Microsoft adopt to try to limit piracy in China? Are there ways of selling software that might make it difficult for piracy to occur?

4. Given the high level of software piracy around the world (see Figure 2.2), to what extent can the threat of trade sanctions be used to force the Chinese to enforce their own intellectual property rights regulations?

5. In the context of the Chinese market, what advantages does the Linux operating system have over Microsoft's Windows 2000? What advantages does Microsoft have over Linux?

Notes

1. Although as we shall see, there is not a strict one-to-one correspondence between political systems and economic systems. A. O. Hirschman, "The On-and-Off Again Connection between Political and Economic Progress," *American Economic Review* 84, no. 2 (1994), pp. 343–48.

2. For a discussion of the roots of collectivism and individualism, see H. W. Spiegel, *The Growth of Economic Thought* (Durham, NC: Duke University Press, 1991). An easily assessable discussion of collectivism and individualism can be found in M. Friedman and R. Friedman, *Free to Choose* (London: Penguin Books, 1980).

3. For a classic summary of the tenets of Marxism details, see A. Giddens, *Capitalism and Modern Social Theory* (Cambridge: Cambridge University Press, 1971).

4. For details see "A Survey of China," *The Economist*, March 18, 1995.

5. J. S. Mill, *On Liberty* (London: Longman's, 1865), p. 6.

6. A. Smith, *The Wealth of Nations, Vol. 1* (London: Penguin Books), p. 325.

7. R. Wesson, *Modern Government—Democracy and Authoritarianism*, 2nd ed. (Englewood Cliffs, NJ: Prentice Hall, 1990).

8. For a detailed but accessible elaboration of this argument, see Friedman and Friedman, *Free to Choose*. Also see P. M. Romer, "The Origins of Endogenous Growth," *Journal of Economic Perspectives* 8, no. 1 (1994), pp. 2–32.

9. M. Borrus, L. A. Tyson, and J. Zysman, "Creating Advantage: How Government Policies Created Trade in the Semiconductor Industry," in *Strategic Trade Policy and the New International Economics*, ed. P. Krugman (Cambridge, MA: MIT Press, 1986).

10. See Lester Thurow, *Head to Head* (New York: Warner Books, 1993).

11. D. North, *Institutions, Institutional Change, and Economic Performance* (Cambridge: Cambridge University Press, 1991).

12. P. Klebnikov, "Russia's Robber Barons," *Forbes*, November 21, 1994, pp. 74–84; C. Mellow, "Russia: Making Cash from Chaos," *Fortune*, April 17, 1995, pp. 145–51; and "Mr Tatum Checks Out," *The Economist*, November 9, 1996, p. 78.

13. "Godfather of the Kremlin?" *Fortune*, December 30, 1996, pp. 90–96.

14. "Mr Tatum Checks Out."

15. K. van Wolferen, *The Enigma of Japanese Power* (New York: Vintage Books, 1990), pp. 100–05.

16. P. Bardhan, "Corruption and Development: A Review of the Issues," *Journal of Economic Literature*, September 1997, pp. 1320–46.

17. K. M. Murphy, A. Shleifer, and R. Vishny, "Why Is Rent Seeking So Costly to Growth," *American Economic Review* 83, no. 2 (1993), pp. 409–14.

18. Keiran Cooke, "Honeypot of as Much as $4 Billion Down the Drain," *Financial Times*, February 26, 1994, p. 4.

19. http://www.transparency.de/.

20. J. Coolidge and S. Rose Ackerman, "High Level Rent Seeking and Corruption in African Regimes," *World Bank Policy Research Working Paper # 1780*, June 1997; and Murphy, Shleifer, and Vishny, "Why Is Rent Seeking So Costly to Growth."

21. For an interesting discussion of strategies for dealing with the low cost of copying and distributing digital information, see the chapter on rights management in C. Shapiro and H. R. Varian, *Information Rules* (Boston: Harvard Business School Press, 1999).

22. Douglass North has argued that the correct specification of intellectual property rights is one factor that lowers the cost of doing business and, thereby, stimulates economic growth and development. See North, *Institutions, Institutional Change, and Economic Performance*.

23. S. Greenberger and C. S. Smith, "CD Piracy Flourishes in China and the West Supplies Equipment," *Wall Street Journal*, April 27, 1997, pp. A1, A4.

24. Business Software Alliance, *Sixth Annual BSA Global Software Piracy Study, May 2001*. Available from http://www.bsa.org.

25. Ibid.

26. "Trade Tripwires," *The Economist*, August 27, 1994, p. 61.

27. The World Bank, *World Development Indicators, 2001* (Oxford: Oxford University Press, 2001).

28. A. Sen, *Development as Freedom* (New York: Alfred A. Knopf, 1999).

29. G. M. Grossman and E. Helpman, "Endogenous Innovation in the Theory of Growth," *Journal of Economic Perspectives* 8, no. 1 (1994),

pp. 23–44, and P. M. Romer, "The Origins of Endogenous Growth," *Journal of Economic Perspectives* 8, no. 1 (1994), pp. 3–22.

30. F. A. Hayek, *The Fatal Conceit: Errors of Socialism* (Chicago: University of Chicago Press, 1989).

31. James Gwartney, Robert Lawson, and Walter Block, *Economic Freedom of the World: 1975–1995* (London: Institute of Economic Affairs, 1996).

32. North, *Institutions, Institutional Change and Economic Performance*. See also Murphy, Shleifer, and Vishny, "Why Is Rent Seeking so Costly to Growth?"

33. Hirschman, "The On-and-Off Again Connection between Political and Economic Progress," and A. Przeworski and F. Limongi, "Political Regimes and Economic Growth," *Journal of Economic Perspectives* 7, no. 3 (1993), pp. 51–59.

34. As an example, see "Why Voting Is Good for You," *The Economist*, August 27, 1994, pp. 15–17.

35. Ibid.

36. For details of this argument, see M. Olson, "Dictatorship, Democracy, and Development," *American Political Science Review*, September 1993.

37. For example, see Jarad Diamond's Pulitzer prize-winning book, *Guns, Germs, and Steel* (New York: W. W. Norton, 1997). Also see J. Sachs, "Nature, Nurture and Growth," *The Economist*, June 14, 1997, pp. 19–22.

38. Sachs, "Nature, Nurture and Growth."

39. "What Can the Rest of the World Learn from the Classrooms of Asia?" *The Economist*, September 21, 1996, p. 24.

40. J. Fagerberg, "Technology and International Differences in Growth Rates," *Journal of Economic Literature* 32 (September 1994), pp. 1147–75.

41. See A. Karatnycky, "Freedom in the World: 2000–2001" and associated materials. Available at http://www.freedomhouse.org/research/freeworld/2001/essay1.

42. Freedom House, "Democracies Century: A Survey of Political Change in the Twentieth Century, 1999." Available at http://www.freedomhouse.org.

43. L. Conners, "Freedom to Connect," *Wired*, August 1997, pp. 105–06.

44. F. Fukuyama, "The End of History," *The National Interest* 16 (Summer 1989), p. 18.

45. S. P. Huntington, *The Clash of Civilizations and the Remaking of World Order* (New York: Simon & Schuster, 1996).

46. Ibid., p. 116.

47. S. Fisher, R. Sahay, and C. A. Vegh, "Stabilization and the Growth in Transition Economies: the Early Experience," *Journal of Economic Perspectives* 10 (Spring 1996), pp. 45–66.

48. G. P. O'Driscoll, K. R. Holmes, and M. Kiroatrick, *2001 Index of Economic Freedom*. (Washington, DC; Heritage Foundation, 2001).

49. International Monetary Fund, *World Economic Outlook: Focus on Transition Economies* (Geneva: IMF, October 2000), and

50. J. C. Brada, "Privatization Is Transition—Is It?" *Journal of Economic Perspectives*, Spring 1996, pp. 67–86.

51. See S. Zahra et al., "Privatization and Entrepreneurial Transformation," *Academy of Management Review* 3, no. 25 (2000), pp. 509–24.

52. Fischer, Sahay, and Vegh, "Stabilization and Growth in Transition Economies."

53. J. Sachs, C. Zinnes, and Y. Eilat, "The Gains from Privatization in Transition Economies: Is Change of Ownership Enough?" CAER Discussion Paper No. 63 (Cambridge, MA: Harvard Institute for International Development, 2000).

54. J. Nellis, "Time to Rethink Privatization in Transition Economies?" *Finance and Development* 36, no. 2 (1999), pp. 16–19.

55. M. S. Borish and M. Noel, "Private Sector Development in the Visegrad Countries," *World Bank*, March 1997.

56. See S. Fisher and R. Sahay, "The Transition Economies after Ten Years," IMF Working Paper 00/30 (Washington: International Monetary Fund, 2000).

57. International Monetary Fund, *World Economic Outlook: Focus on Transition Economies*.

58. "Lessons of Transition," *The Economist*, June 29, 1996, p. 81.

59. Table 3.10 from International Monetary Fund, *World Economic Outlook: Focus on Transition Economies*.

60. Ibid.

61. E. Falcetti, M. Raiser, and P. Sanfey, "Defying the Odds: Initial Conditions, Reforms and Growth in the First Decade of Transition," *European Bank for Reconstruction and Development*, Working Paper Number 55, July 2000.

62. For a discussion of first-mover advantages, see M. Liberman and D. Montgomery, "First-Mover Advantages," *Strategic Management Journal* 9 (Summer Special Issue, 1988), pp. 41–58.

63. S. H. Robock, "Political Risk: Identification and Assessment," *Columbia Journal of World Business*, July/August 1971, pp. 6–20.

64. Steven L. Myers, "Report Says Business Interests Overshadow Rights," *New York Times*, December 5, 1996, p. A8.

65. Jo-Ann Mort, "Sweated Shopping," *The Guardian*, September 8, 1997, p. 11.

66. Bardhan Pranab, "Corruption and Development," *Journal of Economic Literature* 36 (September 1997), pp. 1320–46.

67. A. Shleifer and R. W. Vishny, "Corruption," *Quarterly Journal of Economics*, no. 108 (1993), pp. 599–617.

68. P. Mauro, "Corruption and Growth," *Quarterly Journal of Economics*, no. 110 (1995), pp. 681–712.

Differences in Culture

In 1992, McDonald's Corporation opened its first restaurant in Beijing, China, after a decade of market research. The restaurant, then the largest McDonald's in the world, was located on the corner of Wangfujing Street and the Avenue of Eternal Peace, just two blocks from Tiananmen Square, the very heart of China's capital. The choice of location seemed auspicious, and within two years sales at the restaurant were surpassing all expectations. Then the Beijing city government dropped a bombshell; officials abruptly informed McDonald's that it would have to vacate the location to make way for a commercial, residential, and office complex planned by Hong Kong developer Li Ka-shing. At the time, McDonald's still had 18 years to run on its 20-year lease. A stunned McDonald's did what any good Western company would do—it took the Beijing city government to court to try to enforce the lease. The court refused to enforce the lease, and McDonald's had to move. Chinese observers had a simple explanation for the outcome. McDonald's, they said, lacked the *guanxi* of Li Ka-shing. Given this, how could the company expect to prevail? Company executives should have accepted the decision in good grace and moved on, but instead, McDonald's filed a lawsuit—a move that would only reduce what *guanxi* McDonald's might have with the city government!

This example illustrates a basic difference between doing business in the West and doing business in China. In the advanced economies of the West, business transactions are conducted and regulated by the centuries-old framework of contract law, which specifies the rights and obligations of parties to a business contract and provides mechanisms for seeking to redress grievances should one party in the exchange fail to live up to the legal agreement. In the West, McDonald's could have relied on the courts to enforce its legal contract with the city government. In China, this approach didn't work. China does not have the same legal infrastructure. Personal power and relationships or connections, rather than the rule of law, have always been the key to getting things done in China. Decades of Communist rule stripped away the basic legal infrastructure that did exist to regulate business transactions. Power, relationships, and connections are an important, and some say necessary, influence on getting things done and enforcing business agreements in China. The key to understanding this process is the concept of *guanxi*.

Guanxi literally means relationships, although in business settings it can be better understood as "connec-

tions." McDonald's lost its lease in central Beijing because it lacked the *guanxi* enjoyed by the powerful Li Ka-shing. The concept of *guanxi* is deeply rooted in Chinese culture and particularly the Confucian philosophy of valuing social hierarchy and reciprocal obligations. Confucian ideology has a 2,000-year-old history in China, and over half a century of Communist rule has done little to dent its influence on everyday culture in China. Confucianism stresses the importance of relationships, both within the family and between master and servant. Confucian ideology teaches that people are not created equal. In Confucian thought, loyalty and obligations to one's superiors (or to family) is regarded as a sacred duty, but at the same time, this loyalty has its price. Social superiors are obligated to reward the loyalty of their social inferiors by bestowing "blessings" upon them; thus, the obligations are reciprocal.

Today, Chinese will often cultivate a *guanxiwang,* or "relationship network," for help. Reciprocal obligations are the glue that holds such networks together. If those obligations are not met—if favors done are not paid back or reciprocated—the reputation of the transgressor is tarnished and he or she will be less able to draw on their *guanxiwang* for help in the future. Thus, the implicit threat of social sanctions is often sufficient to ensure that favors are repaid, that obligations are met, and that relationships are honored. In a society that lacks a rule-based legal tradition, and thus legal ways of redressing wrongs such as violations of business agreements, *guanxi* is an important mechanism for building long-term business relationships and getting business done in China. There is a tacit acknowledgment that if you have the right *guanxi,* legal rules can be broken, or at least bent. Li Ka-shing had the right *guanxi;* McDonald's apparently did not.

As they have come to understand this, many Western businesses have tried to build *guanxi* to grease the wheels required to do business in China. Increasingly, *guanxi* has become a commodity that is for sale to foreigners. Many of the sons and daughters of high-ranking government officials have set up "consulting" firms and offered to mobilize their *guanxiwang* or those of their parents to help Western companies navigate their way through Chinese bureaucracy. Taking advantage of such services, however, requires good ethical judgment. There is a fine line between relationship building, which may require doing favors to meet obligations, and bribery. Consider the case of a lucrative business contract that was under consideration for more than a year between a large Chinese state-owned enterprise and two competing multinational firms. After months of negotiations, the Chinese elected to continue discussions with just one of the competitors—the one that had recently hired the son of the principal Chinese negotiator at a significant salary. This occurred even though the favored firm's equipment was less compatible with Chinese equipment already in place than that offered by the multinational that was rejected. The clear implication is that the son of the negotiator had mobilized his *guanxiwang* to help his new employer gain an advantage in the contract negotiations. While hiring the son of the principal negotiator may be viewed as good business practice by some in the context of Chinese culture, others might argue that this action was ethically suspect and could be viewed as little more than a thinly concealed bribe.

Sources: S. D. Seligman, "Guanxi: Grease for the Wheels of China," *China Business Review,* Septmeber/October 1999, pp. 34–38; L. Dana, "Culture Is the Essence of Asia," *Financial Times,* November 27, 2000, p. 12; L. Minder, "McDonald's to Close Original Beijing Store," *USA Today,* December 2, 1996, p. 1A; and M. W. Peng, *Business Strategies in Transition Economies* (Thousand Oaks, CA: Sage Publications, 2000).

Introduction

International business is different because countries are different. In Chapter 2 we saw how national differences in political, economic, and legal systems influence the benefits, costs, and risks associated with doing business in different countries. In this chapter, we will explore how differences in culture across and within countries can affect international business. Several themes run through this chapter.

The first theme is that business success in a variety of countries requires cross-cultural literacy. By cross-cultural literacy, we mean an understanding of how cultural differences across and within nations can affect the way in which business is practiced. In these days of global communications, rapid transportation, and global markets, when the era of the global village seems just around the corner, it is easy to forget just how different various cultures really are. Underneath the veneer of modernism, deep cultural differences often remain. Westerners in general, and Americans in particular, are quick to conclude that because people from other parts of the world also wear blue jeans, listen to Western popular music, eat at McDonald's, and drink Coca-Cola, they also accept the basic tenets of Western (or American) culture. But this is not true. Many of the "Islamic militants" that invaded the U.S. Embassy in Iran after the Iranian revolution that ousted the pro-Western shah of Iran wore blue jeans, but they certainly showed no love of American values.

Increasingly, the Chinese are embracing the material products of modern society. Anyone who has visited Shanghai, for example, cannot fail to be struck by how modern the city seems, with its skyscrapers, department stores, and freeways. But as the opening case demonstrates, beneath the veneer of Western modernism, long-standing cultural traditions rooted in a 2,000-year-old ideology continue to have an important influence on the way business is transacted in China. In China, *guanxi*, or relationships backed by reciprocal obligations, are central to getting business done. As the opening case demonstrates, firms that lack sufficient *guanxi*, as McDonald's apparently did, may find themselves at a disadvantage when doing business in China. In this chapter we shall argue that it is important for foreign businesses to gain an understanding of the culture, or cultures, that prevail in those countries where they do business.

The opening case also illustrates another important theme that we shall develop further in this chapter: The old adage of "when in Rome do as the Romans do" may have ethical ramifications. Prevailing cultural mores in a country may put a foreign business in a difficult ethical position. For example, while it is important to build *guanxi* in China, there is a thin line between giving gifts to support the establishment of relationships, which is culturally normal behavior, and bribery or corruption, which is viewed dimly in the West and against the law in some nations such as the United

States, where the Foreign Corrupt Practices Act makes it illegal for an American company to use bribes of government officials to gain business in a foreign nation.

Another theme developed in this chapter is that a relationship may exist between culture and the cost of doing business in a country or region. Different cultures are more or less supportive of the capitalist mode of production and may increase or lower the costs of doing business. For example, some observers have argued that cultural factors lowered the costs of doing business in Japan and helped to explain Japan's rapid economic assent during the 1960s, 70s, and 80s.[1] By the same token, cultural factors can sometimes raise the costs of doing business. Historically, class divisions were an important aspect of British culture, and for a long time, firms operating in Great Britain found it difficult to achieve cooperation between management and labor. Class divisions led to a high level of industrial disputes in that country during the 1960s and 1970s and raised the costs of doing business in Great Britain relative to the costs in countries such as Switzerland, Norway, Germany, or Japan, where class conflict was historically less prevalent.

The British example, however, brings us to the final theme we will explore in this chapter: Culture is not static. It can and does evolve, although the rate at which culture can change is the subject of some dispute. Some say that aspects of British culture have changed significantly over the past 20 years, and this is reflected in weaker class distinctions and a lower level of industrial disputes. Similarly, there is evidence of changes in the culture of Japan, with the traditional Japanese emphasis on group identification giving way to greater emphasis on individualism.

We open this chapter with a general discussion of what culture is. Then we focus on how differences in social structure, religion, language, and education influence the culture of a country. We then discuss the process of cultural change. The implications for business practice will be highlighted throughout the chapter and summarized in a section at the end.

What Is Culture? ■

Scholars have never been able to agree on a simple definition of culture. In the 1870s, the anthropologist Edward Tylor defined culture as "that complex whole which includes knowledge, belief, art, morals, law, custom, and other capabilities acquired by man as a member of society."[2] Since then hundreds of other definitions have been offered. Geert Hofstede, an expert on cross-cultural differences and management, defined culture as "the collective programming of the mind which distinguishes the members of one human group from another . . . Culture, in this sense, includes systems of values; and values are among the building blocks of culture."[3] Another definition of culture comes from sociologists Zvi Namenwirth and Robert Weber who see culture as a system of ideas and argue that these ideas constitute a design for living.[4]

Here we follow both Hofstede and Namenwirth and Weber by viewing culture as a system of values and norms that are shared among a group of people and that when taken together constitute a design for living. By **values** we mean abstract ideas about what a group believes to be good, right, and desirable. Put differently, values are shared assumptions about how things ought to be.[5] By **norms** we mean the social rules and guidelines that prescribe appropriate behavior in particular situations. We shall use the term **society** to refer to a group of people who share a common set of values and norms. While a society may be equivalent to a country, some countries harbor several "societies" (i.e., they support multiple cultures) and some societies embrace more than one country.

▎Values and Norms

Values form the bedrock of a culture. They provide the context within which a society's norms are established and justified. They may include a society's attitudes toward such concepts as individual freedom, democracy, truth, justice, honesty, loyalty, social obligations, collective responsibility, the role of women, love, sex, marriage, and so on. Values are not just abstract concepts; they are invested with considerable emotional significance. People argue, fight, and even die over values such as freedom. Values also often are reflected in the political and economic systems of a society. As we saw in Chapter 2, democratic free market capitalism is a reflection of a philosophical value system that emphasizes individual freedom.

Norms are the social rules that govern people's actions toward one another. Norms can be subdivided further into two major categories: folkways and mores. **Folkways** are the routine conventions of everyday life. Generally, folkways are actions of little moral significance. Rather, folkways are social conventions concerning things such as the appropriate dress code in a particular situation, good social manners, eating with the correct utensils, neighborly behavior, and the like. While folkways define the way people are expected to behave, violation of folkways is not normally a serious matter. People who violate folkways may be thought of as eccentric or ill-mannered, but they are not usually considered to be evil or bad. In many countries, foreigners may initially be excused for violating folkways.

A good example of folkways concerns attitudes toward time in different countries. People are very time conscious in the United States. Americans tend to arrive a few minutes early for business appointments. When invited for dinner to someone's home, it is considered polite to arrive on time or just a few minutes late. The concept of time can be very different in other countries. It is not necessarily a breach of etiquette to arrive a little late for a business appointment; it might even be considered more impolite to arrive early. Arriving on time for a dinner engagement can be very bad manners. In Great Britain, for example, when someone says, "Come for dinner at 7:00 P.M.," what he means is "come for dinner at 7:30 to 8:00 P.M." The guest who arrives at 7:00 P.M. is likely to find an unprepared and embarrassed host. Similarly, when an Argentinean says, "Come for dinner anytime after 8:00 P.M." what she means is don't come at 8:00 P.M.—it's far too early!

Mores are norms that are seen as central to the functioning of a society and to its social life. They have much greater significance than folkways. Accordingly, violating mores can bring serious retribution. Mores include such factors as indictments against theft, adultery, incest, and cannibalism. In many societies, certain mores have been enacted into law. Thus, all advanced societies have laws against theft, incest, and cannibalism. However, there are also many differences between cultures as to what is perceived as mores. In America, for example, drinking alcohol is widely accepted, whereas in Saudi Arabia the consumption of alcohol is viewed as violating important social mores and is punishable by imprisonment (as some Western citizens working in Saudi Arabia have found out).

Culture, Society, and the Nation-State

We have defined a society as a group of people that share a common set of values and norms; that is, people who are bound together by a common culture. However, there is not a strict one-to-one correspondence between a society and a nation-state. Nation-states are political creations. They may contain a single culture or several cultures. While the French nation can be thought of as the political embodiment of French culture, the nation of Canada has at least three cultures—an Anglo culture, a French-speaking "Quebecois" culture, and a Native American culture. Similarly, many African nations have important cultural differences between tribal groups, as exhibited in the early 1990s when Rwanda dissolved into a bloody civil war between two tribes, the Tutsis and Hutus. Africa is not alone in this regard. India is composed of many distinct cultural groups. During the Gulf War, the prevailing view presented to Western audiences was that Iraq was a homogenous Arab nation. But the chaos that followed the war revealed several different societies within Iraq, each with its own cul-

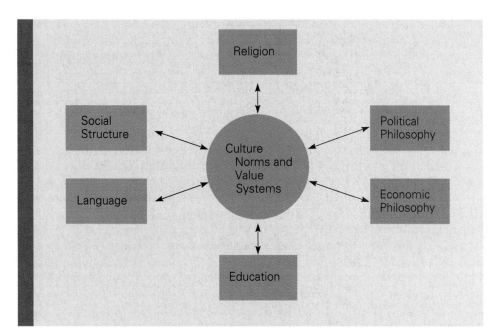

Figure 3.1

The Determinants of
Culture

ture. The Kurds in the north do not view themselves as Arabs and have their own distinct history and traditions. Then there are two Arab societies: the Shiites in the South and the Sunnis who populate the middle of the country and who rule Iraq (the terms *Shiites* and *Sunnis* refer to different sects within the religion of Islam). Among the southern Sunnis is another distinct society of 500,000 "Marsh Arabs" who live at the confluence of the Tigris and Euphrates rivers, pursuing a way of life that dates back 5,000 years.[6]

At the other end of the scale, we can speak of cultures that embrace several nations. Several scholars, for example, argue that we can speak of an Islamic society or culture that is shared by the citizens of many different nations in the Middle East, Asia, and Africa. As you will recall from the last chapter, this view of expansive cultures that embrace several nations underpins Samuel Huntington's view of a world that is fragmented into different civilizations including Western, Islamic, and Sinic (Chinese) civilizations.[7]

To complicate things further, it is also possible to talk about culture at different levels. It is reasonable to talk about "American society" and "American culture," but there are several societies within America, each with its own culture. One can talk about Afro-American culture, Cajun culture, Chinese-American culture, Hispanic culture, Indian culture, Irish-American culture, and Southern culture. The point is that the relationship between culture and country is often ambiguous. One cannot always characterize a country as having a single homogenous culture, and even when one can, one must also often recognize that the national culture is a mosaic of subcultures.

❙The Determinants of Culture

The values and norms of a culture do not emerge fully formed. They are the evolutionary product of a number of factors, including the prevailing political and economic philosophy, the social structure of a society, and the dominant religion, language, and education (see Figure 3.1). We discussed political and economic philosophy at length in Chapter 2. Such philosophy clearly influences the value systems of a society. For example, the values found in the former Soviet Union toward freedom, justice, and individual achievement were clearly different from the values found in the United States, precisely because each society operated according to a different political and economic philosophy. Below we will discuss the influence of social structure, religion, language, and education. Remember that the chain of causation runs both ways. While factors such as social structure and religion clearly influence the values and norms of a society, the values and norms of a society can influence social structure and religion.

Social Structure

A society's "social structure" refers to its basic social organization. Although social structure consists of many different aspects, two dimensions are particularly important when explaining differences between cultures. The first is the degree to which the basic unit of social organization is the individual, as opposed to the group. Western societies tend to emphasize the primacy of the individual, while groups tend to figure much larger in many other societies. The second dimension is the degree to which a society is stratified into classes or castes. Some societies are characterized by a relatively high degree of social stratification and relatively low mobility between strata (e.g., Indian), while other societies are characterized by a low degree of social stratification and high mobility between strata (e.g., American).

Individuals and Groups

A **group** is an association of two or more individuals who have a shared sense of identity and who interact with each other in structured ways on the basis of a common set of expectations about each other's behavior.[8] Human social life is group life. Individuals are involved in families, work groups, social groups, recreational groups, and so on. However, while groups are found in all societies, societies differ according to the degree to which the group is viewed as the primary means of social organization.[9] In some societies, individual attributes and achievements are viewed as being more important than group membership, while in other societies the reverse is true.

The Individual

In Chapter 2, we discussed individualism as a political philosophy. However, individualism is more than just an abstract political philosophy. In many Western societies, the individual is the basic building block of social organization. This is reflected not just in the political and economic organization of society, but also in the way people perceive themselves and relate to each other in social and business settings. The value systems of many Western societies, for example, emphasize individual achievement. The social standing of individuals is not so much a function of whom they work for, as of their individual performance in whatever work setting they choose.

The emphasis on individual performance in many Western societies has both beneficial and harmful aspects. In the United States, the emphasis on individual performance finds expression in an admiration of "rugged individualism" and entrepreneurship. One benefit of this is the high level of entrepreneurial activity in the United States and other Western societies. New products and new ways of doing business (e.g., personal computers, photocopiers, computer software, biotechnology, supermarkets, and discount retail stores) have repeatedly been created in the United States by entrepreneurial individuals. One can argue that the dynamism of the U.S. economy owes much to the philosophy of individualism.

Individualism also finds expression in a high degree of managerial mobility between companies, and this is not always a good thing. While moving from company to company may be good for individual managers, who are trying to build impressive résumés, it is not necessarily a good thing for American companies. The lack of loyalty and commitment to an individual company, and the tendency to move on when a better offer comes along, can result in managers that have good general skills but lack the knowledge, experience, and network of interpersonal contacts that come from years of working within the same company. An effective manager draws on company-specific experience, knowledge, and a network of contacts to find solutions to current problems, and American companies may suffer if their managers lack these attributes.

One positive aspect of high managerial mobility is that executives are exposed to different ways of doing business. The ability to compare business practices helps U.S. executives identify how good practices and techniques developed in one firm might be profitably applied to other firms.

The emphasis on individualism may also make it difficult to build teams within an organization to perform collective tasks. If individuals are always competing with each other on the basis of individual performance, it may be difficult for them to co-operate. One study of U.S. competitiveness by MIT concluded that U.S. firms are being hurt in the global economy by a failure to achieve cooperation both within a company (e.g., between functions; between management and labor) and between companies (e.g., between a firm and its suppliers). Given the emphasis on individualism in the American value system, this failure is not surprising.[10] So the emphasis on individualism in the United States, while helping to create a dynamic entrepreneurial economy, may raise the costs of doing business due to its adverse impact on managerial stability and cooperation.

The Group

In contrast to the Western emphasis on the individual, the group is the primary unit of social organization in many other societies. In Japan, the social status of an individual is determined as much by the standing of the group to which he or she belongs as by his or her individual performance.[11] In traditional Japanese society, the group was the family or village to which an individual belonged. Today the group has frequently come to be associated with the work team or business organization to which an individual belongs. In a now classic study of Japanese society, Nakane has noted how this expresses itself in everyday life:

> When a Japanese faces the outside (confronts another person) and affixes some position to himself socially he is inclined to give precedence to institution over kind of occupation. Rather than saying, "I am a typesetter" or "I am a filing clerk," he is likely to say, "I am from B Publishing Group" or "I belong to S company."[12]

Nakane goes on to observe that the primacy of the group to which an individual belongs often evolves into a deeply emotional attachment in which identification with the group becomes all important in one's life. One central value of Japanese culture is the importance attached to group membership. This may have beneficial implications for business firms. Strong identification with the group is argued to create pressures for mutual self-help and collective action. If the worth of an individual is closely linked to the achievements of the group (e.g., firm), as Nakane maintains is the case in Japan, this creates a strong incentive for individual members of the group to work together for the common good. The failures of cooperation that the MIT study found in many American firms may not be a problem in Japanese firms. Some argue that the success of Japanese enterprises in the global economy is based partly on their ability to achieve close cooperation between individuals within a company and between companies. This finds expression in the widespread diffusion of self-managing work teams within Japanese organizations, the close cooperation between different functions within Japanese companies (e.g., between manufacturing, marketing, and R&D), and the cooperation between a company and its suppliers on issues such as design, quality control, and inventory reduction.[13] In all of these cases, cooperation is driven by the need to improve the performance of the group (i.e., the business firm).

The primacy of the value of group identification also discourages managers and workers from moving from company to company. Lifetime employment in a particular company is the norm in certain sectors of the Japanese economy (estimates suggest that between 20 and 40 percent of all Japanese employees have formal or informal life-time employment guarantees). Over the years, managers and workers build up knowledge, experience, and a network of interpersonal business contacts. All these things can help managers perform their jobs more effectively and achieve cooperation with others.

However, the primacy of the group is not always beneficial. Just as U.S. society is characterized by a great deal of dynamism and entrepreneurship, reflecting the primacy of values associated with individualism, some argue that Japanese society is characterized by a corresponding lack of dynamism and entrepreneurship. Although it is not clear how this will play itself out in the long run, the United States could continue to create more new industries than Japan and continue to be more successful at pioneering radically new products and new ways of doing business.

Social Stratification

All societies are stratified on a hierarchical basis into social categories—that is, into **social strata.** These strata are typically defined on the basis of characteristics such as family background, occupation, and income. Individuals are born into a particular stratum. They become a member of the social category to which their parents belong. Individuals born into a stratum toward the top of the social hierarchy tend to have better life chances than individuals born into a stratum toward the bottom of the hierarchy. They are likely to have a better education, better health, a better standard of living, and better work opportunities. Although all societies are stratified to some degree, they differ in two related ways that are of interest to us here. First, they differ from each other with regard to the degree of mobility between social strata, and second, they differ with regard to the significance attached to social strata in business contexts.

Social Mobility

The term **social mobility** refers to the extent to which individuals can move out of the strata into which they are born. Social mobility varies significantly from society to society. The most rigid system of stratification is a caste system. A caste system is a closed system of stratification in which social position is determined by the family into which a person is born, and change in that position is usually not possible during an individual's lifetime. Often a caste position carries with it a specific occupation. Members of one caste might be shoemakers, members of another caste might be butchers, and so on. These occupations are embedded in the caste and passed down through the family to succeeding generations. Although the number of societies with caste systems has diminished rapidly during the 20th century, one partial example still remains. India has four main castes and several thousand subcastes. Even though the caste system was officially abolished in 1949, two years after India became independent, it is still a powerful force in rural Indian society where occupation and marital opportunities are still partly related to caste.

A **class system** is a less rigid form of social stratification in which social mobility is possible. A class system is a form of open stratification in which the position a person has by birth can be changed through his or her own achievements and/or luck. Individuals born into a class at the bottom of the hierarchy can work their way up, while individuals born into a class at the top of the hierarchy can slip down.

While many societies have class systems, social mobility within a class system varies from society to society. For example, some sociologists have argued that Britain has a more rigid class structure than certain other Western societies, such as the United States.[14] Historically, British society was divided into three main classes: the upper class, which was made up of individuals whose families for generations had wealth, prestige, and occasionally power; the middle class, whose members were involved in professional, managerial, and clerical occupations; and the working class, whose members earned their living from manual occupations. The middle class was further subdivided into the upper-middle class, whose members were involved in important managerial occupations and the prestigious professions (e.g., lawyers, accountants, doctors), and the lower-middle class, whose members were involved in clerical work (e.g., bank tellers) and the less prestigious professions (e.g., schoolteachers).

The British class system exhibited significant divergence between the life chances of members of different classes. The upper and upper-middle classes typically sent their children to a select group of private schools, where they wouldn't mix with lower-class children, and where they picked up many of the speech accents and social norms that marked them as being from the higher strata of society. These same private schools also had close ties with the most prestigious universities, such as Oxford and Cambridge. Until recently, Oxford and Cambridge guaranteed to reserve a certain number of places for the graduates of these private schools. Having been to a prestigious university, the offspring of the upper and upper-middle classes then had an excellent chance of being offered a prestigious job in companies, banks, brokerage firms, and law firms run by members of the upper and upper-middle classes.

In contrast, the members of the British working and lower-middle classes typically went to state schools. The majority left at 16, and those that went on to higher education found it more difficult to get accepted at the best universities. When they did, they found that their lower-class accent and lack of social skills marked them as being from a lower social stratum, which made it more difficult for them to get access to the most prestigious jobs.

As a result of these factors, the class system in Britain tended to perpetuate itself from generation to generation, and mobility was limited. Although upward mobility was possible, it could not normally be achieved in one generation. While an individual from a working class background may have established an income level that was consistent with membership in the upper-middle class, he or she may not have been accepted as such by others of that class due to accent and background. However, by sending his or her offspring to the "right kind of school," the individual could ensure that his or her children were accepted.

According to many politicians and popular commentators, modern British society is now rapidly leaving this class structure behind and moving toward a classless society. However, sociologists continue to dispute this finding and present evidence that this is not the case. For example, a study reported that in 1994, state schools in the London suburb of Islington, which has a population of 175,000, had only 79 candidates for university, while one prestigious private school alone, Eton, sent more than that number to Oxford and Cambridge.[15] This, according to the study's authors, implies that "money still begets money." They argue that a good school means a good university, a good university means a good job, and "merit" only has a limited chance of elbowing its way into this tight little circle.

The class system in the United States is less extreme than in Britain and mobility is greater. Like Britain, the United States has its own upper, middle, and working classes. However, class membership is determined principally by individual economic achievements, as opposed to background and schooling. Thus, an individual can, by his or her own economic achievement, move smoothly from the working class to the upper class in a lifetime. Successful individuals from humble origins are highly respected in American society.

Significance

From a business perspective, the stratification of a society is significant if it affects the operation of business organizations. In American society, the high degree of social mobility and the extreme emphasis on individualism limits the impact of class background on business operations. The same is true in Japan, where most of the population perceives itself to be middle-class. In a country such as Great Britain, however, the relative lack of class mobility and the differences between classes have resulted in the emergence of class consciousness. **Class consciousness** refers to a condition where people tend to perceive themselves in terms of their class background, and this shapes their relationships with members of other classes.

This has been played out in British society in the traditional hostility between upper-middle class managers and their working class employees. Mutual antagonism and lack of respect historically made it difficult to achieve cooperation between management and labor in many British companies and resulted in a relatively high level of industrial disputes. However, the last two decades have seen a dramatic reduction in industrial disputes, which bolsters the arguments of those who claim that the country is moving toward a classless society. An antagonistic relationship between management and labor, and the resulting lack of cooperation and high level of industrial disruption, tends to raise the costs of production in countries characterized by significant class divisions. In turn, this can make it more difficult for companies based in such countries to establish a competitive advantage in the global economy.

Religious and Ethical Systems

Religion may be defined as a system of shared beliefs and rituals that are concerned with the realm of the sacred.[16] **Ethical systems** refer to a set of moral principles, or values, that are used to guide and shape behavior. Most of the world's ethical systems are the product of religions. Thus, we can talk about Christian ethics and Islamic ethics. However, there is a major exception to the principle that ethical systems are grounded in religion. Confucianism and Confucian ethics influence behavior and shape culture in parts of Asia, yet, as we shall see, it is incorrect to characterize Confucianism as a religion.

The relationship between religion, ethics, and society is subtle, complex, and profound. While there are thousands of religions in the world today, four dominate—Christianity, Islam, Hinduism, and Buddhism (see Map 3.1). We review each of these, along with Confucianism, focusing on their business implications. Perhaps the most important business implications of religion center on the extent to which different religions shape attitudes toward work and entrepreneurship and the degree to which the religious ethics affect the costs of doing business in a country.

Christianity

Christianity is the most widely practiced religion in the world. About 1 billion people, approximately 20 percent of the world's population, identify themselves as Christians. The vast majority of Christians live in Europe and the Americas, although their numbers are growing rapidly in Africa. Christianity grew out of Judaism. Like Judaism, it is a monotheistic religion (monotheism is the belief in one god). A religious division in the 11th century led to the establishment of two major Christian organizations—the Roman Catholic church and the Orthodox church. Today the Roman Catholic church accounts for over half of all Christians, most of whom are found in Southern Europe and Latin America. The Orthodox church, while less influential, is still of major importance in several countries (e.g., Greece and Russia). In the 16th century, the Reformation led to a further split with Rome; the result was Protestantism. The nonconformist nature of Protestantism has facilitated the emergence of numerous denominations under the Protestant umbrella (e.g., Baptist, Methodist, Calvinist).

Economic Implications of Christianity: The Protestant Work Ethic

Some sociologists have argued that of the two main branches of Christianity—Catholicism and Protestantism—the latter has the most important economic implications. In 1904, a German sociologist, Max Weber, made a connection between Protestant ethics and "the spirit of capitalism" that has since become famous.[17]

Predominant Religions

Christianity (C)*
- Roman Catholic
- Protestant
- Mormon (LDS)
- Eastern Churches
- Mixed Sects

Islam (M)
- Sunni
- Shi'a

Buddhism (B)
- Hinayanistic
- Lamaistic

Hinduism (H)

Judaism (J)

Sikhism

Animism (Tribal)

Chinese Complex
(Confucianism, Taoism, and Buddhism)

Korean Complex
(Buddhism, Confucianism, Christianity, and Chondogyo)

Japanese Complex
(Shinto and Buddhism)

Vietnamese Complex
(Buddhism, Taoism Confucianism, and Cao Dai)

Unpopulated Regions

* Capital letters indicate the presence of locally important minority adherents of nonpredominant faiths.

Map 3.1

World Religions

Source: From *Student Atlas of World Geography*, Second Edition by John L. Allen. Copyright © 2001 by McGraw-Hill Companies. Reprinted by permission of McGraw-Hill/Dushkin, a division of the McGraw-Hill Companies, Guilford, CT 06437.

Scale: 1 to 180,000,000

0   1000   2000 Miles

0   1000   2000   3000 Kilometers

Weber noted that capitalism emerged in Western Europe. He also noted that in Western Europe:

> Business leaders and owners of capital, as well as the higher grades of skilled labor, and even more the higher technically and commercially trained personnel of modern enterprises, are overwhelmingly Protestant.[18]

According to Weber, there was a relationship between Protestantism and the emergence of modern capitalism. Weber argued that Protestant ethics emphasize the importance of hard work and wealth creation (for the glory of God) and frugality (abstinence from worldly pleasures). According to Weber, this kind of value system was needed to facilitate the development of capitalism. Protestants worked hard and systematically to accumulate wealth. However, their ascetic beliefs suggested that rather than consuming this wealth by indulging in worldly pleasures, they should invest it in the expansion of capitalist enterprises. Thus, the combination of hard work and the accumulation of capital, which could be used to finance investment and expansion, paved the way for the development of capitalism in Western Europe and subsequently in the United States. In contrast, Weber argued that the Catholic promise of salvation in the next world, rather than this world, did not foster the same kind of work ethic.

Protestantism also may have encouraged capitalism's development in another way. By breaking away from the hierarchical domination of religious and social life that characterized the Catholic church for much of its history, Protestantism gave individuals significantly more freedom to develop their own relationship with God. The right to freedom of form of worship was central to the nonconformist nature of early Protestantism. This emphasis on individual religious freedom may have paved the way for the subsequent emphasis on individual economic and political freedoms and the development of individualism as an economic and political philosophy. As we saw in Chapter 2, such a philosophy forms the bedrock on which entrepreneurial free market capitalism is based. Building on this, some scholars claim that there is a connection between individualism, as inspired by Protestantism, and the extent of entrepreneurial activity in a nation.[19]

Islam

With nearly 1 billion adherents, Islam is the second largest of the world's major religions. Islam dates back to 610 A.D. when the prophet Mohammed began spreading the word. Adherents of Islam are referred to as Muslims. Muslims constitute a majority in more than 35 countries and inhabit a nearly contiguous stretch of land from the northwest coast of Africa, through the Middle East, to China and Malaysia in the Far East.

Islam has roots in both Judaism and Christianity (Islam views Jesus Christ as one of God's prophets). Like Christianity and Judaism, Islam is a monotheistic religion. The central principle of Islam is that there is but the one true omnipotent God. Islam requires unconditional acceptance of the uniqueness, power, and authority of God and the understanding that the objective of life is to fulfill the dictates of his will in the hope of admission to paradise. According to Islam, worldly gain and temporal power are an illusion. Those who pursue riches on earth may gain them, but those who forgo worldly ambitions to seek the favor of Allah may gain the greater treasure—entry into paradise. Other major principles of Islam include: (1) honoring and respecting parents, (2) respecting the rights of others, (3) being generous but not a squanderer, (4) avoiding killing except for justifiable causes, (5) not committing adultery, (6) dealing justly and equitably with others, (7) being of pure heart and mind, (8) safeguarding the possessions of orphans, and (9) being humble and unpretentious.[20] There are obvious parallels here with many of the central principles of both Judaism and Christianity.

Islam is an all-embracing way of life governing the totality of a Muslim's being.[21] As God's surrogate in this world, a Muslim is not a totally free agent but is circumscribed by religious principles—by a code of conduct for interpersonal relations—

in social and economic activities. Religion is paramount in all areas of life. The Muslim lives in a social structure that is shaped by Islamic values and norms of moral conduct. The ritual nature of everyday life in a Muslim country is striking to a Western visitor. Among other things, Muslim ritual requires prayer five times a day (it is not unusual for business meetings to be put on hold while the Muslim participants engage in their daily prayer ritual), demands that women should be dressed in a certain manner and subordinate to men, and forbids the consumption of either pig meat or alcohol.

Islamic Fundamentalism

The past two decades have witnessed a surge in what is often referred to as "Islamic fundamentalism."[22] In the West, Islamic fundamentalism is often associated in the media with militants, terrorists, and violent upheavals, such as the bloody conflict occurring in Algeria, the killing of foreign tourists in Egypt, or the September 11, 2001, attracks on the World Trade Center and Pentagon in the United States. This characterization is very misleading. Just as "Christian fundamentalists" in the West are motivated by sincere and deeply held religious values firmly rooted in their faith, so are "Islamic fundamentalists." The violence that the Western media associates with Islamic fundamentalism is perpetrated by a very small minority of radical "fundamentalists" who have highjacked the religion to further their own political ends. The vast majority of Muslims point out that Islam teaches peace, justice and tolerance, not violence and intolerance, and that Islam explicitly repudiates the violence that a radical minority practices.

The rise of fundamentalism has no one cause. In part, it is a response to the social pressures created in traditional Islamic societies by the move toward modernization and by the influence of Western ideas, such as liberal democracy, materialism, equal rights for women, and by Western attitudes toward sex, marriage, and alcohol. In many Muslim countries, modernization has been accompanied by a growing gap between a rich urban minority and an impoverished urban and rural majority. For the impoverished majority, modernization has offered little in the way of tangible economic progress, while threatening the traditional value system. Thus, for a Muslim who cherishes his traditions and feels that his identity is jeopardized by the encroachment of alien Western values, Islamic fundamentalism has become a cultural anchor.

Fundamentalists demand a rigid commitment to traditional religious beliefs and rituals. The result has been a marked increase in the use of symbolic gestures that confirm Islamic values. Women are once again wearing floor-length, long-sleeved dresses and covering their hair; religious studies have increased in universities; the publication of religious tracts has increased; and more religious orations are heard in public.[23] Also, the sentiments of some fundamentalist groups are increasingly anti-Western. Rightly or wrongly, Western influence is blamed for a whole range of social ills, and many fundamentalists' actions are directed against Western governments, cultural symbols, businesses, and even individuals.

In several Muslim countries, fundamentalists have gained political power and have used this to try to make Islamic law (as set down in the Koran, the bible of Islam) the law of the land. There are good grounds for this in Islam. Islam makes no distinction between church and state. It is not just a religion; Islam is also the source of law, a guide to statecraft, and an arbiter of social behavior. Muslims believe that every human endeavor is within the purview of the faith—and this includes political activity—because the only purpose of any activity is to do God's will.[24] (Muslims are not unique in this view; it is also shared by some Christian fundamentalists.) The fundamentalists have been most successful in Iran, where a fundamentalist party has held power since 1979, but they also have a growing influence in many other countries, such as Algeria, Afghanistan, (where the Talaban has established an extreme fundamentalist state), Egypt, Pakistan, the Sudan, and Saudi Arabia.

Economic Implications of Islam

Some explicit economic principles are set down in the Koran.[25] Many of the economic principles of Islam are pro-free enterprise. The Koran speaks approvingly of free enterprise and of earning legitimate profit through trade and commerce (the prophet Mohammed was once a trader). The protection of the right to private property is also embedded within Islam, although Islam asserts that all property is a favor from Allah (God), who created and so owns everything. Those who hold property are regarded as trustees who are entitled to receive profits from it, rather than owners in the Western sense of the word, and they are admonished to use it in a righteous, socially beneficial, and prudent manner. This reflects Islam's concern with social justice. Islam is critical of those who earn profit through the exploitation of others. In the Islamic view of the world, humans are part of a collective in which the wealthy and successful have obligations to help the disadvantaged. Put simply, in Muslim countries, it is fine to earn a profit, so long as that profit is justly earned and not based on the exploitation of others for one's own advantage. It also helps if those making profits undertake charitable acts to help the poor. Furthermore, Islam stresses the importance of living up to contractual obligations, of keeping one's word, and of abstaining from deception.

Given the Islamic proclivity to favor market-based systems, Muslim countries are likely to be receptive to international businesses as long as those businesses behave in a manner that is consistent with Islamic ethics. Businesses that are perceived as making an unjust profit through the exploitation of others, by deception, or by breaking contractual obligations are unlikely to be welcomed in an Islamic state. In addition, in Islamic states where fundamentalism is on the rise, hostility toward Western-owned businesses is likely to increase.

One economic principle of Islam prohibits the payment or receipt of interest, which is considered usury. To the devout Muslim, acceptance of interest payments is seen as a very grave sin. Practitioners of the black art of usury are warned on the pain of hellfire to abstain; the giver and the taker are equally damned. This is not just a matter of theology; in several Islamic states, it is also becoming a matter of law. In 1992, for example, Pakistan's Federal Shariat Court, the highest Islamic law-making body in the country, pronounced interest to be un-Islamic and therefore illegal and demanded that the government amend all financial laws accordingly. In 1999, Pakistan's Supreme Court ruled that Islamic banking methods should be used in the country after July 1, 2001.[26] The accompanying Country Focus looks at how Pakistan's banks are dealing with this issue.

❙Hinduism

Hinduism has approximately 500 million adherents, most of whom are on the Indian subcontinent. Hinduism began in the Indus Valley in India over 4,000 years ago, making it the world's oldest major religion. Unlike Christianity and Islam, its founding is not linked to a particular person. Nor does it have an officially sanctioned sacred book such as the Bible or the Koran. Hindus believe that a moral force in society requires the acceptance of certain responsibilities, called *dharma*. Hindus believe in reincarnation, or rebirth into a different body after death. Hindus also believe in *karma*, the spiritual progression of each person's soul. A person's karma is affected by the way he or she lives. The moral state of an individual's karma determines the challenges he or she will face in their next life. By perfecting the soul in each new life, Hindus believe that an individual can eventually achieve *nirvana*, a state of complete spiritual perfection that renders reincarnation no longer necessary. Many Hindus believe that the way to achieve nirvana is to lead a severe ascetic lifestyle of material and physical self-denial, devoting life to a spiritual rather than material quest.

Economic Implications of Hinduism

Max Weber, who is famous for expounding on the Protestant work ethic, also argued that the ascetic principles embedded in Hinduism do not encourage the kind of en-

Islamic Banking in Pakistan

The Koran clearly condemns interest, which is called *riba* in Arabic, as exploitative and unjust. For many years, banks operating in Islamic countries conveniently ignored this condemnation, but starting about 25 years ago with the establishment of an Islamic bank in Egypt, Islamic banks started to open in predominantly Muslim countries. There are now some 170 Islamic financial institutions worldwide managing over $150 billion in assets and making an average return on capital of over 16 percent. Even conventional banks are entering the market—both Citigroup and HSBC, two of the world's largest financial institutions, now offer Islamic financial services. Until mid-2001, only Iran and the Sudan enforced Islamic banking conventions, but in many other countries, customers could choose between conventional banks and Islamic banks.

In July 2001, Pakistan became the third country to require its banks to adopt Islamic methods. The transition to Islamic banking in Pakistan may determine the fate of Islamic banking elsewhere in the world. Conventional banks make a profit on the spread between the interest rate they have to pay to depositors and the higher interest rate they charge borrowers. Because Islamic banks cannot pay or charge interest, they must find a different way of making money. Pakistan's banks are set to experiment with two different Islamic banking methods—the *mudarabah* and the *murabaha.*

A *mudarabah* contract is similar to a profit-sharing scheme. Under *mudarabah,* when an Islamic bank lends money to a business, rather than charging that business interest on the loan, it takes a share in the profits that are derived from the investment. Similarly, when a business (or individual) deposits money at an Islamic bank in a savings account, the deposit is treated as an equity investment in whatever activity the bank uses the capital for. Thus, the depositor receives a share in the profit from the bank's investment (as opposed to interest payments) according to an agreed-on ratio. Some Muslims claim this is a more efficient system than the Western banking system, since it encourages both long-term savings and long-term investment. However, there is no hard evidence of this, and many believe that a *mudarabah* system is less efficient than a conventional Western banking system.

The second Islamic banking method, the *murabaha* contract, is the most widely used among the world's Islamic banks. It seems set to become the most popular method in Pakistan, primarily because it is the easiest to implement. In a *murabaha contract,* when a firm wishes to purchase something using a loan—let's say a piece of equipment that costs $1,000—the firm tells the bank after having negotiated the price with the equipment manufacturer. The bank then buys the equipment for $1,000, and the borrower buys it back from the bank at some later date for, say, $1,100, a price that includes a $100 markup for the bank. A cynic might point out that such a markup is functionally equivalent to an interest payment, and it is the similarity between this method and conventional banking that makes it so much easier to adopt.

Whichever method is most widely used, observers expect the transition from traditional to Islamic banking to be challenging. One fear is that there could be large-scale withdrawals by depositors, driven by worries that they could suffer in the absence of fixed interest rates. Another concern is that the country needs to have a tight regulatory regime to ensure that unscrupulous borrowers using a *mudarabah* contract do not declare themselves bankrupt, even when their businesses are running a profit. A third concern is that the uncertainty created by the transition will scare off foreign investors, leaving Pakistan starved of capital.

Sources: "Forced Devotion," *The Economist,* February 17, 2001, pp. 76–77; "Islamic Banking Marches On," *The Banker,* February 1, 2000; and F. Bokhari, "Bankers Fear Introduction of Islamic System Will Prompt Big Withdrawals," *Financial Times,* March 6, 2001, p. 4.

trepreneurial activity in pursuit of wealth creation that we find in Protestantism.[27] According to Weber, traditional Hindu values emphasize that individuals should not be judged by their material achievements, but by their spiritual achievements. Hindus perceive the pursuit of material well-being as making the attainment of nirvana more difficult. Given the emphasis on an ascetic lifestyle, Weber thought that devout Hindus would be less likely to engage in entrepreneurial activity than devout Protestants.

Mahatma Gandhi, the famous Indian nationalist and spiritual leader, was certainly the embodiment of Hindu asceticism. It has been argued that the values of Hindu asceticism and self-reliance that Gandhi advocated had a negative impact on the economic development of post-independence India.[28] But one must be careful not to read too much into Weber's arguments. Today, millions of hardworking entrepreneurs form the economic backbone of India's rapidly growing economy.

Hinduism also supports India's caste system. The concept of mobility between castes within an individual's lifetime makes no sense to Hindus. Hindus see mobility between castes as something that is achieved through spiritual progression and reincarnation. An individual can be reborn into a higher caste in his next life if he achieves spiritual development in this life. In so far as the caste system limits individuals' opportunities to adopt positions of responsibility and influence in society, the economic consequences of this religious belief are bound to be negative. For example, within a business organization, the most able individuals may find their route to the higher levels of the organization blocked simply because they come from a lower caste. By the same token, individuals may get promoted to higher positions within a firm as much because of their caste background as because of their ability.

Buddhism

Buddhism was founded in India in the sixth century B.C. by Siddhartha Gautama, an Indian prince who renounced his wealth to pursue an ascetic lifestyle and spiritual perfection. Siddhartha achieved *nirvana* but decided to remain on Earth to teach his followers how they too could achieve this state of spiritual enlightenment. Siddhartha became known as the Buddha (which means "the awakened one"). Today Buddhism has 250 million followers, most of whom are found in Central and Southeast Asia, China, Korea, and Japan. According to Buddhism, life is comprised of suffering. Misery is everywhere and originates in people's desires for pleasure. These desires can be curbed by systematically following the Noble Eightfold Path, which emphasizes right seeing, thinking, speech, action, living, effort, mindfulness, and meditation. Unlike Hinduism, Buddhism does not support the caste system. Nor does Buddhism advocate the kind of extreme ascetic behavior that is encouraged by Hinduism. Nevertheless, like Hindus, Buddhists stress the afterlife and spiritual achievement rather than involvement in this world.

Because of this, the emphasis on wealth creation that is embedded in Protestantism is not found in Buddhism. Thus, in Buddhist societies, we do not see the same kind of cultural stress on entrepreneurial behavior that we see in the Protestant West. But unlike Hinduism, the lack of support for the caste system and extreme ascetic behavior suggests that a Buddhist society may represent a more fertile ground for entrepreneurial activity than a Muslim culture.

Confucianism

Confucianism was founded in the fifth century B.C. by K'ung-Fu-tzu, more generally known as Confucius. For more than 2,000 years until the 1949 Communist revolution, Confucianism was the official ethical system of China. While observance of Confucian ethics has been weakened in China since 1949, more than 150 million people still follow the teachings of Confucius, principally in China, Korea, and Japan. Confucianism teaches the importance of attaining personal salvation through right action. Confucian ideology has become deeply embedded in the culture of these countries over the centuries, and through that, has an impact on the lives of many millions more. Confucianism is built around a comprehensive ethical code that sets down guidelines for relationships with others. The need for high moral and ethical conduct and loyalty to others are central to Confucianism. Unlike religions, Confucianism is not concerned with the supernatural and has little to say about the concept of a supreme being or an afterlife.

Economic Implications of Confucianism

Some maintain that Confucianism may have economic implications as profound as those found in Protestantism, although they are of a different nature.[29] Their basic thesis is that the influence of Confucian ethics on the culture of China, Japan, South Korea, and Taiwan, by lowering the costs of doing business in those countries, may help explain their economic success. In this regard, three values central to the Confucian system of ethics are of particular interest—loyalty, reciprocal obligations, and honesty in dealings with others.

In Confucian thought, loyalty to one's superiors is regarded as a sacred duty—an absolute obligation. In modern organizations based in Confucian cultures, the loyalty that binds employees to the heads of their organization can reduce the conflict between management and labor that we find in more class-conscious societies such as Great Britain. Cooperation between management and labor can be achieved at a lower cost in a culture where the virtue of loyalty is emphasized in the value systems.

However, in a Confucian culture, loyalty to one's superiors, such as a worker's loyalty to management, is not blind loyalty. The concept of reciprocal obligations also comes into play. Confucian ethics stress that superiors are obliged to reward the loyalty of their subordinates by bestowing blessings on them. If these "blessings" are not forthcoming, then neither will be the loyalty. As we saw in the opening case, in China this Confucian ethic is central to the concept of *guanxi*, which refers to relationship networks supported by reciprocal obligations. Similarly, in Japan this ethic finds expression in the concept of lifetime employment. The employees of a Japanese company are loyal to the leaders of the organization, and in return the leaders bestow on them the "blessing" of lifetime employment. The lack of mobility between companies implied by the lifetime employment system suggests that over the years managers and workers build up knowledge, experience, and a network of interpersonal business contacts. All of these can help managers and workers perform their jobs more effectively and cooperate with others in the organization. One result is improved economic performance of the company.

A third concept found in Confucian ethics is the importance attached to honesty. Confucian thinkers emphasize that, although dishonest behavior may yield short-term benefits for the transgressor, in the long run dishonesty does not pay. The importance attached to honesty has major economic implications. When companies can trust each other not to break contractual obligations, the costs of doing business are lowered. Expensive lawyers are not needed to resolve contract disputes. In a Confucian society, there may be less hesitation to commit substantial resources to cooperative ventures than in a society where honesty is less pervasive. When companies adhere to Confucian ethics, they can trust each other not to violate the terms of cooperative agreements. Thus, the costs of achieving cooperation between companies may be lowered in societies such as Japan relative to societies where trust is less pervasive.

For example, it has been argued that the close ties between the automobile companies and their component parts suppliers in Japan are facilitated by a combination of trust and reciprocal obligations. These close ties allow the auto companies and their suppliers to work together on a range of issues, including inventory reduction, quality control, and design. The competitive advantage of Japanese auto companies may in part be explained by such factors.[30] Similarly, the opening case showed how the combination of trust and reciprocal obligations is central to the workings and persistence of *guanxi* networks in China. Someone seeking and receiving help through a *guanxi* network is then obligated to return the favor and faces social sanctions if that obligation is not reciprocated when it is called upon. If they do not return the favor, their reputation will be tarnished and they will be unable to draw on the resources of the network in the future. It is claimed that these relationship-based networks can be more important in helping to enforce agreements between businesses than the Chinese legal system. Some claim that *guanxi* networks are a substitute for the legal system.[31]

Language

One obvious way in which countries differ is language. By language, we mean both the spoken and the unspoken means of communication. Language is one of the defining characteristics of a culture.

Spoken Language

Language does far more than just enable people to communicate with each other. The nature of a language also structures the way we perceive the world. The language of a society can direct the attention of its members to certain features of the world rather than others. The classic illustration of this phenomenon is that whereas the English language has but one word for snow, the language of the Inuit (Eskimos) lacks a general term for it. Instead, because distinguishing different forms of snow is so important in the lives of the Inuit, they have 24 words that describe different types of snow (e.g., powder snow, falling snow, wet snow, drifting snow).[32]

Because language shapes the way people perceive the world, it also helps define culture. In countries with more than one language, one also often finds more than one culture. Canada has an English-speaking culture and a French-speaking culture. Tensions between the two run quite high, with a substantial proportion of the French-speaking minority demanding independence from a Canada "dominated by English speakers." The same phenomenon can be observed in many countries. Belgium is divided into Flemish and French speakers, and tensions between the two groups exist; in Spain, a Basque-speaking minority with its own distinctive culture has been agitating for independence from the Spanish-speaking majority for decades; on the Mediterranean island of Cyprus, the culturally diverse Greek- and Turkish-speaking populations of the island engaged in open conflict in the 1970s, and the island is now partitioned into two parts. While it does not necessarily follow that language differences create differences in culture and, therefore, separatist pressures (e.g., witness the harmony in Switzerland, where four languages are spoken), there certainly seems to be a tendency in this direction.

Chinese is the "mother tongue" of the largest number of people, followed by English and Hindi, which is spoken in India (see Figure 3.2). However, the most widely spoken language in the world is English, followed by French, Spanish, and Chinese (i.e., many people speak English as a second language). English is increasingly becoming the language of international business. When a Japanese and a German businessperson get together to do business, it is almost certain that they will communicate in English. However, while English is widely used, learning the local language yields considerable advantages. Most people prefer to converse in their own language and being able to speak the local language can build rapport, which may be very important for a business deal.

Figure 3.2

Percentage of the World's Population for Whom This Is a First Language

Source: *The Economist Atlas* (London: The Economist Books, 1991), p. 116. Copyright © 1989 and © 1991 The Economist Books, Ltd.

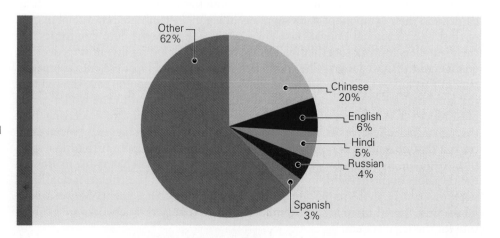

Other
62%

Chinese
20%

English
6%

Hindi
5%

Russian
4%

Spanish
3%

International businesses that do not understand the local language can make major blunders through improper translation. For example, the Sunbeam Corporation used the English words for its "Mist-Stick" mist-producing hair curling iron when it entered the German market, only to discover after an expensive advertising campaign that *mist* means excrement in German. General Motors was troubled by the lack of enthusiasm among Puerto Rican dealers for its new Chevrolet Nova. When literally translated into Spanish, *Nova* meant star. However, when spoken it sounded like "no va," which in Spanish means "it doesn't go." General Motors changed the name of the car to Caribe.[33]

Unspoken Language

Unspoken language refers to nonverbal communication. We all communicate with each other by a host of nonverbal cues. The raising of eyebrows, for example, is a sign of recognition in most cultures, while a smile is a sign of joy. Many nonverbal cues, however, are culturally bound. A failure to understand the nonverbal cues of another culture can lead to a failure of communication. For example, making a circle with the thumb and the forefinger is a friendly gesture in the United States, but it is a vulgar sexual invitation in Greece and Turkey. Similarly, while most Americans and Europeans use the thumbs-up gesture to indicate that "it's all right," in Greece the gesture is obscene.

Another aspect of nonverbal communication is personal space, which is the comfortable amount of distance between you and someone you are talking to. In the United States, the customary distance apart adopted by parties in a business discussion is five to eight feet. In Latin America, it is three to five feet. Consequently, many North Americans unconsciously feel that Latin Americans are invading their personal space and can be seen backing away from them during a conversation. In turn, the Latin American may interpret such backing away as aloofness. The result can be a regrettable lack of rapport between two businesspeople from different cultures.

Education

Formal education plays a key role in a society. Formal education is the medium through which individuals learn many of the language, conceptual, and mathematical skills that are indispensable in a modern society. Formal education also supplements the family's role in socializing the young into the values and norms of a society. Values and norms are taught both directly and indirectly. Schools generally teach basic facts about the social and political nature of a society. They also focus on the fundamental obligations of citizenship. Cultural norms are also taught indirectly at school. Respect for others, obedience to authority, honesty, neatness, being on time, and so on, are all part of the "hidden curriculum" of schools. The use of a grading system also teaches children the value of personal achievement and competition.[34]

From an international business perspective, one important aspect of education is its role as a determinant of national competitive advantage.[35] The availability of a pool of skilled and educated workers seems to be a major determinant of the likely economic success of a country. In analyzing the competitive success of Japan since 1945, for example, Michael Porter notes that after the war, Japan had almost nothing except for a pool of skilled and educated human resources.

With a long tradition of respect for education that borders on reverence, Japan possessed a large pool of literate, educated, and increasingly skilled human resources . . . Japan has benefited from a large pool of trained engineers. Japanese universities graduate many more engineers per capita than in the United States . . . A first-rate primary and secondary education system in Japan operates based on high standards and emphasizes math and science. Primary and secondary education is highly competitive . . . Japanese education provides most students all over Japan with a sound education for later education and training. A Japanese high school graduate knows as much about math as most American college graduates.[36]

Porter's point is that Japan's excellent education system was an important factor explaining the country's postwar economic success. Not only is a good education system a determinant of national competitive advantage, but it is also an important factor guiding the location choices of international businesses. It would make little sense to base production facilities that require highly skilled labor in a country where the education system was so poor that a skilled labor pool wasn't available, no matter how attractive the country might seem on other dimensions. It might make sense to base production operations that require only unskilled labor in such a country.

The general education level of a country is also a good index of the kind of products that might sell in a country and of the type of promotional material that should be used. For example, a country such as Pakistan where more than 70 percent of the population is illiterate is unlikely to be a good market for popular books. Promotional material containing written descriptions of mass-marketed products is unlikely to have an effect in a country where almost three-quarters of the population cannot read. It is far better to use pictorial promotions in such circumstances.

Maps 3.2 and 3.3 provide important data on education worldwide. Map 3.2 shows the percentage of a country's GNP that is devoted to education. Map 3.3 shows illiteracy rates. Although there is not a perfect one-to-one correspondence between the percentage of GNP devoted to education and the quality of education, the overall level of spending indicates a country's commitment to education. Note that the United States spends more of its GNP on education than many other advanced industrialized nations, including Germany and Japan. Despite this, the quality of U.S. education is often argued to be inferior to that offered in many other industrialized countries.

Culture and the Workplace

For an international business with operations in different countries, of considerable importance is how a society's culture affects the values found in the workplace. Management process and practices may need to vary according to culturally determined work-related values. For example, if the cultures of the United States and France result in different work-related values, an international business with operations in both countries should vary its management process and practices to take these differences into account.

Probably the most famous study of how culture relates to values in the workplace was undertaken by Geert Hofstede.[37] As part of his job as a psychologist working for IBM, Hofstede collected data on employee attitudes and values for more than 100,000 individuals from 1967 to 1973. This data enabled him to compare dimensions of culture across 40 countries. Hofstede isolated four dimensions that he claimed summarized different cultures—power distance, uncertainty avoidance, individualism versus collectivism, and masculinity versus femininity.

Hofstede's **power distance** dimension focused on how a society deals with the fact that people are unequal in physical and intellectual capabilities. According to Hofstede, high power distance cultures were found in countries that let inequalities grow over time into inequalities of power and wealth. Low power distance cultures were found in societies that tried to play down such inequalities as much as possible.

The **individualism versus collectivism** dimension focused on the relationship between the individual and his or her fellows. In individualistic societies, the ties between individuals were loose and individual achievement and freedom were highly valued. In societies where collectivism was emphasized, the ties between individuals

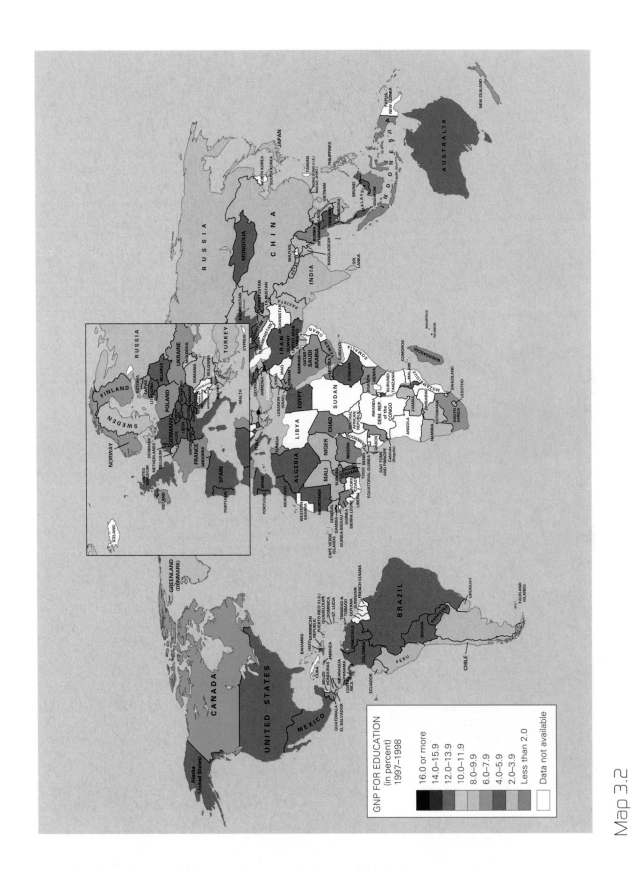

Map 3.2

Percentage of Gross National Product Spent on Education

Source: Map data are from World Bank, *World Development Report 2000–2001*, pp. 284–85.

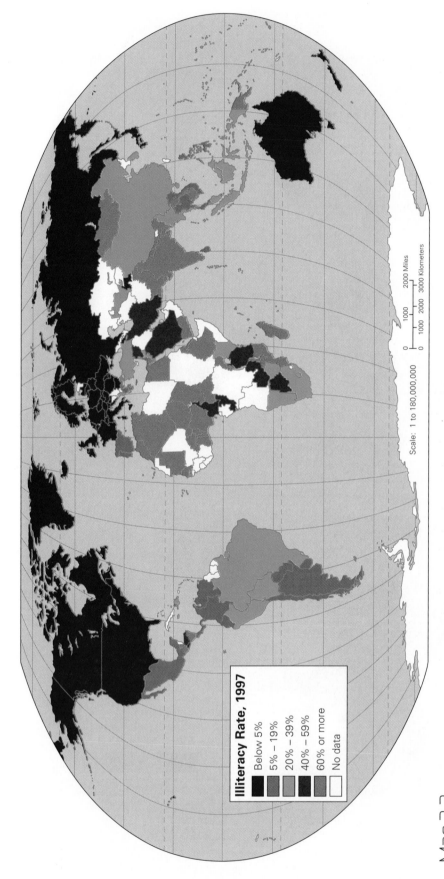

Map 3.3

Illiteracy Rates

Source: From *Student Atlas of World Geography*, Second Edition by John L. Allen. Copyright © 2001 by McGraw-Hill Companies. Reprinted by permission of the McGraw-Hill Companies, a division of the McGraw-Hill/Dushkin, Guilford, CT 06437.

Illiteracy Rate, 1997

Below 5%
5% – 19%
20% – 39%
40% – 59%
60% or more
No data

Scale: 1 to 180,000,000

0   1000   2000   2000 Miles
0   1000   2000   3000 Kilometers

were tight. In such societies, people were born into collectives, such as extended families, and everyone was supposed to look after the interest of his or her collective.

Hofstede's **uncertainty avoidance** dimension measured the extent to which different cultures socialized their members into accepting ambiguous situations and tolerating uncertainty. Members of high uncertainty avoidance cultures placed a premium on job security, career patterns, retirement benefits, and so on. They also had a strong need for rules and regulations; the manager was expected to issue clear instructions, and subordinates' initiatives were tightly controlled. Lower uncertainty avoidance cultures were characterized by a greater readiness to take risks and less emotional resistance to change.

Hofstede's **masculinity versus femininity** dimension looked at the relationship between gender and work roles. In masculine cultures, sex roles were sharply differentiated and traditional "masculine values," such as achievement and the effective exercise of power, determined cultural ideals. In feminine cultures, sex roles were less sharply distinguished, and little differentiation was made between men and women in the same job.

Hofstede created an index score for each of these four dimensions that ranged from 0 to 100 and scored high for high individualism, high power distance, high uncertainty avoidance, and high masculinity. He averaged the score for all employees from a given country. Table 3.1 summarizes this data for 20 selected countries. Western nations such

	Power Distance	Uncertainty Avoidance	Individualism	Masculinity
Argentina	49	86	46	56
Australia	36	51	90	61
Brazil	69	76	38	49
Canada	39	48	80	52
Denmark	18	23	74	16
France	68	86	71	43
Germany (F.R.)	35	65	67	66
Great Britain	35	35	89	66
Indonesia	78	48	14	46
India	77	40	48	56
Israel	13	81	54	47
Japan	54	92	46	95
Mexico	81	82	30	69
Netherlands	38	53	80	14
Panama	95	86	11	44
Spain	57	86	51	42
Sweden	31	29	71	5
Thailand	64	64	20	34
Turkey	66	85	37	45
United States	40	46	91	62

Table 3.1

Work-Related Values for 20 Selected Countries

Source: G. Hofstede, *Culture's Consequences*. Copyright 1980 by Sage Publications. Reprinted by permission of Sage Publications. Cited in G. Hofstede, "The Cultural Relativity of Organizational Practices and Theories," *Journal of International Business Studies* 14 (Fall 1983), pp. 75–89.

as the United States, Canada, and Britain score high on the individualism scale and low on the power distance scale. At the other extreme are a group of Latin American and Asian countries that emphasize collectivism over individualism and score high on the power distance scale. Table 3.1 also reveals that Japan's culture has strong uncertainty avoidance and high masculinity. This characterization fits the standard stereotype of Japan as a country that is male dominant and where uncertainty avoidance exhibits itself in the institution of lifetime employment. Sweden and Denmark stand out as countries that have both low uncertainty avoidance and low masculinity (high emphasis on "feminine" values).

Hofstede's results are interesting for what they tell us in a general way about differences between cultures. Many of Hofstede's findings are consistent with standard Western stereotypes about cultural differences. For example, many people believe Americans are more individualistic and egalitarian than the Japanese (they have a lower power distance), who in turn are more individualistic and egalitarian than Mexicans. Similarly, many might agree that Latin countries such as Mexico place a higher emphasis on masculine value—they are machismo cultures—than the Nordic countries of Denmark and Sweden.

However, one should be careful about reading too much into Hofstede's research. It has been criticized on a number of points.[38] First, Hofstede assumes there is a one-to-one correspondence between culture and the nation-state, but as we saw earlier, many countries have more than one culture. Hofstede's results do not capture this distinction. Second, the research may have been culturally bound. The research team was composed of Europeans and Americans. The questions they asked of IBM employees and their analysis of the answers may have been shaped by their own cultural biases and concerns. So it is not surprising that Hofstede's results confirm Western stereotypes, since it was Westerners who undertook the research!

Third, Hofstede's informants worked not only within a single industry, the computer industry, but also within one company, IBM. At the time, IBM was renowned for its own strong corporate culture and employee selection procedures, making it possible that the employees' values were different in important respects from the values of the cultures from which those employees came. Also, certain social classes (such as unskilled manual workers) were excluded from Hofstede's sample. A final caution is that Hofstede's work is now beginning to look dated. Cultures do not stand still; they evolve, albeit slowly. What was a reasonable characterization in the 1960s and 1970s may not be so today.

Still, just as it should not be accepted without question, Hofstede's work should not be dismissed entirely either. It represents a starting point for managers trying to figure out how cultures differ and what that might mean for management practices. Also, several other scholars have found strong evidence that differences in culture affect values and practices in the workplace, and Hofdstede's basic results have been replicated using more diverse samples of individuals in different settings.[39] Still, managers should use the results with caution, for they are not necessarily accurate.

Hofstede subsequently expanded his original research to include a fifth dimension that he argued captured additional cultural differences not brought out in his earlier work.[40] He referred to this dimension as "Confucian dynamism" (sometimes called "long-term orientation"). According to Hofstede, **Confucian dynamism** captures attitudes toward time, persistence, ordering by status, protection of face, respect for tradition, and reciprocation of gifts and favors. The label refers to these "values" being derived from Confucian teachings. As might be expected, East Asian countries such as Japan, Hong Kong, and Thailand scored high on Confucian dynamism, while nations like the United States and Canada scored low. Hofstede and his associates went on to argue that their evidence suggested that nations with higher economic growth rates scored high on Confucian dynamism and low on individualism—the implication being Confucianism is good for growth. However, subsequent studies have shown that this finding does not hold up under more sophisticated statistical analysis.[41] During the past decade, countries with high individualism and low Confucian dynamics such as the United States have attained high growth rates, while some Confucian cultures such as Japan have had stagnant economic growth. In reality, while culture might have an influence on the economic success of a nation, it is just one of many factors, and while its importance should not be ignored, it should not be overstated either. The factors discussed in Chapter 2—economic, political, and legal systems—are probably more important than culture in explaining differential economic growth rates over time.

Cultural Change

Culture is not a constant; it evolves over time. Changes in value systems can be slow and painful for a society. In the 1960s, for example, American values toward the role of women, love, sex, and marriage underwent significant changes. Much of the social turmoil of that time reflected these changes. Change, however, does occur and can often be quite profound. For example, at the beginning of the 1960s, the idea that women might hold senior management positions in major corporations was not widely accepted. Many scoffed at the idea. Today, it is a reality and few in the mainstream of American society question the development or the capability of women in the business world. American culture has changed. Similarly, the value systems of many ex-Communist states, such as Russia, are undergoing significant changes as those countries move away from values that emphasize collectivism and toward those that emphasize individualism. While social turmoil is an inevitable outcome of such a shift, the shift will still probably occur.

Some claim that a major cultural shift is occurring in Japan, with a move toward greater individualism.[42] The model Japanese office worker, or "salaryman," is pictured as being loyal to his boss and the organization to the point of giving up evenings, weekends, and vacations to serve the organization, which is the collective of which he is a member. However, a new generation of office workers does not seem to fit this model. An individual from the new generation

> is more direct than the traditional Japanese. He acts more like a Westerner, a *gaijian*. He does not live for the company, and will move on if he gets the offer of a better job. He is not keen on overtime, especially if he has a date with a girl. He has his own plans for his free time, and they may not include drinking or playing golf with the boss.[43]

A more detailed example of the changes occurring in Japan is given in the Management Focus, which looks at the impact of Japan's changing culture on Matsushita, one of Japan's most traditional firms. Several studies have suggested that economic advancement and globalization may be important factors in societal change.[44] For example, there is evidence that economic progress is accompanied by a shift in values away from collectivism and toward individualism.[45] Thus, as Japan has become richer, the cultural emphasis on collectivism has declined and greater individualism is being witnessed. One reason for this shift may be that richer societies exhibit less need for social and material support structures built on collectives, whether the collective is the extended family or the paternalistic company. People are better able to take care of their own needs. As a result, the importance attached to collectivism declines, while greater economic freedoms lead to an increase in opportunities for expressing individualism.

The culture of societies may also change as they become richer because economic progress affects a number of other factors, which in turn impact on culture. For example, increased urbanization and improvements in the quality and availability of education are both a function of economic progress, and both can lead to declining emphasis on the traditional values associated with poor rural societies.

Management Focus

Matsushita's and Japan's Changing Culture

Established in 1920, the consumer electronics giant Matsushita was at the forefront of the rise of Japan to the status of major economic power during the 1970s and 1980s. Like many other long-standing Japanese businesses, Matsushita was regarded as a bastion of traditional Japanese values based on strong group identification, reciprocal obligations, and loyalty to the company. Several commentators attributed Matsushita's success, and that of the Japanese economy, to the existence of Confucian values in the workplace. At Matsushita, employees were taken care of by the company from "cradle to the grave." Matsushita provided them with a wide range of benefits including cheap housing, guaranteed lifetime employment, seniority-based pay systems, and generous retirement bonuses. In return, Matsushita expected, and got, loyalty and hard work from its employees. To Japan's postwar generation, struggling to recover from the humiliation of defeat, it seemed like a fair bargain. The employees worked hard for the greater good of Matsushita, and Matsushita reciprocated by bestowing "blessings" on employees.

However, culture does not stay constant. According to some observers, the generation born after 1964 lacked the same commitment to traditional Japanese values as their parents. They grew up in a world that was richer, where Western ideas were beginning to make themselves felt, and where the possibilities seemed greater. They did not want to be tied to a company for life, to be a "salaryman." These trends came to the fore in the 1990s, when the Japanese economy entered an economic slump from which it has yet to recover. As the decade progressed, one Japanese firm after another was forced to change its traditional ways of doing business. Slowly at first, troubled companies started to lay off older workers, effectively abandoning lifetime employment guarantees. As younger people saw this happening, they concluded that loyalty to a company might not be reciprocated, effectively undermining one of the central bargains made in postwar Japan.

Matsushita was one of the last companies to turn its back on Japanese traditions, but in 1998 after years of poor performance, it too bit the bullet and modified traditional practices. First, Matsushita changed the pay scheme for its 11,000 managers. In the past, the traditional twice-a-year bonuses had been based almost entirely on seniority, but now Matsushita said they would be based on performance. In 1999, Matsushita announced that this process would be made transparent; managers would be shown what their performance rankings were and how these fed into pay bonuses. As elementary as this might sound in the West, for Matsushita it represented the beginning of a revolution in human resource practices.

As for globalization, some have argued that advances in transportation and communication technologies, the dramatic increase in trade that we have witnessed since World War II, and the rise of global corporations such as Hitachi, Disney, Microsoft, and Levi Strauss, whose products and operations can be found around the globe, are creating the conditions for the merging of cultures.[46] With McDonald's hamburgers in China, Levi's in India, Sony Walkmans in South Africa, and MTV everywhere helping to foster an ubiquitous youth culture, some argue that the conditions for less cultural variation have been created. At the same time, one must not ignore important countertrends, such as the shift toward Islamic fundamentalism in several countries; the separatist movement in Quebec, Canada; or the continuing ethnic strains and separatist movements in Russia. Such countertrends in many ways are a reaction to the pressures for cultural convergence. In an increasingly modern and materialistic world, some societies are trying to reemphasize their cultural roots and uniqueness. Cultural change is not therefore unidirectional, with national cultures converging toward some homogenous global entity. Also, while some elements of culture change quite rapidly—particularly the use of material symbols—other elements change only slowly if at all. Thus, just because people the world over wear blue jeans and eat at McDonald's, one should not assume that they have also adopted American values—for more often than not, they have not.

About the same time Matsushita took aim at the lifetime employment system and the associated perks. Under the new system, recruits were given the choice of three employment options. First, they could sign on to the traditional option. Under this, they were eligible to live in subsidized company housing, go free to company-organized social events, and buy subsidized services such as banking from group companies. They would also still receive a retirement bonus equal to two years' salary. Under a second scheme, employees could forgo the guaranteed retirement bonus in exchange for higher starting salaries and keep perks such as cheap company housing. Under a third scheme, they would lose both the retirement bonus and the subsidized services, but they would start on a still higher salary. In its first two years of operation, only 3 percent of recruits chose the third option—suggesting there is still a hankering for the traditional paternalistic relationship—but 41 percent took the second option.

In other ways Matsushita's designs are grander still. As the company has moved into new industries such as software engineering and network communications technology, it has begun to sing the praises of democratization of employees and it has sought to encourage individuality, initiative taking, and risk seeking among its younger employees. But while such changes may be easy to articulate, they are hard to implement. For all of its talk, Matsushita has still not changed its lifetime employment commitment to those hired under the traditional system; nor does it seem likely to do so anytime soon. This was underlined in early 2001 when, in response to continued poor performance, Matsushita announced it would close 30 factories in Japan, cut 1,000 marketing jobs, and sell a "huge amount of assets" over the next three years. While this seemed to indicate a final break with the lifetime employment system, the company also said that unneeded marketing staff would not be laid off but instead would be transferred to higher growth areas such as health care.

With so many of its managers a product of the old way of doing things, a skeptic might question the ability of the company to turn its intentions into a reality. As growth has slowed, Matsushita has had to cut back on its hiring, but its continued commitment to long-standing employees means that the average age of its workforce is rising. In the 1960s it was around 25; now it is 35, a trend that might counteract Matsushita's attempts to revolutionize the workplace, for surely those who benefited from the old system will not give way easily to the new.

Sources: "Putting the Bounce Back into Matsushita," *The Economist*, May 22, 1999, pp. 67–68; "In Search of the New Japanese Dream," *The Economist*, February 19, 2000, pp. 59–60; and P. Landers, "Matsushita to Restructure in Bid to Boost Thin Profits," *Wall Street Journal*, December 1, 2000, p. A13.

Implications for Business

International business is different from national business because countries and societies are different. In this chapter, we have seen just how different societies can be. Societies differ because their cultures vary. Their cultures vary because of profound differences in social structure, religion, language, education, economic philosophy, and political philosophy. Three important implications for international business flow from these differences. The first is the need to develop cross-cultural literacy. There is a need not only to appreciate that cultural differences exist, but also to appreciate what such differences mean for international business. A second implication looks at the connection between culture and ethics in decision making. A third implication for international business centers on the connection between culture and national competitive advantage. In this section, we will explore these issues in greater detail.

Cross-Cultural Literacy

One of the biggest dangers confronting a company that goes abroad for the first time is the danger of being ill-informed. International businesses that are ill-informed about the practices of another culture are likely to fail. Doing business in different cultures requires adaptation to conform with the value systems and norms of that culture. Adaptation can embrace all aspects of an international firm's operations in a foreign country. The way in which deals are negotiated, the appropriate incentive pay systems for salespeople, the structure of the organization, the name of a product, the tenor of relations between management and labor, the manner in which the product is promoted, and so on, are all sensitive to cultural differences. What works in one culture might not work in another.

To combat the danger of being ill-informed, international businesses should consider employing local citizens to help them do business in a particular culture. They must also ensure that home-country executives are cosmopolitan enough to understand how differences in culture affect the practice of international business. Transferring executives overseas at regular intervals to expose them to different cultures will help build a cadre of cosmopolitan executives. An international business must also be constantly on guard against the dangers of ethnocentric behavior. **Ethnocentrism** is a belief in the superiority of one's own ethnic group or culture. Hand in hand with ethnocentrism goes a disregard or contempt for the culture of other countries. Unfortunately, ethnocentrism is all too prevalent; many Americans are guilty of it, as are many French people, Japanese people, British people, and so on. Ugly as it is, ethnocentrism is a fact of life, one that international businesses must be on continual guard against.

Culture and Competitive Advantage

One theme that continually surfaced in this chapter is the relationship between culture and national competitive advantage. Put simply, the value systems and norms of a country influence the costs of doing business in that country. The costs of doing business in a country influence the ability of firms to establish a competitive advantage in the global marketplace. We have seen how attitudes toward cooperation between management and labor, toward work, and toward the payment of interest are influenced by social structure and religion. It can be argued that the class-based conflict between workers and management found in British society, when it leads to industrial disruption, raises the costs of doing business in that culture. Similarly, we have seen how the ascetic "other-worldly" ethics of Hinduism may not be as supportive of capitalism as the ethics embedded in Protestantism and Confucianism. Also, Islamic laws banning interest payments may raise the costs of doing business by constraining a country's banking system.

Japan presents us with an interesting example of how culture can influence competitive advantage. Some scholars have argued that the culture of modern Japan lowers the costs of doing business relative to the costs in most Western nations. Japan's emphasis on group affiliation, loyalty, reciprocal obligations, honesty, and education all boost the competitiveness of Japanese companies. The emphasis on group affiliation and loyalty encourages individuals to identify strongly with the companies in which they work. This tends to foster an ethic of hard work and cooperation between management and labor "for the good of the company." Similarly, reciprocal obligations and honesty help foster an atmosphere of trust between companies and their suppliers. This encourages them to enter into long-term relationships with each other to work on inventory reduction, quality control, and joint design—all of which have been shown to improve an organization's competitiveness. This level of cooperation has often been lacking in the West, where the relationship between a company and its suppliers tends to be a short-term one structured around competitive bidding, rather than one based on long-term mutual commitments. In addition, the availability of a pool of highly skilled labor, particularly engineers, has helped Japanese enterprises develop cost-reducing process innovations that have boosted their productivity.[47] Thus, cultural factors may help explain the competitive advantage enjoyed by many Japanese businesses in the global marketplace. The rise of Japan as an economic power during the second half of the 20th century may be in part attributed to the economic consequences of its culture.

It has also been argued that the Japanese culture is less supportive of entrepreneurial activity than, say, American society. In many ways, entrepreneurial activity is a product of an individualistic mind-set, not a classic characteristic of the Japanese. This may explain why American enterprises, rather than Japanese corporations, dominate industries where entrepreneurship and innovation are highly valued, such as computer software and biotechnology. Of course, there are obvious exceptions to this generalization. Masayoshi Son recognized the potential of software far faster than any of Japan's corporate giants; set up his company, Softbank, in 1981; and has since built it into Japan's top software distributor. Similarly, dynamic entrepreneurial individuals established major Japanese companies such as Sony and Matsushita. But these examples may be the exceptions that prove the rule, for as yet there has been no surge in entrepreneurial high-technology enterprises in Japan equivalent to what has occurred in the United States.

For the international business, the connection between culture and competitive advantage is important for two reasons. First, the connection suggests which countries are likely to produce the most viable competitors. For example, one might argue that U.S. enterprises are likely to see continued growth in aggressive, cost-efficient competitors from those Pacific Rim nations where a combination of free market economics, Confucian ideology, group-oriented social structures, and advanced education systems can all be found (e.g., South Korea, Taiwan, Japan, and increasingly China).

Second, the connection between culture and competitive advantage has important implications for the choice of countries in which to locate production facilities and do business. Consider a hypothetical case when a company has to choose between two countries, A and B, for locating a production facility. Both countries are characterized by low labor costs and good access to world markets. Both countries are of roughly the same size (in terms of population) and both are at a similar stage of economic development. In country A, the education system is undeveloped, the society is characterized by a marked stratification between the upper and lower classes, the dominant religion stresses the importance of reincarnation, and there are three major linguistic groups. In country B, the education system is well developed, there is a lack of social stratification, group identification is valued by the culture, the dominant religion stresses the virtue of hard work, and there is only one linguistic group. Which country makes the best investment site?

Country B does. The culture of country B is supportive of the capitalist mode of production and social harmony, whereas the culture of country A is not. In country A, conflict between management and labor, and between different language groups, can be expected to lead to social and industrial disruption, thereby raising the costs of doing business. The lack of a good education system and the dominance of a religion that stresses ascetic behavior as a way of achieving advancement in the next life can also be expected to work against the attainment of business goals.

The same kind of comparison could be made for an international business trying to decide where to push its products, country A or B. Again, country B would be the logical choice because cultural factors suggest that in the long run, country B is the nation most likely to achieve the greatest level of economic growth. In comparison, the culture of country A may produce economic stagnation.

But as important as culture is, it is probably less important than economic, political, and legal systems in explaining differential economic growth between nations. Cultural differences are significant, but we should not overemphasize their importance in the economic sphere. For example, earlier we noted that Max Weber argued that the ascetic principles embedded in Hinduism do not encourage entrepreneurial activity. While this may be the correct academic interpretation, recent years have seen an increase in entrepreneurial activity in India, particularly in the information technology sector where India is rapidly becoming an important global player. The ascetic principles of Hinduism have apparently not held back entrepreneurial activity in this sector!

Culture and Business Ethics

Many ethical principles are universally held across cultures. For example, basic moral principles such as don't kill or don't steal apply everywhere, despite differences in local culture. Similarly, in all cultures it is regarded as unethical to unilaterally and without reason break a business agreement. As Adam Smith pointed out more than 200 years ago, if people cannot trust each other to honor agreements, business activity will not take place, and economic growth will not occur. A certain level of faith that agreements will be honored—that parties to a transaction will do the ethical thing—is required to encourage economic activity no matter what the culture. In the West, our legal system, and particularly our systems of contract law, evolved to help assure people that agreements will be honored, but it is important to recognize that the legal system is designed to deal only with the exceptions to the general principle (which is embedded in our culture) that one should honor agreements. In nations that lack a similar legal tradition, other institutions have emerged to help assure people that business agreements will be honored. As we pointed out earlier, *guanxi* networks may fulfill that role in China (see the opening case). Individuals who break agreements will have their reputation tarnished and will be unable to draw on the *guanxi* network in the future. Whether we are talking about China or the West, however, the basic principle remains the same—it is unethical to break business agreements without good reason, and those that do will face sanctions (either legal or cultural).

Although many ethical principles are universal, some are culturally bound.[48] When this is the case, international businesses may be confronted with difficult ethical dilemmas. For example, *guanxi* networks are often supported by the idea of reciprocal gift giving. But if a Western company gives a "gift" to a government official, as an attempt to build a relationship with that individual that may be useful in the future, that company may subsequently be accused of bribery and supporting corruption. What then is the ethical thing to do?

One response to such a dilemma is to argue that because customs vary from country to country, businesses should adopt the customs (and by extension, ethical practices) of the country in which it is currently doing business. This is the *relativist* or "when in Rome" approach to business ethics. It is also a dangerously flawed approach.[49] It would suggest, for example, that if slavery is practiced in a country, it is OK to practice slavery when doing business in that nation! Obviously, this is not the case. Similarly, as several Western businesses have discovered, just because local sweatshops in parts of Asia employ child labor and pay them below subsistence wages, it doesn't follow that one should adopt the same practices. Ethical values are not like a coat that one puts on in certain seasons and certain places and takes off elsewhere. You cannot leave your ethics behind as you venture around the globe. This suggests that one answer to the question "Whose ethics do you use in international business?" is "Your ethics."[50]

But what should "your ethics" be? The answer is somewhat clearer than it used to be. Organizations such as the United Nations have pushed hard to get countries to ratify agreements that have clear ethical implications. An important example is the Universal Declaration of Human Rights, which has been ratified by almost every country on the planet and lays down basic principles that should always be adhered to irrespective of the culture in which one is doing business. For example, Article 23 of this declaration states that

1. Everyone has the right to work, to free choice of employment, to just and favorable conditions of work and to protection against unemployment.
2. Everyone, without any discrimination, has the right to equal pay for equal work.
3. Everyone who works has the right to just and favorable remuneration ensuring for himself and his family an existence worthy of human dignity, and supplemented, if necessary, by other means of social protection.
4. Everyone has the right to form and to join trade unions for the protection of his interests.

Clearly, the rights to "just and favorable work conditions," "equal pay for equal work," and remuneration that ensures an "existence worthy of human dignity" embodied in Article 23 imply that it is unethical to employ child labor in sweatshop settings and pay less than subsistence wages, even if that happens to be common practice in some countries. But does that mean one should not employ children per se, or buy from suppliers who employ children, even if that is common in a certain country? Here the ethical thing to do becomes less clear. If the choice for the child is between living on the streets and begging for food or working in an apparel factory for subsistence wages, what should a firm do? Should it continue to sanction the employment of child labor as a lesser evil? Again probably not, but neither should the firm simply wash its hands of the situation. If a firm already has a relationship with a supplier who is employing child labor and that fact is suddenly uncovered, walking away from that relationship because of moral outrage may do more harm than good to the children whose interests the firm wishes to protect. In such circumstances, the ethical thing to do may be to find a way of improving the lot of the children. For example, when Levi Strauss found that one of its suppliers employed child labor, it did not terminate the relationship. Instead, it looked into the situation. It discovered that many of the women who worked in the factory brought their children to work with them because there was no local school, and because the pittance that the children earned kept the family's income above subsistence level. So Levi Strauss built a school for the children under 14, and it paid the parents the additional money that their children would otherwise have earned. This was a small price for Levi Strauss to pay, but it made a big difference in the lives of the affected children.

Gray areas will always exist that require managers to use their own moral judgment to solve ethical dilemmas, but those judgments should be made with regard to a high ethical code. Consider again the example of "gift giving" to support relationships. What is the ethical thing to do here? Should one respond to the cultural expectation that a gift should be given, and do so to try to build a relationship that might pay dividends in the future? In nations such as China, where reciprocal gift giving is common and helps to cement *guanxi* relationships, this is not an unreasonable approach, although it may conflict with Western notions of fair play.[51] For example, consider a situation where two Western companies are competing with each other to win a supply contract from a Chinese firm. Imagine that the firm that wins the contract is not the lowest bidder but is the firm that employed the son of the CEO of the Chinese firm as a consultant to advise it on the negotiations. The losing company might believe that principles of fair play have been violated here, but this is not necessarily so. Rather, the winning firm has simply recognized that relationships matter in China and employed an individual with connections to help it win the contract. By employing the son of the CEO, the firm that won the bid helped someone in the CEO's *guanxiwang,* which increased the probability that this "gift" or gesture would be reciprocated.

The practice becomes obviously problematic, however, when government officials are the recipients of the gifts, either directly or indirectly, for then the gifts can be construed as bribery. As was noted in the last chapter, bribery is dangerous, even if it is culturally sanctioned, because the practice can corrupt both the bribe taker and the bribe giver. There is a dividing line between corruption and legitimate gift giving to support business transactions. It is a line that a manager with a strong moral compass should be able to recognize.

Reflecting on such dilemmas, the ethicist Thomas Donaldson has argued that when thinking through ethical problems in international business, firms should be guided by three principles.[52]

1. Respect for core human values (human rights), which determine the absolute moral threshold for all business activities.
2. Respect for local tradition.
3. The belief that context matters when deciding what is right and what is wrong.

Donaldson's point is that respect of core human values must be the starting point for all ethical decisions. Once those are assured, businesses must also respect local cultural differences, which he defines as traditions and context. Thus, Donaldson argues that "gift giving" is not unethical, even though some Western businesses might feel that it is wrong. Gift giving does not violate core human values and is important in the context of some cultures such as China and Japan. By the same token, Donaldson would condemn as unethical decisions that clearly violate core human values. Employing child labor at less than subsistence wages would fall into that category.

Chapter Summary

We have looked at the nature of social culture and studied some implications for business practice. The following points have been made:

1. Culture is a complex whole that includes knowledge, beliefs, art, morals, law, customs, and other capabilities acquired by people as members of society.
2. Values and norms are the central components of a culture. Values are abstract ideals about what a society believes to be good, right, and desirable. Norms are social rules and guidelines that prescribe appropriate behavior in particular situations.
3. Values and norms are influenced by political and economic philosophy, social structure, religion, language, and education.
4. The social structure of a society refers to its basic social organization. Two main dimensions along which social structures differ are the individual–group dimension and the stratification dimension.
5. In some societies, the individual is the basic building block of social organization. These societies emphasize individual achievements above all else. In other societies, the group is the basic building block of social organization. These societies emphasize group membership and group achievements above all else.
6. All societies are stratified into different classes. Class-conscious societies are characterized by low social mobility and a high degree of stratification. Less class-conscious societies are characterized by high social mobility and a low degree of stratification.
7. Religion may be defined as a system of shared beliefs and rituals that is concerned with the realm of the sacred. Ethical systems refer to a set of moral principles, or values, that are used to guide and shape behavior. The world's major religions are Christianity, Islam, Hinduism, and Bud-

dhism. Although not a religion, Confucianism has an impact on behavior that is as profound as that of many religions. The value systems of different religious and ethical systems have different implications for business practice.

8. Language is one defining characteristic of a culture. It has both a spoken and an unspoken dimension. In countries with more than one spoken language, we tend to find more than one culture.

9. Formal education is the medium through which individuals learn skills and are socialized into the values and norms of a society. Education plays an important role in the determination of national competitive advantage.

10. Geert Hofstede studied how culture relates to values in the workplace. Hofstede isolated four dimensions that he claimed summarized different cultures: power distance, uncertainty avoidance, individualism versus collectivism, and masculinity versus femininity.

11. Culture is not a constant; it evolves over time. Economic progress and globalization seem to be two important engines of cultural change.

12. One danger confronting a company that goes abroad for the first time is being ill-informed. To develop cross-cultural literacy, international businesses need to employ host-country nationals, build a cadre of cosmopolitan executives, and guard against the dangers of ethnocentric behavior.

13. The value systems and norms of a country can affect the costs of doing business in that country.

14. Although many ethical principles are universal, some are culturally bounded. What is not ethical in one country might be common in another. Despite this, the "when in Rome" approach to business ethics is dangerous. International businesses need to adhere to a consistent set of ethics derived from a high moral code.

Critical Discussion Questions

1. Outline why the culture of a country might influence the costs of doing business in that country. Illustrate your answer with examples.

2. Do you think that business practices in an Islamic country are likely to differ from business practices in the United States, and if so how?

3. What are the implications for international business of differences in the dominant religion and/or ethical system of a country?

4. Choose two countries that appear to be culturally diverse. Compare the cultures of those countries and then indicate how cultural differences influence (a) the costs of doing business in each country, (b) the likely future economic development of that country, (c) business practices, and (d) business ethics.

5. It is unreasonable to expect Western businesses active in developing nations to adhere to the same ethical standards that they use at home. Discuss!

6. A Western firm is trying to get a license from the government of a developing nation to set up a factory in that country. The firm knows that the factory will bring many benefits to the country. It will provide jobs in an area where unemployment is high and it will produce exports for the country, allowing that nation to earn valuable foreign exchange. So far, the government official with whom the firm is negotiating has been noncommittal, neither rejecting nor approving the request, but simply asking for more and more information. The firm has been told that relationships are important in this country, and that if it hired the daughter of the government official as a consultant, she could use her influence to get the license application approved, to everyone's betterment. What should the firm do?

Disney in France

Closing Case

Until 1992, the Walt Disney Company had experienced nothing but success in the theme park business. Its first park, Disneyland, opened in Anaheim, California, in 1955. Its theme song, "It's a Small World After All," promoted "an idealized vision of America spiced with reassuring glimpses of exotic cultures all calculated to promote heartwarming feelings about living together as one happy family. There were dark tunnels and bumpy rides to scare the children a little but none of the terrors of the real world . . . The Disney characters that everyone knew from the cartoons and comic books were on hand to shepherd the guests and to direct them to the Mickey Mouse watches and Little Mermaid records."[53] The Anaheim park was an instant success.

In the 1970s, the triumph was repeated in Florida, and in 1983, Disney proved the Japanese also have an affinity for Mickey Mouse with the successful opening of Tokyo Disneyland. Having wooed the Japanese, Disney executives in 1986 turned their attention to France and, more specifically, to Paris, the self-proclaimed capital of European high culture and style. "Why did they pick France?" many asked. When word first got out that Disney wanted to build another international theme park, officials from more than 200 locations all over the world descended on Disney with pleas and cash inducements to work the Disney magic in their hometowns. But Paris was chosen because of demographics and subsidies. About 17 million Europeans live less than a two-hour drive from Paris. Another 310 million can fly there in the same time or less. Also, the French government was so eager to attract Disney that it offered the company more than $1 billion in various incentives, all in the expectation that the project would create 30,000 French jobs.

From the beginning, cultural gaffes by Disney set the tone for the project. By late 1986, Disney was deep in negotiations with the French government. To the exasperation of the Disney team, headed by Joe Shapiro, the talks were taking far longer than expected. Jean-Rene Bernard, the chief French negotiator, said he was astonished when Mr. Shapiro, his patience depleted, ran to the door of the room and, in a very un-Gallic gesture, began kicking it repeatedly, shouting, "Get me something to break!" There was also snipping from Parisian intellectuals who attacked the transplantation of Disney's dream world as an assault on French culture; "a cultural Chernobyl," one prominent intellectual called it. The minister of culture announced he would boycott the opening, proclaiming it to be an unwelcome symbol of American clichés and a consumer society. Unperturbed, Disney pushed ahead with the planned summer 1992 opening of the $5 billion park. Shortly after Euro-Disneyland opened, French farmers drove their tractors to the entrance and blocked it. This globally televised act of protest was aimed not at Disney but at the U.S. government, which had been demanding that French agricultural subsidies be cut. Still, it focused world attention on the loveless marriage of Disney and Paris.

Then there were the operational errors. Disney's policy of serving no alcohol in the park, since reversed, caused astonishment in a country where a glass of wine for lunch is a given. Disney thought that Monday would be a light day for visitors and Friday a heavy one and allocated staff accordingly, but the reality was the reverse. Another unpleasant surprise was the hotel breakfast debacle. "We were told that Europeans 'don't take break-

fast,' so we downsized the restaurants," recalled one Disney executive. "And guess what? Everybody showed up for breakfast. We were trying to serve 2,500 breakfasts in a 350-seat restaurant at some of the hotels. The lines were horrendous. Moreover, they didn't want the typical French breakfast of croissants and coffee, which was our assumption. They wanted bacon and eggs." Lunch turned out to be another problem. "Everybody wanted lunch at 12:30. The crowds were huge. Our smiling cast members had to calm down surly patrons and engage in some 'behavior modification' to teach them that they could eat lunch at 11:00 A.M. or 2:00 P.M."

There were major staffing problems too. Disney tried to use the same teamwork model with its staff that had worked so well in America and Japan, but it ran into trouble in France. In the first nine weeks of Euro-Disneyland's operation, roughly 1,000 employees, 10 percent of the total, left. One former employee was a 22-year-old medical student from a nearby town who signed up for a weekend job. After two days of "brainwashing," as he called Disney's training, he left following a dispute with his supervisor over the timing of his lunch hour. Another former employee noted, "I don't think that they realize what Europeans are like . . . that we ask questions and don't think all the same way."

One of the biggest problems, however, was that Europeans didn't stay at the park as long as Disney expected. While Disney succeeded in getting close to 9 million visitors a year through the park gates, in line with its plans, most stayed only a day or two. Few stayed the four to five days that Disney had hoped for. It seems that most Europeans regard theme parks as places for day excursions. A theme park is not seen as a destination for an extended vacation. This was a big shock for Disney. The company had invested billions in building luxury hotels next to the park—hotels that the day-trippers didn't need and that stood half empty most of the time. To make matters worse, the French didn't show up in the expected numbers. In 1994, only 40 percent of the park's visitors were French. One puzzled executive noted that many visitors were Americans living in Europe or, stranger still, Japanese on a European vacation! As a result, by the end of 1994 Euro-Disneyland had cumulative losses of $2 billion. At this point, Euro-Disney changed its strategy. First, the company changed the name to Disneyland Paris in an attempt to strengthen the park's identity. Second, food and fashion offerings changed. To quote one manager, "We opened with restaurants providing French-style food service, but we found that customers wanted self-service like in the U.S. parks. Similarly, products in the boutiques were initially toned down for the French market, but since then the range has changed to give it a more definite Disney image." Third, the prices for day tickets and hotel rooms were cut by one-third. The result was an attendance of 11.7 million in 1996, up from a low of 8.8 million in 1994.

Sources: P. Gumble and R. Turner, "Mouse Trap: Fans Like Euro Disney But Its Parent's Goofs Weigh the Park Down," *Wall Street Journal*, March 10, 1994, p. A1; R. J. Barnet and J. Cavanagh, *Global Dreams* (New York: Touchstone Books, 1994), pp. 33–34; J. Huey, "Eisner Explains Everything," *Fortune*, April 17, 1995, pp. 45–68; R. Anthony, "Euro-Disney: The First 100 Days," Harvard Business School Case # 9-693-013; and Charles Masters, "French Fall for the Charms of Disney," *Sunday Telegraph*, April 13, 1997, p. 21.

Case Discussion Questions

1. What assumptions did Disney make about the tastes and preferences of French consumers? Which of these assumptions were correct? Which were not?

2. How might Disney have had a more favorable initial experience in France? What steps might it have taken to reduce the mistakes associated with the launch of Euro-Disney?

3. In retrospect, was France the best choice for the location of Euro-Disney?

Notes

1. See R. Dore, *Taking Japan Seriously* (Stanford, CA: Stanford University Press, 1987).

2. E. B. Tylor, *Primitive Culture* (London: Murray, 1871).

3. Geert Hofstede, *Culture's Consequences: International Differences in Work Related Values* (Beverly Hills, CA: Sage Publications, 1984), p. 21.

4. J. Z. Namenwirth and R. B. Weber, *Dynamics of Culture* (Boston: Allen & Unwin, 1987), p. 8.

5. R. Mead, *International Management: Cross Cultural Dimensions* (Oxford: Blackwell Business, 1994), p. 7.

6. "Iraq: Down But Not Out," *The Economist*, April 8, 1995, pp. 21–23.

7. S. P. Huntington, *The Clash of Civilizations* (New York, Simon & Schuster, 1996).

8. M. Thompson, R. Ellis, and A. Wildavsky, *Cultural Theory* (Boulder, CO: Westview Press, 1990).

9. M. Douglas, "Cultural Bias," in *Active Voice* (London: Routledge, 1982), pp. 183–254.

10. M. L. Dertouzos, R. K. Lester, and R. M. Solow, *Made in America* (Cambridge, MA: MIT Press, 1989).

11. C. Nakane, *Japanese Society* (Berkeley, CA: University of California Press, 1970).

12. Ibid.

13. For details, see M. Aoki, *Information, Incentives, and Bargaining in the Japanese Economy* (Cambridge: Cambridge University Press, 1988); and Dertouzos, Lester, and Solow, *Made in America*.

14. For an excellent historical treatment of the evolution of the English class system, see E. P. Thompson, *The Making of the English Working Class* (London: Vintage Books, 1966). See also R.

Miliband, *The State in Capitalist Society* (New York: Basic Books, 1969), especially Chapter 2. For more recent studies of class in British societies, see Stephen Brook, *Class: Knowing Your Place in Modern Britain* (London: Victor Gollancz, 1997); A. Adonis and S. Pollard, *A Class Act: The Myth of Britain's Classless Society* (London: 1997); and J. Gerteis and M. Savage, "The Salience of Class in Britain and America: A Comparative Analysis," *British Journal of Sociology*, June 1998.

15. A. Adonis and S. Pollard, *A Class Act: The Myth of Britain's Classless Society* (London: 1997).

16. N. Goodman, *An Introduction to Sociology* (New York: Harper Collins, 1991).

17. M. Weber, *The Protestant Ethic and the Spirit of Capitalism* (New York: Scribner's Sons, 1958, original 1904–1905). For an excellent review of Weber's work, see A. Giddens, *Capitalism and Modern Social Theory* (Cambridge: Cambridge University Press, 1971).

18. Weber, *The Protestant Ethic and the Spirit of Capitalism*, p. 35.

19. A. S. Thomas and S. L. Mueller, "The Case for Comparative Entrepreneurship," *Journal of International Business Studies* 31, no. 2 (2000), pp. 287–302, and S. A. Shane, "Why Do Some Societies Invent More Than Others?" *Journal of Business Venturing* 7 1992 pp. 29–46.

20. See S. M. Abbasi, K. W. Hollman, and J. H. Murrey, "Islamic Economics; Foundations and Practices," *International Journal of Social Economics* 16, no. 5 (1990), pp. 5–17; and R. H. Dekmejian, *Islam in Revolution: Fundamentalism in the Arab World* (Syracuse: Syracuse University Press, 1995).

21. T. W. Lippman, *Understanding Islam* (New York: Meridian Books, 1995).

22. Dekmejian, *Islam in Revolution*.

23. M. K. Nydell, *Understanding Arabs* (Yarmouth, ME: Intercultural Press, 1987).

24. Lippman, *Understanding Islam*.

25. The material in this section is based largely on Abbasi, Hollman, and Murrey, "Islamic Economics; Foundations and Practices."

26. "Islam's Interest," *The Economist*, January 18, 1992, pp. 33–34.

27. For details of Weber's work and views, see Giddens, *Capitalism and Modern Social Theory*.

28. See, for example, the views expressed in "A Survey of India: The Tiger Steps Out," *The Economist*, January 21, 1995.

29. See R. Dore, *Taking Japan Seriously* (Stanford, CA: Stanford University Press, 1987), and C. W. L. Hill, "Transaction Cost Economizing as a Source of Comparative Advantage: The Case of Japan," *Organization Science* 6 (1995).

30. See Aoki, *Information, Incentives, and Bargaining in the Japanese Economy*, and J. P. Womack, D. T. Jones, and D. Roos, *The Machine That Changed the World* (New York: Rawson Associates, 1990).

31. For examples of this line of thinking, see the work by Mike Peng and his associates: M. W. Peng and P. S. Heath, "The Growth of the Firm in Planned Economies in Transition," *Academy of Management Review* 21 (1996), pp. 492–528; M. W. Peng, *Business Strategies in Transition Economies* (Thousand Oaks, CA: Sage, 2000); and M. W. Peng and Y. Luo, "Managerial Ties and Firm Performance in a Transition Economy," *Academy of Management Journal*, June 2000, pp. 486–501.

32. This hypothesis dates back to two anthropologists, Edward Sapir and Benjamin Lee Whorf. See E. Sapir, "The Status of Linguistics as a Science," *Language* 5 (1929), pp. 207–14, and B. L. Whorf, *Language, Thought, and Reality* (Cambridge, MA: MIT Press, 1956).

33. D. A. Ricks, *Big Business Blunders: Mistakes in Multinational Marketing* (Homewood, IL: Dow Jones-Irwin, 1983).

34. N. Goodman, *An Introduction to Sociology* (New York: HarperCollins, 1991).

35. M. E. Porter, *The Competitive Advantage of Nations* (New York: Free Press, 1990).

36. Ibid., pp. 395–97.

37. G. Hofstede, "The Cultural Relativity of Organizational Practices and Theories," *Journal of International Business Studies*, Fall 1983, pp. 75–89.

38. For more a detailed critique, see R. Mead, *International Management: Cross-Cultural Dimensions* (Oxford: Blackwell, 1994), pp. 73–75.

39. For example, see W. J. Bigoness, and G. L. Blakely, "A Cross-National Study of Managerial Values," *Journal of International Business Studies*, December 1996, p. 739; D. H. Ralston, D. H. Holt, R. H. Terpstra, and Y. Kai-Cheng, "The Impact of National Culture and Economic Ideology on Managerial Work Values," *Journal of International Business Studies* 28, no. 1 (1997), pp. 177–208; and P. B. Smith, M. F. Peterson, and Z. Ming Wang, "The Manager as a Mediator of Alternative Meanings," *Journal of International Business Studies* 27, no. 1 (1996), pp. 115–37.

40. G. Hofstede and M. H. Bond, "The Confucius Connection," *Organizational Dynamics* 16, no. 4 (1988), pp. 5–12.

41. R. S. Yeh and J. J. Lawerence, "Individualism and Confucian Dynamism," *Journal of International Business Studies* 26, no. 3 (1995), pp. 655–66.

42. Mead, *International Management: Cross-Cultural Dimensions*, chap. 17.

43. "Free, Young, and Japanese," *The Economist*, December 21, 1991.

44. Namenwirth and Weber, *Dynamics of Culture*.

45. G. Hofstede, "National Cultures in Four Dimensions," *International Studies of Management and Organization* 13, no. 1, pp. 46–74.

46. R. J. Barnet and J. Cavanagh, *Global Dreams: Imperial Corporations and the New World Order* (New York: Touchstone Books, 1994).

47. See Aoki, *Information, Incentives, and Bargaining in the Japanese Economy*; Dertouzos, Lester, and Solow, *Made in America*; and Porter, *The Competitive Advantage of Nations*, pp. 395–97.

48. J. Goodwin and D. Goodwin. "Ethical Judgements Across Cultures," *Journal of Business Ethics* 18, no. 3 (February 1999), pp. 267–81.

49. T. Donaldson, "Values in Tension: Ethics Away from Home," *Harvard Business Review*, September–October 1996.

50. R. T. DeGeorge, "Ethics in International Business—A Contradiction in Terms?" *Business Credit*, September 2000, pp. 50–52.

51. S. Lovett, L. C. Simmons, and R. Kali, "Guanxi versus the Market: Ethics and Efficiency," *Journal of International Business Studies* 30, no. 2 (1999), pp. 231–48.

52. Donaldson, "Values in Tension: Ethics Away from Home."

53. Barnet and Cavanagh, *Global Dreams*, p. 33.

Cases

Enron International in India

Introduction

In 1990, Enron, a Houston-based independent power company, established a subsidiary, Enron International, and gave it the mission of building and running power generation projects in the developing world. Enron's chairman appointed one of his protégés, Rebecca Mark, then only 36 years old, as CEO of the new unit. By 1997, the outspoken and photogenic Mark, who was fast gaining a reputation as one of the most dynamic businesswomen in America, had built Enron International into a global operation with sales of $1.1 billion, annual profits of $220 million, and a backlog of international energy projects worth over $20 billion. The potential jewel in Enron International's crown was a growing presence in India. By the end of 1997, Enron International had plans to invest $20 billion in India. Getting to this point, however, had severely tested Mark's diplomatic skills and political acumen.

Enron's India Strategy

Enron's interests in India date back to 1991, when the country's former prime minister, Narasimha Rao, visited the United States to seek help with India's economic development. Rao asked Enron if it was interested in independent power projects in the country. This request signaled a shift of policy in India. Since independence from Britain in 1947, political opinion in India had largely opposed significant foreign direct investment on anything other than highly favorable terms to the host country. For almost half a century, Indian politics had been strongly influenced by Gandhi's doctrine of *swadeshi*, or self reliance from foreign influence. This had been translated into a presumption against foreign investment and a desire to see India build its own domestic industries under the protection of restrictions on foreign investment and high import tariffs.

However, by the 1990s, the winds of ideological change were blowing through India. The national government seemed to be embracing a free market approach that included substantial deregulation and the loosening of rules on foreign direct investment. Consistent with this, in October 1991, Rao's government liberalized India's domestic power-producing sector, allowing private developers, both Indian and foreign, to build and operate independent power projects with no restrictions on foreign equity ownership.

India's need for power was obvious. A plentiful supply of electric power is a key requirement for economic development, but India was suffering from chronic power shortages. At peak periods, demand for electricity often exceeded available power supply by more than 20 percent. The installed capacity in the early 1990s, which amounted to around 80,000 megawatts, was working at only about 60 percent efficiency. Forecasts suggested that an extra 140,000 megawatts of capacity would be needed by 2005, but public money to finance such massive investments in infrastructure was scarce. In the mid-1990s, about 70 percent of India's electricity supply was being produced by state-owned electricity generation and distribution boards, which collectively were running up losses of over $2 billion per-year. They could not afford to fund the required expansions in capacity.

Mark jumped on Rao's offer, but quickly discovered that India's energy problems involved more than a simple lack of generating capacity. The country also lacked adequate supplies of fuel. To help solve these problems, Mark articulated a strategic vision that was audacious in scope. The vision called for Enron to invest up to $20 billion to become the largest distributor and consumer of liquefied natural gas (LNG) in India by 2010. Under the plan, Enron would set up two LNG terminals and regassification units in India, one at Dabhol in the state of Maharashtra and one at Ennore in the state of Tamil Nadu. The company would construct two gas-based power generating plants near the terminals. Enron would also build a network of pipelines to pipe the gas to its LNG terminals from oil and gas fields near Bombay, and then onward to its own and other power plants around the country. The Bombay fields, however, were not large enough to supply India's projected LNG needs, so the company also planned to import LNG from a facility it was building in the Gulf state of Qatar. The Qatar facility would cost $4 billion to complete and was being funded by a group of investors including the state-owned Qatar Gas & Pipeline Co., Enron International's parent company, and Royal Dutch/Shell. Enron International had promised investors in the Qatar facility a 15 percent annual growth in shareholders' income. Achieving this goal, however, was highly dependent on the success of Mark's India strategy. Without India, Enron might lack sufficient customers to absorb the LNG output from its Qatar facility.

The Dabhol Project

By mid-1992, Mark was moving forward with the first stage of her plan. She was deep in negotiations with the Indian federal government and the government of the state of Maharashtra where Enron's Dabhol power plant was to be constructed. The Dabhol project was bold; Enron was to develop a 2,015 megawatt power plant that would be fired by LNG. The total cost for the project was well over $2 billion, making the Dabhol project the largest foreign investment ever committed to India and the biggest independent power project in the world.

The choice of Dabhol for Enron's first investment in India was dictated by a number of factors. Located on India's western seaboard, the state of Maharashtra and its capital Bombay were enjoying a sustained period of political stability and economic growth. This had enabled the state to attract industry from other areas of India, such as the traditional industrial heartlands of Calcutta and eastern India. Economic growth in these regions had suffered under successive communist governments at the state level. The western seaboard was also closer to the Gulf states, and Qatar in particular, which would lower the costs of shipping LNG. Also, the state of Maharashtra was then governed by the Congress Party, the same party that governed the nation. Rebecca Mark reasoned that Prime Minister Rao would be able to pressure the local state government to approve the project.

Mark was alert to the basic political realities in India. While the federal government in Delhi might in principle approve the project, she realized that Enron would also have to win approval from the Maharashtra state government and cultivate the approval of key players in India's extensive civil service. To get the Dabhol project approved, the company needed to get 170 state and federal permits; sort through 50 complicated legal questions; and deal with a complex web of state and federal taxes. Reflecting on this process, Mark reported:

> I've had tea with every bureaucrat in India . . . People (foreigners) don't understand how to get things done in India. Politicians lay out a plan, but that's different from working through the system. There's only one political level approval—that of the foreign investment board. But then there are all sorts of channels and procedures needed. Politicians will never intervene and force a bureaucrat to make a decision when an issue of process is at stake. This is where companies mess up and are confused.[1]

By early 1995, Enron had received full approval for the project and was proceeding with the initial construction. However, storm clouds were gathering on the political horizon of Maharashtra, and they spelled trouble for Enron. Throughout the negotiations, Maharashtra had been controlled by the Congress Party. Its local leader, Sharad Pawar, was a big supporter of Enron's Dabhol project. Unfortunately, during 1994 and early 1995, the popularity of the Congress Party started to decline. In 1994, a series of ethnic riots swept through Bombay. Anti-Muslim hysteria had been whipped up by Shiv Sena, a local militant Hindu nationalist party. The party was led by Bal Thackery, a former political cartoonist and an admirer of Adolf Hitler. To fight upcoming state elections in February 1995, Shiv Sena formed an alliance with a less extreme Hindu nationalist party,

the BJP. If the alliance won the state elections, Shiv Sena would control the local administration in Maharashtra, while the BJP would occupy any seats won by the alliance in the national parliament.

During the election campaign, Shiv Sena seized on the Dabhol project and used it to attack the Congress Party and its leader, Sharad Pawar. Shiv Sena claimed that Pawar had been bribed by Enron to support the Dabhol project. This played well in the court of public opinion in India, where in the words of one observer, "The popular belief is that any dealings with foreigners are bound to be either crooked or disadvantageous. Maybe 9 times out of 10 this is correct."[2] The BJP also warmed to this theme as the election campaign progressed and began to champion the Gandhi doctrine of *swadeshi* (self-reliance). Both the BJP and Shiv Sena successfully contrasted their defense of Indian rights and Indian self-reliance against what they depicted as the corrupt machinations of Enron, Pawar, and the Congress Party.

Fuel was added to this fire when an Enron official, in testimony before a committee of the U.S. Congress that was dealing with foreign aid allocations, revealed that Enron had spent $20 million to educate Indians about the benefits of its various power projects in the country. (The Enron official made the apparently innocent suggestion that the U.S. government might want to use its foreign aid help with such educational campaigns.) Elements of the Indian press, in concert with Shiv Sena, seized on this "revelation" to claim that the $20 million had been used primarily to "educate" corrupt officials such as Pawar to win approval for the Dabhol project; in other words, that much of the $20 million had been in the form of bribes. In the heat of the election campaign, it apparently mattered little that there was no evidence that Enron had bribed anyone. Mud sticks, and the charges proved to be powerful ammunition. As a result, in February 1995, Pawar and the Congress Party were swept from power in the state of Maharashtra to be replaced by Shiv Sena and its new chief minister, Manohar Joshi.

After the election, the new government set up a committee, under the leadership of Gopinath Munde, the BJP deputy minister in the coalition, to review the Dabhol project. The committee was to review the charges of corruption and abuse that had been leveled at Enron during the election campaign. However, Rebecca Mark felt she was on solid ground. Enron had not done anything wrong, contracts had been signed, construction work on the project was under way, India clearly needed the power, and the agreements protected Enron from any unilateral breach of contract. If the state canceled the project, it would be hit with a $200 million cancellation fee.

In mid-1995, the state government committee reviewing the Dabhol project finished its report. The report was never published, although excerpts in which Enron was accused of deception and cost padding were leaked to the press. Enron vigorously denied these charges. On the cost padding charges, Rebecca Mark later noted,

> In India you are supposed to have a 20 percent import duty on equipment. But when it comes right down to it, very common in a project is that it doesn't end up being 20 percent but whatever the customs inspector wants it to be on the day you get there. So you have to price that risk in.[3]

The implication was that there was a risk premium built into Enron's contract with the state of Maharashtra.

The report also criticized the previous administration for not putting the Dabhol project out to competitive bids. Privately, Enron officials noted that this was an absurd charge. After all, Enron had been invited to the country by Prime Minister Rao, it was Enron that had suggested the Dabhol project, and Enron was the only foreign power producer apparently willing to shoulder the risk associated with such a large investment in the country. Reflecting this, Bob Pender, an independent lawyer who specializes in financing energy projects, noted that the lack of competitive bidding "was the opportunity cost of getting a company to come and create an industry."[4]

Significantly though, the committee was not able to uncover any evidence of corruption by either Enron or Indian political officials. However, after having made such an issue of the project during the election, the Shiv Sena/BJP coalition was not yet ready to back down. On August 3, 1995, the state government issued a work stoppage order on the deal, after Enron had already spent $100 million.

Two days later, Enron served the state government with legal notice that it would pursue arbitration in London. The Maharashtra state government was now facing damages of at least $300 million, with the possibility of another $500 million on top of that. On August 12, Little & Co., which had acted as the lawyers for the Maharashtra state government for the last 20 years, resigned and stated "off the record" that the state's position was indefensible. Top civil servants in the state also reportedly told Munde and Joshi that the government's position was untenable.

Simultaneously, Enron mounted a public relations campaign of its own. Enron ran full-page advertisements in Indian newspapers publicizing the benefits to India of its Dabhol project. It also prevailed on U.S. President Bill Clinton to call the Indian premier to try to get the project started again. By September public opinion polls showed that 80 percent of the people in Maharashtra and 60 percent of those in India wanted the project restarted.

Despite rising pressure to restart the project, the Shiv Sena/BJP coalition government was unwilling to back off without getting something in return. By this point, however, it was clear that the best interests of all parties would be served by a compromise. Enron wanted to get the project back on track. It still had big plans for India, and then there was that plant in Qatar whose output was projected for India. The Maharashtra government, for its part, was facing the potential of heavy damages and was rapidly losing support for its position. At the same time, the government needed evidence that its efforts had not been for naught; it needed to save face.

That fall Rebecca Mark returned to the bargaining table, and a settlement was worked out. Enron agreed to cut the price it charged for power generated by the Dabhol project by 22.6 percent. In return, Enron walked away with a deal for a 2,450 megawatt plant, 450 megawatts bigger than the initial plant. According to Enron, the larger plant would realize much greater scale economies and allow Enron to maintain its projected rate of return on investment while simultaneously cutting prices.

Aftermath

Reflecting on her Indian experience, Mark suggests that the key to Enron's success was its intentions to help India solve a problem and to stay engaged in the country for the long term. She and her colleagues have spent six years coming to India, meeting with the same people, talking about the same projects. Says Mark, "I don't think that anyone who works with us doubts our intentions, goodwill, or long-term commitment to India. We've earned a place on the list of friendlies."[5] Mark also believes that Enron's appeal to the people of India ultimately served the company well. She concludes:

> Our experience tells us that India's a good environment for foreign investment, and a market where foreign investors are seen as necessary. If anything, our experience proves the strength of the system in India to withstand a lot of assaults from different places. Even though the political system is shaky, the judiciary and the business system work.[6]

In February 1997, Enron reaffirmed its commitment to India when it submitted a proposal to build five to seven more power plants in the country for a total cost of $10 billion. As for the Dabhol plant, the first phase of the project, which will generate 740 megawatts of power, was completed in December 1998, three months ahead of schedule.

For India's part, there is little doubt that Enron's experience with the Dabhol project was a public relations setback. Although ultimately the outcome reaffirmed the country's commitment to encouraging foreign direct investment, the perception has been created that the shifting political landscape, bureaucratic rules, and the crosscurrents between national and state governments, make India a difficult place in which to invest. As noted by former U.S. Ambassador to India William Clark, the Dabhol incident "sends the right signals, but unfortunately it sent off the wrong signals for awhile. Just like a retraction in a newspaper, it will take a long time for people to notice."[7]

Case Discussion Questions

1. Why do you think Enron was willing to shoulder the risk of making such a significant investment in India? What long-run benefits did the company foresee? Do you think these benefits compensated for the risks involved?

2. Do you think Enron was correct to build a risk premium into its original pricing of the Dabhol project? Should the company have foreseen that this might have been perceived as cost padding?

3. What lessons about the requirements for successful investment in India can other foreign companies draw from Enron's experience with the Dabhol project?

4. Is former U.S. Ambassador William Clark right when he claims that, in the end, the Dabhol incident sent the right kind of signals about foreign investment in India? What kind of signals do you think it sends about investment in India?

Notes

1. From C. Hill, "How Rebecca Mark Solved India," *Institutional Investor*, January 1998, p. 28G.

2. B. Edwards and M. Shukla, "The Mugging of Enron," *Euromoney*, October 1995, p. 28–33.

3. "You Have to Be Pushy and Aggressive," *Business Week*, February 24, 1997, p. 56.

4. Edwards and Shukla, "The Mugging of Enron."

5. Hill, "How Rebecca Mark Solved India."

6. "It's a Done Deal," *Journal of Commerce*, December, 20, 1996, p. 7B.

7. Ibid.

Sources

1. Edwards, B., and M. Shukla. "The Mugging of Enron." *Euromoney*, October 1995, pp. 28–33.

2. Hill, C. "How Rebecca Mark Solved India." *Institutional Investor*, January 1998, p. 28G.

3. "It's a Done Deal." *Journal of Commerce*, December 20, 1996, p. 7B.

4. Mack, T. "High Finance with a Touch of Theater." *Forbes*, May 18, 1998, pp. 140–54.

5. Nicholson, M. "Dabhol Plant Finally Gets Green Light." *Financial Times*, January 9, 1996, p. 6.

6. Sibbald, P. "You Have to Be Pushy and Aggressive." *Business Week*, February 24, 1997, p. 56.

7. Williams, G. "More Power to India." *Business Week*, January 22, 1996, p. 62.

Royal Dutch/Shell: Human Rights in Nigeria

Introduction

In 1995, a Nigerian military tribunal, in what most observers described as a sham trial, ordered the execution of noted author and playwright Ken Saro-Wiwa and eight other members of the Movement for the Survival of the Ogoni People. The Ogoni are a 500,000-member ethnic group of farmers and fishermen that live in Nigeria's coastal plain. For several years, the Ogoni had been waging a vigorous political campaign against Nigeria's military rulers and the giant oil company Royal Dutch/Shell. They had been seeking greater self-determination, rights to the revenue stemming from oil exploration on traditional Ogoni lands, and compensation for the environmental degradation to their land caused by frequent oil spills from fractured pipelines. Shell had been pumping oil from Ogoni lands since the late 1950s. In 1994, four Ogoni chiefs who advocated cooperation rather than confrontation with Nigeria's military government were lynched by a mob of Ogoni youth. Though he was not present, Saro-Wiwa, a leader of the protest movement, was arrested and subsequently sentenced to death along with eight other Ogoni activists.

Despite intensive international pressure that included appeals to Shell to use its influence in the country to gain clemency for the convicted, the executions went ahead as scheduled on November 10, 1995. After the executions, Shell was criticized in the Western media for its apparent unwillingness to pressure Nigeria's totalitarian regime. The incident started some soul-searching at Shell about the social and environmental responsibility of a multinational corporation in societies such as Nigeria that fall short of Western standards for the protection of human rights and the environment.

Background

The African nation of Nigeria won independence from Britain in 1961. At that time, many believed Nigeria had the potential to become one of the engines of economic growth in Africa. The country was blessed with abundant natural resources, particularly oil and gas; was a net exporter of foodstuffs, and had a large population that by African standards was well educated (today Nigeria has the largest population in Africa, with over 110 million people). By the mid-1990s, it was clear that much of that potential was still to be realized. Thirty-five years after winning independence, Nigeria was still heavily dependent on the oil sector. Oil production accounted for 30 percent of GDP, 95 percent of foreign exchange earnings and about 80 percent of the government's budget revenues. The largely subsistence agricultural sector had failed to keep up with rapid population growth, and Nigeria, once a large net exporter of food, now had to import food. GDP per capita was a paltry $230, one-quarter of what it was in 1981, and the country was creaking under $40 billion of external debt. Nigeria had been unable to garner financial assistance from institutions such as the International Monetary Fund because of the government's unwillingness to account for how it used the revenues from oil taxes.

Political problems partly explained Nigeria's economic malaise. The country has suffered from internal strife among some of the more than 250 ethnic groups that constitute the nation. In the 1960s, the country was racked by a particularly nasty civil war. In December 1983, the civilian government was replaced in a coup by a military regime that ruled by decree. In 1993, democratic elections were held in Nigeria, but the military government nullified the results, declaring there had been widespread ballot fraud.

Royal Dutch/Shell is the main foreign oil producer operating in Nigeria. The company was formed at the turn of the century when Holland's Royal Dutch Company, which had substantial oil operations in Indonesia, merged with Britain's Shell Transport and Trading to create one of the world's first multinational oil companies. Shell is now the world's largest oil company with annual revenues that exceed $130 billion. The company has been operating in Nigeria since 1937, and by the mid-1990s was pumping about half of Nigeria's oil. Nigerian oil accounts for about 11 to 12 percent of the company's global output and generates net income for Shell of about $200 million per year.

Problems in the Ogoni Region

In 1958, Royal Dutch/Shell struck oil on Ogoni lands. By some estimates, the company has extracted some $30 billion worth of oil from the region since then. Despite this, the Ogoni remain desperately poor. Most live in palm-roofed mud huts and practice subsistence agriculture. Of Shell's 5,000 employees in Nigeria, in 1995 only 85 were Ogoni. Because they are a powerless minority among Nigeria's 110 million people, the Ogoni are often

overlooked when it comes to the allocation of jobs either in government or the private sector.

Starting in 1982, the Nigerian government supposedly directed 1.5 percent of the oil revenue it received back to the communities where the oil was produced. In 1992, the percentage was increased to 3 percent. The Ogoni, however, claim they have seen virtually none of this money. Most appears to have been spent in the tribal lands of the ruling majority or has vanished in corrupt deals. Although there were 96 oil wells, two refineries, a petrochemical complex, and a fertilizer plant in the Ogoni region in 1994, the lone hospital was an unfinished concrete husk and the government schools, unable to pay teachers, were rarely open.

In addition to the lack of returns from oil production in their region, the Ogoni claim that their lands have suffered from environmental degradation, much of which could be laid at the feet of Shell. Ogoni activists claim that Shell's poor environmental safeguards have resulted in numerous oil spills and widespread contamination of the soil and groundwater. A Shell spokesman, interviewed in 1994, seemed to acknowledge there might be some basis to these complaints. He stated, "Some of the facilities installed during the last 30 years, whilst acceptable at the time, aren't as we would build them today. Given the age of some of these lines (oil pipelines), regrettably oil spills have occurred from time to time."[1] However, the same spokesman also blamed many of the more recent leaks in the Ogoni region on deliberate sabotage. The sabotage, he stated, had one of two motives—to back up claims for compensation and to support claims of environmental degradation.

On hearing of these claims, Ken Saro-Wiwa called them preposterous. Saro-Wiwa argued that although uneducated youths, frustrated and angry, may have damaged some Shell installations in one or two incidents, "the people would never deliberately spill oil on their land because they know the so-called compensation is paltry and the land is never restored."[2] To support his position, Saro-Wiwa pointed to a spill from the 1960s near a settlement called Ebubu that still had not been cleaned up. In response, Shell stated that the spill occurred during the civil war in the 1960s, and cleanup work was completed in 1990. Subsequently, sunken oil reappeared at the surface, but Shell claims it was unable to do anything about this because of threats made against its employees in the region. In January 1993, out of concern for their safety, Shell barred its employees from entering the region.

In April 1993, the Ogoni organized their first protests against Shell and the government. Ogoni farmers stood in front of earthmoving equipment that was laying a pipeline for Shell through croplands. Although Shell stated that the land had been acquired by legal means and that full compensation had been paid to the farmers and the local community, some of the locals remained unhappy about what they viewed as continuing exploitation of their land. Seeing a threat to the continuity of its oil operations, Shell informed the Nigerian government about the protest. Units from the Nigerian military soon arrived and shots were fired into the crowd of protesters, killing one Ogoni man and wounding several others.

Subsequently, in a series of murky incidents, Nigerian soldiers stormed Ogoni villages, saying they were quelling unrest between neighboring Ogoni tribes. The Ogoni claimed the raids were punishment for obstructing Shell. They stated that the military had orders to use minor land disputes, which had long been settled with little violence, as an excuse to lay entire villages to waste. A feared unit of the mobile police with the nickname "Kill and Go" conducted some of the raids. Although details are sketchy, it has been reported that hundreds of people lost their lives in the violence. The cycle of violence ultimately culminated in the killing of the Ogoni chiefs who argued for compromise with the Nigerian government. This provided the government with the justification they needed to arrest Ken Saro-Wiwa and eight associates in the Movement for the Survival of the Ogoni People.

Nigeria and Shell under Pressure

Saro-Wiwa's arrest achieved the goal that the protests and bloodshed had not; it focused international attention in the plight of the Ogoni people, the heavy-handed policies of the Nigerian government, and Shell's activities in Nigeria. Several human rights organizations immediately pressured Shell to use its influence to gain the release of Saro-Wiwa. They also urged Shell to put on hold plans to start work on a $3.5 billion liquefied natural gas project in Nigeria. The project was structured as a joint venture with the Nigerian government. Shell's central role in the project gave it considerable influence over the government, or so human rights activists believed.

Shell stated that it deplored the heavy-handed approach taken by the Nigerian government to the Ogoni people and regretted pain and loss suffered by Ogoni communities. The company also indicated it was using "discreet diplomacy" to try to bring influence to bear on the Nigerian government. Nigeria's military leadership, however, was in no mood to listen to discreet diplomacy from Shell or anyone else. After a trial by a military tribunal that was derided as nothing more than a kangaroo court, Saro-Wiwa and his associates were sentenced to death by hanging. The sentence was carried out shortly after sunrise on November 10, 1995.

Aftermath

In the wake of Saro-Wiwa's hanging, a storm of protest erupted around the world. The heads of state of the 52-nation British Commonwealth, meeting in New Zealand at the time of Saro-Wiwa's execution, suspended Nigeria and stated they would expel the country if it did not return to democratic rule within two years. U.S. President Bill Clinton recalled the U.S. ambassador to Nigeria and banned the sale of military equipment, on top of aid cuts made in protest at Saro-Wiwa's arrest. British Prime Minister John Major banned arms sales to Nigeria and called for the widest possible embargo. Ambassadors from the 15-nation European Union were recalled, and the EU suspended all aid to Nigeria.

But no country halted purchases of Nigerian oil or sales of oil service equipment to Nigeria. The United States, which imports 40 percent of Nigeria's daily output of 2 million barrels, was silent on the question of an oil embargo. Similarly, no Western country—many of which had national companies working in the Nigerian oil industry—indicated they would impose an embargo on sales to, or purchase from, the Nigerian oil industry. Alone among major public figures, South African President Nelson Mandela called for a ban on Shell. The call was echoed by several environmental groups, including Greenpeace and Friends of the Earth, both of which urged their supporters to boycott Shell products. However, South Africa never enacted a formal ban, and the boycott calls met with only limited success.

For its part, Shell indicated it would go ahead with its plans for a liquefied natural gas operation in Nigeria in partnership with the Nigerian government. In a public notice published in British newspapers, Shell stated, "It has been suggested that Shell should pull out of Nigeria's liquefied natural gas project. But if we do so now, the project will collapse. Maybe forever. So let's be clear who gets hurt if the project gets cancelled. A cancellation would certainly hurt the thousands of Nigerians who will be working on the project, and the tens of thousands benefiting in the local economy."[3]

In November 1996, the Center for Constitutional Rights filed a federal lawsuit in the U.S. District Court in Manhattan on behalf of relatives of Saro-Wiwa who were now residing in the United States. The lawsuit accused Royal Dutch/Shell of being part of a conspiracy that led to Saro-Wiwa's hanging. Shell denied the allegations and stated that they would be refuted in court.

In May 1997, at the annual general meeting of Shell Transport and Trading in London, a group of 18 institutional investors tabled a resolution that would have required Shell to establish an independent external body to monitor its environmental and human rights policies. John Jennings, the outgoing chairman of the company, told reporters after the meeting that proxy votes from shareholders were running 10 to 1 against the resolution.

One reason for the defeat of the shareholder resolution was that the company had already indicated it was taking steps to reform its culture and improve its own monitoring of environmental and human rights policies. Before the shareholder meeting, the company issued its own report on its policies in Nigeria, in which the company admitted that it needed to improve its monitoring of environmental and human rights policies. Under the leadership of its new head, Mark Moody-Stuart, Shell subsequently stated that it expected its companies to express support for fundamental human rights in line with the legitimate role of business and to give proper regard to health, safety, and the environment consistent with their commitment to sustainable development. The company also embraced the UN Universal Declaration of Human Rights, pledged to set up socially responsible management systems, and to develop training procedures to help management deal with human rights dilemmas.

Commenting on these steps, a spokesman for Human Rights Watch stated, "I'm prepared to give them some credit that they realized they had to look at what their own operations were and how to respond. They acknowledged that big companies have social responsibility, and that's a pretty big step for the multinational corporations."[4]

Case Discussion Questions

1. Does Shell bear some responsibility for the problems in the Ogoni region of Nigeria?
2. What steps might Shell have taken to nip some of the protests against it in the bud, or even preempt them?
3. Could the company have done more to gain clemency for Ken Saro-Wiwa? What? Should it have done more?
4. Was the response of Western governments to the execution of Ken Saro-Wiwa about right, too excessive, or too mild? What should have been the appropriate response?
5. In the wake of Saro-Wiwa's execution, was Shell correct to push ahead with the liquefied natural gas project in Nigeria?

6. Do you think it is possible for a company such as Shell to reform itself from within, or would it have been better for Shell to establish an external body to monitor its human rights and environmental policies?

Notes

1. G. Brooks, "Slick Alliance," *The Wall Street Journal*, May 6, 1994, p. A1.
2. Ibid.
3. P. Beckett, "Shell Boldly Defends Its Role in Nigeria," *The Wall Street Journal*, November 27, 1995, p. A9.
4. Ibid.

Sources

1. Beckett, P. "Shell Boldly Defends Its Role in Nigeria." *The Wall Street Journal*, November 27, 1995, p. A9.
2. Brooks, G. "Slick Alliance." *The Wall Street Journal*, May 6, 1994, p. A1.
3. Corzine, R. "Shell Discovers Time and Tide Wait for No Man." *Financial Times*, March 10, 1998, p. 17.
4. Corzine, R., and Boulton. "Shell Defends Its Ethics on Eve of General Meeting." *Financial Times*, May 14, 1997, p. 29.
5. Hamilton, H. "Shell's New Worldview." *Washington Post*, August 2, 1998, p. H1.
6. Hoagland, J. "Shell's Game in Nigeria." *Washington Post*, November 5, 1995, p. C7.
7. Hudson, R., and M. Rose. "Shell Is Pressured to Scrap Its Plans for a New Plant in Nigeria amid Protests." *The Wall Street Journal*, November 14, 1995, p. A11.
8. Kamm, T. "Executions Raise Sanction Threat." *The Wall Street Journal*, November 13, 1995, p. A10.
9. "Multinationals and Their Morals." *The Economist*, December 2, 1995, p. 18.

■ Nike: The Sweatshop Debate

Introduction

Nike is in many ways the quintessential global corporation. Established in 1972 by former University of Oregon track star Phil Knight, Nike is now one of the leading marketers of athletic shoes and apparel on the planet. The company has $10 billion in annual revenues and

sells its products in 140 countries. Nike does not do any manufacturing. Rather, it designs and markets its products, while contracting for their manufacture from a global network of 600 factories scattered around the globe that employ some 550,000 people.[1] This huge corporation has made Knight into one of the richest people in America. Nike's marketing phrase, "Just Do It!" has become as recognizable in popular culture as its "swoosh" logo or the faces of its celebrity sponsors, such as Michael Jordan and Tiger Woods.

For all of its successes, the company has been dogged for more than a decade by repeated and persistent accusations that its products are made in sweatshops where workers, many of them children, slave away in hazardous conditions for less than subsistence wages. Nike's wealth, its detractors claim, has been built on the backs of the world's poor. To many, Nike has become a symbol of the evils of globalization—a rich Western corporation exploiting the world's poor to provide expensive shoes and apparel to the pampered consumers of the developed world. Nike's "Niketown" stores have become standard targets for antiglobalization protesters. Several nongovernmental organizations, such as San Francisco-based Global Exchange, a human rights organization dedicated to promoting environmental, political, and social justice around the world, have targeted Nike for repeated criticism and protests.[2] News programs such as CBS's "48 Hours" hosted by Dan Rather have run exposés on working conditions in foreign factories that supply Nike. Students on the campuses of several major U.S. universities with which Nike has lucrative sponsorship deals have protested against the ties, citing Nike's use of sweatshop labor.

For its part, Nike has taken many steps to try to counter the protests. Yes, it admits, there have been problems in some overseas factories. But the company has signaled a commitment to improving working conditions. It requires that foreign subcontractors meet minimum thresholds for working conditions and pay. It has arranged for independent auditors to examine factories. It has terminated contracts with factories that do not comply with its standards. But for all this effort, the company continues to be a target of protests and a symbol of dissent.

The Case Against Nike

Typical of the exposés against Nike was a "48 Hours," news report that aired October 17, 1996.[3] Reporter Roberta Baskin visited a Nike factory in Vietnam. With a shot of the factory, her commentary began:

> The signs are everywhere of an American invasion in search of cheap labor. Millions of people who are literate, disciplined, and desperate for jobs. This is Nike Town near what use to be called Saigon, one of four factories Nike doesn't own but subcontracts to make a million shoes a month. It takes 25,000 workers, mostly young women, to "Just Do It."
>
> But the workers here don't share in Nike's huge profits. They work six days a week for only $40 a month, just 20 cents an hour.

Baskin interviews one of the workers in the factory, a young woman named Lap. Baskin tells the listener:

> Her basic wage, even as sewing team leader, still doesn't amount to the minimum wage . . . She's down to 85 pounds. Like most of the young women who make shoes, she has little choice but to accept the low wages and long hours. Nike says that it requires all subcontractors to obey local laws; but Lap has already put in much more overtime than the annual legal limit: 200 hours.

Baskin then asks Lap what would happen if she wanted to leave. If she was sick or had something she needed to take care of such as a sick relative, could she leave the factory? Through a translator, Lap replies:

> It is not possible if you haven't made enough shoes. You have to meet the quota before you can go home.

The clear implication of the story was that Nike was at fault here for allowing such working conditions to persist in the Vietnam factory, which was owned by a Korean company.

An earlier attack on Nike's subcontracting practices came in June 1996 from Made in the USA, a foundation largely financed by labor unions and domestic apparel manufacturers that oppose free trade with low-wage countries. According to Joel Joseph, chairman of the foundation; a popular line of high-priced Nike sneakers, the Air Jordans, were made by 11-year-olds in Indonesia making 14 cents per hour. A Nike spokeswoman, Donna Gibbs, countered that this was false. According to Gibbs, the average worker made 240,000 rupiah ($103) a month working a maximum 54-hour week, or about 45 cents per hour. Gibbs noted that Nike had staff members in each factory monitoring conditions to make sure the factory obeyed local minimum wage and child labor laws.[4]

Another example of the criticism against Nike came from a newsletter published by Global Exchange:[5]

> During the 1970s, most Nike shoes were made in South Korea and Taiwan. When workers there gained new freedom to organize and wages began to rise, Nike looked for "greener pastures." It found them in Indonesia and China, where Nike started producing in the 1980s, and most recently in Vietnam.
>
> The majority of Nike shoes are made in Indonesia and China, countries with governments that prohibit independent unions and set the minimum wage at rock bottom. The Indonesian government admits that the minimum wage there does not provide enough to supply the basic needs of one person, let alone a family. In early 1997 the entry-level wage was a miserable $2.46 a day. Labor groups estimate that a livable wage in Indonesia is about $4.00 a day.
>
> In Vietnam the pay is even less—20 cents an hour, or a mere $1.60 a day. But in urban Vietnam, three

simple meals cost about $2.10 a day, and then of course there is rent, transportation, clothing, health care, and much more. According to Thuyen Nguyen of Vietnam Labor Watch, a living wage in Vietnam is at least $3 a day.

In another attack on Nike's practices, Global Exchange in September 1997 published a report on working conditions at four Nike and Reebok subcontractors in southern China.[6] Global Exchange, in conjunction with two Hong Kong human rights groups, had interviewed workers at the factories in 1995 and again in 1997. According to Global Exchange, in one factory, a Korean-owned subcontractor for Nike, workers as young as 13 earning as little as 10 cents an hour toiled up to 17 hours daily in enforced silence. Talking during work was not allowed, with violators fined $1.20 to $3.60, according to the report. The practices violated Chinese labor law, which states that no child under 16 may work in a factory, and the Chinese minimum wage requirement of $1.90 for an eight-hour day. Nike condemned the study as erroneous, saying the report incorrectly stated the wages of workers and made irresponsible accusations.

Global Exchange continued to be a major thorn in Nike's side. In November 1997, the organization obtained and then leaked a confidential report by Ernst & Young of an audit that Nike had commissioned of a factory in Vietnam owned by a Nike subcontractor.[7] The factory had 9,200 workers and made 400,000 pairs of shoes a month. The Ernst & Young report painted a dismal picture of thousands of young women, most under age 25, laboring 10 1/2 hours a day, six days a week, in excessive heat and noise and in foul air, for slightly more than $10 a week. The report also found that workers with skin or breathing problems had not been transferred to departments free of chemicals and that more than half the workers who dealt with dangerous chemicals did not wear protective masks or gloves. It claimed workers were exposed to carcinogens that exceeded local legal standards by 177 times in parts of the plant and that 77 percent of the employees suffered from respiratory problems.

Put on the defensive yet again, Nike called a news conference and pointed out that it had commissioned the report and had acted on it.[8] The company stated it had formulated a plan to deal with the problems cited in the report and had slashed overtime, improved safety and ventilation, and reduced the use of toxic chemicals. The company also asserted that the report showed that its internal monitoring system had performed exactly as it should have. According to one spokesman:

This shows our system of monitoring works . . . We have uncovered these issues clearly before anyone else, and we have moved fairly expeditiously to correct them.

Nike's Responses

Unaccustomed to playing defense, Nike formulated a number of strategies and tactics to deal with the problems of working conditions and pay in subcontractors. In 1996, Nike hired Andrew Young, onetime U.S. ambassador to the United Nations and former Atlanta mayor, to assess working conditions in subcontractors' plants around the world. Young released a mildly critical report of Nike in mid-1997. After completing a two-week tour that covered three countries and inspected 15 factories, Young informed Nike it was doing a good job in treating workers, though it should do better. According to Young, he did not see:

sweatshops, or hostile conditions . . . I saw crowded dorms . . . but the workers were eating at least two meals a day on the job and making what I was told were subsistence wages in those cultures.[9]

Young was widely criticized by human rights and labor groups for not taking his own translators and for doing slipshod inspections, an assertion he repeatedly denied.

In 1996, Nike joined a presidential task force designed to find a way of banishing sweatshops in the shoe and clothing industries. The task force included industry leaders such as Nike, representatives from human rights groups, and labor leaders. In April 1997, the group announced a workers' rights agreement for U.S. companies manufacturing abroad. The accord limited the workweek to 60 hours and called for paying at least the local minimum wage in foreign factories. The task force also agreed to establish an independent monitoring association, later named the Fair Labor Association (FLA), to assess whether companies are abiding by the code.[10]

The FLA now includes among its members the Lawyers Committee for Human Rights, the National Council of Churches, the International Labor Rights Fund, some 135 universities (universities have extensive licensing agreements with sports apparel companies such as Nike), and companies such as Nike, Reebok, and Levi Strauss.

In early 1997, Nike also began to commission independent organizations such as Ernst & Young to audit the factories of its subcontractors. In September 1997, Nike tried to show its critics that it was involved in more than just a public relations exercise when it terminated its relationship with four Indonesian subcontractors, stating that they had refused to comply with the company's standard for wage levels and working conditions. Nike identified one of the subcontractors, Seyon, which manufactured specialty sports gloves for Nike. Nike said that Seyon refused to meet a 10.7 percent increase in the monthly wage, to $70.30, declared by the Indonesian government in April 1997.[11]

On May 12, 1998, in a speech given at the National Press Club, Nike founder Phil Knight spelled out a series of initiatives designed to improve working conditions for the 500,000 people that make products for Nike through subcontractors.12 Among the initiatives, Knight highlighted were the following:

- We have effectively changed our minimum age limits from the ILO (International Labor Organization) standards of 15 in most countries and 14 in developing countries to 18 in all footwear manufacturing and 16 in all other types of manufacturing (apparel, accessories, and equipment.). Existing workers legally employed under the former limits were grandfathered into the new requirements.

- During the past 13 months we have moved to a 100 percent factory audit scheme, where every Nike contract factory will receive an annual check by PricewaterhouseCoopers teams who are specially trained on our Code of Conduct Owner's Manual and audit/monitoring procedures. To date they have performed about 300 such monitoring visits. In a few instances in apparel factories they have found workers under our age standards. Those factories have been required to raise their standards to 17 years of age, to require three documents certifying age, and to redouble their efforts to ensure workers meet those standards through interviews and records checks.

- Our goal was to ensure workers around the globe are protected by requiring factories to have no workers exposed to levels above those mandated by the permissible exposure limits (PELs) for chemicals prescribed in the OSHA (Occupational Safety and Health Administration) air quality standards.

These moves were applauded in the business press, but they were greeted with a skeptical response from Nike's long-term adversaries in the debate over the use of foreign labor. While conceding that's Nike's policies were an improvement, one critic writing in the *New York Times* noted:

Mr. Knight's child labor initiative is . . . a smoke screen. Child labor has not been a big problem with Nike, and Philip Knight knows that better than anyone. But public relations is public relations. So he announces that he's not going to let the factories hire kids, and suddenly that's the headline.

Mr. Knight is like a three-card monte player. You have to keep a close eye on him at all times.

The biggest problem with Nike is that its overseas workers make wretched, below-subsistence wages. It's not the minimum age that needs raising, it's the minimum wage. Most of the workers in Nike factories in China and Vietnam make less than $2 a day, well below the subsistence levels in those countries. In Indonesia the pay is less than $1 a day.

The company's current strategy is to reshape its public image while doing as little as possible for the workers. Does anyone think it was an accident that Nike set up shop in human rights sinkholes, where labor organizing was viewed as a criminal activity and deeply impoverished workers were willing, even eager, to take their places on assembly lines and work for next to nothing?[13]

Other critics question the value of Nike's auditors, *PricewaterhouseCoopers* (PwC). Dara O'Rourke, an assistant professor at MIT, followed the PwC auditors around several factories in China, South Korea, and Vietnam. He concluded that although the auditors found minor violations of labor laws and codes of conduct, they missed major labor practice issues including hazardous working conditions, violations of overtime laws, and violation of wage laws. The problem, according to O'Rourke, was that the auditors had limited training and relied on factory managers for data and to set up interviews with workers, all of which were performed in the factories. The auditors, in other words, were getting an incomplete and somewhat sanitized view of conditions in the factory.[14]

The Controversy Continues

Fueled perhaps by the unforgiving criticisms of Nike that continued after Phil Knight's May 1998 speech, beginning in 1998 and continuing into 2001, a wave of protests against Nike occurred on many university campuses. The moving force behind the protests was United Students Against Sweatshops (USAS). The USAS argued that the Fair Labor Association, which grew out of the presidential task force on sweatshops, was an industry tool and not a truly independent auditor of foreign factories. The USAS set up an alternative independent auditing organization, the Workers Rights Consortium (WRC), charged with auditing factories that produce products under collegiate licensing programs. (Nike is a high-profile supplier of products under these programs.) The WRC is backed, and partly funded, by labor unions and refuses to cooperate with companies, arguing that doing so would jeopardize its independence.

By mid-2000, the WRC had persuaded 48 universities to join the organization, including all nine campuses of the University of California systems, the University of Michigan, and the University of Oregon, Knight's alma mater. When Knight heard the University of Oregon would join the WRC, as opposed to the FLA, he withdrew a planned $30 million donation to the university.[15] Despite this, in November 2000, the University of Washington announced it too would join the WRC, although it would also retain its membership in the FLA.[16]

Nike continued to push forward with its own initiatives, updating progress on its website. In April 2000, in response to accusations it was still hiding substandard conditions, Nike announced it would release the complete reports of all independent audits of its subcontractors' plants. Global Exchange continued to criticize the company, arguing in mid-2001 that the company was not living up to Phil Knight's 1998 promises and that it was intimidating workers from speaking out about abuses.[17]

Case Discussion Questions

1. Should Nike be held responsible for working conditions in foreign factories that it does not own, but where subcontractors make products for Nike?

2. What labor standards regarding safety, working conditions, overtime, and the like, should Nike hold foreign factories to: those prevailing in that country, or those prevailing in the United States?

3. An income of $2.28 a day, the base play of Nike factory workers in Indonesia, is double the daily income of about half the working population. Half of all adults in Indonesia are farmers, who receive less than $1 a day.[18] Given this, is it correct to criticize Nike for the low pay rates of its subcontractors in Indonesia?

4. Could Nike have handled the negative publicity over sweatshops better? What might it have done differently, not just from a public relations perspective but also from a policy perspective?

5. Do you think Nike needs to change its current policy? If so, how? Should Nike make changes even if they hinder the ability of the company to compete?

6. Is the WRC right to argue that the FLA is a tool of industry?

7. If sweatshops are a global problem, what might be a global solution to this problem?

Notes

1. From Nike's corporate website at www.nikebiz.com.

2. www.globalexchange.org.

3. "Boycott Nike," CBS News "48 Hours," October 17, 1996.

4. D. Jones, "Critics Tie Sweatshop Sneakers to 'Air Jordan,'" *USA Today*, June 6, 1996, p. 1B.

5. Global Exchange Special Report: "Nike Just Don't Do It." http://www.globalexchange.org/education/publications/newsltr6.97p2.html#nike.

6. V. Dobnik, "Chinese Workers Abused Making Nikes, Reeboks," *Seattle Times*, September 21, 1997, p. A4.

7. S. Greenhouse, "Nike Shoe Plant in Vietnam Is Called Unsafe for Workers," *New York Times*, November 8, 1997.

8. Ibid.

9. Quoted in Dobnik, "Chinese Workers Abused Making Nikes, Reeboks."

10. W. Bounds and H. Stout, "Sweatshop Pact: Good Fit or Threadbare?" *Wall Street Journal*, April 10, 1997, p. A2.

11. "Nike Gives Four Factories the Boot," *Los Angeles Times*, September 23, 1997, p. 20.

12. Archived at http://www.nikebiz.com/labor/speech trans.shtml.

13. B. Herbet, "Nike Blinks," *New York Times*, May 21st, 1998.

14. Dara O'Rourke, "Monitoring the Monitors: A Critique of the PricewaterhouseCoopers (PwC) Labor Monitoring," Department of Urban Studies and Planning, MIT.

15. L. Lee and A. Bernstein, "Who Says Student Protests Don't Matter?" *Business Week*, June 12, 2000, p. 94–96.

16. R. Deen, "UW to Join Anti-Sweatshop Group," *Seattle Post-Intelligencer.* November 20, 2000, p. B2.

17. "Rights Group Says Nike Isn't Fulfilling Promises," *Wall Street Journal*, May 16, 2001.

18. Figures from P. Kenel, "The Sweatshop Dilemma," *Christian Science Monitor*, August 21, 1996, p. 20.

Part 3

The Global Trade and Investment Environment

International
Trade Theory

Living standards in Ghana and South Korea were roughly comparable in 1970. Ghana's 1970 gross national product (GNP) per head was $250, and South Korea's was $260. By 1998 the situation had changed dramatically. South Korea had a GNP per head of $8,600 and boasted the world's 12th largest economy. Ghana's GNP per capita in 1998 was only $390, while its economy ranked 96 in the world. These differences in economic circumstances were due to vastly different economic growth rates since 1970. Between 1968 and 1998, the average annual growth rate in Ghana's GNP was less than 1.5 percent. In contrast, South Korea achieved a rate of more than 8 percent annually between 1968 and 1998.

While no simple explanation addresses the difference in growth rates between Ghana and South Korea, part of the answer may be found in the countries' attitudes toward international trade. A now classic study by the World Bank suggests that whereas the South Korean government implemented policies that encouraged companies to engage in international trade, the actions of the Ghanaian government discouraged domestic producers from becoming involved in international trade. As a consequence, in 1980 trade accounted for 18 percent of Ghana's GNP by value compared to 74 percent of South Korea's GNP.

In 1957, Ghana became the first of Great Britain's West African colonies to gain independence. Its first president, Kwame Nkrumah, influenced the rest of the continent with his theories of pan-African socialism. For Ghana this meant the imposition of high tariffs on many imports, an import substitution policy aimed at fostering Ghana self-sufficiency in certain manufactured goods, and the adoption of policies that discouraged Ghana's enterprises from engaging in exports. The results were an unmitigated disaster that transformed one of Africa's most prosperous nations into one of the world's poorest.

As an illustration of how Ghana's antitrade policies destroyed the Ghanaian economy, consider the Ghanaian government's involvement in the cocoa trade. A combination of favorable climate, good soils, and ready access to world shipping routes has given Ghana an absolute advantage in cocoa production. Quite simply, it is one of the best places in the world to grow cocoa. As a consequence, Ghana was the world's largest producer and exporter of cocoa in 1957. Then the government of the newly independent nation created a state-controlled cocoa marketing board. The board was given the authority to fix prices for cocoa and was designated the sole buyer of all cocoa grown in Ghana. The board held down the prices that it paid farmers for cocoa, while selling the cocoa that it bought from them on the world market at world prices. Thus, it might buy cocoa from farmers at 25 cents a pound and sell it on the world market for the world price of 50 cents a pound. In effect, the board was taxing exports by paying farmers considerably less for their cocoa than it was worth on the world market and putting the difference into government coffers. This money was used to fund the government policy of nationalization and industrialization.

One result of the cocoa policy was that between 1963 and 1979 the price paid by the cocoa marketing board to Ghana's farmers increased by a factor of 6, while the price of consumer goods in Ghana increased by a factor of 22, and while the price of cocoa in neighboring countries increased by a factor of 36! In real terms, the Ghanaian farmers were paid less every year for their cocoa by the cocoa marketing board, while the world price increased significantly. Ghana's farmers responded by switching to the production of subsistence foodstuffs that could be sold within Ghana, and the country's production and exports of cocoa plummeted by more than one-third in seven years. At the same time, the Ghanaian government's attempt to build an industrial base through state-run enterprises was a complete failure. The resulting drop in Ghana's export earnings plunged the country into recession, led to a decline in its foreign currency reserves, and severely limited its ability to pay for necessary imports.

In essence, what happened in Ghana is that the inward-oriented trade policy of the Ghanaian government resulted in a shift of that country's resources away from the profitable activity of growing cocoa—where it had an absolute advantage in the world economy—and toward growing subsistence foods and manufacturing, where it had no advantage. This inefficient use of the country's resources severely damaged the Ghanaian economy and held back the country's economic development.

In contrast, consider the trade policy adopted by the South Korean government. The World Bank has characterized the trade policy of South Korea as "strongly outward-oriented." Unlike in Ghana, the policies of the South Korean government emphasized low import barriers on manufactured goods (but not on agricultural goods) and incentives to encourage South Korean firms to export. Beginning in the late 1950s, the South Korean government progressively reduced import tariffs from an average of 60 percent of the price of an imported good to less than 20 percent in the mid-1980s. On most nonagricultural goods, import tariffs were reduced to zero. In addition, the number of imported goods subjected to quotas was reduced from more than 90 percent in the late 1950s to zero by the early 1980s. Over the same period, South Korea progressively reduced the subsidies given to South Korean exporters from an average of 80 percent of their sales price in the late 1950s to an average of less than 20 percent of their sales price in 1965 and down to zero in 1984. Put another way, with the exception of the agricultural sector (where a strong farm lobby maintained import controls), South Korea moved progressively toward a free trade stance.

South Korea's outward-looking orientation has been rewarded by a dramatic transformation of its economy. Initially, South Korea's resources shifted from agriculture to the manufacture of labor-intensive goods, especially textiles, clothing, and footwear. An abundant supply of cheap but well-educated labor helped form the basis of South Korea's comparative advantage in labor-intensive manufacturing. More recently, as labor costs have risen, the growth areas in the economy have been in the more capital-intensive manufacturing sectors, especially motor vehicles, semiconductors, consumer electronics, and advanced materials. As a result of these developments, South Korea has gone through some dramatic changes. In the late 1950s, 77 percent of the country's employment was in the agricultural sector; today the figure is less than 20 percent. Over the same period the percentage of its GNP accounted for by manufacturing increased from less than 10 percent to more than 30 percent, while the overall GNP grew at an annual rate of more than 9 percent.

Sources: "Poor Man's Burden: A Survey of the Third World," *The Economist*, September 23, 1989; World Bank, *World Development Report, 2000* (Oxford: Oxford University Press, 2000), Table 1; J. Wha-Lee, "International Trade, Distortions, and Long-Run Economic Growth," *International Monetary Fund Staff Papers* 40, no. 2 (June 1993), p. 299.

▌ Introduction

The opening case illustrates the gains that come from international trade. For a long time the economic policies of the Ghanaian government discouraged trade with other nations. The result was a shift in Ghana's resources away from productive uses (growing cocoa) and toward unproductive uses (subsistence agriculture). The economic policies of the South Korean government encouraged trade with other nations. The result was a shift in South Korea's resources away from uses where it had no comparative advantage in the world economy (agriculture) and toward more productive uses (labor-intensive manufacturing). As a direct result of their policies toward international trade, Ghana's economy declined while South Korea's grew.

This chapter has two goals that are related to the story of Ghana and South Korea. The first is to review a number of theories that explain why it is beneficial for a country to engage in international trade. The second goal is to explain the pattern of international trade that we observe in the world economy. With regard to the pattern of trade, we will be primarily concerned with explaining the pattern of exports and imports of products between countries. We will not be concerned with the pattern of foreign direct investment between countries; that is discussed in Chapter 7.

▌ An Overview of Trade Theory

We open this chapter with a discussion of mercantilism. Propagated in the 16th and 17th centuries, mercantilism advocated that countries should simultaneously encourage exports and discourage imports. Although mercantilism is an old and largely discredited doctrine, its echoes remain in modern political debate and in the trade policies of many countries. Next we will look at Adam Smith's theory of absolute advantage. Proposed in 1776, Smith's theory was the first to explain why unrestricted free trade is beneficial to a country. **Free trade** refers to a situation where a government does not attempt to influence through quotas or duties what its citizens can buy from another country, or what they can produce and sell to another country. Smith argued that the invisible hand of the market mechanism, rather than government policy, should determine what a country imports and what it exports. His arguments imply that such a laissez-faire stance toward trade was in the best interests of a country. Building on Smith's work are two additional theories that we shall review. One is the theory of comparative advantage, advanced by the 19th century English economist David Ricardo. This theory is the intellectual basis of the modern argument for unrestricted free trade. In the 20th century Ricardo's work was refined by two Swedish economists, Eli Heckscher and Bertil Ohlin, whose theory is known as the Heckscher-Ohlin theory.

The Benefits of Trade

The great strength of the theories of Smith, Ricardo, and Heckscher-Ohlin is that they identify with precision the specific benefits of international trade. Common sense suggests that some international trade is beneficial. For example, nobody would suggest that Iceland should grow its own oranges. Iceland can benefit from trade by exchanging some of the products that it can produce at a low cost (fish) for some products that it cannot produce at all (oranges). Thus, by engaging in international trade, Icelanders are able to add oranges to their diet of fish.

The theories of Smith, Ricardo, and Heckscher-Ohlin go beyond this common-sense notion, however, to show why it is beneficial for a country to engage in international trade *even for products it is able to produce for itself*. This is a difficult concept for people to grasp. For example, many people in the United States believe that American consumers should buy products produced in the United States by American companies whenever possible to help save American jobs from foreign competition. Such thinking apparently underlay a 1997 decision by the International Trade Commission to protect the Louisiana crawfish industry from inexpensive Chinese imports (see the accompanying Country Focus).

The same kind of nationalistic sentiments can be observed in many other countries. However, the theories of Smith, Ricardo, and Heckscher-Ohlin tell us that a country's economy may gain if its citizens buy certain products from other nations that could be produced at home. The gains arise because international trade allows a country to specialize in the manufacture and export of products that can be produced most efficiently in that country, while importing products that can be produced more efficiently in other countries. So it may make sense for the United States to specialize in the production and export of commercial jet aircraft, since the efficient production of commercial jet aircraft requires resources that are abundant in the United States, such as a highly skilled labor force and cutting-edge technological know-how. On the other hand, it may make sense for the United States to import textiles from India since the efficient production of textiles requires a relatively cheap labor force—and cheap labor is not abundant in the United States.

Of course, this economic argument is often difficult for segments of a country's population to accept. With their future threatened by imports, American textile companies and their employees have tried hard to persuade the U.S. government to limit the importation of textiles by demanding quotas and tariffs. Similarly, as the Country Focus illustrates, with their future threatened by imports, the Louisiana crawfish industry succeeded in persuading the government to limit imports of crawfish from China. Although such import controls may benefit particular groups, such as American textile businesses and their employees or Louisiana crawfish farmers, the theories of

Crawfish Wars

Once upon a time, Louisiana was owned by the French. Napoleon sold the territory to the United States when Thomas Jefferson was president, but many of the French stayed on. Over time, their descendants developed the distinctive Cajun culture that today is celebrated in the United States for its unique cuisine and music. At the heart of that cuisine can be found the venerable crawfish, as Louisianians call the crayfish. The crawfish is a fresh-water crustacean native to the bayous of Louisiana. A central ingredient of crawfish pie, bisque, etouffee, and gumbo, the crawfish is to Cajun Louisiana what wine is to France: a culinary symbol of its culture. It is also a major industry that generates $300 million per year in revenues for Louisiana crawfish farmers—or at least it did until the Chinese appeared.

In the early 1990s, development of the Chinese industry was encouraged by Louisiana importers to meet the growing demand for crawfish. In China, the crawfish industry proved to be attractive for entrepreneurial farmers. Chinese crawfish first started to appear on the Louisiana scene in 1991. Although old-time Cajuns were quick to claim that the Chinese crawfish had a markedly inferior taste, consumers didn't seem to notice the difference. More importantly perhaps, they liked the price, which ran between $2 and $3 per pound depending on the season, compared to $5 to $8 per pound for native Louisiana crawfish. With the significant price advantage, sales of Chinese imports skyrocketed from 353,000 pounds in 1992 to 5.5 million pounds in 1996. By 1996, Louisiana state officials estimated that 3,000 jobs had been lost in the local industry, mostly minimum-wage crawfish peelers, due to market share gains made by the Chinese.

This was too much for the Louisiana industry to stomach. In 1996, Louisiana's Crawfish Promotion and Research Board filed a petition with the International Trade Commission, an arm of the U.S. government, requesting an antidumping action. The petition claimed that Chinese crawfish producers were dumping their product, selling at below cost to drive Louisiana producers out of business. The industry requested that a 200 percent to 300 percent import tax be placed on Chinese crawfish. The State of Louisiana appropriated $350,000 from state funds to support the action.

Lawyers representing the Chinese crawfish industry claimed that lower production costs in China were the reason for the low prices—not dumping. One Louisiana-based importer of Chinese crawfish pointed out that 27 processing plants in China supplied his company. Workers at these plants were given housing and other amenities and paid 15 cents per hour, or $9 for a 60-hour week. The lawyers also said Chinese crawfish have been good for American consumers, who have saved money and benefited from a steadier supply, and good for Louisiana cuisine, because it is has become less expensive to cook. The lawyers pointed out that the action was not in the interests of American consumers, since it was nothing more than an attempt by Louisiana producers to reestablish their lucrative monopoly on the production of crawfish, a monopoly that would enable them to extract higher prices from consumers.

However, the International Trade Commission was deaf to such arguments. The commission deemed that China was a "nonmarket economy" since it was not yet a member of the World Trade Organization (something that changed in 2001). The commission then used prices in a "market economy," Spain, to establish a benchmark for a "fair market value" for crawfish. Since Spanish crawfish sell for approximately twice the price of Chinese crawfish and about the same price as Louisiana crawfish, the commission concluded that the Chinese were dumping (selling below costs of production). In August 1997, the commission levied a 110 to 123 percent duty on imports of Chinese crawfish, effectively negating the price advantage enjoyed by Chinese producers. In the interests of protecting American jobs, the commission sided with Louisiana producers and against American consumers, who would now have to pay higher prices for crawfish. Under commission regulations, the ruling would stay in place for five years, after which the legitimacy of the import duty must be reevaluated.

Sources: Donna St. George, "Crawfish Wars: Cajun Country Vs China," New York Times, May 7, 1997, pp. B1, B10; P. Passell, "Protecting America's Shores from Those Chinese Crawfish," New York Times, August 28, 1997, p. D2; N. Dunne, "Shellfish Imports Stick in the Cajun Craw," Financial Times, August 21, 1997, p. 16; and B. Thevenot, "Getting Pinched," The Times Picayune, March 11, 2000, p. C1.

Smith, Ricardo, and Heckscher-Ohlin suggest that the economy as a whole is hurt by this kind of action. Limits on imports are often in the interests of domestic producers, but not domestic consumers.

The Pattern of International Trade

The theories of Smith, Ricardo, and Heckscher-Ohlin also help to explain the pattern of international trade that we observe in the world economy. Some aspects of the pattern are easy to understand. Climate and natural-resource endowments explain why Ghana exports cocoa, Brazil exports coffee, Saudi Arabia exports oil, and China exports crawfish. But much of the observed pattern of international trade is more difficult to explain. For example, why does Japan export automobiles, consumer electronics, and machine tools? Why does Switzerland export chemicals, watches, and jewelry? David Ricardo's theory of comparative advantage offers an explanation in terms of international differences in labor productivity. The more sophisticated Heckscher-Ohlin theory emphasizes the interplay between the proportions in which the factors of production (such as land, labor, and capital) are available in different countries and the proportions in which they are needed for producing particular goods. This explanation rests on the assumption that countries have varying endowments of the various factors of production. Tests of this theory, however, suggest that it is a less powerful explanation of real-world trade patterns than once thought.

One early response to the failure of the Heckscher-Ohlin theory to explain the observed pattern of international trade was the *product life-cycle theory.* Proposed by Raymond Vernon, this theory suggests that early in their life cycle, most new products are produced in and exported from the country in which they were developed. As a new product becomes widely accepted internationally, however, production starts in other countries. As a result, the theory suggests, the product may ultimately be exported back to the country of its original innovation.

In a similar vein, during the 1980s economists such as Paul Krugman of Massachusetts Institute of Technology developed what has come to be known as the *new trade theory.* New trade theory stresses that in some cases countries specialize in the production and export of particular products not because of underlying differences in factor endowments, but because in certain industries the world market can support only a limited number of firms. (This is argued to be the case for the commercial aircraft industry.) In such industries, firms that enter the market first are able to build a competitive advantage that is subsequently difficult to challenge. Thus, the observed pattern of trade between nations may be due in part to the ability of firms within a given nation to capture first-mover advantages. The United States dominates in the export of commercial jet aircraft because American firms such as Boeing were first movers in the world market. Boeing built a competitive advantage that has subsequently been difficult for firms from countries with equally favorable factor endowments to challenge.

In a work related to the new trade theory, Michael Porter of the Harvard Business School developed a theory, referred to as the theory of national competitive advantage, that attempts to explain why particular nations achieve international success in particular industries. Like the new trade theorists, in addition to factor endowments, Porter points out the importance of country factors such as domestic demand and domestic rivalry in explaining a nation's dominance in the production and export of particular products.

Trade Theory and Government Policy

Although all these theories agree that international trade is beneficial to a country, they lack agreement in their recommendations for government policy. Mercantilism makes a crude case for government involvement in promoting exports and limiting imports. The theories of Smith, Ricardo, and Heckscher-Ohlin form part of the case for unrestricted free trade. The argument for unrestricted free trade is that both import controls and export incentives (such as subsidies) are self-defeating and result in wasted resources. Both the new trade theory and Porter's theory of national competitive advantage can be interpreted as justifying some limited government intervention to support the development of certain export-oriented industries. We will discuss the pros and cons of this argument, known as strategic trade policy, as well as the pros and cons of the argument for unrestricted free trade in Chapter 5.

■ Mercantilism

The first theory of international trade emerged in England in the mid-16th century. Referred to as *mercantilism*, its principle assertion was that gold and silver were the mainstays of national wealth and essential to vigorous commerce. At that time, gold and silver were the currency of trade between countries; a country could earn gold and silver by exporting goods. By the same token, importing goods from other countries would result in an outflow of gold and silver to those countries. The main tenet of **mercantilism** was that it was in a country's best interests to maintain a trade surplus, to export more than it imported. By doing so, a country would accumulate gold and silver and, consequently, increase its national wealth and prestige. As the English mercantilist writer Thomas Mun put it in 1630:

> The ordinary means therefore to increase our wealth and treasure is by foreign trade, wherein we must ever observe this rule: to sell more to strangers yearly than we consume of theirs in value.[1]

Consistent with this belief, the mercantilist doctrine advocated government intervention to achieve a surplus in the balance of trade. The mercantilists saw no virtue in a large volume of trade per se. Rather, they recommended policies to maximize exports and minimize imports. To achieve this, imports were limited by tariffs and quotas, while exports were subsidized.

The classical economist David Hume pointed out an inherent inconsistency in the mercantilist doctrine in 1752. According to Hume, if England had a balance-of-trade surplus with France (it exported more than it imported) the resulting inflow of gold and silver would swell the domestic money supply and generate inflation in England. In France, however, the outflow of gold and silver would have the opposite effect. France's money supply would contract, and its prices would fall. This change in relative prices between France and England would encourage the French to buy fewer English goods (because they were becoming more expensive) and the English to buy more French goods (because they were becoming cheaper). The result would be a deterioration in the English balance of trade and an improvement in France's trade balance, until the English surplus was eliminated. Hence, according to Hume, in the long run no country could sustain a surplus on the balance of trade and so accumulate gold and silver as the mercantilists had envisaged.

The flaw with mercantilism was that it viewed trade as a zero-sum game. (A **zero-sum game** is one in which a gain by one country results in a loss by another.) It was left to Adam Smith and David Ricardo to show the shortsightedness of this approach and to demonstrate that trade is a **positive-sum game,** or a situation in which all countries can benefit. The mercantilist doctrine is by no means dead.[2] For example, Jarl Hagelstam, a director at the Finnish Ministry of Finance, has observed that in most trade negotiations:

> The approach of individual negotiating countries, both industrialized and developing, has been to press for trade liberalization in areas where their own comparative competitive advantages are the strongest, and to resist liberalization in areas where they are less competitive and fear that imports would replace domestic production.[3]

Hagelstam attributes this strategy by negotiating countries to a neomercantilist belief held by the politicians of many nations. This belief equates political power with economic power and economic power with a balance-of-trade surplus. Thus, the trade strategy of many nations is designed to simultaneously boost exports and limit imports.

Absolute Advantage ◼

In his 1776 landmark book *The Wealth of Nations*, Adam Smith attacked the mercantilist assumption that trade is a zero-sum game. Smith argued that countries differ in their ability to produce goods efficiently. In his time, the English, by virtue of their superior manufacturing processes, were the world's most efficient textile manufacturers. Due to the combination of favorable climate, good soils, and accumulated expertise, the French had the world's most efficient wine industry. The English had an *absolute advantage* in the production of textiles, while the French had an *absolute advantage* in the production of wine. Thus, a country has an **absolute advantage** in the production of a product when it is more efficient than any other country in producing it.

According to Smith, countries should specialize in the production of goods for which they have an absolute advantage and then trade these for goods produced by other countries. In Smith's time, this suggested that the English should specialize in the production of textiles while the French should specialize in the production of wine. England could get all the wine it needed by selling its textiles to France and buying wine in exchange. Similarly, France could get all the textiles it needed by selling wine to England and buying textiles in exchange. Smith's basic argument, therefore, is that you should never produce goods at home that you can buy at a lower cost from other countries. Smith demonstrates that by specializing in the production of goods in which each has an absolute advantage, both countries benefit by engaging in trade.

Consider the effects of trade between Ghana and South Korea. The production of any good (output) requires resources (inputs) such as land, labor, and capital. Assume that Ghana and South Korea both have the same amount of resources and that these resources can be used to produce either rice or cocoa. Assume further that 200 units of resources are available in each country. Imagine that in Ghana it takes 10 resources to produce one ton of cocoa and 20 resources to produce one ton of rice. Thus, Ghana could produce 20 tons of cocoa and no rice, 10 tons of rice and no cocoa, or some combination of rice and cocoa between these two extremes. The different combinations that Ghana could produce are represented by the line GG′ in Figure 4.1. This is referred to as Ghana's production possibility frontier (PPF). Similarly, imagine that in South Korea it takes 40 resources to produce one ton of cocoa and 10 resources to produce one ton of rice. Thus, South Korea could produce 5 tons of cocoa and no rice, 20 tons of rice and no cocoa, or some combination between these two extremes. The different combinations available to South Korea are represented by the line KK′ in Figure 4.1, which is South Korea's PPF. Clearly, Ghana has an absolute advantage in the production of cocoa. (More resources are needed to produce a ton of cocoa in South Korea than in Ghana.) By the same token, South Korea has an absolute advantage in the production of rice.

Now consider a situation in which neither country trades with any other. Each country devotes half of its resources to the production of rice and half to the production of cocoa. Each country must also consume what it produces. Ghana would be able to produce 10 tons of cocoa and 5 tons of rice (point A in Figure 4.1), while South Korea would be able to produce 10 tons of rice and 2.5 tons of cocoa. Without trade, the combined production of both countries would be 12.5 tons of cocoa (10 tons in Ghana plus 2.5 tons in South Korea) and 15 tons of rice (5 tons in Ghana and 10 tons in South Korea). If each country were to specialize in producing the good for which it had an absolute advantage and then trade with the other for the good it lacks, Ghana could produce 20 tons of cocoa, and South Korea could produce 20 tons of rice. Thus, by specializing, the production of both goods could be increased. Production of cocoa would increase from 12.5 tons to 20 tons, while production of rice would increase from 15 tons to 20 tons. The increase in production that would result from specialization is therefore 7.5 tons of cocoa and 5 tons of rice. Table 4.1 summarizes these figures.

Figure 4.1

The Theory of Absolute
Advantage

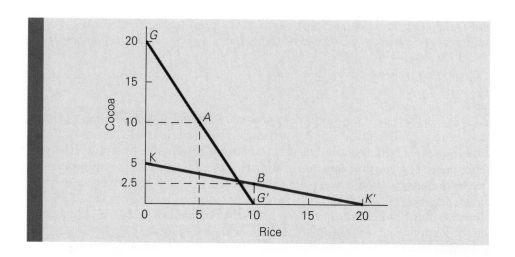

Table 4.1

Absolute Advantage and
the Gains from Trade

Resources Required to Produce 1 Ton of Cocoa and Rice		
	Cocoa	**Rice**
Ghana	10	20
South Korea	40	10
Production and Consumption without Trade		
	Cocoa	**Rice**
Ghana	10.0	5.0
South Korea	2.5	10.0
Total production	12.5	15.0
Production with Specialization		
	Cocoa	**Rice**
Ghana	20.0	0.0
South Korea	0.0	20.0
Total production	20.0	20.0
Consumption After Ghana Trades 6 Tons of Cocoa for 6 Tons of South Korean Rice		
	Cocoa	**Rice**
Ghana	14.0	6.0
South Korea	6.0	14.0
Increase in Consumption as a Result of Specialization and Trade		
	Cocoa	**Rice**
Ghana	4.0	1.0
South Korea	3.5	4.0

By engaging in trade and swapping one ton of cocoa for one ton of rice, producers in both countries could consume more of both cocoa and rice. Imagine that Ghana and South Korea swap cocoa and rice on a one-to-one basis; that is, the price of one ton of cocoa is equal to the price of one ton of rice. If Ghana decided to export 6 tons of cocoa to South Korea and import 6 tons of rice in return, its final consumption after trade would be 14 tons of cocoa and 6 tons of rice. This is 4 tons more cocoa than it could have consumed before specialization and trade and 1 ton more rice. Similarly, South Korea's final consumption after trade would be 6 tons of cocoa and 14 tons of rice. This is 3.5 tons more cocoa than it could have consumed before specialization and trade and 4 tons more rice. Thus, as a result of specialization and trade, output of both cocoa and rice would be increased, and consumers in both nations would be able to consume more. Thus, we can see that trade is a positive-sum game; it produces net gains for all involved.

Comparative Advantage

David Ricardo took Adam Smith's theory one step further by exploring what might happen when one country has an absolute advantage in the production of all goods.[4] Smith's theory of absolute advantage suggests that such a country might derive no benefits from international trade. In his 1817 book *Principles of Political Economy*, Ricardo showed that this was not the case. According to Ricardo's theory of **comparative advantage,** it makes sense for a country to specialize in the production of those goods that it produces most efficiently and to buy the goods that it produces less efficiently from other countries, even if this means buying goods from other countries that it could produce more efficiently itself.[5] While this may seem counterintuitive, the logic can be explained with a simple example.

Assume that Ghana is more efficient in the production of both cocoa and rice; that is, Ghana has an absolute advantage in the production of both products. In Ghana it takes 10 resources to produce one ton of cocoa and $13\frac{1}{3}$ resources to produce one ton of rice. Thus, given its 200 units of resources, Ghana can produce 20 tons of cocoa and no rice, 15 tons of rice and no cocoa, or any combination in between on its PPF (the line GG′ in Figure 4.2). In South Korea it takes 40 resources to produce one ton of cocoa and 20 resources to produce one ton of rice. Thus, South Korea can produce 5 tons of cocoa and no rice, 10 tons of rice and no cocoa, or any combination on its PPF (the line KK′ in Figure 4.2). Again assume that without trade, each country uses half of its resources to produce rice and half to produce cocoa. Thus, without trade, Ghana will

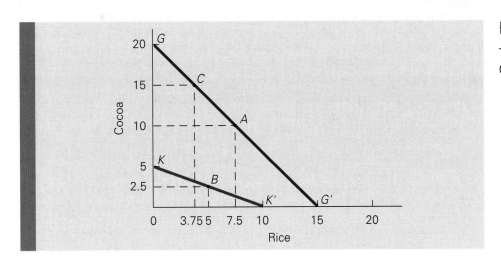

Figure 4.2

The Theory of Comparative Advantage

produce 10 tons of cocoa and 7.5 tons of rice (point A in Figure 4.2), while South Korea will produce 2.5 tons of cocoa and 5 tons of rice (point B in Figure 4.2).

In light of Ghana's absolute advantage in the production of both goods, why should it trade with South Korea? Although Ghana has an absolute advantage in the production of both cocoa and rice, it has a comparative advantage only in the production of cocoa: Ghana can produce 4 times as much cocoa as South Korea, but only 1.5 times as much rice. Ghana is *comparatively* more efficient at producing cocoa than it is at producing rice.

Without trade the combined production of cocoa will be 12.5 tons (10 tons in Ghana and 2.5 in South Korea), and the combined production of rice will also be 12.5 tons (7.5 tons in Ghana and 5 tons in South Korea). Without trade each country must consume what it produces. By engaging in trade, the two countries can increase their combined production of rice and cocoa, and consumers in both nations can consume more of both goods.

The Gains from Trade

Imagine that Ghana exploits its comparative advantage in the production of cocoa to increase its output from 10 tons to 15 tons. This uses up 150 units of resources, leaving the remaining 50 units of resources to use in producing 3.75 tons of rice (point C in Figure 4.2). Meanwhile, South Korea specializes in the production of rice, producing 10 tons. The combined output of both cocoa and rice has now increased. Before specialization, the combined output was 12.5 tons of cocoa and 12.5 tons of rice. Now it is 15 tons of cocoa and 13.75 tons of rice (3.75 tons in Ghana and 10 tons in South Korea). The source of the increase in production is summarized in Table 4.2.

Not only is output higher, but also both countries can now benefit from trade. If Ghana and South Korea swap cocoa and rice on a one-to-one basis, with both countries choosing to exchange 4 tons of their export for 4 tons of the import, both countries are able to consume more cocoa and rice than they could before specialization and trade (see Table 4.2). Thus, if Ghana exchanges 4 tons of cocoa with South Korea for 4 tons of rice, it is still left with 11 tons of rice, which is 1 ton more than it had before trade. The 4 tons of rice it gets from South Korea in exchange for its 4 tons of cocoa, when added to the 3.75 tons it now produces domestically, leaves it with a total of 7.75 tons of rice, which is .25 of a ton more than it had before specialization. Similarly, after swapping 4 tons of rice with Ghana, South Korea still ends up with 6 tons of rice, which is more than it had before specialization. In addition, the 4 tons of cocoa it receives in exchange is 1.5 tons more than it produced before trade. Thus, consumption of cocoa and rice can increase in both countries as a result of specialization and trade.

The basic message of the theory of comparative advantage is that *potential world production is greater with unrestricted free trade than it is with restricted trade*. Ricardo's theory suggests that consumers in all nations can consume more if there are no restrictions on trade. This occurs even in countries that lack an absolute advantage in the production of any good. In other words, to an even greater degree than the theory of absolute advantage, *the theory of comparative advantage suggests that trade is a positive-sum game in which all countries that participate realize economic gains*. As such, this theory provides a strong rationale for encouraging free trade. So powerful is Ricardo's theory that it remains a major intellectual weapon for those who argue for free trade.

Qualifications and Assumptions

The conclusion that free trade is universally beneficial is a rather bold one to draw from such a simple model. Our simple model includes many unrealistic assumptions:

1.   We have assumed a simple world in which there are only two countries and two goods. In the real world, there are many countries and many goods.

Resources Required to Produce 1 Ton of Cocoa and Rice

	Cocoa	Rice
Ghana	10	13.33
South Korea	40	20

Production and Consumption without Trade

	Cocoa	Rice
Ghana	10.0	7.5
South Korea	2.5	5.0
Total production	12.5	12.5

Production with Specialization

	Cocoa	Rice
Ghana	15.0	3.75
South Korea	0.0	10.0
Total production	15.0	13.75

Consumption After Ghana Trades 4 Tons of Cocoa for 4 Tons of South Korean Rice

	Cocoa	Rice
Ghana	11.0	7.75
South Korea	4.0	6.0

Increase in Consumption as a Result of Specialization and Trade

	Cocoa	Rice
Ghana	1.0	0.25
South Korea	1.5	1.0

Table 4.2

Comparative Advantage and the Gains from Trade

2. We have assumed away transportation costs between countries.

3. We have assumed away differences in the prices of resources in different countries. We have said nothing about exchange rates, simply assuming that cocoa and rice could be swapped on a one-to-one basis.

4. We have assumed that resources can move freely from the production of one good to another within a country. In reality, this is not always the case.

5. We have assumed constant returns to scale; that is, that specialization by Ghana or South Korea has no effect on the amount of resources required to produce one ton of cocoa or rice. In reality, both diminishing and increasing returns to specialization exist. The amount of resources required to produce a good might decrease or increase as a nation specializes in production of that good.

6. We have assumed that each country has a fixed stock of resources and that free trade does not change the efficiency with which a country uses its resources. This static assumption makes no allowances for the dynamic changes in a country's stock of resources and in the efficiency with which the country uses its resources that might result from free trade.

7. We have assumed away the effects of trade on income distribution within a country.

Given these assumptions, can the conclusion that free trade is mutually beneficial be extended to the real world of many countries, many goods, positive transportation costs, volatile exchange rates, immobile domestic resources, nonconstant returns to specialization, and dynamic changes? Although a detailed extension of the theory of comparative advantage is beyond the scope of this book, economists have shown that the basic result derived from our simple model can be generalized to a world composed of many countries producing many different goods.[6] Despite the shortcomings of the Ricardian model, research suggests that the basic proposition that countries will export the goods that they are most efficient at producing is borne out by the data.[7] However, once all the assumptions are dropped, the case for unrestricted free trade, while still positive, has been argued by some economists associated with the "new trade theory" to lose some of its strength.[8] We return to this issue later in this chapter and in the next.

Simple Extensions of the Ricardian Model

Let us explore the effect of relaxing three of the assumptions identified above in the simple comparative advantage model. Below we relax the assumption that resources move freely from the production of one good to another within a country, the assumption of constant returns to specialization, and the assumption that trade does not change a country's stock of resources or the efficiency with which those resources are utilized.

Immobile Resources

In our simple comparative model of Ghana and South Korea, we assumed that producers (farmers) could easily convert land from the production of cocoa to rice, and vice versa. While this assumption may hold for some agricultural products, resources do not always shift quite so easily from producing one good to another. A certain amount of friction is involved. For example, embracing a free trade regime for an advanced economy such as the United States often implies that the country will produce less of some labor-intensive goods, such as textiles, and more of some knowledge-intensive goods, such as computer software or biotechnology products. Although the country as a whole will gain from such a shift, textile producers will lose. A textile worker in South Carolina is probably not qualified to write software for Microsoft. Thus, the shift to free trade may mean that she becomes unemployed or has to accept another less attractive job, such as working at a fast-food restaurant. For an example of how the shift toward free trade can impact an individual enterprise and its employees, look at the Management Focus profiling how the outdoor equipment cooperative REI is adjusting its own production activities to deal with a move toward greater free trade in textiles in the U.S. economy.

Resources do not always move easily from one economic activity to another. The process creates friction and human suffering too. While the theory predicts that the benefits of free trade outweigh the costs by a significant margin, this is of cold comfort to those who bear the costs. Accordingly, political opposition to the adoption of a free trade regime typically comes from those whose jobs are most at risk. In the United States, for example, textile workers and their unions have long opposed the move toward free trade precisely because this group has much to lose from free trade. Governments often ease the transition toward free trade by helping to retrain those who lose their jobs as a result. The pain caused by the movement toward a free trade regime is a short-term phenomenon, while the gains from trade once the transition has been made are both significant and enduring.

Diminishing Returns

The simple comparative advantage model developed above assumes constant returns to specialization. By **constant returns to specialization** we mean the units of resources

Management Focus

Free Trade and REI

Recreational Equipment Inc. (REI) is a buyer's cooperative that has grown into one of the major suppliers of outdoor equipment in the United States and has a rapidly growing international business. Started in Seattle in 1938 by Lloyd Anderson, the company provided high-quality climbing gear at a low price to members of the cooperative. For its first 37 years, REI operated a single store in Seattle, but in 1975 the cooperative started opening stores in other cities. Today REI has become a $621 million a year business with 60 stores worldwide, 6,600 employees, revenue growth of 8 to 10 percent annually, and a goal of opening up three to five retail outlets per year. Despite the growth, REI is still organized as a cooperative with 1.7 million active members. All members receive a dividend check at the end of each year that amounts to about 10 percent of the value of their purchases during the year (one does not have to be a member to shop at REI). REI also has one of the fastest growing, and most profitable, Internet sites in the retail industry, which registered revenues of $412 million in 1999, up 300 percent from a year earlier.

To supply some of its own product needs, REI has two subsidiaries. One of these, Thaw, has been supplying REI with a range of gear, including tents, backpacks, sleeping bags, and clothing, for 33 years. In recent years, Thaw has concentrated on producing clothing items made out of fleece for REI's stores. Unfortunately for Thaw's 200 employees, the economics of manufacturing garments in the United States have been changing for several years. Following passage of the North American Free Trade Agreement (NAFTA) in 1993, all tariffs on trade in textile garments between the United States and Mexico were dropped (a tariff is a tax on imports). In the following years, an increasing number of textile operations shut down in the United States and moved to Mexico, attracted by lower labor costs. Wage rates for textile workers in Mexico run about $5 to $10 a day, compared to $8 to $10 an hour at Thaw's operation. For a labor-intensive operation such as garment production, these wage differentials are significant.

Given these economics, in mid-2000 REI announced it would be closing its Thaw subsidiary and sourcing its fleece products from Mexico. By shifting its production to Mexico, REI expects to reduce the cost of its fleece items by 20 percent. That means lower prices for REI's members and other customers and bigger profits for REI, which translates into larger dividend checks for REI's members. It also means that its employees at Thaw will be out of a job. To assist its former employees at Thaw, REI has added funds to federal money to assist with job retraining, unemployment benefits, and health insurance.

The events at Thaw are being repeated across the country. Since 1993, about 450,000 jobs have been lost in the U.S. garment industry as production has moved to low-wage countries such as Mexico. Former textile workers, most of whom are low skilled, have found it difficult to find alternative full-time employment. The Department of Labor estimates that between 1995 and 1997, 58 percent of unemployed textile workers failed to find full-time jobs, while for the 42 percent that did, their average wage dropped by some 20 percent. As painful as this has been for textile workers, the American consumer has gained from lower prices, and American companies in many other industries have seen their sales to Mexico boom as trade barriers have come down. Thus, while a strong case can be made that NAFTA has benefited the majority of Americans and Mexicans alike, it has inflicted pain on some groups, such as U.S. textile workers, and forces some companies, such as REI, to make difficult managerial decisions.

Sources: R. T. Nelson, "REI's Globalization," *SeattleTimes*, May 14, 2000, pp. D1, D2, and E. Chabrow, "REI Gets Head Start in Clicks and Mortar Race," *Information Week*, May 1, 2000.

required to produce a good (cocoa or rice) are assumed to remain constant no matter where one is on a country's production possibility frontier (PPF). Thus, we assumed that it always took Ghana 10 units of resources to produce one ton of cocoa. However, it is more realistic to assume diminishing returns to specialization. **Diminishing returns to specialization** occurs when more units of resources are required to produce each additional unit. While 10 units of resources may be sufficient to increase Ghana's output of cocoa from 12 tons to 13 tons, 11 units of resources may be needed to increase output from 13 to 14 tons, 12 units of resources to increase output from 14 tons

Figure 4.3

Ghana's PPF under
Diminishing Returns

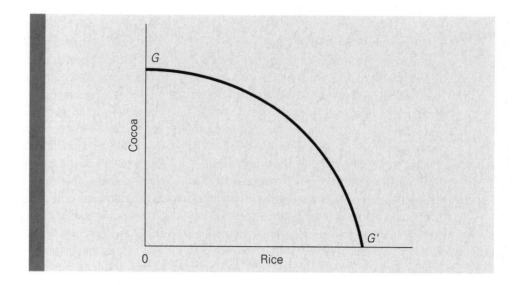

to 15 tons, and so on. Diminishing returns implies a convex PPF for Ghana (see Figure 4.3), rather than the straight line depicted in Figure 4.2.

It is more realistic to assume diminishing returns for two reasons. First, not all resources are of the same quality. As a country tries to increase its output of a certain good, it is increasingly likely to draw on more marginal resources whose productivity is not as great as those initially employed. The result is that it requires ever more resources to produce an equal increase in output. For example, some land is more productive than other land. As Ghana tries to expand its output of cocoa, it might have to utilize increasingly marginal land that is less fertile than the land it originally used. As yields per acre decline, Ghana must use more land to produce one ton of cocoa.

A second reason for diminishing returns is that different goods use resources in different proportions. For example, imagine that growing cocoa uses more land and less labor than growing rice, and that Ghana tries to transfer resources from rice production to cocoa production. The rice industry will release proportionately too much labor and too little land for efficient cocoa production. To absorb the additional resources of labor and land, the cocoa industry will have to shift toward more labor-intensive methods of production. The effect is that the efficiency with which the cocoa industry uses labor will decline, and returns will diminish.

Diminishing returns show that it is not feasible for a country to specialize to the degree suggested by the simple Ricardian model outlined earlier. Diminishing returns to specialization suggest that the gains from specialization are likely to be exhausted before specialization is complete. In reality, most countries do not specialize, but instead, produce a range of goods. However, the theory predicts that it is worthwhile to specialize until that point where the resulting gains from trade are outweighed by diminishing returns. Thus, the basic conclusion that unrestricted free trade is beneficial still holds, although because of diminishing returns, the gains may not be as great as suggested in the constant returns case.

Dynamic Effects and Economic Growth

Our simple comparative advantage model assumed that trade does not change a country's stock of resources or the efficiency with which it utilizes those resources. This static assumption makes no allowances for the dynamic changes that might result from trade. If we relax this assumption, it becomes apparent that opening an economy to trade is likely to generate dynamic gains of two sorts.[9] First, free trade might increase

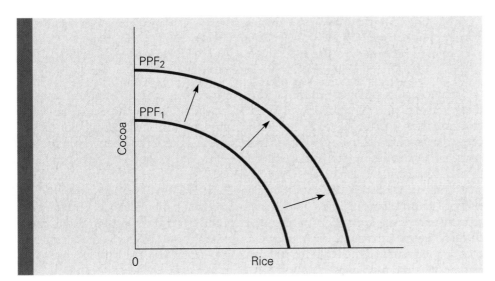

Figure 4.4

The Influence of Free Trade on the PPF

a country's stock of resources as increased supplies of labor and capital from abroad become available for use within the country. This is occurring now in Eastern Europe, where many Western businesses are investing large amounts of capital in the former Communist countries.

Second, free trade might also increase the efficiency with which a country uses its resources. Gains in the efficiency of resource utilization could arise from a number of factors. For example, economies of large-scale production might become available as trade expands the size of the total market available to domestic firms. Trade might make better technology from abroad available to domestic firms; better technology can increase labor productivity or the productivity of land. (The so-called green revolution had this effect on agricultural outputs in developing countries.) Also, opening an economy to foreign competition might stimulate domestic producers to look for ways to increase their efficiency. Again, this phenomenon is arguably occurring in the once-protected markets of Eastern Europe, where many former state monopolies are increasing the efficiency of their operations to survive in the competitive world market.

Dynamic gains in both the stock of a country's resources and the efficiency with which resources are utilized will cause a country's PPF to shift outward. This is illustrated in Figure 4.4, where the shift from PPF_1 to PPF_2 results from the dynamic gains that arise from free trade. As a consequence of this outward shift, the country in Figure 4.4 can produce more of both goods than it did before introduction of free trade. The theory suggests that opening an economy to free trade not only results in static gains of the type discussed earlier, but also results in dynamic gains that stimulate economic growth. If this is so, the case for free trade becomes stronger.

Evidence for the Link between Trade and Growth

Many economic studies have looked at the relationship between trade and economic growth. In general, these studies suggest that, as predicted by the theory, countries that adopt a more open stance toward international trade enjoy higher growth rates than those that close their economies to trade. Jeffrey Sachs and Andrew Warner created a measure of how "open" to international trade an economy was and then looked at the relationship between "openness" and economic growth for a sample of more than 100 countries for the years 1970 to 1990.[10] Among other findings, they reported:

> We find a strong association between openness and growth, both within the group of developing and the group of developed countries. Within the group of

developing countries, the open economies grew at 4.49 percent per year, and the closed economies grew at 0.69 percent per year. Within the group of developed economies, the open economies grew at 2.29 percent per year, and the closed economies grew at 0.74 percent per year.[11]

The message of this study seems clear: Adopt an open economy and embrace free trade, and over time your nation will be rewarded with higher economic growth rates. Higher growth will raise income levels and living standards. This last point has recently been confirmed by a study that looked at the relationship between trade and growth in incomes. The study, undertaken by Jeffrey Frankel and David Romer, found that on average, a one percentage point increase in the ratio of a country's trade to its gross domestic product increases income per person by at least one-half percent.[12] For every 10 percent increase in the importance of international trade in an economy, average income levels will rise by at least 5 percent. Despite the short-term adjustment costs associated with adopting a free trade regime, trade would seem to produce greater economic growth and higher living standards in the long run, just as the theory of Ricardo would lead us to expect.[13]

Heckscher-Ohlin Theory

Ricardo's theory stresses that comparative advantage arises from differences in productivity. Thus, whether Ghana is more efficient than South Korea in the production of cocoa depends on how productively it uses its resources. Ricardo stressed labor productivity and argued that differences in labor productivity between nations underlie the notion of comparative advantage. Swedish economists Eli Heckscher (in 1919) and Bertil Ohlin (in 1933) put forward a different explanation of comparative advantage.[14] They argued that comparative advantage arises from differences in national factor endowments.[14] By factor endowments they meant the extent to which a country is endowed with such resources as land, labor, and capital. Nations have varying factor endowments, and different factor endowments explain differences in factor costs. The more abundant a factor, the lower its cost. The Heckscher-Ohlin theory predicts that countries will export those goods that make intensive use of factors that are locally abundant, while importing goods that make intensive use of factors that are locally scarce. Thus, the Heckscher-Ohlin theory attempts to explain the pattern of international trade that we observe in the world economy. Like Ricardo's theory, the Heckscher-Ohlin theory argues that free trade is beneficial. Unlike Ricardo's theory, however, the Heckscher-Ohlin theory argues that the pattern of international trade is determined by differences in factor endowments, rather than differences in productivity.

The Heckscher-Ohlin theory also has commonsense appeal. For example, the United States has long been a substantial exporter of agricultural goods, reflecting in part its unusual abundance of arable land. In contrast, China excels in the export of goods produced in labor-intensive manufacturing industries, such as textiles and footwear. This reflects China's relative abundance of low-cost labor. The United States, which lacks abundant low-cost labor, has been a primary importer of these goods. Note that it is relative, not absolute, endowments that are important; a country may have larger absolute amounts of land and labor than another country, but be relatively abundant in one of them.

The Leontief Paradox

The Heckscher-Ohlin theory has been one of the most influential theoretical ideas in international economics. Most economists prefer the Heckscher-Ohlin theory to Ricardo's theory because it makes fewer simplifying assumptions. Because of its influence, the theory has been subjected to many empirical tests. Beginning with a famous study published in 1953 by Wassily Leontief (winner of the Nobel Prize in economics in 1973), many of these tests have raised questions about the validity of the Heckscher-Ohlin theory.[15] Using the Heckscher-Ohlin theory, Leontief postulated that since the United States was relatively abundant in capital compared to other nations, the United States would be an exporter of capital-intensive goods and an importer of labor-intensive goods. To his surprise, however, he found that U.S. exports were less capital intensive than U.S. imports. Since this result was at variance with the predictions of the theory, it has become known as the Leontief paradox.

No one is quite sure why we observe the Leontief paradox. One possible explanation is that the United States has a special advantage in producing new products or goods made with innovative technologies. Such products may be less capital intensive than products whose technology has had time to mature and become suitable for mass production. Thus, the United States may be exporting goods that heavily use skilled labor and innovative entrepreneurship, such as computer software, while importing heavy manufacturing products that use large amounts of capital. Some more recent empirical studies tend to confirm this.[16] Recent tests of the Heckscher-Ohlin theory using data for a large number of countries tend to confirm the existence of the Leontief paradox.[17]

This leaves economists with a difficult dilemma. They prefer the Heckscher-Ohlin theory on theoretical grounds, but it is a relatively poor predictor of real-world international trade patterns. On the other hand, the theory they regard as being too limited, Ricardo's theory of comparative advantage, actually predicts trade patterns with greater accuracy. The best solution to this dilemma may be to return to the Ricardian idea that trade patterns are largely driven by international differences in productivity. Thus, one might argue that the United States exports commercial aircraft and imports automobiles not because its factor endowments are especially suited to aircraft manufacture and not suited to automobile manufacture, but because the United States is more efficient at producing aircraft than automobiles. A key assumption in the Heckscher-Ohlin theory is that technologies are the same across countries. This may not be the case, and differences in technology may lead to differences in productivity, which in turn, drives international trade patterns.[18] Thus, Japan's success in exporting automobiles in the 1970s and 1980s was based not just on the relative abundance of capital, but also on its development of innovative manufacturing technology that enabled it to achieve higher productivity levels in automobile production than other countries that also had abundant capital.

The Product Life-Cycle Theory

Raymond Vernon initially proposed the product life-cycle theory in the mid-1960s.[19] Vernon's theory was based on the observation that for most of the 20th century a very large proportion of the world's new products had been developed by U.S. firms and sold first in the U.S. market (e.g., mass-produced automobiles, televisions, instant cameras, photocopiers, personal computers, and semiconductor chips). To explain this, Vernon argued that the wealth and size of the U.S. market gave U.S. firms a strong incentive to develop new consumer products. In addition, the high cost of U.S. labor gave U.S. firms an incentive to develop cost-saving process innovations.

Just because a new product is developed by a U.S. firm and first sold in the U.S. market, it does not follow that the product must be produced in the United States. It could be produced abroad at some low-cost location and then exported back into the United States. However, Vernon argued that most new products were initially produced in America. Apparently, the pioneering firms believed it was better to keep production facilities close to the market and to the firm's center of decision making, given the uncertainty and risks inherent in introducing new products. Also, the demand for most new products tends to be based on nonprice factors. Consequently, firms can charge relatively high prices for new products, which obviates the need to look for low-cost production sites in other countries.

Vernon went on to argue that early in the life cycle of a typical new product, while demand is starting to grow rapidly in the United States, demand in other advanced countries is limited to high-income groups. The limited initial demand in other advanced countries does not make it worthwhile for firms in those countries to start producing the new product, but it does necessitate some exports from the United States to those countries.

Over time, demand for the new product starts to grow in other advanced countries (e.g., Great Britain, France, Germany, and Japan). As it does, it becomes worthwhile for foreign producers to begin producing for their home markets. In addition, U.S. firms might set up production facilities in those advanced countries where demand is growing. Consequently, production within other advanced countries begins to limit the potential for exports from the United States.

As the market in the United States and other advanced nations matures, the product becomes more standardized, and price becomes the main competitive weapon. As this occurs, cost considerations start to play a greater role in the competitive process. Producers based in advanced countries where labor costs are lower than in the United States (e.g., Italy, Spain) might now be able to export to the United States.

If cost pressures become intense, the process might not stop there. The cycle by which the United States lost its advantage to other advanced countries might be repeated once more, as developing countries (e.g., Thailand) begin to acquire a production advantage over advanced countries. Thus, the locus of global production initially switches from the United States to other advanced nations and then from those nations to developing countries.

The consequence of these trends for the pattern of world trade is that over time the United States switches from being an exporter of the product to an importer of the product as production becomes concentrated in lower-cost foreign locations. Figure 4.5 shows the growth of production and consumption over time in the United States, other advanced countries, and developing countries.

Evaluating the Product Life-Cycle Theory

Historically, the product life-cycle theory is an accurate explanation of international trade patterns. Consider photocopiers; the product was first developed in the early 1960s by Xerox in the United States and sold initially to U.S. users. Originally Xerox exported photocopiers from the United States, primarily to Japan and the advanced countries of Western Europe. As demand began to grow in those countries, Xerox entered into joint ventures to set up production in Japan (Fuji-Xerox) and Great Britain (Rank-Xerox). In addition, once Xerox's patents on the photocopier process expired, other foreign competitors began to enter the market (e.g., Canon in Japan, Olivetti in Italy). As a consequence, exports from the United States declined, and U.S. users began to buy some of their photocopiers from lower-cost foreign sources, particularly Japan. More recently, Japanese companies have found that manufacturing costs are too high in their own country, so they have begun to switch production to developing countries such as Singapore and Thailand. As a result, initially the United States and now several other advanced countries (e.g., Japan and Great Britain) have switched from being exporters of photocopiers to being importers. This evolution in the pattern of international trade in photocopiers is consistent with the predictions of the product life-cycle theory that mature industries tend to go out of the United States and into low-cost assembly locations.

However, the product life-cycle theory is not without weaknesses. Viewed from an Asian or European perspective, Vernon's argument that most new products are devel-

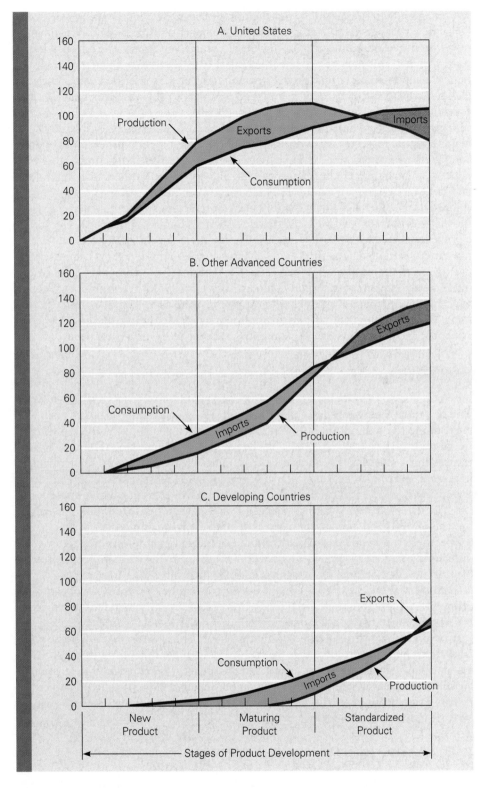

Figure 4.5

The Product Life-Cycle
Theory

Source: Adapted from R. Vernon
and L. T. Wells, *The Economic
Environment of International Business,*
4th ed. (Englewood Cliffs, NJ:
Prentice Hall, 1986).

oped and introduced in the United States seems ethnocentric. Although it may be true
that during U.S. global dominance (from 1945 to 1975), most new products were
introduced in the United States, there have always been important exceptions. These
exceptions appear to have become more common in recent years. Many new products
are now introduced in Japan (e.g., videogame consoles). With the increased global-

ization and integration of the world economy discussed in Chapter 1, a growing number of new products (e.g., laptop computers, compact disks, and digital cameras) are now introduced simultaneously in the United States, Japan, and the advanced European nations. This may be accompanied by globally dispersed production, with particular components of a new product being produced in those locations around the globe where the mix of factor costs and skills is most favorable (as predicted by the theory of comparative advantage).

Consider laptop computers, which were introduced simultaneously in a number of major national markets by Toshiba. Although various components for Toshiba laptop computers are manufactured in Japan (e.g., display screens, memory chips), other components are manufactured in Singapore and Taiwan and still others (e.g., hard drives and microprocessors) are manufactured in the United States. All the components are shipped to Singapore for final assembly, and the completed product is then shipped to the major world markets (the United States, Western Europe, and Japan). The pattern of trade associated with this new product is both different from and more complex than the pattern predicted by Vernon's model. Trying to explain this pattern using the product life-cycle theory would be very difficult. The theory of comparative advantage might better explain why certain components are produced in certain locations and why the final product is assembled in Singapore. Although Vernon's theory may be useful for explaining the pattern of international trade during the brief period of American global dominance, its relevance in the modern world is limited.

The New Trade Theory

The new trade theory began to emerge in the 1970s when a number of economists were questioning the assumption of diminishing returns to specialization used in international trade theory (see Figure 4.3).[20] They argued that increasing returns to specialization might exist in some industries. Economies of scale represent one particularly important source of increasing returns. **Economies of scale** are unit cost reductions associated with a large scale of output. If international trade results in a country specializing in the production of a certain good, and if there are economies of scale in producing that good, then as output of that good expands, unit costs will fall. In such a case, there will be increasing returns to specialization, not diminishing returns! Put differently, as a country produces more of the good, due to the realization of economies of scale, productivity will increase and unit costs will fall.

New trade theory also argues that if the output required to realize significant scale economies represents a substantial proportion of total world demand for that product, the world market may be able to support only a limited number of firms based in a limited number of countries producing that product. Those firms that enter the world market first may gain an advantage that may be difficult for other firms to match. Thus, a country may dominate in the export of a particular product where scale economies are important, and where the volume of output required to gain scale economies represents a significant proportion of world output, because it is home to a firm that was an early mover in this industry.

The Aerospace Example

The commercial aerospace industry, which is currently dominated by just two firms, Boeing and Airbus (although there are several niche players), is a good example of this theory. Economies of scale in this industry come from the ability to spread fixed costs over a large output. The fixed costs of developing a new commercial jet airliner are astronomical. Boeing spent an estimated $5 billion to develop its Boeing 777 jetliner. A major source of scale economies is the ability to spread these fixed costs over a large output.

If Boeing only makes 100 of the Boeing 777, its fixed costs will amount to $50 million per unit (i.e., $5 billion divided by 100). If the variable costs such as labor, equipment, and parts equal $80 million per aircraft, the total cost of each aircraft would be $130 million (i.e., $80 million in per unit variable costs plus $50 million in per unit fixed costs). If Boeing makes 500 of these aircraft, the fixed costs fall to $10 million per unit (i.e., $5 billion divided by 500), bringing the total cost of each aircraft to just $90 million (i.e., $80 million plus $10 million). The economies of scale here are significant, with average unit costs falling by $40 million as output expands from 100 units to 500 units.

In addition to economies of scale, learning effects also exist in this industry. These too may result in increasing returns to specialization. **Learning effects** are cost savings that come from learning by doing. Labor, for example, learns by repetition how best to carry out a task. Labor productivity increases over time and variable unit costs fall as individuals learn the most efficient way to perform a particular task. Learning effects tend to be more significant when a technologically complex task is repeated because there is more to learn. Thus, learning effects will be more significant in an assembly process involving 1,000 complex steps than in an assembly process involving 100 simple steps—and assembling a commercial jetliner involves more complex steps than perhaps any other product. Learning effects were first documented in the aerospace industry where it was found that each time accumulated output of airframes was doubled, unit costs declined to 80 percent of their previous level.[21] Thus, the fourth airframe typically cost only 80 percent of the second airframe to produce, the eighth airframe only 80 percent of the fourth, the 16th only 80 percent of the eighth, and so on. This observation implies that the $80 million in per unit variable costs required to build a 777 will decline over time as output expands, primarily because of gains in labor productivity. Thus, while variable costs per unit might be $80 million by the time 100 aircraft have been manufactured, by the time 500 aircraft have been manufactured, they may have fallen to $60 million per unit.

Combine learning effects with our earlier calculation of the decline in unit fixed costs, and our analysis suggests that as output of 777s expands from 100 to 500 units, unit costs will fall from $130 million ($80 million variable costs and $50 million fixed costs per unit), to $70 million ($60 million variable costs plus $10 million fixed costs per unit). Obviously, increasing returns to specialization are very important in this industry. Just how important they are can be appreciated by the fact that the list price for a new Boeing 777 is about $120 million. Thus, if Boeing sells only 100 aircraft it will not make any money on this product. If it sells 500 aircraft, due to scale economies and learning effects it will make acceptable profits.

World demand is large enough to support only a limited number of aircraft producers at high output levels. Forecasts suggest that the global market for long-range aircraft with a seating capacity of about 300, such as the 777, will be about 1,500 aircraft between 1997 and 2008. If we assume that Boeing has to sell about 500 aircraft to make a decent return on its investment, this suggests that the world market is large enough to support only three producers profitably!

Implications

New trade theory has important implications. The theory suggests that a country may predominate in the export of a good simply because it was lucky enough to have one or more firms among the first to produce that good. Underpinning this argument is the notion of **first-mover advantages,** which are the economic and strategic advantages that accrue to early entrants into an industry.[22] Because they are able to gain economies of scale and learning effects, the early entrants in an industry may get a lock on the world market that discourages subsequent entry. First movers' ability to benefit from increasing returns creates a barrier to entry. In the commercial aircraft industry, for example, the fact that Boeing and Airbus are already in the industry and have the benefits of economies of scale and learning effects discourages new entry and reen-forces the dominance of America and Europe in the trade of commercial jet aircraft. This dominance is further reenforced because global demand may not be sufficient to profitably support another producer in the industry. So although Japanese firms might be able to compete in the market, they have decided not to enter the industry but to ally themselves as major subcontractors with primary producers (e.g., Mitsubishi Heavy Industries is a major subcontractor for Boeing on the 767 and 777 programs).

New trade theory is at variance with the Heckscher-Ohlin theory, which suggests that a country will predominate in the export of a product when it is particularly well endowed with those factors used intensively in its manufacture. New trade theorists argue that the United States leads in exports of commercial jet aircraft not because it is better endowed with the factors of production required to manufacture aircraft, but because one of the first movers in the industry, Boeing, was a U.S. firm. The new trade theory is not at variance with the theory of comparative advantage. Economies of scale and learning effects both increase the efficiency of resource utilization, and hence in-crease productivity. Thus, the new trade theory identifies an important source of com-parative advantage.

It is perhaps too early to say how useful this theory is in explaining trade patterns. The theory is so new that little supporting empirical work has been done. Consistent with the theory, however, a study by Harvard business historian Alfred Chandler suggests the ex-istence of first-mover advantages is an important factor in explaining the dominance of firms from certain nations in certain industries.[23] The number of firms is very limited in many global industries, including the chemical industry, the heavy construction-equipment industry, the heavy truck industry, the tire industry, the consumer electron-ics industry, the jet engine industry, and the computer software industry.

Perhaps the most contentious implication of the new trade theory is the argument that it generates for government intervention and strategic trade policy.[24] New trade theorists stress the role of luck, entrepreneurship, and innovation in giving a firm first-mover advantages. According to this argument, the reason Boeing was the first mover in commercial jet aircraft manufacture—rather than firms like Great Britain's De-Havilland and Hawker Siddely, or Holland's Fokker, all of which could have been—was that Boeing was both lucky and innovative. One way Boeing was lucky is that DeHavilland shot itself in the foot when its Comet jet airliner, introduced two years earlier than Boeing's first jet airliner, the 707, was found to be full of serious techno-logical flaws. Had DeHavilland not made some serious technological mistakes, Great Britain might now be the world's leading exporter of commercial jet aircraft! Boeing's innovativeness was demonstrated by its independent development of the technologi-cal know-how required to build a commercial jet airliner. Several new trade theorists have pointed out, however, that Boeing's R&D was largely paid for by the U.S. gov-ernment; the 707 was a spinoff from a government-funded military program. Herein lies a rationale for government intervention. By the sophisticated and judicious use of subsidies, could a government increase the chances of its domestic firms becoming first movers in newly emerging industries, as the U.S. government apparently did with Boe-ing? If this is possible, and the new trade theory suggests it might be, then we have an economic rationale for a proactive trade policy that is at variance with the free trade prescriptions of the trade theories we have reviewed so far. We will consider the pol-icy implications of this issue in Chapter 5.

National Competitive Advantage: Porter's Diamond

In 1990, Michael Porter of the Harvard Business School published the results of an intensive research effort that attempted to determine why some nations succeed and others fail in international competition.[25] Porter and his team looked at 100 indus-

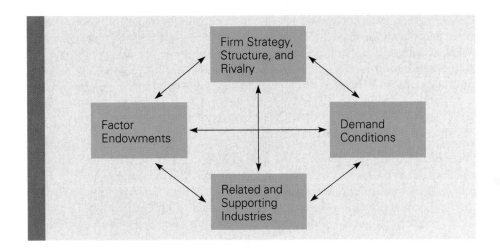

Figure 4.6

Determinants of National
Competitive Advantage:
Porter's Diamond

tries in 10 nations. The book that contains the results of this work, *The Competitive Advantage of Nations*, has made an important contribution to thinking about trade. Like the work of the new trade theorists, Porter's work was driven by a belief that existing theories of international trade told only part of the story. For Porter, the essential task was to explain why a nation achieves international success in a particular industry. Why does Japan do so well in the automobile industry? Why does Switzerland excel in the production and export of precision instruments and pharmaceuticals? Why do Germany and the United States do so well in the chemical industry? These questions cannot be answered easily by the Heckscher-Ohlin theory, and the theory of comparative advantage offers only a partial explanation. The theory of comparative advantage would say that Switzerland excels in the production and export of precision instruments because it uses its resources very productively in these industries. Although this may be correct, this does not explain why Switzerland is more productive in this industry than Great Britain, Germany, or Spain. Porter tries to solve this puzzle.

Porter theorizes that four broad attributes of a nation shape the environment in which local firms compete and these attributes promote or impede the creation of competitive advantage (see Figure 4.6). These attributes are

- *Factor endowments*—a nation's position in factors of production such as skilled labor or the infrastructure necessary to compete in a given industry.
- *Demand conditions*—the nature of home demand for the industry's product or service.
- *Relating and supporting industries*—the presence or absence of supplier industries and related industries that are internationally competitive.
- *Firm strategy, structure, and rivalry*—the conditions governing how companies are created, organized, and managed and the nature of domestic rivalry.

Porter speaks of these four attributes as constituting the *diamond*. He argues that firms are most likely to succeed in industries or industry segments where the diamond is most favorable. He also argues that the diamond is a mutually reinforcing system. The effect of one attribute is contingent on the state of others. For example, Porter argues favorable demand conditions will not result in competitive advantage unless the state of rivalry is sufficient to cause firms to respond to them.

Porter maintains that two additional variables can influence the national diamond in important ways: chance and government. Chance events, such as major innovations, can reshape industry structure and provide the opportunity for one nation's firms to supplant another's. Government, by its choice of policies, can detract from or improve national advantage. For example, regulation can alter home demand conditions, antitrust policies can influence the intensity of rivalry within an industry, and government investments in education can change factor endowments.

Factor Endowments

Factor endowments lie at the center of the Heckscher-Ohlin theory. While Porter does not propose anything radically new, he does analyze the characteristics of factors of production. He recognizes hierarchies among factors, distinguishing between basic factors (e.g., natural resources, climate, location, and demographics) and advanced factors (e.g., communication infrastructure, sophisticated and skilled labor, research facilities, and technological know-how). He argues that advanced factors are the most significant for competitive advantage. Unlike the naturally endowed basic factors, advanced factors are a product of investment by individuals, companies, and governments. Thus, government investments in basic and higher education, by improving the general skill and knowledge level of the population and by stimulating advanced research at higher education institutions, can upgrade a nation's advanced factors.

The relationship between advanced and basic factors is complex. Basic factors can provide an initial advantage that is subsequently reinforced and extended by investment in advanced factors. Conversely, disadvantages in basic factors can create pressures to invest in advanced factors. An obvious example of this phenomenon is Japan, a country that lacks arable land and mineral deposits and yet through investment has built a substantial endowment of advanced factors. Porter notes that Japan's large pool of engineers (reflecting a much higher number of engineering graduates per capita than almost any other nation) has been vital to Japan's success in many manufacturing industries.

Demand Conditions

Porter emphasizes the role home demand plays in upgrading competitive advantage. Firms are typically most sensitive to the needs of their closest customers. Thus, the characteristics of home demand are particularly important in shaping the attributes of domestically made products and in creating pressures for innovation and quality. Porter argues that a nation's firms gain competitive advantage if their domestic consumers are sophisticated and demanding. Such consumers pressure local firms to meet high standards of product quality and to produce innovative products. Porter notes that Japan's sophisticated and knowledgeable buyers of cameras helped stimulate the Japanese camera industry to improve product quality and to introduce innovative models. A similar example can be found in the wireless telephone equipment industry, where sophisticated and demanding local customers in Scandinavia helped push Nokia of Finland and Ericsson of Sweden to invest in cellular phone technology long before demand for cellular phones took off in other developed nations. As a result, Nokia and Ericsson, together with Motorola, today are dominant players in the global cellular telephone equipment industry. Finland has the highest penetration rate for mobile phones in the world with more than 70 percent of Finns owning a wireless handset. The case of Nokia is reviewed in more depth in the accompanying Management Focus.

 ## Related and Supporting Industries

The third broad attribute of national advantage in an industry is the presence of suppliers or related industries that are internationally competitive. The benefits of investments in advanced factors of production by related and supporting industries can spill over into an industry, thereby helping it achieve a strong competitive position internationally. Swedish strength in fabricated steel products (e.g., ball bearings and cutting tools) has drawn on strengths in Sweden's specialty steel industry. Technological leadership in the U.S. semiconductor industry until the mid-1980s provided the basis for U.S. success in personal computers and several other technically advanced electronic products. Similarly, Switzerland's success in pharmaceuticals is closely related to its previous international success in the technologically related dye industry.

One consequence of this process is that successful industries within a country tend to be grouped into clusters of related industries. This was one of the most pervasive findings of Porter's study. One such cluster is the German textile and apparel sector, which includes high-quality cotton, wool, synthetic fibers, sewing machine needles, and a wide range of textile machinery. Such clusters are important, because valuable knowledge can flow between the firms within a geographic cluster, benefiting all within that cluster. Knowledge flows occur when employees move between firms within a region and when national industry associations bring employees from different companies together for regular conferences or workshops.[26]

Firm Strategy, Structure, and Rivalry

The fourth broad attribute of national competitive advantage in Porter's model is the strategy, structure, and rivalry of firms within a nation. Porter makes two important points here. First, different nations are characterized by different management ideologies, which either help them or do not help them to build national competitive advantage. For example, Porter notes the predominance of engineers in top management at German and Japanese firms. He attributes this to these firms' emphasis on improving manufacturing processes and product design. In contrast, Porter notes a predominance of people with finance backgrounds leading many U.S. firms. He links this to U.S. firms' lack of attention to improving manufacturing processes and product design, particularly during the 1970s and 80s. He also argues that the dominance of finance has led to a corresponding overemphasis on maximizing short-term financial returns. According to Porter, one consequence of these different management ideologies has been a relative loss of U.S. competitiveness in those engineering-based industries where manufacturing processes and product design issues are all-important (e.g., the automobile industry).

Porter's second point is that there is a strong association between vigorous domestic rivalry and the creation and persistence of competitive advantage in an industry. Vigorous domestic rivalry induces firms to look for ways to improve efficiency, which makes them better international competitors. Domestic rivalry creates pressures to innovate, to improve quality, to reduce costs, and to invest in upgrading advanced factors. All this helps to create world-class competitors. Porter cites the case of Japan:

> Nowhere is the role of domestic rivalry more evident than in Japan, where it is all-out warfare in which many companies fail to achieve profitability. With goals that stress market share, Japanese companies engage in a continuing struggle to outdo each other. Shares fluctuate markedly. The process is prominently covered in the business press. Elaborate rankings measure which companies are most popular with university graduates. The rate of new product and process development is breathtaking.[27]

A similar point about the stimulating effects of strong domestic competition can be made with regard to the rise of Nokia of Finland to global preeminence in the market for cellular telephone equipment. For details, see the Management Focus.

Evaluating Porter's Theory

Porter contends that the degree to which a nation is likely to achieve international success in a certain industry is a function of the combined impact of factor endowments, domestic demand conditions, related and supporting industries, and domestic rivalry. He argues that the presence of all four components is usually required for this diamond to boost competitive performance (although there are exceptions). Porter also contends that government can influence each of the four components of the diamond

The Rise of Finland's Nokia

The mobile telephone equipment industry is one of the great growth stories of recent years. The number of wireless subscribers has been expanding rapidly. By the end of 2000, there were over 550 million wireless subscribers worldwide, up from less than 10 million in 1990. Forecasts suggest that by 2004, the number could reach 1.4 billion. Three firms currently dominate the global market for wireless equipment (e.g., wireless phones, base station equipment, digital switches): Motorola, Nokia, and Ericsson. Nokia leads the market in mobile telephone sales and is gaining rapidly on Motorola in the network equipment segment.

Nokia's roots are in Finland, not normally a country that comes to mind when one talks about leading-edge technology companies. In the 1980s, Nokia was a rambling Finnish conglomerate with activities that embraced tire manufacturing, paper production, consumer electronics, and telecommunication equipment. By 2000 it had transformed itself into a focused telecommunications equipment manufacturer with a global reach, sales of $24 billion, and earnings of $4.5 billion. How has this former conglomerate emerged to take a global leadership position in wireless telecommunication equipment? Much of the answer lies in the history, geography, and political economy of Finland and its Nordic neighbors.

The story starts in 1981 when the Nordic nations got together to create the world's first international mobile telephone network. They had good reason to become pioneers; in the sparsely populated and inhospitably cold areas, it cost far too much to lay down a traditional wireline telephone service. Yet the same geographic features make telecommunications all the more valuable; people driving through the Arctic winter and owners of remote northern houses need a telephone to summon help if things go wrong. As a result, Sweden, Norway, and Finland became the first nations to take wireless telecommunications seriously. They found, for example, that while it cost up to $800 per subscriber to bring a traditional wireline service to remote locations in the far north, the same locations could be linked by wireless telephones for only $500 per person. As a consequence, by 1994, 12 percent of people in Scandinavia owned wireless phones, compared with less than 6 percent in the United States, the world's second most developed market. This leadership has continued. In mid-2000 some 70 percent of the population in Finland owned a wireless phone, compared with 30 percent in the United States.

either positively or negatively. Factor endowments can be affected by subsidies, policies toward capital markets, policies toward education, and so on. Government can shape domestic demand through local product standards or with regulations that mandate or influence buyer needs. Government policy can influence supporting and related industries through regulation and influence firm rivalry through such devices as capital market regulation, tax policy, and antitrust laws.

If Porter is correct, we would expect his model to predict the pattern of international trade that we observe in the real world. Countries should be exporting products from those industries where all four components of the diamond are favorable, while importing in those areas where the components are not favorable. Is he correct? We simply do not know. Porter's theory has not yet been subjected to independent empirical testing. Much about the theory rings true, but the same can be said for the new trade theory, the theory of comparative advantage, and the Heckscher-Ohlin theory. It may be that each of these theories, which complement each other, explains something about the pattern of international trade.

Implications for Business

Why does all this matter for business? There are at least three main implications for international businesses of the material discussed in this chapter: location implications, first-mover implications, and policy implications.

Nokia, as a long-time telecommunication equipment supplier, was well positioned to take advantage of this development. Other forces were also at work in Finland that helped Nokia develop its competitive edge. Unlike virtually every other developed nation, Finland has never had a national telephone monopoly. Instead, the country's telephone services have long been provided by about 50 autonomous local telephone companies, whose elected boards set prices by referendum (which naturally means low prices). This army of independent and cost-conscious telephone service providers prevented Nokia from taking anything for granted in its home country. With typical Finnish pragmatism, they were willing to buy from the lowest-cost supplier, whether that was Nokia, Ericsson, Motorola, or someone else. This situation contrasted sharply with that prevailing in most developed nations until the late 1980s and early 1990s; domestic telephone monopolies typically purchased equipment from a dominant local supplier or made it themselves. Nokia responded to this competitive pressure by doing everything possible to drive down its manufacturing costs while still staying at the leading edge of wireless technology.

The consequences of these forces are clear. Nokia is now the leader in digital wireless technology, which is the wave of the future. Many now regard Finland as the lead market for wireless telephone services. If you want to see the future of wireless, you don't go to New York or San Francisco, you go to Helsinki, where Finns use their wireless handsets not just to talk to each other, but also to browse the Web, execute e-commerce transactions, control household heating and lighting systems, or purchase Coke from a wireless-enabled vending machine. Nokia has gained this lead because Scandinavia started switching to digital technology five years before the rest of the world. Spurred on by its cost-conscious Finnish customers, Nokia now has the lowest cost structure of any cellular phone equipment manufacturer in the world, making it a more profitable enterprise than Motorola, its leading global rival. Nokia's operating margins in 2000 were 20 percent, compared with 6.4 percent at Motorola.

Sources: "Lessons from the Frozen North," *The Economist*, October 8, 1994, pp. 76–77; G. Edmondson, "Grabbing Markets from the Giants," *Business Week, Special Issue: 21st Century Capitalism*, 1995, pp. 156; company news releases; "A Finnish Fable," *The Economist*, October 14, 2000; "To the Finland Base Station," *The Economist*, October 9, 1999, pp. 23–27; and "A Survey of Telecommunications," *The Economist*, October 9, 1999.

Location Implications

Underlying most of the theories we have discussed is the notion that different countries have particular advantages in different productive activities. Thus, from a profit perspective, it makes sense for a firm to disperse its productive activities to those countries where, according to the theory of international trade, they can be performed most efficiently. If design can be performed most efficiently in France, that is where design facilities should be located; if the manufacture of basic components can be performed most efficiently in Singapore, that is where they should be manufactured; and if final assembly can be performed most efficiently in China, that is where final assembly should be performed. The result is a global web of productive activities, with different activities being performed in different locations around the globe depending on considerations of comparative advantage, factor endowments, and the like. If the firm does not do this, it may find itself at a competitive disadvantage relative to firms that do.

Consider the production of a laptop computer, a process with four major stages: (1) basic research and development of the product design, (2) manufacture of standard electronic components (e.g., memory chips), (3) manufacture of advanced components (e.g., flat-top color display screens and microprocessors), and (4) final assembly. Basic R&D requires a pool of highly skilled and educated workers with good backgrounds in microelectronics. The two countries with a comparative advantage in basic microelectronics R&D and design are Japan and the United States, so most producers of laptop computers locate their R&D facilities in one, or both, of these countries. (Apple, IBM, Motorola,

Texas Instruments, Toshiba, and Sony all have major R&D facilities in both Japan and the United States.)

The manufacture of standard electronic components is a capital-intensive process requiring semiskilled labor, and cost pressures are intense. The best locations for such activities today are places such as Singapore, Taiwan, Malaysia, and South Korea. These countries have pools of relatively skilled, low-cost labor. Thus, many producers of laptop computers have standard components, such as memory chips, produced at these locations.

The manufacture of advanced components such as microprocessors and display screens is a capital-intensive process requiring skilled labor. Because cost pressures are not so intense at this stage, these components can be—and are—manufactured in countries with high labor costs that also have pools of highly skilled labor (primarily Japan and the United States).

Finally, assembly is a relatively labor-intensive process requiring only low-skilled labor, and cost pressures are intense. As a result, final assembly may be carried out in a country such as Mexico, which has an abundance of low-cost, low-skilled labor.

A laptop computer produced by a U.S. manufacturer may be designed in California, have its standard components produced in Taiwan and Singapore, its advanced components produced in Japan and the United States, its final assembly in Mexico, and be sold in the United States or elsewhere in the world. By dispersing production activities to different locations around the globe, the U.S. manufacturer is taking advantage of the differences between countries identified by the various theories of international trade.

First-Mover Implications

According to the new trade theory, firms that establish a first-mover advantage with regard to the production of a particular new product may subsequently dominate global trade in that product. This is particularly true in industries where the global market can profitably support only a limited number of firms, such as the aerospace market, but early commitments also seem to be important in less concentrated industries such as the market for cellular telephone equipment (see the Management Focus on Nokia). For the individual firm, the clear message is that it pays to invest substantial financial resources in trying to build a first-mover, or early-mover, advantage, even if that means several years of substantial losses before a new venture becomes profitable. Although the details of how to achieve this are beyond the scope of this book, many publications offer strategies for exploiting first-mover advantages.[28]

Policy Implications

The theories of international trade also matter to international businesses because firms are major players on the international trade scene. Business firms produce exports, and business firms import the products of other countries. Because of their pivotal role in international trade, businesses can exert a strong influence on government trade policy, lobbying to promote free trade or trade restrictions. The theories of international trade claim that promoting free trade is generally in the best interests of a country, although it may not always be in the best interest of an individual firm. Many firms recognize this and lobby for open markets.

For example, when the U.S. government announced in 1991 its intention to place a tariff on Japanese imports of liquid crystal display (LCD) screens, IBM and Apple Computer protested strongly. Both IBM and Apple pointed out that (1) Japan was the lowest-cost source of LCD screens, (2) they used these screens in their own laptop computers, and (3) the proposed tariff, by increasing the cost of LCD screens, would increase the cost of laptop computers produced by IBM and Apple, thus making them less competitive in the world market. In other words, the tariff, designed to protect U.S. firms, would be self-defeating. In response to these pressures, the U.S. government reversed its posture.

Unlike IBM and Apple, however, businesses do not always lobby for free trade. In the United States, for example, restrictions on imports of automobiles, machine tools, textiles, and steel are the result of direct pressure by U.S. firms on the government. In some cases, the government responded by getting foreign companies to agree to "voluntary" restrictions on their imports, using the implicit threat of more comprehensive formal trade barriers to get them to adhere to these agreements. In other cases, the government used what are called "antidumping" actions to justify tariffs on imports from other nations (these mechanisms will be discussed in detail in the next chapter).

As predicted by international trade theory, many of these agreements have been self-defeating, such as the voluntary restriction on machine tool imports agreed to in 1985. Due to limited import competition from more efficient foreign suppliers, the prices of machine tools in the United States rose to higher levels than would have prevailed under free trade. Because machine tools are used throughout the manufacturing industry, the result was to increase the costs of U.S. manufacturing in general, creating a corresponding loss in world market competitiveness. Shielded from international competition by import barriers, the U.S. machine tool industry had no incentive to increase its efficiency. Consequently, it lost many of its export markets to more efficient foreign competitors. As a consequence of this misguided action, the U.S. machine tool industry shrunk during the period when the agreement was in force. For anyone schooled in international trade theory, this was not surprising.[29]

Finally, Porter's theory of national competitive advantage also contains policy implications. Porter's theory suggests that it is in the best interest of business for a firm to invest in upgrading advanced factors of production; for example, to invest in better training for its employees and to increase its commitment to research and development. It is also in the best interests of business to lobby the government to adopt policies that have a favorable impact on each component of the national diamond. Thus, according to Porter, businesses should urge government to increase investment in education, infrastructure, and basic research (since all these enhance advanced factors) and to adopt policies that promote strong competition within domestic markets (since this makes firms stronger international competitors, according to Porter's findings).

Chapter Summary

This chapter has reviewed a number of theories that explain why it is beneficial for a country to engage in international trade and has explained the pattern of international trade that we observe in the world economy. We have seen how the theories of Smith, Ricardo, and Heckscher-Ohlin all make strong cases for unrestricted free trade. In contrast, the mercantilist doctrine and, to a lesser extent, the new trade theory can be interpreted to support government intervention to promote exports through subsidies and to limit imports through tariffs and quotas.

In explaining the pattern of international trade, the second objective of this chapter, we have seen that with the exception of mercantilism, which is silent on this issue, the different theories offer largely complementary explanations. Although no one theory may explain the apparent pattern of international trade, taken together, the theory of comparative advantage, the Heckscher-Ohlin theory, the product life-cycle theory, the new trade theory, and Porter's theory of national competitive advantage do suggest which factors are important. Comparative advantage tells us that productivity differences are important; Heckscher-Ohlin tells us that factor endowments matter; the product life-cycle theory tells us that where a new product is introduced is important; the new trade theory tells us that increasing returns to specialization and first-mover advantages matter; and Porter tells us that all these factors may be important insofar as they impact the four components of the national diamond.

The following points have been made in this chapter:

1. Mercantilists argued that it was in a country's best interests to run a balance-of-trade surplus. They viewed trade as a zero-sum game, in which one country's gains cause losses for other countries.

2. The theory of absolute advantage suggests that countries differ in their ability to produce goods efficiently. The theory suggests that a country should specialize in producing goods in areas where it has an absolute advantage and import goods in areas where other countries have absolute advantages.

3. The theory of comparative advantage suggests that it makes sense for a country to specialize in producing those goods that it can produce most efficiently, while buying goods that it can produce relatively less efficiently from other countries—even if that means buying goods from other countries that it could produce more efficiently itself.

4. The theory of comparative advantage suggests that unrestricted free trade brings about increased world production; that is, that trade is a positive-sum game.

5. The theory of comparative advantage also suggests that opening a country to free trade stimulates economic growth, which creates dynamic gains from trade. The empirical evidence seems to be consistent with this claim.

6. The Heckscher-Ohlin theory argues that the pattern of international trade is determined by differences in factor endowments. It predicts that countries will export those goods that make intensive use of locally abundant factors and will import goods that make intensive use of factors that are locally scarce.

7. The product life-cycle theory suggests that trade patterns are influenced by where a new product is introduced. In an increasingly integrated global economy, the product life-cycle theory seems to be less predictive than it was between 1945 and 1975.

8. The new trade theory argues that in those industries where substantial economies of scale imply that the world market will profitably support only a few firms, countries may predominate in the export of certain products simply because they had a firm that was a first mover in that industry.

9. Some new trade theorists have promoted the idea of strategic trade policy. The argument is that government, by the sophisticated and judicious use of subsidies, might be able to increase the chances of domestic firms becoming first movers in newly emerging industries.

10. Porter's theory of national competitive advantage suggests that the pattern of trade is influenced by four attributes of a nation: (a) factor endowments, (b) domestic demand conditions, (c) relating and supporting industries, and (d) firm strategy, structure, and rivalry.

11. Theories of international trade are important to an individual business firm primarily because they can help the firm decide where to locate its various production activities.

12. Firms involved in international trade can and do exert a strong influence on government policy toward trade. By lobbying government, business firms can promote free trade or trade restrictions.

Critical Discussion Questions

1. Mercantilism is a bankrupt theory that has no place in the modern world. Discuss.

2. China is a neomercantilist nation. It protects industries where it has no competitive advantage in the world economy, while demanding that other countries open up those markets where Chinese producers have a competitive advantage. Discuss this statement.

3. Unions in developed nations often oppose imports from low-wage countries and advocate trade barriers to protect jobs from what they often characterize as "unfair" import competition. Is such competition "unfair"? Do you think that this argument is in the best interests of (a) the unions, (b) the people they represent, and/or (c) the country as a whole?

4. Drawing on the theory of comparative advantage to support your arguments, outline the case for free trade.

5. What are the potential costs of adopting a free trade regime? Do you think governments should do anything to reduce these costs? What?

6. Using the new trade theory and Porter's theory of national competitive advantage, outline the case for government policies that would build national competitive advantage in a particular industry.

What kinds of policies would you recommend that the government adopt? Are these policies at variance with the basic free trade philosophy?

7. The world's poorest countries are at a competitive disadvantage in every sector of their economies. They have nothing to export. They have no capital; their land is of poor quality; they often have too many people given available work opportunities; and they are poorly educated. Free trade cannot possibly be in the interests of such nations! Discuss.

8. In general, policies designed to limit competition from low-cost foreign competitors do not help a country to achieve greater economic growth. Discuss this statement.

The Rise of the Indian Software Industry

Closing Case

As a relatively poor country, India is not normally thought off as a nation capable of building a major presence in a high-technology industry, such as computer software. In little over a decade, however, the Indian software industry has astounded its skeptics and emerged from obscurity to become an important force in the global software industry. Between 1991–1992 and 1999–2000, sales of Indian software companies grew at a compound rate in excess of 60 percent annually. In 1991–1992, the industry had sales totaling $388 million. By 2000 they were around $6 billion. By the late 1990s, more than 900 software companies in India employed 200,000 software engineers, the third largest concentration of such talent in the world.

Much of this growth was powered by exports. In 1985, Indian software exports were worth less than $10 million. They surged to $1.8 billion in 1997 and hit a record $4 billion in 2000. The future looks very bright. Powered by continued export-led growth, India's National Association of Software and Service Companies projects that total software revenues generated by Indian companies will hit $28 billion by 2004–2005 and $87 billion by 2007–2008. As a testament to this growth, many foreign software companies are now investing heavily in Indian software development operations including Microsoft, IBM, Oracle, and Computer Associates, the four largest U.S.-based software houses. Equally significantly, two out of every five global companies now source their software services from India.

Most of the current growth of the Indian software industry has been based on contract or project-based work for foreign clients. Many Indian companies, for example, maintain applications for their clients, convert code, or migrate software from one platform to another. Increasingly, Indian companies are also involved in important

development projects for foreign clients. For example, TCS, India's largest software company, has an alliance with Ernst & Young under which TCS will develop and maintain customized software for Ernst & Young's global clients. TCS also has a development alliance with Microsoft under which the company developed a paperless National Share Depositary system for the Indian stock market based on Microsoft's Windows NT operating system and SQL Server database technology. Indian companies are also moving aggressively into e-commerce projects. From almost zero in 1997, e-commerce or e-business projects now account for about 10 percent of all software development and service work in India and are projected to reach 20 percent within two years.

The Indian software industry has emerged despite a poor information technology infrastructure. The installed base of personal computers in India stood at just 3 million in 1999, and this in a nation of nearly 1 billion people. With just 22 telephone lines per 1,000 people, India has one of the lowest penetration rates for fixed telephone lines in Asia, if not the world. Internet connections numbered less than 100,000 in 1998, compared to 60 million in the United States. But sales of personal computers are starting to take off, and the rapid growth of mobile telephones in India's main cities is to some extent compensating for the lack of fixed telephone lines.

In explaining the success of their industry, India's software entrepreneurs point to a number of factors. Although the general level of education in India is low, India's important middle class is highly educated and its top educational institutions are world class. Also, India has always emphasized engineering. Another great plus from an international perceptive is that English is the working language throughout much of middle-class India —a remnant from the days of the British raja. Then there is the wage rate. American software engineers are increasingly scarce, and the basic salary has been driven up to one of the highest for any occupational group in the country, with entry-level programmers earning $70,000 per year. An entry-level programmer in India, in contrast, starts at around $5,000 per year, which is very low by international standards but high by Indian standards. Salaries for programmers are rising rapidly in India, but so is productivity. In 1992, productivity was around $21,000 per software engineer. By 1997, the figure had risen to $45,000. As a consequence of these factors, by 2000 work done in India for U.S. software companies amounted to $25 to $35 an hour, compared to $75 to $100 per hour for software development done in the United States.

Another factor helping India is that satellite communications have removed distance as an obstacle to doing business for foreign clients. Because software is nothing more than a stream of zeros and ones, it can be transported at the speed of light and negligible cost to any point in the world. In a world of instant communication, India's geographical position between Europe and the United States has given it a time zone advantage. Indian companies have been able to exploit the rapidly expanding international market for outsourced software services, including the expanding market for remote maintenance. Indian engineers can fix software bugs, upgrade systems, or process data overnight while their users in Western companies are asleep.

To maintain their competitive position, Indian software companies are now investing heavily in training and leading-edge programming skills. They have also been enthusiastic adopters of international quality standards, particularly ISO 9000 certification. Indian companies are also starting to make forays into the application and shrink-wrapped software business, primarily with applications aimed at the domestic market. It may only be a matter of time, however, before Indian companies start to compete head to head with companies such as Microsoft, Oracle, PeopleSoft, and SAP in the applications business.

Sources: P. Taylor, "Poised for Global Growth," *Financial Times: India's Software Industry*, December 3, 1997, pp. 1, 8; P. Taylor, "An Industry on the Up and Up," *Financial Times: India's Software Industry*, December 3, 1997, p. 3; Krishna Guha, "Strategic Alliances with Global Partners," *Financial Times: India's Software Industry*, December 3, 1997, p. 6; "Indian SW Industry to Touch $13 Billion in 2001–02," *Computers Today*, December 15, 2000, pp. 14–17; and United Nations, *Human Development Report*, (New York: Oxford University Press, 2000), and Table 12.

Case Discussion Questions

1. To what extent does the theory of comparative advantage explain the rise of the Indian software industry?

2. To what extent does the Heckscher-Ohlin theory explain the rise of the Indian software industry?

3. Use Michael Porter's diamond to analyze the rise of the Indian software industry. Does this analysis help explain the rise of this industry?

4. Which of the above theories—comparative advantage, Heckscher-Ohlin, or Porter's—gives the best explanation of the rise of the Indian software industry? Why?

Notes

1. H. W. Spiegel, *The Growth of Economic Thought* (Durham, NC: Duke University Press, 1991).

2. G. de Jonquieres, "Mercantilists Are Treading on Thin Ice," *Financial Times*, July 3, 1994, p. 16.

3. Jarl Hagelstam, "Mercantilism Still Influences Practical Trade Policy at the End of the Twentieth Century," *Journal of World Trade*, 1991, pp. 95–105.

4. S. Hollander, *The Economics of David Ricardo* (Buffalo: The University of Toronto Press, 1979).

5. D. Ricardo, *The Principles of Political Economy and Taxation* (Homewood, IL: Irwin, 1967, first published in 1817).

6. For example, R. Dornbusch, S. Fischer, and P. Samuelson, "Comparative Advantage: Trade and Payments in a Ricardian Model with a Continuum of Goods," *American Economic Review* 67 (December 1977), pp. 823–39.

7. B. Balassa, "An Empirical Demonstration of Classic Comparative Cost Theory," *Review of Economics and Statistics*, 1963, pp. 231–38.

8. See P. R. Krugman, "Is Free Trade Passé?" *Journal of Economic Perspectives* 1 (Fall 1987), pp. 131–44.

9. P. Samuelson, "The Gains from International Trade Once Again," *Economic Journal* 72 (1962), pp. 820–29.

10. J. D. Sachs and A. Warner, "Economic Reform and the Process of Global Integration," *Brookings Papers on Economic Activity*, 1995, pp. 1–96.

11. Sachs and Warner, "Economic Reform and the Process of Global Integration," pp. 35–36.

12. J. A. Frankel and D. Romer, "Does Trade Cause Growth?" *American Economic Review* 89, no. 3 (June 1999), pp. 379–99.

13. A recent skeptical review of the empirical work on the relationship between trade and growth questions these results. See Francisco Rodriguez and Dani Rodrik, "Trade Policy and Economic Growth: A Skeptics Guide to the Cross-National Evidence," *National Bureau of Economic Research*, Working Paper Series Number 7081, April 1999. Even these authors, however, cannot find any evidence that trade hurts economic growth or income levels.

14. B. Ohlin, *Interregional and International Trade* (Cambridge: Harvard University Press, 1933). For a summary, see R. W. Jones and J. P. Neary, "The Positive Theory of International Trade," in *Handbook of International Economics*, R. W. Jones and P. B. Kenen, eds. (Amsterdam: North Holland, 1984).

15. W. Leontief, "Domestic Production and Foreign Trade: The American Capital Position Re-Examined," *Proceedings of the American Philosophical Society* 97 (1953), pp. 331–49.

16. R. M. Stern and K. Maskus, "Determinants of the Structure of U.S. Foreign Trade," *Journal of International Economics* 11 (1981), pp. 207–44.

17. See H. P. Bowen, E. E. Leamer, and L. Sveikayskas, "Multicountry, Multifactor Tests of the Factor Abundance Theory," *American Economic Review* 77 (1987), pp. 791–809.

18. D. Trefler, "The Case of the Missing Trade and Other Mysteries," *American Economic Review* 85 (December 1995), pp. 1029–46.

19. R. Vernon, "International Investments and International Trade in the Product Life Cycle," *Quarterly Journal of Economics*, May 1966, pp. 190–207, and R. Vernon and L. T. Wells, *The Economic Environment of International Business*, 4th ed. (Englewood Cliffs, NJ: Prentice Hall, 1986).

20. For a good summary of this literature, see E. Helpman and P. Krugman, *Market Structure and Foreign Trade: Increasing Returns, Imperfect Competition, and the International Economy* (Boston: MIT Press, 1985). Also see P. Krugman, "Does the New Trade Theory Require a New Trade Policy?" *World Economy* 15, no. 4, (1992), pp. 423–41.

21. A. A. Alchian, "Reliability of Progress Curves in Airframe Production," *Econometrica* 31 (1963), pp. 679–93.

22. M. B. Lieberman and D. B. Montgomery "First-Mover Advantages," *Strategic Management Journal* 9 (Summer 1988), pp. 41–58.

23. A. D. Chandler, *Scale and Scope* (New York: Free Press, 1990).

24. Krugman, "Does the New Trade Theory Require a New Trade Policy?"

25. M. E. Porter, *The Competitive Advantage of Nations* (New York: Free Press, 1990). For a good review of this book, see R. M. Grant, "Porter's Competitive Advantage of Nations: An Assessment," *Strategic Management Journal* 12 (1991), pp. 535–48.

26. B. Kogut, ed., *Country Competitiveness: Technology and the Organizing of Work* (New York: Oxford University Press, 1993).

27. Porter, *The Competitive Advantage of Nations*, p. 121.

28. Lieberman and Montgomery, "First-Mover Advantages."

29. C. A. Hamilton, "Building Better Machine Tools," *Journal of Commerce*, October 30, 1991, p. 8, and "Manufacturing Trouble," *The Economist*, October 12, 1991, p. 71.

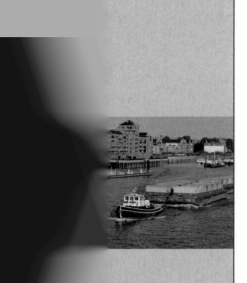

The Political
Economy of
International
Trade

Under the terms of a long-standing agreement, banana producers from 71 countries in Africa, the Caribbean, and the Pacific have been granted preferential access to the European Union (EU) market. Most of the countries are former colonies of either Great Britain or France, both members of the EU. The original goal of the agreement was to help these developing nations by making it easier for them to sell bananas in the EU. Some of the developing nations that have benefited from this arrangement are highly dependent on banana exports and claim their economies would be devastated without the agreement, which requires the EU to erect trade barriers against imports from other nations, particularly those in Latin America. Under the agreement, up to 875,000 tons of Caribbean, African, and Pacific bananas can enter the EU each year duty free. In contrast, the EU has imposed tariffs of 15 to 20 percent by value on the first 2.5 million tons of banana imports from Latin America. The EU has also placed prohibitive tariffs on any imports from Latin America in excess of 2.5 million tons, in effect capping imports at that amount. These tariffs result in consumers within the EU paying higher prices for bananas. According to a study by one French economist, restrictions on banana imports cost European consumers up to $2 billion a year, or 55 cents per kilogram of bananas, some two-thirds of which ends up as bigger profits for European fruit distributors.

Two leading U.S.-based growers and marketers of bananas, Chiquita Brands and Dole Food Co., complained to the U.S. government in 1995 that the EU's preferential banana agreement violated World Trade Organization rules and shut them out of the lucrative EU market. The U.S. government agreed to appeal on behalf of the banana industry to the WTO. The United States was joined in its complaint by four banana-producing nations in Latin America—Ecuador, Guatemala, Honduras, and Mexico. Under the terms of the 1995 global trade agreement that established the World Trade Organization, the WTO has the right to review complaints bought by one member state against another. If a WTO arbitration panel finds that a nation's trade policies violate WTO rules, it can recommend changes in those policies. If those recommenda-

tions are not adopted, the injured party has the right to impose punitive tariffs on imports from the violating nation or, in this case, trade bloc. This dispute was the first to involve the United States and the EU. It was widely seen as a test of the WTO's credibility. Would the WTO issue an unbiased ruling? More importantly, would it be able to make the ruling stick?

Defenders of the agreement claimed the EU was lending a helping hand to impoverished developing nations. They painted the dispute as a confrontation that unjustly pitted the interests of U.S. banana multinationals against the interests of these developing nations (ignoring the fact that European consumers are also hurt by these restrictions). The WTO arbitration panel was not convinced by these arguments. It issued its first ruling on the banana issue in late 1997. The EU banana agreement was found to be in violation of WTO rules and would have to be changed. The EU was given until January 1, 1999, to bring its regime in line with WTO rules. Although the EU did make some changes, neither the United States nor several of its Latin American partners saw these as going far enough. Nor did most independent observers. In February 1999, the United States sought WTO permission to use retaliatory trade measures against the EU, hoping to put economic pressure on the EU to change the banana agreement. When the EU failed to move on the issue, the WTO authorized the United States to impose sanctions of $191.4 million annually on European imports into the United States. These took the form of import tariffs amounting to 100 percent of the value of a range of European goods including salt, cashmere clothing items, packaging products, and lead acid batteries.

A year later the sanctions were still in force. While the EU made some effort to change its banana agreement to bring it in line with WTO rules, internal political conflicts within the EU had stalled progress. In the meantime, developing nations allied with the EU continued to be given preferential access to the EU market, while Latin American banana producers are facing the same hurdles they did in 1995. In November 2000, Beamglow, a small British packaging company, announced it would sue the EU Commission for damages after losing one-third of its U.S.

sales due to the imposition of the 100 percent punitive tariff. About the same time, a number of small companies that sold cashmere products to the United States were also said to be considering similar legal action.

Sources: L. Kemeny, "Banana War Slips into the Courts," *Sunday Times,* November 5, 2000; E. Drew, "Deadlock Continues in Banana Wars," *African Business,* June 2000; "The Beef over Bananas," *The Economist,* March 6, 1999, pp. 65–67; "Stealing from the Poor," *The Economist,* April 24, 1999, pp. 70–71; and "Europe's Burden," *The Economist,* May 22, 1999, pp. 84–85.

▮ Introduction

Our review of the classical trade theories of Smith, Ricardo, and Heckscher-Ohlin in Chapter 4 showed us that, in a world without trade barriers, trade patterns are determined by the relative productivity of different factors of production in different countries. Countries will specialize in products that they can make most efficiently, while importing products that they can produce less efficiently. Chapter 4 also laid out the intellectual case for free trade. Remember, **free trade** refers to a situation where a government does not attempt to restrict what its citizens can buy from another country or what they can sell to another country. As we saw in Chapter 4, the theories of Smith, Ricardo, and Heckscher-Ohlin predict that the consequences of free trade include both static economic gains (because free trade supports a higher level of domestic consumption and more efficient utilization of resources) and dynamic economic gains (because free trade stimulates economic growth and the creation of wealth).

In this chapter we look at the political reality of international trade. The political reality is that while many nations are nominally committed to free trade, they tend to intervene in international trade to protect the interests of politically important groups. The opening case illustrates the nature of such political realities. The case describes how the European Union (EU) erected trade barriers against the importation of bananas from Latin America, most of which are marketed by U.S. multinational enterprises. The EU erected these barriers for political reasons. It wanted to help a number of developing countries that were once former colonies of two prominent members of the EU: Great Britain and France. However, the EU is also a member of the World Trade Organization and has to abide by its rules if it wants to enjoy the benefits of membership. Unfortunately for the EU, the WTO ruled that the banana tariff is illegal. This decision placed the EU between a rock and a hard place. On the one hand, the EU is under considerable pressure from powerful political interests within Europe to maintain the ban. On the other hand, the EU would like to abide by the rules of the WTO— rules that have brought significant benefits to the EU (as we shall discuss later in this chapter). For now, the EU has chosen to live with this dilemma and bear the costs in terms of the punitive retaliatory tariffs on EU imports into the United States that have been authorized by the WTO. This decision undermines the authority of the World Trade Organization and raises trade tensions between the United States and the EU, tensions that some fear might lead to a trade war between the two entities.

In this chapter, we explore the political and economic reasons that governments have for intervening in international trade. When governments intervene, they often do so by restricting imports of goods and services into their nation, while adopting policies that promote exports. Normally their motives are to protect domestic producers and jobs from foreign competition while increasing the foreign market for products of domestic producers. However, in recent years, "social" issues have intruded into the decision-making calculus. In the United States, for example, there is a movement to try to ban imports of goods from countries that do not abide by the same labor, health, and environmental regulations as the United States.

We start this chapter by describing the range of policy instruments that governments use to intervene in international trade. This is followed by a detailed review of the various political and economic motives that governments have for intervention.

In the third section of this chapter we consider how the case for free trade stands up in view of the various justifications given for government intervention in international trade. Then we look at the emergence of the modern international trading system, which is based on the General Agreement on Tariffs and Trade (GATT) and its successor, the World Trade Organization (WTO). The GATT and WTO are the creations of a series of multinational treaties. The most recent was completed in 1995, involved more than 120 countries, and resulted in the creation of the WTO. The purpose of these treaties has been to lower barriers to the free flow of goods and services between nations. Like the GATT before it, the WTO promotes free trade by limiting the ability of national governments to adopt policies that restrict imports into their nations. In the final section of this chapter, we discuss the implications of this material for business practice.

Instruments of Trade Policy

Trade policy uses seven main instruments: tariffs, subsidies, import quotas, voluntary export restraints, local content requirements, administrative policies, and antidumping duties. Tariffs are the oldest and simplest instrument of trade policy. As we shall see later in this chapter, they are also the instrument that GATT and WTO have been most successful in limiting. A fall in tariff barriers in recent decades has been accompanied by a rise in nontariff barriers, such as subsidies, quotas, voluntary export restraints, and antidumping duties.

Tariffs

A **tariff** is a tax levied on imports. Tariffs fall into two categories. **Specific tariffs** are levied as a fixed charge for each unit of a good imported (for example, $3 per barrel of oil). **Ad valorem tariffs** are levied as a proportion of the value of the imported good. The European Union has imposed such a tariff on imports of bananas from Latin America; the tariff amounts to 15 to 20 percent by value on the first 2.5 million tons of imports of bananas from Latin America (see the opening case).

A tariff raises the cost of imported products. In most cases, tariffs are put in place to protect domestic producers from foreign competition. In the mid-1980s when the U.S. automobile industry was losing share to Japanese competitors, the U.S. government placed a 25 percent by value tariff on the importation of light trucks into the United States (light trucks include sport utility vehicles). The tariff raised the price of light trucks imported into the United States and gave U.S. automobile companies some protection from foreign competition (although a cynic might note that all the tariff did was speed up the plans of European and Japanese automobile companies to build light trucks in the United States). While the principal objective of most tariffs is to protect domestic producers and employees against foreign competition, they also raise revenue for the government. Until the income tax was introduced, for example, the U.S. government raised most of its revenues from tariffs.

The important thing to understand about a tariff is who suffers and who gains. The government gains, because the tariff increases government revenues. Domestic producers gain, because the tariff affords them some protection against foreign competitors by increasing the cost of imported foreign goods. Consumers lose because they must pay more for certain imports. Whether the gains to the government and domestic producers exceed the loss to consumers depends on various factors such as the amount of the tariff, the importance of the imported good to domestic consumers, the number of jobs saved in the protected industry, and so on.

Although detailed consideration of these issues is beyond the scope of this book, two conclusions that can be derived from a more advanced analysis.[1] First, tariffs are unambiguously pro-producer and anti-consumer. While they protect producers from foreign competitors, this restriction of supply also raises domestic prices. Thus, as noted in the opening case, the tariff on banana imports into the European Union has raised prices for bananas in the EU, and cost consumers some $2 billion a year. Another study by Japanese economists calculated that tariffs on imports of foodstuffs, cosmetics, and chemicals into Japan in 1989 cost the average Japanese consumer about $890 per year in the form of higher prices.[2] Almost all studies that have looked at this issue find that import tariffs impose significant costs on domestic consumers in the form of higher prices.[3] For another example, see the accompanying Country Focus, which looks at the cost to U.S. consumers of tariffs on imports into the United States.

Second, tariffs reduce the overall efficiency of the world economy. They reduce efficiency because a protective tariff encourages domestic firms to produce products at home that, in theory, could be produced more efficiently abroad. The consequence is an inefficient utilization of resources. For example, tariffs on the importation of rice into South Korea have caused the land of South Korean rice farmers to be used in an unproductive manner. It would make more sense for the South Koreans to purchase their rice from lower-cost foreign producers and to utilize the land now employed in rice production in some other way, such as growing foodstuffs that cannot be produced more efficiently elsewhere or for residential and industrial purposes.

Subsidies

A **subsidy** is a government payment to a domestic producer. Subsidies take many forms including cash grants, low-interest loans, tax breaks, and government equity participation in domestic firms. By lowering production costs, subsidies help domestic producers in two ways: they help them compete against foreign imports and they help them gain export markets.

Agriculture tends to be one of the largest beneficiaries of subsidies in most countries. In 1998, for example, developed countries paid some $360 billion in support to farmers. In Japan, agricultural subsidies amounted to a staggering 62 percent of the value of gross farm receipts, or $21,000 per farmer. In the European Union, where the Common Agricultural Policy (CAP) has long provided subsidies to help farmers stay in business, subsidies amounted to 43 percent of the value of gross farm receipts, or $19,000 per farmer. In the United States, subsidies were 22 percent of gross farm receipts, which again amounts to $19,000 per farmer. In Canada, subsidies were 18 percent of gross farm receipts, or $8,000 per farmer.[4]

Outside of agriculture, subsidies are much lower, but they are still significant. One study found that government subsidies to manufacturing industries in most industrialized countries amounted to between 2 percent and 3.5 percent of the value of industrial output. The average rate of subsidy in the United States was 0.5 percent; in Japan it was 1 percent, and in Europe it ranged from just below 2 percent in Great Britain and West Germany to as much as 6 to 7 percent in Sweden and Ireland.[5] These figures, however, almost certainly underestimate the true value of subsidies, since they are based only on cash grants and ignore other kinds of subsidies (e.g., equity participation or low-interest loans).

The main gains from subsidies accrue to domestic producers, whose international competitiveness is increased as a result of them. Advocates of strategic trade policy (which, as you will recall from Chapter 4, is an outgrowth of the new trade theory) favor subsidies to help domestic firms achieve a dominant position in those industries where economies of scale are important and the world market is not large enough to profitably support more than a few firms (e.g., aerospace, semiconductors). According to this argument, subsidies can help a firm achieve a first-mover advantage in an emerging industry (just as U.S. government subsidies, in the form of substantial R&D grants, allegedly helped Boeing). If this is achieved, further gains to the domestic economy arise from the employment and tax revenues that a major global company can generate.

Country Focus

The Costs of Protectionism in the United States

The United States likes to think of itself as a nation committed to unrestricted free trade. In their negotiations with trading partners such as China, the European Union, and Japan, U.S. trade representatives can often be heard claiming that the U.S. economy is an open one with few import tariffs. However, while it is true that tariffs on the importation of goods into the United States are low when compared to those found in many other nations, they still exist. One study concluded that these tariffs cost U.S. consumers about $32 billion per year during the 1980s. A more recent study suggested that in 1996, import protection cost U.S. consumers $223.4 billion in higher prices.

Gary Hufbauer and Kim Elliott of the Institute for International Economics undertook the first study. They looked at the effect of import tariffs on economic activity in 21 industries with annual sales of $1 billion or more that the U.S. protected most heavily from foreign competition. The industries included apparel, ceramic tiles, luggage, and sugar. In most of these industries, import tariffs had originally been imposed to protect U.S. firms and employees from the effects of low-cost foreign competitors. The typical reasoning behind the tariffs was that without such protection, U.S. firms in these industries would go out of business and substantial unemployment would result. So the tariffs were presented as having positive effects for the U.S. economy, not to mention the U.S. Treasury, which benefited from the associated revenues.

The study found, however, that while these import tariffs saved about 200,000 jobs in the protected industries that would otherwise have been lost to foreign competition, they also cost American consumers about $32 billion per year in the form of higher prices. Even when the proceeds from the tariff that accrued to the U.S. Treasury were added into the equation, the total cost to the nation of this protectionism still amounted to $10.2 billion per year, or over $50,000 per job saved.

The two economists argued that these figures understated the tariffs' true cost to the nation. They maintained that by making imports less competitive with American-made products, tariffs allowed domestic producers to charge more than they might otherwise because they did not have to compete with low-priced imports. By dampening competition, these tariffs removed an incentive for firms in the protected industries to become more efficient, thereby retarding economic progress. Further, the study's authors noted that if the tariffs had not been imposed, some of the $32 billion freed up every year would have been spent on other goods and services, and growth in these areas would have created additional jobs, thereby offsetting the loss of 200,000 jobs in the protected industries.

In a 1999 study, Howard Wall used a different methodology to provide updated estimates on the impact of protectionism on trade volume and prices. Wall found that while the United States imported more than $723 billion in merchandise from countries outside of NAFTA in 1996, it would have imported over $111 billion more if it had a policy of pure free trade. (NAFTA is the North American Free Trade Agreement signed by Canada, Mexico, and the United States.) Wall concluded that the higher prices resulting from import protection cost U.S. consumers some $223.4 billion in 1996, or 3.4 percent of GDP. However, Wall's estimates also suggest that the United States suffered from trade barriers in other countries. While the United States exported $499 billion of goods in 1996, according to Wall, it would have exported an additional $130 billion of goods to non-NAFTA countries had those countries not had trade barriers.

Sources: G. Hufbauer and K. A. Elliott, *Measuring the Costs of Protectionism in the United States* (Washington, DC: Institute for International Economics, 1993), and H. J. Wall, "Using the Gravity Model to Estimate the Costs of Protectionism," *Federal Reserve Bank of St. Louis Review*, January–February, 1999, pp. 33–40.

But subsidies must be paid for. Governments typically pay for subsidies by taxing individuals. Therefore, whether subsidies generate national benefits that exceed their national costs is debatable. In practice, many subsidies are not that successful at increasing the international competitiveness of domestic producers. Rather, they tend to protect the inefficient, rather than promoting efficiency, and promote excess production. Agricultural subsidies (1) allow inefficient farmers to stay in business,

(2) encourage countries to overproduce heavily subsidized agricultural products, (3) encourage countries to produce products that could be grown more cheaply elsewhere and imported, and, therefore, (4) reduce international trade in agricultural products. One recent study estimated that if advanced countries abandoned subsidies to farmers, global trade in agricultural products would be 50 percent higher and the world as a whole would be better off to the tune of $160 billion.[6] This increase in wealth arises from the more efficient use of agricultural land.

Import Quotas and Voluntary Export Restraints

An **import quota** is a direct restriction on the quantity of some good that may be imported into a country. The restriction is usually enforced by issuing import licenses to a group of individuals or firms. For example, the United States has a quota on cheese imports. The only firms allowed to import cheese are certain trading companies, each of which is allocated the right to import a maximum number of pounds of cheese each year. In some cases the right to sell is given directly to the governments of exporting countries. This is the case for sugar and textile imports in the United States.

A variant on the import quota is the voluntary export restraint (VER). A **voluntary export restraint** is a quota on trade imposed by the exporting country, typically at the request of the importing country's government. One of the most famous examples is the limitation on auto exports to the United States enforced by Japanese automobile producers in 1981. A response to direct pressure from the U.S. government, this VER limited Japanese imports to no more than 1.68 million vehicles per year. The agreement was revised in 1984 to allow 1.85 million Japanese vehicles per year. The agreement was allowed to lapse in 1985, but the Japanese government indicated its intentions at that time to continue to restrict exports to the United States to 1.85 million vehicles per year.[7] Foreign producers agree to VERs because they fear far more damaging punitive tariffs or import quotas might follow if they do not. Agreeing to a VER is seen as a way of making the best of a bad situation by appeasing protectionist pressures in a country.

As with tariffs and subsidies, both import quotas and VERs benefit domestic producers by limiting import competition. As with all restrictions on trade, quotas do not benefit consumers. An import quota or VER always raises the domestic price of an imported good. When imports are limited to a low percentage of the market by a quota or VER, the price is bid up for that limited foreign supply. In the case of the automobile industry, for example, the VER increased the price of the limited supply of Japanese imports. According to a study by the U.S. Federal Trade Commission, the automobile industry VER cost U.S. consumers about $1 billion per year between 1981 and 1985. That $1 billion per year went to Japanese producers in the form of higher prices.[8] The extra profit that producers make when supply is artificially limited by an import quota is referred to as a **quota rent.**

If a domestic industry lacks the capacity to meet demand, an import quota can raise prices for *both* the domestically produced and imported good. This happened in the U.S. sugar industry, where an import quota has long limited the amount foreign producers can sell in the U.S. market. According to one study, as a result of import quotas the price of sugar in the United States has been as much as 40 percent greater than the world price.[9] These higher prices have translated into greater profits for U.S. sugar producers, who have lobbied politicians to keep the lucrative agreement in place. They argue that U.S. jobs in the sugar industry will be lost to foreign producers if the quota system is scrapped.

Another industry that has long operated with import quotas is the textile industry, which has a complex set of multinational agreements that govern the amount one country can export to others. In this industry, quotas on imports into the United States have restricted the supply of certain apparel products and increased their price by as much as 70 percent.[10] Quotas also encourage firms to engage in strategic actions de-

Management Focus

Navigating Around Import Quotas

The Hong Kong-based Esquel Group, founded in 1976, is the world's largest manufacturer of men's cotton shirts, with annual sales of about $500 million. Esquel produces about 48 million shirts and 5 million pairs of pants a year. Its customers include the premier brands in the United States—Polo Ralph Lauren, Tommy Hilfiger, Brooks Brothers, Hugo Boss, Nordstrom, Eddie Bauer, Abercrombie and Fitch, and Lands' End.

Shortly after it began production, Esquel found its growth opportunities limited by Hong Kong's quota rights. A quota right is a right to export a prespecified amount of a certain product into a country. Hong Kong's total quota right for shirts in 2000 was 36 million, meaning that it could export 36 million shirts to other countries. With growth limited by restrictive quota rights, Esquel switched production to mainland China, which at the time did not have any quota restrictions. In no time, Esquel was shipping 12 million shirts per year from China to Europe and the United States. However, as Chinese textile products began to grab an ever-larger share of the European and U.S. markets, domestic U.S. and European producers lobbied for and got quotas imposed on imports from China. For Esquel this meant it was time to shift production location yet again, this time to Malaysia, which had quota rights that exceeded domestic production. Esquel quickly built up a large export position in men's and woman's shirts, but, as Malaysian textiles began to make inroads into the U.S. market, the United States placed tight quota restrictions on Malaysia too. So Esquel made another shift in production location, this time to Mauritius, an island in the Indian Ocean that had unused quota rights.

Mauritius is so far from anywhere that under normal circumstances, no one would think of locating major production facilities there, but its unused quota rights made it a valuable location. Currently, Esquel grows extra-long staple cotton in western China and spins the yarn there and in Guangdong, Southern China. It then loads the fiber and accessories on boats to Mauritius, where it is assembled into products for the United States and Europe. One drawback with Mauritius, apart from its geographic isolation, is that although it is rich in quota rights, it is short in labor to exploit those rights. So Esquel imported 2,000 factory workers from China to Mauritius to make its textile products.

This is not the last word in Esquel's efforts to exploit quota rights. Under the 1994 North American Free Trade Agreement, Mexico has quota-free and duty-free access to the U.S. market. Under another law, Caribbean countries have unlimited access to the U.S. market for apparel for fabric made and woven in the United States. Esquel has yet to take advantage of the Mexican opening, although it is weighing its options, but it has already taken advantage of the Caribbean opening. The company built a plant in Jamaica, and, finding the local labor inadequate, imported 700 workers from China to staff the plant. Next stop is Maldives, another island nation in the Indian Ocean with unused quota rights. Esquel plans to produce 200,000 knit shirts and cotton pants in Maldives for export to the United States and Europe, again using imported Chinese labor.

Source: A. Tanzer, "The Great Quota Hustle," *Forbes*, March 6, 2000, pp. 119–25.

---

signed to circumvent quotas. The accompanying Management Focus looks at how one company, Hong Kong-based Esquel, has altered the geographic distribution of its production system to circumvent quotas on the importation of certain textile products into the United States. The United States is not alone in imposing quotas on textile imports. Most other developed nations have similar quotas. Under a World Trade Organization agreement struck in 1995, many of the quotas on textile products are scheduled to be phased out by 2005.

Local Content Requirements

A **local content requirement** is a requirement that some specific fraction of a good be produced domestically. The requirement can be expressed either in physical terms (e.g., 75 percent of component parts for this product must be produced locally) or in value terms (e.g., 75 percent of the value of this product must be produced locally).

Local content regulations have been widely used by developing countries to shift their manufacturing base from the simple assembly of products whose parts are manufactured elsewhere into the local manufacture of component parts. They have also been used in developed countries to try to protect local jobs and industry from foreign competition. For example, a little-known law in the United States, the Buy America Act, specifies that government agencies must give preference to American products when putting contracts for equipment out to bid unless the foreign products have a significant price advantage. The law specifies a product as "American" if 51 percent of the materials by value are produced domestically. This amounts to a local content requirement. If a foreign company, or an American one for that matter, wishes to win a contract from a U.S. government agency to provide some equipment, it must ensure that at least 51 percent of the product by value is manufactured in the United States.

From the point of view of a domestic producer of parts going into a final product, local content regulations provide protection in the same way an import quota does: by limiting foreign competition. The aggregate economic effects are also the same; domestic producers benefit, but the restrictions on imports raise the prices of imported components. In turn, higher prices for imported components are passed on to consumers of the final product in the form of higher final prices. So as with all trade policies, local content regulations tend to benefit producers and not consumers.

Administrative Policies

In addition to the formal instruments of trade policy, governments of all types sometimes use informal or administrative policies to restrict imports and boost exports. **Administrative trade policies** are bureaucratic rules that are designed to make it difficult for imports to enter a country. Some would argue that the Japanese are the masters of this kind of trade barrier. In recent years Japan's formal tariff and nontariff barriers have been among the lowest in the world. However, critics charge that the country's informal administrative barriers to imports more than compensate for this. For example, the Netherlands exports tulip bulbs to almost every country in the world except Japan. In Japan, customs inspectors insist on checking every tulip bulb by cutting it vertically down the middle, and even Japanese ingenuity cannot put them back together again! Federal Express has had a tough time expanding its global express shipping services into Japan because Japanese customs inspectors insist on opening a large proportion of express packages to check for pornography, a process that can delay an "express" package for days. Japan is not the only country that engages in such policies. France required that all imported videotape recorders arrive through a small customs entry point that was both remote and poorly staffed. The resulting delays kept Japanese VCRs out of the French market until a VER agreement was negotiated.[11] As with all instruments of trade policy, administrative instruments benefit producers and hurt consumers, who are denied access to possibly superior foreign products.

Antidumping Policies

In the context of international trade, **dumping** is variously defined as selling goods in a foreign market at below their costs of production, or as selling goods in a foreign market at below their "fair" market value. There is a difference between these two definitions; the "fair" market value of a good is normally judged to be greater than the costs of producing that good because the former includes a "fair" profit margin. Dumping is viewed as a method by which firms unload excess production in foreign markets. Some dumping may be the result of predatory behavior, with producers using substantial profits from their home markets to subsidize prices in a foreign market with a view to driving indigenous competitors out of that market. Once this has been achieved, so the argument goes, the predatory firm can raise prices and earn substantial profits.

An alleged example of dumping occurred in 1997, when two South Korean manufacturers of semiconductors, LG Semicon and Hyundai Electronics, were accused of selling dynamic random access memory chips (DRAMs) in the U.S. market at below their costs of production. This action occurred in the middle of a worldwide glut of chip-making capacity. It was alleged that the firms were trying to unload their excess production in the United States.

Antidumping policies are designed to punish foreign firms that engage in dumping. The ultimate objective is to protect domestic producers from "unfair" foreign competition. Although antidumping policies vary somewhat from country to country, the majority are similar to the policies used in the United States. If a domestic producer believes that a foreign firm is dumping production in the U.S. market, it can file a petition with two government agencies, the Commerce Department and the International Trade Commission. In the Korean DRAM case, Micron Technology, a U.S. manufacturer of DRAMs, filed the petition. The government agencies then investigated the complaint. If they find it has merit, the Commerce Department may impose an antidumping duty on the offending foreign imports (antidumping duties are often called **countervailing duties**). These duties, which represent a special tariff, can be fairly substantial and stay in place for up to five years. For example, after reviewing Micron's complaint, the Commerce Department imposed 9 percent and 4 percent countervailing duties on LG Semicon and Hyundai DRAM chips, respectively.

The Case for Government Intervention

Now that we have reviewed the various instruments of trade policy that governments can use, it is time to take a more detailed look at the case for government intervention in international trade. Arguments for government intervention take two paths—political and economic. Political arguments for intervention are concerned with protecting the interests of certain groups within a nation (normally producers), often at the expense of other groups (normally consumers). Economic arguments for intervention are typically concerned with boosting the overall wealth of a nation (to the benefit of all, both producers and consumers).

Political Arguments for Intervention

Political arguments for government intervention cover a range of issues including protecting jobs, protecting industries deemed important for national security, retaliating to unfair foreign competition, protecting consumers from "dangerous" products, furthering the goals of foreign policy, and protecting the human rights of individuals in exporting countries.

Protecting Jobs and Industries

Perhaps the most common political argument for government intervention is that it is necessary for protecting jobs and industries from foreign competition. The voluntary export restraints that offered some protection to the U.S. automobile, machine tool, and steel industries during the 1980s were motivated by such considerations. Similarly, Japan's quotas on imports of rice are aimed at protecting jobs in that country's agricultural sector. The same motive underlay establishment of the Common Agricultural Policy (CAP) by the European Union. The CAP was designed to protect the jobs of Europe's politically powerful farmers by restricting imports and guaranteeing prices. However, the higher prices that resulted from the CAP have cost Europe's consumers dearly. This is true of most attempts to protect jobs and industries through government intervention. As we saw earlier in the chapter, the VER in the automobile industry raised the price of Japanese imports, at a cost of $1 billion per year to U.S. consumers.

In addition to hurting consumers, trade controls may sometimes hurt the very producers they are intended to protect. The VER agreement in the U.S. machine tool industry turned out to be self-defeating. By limiting Japanese and Taiwanese machine tool imports, the VER raised the prices of machine tools purchased by U.S. manufacturers to levels above those prevailing in the world market. In turn, this raised the capital costs of the U.S. manufacturing industry in general, thereby decreasing its international competitiveness.

National Security

Countries sometimes argue that it is necessary to protect certain industries because they are important for national security. Defense-related industries often get this kind of attention (e.g., aerospace, advanced electronics, semiconductors, etc.). Although not as common as it used to be, this argument is still made. Those in favor of protecting the U.S. semiconductor industry from foreign competition, for example, argue that semiconductors are now such important components of defense products that it would be dangerous to rely primarily on foreign producers for them. In 1986, this argument helped persuade the federal government to support Sematech, a consortium of 14 U.S. semiconductor companies that accounts for 90 percent of the U.S. industry's revenues. Sematech's mission is to conduct joint research into manufacturing techniques that can be parceled out to members. The government saw the venture as so critical that Sematech was specially protected from antitrust laws. Initially, the U.S. government provided Sematech with $100 million per year in subsidies. By the mid-1990s, however, the U.S. semiconductor industry had regained its leading market position, largely through the personal computer boom and demand for microprocessor chips made by Intel. In 1994, the consortium's board voted to seek an end to federal funding, and since 1996 the consortium has been funded entirely by private money.[12]

Retaliation

Some argue that governments should use the threat to intervene in trade policy as a bargaining tool to help open up foreign markets and force trading partners to "play by the rules of the game." The U.S. government has successfully used the threat of punitive trade sanctions to get the Chinese government to enforce its intellectual property laws. Lax enforcement of these laws had given rise to massive copyright infringements in China that have been costing U.S. companies such as Microsoft hundreds of millions of dollars per years in lost sales revenues. After the United States threatened to impose 100 percent tariffs on a range of Chinese imports, and after harsh words between officials from the two countries, the Chinese agreed to tighter enforcement of intellectual property regulations.[13]

If it works, such a politically motivated rationale for government intervention may liberalize trade and bring with it resulting economic gains. It is a risky strategy, however. A country that is being pressured may not back down and instead may respond to the imposition of punitive tariffs by raising trade barriers of its own. This is exactly what the Chinese government threatened to do when pressured by the United States, although it ultimately did back down. If a government does not back down, however, the results could be higher trade barriers all around and an economic loss to all involved.

Protecting Consumers

Many governments have long had regulations in place to protect consumers from "unsafe" products. The indirect effect of such regulations often is to limit or ban the importation of such products. In 1998, the Clinton administration decided to permanently ban imports into the United States of 58 types of military-style assault weapons. (The United States already prohibited the sale of such weapons in the United States by U.S.-based firms.) The ban was motivated by a desire to increase public safety. It followed on the heels of a rash of random and deadly shootings by deranged

Trade in Hormone-Treated Beef

In the 1970s, scientists discovered how to synthesize certain hormones and use them to promote the growth rate of livestock animals, reduce the fat content of meat, and increase milk production. Bovine somatotropin (BST), a growth hormone produced by beef cattle, was first synthesized by the biotechnology firm Genentech. Injections of BST could be used to supplement an animal's own hormone production and increase its growth rate. These hormones soon became popular among farmers, who found that they could cut costs and help satisfy consumer demands for leaner meat. Although several of these hormones occurred naturally in animals, consumer groups in several countries soon raised concerns about the practice. They argued that the use of hormone supplements was unnatural and that the health consequences of consuming hormone-treated meat were unknown but might include hormonal irregularities and cancer.

The European Union (EU) responded to these concerns in 1989 by banning the use of growth-promoting hormones in the production of livestock and the importation of hormone-treated meat. The ban was controversial because a reasonable consensus existed among scientists that the hormones posed no health risk. Before the ban, a number of these hormones had passed licensing procedures in several EU countries. As part of this process, research had been assembled that appeared to show that consuming hormone-treated meat had no effect on human health. Although the EU banned hormone-treated meat, many other countries did not, including big meat-producing countries such as Australia, Canada, New Zealand, and the United States. The use of hormones soon became widespread in these countries. According to trade officials outside the EU, the European ban constituted an unfair restraint on trade. As a result of this ban, exports of meat to the EU fell. For example, U.S. red meat exports to the EU declined from $231 million in 1988 to $98 million in 1994. The complaints of meat exporters were bolstered in 1995 when Codex Alimentarius, the international food standards body of the UN's Food and Agriculture Organization and the World Health Organization, approved the use of growth hormones. In making this decision, Codex reviewed the scientific literature and found no evidence of a link between the consumption of hormone-treated meat and human health problems, such as cancer.

Fortified by such decisions, in 1995 the United States pressed the EU to drop the ban on the import of hormone-treated beef. The EU refused, citing "consumer concerns about food safety." In response, both Canada and the United States independently filed formal complaints with the World Trade Commission. The United States was joined in its complaint by a number of other countries, including Australia and New Zealand. The WTO created a trade panel of three independent experts. After reviewing evidence and hearing from a range of experts and representatives of both parties, the panel in May 1997 ruled that the EU ban on hormone-treated beef was illegal because it had no scientific justification. The panel also noted that the EU was inconsistent in its application of the ban. The EU takes a very strict view on the use of growth-promoting hormones in the beef sector, where it has a substantial surplus and is not internationally competitive, while it still allows the use of some growth hormones for pig-meat production where the EU has no substantial surplus and does not compete in international markets. The EU immediately indicated it would appeal the finding to the WTO court of appeals. The WTO court heard the appeal in November 1997 and in February 1998 agreed with the findings of the trade panel that the EU had not presented any scientific evidence to justify the hormone ban.

This ruling left the EU in a difficult position. Legally, the EU had to lift the ban or face punitive sanctions, but the ban had wide public support in Europe. The EU feared that lifting the ban could produce a consumer backlash. Instead the EU did nothing, so in February 1999 the United States asked the WTO for permission to impose punitive sanctions on the EU. About the same time, the United States also asked the WTO for permission to place sanctions on the EU for its failure to adjust quotas and tariffs on banana imports (see the opening case). The WTO responded by allowing the United States to impose punitive tariffs valued at $191.4 million on EU exports to the United States.

Sources: C. Southey, "Hormones Fuel a Meaty EU Row," *Financial Times,* September 7, 1995, p. 2; E. L. Andrews, "In Victory for U.S., European Ban on Treated Beef Is Ruled Illegal," *New York Times,* May 9, 1997, p. A1; F. Williams and G. de Jonquieres, "WTO's Beef Rulings Give Europe Food for Thought," *Financial Times,* February 13, 1998, p. 5; and World Trade Organization, *EC Measures Concerning Meat and Meat Products,* August 18, 1997.

individuals using such weapons, including one in the president's home state of Arkansas that left four children and a schoolteacher dead.[14]

The accompanying Country Focus describes how the European Union banned the sale and importation of hormone-treated beef. The ban was motivated by a desire to protect European consumers from the possible health consequences of meat treated with growth hormones.

The conflict over the importation of hormone-treated beef into the European Union may prove to be a taste of things to come. In addition to the use of hormones to promote animal growth and meat production, the science of biotechnology has made it possible to genetically alter many crops so that they are resistant to common herbicides, produce proteins that are natural insecticides, have dramatically improved yields, or can withstand inclement weather conditions. A new breed of genetically modified tomatoes has an antifreeze gene inserted into its genome and can thus be grown in colder climates than hitherto possible. Another example is a genetically engineered cotton seed produced by Monsanto. The seed has been engineered to express a protein that provides protection against three common insect pests: the cotton bollworm, tobacco budworm, and pink bollworm. Use of this seed reduces or eliminates the need for traditional pesticide applications for these pests. As enticing as such innovations sound, they have met with intense resistance from consumer groups, particularly in Europe. The fear is that the widespread use of genetically altered seed corn could have unanticipated and harmful effects on human health and may result in "genetic pollution." (An example of genetic pollution would be when the widespread use of crops that produce "natural pesticides" stimulates the evolution of "super-bugs" that are resistant to those pesticides.) Such concerns have led Austria and Luxembourg to outlaw the importation, sale, or use of genetically altered organisms. Sentiment against genetically altered organisms also runs strongly in several other European countries, most notably Germany and Switzerland. It seems likely, therefore, that the World Trade Organization will be drawn into the conflict between those that want to expand the global market for genetically altered organisms, such as Monsanto, and those that want to limit it, such as Austria and Luxembourg.[15]

Furthering Foreign Policy Objectives

Governments sometimes use trade policy to support their foreign policy objectives.[16] A government may grant preferential trade terms to a country it wants to build strong relations with. Trade policy has also been used several times to pressure or punish "rogue states" that do not abide by international law or norms. Iraq has labored under extensive trade sanctions since the UN coalition defeated the country in the 1991 Gulf War. The theory is that such pressure might persuade the "rogue state" to mend its ways or it might hasten a change of government. In the case of Iraq, the sanctions are seen as a way of forcing that country to comply with several UN resolutions. In another example, the United States has maintained long-running trade sanctions against Cuba. Their principal function is to impoverish Cuba in the hope that the resulting economic hardship will lead to the downfall of Cuba's Communist government and its replacement with a more democratically inclined (and pro-U.S.) regime. The United States also has trade sanctions in place against Libya and Iran, both of which it accuses of supporting terrorist action against U.S. interests.

Other countries can undermine any unilateral trade sanctions. The U.S. sanctions against Cuba, for example, have not stopped other Western countries from trading with Cuba. The U.S. sanctions have done little more than help create a vacuum into which other trading nations, such as Canada and Germany, can and have stepped. In an attempt to put a halt to this and further tighten the screws on Cuba, in 1996 the U.S. Congress passed the **Helms-Burton Act.** This act allows Americans to sue foreign firms that use property in Cuba confiscated from them after the 1959 revolution. A similar act, the **D'Amato Act,** aimed at Libya and Iran was also passed that year.

The passage of Helms-Burton elicited howls of protest from America's trading partners, including the European Union, Canada, and Mexico, all of which claim the law violates their sovereignty and is illegal under World Trade Organization rules. For example, Canadian companies that have been doing business in Cuba for years see no reason why they should suddenly be sued in U.S. courts when Canada does not restrict trade with Cuba. They are not violating Canadian law and they are not U.S. companies, so why should they be subject to U.S. law? Despite such protests, the law is still on the books in the United States, although the U.S. government has been less than enthusiastic about enforcing it—probably because it is unenforceable. President Clinton regularly used his executive power to suspend items in the act, essentially rendering it toothless. The fuss over Helms-Burton illustrates that trade policy is a rather blunt and sometimes counterproductive instrument of foreign policy.

Protecting Human Rights

Protecting and promoting human rights in other countries is an important element of foreign policy for many democracies. Governments sometimes use trade policy to try to improve the human rights policies of trading partners. For years the most obvious example of this was the annual debate in the United States over whether to grant most favored nation (MFN) status to China. MFN status allows countries to export goods to the United Status under favorable terms. Under MFN rules, the average tariff on Chinese goods imported into the United States is 8 percent. If China's MFN status were rescinded, tariffs would probably rise to about 40 percent. Trading partners who are signatories of the World Trade Organization, as most are, automatically receive MFN status. However, China did not join the WTO until 2001, so historically the decision of whether to grant MFN status to China was a real one. The decision was made more difficult by the perception that China had a poor human rights record. As indications of the country's disregard for human rights, critics of China often point to the 1989 Tiananmen Square massacre, China's continuing subjugation of Tibet (which China occupied in the 1950s), and the squashing of political dissent in China (there are an estimated 1,700 political prisoners in China).[17] These critics argued that it was wrong for the United States to grant MFN status to China, and that instead, the United States should withhold MFN status until China showed measurable improvement in its human rights record. Put differently, the critics argued that trade policy should be used as a political weapon to force China to change its internal policies toward human rights.

But others contend that limiting trade with such countries would make matters worse, not better. They argue that the best way to change the internal human rights stance of a country is to engage it through international trade. At its core, the argument is simple: Growing bilateral trade raises the income levels of both countries, and as a state becomes richer, its people begin to demand—and generally receive—better treatment with regard to their human rights. This is a variant of the argument in Chapter 2 that economic progress begets political progress (if political progress is measured by the adoption of a democratic government that respects human rights). This argument ultimately won the day in 1999 when the Clinton administration blessed China's application to join the WTO and announced that trade and human rights issues should be decoupled.

Economic Arguments for Intervention

With the development of the new trade theory and strategic trade policy (see Chapter 4), the economic arguments for government intervention have undergone a renaissance in recent years. Until the early 1980s, most economists saw little benefit in government intervention and strongly advocated a free trade policy. This position has changed at the margins with the development of strategic trade policy, although as we will see in the next section, there are still strong economic arguments for sticking to a free trade stance.

The Infant Industry Argument

The infant industry argument is by far the oldest economic argument for government in- tervention. Alexander Hamilton first proposed it in 1792. According to this argument, many developing countries have a potential comparative advantage in manufacturing, but new manufacturing industries cannot initially compete with well-established indus- tries in developed countries. To allow manufacturing to get a toehold, the argument is that governments should temporarily support new industries (with tariffs, import quotas, and subsidies) until they have grown strong enough to meet international competition.

This argument has had substantial appeal for the governments of developing na- tions during the past 40 years, and the GATT has recognized the infant industry ar- gument as a legitimate reason for protectionism. Nevertheless, many economists remain very critical of this argument. They make two main points. First, protection of manufacturing from foreign competition does no good unless the protection helps make the industry efficient. In case after case, however, protection seems to have done little more than foster the development of inefficient industries that have little hope of ever competing in the world market. Brazil, for example, built up the world's 10th largest auto industry behind tariff barriers and quotas. Once those barriers were re- moved in the late 1980s, however, foreign imports soared and the industry was forced to face up to the fact that after 30 years of protection, the Brazilian industry was one of the world's most inefficient.[18]

Second, the infant industry argument relies on an assumption that firms are unable to make efficient long-term investments by borrowing money from the domestic or in- ternational capital market. Consequently, governments have been required to subsidize long-term investments. Given the development of global capital markets over the past 20 years, this assumption no longer looks as valid as it once did (see Chapter 11 for de- tails). Today, if a developing country really does have a potential comparative advan- tage in a manufacturing industry, firms in that country should be able to borrow money from the capital markets to finance the required investments. Given financial support, firms based in countries with a potential comparative advantage have an incentive to go through the necessary period of initial losses in order to make long-run gains with- out requiring government protection. Many Taiwanese and South Korean firms did this in industries such as textiles, semiconductors, machine tools, steel, and shipping. Thus, given efficient global capital markets, the only industries that would require govern- ment protection would be those that are not worthwhile.

Strategic Trade Policy

Some new trade theorists have proposed the strategic trade policy argument.[19] We re- viewed the basic argument in Chapter 4 when we considered the new trade theory. The new trade theory argues that in industries where the existence of substantial scale economies implies that the world market will profitably support only a few firms, coun- tries may predominate in the export of certain products simply because they had firms that were able to capture first-mover advantages. The dominance of Boeing in the commercial aircraft industry is attributed to such factors.

There are two components to the strategic trade policy argument. First, it is argued that by appropriate actions, a government can help raise national income if it can somehow ensure that the firm or firms to gain first-mover advantages in such an in- dustry are domestic rather than foreign enterprises. Thus, according to the strategic trade policy argument, a government should use subsidies to support promising firms that are active in newly emerging industries. Advocates of this argument point out that the substantial R&D grants that the U.S. government gave Boeing in the 1950s and 60s probably helped tilt the field of competition in the newly emerging market for jet passenger planes in Boeing's favor. (Boeing's 707 jet airliner was derived from a mil- itary plane.) Similar arguments are now made with regard to Japan's dominance in the production of liquid crystal display screens (used in laptop computers). Although these screens were invented in the United States, the Japanese government, in cooperation with major electronics companies, targeted this industry for research support in the late 1970s and early 80s. The result was that Japanese firms, not U.S. firms, subsequently captured the first-mover advantages in this market.

The second component of the strategic trade policy argument is that it might pay government to intervene in an industry if it helps domestic firms overcome the barriers to entry created by foreign firms that have already reaped first-mover advantages. This argument underlies government support of Airbus Industrie, Boeing's major competitor. Formed in 1966 as a consortium of four companies from Great Britain, France, Germany, and Spain, Airbus had less than 5 percent of the world commercial aircraft market when it began production in the mid-1970s. By 2000 it had increased its share to about 45 percent and was threatening Boeing's dominance. How did Airbus achieve this? According to the U.S. government, the answer is a $13.5 billion subsidy from the governments of Great Britain, France, Germany, and Spain.[20] Without this subsidy, Airbus would have never been able to break into the world market. In another example, the rise to dominance of the Japanese semiconductor industry, despite the first-mover advantages enjoyed by U.S. firms, is attributed to intervention by the Japanese government. In this case the government did not subsidize the costs of domestic manufacturers. Rather, it protected the Japanese home market while pursuing policies that ensured Japanese companies got access to the necessary manufacturing and product know-how.

If these arguments are correct, they clearly suggest a rationale for government intervention in international trade. Governments should target technologies that may be important in the future and use subsidies to support development work aimed at commercializing those technologies. Furthermore, government should provide export subsidies until the domestic firms have established first-mover advantages in the world market. Government support may also be justified if it can help domestic firms overcome the first-mover advantages enjoyed by foreign competitors and emerge as viable competitors in the world market (as in the Airbus and semiconductor examples). In this case, a combination of home-market protection and export-promoting subsidies may be called for.

The Revised Case for Free Trade

The strategic trade policy arguments of the new trade theorists suggest an economic justification for government intervention in international trade. This justification challenges the rationale for unrestricted free trade found in the work of classic trade theorists such as Adam Smith and David Ricardo. In response to this challenge to economic orthodoxy, a number of economists—including some of those responsible for the development of the new trade theory, such as Paul Krugman of MIT—have been quick to point out that although strategic trade policy looks nice in theory, in practice it may be unworkable. This response to the strategic trade policy argument constitutes the revised case for free trade.[21]

Retaliation and Trade War

Krugman argues that a strategic trade policy aimed at establishing domestic firms in a dominant position in a global industry is a beggar-thy-neighbor policy that boosts national income at the expense of other countries. A country that attempts to use such policies will probably provoke retaliation. In many cases, the resulting trade war between two or more interventionist governments will leave all countries involved worse off than if a hands-off approach had been adopted in the first place. If the U.S. government were to respond to the Airbus subsidy by increasing its own subsidies to Boeing, for example, the result might be that the subsidies would cancel each other out. In the process, both European and U.S. taxpayers would end up supporting an expensive and pointless trade war, and both Europe and the United States would be worse off.

Krugman may be right about the danger of a strategic trade policy leading to a trade war. The problem, however, is how to respond when one's competitors are already being supported by government subsidies; that is, how should Boeing and the United States respond to the subsidization of Airbus? According to Krugman, the answer is probably not to engage in retaliatory action, but to help establish rules of the game that minimize the use of trade-distorting subsidies. This is what the World Trade Organization seeks to do.

Domestic Politics

Governments do not always act in the national interest when they intervene in the economy; politically important interest groups often influence them. The European Union's support for the Common Agricultural Policy (CAP), which arose because of the political power of French and German farmers, is an example. The CAP benefited inefficient farmers and the politicians who relied on the farm vote, but not consumers in the EU, who end up paying more for their foodstuffs. Thus, a further reason for not embracing strategic trade policy, according to Krugman, is that such a policy is almost certain to be captured by special interest groups within the economy, who will distort it to their own ends. Krugman concludes that in the United States:

> To ask the Commerce Department to ignore special-interest politics while formulating detailed policy for many industries is not realistic: to establish a blanket policy of free trade, with exceptions granted only under extreme pressure, may not be the optimal policy according to the theory but may be the best policy that the country is likely to get.[22]

Development of the World Trading System

There are strong economic arguments for supporting unrestricted free trade. While many governments have recognized the value of these arguments, they have been unwilling to unilaterally lower their trade barriers for fear that other nations might not follow suit. Consider the problem that two neighboring countries, say France and Italy, face when considering whether to lower barriers to trade between them. In principle, the government of Italy might be in favor of lowering trade barriers, but it might be unwilling to do so for fear that France will not do the same. Instead, the government might fear that the French will take advantage of Italy's low barriers to enter the Italian market, while at the same time continuing to shut Italian products out of their market through high trade barriers. The French government might feel that it faces exactly the same dilemma. The essence of the problem is a lack of trust. Both governments recognize that their respective nations will benefit from lower trade barriers between them, but neither government is willing to lower barriers for fear that the other might not follow.[23]

Such a deadlock can be resolved if both countries negotiate a set of rules to govern cross-border trade and lower trade barriers. But who is to monitor the governments to make sure that they are playing by the trade rules? And who is to impose sanctions on a government that cheats? Both governments could set up an independent body whose function is to act as a referee. This referee could monitor trade between the countries, make sure that no side cheats, and impose sanctions on a country if it does cheat in the trade game.

While it might sound unlikely that any government would compromise its national sovereignty by submitting to such an arrangement, since World War II an international trading framework has evolved that has exactly these features. For its first 50 years, this framework was known as the General Agreement on Tariffs and Trade (the

GATT). Since 1995, it has been known as the World Trade Organization (WTO). Here we look at the evolution and workings of the GATT and WTO. We set the scene with a brief discussion of the pre-GATT history of world trade.

From Smith to the Great Depression

As we saw in Chapter 4, the theoretical case for free trade dates to the late 18th century and the work of Adam Smith and David Ricardo. Free trade as a government policy was first officially embraced by Great Britain in 1846, when the British Parliament repealed the Corn Laws. The Corn Laws placed a high tariff on imports of foreign corn. The objectives of the Corn Laws tariff were to raise government revenues and to protect British corn producers. There had been annual motions in Parliament in favor of free trade since the 1820s when David Ricardo was a member. However, agricultural protection was withdrawn only as a result of a protracted debate when the effects of a harvest failure in Great Britain were compounded by the imminent threat of famine in Ireland. Faced with considerable hardship and suffering among the populace, Parliament narrowly reversed its long-held position.

During the next 80 years or so, Great Britain, as one of the world's dominant trading powers, pushed the case for trade liberalization; but the British government was a voice in the wilderness. Its major trading partners did not reciprocate the British policy of unilateral free trade. The only reason Britain kept this policy for so long was that, as the world's largest exporting nation, it had far more to lose from a trade war than did any other country.

By the 1930s, however, the British attempt to stimulate free trade was buried under the economic rubble of the Great Depression. The Great Depression had roots in the failure of the world economy to mount a sustained economic recovery after the end of World War I in 1918. Things got worse in 1929 with the U.S. stock market collapse and the subsequent run on the U.S. banking system. Economic problems were compounded in 1930 when the U.S. Congress passed the Smoot-Hawley tariff. Aimed at avoiding rising unemployment by protecting domestic industries and diverting consumer demand away from foreign products, the Smoot-Hawley tariff erected an enormous wall of tariff barriers. Almost every industry was rewarded with its "made-to-order" tariff. A particularly odd aspect of the Smoot-Hawley tariff-raising binge was that the United States was running a balance-of-payment surplus at the time and it was the world's largest creditor nation. The Smoot-Hawley tariff had a damaging effect on employment abroad. Other countries reacted to the U.S. action by raising their own tariff barriers. U.S. exports tumbled in response, and the world slid further into the Great Depression.[24]

1947–1979: GATT, Trade Liberalization, and Economic Growth

The economic damage caused by the beggar-thy-neighbor trade policies that the Smoot-Hawley Act ushered in exerted a profound influence on the economic institutions and ideology of the post-World War II world. The United States emerged from the war both victorious and economically dominant. After the debacle of the Great Depression, opinion in the U.S. Congress had swung strongly in favor of free trade. Under U.S. leadership, GATT was established in 1947.

The GATT was a multilateral agreement whose objective was to liberalize trade by eliminating tariffs, subsidies, import quotas, and the like. From its foundation in 1947 until it was superseded by the WTO, the GATT's membership grew from 19 to more than 120 nations. The GATT did not attempt to liberalize trade restrictions in one fell swoop; that would have been impossible. Rather, tariff reduction was spread over eight rounds. The most recent, the Uruguay Round, was launched in 1986 and completed in December 1993. In these rounds, mutual tariff reductions were negotiated among all members, who then committed themselves not to raise import tariffs above negotiated rates. GATT regulations were enforced by a mutual monitoring mechanism. If a country felt that one of its trading partners was violating a GATT regulation, it could ask the Geneva-based bureaucracy that administered the GATT to investigate. If GATT investigators found the complaints to be valid, member countries could be asked to pressure the offending party to change its policies. In general, such pressure was always sufficient to get an offending country to change its policies. If it were not, the offending country could have been expelled from the GATT.

In its early years, the GATT was by most measures very successful. For example, the average tariff declined by nearly 92 percent in the United States between the Geneva Round of 1947 and the Tokyo Round of 1973–79. Consistent with the theoretical arguments first advanced by Ricardo and reviewed in Chapter 4, the move toward free trade under the GATT appeared to stimulate economic growth. From 1953 to 1963, world trade grew at an annual rate of 6.1 percent, and world income grew at an annual rate of 4.3 percent. Performance from 1963 to 1973 was even better; world trade grew at 8.9 percent annually, and world income grew at 5.1 percent annually.[25]

1980–1993: Disturbing Trends

During the 1980s and early 1990s, the world trading system erected by the GATT came under strain as pressures for greater protectionism increased around the world. Three reasons caused the rise in such pressures during the 1980s. First, the economic success of Japan strained the world trading system. Japan was in ruins when the GATT was created. By the early 1980s, however, it had become the world's second largest economy and its largest exporter. Japan's success in such industries as automobiles and semiconductors by itself might have been enough to strain the world trading system. Things were made worse, however, by the widespread perception in the West that despite low tariff rates and subsidies, Japanese markets were closed to imports and foreign investment by administrative trade barriers.

Second, the world trading system was strained by the persistent trade deficit in the world's largest economy, the United States. Although the deficit peaked in 1987 at more than $170 billion, by the end of 1992 the annual rate was still running about $80 billion. From a political perspective, the matter was worsened in 1992 by the United States' $45 billion trade deficit with Japan, a country perceived as not playing by the rules. The consequences of the U.S. deficit included painful adjustments in industries such as automobiles, machine tools, semiconductors, steel, and textiles, where domestic producers steadily lost market share to foreign competitors. The resulting unemployment gave rise to renewed demands in the U.S. Congress for protection against imports.

A third reason for the trend toward greater protectionism was that many countries found ways to get around GATT regulations. Bilateral voluntary export restraints (VERs) circumvent GATT agreements, because neither the importing country nor the exporting country complain to the GATT bureaucracy in Geneva—and without a complaint, the GATT bureaucracy can do nothing. Exporting countries agreed to VERs to avoid more damaging punitive tariffs. One of the best-known examples is the VER between Japan and the United States, under which Japanese producers promised to limit their auto imports into the United States as a way of defusing growing trade tensions. According to a World Bank study, 13 percent of the imports of industrialized countries in 1981 were subjected to nontariff trade barriers such as VERs. By 1986, this figure had increased to 16 percent. The most rapid rise was in the United States, where the value of imports affected by nontariff barriers (primarily VERs) increased by 23 percent between 1981 and 1986.[26]

The Uruguay Round and the World Trade Organization

Against the background of rising pressures for protectionism, in 1986 the GATT members embarked on their eighth round of negotiations to reduce tariffs, the Uruguay Round (so named because it occurred in Uruguay). This was the most difficult round of negotiations yet, primarily because it was also the most ambitious. Until then, GATT rules had applied only to trade in manufactured goods and commodities. In the Uruguay Round, member countries sought to extend GATT rules to cover trade in services. They also sought to write rules governing the protection of intellectual property, to reduce agricultural subsidies, and to strengthen the GATT's monitoring and enforcement mechanisms.

The Uruguay Round dragged on for seven years before an agreement was reached December 15, 1993. The agreement was formally signed by member states at a meeting in Marrakech, Morocco, on April 15, 1994. It went into effect July 1, 1995. The Uruguay Round contained the following provisions: (1) tariffs on industrial goods were to be reduced by more than one-third, and tariffs were to be scrapped on over 40 percent of manufactured goods; (2) average tariff rates imposed by developed nations on manufactured goods were to be reduced to less than 4 percent of value, the lowest level in modern history; (3) there was to be a substantial reduction in agricultural subsidies; (4) for the first time GATT fair trade and market access rules were to be extended to cover a wide range of services; (5) GATT rules were also to be extended to provide enhanced protection for patents, copyrights, and trademarks (intellectual property); (6) barriers on trade in textiles were to be significantly reduced over 10 years; and (7) a World Trade Organization (WTO) was to be created to implement the GATT agreement.

Services and Intellectual Property

In the long run, the extension of GATT rules to cover services and intellectual property may be particularly significant. Until 1995, GATT rules applied only to industrial goods (i.e., manufactured goods and commodities). In 1999, world trade in services amounted to $1,340 billion (compared to world trade in goods of $5,460 billion).[27] Extension of GATT rules to this important trading arena could significantly increase both the total share of world trade accounted for by services and the overall volume of world trade. The extension of GATT rules to cover intellectual property will make it much easier for high-technology companies to do business in developing nations where intellectual property rules have historically been poorly enforced (see Chapter 2 for details). High-technology companies now have a mechanism to force countries to prohibit the piracy of intellectual property.

The World Trade Organization

The clarification and strengthening of GATT rules and the creation of the World Trade Organization also hold out the promise of more effective policing and enforcement of GATT rules. The WTO acts as an umbrella organization that encompasses the GATT along with two new sister bodies, one on services and the other on intellectual property. The WTO has taken over responsibility for arbitrating trade disputes and monitoring the trade policies of member countries. While the WTO operates on the basis of consensus as the GATT did, in the area of dispute settlement member countries will no longer be able to block adoption of arbitration reports. Arbitration panel reports on trade disputes between member countries will be automatically adopted by the WTO unless there is a consensus to reject them. Countries that have been found by the arbitration panel to violate GATT rules may appeal to a permanent appellate body, but its verdict is binding. If offenders fail to comply with the recommendations of the arbitration panel, trading partners have the right to compensation or, in the last resort, to impose (commensurate) trade sanctions (for an example, see the opening case on the banana wars). Every stage of the procedure is subject to strict time limits. Thus, the WTO has something that the GATT never had—teeth.[28]

WTO: Experience to Date

By 2000, the WTO had 140 members and another 29 countries, including China, the Russian Federation, and Saudi Arabia, negotiating for membership into the organization.

Since its formation, the WTO has remained at the forefront of efforts to promote global free trade. Its creators expressed the hope that the enforcement mechanisms granted to the WTO would make it a more effective policeman of global trade rules than the GATT had been. The great hope was that the WTO might emerge as an effective advocate and facilitator of future trade deals, particularly in areas such as services. The experience so far has been encouraging, although the collapse of WTO talks in Seattle in late 1999 has raised a number of questions about the future direction of the WTO.

WTO as a Global Policeman

The first few years in the life of the WTO suggest that its policing and enforcement mechanisms are having a positive effect. Between 1995 and late 2000, 213 trade disputes between member countries were brought to the WTO.[29] This record compares with a total of 196 cases handled by the GATT over almost half a century. Of the cases brought to the WTO, three-fourths had been resolved by late 2000 following informal consultations between the disputing countries. Resolving the remainder has involved more formal procedures, but these have been largely successful. In general, the countries involved have adopted the WTO's recommendations. Only a handful of cases so far have yet to be resolved by the WTO, including highly contentious disputes between the United States and the European Union over bananas and hormone-treated beef. The fact that countries are using the WTO represents an important vote of confidence in the organization's dispute resolution procedures. Reflecting this success, in its 1999 annual report the WTO noted:

> The state of the world trading system is generally sound . . . there were no major trade policy reversals in 1998 and 1999 and . . . there is no evidence of a return to protectionist measures. On the contrary, a number of countries have undertaken concrete measures to further liberalize their economic and trade regimes.[30]

Expanding Trade Agreements

As explained above, the Uruguay Round of GATT negotiations extended global trading rules to cover trade in services. The WTO was given the role of brokering future agreements to open up global trade in services. The WTO was also encouraged to extend its reach to encompass regulations governing foreign direct investment, something the GATT had never done. Two of the first industries targeted for reform were the global telecommunication and financial services industries.

The WTO came close to reaching an agreement to liberalize global telecommunication services in early 1996, but ultimately failed to close a deal when the United States declined to sanction the draft agreement, arguing that it did not do enough to open national markets to foreign investment. The WTO tried again to reach an agreement in February 1997. Given its importance in the global economy, the telecommunication service industry was clearly a very important target for reform. The goal of the WTO was to get countries to agree to open their telecommunication markets to competition, allowing foreign operators to purchase ownership stakes in domestic telecommunication providers and establishing a set of common rules for fair competition. The benefits claimed for such agreements where threefold.

First, advocates argued that inward investment and increased competition would stimulate the modernization of telephone networks around the world and lead to higher quality service. Second, supporters maintained that the increased competition would benefit customers through lower prices. Estimates suggested that a deal would soon reduce the average cost of international telephone calls by 80 percent and save users $1,000 billion over three years.[31] Third, the WTO argued that trade in other goods and services invariably depends on flows of information matching buyers to sellers. As telecommunication services improve in quality and decline in price, international trade increases in volume and becomes less costly for traders. Telecommunication reform, therefore, should promote cross-border trade in other goods and services.

After some last-minute hedging by the United States, a deal was reached February 15, 1997. Under the pact, 68 countries accounting for more than 90 percent of world telecommunication revenues pledged to start opening their markets to foreign competition and to abide by common rules for fair competition in telecommunications. Most of the world's biggest markets, including the United States, European Union, and Japan, were fully liberalized by January 1, 1998, when the pact went into effect. All forms of basic telecommunication service are covered, including voice telephony, data and fax transmissions, and satellite and radio communications. Many telecommunication companies responded positively to the deal, pointing out that it would give them a much greater ability to offer their business customers "one-stop shopping"—a global, seamless service for all their corporate needs and a single bill.[32]

Fresh from success in brokering a telecommunication agreement, in 1997 the WTO embarked on a series of negotiations to liberalize the global financial services industry. The financial services industry includes banking, securities businesses, insurance, asset management services, and the like. As with telecommunications, the first attempt at reaching a global deal in 1995 failed when the United States refused to join a pact. The negotiations stalled because the United States felt developing countries were not prepared to make enough concessions.

The global financial services industry is enormous. The sector executes $1.2 trillion a day in foreign exchange transactions. International financing extended by banks around the world reporting to the Bank for International Settlements is estimated at $6.4 trillion, including $4.6 trillion net international lending. Total world banking assets are put at more than $20 trillion, insurance premiums at $2 trillion, stock market capitalization at over $10 trillion, and market value of listed bonds at around $10 trillion. In addition, practically every international trade in goods or services requires credit, capital, foreign exchange, and insurance.[33]

Participants in the negotiations wanted to see more competition in the sector, both to allow firms greater opportunities abroad and to encourage greater efficiency. Developing countries need the capital and financial infrastructure for their development. But governments also have to ensure that the system is sound and stable because of the economic shocks that can be caused if exchange rates, interest rates, or other market conditions fluctuate excessively. They also have to avoid economic crises caused by bank failures. Therefore, government intervention in prudential safeguards is an important condition underpinning financial market liberalization.

An agreement was reached December 14, 1997.[34] The deal covers more than 95 percent of the world's financial services market. Under the agreement, which took effect at the beginning of March 1999, 102 countries pledged to open to varying degrees their banking, securities, and insurance sectors to foreign competition. In common with the telecommunication deal, the accord covers not just cross-border trade but also foreign direct investment. A total of 70 countries agreed to dramatically lower or eradicate barriers to foreign direct investment in their financial services sector. The United States and the European Union, with minor exceptions, are fully open to inward investment by foreign banks, insurance, and securities companies. As part of the deal, many Asian countries made important concessions that allow, for the first time, significant foreign participation in their financial services sectors.

The WTO in Seattle: A Watershed?

At the end of November 1999, representatives from the WTO's member states met in Seattle, Washington. The goal of the meeting was to launch a new round of talks—dubbed "the millennium round"—aimed at further reducing barriers to cross-border trade and investment. This round of talks was to be the ninth since 1947. Expectations were high that after the normal amount of haggling, posturing, and last-minute brinkmanship, the talks would yield agreement on major goals for the next round of talks, which were scheduled to begin soon after. Prominent on the agenda was an attempt to get the assembled countries to agree to work toward the reduction of barriers

Shrimps, Turtles, and the WTO

There are seven species of sea turtles in the world; six of them are on the list of endangered species in the United States. A major cause of the decline of sea turtles has been poor fishing practices, particularly by shrimp boats. An estimated 150,000 sea turtles are trapped and drown in the nets of shrimp boats each year. In an effort to limit this carnage, in 1989 the U.S. Congress passed a law that required shrimp boats to be equipped with a turtle-excluder device. This is a simple grate that fits over the mouth of shrimp trawling nets and prevents sea turtles from becoming trapped. The law also banned the importation of shrimp from countries that fail to mandate the use of turtle-excluder devices.

As with many such laws, the U.S. government dragged its heels on enforcing the import ban. It wasn't until 1996 that the United States placed an embargo on the importation of shrimp from countries that failed to mandate the use of excluder devices. Even then, it did so only because environmental groups in the United States had brought a lawsuit against the government to compel it to enforce its own law. Three countries were targeted by the 1996 ban—India, Pakistan, and Malaysia. The three responded to the ban by filing a complaint with the World Trade Organization. They were joined by Thailand, which decided as a matter of principle to pursue the WTO case (Thailand had already satisfied the United States that its turtle protection methods were adequate).

As is normal in such cases, the WTO formed an independent arbitration panel composed of three experts from countries not involved in the dispute. The panel was charged with reviewing the U.S. position to see whether it did conflict with WTO rules. In its defense, the United States claimed there are provisions in the WTO rules for taking restrictive measures if they are related "to the conservation of exhaustible natural resources and if such measures are made effective in conjunction with restrictions on domestic production or consumption." The United States was supported in its case by a number of environmental organizations, including the World Wildlife Fund (WWF). In a brief submitted to the panel, the WWF argued that marine turtles are migratory animals, a global resource that should be subject to stewardship by international society. Even though no multilateral body or resolution had authorized the United States to enact its ban, the WWF claimed that the United States acted in a manner consistent with its obligations and took reasonable measures that reflected the will of the international community.

For their part, the four countries that brought the complaint argued that the U.S. ban represented an unfair restraint on trade that was illegal under WTO rules. According to these countries, the United States was violating WTO rules by applying domestic legislation outside of its boundaries and by applying it in a discriminatory manner. Influential voices in all these countries accused the United States of hypocrisy. An

to cross-border trade in agricultural products and cross-border trade and investment in services.

These expectations were dashed on the rocks of a hard and unexpected reality. The talks ended December 3, 1999, without any agreement being reached. Inside the meeting rooms, the problem was an inability to reach consensus on the primary goals for the next round of talks. A major stumbling block was friction between the United States and the European Union over whether to endorse the aim of ultimately eliminating subsidies to agricultural exporters. The United States wanted the elimination of such subsidies to be a priority. The EU, with its politically powerful farm lobby and long history of farm subsidies, was unwilling to take this step. Another stumbling block was related to efforts by the United States to write "basic labor rights" into the law of the world trading system. The United States wanted the WTO to allow governments to impose tariffs on goods imported from countries that did not abide by what the United States saw as fair labor practices. Representatives from developing nations reacted angrily to this proposal, suggesting that it was simply an attempt by the United States to find a legal way of restricting imports from poorer nations.

While the disputes inside the meeting rooms were acrimonious enough, it was events outside that captured the attention of the world press. The WTO talks proved article in *The Hindu,* an Indian newspaper, stated, "Compared to what the U.S. as a nation is doing to another global shared resource, the world's climate and atmosphere, what complainant nations like India are doing to the marine turtle is a contemptuously small problem . . . The U.S. leadership has, unfortunately, always put its national interests before global concerns in its global environmental policies. Its behavior on the climate change issue is one example. Its refusal to sign the bio-diversity treaty is another. Its refusal to pay dues to the United Nations is yet another."

The World Trade Organization panel on April 6, 1998, ruled that the ban was in violation of WTO rules and would need to be amended. According to the WTO, by enacting a targeted ban against just three countries, the United States had acted in a discriminatory manner, which was in violation of WTO accords. Further, the WTO stated that if the United States wished to impose such a ban, it should be a blanket ban against imports from all countries that fail to use turtle-excluder device, not just a targeted list of countries.

The environmental movement reacted to the WTO ruling with dismay. A Sierra Club spokesman noted that "This is the clearest slap at environmental protection to come out of the WTO to date." Similarly, a spokeswoman for the Washington, D.C. based Center for Marine Conservation stated "It is unthinkable that we should not be allowed to mitigate the impacts of our own shrimp markets on endangered sea turtles.

This entire life form is threatened with extinction." However, this reaction, which was widely reported in the press, seems to have been based on a failure to read and/or understand the WTO's ruling. The ruling actually stated that under certain circumstance it was all right for the United States to restrict imports for environmental reasons, but only if such restrictions were applied in a nondiscriminatory manner. The problem with the U.S. ban as it stood was that it had targeted a select group of countries—it was discriminatory.

In response, the United States revised the law so that it restricted shrimp imports from any country that failed to use a turtle-excluder device on its shrimp boats. The import ban, however, stayed in place. Malaysia responded by filing a complaint in October 2000 with the WTO, arguing that the United States was still in violation of WTO rules. In October 2001, the WTO rejected Malaysia's complaint, effectively confirming that the amended U.S. ban was consistent with WTO rules.[36]

Sources: A. Aggarwal and S. Narain. Politics of Conservation. *The Hindu,* October 26, 1997, p. 26.; J. H. Cushman. Trade Group Strikes a Blow at U.S. Environmental Law. *New York Times,* April 7, 1998, page D1.; Staff Writer. WTO Ruling in Turtle Protection Dispute. *Bangkok Post,* March 18, 1998.; J. Maggs. WTO Shrimp Ruling Heightens Environment vs. Trade Debate. *Journal of Commerce,* April 7, 1998, page 3A.; Malaysia Swims Against the Tide Over U.S. Shrimps Import Ban. *New Straits Times Press* (Malaysia), October 25, 2001, page 2.

to be a lightning rod for a diverse collection of organizations from environmentalists and human rights groups to labor unions. For various reasons, these groups are opposed to free trade. All these organizations argued that the WTO is an undemocratic institution that was usurping the national sovereignty of member states and making decisions of great importance behind closed doors. They took advantage of the Seattle meetings to voice their opposition, which the world press recorded. Environmentalists expressed concern about the impact that free trade in agricultural products might have on the rate of global deforestation. They argued that lower tariffs on imports of lumber from developing nations will stimulate demand and accelerate the rate at which virgin forests are logged, particularly in nations such as Malaysia and Indonesia. They also pointed to the adverse impact that some WTO rulings have had on environmental policies. For example, the WTO recently blocked a U.S. rule that ordered shrimp nets be equipped with a device that allows endangered sea turtles to escape. The WTO found the rule discriminated against foreign importers who lacked such nets.[35] Environmentalist argued that the rule was necessary to protect the turtles from extinction (see the accompanying Country Focus for details).

Human rights activists see WTO rules as outlawing the ability of nations to stop imports from countries where child labor is used or working conditions are hazardous.

193

Similarly, labor unions oppose trade laws that allow imports from low-wage countries and result in a loss of jobs in high-wage countries. They buttress their position by arguing that American workers are losing their jobs to imports from developing nations that do not have adequate labor standards.

Supporters of the WTO and free trade are quick to dismiss these concerns. They have repeatedly pointed out that the WTO exists to serve the interests of its member states, not subvert them. The WTO lacks the ability to force any member nation to take an action that it is opposed to. The WTO can allow member nations to impose retaliatory tariffs on countries that do not abide by WTO rules, but that is the limit of its power. Furthermore, supporters argue, it is rich countries that pass strict environmental laws and laws governing labor standards, not poor ones. In their view, free trade, by raising living standards in developing nations, will be followed by the passage of such laws in these nations. Using trade regulations to try to impose such practices on developing nations, they believe, will produce a self-defeating backlash.

Many representatives from developing nations, who make up about 105 of the WTO's 140 members, also reject the position taken by environmentalists and advocates of human and labor rights. Poor countries, which depend on exports to boost their economic growth rates and work their way out of poverty, fear that rich countries will use environmental concerns, human rights, and labor-related issues to erect barriers to the products of the developing world. They believe that attempts to incorporate language about the environment or labor standards in future trade agreements will amount to little more than trade barriers by another name.[37] If this were to occur, they argue that the effect would be to trap the developing nations of the world in a grinding cycle of poverty and debt.

Such pro-trade arguments fell on deaf ears. As the WTO representatives gathered in Seattle, environmentalists, human rights activists, and labor unions marched in the streets. Some of the more radical elements in these organizations, together with groups of anarchists who were philosophically opposed to "global capitalism" and "the rape of the world by multinationals," succeeded not only in shutting down the opening ceremonies of the WTO, but also in sparking violence in the normally peaceful streets of Seattle. Against the wishes of the vast majority of protesters, a number of demonstrators engaged in property damage and looting. The police responded with tear gas, rubber bullets, pepper spray, and baton charges. When it was all over, 600 demonstrators had been arrested, millions of dollars in property had been damaged in downtown Seattle, and the global news media had their headline: "WTO talks collapse amid violent demonstrations."

The question that now must be asked is whether the events in Seattle portray an end to half a century of trade liberalization, or whether they represent nothing more than a bump in the road. History suggests that the WTO will ultimately get the next round of talks under way. The last round of global trade talks—the Uruguay Round—also took several years to initiate. However, Seattle may have been a watershed of sorts. In the past, previous trade talks were pursued in relative obscurity with only interested economists, politicians, and businesspeople paying much attention. Seattle demonstrated that the issues surrounding the global trend toward free trade have moved to center stage in the popular consciousness. The debate on the merits of free trade and globalization has become mainstream. Whether further liberalization occurs, therefore, may depend on the importance that popular opinion in countries such as the United States attaches to issues such as human rights and labor standards, job security, environmental policies, and national sovereignty. It will also depend on the ability of advocates of free trade to articulate in a clear and compelling manner the argument that, in the long run, free trade is the best way of promoting adequate labor standards, of providing more jobs, and of protecting the environment. Exactly how this debate will play out remains to be seen, but given recent trends it would not be surprising if labor rights and environmental considerations played a much larger role in the next round of global trade talks when they finally get started (which, despite the breakdown of the Seattle meeting, seems likely to occur within the next two to three years).

The Future: Unresolved Issues

The 1994 GATT deal still leaves a lot to be done on the international trade front. Substantial trade barriers still remain in areas such as broadcast entertainment, although these seem likely to be reduced eventually. More significantly, there is still a whole range of issues that the GATT and now the WTO have yet to deal with but increasingly will need to. Three of the most important areas for future development are in the areas of environmentalism, worker rights, and foreign direct investment.[38]

High on the list of the WTO's future concerns will be the interaction of environmental and trade policies and the issue of how best to promote sustainable development and ecological well-being without resorting to protectionism. The WTO will have to find ways to deal with the increasingly vigorous claims by environmentalists that expanded international trade encourages companies to locate factories in areas of the world where they are freer to pollute and degrade the environment. Also, the WTO will now have to deal with concerns that free trade encourages firms to shift their production to countries with low labor rates where workers' rights are routinely violated.

GATT regulations have never been extended to embrace foreign direct investment (investment by a firm based in one country in productive facilities in another country). Given the globalization of production that we are now witnessing in the world economy, barriers to foreign direct investment seem antiquated, and yet they are still widespread (we will discuss these in detail in Chapter 7). Currently many countries limit investment by foreign companies in their economies (e.g., local content requirements, local ownership rules, and even outright prohibition).

A final issue of concern has been the proliferation of antidumping actions in recent years. WTO rules allow countries to impose antidumping duties on foreign goods that are being sold cheaper than at home, or below their cost of production, when domestic producers can show that they are being harmed. The rather vague definition of what constitutes "dumping" has proved to be a loophole, which many countries are exploiting to pursue protectionism. In the United States, for example, 26 antidumping cases were launched in 1998, up from 16 in the previous year. In the first six months of 1999, the United States launched another 28 antidumping actions. There has also been a rise in cases filed by the European Union. As of 2000, WTO members had reported implementation of some 1,097 antidumping actions to the WTO. The United States had the largest number of antidumping actions, with some 336, followed by the EU with 183. When an industry faces strong foreign competition, the first response of some firms in that industry seems to be to cry foul and accuse the foreign producers of dumping. The process can then become politicized, as representatives of businesses and their employees lobby government officials to "protect domestic jobs from unfair foreign competition." If this trend continues, the WTO likely will try to strengthen the regulations governing the imposition of antidumping duties.

Implications for Business

What are the implications of all of this for business practice? Why should the international manager care about the political economy of free trade or about the relative merits of arguments for free trade and protectionism? There are two answers to this question. The first concerns the impact of trade barriers on a firm's strategy. The second concerns the role that business firms can play in promoting free trade and/or trade barriers.

Trade Barriers and Firm Strategy

To understand how trade barriers affect a firm's strategy, consider first the material we covered in Chapter 4. Drawing on the theories of international trade, we discussed how it makes sense for the firm to disperse its various production activities to those countries around the globe where they can be performed most efficiently. Thus, it may make sense for a firm to design and engineer its product in one country, to manufacture components in another, to perform final assembly operations in yet another country, and then export the finished product to the rest of the world.

Clearly, trade barriers are a constraint on a firm's ability to disperse its productive activities in such a manner. First, and most obviously, tariff barriers raise the costs of exporting products to a country (or of exporting partly finished products between countries). This may put the firm at a competitive disadvantage vis-à-vis indigenous competitors in that country. In response, the firm may then find it economical to locate production facilities in that country so that it can compete on an even footing with indigenous competitors. Second, quotas and voluntary export restraints may limit a firm's ability to serve a country from locations outside of that country. Again, the response by the firm might be to set up production facilities in that country—even though it may result in higher production costs. Such reasoning was one of the factors behind the rapid expansion of Japanese automaking capacity in the United States during the 1980s. This followed the establishment of a VER agreement between the United States and Japan that limited U.S. imports of Japanese automobiles.

Third, to conform to local content regulations, a firm may have to locate more production activities in a given market than it would otherwise. Again, from the firm's perspective, the consequence might be to raise costs above the level that could be achieved if each production activity was dispersed to the optimal location for that activity. And finally, even when trade barriers do not exist, the firm may still want to locate some production activities in a given country to reduce the threat of trade barriers being imposed in the future.

All the above effects are likely to raise the firm's costs above the level that could be achieved in a world without trade barriers. The higher costs that result need not translate into a significant competitive disadvantage relative to other foreign firms, however, if the countries imposing trade barriers do so to the imported products of all foreign firms, irrespective of their national origin. But when trade barriers are targeted at exports from a particular nation, firms based in that nation are at a competitive disadvantage to firms of other nations. The firm may deal with such targeted trade barriers by moving production into the country imposing barriers. Another strategy may be to move production to countries whose exports are not targeted by the specific trade barrier, which is what the Esquel Group did to circumvent quota limits (see the Management Focus).

Finally, the threat of antidumping action limits the ability of a firm to use aggressive pricing to gain market share in a country. Firms in a country can also make strategic use of antidumping measures to limit aggressive competition from low-cost foreign producers. For example, the U.S. steel industry has been very aggressive in bringing antidumping actions against foreign steelmakers, particularly in times of weak global demand for steel and excess capacity. For example, in 1998 and 1999 the United States faced a surge in low-cost steel imports as a severe recession in Asia left producers there with excess capacity. The U.S. producers filed several complaints with the International Trade Commission. One argued that Japanese producers of hot rolled steel were selling it at below cost in the United States. The ITC agreed and levied tariffs ranging from 18 percent to 67 percent on imports of certain steel products from Japan.[39]

Policy Implications

As noted in Chapter 4, business firms are major players on the international trade scene. Because of their pivotal role in international trade, firms can and do exert a strong influence on government policy toward trade. This influence can encourage protectionism or it can encourage the government to support the

WTO and push for open markets and freer trade among all nations. Government policies with regard to international trade can have a direct impact on business.

Consistent with strategic trade policy, examples can be found of government intervention in the form of tariffs, quotas, antidumping actions, and subsidies helping firms and industries establish a competitive advantage in the world economy. In general, however, the arguments contained in this chapter and in Chapter 4 suggest that government intervention has three drawbacks. Intervention can be self-defeating, since in practice it tends to protect the inefficient rather than help firms become efficient global competitors. Intervention is dangerous; it may invite retaliation and trigger a trade war. Finally, intervention is unlikely to be well-executed, given the opportunity for such a policy to be captured by special interest groups. Does this mean, then, that business should simply encourage government to adopt a *laissez-faire* free trade policy?

Most economists would probably argue that the best interests of international business are served by a free trade stance, but not a laissez-faire stance. It is probably in the best long-run interests of the business community to encourage the government to aggressively promote greater free trade by, for example, strengthening the WTO. Business probably has much more to gain from government efforts to open protected markets to imports and foreign direct investment than from government efforts to support certain domestic industries in a manner consistent with the recommendations of strategic trade policy.

This conclusion is reinforced by a phenomenon we touched on in Chapter 1— the increasing integration of the world economy and internationalization of production that has occurred over the past two decades. We live in a world where many firms of all national origins increasingly depend for their competitive advantage on globally dispersed production systems. Such systems are the result of freer trade. Freer trade has brought great advantages to firms that have exploited it and to consumers who benefit from the resulting lower prices. Given the danger of retaliatory action, business firms that lobby their governments to engage in protectionism must realize that by doing so they may be denying themselves the opportunity to build a competitive advantage by constructing a globally dispersed production system. By encouraging their governments to engage in protectionism, their own activities and sales overseas may be jeopardized if other governments retaliate. This does not mean that a firm should never seek protection in the form of antidumping actions and the like, but it should review its options carefully and think through the larger consequences.

Chapter Summary

The objective of this chapter was to describe how the reality of international trade deviates from the theoretical ideal of unrestricted free trade reviewed in Chapter 4. Consistent with this objective, in this chapter we have reported the various instruments of trade policy, reviewed the political and economic arguments for government intervention in international trade, reexamined the economic case for free trade in light of the strategic trade policy argument, and looked at the evolution of the world trading framework. While a policy of free trade may not always be the theoretically optimal policy (given the arguments of the new trade theorists), in practice it is probably the best policy for a government to pursue. In particular, the long-run interests of business and consumers may be best served by strengthening international institutions such as the WTO. Given the danger that isolated protectionism might escalate into a trade war, business probably has far more to gain from government efforts to open protected markets to imports and foreign direct investment (through the WTO) than from government efforts to protect domestic industries from foreign competition.

In this chapter the following points have been made:

1. The effect of a tariff is to raise the cost of imported products. Gains accrue to the government (from revenues) and to producers (who are protected

from foreign competitors). Consumers lose because they must pay more for imports.

2. By lowering costs, subsidies help domestic producers to compete against low-cost foreign imports and to gain export markets. However, subsidies must be paid for by taxpayers. They also tend to be captured by special interests that use them to protect the inefficient.

3. An import quota is a direct restriction imposed by an importing country on the quantity of some good that may be imported. A voluntary export restraint (VER) is a quota on trade imposed from the exporting country's side. Both import quotas and VERs benefit domestic producers by limiting import competition, but they result in higher prices, which hurts consumers.

4. A local content requirement calls for some specific fraction of a good to be produced domestically. Local content requirements benefit the producers of component parts, but they raise prices of imported components, which hurts consumers.

5. An administrative policy is an informal instrument or bureaucratic rule that can be used to restrict imports and boost exports. Such policies benefit producers but hurt consumers, who are denied access to possibly superior foreign products.

6. There are two types of arguments for government intervention in international trade: political and economic. Political arguments for intervention are concerned with protecting the interests of certain groups, often at the expense of other groups, or with promoting goals with regard to foreign policy, human rights, consumer protection, and the like. Economic arguments for intervention are about boosting the overall wealth of a nation.

7. The most common political argument for intervention is that it is necessary to protect jobs. However, political intervention often hurts consumers and it can be self-defeating.

8. Countries sometimes argue that it is important to protect certain industries for reasons of national security.

9. Some argue that government should use the threat to intervene in trade policy as a bargaining tool to open up foreign markets. This can be

a risky policy; if it fails, the result can be higher trade barriers.

10. The infant industry argument for government intervention contends that to let manufacturing get a toehold, governments should temporarily support new industries. In practice, however, governments often end up protecting the inefficient.

11. Strategic trade policy suggests that with subsidies, government can help domestic firms gain first-mover advantages in global industries where economies of scale are important. Government subsidies may also help domestic firms overcome barriers to entry into such industries.

12. The problems with strategic trade policy are twofold: (a) such a policy may invite retaliation, in which case all will lose, and (b) strategic trade policy may be captured by special interest groups, which will distort it to their own ends.

13. The Smoot-Hawley tariff, introduced in 1930, erected an enormous wall of tariff barriers to imports. Other countries responded by adopting similar tariffs, and the world slid further into the Great Depression

14. The GATT was a product of the post-war free trade movement. The GATT was successful in lowering trade barriers on manufactured goods and commodities. The move toward greater free trade under the GATT appeared to stimulate economic growth.

15. The completion of the Uruguay Round of GATT talks and the establishment of the World Trade Organization have strengthened the world trading system by extending GATT rules to services, increasing protection for intellectual property, reducing agricultural subsidies, and enhancing monitoring and enforcement mechanisms.

16. Trade barriers act as a constraint on a firm's ability to disperse its various production activities to optimal locations around the globe. One response to trade barriers is to establish more production activities in the protected country.

17. Business may have more to gain from government efforts to open protected markets to imports and foreign direct investment, than from government efforts to protect domestic industries from foreign competition.

Critical Discussion Questions

1. Do you think governments should take human rights considerations into account when granting preferential trading rights to countries? What are the arguments for and against taking such a position?

2. Whose interests should be the paramount concern of government trade policy—the interests of producers (businesses and their employees) or those of consumers?

3. Given the arguments relating to the new trade theory and strategic trade policy, what kind of trade policy should business be pressuring government to adopt?

4. You are an employee of a U.S. firm that produces personal computers in Thailand and then exports them to the United States and other countries for sale. The personal computers were originally produced in Thailand to take advantage of relatively low labor costs and a skilled workforce. Other possible locations considered at the time were Malaysia and Hong Kong. The U.S. government decides to impose punitive 100 percent ad valorem tariffs on imports of computers from Thailand to punish the country for administrative trade barriers that restrict U.S. exports to Thailand. How do you think your firm should respond? What does this tell you about the use of targeted trade barriers?

Is a Tax Break an Export Subsidy?

Closing Case

The U.S. economy was facing a surging trade deficit in 1971. Alarmed by this, then-President Nixon concocted a special income tax break for U.S. exporters. The corporate deduction, known as the Foreign Sales Corporation (FSC), produced large tax savings for U.S. exporters, although it is questionable as to whether those had an impact on the trade deficit. In 1999 and 2000, however, the FCS moved to center stage in a trade dispute between the United States and the European Union, which the World Trade Organization is trying to resolve.

The FSC tax break allows exporters to avoid paying corporate income tax on exports of manufactured goods, the sales of which are channeled through shell companies, known as Foreign Sales Corporations, which are registered in offshore tax havens such as Bermuda. While this sounds fairly arcane, the benefits are not. Estimates suggest that some 6,000 U.S. companies saved about $3.5 billion in income taxes in 1998 as a result of the FSC. Two of the major beneficiaries include Boeing and General Electric. Boeing saved $130 million in taxes in 1998 as a result of the FSC, 12 percent of its total earnings that year, while General Electric saved $150 million.

In 1998, the European Union filed a complaint with the WTO claiming that the FSC constituted an illegal export subsidy that was in clear violation of WTO rules. The United States was a bit taken aback by this action, arguing that it had an unwritten "gentleman's agreement" with the EU that neither entity would attack each other's tax systems in trade courts. Furthermore, the United States stated that tax codes had always been seen as "internal matters" that fell outside the jurisdiction of trade policy. The EU replied that this was a hypocritical stance. The United States had already challenged the EU at the WTO on other policies that are normally considered "internal matters," such as food safety and envi-

ronmental regulations. (The United States had complained to the WTO about the EU policy to ban hormone-treated beef, which the EU implemented for safety and environmental reasons.) Given this, why should tax codes be any different?

After hearing the evidence, a WTO arbitration panel in February 2000 agreed with the EU, arguing that the tax break was illegal because it applied just to exports and was thus technically an export subsidy and in violation of WTO rules. The United States was given until October 1, 2000, to revise the code or face the possibility of punitive sanctions. The prospect of trade sanctions sent Treasury officials, tax lawyers, members of Congress, and business lobbyists into a frenzy to fashion a fix for the FSC. After working in secret for several months, the Ways and Means Committee of the House of Representatives formulated a bill to amend the FSC. While the bill did scrap many of the FSC provisions, it not only retained the tax break given to export sales, but it also expanded the break, adding $1.5 billion to the projected $25 billion cost of the tax write-off to the U.S. Treasury. In reaching this decision, the politicians argued that the reason for retaining the tax break was to compensate for the EU practice of granting European exporters a rebate on the value-added taxes they normally have to pay.

The Europeans were quick to point out that trade rules allow rebates on consumption taxes such as the European value-added tax and on U.S. excise taxes and state sales taxes, but specifically not on income tax. Moreover, the Europeans do not exempt their corporations from paying income tax on export revenue. The EU signaled that if the revised FSC code were passed, it would challenge it in the WTO and seek permission to impose punitive tariffs worth $4.04 billion on U.S. exports to the EU. That threat got the attention of Congress, which scrambled to amend the legislation.

In mid-November 2000, the U.S. Congress passed an amended bill that repealed the FSC, but replaced it with a new system that offered up to $6 billion a year in tax breaks to large exporters such as Boeing and Microsoft. The United States claimed the new scheme would bring it into compliance with WTO rules. The EU countered that the new code was no better than the FSC, since it still maintained a tax break for export income. Two days later it filed a brief with the WTO seeking permission to impose punitive tariffs of $4.04 billion on U.S. exports.

In late December 2000, the WTO agreed to set up a panel to review the new U.S. tax code, signaling that it would issue a ruling in 90 days on the legality of the code. At the same time, the WTO gave the EU permission to impose sanctions against the United States if the revised code is found to be in violation of WTO rules. Suddenly, an arcane debate over tax codes had moved to center stage in the trade debate and risked sparking a trade war between the world's two largest trading entities.

Sources: A. Entous, "Congress Oks Bill to Avert Trade War with EU," Reuters, November 14, 2000; G. Winestock, "EU Aims for Huge Sanctions on the U.S.," *Wall Street Journal*, November 20, 2000, p. A2; and P. Magnusson, "The Tax Break Could Trigger a Trade War," *Business Week*, September 4, 2000, pp. 103–04.

Case Discussion Questions

1. How does the FSC item in the U.S. tax code constitute an export subsidy?

2. Do you think that "internal matters" such as tax codes and food safety laws should be excluded from consideration by the World Trade Organization?

3. Why do you think the U.S. Congress is apparently so reluctant to scrap the FSC?

4. Can you see a solution to this trade dispute? What is it?

5. What do you think might occur if the trade dispute is not resolved?

References

1. For a detailed welfare analysis of the effect of a tariff, see P. R. Krugman and M. Obstfeld, *International Economics: Theory and Policy* (New York: Harper Collins, 2000), chap. 8.

2. Y. Sazanami, S. Urata, and H. Kawai, *Measuring the Costs of Protection in Japan* (Washington, DC: Institute for International Economics, 1994).

3. J. Bhagwati, *Protectionism* (Cambridge, MA: MIT Press, 1988) and "Costs of Protection," *Journal of Commerce*, September 25, 1991, p. 8A.

4. "A Not So Perfect Market," *The Economist: Survey of Agriculture and Technology*, March 25, 2000, pp. 8–10.

5. "From the Sublime to the Subsidy," *The Economist*, February 24, 1990, p. 71

6. The study was undertaken by Kym Anderson of the University of Adelaide. See "A Not So Perfect Market."

7. R. W. Crandall, *Regulating the Automobile* (Washington, DC: Brookings Institute, 1986).

8. Quoted in Krugman and Obstfeld, *International Economics*.

9. Hufbauer and Elliott, *Measuring the Costs of Protectionism in the United States*.

10. A. Tanzer, "The Great Quota Hustle," *Forbes*, March 6, 2000, pp. 119–25.

11. Bhagwati, *Protectionism*, and "Japan to Curb VCR Exports," *New York Times*, November 21, 1983, p. D5.

12. Alan Goldstein, "Sematech Members Facing Dues Increase; 30% Jump to Make Up for Loss of Federal Funding," *Dallas Morning News*," July 27, 1996, p. 2F.

13. N. Dunne and R. Waters, "US Waves a Big Stick at Chinese Pirates," *Financial Times*, January 6, 1995, p. 4.

14. John Broder, "Clinton to Impose Ban on 58 Types of Imported Guns," *New York Times*, April 6, 1998, p. A1.

15. Bill Lambrecht, "Monsanto Softens Its Stance on Labeling in Europe," *St. Louis Post-Dispatch*, March 15, 1998, p. E1.

16. Peter S. Jordan, "Country Sanctions and the International Business Community," *American Society of International Law Proceedings of the Annual Meeting 20* no. 9, (1997), pp. 333–42.

17. "Waiting for China; Human Rights and International Trade," *Commonwealth*, March 11, 1994; and "China: The Cost of Putting Business First," *Human Rights Watch*, July 1996.

18. "Brazil's Auto Industry Struggles to Boost Global Competitiveness," *Journal of Commerce*, October 10, 1991, p. 6A.

19. For reviews, see J. A. Brander, "Rationales for Strategic Trade and Industrial Policy," in *Strategic Trade Policy and the New International Economics*, ed. P. R. Krugman (Cambridge, MA: MIT Press, 1986); P. R. Krugman, "Is Free Trade

Passé?" *Journal of Economic Perspectives* 1 (1987), pp. 131–44; and P. R. Krugman, "Does the New Trade Theory Require a New Trade Policy?" *World Economy* 15, no. 4 (1992), pp. 423–41.

20. "Airbus and Boeing: The Jumbo War," *The Economist,* June 15, 1991, pp. 65–66.

21. For details see Krugman, *Is Free Trade Passé?* and Brander, "Rationales for Strategic Trade and Industrial Policy."

22. Krugman, *"Is Free Trade Passé?"*

23. This dilemma is a variant of the famous prisoner's dilemma, which has become a classic metaphor for the difficulty of achieving cooperation between self-interested and mutually suspicious entities. For a good general introduction, see A. Dixit and B. Nalebuff, *Thinking Strategically: The Competitive Edge in Business, Politics, and Everyday Life* (New York: W.W. Norton & Co., 1991).

24. Note that the Smoot-Hawley tariff did not cause the Great Depression. However, the beggar-thy-neighbor trade policies that it ushered in certainly made things worse. See Bhagwati, *Protectionism.*

25. Ibid.

26. World Bank, *World Development Report* (New York: Oxford University Press, 1987).

27. World Trade Organization, *Annual Report 2000* Geneva; WTO, 2000).

28. Frances Williams, "WTO—New Name Heralds New Powers," *Financial Times,* December 16, 1993, p. 5, and Frances Williams, "Gatt's Successor to Be Given Real Clout," *Financial Times,* April 4, 1994, p. 6.

29. "Overview of Developments in the International Trading Environment," *Annual Report by the Director General,* World Trade Organization, November 22, 2000.

30. *World Trade Organization 1999 Annual Report* (Geneva: WTO, 1999).

31. Alan Cane, "Getting Through: Why Telecommunications Talks Matter," *Financial Times,* February 14, 1997.

32. Frances Williams, "Telecoms: World Pact Set to Slash Costs of Calls," *Financial Times,* February 17, 1997.

33. WTO press brief, Financial Services, September 1996.

34. G. De Jonquieres, "Happy End to a Cliff Hanger," *Financial Times,* December 15, 1997, p. 15.

35. Jim Carlton, "Greens Target WTO Plan for Lumber," *Wall Street Journal,* November 24, 1999, p. A2.

36. Sources: A. Aggarwal and S. Narain. "Politics of Conservation," *The Hindu,* October 26, 1997, p. 26; J. H. Cushman, "Trade Group Strikes a Blow at U.S. Environmental Law," *New York Times,* April 7, 1998, p. D1; "WTO Ruling in Turtle Protection Dispute," *Bangkok Post,* March 18, 1998; and J. Maggs, "WTO Shrimp Ruling Heightens Environment vs. Trade Debate," *Journal of Commerce,* April 7, 1998, p. 3A.

37. Kari Huus, "WTO Summit Leaves Only Discontent," MSNBC, December 3, 1999 (www.msnbc.com).

38. "A Disquieting New Agenda for Trade," *The Economist,* July 16, 1994, pp. 55–56, and Frances Williams, "Trade Round Like This May Never Be Seen Again," *Financial Times,* December 16, 1993, p. 7.

39. "Punitive Tariffs Are Approved on Imports of Japanese Steel," *New York Times,* June 12, 1999, p. A3.

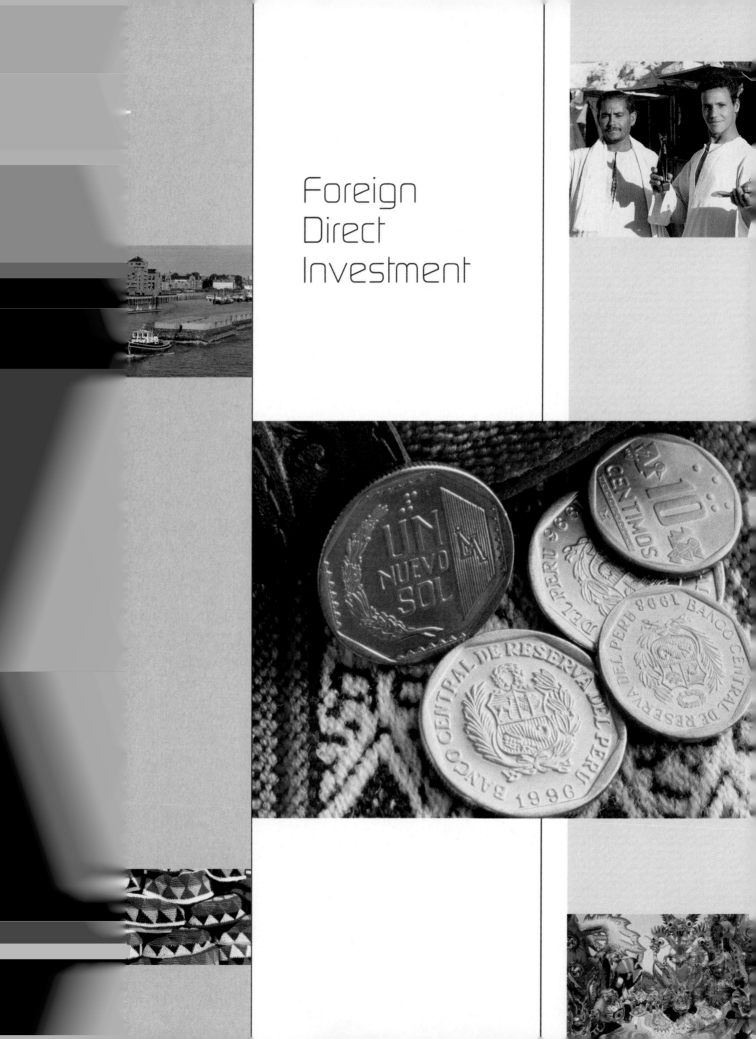

Foreign
Direct
Investment

Thirty years ago Starbucks was a single store in Seattle's Pike Place Market selling premium roasted coffee. Today it is a global roaster and retailer of coffee with over 3,500 stores, an increasing proportion of which are to be found outside the United States. Starbucks Corporation set out on its current course in the 1980s when the company's director of marketing, Howard Schultz, came back from a trip to Italy enchanted with the Italian coffeehouse experience. Schultz, who later became CEO, persuaded the company's owners to experiment with the coffeehouse format—and the Starbucks' experience was born. The basic strategy was to sell the company's own premium roasted coffee, along with freshly brewed espresso-style coffee beverages, a variety of pastries, coffee accessories, teas, and other products, in a tastefully designed coffeehouse setting. The company also stressed providing superior customer service. Reasoning that motivated employees provide the best customer service, Starbucks' executives devoted a lot of attention to employee hiring and training programs and progressive compensation policies that gave even part-time employees stock option grants and medical benefits. The formula met with spectacular success in the United States, where Starbucks went from obscurity to one of the best known brands in the country in a decade.

In 1995, with almost 700 stores across the United States, Starbucks began exploring foreign opportunities. Its first target market was Japan. Although Starbucks had resisted a franchising strategy in North America, where its stores are company owned, Starbucks initially decided to license its format in Japan. However, the company also realized that a pure licensing agreement would not give Starbucks the control needed to ensure that the Japanese licensees closely followed Starbucks' successful formula. So the company established a joint venture with a local retailer, Sazaby Inc. Each company held a 50 percent stake in the venture, Starbucks Coffee of Japan. Starbucks initially invested $10 million in this venture, its first foreign direct investment. The Starbucks' format was then licensed to the venture, which was charged with taking over responsibility for growing Starbucks' presence in Japan.

To make sure the Japanese operations replicated the "Starbucks' experience" in North America, Starbucks transferred some employees to the Japanese operation. The licensing agreement required all Japanese store managers and employees to attend training classes simi-

lar to those given to U.S. employees. The agreement also required that stores adhere to the design parameters established in the United States. In 2001, the company introduced a stock option plan for all Japanese employees, making it the first company in Japan to do so. Skeptics doubted that Starbucks would be able to replicate its North American success overseas, but by 2001, Starbucks had more than 150 stores in Japan and plans to continue opening them at a brisk pace.

After getting its feet wet in Japan, the company embarked on an aggressive foreign investment program. In 1998, it purchased Seattle Coffee, a British coffee chain with 60 retail stores, for $84 million. An American couple, originally from Seattle, had started Seattle Coffee with the intention of establishing a Starbucks-like chain in Britain. In the late 1990s, Starbucks opened stores in Taiwan, China, Singapore, Thailand, New Zealand, South Korea, and Malaysia.

In Asia, Starbucks' most common strategy was to license its format to a local operator in return for initial licensing fees and royalties on store revenues. Starbucks also sold coffee and related products to the local licensees, who then resold them to customers. As in Japan, Starbucks insisted on an intensive employee training program and strict specifications regarding the format and layout of the store. However, Starbucks became disenchanted with some of the straight licensing arrangements and converted several into joint-venture arrangements or wholly owned subsidiaries. In Thailand, for example, Starbucks initially entered into a licensing agreement with Coffee Partners, a local Thai company. Under the terms of the licensing agreement, Coffee Partners was required to open at least 20 Starbucks coffee stores in Thailand within five years. However, Coffee Partners found it difficult to raise funds from Thai banks to finance this expansion. In July 2000, Starbucks acquired Coffee Partners for about $12 million. Its goal was to gain tighter control over the expansion strategy in Thailand. A similar development occurred in South Korea, where Starbucks initially licensed its format to ESCO Korea Ltd. in 1999. Although ESCO soon had 10 very successful stores open, Starbucks felt that ESCO would not be able to achieve the company's aggressive growth targets, so in December 2000 it converted its licensing arrangement into a joint venture with Shinsegae, the parent company of ESCO. The joint venture enabled Starbucks to exercise greater control over the growth strategy in South Korea and to help fund that operation, while gaining the benefits of a local operating partner. By October 2000, Starbucks had invested some $52 million in foreign joint ventures.

By 2001, Starbucks had more than 600 stores in 20 countries outside of North America and was contemplating aggressive expansion plans into mainland Europe. The company's plans called for opening some 650 stores in six European countries, including the coffee cultures of France and Italy, by 2005. As its first entry point on the European mainland (Starbucks had 150 stores in Great Britain), Starbucks chose Switzerland. Drawing on its experience in Asia, the company entered into a joint venture with a Swiss company, Bon Appetit Group, Switzerland's largest food service company. Bon Appetit was to hold a majority stake in the venture, and Starbucks would license its format to the Swiss company using a similar agreement to those it had used successfully in Asia.

Sources: Starbucks 10K, various years; C. McLean, "Starbucks Set to Invade Coffee-Loving Continent," *Seattle Times,* October 4, 2000, p. E1; J. Ordonez, "Starbucks to Start Major Expansion in Overseas Market," *Wall Street Journal,* October 27, 2000, p. B10.

▮ Introduction

This chapter is concerned with foreign direct investment (FDI). **Foreign direct investment** occurs when a firm invests directly in facilities to produce and/or market a product in a foreign country. When Starbucks invested $10 million in Starbucks Coffee of Japan in 1996, it was engaging in its first foreign direct investment. By the end of 2000, the company had made cumulative foreign investments of some $150 million, including its $84 million purchase of British retailer Seattle Coffee, its $12 million purchase of Coffee Partners in Thailand, and cumulative investments of $52 million in various joint ventures. According to the U.S. Department of Commerce, FDI occurs whenever a U.S. citizen, organization, or affiliated group takes an interest of 10 percent or more in a foreign business entity (all of Starbucks' foreign investments were for more than 10 percent of the equity of a business). Once a firm undertakes FDI, it becomes a **multinational enterprise** (the meaning of multinational being "more than one country").

FDI takes on two main forms; the first is a **green-field investment,** which involves the establishment of a wholly new operation in a foreign country. The second involves acquiring or merging with an existing firm in the foreign country. Acquisitions can be a minority (where the foreign firm takes a 10 percent to 49 percent interest in the firm's voting stock), majority (foreign interest of 50 percent to 99 percent), or full outright stake (foreign interest of 100 percent).[1] There is an important distinction between FDI and **foreign portfolio investment** (FPI). Foreign portfolio investment is investment by individuals, firms, or public bodies (e.g., national and local governments) in foreign financial instruments (e.g., government bonds, foreign stocks). FPI does not involve taking a significant equity stake in a foreign business entity (i.e., the equity stake is less than 10 percent). FPI is determined by different factors than FDI and raises different issues. Accordingly, we discuss FPI in Chapter 11 in our review of the international capital market.

In Chapter 4, we considered several theories that sought to explain the pattern of trade between countries. These theories focus on why countries export some products and import others. None of these theories addresses why a firm might decide to invest directly in production facilities in a foreign country, rather than exporting its domestic production to that country or licensing a foreign entity to produce its product in return for licensing fees. The theories we reviewed in Chapter 4 do not explain the pattern of foreign direct investment between countries. They do not explain, for example, why Starbucks chose to acquire Seattle Coffee in Great Britain, rather than simply license the Starbucks formula to a British firm. The theories we explore in this chapter seek to do just this.

Our central objective will be to identify the economic rationale that underlies foreign direct investment. Firms often view exports and FDI as substitutes for each other.

For example, when deciding to serve the North American market, Toyota had to choose between exporting and foreign direct investment in North American production facilities. Although Toyota initially served the North American market through exports, increasingly it has turned to FDI. Toyota now has the capability to produce 400,000 cars a year in North America. This chapter attempts to understand the conditions under which firms such as Toyota prefer FDI to exporting. We will review various theories regarding these conditions.

These theories also need to explain why it is preferable for a firm to engage in FDI rather than licensing. **Licensing** occurs when a domestic firm, the licensor, licenses to a foreign firm, the licensee, the right to produce its product, to use its production processes, or to use its brand name or trademark. In return for giving the licensee these rights, the licensor collects royalty fees on every unit the licensee sells or on total licensee revenues. The advantage claimed for licensing over FDI is that the licensor does not have to pay for opening a foreign market; the licensee does that. Nor does the licensor have to bear the risks associated with opening a foreign market. However, despite these attractions, many firms are reluctant to engage in straight licensing arrangements, preferring to make some kind of foreign direct investment. Thus, in the opening case we saw that Starbucks originally considered a straight licensing strategy for entering the Japanese market but ultimately entered through a joint venture, which required some direct investment. Similarly, while the company did initially license its format in several Asian countries, such as Thailand and South Korea, there too it has switched to a direct investment strategy, acquiring its Thai licensee and entering into a joint venture with its South Korean licensee. What is the theoretical rationale for such a decision? The opening case hints that the need for control was a consideration. We shall develop the theoretical explanation in this chapter, and as we shall see, the need for control is an important factor in explaining the decision.

In the remainder of the chapter, we first look at the growing importance of FDI in the world economy. Next we look at the theories that have been used to explain horizontal foreign direct investment. **Horizontal foreign direct investment** is FDI in the same industry in which a firm operates at home. Starbucks' acquisition of Seattle Coffee in Britain is an example of horizontal FDI. After reviewing horizontal FDI, we consider the theories that help to explain vertical foreign direct investment. **Vertical foreign direct investment** is FDI in an industry that provides inputs for a firm's domestic operations, or it may be FDI in an industry abroad that sells the outputs of a firm's domestic operations. Finally, we review the implications of these theories for business practice.

Foreign Direct Investment in the World Economy ∎

When discussing foreign direct investment, it is important to distinguish between the flow of FDI and the stock of FDI. The **flow of FDI** refers to the amount of FDI undertaken over a given time period (normally a year). The **stock of FDI** refers to the total accumulated value of foreign-owned assets at a given time. We also talk of outflows of FDI, meaning the flow of FDI out of a country, and inflows of FDI, meaning the flow of FDI into a country.

∎The Growth of FDI

The past 20 years have seen a marked increase in both the flow and stock of FDI in the world economy. The average yearly outflow of FDI increased from about $25 billion in 1975 to a record $1.3 trillion in 2000 (see Figure 6.1).[2] The flow of FDI not only accelerated over the last quarter century, but it also accelerated faster than the growth in world trade. For example, between 1990 and 2000, the total flow of FDI from all countries increased about fivefold, while world trade grew by some 82 percent and

Figure 6.1

FDI Outflows 1982–2000
($ billions)

Source: United Nations, *World Investment Report, 2001* (New York and Geneva: United Nations, 2001).

Figure 6.2

FDI Flows by Region

Sources: World Trade Organization, *Annual Report, 2001* (Geneva: WTO, 2001), and United Nations, *World Investment Report, 2001* (New York and Geneva; United Nations, 2001).

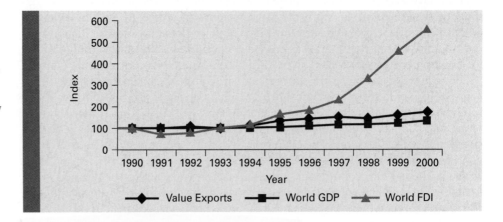

world output by 23 percent (see Figure 6.2).[3] As a result of the strong FDI flow, by 2000 the global stock of FDI exceeded $5.7 trillion. In total, 63,000 parent companies had 690,000 affiliates in foreign markets that collectively produced an estimated $14 trillion in global sales, nearly twice as high as the value of global exports.[4]

FDI is growing more rapidly than world trade and world output for several reasons. Despite the general decline in trade barriers that we have witnessed over the past 30 years, business firms still fear protectionist pressures. Executives see FDI as a way of circumventing future trade barriers. Much of the Japanese automobile companies' investment in the United States during the 1980s and early 1990s was driven by a desire to reduce exports from Japan, thereby alleviating trade tensions between the two nations. Also, much of the recent increase in FDI is being driven by the dramatic political and economic changes that have been occurring in many of the world's developing nations. The general shift toward democratic political institutions and free market economies that we discussed in Chapter 2 has encouraged FDI. Across much of Asia, Eastern Europe, and Latin America, economic growth, economic deregulation, privatization programs that are open to foreign investors, and the removal of many restrictions on FDI have all made these countries more attractive to foreign investors. According to the United Nations, some 94 percent of the 1,035 changes made between 1991 and 2000 worldwide in the laws governing foreign direct investment created a more favorable environment for FDI. The desire of governments to facilitate FDI has also been reflected in a dramatic increase in the number of bilateral investment treaties designed to protect and promote investment between two countries. As of January 1, 2000, there were 1,856 such treaties in the world involving more than 160 countries, a tenfold increase from the 181 treaties that existed in 1980.[5]

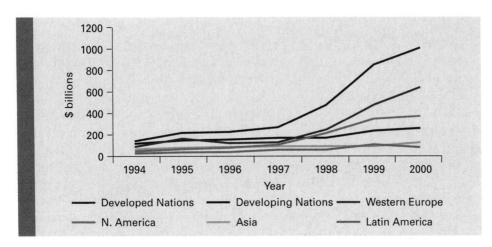

Figure 6.3

FDI into Developed and
Developing Nations
1994-2000

Source: United Nations, *World
Investment Report, 2001* (New York
and Geneva: United Nations, 2001).

The globalization of the world economy, a phenomenon that we first discussed in Chapter 1, is also having a positive impact on the volume of FDI. Firms such as Starbucks now see the whole world as their market, and they are undertaking FDI in an attempt to make sure they have a significant presence in many regions of the world. For reasons that we shall explore later in this book, many firms now believe it is important to have production facilities based close to their major customers. This, too, is creating pressures for greater FDI.

The Direction of FDI

Historically, most FDI has been directed at the developed nations of the world as firms based in advanced countries invested in the others' markets (see Figure 6.3). The United States has often been the favorite target for FDI inflows. This trend continued in the late 1990s, when the United States remained the largest recipient of foreign direct investment.[6] In 2000, the United States was again the largest recipient of FDI, accounting for $281 billion of the $1.3 trillion in global FDI, while Western Europe was the largest single regional recipient of FDI, with $633 billion in inflows.[7] The United States is attractive because of its large and wealthy domestic markets, its dynamic and stable economy, a favorable political environment, and the openness of the country to FDI. Investors have included firms based in the United Kingdom, Japan, Germany, Holland, and France.

Although developed nations in general, and the United States in particular, still account for the largest share of FDI inflows, there has been some increase of FDI into the world's developing nations (see Figure 6.3). From 1985 to 1990, the annual inflow of FDI into developing nations averaged $27.4 billion, or 17.4 percent of the total global flow. By 1997, the inflow into developing nations had risen to $149 billion, or 37 percent of the total. However, it fell back to 19 percent of the total in 2000. Most recent inflows into developing nations have been targeted at the emerging economies of South, East, and Southeast Asia. Driving much of the increase has been the growing importance of China as a recipient of FDI. In 2000, China received direct investments valued at about $40 billion, and that investment increased in 2001 as China prepared to join the World Trade Organization. The reasons for the strong flow of investment into China are discussed in the accompanying Country Focus.

Latin America emerged as the next most important region in the developing world for FDI inflows. In 2000, total inward investments into this region reached about $86 billion. About $34 billion of this total was invested in Brazil, with another $13 billion targeted at Mexico. Much of this investment was a response to reforms in the region, including privatization, the liberalization of regulations governing FDI, and the growing importance of regional free trade areas such as MERCOSUR and NAFTA (which

Foreign Direct Investment in China

Beginning in late 1978, China's leadership decided to move the economy away from a centrally planned system to one that was more market driven, while still maintaining the rigid political framework of Communist party control. The strategy had a number of key elements, including a switch to household responsibility in agriculture instead of the old collectivization, increases in the authority of local officials and plant managers in industry, establishment of small- to medium-scale private enterprises in services and light manufacturing, and increased foreign trade and investment. The result has been two decades of sustained high economic growth rates of between 10 and 11 percent annually compounded.

Starting from a tiny base, foreign investment surged to an annual average rate of $2.7 billion between 1985 and 1990 and then exploded to reach a record $45.2 billion in 1997, making China the second biggest recipient of FDI inflows in the world after the United States. Since then it has trended down slightly, declining to $40 billion in 2000, but even at this level, China is the largest recipient of FDI in the developing world, accounting for about 21 percent of the total in 2000. Over the past 20 years, this inflow has resulted in establishment of 170,000 foreign-funded enterprises in China. The total stock of FDI in China had grown to $346 billion in 2000 ($470 billion in Hong Kong is added to this figure), amounting to 28 percent of China's total GDP and over 14 percent of annualized gross fixed capital formation between 1994 and 2000. FDI inflows have been a major source of investment and economic growth in China since liberalization began, accounting for perhaps as much as 30 percent of the country's growth.

The reasons for the rise in investment are fairly obvious. With a population of 1.5 billion people, China represents the largest potential market in the world. Import tariffs have made it difficult to serve this market via exports, so FDI was required if a company wanted to tap into the huge potential of the country. Although China now seems set to join the World Trade Organization, import tariffs will be reduced over a number of years, so this motive for investing in China will persist. Also, many foreign firms believe that doing business in China requires a substantial presence in the country to build *guanxi*, the crucial relationship networks (see Chapter 3 for details). Furthermore, a combination of cheap labor and tax incentives, particularly for enterprises that establish themselves in special economic zones, makes China an attractive base from which to serve Asian or world markets with exports.

Less obvious, at least to begin with, was how difficult it would be for foreign firms to do business in China. Blinded by the size and potential of China's market, many firms have paid scant attention to the complexities of operating a business in this country until after the investment has been made. China may have a huge population, but despite two decades of rapid growth, it is still a poor country where the average income is little more than $750 per year. This lack of purchasing power translates into a weak market for many Western consumer goods from automobiles to household appliances. Another problem is the lack of a well-developed transportation infrastructure or distribution system. PepsiCo discovered this problem at its subsidiary in Chongqing. Perched above the Yangtze River in southwest Sichuan province, Chongqing lies at the heart of China's massive hinterland. The Chongqing municipality, which includes the city and its surrounding regions, contains over 30 million people, but according to Steve Chen, the manager of the Pepsi subsidiary, the lack of well-developed road and distribution systems means he can reach only about half of this population with his product.

Other problems include a highly regulated environment that can make it problematic to conduct business transactions and shifting tax and regulatory regimes. For example, in 1997, the Chinese government suddenly scrapped a tax credit scheme that had

will be discussed in Chapter 8). At the other end of the scale, Africa received the smallest amount of inward investment, around $8 billion in 2000. The inability of Africa to attract greater investment is in part a reflection of the political unrest, armed conflict, and frequent changes in economic policy in the region.

Another way of looking at the importance of FDI inflows is to express them as a percentage of gross fixed capital formation. **Gross fixed capital formation** summarizes the total amount of capital invested in factories, stores, office buildings, and the like.

Country Focus

made it attractive to import capital equipment into China. This immediately made it more expensive to set up operations in the country.

There are also difficulties finding qualified personnel to staff operations. The cultural revolution produced a generation of people who lack the basic educational background that is taken for granted in the West. Because of the country's past, few local people understand the complexities of managing a modern industrial enterprise.

There are also problems with local joint-venture partners who are inexperienced, opportunistic, or simply operate according to different goals. One U.S. manager explained that when he laid off 200 people to reduce costs, his Chinese partner hired them all back the next day. When he inquired why they had been hired back, the Chinese partner, which was government owned, explained that as an agency of the government, it had an "obligation" to reduce unemployment.

Increased investment in China's coastal regions has raised another source of concern. Serious overcapacity now looms in certain sectors, with negative implications for prices and profits.

Reflecting the growing awareness of these problems, Western enterprises' rate of investment into China slowed in the late 1990s. In July 1997, Chrysler said it would close its sales office in Beijing, citing overcapacity in the automobile market and lower than expected demand for cars. Chrysler also announced that, while it will maintain its joint venture in Shanghai to make Jeeps, it will not be looking for new investments in China. Similarly, in August 1997, Chicago-based Ameritech Corp. stated that because of regulatory problems it would drop out of its telecommunication joint venture and pull out of China. About the same time, Caterpillar Inc. stated it would be closing a joint venture in China because there was little demand for the engines produced by the venture. To compound matters further, the financial crisis that swept through Asia in late 1997 and early 1998 curtailed the flow of investment money from other Asian countries, a source that historically had been of major importance. Because of these factors, initial projections called for FDI inflows into China to decline in 1998 to $35 billion. But the steep decline didn't happen. The positives were too compelling. FDI totaled almost $44 billion in 1998, and although it declined to $40 billion in 1999 and 2000, initial projections suggested it would once more resume an upward path in 2001 as Western and Asian firms invest in China to take advantage of the country's entry into the World Trade Organization.

To continue to attract foreign investment, the Chinese government has committed itself to invest more than $800 billion in infrastructure projects over the next 10 years, which should improve the nation's poor highway system. By giving preferential tax breaks to companies that invest in special regions, such as that around Chongqing, the Chinese have created incentives for foreign companies to invest in China's vast interior where markets are underserved. They have been pursuing a macroeconomic policy that includes an emphasis on maintaining steady economic growth, low inflation, and a stable currency, all of which are attractive to foreign investors. And to deal with the lack of qualified personnel, in 1997 the government instructed universities to establish 30 business schools to train Chinese in basic skills such as accounting, finance, and human resource management. Given these developments, it seems likely that the country will continue to be an important magnet for foreign investors well into the future.

Sources: Interviews by the author while in China, March 1998; L. Sly, "China Losing Its Golden Glow," *Chicago Tribune*, September 15, 1997, p. 1; M. Miller, "Search for Fresh Capital Widens," *South China Morning Post*, April 9, 1998, p. 1; S. Mufson, "China Says Asian Crisis Will Have an Impact," *Washington Post*, March 8, 1998, p. A27; and United Nations, *World Investment Report, 2000* (New York and Geneva: United Nations, 2001).

Other things being equal, the greater the capital investment in an economy, the more favorable its future growth prospects are likely to be. Viewed this way, FDI can be seen as an important source of capital investment and a determinant of the future growth rate of an economy. Figure 6.4 summarizes inward flows of FDI as a percentage of gross fixed capital formation by region for 1999 (the latest year for which data are available).[8] In general, FDI now accounts for about 16 percent of worldwide gross fixed capital formation and as much as 27 percent in Latin America and 27 percent in Western

Figure 6.4

Inward FDI Flows as a
Percentage of Gross Fixed
Capital Formation, 1999

Source: United Nations, *World
Investment Report, 2001* (New York
and Geneva; United Nations, 2001).

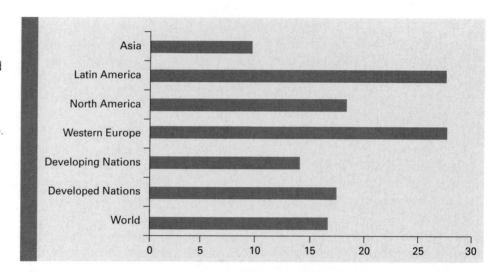

Europe. In the early 1990s, the figure was only around 4 percent worldwide. It has been moving upward since, suggesting that FDI is becoming an increasingly important source of investment in the world's economies.

These gross figures hide important individual country differences. For example, in 1999 inward FDI accounted for some 92 percent of gross fixed capital formation in Ireland, 33 percent in the United Kingdom, and 31 percent in Brazil, but only 2.4 percent in India, 3.1 percent in Italy, and 1.1 percent in Japan—suggesting that FDI is an important source of investment, and thus economic growth, in the first three countries, but not the latter three. These differences can be explained by several factors, including the perceived ease and attractiveness of investing in a nation. To the extent that burdensome regulations limit the opportunities for foreign investment in countries such as Japan and India, these nations may be hurting themselves by limiting their access to needed capital investments. We shall return to and discuss this issue in more detail in Chapter 7.

The Source of FDI

Since World War II, the United States has traditionally been by far the largest source country for FDI. During the late 1970s the United States still accounted for about 47 percent of all FDI outflows from industrialized countries, while the second-place United Kingdom accounted for about 18 percent. U.S. firms so dominated the growth of FDI in the 1960s and 70s, that the words *American* and *multinational* became almost synonymous. By 1980, 178 of the world's largest 382 multinationals were U.S. firms, and 40 of them were British.[9] However, during 1985–90 the United States slipped to third place behind Japan and the United Kingdom. Since then, as Figure 6.5 illustrates, the United States regained its dominant position in every year but 1999 and 2000, when the United Kingdom was the largest source country. However, as a percentage of total outward FDI flows, the U.S. share declined to less than 20 percent by the end of the 1990s. The source of FDI by country remains highly concentrated, with the largest six countries accounting for about 75 percent of all foreign direct investment outflows in 2000. With the exception of Spain, the countries illustrated in Figure 6.5 have dominated foreign direct investment outflows for much of the last two decades. As might be expected, these countries also predominate in rankings of the world's largest multinationals. As of 2000, 26 percent of the world's 100 largest multinationals were U.S. enterprises; 17 percent were Japanese; 12 percent were French; 12 percent, German; and 10 percent, British.[10]

The high level of FDI outflows from the United States has been driven by a combination of factors including a strong U.S. economy; strong corporate profits and cash

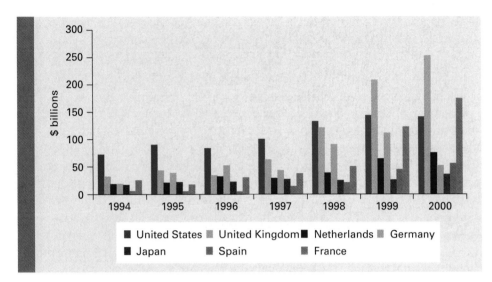

Figure 6.5

FDI Outflows by Select
Country, 1994–2000

Source: United Nations, *World
Investment Report, 2001* (New York
and Geneva; United Nations, 2001).

flow, which have given firms the capital to invest abroad; and a relatively strong currency, particularly since 1995. Similar factors explain the continued growth of FDI
outflows from the United Kingdom during the 1990s. The recent growth of foreign direct investment from Spain reflects the fact that countries from that nation have become among the largest investors in Latin America. Although a handful of developed
nations still account for the bulk of foreign direct investment outflows, some developing nations are starting to get in on the act, most notably China, which accounted
for almost $20 billion of outward foreign direct investment flows in 1999 and 2000, al-
though the majority of that came from Hong Kong–based enterprises.

The Form of FDI: Acquisitions versus Green-Field Investments

As noted earlier, FDI can take the form of a green-field investment in a new facility or
an acquisition of or a merger with an existing local firm. The data suggest the majority of cross-border investment is in the form of mergers and acquisitions rather than
green-field investments. UN estimates indicate that in 1999 some 80 percent of all
FDI inflows was in the form of mergers and acquisitions. There is a marked difference,
however, between FDI flows into developed and developing nations. Between 1987
and 1999, the value of cross-border mergers and acquisitions into *developed* countries
grew at 20 percent annually and was never less than 77 percent of all FDI flows into
developed countries. In the case of *developing* nations, the ratio of the value of cross-
border mergers and acquisitions to FDI was about 33 percent in 1999, although this
represented an increase from about 10 percent a decade earlier. The lower percentage
of FDI inflows that is in the form of mergers and acquisitions may simply reflect the
fact that there are fewer target firms to acquire in developing nations.

When contemplating FDI, why do firms apparently prefer to acquire existing assets
rather than undertake green-field investments? We shall return to this and consider it
in much greater depth in Chapter 14, so for now we will make only a few basic obser-
vations. First, mergers and acquisitions are quicker to execute than green-field investments. This is an important consideration in the modern business world where
markets evolve very rapidly. Many firms apparently believe that if they do not acquire
a desirable target firm, then their global rivals will. The case of Cemex in the accompanying Management Focus illustrates this. Cemex is the world's third largest cement
company and Mexico's largest multinational company. Cemex's rise to global status
took less than a decade and has been driven primarily by acquisitions. If Cemex had
relied on green-field investments, it could not have become so large so fast.

Cemex's Foreign Acquisitions

In little more than a decade, Mexico's largest cement manufacturer, Cemex, has transformed itself from a primarily Mexican operation into the third largest cement company in the world behind Holderbank of Switzerland and Lafarge Group of France. Cemex has long been a powerhouse in Mexico and currently controls more than 60 percent of the market for cement in that country. Cemex's domestic success has been based in large part on an obsession with efficient manufacturing and a focus on customer service that is second to none in the industry.

Cemex is a leader in using information technology to match production with consumer demand. The company sells ready mixed cement that can survive for only about 90 minutes before solidifying, so precise delivery is important. But Cemex can never predict with total certainty what demand will be on any given day, week, or month. To better manage unpredictable demand patterns, Cemex developed a system of seamless information technology, including truck-mounted global positioning systems, radio transmitters, satellites, and computer hardware, that allows Cemex to control the production and distribution of cement like no other company can, responding quickly to unanticipated changes in demand and reducing waste. The results are lower costs and superior customer service, both differentiating factors for Cemex.

The company also pays lavish attention to its distributors—some 5,000 in Mexico alone—who can earn points toward rewards for hitting sales targets. Those points can then be converted into Cemex stock. High-volume distributors can purchase trucks and other supplies through Cemex at significant discounts. Cemex also is known for its marketing drives that focus on end users, the builders themselves. For example, Cemex trucks drive around local Mexican building sites, and if Cemex cement is being used, the construction crews win soccer balls, caps, and T-shirts.

Cemex's international expansion strategy was driven by a number of factors. First, the company wished to reduce its reliance on the Mexican construction market, which was characterized by very volatile demand. Second, the company realized there was tremendous demand for cement in many devel-

Second, foreign firms are acquired because those firms have valuable strategic assets, such as brand loyalty, customer relationships, trademarks or patents, distribution systems, production systems, and the like. It is easier and perhaps less risky for a firm to acquire those assets than to build them from the ground up through a green-field investment. Cemex's acquisition in late 2000 of Houston-based cement maker Southland for $2.5 billion is a good example. Cemex wanted quick entry to the growing U.S. construction market, and Southland's production and distribution assets enabled Cemex to achieve this.

Third, firms make acquisitions because they believe they can increase the efficiency of the acquired unit by transferring capital, technology, or management skills. For example, Cemex has developed the best information systems in the global cement industry, which has enabled it to better meet customer needs (see the Management Focus for details). Cemex can increase the efficiency of its acquired units, such as Southland, by transferring its technological know-how to those units after the acquisition. Thus, there are some fairly compelling arguments for favoring mergers and acquisitions over green-field investments. But many mergers and acquisitions fail to realize their anticipated gains.[11] Chapter 14 further studies this issue.

Horizontal Foreign Direct Investment

Horizontal FDI is investment in the same industry abroad as a firm operates in at home. We need to understand why firms go to the trouble of acquiring or establishing operations abroad, when the alternatives of exporting and licensing are available. Other things being equal, FDI is expensive and risky compared to exporting or licensing. FDI is expensive because a firm must bear the costs of establishing production faoping countries, where significant construction was being undertaken or needed. Third, the company believed that it understood the needs of construction businesses in developing nations better than the established multinational cement companies, all of which were from developed nations. Fourth, Cemex believed that it could create significant value by acquiring cement companies in other markets and transferring its skills in customer service, marketing, information technology, and production management to those units.

The company embarked in earnest on its international expansion strategy in the early 1990s. Initially Cemex targeted other developing nations, acquiring established cement makers in Venezuela, Colombia, Indonesia, the Philippines, Egypt, and several other countries. It also purchased two stagnant companies in Spain and turned them around. Then in 2000 it undertook its largest purchase, the $2.5 billion acquisition of Houston-based Southland, one of the largest cement companies in the United States. Cemex entered 2001 with 56 cement plants in 30 countries, most of which were gained through acquisitions. In all cases, Cemex

has devoted great attention to transferring its technological, management, and marketing know-how to acquired units, thereby improving their performance.

The benefits of this strategy have flowed through to the bottom line. From 1991 to 2000, the company's earnings before interest, tax, and depreciation when measured in U.S. dollars grew by more than 20 percent annually. Cash earnings per share also grew by 20 percent a year, while sales grew by 17 percent. Since profits have grown faster than sales, the company must be realizing significant efficiency gains in its acquired units. By 2000, Cemex was number one among the world's four largest cement manufacturers on most measures of financial performance, suggesting that its strategy of entering foreign markets through acquisitions was paying dividends.

Sources: C. Piggott, "Cemex's Stratospheric Rise," *Latin Finance*, March 2001, p. 76; J. F. Smith, "Making Cement a Household Word," *Los Angeles Times*, January 16, 2000, p. C1; and D. Helft, "Cemex Attempts to Cement Its Future," *The Industry Standard*, November 6, 2000.

cilities in a foreign country or of acquiring a foreign enterprise. FDI is risky because of the problems associated with doing business in another culture where the "rules of the game" may be very different. Relative to firms native to a culture, there is a greater probability that a firm in a foreign culture will make costly mistakes due to ignorance. When a firm exports, it need not bear the costs of FDI, and the risks associated with selling abroad can be reduced by using a native sales agent. Similarly, when a firm licenses its know-how, it need not bear the costs or risks of FDI. So why do so many firms apparently prefer FDI over either exporting or licensing?

The quick answer is that other things are not equal! A number of factors can alter the relative attractiveness of exporting, licensing, and FDI. We will consider these factors: (1) transportation costs, (2) market imperfections, (3) following competitors, (4) strategic behavior, and (5) location advantages.

Transportation Costs

When transportation costs are added to production costs, it becomes unprofitable to ship some products a long distance. This is particularly true of products that have a low value-to-weight ratio and can be produced in almost any location (e.g., cement, soft drinks, etc.). For such products, relative to either FDI or licensing, the attractiveness of exporting decreases. Thus, transportation costs alone help explain why Cemex has undertaken FDI rather than exporting (see the Management Focus). For products with a high value-to-weight ratio, however, transport costs are normally a very minor component of total landed cost (e.g., electronic components, personal computers, medical equipment, computer software, etc.). In such cases, transportation costs have little impact on the relative attractiveness of exporting, licensing, and FDI.

Market Imperfections (Internalization Theory)

Market imperfections provide a major explanation of why firms may prefer FDI to either exporting or licensing. **Market imperfections** are factors that inhibit markets from working perfectly. The market imperfections explanation of FDI is the one favored by most economists.[12] In the international business literature, the marketing imperfection approach to FDI is typically referred to as **internalization theory.**

With regard to horizontal FDI, market imperfections arise in two circumstances: when there are impediments to the free flow of products between nations, and when there are impediments to the sale of know-how. (Licensing is a mechanism for selling know-how.) Impediments to the free flow of products between nations decrease the profitability of exporting, relative to FDI and licensing. Impediments to the sale of know-how increase the profitability of FDI relative to licensing. Thus, the market imperfections explanation predicts that FDI will be preferred whenever there are impediments that make both exporting and the sale of know-how difficult and/or expensive.

Impediments to Exporting

Governments are the main source of impediments to the free flow of products between nations. By placing tariffs on imported goods, governments increase the cost of exporting relative to FDI and licensing. Similarly, by limiting imports through the imposition of quotas, governments increase the attractiveness of FDI and licensing. For example, the wave of FDI by Japanese auto companies in the United States during the 1980s was partly driven by protectionist threats from Congress and by quotas on the importation of Japanese cars. For Japanese auto companies, these factors have decreased the profitability of exporting and increased the profitability of FDI.

Impediments to the Sale of Know-How

The competitive advantage that many firms enjoy comes from their technological, marketing, or management know-how. Technological know-how can enable a company to build a better product; for example, Xerox's technological know-how enabled it to build the first photocopier, and Nokia's technological know-how has given it a strong competitive position in the global market for wireless telephone equipment. Alternatively, technological know-how can improve a company's production process vis-á-vis competitors. For example, many claim that Toyota's competitive advantage comes from its superior production system. Marketing know-how can enable a company to better position its products in the marketplace; the competitive advantage of such companies as Kellogg, H. J. Heinz, and Procter & Gamble seems to come from superior marketing know-how. Management know-how with regard to factors such as organizational structure, human relations, control systems, planning systems, inventory management, and so on can enable a company to manage its assets more efficiently than competitors. The competitive advantage of Starbucks, which was profiled in the opening case, seems to come from valuable management knowledge related to the branding and operations of retail coffee stores. Similarly, Cemex has used its technological know-how to better manage customer demand and improve operating efficiencies and its marketing knowledge to build a well-earned reputation for being very customer focused (see Management Focus).

If we view know-how (expertise) as a competitive asset, it follows that the larger the market in which that asset is applied, the greater the profits that can be earned from the asset. Nokia can earn greater returns on its know-how by selling its wireless telephone equipment worldwide than by selling it only in its native Finland. However, this alone does not explain why Nokia undertakes FDI (the company has production locations around the world). For Nokia to favor FDI, two conditions must hold. First, transportation costs and/or impediments to exporting must rule out exporting as an option. Second, there must be some reason Nokia cannot sell its wireless know-how to foreign producers. Since licensing is the main mechanism by which firms sell their know-how, there must be some reason Nokia is not willing to license a foreign firm to manufacture and market its cellular telephone equipment. Other things being equal, licensing might look attractive to such a firm, since it would not have to bear the costs and risks associated with FDI yet it could still earn a good return from its know-how in the form of royalty fees.

According to economic theory, there are three reasons the market does not always work well as a mechanism for selling know-how, or why licensing is not as attractive as it initially appears. First, licensing may result in a firm's giving away its know-how to a potential foreign competitor. For example, in the 1960s, RCA licensed its leading-edge color television technology to a number of Japanese companies, including Matsushita and Sony. At the time, RCA saw licensing as a way to earn a good return from its technological know-how in the Japanese market without the costs and risks associated with FDI. However, Matsushita and Sony quickly assimilated RCA's technology and used it to enter the U.S. market to compete directly against RCA. As a result, RCA is now a minor player in its home market, while Matsushita and Sony have a much bigger market share.

Second, licensing does not give a firm the tight control over manufacturing, marketing, and strategy in a foreign country that may be required to profitably exploit its advantage in know-how. With licensing, control over production, marketing, and strategy is granted to a licensee in return for a royalty fee. However, for both strategic and operational reasons, a firm may want to retain control over these functions. For example, a firm might want its foreign subsidiary to price and market very aggressively, but the licensee may be unable to do this. The opening case showed how this became an issue with Starbucks, which originally pursued a licensing strategy in Thailand, but then acquired the Thai operation because it thought the licensee was not aggressive enough in growing the market and was capital-constrained. In another case, the firm might want the licensee to price and market very aggressively to keep a global competitor in check, but the licensee, which has to make a profit, may be unwilling to do this for the greater good of the licensor. For example, Kodak has used its Japanese subsidiary to launch aggressive attacks against its global competitor, Fuji Film. The idea has been to keep Fuji busy defending its home market, which limits Fuji's ability to launch aggressive attacks in the United States. While Kodak's Japanese subsidiary, which is wholly owned, has to accept such strategic direction from the center, a licensee would be unlikely to accept such an imposition, since such a strategy would allow the licensee to make only a low profit or even take a loss.

Or a firm may want control over the operations of a foreign entity to take advantage of differences in factor costs among countries, producing only part of its final product in a given country, while importing other parts from where they can be produced at lower cost. Again, a licensee would be unlikely to accept such an arrangement because it would limit the licensee's autonomy. When tight control over a foreign entity is desirable, horizontal FDI is preferable to licensing.

Third, a firm's know-how may not be amenable to licensing. This is particularly true of management and marketing know-how. It is one thing to license a foreign firm to manufacture a particular product, but quite another to license the way a firm does business—how it manages its process and markets its products. Consider Toyota, a company whose competitive advantage in the global auto industry is acknowledged to come from its superior ability to manage the overall process of designing, engineering, manufacturing, and selling automobiles; that is, from its management and organizational know-how. Toyota is credited with pioneering the development of a new production process, known as lean production, that enables it to produce higher-quality automobiles at a lower cost than its global rivals.[13] Although Toyota has certain products that can be licensed, its real competitive advantage comes from its management and process know-how. These kinds of skills are difficult to articulate or codify; they cannot be written down in a simple licensing contract. They are organizationwide and have been developed over years. They are not embodied in any one individual, but instead are widely dispersed throughout the company. Toyota's skills are embedded in its organizational culture, and culture is something that cannot be licensed. Thus, as Toyota moves away from its traditional exporting strategy, it has increasingly pursued a strategy of FDI, rather than licensing foreign enterprises to produce its cars.

The same is true of Cemex, which was profiled in the accompanying Management Focus. Because it is embedded in organizational processes and managerial skills, Cemex's know-how with regard to management, marketing, and technology might all be difficult to transfer via a licensing contract. Thus, FDI became the logical way for Cemex to expand internationally. Starbucks may also have found it difficult to transfer its management and marketing know-how via a licensing strategy, hence its recent preference for FDI in the form of acquisitions or joint ventures over straight licensing deals (see the opening case).

All of this suggests that when one or more of the following conditions holds, markets fail as a mechanism for selling know-how and FDI is more profitable than licensing: (1) when the firm has valuable know-how that cannot be adequately protected by a licensing contract, (2) when the firm needs tight control over a foreign entity to maximize its market share and earnings in that country, and (3) when a firm's skills and know-how are not amenable to licensing.

Strategic Behavior

Another theory used to explain FDI is based on the idea that FDI flows are a reflection of strategic rivalry between firms in the global marketplace. An early variant of this argument was expounded by F. T. Knickerbocker, who looked at the relationship between FDI and rivalry in oligopolistic industries.[14] An **oligopoly** is an industry composed of a limited number of large firms (e.g., an industry in which four firms control 80 percent of a domestic market would be defined as an oligopoly). A critical competitive feature of such industries is interdependence of the major players: What one firm does can have an immediate impact on the major competitors, forcing a response in kind. If one firm in an oligopoly cuts prices, this can take market share away from its competitors, forcing them to respond with similar price cuts to retain their market share.

This kind of imitative behavior can take many forms in an oligopoly. One firm raises prices, the others follow; someone expands capacity, and the rivals imitate lest they be left at a disadvantage in the future. Knickerbocker argued that the same kind of imitative behavior characterizes FDI. Consider an oligopoly in the United States in which three firms—A, B, and C—dominate the market. Firm A establishes a subsidiary in France. Firms B and C decide that if this investment is successful, it may knock out their export business to France and give firm A a first-mover advantage. Furthermore, firm A might discover some competitive asset in France that it could repatriate to the United States to torment firms B and C on their native soil. Given these possibilities, firms B and C decide to follow firm A and establish operations in France.

Studies that looked at FDI by U.S. firms during the 1950s and 60s show that firms based in oligopolistic industries tended to imitate each other's FDI.[15] The same phenomenon has been observed with regard to FDI undertaken by Japanese firms during the 1980s.[16] For example, Toyota and Nissan responded to investments by Honda in the United States and Europe by undertaking their own FDI in the United States and Europe.

Knickerbocker's theory can be extended to embrace the concept of multipoint competition. **Multipoint competition** arises when two or more enterprises encounter each other in different regional markets, national markets, or industries. Economic theory suggests that rather like chess players jockeying for advantage, firms will try to match each other's moves in different markets to try to hold each other in check. The idea is to ensure that a rival does not gain a commanding position in one market and then use the profits generated there to subsidize competitive attacks in other markets. Kodak and Fuji Photo Film Co., for example, compete against each other around the world. If Kodak enters a particular foreign market, Fuji will not be far behind. Fuji feels compelled to follow Kodak to ensure that Kodak does not gain a dominant position in the foreign market that it could then leverage to gain a competitive advantage elsewhere. The converse also holds, with Kodak following Fuji when the Japanese firm is the first to enter a foreign market.

Although Knickerbocker's theory and its extensions can help to explain imitative FDI behavior by firms in oligopolistic industries, it does not explain why the first firm in an oligopoly decides to undertake FDI, rather than to export or license. In contrast, the market imperfections explanation addresses this phenomenon. The imitative theory also does not address the issue of whether FDI is more efficient than exporting or licensing for expanding abroad. Again, the market imperfections approach addresses the efficiency issue. For these reasons, many economists favor the market imperfections explanation for FDI, although most would agree that the imitative explanation tells part of the story.

The Product Life Cycle

Raymond Vernon's product life-cycle theory, described in Chapter 4, also is used to explain FDI. Vernon argued that often the same firms that pioneer a product in their home markets undertake FDI to produce a product for consumption in foreign markets. Thus, Xerox introduced the photocopier in the United States, and it was Xerox that set up production facilities in Japan (Fuji-Xerox) and Great Britain (Rank-Xerox) to serve those markets. Vernon's view is that firms undertake FDI at particular stages in the life cycle of a product they have pioneered. They invest in other advanced countries when local demand in those countries grows large enough to support local production (as Xerox did). They subsequently shift production to developing countries when product standardization and market saturation give rise to price competition and cost pressures. Investment in developing countries, where labor costs are lower, is seen as the best way to reduce costs.

Vernon's theory has merit. Firms do invest in a foreign country when demand in that country will support local production, and they do invest in low-cost locations (e.g., developing countries) when cost pressures become intense.[17] However, Vernon's theory fails to explain why it is profitable for a firm to undertake FDI at such times, rather than continuing to export from its home base and rather than licensing a foreign firm to produce its product. Just because demand in a foreign country is large enough to support local production, it does not necessarily follow that local production is the most profitable option. It may still be more profitable to produce at home and export to that country (to realize the scale economies that arise from serving the global market from one location). Alternatively, it may be more profitable for the firm to license a foreign company to produce its product for sale in that country. The product life-cycle theory ignores these options and, instead, simply argues that once a foreign market is large enough to support local production, FDI will occur. This limits its explanatory power and its usefulness to business in that it fails to identify when it is profitable to invest abroad.

Location-Specific Advantages

The British economist John Dunning has argued that in addition to the various factors discussed above, location-specific advantages can help explain the nature and direction of FDI.[18] By **location-specific advantages,** Dunning means the advantages that arise from using resource endowments or assets that are tied to a particular foreign location and that a firm finds valuable to combine with its own unique assets (such as the firm's technological, marketing, or management know-how). Dunning accepts the internalization argument that market failures make it difficult for a firm to license its own unique assets (know-how). Therefore, he argues that combining location-specific assets or resource endowments and the firm's own unique assets often requires FDI. It requires the firm to establish production facilities where those foreign assets or resource endowments are located (Dunning refers to this argument as the **eclectic paradigm**).

An obvious example of Dunning's arguments is natural resources, such as oil and other minerals, which are specific to certain locations. Dunning suggests that a firm must undertake FDI to exploit such foreign resources. This explains the FDI undertaken by many of the world's oil companies, which have to invest where oil is located to combine their technological and managerial knowledge with this valuable location-specific resource. Another example is valuable human resources, such as low-cost highly skilled labor. The cost and skill of labor varies from country to country. Since labor is not internationally mobile, according to Dunning it makes sense for a firm to locate production facilities where the cost and skills of local labor are most suited to its particular production processes.

However, the implications of Dunning's theory go beyond basic resources such as minerals and labor. Consider Silicon Valley, which is the world center for the computer and semiconductor industry. Many of the world's major computer and semiconductor companies, such as Apple Computer, Silicon Graphics, and Intel, are located close to each other in the Silicon Valley region of California. As a result, much of the cutting-edge research and product development in computers and semiconductors occurs here. According to Dunning's arguments, knowledge being generated in Silicon Valley with regard to the design and manufacture of computers and semiconductors is available nowhere else in the world. As it is commercialized, that knowledge diffuses throughout the world, but the leading edge of knowledge generation in the computer and semiconductor industries is to be found in Silicon Valley. In Dunning's language, this means Silicon Valley has a location-specific advantage in the generation of knowledge related to the computer and semiconductor industries. In part, this advantage comes from the sheer concentration of intellectual talent in this area, and in part it arises from a network of informal contacts that allows firms to benefit from each other's knowledge generation. Economists refer to such knowledge "spillovers" as **externalities,** and one well-established theory suggests that firms can benefit from such externalities by locating close to their source.[19]

In so far as this is the case, it makes sense for foreign computer and semiconductor firms to invest in research and (perhaps) production facilities so they too can learn about and utilize valuable new knowledge before those based elsewhere, thereby giving them a competitive advantage in the global marketplace.[20] Evidence suggests that European, Japanese, South Korean, and Taiwanese computer and semiconductor firms are investing in the Silicon Valley region, precisely because they wish to benefit from the externalities that arise there.[21] Others have argued that direct investment by foreign firms in the U.S. biotechnology industry has been motivated by desires to gain access to the unique location-specific technological knowledge of U.S. biotechnology firms.[22] Dunning's theory, therefore, seems to be a useful addition to those outlined above, for it helps explain like no other how location factors affect the direction of FDI.

Vertical Foreign Direct Investment

Vertical FDI takes two forms. There is **backward vertical FDI** into an industry abroad that provides inputs for a firm's domestic production processes. Historically, most backward vertical FDI has been in extractive industries (e.g., oil extraction, bauxite mining, tin mining, copper mining). The objective has been to provide inputs into a firm's downstream operations (e.g., oil refining, aluminum smelting and fabrication, tin smelting and fabrication). Firms such as Royal Dutch/Shell, British Petroleum (BP), RTZ, Consolidated Gold Field, and Alcoa are among the classic examples of such vertically integrated multinationals.

A second form of vertical FDI is **forward vertical FDI** in which an industry abroad sells the outputs of a firm's domestic production processes. Forward vertical FDI is less common than backward vertical FDI. For example, when Volkswagen entered the U.S. market, it acquired a large number of dealers rather than distribute its cars through independent U.S. dealers.

With both horizontal and vertical FDI, the question that must be answered is why would a firm go to all the trouble and expense of setting up operations in a foreign country? Why, for example, did petroleum companies such as BP and Royal Dutch/Shell vertically integrate backward into oil production abroad? The location-specific advantages argument helps explain the direction of such FDI; vertically integrated multinationals in extractive industries invest where the raw materials are. However, this argument does not clarify why they did not simply import raw materials extracted by local producers. And why do companies such as Volkswagen feel it is necessary to acquire their own dealers in foreign markets, when in theory it might seem less costly to rely on foreign dealers? There are two basic answers to these kinds of questions. The first is a strategic behavior argument, and the second draws on the market imperfections approach.

Strategic Behavior

According to economic theory, by vertically integrating backward to gain control over the source of raw material, a firm can raise entry barriers and shut new competitors out of an industry.[23] Such strategic behavior involves vertical FDI if the raw material is found abroad. An example occurred in the 1930s, when commercial smelting of aluminum was pioneered by North American firms such as Alcoa and Alcan Aluminum Ltd. Aluminum is derived by smelting bauxite. Although bauxite is a common mineral, the percentage of aluminum in bauxite is typically so low that it is not economical to mine and smelt. During the 1930s, only one large-scale deposit of bauxite with an economical percentage of aluminum had been discovered, and it was on the Caribbean island of Trinidad. Alcoa and Alcan vertically integrated backward and acquired ownership of the deposit. This action created a barrier to entry into the aluminum industry. Potential competitors were deterred because they could not get access to high-grade bauxite—it was all owned by Alcoa and Alcan. Those that did enter the industry had to use lower-grade bauxite than Alcan and Alcoa and found themselves at a cost disadvantage. This situation persisted until the 1950s and 1960s, when new high-grade deposits were discovered in Australia and Indonesia.

However, despite the bauxite example, the opportunities for barring entry through vertical FDI seem far too limited to explain the incidence of vertical FDI among the world's multinationals. In most extractive industries, mineral deposits are not as concentrated as in the case of bauxite in the 1930s; new deposits are constantly being discovered. Consequently, any attempt to monopolize all viable raw material deposits is bound to prove very expensive if not impossible.

Another strand of the strategic behavior explanation of vertical FDI sees such investment not as an attempt to build entry barriers, but as an attempt to circumvent the barriers established by firms already doing business in a country. This may explain Volkswagen's decision to establish its own dealer network when it entered the North American auto market. The market was then dominated by GM, Ford, and Chrysler. Each firm had its own network of dealers. Volkswagen felt that the only way to get quick access to the United States was to promote its cars through company owned dealerships.

Market Imperfections

As in the case of horizontal FDI, a more general explanation of vertical FDI can be found in the market imperfections approach.[24] The market imperfections approach offers two explanations for vertical FDI. As with horizontal FDI, the first explanation revolves around the idea that there are impediments to the sale of know-how through the market mechanism. The second explanation is based on the idea that investments in specialized assets expose the investing firm to hazards that can be reduced only through vertical FDI.

Impediments to the Sale of Know-How

Consider the case of oil refining companies such as British Petroleum and Royal Dutch/Shell. Historically, these firms pursued backward vertical FDI to supply their British and Dutch oil refining facilities with crude oil. When this occurred in the early decades of this century, neither Great Britain nor the Netherlands had domestic oil supplies. However, why did these firms not just import oil from firms in oil-rich countries such as Saudi Arabia and Kuwait?

Originally, there were no Saudi Arabian or Kuwaiti firms with the technological expertise for finding and extracting oil. BP and Royal Dutch/Shell had to develop this know-how themselves to get access to oil. This alone does not explain FDI, however, for once BP and Shell had developed the necessary know-how they could have licensed it to Saudi Arabian or Kuwaiti firms. However, as we saw in the case of horizontal FDI, licensing can be self-defeating as a mechanism for the sale of know-how. If the oil refining firms had licensed their prospecting and extraction know-how to Saudi Arabian or Kuwaiti firms, they would have risked giving away their technological know-how to those firms, creating future competitors in the process. Once they had the know-how, the Saudi and Kuwaiti firms might have gone prospecting for oil in other parts of the world, competing directly against BP and Royal Dutch/Shell. Thus, it made more sense for these firms to undertake backward vertical FDI and extract the oil themselves instead of licensing their hard-earned technological expertise to local firms.

Generalizing from this example, the prediction is that backward vertical FDI will occur when a firm has the knowledge and the ability to extract raw materials in another country and there is no efficient producer in that country that can supply raw materials to the firm.

Investment in Specialized Assets

Another strand of the market imperfections argument predicts that vertical FDI will occur when a firm must invest in specialized assets whose value depends on inputs provided by a foreign supplier. In this context, a specialized asset is an asset designed to perform a specific task and whose value is significantly reduced in its next-best use. Consider the case of an aluminum refinery, which is designed to refine bauxite ore and produce aluminum. Bauxite ores vary in content and chemical composition from deposit to deposit. Each type of ore requires a different type of refinery. Running one type of bauxite through a refinery designed for another type increases production costs by 20 to 100 percent.[25] Thus, the value of an investment in an aluminum refinery depends on the availability of the desired kind of bauxite ore.

Imagine that a U.S. aluminum company must decide whether to invest in an aluminum refinery designed to refine a certain type of ore. Assume further that this ore is available only through an Australian mining firm at a single bauxite mine. Using a different type of ore in the refinery would raise production costs by at least 20 percent. Therefore, the value of the U.S. company's investment depends on the price it must pay the Australian firm for this bauxite. Recognizing this, once the U.S. company has invested in a new refinery, what is to stop the Australian firm from raising bauxite prices? Absolutely nothing; and once it has made the investment, the U.S. firm is locked into its relationship with the Australian supplier. The Australian firm can increase bauxite prices, secure in the knowledge that as long as the increase in the total production costs is less than 20 percent, the U.S. firm will continue to buy from it. (It would become economical for the U.S. firm to buy from another supplier only if total production costs increased by more than 20 percent.)

The U.S. firm can reduce the risk of the Australian firm opportunistically raising prices in this manner by buying out the Australian firm. If the U.S. firm can buy the Australian firm, or its bauxite mine, it need no longer fear that bauxite prices will be increased after it has invested in the refinery. In other words, it would make economic sense for the U.S. firm to engage in vertical FDI. In practice, these kinds of considerations have driven aluminum firms to pursue vertical FDI to such a degree that in 1976, 91 percent of the total volume of bauxite was transferred within vertically integrated firms.[26]

Implications for Business

The implications of the theories of horizontal and vertical FDI for business practice are relatively straightforward. First, the location-specific advantages argument associated with John Dunning helps explain the direction of FDI, both with regard to horizontal and vertical FDI. However, the argument does not explain why firms prefer FDI to licensing or to exporting. In this regard, from both an explanatory and a business perspective, perhaps the most useful theory is the market imperfections approach. With regard to horizontal FDI, this approach identifies with some precision how the relative rates of return associated with horizontal FDI, exporting, and licensing vary with circumstances. The theory suggests that exporting is preferable to licensing and horizontal FDI as long as transport costs are minor and tariff barriers are trivial. As transport costs and/or tariff barriers increase, exporting becomes unprofitable, and the choice is between horizontal FDI and licensing. Since horizontal FDI is more costly and more risky than licensing, other things being equal, the theory argues that licensing is preferable to horizontal FDI. Other things are seldom equal, however. Although licensing may work, it is not an attractive option when one or more of the following conditions exist: *(a)* the firm has valuable know-how that cannot be adequately protected by a licensing contract, *(b)* the firm needs tight control over a foreign entity to maximize its market share and earnings in that country, and *(c)* a firm's skills and know-how are not amenable to licensing. Figure 6.6 presents these considerations as a decision tree.

Firms for which licensing is not a good option tend to be clustered in three types of industries:

1. High-technology industries where protecting firm-specific expertise is of paramount importance and licensing is hazardous.
2. Global oligopolies, where competitive interdependence requires that multinational firms maintain tight control over foreign operations so that they have the ability to launch coordinated attacks against their global competitors (as Kodak has done with Fuji).
3. Industries where intense cost pressures require that multinational firms maintain tight control over foreign operations (so they can disperse manufacturing to locations around the globe where factor costs are most favorable to minimize costs).

The majority of the limited evidence seems to support these conjectures.[27] In addition, licensing is not a good option if the competitive advantage of a firm is based upon managerial or marketing knowledge that is embedded in the routines of the firm, and/or the skills of its managers, and is difficult to codify in a "book of blueprints." This would seem to be the case for firms based in a fairly wide range of industries, and as we have seen from examples in this chapter, includes the likes of Starbucks and Cemex.

Firms for which licensing is a good option tend to be in industries whose conditions are opposite to those specified above. Licensing tends to be more

Figure 6.6

A Decision Framework

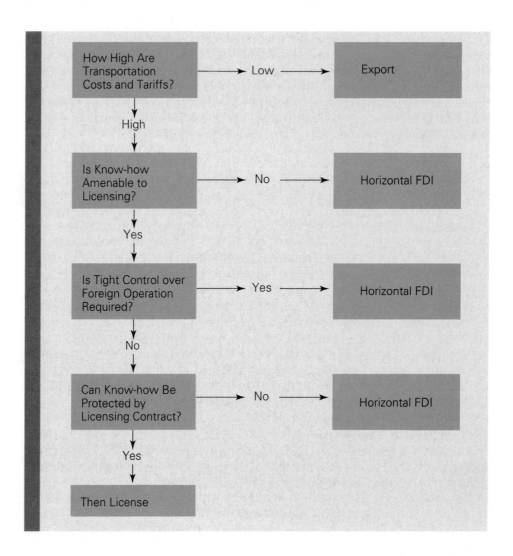

common (and more profitable) in fragmented, low-technology industries in which globally dispersed manufacturing is not an option. Licensing is also easier if the knowledge to be transferred is relatively easy to codify. A good example of an industry where these conditions seem to exist is the fast-food industry. McDonald's has expanded globally by using a franchising strategy. Franchising is essentially the service-industry version of licensing—although it normally involves much longer-term commitments than licensing. With franchising, the firm licenses its brand name to a foreign firm in return for a percentage of the franchisee's profits. The franchising contract specifies the conditions that the franchisee must fulfill if it is to use the franchisor's brand name. Thus, McDonald's allows foreign firms to use its brand name as long as they agree to run their restaurants on exactly the same lines as McDonald's restaurants elsewhere in the world. This strategy makes sense for McDonald's because (a) like many services, fast food cannot be exported, (b) franchising economizes the costs and risks associated with opening foreign markets, (c) unlike technological know-how, brand names are relatively easy to protect using a contract, (d) there is no compelling reason for McDonald's to have tight control over franchisees, and (e) McDonald's know-how, in terms of how to run a fast-food restaurant, is amenable to being specified in a written contract (e.g., the contract specifies the details of how to run a McDonald's restaurant). Having said this, it is worth noting that McDonald's does undertake some FDI to establish "master franchisors" in each country in which it does business. These master franchisors are normally joint ventures with local companies, and their task is to manage McDonald's franchisees within a particular country.

In contrast to the market imperfections approach, the product life-cycle theory and Knickerbocker's theory of horizontal FDI tend to be less useful from a business perspective. These two theories are descriptive rather than analytical. They do a good job of describing the historical pattern of FDI, but they do a relatively poor job of identifying the factors that influence the relative profitability of FDI, licensing, and exporting. The issue of licensing as an alternative to FDI is ignored by both these theories.

Finally, with regard to vertical FDI, both the market imperfections approach and the strategic behavior approach have some useful implications for business practice. The strategic behavior approach points out that vertical FDI may be a way of building barriers to entry into an industry. The strength of the market imperfections approach is that it points out the conditions under which vertical FDI might be preferable to the alternatives. Most importantly, the market imperfections approach points to the importance of investments in specialized assets and imperfections in the market for know-how as factors that increase the relative attractiveness of vertical FDI.

Chapter Summary

This chapter reviewed theories that attempt to explain the pattern of FDI between countries. This objective takes on added importance in light of the expanding volume of FDI in the world economy. As we saw early in the chapter, the volume of FDI has grown more rapidly than the volume of world trade in recent years. We also noted that any theory seeking to explain FDI must explain why firms go to the trouble of acquiring or establishing operations abroad when the alternatives of exporting and licensing are available.

We reviewed a number of theories that attempt to explain horizontal and vertical FDI. With regard to horizontal FDI, it was argued that the market imperfections and location-specific advantages approaches might have the greatest explanatory power and therefore be most useful for business practice. This is not to belittle the explanations for horizontal FDI put forward by Vernon and Knickerbocker, since these theories also have value in explaining the pattern of FDI in the world economy. Still, both theories are weakened by their failure to explicitly consider the factors that drive the choice among exporting, licensing, and FDI. Finally, with regard to vertical FDI, it was argued that the strategic behavior and market imperfections approaches both have a certain amount of explanatory power.

This chapter made the following points:

1. Foreign direct investment occurs when a firm invests directly in facilities to produce a product in a foreign country. It also occurs when a firm buys an existing enterprise in a foreign country.

2. Horizontal FDI is FDI in the same industry abroad as a firm operates at home. Vertical FDI is FDI in an industry abroad that provides inputs into or sells outputs from a firm's domestic operations.

3. Any theory seeking to explain FDI must explain why firms go to the trouble of acquiring or establishing operations abroad when the alternatives of exporting and licensing are available.

4. Several factors characterized FDI trends over the past 20 years; (*a*) there has been a rapid increase in the total volume of FDI undertaken; (*b*) there has been some decline in the relative importance of the United States as a source for FDI, while several other countries have increased their share of total FDI outflows; (*c*) an increasing share of FDI seems to be directed at the developing nations of Asia and Eastern Europe, while the United States has become a major recipient of FDI; and (*d*) there has been an increase in the amount of FDI undertaken by firms based in developing nations.

5. High transportation costs and/or tariffs imposed on imports help explain why many firms prefer horizontal FDI or licensing over exporting.

6. Impediments to the sale of know-how explain why firms prefer horizontal FDI to licensing. These impediments arise when: (*a*) a firm has valuable know-how that cannot be adequately protected by a licensing contract, (*b*) a firm needs tight control over a foreign entity to maximize its market share and earnings in that country, and (*c*) a firm's skills and know-how are not amenable to licensing.

7. Knickerbocker's theory suggests that much FDI is explained by imitative strategic behavior by

rival firms in an oligopolistic industry. However, this theory does not address the issue of whether FDI is more efficient than exporting or licensing for expanding abroad.

8. Vernon's product life-cycle theory suggests that firms undertake FDI at particular stages in the life cycle of products they have pioneered. However, Vernon's theory does not address the issue of whether FDI is more efficient than exporting or licensing for expanding abroad.

9. Dunning has argued that location-specific advantages are of considerable importance in explaining the nature and direction of FDI. According to Dunning, firms undertake FDI to exploit resource endowments or assets that are location-specific.

10. Backward vertical FDI may be explained as an attempt to create barriers to entry by gaining control over the source of material inputs into the downstream stage of a production process. Forward vertical FDI may be seen as an attempt to circumvent entry barriers and gain access to a national market.

11. The market imperfections approach suggests that vertical FDI is a way of reducing a firm's exposure to the risks that arise from investments in specialized assets.

12. From a business perspective, the most useful theory is probably the market imperfections approach, because it identifies how the relative profit rates associated with horizontal FDI, exporting, and licensing vary with circumstances.

Critical Discussion Questions

1. In 1999 inward FDI accounted for some 45 percent of gross fixed capital formation in Ireland, but only 0.3 percent in Japan. What do you think explains this difference in FDI inflows into the two countries?

2. Compare and contrast these explanations of horizontal FDI: the market imperfections approach, Vernon's product life-cycle theory, and Knickerbocker's theory of FDI. Which theory do you think offers the best explanation of the historical pattern of horizontal FDI? Why?

3. Read the opening case on Starbucks. Using the market imperfections approach to FDI, explain Starbucks' approach to expanding its presence in Thailand, Great Britain, and Japan.

4. Compare and contrast these explanations of vertical FDI: the strategic behavior approach and the market imperfections approach. Which theory do you think offers the better explanation of the historical pattern of vertical FDI? Why?

5. You are the international manager of a U.S. business that has just developed a revolutionary new personal computer that can perform the same functions as existing PCs but costs only half as much to manufacture. Several patents protect the unique design of this computer. Your CEO has asked you to formulate a recommendation for how to expand into Western Europe. Your options are (a) to export from the United States, (b) to license a European firm to manufacture and market the computer in Europe, and (c) to set up a wholly owned subsidiary in Europe. Evaluate the pros and cons of each alternative and suggest a course of action to your CEO.

Closing Case

Electrolux

With sales of around SKr120 billion ($14 billion), Electrolux is the world's largest manufacturer of household appliances (washing machines, dishwashers, refrigerators, vacuum cleaners, and so on). A Swedish company with a small home market, Electrolux has always had to look to other markets for its growth. By 2000, the company was generating more than 85 percent of its sales outside of Sweden. A little over 50 percent of sales are in Western Europe, with another 30 percent in North America. In recent years, the most rapid growth has come from Asia, Eastern Europe, and Latin America (6.4 percent of revenues). As of early 2001 the company employed approximately 85,000 people worldwide, had 150 factories and 300 warehouses located in 60 countries, and sold about 55 million products per year in 150 countries.

Electrolux's expansion into Asia, Eastern Europe, and Latin America dates from an early 1990s planning review, which concluded that demand for household appliances was mature in Western Europe and North America. The company conjectured that growth in these regions would be limited to replacement demand and the growth in population and would be unlikely to exceed 2 to 3 percent annually. Leif Johansson, then the CEO of Electrolux, decided the company was too dependent on these mature markets. He reasoned that the company would have to expand aggressively into the emerging markets of the developing world if it was to maintain its historic growth rate. The company estimated that demand for household appliances in Asia, Eastern Europe, and Latin America could grow at 20 percent annually for at least the next decade, and probably beyond. In 1994, he set an ambitious goal for Electrolux: the company would have to double its sales in these emerging markets from the $1.35 billion it achieved in 1994 to $2.7 billion by 1997 (this target was exceeded). As an additional goal, he stated that Electrolux should become one of the top three suppliers of household goods in Southeast Asia by the year 2000.

In addition to the obvious growth potential, another consideration for Electrolux was that its main global competitors, General Electric and Whirlpool of the United States and Germany's Bosch-Siemens, had recently announced similar plans. Electrolux thought it better move quickly so as not to be left out in the race to profit from these emerging markets.

Having committed itself to expansion, Electrolux had to decide how to achieve its ambitious goals. A combination of cost considerations and import barriers made direct exporting from its Western European and North American plants uneconomical. Instead, various approaches were adopted for different regions and countries. Acquisitions of going concerns, green-field developments, joint ventures, and enhanced marketing were all considered. Electrolux stated that it was prepared to spend $200 million per year to increase its presence in these emerging markets.

Electrolux made its first move into Eastern Europe in 1991 when it acquired Lehel, Hungary's largest manufacturer of household appliances. In addition, Electrolux decided to establish wholly owned operating companies in Russia, Poland, and the Czech Republic. Each of these operating subsidiaries was a green-field development.

Asia demands a much greater need to adapt to local conditions. Regulations concerning foreign ownership in India and China, for example, virtually compel Electrolux to work through joint ventures with local partners. In China, the world's fastest-growing market, the company already had joint ventures in compressors, vacuum cleaners, and water purification equipment in 1994. Between 1994 and 1997, the company spent another $300 million to build five manufacturing plants in that

country. In Southeast Asia, the emphasis is on the marketing of goods imported from China, rather than on local production.

In Latin America, the company expanded through acquisitions, including its 1996 acquisition of Refripar, the largest producer of refrigerator products in Brazil. Electrolux's goal is to turn Refripar into its Latin American base for the production of household products.

Although Electrolux has been largely successful in its attempt to globalize its production and sales base, the expansion has not been without problems. In 1997, the company suffered a significant drop in profit due to deteriorating market conditions in Brazil and the Asian Pacific region. The profit slump exposed serious weaknesses that had developed in Electrolux's global production system. Although the company had expanded rapidly via acquisitions since the early 1990s, it had not rationalized its production operations. Consequently, there was often considerable duplication of facilities within regions. In early 1998, the company's new CEO, Michael Treschow, announced a restructuring plan that called for the loss of 12,000 jobs and the closure of 25 factories and 50 warehouses worldwide. At the same time, however, Treschow reaffirmed Electrolux's commitment to building a global corporation with significant operations in the world's developing markets.

Sources: C. Brown-Humes, "Electrolux Plugs into Households All over Asia," *Financial Times*, April 27, 1995, p. 15; C. Brown-Humes, "Electrolux Buys Control of Brazilian Group," *Financial Times*, January 11, 1996, p. 30; G. McIvor, "Electrolux Comes under the Scalpel," *Financial Times*, October 29, 1997, p. 27; Electrolux's website, *http://www.electrolux.com*; and M. Treschow, "What Does a Knife Do When the Cutting's Done?" *Business Week*, October 23, 2000, p. 148.

Case Discussion Questions

1. What were the primary motivating factors behind Electrolux's decision to expand aggressively into Asia, Eastern Europe, and Latin America in the 1990s?

2. Why do you think Electrolux acquired Lehel in Hungary, but opted for green-field investments to enter many other Eastern European countries?

3. The company has generally preferred FDI to exports as a mode of entry into foreign markets. Why do you think this is the case?

4. What theory, or theories, best explains Electrolux's FDI decisions during the 1990s: (*a*) the market imperfections approach, (*b*) the strategic behavior approach, (*c*) the product life-cycle approach, or (*d*) the location-specific advantages approach?

Notes

1. United Nations, *World Investment Report, 2000* (New York and Geneva: United Nations, 2001).

2. Ibid, and UN press release, "World FDI Flows Exceed US $1.1 trillion in 2000," December 7, 2000.

3. World Trade Organization, *Annual Report, 2000* (Geneva: WTO, 2000), and United Nations, *World Investment Report, 2000* (New York and Geneva: United Nations, 2000).

4. United Nations, *World Investment Report, 2000*.

5. Ibid.

6. Ibid.

7. United Nations, *World Investment Report, 2001*.

8. United Nations, *World Investment Report, 2001*.

9. M. Kidron and R. Segal, *The New State of the World Atlas* (New York: Simon & Schuster, 1987).

10. United Nations, *World Investment Report, 2001*.

11. See D. J. Ravenscraft and F. M. Scherer, *Mergers, Selloffs and Economic Efficiency* (Washington, DC: The Brookings Institution, 1987).

12. For example, see S. H. Hymer, *The International Operations of National Firms: A Study of Direct Foreign Investment* (Cambridge, MA: MIT Press, 1976); A. M. Rugman, *Inside the Multinationals: The Economics of Internal Markets* (New York: Columbia University Press, 1981); D. J. Teece, "Multinational Enterprise, Internal Governance, and Industrial Organization," *American Economic Review* 75 (May 1983), pp. 233–38; and C. W. L. Hill and W. C. Kim, "Searching for a Dynamic Theory of the Multinational Enterprise: A Transaction Cost Model," *Strategic Management Journal* (special issue) 9 (1988), pp. 93–104.

13. J. P. Womack, D. T. Jones, and D. Roos, *The Machine That Changed the World* (New York: Rawson Associates, 1990).

14. The argument is most often associated with F. T. Knickerbocker, *Oligopolistic Reaction and Multinational Enterprise* (Boston: Harvard Business School Press, 1973).

15. The studies are summarized in R. E. Caves, *Multinational Enterprise and Economic Analysis,* 2nd ed. (Cambridge, UK: Cambridge University Press, 1996).

16. See R. E. Caves, "Japanese Investment in the US: Lessons for the Economic Analysis of Foreign Investment," *The World Economy* 16 (1993), pp. 279–300; B. Kogut and S. J. Chang, "Technological Capabilities and Japanese Direct Investment in the United States," *Review of Economics and Statistics* 73 (1991), pp. 401–43; and J. Anand and B. Kogut, "Technological Capabilities of Countries, Firm Rivalry, and Foreign Direct Investment," *Journal of International Business Studies*, Third Quarter (1997), pp. 445–65.

17. For the use of Vernon's theory to explain Japanese direct investment in the United States and Europe, see S. Thomsen, "Japanese Direct Investment in the European Community," *The World Economy* 16 (1993), pp. 301–15.

18. J. H. Dunning, *Explaining International Production* (London: Unwin Hyman, 1988).

19. P. Krugman, "Increasing Returns and Economic Geography," *Journal of Political Economy* 99, no. 3 (1991), pp. 483–99.

20. J. M. Shaver and F. Flyer. "Agglomeration Economies, Firm Heterogeneity, and Foreign Direct Investment in the United States," *Strategic Management Journal* 21 (2000), pp. 1175–93.

21. J. H. Dunning and R. Narula, "Transpacific Foreign Direct Investment and the Investment Development Path," *South Carolina Essays in International Business* 10 (May 1995).

22. W. Shan and J. Song, "Foreign Direct Investment and the Sourcing of Technological Advantage: Evidence from the Biotechnology Industry," *Journal of International Business Studies,* Second Quarter (1997), pp. 267–84.

23. Caves, *Multinational Enterprise and Economic Analysis.*

24. J. F. Hennart, "Upstream Vertical Integration in the Aluminum and Tin Industries," *Journal of Economic Behavior and Organization* 9 (1988), pp. 281–99; and O. E. Williamson, *The Economic Institutions of Capitalism* (New York: Free Press, 1985).

25. Hennart, "Upstream Vertical Integration."

26. Ibid.

27. See Caves, *Multinational Enterprise and Economic Analysis.*

The Political Economy of Foreign Direct Investment

For years South Africa was an international pariah. The white minority government practiced apartheid, disenfranchising the country's black majority, many of whom lived in poverty. The main political voice of the black majority, the African National Congress (ANC), was outlawed. Many of the ANC's leaders, including Nelson Mandela, were imprisoned, while the remainder lived in exile. To put economic pressure on South Africa to change its racist ways, the U.S. government placed trade sanctions on South Africa and encouraged U.S. companies to divest themselves of any assets in the country. Many responded, with 240 of 360 U.S. companies with investments in South Africa leaving between 1986 and 1994. These included Ford, General Motors, IBM, and Kodak, all of which sold their South African assets during this period. The economic pressure contributed to the abandonment of apartheid in 1994, when the country held its first democratic elections. The ANC won the elections, and Nelson Mandela was elected president.

Although former Communists had a strong presence in the ANC, the new South African government embraced an economic program that had many elements of free market economics. A privatization program was initiated, and policies were enacted to open the country to foreign trade and investment. The government also adopted disciplined fiscal and monetary policies, cutting the national budget deficit from 8 percent of GDP in 1994 to less than 2 percent by 2000 and reducing the inflation rate from 10 percent to under 6 percent over the same period. One main goal was to create an environment that would entice foreign companies to invest in the newly democratic South Africa. The South African government believed that the country would be rewarded for doing the right things by a surge in foreign direct investment. After all, South Africa was the largest economy in Africa with 41 million people; good communications, power, and transportation infrastructures; and a gross national product per capita in excess of $3,000, which put the country in the same league as many emerging Asian economies such as Thailand and Malaysia. There was a belief that foreign investment inflows would help to revitalize the economy, infusing the country with much-needed capital, jobs, skills, and technology, all of which would boost employment, exports, and economic growth. Of particular concern was the high level of unemployment among the black majority, which according to some estimates ran as high as 40 percent. Foreign investment was seen as the key to reducing this.

But the government was disappointed. Foreign direct investment did increase from an average of just $22 million annually between 1988 and 1993 to hit a peak of $3.8 billion in 1997, but it fell back to less than $2 billion in 2000. By the standards of other developing countries, South Africa lured relatively little foreign direct investment during this period: $32 per capita between 1994 and 1999, compared with $106 for Brazil, $252 for Argentina, and $333 for Chile. While South Africa attracted $1.4 billion in FDI in 1999, Thailand and Singapore, both still reeling from the Asian economic crisis, attracted in excess of $6 billion apiece, while Chile snagged $9 billion and Brazil $31 billion. Partly due to the anemic inflow of foreign capital, unemployment among South African blacks remained persistently high—about 35 percent by some estimates in 2001—creating what some see as a "human time bomb." Economic growth also stalled, averaging less than 1 percent a year between 1995 and 2000.

Why did more foreign capital not flow into South Africa after the end of apartheid in 1994? There seem to be several reasons. One problem was the perception that despite high unemployment, labor in South Africa was relatively expensive, lacked skills, and was not particularly productive. Basic wage rates were often higher than elsewhere in southern Africa and Southeast Asia, while productivity was hurt by a relatively high level of days lost due to industrial disputes. Restrictive labor laws also gave foreign investors cause for concern. For example, in January 2001 Volkswagen was ordered to reinstate 1,300 employees that were sacked in an illegal strike in 2000.

Another problem is that many companies that pulled out of South Africa before 1994 now feel that they are not being rewarded for their efforts and are thus less likely to reinvest. While South Africa has a number of incentives to attract foreign investors, such as tax breaks, there is no preferential treatment for companies that divested in protest against apartheid. When Kodak pulled out in 1986, it commanded more that 60 percent of the South African market for film products. When Kodak returned to South Africa in 1996, not only was there no red carpet, no thanks, and, most importantly, no differential incentives, there was no business. Foreign companies that had not divested now dominated the film market, and Kodak had to spend heavily to regain market share. Four years later, Kodak still had less than 30 percent of the South African film market.

A third problem is political. South Africa is being damned for association with some of its neighbors and has been punished for some of the rather outlandish statements of its current president, Thabo Mbeki. In neighboring Zimbabwe, President Robert Mugabe has actively encouraged landless blacks to illegally seize land from long-term white owners, using violence to evict them if they resist. President Mbeki's failure to quickly condemn Mugabe led some to question his judgment and raised fears that South Africa might slip toward this kind of anarchy. Mbeki's critics gained more ammunition when he proclaimed that the HIV virus did not cause AIDS and questioned the efficacy of drugs used to treat the disease. Mbeki told an ANC parliamentary caucus that the United States and pharmaceutical companies have conspired to establish a false link between HIV and AIDS to promote the sales of antiretroviral drugs produced by U.S. pharmaceutical companies. The issue is serious for two reasons. First, some 11 percent of South Africa's 45 million people are estimated to be infected with the HIV virus, making it a health crisis of huge proportions. Second, Mbeki's statements have added to the perception that the leadership is not particularly stable, and this has unnerved skittish foreign investors, who have turned their attention to more politically stable countries.

Another problem concerns South Africa's crime rate. The combination of high unemployment, weak policing, and the easy and wide availability of guns has made South Africa one of the murder capitals of the world. With more than 140 murders or attempted murders everyday, South Africa has a murder rate per capita that is eight times that in the United States. This alone is enough to put off many foreign investors. Finally, perception is widespread in South Africa that the government suffers from endemic corruption. As with the crime rate and President Mbeki's statements regarding AIDS, this adds to the general impression that South Africa is becoming politically unstable and less attractive as a draw for foreign investors, particularly when there are so many other attractive locations for direct investment around the world.

Sources: R. Block, "African Leaders Seek More Investment," *Wall Street Journal,* January 9, 2001, p. A16; "Jobless and Joyless," *The Economist,* February 24, 2001, pp. S11–S13; Roger Thurow, "South Africans Who Fought for Sanctions Now Scrap for Investors," *Wall Street Journal,* February 11, 2000, p. A1; and Henri Cauvin, "South Africa's Economic Lament," *New York Times,* November 11, 2000, pp. B1, B2.

▓ Introduction

Chapter 6 looked at the phenomenon of foreign direct investment (FDI) and reviewed several theories that attempt to explain the economic rationale for FDI, but it did not discuss the role of governments in FDI. Through their choice of policies and their statements and actions, governments can both encourage and restrict FDI. Host governments can encourage FDI by providing incentives for foreign firms to invest in their economies, and they can restrict or discourage FDI through a variety of laws, policies, and statements. In the opening case we saw how a newly democratic South Africa tried to encourage FDI to gain access to capital and technology and to increase jobs. However, the case also illustrates how labor policies and the somewhat outlandish statements of South African President Thabo Mbeki may have had the unintended consequence of discouraging FDI.

The government of a source country for FDI also can encourage or restrict FDI by domestic firms. In recent years, the Japanese government has pressured many Japanese firms to undertake FDI. The Japanese government sees FDI as a substitute for exporting and thus as a way of reducing Japan's politically embarrassing balance of payments surplus. In contrast, the U.S. government has, for political reasons, from time to time restricted FDI by domestic firms. For example, in response to a belief that the Iranian government actively supports terrorist organizations, the U.S. government has prohibited U.S. firms from investing in or exporting to Iran. As discussed in the opening case, the U.S. government also discouraged firms from investing in South Africa before 1994, when the white minority government operated an apartheid regime.

Historically, one important determinant of a government's policy toward FDI has been its political ideology. Accordingly, this chapter opens with a discussion of how political ideology influences government policy. To a greater or lesser degree, the officials of many governments tend to be pragmatic nationalists who weigh the benefits and costs of FDI and vary their stated policy on a case-by-case basis. After discussing political ideology, we will consider the benefits and costs of FDI. Then we will look at the various policies home and host governments adopt to encourage and/or restrict FDI. The chapter closes with a detailed discussion of the implications of government policy for the business firm. In this closing section, we examine the factors that determine the relative bargaining strengths of a host government and a firm contemplating FDI. We will look at how the negotiations between firm and government are often played out and at how firms can use this knowledge to their advantage.

Political Ideology and Foreign Direct Investment ▮

Historically, ideology toward FDI has ranged from a dogmatic radical stance that is hostile to all FDI at one extreme to an adherence to the noninterventionist principle of free market economics at the other. Between these two extremes is an approach that might be called pragmatic nationalism.

▎The Radical View

The radical view traces its roots to Marxist political and economic theory. Radical writers argue that the multinational enterprise (MNE) is an instrument of imperialist domination. They see the MNE as a tool for exploiting host countries to the exclusive benefit of their capitalist-imperialist home countries. They argue that MNEs extract profits from the host country and take them to their home country, giving nothing of value to the host country in exchange. They note, for example, that key technology is tightly controlled by the MNE, and that important jobs in the foreign subsidiaries of MNEs go to home-country nationals rather than to citizens of the host country. Because of this, according to the radical view, FDI by the MNEs of advanced capitalist nations keeps the less developed countries of the world relatively backward and dependent on advanced capitalist nations for investment, jobs, and technology. Thus, according to the extreme version of this view, no country should ever permit foreign corporations to undertake FDI, since they can never be instruments of economic development, only of economic domination. Where MNEs already exist in a country, they should be immediately nationalized.[1]

From 1945 until the 1980s, the radical view was very influential in the world economy. Until the collapse of communism between 1989 and 1991, the countries of Eastern Europe were opposed to FDI. Similarly, Communist countries elsewhere, such as China, Cambodia, and Cuba, were all opposed in principle to FDI (although in practice the Chinese started to allow FDI in mainland China in the 1970s). Many socialist countries, particularly in Africa where one of the first actions of many newly independent states was to nationalize foreign-owned enterprises, also embraced the radical position. Countries whose political ideology was more nationalistic than socialistic further embraced the radical position. This was true in Iran and India, for example, both of which adopted tough policies restricting FDI and nationalized many foreign-owned enterprises. Iran is particularly interesting because its Islamic government, while rejecting Marxist theory, has essentially embraced the radical view that FDI by MNEs is an instrument of imperialism.

By the end of the 1980s, however, the radical position was in retreat almost everywhere. There seem to be three reasons for this: (1) the collapse of communism in Eastern Europe; (2) the generally abysmal economic performance of those countries that embraced the radical position, and a growing belief by many of these countries that FDI can be an important source of technology and jobs and can stimulate economic growth; and (3) the strong economic performance of those developing countries that embraced capitalism rather than radical ideology (e.g., Singapore, Hong Kong, and Taiwan). For example, even though the governing African National Congress party in South Africa contains many former Communists, the government has not adopted a radical stance and is actively encouraging foreign firms to undertake FDI (see the opening case). Twenty years ago this would not have occurred, but in the new world order ushered in by the collapse of communism it is a common position.

The Free Market View

The free market view traces its roots to classical economics and the international trade theories of Adam Smith and David Ricardo (see Chapter 4). The intellectual case for this view has been strengthened by the market imperfections explanation of horizontal and vertical FDI that we reviewed in Chapter 6. The free market view argues that international production should be distributed among countries according to the theory of comparative advantage. Countries should specialize in the production of those goods and services that they can produce most efficiently. Within this framework, the MNE is an instrument for dispersing the production of goods and services to the most efficient locations around the globe. Viewed this way, FDI by the MNE increases the overall efficiency of the world economy.

Consider a well-publicized decision by IBM in the mid-1980s to move assembly operations for many of its personal computers from the United States to Guadalajara, Mexico. IBM invested about $90 million in an assembly facility with the capacity to produce 100,000 PCs per year, 75 percent of which were exported back to the United States.[2] According to the free market view, moves such as this can be seen as increasing the overall efficiency of resource utilization in the world economy. Mexico, due to its low labor costs, has a comparative advantage in the assembly of PCs. According to the free market view, by moving the production of PCs from the United States to Mexico, IBM frees U.S. resources for use in activities in which the United States has a comparative advantage (e.g., the design of computer software, the manufacture of high-value-added components such as microprocessors, or basic R&D). Also, consumers benefit because the PCs cost less than they would if they were produced domestically. In addition, Mexico gains from the technology, skills, and capital that IBM transfers with its FDI. Contrary to the radical view, the free market view stresses that such resource transfers benefit the host country and stimulate its economic growth. Thus, the free market view argues that FDI is a benefit to both the source country and the host country.

For reasons explored earlier in this book (see Chapter 2), the free market view has been ascendant worldwide in recent years, spurring a global move toward the removal of restrictions on inward and outward foreign direct investment. An example is South Korea, which started dismantling its restrictive regulations governing inward FDI in the mid-1990s. As described in the accompanying Management Focus, foreign firms are starting to affect competition in certain sectors of the South Korean economy.

As noted earlier in this book, according to the United Nations, between 1991 and 2000 some 94 percent of the 1,035 changes worldwide in the laws governing foreign direct investment created a more favorable environment for FDI. The desire of governments to

ManagementFocus

Volvo's FDI in South Korea

Historically, South Korea has been largely closed to foreign direct investment. During its 30-year dash from one of the world's poorest nations to one of its richest, South Korea closely adhered to the Japanese model of development, severely restricting foreign ownership of industrial and commercial activities. The walls of fortress Korea began to crumble in the mid-1990s when the government lifted almost all restrictions on foreign entry into the country's retail sector. The move was prompted by a belief that foreign entry would provide much-needed competition and lower prices in the retail sector. Over the next few years, a wave of foreign discounters entered the country, opening 22 large discount stores by the end of 1999. These discounters included Carrefour and Promodes from France, Wal-Mart and Costco from the United States, and Tesco from the United Kingdom. They provide a new source of competition for South Korea's indigenous discounters, which included E-Mart and Magnet. The entry of foreign competitors with access to significant capital resources stimulated E-Mart and Magnet to increase their operating efficiency and lower prices to keep the foreigners at bay. The main beneficiaries of this development have been South Korean consumers, who now enjoy more choice and lower prices.

Liberalization of the retail sector, however, was just the first wave of opening South Korea to foreign direct investment. In 1997, South Korea's long period of economic expansion came to an abrupt end when a financial crisis swept across Asia. This produced a sharp drop in economic activity in South Korea. The South Korean currency slumped against the dollar, requiring the government to seek $58 billion in aid from the International Monetary Fund. As demand for their products plummeted, dozens of highly leveraged South Korean companies found themselves unable to service the debt they had taken on during the boom years to finance their expansion. Many teetered on the edge of bankruptcy. The South Korean government responded by removing many of the restrictions to foreign direct investment, including regulations that prohibited foreign firms from making hostile takeovers of South Korean enterprises.

The impact was dramatic. FDI in the South Korean economy surged from $3 billion in 1997 to $10.3 billion in 1999. The total stock of foreign investment in South Korea soared from $5.2 billion in 1990 to $28 billion by the end of the decade. While many Koreans initially viewed the new wave of foreign investment with deep suspicion, and the radical press demonized foreign companies as unwelcome guests feeding off the local market like leeches, it quickly became apparent that the reality was something else. Samsung's money-losing construction equipment division was acquired by Sweden's Volvo in February 1998 for $572 million. This was South Korea's first major sale of a distressed company to a foreign investor, and both the public and Samsung employees greeted the sale with deep apprehension. Two years later, however, most of those fears had been put to rest.

Volvo immediately launched an ambitious investment program, committing another $200 million to the plant in an attempt to turn the ex-Samsung facility into its main global base for excavators and other construction equipment. The company transferred leading-edge manufacturing technology to the plant, moved in some of its best managers to oversee the operations, and made the facility its global center for R&D in excavators. Volvo even closed its excavator plant in Sweden, signaling the company's commitment to the South Korean facility. Although some 13 percent of the 1,655 employees at the plant left after the Volvo acquisition, these job reductions were achieved through attrition and not layoffs. Volvo refocused the production of the plant, emphasizing higher quality and higher priced machines that promise better profit margins. The old South Korean emphasis on sales volume and market share has been replaced by a focus on product quality, operating efficiency, and profitability. The management hierarchy was significantly reduced, much of the bureaucracy was removed, and decision-making responsibilities were pushed down the line to self-managing work teams. By 2000, the plant was making a profit and capacity utilization had increased from 50 percent to about 70 percent. The ultimate goal is to export 60 to 70 percent of the output from the plant, up from 35 percent of production when Samsung owned the plant.

Sources: Charles S. Lee. "Foreign Affair," *Far Eastern Economic Review*, April 29, 1999, pp. 58–60; S. W. Park, "Foreign Retail Chains Take Root in Korea," *Business Korea*, December 1999, pp. 42–43; and M. Schuman, "South Korea Enjoys Foreign Investment Boom," *Wall Street Journal*, November 26, 1999, p. A8.

facilitate FDI has also been reflected in a dramatic increase in the number of bilateral investment treaties designed to protect and promote investment between two countries. As of January 1, 2000, there were 1,856 such treaties in the world involving over 160 countries, a tenfold increase from the 181 treaties that existed in 1980.[3] However, in practice no country has adopted the free market view in its pure form (just as no country has adopted the radical view in its pure form). Countries such as Great Britain and the United States are among the most open to FDI, but the governments of both countries intervene. Great Britain does so by reserving the right to block foreign takeovers of domestic firms if the takeovers are seen as "contrary to national security interests" or if they have the potential for "reducing competition." (In practice this right is rarely exercised.) U.S. controls on FDI are more limited and largely informal. As noted earlier, for political reasons, the United States will occasionally restrict U.S. firms from undertaking FDI in certain countries (e.g., Cuba and Iran). In addition, there are some limited restrictions on inward FDI. For example, foreigners are prohibited from purchasing more than 25 percent of any U.S. airline or from acquiring a controlling interest in a U.S. television broadcast network. Since 1989, the government has had the right to review foreign investment on the grounds of "national security."

❙ Pragmatic Nationalism

In practice, many countries have adopted neither a radical policy nor a free market policy toward FDI, but instead a policy that can best be described as pragmatic nationalism. The pragmatic nationalist view is that FDI has both benefits and costs. FDI can benefit a host country by bringing capital, skills, technology, and jobs, but those benefits often come at a cost. When a foreign company rather than a domestic company produces products, the profits from that investment go abroad. Many countries are also concerned that a foreign-owned manufacturing plant may import many components from its home country, which has negative implications for the host country's balance-of-payments position.

Recognizing this, countries adopting a pragmatic stance pursue policies designed to maximize the national benefits and minimize the national costs. According to this view, FDI should be allowed only if the benefits outweigh the costs. Japan offers one of the more extreme examples of pragmatic nationalism. Until the 1980s, Japan's policy was probably one of the most restrictive among countries adopting a pragmatic nationalist stance. This was due to Japan's perception that direct entry of foreign (especially U.S.) firms with ample managerial resources into the Japanese markets could hamper the development and growth of their own industry and technology.[4] This belief led Japan to block the majority of applications to invest in Japan. However, there were always exceptions to this policy. Firms that had important technology were often permitted to undertake FDI if they insisted that they would neither license their technology to a Japanese firm nor enter into a joint venture with a Japanese enterprise. IBM and Texas Instruments were able to set up wholly owned subsidiaries in Japan by adopting this negotiating position. From the perspective of the Japanese government, the benefits of FDI in such cases—the stimulus that these firms might impart to the Japanese economy—outweighed the perceived costs.

Another aspect of pragmatic nationalism is the tendency to aggressively court FDI believed to be national interests by, for example, offering subsidies to foreign MNEs in the form of tax breaks or grants. The countries of the European Union often seem to be competing with each other to attract U.S. and Japanese FDI by offering large tax breaks and subsidies. Great Britain has been the most successful at attracting Japanese investment in the automobile industry. Nissan, Toyota, and Honda now have major assembly plants in Great Britain and use the country as their base for serving the rest of Europe—with obvious employment and balance-of-payments benefits for Britain.

Ideology	Characteristics	Host-Government Policy Implications
Radical	Marxist roots Views the MNE as an instrument of imperialist domination	Prohibit FDI Nationalize subsidiaries of foreign-owned MNEs
Free market	Classical economic roots (Smith) Views the MNE as an instrument for allocating production to most efficient locations	No restrictions on FDI
Pragmatic nationalism	Views FDI as having both benefits and costs	Restrict FDI where costs outweigh benefits Bargain for greater benefits and fewer costs Aggressively court beneficial FDI by offering incentives

Table 7.1

Political Ideology toward FDI

Summary

The three main ideological positions regarding FDI are summarized in Table 7.1. Recent years have seen a marked decline in the number of countries that adhere to a radical ideology. Although no countries have adopted a pure free market policy stance, an increasing number of countries are gravitating toward the free market end of the spectrum and have liberalized their foreign investment regime. This includes many countries that only a few years ago were firmly in the radical camp (e.g., the former Communist countries of Eastern Europe and many of the socialist countries of Africa) and several countries that until recently could best be described as pragmatic nationalists with regard to FDI (e.g., Japan, South Korea, Italy, Spain, and most Latin American countries). One result has been the surge in the volume of FDI worldwide, which, as we noted in Chapter 6, has been growing twice as fast as the growth in world trade. Another result has been a dramatic increase in the volume of FDI directed at countries that have recently liberalized their FDI regimes, such as China, India, and Vietnam.

The Benefits of FDI to Host Countries ▮

In this section, we explore the four main benefits of FDI to a host country: the resource-transfer effect, the employment effect, the balance-of-payments effect, and the effect on competition and economic growth. In the next section, we will explore the costs of FDI to host countries. Economists who favor the free market view argue that the benefits of FDI to a host country so outweigh the costs that pragmatic nationalism is a misguided policy. According to the free market view, in a perfect world the best policy would be for all countries to forgo intervening in the investment decisions of MNEs.[5]

Resource-Transfer Effects

Foreign direct investment can make a positive contribution to a host economy by supplying capital, technology, and management resources that would otherwise not be available and thus boost that country's economic growth rate. The accompanying Country Focus describes how the Venezuelan government has been encouraging FDI in its petroleum industry in an attempt to benefit from resource-transfer effects. The transfer of capital, technology, and management resources was also an important feature of Volvo's acquisition of Samsung's excavation business (see the Management Focus) and is one of the reasons that the South African government has been so keen to encourage FDI (see the opening case).

Capital

Many MNEs, by virtue of their large size and financial strength, have access to financial resources not available to host-country firms. These funds may be available from internal company sources, or, because of their reputation, large MNEs may find it easier to borrow money from capital markets than host-country firms would. This consideration was a factor in the Venezuelan government's decision to invite foreign oil companies to enter into joint ventures with PDVSA, the state-owned Venezuelan oil company, to develop Venezuela's oil industry. Similarly, the desire of the South African government to encourage FDI by foreign firms is partly based on the belief that they have access to capital resources that South Africa needs (see the opening case).

Technology

As we saw in Chapter 2, the crucial role played by technological progress in economic growth is now widely accepted.[6] Technology can stimulate economic development and industrialization. It can take two forms, both of which are valuable. Technology can be incorporated in a production process (e.g., the technology for discovering, extracting, and refining oil) or it can be incorporated in a product (e.g., personal computers). However, many countries lack the research and development resources and skills required to develop their own indigenous product and process technology. This is particularly true of the world's less developed nations. Such countries must rely on advanced industrialized nations for much of the technology required to stimulate economic growth, and FDI can provide it. As we see in the Country Focus on Venezuela, a lack of relevant technological know-how with regard to the discovery, extraction, and refining of oil was one factor behind the Venezuelan government's decision to invite foreign oil companies into Venezuela.

FDI is not the only way to access advanced technology. Another option is to license that technology from foreign MNEs. The Japanese government, in particular, has long favored this strategy. The Japanese government believes that, in the case of FDI, the technology is still ultimately controlled by the foreign MNE. Consequently, it is difficult for indigenous Japanese firms to develop their own, possibly better, technology because they are denied access to the basic technology. With this in mind, the Japanese government has insisted in the past that technology be transferred to Japan through licensing agreements, rather than through FDI. The advantage of licensing is that in return for royalty payments, host-country firms are given direct access to valuable technology.

The licensing option is generally less attractive to the MNE, however. By licensing its technology to foreign companies, an MNE risks creating a future competitor—as many U.S. firms have learned at great cost in Japan. Given this tension, the mode for transferring technology—licensing or FDI—can be a major negotiating point between an MNE and a host government. Whether the MNE gets its way depends on the relative bargaining powers of the MNE and the host government. In addition to this issue, it can be difficult to transfer technology using a licensing agreement, particularly when the technology is complex and making the technology operational requires substantial experience. In such cases, direct investment is usually preferred to licensing (this was discussed in more detail in Chapter 6).

Much research supports the view that multinational firms often do transfer significant technology when they invest in a foreign country.[7] For example, a study of FDI in Sweden found that foreign firms increased both the labor and total factor productivity of Swedish firms that they acquired, suggesting that significant technology transfers had taken place (technology typically boosts productivity).[8] A study of FDI by the Organization for Economic Cooperation and Development (OECD) found that foreign investors invested significant amounts of capital in R&D in the countries in which they invested, suggesting that not only were they transferring technology to those countries, but they may also have been upgrading existing technology or creating new technology in those countries.[9]

Management

Foreign management skills acquired through FDI may also produce important benefits for the host country. Foreign managers trained in the latest management techniques can often help to improve the efficiency of operations in the host country, whether those operations are acquired or green-field developments. This was a factor in Volvo's acquisition of Samsung excavation business, when Volvo's managers improved the operations and efficiency of the acquired unit (see the Management Focus). Beneficial spin-off effects may also arise when local personnel who are trained to occupy managerial, financial, and technical posts in the subsidiary of a foreign MNE leave the firm and help to establish indigenous firms. Similar benefits may arise if the superior management skills of a foreign MNE stimulate local suppliers, distributors, and competitors to improve their own management skills.

The benefits may be considerably reduced if most management and highly skilled jobs in the subsidiaries are reserved for home-country nationals. The percentage of management and skilled jobs that go to citizens of the host country can be a major negotiating point between an MNE wishing to undertake FDI and a potential host government. In recent years, most MNEs have responded to host-government pressures on this issue by agreeing to reserve a large proportion of management and highly skilled jobs for citizens of the host country.

Employment Effects

Another beneficial employment effect claimed for FDI is that it brings jobs to a host country that would otherwise not be created there. As we saw in the opening case, the government of South Africa has been encouraging FDI in part to help reduce high unemployment, which stands at around 35 percent. The effects of FDI on employment are both direct and indirect. Direct effects arise when a foreign MNE employs a number of host-country citizens. Indirect effects arise when jobs are created in local suppliers as a result of the investment and when jobs are created because of increased local spending by employees of the MNE. The indirect employment effects are often as large as, if not larger than, the direct effects. For example, when Toyota opened a new auto plant in France in 1997, estimates suggested the plant would create 2,000 direct jobs and perhaps another 2,000 jobs in support industries.[10]

Cynics argue that not all the "new jobs" created by FDI represent net additions in employment. In the case of FDI by Japanese auto companies in the United States, some argue that the jobs created by this investment have been more than offset by the jobs lost in U.S.-owned auto companies, which have lost market share to their Japanese competitors. As a consequence of such substitution effects, the net number of new jobs created by FDI may not be as great as initially claimed by an MNE. The issue of the likely net gain in employment may be a major negotiating point between an MNE wishing to undertake FDI and the host government.

When FDI takes the form of an acquisition of an established enterprise in the host economy, as opposed to a green-field investment, the immediate effect may be to reduce employment as the multinational tries to restructure the operations of the acquired unit to improve its operating efficiency (this was the case in Volvo's acquisition of the Samsung division as detailed in the Management Focus). However, even in such cases, research suggests that after the initial restructuring, enterprises acquired by foreign firms tend to grow their employment base at a faster rate than domestic rivals. For

Foreign Direct Investment in Venezuela's Petroleum Industry

Country Focus

Venezuela nationalized its oil industry in 1976, effectively closing the sector to foreign investors. The stated goal at the time was to control this important natural resource for the benefit of Venezuela, as opposed to foreign oil companies. The results, however, fell short of expectations. The country's state-owned oil monopoly, Petroleos de Venezuela SA (PDVSA), failed to develop new oil fields to replace the depletion of existing reserves, and the country's oil output was falling by the mid-1980s.

Faced with the prospect of declining export revenues from oil, Venezuela reversed its policy in 1991 and began to open its oil industry to foreign investors. The Venezuelan government turned to foreign investors for three reasons. First, it recognized that PDVSA did not have the capital required to undertake the investment alone. Second, it realized that PDVSA lacked the technological resources and skills of many of the world's major oil companies, particularly in the areas of oil exploration, oil field development, and sophisticated refining. The government understood that if PDVSA was to develop many of Venezuela's oil fields in a timely fashion, it had no alternative but to turn to foreign companies for help. Third, the government believed that PDVSA would be able to use joint ventures with foreign oil companies as a vehicle for learning about modern management techniques in the industry. PDVSA could then use this knowledge to improve the efficiency of its own operations.

The original plan called for the investment of $73 billion in the oil industry. The plan, as outlined by Gustavo Roosen, president of PDVSA, is to develop a crude oil production potential of 4 million barrels per day by 2002 and 7 million barrels per day by 2007 (the country produced about 2.6 million barrels per day in 1991). Of the $73 billion in projected capital spending, PDVSA planned to invest about $45 billion, while foreign oil companies were expected to supply the remaining $28 billion. The first FDI agreement was signed in 1992 with British Petroleum

(BP). BP agreed to invest $60 million by 1995 to develop a marginal oil field that it would then be given the rights to for 20 years. Using a BP study, PDVSA identified sectors in eastern Venezuela with strong prospects for large discoveries of crude oil and entered into several ventures with other foreign partners to develop these zones. If commercial quantities of oil are discovered, PDVSA will share future production with its partners. Under the terms of most agreements, PDVSA will receive 35 percent of the earnings from any successful exploration venture. Also, with foreign investors such as Conoco and Total Oil Company, PDVSA is investing in state-of-the-art refining facilities that can be used to convert heavy crude oil into a lighter, high-value crude oil for export. Finally, PDVSA, Shell, Exxon, and Mitsubishi have entered into a $5.6 billion joint venture to produce liquefied natural gas for export.

By 1997, over 40 development projects were under way in Venezuela involving cooperation between PDVSA and foreign oil companies. Almost all of the world's major oil companies now had some activities in the country, compared to none before 1991. The country's oil output was also expanding, reaching 3.5 million barrels per day in 1997, up from a low of 1.7 million barrels per day in 1985. By 1999, the once marginally profitable enterprise earned profits of $24 billion, boosted in part by higher oil prices and in part by a 20 percent reduction in operating costs due to productivity gains. In 2000, PDVSA launched another 10-year plan. The plan called for the investment of another $53 billion between 2000 and 2010, with some $31 billion coming from the private sector, and the majority of that from foreign investors.

Sources: J. Mann, "A Little Help from Their Friends," *Financial Times,* November 10, 1993, p. 28; "Venezuela: A Survey," *The Economist,* October 14, 1994; E. Luce, "Oil: Foreign Investment: Finding a Balanced Approach," *Financial Times,* October 21, 1997, p. 6; and "PDVSA Projects $53 Billion in Outlays for 10 Year Plan," *Oil & Gas Journal,* April 17, 2000, pp. 26–27.

example, an OECD study found that between 1989 and 1996 foreign firms created new jobs at a faster rate than their domestic counterparts.[11] In the United States, the work force of foreign firms grew by 1.4 percent per year, compared to 0.8 percent per year for domestic firms. In Great Britain and France, the workforce of foreign firms grew at 1.7 percent per year, while employment at domestic firms fell by 2.7 percent per year. The same study found that foreign firms tended to pay higher wage rates than domestic firms, suggesting that the quality of employment was better. Another study looking at FDI in Eastern European transition economies found that although employment fell following the acquisition of an enterprise by a foreign firm, often those enterprises were in competitive difficulties and would not have survived if they had not been acquired. After an initial period of adjustment and retrenchment, employment downsizing was often followed by new investments and employment either remained stable or increased.[12]

Balance-of-Payments Effects

FDI's effect on a country's balance-of-payments accounts is an important policy issue for most host governments. To understand this concern, we must first familiarize ourselves with balance-of-payments accounting. Then we will examine the link between FDI and the balance-of-payments accounts.

Balance-of-Payments Accounts

A country's balance-of-payments accounts keep track of both its payments to and its receipts from other countries. A summary of the U.S. balance-of-payments accounts for 2000 is given in Table 7.2. Any transaction resulting in a payment to other countries is entered in the balance-of-payments accounts as a debit and given a negative (−) sign. Any transaction resulting in a receipt from other countries is entered as a credit and given a positive (+) sign. Balance-of-payments accounts are divided into two main sections: the current account and the capital account. The **current account** records transactions that pertain to three categories, all of which can be seen in Table 7.2. The first category, merchandise, refers to the export or import of physical goods (e.g., autos, computers, chemicals). The second category is the export or import of services (e.g., intangible products such as banking and insurance services). The third category, investment income, refers to income from foreign investments and payments that have to be made to foreigners investing in a country. For example, if a U.S. citizen owns a share of a

Current Account	Credits	Debits
Exports of goods, services, and income	$1,069,531	
Merchandise	773,304	
Services	296,227	
Income receipts on investments	345,394	
Imports of goods, services, and income		−$1,797,061
Merchandise		−1,222,772
Services		−215,239
Income payments on investments		−359,050
Unilateral transfers		−53,241
Balance of current account		−435,377
Capital Account		
U.S. assets abroad		−553,349
Foreign assets in United States	952,430	
Balance on capital account	399,081	
Statistical discrepancy	35,616	

Table 7.2

U.S. Balance of Payments Accounts for 2000 (figures in $ millions)

Source: U.S. Department of Commerce.

Finnish company and receives a dividend payment of $5, that payment shows up on the U.S. current account as the receipt of $5 of investment income.

A **current account deficit** occurs when a country imports more goods, services, and income than it exports. A **current account surplus** occurs when a country exports more goods, services, and income than it imports. In recent years, the United States has run a persistent trade deficit. Table 7.2 shows that in 2000 the current account deficit was −$435,377 million.

The **capital account** records transactions that involve the purchase or sale of assets. Thus, when a German firm purchases stock in a U.S. company, the transaction enters the U.S. balance of payments as a credit on the capital account. This is because capital is flowing into the country. When capital flows out of the United States, it enters the capital account as a debit.

A basic principle of balance-of-payments accounting is double-entry bookkeeping. Every international transaction automatically enters the balance of payments twice— once as a credit and once as a debit. Imagine that you purchase a car produced in Japan by Toyota for $20,000. Since your purchase represents a payment to another country for goods, it will enter the balance of payments as a debit on the current account. Toyota now has the $20,000 and must do something with it. If Toyota deposits the money at a U.S. bank, Toyota has purchased a U.S. asset—a bank deposit worth $20,000— and the transaction will show up as a $20,000 credit on the capital account. Or Toyota might deposit the cash in a Japanese bank in return for Japanese yen. Now the Japanese bank must decide what to do with the $20,000. Any action that it takes will ultimately result in a credit for the U.S. balance of payments. For example, if the bank lends the $20,000 to a Japanese firm that uses it to import personal computers from the United States, then the $20,000 must be credited to the U.S. balance-of-payments current account. Or the Japanese bank might use the $20,000 to purchase U.S. government bonds, in which case it will show up as a credit on the U.S. balance-of-payments capital account.

Thus, any international transaction automatically gives rise to two offsetting entries in the balance of payments. Because of this, the current account balance and the capital account balance should always add up to zero. (In practice, this does not always occur due to the existence of statistical discrepancies that need not concern us here.)

Governments normally are concerned when their country is running a deficit on the current account of their balance of payments.[13] When a country runs a current account deficit, the money that flows to other countries is then used by those countries to purchase assets in the deficit country. Thus, when the United States runs a trade deficit with Japan, the Japanese use the money that they receive from U.S. consumers to purchase U.S. assets such as stocks, bonds, and the like. A deficit on the current account is financed by selling assets to other countries; that is, by a surplus on the capital account. Thus, the U.S. current account deficit during the 1980s and 90s was financed by a steady sale of U.S. assets (stocks, bonds, real estate, and whole corporations) to other countries. Countries that run current account deficits become net debtors.

For example, as a result of financing its current account deficit through asset sales, the United States must deliver a stream of interest payments to foreign bondholders, rents to foreign landowners, and dividends to foreign stockholders. Such payments to foreigners drain resources from a country and limit the funds available for investment within the country. Since investment within a country is necessary to stimulate economic growth, a persistent current account deficit can choke a country's future economic growth.

FDI and the Balance of Payments

Given the concern about current account deficits, the balance-of-payments effects of FDI can be an important consideration for a host government. There are three potential balance-of-payments consequences of FDI. First, when an MNE establishes a foreign subsidiary, the capital account of the host country benefits from the initial capital inflow. (A debit will be recorded in the capital account of the MNE's home country, since capital is flowing out of the home country.) However, this is a one-time-only effect. Set against this must be the outflow of earnings to the foreign parent company, which will be recorded as a debit on the current account of the host country.

Second, if the FDI is a substitute for imports of goods or services, it can improve the current account of the host country's balance of payments. Much of the FDI by Japanese automobile companies in the United States and United Kingdom, for example, can be seen as substituting for imports from Japan. Thus, the current account of the U.S. balance of payments has improved somewhat because many Japanese companies are now supplying the U.S. market from production facilities in the United States, as opposed to facilities in Japan. Insofar as this has reduced the need to finance a current account deficit by asset sales to foreigners, the United States has clearly benefited from this.

A third potential benefit to the host country's balance-of-payments position arises when the MNE uses a foreign subsidiary to export goods and services to other countries. There are some striking examples of this phenomenon. In the Czech Republic, Skoda, the national automobile company, was a well-established producer and exporter. After its sale to Volkswagen in 1992, however, exports boomed as the new owners redirected the company's sales efforts toward the European Union. The share of exports in Skoda's sales increased from 34 percent in 1990 to 52 percent in 1995 and 80 percent in 1999. The Management Focus provided another example of this phenomenon. After acquiring Samsung's excavation division, Volvo made it the global center for its excavation business and redirected its attention toward exports.

Effect on Competition and Economic Growth

Economic theory tells us that the efficient functioning of markets depends on an adequate level of competition between producers. When FDI takes the form of a greenfield investment, the result is to establish a new enterprise, increasing the number of players in a market and thus consumer choice. In turn, this can increase competition in a national market, thereby driving down prices and increasing the economic welfare of consumers. Increased competition tends to stimulate capital investments by firms in plant, equipment, and R&D as they struggle to gain an edge over their rivals. The long-term results may include increased productivity growth, product and process innovations, and greater economic growth. Such beneficial effects seem to have occurred in the South Korean retail sector following the liberalization of FDI regulations in 1996. FDI by large Western discount stores, including Wal-Mart, Costco, Carrefour, and Tesco, seems to have encouraged indigenous South Korean discounters such as E-Mart to improve the efficiency of their own operations. The results have included more competition and lower prices, which benefits South Korean consumers.

FDI's impact on competition in domestic markets may be particularly important in the case of services, such as telecommunications, retailing, and many financial services, where exporting is often not an option because the service has to be produced where it is delivered.[14] For example, under a 1997 agreement sponsored by the World Trade Organization, 68 countries accounting for more than 90 percent of world telecommunications revenues pledged to start opening their markets to foreign investment and competition and to abide by common rules for fair competition in telecommunications. Before this agreement, most of the world's telecommunications markets were closed to foreign competitors, and in most countries the market was monopolized by a single carrier, which was often a state-owned enterprise. The agreement has dramatically increased the level of competition in many national telecommunications markets.

Three benefits from this agreement have started to occur. First, inward investment has increased competition and stimulated investment in the modernization of telephone networks around the world, leading to better service. Second, the increased competition has resulted in lower prices. Third, trade in other goods and services depends on flows of information matching buyers to sellers. As telecommunication service improves in quality and declines in price, international trade increases in volume and becomes less costly for traders. Telecommunication reform, therefore, should promote cross-border trade in other goods and services. Renato Ruggiero, the director general of the WTO, has argued:

> Telecommunications liberalization could mean global income gains of some $1 trillion over the next decade or so. This represents about 4 percent of world GDP at today's prices.[15]

The Costs of FDI to Host Countries

Three costs of FDI concern host countries. They arise from possible adverse effects on competition within the host nation, adverse effects on the balance of payments, and the perceived loss of national sovereignty and autonomy.

Adverse Effects on Competition

Although we have just outlined how foreign direct investment can boost competition, host governments sometimes worry that the subsidiaries of foreign MNEs may have greater economic power than indigenous competitors. If it is part of a larger international organization, the foreign MNE may be able to draw on funds generated elsewhere to subsidize its costs in the host market, which could drive indigenous companies out of business and allow the firm to monopolize the market. (Once the market was monopolized, the foreign MNE could raise prices above those that would prevail in competitive markets, with harmful effects on the economic welfare of the host nation.) This concern tends to be greater in countries that have few large firms of their own (generally less developed countries). It tends to be a relatively minor concern in most advanced industrialized nations.

While FDI in the form of green-field investments should increase competition, it is less clear that this is the case when the FDI takes the form of acquisitions of an established enterprise in the host nation, as was the case when Volvo acquired Samsung's excavation division (see the Management Focus). Because an acquisition does not result in a net increase in the number of players in a market, the effect on competition may be neutral. When a foreign investor acquires two or more firms in a host country, and subsequently merges them, the effect may be to reduce the level of competition in that market, create monopoly power for the foreign firm, reduce consumer choice, and raise prices. For example, Hindustan Lever Ltd., the Indian subsidiary of Unilever, acquired its main local rival, Tata Oil Mills, to assume a dominant position in the bath soap (75 percent) and detergents (30 percent) markets in India. Hindustan Lever also acquired several local companies in other markets, such as the ice cream makers Dollops, Kwality, and Milkfood. By combining these companies, Hindustan Lever jumped from zero in the Indian ice cream market in 1992 to 74 percent in 1997.[16] However, there is little evidence that such developments are widespread. In many nations, domestic competition authorities have the right to review and block any mergers or acquisitions that they view as having a detrimental impact on competition. If such institutions are operating effectively, this should be sufficient to make sure that foreign entities do not monopolize a country's markets.

Adverse Effects on the Balance of Payments

The possible adverse effects of FDI on a host country's balance-of-payments position have been hinted at earlier. There are two main areas of concern with regard to the balance of payments. First, as mentioned earlier, set against the initial capital inflow

that comes with FDI must be the subsequent outflow of earnings from the foreign subsidiary to its parent company. Such outflows show up as a debit on the capital account.
Some governments have responded to such outflows by restricting the amount of earnings that can be repatriated to a foreign subsidiary's home country.

A second concern arises when a foreign subsidiary imports a substantial number of
its inputs from abroad, which results in a debit on the current account of the host
country's balance of payments. One criticism leveled against Japanese-owned auto assembly operations in the United States, for example, is that they tend to import many
component parts from Japan. Because of this, the favorable impact of this FDI on the
current account of the U.S. balance-of-payments position may not be as great as initially supposed. The Japanese auto companies have responded to these criticisms by
pledging to purchase 75 percent of their component parts from U.S.-based manufacturers (but not necessarily U.S.-owned manufacturers). When the Japanese auto company Nissan invested in the United Kingdom, it responded to concerns about local
content by pledging to increase the proportion of local content to 60 percent and by
subsequently raising it to over 80 percent.

National Sovereignty and Autonomy

Many host governments worry that FDI is accompanied by some loss of economic independence. The concern is that key decisions that can affect the host country's economy will be made by a foreign parent that has no real commitment to the host country
and over which the host country's government has no real control. A quarter of a century ago this concern was expressed by several European countries, who feared that
FDI by U.S. MNEs was threatening their national sovereignty. The same concerns
have surfaced in the United States with regard to European and Japanese FDI. The
main fear seems to be that if foreigners own assets in the United States, they can somehow "hold the country to economic ransom." Twenty-five years ago when officials in
the French government were making similar complaints about U.S. investments in
France, many U.S. politicians dismissed the charge as silly. Now that the shoe is on
the other foot, some U.S. politicians no longer think the notion is silly. However, most
economists dismiss such concerns as groundless and irrational. Political scientist
Robert Reich has noted that such concerns are the product of outmoded thinking because
they fail to account for the growing interdependence of the world economy.[17] In a
world where firms from all advanced nations are increasingly investing in each other's
markets, it is not possible for one country to hold another to "economic ransom" without hurting itself.

The Benefits and Costs of FDI to Home Countries

FDI also produces costs and benefits to the home (or source) country. Does the U.S.
economy benefit or lose from investments by its firms in foreign markets? Does the
Swedish economy lose or gain from Volvo's investment in South Korea? Some argue
that FDI is not always in the home country's national interest and should be restricted.
Others argue that the benefits far outweigh the costs and any restrictions would be
contrary to national interests. To understand why people take these positions, let us
look at the benefits and costs of FDI to the home (source) country.[18]

Benefits of FDI to the Home Country

The benefits of FDI to the home country arise from three sources. First, and perhaps
most important, the capital account of the home country's balance-of-payments benefits from the inward flow of foreign earnings. Thus, one benefit to Sweden from
Volvo's investment in South Korea is the earnings that are subsequently repatriated to
Sweden from South Korea. FDI can also benefit the current account of the home

country's balance of payments if the foreign subsidiary creates demands for home-country exports of capital equipment, intermediate goods, complementary products, and the like.

Second, benefits to the home country from outward FDI arise from employment effects. As with the balance of payments, positive employment effects arise when the foreign subsidiary creates demand for home-country exports of capital equipment, intermediate goods, complementary products, and the like. Thus, Toyota's investment in auto assembly operations in Europe has benefited both the Japanese balance-of-payments position and employment in Japan because Toyota imports some component parts for its European-based auto assembly operations directly from Japan.

Third, benefits arise when the home-country MNE learns valuable skills from its exposure to foreign markets that can be transferred back to the home country. This amounts to a reverse resource-transfer effect. Through its exposure to a foreign market, an MNE can learn about superior management techniques and superior product and process technologies. These resources can then be transferred back to the home country, contributing to the home country's economic growth rate.[19] For example, one reason General Motors and Ford invested in Japanese automobile companies (GM owns part of Isuzu, and Ford owns part of Mazda) was to learn about their production processes. If GM and Ford are successful in transferring this know-how back to their U.S. operations, the result may be a net gain for the U.S. economy.

Costs of FDI to the Home Country

Against these benefits must be set the apparent costs of FDI for the home (source) country. The most important concerns center around the balance-of-payments and employment effects of outward FDI. The home country's balance of payments may suffer in three ways. First, the capital account of the balance of payments suffers from the initial capital outflow required to finance the FDI. This effect, however, is usually more than offset by the subsequent inflow of foreign earnings. Second, the current account of the balance of payments suffers if the purpose of the foreign investment is to serve the home market from a low-cost production location. Third, the current account of the balance of payments suffers if the FDI is a substitute for direct exports. Thus, insofar as Toyota's assembly operations in the United States are intended to substitute for direct exports from Japan, the current account position of Japan will deteriorate.

With regard to employment effects, the most serious concerns arise when FDI is seen as a substitute for domestic production. This was the case with Volvo's investment in South Korea and Toyota's investments in Europe. One obvious result of such FDI is reduced home-country employment. If the labor market in the home country is already very tight, with little unemployment, this concern may not be that great. However, if the home country is suffering from unemployment, concern about the export of jobs may arise. For example, one objection frequently raised by U.S. labor leaders to the free trade pact between the United States, Mexico, and Canada (see the next chapter) is that the United States will lose hundreds of thousands of jobs as U.S. firms invest in Mexico to take advantage of cheaper labor and then export back to the U.S. market.[20]

International Trade Theory and FDI

When assessing the costs and benefits of FDI to the home country, keep in mind the lessons of international trade theory (see Chapter 4). International trade theory tells us that home-country concerns about the negative economic effects of offshore production may be misplaced. The term *offshore production* refers to FDI undertaken to serve the home market. Far from reducing home-country employment, such FDI may actually stimulate economic growth (and hence employment) in the home country by freeing home-country resources to concentrate on activities where the home country has a comparative advantage. In addition, home-country consumers benefit if the price of the particular product falls as a result of the FDI. Also, if a company were prohibited from making such investments on the grounds of negative employment effects while its international competitors reaped the benefits of low-cost production locations, it would undoubtedly lose market share to its international competitors. Under such a scenario, the adverse long-run economic effects for a country would probably outweigh the relatively minor balance-of-payments and employment effects associated with offshore production.

Government Policy Instruments and FDI

Before tackling the important issue of bargaining between the MNE and the host government, we need to discuss the policy instruments that governments use to regulate FDI activity by MNEs. Both home (source) countries and host countries have a range of policy instruments that they can use. We will look at each in turn.

Home-Country Policies

Through their choice of policies, home countries can both encourage and restrict FDI by local firms. We look at policies designed to encourage outward FDI first. These include foreign risk insurance, capital assistance, tax incentives, and political pressure. Then we will look at policies designed to restrict outward FDI.

Encouraging Outward FDI

Many investor nations now have government-backed insurance programs to cover major types of foreign investment risk. The types of risks insurable through these programs include the risks of expropriation (nationalization), war losses, and the inability to transfer profits back home. Such programs are particularly useful in encouraging firms to undertake investments in politically unstable countries.[21] In addition, several advanced countries also have special funds or banks that make government loans to firms wishing to invest in developing countries. As a further incentive to encourage domestic firms to undertake FDI, many countries have eliminated double taxation of foreign income (i.e., taxation of income in both the host country and the home country). Last, and perhaps most significant, a number of investor countries (including the United States) have used their political influence to persuade host countries to relax their restrictions on inbound FDI. For example, in response to direct U.S. pressure, Japan relaxed many of its formal restrictions on inward FDI in the 1980s. Now, in response to further U.S. pressure, Japan moved toward relaxing its informal barriers to inward FDI. One beneficiary of this trend has been Toys "Я" Us, which, after five years of intensive lobbying by company and U.S. government officials, opened its first retail stores in Japan in December 1991. By 2000, Toys "Я" Us had more than 150 stores in Japan and its Japanese operation, in which the company retained a controlling stake, and had a listing on the Japanese stock exchange.

Restricting Outward FDI

Virtually all investor countries, including the United States, have exercised some control over outward FDI from time to time. One common policy has been to limit capital outflows out of concern for the country's balance of payments. From the early 1960s until 1979, for example, Great Britain had exchange-control regulations that limited the amount of capital a firm could take out of the country. Although the main intent of such policies was to improve the British balance of payments, an important secondary intent was to make it more difficult for British firms to undertake FDI.

In addition, countries have occasionally manipulated tax rules to try to encourage their firms to invest at home. The objective behind such policies is to create jobs at home rather than in other nations. At one time these policies were also adopted by Great Britain. The British advanced corporation tax system taxed British companies' foreign earnings at a higher rate than their domestic earnings. This tax code created an incentive for British companies to invest at home.

Finally, countries sometimes prohibit firms from investing in certain countries for political reasons. Such restrictions can be formal or informal. For example, formal rules prohibited U.S. firms from investing in countries such as Cuba, Libya, and Iran, whose political ideology and actions are judged to be contrary to U.S. interests. Similarly, during the 1980s, informal pressure was applied to dissuade U.S. firms from investing in South Africa. In this case, the objective was to put pressure on South Africa to change its apartheid laws, which occurred during the early 1990s (see the opening case). Thus, this policy was successful.

Host-Country Policies

Host countries adopt policies designed both to restrict and to encourage inward FDI. As noted earlier in this chapter, political ideology has determined the type and scope of these policies in the past. In the last decade of the 20th century, many countries moved quickly away from adhering to some version of the radical stance and prohibiting much FDI and toward a combination of free market objectives and pragmatic nationalism.

Encouraging Inward FDI

It is increasingly common for governments to offer incentives to foreign firms to invest in their countries. Such incentives take many forms, but the most common are tax concessions, low-interest loans, and grants or subsidies. Incentives are motivated by a desire to gain from the resource-transfer and employment effects of FDI. They are also motivated by a desire to capture FDI away from other potential host countries. For example, in the mid-1990s the governments of Great Britain and France competed with each other on the incentives they offered Toyota to invest in their respective countries. In the United States, state governments often compete with each other to attract FDI. For example, Kentucky offered Toyota an incentive package worth $112 million to persuade it to build its U.S. automobile assembly plants there. The package included tax breaks, new state spending on infrastructure, and low-interest loans.[22]

Restricting Inward FDI

Host governments use a wide range of controls to restrict FDI in one way or another. The two most common are ownership restraints and performance requirements. Ownership restraints can take several forms. In some countries, foreign companies are excluded from specific fields. For example, they are excluded from tobacco and mining in Sweden and from the development of certain natural resources in Brazil, Finland, and Morocco. In other industries, foreign ownership may be permitted although a significant proportion of the equity of the subsidiary must be owned by local investors. For example, foreign ownership is restricted to 25 percent or less of an airline in the United States.

Foreign firms are often excluded from certain sectors on the grounds of national security or competition. Particularly in less developed countries, the feeling seems to be that local firms might not be able to develop unless foreign competition is restricted by a combination of import tariffs and controls on FDI. This is really a variant of the infant industry argument discussed in Chapter 5.

Also, ownership restraints seem to be based on a belief that local owners can help to maximize the resource-transfer and employment benefits of FDI for the host country. Until the early 1980s, the Japanese government prohibited most FDI but allowed joint ventures between Japanese firms and foreign MNEs if the MNE had a valuable technology. The Japanese government clearly believed such an arrangement would speed up the subsequent diffusion of the MNE's valuable technology throughout the Japanese economy.

Performance requirements can also take several forms. Performance requirements are controls over the behavior of the MNE's local subsidiary. The most common performance requirements are related to local content, exports, technology transfer, and local participation in top management. As with certain ownership restrictions, the logic underlying performance requirements is that such rules help to maximize the benefits and minimize the costs of FDI for the host country. Virtually all countries employ some form of performance requirements when it suits their objectives. However, performance requirements tend to be more common in less developed countries than in advanced industrialized nations. For example, one study found that some 30 percent of the affiliates of U.S. MNEs in less developed countries were subject to performance requirements, while only 6 percent of the affiliates in advanced countries were faced with such requirements.[23]

International Institutions and the Liberalization of FDI

Until the 1990s there was no consistent involvement by multinational institutions in the governing of FDI. This changed with the formation of the World Trade Organization in 1995. As noted in Chapter 5, the role of the WTO embraces the promotion of international trade in services. Since many services have to be produced where they are sold, exporting is not an option (for example, one cannot export McDonald's hamburgers or consumer banking services). Given this, the WTO has become involved in regulations governing FDI. As might be expected for an institution created to promote free trade, the thrust of the WTO's efforts has been to push for the liberalization of regulations governing FDI, particularly in services. Under the auspices of the WTO, two extensive multinational agreements were reached in 1997 to liberalize trade in telecommunications and financial services. Both these agreements contained detailed clauses that require signatories to liberalize their regulations governing inward FDI, essentially opening their markets to foreign telecommunication and financial services companies.

However, the WTO has had less success trying to initiate talks aimed at establishing a universal set of rules designed to promote the liberalization of FDI. Led by Malaysia and India, developing nations have so far rejected any attempts by the WTO to start such discussions. In an attempt to make some progress on this issue, the Organization for Economic Cooperation and Development (OECD) in 1995 initiated talks between its members. (The OECD is a Paris-based intergovernmental organization of "wealthy" nations whose purpose is to provide its 29 member states with a forum in which governments can compare their experiences, discuss the problems they share, and seek solutions that can then be applied within their own national contexts. The members include most European Union countries, the United States, Canada, Japan, and South Korea). The aim of the talks was to draft a Multilateral Agreement on Investment (MAI) that would make it illegal for signatory states to discriminate against foreign investors. This would liberalize rules governing FDI between OECD states. Unfortunately for those promoting the agreement, the talks broke down in early 1998, primarily because the United States refused to sign the agreement. According to the United States, the proposed agreement contained too many exceptions that would weaken its powers. For example, the proposed agreement would not have barred discriminatory taxation of foreign-owned companies, and it would have allowed countries to restrict foreign television programs and music in the name of preserving culture. Also campaigning against the MAI were environmental and labor groups, who criticized the proposed agreement on the grounds that it contained no binding environmental or labor agreements. Despite these problems, negotiations on a revised

MAI treaty may be restarted. Also, as noted earlier, individual nations have continued to unilaterally remove restrictions to inward FDI as a wide range of countries from South Korea to South Africa try to encourage foreign firms to invest in their economies.[24]

Implications for Business

A number of fairly obvious implications for business are in the material discussed in this chapter. For a start, a host government's attitude toward FDI should be an important variable in deciding where to locate foreign production facilities and where to make a foreign direct investment. Other things being equal, investing in countries that have permissive policies toward FDI is clearly preferable to investing in countries that restrict FDI.

Generally, however, the issue is not this straightforward. Despite the move toward a free market stance in recent years, many countries still have a rather pragmatic stance toward FDI.[25] In such cases, a firm considering FDI may have to negotiate the specific terms of the investment with the host country's government. Such negotiations often center on two broad issues. If the host government is trying to attract FDI, the central issue is likely to be the kind of incentives the host government is prepared to offer to the MNE and what the firm will commit in exchange. If the host government is uncertain about the benefits of FDI and might restrict access, the central issue is likely to be the concessions the firm must make to go forward with a proposed investment.

In the remainder of this section, we will focus on negotiating with a host government. Before moving on, however, note that negotiations between MNEs and host governments increasingly are occurring within the framework of broad multilateral agreements to which the host and home countries are signatories.[26] For example, when an American firm is considering investment in the Brazilian telecommunications sector, the 1997 WTO telecommunication agreement sets the parameters under which negotiations can proceed. Because the agreement has removed most impediments to cross-border investments in telecommunications, the scope for bargaining between the MNE and the host government is significantly reduced. The same is true of much cross-border investment in financial services, again due to the establishment of a WTO agreement. In additional, extensive regional agreements such as the European Union (EU) and the North American Free Trade Agreement (NAFTA) now govern FDI flows between countries that are members of the same regional bloc (we discuss these agreements in depth in the next chapter). NAFTA, for example, sets the parameters that govern the conditions under which firms from Canada, Mexico, and the United States can invest in each other's markets. These parameters, which are generally very liberal and remove most restrictions on FDI flows between member states, significantly limit the scope for bargaining. Still, given the failure of both the WTO and the OECD to establish extensive multilateral agreements governing FDI, negotiations between MNEs and host governments remain an important issue in many instances.

The Nature of Negotiation

The objective of any negotiation is to reach an agreement that benefits both parties. Negotiation is both an art and a science. The science of it requires analyzing the relative bargaining strengths of each party and the different strategic options available to each party and assessing how the other party might respond to various bargaining ploys.[27] The art of negotiation incorporates "interpersonal skills, the ability to convince and be convinced, the ability to

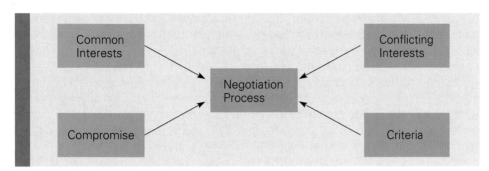

Figure 7.1

The Context of
Negotiation—the Four Cs

employ a basketful of bargaining ploys, and the wisdom to know when and how to use them."[28] In the context of international business, the art of negotiation also includes understanding the influence of national norms, value systems, and culture on the approach and likely negotiating tactics of the other party as well as sensitivity to such factors in shaping a firm's approach to negotiations with a foreign government. For example, negotiating with the Japanese government for access is likely to be very different from negotiating with the British government. Consequently, it requires different interpersonal skills and bargaining ploys. The national differences in society and culture discussed in Chapter 3 are important factors in negotiations.

The negotiation process has been characterized as occurring within the context of "the four Cs": common interests, conflicting interests, compromise, and criteria (see Figure 7.1).[29] To explore this concept, consider the negotiation between IBM and Mexico that occurred in 1984 and 1985 when IBM tried to get permission to establish a facility to manufacture personal computers in Guadalajara, Mexico. At that time, Mexican law required foreign investors to agree to a minimum of 51 percent local ownership of any production facilities established in Mexico (the law was repealed as part of the 1994 North American Free Trade Agreement). The rationale for this law was Mexico's desire to reduce its economic dependence on foreign-owned enterprises, thereby preserving its national sovereignty. As with many such laws, in practice it was used as a bargaining chip by the Mexican government to extract concessions from foreign firms wishing to establish production facilities in Mexico. The government was often willing to waive the 51 percent ownership requirement if a foreign firm would make concessions that increased the beneficial impact of its investment on the Mexican economy.

IBM proposed to invest about $40 million in a state-of-the-art production facility with the capacity to produce 100,000 PCs per year, 75 percent of which would be exported (primarily to the United States). IBM's objective was to take advantage of Mexico's low labor costs to reduce the cost of manufacturing PCs. Given the proprietary nature of the product and process technology involved in the design and manufacture of PCs, IBM wanted to maintain 100 percent ownership of the Guadalajara facility. IBM believed that if it entered into a joint venture with a Mexican firm to produce PCs, as required under Mexican law, it would risk giving away valuable technology to a potential future competitor.

When presenting its case to the Mexican government, IBM stressed the benefits of the proposed investment for the Mexican economy. These included the creation of 80 direct jobs and 800 indirect ones, the transfer of high-technology job skills to Mexico, new direct investment of $7 million (the remaining $33 million required to finance the investment would be raised from the Mexican capital market), and exports of 75,000 personal computers per year. The Mexican government rejected the proposal on the grounds that IBM did not propose to use sufficient local content in the plant and would thus be importing too many parts and materials. IBM twice resubmitted its proposal. Maintaining its insistence on 100 percent ownership, IBM with each proposal increased its commitment to purchase local parts, increased the level of its direct investment, and raised its planned level of exports. The Mexican government agreed to the third proposal, which had extracted significant concessions from IBM. The final agreement required IBM to invest $91 million (up from $40 million). This money was distributed among expansion of the Guadalajara plant ($7 million), investment in local R&D ($35 million), development of local part suppliers ($20 million), expansion of its purchasing and distribution network ($13 million), contributions to a Mexican government-sponsored semiconductor technology center ($12 million), and various other minor investments. In addition, IBM agreed to achieve 82 percent local content by the fourth year of operation and to export 92 percent of the PCs produced in Mexico. In exchange, the Mexican government waived its 51 percent local ownership requirement and allowed IBM to maintain 100 percent control.[30]

In this example, the common interest of both IBM and Mexico is establishing a new enterprise in Mexico. Conflicting interests arise from such issues as the proportion of component parts that will be procured locally rather than imported, the total amount of investment, the total number of jobs created, and the proportion of output that will be exported. Compromise involves reaching a decision that brings benefits to both parties, even though neither will get all of what it wants. IBM's criteria or objectives are to achieve satisfactory profits and to maintain 100 percent ownership. Mexico's criteria are to achieve satisfactory net benefits from the resource-transfer, employment, and balance-of-payments effects of the investment.

Bargaining Power

The outcome of any negotiated agreement depends on the relative bargaining power of both parties. Each side's bargaining power depends on three factors (see Table 7.3):

- The value each side places on what the other has to offer.
- The number of comparable alternatives available to each side.
- Each party's time horizon.

From the perspective of a firm negotiating the terms of an investment with a host government, the firm's bargaining power is high when the host government places a high value on what the firm has to offer, the number of comparable alternatives open to the firm is great, and the firm has a long time in which to complete the negotiations. The converse also holds. The firm's bargaining power is low when the host government places a low value on what the firm has to offer, few comparable alternatives are open to the firm, and the firm has a short time in which to complete the negotiations.

Consider again the case of IBM and Mexico. IBM was in a fairly strong bargaining position, primarily because Mexico was suffering from a flight of capital out of the country at the time (1985 and 1986), which made the

Table 7.3

Determinants of Bargaining Power

	Bargaining Power of Firm	
	High	**Low**
Firm's time horizon	Long	Short
Comparable alternatives open to firm	Many	Few
Value placed by host government on investment	High	Low

government eager to attract new foreign investment. But IBM's bargaining power was moderated somewhat by three things. First, despite its symbolic importance, the size of the proposed investment was unlikely to have more than a marginal impact on the Mexican economy, so the economic value placed by Mexico on the investment was not that great. Second, IBM was looking for a low-labor-cost, politically stable location close to the United States. Mexico was obviously the most desirable location given these criteria. Greater distance and higher transportation costs made alternative low-labor-cost locations, such as Taiwan or Singapore, relatively less attractive, while other potential locations in Central America were ruled out by political instability. Third, given the profusion of low-cost competitors moving into the U.S. personal computer market during the mid-1980s, IBM probably felt it needed to move quickly to establish its own low-cost production facilities. But there was no compelling reason for Mexico to close a deal quickly. Due to all these factors, the Mexican government also held some bargaining power in the negotiations and was able to extract some concessions from IBM. On the other hand, IBM's strong position allowed it to insist that it maintain 100 percent ownership of its Mexican subsidiary. This represented a significant concession from the Mexican government; IBM was the first major company for which Mexico waived its prohibition of majority ownership.

In a similar case during the 1960s, IBM was one of the few firms to get the Japanese government to waive the restriction on FDI that would allow it to establish a wholly owned subsidiary in Japan. IBM was able to do this because it was the only major source of mainframe computer technology at the time, and numerous Japanese companies needed that technology for data processing. The lack of comparable alternatives available to the Japanese enabled IBM to pry open the Japanese market. Similarly, during the 1980s, Toyota extracted significant concessions from the state of Kentucky in the form of tax breaks, low-interest loans, and grants, and Honda received similar concessions from the state of Ohio. At that time, both states were suffering from high unemployment, and the proposed auto assembly plants promised to have a substantial impact on employment. Also, both companies had a number of states from which to choose. Thus, the high value placed by state governments on the proposed investment and the number of comparable alternatives open to each company considerably strengthened the bargaining power of both companies relative to that of the state governments.

Chapter Summary

This chapter examined governments' influence on firms' decisions to invest in foreign countries. By their choice of policies, both host-country and home-country governments encourage and restrict FDI. We also explored the factors that influence negotiations between a host-country government and a firm contemplating FDI. The chapter made the following points:

1. An important determinant of government policy toward FDI is political ideology. Political ideology ranges from a radical stance that is hostile to FDI to a noninterventionist, free market stance. Between the two extremes is an approach best described as pragmatic nationalism.

2. The radical view sees the MNE as an imperialist tool for exploiting host countries. According to this view, no country should allow FDI. Due to

the collapse of communism, the radical view was in retreat everywhere by the end of the 1990s.

3. The free market view sees the MNE as an instrument for increasing the overall efficiency of resource utilization in the world economy. FDI can be viewed as a way of dispersing the production of goods and services to those locations around the globe where they can be produced most efficiently.

4. Pragmatic nationalism views FDI as having both benefits and costs. Countries adopting a pragmatic stance pursue policies designed to maximize the benefits and minimize the costs of FDI.

5. The benefits of FDI to a host country arise from resource-transfer effects, employment effects, balance-of-payments effects, and its ability to promote competition.

6. FDI can make a positive contribution to a host economy by supplying capital, technology, and management resources that would otherwise not be available. Such resource transfers can stimulate the economic growth of the host economy.

7. Employment effects arise from the direct and indirect creation of jobs by FDI.

8. Balance-of-payments effects arise from the initial capital inflow to finance FDI, from import substitution effects, and from subsequent exports by the new enterprise.

9. By increasing consumer choice, foreign direct investment can help to increase the level of competition in national markets, thereby driving down prices and increasing the economic welfare of consumers.

10. The costs of FDI to a host country include adverse effects on competition and balance of payments and a perceived loss of national sovereignty.

11. Host governments are concerned that foreign MNEs may have greater economic power than indigenous companies and that they may be able to monopolize the market.

12. Adverse effects on the balance of payments arise from the outflow of a foreign subsidiary's earnings and from the import of inputs from abroad.

13. National sovereignty concerns are raised by FDI because key decisions that affect the host country will be made by a foreign parent that may have no real commitment to the host country and the host government will have no control over them.

14. The benefits of FDI to the home (source) country include improvement in the balance of payments as a result of the inward flow of foreign earnings, positive employment effects when the foreign subsidiary creates demand for home-country exports, and benefits from a reverse resource-transfer effect. A reverse resource-transfer effect arises when the foreign subsidiary learns valuable skills abroad that can be transferred back to the home country.

15. The costs of FDI to the home country include adverse balance-of-payments effects that arise from the initial capital outflow and from the export substitution effects of FDI. Costs also arise when FDI exports jobs abroad.

16. Home countries can adopt policies designed to both encourage and restrict FDI. Host countries try to attract FDI by offering incentives and try to restrict FDI by dictating ownership restraints and requiring that foreign MNEs meet specific performance requirements.

17. A firm considering FDI usually must negotiate the terms of the investment with the host government. The object of any negotiation is to reach an agreement that benefits both parties. Negotiation inevitably involves compromise.

18. The outcome of negotiation is typically determined by the relative bargaining powers of the foreign MNE and the host government. Bargaining power depends on the value each side places on what the other has to offer, the number of comparable alternatives available to each side, and each party's time horizon.

Critical Discussion Questions

1. Read the opening case on FDI in South Africa. Potentially how important is FDI to the health of the South African economy? Why do you think that the level of FDI into South Africa has fallen short of expectations? What steps do you think the South African government might take to increase the level of FDI inflows?

2. Explain how the political ideology of a host government might influence the negotiations between the host government and a foreign MNE.

3. Under what circumstances is an MNE in a powerful negotiating position vis-à-vis a host government? What kind of concessions is a firm likely to win in such situations?

4. Under what circumstances is an MNE in a weak negotiating position vis-à-vis a host government? What kind of concessions is a host government likely to win in such situations?

5. Inward FDI is bad for (a) a developing economy and (b) a developed economy and should be subjected to strict controls! Discuss.

6. Firms should not be investing abroad when there is a need for investment to create jobs at home! Discuss.

7. Do you think the successful conclusion of a multilateral agreement to liberalize regulations governing FDI will benefit the world economy? Why?

Toyota in France

The French have always been somewhat ambivalent toward foreign direct investment. In the 1960s and 1970s, successive French governments used a mixture of socialist and nationalist rhetoric to spurn foreign investment proposals by companies such as General Motors. These governments took the view that direct investment by foreign multinational enterprises would damage the French economy. Government officials believed strongly in the need for France to build its own indigenous enterprises. They argued that the economic power enjoyed by foreign multinationals gave them the ability to dominate any markets they entered, at the expense of locally grown enterprises. Successive socialist governments in France expressed a desire to control economic activity through extensive planning and the nationalization of private businesses. Letting foreign multinationals into the country was thought to be inconsistent with this goal.

France's policy toward inward foreign direct investment began to change in the early 1980s. Although France's socialist president, Francois Mitterrand, remained suspicious of direct investment by foreign firms, his successive administrations reduced the bureaucratic obstacles to foreign investment and created a more coherent mechanism for luring inward investment. The change in policy reflected the growing realization that inward investment could have substantial benefits for the French economy, including the creation of jobs, the transfer of valuable technology, and the increase of exports that would bolster France's balance-of-payments position. The shift toward a more liberal attitude accelerated under Mitterrand's successor, Gaullist Jacques Chirac. Chirac, who espoused a free market philosophy with a unique French twist, made encouraging inward investment a priority. The results have been striking. According to UN data, FDI inflows into France surged from an annual average of $13.9 billion between 1988 and 1993 to a record $21.9 billion in 1996, and $39.1 billion in 1999. The cumulative stock of FDI in France grew from $86 billion in 1990 to $182 billion by decade's end. Among the foreign companies that made major investments in France over this time period were Toyota, IBM, Motorola, and Federal Express Corp.

One noteworthy inward investment in recent years was Toyota's December 1997 decision to invest $656.8 million in a car plant in France to produce 150,000 vehicles per year. The investment represents the Japanese company's second major commitment to Europe. Toyota already has extensive operations in the United Kingdom. The decision to locate in France was taken despite intense lobbying from British government officials, who wanted Toyota to expand its UK operations. The investment represents a continuation of Toyota's strategy to replace exports from Japan with direct production in important regional markets. This strategy was originally undertaken to reduce European demands for trade barriers to limit the "flood" of Japanese automobile imports.

Plans called for the car to be produced at Toyota's French plant to have 60 percent European content, thus qualifying it to be classified as "European" under European Union regulations and allowing Toyota to circumvent import duties. By 2001, some 2,000 people were employed at the new plant, and an additional 2,000 jobs are estimated to have been created among suppliers. Toyota has been exporting output from the plant to other countries within the European Union, helping France's balance-of-trade position.

A number of factors motivated Toyota's choice of France as a location for the plant. First, the company hoped that its new plant would help it to increase its market share in France from 1.1 percent in 1997 to around 5 percent. Second, Toyota picked France because the country has long had an indigenous automobile industry, which yields an adequate supply of trained labor and technical expertise, along with a network of experienced subcontractors. Third, the French government reportedly offered considerable subsidies to induce Toyota to invest in the country. These included tax breaks, the waiving of some social security contributions, and financial aid for training the workforce. In addition, the city of Valenciennes, where the plant is located, waived or significantly reduced the annual property tax on the site. Estimates suggest that these subsidies reached 10 percent of the value of the investment. Fourth, one of the most important attractions of France was the priority of establishing a presence not only within Europe's single market, but also within the euro single currency zone. The United Kingdom's continued ambivalence to monetary (and currency) union with other European Union countries was a big hindrance to Toyota investing further in the United Kingdom. As of January 1999, the exchange rate for the French franc was locked against that of several other currencies—including that of Germany—in advance of full monetary union and currency union in 2002.

Sources: A. Jack, "French Consider Takeover Defences," *Financial Times*, November 15, 1997, p. 2; R. Graham and H. Simonian,

"Toyota Picks France for New Plant," *Financial Times*, December 10, 1997, p. 6; and A. Jack, "French Go into Overdrive to Win Investors," *Financial Times*, December 10, 1997, p. 6.

Case Discussion Questions

1. How would you characterize the shift in French attitudes and policies toward FDI? What do you think has driven this change in attitudes and policies?

2. What are the benefits to the French economy of Toyota's investment in France?

3. How do you think European Union regulations affected Toyota's decision to invest in France?

4. Why do you think Toyota chose France over the United Kingdom as a location for its new plant?

5. Can you see any downside for France of Toyota's investment?

Notes

1. For elaboration, see S. Hood and S. Young, *The Economics of the Multinational Enterprise* (London: Longman, 1979), and P. M. Sweezy and H. Magdoff, *The Dynamics of U.S. Capitalism* (New York: Monthly Review Press, 1972).

2. S. Weiss, "The Long Path to the IBM-Mexico Agreement: An Analysis of Micro-Computer Investment Decisions," working paper 3, NYU School of Business, 1989.

3. Ibid.

4. M. Itoh and K. Kiyono, "Foreign Trade and Direct Investment," in *Industrial Policy of Japan*, ed. R. Komiya, M. Okuno, and K. Suzumura (Tokyo: Academic Press, 1988).

5. See Hood and Young, *The Economics of the Multinational Enterprise*. Also, chap. 6 in United Nations, *World Investment Report, 2000* (New York & Geneva: United Nations, 2000).

6. P. M. Romer, "The Origins of Endogenous Growth," *Journal of Economic Perspectives* 8, no. 1 (1994), pp. 3–22.

7. X. J. Zhan, and T. Ozawa, *Business Restructuring in Asia: Cross Border M&As in Crisis Affected Countries* (Copenhagen: Copenhagen Business School, 2000).

8. K. M. Moden, "Foreign Acquisitions of Swedish Companies: Effects on R&D and Productivity," Stockholm: Research Institute of International Economics, mimeo, 1998.

9. "Foreign Friends," *The Economist*, January 8, 2000, pp. 71–72.

10. A. Jack, "French Go into Overdrive to Win Investors," *Financial Times*, December 10, 1997, p. 6.

11. "Foreign Friends."

12. G. Hunya and K. Kalotay, *Privatization and Foreign Direct Investment in Eastern and Central Europe* (Geneva: UNCTAD, 2001).

13. P. Krugman, *The Age of Diminished Expectations* (Cambridge, MA: MIT Press, 1990).

14. United Nations, *World Investment Report, 1998* (New York and Geneva: United Nations, 1997).

15. "Ruggiero Congratulates Governments on Landmark Telecommunications Agreement," World Trade Organization Press Release, February 17, 1997.

16. United Nations, *World Investment Report, 2000* (New York & Geneva: United Nations, 2000).

17. R. B. Reich, *The Work of Nations: Preparing Ourselves for the 21st Century* (New York: Alfred A. Knopf, 1991).

18. For a review, see J. H. Dunning, "Re-Evaluating the Benefits of Foreign Direct Investment," *Transnational Corporations* 3, no. 1 (February 1994), pp. 23–51.

19. This idea has recently been articulated, although not quite in this form, by C. A. Bartlett and S. Ghoshal, *Managing across Borders: The Transnational Solution* (Boston: Harvard Business School Press, 1989).

20. P. Magnusson, "The Mexico Pact: Worth the Price?" *Business Week*, May 27, 1991, pp. 32–35.

21. C. Johnston, "Political Risk Insurance," in *Assessing Corporate Political Risk*, ed. D. M. Raddock (Totowa, NJ: Rowan & Littlefield, 1986).

22. M. Tolchin and S. Tolchin, *Buying into America: How Foreign Money Is Changing the Face of Our Nation* (New York: Times Books, 1988).

23. J. Behrman and R. E. Grosse, *International Business and Government: Issues and Institutions* (Columbia: University of South Carolina Press, 1990).

24. G. De Jonquiers and S. Kuper, "Push to Keep Alive Effort to Draft Global Investment Rules," *Financial Times*, April 29, 1988, p. 5.

25. J. H. Dunning, "An Overview of Relations with National Governments," *New Political Economy* 3, no. 2, (1998), pp. 280–84.

26. R. Ramamurti, "The Obsolescing Bargaining Model? MNC-Host Developing Country Relations Revisited," *Journal of International Business Studies* 32, no. 1, (2001), pp. 23–39.

27. For a good introduction, see M. H. Bazerman, *Negotiating Rationally* (New York: Free Press, 1997), and A. Dixit and B. Nalebuff, *Thinking Strategically: The Competitive Edge in Business, Politics, and Everyday Life* (New York: W. W. Norton, 1991).

28. H. Raiffa, *The Art and Science of Negotiation* (Cambridge, MA: Harvard University Press, 1982).

29. J. Fayerweather and A. Kapoor, *Strategy and Negotiation for the International Corporation* (Cambridge, MA: Ballinger, 1976).

30. J. Behrman and R. E. Grosse, *International Business and Government: Issues and Institutions* (Columbia, SC: University of South Carolina Press, 1990); and S. Weiss, "The Long Path to the IBM-Mexico Agreement: An Analysis of Microcomputer Investment Negotiations, 1983–1986," working paper 3, NYU School of Business, 1989.

Regional
Economic
Integration

During the late 1990s a wave of mergers swept through the insurance industry in the European Union. The mergers were the result of a process begun January 1, 1993, when the Single European Act became law among the member states of the European Union. The goal of the Single European Act was to remove barriers to cross-border trade and investment within the confines of the EU, thereby creating a single market instead of a collection of distinct national markets.

Under the act, the EU insurance industry was deregulated and liberalized in mid-1994. Before that, wide variations in competitive conditions, regulations, and prices existed among the different national insurance markets. For example, in early 1994, a simple 10-year life insurance policy in Portugal cost three times more than the same policy in France, while automobile insurance for an experienced driver cost twice as much in Ireland as in Italy and four times as much as in Great Britain. The new rules did two main things. First, they made cross-border trade possible by allowing insurance companies to sell their products anywhere in the EU on the basis of regulations in their home state, the so-called single license. Second, insurers throughout the EU were allowed to set their own rates for all classes of insurance policies. They no longer needed to submit policy wordings to local officials for approval, thereby dismantling the highly regulated regime behind which much of the industry had sheltered. Among the expected outcomes of these changes were an increase in competition and downward pressure on prices.

In 1999, the move toward a single market in the EU was given a further push by the adoption of a common currency, the euro, among a majority of the EU's member states. On January 1, 1999, 11 of the EU's 15 member states locked in their currency exchange rates against each other and began handing over responsibility for monetary policy to the newly created European Central Bank. On January 1, 2002, the currencies of the participating states were formally abolished and replaced by a common monetary unit, the euro. The introduction of the euro has made it easier for consumers to compare the insurance products offered by companies based in different EU states. This should increase competition and lower prices. Also, the spread of the Internet has made it much easier for consumers to comparison shop. Insurance policies are well suited to being sold over the Internet, and the spread of this communication technology has now made it practical for a French citizen, for example, to use the Internet to buy an insurance policy from a Dutch company and pay for that policy in euros.

The initial response to the actual and impending changes in the competitive environment of the insurance industry was muted. However, by mid-1996, insurance companies were beginning to realize they needed to reposition themselves to compete more effectively in a single market dominated by a single currency. This realization resulted in a wave of mergers between firms within nations as they tried to attain the scale economies necessary to compete on a larger European playing field. In 1996, Axa and UAP, two French insurance companies, merged to create the largest European insurance company. As part of the deal, Axa gained control over several subsidiary companies that UAP had acquired in Germany in 1994, allowing Axa to increase its presence in this important market. Two large British insurance companies, Royal Insurance and Sun Alliance, also joined forces in 1996. This was followed in 1997 and early 1998 by a number of cross-border mergers, the most notable of which was between Germany's Allianz and AGF, a large French insurance company. The merger between Allianz and AGF was prompted by a takeover bid for AGF launched by the large Italian insurance company Generali. Generali wanted to acquire AGF to expand its presence in France. The bid spurred Allianz into action. Allianz, which dominates the German insurance market, had been feeling threatened by increased competition in its home market arising in part from a merger between Munich-based Hamburg–Mannheimer and Britain's Victoria Insurance and in part from the increased strength of the Axa–UAP combination. Displaying a sensitivity for French sentiments that Generali lacked, Allianz promised that AGF's management would remain French and that Allianz executives would be in the minority on the board of the merged company. Unwilling to make such concessions, Generali eventually withdrew its counter-bid for AGF, but not before it had won a significant concession from Allianz and AGF. In return for withdrawing its bid, the German and French companies agreed to sell several important subsidiaries to the Italian insurer, boosting Generali's premiums by more than half and giving it a sizable presence in both Germany and Italy.

As a result of these developments, the shape of the EU insurance industry had been substantially altered by early 2000. Allianz had emerged as the largest pan-European insurer, with $64 billion in total premium income. In addition to its leading position in Germany, Allianz had become one of the top five insurers in Belgium, Spain, and France. The Axa–UAP combination had become the second largest European insurer with significant activities in France and Germany, while Italy's Generali with premium income of $31 billion was now the third largest pan-European insurance company. The insurance market in the EU had become much more concentrated. According to one study, the seven largest insurance companies in Europe had increased their share of the EU insurance market from under 20 percent in 1990 to over 40 percent by 2000, with much of the increase in concentration coming about due to mergers and acquisitions. Meanwhile, companies that have remained focused on individual national markets within Europe have seen their market share decline.

Despite these changes the EU is still some way off from having a truly single European insurance market. According to the European Commission, onerous obligations laid on by regulators in individual member states continue to make it difficult for insurance companies to market the same policy across the region. For example, various EU member states still have different policies for taxing insurance premiums, making the use of a single policy complex. As a result, while the EU insurance industry has consolidated, and pan-European companies have emerged, most policies that are written are still local. In an effort to change this, the European Commission is now pushing member states to harmonize regulations, thereby removing the last legal impediment to the emergence of a truly pan-European insurance market.

Sources: R. Lapper, "Hard Work to Be Free and Single," *Financial Times*, July 1, 1994, p. 19; "A Singular Market. In the European Union: A Survey," *The Economist*, October 22, 1994, pp. 10–16; "Insurance: Can the Empire Strike Back?" *The Economist*, April 25, 1998, p. 76; C. Adams, A. Jack, and A. Fisher, "Allianz Bid Mirrors Its Global Ambitions," *Financial Times*, November 11, 1997, p. 20; S. Shapiro, "Cross-Border Freedom Upheld," *Business Insurance*, February 21, 2000, pp. 39–41; and J. Croft, "Big Push for More Growth in Europe," *Financial Times*, April 27, 2001, p. 4.

Introduction

One notable trend in the global economy in recent years has been the accelerated movement toward regional economic integration. By **regional economic integration,** we mean agreements among countries in a geographic region to reduce, and ultimately remove, tariff and non-tariff barriers to the free flow of goods, services, and factors of production between each other. The last few years have witnessed an unprecedented proliferation of regional trade arrangements. World Trade Organization members are required to notify the WTO of any regional trade agreements in which they participate. By 2001, nearly all of the WTO's 136 members had notified the organization of participation in one or more regional trade agreements. From 1948 to 1994, there were 124 notifications to the GATT of regional trade agreements. Since the creation of the WTO in 1995, 90 additional arrangements covering trade in goods or services have

Figure 8.1

Regional Trade
Agreements Notified to
GATT and the WTO,
1948–1999

Source: World Trade Organization.

been created. Not all regional trade agreements notified in the last half century are still in force. Most of the discontinued agreements, however, have been superseded by re-designed agreements among the same signatories. Out of the 214 agreements or enlargements so far notified to the GATT and the WTO, 134 are deemed to be currently in force (see Figure 8.1).[1]

Consistent with the predictions of international trade theory, particularly the theory of comparative advantage (see Chapter 4), the belief has been that agreements designed to promote freer trade within regions will produce gains from trade for all member countries. As we saw in Chapter 5, the General Agreement on Tariffs and Trade and its successor, the World Trade Organization, also seek to reduce trade barriers. With more than 120 member-states, the WTO has a worldwide perspective. By entering into regional agreements, groups of countries aim to reduce trade barriers more rapidly than can be achieved under the auspices of the WTO.

Nowhere has the movement toward regional economic integration been more successful than in Europe. As noted in the opening case, on January 1, 1993, the European Union effectively became a single market with 340 million consumers. But the EU is not stopping there. The member-states of the EU are launching a single currency, they are moving toward a closer political union, and they are discussing enlarging the EU from the current 15 countries to ultimately include another 15 Eastern European states.

Similar moves toward regional integration are being pursued elsewhere in the world. Canada, Mexico, and the United States have implemented the North American Free Trade Agreement (NAFTA). This promises to ultimately remove all barriers to the free flow of goods and services between the three countries. Argentina, Brazil, Paraguay, and Uruguay have implemented a 1991 agreement to start reducing barriers to trade between themselves. Known as MERCOSUR, this free trade area is viewed by some as the first step in a move toward creation of a South American Free Trade Area (SAFTA). There is also talk of establishing a hemispherewide Free Trade Agreement of the Americas (FTAA). Along similar lines, 18 Pacific Rim countries, including the NAFTA member states, Japan, and China, have been discussing a possible pan-Pacific free trade area under the auspices of the Asia Pacific Economic Cooperation forum (APEC). There are also active attempts at regional economic integration in Central America, the Andean Region of South America, Southeast Asia, and parts of Africa.

As the opening case on the European insurance industry demonstrates, a move toward greater regional economic integration can potentially deliver important benefits to consumers and present firms with new challenges. In the European insurance industry, creation of a single EU insurance market opened formerly protected national markets to increased competition, which should result in lower prices for insurance products. This will benefit consumers, who will have more money to spend on other goods and services. As for insurance companies, the increase in competition and greater price pressure that has followed the creation of a single market has forced them to look for cost savings from economies of scale. They have also sought to increase their presence in different nations. The mergers occurring in the European insurance industry are seen as a way of achieving both these goals. As the opening case makes clear, however, the promise of a single market has yet to be fully attained due to the lingering persistence of regulatory differences between member states of the EU. The European Commission is currently tackling this issue.

The rapid spread of regional trade agreements raises the fear among some of a world in which regional trade blocs compete against each other. In this scenario of the future, free trade will exist within each bloc, but each bloc will protect its market from outside competition with high tariffs. The specter of the EU and NAFTA turning into "economic fortresses" that shut out foreign producers with high tariff barriers is worrisome to those who believe in unrestricted free trade. If such a scenario were to materialize, the resulting decline in trade between blocs could more than offset the gains from free trade within blocs.

With these issues in mind, the main objectives of this chapter are as follows: (1) to explore the economic and political debate surrounding regional economic integration, paying particular attention to the economic and political benefits and costs of integration; (2) to review progress toward regional economic integration around the world; and (3) to map the important implications of regional economic integration for the practice of international business. Before tackling these objectives, however, we first need to examine the levels of integration that are theoretically possible.

▌ Levels of Economic Integration

Several levels of economic integration are possible in theory (see Figure 8.2). From least integrated to most integrated, they are a free trade area, a customs union, a common market, an economic union, and, finally, a full political union.

In a free trade area, all barriers to the trade of goods and services among member countries are removed. In the theoretically ideal free trade area, no discriminatory tariffs, quotas, subsidies, or administrative impediments are allowed to distort trade between members. Each country, however, is allowed to determine its own trade policies

Figure 8.2

Levels of Economic Integration

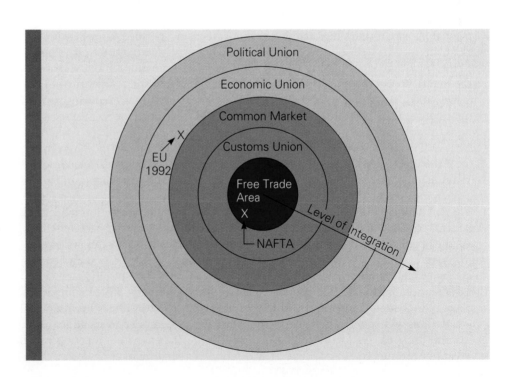

with regard to nonmembers. Thus, for example, the tariffs placed on the products of nonmember countries may vary from member to member.

The most enduring free trade area in the world is the European Free Trade Association (EFTA). Established in January 1960, EFTA currently joins four countries—Norway, Iceland, Liechtenstein, and Switzerland—down from seven in 1995 (three EFTA members, Austria, Finland, and Sweden, joined the EU on January 1, 1996). EFTA was founded by those Western European countries that initially decided not to be part of the European Community (the forerunner of the EU). Its original members included Austria, Great Britain, Denmark, Finland, and Sweden, all of which are now members of the EU. The emphasis of EFTA has been on free trade in industrial goods. Agriculture was left out of the arrangement, each member being allowed to determine its own level of support. Members are also free to determine the level of protection applied to goods coming from outside EFTA. Other free trade areas include the North American Free Trade Agreement (NAFTA), which we shall discuss in depth later in the chapter.

The customs union is one step further along the road to full economic and political integration. A customs union eliminates trade barriers between member countries and adopts a common external trade policy. Establishment of a common external trade policy necessitates significant administrative machinery to oversee trade relations with nonmembers. Most countries that enter into a customs union desire even greater economic integration down the road. The EU began as a customs union and has moved beyond this stage. Other customs unions around the world include the current version of the Andean Pact (between Bolivia, Colombia, Ecuador, and Peru). The Andean Pact established free trade between member countries and imposes a common tariff, of 5 to 20 percent, on products imported from outside.[2]

Like a customs union, the theoretically ideal common market has no barriers to trade between member countries and a common external trade policy. Unlike a customs union, a common market also allows factors of production to move freely between members. Labor and capital are free to move because there are no restrictions on immigration, emigration, or cross-border flows of capital between member countries. Establishing a common market demands a significant degree of harmony and cooperation on fiscal, monetary, and employment policies. Achieving this degree of cooperation has proven very difficult. For years the European Union functioned as a common market, although it has now moved beyond this stage. MERCOSUR, the South America grouping of Argentina, Brazil, Paraguay, and Uruguay, hopes to eventually establish itself as a common market.

An economic union entails even closer economic integration and cooperation than a common market. Like the common market, an economic union involves the free flow of products and factors of production between member countries and the adoption of a common external trade policy. Unlike a common market, a full economic union also requires a common currency, harmonization of members' tax rates, and a common monetary and fiscal policy. Such a high degree of integration demands a coordinating bureaucracy and the sacrifice of significant amounts of national sovereignty to that bureaucracy. The EU is an economic union, although an imperfect one since not all members of the EU have adopted the euro, the currency of the EU, and differences in tax rates across countries still remain.

The move toward economic union raises the issue of how to make a coordinating bureaucracy accountable to the citizens of member nations. The answer is through political union. The EU is on the road toward political union. The European Parliament, which is playing an ever more important role in the EU, has been directly elected by citizens of the EU countries since the late 1970s. In addition, the Council of Ministers (the controlling, decision-making body of the EU) is composed of government ministers from each EU member. Canada and the United States provide examples of even closer degrees of political union; in each country, independent states were effectively combined into a single nation. Ultimately, the EU may move toward a similar federal structure.

The Case for Regional Integration

The case for regional integration is both economic and political. The case for integration is typically not accepted by many groups within a country, which explains why most attempts to achieve regional economic integration have been contentious and halting. In this section, we examine the economic and political cases for integration and two impediments to integration. In the next section, we look at the case against integration.

The Economic Case for Integration

The economic case for regional integration is relatively straightforward. We saw in Chapter 4 how economic theories of international trade predict that unrestricted free trade will allow countries to specialize in the production of goods and services that they can produce most efficiently. The result is greater world production than would be possible with trade restrictions. We also saw in that chapter how opening a country to free trade stimulates economic growth in the country, which creates dynamic gains from trade. Further, we saw in Chapter 6 how foreign direct investment (FDI) can transfer technological, marketing, and managerial know-how to host nations. Given the central role of knowledge in stimulating economic growth, opening a country to FDI also is likely to stimulate economic growth. In sum, economic theories suggest that free trade and investment is a positive-sum game, in which all participating countries stand to gain.

Given this, the theoretical ideal is a total absence of barriers to the free flow of goods, services, and factors of production among nations. However, as we saw in Chapters 5 and 7, a case can be made for government intervention in international trade and FDI. Because many governments have accepted part or all of the case for intervention, unrestricted free trade and FDI have proved to be only an ideal. Although international institutions such as GATT and the WTO have been moving the world toward a free trade regime, success has been less than total. In a world of many nations and many political ideologies, it is very difficult to get all countries to agree to a common set of rules.

Against this background, regional economic integration can be seen as an attempt to achieve additional gains from the free flow of trade and investment between countries beyond those attainable under international agreements such as GATT and the WTO. It is easier to establish a free trade and investment regime among a limited number of adjacent countries than among the world community. Problems of coordination and policy harmonization are largely a function of the number of countries that seek agreement. The greater the number of countries involved, the greater the number of perspectives that must be reconciled, and the harder it will be to reach agreement. Thus, attempts at regional economic integration are motivated by a desire to exploit the gains from free trade and investment.

The Political Case for Integration

The political case for regional economic integration has also loomed large in most attempts to establish free trade areas, customs unions, and the like. By linking neighboring economies and making them increasingly dependent on each other, incentives are created for political cooperation between the neighboring states. In turn, the potential for violent conflict between the states is reduced. In addition, by grouping their economies, the countries can enhance their political weight in the world.

These considerations underlay establishment of the European Community (EC) in 1957 (the EC was the forerunner of the EU). Europe had suffered two devastating wars in the first half of the century, both arising out of the unbridled ambitions of nation-states. Those who have sought a united Europe have always had a desire to make another outbreak of war in Europe unthinkable. Many Europeans also felt that after World War II the European nation-states were no longer large enough to hold their own in world markets and world politics. The need for a united Europe to deal with the United States and the politically alien Soviet Union certainly loomed large in the minds of many of the EC's founders.[3] A long-standing joke in Europe is that the European Commission should erect a statue to Joseph Stalin, for without the aggressive policies of the former dictator of the old Soviet Union, the countries of Western Europe may have lacked the incentive to cooperate and form the EC.

Impediments to Integration

Despite the strong economic and political arguments for integration, it has never been easy to achieve or sustain for two main reasons. First, although economic integration benefits the majority, it has its costs. While a nation as a whole may benefit significantly from a regional free trade agreement, certain groups may lose. Moving to a free trade regime involves some painful adjustments. For example, as a result of the 1994 establishment of NAFTA, some Canadian and U.S. workers in such industries as textiles, which employ low-cost, low-skilled labor, will certainly lose their jobs as Canadian and U.S. firms move production to Mexico. The promise of significant net benefits to the Canadian and U.S. economies as a whole is little comfort to those who will lose as a result of NAFTA. It is understandable then, that such groups were in the forefront of opposition to NAFTA and will continue to oppose any widening of the agreement (see the accompanying Country Focus).

A second impediment to integration arises from concerns over national sovereignty. For example, Mexico's concerns about maintaining control of its oil interests resulted in an agreement with Canada and the United States to exempt the Mexican oil industry from any liberalization of foreign investment regulations achieved under NAFTA. Concerns about national sovereignty arise because close economic integration demands that countries give up some degree of their control over such key policy issues as monetary policy, fiscal policy (e.g., tax policy), and trade policy. This has been a major stumbling block in the EU. To achieve full economic union, the EU introduced a common currency to be controlled by a central EU bank. Although most member states have signed on to such a deal, Great Britain remains an important holdout. A politically important segment of public opinion in that country opposes a common currency on the grounds that it would require relinquishing control of the country's monetary policy to the EU, which many British perceive as a bureaucracy run by foreigners. In 1992, the British won the right to opt out of any single currency agreement, and as of 2001, there was little sign that the British government would reverse its decision.

The Case against Regional Integration

Although the tide has been running strongly in favor of regional free trade agreements in recent years (see Figure 8.1), some economists have expressed concern that the benefits of regional integration have been oversold, while the costs have often been ignored.[4] They point out that the benefits of regional integration are determined by the extent of trade creation, as opposed to trade diversion. **Trade creation** occurs when high-cost domestic producers are replaced by low-cost producers within the free trade area. It may also occur when higher-cost external producers are replaced by lower-cost external producers within the free trade area (see the accompanying Country Focus for an example). **Trade diversion** occurs when lower-cost external suppliers are replaced by higher-cost suppliers within the free trade area. A regional free trade agreement will benefit the world only if the amount of trade it creates exceeds the amount it diverts.

Suppose the United States and Mexico imposed tariffs on imports from all countries, and then they set up a free trade area, scrapping all trade barriers between

NAFTA and the U.S. Textile Industry

When the North American Free Trade Agreement went into effect in 1994, many expressed fears that one consequence would be large job losses in the U.S. textile industry as companies moved production from the United States to Mexico. Opponents of NAFTA argued passionately, but unsuccessfully, that the treaty should not be adopted because of the negative impact it would have on employment in the United States.

A quick glance at the data seven years after the passage of NAFTA suggests the critics had a point. Between 1993 and 2000, employment in the U.S. textile industry fell from about 1 million to 560,000, a 45 percent reduction. Over the same period, exports of garments from Mexico to the United States surged from $1.6 billion to $8.3 billion (see Figure 8.3). Such data seem to indicate that the job losses have been due to apparel production migrating from the United States to Mexico. Examples are plentiful. In 1995, Fruit of the Loom Inc., the largest manufacturer of underwear in the United States, said it would close six of its domestic plants and cut back operations at two others, laying off about 3,200 workers, or 12 percent of its U.S. workforce. The company announced the closures were part of its drive to move its operations to cheaper plants abroad, particularly in Mexico. Before the closures, less than 30 percent of its sewing was

done outside the United States, but Fruit of the Loom planned to move the majority of that work to Mexico. Similarly, fabric makers have been moving production to Mexico. Cone Mills of South Carolina, one of the country's largest producers of denim fabric, has reduced its U.S. employment by one-third since 1994, while investing $200 million in two new factories in Mexico. Similarly, Burlington Industries in 1999 eliminated 2,900 jobs in its North Carolina fabric plants, or 17 percent of its total workforce, while investing heavily in Mexican manufacturing capability.

For textile manufactures, the advantages of locating in Mexico include cheap labor and cheap inputs. Labor rates in Mexico average between $10 and $20 a day, compared to $10 to $12 an hour for U.S. textile workers. Another advantage for denim makers such as Cone Mills is cheap water (water is essential for dyeing cotton yarn with indigo). In Mexico, Cone Mills pays about 30 cents per cubic meter for water, about one-fifth of the rate in South Carolina. In addition, Cone Mills and other fabric makers have been locating in Mexico because many of their customers—garment makers—have already located there and being in the same region reduces transportation costs.

However, job losses in the U.S. textile industry do not mean that the overall effects of NAFTA have been negative. Clothing prices in the United States have also fallen since 1994 as textile production shifted

Figure 8.3

U.S. Mexican Trade in Textiles, 1993–2000

Source: U.S. Department of Commerce.

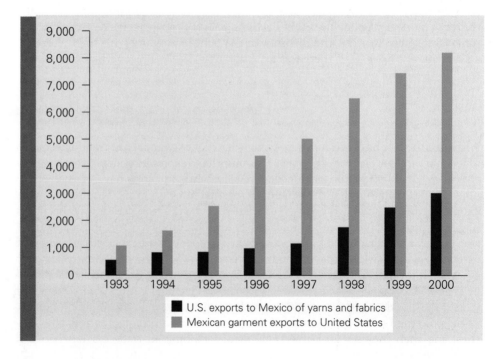

Legend:
■ U.S. exports to Mexico of yarns and fabrics
■ Mexican garment exports to United States

from high-cost U.S. producers to lower-cost Mexican producers. This benefits consumers, who now have more money to spend on other items. Denim fabric, which used to sell for $3.20 per yard, now sells for $2.40 per yard. The cost of a typical pair of designer jeans, for example, fell from $55 in 1994 to around $48 today. In 1994, blank T-shirts wholesaled for $24 a dozen. Now they sell for $14 a dozen. Nor is the fall in prices simply a result of the movement of production from the United States to Mexico. NAFTA has also resulted in textile production being moved from Asia to Mexico. In 1980, 83 percent of all U.S. textile imports came from Asia. By 1997, Asia accounted for 41 percent of U.S. textile imports as companies switched their source of textiles from Asia to Mexico.

In addition to lower prices, the shift in textile production to Mexico has also benefited the U.S. economy in other ways. First, despite the shift of fabric and apparel production to Mexico, there has been a surge in exports from U.S. fabric and yarn makers, many of which are in the chemical industry. Before the passage of NAFTA, U.S. yarn producers, such as E.I. du Pont, supplied only small amounts of fabric and yarn to Asian producers. However, as apparel production has moved from Asia to Mexico, exports of fabric and yarn to that country have surged. U.S. producers supply 70 percent of the raw material going to Mexican sewing shops. Between 1994 and 2000, U.S. fabric and yarn exports to Mexico, mostly in the form of cut pieces ready for sewing, grew from $760 million to $3 billion. In addition, U.S. manufacturers of textile equipment have also seen an increase in their sales as apparel factories in Mexico order textile equipment. Exports of textile equipment to Mexico nearly doubled in 2000 over the 1994 level, to $35.5 million.

Although there have been job losses in the U.S. textile industry, advocates of NAFTA argue that there have been benefits to the U.S. economy in the form of lower clothing prices and an increase in exports from fabric and yarn producers and from producers of textile machinery, to say nothing of the gains in other sectors of the U.S. economy. Trade has been created as a result of NAFTA. The gains from trade are being captured by U.S. consumers and by producers in certain sectors. As always, the establishment of a free trade area creates winners and losers—and the losers have been employees in the textile industry—but advocates argue that the gains outweigh the losses.

Sources: C. Burritt, "Seven Years into NAFTA, Textile Makers Seek a Payoff in Mexico," *Atlanta Journal-Constitution*, December 17, 2000, p. Q1; I. McAllister, "Trade Agreements: How They Affect U.S. Textile," *Textile World*, March 2000, pp. 50–54; and J. Millman, "Mexico Weaves More Ties," *Wall Street Journal*, August 21, 2000, p. A12.

themselves but maintaining tariffs on imports from the rest of the world. If the United States began to import textiles from Mexico, would this change be for the better? If the United States previously produced all its own textiles at a higher cost than Mexico, then the free trade agreement has shifted production to the cheaper source. According to the theory of comparative advantage, trade has been created within the regional grouping, and there would be no decrease in trade with the rest of the world. Clearly, the change would be for the better. If, however, the United States previously imported textiles from Costa Rica, which produced them more cheaply than either Mexico or the United States, then trade has been diverted from a low-cost source—a change for the worse.

In theory, WTO rules should ensure that a free trade agreement does not result in trade diversion. These rules allow free trade areas to be formed only if the members set tariffs that are not higher or more restrictive to outsiders than the ones previously in effect. However, as we saw in Chapter 5, GATT and the WTO do not cover some nontariff barriers. As a result, regional trade blocs could emerge whose markets are protected from outside competition by high nontariff barriers. In such cases, the trade diversion effects might outweigh the trade creation effects. The only way to guard against this possibility, according to those concerned about this potential, is to increase the scope of the WTO so it covers nontariff barriers to trade. There is no sign that this is going to occur anytime soon, however; so the risk remains that regional economic integration will result in trade diversion.

Regional Economic Integration in Europe

Europe has two trade blocs—the European Union and the European Free Trade Association. Of the two, the EU is by far the more significant, not just in terms of membership (the EU has 15 members, and EFTA has 4), but also in terms of economic and political influence in the world economy. Many now see the EU as an emerging economic and political superpower of the same order as the United States and Japan. Accordingly, we will concentrate our attention on the EU.[5]

Evolution of European Union

The EU is the product of two political factors: (1) the devastation of two world wars on Western Europe and the desire for a lasting peace, and (2) the European nations' desire to hold their own on the world's political and economic stage. In addition, many Europeans were aware of the potential economic benefits of closer economic integration of the countries.

The original forerunner of the EU, the European Coal and Steel Community, was formed in 1951 by Belgium, France, West Germany, Italy, Luxembourg, and the Netherlands. Its objective was to remove barriers to intragroup shipments of coal, iron, steel, and scrap metal. With the signing of the Treaty of Rome in 1957, the European Community was established. The name changed again in 1994 when the *European Community* became the *European Union* following the ratification of the Maastricht Treaty (discussed later).

The Treaty of Rome provided for the creation of a common market. Article 3 of the treaty laid down the key objectives of the new community, calling for the elimination of internal trade barriers and the creation of a common external tariff and requiring member states to abolish obstacles to the free movement of factors of production among the members. To facilitate the free movement of goods, services, and factors of production, the treaty provided for any necessary harmonization of the member states' laws. Furthermore, the treaty committed the EC to establish common policies in agriculture and transportation.

The community grew in 1973, when Great Britain, Ireland, and Denmark joined. These three were followed in 1981 by Greece, in 1986 by Spain and Portugal, and in 1996 by Austria, Finland, and Sweden (see Map 8.1) bringing the total membership to 15 (East Germany became part of the EC after the reunification of Germany in 1990). With a population of 350 million and a GDP greater than that of the United States, these enlargements made the EU a potential global superpower. Another 12 countries have applied to join the EU, although the EU seems to be in no hurry to expand.

Political Structure of the European Union

The economic policies of the EU are formulated and implemented by a complex and still-evolving political structure. The five main institutions in this structure are the European Council, the Council of Ministers, the European Commission, the European Parliament, and the Court of Justice.[6]

The European Council is composed of the heads of state of the EU's member nations and the president of the European Commission. Each head of state is normally accompanied by a foreign minister to these meetings. The European Council meets at least twice a year and often resolves major policy issues and sets policy directions.

The European Commission is responsible for proposing EU legislation, implementing it, and monitoring compliance with EU laws by member states. Headquartered in Brussels, Belgium, the commission has more than 10,000 employees. It is run by a group of 20 commissioners appointed by each member country for four-year renewable terms. Most countries appoint only one commissioner, although the most populated

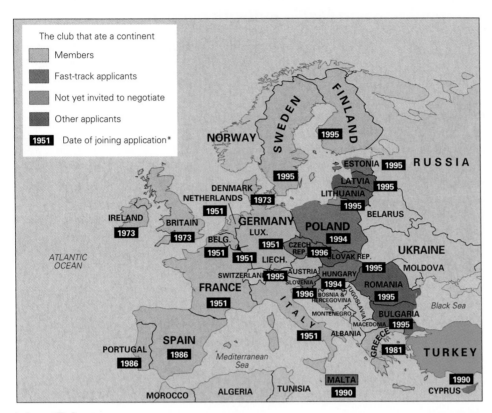

The club that ate a continent
- Members
- Fast-track applicants
- Not yet invited to negotiate
- Other applicants
- 1951 Date of joining application*

Map 8.1

The European Union

Source: *The Economist*, October 23, 1999, p. 4.

states—Great Britain, France, Germany, Italy, and Spain—appoint two each. A president and six vice presidents are chosen from among these commissioners for two-year renewable terms. The commission has a monopoly in proposing European Union legislation. The commission starts the legislative ball rolling by making a proposal, which goes to the Council of Ministers and then to the European Parliament. The Council of Ministers cannot legislate without a commission proposal in front of it. The commission is also responsible for implementing aspects of EU law, although in practice much of this must be delegated to member states. Another responsibility of the commission is to monitor member states to make sure they are complying with EU laws. In this policing role, the commission will normally ask a state to comply with any EU laws that are being broken. If this persuasion is not sufficient, the commission can refer a case to the Court of Justice.

The European Commission's role in competition policy has become increasingly important to business in recent years. Since 1990 when the office was formally assigned a role in competition policy, the EU's competition commissioner has been steadily gaining influence as the chief regulator of competition policy in the 15 member nations of the EU. As with antitrust authorities in the United States, which include the Federal Trade Commission and the Department of Justice, the role of the competition commissioner is to ensure that no one enterprise uses its market power to drive out competitors and monopolize markets. The commissioner also reviews proposed mergers and acquisitions to make sure they do not create a dominant enterprise with substantial market power. Between 1990 and 2000, the commission reviewed some 1,500 merger cases. Of these, 13 were rejected, and another 13 were withdrawn after the commission raised substantial objections.[7] For example, in 2000 a proposed

ManagementFocus

The European Commission and Media Industry Mergers

In late 1999, U.S. Internet giant AOL announced it would merge with the music and publishing conglomerate Time Warner. Although both companies were American, both also had substantial operations in Europe. The European Commissioner for Competition Mario Monti announced that the commission would investigate the impact of the merger on competition in Europe.

The investigation took on a new twist when Time Warner subsequently announced it would form a joint venture with British-based EMI. Time Warner and EMI are two of the top five music publishing companies in the world. The proposed joint venture would have been three times as large as its nearest global competitor. The European Commission now had two concerns. The first was that the joint venture between EMI and Time Warner would reduce the level of competition in the music publishing industry. The second was that a combined AOL–Time Warner would dominate the emerging market for downloading music over the Internet, particularly given the fact that AOL would be able to gain preferential access to the music libraries of both Warner and EMI. This would potentially put other online service providers at a disadvantage. The commission was also concerned that AOL Europe was a joint venture between AOL and Bertelsmann, a German media company that also had considerable music publishing interests. Accordingly, the commission announced it would undertake a separate investigation of the proposed deal between Time Warner and EMI.

Yet another twist occurred in mid-2000 while the AOL, Time Warner, EMI combinations were still under investigation. Vivendi, a French media conglomerate with significant music publishing, television, and Internet activities, announced it was in talks to acquire Seagram, a Canadian company that owned Universal Studios and Polygram Records, along with an alcoholic beverage business. Vivendi's plan was to sell the beverage business and hold on to Universal. Vivendi announced that its proposed acquisition would be a competitive answer to the AOL–Time Warner combination. The European Commission, however, was concerned that Vivendi, which owned Europe's largest pay television service, Canal Plus, and had a 20 percent ownership stake in British Sky Broadcasting, a satellite TV venture, would use its power to dominate the pay television market and dictate the use of Universal films and music, thereby putting competitors in the film and music business at a disadvantage. Thus, Monti announced that the European Commission would also investigate this deal.

These investigations continued into late 2000 and were resolved by a series of concessions extracted by the European Commission from the various players. First, under pressure from the commission, Time Warner and EMI agreed to drop their proposed joint venture, thereby maintaining the level of competition in the music publishing business. Second, AOL and Time Warner agreed to allow rival Internet service providers access to online music on the same terms as AOL would receive from Warner Music Group for the next five years. Third, AOL agreed to sever all ties with Bertelsmann, and the German company agreed to withdraw from AOL Europe. These developments alleviated the commission's concern that the AOL–Time Warner combination would dominate the emerging market for the digital download of music. With these concessions in hand, the commission approved the AOL–Time Warner merger in early October 2000.

The commission then turned its attention to the proposed deal between Vivendi and Seagram. The commission appeared to buy the argument that the Vivendi–Universal combination was a competitive response to the AOL–Time Warner action, but still it extracted several concessions from Vivendi to ensure that the enlarged company did not abuse its market power. Most importantly, the commission agreed that the proposed acquisition could proceed as long as Vivendi agreed to sell its 20 percent ownership stake in British Sky Broadcasting, a condition to which Vivendi readily agreed.

By late 2000, all these transactions had been completed. The shape of the media business, both in Europe and worldwide, now looked very different, and the European Commission had played a pivotal role in determining the outcome. Its demand for concessions had altered the strategy of several of the players, led to somewhat different combination than those originally planned, and, the Commission believed, preserved competition in the global media business.

Sources: W. Drozdiak, "EU Allows Vivendi Media Deal," *Washington Post,* October 14, 2000, p. E2; D. Hargreaves, "Business as Usual in the New Economy," *Financial Times,* October 6, 2000, p. 1; and D. Hargreaves, "Brussels Clears AOL-Time Warner Deal," *Financial Times,* October 12, 2000, p. 12.

merger between Time Warner of the United States and EMI of the United Kingdom, both music recording companies, was withdrawn after the commission expressed concerns that the merger would reduce the number of major record companies from five to four and create a dominant player in the $40 billion global music industry. Similarly, the commission blocked a proposed merger between two U.S. telecommunication companies, WorldCom and Sprint, because their combined holdings of Internet infrastructure in Europe would give the merged companies so much market power that the commission argued the combined company would dominate that market. Another example of the commission's influence over business combinations is given in the accompanying Management Focus, which looks at the commission's role in shaping mergers and joint ventures in the media industry.

The Council of Ministers represents the interests of member states. It is clearly the ultimate controlling authority within the EU since draft legislation from the commission can become EU law only if the council agrees. The council is composed of one representative from the government of each member state. The membership, however, varies depending on the topic being discussed. When agricultural issues are being discussed, the agriculture ministers from each state attend council meetings; when transportation is being discussed transportation ministers attend, and so on. Before 1993, all council issues had to be decided by unanimous agreement between member states. This often led to marathon council sessions and a failure to make progress or reach agreement on proposals submitted from the commission. In an attempt to clear the resulting logjams, the Single European Act formalized the use of majority voting rules on issues "which have as their object the establishment and functioning of a single market." Most other issues, however, such as tax regulations and immigration policy, still require unanimity among council members if they are to become law.

The European Parliament, which now has about 630 members, is directly elected by the populations of the member states. The parliament, which meets in Strasbourg, France, is primarily a consultative rather than legislative body. It debates legislation proposed by the commission and forwarded to it by the council. It can propose amendments to that legislation, which the commission and ultimately the council are not obliged to take up but often will. The power of the parliament recently has been increasing, although not by as much as parliamentarians would like. The European Parliament now has the right to vote on the appointment of commissioners, as well as veto power over some laws (such as the EU budget and single-market legislation). One major debate now being waged in Europe is whether the council or the parliament should ultimately be the most powerful body in the EU. There is concern in Europe over the democratic accountability of the EU bureaucracy. Some think the answer to this apparent democratic deficit lies in increasing the power of the parliament, while others think that true democratic legitimacy lies with elected governments, acting through the Council of Ministers.[8]

The Court of Justice, which is comprised of one judge from each country, is the supreme appeals court for EU law. Like commissioners, the judges are required to act as independent officials, rather than as representatives of national interests. The commission or a member country can bring other members to the court for failing to meet treaty obligations. Similarly, member countries, companies, or institutions can bring the commission or council to the court for failure to act according to an EU treaty.

❙ The Single European Act

Two revolutions occurred in Europe in the late 1980s. The first was the collapse of communism in Eastern Europe. The second revolution was much quieter, but its impact on Europe and the world may have been just as profound as the first. It was the adoption of the Single European Act by the member nations of the EC in 1987. This act committed the EC countries to work toward establishment of a single market by December 31, 1992.

The Stimulus for the Single European Act

The Single European Act was born of a frustration among EC members that the community was not living up to its promise. By the early 1980s, it was clear that the EC had fallen short of its objectives to remove barriers to the free flow of trade and investment between member countries and to harmonize the wide range of technical and legal standards for doing business. At the end of 1982, the European Commission found itself inundated with 770 cases of intra-EC protectionism to investigate. In addition, some 20 EC directives setting common technical standards for a variety of products ranging from cars to thermometers were deadlocked. Many companies considered the disharmony of the members' technical, legal, regulatory, and tax standards as the EC's main problem. The "rules of the game" differed substantially from country to country, which stalled the creation of a true single internal market. For example, in violation of Article 3 of the Treaty of Rome, each country had adopted its own trade policy with regard to automobile imports (e.g., whereas Japanese imports were not restricted in Belgium, they were limited to 11 percent of the car market in Great Britain and to less than 2 percent in France and Italy). These divisions resulted in substantial price differentials between countries. In 1989, the prices of the same model of car were, on average, 31 percent higher in the United Kingdom and 11 percent higher in Germany than in Belgium.[9]

Against this background, many of the EC's prominent businesspeople mounted an energetic campaign in the early 1980s to end the EC's economic divisions. The EC responded by creating the Delors Commission. Under the chairmanship of Jacques Delors, the former French finance minister and president of the EC Commission, the Delors Commission produced a discussion paper in 1985. This proposed that all impediments to the formation of a single market be eliminated by December 31, 1992. The result was the Single European Act, which was independently ratified by the parliaments of each member country and became EC law in 1987.

The Objectives of the Act

The purpose of the Single European Act was to have a single market in place by December 31, 1992. The act proposed the following changes:[10]

- Remove all frontier controls between EC countries, thereby abolishing delays and reducing the resources required for complying with trade bureaucracy.
- Apply the principle of "mutual recognition" to product standards. A standard developed in one EC country should be accepted in another, provided it meets basic requirements in such matters as health and safety.
- Open public procurement to nonnational suppliers, reducing costs directly by allowing lower-cost suppliers into national economies and indirectly by forcing national suppliers to compete.
- Lift barriers to competition in the retail banking and insurance businesses, which should drive down the costs of financial services, including borrowing, throughout the EC.
- Remove all restrictions on foreign exchange transactions between member countries by the end of 1992.
- Abolish restrictions on cabotage—the right of foreign truckers to pick up and deliver goods within another member state's borders—by the end of 1992. Estimates suggested this would reduce the cost of haulage within the EC by 10 to 15 percent.

All those changes were predicted to lower the costs of doing business in the EC, but the single-market program was also expected to have more complicated supply-side effects. For example, the expanded market was predicted to give EC firms greater opportunities to exploit economies of scale. In addition, it was thought that the increase in competitive intensity brought about by removing internal barriers to trade and investment would force EC firms to become more efficient. To signify the importance of the Single European Act, the European Community also decided to change its name to the European Union once the act took effect.

Implications

The implications of the Single European Act are potentially enormous. If the EU is successful in establishing a single market, the member countries can expect significant gains from the free flow of trade and investment. These gains may be greater than those predicted by standard trade theory that accrue when regions specialize in producing those goods and services that they produce most efficiently. The lower costs of doing business implied by the Single European Act should benefit EU firms, as will the economies of scale inherent in serving a single market of 360 million consumers. On the other hand, as a result of the Single European Act, many EU firms are facing increased competitive pressure. Countries such as France and Italy have long used administrative trade barriers and subsidies to protect their home markets from foreign competition. Removal of these barriers has increased competition, and some firms may go out of business. Ultimately, however, both consumers and EU firms will benefit from this. Consumers will benefit from the lower prices implied by a more competitive market. EU firms will benefit if the increased competitive pressure forces them to become more efficient, thereby transforming them into more effective international competitors capable of going head to head with U.S. and Asian rivals in the world marketplace.

The Establishment of the Euro

In December 1991, leaders of the EC member-states met in Maastricht, the Netherlands, to discuss the next steps for the EC. The results of the Maastricht meeting surprised both Europe and the rest of the world. For months the countries of the EC had been fighting over the issue of a common currency. Although many economists believed a common currency was required to cement a closer economic union, deadlock had been predicted. The British in particular had opposed any attempt to establish a common currency. Instead, the 12 members signed a treaty that committed them to adopting a common currency by January 1, 1999, and paved the way for closer political cooperation.

The treaty laid down the main elements, if only in embryo, of a future European government: a single currency—the euro—a common foreign and defense policy, a common citizenship, and an EU parliament with teeth. It is now just a matter of waiting, some believe, for history to take its course and a "United States of Europe" to emerge. Of more immediate interest are the implications for business of the establishment of a single currency.[11]

The euro is a currency unit now used by 11 of the 15 member states of the European Union; these 11 states are now members of what is often referred to as the euro zone. The establishment of the euro has rightly been described as an amazing political feat. There are few historic precedents for what the Europeans are doing. Establishing the euro required the participating national governments not only to give up their own currencies, but also to give up control over monetary policy. Governments do not routinely sacrifice national sovereignty for the greater good, indicating the importance that the Europeans attach to the euro. By adopting the euro, the EU has created the second largest currency zone in the world after that of the U.S. dollar. Some believe that ultimately the euro could come to rival the dollar as the most important currency in the world.

According to the Maastricht Treaty, to join the euro zone member countries had to achieve low inflation rates, low long-term interest rates, a stable exchange rate, public debt limited to no more than 60 percent of a country's gross domestic product, and current budget deficits of no more than 3 percent of GDP. Initially, there was considerable skepticism that this would be possible. However, by the spring of 1998 it was clear that of the 12 countries that had signaled their intention to join the euro zone, only Greece would not make the criteria. For now three EU countries, Britain, Denmark, and Sweden, are still sitting on the sidelines, although there is speculation that Great Britain and Sweden may join. The 11 countries that made the grade and agreed to the euro locked their exchange rates against each other January 1, 1999. Euro notes and coins were not actually issued until January 1, 2002. In the interim, national currencies circulated in each of the 11 countries. However, in each participating state the national currency stood for a defined amount of euros. After January 1, 2002, euro notes and coins were issued and the national currencies were taken out of circulation. By mid-2002, all prices and routine economic transactions within the euro zone were in euros.

Benefits of the Euro

Europeans decided to establish a single currency in the EU for a number of reasons. First, they believe that business and individuals will realize significant savings from having to handle one currency, rather than many. These savings come from lower foreign exchange and hedging costs. For example, people going from Germany to France will no longer have to pay a commission to a bank to change deutsche marks into francs. Instead, they will be able to use euros. According to the European Commission, such savings could amount to 0.5 percent of the European Union's GDP, or about $40 billion a year.

Second, and perhaps more importantly, the adoption of a common currency will make it easier to compare prices across Europe. This should increase competition because it will be much easier for consumers to shop around. For example, if a German finds that cars sell for less in France than Germany, he may be tempted to purchase from a French car dealer rather than his local car dealer. Alternatively, traders may engage in arbitrage to exploit such price differentials, buying cars in France and reselling them in Germany. The only way that German car dealers will be able to hold onto business in the face of such competitive pressures will be to reduce the prices they charge for cars. As a consequence of such pressures, the introduction of a common currency should lead to lower prices. This should translate into substantial gains for European consumers

Third, faced with lower prices European producers will be forced to look for ways to reduce their production costs to maintain their profit margins. The introduction of a common currency, by increasing competition, should ultimately produce long-run gains in the economic efficiency of European companies.

Fourth, the introduction of a common currency should give a strong boost to the development of a highly liquid pan-European capital market. The development of such a capital market should lower the cost of capital and lead to an increase in both the level of investment and the efficiency with which investment funds are allocated. This could be especially helpful to smaller companies that have historically had difficulty borrowing money from domestic banks. For example, the capital market of Portugal is very small and illiquid, which makes it extremely difficult for bright Portuguese entrepreneurs with a good idea to borrow money at a reasonable price. However, in theory, such companies should soon be able tap a much more liquid pan-European capital market. Right now Europe has no continentwide capital market, such as the NASDAQ market in the United States, that funnels investment capital to dynamic young growth companies. The euro's introduction could facilitate establishment of such a market. The long-run benefits of such a development should not be underestimated.

Finally, the development of a pan-European euro-denominated capital market will increase the range of investment options open to both individuals and institutions. For example, it will now be much easier for individuals and institutions based in, let's say, Holland to invest in Italian or French companies. This will enable European investors to better diversify their risk, which again lowers the cost of capital, and should also increase the efficiency with which capital resources are allocated. [12]

1. $\left(\dfrac{S_1 - S_2}{S_2}\right)(100) = I_1 - I_2 \quad = 1165$

2. a. $\dfrac{2.8}{3.70} = .76$ ✓

   $\$/\pounds$

   b. $\dfrac{3.10}{4.65} = .67$ —

   inflation ↑ $\$$ ↓

   c. fisher effect

   $$\dfrac{S_1 - S_2}{S_2}(100) = I_1 - I_2$$

   $$\dfrac{.76 - .67}{.67}(100) = I_1 - 10 \quad \text{Solve} \quad 23.4$$

   100

   $\$/\pounds \quad \dfrac{S_1 \;\; \frac{\$}{\pounds}}{S_2}(100) = I_1^{\$} - I_2^{\$l}$

Costs of the Euro

The drawback, for some, of a single currency is that national authorities have lost control over monetary policy. Thus, it is crucial to ensure that the EU's monetary policy is well managed. The Maastricht Treaty called for establishment of an independent European Central Bank (ECB), similar in some respects to the U.S. Federal Reserve, with a clear mandate to manage monetary policy so as to ensure price stability. The ECB, based in Frankfurt, is meant to be independent from political pressure—although critics question this. Among other things, the ECB sets interest rates and determines monetary policy across the euro zone. The implied loss of national sovereignty to the ECB underlies the decision by Great Britain, Denmark, and Sweden to stay out of the euro zone for now. In these countries, many are suspicious of the ability of the ECB to remain free from political pressure and to keep inflation under tight control. In theory, the design of the ECB should ensure that it remains free of political pressure. The ECB is modeled on the German Bundesbank, which historically has been the most independent and successful central bank in Europe. The Maastricht Treaty prohibits the ECB from taking orders from politicians. The executive board of the bank, which consists of a president, vice president, and four other members, carries out policy by issuing instructions to national central banks. The policy itself is determined by the governing council, which consists of the executive board plus the central bank governors from the 11 euro zone countries. The governing council votes on interest rate changes. Members of the executive board are appointed for eight-year nonrenewable terms, insulating them from political pressures to get reappointed. Nevertheless, the jury is still out on the issue of the ECB's independence, and it will take some time for the bank to establish its inflation-fighting credentials.

According to critics, another drawback of the euro is that the EU is not what economists would call an *optimal currency area*. In an optimal currency area, similarities in the underlying structure of economic activity make it feasible to adopt a single currency and use a single exchange rate as an instrument of macroeconomic policy. Many of the European economies in the euro zone, however, are very dissimilar. For example, Finland and Portugal are very dissimilar economies. The structure of economic activity within each country is very different. They have different wage rates and tax regimes, different business cycles, and may react very differently to external economic shocks. A change in the euro exchange rate that helps Finland may hurt Portugal. Obviously, such differences complicate macroeconomic policy. For example, when euro economies are not growing in unison, a common monetary policy may mean that interest rates are too high for depressed regions and too low for booming regions. It will be interesting to see how the EU copes with the strains caused by such divergent economic performance.

One way of dealing with such divergent effects within the euro zone might be for the EU to engage in fiscal transfers, taking money from prosperous regions and pumping it into depressed regions. Such a move, however, would open a political can of worms. Would the citizens of Germany forgo their "fair share" of EU funds to create jobs for underemployed Portuguese workers?

Several critics believe that the euro puts the economic cart before the political horse. In their view, a single currency should follow, not precede, political union. They argue that the euro will unleash enormous pressures for tax harmonization and fiscal transfers from the center, both policies that cannot be pursued without the appropriate political structure. The most apocalyptic vision that flows from these negative views is that far from stimulating economic growth, as its advocates claim, the euro will lead to lower economic growth and higher inflation within Europe. To quote one critic:

> Imposing a single exchange rate and an inflexible exchange rate on countries that are characterized by different economic shocks, inflexible wages, low labor mobility, and separate national fiscal systems without significant cross-border

fiscal transfers will raise the overall level of cyclical unemployment among EMU members. The shift from national monetary policies dominated by the (German) Bundesbank within the European Monetary System to a European Central Bank governed by majority voting with a politically determined exchange rate policy will almost certainly raise the average future rate of inflation.[13]

The Early Experience

In the first two years of its existence, the euro did not live up to expectations of all its supporters. In January 1999, the euro was trading at 1 euro = $1.17. By late November of that year, the value of the euro had slumped to 1 euro = $1. Although it recovered slightly in December, by the end of the year the euro had still lost 15 percent of its value against the U.S. dollar and was also down significantly against the Japanese yen. The slide continued in 2000, and by fall 2000 the euro was trading at 0.88=$1, representing a decline against the dollar of more than 20 percent. It stayed in that range during much of 2001.

Critics were quick to claim that the fall in the euro demonstrated the foreign exchange market's lack of confidence in the ability of the ECB to effectively manage monetary policy. However, there are no signs that the ECB is mismanaging monetary policy in the euro zone.[14] Inflationary pressures seem to be under control, the ECB seems to have managed interest rates with some skill, and there is no sign that the ECB is bowing to political pressure. Initially the decline in the value of the euro was attributed to two factors: the growth differential and the interest rate differential between the United States and the European Union.[15] During 1999 and 2000, U.S. economic growth was higher than growth in the euro zone, while U.S. interest rates were higher than interest rates on euros. Given the growth and interest rate differential, internationally mobile capital flowed out of Europe and toward the United States in anticipation of higher returns. This increased demand for dollars, decreased demand for euros, and resulted in a depreciation of the euro against the dollar.

However, by mid-2001 these factors were no longer relevant. Economic growth in the United States had slowed to less than that in Europe, and the Federal Reserve had aggressively reduced U.S. interest rates, and yet the dollar remained strong relative to the euro. Why? One explanation is that in times of economic uncertainty, the dollar retains its role as a "safe haven" currency, and 2001 was a time of significant economic uncertainty with some predicting the world was entering a recession. Another explanation is that investors still expect the U.S. economy to emerge from the 2001 economic slowdown ahead of Europe, and so they continue to hold dollars.[16] Whatever the reason for the decline in the value of the euro, one thing remains clear—it is still too early to judge whether the ECB is doing a good job, and whether the euro is a success. That will take several more years.

Enlargement of the European Union

The other big issue the EU must now grapple with is enlargement. After a bitter dispute among the existing 12 members, they agreed in March 1994 to enlarge the EU to include Austria, Finland, Sweden, and Norway. Most of the opposition to enlargement came from Great Britain, which worried that enlargement and a subsequent reduction in its voting power in the EU's top decision-making body, the Council of Ministers, would limit its ability to block EU developments that it did not like. Great Britain backed down in the face of strong opposition from other EU members and agreed to enlargement.

Voters in the four countries went to the polls in late 1994. Austria, Finland, and Sweden all voted to join the EU, but Norway voted to stay out. Thus, the EU of 12 became the EU of 15 on January 1, 1996. Next the EU had to deal with membership applications from Hungary, Poland, the Czech Republic, Estonia, Slovenia, Malta,

Cyprus, and Turkey.[17] In 1997, the EU responded by formally inviting five former Communist states, Estonia, Poland, the Czech Republic, Slovenia, and Hungary, to join. Another country, Turkey, was invited to join in December 1999; however, the timetable remains uncertain. All these countries still have a long way to go before their economies reach the level enjoyed by current EU members. For example, according to the European Commission, Poland, the country with the largest population among the five, needs to modernize its agricultural sector, speed up its sluggish privatization efforts, and bring its inflation rate down from around 20 percent to 3 percent.[18]

Fortress Europe?

One concern often voiced by commentators in the United States and Asian countries is that the EU at some point will impose new barriers on imports from outside the EU. The fear is that the EU might increase external protection as weaker member states attempt to offset their loss of protection against other EU countries by arguing for limitations on outside competition.

In theory, given the free market philosophy that underpins the Single European Act, this should not occur. In October 1988, the European Commission debated external trading policy and published a detailed statement of the EC's trading intentions in the post-1992 era.[19] The commission stressed the EC's interests in vigorous external trade. In 2000, exports by EU countries to non-EU countries accounted for 19 percent of total world exports, compared to 16.4 percent for the United States and 10 percent for Japan. These external exports are equivalent to 10.6 percent of the EU's GDP, compared to 8.8 percent for the United States and 10 percent for Japan. It is not in the EU's interests to adopt a protectionist stance, given the reliance on external trade. The commission has also promised loyalty to GATT and WTO rules on international trade. As for the types of trade not covered by the WTO, the EU states it will push for reciprocal access. The EU has stated that in certain cases it might replace individual national trade barriers with EU protection against imports, but it also has promised that the overall level of protection would not rise.

Despite such reassurances, there is no guarantee that the EU will not adopt a protectionist stance toward external trade. However, in a published report on the issue, the WTO stated that the growth of regional trade groups such as the EU has not impeded the growth of freer world trade, as some fear, and may have helped to promote it.[20]

Regional Economic Integration in the Americas ▪

No other attempt at regional economic integration comes close to the EU in its boldness or its potential implications for the world economy, but regional economic integration is on the rise in the Americas. The most significant attempt is the North American Free Trade Agreement. In addition to NAFTA, several other trade blocs are in the offing in the Americas (see Map 8.2), the most significant of which appear to be the Andean Group and MERCOSUR. There are also plans to establish a hemispherewide Free Trade Area of the Americas (FTAA) by late 2005.

The North American Free Trade Agreement

The governments of the United States and Canada in 1988 agreed to enter into a free trade agreement, which took effect January 1, 1989. The goal of the agreement was to eliminate all tariffs on bilateral trade between Canada and the United States by 1998. This was followed in 1991 by talks among the United States, Canada, and Mexico aimed at establishing a North American Free Trade Agreement for the three countries. The talks concluded in August 1992 with an agreement in principle and by late 1993, the agreement had been ratified by the governments of all three countries.

Map 8.2

Economic Integration
in the Americas

Source: *The Economist*, April 21,
2001, p. 20.

Continental Commerce
2000, $bn*

■ NAFTA
■ MERCOSUR
■ Andean community
■ Central America
■ Caribbean community
$5.4 Intraregional trade*
$0.4 Interregional trade
flows*

*Preliminary estimates †1999 estimates

NAFTA's Contents

The agreement became law January 1, 1994.[21] The contents of NAFTA include the following:

- Abolition within 10 years of tariffs on 99 percent of the goods traded between Mexico, Canada, and the United States.
- Removal of most barriers on the cross-border flow of services, allowing financial institutions, for example, unrestricted access to the Mexican market by 2000.
- Protection of intellectual property rights.
- Removal of most restrictions on foreign direct investment between the three member countries, although special treatment (protection) will be given to Mexican energy and railway industries, American airline and radio communications industries, and Canadian culture.
- Application of national environmental standards, provided such standards have a scientific basis. Lowering of standards to lure investment is described as being inappropriate.
- Establishment of two commissions with the power to impose fines and remove trade privileges when environmental standards or legislation involving health and safety, minimum wages, or child labor are ignored.

Arguments for NAFTA

Opinions remain divided as to the consequences of NAFTA. Proponents argue that NAFTA should be viewed as an opportunity to create an enlarged and more efficient productive base for the entire region. One likely effect of NAFTA will be that many U.S. and Canadian firms will move some production to Mexico to take advantage of lower labor costs. (In 2000, the average hourly labor cost in Mexico was still one-tenth of that in the United States and Canada.) Movement of production to Mexico is most likely to occur in low-skilled, labor-intensive manufacturing industries where Mexico might have a comparative advantage (e.g., textiles; see the Country Focus). Many will benefit from such a trend. Mexico benefits because it gets much-needed investment and employment. The United States and Canada should benefit because the increased incomes of the Mexicans will allow them to import more U.S. and Canadian goods, thereby increasing demand and making up for the jobs lost in industries that moved production to Mexico. U.S. and Canadian consumers will benefit from the lower prices of products produced in Mexico. In addition, the international competitiveness of U.S. and Canadian firms that move production to Mexico to take advantage of lower labor costs will be enhanced, enabling them to better compete with Asian and European rivals.

Arguments against NAFTA

Those who opposed NAFTA claimed that ratification would be followed by a mass exodus of jobs from the United States and Canada into Mexico as employers sought to profit from Mexico's lower wages and less strict environmental and labor laws. According to one extreme opponent, Ross Perot, up to 5.9 million U.S. jobs would be lost to Mexico after NAFTA. Most economists, however, dismissed these numbers as being absurd and alarmist. They argued that Mexico would have to run a bilateral trade surplus with the United States of close to $300 billion for job loss on such a scale to occur—and $300 billion is about the size of Mexico's present GDP. In other words, such a scenario is implausible.

More sober estimates of the impact of NAFTA ranged from a net creation of 170,000 jobs in the United States (due to increased Mexican demand for U.S. goods and services) and an increase of $15 billion per year to the U.S. and Mexican GDP, to a net loss of 490,000 U.S. jobs. To put these numbers in perspective, employment in the U.S. economy was predicted to grow by 18 million from 1993 to 2003. As most economists repeatedly stressed, NAFTA would have a small impact on both Canada and the United States. It could hardly be any other way, since the Mexican economy is only 5 percent of the size of the U.S. economy. Signing NAFTA required the largest leap of economic faith from Mexico rather than Canada or the United States. Falling trade barriers are exposing Mexican firms to highly efficient U.S. and Canadian competitors that, when compared to the average Mexican firm, have far greater capital resources, access to highly educated and skilled workforces, and much greater technological sophistication. The short-run outcome is bound to be painful economic restructuring and unemployment in Mexico. But if economic theory is any guide, there should be dynamic gains in the long run in the efficiency of Mexican firms as they adjust to the rigors of a more competitive marketplace. To the extent that this happens, an acceleration of Mexico's long-run rate of economic growth will follow, and Mexico might yet become a major market for Canadian and U.S. firms.[22]

Environmentalists have also voiced concerns about NAFTA. They point to the sludge in the Rio Grande River and the smog in the air over Mexico City and warn that Mexico could degrade clean air and toxic waste standards across the continent. They claim the lower Rio Grande is the most polluted river in the United States, increasing in chemical waste and sewage along its course from El Paso, Texas, to the Gulf of Mexico.

There is also continued opposition in Mexico to NAFTA from those who fear a loss of national sovereignty. Mexican critics argue that their country will be dominated by U.S. firms that will not really contribute to Mexico's economic growth, but instead will use Mexico as a low-cost assembly site, while keeping their high-paying, high-skilled jobs north of the border.

The Early Experience

The first year after NAFTA turned out to be a largely positive experience for all three countries. U.S. trade with Canada and Mexico expanded at about twice the rate of trade with non-NAFTA countries in the first nine months of 1994, compared with the same period in 1993. U.S. exports to Mexico grew by 22 percent, while Mexican exports to the United States grew by 23 percent. Anti-NAFTA campaigners had warned of doom for the U.S. auto industry, but exports of autos to Mexico increased by nearly 500 percent in the first nine months of 1993. The U.S. Commerce Department estimated that the surge in exports to Mexico secured about 130,000 U.S. jobs, while only 13,000 people applied for aid under a program designed to help workers displaced by the movement of jobs to Mexico, suggesting that job losses from NAFTA had been small.[23]

However, the early euphoria over NAFTA was snuffed out in December 1994 when the Mexican economy was shaken by a financial crisis. Through 1993 and 1994, Mexico's trade deficit with the rest of the world had grown sharply, while Mexico's inflation rate had started to accelerate. This put increasing pressure on the Mexican currency, the peso. Traders in the foreign exchange markets, betting that there would be a large decline in the value of the peso against the dollar, began to sell pesos and buy dollars. As a result, in December 1994, the Mexican government was forced to devalue the peso by about 35 percent against the dollar. This effectively increased the cost of imports from the United States by 35 percent. The devaluation of the peso was followed quickly by a collapse in the value of the Mexican stock market, and the country suddenly and unexpectedly appeared to be in the midst of a major economic crisis. Soon afterward, the Mexican government introduced an austerity program designed to rebuild confidence in the country's financial institutions and rein in growth and inflation. The program was backed by a $20 billion loan guarantee from the U.S. government.[24]

One result of this turmoil was a sharp decline in Canadian and U.S. exports to Mexico. Many companies also reduced or postponed their plans to expand into Mexico. NAFTA critics seized on Mexico's financial crisis to crow that they had been right. But in reality, just as the celebrations of NAFTA's success were premature, so were claims of its sudden demise. By the late 1990s, Mexico had recovered from its crisis, its economy was growing again, and the volume of trade with its NAFTA partners was once more expanding.

Early studies of NAFTA's impact suggest that so far at least, its effects have been at best muted.[25] The most comprehensive study to date was undertaken by researchers at the University of California, Los Angeles, and funded by various departments of the U.S. government.[26] Their findings are enlightening. First, they conclude that the growth in trade between Mexico and the United States began to change nearly a decade before the implementation of NAFTA when Mexico unilaterally started to liberalize its own trade regime to conform with GATT standards. The period since NAFTA took effect has had little impact on trends already in place. The study found that trade growth in those sectors that underwent tariff liberalization in the first two and a half years of NAFTA was only marginally higher than trade growth in sectors not yet liberalized. For example, between 1993 and 1996, U.S. exports to Mexico in sectors liberalized under NAFTA grew by 5.83 percent annually, while exports in sectors not liberalized under NAFTA grew by 5.35 percent. In short, the authors argue that NAFTA has so far had only a marginal impact on the level of trade between the United States and Mexico.

As for NAFTA's much-debated impact on jobs in the United States, the study concluded the impact was positive but very small. The study found that while NAFTA created 31,158 new jobs in the United States, 28,168 jobs were also lost due to imports from Mexico, for a net job gain of around 3,000 in the first two years of the NAFTA regime.

However, as the authors of the report point out, trade flows and employment in 1995 and 1996 were significantly affected by the peso devaluation and subsequent economic crisis that gripped Mexico in early 1995. Given this, it is probably too early to draw conclusions about the true impact of NAFTA on trade flows and employment. It will be some time before any meaningful conclusions can be stated. The most that can be said at this juncture is that while the optimistic picture of job creation painted by NAFTA's advocates has not yet come to pass, neither has the apocalyptic vision of widespread job losses in the United States and Canada propagated by NAFTA's opponents.

Enlargement

One big issue now confronting NAFTA is that of enlargement. A number of other Latin American countries have indicated their desire to eventually join NAFTA. The governments of both Canada and the United States are adopting a wait-and-see attitude with regard to most countries. Getting NAFTA approved was a bruising political experience, and neither government is eager to repeat the process soon. Nevertheless, the Canadian, Mexican, and U.S. governments began talks in 1995 regarding Chile's possible entry into NAFTA. As of 2001, however, these talks have yielded little progress, primarily because of political opposition in the U.S. Congress to expanding NAFTA.

The Andean Pact

The Andean Pact was formed in 1969 when Bolivia, Chile, Ecuador, Colombia, and Peru signed the Cartagena Agreement. The Andean Pact was largely based on the EU model, but it has been far less successful at achieving its stated goals. The integration steps begun in 1969 included an internal tariff reduction program, a common external tariff, a transportation policy, a common industrial policy, and special concessions for the smallest members, Bolivia and Ecuador.

By the mid-1980s, the Andean Pact had all but collapsed and had failed to achieve any of its stated objectives. There was no tariff-free trade between member countries, no common external tariff, and no harmonization of economic policies. Political and economic problems seem to have hindered cooperation between member countries. The countries of the Andean Pact have had to deal with low economic growth, hyperinflation, high unemployment, political unrest, and crushing debt burdens. In addition, the dominant political ideology in many of the Andean countries during this period tended toward the radical/socialist end of the political spectrum. Since such an ideology is hostile to the free market economic principles on which the Andean Pact was based, progress toward closer integration could not be expected.

The tide began to turn in the late 1980s when, after years of economic decline, the governments of Latin America began to adopt free market economic policies. In 1990, the heads of the five current members of the Andean Pact—Bolivia, Ecuador, Peru, Colombia, and Venezuela—met in the Galápagos Islands. The resulting Galápagos Declaration effectively relaunched the Andean Pact. The declaration's objectives included the establishment of a free trade area by 1992, a customs union by 1994, and a common market by 1995.

This last milestone has not been reached. However, there are some grounds for cautious optimism. For the first time, the controlling political ideology of the Andean countries is at least consistent with the free market principles underlying a common market. In addition, since the Galápagos Declaration, internal tariff levels have been reduced by all five members, and a customs union with a common external tariff was established in mid-1994, six months behind schedule.

Significant differences between member countries still exist that may make harmonization of policies and close integration difficult. For example, Venezuela's GNP per person is four times that of Bolivia's, and Ecuador's tiny production-line industries cannot compete with Colombia's and Venezuela's more advanced industries. Such differences are a recipe for disagreement and suggest that many of the adjustments required to achieve a true common market will be painful, even though the net benefits will probably outweigh the costs.[27] To complicate matters even further, in recent years

Peru and Ecuador have fought a border war, Venezuela has remained aloof during a banking crisis, and Colombia has suffered from domestic political turmoil and problems related to its drug trade. This has led some to argue that the pact is more "formal than real."[28] The outlook for the Andean Pact started to change in 1998 when the group entered into negotiations with MERCOSUR to establish a South American free trade area. However, these negotiations broke down in 1999, and there has been no progress since.

MERCOSUR

MERCOSUR originated in 1988 as a free trade pact between Brazil and Argentina. The modest reductions in tariffs and quotas accompanying this pact reportedly helped bring about an 80 percent increase in trade between the two countries in the late 1980s.[29] Encouraged by this success, the pact was expanded in March 1990 to include Paraguay and Uruguay. The initial aim was to establish a full free trade area by the end of 1994 and a common market sometime thereafter. The four countries of MERCOSUR have a combined population of 200 million. With a market of this size, MERCOSUR could have a significant impact on the economic growth rate of the four economies. In December 1995, MERCOSUR's members agreed to a five-year program under which they hoped to perfect their free trade area and move toward a full customs union.[30]

For its first eight years or so, MERCOSUR seemed to be making a positive contribution to the economic growth rates of its member states. Trade between MERCOSUR's four core members quadrupled between 1990 and 1998. The combined GDP of the four member states grew at an annual average rate of 3.5 percent between 1990 and 1996, a performance that is significantly better than the four attained during the 1980s.[31]

However, MERCOSUR has its critics, including Alexander Yeats, a senior economist at the World Bank, who wrote a stinging critique of MERCOSUR that was "leaked" to the press in October 1996.[32] According to Yeats, the trade diversion effects of MERCOSUR outweigh its trade creation effects. Yeats points out that the fastest-growing items in intra-MERCOSUR trade are cars, buses, agricultural equipment, and other capital-intensive goods that are produced relatively inefficiently in the four member countries. In other words, MERCOSUR countries, insulated from outside competition by tariffs that run as high as 70 percent of value on motor vehicles, are investing in factories that build products that are too expensive to sell to anyone but themselves. The result, according to Yeats, is that MERCOSUR countries might not be able to compete globally once the group's external trade barriers come down. In the meantime, capital is being drawn away from more efficient enterprises. In the near term, countries with more efficient manufacturing enterprises lose because MERCOSUR's external trade barriers keep them out of the market.

The leak of Yeats's report caused a storm at the World Bank, which typically does not release reports that are critical of member states (the MERCOSUR countries are members of the World Bank). It also drew strong protests from Brazil, one of the primary targets of the critique. Still, in tacit admission that at least some of Yeats's arguments have merit, a senior MERCOSUR diplomat let it be known that external trade barriers will gradually be reduced, forcing member countries to compete globally. Many external MERCOSUR tariffs, which average 14 percent, are lower than they were before the group's creation, and there are plans for a hemispheric Free Trade Area of the Americas to be established by 2005 (which will combine MERCOSUR, NAFTA, and other American nations). If that occurs, MERCOSUR will have no choice but to reduce its external tariffs further.

MERCOSUR hit a significant roadblock in 1998, when its member states slipped into recession and intra-bloc trade slumped. Trade fell further in 1999 following a financial crisis in Brazil that led to the devaluation of the Brazilian real, which immediately made the goods of other MERCOSUR members 40 percent more expensive in Brazil, their largest export market. At this point, progress toward establishing a customs union all but came to a halt. Things deteriorated further in 2001 when Argentina, beset by economic stresses, suggested that the customs union be "temporarily suspended." Argentina wanted to suspend MERCOSUR's tariff so that it could abolish duties on imports of capital equipment, while raising those on consumer goods to 35 percent (MERCOSUR had established a 14 percent import tariff on both sets of goods). Brazil agreed to this request, effectively putting an end for now to MERCOSUR's quest to become a fully functioning customs union.[33]

Central American Common Market and CARICOM

Two other trade pacts in the Americas have not made much progress yet. In the early 1960s, Costa Rica, El Salvador, Guatemala, Honduras, and Nicaragua attempted to set up a Central American common market. It collapsed in 1969 when war broke out between Honduras and El Salvador after a riot at a soccer match between teams from the two countries. Now the five countries are trying to revive their agreement, although no definite progress has been made.

A customs union was to have been created in 1991 between the English-speaking Caribbean countries under the auspices of the Caribbean Community. Referred to as CARICOM, it was established in 1973. However, it has repeatedly failed to progress toward economic integration. A formal commitment to economic and monetary union was adopted by CARICOM's member states in 1984, but since then little progress has been made. In October 1991, the CARICOM governments failed, for the third consecutive time, to meet a deadline for establishing a common external tariff.

Free Trade Area of the Americas

At a hemispherewide "Summit of the Americas" in December 1994, a Free Trade Area of the Americas (FTAA) was proposed. It took more than three years for talks to be begin, but in April 1998, 34 heads of state traveled to Santiago, Chile, for the second Summit of the Americas where they formally inaugurated talks to establish an FTAA by 2005. The continuing talks will address a wide range of economic, political, and environmental issues related to cross-border trade and investment. Although the United States was an early advocate of an FTAA, support from the United States seems to be mixed at this point. Since the United States has by far the largest economy in the region, strong U.S. support is a precondition for establishment of an FTAA. Canada is chairing the crucial first stage of negotiations and hosted the second Summit of the Americas in early 2001. If an FTAA established, it will have major implications for cross-border trade and investment flows within the hemisphere. The FTAA would open a free trade umbrella over nearly 800 million people who accounted for more than $11 trillion in GDP in 2000. At this point, however, any definitive agreement is still several years away.

Regional Economic Integration Elsewhere ▮

Outside of Western Europe and the Americas, there have been numerous attempts at regional economic integration throughout Asia and Africa. However, few exist in anything other than name. Perhaps the most significant is the Association of Southeast Asian Nations (ASEAN). In addition, the Asia Pacific Economic Cooperation (APEC) forum has recently emerged as the seed of a potential free trade region.

Association of Southeast Asian Nations

Formed in 1967, ASEAN includes Brunei, Indonesia, Laos, Malaysia, Myanmar, Philippines, Singapore, Thailand, and Vietnam. Laos, Myanmar, and Vietnam have all

Map 8.3

Asia Pacific Economic Cooperation

Source: APEC.

joined recently, and their inclusion complicates matters because their economies are a long way behind those of the original members. The basic objectives of ASEAN are to foster freer trade between member countries and to achieve cooperation in their industrial policies. Progress has been very limited, however. For example, only 5 percent of intra-ASEAN trade currently consists of goods whose tariffs have been reduced through an ASEAN preferential trade arrangement. Future progress seems limited because the financial crisis that swept through Southeast Asia in 1997 hit several ASEAN countries particularly hard, most notably Indonesia, Malaysia, and Thailand. Until these countries can get back on their economic feet, it is unlikely that much progress will be made.

Asia Pacific Economic Cooperation

Asia Pacific Economic Cooperation (APEC) was founded in 1990 at the suggestion of Australia. APEC currently has 18 member states including such economic powerhouses as the United States, Japan, and China (see Map 8.3). Collectively the 18 member states account for half of the world's GNP, 40 percent of world trade, and most of the growth in the world economy. The stated aim of APEC is to increase multilateral cooperation in view of the economic rise of the Pacific nations and the growing interdependence within the region. U.S. support for APEC was also based on the belief that it might prove a viable strategy for heading off any moves to create Asian groupings from which it would be excluded.

Interest in APEC was heightened considerably in November 1993 when the heads of APEC member states met for the first time at a two-day conference in Seattle. Debate before the meeting speculated on the likely future role of APEC. One view was that APEC should commit itself to the ultimate formation of a free trade area. Such a move would transform the Pacific Rim from a geographical expression into the world's largest free trade area. Another view was that APEC would produce no more than hot air and lots of photo opportunities for the leaders involved. As it turned out, the APEC meeting produced little more than some vague commitments from member states to work together for greater economic integration and a general lowering of trade barriers. However, significantly, member states did not rule out the possibility of closer economic cooperation in the future.[34]

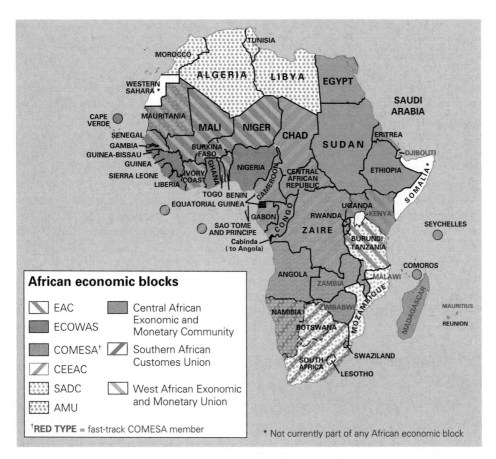

African economic blocks

- EAC
- ECOWAS
- COMESA†
- CEEAC
- SADC
- AMU
- Central African Exonomic and Monetary Community
- Southern African Customes Union
- West African Exonomic and Monetary Union

†**RED TYPE** = fast-track COMESA member

* Not currently part of any African economic block

Map 8.4

Trade Blocs in Africa

Source: *The Economist*, February 10, 2001, p. 77.

The heads of state met again in November 1994 in Jakarta, Indonesia. This time they agreed to take more concrete steps, and the joint statement at the end of the meeting formally committed APEC's industrialized members to remove their trade and investment barriers by 2010 and for developing economies to do so by 2020. They also called for a detailed blueprint charting how this might be achieved. This blueprint was presented and discussed at the next APEC summit, held in Osaka, Japan, in November 1995.[35] This was followed by further annual meetings. At the 1997 meeting, member states formally endorsed proposals designed to remove trade barriers in 15 sectors, ranging from fish to toys. However, the plan is vague and commits APEC to doing no more than holding further talks. Commenting on the vagueness of APEC pronouncements, the influential Brookings Institution, a U.S.-based economic policy institution, noted that APEC "is in grave danger of shrinking into irrelevance as a serious forum." Despite the slow progress, APEC is worth watching. If it eventually does transform itself into a free trade area, it will probably be the world's largest.[36]

Regional Trade Blocs in Africa

African countries have been experimenting with regional trade blocs for half a century. There are now 9 trade blocs on the African continent (see Map 8.4). Many countries are members of more than one group. Although the number of trade groups is impressive, progress toward the establishment of meaningful trade blocs has been slow.

Many of these groups have been dormant for years. Significant political turmoil in several African nations has been a persistent impediment to any meaningful progress. Also, deep suspicion of free trade exists in several African countries. The argument most frequently heard is that since these countries have less developed and less diversified economies, they need to be "protected" by tariff barriers from unfair foreign competition. Given the prevalence of this argument, it has been hard to establish free trade areas or customs unions.

The most recent attempt to reenergize the free trade movement in Africa occurred in early 2001, when Kenya, Uganda, and Tanzania, member states of the East African Community (EAC), committed themselves to relaunching their bloc, 24 years after it collapsed. The three countries, with 80 million inhabitants, intend to establish a customs union, regional court, legislative assembly, and, eventually, a political federation. Their program includes cooperation on immigration, road and telecommunication networks, investment, and capital markets. However, while local business leaders welcomed the relaunch as a positive step, they were critical of the EAC's failure in practice to make progress on free trade. At the EAC treaty's signature in November 1999, members gave themselves four years to negotiate a customs union, with a draft now slated for the end of 2001. But that fell far short of earlier plans for an immediate free trade zone, shelved after Tanzania and Uganda, fearful of Kenyan competition, expressed concerns that the zone could create imbalances similar to those that contributed to the breakup of the first community.[37] It remains to be seen if these countries can have great success this time, but if history is any guide, it will be an uphill road.

Implications for Business

Currently the most significant developments in regional economic integration are occurring in the EU and NAFTA. Although some of the Latin American trade blocs and APEC may have greater economic significance in the future, at present the EU and NAFTA have more profound and immediate implications for business practice. Accordingly, in this section we will concentrate on the business implications of those two groups. Similar conclusions, however, could be drawn with regard to the creation of a single market anywhere in the world.

Opportunities

The creation of a single market offers significant opportunities because markets that were formerly protected from foreign competition are opened. For example, in Europe before 1992 the large French and Italian markets were among the most protected. These markets are now much more open to foreign competition in the form of both exports and direct investment. Nonetheless, the specter of "Fortress Europe" suggests that to fully exploit such opportunities, it will pay non-EU firms to set up EU subsidiaries. Many major U.S. firms have long had subsidiaries in Europe. Those that do not would be advised to consider establishing them now, lest they run the risk of being shut out of the EU by nontariff barriers. In fact, non-EU firms rapidly increased their direct investment in the EU in anticipation of the creation of a single market. Between 1985 and 1989, for example, approximately 37 percent of the FDI inflows into industrialized countries was directed at the EC. By 1991, this figure had risen to 66 percent.[38]

Additional opportunities arise from the inherent lower costs of doing business in a single market—as opposed to 15 national markets in the case of the EU or 3 national markets in the case of NAFTA. Free movement of goods across borders, harmonized product standards, and simplified tax regimes make it possible for firms based in the EU and the NAFTA countries to realize potentially enormous cost economies by centralizing production in those EU and NAFTA locations where the mix of factor costs and skills is optimal. Rather than producing a product in each of the 15 EU countries or the 3 NAFTA countries, a firm may be able to serve the whole EU or North American market from a single location. This location must be chosen carefully, of course, with an eye on local factor costs and skills.

For example, in response to the changes created by EU after 1992, the St. Paul-based 3M Company has been consolidating its European manufacturing and distribution facilities to take advantage of economies of scale. Thus, a plant in Great Britain now produces 3M's printing products and a German factory its reflective traffic control materials for all of the EU. In each case, 3M chose a location for centralized production after carefully considering the likely production costs in alternative locations within the EU. The ultimate goal of 3M is to dispense with all national distinctions, directing R&D, manufacturing, distribution, and marketing for each product group from an EU headquarters.[39] Similarly, Unilever, one of Europe's largest companies, began rationalizing its production in advance of 1992 to attain scale economies. Unilever concentrated its production of dishwashing powder for the EU in one plant, bath soap in another, and so on.[40]

Even after the removal of barriers to trade and investment, enduring differences in culture and competitive practices often limit the ability of companies to realize cost economies by centralizing production in key locations and producing a standardized product for a single multicountry market. Consider the case of Atag Holdings NV, a Dutch maker of kitchen appliances that is profiled in the accompanying Management Focus. Due to enduring differences between nations within the EU's single market, Atag still has to produce various "national brands," which clearly limits the company's ability to attain scale economies.

Threats

Just as the emergence of single markets in the EU and America creates opportunities for business, it also presents a number of threats. For one thing, the business environment within each grouping will become more competitive. The lowering of barriers to trade and investment between countries is likely to lead to increased price competition throughout the EU and NAFTA. For example, before 1992 a Volkswagen Golf cost 55 percent more in Great Britain than in Denmark and 29 percent more in Ireland than in Greece.[41] Such price differentials will vanish in a single market. This is a direct threat to any firm doing business in EU or NAFTA countries. To survive in the tougher single-market environment, firms must take advantage of the opportunities offered by the creation of a single market to rationalize their production and reduce their costs. Otherwise, they will be severely disadvantaged.

A further threat to firms outside these trading blocs arises from the likely long-term improvement in the competitive position of many firms within the areas. This is particularly relevant in the EU, where many firms are currently limited by a high cost structure in their ability to compete globally with North American and Asian firms. The creation of a single market and the resulting increased competition in the EU is beginning to produce serious attempts by many EU firms to reduce their cost structure by rationalizing production. This could transform many EU companies into efficient global competitors. The message for non-EU businesses is that they need to prepare for the emergence of more capable European competitors by reducing their own cost structures.

Another threat to firms outside of trading areas is the threat of being shut out of the single market by the creation of a "trade fortress." The charge that regional economic integration might lead to a fortress mentality is most often leveled at the EU. As noted earlier in the chapter, although the free trade philosophy underpinning the EU theoretically argues against the creation of any fortress in Europe, there are signs that the EU may raise barriers to imports and investment in certain "politically sensitive" areas, such as autos. Non-EU firms

Management Focus

Atag Holdings

Atag Holdings NV is a Dutch company whose main business is kitchen appliances. Atag thought it was well placed to benefit from the single market, but so far it has found it tough going. Atag's plant is just one mile from the German border and near the center of the EU's population. The company thought that it could cater to both the "potato" and "spaghetti" belts—marketers' terms for consumers in Southern and Northern Europe—by producing two main product lines and selling these standardized "euro-products" to "euro-consumers." The main benefit of doing so is the economy of scale derived from mass production of a standardized range of products.

Unfortunately, Atag quickly discovered that the "euro-consumer" is a myth. Consumer preferences vary much more across nations than Atag had thought. Consider ceramic stove tops; Atag planned to market just 2 varieties throughout the EU but has found it needs 11. Belgians, who cook in huge pots, require extra-large burners. Germans like oval pots and burners to fit. The French need small burners and very low temperatures for simmering sauces and broths. Ger-

mans like oven knobs on the top; the French want them on the front. Most Germans and French prefer black and white cookers; the British demand a range of colors including peach, pigeon blue, and mint green.

Despite these problems, foreign sales of Atag's kitchenware increased from 4 percent of total revenues in 1985 to 25 percent a few years after the formation of Europe's single market. But the company now has a much more realistic assessment of the benefits of a single market among a group of countries whose cultures and traditions still differ in deep and often profound ways. Atag now believes its range of designs and product quality, rather than the magic bullet of a "euro-product" designed for a "euro-consumer," will keep the company competitive. At the same time, Atag has to cope with higher costs than would have been the case were it possible to pursue greater product standardization.

Sources: T. Horwitz, "Europe's Borders Fade," *Wall Street Journal*, May 18, 1993, pp. A1, A12; "A Singular Market," *The Economist*, October 22, 1994, pp. 10–16; and "Something Dodgy in Europe's Single Market," *The Economist*, May 21, 1994, pp. 69–70.

might be well advised, therefore, to set up their own EU operations as quickly as possible. This could also occur in the NAFTA countries, but it seems less likely.

Finally, the emerging role of the European Commission in competition policy suggests the EU is increasingly willing and able to intervene and impose conditions on companies proposing mergers and acquisitions. This is a threat insofar as it limits the ability of firms to pursue the corporate strategy of their choice. As we saw in the Management Focus on the media industry mergers, the commission may require significant concessions from businesses as a precondition for allowing proposed mergers and acquisitions to proceed. While this constrains the strategic options for firms, it should be remembered that in taking such action, the commission is trying to maintain the level of competition in Europe's single market, which should benefit consumers.

Chapter Summary

This chapter pursued three main objectives: to examine the economic and political debate surrounding regional economic integration; to review the progress toward regional economic integration in Europe, the Americas, and elsewhere; and to distinguish the important implications of regional economic integration for the practice of international business. This chapter made the following points:

1. A number of levels of economic integration are possible in theory. In order of increasing inte-

gration, they include a free trade area, a customs union, a common market, an economic union, and full political union.

2. In a free trade area, barriers to trade between member countries are removed, but each country determines its own external trade policy. In a customs union, internal barriers to trade are removed and a common external trade policy is adopted. A common market is similar to a customs union, ex-

cept that a common market also allows factors of production to move freely between countries. An economic union involves even closer integration, including the establishment of a common currency and the harmonization of tax rates. A political union is the logical culmination of attempts to achieve ever-closer economic integration.

3. Regional economic integration is an attempt to achieve economic gains from the free flow of trade and investment between neighboring countries.

4. Integration is not easily achieved or sustained. Although integration brings benefits to the majority, it is never without costs for the minority. Concerns over national sovereignty often slow or stop integration attempts.

5. Regional integration will not increase economic welfare if the trade creation effects in the free trade area are outweighed by the trade diversion effects.

6. The Single European Act sought to create a true single market by abolishing administrative barriers to the free flow of trade and investment between EU countries.

7. The Maastricht Treaty aims to take the EU even further along the road to economic union by establishing a common currency. The economic gains from a common currency come from reduced exchange costs, reduced risk associated with currency fluctuations, and increased price competition within the EU.

8. Increasingly, the European Commission is taking an activist stance with regard to competition policy, intervening to restrict mergers and acquisitions that it believes will reduce competition in the EU.

9. Although no other attempt at regional economic integration comes close to the EU in terms of potential economic and political significance, various other attempts are being made in the world. The most notable include NAFTA in North America, the Andean Pact and MERCOSUR in Latin America, ASEAN in Southeast Asia, and perhaps APEC.

10. The creation of single markets in the EU and North America means that many markets that were formerly protected from foreign competition are now more open. This creates major investment and export opportunities for firms within and outside these regions.

11. The free movement of goods across borders, the harmonization of product standards, and the simplification of tax regimes make it possible for firms based in a free trade area to realize potentially enormous cost economies by centralizing production in those locations within the area where the mix of factor costs and skills is optimal.

12. The lowering of barriers to trade and investment between countries within a trade group will probably be followed by increased price competition.

Critical Discussion Questions

1. NAFTA is likely to produce net benefits for the Canadian, Mexican, and U.S. economies. Discuss.

2. What are the economic and political arguments for regional economic integration? Given these arguments, why don't we see more integration in the world economy?

3. What effect is creation of a single market and a single currency within the EU likely to have on competition within the EU? Why?

4. Do you think it is correct for the European Commission to restrict mergers between American companies that do business in Europe? (For example, the European Commission vetoed the proposed merger between WorldCom and Sprint, both U.S. companies, and it carefully reviewed the merger between AOL and Time Warner, again both U.S. companies.)

5. How should a U.S. firm that currently exports only to Western Europe respond to the creation of a single market?

6. How should a firm with self-sufficient production facilities in several EU countries respond to the creation of a single market? What are the constraints on its ability to respond in a manner that minimizes production costs?

7. After a promising start, in the last few years MERCOSUR, the major Latin American trade agreement, has faltered and by 2001 seemed to be in trouble. What problems are hurting MERCOSUR? What can be done to solve these problems?

8. Would establishment of a Free Trade Area of the Americas (FTAA) in 2005 be good for the two most advanced economies in the hemisphere, the United States and Canada? How might the establishment of the FTAA impact the strategy of North American firms?

Deutsche Bank's pan-European Retail Banking Strategy

In March 2000, Deutsche Bank, Germany's largest bank, announced it would merge with Dresdner Bank, Germany's third largest bank. The stated strategic goal of the merger was to create a European investment and asset management institution that would have the economies of scale required to compete with the top global investment banks, including Citicorp and Merrill Lynch. An important component of the proposed merger was a plan by Deutsche Bank and Dresdner to combine their retail bank operations into Deutsche Bank's retail banking division, Bank 24, and then spin off Bank 24 as an independent entity in which the merged company would have no more than a 10 percent ownership stake. At the time, Bank 24 had some 11 million customers, the majority in Germany but 1.5 million in Italy and another 600,000 in Spain. In addition to its 2,000 retail branches, Bank 24 had also been a pioneer in using the Internet to sell banking services, and by 2000 some 20 percent of all transactions were online. The plan to spin off Bank 24 indicated the two banks had decided to withdraw from retail banking, instead concentrating on the wholesale side of the business (investment banking and money management). Most analysts applauded the proposed deal, noting that retail banking in Germany was a low-margin business that held few attractions, while investment banking was a high-margin business.

By April 2000, however, the proposed deal had collapsed following significant disagreements between management teams at the two companies. Initially, few thought that this would lead to a change in strategy at Deutsche Bank, but six months later the bank announced it had rethought its retail strategy. Suddenly, Bank 24 was at the heart of a new strategy by Deutsche Bank to build a pan-European retail channel. The change of strategy stemmed from a growing realization that Deutsche Bank's branch and online banking platform provided a powerful sales channel to a rapidly growing "money class"—Europe's highly educated and prosperous 30- and 40-year-olds. Deutsche Bank estimated there are more than 60 million people in this demographic with the European Union. Increasingly, this group is switching their savings from deposit accounts into equities and investment funds as they begin to plan for their retirement. Deutsche Bank realized it could use its retail branch network to sell the investment products churned out by its investment banking and asset management operations. Deutsche Bank also realized that with the advent of the euro, the impedi-

ments to the cross-border sale of money management products had been significantly reduced, at least within the euro zone.

To implement the strategy, Deutsche Bank plans to weld Bank 24's operations, which are scattered across seven European countries, into a coherent whole. The model in each country will be the same. The basic idea will be to offer a full range of financial services via branch offices, telephones, and increasingly the Internet. But in an effort to curb costs, the emphasis is likely to be the Internet. Thus, the company wants to grow its retail customer base to 14 million by 2004, while keeping the number of branches constant at 2,000 and reducing total employment by about 10 percent. The geographical distribution of branches will change, however, with some branches in Germany being consolidated or closed, while retail branches are opened in other European countries. The initial plans call for further expansion in Italy, Spain, France, and Belgium, where Bank 24 already has a presence. The company, however, also states that if the concept works, it will move into the Netherlands and the United Kingdom, as well as some non-EU countries, such as Poland and the Czech Republic (both of which have applied to enter the EU). Deutsche Bank also indicated that Bank 24 might make selected acquisitions to establish a larger retail presence in other EU nations.

Another element of the strategy calls for Deutsche Bank to expand the reach of its online brokerage unit, Maxblue, into a pan-European discount broker. Bank 24 will be used to market Maxblue. In late 2000, Maxblue had some 300,000 client accounts, the majority in Germany. The plan calls for this number to grow to 1.5 million by 2004, many of whom would be outside of Germany. If attained, this would give Deutsche Bank a 30 percent share of the online market that is expected to exist by 2004.

Implementing this strategy will require heavy investments, particularly in information technology. Before the change in strategy, Deutsche Bank had budgeted some $110 million for building up Bank 24, including redesigning branches abroad, unifying information technology, and marketing the new look. Now estimates suggest it will take some $250 million of marketing expenditure just to achieve brand recognition across Europe, and significant additional investments will be required in information technology. Despite this investment, Deutsche Bank claims the shift in strategy will boost Bank 24's profits from euro 400 million in 2000 to euro 1 billion by 2004.

Sources: "German Banking," *The Economist*, April 8, 2000; M. Walker, "Deutsche Bank Plans to Make Its Retail Unit a Stock

Outlet," *Wall Street Journal*, October 23, 2000, p. A25; and T. Major, "DB24 Reprived to Target Europe's Forty Somethings," *Financial Times*, November 17, 2000, p. 33.

Case Discussion Questions

1. What are the main elements of Deutsche Bank's strategy for Bank 24? Does this strategy hold appeal given (a) the creation of a single market in the European Union and (b) the introduction of the euro?

2. What potential impediments do you think might get in the way of Deutsche Bank's aspirations to establish a pan-European retail presence and a pan-European discount brokerage?

3. How easy do you think it might be for other European banks to adopt a similar strategy and for American banks to enter Europe and go after the same "money class"? Given this, how competitive do you think this market is likely to be?

4. Deutsche Bank estimates it can more than double the profits of Bank 24 by 2004, while holding the number of branches roughly constant and increasing its customer base from 11 million to 14 million. How realistic do you think this profit goal is given your answers to questions 2 and 3 and the investments apparently required to implement the strategy?

Notes

1. World Trade Organization.

2. The Andean Pact has been through a number of changes since its inception. The latest version was established in 1991. See "Free-Trade Free for All," *The Economist*, January 4, 1991, p. 63.

3. D. Swann, *The Economics of the Common Market*, 6th ed. (London: Penguin Books, 1990).

4. See J. Bhagwati, "Regionalism and Multilateralism: An Overview," Columbia University discussion paper 603, Department of Economics, Columbia University, New York; A. de la Torre and M. Kelly, "Regional Trade Arrangements," occasional paper 93, Washington, DC: International Monetary Fund, March 1992; and J. Bhagwati, "Fast Track to Nowhere," *The Economist*, October 18, 1997, pp. 21–24.

5. N. Colchester and D. Buchan, *Europower: The Essential Guide to Europe's Economic Transformation in 1992* (London: The Economist Books, 1990); and Swann, *Economics of the Common Market*.

6. Swann, *Economics of the Common Market*; Colchester and Buchan, *Europower: The Essential Guide to Europe's Economic Transformation in 1992*; "The European Union: A Survey," *The Economist*, October 22, 1994; and "The European Community: A Survey," *The Economist*, July 3, 1993.

7. B. Roughton and M. Geewax, "European Union Regulators Gaining Influence over U.S. Mergers," *Atlanta Journal-Constitution*, October 8, 2000, p. Q1.

8. "The European Community: A Survey."

9. Colchester and Buchan, *Europower*.

10. "One Europe, One Economy," *The Economist*, November 30, 1991, pp. 53–54, and "Market Failure: A Survey of Business in Europe," *The Economist*, June 8, 1991, pp. 6–10.

11. See C. Wyploze, "EMU: Why and How It Might Happen," *Journal of Economic Perspectives* 11 (1997), pp. 3–22, and M. Feldstein, "The Political Economy of the European Economic and Monetary Union," *Journal of Economic Perspectives* 11 (1997), pp. 23–42.

12. "One Europe, One Economy," and Feldstein, "The Political Economy of the European Economic and Monetary Union."

13. Feldstein, "The Political Economy of the European Economic and Monetary Union."

14. "The Confused Muddle," *The Economist*, December 11, 1999, pp. 44–45, and "Currency Crossroads," *The Economist*, December 4, 1999, pp. 17–18.

15. International Monetary Funds, *World Economic Outlook*, October 2000.

16. "The Darling Dollar," *The Economist*, April 7, 2001.

17. "From the Arctic to the Mediterranean," *The Economist*, March 5, 1994, pp. 52, 57; L. Barber, "More Does Not Mean Merrier," *Financial Times*, March 14, 1994, p. 13; and L. Barber, "Hopes of Wider Union Turn to Fear of No Union," *Financial Times*, December 9, 1994, p. 2.

18. J. Perles, "Europe Invites 5 Ex-Communist Nations to Join," *New York Times*, July 17, 1997, p. A6.

19. "What Are They Building? Survey of Europe's Internal Market," *The Economist*, July 8, 1989, pp. 5–7, and Colchester and Buchan, *Europower*.

20. World Trade Organization, *Regionalism and the World Trading System* (Geneva: World Trade Organization, 1995).

21. "What Is NAFTA?" *Financial Times*, November 17, 1993, p. 6, and S. Garland, "Sweet Victory," *Business Week*, November 29, 1993, pp. 30–31.

22. "NAFTA: The Showdown," *The Economist*, November 13, 1993, pp. 23–36.

23. "Happy Ever NAFTA?" *The Economist*, December 10, 1994, pp. 23–24, and D. Harbrecht, "What Has NAFTA Wrought? Plenty of Trade?" *Business Week*, November 21, 1994, pp. 48–49.

24. P. B. Carroll and C. Torres, "Mexico Unveils Program of Harsh Fiscal Medicine," *Wall Street Journal*, March 3, 1995, pp. A1, A6.

25. N. C. Lustog, "NAFTA: Setting the Record Straight," *The World Economy*, 1997, pp. 605–14.

26. R. H. Ojeda, C. Dowds, R. McCleery, S. Robinson, D. Runsten, C. Wolff, and G. Wolff, "NAFTA—How Has It Done? North American Integration Three Years after NAFTA," North American Integration and Development Center at UCLA, December 1996.

27. "NAFTA Is Not Alone," *The Economist*, June 18, 1994, pp. 47–48; B. Sweeney, "First Latin American Customs Union Looms over Venezuela," *Journal of Commerce*, September 26, 1991, p. 5A; and "The Business of the American Hemisphere," *The Economist*, August 24, 1991, pp. 37–38.

28. The comment was made by the Colombian ambassador. See K. G. Hall, "Andean Pact Nations to Work Together at Talks," *Journal of Commerce*, April 8, 1998, p. 2A.

29. "Business of the American Hemisphere."

30. "NAFTA Is Not Alone."

31. "Murky MERCOSUR," *The Economist*, July 26, 1997, pp. 66–67.

32. See M. Philips, "South American Trade Pact Under Fire," *Wall Street Journal*, October 23, 1996, p. A2; A. J. Yeats, *Does MERCOSUR's Trade Performance Justify Concerns about the Global Welfare-Reducing Effects of Free Trade Arrangements? Yes!* (Washington, DC: World Bank, 1996); and D. M. Leipziger et al., "MERCOSUR: Integration and Industrial Policy," *The World Economy*, 1997, pp. 585–604.

33. "Another Blow to MERCOSUR," *The Economist*, March 31, 2001, pp. 33–34.

34. "Aimless in Seattle," *The Economist*, November 13, 1993, pp. 35–36.

35. G. de Jonquieres, "Different Aims, Common Cause," *Financial Times*, November 18, 1995, p. 14.

36. G. de Jonquieres, "APEC Grapples with Market Turmoil," *Financial Times*, November 21, 1997, p. 6; and G. Baker, "Clinton Team Wins Most of the APEC Tricks," *Financial Times*, November 27, 1997, p. 5.

37. M. Turner, "Trio Revives East African Union," *Financial Times*, January 16, 2001, p. 4.

38. "World Economic Survey," *The Economist*, September 19, 1992, p. 17.

39. P. Davis, "A European Campaign: Local Companies Rush for a Share of EC Market While Barriers Are Down," *Minneapolis-St. Paul City Business*, January 8, 1990, p. 1.

40. "The Business of Europe," *The Economist*, December 7, 1991, pp. 63–64.

41. E. G. Friberg, "1992: Moves Europeans Are Making," *Harvard Business Review*, May–June 1989, pp. 85–89.

Cases

Protecting U.S. Steel

Introduction

"Open trade is not just an economic opportunity, it is a moral imperative."[1] So said President George W. Bush on May 7, 2001, in a speech before the Council of the Americas. Both before his election and since taking office, Bush has repeatedly voiced strong support for free trade, often in stirring terms. It was surprising to many, therefore, when on June 5, 2001, the same President Bush stated he would ask the U.S. trade representative in his cabinet, Bob Zoellick, to invoke Section 201 of the 1974 Trade Act to determine whether the steel industry had been "seriously injured" or "threatened by serious injury" from imports.

Section 201 cases are investigated by the U.S. International Trade Commission (ITC), which must deliver its report and recommendation within six months. The president then has 60 days to determine the remedies, if any, against foreign importers. If the ITC does find damage, among other remedies President Bush can impose import quotas or prohibitively high tariffs on foreign steel imports.

The Steel Industry

Steel is the most basic and widely used metal in industry. The U.S. steel products industry generates $50 billion annually, employs some 150,000 workers, and produces around 100 million tons of steel per year.[2] Once by far the world's largest producer, the U.S. steel industry is now just another player in a global industry, accounting for about 12 percent of worldwide steel production. Other major producing nations include China, Japan,

Russia, Germany, South Korea, Ukraine, and Brazil. The largest U.S. producer, USX Corporation, ranked 14th in the world in 1999 in terms of production with 10.7 million metric tons of output. Nucor, the next largest U.S. firm in 1999, produced 10 million metric tons and ranked 16th. In contrast, Nippon Steel of Japan produced 28.4 million metric tons, making it the world's largest producer. POSCO of South Korea, the world's second largest steel firm, produced 27.7 million metric tons. Thyssen Krupp of Germany produced 17.7 million tons, as did Shanghai Baosteel of China.

In 1999, some 40 percent of all steel produced was traded internationally, up from 26 percent in 1990. Exports and imports of steel for 1999 are given in Table 1. As can be seen, the United States was the world's largest importer in 1999.

The most basic fact about the global steel industry for the last 30 years has been persistent excess capacity. Supply has often exceeded demand by 20 percent, and during the late 1990s this figure rose to 30 percent. Persistent global excess capacity in the steel industry has caused downward pressure on prices and resulted in ongoing losses for many of the world's steel companies. By 2001, prices were at their lowest levels in 20 years. In America, no fewer than 18 steel firms filed for bankruptcy protection from 1997 to 2001, and some 23,500 steelworkers lost their jobs.[3]

Steel firms worldwide have responded to the combination of excess capacity and pricing pressures by trying to reduce their operating costs so they can maintain profitability in a harsh environment. To a large extent they have successfully reduced costs, but the losses have continued. Between 1990 and 2000, crude steel output per

[1]Brink Lindsey, "Steel Trap," *National Review*, July 9, 2001, p. 22.
[2]All statistics from the International Iron and Steel Institute. Go to http://www.worldsteel.org/.

[3]"A Tricky Business," *The Economist*, June 30, 2001, pp. 55–56.

	Country	Exports		Country	Imports
1	Russia	27.3	1	United States	32.7
2	Japan	26.1	2	Germany	17.7
3	Germany	20.9	3	China	17.0
4	Belgium-Luxembourg	20.7	4	Italy	15.9
5	Ukraine	19.0	5	France	15.3
6	France	16.2	6	Taiwan	13.1

Table 1

Exports and Imports of Steel, 1999 (millions of metric tons)

worker increased from under 400 tons to 600 tons in the European Union, Japan, and the United States, indicating significant productivity gains.[4] However, little capacity was removed from the market. Global demand remained flat during the 1990s at around 780 million metric tons a year, despite a 30 percent expansion in world GDP, while capacity remained at around 1,150 million metric tons. Hence, the excess capacity persisted. The combination of a 50 percent increase in worker productivity with zero demand growth meant that something had to give. But it was not capacity, it was employment. Between 1990 and 2000 employment in the global steel industry fell from 1.388 million to 0.84 million.

Causes of Global Excess Capacity

There are several explanations for why capacity has remained so high in the global steel industry, despite poor demand fundamentals. One is that while capacity has been reduced in high-cost locations, such as the United States and Western Europe, new steelmakers have entered the global market, keeping the overall level of capacity constant. South Korea, Brazil, and now Eastern Europe have added capacity to the global marketplace, making up for reductions elsewhere. In several of these countries, steel has been viewed as a "strategic industry" that is vital for national security and supported by the state with subsidies.

Another source of additional capacity has been the expansion of steel mini-mills. In contrast to traditional steelmakers, which employ basic oxygen furnaces to produce steel, mini-mills use electric arc furnaces to smelt and process scrap steel. Only commercialized in the 1960s, electric arc technology has increased significantly in its efficiency over the past three decades, allowing firms employing this technology to grow capacity, and make profits, even while more traditional producers have struggled to stay afloat. One of the most successful of the mini-mill producers, Nucor Corporation, did not enter the industry until 1968. Since then it has built eight steel mills, bringing 12.9 million metric tons of new capacity onto the market, and added some 6,000 employees.[5] By 2001, Nucor was the largest steel producer in the United States and one of the top 10 producers in the world. Starting from nothing in the late 1960s, steel mini-mills had gained a 40 percent share of the U.S. steel market in 2000, all produced from capacity that had been added over the past three decades.[6] In

contrast to most traditional steelmakers, Nucor and other mini-mill companies have been profitable for most of their operating history. Even in 2000, a dreadful year for the U.S. steel industry, Nucor remained profitable, earning $213 million in after-tax profits on sales of $4.9 billion. In contrast, USX, the largest traditional steelmaker in the United States, lost $147 million on sales of $6.4 billion in 2000.

Another important reason for persistent excess capacity is government interventions have distorted the market process, making the shedding of excess capacity a painfully slow affair. In Europe, for example, governments responded to problems in the steel industry by privatizing troubled state-owned steel companies, mostly in the early 1990s. Many of these companies, which had been bankrolled by taxpayers for decades, were given clean balance sheets to make them financially viable. Governments wrote off billions of dollars in accumulated debt, constituting a massive hidden subsidy to formerly state-owned steelmakers. Even with such hidden subsidies, however, these companies have struggled to break even. Many are now losing money, but as long as they are covering their variable production costs and making some contribution toward their fixed costs, it pays them to stay in business in the hope that demand will improve.

America has not been an innocent bystander in this process either. The U.S. steel industry has a powerful political lobbying group. The Congressional Steel Caucus has more than 100 members in the House of Representatives and 33 in the Senate. It has been and remains a strong advocate of steel industry and steel union interests. Many in this caucus advocate protection for battered American steelmakers from foreign competitors who are accused of dumping steel on the U.S. market at below the prices that prevail in their home markets or, worse still, below their costs of production.[7]

The American steel industry has proven itself adept at using trade legislation, and particularly Section 201, to gain relief from foreign competitors. Although steel accounts for only 2 percent of U.S. imports, some 46 percent of antidumping quotas and tariffs imposed by the International Trade Commission and in force in 2001 are on steel products.[8] About one-third of all antidumping cases launched in the United States between 1980 and 1995 were steel cases. Steel imports from nearly every country are now subject to one or more antidumping or countervailing duty actions. These actions cover 44 percent of finished steel imports from countries outside of the North American Free Trade Agreement and 11 percent of finished steel imports from Canada and Mexico.[9]

[4]G. C. Hufbauer and B. Goodrich, "Steel: Big Problems, Better Solutions," Institute for International Economics, Policy Brief, Number 01-9, July 2001.
[5]Nucor Corporation, *Annual 10K Report*, 2001.
[6]"A Tricky Business."

[7]B. Lindsey, "Steel Trap," *National Review*, July 9, 2001, pp. 22–24.
[8]"A Tricky Business."
[9]Hufbauer and Goodrich, "Steel: Big Problems, Better Solutions."

Is More Protectionism the Answer?

Given the history of persistent excess capacity in the global steel industry, and given the failure of a long history of antidumping and tariff measures to protect America's ailing traditional steelmakers from foreign competition, should the government adopt additional measures designed to further protect the steel industry? This is the question that the ITC and President Bush must grapple with.

Many argue that the American industry is facing unfair competition from foreign producers, many of which are subsidized by their respective governments and are dumping steel in the United States at below-market prices. They argue that protectionism is necessary to protect not only American jobs but also an industry that is vital to national security. To quote one representative of this perspective, Roger Phillips, the chairman and CEO of U.S. steelmaker Ipsco Steel, Inc:

> People who claim that we should shut down American capacity are really arguing that we should allow foreigners a greater share of our market—foreign countries that as a national policy deliberately run their own steelmaking industries at levels in excess of their needs. If we were to shut down capacity every time there was a global surplus, we would soon have no domestic capacity at all. Absent any conclusive economic reason, the need to secure supply of such an important raw material would dictate that we maintain domestic capacity roughly in line with our needs. Rather than possessing too much steelmaking capacity, this reasoning suggests we need more![10]

But others argue that the trade barriers are counterproductive. Free traders argue that the United States should not complain when other countries export their steel at bargain prices, whatever the reason—dumping, subsidization, or just plain low costs. Instead, the country should recognize such imports for what they are—a bargain that frees dollars for investment and consumption elsewhere in the economy. If foreign governments want to subsidize the living standards of American consumers by supplying steel at below the costs of production, so be it! Besides, they argue, there is little evidence that import barriers get foreign governments to correct their own market distortions.

Free traders also argue that import barriers on steel may cause more job losses in U.S. industries that consume steel—such as automobiles, heavy equipment, and machinery—than the number of jobs saved in steel mills. An increase in steel prices that would follow the imposition of trade barriers would ultimately be passed on to consumers in the form of a multitude of small markups for cars, washing machines, buildings, and so on. Thus, while steel producers would undoubtedly benefit from import barriers, American consumers would lose. Also, by protecting U.S. steelmakers from market forces, protectionism would reduce their incentive to invest in technologies that improve the productivity of steelmaking.[11]

Other voices argue that solving the problem of dumping in the steel industry is best done through multinational trade agreements and negotiations, not unilateral national measures. History has shown that unilateral measures rarely work as intended and are often counterproductive. The imposition of trade barriers can invite retaliation and escalate into a trade war in which all parties lose. Supporters of multilateral measures argue the World Trade Organization exists to police global trade. Expanding the scope of the WTO so that its dispute resolution procedures can better deal with distortions in trade arising from government subsidies and dumping would be the way to go, they say, not protectionism.

Case Discussion Questions

1. What are the reasons for persistent excess capacity in the global steel industry? What would it take for this capacity to be eradicated?

2. Do you think the steel industry is vital to the national security interests of the United States? If so, is it important to protect this industry from low-cost foreign producers?

3. Do you think it's correct to assert, as advocates of free trade do, that protectionism is self-defeating and harms consumers?

4. What do you think would happen to American steelmakers if the U.S. government decided to unilaterally remove all barriers to foreign steel imports? Would the U.S. steel industry become extinct?

5. What do you think President Bush should do in this case? Why?

---

[10]Roger Phillips, "The Value of 201," *Iron Age New Steel*, August 2001, pp. 36–38.

[11]Hufbauer and Goodrich, "Steel: Big Problems, Better Solutions."

Boeing versus Airbus: Trade Disputes

Introduction

For years the commercial aircraft industry has been an American success story. Until 1980, U.S. manufacturers held a virtual monopoly. Despite the rise of the European-based Airbus Industrie, this persisted through the mid-1990s, when two U.S. firms, Boeing and McDonnell Douglas, accounted for over two-thirds of world market share. In late 1996, many analysts thought that U.S. dominance in this industry would be further strengthened when Boeing announced a decision to acquire McDonnell Douglas for $13.3 billion, creating an aerospace behemoth nearly twice the size of its nearest competitor.

The industry is routinely the largest net contributor to the U.S. balance of trade, and Boeing is the largest U.S. exporter. In the 1990s, the U.S. commercial aircraft industry regularly ran a substantial positive trade balance with the rest of the world of $12 billion to $15 billion per year. The impact of the industry on U.S. employment is also enormous. In 2000, Boeing directly employed over 120,000 people in the Seattle area and another 100,000 elsewhere in the nation. The company also indirectly supported a further 600,000 jobs nationwide in related industries (e.g., subcontractors) and through the impact of Boeing wages on the general level of economic activity.

Despite Boeing's formidable reach, since the mid-1980s U.S. dominance in the commercial aerospace industry has been threatened by the rise of Airbus Industrie. Airbus is a consortium of four European aircraft manufacturers: one British (20.0 percent ownership stake), one French (37.9 percent ownership), one German (37.9 percent ownership), and one Spanish (4.2 percent ownership). Founded in 1970, Airbus was initially a marginal competitor and was regarded as unlikely to challenge U.S. dominance. Since 1981, however, Airbus has confounded its critics and emerged as the world's second largest aircraft manufacturer. By the early 1990s, Airbus's share of aircraft orders in any one year stood between 20 percent and 30 percent, up from 14 percent in 1981. In 1994, Airbus captured more orders than Boeing for the first time in history (Airbus garnered 122 orders against Boeing's 121). However, most analysts point out that this was an aberration, given the extremely low level of aircraft orders in that year. In 1995, Boeing captured over 70 percent of all new aircraft orders, leaving Airbus with less than a 25 percent share. Nevertheless, Airbus set its sights on gaining a 50 percent share of all new orders for commercial jet aircraft of more than 100 seats by 2000. In 1998, Airbus moved closer to attaining this goal when it snagged 46 percent of the record 1,212 large commercial jet aircraft ordered that year, leaving Boeing with 54 per-

cent of the market. Since then, Airbus and Boeing have roughly split the market for new aircraft orders.

Over the years, many in the United States have responded to the success of Airbus by crying foul. It has been repeatedly claimed that Airbus is heavily subsidized by the governments of Great Britain, France, Germany, and Spain. Airbus has responded by pointing out that both Boeing and McDonnell Douglas have benefited for years from hidden U.S. government subsidies. In 1992, the two sides appeared to reach an agreement that put to rest their long-standing trade dispute. However, the dispute has surfaced twice since then. First in 1997, when the European Union decided to challenge the merger between Boeing and McDonnell Douglas on the grounds that it limited competition. Then again in 2000, when Airbus announced it would build a super-jumbo jet to compete with Boeing's lucrative monopoly in the jumbo jet market. Boeing stated it would be watching the development closely to make sure that European governments did not exceed the ceilings of launch aid subsidies agreed to in 1992. In this case, we examine the debate between the two sides in this on-again, off-again trade dispute. First, however, let us look at the competitive structure of the commercial aircraft industry.

Industry Competitive Dynamics

Competitive dynamics in the commercial aircraft industry are driven by a number of key factors. Perhaps foremost among these is that the costs of developing a new airliner are enormous. Boeing spent a reported $5 billion developing and tooling up to produce the 777 wide-bodied jetliner that it introduced in 1994. The development costs for Airbus's new aircraft, the 555-seat A380 "super-jumbo," are estimated to be anywhere between $10 billion and $15 billion. (The A380 is Airbus's direct competitor to Boeing's profitable 747 model line.)

Given such enormous development costs, a company must capture a significant share of world demand to break even. In the case of the 777, for example, Boeing needed to sell more than 200 aircraft to break even, a figure that represented about 15 percent of predicted industry sales for this class of aircraft between 1994 and 2004. Given the volume of sales required to break even, it can take up to 10 to 14 years of production for an aircraft model to turn a profit, and this is on top of the 5 to 6 years of negative cash flows during development.

On the manufacturing side, a significant experience curve exists in aircraft production. Due to learning effects, on average, unit cost falls by about 20 percent with each doubling of accumulated output. A company that fails to move along the experience curve faces a significant unit-cost disadvantage. A company that achieves only half of the market share required to break even will suffer a 20 percent unit-cost disadvantage.

Another feature of the industry is that demand for aircraft is highly volatile. This makes long-run planning difficult and raises the risks involved in producing aircraft. The commercial airline business is prone to boom-and-bust cycles. During the early 1990s, many major airlines experienced financial trouble. Pan Am, Eastern, Braniff, and TWA were all either in Chapter 11 bankruptcy protection or had recently folded. Many other airlines were losing money. In response, airlines slowed their ordering of new aircraft, pushed back delivery dates for aircraft already on firm order, and decided not to convert their options on future aircraft deliveries to firm orders. Thus, although both Boeing and Airbus both entered the 1990s with record orders, the troubles in the airline business spread to them. The low point was reached in 1994 when 260 large (100-seat plus) commercial jet aircraft were ordered worldwide. A significant recovery occurred in 1995, with close to 500 aircraft orders. The growth in demand continued during the next three years. In 1998, 1,212 large commercial jet aircraft were ordered, a record. However, orders have trended down since then, reflecting a slowdown in the global economy, and the entire industry may book less than 600 orders in 2001.

The combination of high development costs, break-even levels that constitute a significant percentage of world demand, substantial experience curve levels, and volatile demand makes for an industry that can support only a few major players. Analysts seem to agree that the large jet commercial aircraft market can profitably support only two, or possibly three, major producers. By 1998, there were only two major players in the industry, McDonnell Douglas having been absorbed by Boeing. This, combined with the strong production and order levels reached that year, should have boded well for productivity. However, Boeing's profits were poor during 1997 and 1998 as it struggled to cope with a poorly managed ramp-up of its aircraft production rates, the effects of unexpectedly high manufacturing costs, and intense price competition from an increasingly aggressive Airbus.

Trade Frictions before 1992

In the 1980s and early 1990s, both Boeing and McDonnell Douglas argued that Airbus had an unfair competitive advantage due to the level of subsidy it received from the governments of Great Britain, France, Germany, and Spain. They argued that the subsidies allow Airbus to set unrealistically low prices, to offer concessions and attractive financing terms to airlines, to write off development costs, and to use state-owned airlines to obtain orders. In making these claims, Boeing and McDonnell Douglas had the support of the U.S. government. According to a study by the Department of Commerce, Airbus received more than $13.5 billion in government subsidies between 1970 and 1990 ($25.9 billion if commercial interest rates are applied). Most of these subsidies were in the form of loans at below-market interest rates and tax breaks. The subsidies financed research and development and provided attractive financing terms for Airbus's customers. For most of its customers, Airbus is believed to have financed 80 percent of the cost of aircraft for a term of 8 to 10 years at an annual interest rate of approximately 7 percent. In contrast, the U.S. Export-Import Bank required 20 percent down payments from Boeing and McDonnell Douglas customers, financed only 40 percent of the cost of an aircraft directly, and guaranteed the financing of the remaining 40 percent by private banks at an average interest rate of 8.4 percent to 8.5 percent for a period of 10 years.

Airbus's response to these charges was to point out that its success is not due to subsidies but to a good product and a good strategy. Most observers agree that Airbus's aircraft incorporate state-of-the-art technology, particularly in materials applications, systems for flight control and safety, and aerodynamics. Airbus gained ground initially by targeting market segments not served by new aircraft or not served at all. Thus, Airbus has taken the initiative in targeting two segments of the market with wide-bodied twin-engine aircraft, then in developing a new generation of aircraft for the 150-seat market, and going after the market below the 747 for a 250- to 300-seat airliner with its A330 and A340 models (to which Boeing's 777 is a belated but apparently successful competitive response).

Airbus also argued that both Boeing and McDonnell Douglas have benefited from U.S. government aid for a long time and that the aid it has received has merely leveled the playing field. In the United States, planes were built under government contract during World War I, and the construction of mail planes was subsidized between the world wars. Almost all production was subsidized during World War II, and subsidies continued at a high level after the war. The Boeing 707, for example, is a derivative of a military transport program that was subsidized by the U.S. government. Boeing's subsidized programs include the B-17, B-29, B-47, B-52, and K-135, just to name a few. Its nonairline programs have included the Minuteman missile, Apollo-Saturn, and space station programs.

A 1991 European Commission study attempted to estimate the amount of subsidies received by the U.S. industry. The study contended that Boeing and McDonnell Douglas received $18 billion to $22 billion in indirect government aid between 1976 and 1990. The report claimed that commercial aircraft operations benefited through Defense Department contracts by as much as $6.34 billion during the 1976–90 period. In addition, the report claimed that NASA pumped at least $8 billion into commercial aircraft production over the same period, and that tax exemptions have given an additional $1.7 billion to Boeing and $1.4 billion to McDonnell Douglas.

Boeing rejected the claims of the European Commission report. The company pointed out that the report's assumption that Boeing receives direct government grants in the form of an additional 5 percent for commercial work with every military or space contract it receives was false. The company also argued that during the 1980s only 3 percent of Boeing's R&D spending came from Department of Defense funding and only 4 percent from NASA funding. Boeing also argued that since the four companies in the Airbus consortium do twice as much military and space work as Boeing, they must receive much larger indirect subsidies.

The 1992 Agreement and Its Aftermath

In mid-1992, the United States and the four European governments involved agreed to a pact that seemed likely to end the long-standing dispute. The 1992 pact, which was negotiated by the European Union on behalf of the four member states, limited direct European government subsidies to each Airbus partner to 33 percent of new development costs and specified that future subsidies must be repaid with interest. The agreement also limited indirect subsidies, such as military research that has applications to commercial aircraft, to 5 percent of development costs for commercial aircraft. Although Airbus officials say the controversy has been resolved, Boeing officials say they will be competing for years against subsidized products.

In February 1993, it looked as if the trade dispute was about to reemerge. Newly elected President Clinton repeatedly blasted the European Union for allowing subsidies of Airbus to continue, blamed job losses in the U.S. aerospace industry on the subsidies, and called for the EU to renegotiate the 1992 deal.

To the surprise of the administration, however, this renewed attack on Airbus subsidies was greeted with conspicuous silence from the U.S. industry. Many analysts theorized that this was because a renewed dispute could prompt damaging retaliation from Europe. For one thing, Airbus equips its aircraft with engines made by two U.S. companies—Pratt & Whitney and General Electric—and with avionics made by U.S. companies. In addition, many state-owned airlines in Europe purchase aircraft from Boeing and McDonnell Douglas. Many in the U.S. industry apparently believed that this lucrative business would be put at risk if the government reopened the trade dispute so soon after the 1992 agreement.

A similar cool response from the U.S. industry greeted attempts by two senators, John C. Danforth of Missouri and Max Baucus of Montana, to reopen the trade dispute with Airbus. In early 1993, Danforth and Baucus cosponsored legislation requiring the U.S. government to launch a trade case against Airbus on charges of unfair subsidies. They also sponsored a bill to create an aerospace industry consortium called Aerotech that would finance aerospace research, with half of the funds coming from industry and half from the U.S. government. Vice President Al Gore called the establishment of Aerotech "an administration priority," but a Boeing spokesman said the company was "very guarded about Aerotech" because it could violate the 1992 accord. Both Danforth/Baucus bills died in committee hearings, and the Clinton administration quietly dropped all talk of reopening the trade dispute.

The Boeing–McDonnell Douglas Merger

In December 1996, Boeing stunned the aerospace industry by announcing it would merge with longtime rival McDonnell Douglas in a deal estimated to be worth $13.3 billion. The merger, completed in 1997, was driven by Boeing's desire to strengthen its presence in the defense and space side of the aerospace business areas where McDonnell Douglas was traditionally strong. On the commercial side of the aerospace business, Douglas had been losing market share since the 1970s. By 1996, Douglas accounted for less than 10 percent of production in the large commercial jet aircraft market and only 3 percent of new orders placed that year. The dearth of new orders meant the long-term outlook for Douglas's commercial business was increasingly murky. With or without the merger, many analysts felt that it was only a matter of time before McDonnell Douglas would be forced to exit from the commercial jet aircraft business. In their view, the merger with Boeing merely accelerated that process.

Because the merger would reduce the number of players in the commercial aerospace industry from three to two, Boeing and McDonnell Douglas officials expected both the U.S. Federal Trade Commission (FTC) and the Competition Commission of the European Union to investigate the merger to assess its effects on competition. Boeing executives believed that the FTC would approve the proposed merger. Boeing's argument was that the Boeing–McDonnell Douglas combination was necessary to create a strong U.S. entrant in a competitive global marketplace. U.S. antitrust authorities have been sympathetic to this argument in recent years. Boeing executives also pointed out that since the end of the Cold War, the U.S. government had been arguing for consolidation in the defense industry to eliminate excess capacity. The Boeing–McDonnell Douglas merger helped to achieve that goal and thus should receive government support.

As for the Europeans, here too Boeing executives believed there would be little opposition to the merger. In the words of Harry Stonecipher, CEO of McDonnell Douglas, "My good friend Jean Pierson, head of Airbus, has been saying at airshows lately, 'Douglas is not a factor in the commercial industry' so the deal is apparently a non-event."[1] Initially, Airbus officials seemed to indicate they agreed with this assessment and would not oppose the merger. However, within days of the merger announcement, Karl Van Miert, the EU competition commissioner, signaled that the EU would launch a probe of the merger. Van Miert stated the EU would oppose the merger if it thought doing so was necessary to preserve competition. In justifying the probe, he expressed the concern that if the number of players in the market for large commercial jet aircraft were reduced to two, they might engage in tacit collusion, raising prices above the level that would prevail in more competitive market situations.

Van Miert's statements raised hackles in the United States. Government officials and Boeing executives were heard wondering out loud what authority a European body would have over a merger between two U.S. companies that did almost all their manufacturing in the United States and had few assets in Europe. Van Miert stated that EU law required him to evaluate the merger and entitled the EU to block the merger if it was found to be anticompetitive. While Van Miert acknowledged that the EU could not actually stop the merger, under EU competition law, the commission could declare the merger illegal, restrict its business in Europe, and fine it up to 10 percent of its estimated $48 billion annual sales. Boeing executives argued that if this were the outcome, it would provoke a trade war between the United States and the EU. Some U.S. politicians claimed that the stance adopted by the EU amounted to nothing less than a flagrant violation of U.S. national sovereignty.

Complicating the issue further was Boeing's success in inking long-term exclusive supply contracts with three major U.S.-based airlines: American Airlines, Delta, and Continental. The American Airlines deal was signed in late 1996 and the two others in the first half of 1997. All three deals named Boeing the exclusive supplier of each airlines' aircraft needs for 20 years. Van Miert argued that these agreements were anticompetitive and reinforced his concerns about the market power of a Boeing–McDonnell Douglas combination. These agreements seemed to promote a change of heart among Airbus executives. After originally stating that they had no objections to the merger, Airbus executives became increasingly vocal in their opposition. In March 1997, Jean Pierson, the head of the consortium, warned that the proposed merger could give Boeing a "structural hold" on the industry, spanning the supply of aircraft, servicing, and spare parts. Similarly, commenting on the exclusive supplier deals, Airbus spokesman David Venz argued that the Boeing–McDonnell Douglas combination would "have a locked-in captive customer for 29 years. They have effectively removed choice from the airline who signs those contracts."[2]

In mid-May 1997, the European Commission gave Boeing and McDonnell Douglas its official statement of objections to the planned merger and asked the two U.S. groups to respond before June 12, when hearings on the subject were scheduled in Brussels. The commission stated that the merger raised three principal concerns. First, it would restrict competition in the market for large commercial jet aircraft. Second, McDonnell Douglas's extensive defense and space activities raised the possibility that U.S. government funding for defense and space programs would be used to fund the development of commercial jet aircraft. Third, the sole supplier agreements with American Airlines, Delta, and Continental restricted competition in the commercial aerospace market.

In commenting on these concerns, Boeing CEO Phil Condit noted that since McDonnell Douglas accounted for only 3 percent of commercial sales in 1996, one could hardly argue that the merger would have a restrictive effect on competition. Condit stated that there was no question of defense research funding being used for civil programs, since the issue was already regulated by the 1992 bilateral trade agreement. As for the sole supplier agreements, Condit noted that the deals were struck at the initiative of the airlines.

On June 30, 1997, the Federal Trade Commission issued its own ruling on the merger. In a 4-to-1 decision, an FTC panel recommended that the merger be given unconditional approval. Before reaching its decision, the FTC interviewed 40 executives of airlines to find out whether they thought the merger would cause higher prices from Boeing. While some airlines expressed a preference that McDonnell Douglas remain in the bidding, they were virtually unanimous in acknowledging that they were unlikely to buy from that company because it appeared not to be making the investment required to

[1]John Mintz, "Boeing to Buy McDonnell Douglas," *Washington Post*, December 16, 1996, p. A1.

[2]M. Kayal, "Boeing May Be Flying into Antitrust Territory," *Journal of Commerce*, March 25, 1997, p. 3A.

remain viable. In short, the FTC concluded that Mc-Donnell Douglas was no longer a viable competitor in the large commercial jet market, and therefore, the merger would not have a detrimental effect on competition. At the same time, the FTC did note that the sole supplier agreements that Boeing had reached were "potentially troubling." Although the three agreements reached by July 1997 accounted for only 11 percent of the global market, the FTC signaled that it would be concerned if more occurred.

On July 18, senior EU officials stated publicly that they planned to declare the merger illegal, insisting it would harm competition in Europe. In announcing this intention, Van Miert stated he was particularly concerned about the exclusive supplier contracts, which unfairly closed Airbus out of an important segment of the global market.

In a last-minute bid to stop the European Commission from declaring the merger illegal, Boeing blinked and stated it would not enforce provisions in the 20-year supplier contracts with American, Delta, and Continental. With this concession in hand, on July 23, a triumphant Van Miert announced the European Commission would now approve the merger. Across Europe, newspapers sang Van Miert's praise, depicting him as the man who had taken on the American colossus and won. "You have to hand it to him," stated one EU official, "he took them on and won. He showed them that the European Commission is a force to be reckoned with."[3]

Boeing and Airbus in the New Millennium

The first year of the new millennium was an eventful one for Airbus. In mid-2000, three of the four partners in Airbus merged to form European Aeronautic Defense and Space company (EADS). The merger brought together DaimlerChrysler Aerospace of Germany, Aerospatiale Matra of France, and Construcciones Aeronauticas of Spain to form a group with interests in commercial aircraft, defense, and space that could compete globally with the new Boeing. Within this new company, Airbus was set up as a division in which EADS held 80 percent of the equity, and BEA systems of the United Kingdom, the remaining Airbus partner, held 20 percent.

With this merger, Airbus moved from being a consortium to a single corporate entity with a single set of consolidated financial accounts. The new Airbus entity has 40,000 employees in Germany, France, Spain, and the United Kingdom and will take over all Airbus engineering and manufacturing operations. EADS disclosed that on a pro forma basis, Airbus made operating profits of euro 1.03 billion on sales of euro 15.7 billion in 1999. By consolidating operations, EADS stated it aimed to reduce annual operating costs by some euros 350 million by 2004, while boosting its net profit margin to 10 percent, up from 8 percent in 2000.

Also in 2000, Airbus announced it would build a competitor to Boeing's 747. Airbus's super-jumbo, the A380, would be the world's largest commercial jet aircraft with over 550 seats. It will cost an estimated $12 billion to build and should enter service in 2006. By mid-2001, Airbus had amassed 62 firm orders for the super-jumbo and some 40 options that could be converted into orders in the future. Estimates suggest that Airbus must sell some 230 A380s over the next 20 years to break even on its investment and some 780 A380s to make a decent return on its investment. Airbus estimates the 20-year market for the super-jumbo at 1,500 aircraft. Boeing believes this is a vast overstatement and estimates that there is a market for only 500 very large aircraft over that time period. Underlying these different forecasts are different assumptions about the future of air travel. Airbus assumes that most travelers will continue to fly through major international hubs, such as London, New York, and Tokyo, which will increase demand for very large aircraft. Boeing assumes that increasingly, airlines will bypass congested hubs and instead fly point to point.

Based on its analysis of future demand, Boeing decided not to build a new version of its own jumbo jet, the 747. Instead, the company plans to develop a smaller aircraft, the 250-seat sonic cruiser, that will fly at close to the speed of sound, cutting hours off transoceanic travel times. In addition, Boeing has signaled that it will keep a close eye on the level of subsidies given to Airbus to support the development of the A380. Boeing calculates that subsidies will account for some $4 billion of the $12 billion required to develop the A380. Under the 1992 agreement, such "launch aid" is allowed if it is paid back to the governments that provided it at commercial rates.

Case Discussion Questions

1. Do you believe Airbus could have become a viable competitor without subsidies?

2. Why do you think the four European governments agreed to subsidize the establishment of Airbus?

3. Is Airbus's position with regard to the dispute over subsidies reasonable?

4. Given the 1992 agreement, what additional action (if any) should the U.S. government take with respect to Airbus?

5. Why do you think the U.S. industry reacted with caution to attempts by politicians to reopen the trade dispute in 1993?

[3]Emma Tucker, "Van Miert's Finest Hour," *Financial Times*, July 24, 1997, p. 23.

6. In an era of global competition, what is the case for antitrust authorities to permit the formation of large domestic firms through mergers and acquisitions?

7. Was the threat by EU authorities to declare the Boeing–McDonnell Douglas merger illegal a violation of U.S. sovereignty?

8. Do you think the EU Commission had a strong case in its attempts to wring concessions from Boeing regarding the merger with McDonnell Douglas? Was Boeing right to make significant concessions to the EU? What might have occurred if the concessions were not made?

9. Airbus has now become a corporate entity that is 80 percent owned by EADS. How do you think that this new corporate structure might change the long-standing dispute between Boeing and Airbus over subsidies?

Sources

1. "A Phony War." *The Economist*, May 5, 2001.
2. Barnard, B. "Battle over Boeing Shifts to Subsidies." *Journal of Commerce*, July 25, 1997, p. 1A.
3. Cohen, R. "France Pledges Subsidy to Aerospace Group." *New York Times*, February 3, 1994, p. 5.
4. Coleman, B. "GATT to Rule against German Aid to Airbus." *Wall Street Journal*, January 16, 1992, p. 5.
5. Core, O. C. "Airbus Arrives." *Seattle Times*, July 21, 1992, pp. C1–C3.
6. Davis, B., and B. Ingersoll. "Cloudy Issue." *Wall Street Journal*, March 8, 1993, p. A1.
7. De Jonquieres, G. "Storm over the Atlantic." *Financial Times*, May 22, 1997, p. 17.
8. Dertouzos, M. L.; R. K. Lester; and R. M. Solow. *Made in America*. Cambridge, MA: MIT Press, 1989.
9. "Dissecting Airbus." *The Economist*, February 16, 1991, pp. 51–52.
10. Gow, D. "Airbus Warns on Sales." *The Guardian*, January 14, 1999, p. 22.
11. Grimaldi, J. "FTC Approves Boeing Merger." *Seattle Times*, July 1, 1997, p. A1.
12. "The Jumbo War." *The Economist*, June 15, 1991, pp. 65–66.
13. Kayal, M. "Boeing May Be Flying into Antitrust Territory." *Journal of Commerce*, March 25, 1997, p. 3A.
14. Kayal, M. "The Boeing-McDonnell Merger Looks Very Different through European Eyes." *Journal of Commerce*, July 21, 1997, p. 1A.
15. Klepper, G. "Entry into the Market for Large Transport Aircraft." *European Economic Review* 34 (1990), pp. 775–803.
16. Lane, P. "Study Complains of Alleged Subsidies." *Seattle Times*, December 4, 1991, p. G2.
17. Mintz, J. "Boeing to Buy McDonnell Douglas." *Washington Post*, December 16, 1996, p. A1.
18. Skapinker, M. "EU Sets out Objections to Boeing Merger." *Financial Times*, May 23, 1997, p. 6.
19. Stroud, M. "Worries over a Technology Shift Follow McDonnell-Taiwan Accord." *Investor's Business Daily*, November 21, 1991, p. 36.
20. "Super Jumbo Trade War Ahead." *The Economist*, May 6, 2000.
21. Toy, S., et al. "Zoom! Airbus Comes on Strong." *Business Week*, April 22, 1991, pp. 48–50.
22. Tucker, E. "Van Miert's Finest Hour." *Financial Times*, July 24, 1997, p. 23.

The Rise and Fall of the Japanese Semiconductor Industry, 1970–2001

Introduction

The semiconductor industry was born with the invention of the transistor at Bell Telephone laboratories in 1947. The transistor was first commercialized in the 1950s by U.S. firms, and it soon became a major component of electronic products. In the 1960s, the transistor was replaced by the integrated circuit. Like the transistor, the integrated circuit was first developed and commercialized by U.S. firms. Today, semiconductors are the main components of numerous electronic products including computers, photo-copiers, and telecommunication equipment. In addition, they are increasingly finding their way into a host of other products from automobiles to machine tools.

Semiconductors can be divided into several broad product groups, the most important of which are memory devices, such as DRAMs (dynamic random access memory chips), and logic chips, such as the microprocessors and microcontrollers. The total world market for semiconductors stood at $35 billion in 1988, reached $91.5 billion in 1994, increased to $122 billion in 1998, and hit $204 billion in 2000.

U.S. enterprises dominated the world market from the 1950s until the early 1980s. At the height of U.S. success in the mid-1970s, U.S. firms held close to 70 percent of the world market. During the 1980s, however, the market share of U.S. firms plummeted, falling to 29 percent by 1990, while the share held by Japanese producers rose from 24 percent at the end of the 1970s to 49 percent by 1990. By the end of the 1980s, the United States was a net importer of semiconductors, while 5 of the 10 largest semiconductor producers were Japanese. More significantly still, by 1988 Japanese firms had captured more than 80 percent of the world market for the most widely used integrated circuit in digital equipment, the DRAM. Invented by Intel and once produced exclusively by U.S. firms, as of 1988 only two U.S. firms were in the DRAM market, Micron Technologies and Texas Instruments, and Texas Instruments was manufacturing most of its DRAMs in Japan.

However, the late 1980s may have been something of a high-water mark in the global success of Japanese semiconductor firms. By the mid-1990s, the U.S. industry was again gaining global market share. By 1994, U.S. manufacturers had increased their share of the world semiconductor market to 42 percent, while the share taken by Japanese firms stood at 41 percent, down almost 10 percentage points from their high. Also, foreign firms held 22.4 percent of the Japanese semiconductor market in 1994, up from about 14 percent in 1990. As the 1990s progressed, Japan's share of the global market continued to decline. In this case we explore some reasons for the rise of Japan's semiconductor industry and for the subsequent decline in its growth in global market share.

Japan's Industrial Policy

Why were the Japanese so successful in the global semiconductor industry between the 1970s and late 1980s? One argument is that the industrial policy of the Japanese government was the driving force behind that success. During the 1960s and 1970s, the Japanese government, principally through the Ministry of International Trade and Industry (MITI), sought to build a competitive semiconductor industry by limiting foreign competition in the domestic market and acquiring foreign technology and know-how. The foreign investment laws created after World War II (by the U.S. occupation government) required the Japanese government to approve all applications for foreign direct investment in Japan. MITI consistently rejected all applications by U.S. semiconductor firms to set up wholly owned subsidiaries in Japan, to set up joint ventures in which the U.S. partner would have a majority stake, or to acquire equity in Japanese semiconductor firms. At the same time, the government limited foreign import penetration of the Japanese market through a combination of high tariffs and restrictive quotas. Import penetration of the Japanese market was also limited by requirements that Japanese companies get permission from MITI before buying advanced integrated circuits from foreign companies. For example, until 1974, integrated circuits that contained more than 200 circuit elements could not be imported without special permission.

Because U.S. producers were denied direct access to the Japanese semiconductor market, they typically sought indirect access by licensing their product and process know-how to Japanese enterprises. This too was regulated by MITI. MITI's policy was to insist that if a foreign firm were going to license technology in Japan, that technology had to be licensed to all Japanese firms that requested access. In other words, U.S. firms were not able to discriminate between licensees. MITI also conditioned approval of certain deals on the willingness of the involved Japanese firms to diffuse their technological developments, through sublicensing agreements, to other Japanese firms. The net result of these policies was to encourage the rapid diffusion of advanced semiconductor product and process technology throughout the Japanese semiconductor industry.

U.S. firms went along with this policy because it was their only way to get access to the Japanese market. Initially, licensing was a very lucrative arrangement. By the end of the 1960s, Japanese semiconductor firms were reportedly paying at least 10 percent of their sales revenues as royalties to U.S. firms: 2 percent to General Electric, 4.5 percent to Fairchild, and 3.5 percent to Texas Instruments. The most notable long-run consequence, however, was a transfer of U.S. technological know-how to a number of emerging Japanese competitors. Shielded from foreign competition by import barriers and restrictions on foreign direct investment and armed with state-of-the-art technological know-how, the Japanese firms had only each other to compete with for a share of the rapidly growing Japanese semiconductor market. Stimulated by MITI's insistence that technology be shared among all Japanese semiconductor firms, this competition was intense and based primarily on cost (since everyone had the same technology). The firms that rose to the top in this tough environment, such as NEC, were more than capable of going head to head with U.S. semiconductor firms by the mid-1970s.

Trade Agreements

By the mid-1980s, the changing fortunes of the Japanese and U.S. semiconductor industries had given birth to a bitter trade dispute between the two countries. After incurring heavy losses, U.S. firms claimed they were facing unfair competition from Japan. They accused the Japanese of selling semiconductors, and especially DRAMs, in the United States for less than their fair market value while simultaneously shutting U.S. firms out of the important and lucrative Japanese semiconductor market. The dispute was settled by a 1986 trade agreement between the United States and Japan. The agreement specified a fair market value for semiconductors. Japanese companies were not supposed to sell their semiconductors for less than this price outside of Japan. The agreement also sought to increase foreign access to Japan's domestic semiconductor market. In a non-binding side letter, the Japanese government agreed to help ensure that foreign manufacturers gained more than 20 percent of the Japanese market by the end of 1991, a significant increase from the 8.6 percent share held in 1986.

Although the agreement led to an increase in prices for semiconductors in the United States, foreign producers were still not able to capture a major share of Japan's semiconductor market. By early 1991 when the 1986 agreement was close to expiration, the American Semiconductor Industry Association claimed that foreigners held only a 12 percent share of the Japanese market (the Japanese claimed the foreign share was closer to 17 percent).

In June 1991, the United States and Japan signed a new five-year pact to replace the 1986 agreement. Unlike the previous agreement, this pact formally committed the Japanese to ensuring that foreign producers gained a 20 percent share of their semiconductor market by the end of 1992. In return, the United States agreed to abolish the fair market value system created under the 1986 pact.

This new agreement was greeted with a mixed reception on both sides. While most U.S. semiconductor manufacturers approved of the agreement, some analysts and politicians argued that the government should not have abolished the fair market value system. House Democratic Leader Richard Gephardt, for example, criticized the agreement for its lack of specific commitments by Japan to widen its chip market to foreign sellers. Similarly, Clyde Prestowitz, a former U.S. trade official who helped to craft the 1986 agreement, called the pact a step backward, primarily because it abolished the fair market value system. The Japanese, in contrast, expressed pleasure that the fair market value system had been removed, but many criticized the formal commitment to a 20 percent market share for foreign companies. For example, a senior official at Toshiba, one of Japan's largest semiconductor manufacturers, noted, "We believe that the agreement infringes the principles of free trade, which shouldn't be limited by an agreement of any kind." Similarly, a senior official from the NEC Corporation said, "As you know, the semiconductor was invented in the U.S. and the U.S. was number one in the world for a long time in semiconductors. The U.S. might be a little complacent about what it has achieved. There has been a lack of effort."

Despite such misgivings, the pact seemed to deliver what it promised. The foreign share of the Japanese semiconductor market reached 20 percent in the fourth quarter of 1992. Although it fell back somewhat in the first half of 1993, foreign producers again gained share in the fourth quarter, pushing their total share for the year to 19.4 percent, up from an average of 16.7 percent for all of 1992. The performance of foreigners was even better in 1994, when they captured over 22 percent of the Japanese market. In the fourth quarter of 1994, foreign producers gained a record 23.7 percent market share. However, some analysts wondered whether the pact had much to do with the foreign success. They pointed out that the value of the Japanese yen had strengthened by about 40 percent against the U.S. dollar since 1991. With the yen this high, the terms of trade in the Japanese semiconductor market had swung sharply toward foreign producers, who now had a distinct cost advantage over their Japanese rivals.

Critics note that in the important DRAM market there has been only a limited U.S. resurgence (in contrast to the market for logic chips, where Intel, Motorola, and others continue to dominate). While both Micron Technology and Texas Instruments—the lone two U.S. DRAM manufacturers—did extremely well during 1994 and 1995, much of the DRAM market share gain in Japan has been made by South Korean firms, particularly Samsung. Samsung, which didn't even produce DRAMs in 1988, accounted for 12.7 percent of the world DRAM market in 1994, ahead of Japan's Hitachi Corp. and NEC, which accounted for 9.7 percent and 9.2 percent, respectively. The Japanese share of the world DRAM market was cut in half between 1988 and 1994 as customers switched to low-cost producers such as market leader Samsung and Micron Technology (which enjoyed a 4.5 percent market share in 1994). As of 1995, these trends showed no sign of slowing. One 1995 estimate suggested that South Korean firms were reinvesting 30 percent to 55 percent of their semiconductor revenues in new plants and equipment, the Americans were reinvesting 22 percent, while the Japanese were reinvesting only 15 percent. Also, a number of Taiwanese firms had announced aggressive plans to expand their presence in the DRAM business. In the face of this rapid investment in capacity by non-Japanese firms and the apparent reluctance of Japanese firms to invest, many thought it would be difficult for the Japanese producers to keep their 37 percent share of the global DRAM market.

In the summer of 1996, representatives from Japan and the United States met again to renegotiate the 1991 semiconductor agreement, which was due to expire July 31, 1996. This time, the Japanese were determined to oppose any attempt by the U.S. side to continue to impose numerical targets or otherwise interfere in the market mechanism. In making their case, the Japanese

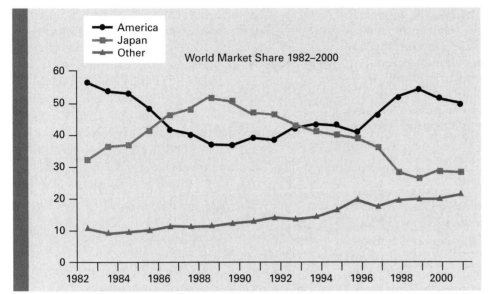

Figure 1

World Market Share, 1982–2000

Source: Semiconductor Industry Association statistics; www.semichips.org.

pointed out that during the first six months of 1996, the foreign share of the Japanese semiconductor market had risen to over 30 percent and that two-thirds of that share had been taken by American firms. In the wider global market, Japanese producers were seeing their share being taken by aggressive competitors from South Korea and now Taiwan. In the DRAM sector in particular, the rise in the value of the Japanese yen had made it increasingly difficult for Japanese firms to compete against the South Koreans and Taiwanese.

Publicly, the Americans declared that they would push for another agreement, and they voiced concerns that without some kind of deal, the Japanese market would once more be closed to foreign competition. Privately, however, government officials admitted that Japan's semiconductor industry seemed to be on the wane, and that it would be difficult to renew the agreement, particularly given the rise of new competitors and the profit boom being enjoyed by some of America's own semiconductor companies.

After the customary hard bargaining, which went down to the wire as so many trade deals seem to, an agreement was reached that enabled the American side to save face while basically giving the Japanese what they wanted. Under the deal, U.S. and Japanese industry associations agreed to create an entity to collect data about the sector and deliver it to their governments, which would meet annually to discuss the industry. In the words of one observer, the deal represented "the tiniest of fig leaves . . . The idea that there will be government meetings yearly to review semiconductor trade but with no power to do anything about it means that everyone has decided to smile and go home."[1]

[1]M. Nakamoto, "Tough Poker Game for Barshefsky," *Financial Times*, August 5, 1996, p. 3.

Aftermath

The years after the 1996 agreement were not kind to the semiconductor industry. In 1997, a glut of new capacity in South Korea and Taiwan produced excess capacity in memory chips. Prices for DRAMs fell by as much as 70 percent, and most of the world's major producers of memory chips posted significant losses. Among those worst hit were the big five Japanese semiconductor companies—NEC, Toshiba, Hitachi, Fujitsu, and Mitsubishi Electric. Throughout 1997–98, the yen continued to gain strength against the currencies of South Korea and Taiwan (the former collapsed in value in late 1997), effectively pricing Japanese firms out of the DRAM market. By late 1998, Japan's share of the global market for DRAMs had shrunk to 30 percent, down from a peak of 80 percent 10 years earlier, and Japan's share was forecast to fall to 20 percent by 2000. News reports suggested that Hitachi, Fujitsu, and Mitsubishi Electric were contemplating leaving the DRAM market and focusing on niches within the market for logic chips. The big gainers in the DRAM market were Taiwanese firms. Japan's share of the total semi-conductor market (memory plus logic chips) fell from 36 percent in 1996 to 26.4 percent in 1998, while American firms saw their share of the total increase from 46.2 percent to 53.4 percent over the same period due to strong sales of logic chips (see Figure 1).

The global semiconductor industry quickly recovered from the 1997–98 slowdown, and in 1999 and 2000 global sales surged, hitting a record $204 billion in 2000. However, this boom was short lived. A global economic slowdown in 2001 precipitated a collapse in prices for semiconductors, and global sales contracted by more than 14 percent to $175 billion. Japanese firms were again particularly hard hit. NEC announced 4,000 job cuts and stated it would exit the DRAM business in 2003. Fujitsu reported losses of $1.6 billion in its semiconductor business. Meanwhile, foreigners continued to hold onto their about 30 percent of Japan's semiconductor market in the 1996–2000 period. In the North American market, the share of Japanese firms stood at 11.6 percent in 2000, down from 19 percent in 1996. American firms accounted for 70.2 percent of the market, up from 67.6 percent in 1996.

Case Discussion Questions

1. What factors account for the rise of Japan's semiconductor manufacturers during the 1970s and 1980s?

2. Does the rise of Japanese semiconductor companies during the 1970s and 1980s indicate that government industrial policy can play an important role in facilitating national competitiveness in industries targeted by that policy?

3. What explains the relative decline of Japanese semiconductor firms since 1988? Can it be attributed to the 1991 semiconductor pact or to other economic factors?

4. What are the implications of your answer to question 3 for national trade policy?

Sources

1. Semiconductor Industry Association statistics and forecasts. http://www.semichips.org.

2. "And Then There Were Two." *The Economist,* January 23, 1999, pp. 58–59.

3. Borrus, M.; L. A. Tyson; and J. Zysman. "Creating Advantage: How Government Policies Created Trade in the Semiconductor Industry." In *Strategic Trade Policy and the New International Economics,* ed. P. Krugman. Cambridge, MA: MIT Press, 1986.

4. Chao, J., and D. Hamilton. "Bad Times Are Just a Memory for DRAM Chip Makers." *Wall Street Journal,* August 28, 1995, p. B4.

5. Davis, B. "Chip Report Eases U.S.-Japan Conflict." *Wall Street Journal,* March 21, 1994, p. A2.

6. Darlin, D. "South Korean Chip Firms Play Catch-Up." *Wall Street Journal,* July 29, 1991, p. A5.

7. Dertouzos, M. L.; R. K. Lester; and R. M. Solow. *Made in America.* Cambridge, MA: MIT Press, 1989.

8. Dunne, N. "US and Japan in Agreement on Chips." *Financial Times,* August 3, 1996, p. 3.

9. "Global Sales Heading for 9% Growth Next Year." *Financial Times,* November 13, 1998, p. 6.

10. Nakamoto, M. "Tough Poker Game for Barshefsky." *Financial Times,* August 5, 1996, p. 3.

11. Schlesinger, J. "As U.S. Firms Hail Semiconductor Pact, Some Japan Concerns Have Reservations." *Wall Street Journal,* June 6, 1991, p. A14.

12. "Semiconductor Trade: A Wafer Thin Case." *The Economist,* July 27, 1996, p. 53.

13. "Standard & Poors Industry Surveys." *Electronics,* August 3, 1995.

14. Yamamura, K. "Caveat Emptor: The Industrial Policy of Japan." In *Strategic Trade Policy and the New International Economics,* ed. P. Krugman. Cambridge, MA: MIT Press, 1986.

The Global
Monetary System

The Foreign Exchange Market

Foreign Exchange Losses at JAL

One of the world's largest airlines, Japan Airlines (JAL), is also one of the best customers of Boeing, the world's biggest manufacturer of commercial airplanes. Every year JAL needs to raise about $800 million to purchase aircraft from Boeing. Boeing aircraft are priced in U.S. dollars, with prices ranging from about $35 million for a 737 to $160 million for a top-of-the-line 747-400. JAL orders an aircraft two to six years before the plane is actually needed and normally pays Boeing a 10 percent deposit when ordering. The bulk of the payment is made when the aircraft is delivered.

The long lag between placing an order and making a final payment presents a conundrum for JAL. Most of JAL's revenues are in Japanese yen, not U.S. dollars (which is not surprising for a Japanese airline). When purchasing Boeing aircraft, JAL must change its yen into dollars to pay Boeing. In the interval between placing an order and making final payment, the value of the yen against the dollar may change. This can increase or decrease the cost of an aircraft. Consider an order placed for a 747 aircraft that was to be delivered in five years. The dollar value of this order was $100 million. Suppose the prevailing exchange rate at the time of ordering was $1 = ¥240 (i.e., one dollar was worth 240 yen), making the price of the 747 ¥2.4 billion. When final payment is due, however, the dollar/yen exchange rate might have changed. The yen might have declined in value against the dollar. For example, the dollar/yen exchange rate might be $1=¥300. If this occurs, the price of the 747 would go from ¥2.4 billion to ¥3.0 billion, a 25 percent increase. Another (more favorable) scenario is that the yen might rise in value against the dollar to $1=¥200. If this occurs, the yen price of the 747 would fall 16.7 percent to ¥2.0 billion.

JAL has no way of knowing what the value of the yen will be against the dollar in five years. However, JAL can enter into a contract with foreign exchange traders to purchase dollars five years hence based on the assessment of those traders as to what they think the dollar/yen exchange rate will be then. This is called entering into a forward exchange contract. The advantage of entering into a forward exchange contract is that JAL knows now what it will have to pay for the 747 in five years. For example, if the value of the yen is expected to increase against the dollar, foreign exchange traders might offer a forward exchange contract that allows JAL to purchase dollars at a rate of $1=¥185 in five years, instead of the $1=¥240 rate that prevailed at the time of ordering. At this forward exchange rate, the 747 would only cost ¥1.85 billion, a 23 percent saving over the yen price implied at time of ordering.

JAL was confronted with just this scenario in 1985 when it entered into a 10-year forward exchange contract with a total value of about $3.6 billion. This contract gave JAL the right to buy U.S. dollars from a consortium of foreign exchange traders at various points during the next 10 years for an average exchange rate of $1=¥185. This looked like a great deal to JAL given the 1985 exchange rate of $1=¥240. However, by September 1994 when the bulk of the contract had been executed, it no longer looked like a good deal. To everyone's surprise, the value of the yen had surged against the dollar. By 1992, the exchange rate stood at $1=¥120, and by 1994, it was $1=¥99. Unfortunately, JAL could not take advantage of this more favorable exchange rate. Instead, JAL was bound by the terms of the contract to purchase dollars at the contract rate of $1=¥185, a rate that by 1994 looked outrageously expensive. This misjudgment cost JAL dearly. In 1994, JAL was paying 86 percent more than it needed to for each Boeing aircraft bought with dollars purchased via the forward exchange contract! In October 1994, JAL admitted publicly that the loss in its most recent financial year from this misjudgment amounted to $450 million, or ¥45 billion. Furthermore, foreign exchange traders speculated that JAL had probably lost ¥155 billion ($1.5 billion) on this contract since 1988.

Sources: W. Dawkins, "JAL to Disclose Huge Currency Hedge Loss," *Financial Times,* October 4, 1994, p. 19; and W. Dawkins, "Tokyo to Lift Veil on Currency Risks," *Financial Times,* October 5, 1994, p. 23.

Introduction

This chapter has three main objectives. The first is to explain how the foreign exchange market works. The second is to examine the forces that determine exchange rates and to discuss the degree to which it is possible to predict future exchange rate movements. The third objective is to map the implications for international business of exchange rate movements and the foreign exchange market. This chapter is the first of three that deal with the international monetary system and its relationship to international business. In Chapter 10, we will explore the institutional structure of the international monetary system. The institutional structure is the context within which the foreign exchange market functions. As we shall see, changes in the institutional structure of the international monetary system can exert a profound influence on the development of foreign exchange markets. In Chapter 11, we will look at the recent evolution of global capital markets and discuss the implications of this development for international businesses.

The **foreign exchange market** is a market for converting the currency of one country into that of another country. An **exchange rate** is simply the rate at which one currency is converted into another. We saw in the opening case how JAL used the foreign exchange market to convert Japanese yen into U.S. dollars. Without the foreign exchange market, international trade and international investment on the scale that we see today would be impossible; companies would have to resort to barter. The foreign exchange market is the lubricant that enables companies based in countries that use different currencies to trade with each other.

We know from earlier chapters that international trade and investment have their risks. As the opening case illustrates, some of these risks exist because future exchange rates cannot be perfectly predicted. The rate at which one currency is converted into another typically changes over time. One function of the foreign exchange market is to provide some insurance against the risks that arise from changes in exchange rates, commonly referred to as **foreign exchange risk.** Although the foreign exchange market offers some insurance against foreign exchange risk, it cannot provide complete insurance. JAL's loss of $1.5 billion on foreign exchange transactions is an extreme example of what can happen, but it is not unusual for international businesses to suffer losses because of unpredicted changes in exchange rates. Currency fluctuations can make seemingly profitable trade and investment deals unprofitable, and vice versa. The opening case contains an example of this.

In addition to altering the value of trade deals and foreign investments, currency movements can also open or close export opportunities and alter the attractiveness of imports. For example, consider what occurred following the introduction of the euro in January 2000 to the profits and sales of many U.S. companies that made substantial exports to Europe. Initially the euro/dollar exchange rate was E1=$1.08, signifying that one euro was worth about 8 percent more than one dollar. Over the next few months the value of the euro fell sharply, and by late 2000 one euro was worth only about 82 cents (E1=$0.82), a 25 percent decline in value. The products that U.S. companies were exporting to Europe, while having stable prices in terms of dollars, had increased in price by about 25 percent when converted into euros. As a consequence, European consumers, paying in euros, cut back their purchases of U.S. products, and by late 2000 a number of U.S. companies were reporting that their profits and sales would be below expectations, primarily due to weak export sales to Europe. For example, Stern Pinball, a manufacturer of pinball machines based in Illinois, reported 1999 sales of about $30 million, of which some $15 million were exports to European Union countries. Following the fall in the value of the euro against the dollar during 2000, Stern's export sales to Europe fell by some 50 percent.[1]

While the existence of foreign exchange markets is a necessary precondition for large-scale international trade and investment, as suggested by this example and the opening case, the movement of exchange rates introduces many risks into international trade and investment. Some of these risks can be insured against by using instruments offered by the foreign exchange market, such as the forward exchange contracts discussed in the opening case; others cannot be.

We begin this chapter by looking at the functions and the form of the foreign exchange market. This includes distinguishing among spot exchanges, forward exchanges, and currency swaps. Then we will consider the factors that determine exchange rates. We will also look at how foreign trade is conducted when a country's currency cannot be exchanged for other currencies; that is, when its currency is not convertible. The chapter closes with a discussion of these things in terms of their implications for business.

The Functions of the Foreign Exchange Market ■

The foreign exchange market serves two main functions. The first is to convert the currency of one country into the currency of another. The second is to provide some insurance against foreign exchange risk, by which we mean the adverse consequences of unpredictable changes in exchange rates.[2]

❙ Currency Conversion

Each country has a currency in which the prices of goods and services are quoted. In the United States, it is the dollar ($); in Great Britain, the pound (£); in France, Germany, and other members of the euro zone it is the euro (E); in Japan, the yen (¥); and so on. In general, within the borders of a particular country, one must use the national currency. A U.S. tourist cannot walk into a store in Edinburgh, Scotland, and use U.S. dollars to buy a bottle of Scotch whisky. Dollars are not recognized as legal tender in Scotland; the tourist must use British pounds. Fortunately, the tourist can go to a bank and exchange her dollars for pounds. Then she can buy the whisky.

When a tourist changes one currency into another, she is participating in the foreign exchange market. The exchange rate is the rate at which the market converts one currency into another. For example, an exchange rate of $1 = ¥120 specifies that one U.S. dollar has the equivalent value of 120 Japanese yen. The exchange rate allows us to compare the relative prices of goods and services in different countries. Our U.S. tourist wishing to buy a bottle of Scotch whisky in Edinburgh, may find that she must pay £30 for the bottle, knowing that the same bottle costs $40 in the United States. Is this a good deal? Imagine the current pound/dollar exchange rate is £1.00 = $1.50. Our intrepid tourist takes out her calculator and converts £30 into dollars. (The calculation is 25 × 1.5) She finds that the bottle of Scotch costs the equivalent of $45. She is surprised that a bottle of Scotch whisky could cost less in the United States than in Scotland. (This is true; alcohol is taxed heavily in Great Britain.)

Tourists are minor participants in the foreign exchange market; companies engaged in international trade and investment are major ones. International businesses have four main uses of foreign exchange markets. First, the payments a company receives for its exports, the income it receives from foreign investments, or the income it receives from licensing agreements with foreign firms may be in foreign currencies. To use those funds in its home country, the company must convert them to its home country's currency. Consider the Scotch distillery that exports its whisky to the United States. The distillery is paid in dollars, but since those dollars cannot be spent in Great Britain, they must be converted into British pounds.

Second, international businesses use foreign exchange markets when they must pay a foreign company for its products or services in its country's currency. For example, our friend Michael runs a company called NST, a large British travel service for school groups. Each year Michael's company arranges vacations for thousands of British

George Soros—The Man Who Moved Currency Markets

George Soros, a Hungarian-born financier, is the principal partner of the Quantum Group, which controls a series of hedge funds with assets of about $15 billion. A **hedge fund** is an investment fund that not only buys financial assets (such as stocks, bonds, and currencies) but also sells them short. **Short selling** occurs when an investor places a speculative bet that the value of a financial asset will decline and then profits from that decline. A common variant of short selling occurs when an investor borrows stock from his broker and sells that stock. The short seller has to ultimately pay back that stock to his broker. However, he hopes that in the intervening period the value of the stock will decline so that the cost of repurchasing the stock to pay back the broker is significantly less than the income he received from the initial sale of the stock. For example, imagine that a short seller borrows 100 units of IBM stock and sells it in the market at $150 per share, yielding a total income of $15,000. In one year, the short seller has to give the 100 units of IBM stock back to his broker. In the intervening period, the value of the IBM stock falls to $50. Consequently, it now costs the short seller only $5,000 to repurchase the 100 units of IBM stock for his broker. The difference between the initial sales price ($150) and the repurchase price ($50) repre-

sents the short seller's profit, which in this case is $100 per unit of stock for a total profit of $10,000. Short selling was originally developed as a means of reducing risk (of hedging), but it is often used for speculation.

Along with other hedge funds, Soros's Quantum Fund often takes a short position in currencies that he expects to decline in value. For example, if Soros expects the British pound to decline against the U.S. dollar, he may borrow 1 billion pounds from a currency trader and immediately sell those for U.S. dollars. Soros will then hope that the value of the pound will decline against the dollar, so that when he has to repay the 1 billion pounds it will cost him considerably less (in U.S. dollars) than he received from the initial sale.

Since the 1970s, Soros has consistently earned huge returns by making such speculative bets. His most spectacular triumph came in September 1992. He believed the British pound was likely to decline in value against major currencies, particularly the German deutsche mark. The prevailing exchange rate was £1=DM2.80. The British government was obliged by a European Union agreement on monetary policy to try to keep the pound above DM2.77. Soros doubted that the British could do this, so he shorted the pound, borrowing billions of pounds (using the assets of the Quantum Fund as collateral)

schoolchildren and their teachers in France. French hotel proprietors demand payment in euros, so Michael must convert large sums of money from pounds into euros to pay them.

Third, international businesses use foreign exchange markets when they have spare cash that they wish to invest for short terms in money markets. For example, consider a U.S. company that has $10 million it wants to invest for three months. The best interest rate it can earn on these funds in the United States may be 8 percent. Investing in a South Korean money market account, however, may earn 12 percent. Thus, the company may change its $10 million into Korean won and invest it in South Korea. Note, however, that the rate of return it earns on this investment depends not only on the Korean interest rate, but also on the changes in the value of the Korean won against the dollar in the intervening period.

Finally, currency speculation is another use of foreign exchange markets. **Currency speculation** typically involves the short-term movement of funds from one currency to another in the hopes of profiting from shifts in exchange rates. Consider again the U.S. company with $10 million to invest for three months. Suppose the company suspects that the U.S. dollar is overvalued against the Japanese yen. That is, the company expects the value of the dollar to depreciate against that of the yen. Imagine the current dollar/yen exchange rate is $1 = ¥120. The company exchanges its $10 million into yen, receiving ¥1.2 billion. Over the next three months, the value of the dollar depreciates and immediately began selling them for German deutsche marks. His simultaneous sale of pounds and purchase of marks were so large that it helped drive down the value of the pound against the mark. Other currency traders, seeing Soros's market moves and knowing his reputation for making successful currency bets, jumped on the bandwagon and started to sell pounds short and buy deutsche marks. The resulting bandwagon effect put enormous pressure on the pound. The British Central Bank, at the request of the British government, spent about 20 billion pounds on September 16, 1992, to try to prop up the value of the pound against the deutsche mark (by selling marks and buying pounds), but to no avail. The pound continued to fall and on September 17, the British government gave up and let the pound decline (it actually fell to £1=DM2.00). Soros made a $1 billion profit in four weeks!

Like all currency speculators, however, George Soros has had his losses. In February 1994, he bet that the Japanese yen would decline in value against the U.S. dollar and promptly shorted the yen. However, the yen defied his expectations and continued to rise, costing his Quantum Fund $600 million. Similarly, a series of incorrect bets in 1987 resulted in losses of more than $800 million for Quantum. Despite such defeats, however, the Quantum Fund has earned an average annual rate of return of over 40 percent since 1970.

Soros has gained a reputation for being able to move currency markets by his actions. This is the consequence not so much of the money that Soros puts into play, but of the bandwagon effect that results when other speculators follow his lead. This reputation has resulted in Soros being depicted as the archvillain of the 1997 Asian currency crisis. In 1997, the currencies of Thailand, Malaysia, South Korea, and Indonesia all lost between 50 percent and 70 percent of their value against the U.S. dollar. While the reasons for the crisis are complex, a common feature was excessive borrowing by firms based in these countries. Several Asian leaders, however, most notably Mahathir bin Mohamad, the prime minister of Malaysia, instead blamed the crisis on "criminal speculation" by Soros, who had been intent on impoverishing Asian nations. Soros denied that his fund had been involved in shorting Asian currencies.

Sources: P. Harverson, "Billion Dollar Man the Money Markets Fear," *Financial Times*, September 30, 1994, p. 10; "A Quantum Dive," *The Economist*, March 15, 1994, pp. 83–84; B. J. Javetski, "Europe's Money Mess," *Business Week*, September 28, 1992, pp. 30–31; "Meltdown," *The Economist*, September 19, 1992, p. 69; and T. L. Friedman, "Mahathir's Wrath," *New York Times*, December 18, 1997, p. 27.

until $1 = ¥100$. Now the company exchanges its ¥1.2 billion back into dollars and finds that it has $12 million. The company has made a $2 million profit on currency speculation in three months on an initial investment of $10 million.

One of the most famous currency "speculators" is George Soros, whose Quantum Group of "hedge funds" controls about $15 billion in assets. The activities of Soros, who has been spectacularly successful, are profiled in the accompanying Management Focus. In general, however, companies should beware of speculation for it is a very risky business. The company cannot know for sure what will happen to exchange rates. While a speculator may profit handsomely if his speculation about future currency movements turns out to be correct, he can also lose vast amounts of money if it turns out to be wrong. For example, in 1991, Clifford Hatch, the finance director of the British food and drink company Allied-Lyons, bet large amounts of the company's funds on the speculation that the British pound would rise in value against the U.S. dollar. Over the previous three years, Hatch had made over $25 million for Allied-Lyons by placing similar currency bets. His 1991 bet, however, went spectacularly wrong when the British pound plummeted in value against the U.S. dollar. In February 1991, one pound bought $2; by April it bought less than $1.75. The total loss to Allied-Lyons from this speculation was a staggering $269 million, more than the company was to earn from all of its food and drink activities during 1991![3]

Table 9.1

Foreign Exchange
Quotations

Source: *Wall Street Journal*,
November 29, 2001, p. C14.

CURRENCY TRADING

Wednesday, November 28, 2001

EXCHANGE RATES

The New York foreign exchange mid-range rates below apply to trading among banks in amounts of $1 million and more, as quoted at 4 p.m. Eastern time by Reuters and other sources. Retail transactions provide fewer units of foreign currency per dollar. Rates for the 12 Euro currency countries are derived from the latest dollar-euro rate using the exchange ratios set 1/1/99.

Country	U.S. $ EQUIV.		CURRENCY PER U.S. $	
	Wed	Tue	Wed	Tue
Argentina (Peso)	1.0016	1.0011	.9984	.9989
Australia (Dollar)	.5215	.5225	1.9174	1.9137
Austria (Schilling)	.06456	.06420	15.489	15.577
Bahrain (Dinar)	2.6525	2.6525	.3770	.3770
Belgium (Franc)	.0220	.0219	45.4074	45.6644
Brazil (Real)	.4029	.4047	2.4820	2.4710
Britain (Pound)	1.4261	1.4153	.7012	.7066
1-month forward	1.4238	1.4130	.7023	.7077
3-months forward	1.4195	1.4088	.7045	.7098
6-months forward	1.4130	1.4027	.7077	.7129
Canada (Dollar)	.6312	.6274	1.5842	1.5939
1-month forward	.6311	.6273	1.5846	1.5942
3-months forward	.6309	.6271	1.5850	1.5947
6-months forward	.6308	.6270	1.5852	1.5950
Chile (Peso)	.001479	.001490	676.25	670.95
China (Renminbi)	.1208	.1208	8.2772	8.2770
Colombia (Peso)	.0004333	.0004324	2308.05	2312.50
Czech. Rep. (Koruna)				
Commercial rate	.02668	.02665	37.480	37.525
Denmark (Krone)	.1194	.1187	8.3755	8.4230
Ecuador (US Dollar)-e	1.0000	1.0000	1.0000	1.0000
Finland (Markka)	.1494	.1486	6.6926	6.7305
France (Franc)	.1354	.1347	7.3836	7.4254
1-month forward	.1353	.1345	7.3911	7.4332
3-months forward	.1350	.1343	7.4075	7.4487
6-months forward	.1347	.1340	7.4264	7.4652
Germany (Mark)	.4542	.4517	2.2015	2.2140
1-month forward	.4538	.4512	2.2038	2.2163
3-months forward	.4528	.4503	2.2087	2.2209
6-months forward	.4516	.4493	2.2143	2.2259
Greece (Drachma)	.002607	.002593	383.64	385.73
Hong Kong (Dollar)	.1282	.1282	7.7985	7.7988
Hungary (Forint)	.003551	.003508	281.58	285.10
India (Rupee)	.02084	.02085	47.990	47.970
Indonesia (Rupiah)	.0000962	.0000959	10400	10430
Ireland (Punt)	1.1280	1.1217	.8865	.8915
Israel (Shekel)	.2362	.2361	4.2330	4.2360
Italy (Lira)	.0004588	.0004562	2179.50	2191.84

Country	U.S. $ EQUIV.		CURRENCY PER U.S. $	
	Wed	Tue	Wed	Tue
Japan (Yen)	.008123	.008067	123.11	123.96
1-month forward	.008136	.008080	122.91	123.76
3-months forward	.008164	.008109	122.49	123.32
6-months forward	.008207	.008150	121.85	122.71
Jordan (Dinar)	1.4088	1.4088	.7098	.7098
Kuwait (Dinar)	3.2637	3.2605	.3064	.3067
Lebanon (Pound)	.0006606	.0006606	1513.75	1513.75
Malaysia (Ringgit)-b	.2632	.2632	3.8000	3.8000
Malta (Lira)	2.2134	2.1935	.4518	.4559
Mexico (Peso)				
Floating rate	.1079	.1080	9.2695	9.2615
Netherlands (Guilder)	.4031	.4009	2.4805	2.4946
New Zealand (Dollar)	.4148	.4150	2.4108	2.4096
Norway (Krone)	.1117	.1110	8.9549	9.0104
Pakistan (Rupee)	.01645	.01645	60.800	60.800
Peru (new Sol)	.2912	.2911	3.4335	3.4354
Philippines (Peso)	.01925	.01921	51.950	52.050
Poland (Zloty)-d	.2458	.2450	4.0679	4.0813
Portugal (Escudo)	.004431	.004406	225.67	226.94
Russia (Ruble)-a	.03339	.03339	29.945	29.945
Saudi Arabia (Riyal)	.2666	.2666	3.7504	3.7504
Singapore (Dollar)	.5460	.5454	1.8315	1.8335
Slovak Rep. (Koruna)	.02050	.02041	48.779	49.005
South Africa (Rand)	.1014	.1004	9.8588	9.9613
South Korea (Won)	.0007893	.0007937	1267.00	1260.00
Spain (Peseta)	.005339	.005309	187.29	188.35
Sweden (Krona)	.0939	.0944	10.6474	10.5966
Switzerland (Franc)	.6075	.6039	1.6460	1.6560
1-month forward	.6075	.6038	1.6461	1.6561
3-months forward	.6075	.6038	1.6461	1.6561
6-months forward	.6076	.6040	1.6458	1.6555
Taiwan (Dollar)	.02908	.02906	34.390	34.410
Thailand (Baht)	.02268	.02271	44.095	44.040
Turkey (Lira)-f	.00000067	.00000068	1482500	1475000
United Arab (Dirham)	.2723	.2723	3.6730	3.6730
Uruguay (New Peso)				
Financial	.07231	.07241	13.830	13.810
Venezuela (Bolivar)	.001340	.001341	746.00	745.50
SDR	1.2628	1.2588	.7919	.7944
Euro	.8884	.8834	1.1256	1.1320

Special Drawing Rights (SDR) are based on exchange rates for the U.S., German, British, French , and Japanese currencies. Source: International Monetary Fund.

a-Russian Central Bank rate. b-Government rate. d-Floating rate; trading band suspended on 4/11/00. e-Adopted U.S. dollar as of 9/11/00. f-Floating rate, eff. Feb. 22.

▌Insuring against Foreign Exchange Risk

A second function of the foreign exchange market is to provide insurance to protect against the possible adverse consequences of unpredictable changes in exchange rates (foreign exchange risk). To explain how the market performs this function, we must first distinguish among spot exchange rates, forward exchange rates, and currency swaps.

Spot Exchange Rates

When two parties agree to exchange currency and execute the deal immediately, the transaction is referred to as a spot exchange. Exchange rates governing such "on the spot" trades are referred to as spot exchange rates. The **spot exchange rate** is the rate at which a foreign exchange dealer converts one currency into another currency on a particular day. Thus, when our U.S. tourist in Edinburgh goes to a bank to convert her dollars into pounds, the exchange rate is the spot rate for that day. Spot exchange rates are reported daily in the financial pages of newspapers. Table 9.1 shows the dollar exchange rates for currencies traded in the New York Foreign Exchange market as of 4 P.M. May 18, 2001. An exchange rate can be quoted in two ways: as the price of the foreign currency in terms of dollars (for example, $0.008095 per yen; $0.8808 per euro) or as the price of dollars in terms of the foreign currency (for example, ¥123.54 per dollar; E1.1353 per dollar). The first of these exchange rate quotations (dollar per foreign currency) is said to be in *direct* (or American) terms, the second (foreign currency units per dollar) in *indirect* terms.

Spot rates change continually, often on a day-by-day basis (although the magnitude of the changes over such short time periods will be small). The value of a currency is determined by the interaction between the demand and supply of that currency relative to the demand and supply of other currencies. For example, if lots of people want U.S. dollars and dollars are in short supply, and few people want British pounds and pounds are in plentiful supply, the spot exchange rate for converting dollars into pounds will change. The dollar is likely to appreciate against the pound (or, conversely, the pound will depreciate against the dollar). Imagine the spot exchange rate is £1 = $1.50 when the market opens. As the day progresses, dealers demand more dollars and fewer pounds. By the end of the day, the spot exchange rate might be £1 = $1.48. The dollar has appreciated, and the pound has depreciated.

Forward Exchange Rates

The fact that spot exchange rates change continually as determined by the relative demand and supply for different currencies can be problematic for an international business. A U.S. company that imports laptop computers from Japan knows that in 30 days it must pay yen to a Japanese supplier when a shipment arrives. The company will pay the Japanese supplier ¥200,000 for each laptop computer, and the current dollar/yen spot exchange rate is $1 = ¥120. At this rate, each computer costs the importer $1,667 (i.e., 1,667 = 200,000/120). The importer knows she can sell the computers the day they arrive for $2,000 each, which yields a gross profit of $333 on each computer ($2,000 − $1667). However, the importer will not have the funds to pay the Japanese supplier until the computers have been sold. If over the next 30 days the dollar unexpectedly depreciates against the yen, say to $1 = ¥95, the importer will still have to pay the Japanese company ¥200,000 per computer, but in dollar terms that would be equivalent to $2,105 per computer, which is more than she can sell the computers for. A depreciation in the value of the dollar against the yen from $1 = ¥120 to $1 = ¥95 would transform a profitable deal into an unprofitable one.

To avoid this risk, the U.S. importer might want to engage in a forward exchange. A **forward exchange** occurs when two parties agree to exchange currency and execute the deal at some specific date in the future. Exchange rates governing such future transactions are referred to as **forward exchange rates.** For most major currencies, forward exchange rates are quoted for 30 days, 90 days, and 180 days into the future. (Forward exchange rate quotations appear in Table 9.1.) In some cases, it is possible to get forward exchange rates for several years into the future. The opening case, for example, reported how JAL entered into a contract that predicted forward exchange rates up to 10 years in the future. Returning to our computer importer example, let us assume the 30-day forward exchange rate for converting dollars into yen is $1 = ¥110. The importer enters into a 30-day forward exchange transaction with a foreign exchange dealer at this rate and is guaranteed that she will have to pay no more than $1,818 for each computer (1,818 = 200,000/110). This guarantees her a profit of $182 per computer ($2,000 − $1,818). She also insures herself against the possibility that an unanticipated change in the dollar/yen exchange rate will turn a profitable deal into an unprofitable one.

In this example, the spot exchange rate ($1 = ¥120) and the 30-day forward rate ($1 = ¥110) differ. Such differences are normal; they reflect the expectations of the foreign exchange market about future currency movements. In our example, the fact that $1 bought more yen with a spot exchange than with a 30-day forward exchange indicates foreign exchange dealers expected the dollar to depreciate against the yen in the next 30 days. When this occurs, we say the dollar is selling at a discount on the

30-day forward market (i.e., it is worth less than on the spot market). Of course, the opposite can also occur. If the 30-day forward exchange rate were $1 = ¥130, for example, $1 would buy more yen with a forward exchange than with a spot exchange. In such a case, we say the dollar is selling at a premium on the 30-day forward market. This reflects the foreign exchange dealers' expectations that the dollar will appreciate against the yen over the next 30 days.

Currency Swaps

The above discussion of spot and forward exchange rates might lead you to conclude that the option to buy forward is very important to companies engaged in international trade—and you would be right. By 1998, the last year for which international data are available, forward instruments accounted for some 60 percent of all foreign exchange transactions, while spot exchanges accounted for 40 percent.[4] However, the vast majority of these forward exchanges were not forward exchanges of the type we have been discussing, but rather a more sophisticated instrument known as currency swaps.

A **currency swap** is the simultaneous purchase and sale of a given amount of foreign exchange for two different value dates. Swaps are transacted between international businesses and their banks, between banks, and between governments when it is desirable to move out of one currency into another for a limited period without incurring foreign exchange risk. A common kind of swap is spot against forward. Consider a company such as Apple Computer. Apple assembles laptop computers in the United States, but the screens are made in Japan. Apple also sells some of the finished laptops in Japan. So, like many companies, Apple both buys from and sells to Japan. Imagine Apple needs to change $1 million into yen to pay its supplier of laptop screens today. Apple knows that in 90 days it will be paid ¥120 million by the Japanese importer that buys its finished laptops. It will want to convert these yen into dollars for use in the United States. Let us say today's spot exchange rate is $1 = ¥120 and the 90-day forward exchange rate is $1 = ¥110. Apple sells $1 million to its bank in return for ¥120 million. Now Apple can pay its Japanese supplier. At the same time, Apple enters into a 90-day forward exchange deal with its bank for converting ¥120 million into dollars. Thus, in 90 days Apple will receive $1.09 million (¥120 million/110 = $1.09 million). Since the yen is trading at a premium on the 90-day forward market, Apple ends up with more dollars than it started with (although the opposite could also occur). The swap deal is just like a conventional forward deal in one important respect: It enables Apple to insure itself against foreign exchange risk. By engaging in a swap, Apple knows today that the ¥120 million payment it will receive in 90 days will yield $1.09 million.

The Nature of the Foreign Exchange Market

So far we have dealt with the foreign exchange market only as an abstract concept. It is now time to take a closer look at the nature of this market. The foreign exchange market is not located in any one place. It is a global network of banks, brokers, and foreign exchange dealers connected by electronic communications systems. When companies wish to convert currencies, they typically go through their own banks rather than entering the market directly. The foreign exchange market has been growing at a rapid pace, reflecting a general growth in the volume of cross-border trade and investment (see Chapter 1). In March 1986, the average total value of global foreign exchange trading was about $200 billion per day. By April 1995 it was over $1,200 billion per day, and by April 1998 it reached $1,490 billion per day. However, it fell back to $1,210 billion per day in April 2001, largely due to the introduction of the euro, which reduced the number of major trading currencies in the world.[5] The most important

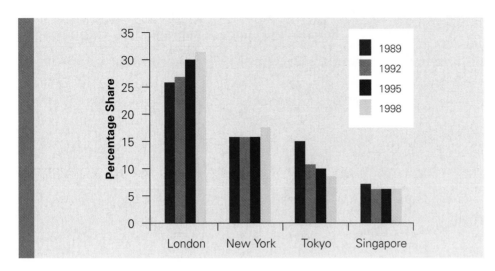

Figure 9.1

Geographical Distribution of Global Foreign Exchange Activity (percentage share of total average daily turnover)

Source: Bank for International Settlements, *Central Bank Survey of Foreign Exchange and Derivatives Market Activity, April 2001* (Basle, Switzerland: BIS, 2001).

trading centers are London (31 percent of activity), New York (16 percent of activity), Tokyo (9 percent of activity) and Singapore (6 percent of activity).[6] Major secondary trading centers include Zurich, Frankfurt, Paris, Hong Kong, San Francisco, and Sydney (see Figure 9.1).

London's dominance in the foreign exchange market is due to both history and geography. As the capital of the world's first major industrial trading nation, London had become the world's largest center for international banking by the end of the 19th century, a position it has retained. Today London's central position between Tokyo and Singapore to the east and New York to the west has made it the critical link between the East Asian and New York markets. Due to the particular differences in time zones, London opens soon after Tokyo closes for the night and is still open for the first few hours of trading in New York. However, some now argue that the failure of Great Britain to join the first round of the European monetary union might lead to the demise of London as the center of global foreign exchange trading. This is particularly likely to occur if the euro emerges as a major currency unit after 2002, and if Great Britain stays out of the euro zone (see Chapter 8 for details).

Two features of the foreign exchange market are of particular note. The first is that the market never sleeps. Tokyo, London, and New York are all shut for only 3 hours out of every 24. During these three hours, trading continues in a number of minor centers, particularly San Francisco and Sydney, Australia. The second feature of the market is the extent of integration of the various trading centers. High-speed computer linkages between trading centers around the globe have effectively created a single market. The integration of financial centers implies there can be no significant difference in exchange rates quoted in the trading centers. For example, if the yen/dollar exchange rate quoted in London at 3 P.M. is ¥120 = $1, the yen/dollar exchange rate quoted in New York at the same time (10 A.M. New York time) will be identical. If the New York yen/dollar exchange rate were ¥125 = $1, a dealer could make a profit through **arbitrage,** buying a currency low and selling it high. For example, if the prices differed in London and New York as given, a dealer in New York could take $1 million and use that to purchase ¥125 million. She could then immediately sell the ¥125 million for dollars in London, where the transaction would yield $1.046666 million, allowing the trader to book a profit of $46,666 on the transaction. If all dealers tried to cash in on the opportunity, however, the demand for yen in New York would rise, resulting in an appreciation of the yen against the dollar such that the price differential

Table 9.2

Currency Use on One Side
of a Foreign Exchange
Transaction

Source: Bank for International
Settlements, *Central Bank Survey of
Foreign Exchange and Derivatives
Market Activity in April 2001* (Basle,
Switzerland: BIS, 2001).

*The Deutsche mark was replaced by
the euro in 2000, and the ECU
became the euro.

†NA: Not applicable.

Currency	Percentage share of average daily turnover			
	April 1992	April 1995	April 1998	April 2001
U.S. dollar	82	83	87	90
Deutsche mark*	40	37	30	NA†
Japanese yen	23	24	21	NA
Pound sterling	14	10	11	13.2
Swiss franc	9	7	7	6.1
Canadian dollar	3	3	4	4.5
Australian dollar	2	3	3	4.2
ECU* and other EMS currencies	12	15	17	NA
Euro	NA	NA	NA	38

between New York and London would quickly disappear. Since foreign exchange dealers are continually watching their computer screens for arbitrage opportunities, the few that arise tend to be small, and they disappear in minutes.

Another feature of the foreign exchange market is the important role played by the U.S. dollar. Although a foreign exchange transaction can in theory involve any two currencies, most transactions involve dollars. This is true even when a dealer wants to sell a nondollar currency and buy another. A dealer wishing to sell Korean won for Brazilian real, for example, will usually sell the won for dollars and then use the dollars to buy real. Although this may seem a roundabout way of doing things, it is actually cheaper than trying to find a holder of real who wants to buy won. Because the volume of international transactions involving dollars is so great, it is not hard to find dealers who wish to trade dollars for won or real.

Due to its central role in so many foreign exchange deals, the dollar is a vehicle currency. Table 9.2 shows that in April 2001, 90 percent of all foreign exchange transactions involved dollars. After the dollar, the most important vehicle currencies were the euro and the British pound—reflecting the importance of these trading entities in the world economy. Since the implementation of the euro, it has replaced the mark as the world's second most important vehicle currency. The British pound used to be second in importance to the dollar as a vehicle currency, but its importance has diminished in recent years. Despite this, London has retained its leading position in the global foreign exchange market, which suggests that the introduction of the euro might not have the negative impact suggested by critics of Great Britain's decision to stay out of the euro zone.

Economic Theories of Exchange Rate Determination

At the most basic level, exchange rates are determined by the demand and supply of one currency relative to the demand and supply of another. For example, if the demand for dollars outstrips the supply of them and if the supply of Japanese yen is greater than the demand for them, the dollar–yen exchange rate will change. The dollar will appreciate against the yen (or the yen will depreciate against the dollar). However, while differences in relative demand and supply explain the determination of exchange rates, they do so only in a superficial sense. This simple explanation does not tell us what factors underlie the demand for and supply of a currency. Nor does it tell us when the demand for dollars will exceed the supply (and vice versa) or when the supply of Japanese yen will exceed demand for them (and vice versa). Neither does it tell us under what conditions a currency is in demand or under what conditions it is not demanded. In this section, we will review economic theory's answers to these questions. This will give us a deeper understanding of how exchange rates are determined.

If we understand how exchange rates are determined, we may be able to forecast exchange rate movements. Since future exchange rate movements influence export opportunities, the profitability of international trade and investment deals, and the price competitiveness of foreign imports, this is valuable information for an international business. Unfortunately, there is no simple explanation. The forces that determine exchange rates are complex, and no theoretical consensus exists, even among academic economists who study the phenomenon every day. Nonetheless, most economic theories of exchange rate movements seem to agree that three factors have an important impact on future exchange rate movements in a country's currency: the country's price inflation, its interest rate, and market psychology.[7]

Prices and Exchange Rates

To understand how prices are related to exchange rate movements, we first need to discuss an economic proposition known as the law of one price. Then we will discuss the theory of purchasing power parity (PPP), which links changes in the exchange rate between two countries' currencies to changes in the countries' price levels.

The Law of One Price

The **law of one price** states that in competitive markets free of transportation costs and barriers to trade (such as tariffs), identical products sold in different countries must sell for the same price when their price is expressed in terms of the same currency.[8] For example, if the exchange rate between the British pound and the dollar is £1=$1.50, a jacket that retails for $75 in New York should sell for £50 in London. Consider what would happen if the jacket cost £40 in London ($60 in U.S. currency). At this price, it would pay a trader to buy jackets in London and sell them in New York (an example of arbitrage). The company initially could make a profit of $15 on each jacket by purchasing it for £40 ($60) in London and selling it for $75 in New York (we are assuming away transportation costs and trade barriers.) However, the increased demand for jackets in London would raise their price in London, and the increased supply of jackets in New York would lower their price there. This would continue until prices were equalized. Thus, prices might equalize when the jacket cost £44 ($66) in London and $66 in New York (assuming no change in the exchange rate of £1 = $1.50).

Purchasing Power Parity

If the law of one price were true for all goods and services, the purchasing power parity (PPP) exchange rate could be found from any individual set of prices. By comparing the prices of identical products in different currencies, it would be possible to determine the "real" or PPP exchange rate that would exist if markets were efficient. (An **efficient market** has no impediments to the free flow of goods and services, such as trade barriers.)

A less extreme version of the PPP theory states that given **relatively efficient markets**— that is, markets in which few impediments to international trade exist—the price of a "basket of goods" should be roughly equivalent in each country. To express the PPP theory in symbols, let $P_\$$ be the U.S. dollar price of a basket of particular goods and P_Y be the price of the same basket of goods in Japanese yen. The PPP theory predicts that the dollar/yen exchange rate, $E_{\$/Y}$, should be equivalent to:

$$E_{\$/Y} = P_\$/P_Y$$

Thus, if a basket of goods costs $200 in the United States and ¥20,000 in Japan, PPP theory predicts that the dollar/yen exchange rate should be $200/¥20,000 or $0.01 per Japanese yen (i.e. $1=¥100).

Every year, the newsmagazine *The Economist* publishes its own version of the PPP theorem, which it refers to as the "Big Mac Index." *The Economist* has selected McDonald's "Big Mac" as a proxy for a "basket of goods" because it is produced according to more or less the same recipe in about 120 countries. The Big Mac PPP is the exchange rate that would leave hamburgers costing the same in each country. According to *The Economist,* comparing a country's actual exchange rate with the one predicted by the PPP theorem based on relative prices of Big Macs is a test on whether a currency is undervalued or not. This is not a totally serious exercise, as *The Economist* admits, but it does provide us with a useful illustration of the PPP theorem.

The Big Mac index for April 2001 is reproduced in Table 9.3. The first column of the table shows local currency prices of a Big Mac; the second converts them into dollars. The average price of a Big Mac in the United States is $2.54; in Japan it is ¥294, or $2.38 at April 2001 exchange rates. The third column shows the PPP exchange rate implied by these different prices. Thus, the PPP exchange rate for the dollar and yen implied by comparing the prices for Big Macs in Japan and the United States is $1=¥116. Column four gives the actual exchange rate on April 17, 2001 ($1=¥124). Column five compares this to the exchange rate predicted by PPP. This tells us that the Japanese yen is 6 percent undervalued against the dollar and should appreciate against the dollar by that amount according to the PPP theorem. If the Big Mac index were an accurate indicator of PPPs, which it is not, a glance down column five suggests that the U.S. dollar was significantly overvalued against the majority of currencies in early 2001 and would be expected to depreciate in value over the next few months.

The next step in the PPP theory is to argue that the exchange rate will change if relative prices change. For example, imagine there is no price inflation in the United States, while prices in Japan are increasing by 10 percent a year. At the beginning of the year, a basket of goods costs $200 in the United States and ¥20,000 in Japan, so the dollar/yen exchange rate, according to PPP theory, should be $1 = ¥100. At the end of the year, the basket of goods still costs $200 in the United States, but it costs ¥22,000 in Japan. PPP theory predicts that the exchange rate should change as a result. More precisely, by the end of the year:

$$E_{\$/¥} = \$200/¥22,000$$

Thus, ¥1 = $0.0091 (or $1=¥110). Because of 10 percent price inflation, the Japanese yen has depreciated by 10 percent against the dollar. One dollar will buy 10 percent more yen at the end of the year than at the beginning.

Money Supply and Price Inflation

In essence, PPP theory predicts that changes in relative prices will result in a change in exchange rates. Theoretically, a country in which price inflation is running wild should expect to see its currency depreciate against that of countries in which inflation rates are lower. If we can predict what a country's future inflation rate is likely to be, we can also predict how the value of its currency relative to other currencies—its exchange rate—is likely to change. The growth rate of a country's money supply determines its likely future inflation rate.[9] Thus, in theory at least, we can use information about the growth in money supply to forecast exchange rate movements.

Inflation is a monetary phenomenon. It occurs when the quantity of money in circulation rises faster than the stock of goods and services; that is, when the money supply increases faster than output increases. Imagine what would happen if everyone in the country was suddenly given $10,000 by the government. Many people would rush out to spend their extra money on those things they had always wanted—new cars, new furniture, better clothes, and so on. There would be a surge in demand for goods and services. Car dealers, department stores, and other providers of goods and services would respond to this upsurge in demand by raising prices. The result would be price inflation.

	Big Mac prices		Implied PPP* of the Dollar	Actual $ Exchange Rate 17/04/01	Under(−)/ over(+) Valuation against the Dollar, %
	in Local Currency	in Dollars			
United States[†]	$2.54	2.54	—	—	—
Argentina	Peso2.50	2.50	0.98	1.00	−2
Australia	A$3.00	1.52	1.18	1.98	−40
Brazil	Real3.60	1.64	1.42	2.19	−35
Britain	£1.99	2.85	1.28[‡]	1.43[‡]	12
Canada	C$3.33	2.14	1.31	1.56	−16
Chile	Peso1260	2.10	496	601	−17
China	Yuan9.90	1.20	3.90	8.28	−53
Czech Rep	Koruna56.00	1.43	22.0	39.0	−44
Denmark	DKr24.75	2.93	9.74	8.46	15
Euro area	€2.57	2.27	0.99[§]	0.88[§]	−11
France	FFr18.5	2.49	7.28	7.44	−2
Germany	DM5.10	2.30	2.01	2.22	−9
Italy	Lire4300	1.96	1693	2195	−23
Spain	Pta395	2.09	156	189	−18
Hong Kong	HK$10.70	1.37	4.21	7.80	−46
Hungary	Forint399	1.32	157	303	−48
Indonesia	Rupiah14700	1.35	5787	10855	−47
Japan	¥294	2.38	116	124	−6
Malaysia	M$4.52	1.19	1.78	3.80	−53
Mexico	Peso21.9	2.36	8.62	9.29	−7
New Zealand	NZ$3.60	1.46	1.42	2.47	−43
Philippines	Peso59.00	1.17	23.2	50.3	−54
Poland	Zloty5.90	1.46	2.32	4.03	−42
Russia	Roule35.00	1.21	13.8	28.9	−52
Singapore	S$3.30	1.82	1.30	1.81	−28
South Africa	Rand9.70	1.19	3.82	8.13	−53
South Korea	Won3000	2.27	1181	1325	−11
Sweden	SKr24.0	2.33	9.45	10.28	−8
Switzerland	SFr6.30	3.65	2.48	1.73	44
Taiwan	NT$70.0	2.13	27.6	32.9	−16
Thailand	Baht55.0	1.21	21.7	45.5	−52

Table 9.3

Big Mac Index for April 2001

*Purchasing-power parity: local price divided by price in United States

[†]Average of New York, Chicago, San Francisco, and Atlanta

[dd]Dollars per pound

[§]Dollars per euro

Source: McDonald's; *The Economist*, April 21, 2001, p. 74.

A government increasing the money supply is analogous to giving people more money. An increase in the money supply makes it easier for banks to borrow from the government and for individuals and companies to borrow from banks. The resulting increase in credit causes increases in demand for goods and services. Unless the output of goods and services is growing at a rate similar to that of the money supply, the result will be inflation. This relationship has been observed time after time in country after country.

So now we have a connection between the growth in a country's money supply, price inflation, and exchange rate movements. Put simply, when the growth in a country's money supply is faster than the growth in its output, price inflation is fueled. The PPP theory tells us that a country with a high inflation rate will see a depreciation in its currency exchange rate. In the mid-1980s, Bolivia experienced hyperinflation—an explosive and seemingly uncontrollable price inflation in which money loses value very rapidly. Table 9.4 presents data on Bolivia's money supply, inflation rate, and its peso's exchange rate with the U.S. dollar during the period of hyperinflation. The exchange rate is actually the "black market" exchange rate, as the Bolivian government prohibited converting the peso to other currencies during the period. The data show that the growth in money supply, the rate of price inflation, and the depreciation of the peso against the dollar all moved in step with each other. This is just what PPP

Table 9.4

Macroeconomic Data for Bolivia, April 1984– October 1985

Source: Juan-Antino Morales, "Inflation Stabilization in Bolivia," in *Inflation Stabilization: The Experience of Israel, Argentina, Brazil, Bolivia, and Mexico,* ed. Michael Bruno et al. (Cambridge, MA: MIT Press, 1988).

Month	Money Supply (billions of pesos)	Price Level Relative to 1982 (average = 1)	Exchange Rate (pesos per dollar)
1984			
April	270	21.1	3,576
May	330	31.1	3.512
June	440	32.3	3,342
July	599	34.0	3,570
August	718	39.1	7,038
September	889	53.7	13,685
October	1,194	85.5	15,205
November	1,495	112.4	18,469
December	3,296	180.9	24,515
1985			
January	4,630	305.3	73,016
February	6,455	863.3	141,101
March	9,089	1,078.6	128,137
April	12,885	1,205.7	167,428
May	21,309	1,635.7	272,375
June	27,778	2,919.1	481,756
July	47,341	4,854.6	885,476
August	74,306	8,081.0	1,182,300
September	103,272	12,647.6	1,087,440
October	132,550	12,411.8	1,120,210

theory and monetary economics predict. Between April 1984 and July 1985, Bolivia's money supply increased by 17,433 percent, prices increased by 22,908 percent, and the value of the peso against the dollar fell by 24,662 percent! In October 1985, the Bolivian government instituted a dramatic stabilization plan—which included the introduction of a new currency and tight control of the money supply—and by 1987 the country's annual inflation rate was down to 16 percent.[10]

Another way of looking at the same phenomenon is that an increase in a country's money supply, which increases the amount of currency available, changes the relative demand and supply conditions in the foreign exchange market. If the U.S. money supply is growing more rapidly than U.S. output, dollars will be relatively more plentiful than the currencies of countries where monetary growth is closer to output growth. As a result of this relative increase in the supply of dollars, the dollar will depreciate on the foreign exchange market against the currencies of countries with slower monetary growth.

Government policy determines whether the rate of growth in a country's money supply is greater than the rate of growth in output. A government can increase the money supply simply by telling the country's central bank to print more money. Governments tend to do this to finance public expenditure (building roads, paying government workers, paying for defense, etc.). A government could finance public expenditure by raising taxes, but since nobody likes paying more taxes and since politicians do not like to be unpopular, they have a natural preference for printing money. Unfortunately, there is no magic money tree. The inevitable result of excessive growth in money supply is price inflation. However, this has not stopped governments around the world from printing money, with predictable results. If an international business is attempting to predict future movements in the value of a country's currency on the foreign exchange market, it should examine that country's policy toward monetary growth. If the government seems committed to controlling the rate of growth in money supply, the country's future inflation rate may be low (even if the current rate is high) and its currency should not depreciate too much on the foreign exchange market. If the government seems to lack the political will to control the rate of growth in money supply, the future inflation rate may be high, which is likely to cause its currency to depreciate. Historically, many Latin American governments have fallen into this latter category, including Argentina, Bolivia, and Brazil. More recently, many of the newly democratic states of Eastern Europe made the same mistake.

Empirical Tests of PPP Theory

PPP theory predicts that exchange rates are determined by relative prices, and that changes in relative prices will result in a change in exchange rates. A country in which price inflation is running wild should expect to see its currency depreciate against that of countries with lower inflation rates. This is intuitively appealing, but is it true in practice? There are several good examples of the connection between a country's price inflation and exchange rate position (such as Bolivia). However, extensive empirical testing of PPP theory has yielded mixed results.[11] While PPP theory seems to yield relatively accurate predictions in the long run, it does not appear to be a strong predictor of short-run movements in exchange rates covering time spans of five years or less.[12] In addition, the theory seems to best predict exchange rate changes for countries with high rates of inflation and underdeveloped capital markets. The theory is less useful for predicting short-term exchange rate movements between the currencies of advanced industrialized nations that have relatively small differentials in inflation rates.

The failure to find a strong link between relative inflation rates and exchange rate movements has been referred to as the *purchasing power parity puzzle*. Several factors may explain the failure of PPP theory to predict exchange rates more accurately.[13] PPP theory assumes away transportation costs and barriers to trade. In practice, these factors are significant and they tend to create significant price differentials between countries. Transportation costs are certainly not trivial for many goods. Moreover, as we saw in Chapters 5 and 7, governments routinely intervene in international trade, creating tariff and nontariff barriers to cross-border trade. Barriers to trade limit the ability of traders to use arbitrage to equalize prices for the same product in different countries, which is required for the law of one price to hold. Government intervention in cross-border trade, by violating the assumption of efficient markets, weakens the link between relative price changes and changes in exchange rates predicted by PPP theory.

In addition, the PPP theory may not hold if many national markets are dominated by a handful of multinational enterprises that have sufficient market power to be able to exercise some influence over prices, control distribution channels, and differentiate their product offerings between nations.[14] In fact, this situation does seem to prevail in a number of industries. In the detergent industry, two companies, Unilever and Procter & Gamble, dominate the market in nation after nation. In heavy earthmoving equipment, Caterpillar Inc. and Komatsu are global market leaders. In the market for semiconductor equipment, Applied Materials has a commanding market share lead in almost every important national market. Microsoft dominates the market for personal computer operating systems and applications systems around the world, and so on. In such cases, dominant enterprises may be able to exercise a degree of pricing power, setting different prices in different markets to reflect varying demand conditions. This is referred to as price discrimination (we consider the topic from a strategic perspective in Chapter 17). For price discrimination to work, arbitrage must be limited. According to this argument, enterprises with some market power may be able to control distribution channels and therefore limit the unauthorized resale (arbitrage) of products purchased in another national market. They may also be able to limit resale (arbitrage) by differentiating otherwise identical products among nations along some line, such as design or packaging. For example, even though the version of Microsoft Office sold in China may be less expensive than the version sold in the United States, the use of arbitrage to equalize prices may be limited because few Americans would want a version that was based on Chinese characters. The design differentiation between Microsoft Office for China and for the United States means that the law of one price would not work for Microsoft Office, even if transportation costs were trivial and tariff barriers between the United States and China did not exist. If the inability to practice arbitrage were widespread enough, it would break the connection between changes in relative prices and exchange rates predicted by the PPP theorem and help explain the limited empirical support for this theory.

Another factor of some importance is that governments also intervene in the foreign exchange market in attempting to influence the value of their currencies. We will look at why and how they do this in Chapter 10. For now, the important thing to note is that governments regularly intervene in the foreign exchange market, and this further weakens the link between price changes and changes in exchange rates. One more factor explaining the failure of PPP theory to predict short-term movements in foreign exchange rates is the impact of investor psychology and other factors on currency purchasing decisions and exchange rate movements. We will discuss this issue in more detail later in this chapter.

Interest Rates and Exchange Rates

Economic theory tells us that interest rates reflect expectations about likely future inflation rates. In countries where inflation is expected to be high, interest rates also will be high, because investors want compensation for the decline in the value of their money. This relationship was first formalized by economist Irvin Fisher and is referred to as the Fisher Effect. The Fisher Effect states that a country's "nominal" interest rate (i) is the sum of the required "real" rate of interest (r) and the expected rate of inflation over the period for which the funds are to be lent (I). More formally,

$$i = r + I$$

For example, if the real rate of interest in a country is 5 percent and annual inflation is expected to be 10 percent, the nominal interest rate will be 15 percent. As predicted by the Fisher Effect, a strong relationship seems to exist between inflation rates and interest rates.[15]

We can take this one step further and consider how it applies in a world of many countries and unrestricted capital flows. When investors are free to transfer capital between countries, real interest rates will be the same in every country. If differences in real interest rates did emerge between countries, arbitrage would soon equalize them. For example, if the real interest rate in Japan was 10 percent and only 6 percent in the United States, it would pay investors to borrow money in the United States and invest it in Japan. The resulting increase in the demand for money in the United States would raise the real interest rate there, while the increase in the supply of foreign money in Japan would lower the real interest rate there. This would continue until the two sets of real interest rates were equalized. (In practice, differences in real interest rates may persist due to government controls on capital flows; investors are not always free to transfer capital between countries.)

It follows from the Fisher Effect that if the real interest rate is the same worldwide, any difference in interest rates between countries reflects differing expectations about inflation rates. Thus, if the expected rate of inflation in the United States is greater than that in Japan, U.S. nominal interest rates will be greater than Japanese nominal interest rates.

Since we know from PPP theory that there is a link (in theory at least) between inflation and exchange rates, and since interest rates reflect expectations about inflation, it follows that there must also be a link between interest rates and exchange rates. This link is known as the International Fisher Effect (IFE). The **International Fisher Effect** states that for any two countries, the spot exchange rate should change in an equal amount but in the opposite direction to the difference in nominal interest rates between the two countries. Stated more formally, the change in the spot exchange rate between the United States and Japan, for example, can be modeled as follows:

$$(S_1 - S_2)/S_2 \times 100 = i_\$ - i_¥$$

where $i_\$$ and $i_¥$ are the respective nominal interest rates in the United States and Japan, S_1 is the spot exchange rate at the beginning of the period, and S_2 is the spot exchange rate at the end of the period. If the U.S. nominal interest rate is higher than Japan's, reflecting greater expected inflation rates, the value of the dollar against the yen should fall by that interest rate differential in the future. So if the interest rate in the United States is 10 percent and in Japan it is 6 percent, we would expect the value of the dollar to depreciate by 4 percent against the Japanese yen.

Do interest rate differentials help predict future currency movements? The evidence is mixed; as in the case of PPP theory, in the long run, there seems to be a relationship between interest rate differentials and subsequent changes in spot exchange rates. However, considerable short-run deviations occur. Like PPP, the International Fisher Effect is not a good predictor of short-run changes in spot exchange rates.[16]

Investor Psychology and Bandwagon Effects

Empirical evidence suggests that neither PPP theory nor the International Fisher Effect are particularly good at explaining short-term movements in exchange rates. One reason may be the impact of investor psychology on short-run exchange rate movements. Increasing evidence reveals that various psychological factors play an important role in determining the expectations of market traders as to likely future exchange rates.[17] In turn, expectations have a tendency to become self-filling prophecies. We discussed a good example of this mechanism in the Management Focus about George Soros. When George Soros shorted the British pound in September 1992, many foreign exchange traders jumped on the bandwagon and did likewise, selling British pounds and purchasing German marks. As the

Why Did the Korean Won Collapse?

In early 1997, South Korea could look back with pride on a 30-year "economic miracle" that had raised the country from the ranks of the poor and given it the world's 11th largest economy. By the end of 1997, the Korean currency, the won, had lost a staggering 67 percent of its value against the U.S. dollar, the South Korean economy lay in tatters, and the International Monetary Fund was overseeing a $55 billion rescue package. This sudden turn of events had its roots in investments made by South Korea's large industrial conglomerates, or *chaebol*, during the 1990s, often at the bequest of politicians. In 1993, Kim Young-Sam, a populist politician, became president of South Korea. Mr. Kim took office during a mild recession and promised to boost economic growth by encouraging investment in export-oriented industries. He urged the *chaebol* to invest in new factories. South Korea enjoyed an investment-led economic boom in 1994–95, but at a cost. The *chaebol*, always reliant on heavy borrowing, built up massive debts that were equivalent, on average, to four times their equity.

As might be expected, as the volume of investments ballooned during the 1990s, the quality of many of these investments declined significantly. The investments often were made on the basis of unrealistic projections about future demand conditions. This resulted in significant excess capacity and falling prices. An example is investments made by South Korean *chaebol* in semiconductor factories. Investments in such facilities surged in 1994 and 1995 when a temporary global shortage of dynamic random access memory chips (DRAMs) led to sharp price increases for this product. However, supply shortages had disappeared by 1996 and excess capacity was beginning to make itself felt, just as the South Koreans started to bring new DRAM factories on stream. The results were predictable; prices for DRAMs plunged and the earnings of South Korean DRAM manufacturers fell by 90 percent, which meant it was difficult for them to make scheduled payments on the debt they had taken on to build the extra capacity. The risk of corporate bankruptcy increased significantly, and not just in the semiconductor industry. South Korean companies were also investing heavily in a wide range of other industries, including automobiles and steel.

Matters were complicated further because much of the borrowing had been in U.S. dollars, as opposed to Korean won. This had seemed like a smart move at the time. The dollar/won exchange rate had been stable at around $1=W850. Interest rates on dollar borrowings were two to three percentage points lower than rates on borrowings in Korean won. Much of this borrowing was in the form of short-term dollar-denominated debt that had to be paid back to the lending institution within one year. While the borrowing strategy seemed to make sense, there was a risk here. If the won were to depreciate against the dollar, this would increase the size of the debt burden that South Korean companies would have to service, when measured in the local currency. Currency depreciation would raise borrowing costs, depress corporate earnings, and increase the risk of bankruptcy. This is exactly what happened.

By mid-1997, foreign investors had become alarmed at the rising debt levels of South Korean com-

bandwagon effect gained momentum, with more traders selling British pounds and purchasing deutsche marks in expectation of a decline in the pound, their expectations became a self-fulfilling prophecy with massive selling forcing down the value of the pound against the deutsche mark. In other words, the pound declined in value not because of any major shift in macroeconomic fundamentals, but because investors moved in a herd in re-

a major role in determining short-run ... fects can be hard to predict. Investor psychology can be influenced by political factors and by microeconomic events, such as the investment decisions of individual firms, many of which are only loosely linked to macroeconomic fundamentals, such as relative inflation rates. Also, bandwagon effects can be both triggered and exacerbated by the idiosyncratic behavior of politicians. Something like this seems to have occurred in Southeast Asia during 1997 when one after another, the currencies of Thailand, Malaysia, South Korea, and Indonesia lost between 50 percent and 70 percent of their panies, particularly given the emergence of excess capacity and plunging prices in several areas where the companies had made huge investments, including semiconductors, automobiles, and steel. Given increasing speculation that many South Korean companies would not be able to service their debt payments, foreign investors began to withdraw their money from the Korean stock and bond markets. In the process, they sold Korean won and purchased U.S. dollars. The selling of won accelerated in mid-1997 when two of the smaller *chaebol* filed for bankruptcy, citing their inability to meet scheduled debt payments. The increased supply of won and the increased demand for U.S. dollars pushed down the price of won in dollar terms from around won 840=$1 to won 900=$1.

At this point, the South Korean central bank stepped into the foreign exchange market to try to keep the exchange rate above won 1,000=$1. It used dollars that it held in reserve to purchase won. The idea was to try to push up the price of the won in dollar terms and restore investor confidence in the stability of the exchange rate. This action, however, did not address the underlying debt problem faced by South Korean companies. Against a backdrop of more corporate bankruptcies in South Korea, and the government's stated intentions to take some troubled companies into state ownership, Standard & Poor's, the U.S. credit rating agency, downgraded South Korea's sovereign debt. This caused the Korean stock market to plunge 5.5 percent, and the Korean won to fall to won 930 = $1. According to S&P, "The downgrade of . . . ratings reflects the escalating cost to the government of supporting the country's ailing corporate and financial sectors."

The S&P downgrade triggered a sharp sale of the Korean won. In an attempt to protect the won against what was fast becoming a classic bandwagon effect, the South Korean central bank raised short-term interest rates to over 12 percent, more than double the inflation rate. The bank also stepped up its intervention in the currency exchange markets, selling dollars and purchasing won in an attempt to keep the dollar/won exchange rate above $1=W1,000. The main effect of this action, however, was to rapidly deplete South Korea's foreign exchange reserves. These stood at $30 billion on November 1, but fell to only $15 billion two weeks later. With its foreign exchange reserves almost exhausted, the South Korean central bank gave up its defense of the won November 17. Immediately, the price of won in dollars plunged to around won 1,500=$1, effectively increasing by 60 to 70 percent the amount of won heavily indebted Korean companies had to pay to meet scheduled payments on their dollar-denominated debt. These losses, due to adverse changes in foreign exchange rates, depressed the profits of many firms. South Korean firms suffered foreign exchange losses of more than $15 billion in 1997.

Sources: J. Burton and G. Baker, "The Country That Invested Its Way into Trouble," *Financial Times*, January 15, 1998, p. 8; J. Burton, "South Korea's Credit Rating is Lowered," *Financial Times*, October 25, 1997, p. 3; J. Burton, "Currency Losses Hit Samsung Electronics," *Financial Times*, March 20, 1998, p. 24; and "Korean Firms' Foreign Exchange Losses Exceed US $15 Billion," *Business Korea*, February 1998, p. 55.

value against the U.S. dollar in a few months. For a detailed look at what occurred in South Korea, see the accompanying Country Focus. The collapse in the value of the Korean currency did not occur because South Korea had a higher inflation rate than the U the cause of an excessive buildup of dollar-denominated de h

Relati nal interest rate differentials are all mo run changes in exchange rates. They are poor predictors of short-run changes in exchange rates, however, perhaps because of the impact of psychological factors, investor expectations, and bandwagon effects on short-term currency movements. This information is useful for an international business. Insofar as the long-term profitability of foreign investments, export opportunities, and the price competitiveness of foreign imports are all influenced by long-term movements in exchange rates, international businesses would be advised to pay attention to countries' differing monetary growth, inflation, and interest rates. International businesses that engage in foreign exchange transactions on a day-to-day basis could benefit by knowing some predictors of short-term foreign exchange rate movements. Unfortunately, short-term exchange rate movements are difficult to predict.

Exchange Rate Forecasting

A company's need to predict future exchange rate variations raises the issue of whether it is worthwhile for the company to invest in exchange rate forecasting services to aid decision making. Two schools of thought address this issue. The efficient market school argues that forward exchange rates do the best possible job of forecasting future spot exchange rates, and, therefore, investing in forecasting services would be a waste of money. The other school of thought, the inefficient market school, argues that companies can improve the foreign exchange market's estimate of future exchange rates (as contained in the forward rate) by investing in forecasting services. In other words, this school of thought does not believe the forward exchange rates are the best possible predictors of future spot exchange rates.

The Efficient Market School

Forward exchange rates represent market participants' collective predictions of likely spot exchange rates at specified future dates. If forward exchange rates are the best possible predictor of future spot rates, it would make no sense for companies to spend additional money trying to forecast short-run exchange rate movements. Many economists believe the foreign exchange market is efficient at setting forward rates.[19] An **efficient market** is one in which prices reflect all available public information. (If forward rates reflect all available information about likely future changes in exchange rates, there is no way a company can beat the market by investing in forecasting services.)

If the foreign exchange market is efficient, forward exchange rates should be unbiased predictors of future spot rates. This does not mean the predictions will be accurate in any specific situation. It means inaccuracies will not be consistently above or below future spot rates; they will be random. Many empirical tests have addressed the efficient market hypothesis. Although most of the early work seems to confirm the hypothesis (suggesting that companies should not waste their money on forecasting services), more recent studies have challenged it.[20] There is some evidence that forward rates are not unbiased predictors of future spot rates, and that more accurate predictions of future spot rates can be calculated from publicly available information.[21]

The Inefficient Market School

Citing evidence against the efficient market hypothesis, some economists believe the foreign exchange market is inefficient. An inefficient market is one in which prices do not reflect all available information. In an inefficient market, forward exchange rates will not be the best possible predictors of future spot exchange rates.

If this is true, it may be worthwhile for international businesses to invest in forecasting services (as many do). The belief is that professional exchange rate forecasts might provide better predictions of future spot rates than forward exchange rates do. However, the track record of professional forecasting services is not that good. An analysis of the forecasts of 12 major forecasting services between 1978 and 1982 concluded the forecasters in general did not provide better forecasts than the forward exchange rates.[22] Also, forecasting services did not predict the 1997 currency crisis that swept through Southeast Asia.

Approaches to Forecasting

Assuming the inefficient market school is correct that the foreign exchange market's estimate of future spot rates can be improved, on what basis should forecasts be prepared? Here again, there are two schools of thought. One adheres to fundamental analysis, while the other uses technical analysis.

Fundamental Analysis

Fundamental analysis draws on economic theory to construct sophisticated econometric models for predicting exchange rate movements. The variables contained in these models typically include those we have discussed, such as relative money supply growth rates, inflation rates, and interest rates. In addition, they may include variables related to balance-of-payments positions.

Running a deficit on a balance-of-payments current account (a country is importing more goods and services than it is exporting), creates pressures that result in the depreciation of the country's currency on the foreign exchange market.[23] (For background on the balance of payments, see Chapter 7.) Consider what might happen if the United States was running a persistent current account balance-of-payments deficit. Since the United States would be importing more than it was exporting, people in other countries would be increasing their holdings of U.S. dollars. If these people were willing to hold their dollars, the dollar's exchange rate would not be influenced. However, if these people converted their dollars into other currencies, the supply of dollars in the foreign exchange market would increase (as would demand for the other currencies). This shift in demand and supply would create pressures that could lead to the depreciation of the dollar against other currencies.

This argument hinges on whether people in other countries are willing to hold dollars. This depends on such factors as U.S. interest rates and inflation rates. So, in a sense, the balance-of-payments position is not a fundamental predictor of future exchange rate movements. For example, between 1998 and 2001, the U.S. dollar appreciated against most major currencies despite a growing balance-of-payments deficit. Relatively high real interest rates in the United States made the dollar very attractive to foreigners, so they did not convert their dollars into other currencies. Given this, we are back to the argument that the fundamental determinants of exchange rates are monetary growth, inflation rates, and interest rates.

Technical Analysis

Technical analysis uses price and volume data to determine past trends, which are expected to continue into the future. This approach does not rely on a consideration of economic fundamentals. Technical analysis is based on the premise that there are analyzable market trends and waves and that previous trends and waves can be used to predict future trends and waves. Since there is no theoretical rationale for this assumption of predictability, many economists compare technical analysis to fortune-telling. Despite this skepticism, technical analysis has gained favor in recent years.[24]

Currency Convertibility

Until this point we have assumed that the currencies of various countries are freely convertible into other currencies. This assumption is invalid. Many countries restrict the ability of residents and nonresidents to convert the local currency into a foreign currency, making international trade and investment more difficult. Many international businesses have used "countertrade" practices to circumvent problems that arise when a currency is not freely convertible.

Convertibility and Government Policy

Due to government restrictions, a significant number of currencies are not freely convertible into other currencies. A country's currency is said to be **freely convertible** when the country's government allows both residents and nonresidents to purchase unlimited amounts of a foreign currency with it. A currency is said to be **externally convertible** when only nonresidents may convert it into a foreign currency without any limitations. A currency is **nonconvertible** when neither residents nor nonresidents are allowed to convert it into a foreign currency.

Free convertibility is the exception rather than the rule. Many countries place some restrictions on their residents' ability to convert the domestic currency into a foreign currency (a policy of external convertibility). Restrictions range from the relatively minor (such as restricting the amount of foreign currency they may take with them out of the country on trips) to the major (such as restricting domestic businesses' ability to take foreign currency out of the country). External convertibility restrictions can limit domestic companies' ability to invest abroad, but they present few problems for foreign companies wishing to do business in that country. For example, even if the Japanese government tightly controlled the ability of its residents to convert the yen into U.S. dollars, all U.S. businesses with deposits in Japanese banks may at any time convert all their yen into dollars and take them out of the country. Thus, a U.S. company with a subsidiary in Japan is assured that it will be able to convert the profits from its Japanese operation into dollars and take them out of the country.

Serious problems arise, however, under a policy of nonconvertibility. This was the practice of the former Soviet Union, and it continued to be the practice in Russia until recently. When strictly applied, nonconvertibility means that although a U.S. company doing business in a country such as Russia may be able to generate significant ruble profits, it may not convert those rubles into dollars and take them out of the country. Obviously this is not desirable for international business.

Governments limit convertibility to preserve their foreign exchange reserves. A country needs an adequate supply of these reserves to service its international debt commitments and to purchase imports. Governments typically impose convertibility restrictions on their currency when they fear that free convertibility will lead to a run on their foreign exchange reserves. This occurs when residents and nonresidents rush to convert their holdings of domestic currency into a foreign currency—a phenomenon generally referred to as capital flight. **Capital flight** is most likely to occur when the value of the domestic currency is depreciating rapidly because of hyperinflation, or when a country's economic prospects are shaky in other respects. Under such circumstances, both residents and nonresidents tend to believe that their money is more likely to hold its value if it is converted into a foreign currency and invested abroad. Not only will a run on foreign exchange reserves limit the country's ability to service its international debt and pay for imports, but it will also lead to a precipitous depreciation in the exchange rate as residents and nonresidents unload their holdings of domestic currency on the foreign exchange markets (thereby increasing the market supply of the country's currency). Governments fear that the rise in import prices resulting from currency depreciation will lead to further increases in inflation. This fear provides another rationale for limiting convertibility.

Countertrade

Companies can deal with the nonconvertibility problem by engaging in countertrade. Countertrade is discussed in detail in Chapter 15, so we will merely introduce the concept here. **Countertrade** refers to a range of barterlike agreements by which goods and services can be traded for other goods and services. Countertrade can make sense when a country's currency is nonconvertible. For example, consider the deal that General Electric struck with the Romanian government in 1984, when that country's currency was nonconvertible. When General Electric won a contract for a $150 million generator project in Romania, it agreed to take payment in the form of Romanian goods that could be sold for $150 million on international markets. In a similar case, the Venezuelan government negotiated a contract with Caterpillar in 1986 under which Venezuela would trade 350,000 tons of iron ore for Caterpillar heavy construction equipment. Caterpillar subsequently traded the iron ore to Romania in exchange for Romanian farm products, which it then sold on international markets for dollars.[25]

How important is countertrade? One estimate is that 20 to 30 percent of world trade in 1985 involved some form of countertrade agreements. Since then, however, more currencies have become freely convertible, and the percentage of world trade that involves countertrade has fallen to between 10 percent and 20 percent.[26]

Implications for Business

This chapter contains a number of clear implications for business. First, it is critical that international businesses understand the influence of exchange rates on the profitability of trade and investment deals. Adverse changes in exchange rates can make apparently profitable deals unprofitable. The risk introduced into international business transactions by changes in exchange rates is referred to as foreign exchange risk. Means of hedging against foreign exchange risk are available. Forward exchange rates and currency swaps allow companies to insure against this risk.

International businesses must also understand the forces that determine exchange rates. This is particularly true in light of the increasing evidence that forward exchange rates are not unbiased predictors. If a company wants to know how the value of a particular currency is likely to change over the long term on the foreign exchange market, it should look closely at those economic fundamentals that appear to predict long-run exchange rate movements (i.e., the growth in a country's money supply, its inflation rate, and its nominal interest rates). For example, an international business should be very cautious about trading with or investing in a country with a recent history of rapid growth in its domestic money supply. The upsurge in inflation that is likely to follow such rapid monetary growth could lead to a sharp drop in the value of the country's currency on the foreign exchange market, which could transform a profitable deal into an unprofitable one. This is not to say that an international business should not trade with or invest in such a country. Rather, it means an international business should take some precautions before doing so, such as buying currency forward on the foreign exchange market or structuring the deal around a countertrade arrangement.

Complicating this picture is the issue of currency convertibility. The proclivity that many governments seem to have to restrict currency convertibility suggests that the foreign exchange market does not always provide the lubricant necessary to make international trade and investment possible. Given this, international businesses need to explore alternative mechanisms for facilitating international trade and investment that do not involve currency conversion. Countertrade seems the obvious mechanism. We return to the topic of countertrade and discuss it in depth in Chapter 15.

Chapter Summary

This chapter explained how the foreign exchange market works, examined the forces that determine exchange rates, and then discussed the implications of these factors for international business. Given that changes in exchange rates can dramatically alter the profitability of foreign trade and investment deals, this is an area of major interest to international business. This chapter made the following points:

1. One function of the foreign exchange market is to convert the currency of one country into the currency of another.

2. International businesses participate in the foreign exchange market to facilitate international trade and investment, to invest spare cash in short-term money market accounts abroad, and to engage in currency speculation.

3. A second function of the foreign exchange market is to provide insurance against foreign exchange risk.

4. The spot exchange rate is the exchange rate at which a dealer converts one currency into another currency on a particular day.

5. Foreign exchange risk can be reduced by using forward exchange rates. A forward exchange rate is an exchange rate governing future transactions.

6. Foreign exchange risk can also be reduced by engaging in currency swaps. A swap is the simultaneous purchase and sale of a given amount of foreign exchange for two different value dates.

7. The law of one price holds that in competitive markets that are free of transportation costs and barriers to trade, identical products sold in different countries must sell for the same price when their price is expressed in the same currency.

8. Purchasing power parity (PPP) theory states the price of a basket of particular goods should be roughly equivalent in each country. PPP theory predicts that the exchange rate will change if relative prices change.

9. The rate of change in countries' relative prices depends on their relative inflation rates. A country's inflation rate seems to be a function of the growth in its money supply.

10. The PPP theory of exchange rate changes yields relatively accurate predictions of long-term trends in exchange rates, but not of short-term movements. The failure of PPP theory to predict exchange rate changes more accurately may be due to the existence of transportation costs, barriers to trade and investment, and the impact of psychological factors such as bandwagon effects on market movements and short-run exchange rates.

11. Interest rates reflect expectations about inflation. In countries where inflation is expected to be high, interest rates also will be high.

12. The International Fisher Effect states that for any two countries, the spot exchange rate should change in an equal amount but in the opposite direction to the difference in nominal interest rates.

13. The most common approach to exchange rate forecasting is fundamental analysis. This relies on variables such as money supply growth, inflation rates, nominal interest rates, and balance-of-payments positions to predict future changes in exchange rates.

14. In many countries, the ability of residents and nonresidents to convert local currency into a foreign currency is restricted by government policy. A government restricts the convertibility of its currency to protect the country's foreign exchange reserves and to halt any capital flight.

15. Particularly bothersome for international business is a policy of nonconvertibility, which prohibits residents and nonresidents from exchanging local currency for foreign currency. A policy of nonconvertibility makes it very difficult to engage in international trade and investment in the country.

16. One way of coping with the nonconvertibility problem is to engage in countertrade—to trade goods and services for other goods and services.

Critical Discussion Questions

1. The interest rate on South Korean government securities with one-year maturity is 4 percent, and the expected inflation rate for the coming year is 2 percent. The interest rate on U.S. government securities with one-year maturity is 7 percent, and the expected rate of inflation is 5 percent. The current spot exchange rate for Korean won is $1 = W1,200. Forecast the spot exchange rate one year from today. Explain the logic of your answer.

2. Two countries, Great Britain and the United States, produce just one good: beef. Suppose the

price of beef in the United States is $2.80 per pound and in Britain it is £3.70 per pound.

a. According to PPP theory, what should the $/£ spot exchange rate be?

b. Suppose the price of beef is expected to rise to $3.10 in the United States and to £4.65 in Britain. What should the one-year forward $/£ exchange rate be?

c. Given your answers to parts a and b, and given that the current interest rate in the United States is 10 percent, what would you expect the current interest rate to be in Britain?

3. You manufacture wine goblets. In mid-June you receive an order for 10,000 goblets from Japan. Payment of ¥400,000 is due in mid-December. You expect the yen to rise from its present rate of $1 = ¥130 to $1 = ¥100 by December. You can borrow yen at 6 percent a year. What should you do?

Closing Case

The Collapse of the Thai Baht in 1997

During the 1980s and 1990s, Thailand emerged as one of Asia's most dynamic tiger economies. From 1985 to 1995, Thailand achieved an annual average economic growth rate of 8.4 percent, while keeping its annual inflation rate at only 5 percent (comparable figures for the United States over this period were 1.3 percent for economic growth and 3.2 percent for inflation). Much of Thailand's economic growth was powered by exports. From 1990 to 1996, for example, the value of exports from Thailand grew by 16 percent per year compounded. The wealth created by export-led growth fueled an investment boom in commercial and residential property, industrial assets, and infrastructure. As demand for property increased, the value of commercial and residential real estate in Bangkok soared. This fed a building boom the likes of which had never been seen in Thailand. Office and apartment buildings were going up all over the city. Heavy borrowing from banks financed much of this construction, but as long as property values continued to rise, the banks were happy to lend to property companies.

By early 1997, however, it was clear that the boom had produced excess capacity in residential and commercial property. An estimated 365,000 apartment units were unoccupied in Bangkok in late 1996. With another 100,000 units scheduled to be completed in 1997, years of excess demand in the Thai property market had been replaced by excess supply. By one estimate, Bangkok's building boom by 1997 had produced enough excess space to meet its residential and commercial needs for at least five years.

At the same time, Thailand's investments in infrastructure, industrial capacity, and commercial real estate were sucking in foreign goods at unprecedented rates. To build infrastructure, factories, and office buildings, Thailand was purchasing capital equipment and materials from America, Europe, and Japan. As a consequence, the current account of the balance of payments shifted strongly into the red during the mid-1990s. Despite strong export growth, imports grew faster. By 1995, Thailand was running a current account deficit equivalent to 8.1 percent of its GDP.

Things started to fall apart February 5, 1997, when Somprasong Land, a Thai property developer, announced it had failed to make a scheduled $3.1 million interest payment on an $80 billion eurobond loan, effectively entering into default. Somprasong Land was the first victim of speculative overbuilding in the Bangkok property market. The Thai stock market had already declined by 45 percent since its high in early 1996, primarily on concerns that several property companies might be forced into bankruptcy. Now one had been. The stock market fell another 2.7 percent on the news, but it was only the beginning. In the aftermath of Somprasong's default, it became clear that, along with several other property developers, many of the country's financial institutions, including Finance One, were also on the brink of default. Finance One, the country's largest financial institution, had pioneered a practice that had become widespread among Thai institutions—issuing bonds denominated in U.S. dollars and using the proceeds to finance lending to the country's booming property developers. In theory, this practice made sense because Finance One was able to exploit the interest rate differential between dollar-denominated debt and Thai debt (i.e., Finance One borrowed in U.S. dollars at a low interest rate and lent in Thai baht at high interest rates). The only problem with this financing strategy was that when the Thai property market began to unravel in 1996 and 1997, the property developers could no longer pay back the cash they had borrowed from Finance One. This made it difficult for Finance One to pay back its creditors. As the effects of overbuilding became evident in 1996, Finance One's nonperforming loans doubled, then doubled again in the first quarter of 1997.

In February 1997, trading in the shares of Finance One was suspended while the government tried to arrange for the troubled company to be acquired by a small Thai bank, in a deal sponsored by the Thai central bank. It didn't work, and when trading resumed in Finance One shares in May, they fell 70 percent in a single day. By this time bad loans in the Thai property market were swelling daily and had risen to more than $30 billion. Finance One was bankrupt, and it was feared that others would follow.

It was at this point that currency traders began a concerted attack on the Thai currency. For the previous 13 years, the Thai baht had been pegged to the U.S. dollar at an exchange rate of about $1=Bt25. This peg, however, had become increasingly difficult to defend. Currency traders looking at Thailand's growing current account deficit and dollar-denominated debt burden, reasoned that demand for dollars in Thailand would rise while demand for baht would fall. (Businesses and financial institutions would be exchanging baht for dollars to service their debt payments and purchase imports.) There were several attempts to force a devaluation of the baht in late 1996 and early 1997. These speculative attacks typically involved traders selling baht short to profit from a future decline in the value of the baht against the dollar. In this context, short selling involves a currency trader borrowing baht from a financial institution and immediately reselling those baht in the foreign exchange market for dollars. The theory is that if the value of the baht subsequently falls against the dollar, then when the trader has to buy the baht back to repay the financial institution, it will cost her fewer dollars than she received from the initial sale of baht. For example, a trader might borrow Bt100 from a bank for six months. The trader then exchanges the Bt100 for $4 (at an exchange rate of $1=Bt25). If the exchange rate subsequently declines to $1=Bt50, it will cost the trader only $2 to repurchase the Bt100 in six months and pay back the bank, leaving the trader with a 100 percent profit!

In May 1997, short sellers were swarming over the Thai baht. In an attempt to defend the peg, the Thai government used its foreign exchange reserves (which were denominated in U.S. dollars) to purchase baht. It cost the Thai government $5 billion to defend the baht, which reduced its "officially reported" foreign exchange reserves to a two-year low of $33 billion. In addition, the Thai government raised key interest rates from 10 percent to 12.5 percent to make holding baht more attractive, but because this also raised corporate borrowing costs it exacerbated the debt crisis. What the world financial community did not know at this point, was that with the blessing of his superiors, a foreign exchange trader at the Thai central bank had locked up most of Thailand's foreign exchange reserves in forward contracts. The reality was that Thailand had only $1.14 billion in available foreign exchange reserves left to defend the dollar peg. Defending the peg was now impossible.

On July 2, 1997, the Thai government bowed to the inevitable and announced it would allow the baht to float freely against the dollar. The baht immediately lost 18 percent of its value and started a slide that would bring the exchange rate down to $1=Bt55 by January 1998. As the baht declined, the Thai debt bomb exploded. A 50 percent decline in the value of the baht against the dollar doubled the amount of baht required to serve the dollar-denominated debt commitments taken on by Thai financial institutions and businesses. This made more bankruptcies and further pushed down the battered Thai stock market. The Thailand Set stock market index ultimately declined from 787 in January 1997 to a low of 337 in December of that year, and this on top of a 45 percent decline in 1996!

Sources: "Bitter Pill for the Thais," *Straits Times,* July 5, 1997, p. 46; World Bank, *1997 World Development Report* (New York: World Bank), Table 2; T. Bardacke, "Somprasong Defaults on $80 Million Eurobond," *Financial Times,* February 6, 1997, p. 25; and T. Bardacke, "The Day the Miracle Came to an End," *Financial Times,* January 12, 1998, pp. 6–7.

Case Discussion Questions

1. Identify the main factors that led to the collapse of the Thai baht in 1997.

2. Do you think the sudden collapse of the Thai baht can be explained by the purchasing power parity theorem?

3. What role did speculators play in the fall of the Thai baht? Did they cause its fall?

4. What steps might the Thai government have taken to preempt the financial crisis that swept the nation in 1997?

5. How will the collapse of the Thai baht affect businesses in Thailand, particularly those that purchase inputs from abroad or export finished products?

6. Do you notice any similarities between the collapse of the Thai baht in 1997 and the collapse of the Korean won around the same time (see the Country Focus in this chapter)? What are these similarities? Do you think these two events were related? How?

Notes

1. C. Cooper, "Euro's Drop Is Hardest for Smallest," *Wall Street Journal*, October 2, 2000, p. A21.

2. For a good general introduction to the foreign exchange market, see R. Weisweiller, *How the Foreign Exchange Market Works* (New York: New York Institute of Finance, 1990). A detailed description of the economics of foreign exchange markets can be found in P. R. Krugman and M. Obstfeld, *International Economics: Theory and Policy* (New York: Harper-Collins, 1994).

3. C. Forman, "Allied-Lyons to Post $269 Million Loss from Foreign Exchange as Dollar Soars," *Wall Street Journal*, March 20, 1991, p. A17.

4. Bank for International Settlements, *Central Bank Survey of Foreign Exchange and Derivatives Market Activity, April 2001* (Basle, Switzerland: BIS, 2001).

5. Ibid.

6. Ibid.

7. For a comprehensive review see M. Taylor, "The Economics of Exchange Rates," *Journal of Economic Literature* 33, (1995), pp. 13–47.

8. Krugman and Obstfeld, *International Economics: Theory and Policy.*

9. M. Friedman, *Studies in the Quantity Theory of Money* (Chicago: University of Chicago Press, 1956). For an accessible explanation, see M. Friedman and R. Friedman, *Free to Choose* (London: Penguin Books, 1979), chap. 9.

10. Juan-Antino Morales, "Inflation Stabilization in Bolivia," in *Inflation Stabilization: The Experience of Israel, Argentina, Brazil, Bolivia, and Mexico*, ed. Michael Bruno et al. (Cambridge, MA: MIT Press, 1988); and The Economist, *World Book of Vital Statistics* (New York: Random House, 1990).

11. For reviews and recent articles, see L. H. Officer, "The Purchasing Power Parity Theory of Exchange Rates: A Review Article," International Monetary Fund staff papers, March 1976, pp. 1–60; Taylor, "The Economics of Exchange Rates"; H. J. Edison, J. E. Gagnon, and W. R. Melick, "Understanding the Empirical Literature on Purchasing Power Parity," *Journal of International Money and Finance* 16 (February 1997), pp. 1–18; J. R. Edison, "Multi-Country Evidence on the Behavior of Purchasing Power Parity under the Current Float," *Journal of International Money and Finance* 16 (February 1997), pp. 19–36; and K. Rogoff, "The Purchasing Power Parity Puzzle," *Journal of Economic Literature* 34 (1996), pp. 647–68.

12. M. Obstfeld and K. Rogoff. "The Six Major Puzzles in International Economics," National Bureau of Economic Research working paper 7777, July 2000.

13. Ibid.

14. See M. Devereux and C. Engel. "Monetary Policy in the Open Economy Revisited: Price Setting and Exchange Rate Flexibility," National Bureau of Economic Research working paper 7665, April 2000. Also P. Krugman. "Pricing to Market When the Exchange Rate Changes," in: *Real Financial Economics*, S. Arndt and J. Richardson (eds). Cambridge, MA: MIT Press.

15. For a summary of the evidence, see the survey by Taylor, "The Economics of Exchange Rates."

16. R. E. Cumby and M. Obstfeld, "A Note on Exchange Rate Expectations and Nominal Interest Differentials: A Test of the Fisher Hypothesis," *Journal of Finance*, June 1981, pp. 697–703.

17. Taylor, "The Economics of Exchange Rates."

18. See, H. L. Allen and M. P. Taylor, "Charts, Noise, and Fundamentals in the Foreign Exchange Market," *Economic Journal* 100 (1990), pp. 49–59, and T. Ito, "Foreign Exchange Rate Expectations: Micro Survey Data," *American Economic Review* 80 (1990), pp. 434–49.

19. For example, see E. Fama, "Forward Rates as Predictors of Future Spot Rates," *Journal of Financial Economics*, October 1976, pp. 361–77.

20. R. M. Levich, "The Efficiency of Markets for Foreign Exchange," in *International Finance*, ed. G. D. Gay and R. W. Kold (Richmond, VA: Robert F. Dane, Inc., 1983).

21. J. Williamson, *The Exchange Rate System* (Washington, DC: Institute for International Economics, 1983).

22. R. M. Levich, "Currency Forecasters Lose Their Way," *Euromoney*, August 1983, p. 140.

23. Rogoff, "The Purchasing Power Parity Puzzle."

24. C. Engel and J. D. Hamilton, "Long Swings in the Dollar: Are They in the Data and Do Markets Know It?" *American Economic Review*, September 1990, pp. 689–713.

25. J. R. Carter and J. Gagne, "The Do's and Don'ts of International Countertrade," *Sloan Management Review*, Spring 1988, pp. 31–37.

26. D. S. Levine, "Got a Spare Destroyer Lying Around?" *World Trade* 10 (June 1997), pp. 34–35, and Dan West, "Countertrade," *Business Credit*, April 2001, pp. 64–67.

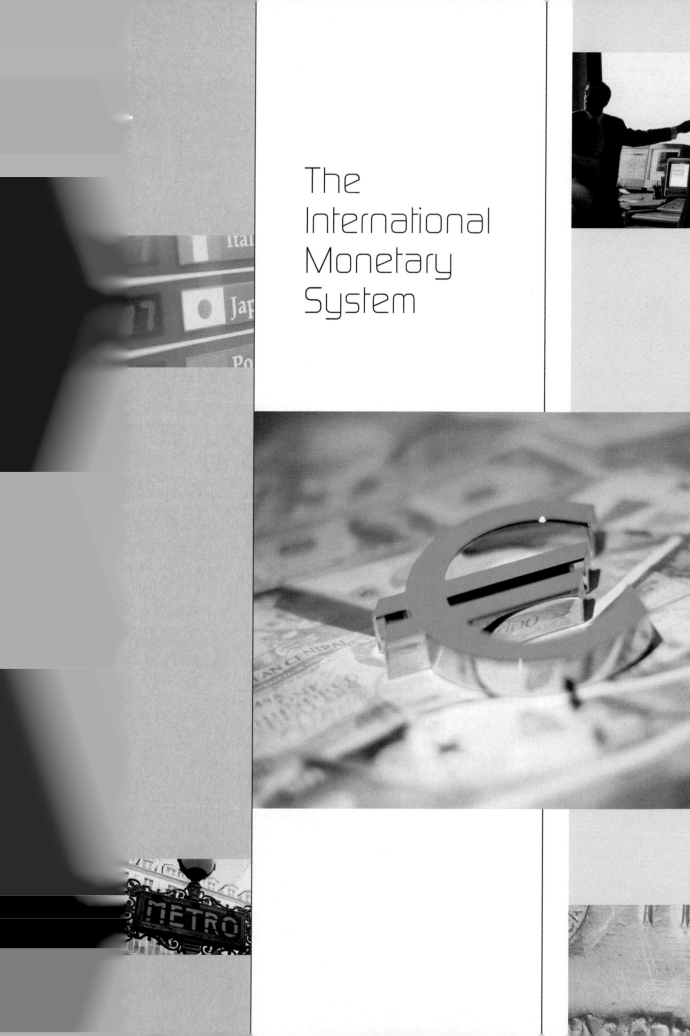

The International Monetary System

In May 2001, the International Monetary Fund (IMF) agreed to lend $8 billion to Turkey to help the country stabilize its economy and halt a sharp slide in the value of its currency. This was the third time in two years that the international lending institution had put together a loan program for Turkey, and it was the 18th program since Turkey became a member of the IMF in 1958.

Many of Turkey's problems stemmed from a large and inefficient state sector and heavy subsidies to various private sectors of the economy such as agriculture. Although the Turkish government started to privatize state-owned companies in the late 1980s, the programs proceeded at a glacial pace, hamstrung by political opposition within Turkey. Instead of selling state-owned assets to private investors, successive governments increased support to unprofitable state-owned industries and raised the wage rates of state employees. Nor did the government cut subsidies to politically powerful private sectors of the economy, such as agriculture. To support state industries and finance subsidies, Turkey issued significant amounts of government debt. To limit the amount of debt, the government simply printed money to finance spending. The result, predictably, was rampant inflation and high interest rates. During the 1990s, inflation averaged over 80 percent a year while real interest rates rose to more than 50 percent on a number of occasions. Despite this, the Turkish economy continued to grow at a healthy pace of 6 percent annually in real terms, a remarkable achievement given the high inflation rates and interest rates.

By the late 1990s, however, the "Turkish miracle" of sustained growth in the face of high inflation and interest rates was running out of steam. Government debt had risen to 60 percent of gross domestic product, government borrowing was leaving little capital for private enterprises, and the cost of financing government debt was spiraling out of control. Rampant inflation was putting pressure on the Turkish currency, the lira, which at the time was pegged in value to a basket of other currencies.

Realizing that it needed to drastically reform its economy, the Turkish government sat down with the IMF in late 1999 to work out a recovery program, adopted in January 2000.

As with most IMF programs, the focus was on bringing down the inflation rate, stabilizing the value of the Turkish currency, and restructuring the economy to reduce government debt. The Turkish government committed itself to reducing government debt by taking a number of steps. These included an accelerated privatization program, using the proceeds to pay down debt; the reduction of agricultural subsidies; reform to make it more difficult for people to qualify for public pension programs; and tax increases. The government also agreed to rein in the growth in the money supply to better control inflation. To limit the possibility of speculative attacks on the Turkish currency in the foreign exchange markets, the Turkish government and IMF announced that Turkey would peg the value of the lira against a basket of currencies and devalue the lira by a predetermined amount each month throughout 2000, bringing the total devaluation for the year to 25 percent. To ease the pain, the IMF agreed to provide the Turkish government with $5 billion in loans that could be used to support the value of the lira.

Initially the program seemed to be working. Inflation fell to 35 percent in 2000, while the economy grew by 6 percent. By the end of 2000, however, the program was in trouble. Burdened with nonperforming loans, a number of Turkish banks faced default and had been taken into public ownership by the government. When a criminal fraud investigation uncovered evidence that several of these banks had been pressured by politicians into providing loans at below-market interest rates, foreign investors, worried that more banks might be involved, started to pull their money out of Turkey. This sent the Turkish stock market into a tailspin and put enormous pressure on the Turkish lira. Sensing that the government might be forced to devalue the lira at a faster rate than planned, traders in the foreign exchange market started to sell the lira short, while the flow of foreign capital out of Turkey increased to a flood, which put even more pressure on the lira. The government raised Turkish overnight interbank lending rates to as high as 1,950 percent to try to stem the outflow of capital, but it was clear that Turkey alone could not halt the flow.

The IMF stepped once more into the breach, December 6, 2000, announcing a quickly arranged $7.5 billion loan program for the country. In return for the loan, the IMF required the Turkish government to close 10 insolvent banks, speed up its privatization plans (which had once more stalled), and cap any pay increases for government workers. The IMF also reportedly urged the Turkish government to let its currency float freely in the foreign exchange markets, but the government refused, arguing that the result would be a rapid devaluation in the lira, which would raise import prices and fuel price inflation. The government insisted that reducing inflation should be its first priority.

This plan started to come apart in February 2001. A surge in inflation and a rapid slowdown in economic growth once more spooked foreign investors. Into this explosive mix waded Turkey's prime minister and president, who engaged in a highly public argument about economic policy and political corruption. This triggered a rapid outflow of capital. The government raised the overnight interbank lending rate to 7,500 percent to try to persuade foreigners to leave their money in the country, but to no avail. Realizing that it would be unable to keep the lira within its planned monthly devaluation range without raising interest rates to absurd levels or seriously depleting the country's foreign exchange reserves, on February 23, 2001, the Turkish government decided to let the lira float freely. The lira immediately dropped 50 percent in value against the U.S. dollar, but ended the day down some 28 percent.

Over the next two months, the Turkish economy continued to weaken as a global economic slowdown affected the nation. Inflation stayed high, and progress at reforming the country's economy remained bogged down by political considerations. By early April the lira had fallen 40 percent against the dollar since February 23, and the country was teetering on the brink of an economic meltdown. For the third time in 18 months, the IMF stepped in, arranging for another $8 billion in loans. Once more, the IMF insisted that the Turkish government accelerate privatization, close insolvent banks, deregulate its market, and cut government spending. Critics of the IMF, however, claimed this "austerity program" would only slow the Turkish economy and make matters worse, not better. These critics advocated a mix of sound monetary policy and tax cuts to boost Turkey's economic growth.

Sources: P. Blustein, "Turkish Crisis Weakens the Case for Intervention," *Washington Post*, March 2, 2001, p. E1; H. Pope, "Can Turkey Finally Mend Its Economy?" *Wall Street Journal*, May 22, 2001, p. A18; "Turkish Bath," *Wall Street Journal*, February 23, 2001, p. A14; E. McBride, "Turkey—Fingers Crossed," *The Economist*, June 10, 2000, p. SS16–SS17; and "Turkey and the IMF," *The Economist*, December 9, 2000, pp. 81–82.

▉ Introduction

The **international monetary system** refers to the institutional arrangements that countries adopt to govern exchange rates. In Chapter 9 we assumed the foreign exchange market was the primary institution for determining exchange rates and the impersonal market forces of demand and supply determined the relative value of any two currencies (i.e., their exchange rate). Furthermore, we explained that the demand and supply of currencies is influenced by their respective countries' relative inflation rates and interest rates. When the foreign exchange market determines the relative value of a currency, we say that the country is adhering to a **floating exchange rate** regime. The world's four major trading currencies—the U.S. dollar, the European Union's euro, the Japanese yen, and the British pound—are all free to float against each other. Thus, their exchange rates are determined by market forces and fluctuate against each other on a day-to-day, if not minute-to-minute, basis. However, the exchange rates of many currencies are not determined by the free play of market forces; other institutional arrangements are adopted.

In the opening case, for example, we learned that until recently, the value of the Turkish lira was pegged to a basket of currencies. Many of the world's smaller nations peg their currencies, primarily to the dollar or the euro. A **pegged exchange rate** means the value of the currency is fixed relative to a reference currency, such as the U.S. dollar, and then the exchange rate between that currency and other currencies is determined by the reference currency exchange rate. Thus, Belize pegs its currency to the dollar, and the exchange rate between the Belizean currency and the euro is determined by the U.S. dollar/euro exchange rate.

Other countries, while not adopting a formal pegged rate, try to hold the value of their currency within some range against an important reference currency such as the U.S. dollar. This is often referred to as a **dirty float.** It is a float because in theory, the value of the currency is determined by market forces, but it is a dirty float (as opposed to a clean float) because the central bank of a country will intervene in the foreign exchange market to try to maintain the value of its currency if it depreciates too rapidly against an important reference currency.

Still other countries have operated with a **fixed exchange rate** system, in which the values of a set of currencies are fixed against each other at some mutually agreed on exchange rate. Before the introduction of the euro in 2000, several member states of the European Union operated with fixed exchange rates within the context of the European Monetary System (EMS). For a quarter of a century after World War II, the world's major industrial nations participated in a fixed exchange rate system. Although this system collapsed in 1973, some still argue that the world should attempt to reimpose it.

Pegged exchange rates, dirty floats, and fixed exchange rate systems all require some degree of government intervention in the foreign exchange market to maintain the value of a currency. A currency may come under pressure when there are significant economic problems in the nation. In the case of Turkey, for example, these included high inflation, excessive government debt, and a crisis in the banking system (see the opening case). A government can try to maintain the value of its currency by using foreign currency held in reserve (foreign exchange reserves) to buy its currency in the market, thereby increasing demand for the currency and raising its price. Thus, as the Turkish lira began to depreciate rapidly in late 2000, the Turkish central bank entered the foreign exchange market, using foreign currency it held in reserve, such as U.S. dollars, Japanese yen, and euros, to purchase lira in an attempt to halt the depreciation in the exchange rate. However, since governments may not have sufficient foreign exchange reserves to defend the value of their currency, they sometimes call on a powerful multinational institution, the International Monetary Fund (IMF), for loans to help them do this. The IMF is another important player in the international monetary system. As we saw in the opening case, the IMF does not simply lend money to a country in trouble. In exchange for the loan, it requires that the government adopt policies designed to correct whatever economic problems caused the depreciation in the nation's currency. Thus, the IMF insisted that Turkey take steps to reduce its inflation rate and government debt and to resolve problems in the country's banking system.

In this chapter we will explain how the international monetary system works and point out its implications for international business. To understand how the international monetary system works, we must review the system's evolution. We will begin with a discussion of the gold standard and its breakup during the 1930s. Then we will discuss the 1944 Bretton Woods conference. This established the basic framework for the post–World War II international monetary system. The Bretton Woods system called for fixed exchange rates against the U.S. dollar. Under this fixed exchange rate system, the value of most currencies in terms of U.S. dollars was fixed for long periods and allowed to change only under a specific set of circumstances. The Bretton Woods conference also created two major international institutions that play a role in the international monetary system—the International Monetary Fund (IMF) and the World

Bank. The IMF was given the task of maintaining order in the international monetary system; the World Bank's role was to promote development.

Today, both these institutions continue to play major roles in the world economy. In 1997 and 1998, for example, the IMF helped several Asian countries deal with the dramatic decline in the value of their currencies that occurred during the Asian financial crisis that started in 1997. By early 2001, the IMF had programs in more than 70 countries. There is, however, a growing debate about the role of the IMF and to a lesser extent the World Bank and the appropriateness of their policies for many developing nations. In the case of Turkey, several prominent critics claim that IMF policy might make things worse, not better, and they point out that despite successive IMF-sponsored "austerity programs" over the years, the country still has serious economic problems. The debate over the role of the IMF took on new urgency given the institution's extensive involvement in the economies of Asia and Eastern Europe during the latter part of the 1990s. Accordingly, we shall discuss the issue in depth.

The Bretton Woods system of fixed exchange rates collapsed in 1973. Since then, the world has operated with a mixed system in which some currencies are allowed to float freely, but many are either managed by government intervention or pegged to another currency. We will explain the reasons for the failure of the Bretton Woods system as well as the nature of the present system. We will also discuss how pegged exchange rate systems work. Two decades after the breakdown of the Bretton Woods system, the debate continues over what kind of exchange rate regime is best for the world. Some economists advocate a system in which major currencies are allowed to float against each other. Others argue for a return to a fixed exchange rate regime similar to the one established at Bretton Woods. This debate is intense and important, and we will examine the arguments of both sides.

Finally, we will discuss the implications of all this material for international business. We will see how the exchange rate policy adopted by a government can have an important impact on the outlook for business operations in a given country. If government exchange rate policies result in a currency devaluation, for example, exporters based in that country may benefit as their products become more price competitive in foreign markets. Alternatively, importers will suffer from an increase in the price of their products. We will also look at how the policies adopted by the IMF can have an impact on the economic outlook for a country and, accordingly, on the costs and benefits of doing business in that country.

The Gold Standard

The gold standard had its origin in the use of gold coins as a medium of exchange, unit of account, and store of value—a practice that dates to ancient times. When international trade was limited in volume, payment for goods purchased from another country was typically made in gold or silver. However, as the volume of international trade expanded in the wake of the Industrial Revolution, a more convenient means of financing international trade was needed. Shipping large quantities of gold and silver around the world to finance international trade seemed impractical. The solution adopted was to arrange for payment in paper currency and for governments to agree to convert the paper currency into gold on demand at a fixed rate.

Mechanics of the Gold Standard

Pegging currencies to gold and guaranteeing convertibility is known as the **gold standard.** By 1880, most of the world's major trading nations, including Great Britain, Germany, Japan, and the United States, had adopted the gold standard. Given a common gold standard, the value of any currency in units of any other currency (the exchange rate) was easy to determine.

For example, under the gold standard, one U.S. dollar was defined as equivalent to 23.22 grains of "fine" (pure) gold. Thus, one could, in theory, demand that the U.S. government convert that one dollar into 23.22 grains of gold. Since there are 480 grains in an ounce, one ounce of gold cost $20.67 (480/23.22). The amount of a currency needed to purchase one ounce of gold was referred to as the gold par value. The British pound was defined as containing 113 grains of fine gold. In other words, one ounce of gold cost £4.25 (480/113). From the gold par values of pounds and dollars, we can calculate what the exchange rate was for converting pounds into dollars; it was £1=$4.87 (i.e., $20.67/£4.25).

Strength of the Gold Standard

The great strength claimed for the gold standard was that it contained a powerful mechanism for achieving balance-of-trade equilibrium by all countries.[1] A country is said to be in balance-of-trade equilibrium when the income its residents earn from exports is equal to the money its residents pay to people in other countries for imports (the current account of its balance of payments is in balance). Suppose there are only two countries in the world, Japan and the United States. Imagine Japan's trade balance is in surplus because it exports more to the United States than it imports from the United States. Japanese exporters are paid in U.S. dollars, which they exchange for Japanese yen at a Japanese bank. The Japanese bank submits the dollars to the U.S. government and demands payment of gold in return. (This is a simplification of what would occur, but it will make our point.)

Under the gold standard, when Japan has a trade surplus, there will be a net flow of gold from the United States to Japan. These gold flows automatically reduce the U.S. money supply and swell Japan's money supply. As we saw in Chapter 9, there is a close connection between money supply growth and price inflation. An increase in money supply will raise prices in Japan, while a decrease in the U.S. money supply will push U.S. prices downward. The rise in the price of Japanese goods will decrease demand for these goods, while the fall in the price of U.S. goods will increase demand for these goods. Thus, Japan will start to buy more from the United States, and the United States will buy less from Japan, until a balance-of-trade equilibrium is achieved.

This adjustment mechanism seems so simple and attractive that even today, more than 60 years after the final collapse of the gold standard, some people believe the world should return to a gold standard.

The Period between the Wars: 1918–1939

The gold standard worked reasonably well from the 1870s until the start of World War I in 1914, when it was abandoned. During the war, several governments financed part of their massive military expenditures by printing money. This resulted in inflation, and by the war's end in 1918, price levels were higher everywhere. The United States returned to the gold standard in 1919, Great Britain in 1925, and France in 1928.

Great Britain returned to the gold standard by pegging the pound to gold at the prewar gold parity level of £4.25 per ounce, despite substantial inflation between 1914 and 1925. This priced British goods out of foreign markets, which pushed the country into a deep depression. When foreign holders of pounds lost confidence in Great Britain's commitment to maintaining its currency's value, they began converting their holdings of pounds into gold. The British government saw that it could not satisfy the demand for gold without seriously depleting its gold reserves, so it suspended convertibility in 1931.

The United States followed suit and left the gold standard in 1933 but returned to it in 1934, raising the dollar price of gold from $20.67 per ounce to $35 per ounce. Since more dollars were needed to buy an ounce of gold than before, the implication was that the dollar was worth less. This effectively amounted to a devaluation of the dollar relative to other currencies. Thus, before the devaluation the pound/dollar exchange rate was £1 = $4.87, but after the devaluation it was £1 = $8.24. By reducing the price of U.S. exports and increasing the price of imports, the government was trying to create employment in the United States by boosting output. However, a number of other countries adopted a similar tactic, and in the cycle of competitive devaluations that soon emerged, no country could win.

The net result was the shattering of any remaining confidence in the system. With countries devaluing their currencies at will, one could no longer be certain how much gold a currency could buy. Instead of holding onto another country's currency, people often tried to change it into gold immediately, lest the country devalue its currency in the intervening period. This put pressure on the gold reserves of various countries, forcing them to suspend gold convertibility. By the start of World War II in 1939, the gold standard was dead.

The Bretton Woods System

In 1944, at the height of World War II, representatives from 44 countries met at Bretton Woods, New Hampshire, to design a new international monetary system. With the collapse of the gold standard and the Great Depression of the 1930s fresh in their minds, these statesmen were determined to build an enduring economic order that would facilitate postwar economic growth. There was general consensus that fixed exchange rates were desirable. In addition, the conference participants wanted to avoid the senseless competitive devaluations of the 1930s, and they recognized that the gold standard would not assure this. The major problem with the gold standard as previously constituted was that no multinational institution could stop countries from engaging in competitive devaluations.

The agreement reached at Bretton Woods established two multinational institutions—the International Monetary Fund (IMF) and the World Bank. The task of the IMF would be to maintain order in the international monetary system and that of the World Bank would be to promote general economic development. The Bretton Woods agreement also called for a system of fixed exchange rates that would be policed by the IMF. Under the agreement, all countries were to fix the value of their currency in terms of gold but were not required to exchange their currencies for gold. Only the dollar remained convertible into gold—at a price of $35 per ounce. Each country decided what it wanted its exchange rate to be vis-à-vis the dollar and then calculated the gold par value of the currency based on that selected dollar exchange rate. All participating countries agreed to try to maintain the value of their currencies within 1 percent of the par value by buying or selling currencies (or gold) as needed. For example, if foreign exchange dealers were selling more of a country's currency than they demanded, the government of that country would intervene in the foreign exchange markets, buying its currency in an attempt to increase demand and maintain its gold par value.

Another aspect of the Bretton Woods agreement was a commitment not to use devaluation as a weapon of competitive trade policy. However, if a currency became too weak to defend, a devaluation of up to 10 percent would be allowed without any formal approval by the IMF. Larger devaluations required IMF approval.

The Role of the IMF

The IMF Articles of Agreement were heavily influenced by the worldwide financial collapse, competitive devaluations, trade wars, high unemployment, hyperinflation in Germany and elsewhere, and general economic disintegration that occurred between the two world wars. The aim of the Bretton Woods agreement, of which the IMF was the main custodian, was to try to avoid a repetition of that chaos through a combination of discipline and flexibility.

Discipline

A fixed exchange rate regime imposes discipline in two ways. First, the need to maintain a fixed exchange rate puts a brake on competitive devaluations and brings stability to the world trade environment. Second, a fixed exchange rate regime imposes monetary discipline on countries, thereby curtailing price inflation. For example, consider what would happen under a fixed exchange rate regime if Great Britain rapidly increased its money supply by printing pounds. As explained in Chapter 9, the increase in money supply would lead to price inflation. Given fixed exchange rates, inflation would make British goods uncompetitive in world markets, while the prices of imports would become more attractive in Great Britain. The result would be a widening trade deficit in Great Britain, with the country importing more than it exports. To correct this trade imbalance under a fixed exchange rate regime, Great Britain would be required to restrict the rate of growth in its money supply to bring price inflation back under control. Thus, fixed exchange rates are seen as a mechanism for controlling inflation and imposing economic discipline on countries.

Flexibility

Although monetary discipline was a central objective of the Bretton Woods agreement, it was recognized that a rigid policy of fixed exchange rates would be too inflexible. It would probably break down just as the gold standard had. In some cases, a country's attempts to reduce its money supply growth and correct a persistent balance-of-payments deficit could force the country into recession and create high unemployment. The architects of the Bretton Woods agreement wanted to avoid high unemployment, so they built limited flexibility into the system. Two major features of the IMF Articles of Agreement fostered this flexibility: IMF lending facilities and adjustable parities.

The IMF stood ready to lend foreign currencies to members to tide them over during short periods of balance-of-payments deficits, when a rapid tightening of monetary or fiscal policy would hurt domestic employment. A pool of gold and currencies contributed by IMF members provided the resources for these lending operations. A persistent balance-of-payments deficit can lead to a depletion of a country's reserves of foreign currency, forcing it to devalue its currency. By providing deficit-laden countries with short-term foreign currency loans, IMF funds would buy time for countries to bring down their inflation rates and reduce their balance-of-payments deficits. The belief was that such loans would reduce pressures for devaluation and allow for a more orderly and less painful adjustment.

Countries were to be allowed to borrow a limited amount from the IMF without adhering to any specific agreements. However, extensive drawings from IMF funds would require a country to agree to increasingly stringent IMF supervision of its macroeconomics policies. Heavy borrowers from the IMF must agree to monetary and fiscal conditions set down by the IMF, which typically included IMF-mandated targets on domestic money supply growth, exchange rate policy, tax policy, government spending, and so on.

The system of adjustable parities allowed for the devaluation of a country's currency by more than 10 percent if the IMF agreed that a country's balance of payments was in "fundamental disequilibrium." The term *fundamental disequilibrium* was not defined in the IMF's Articles of Agreement, but it was intended to apply to countries that had suffered permanent adverse shifts in the demand for their products. Without devaluation, such a country would experience high unemployment and a persistent trade deficit until the domestic price level had fallen far enough to restore a balance-of-payments equilibrium. The belief was that devaluation could help sidestep a painful adjustment process in such circumstances.

The Role of the World Bank

The official name for the World Bank is the International Bank for Reconstruction and Development (IBRD). When the Bretton Woods participants established the World

Bank, the need to reconstruct the war-torn economies of Europe was foremost in their minds. The bank's initial mission was to help finance the building of Europe's economy by providing low-interest loans. As it turned out, the World Bank was overshadowed in this role by the Marshall Plan, under which the United States lent money directly to European nations to help them rebuild. So the bank turned its attention to "development" and began lending money to Third World nations. In the 1950s, the bank concentrated on public-sector projects. Power stations, road building, and other transportation investments were much in favor. During the 1960s, the bank also began to lend heavily in support of agriculture, education, population control, and urban development.

The bank lends money under two schemes. Under the IBRD scheme, money is raised through bond sales in the international capital market. Borrowers pay what the bank calls a market rate of interest—the bank's cost of funds plus a margin for expenses. This "market" rate is lower than commercial banks' market rate. Under the IBRD scheme, the bank offers low-interest loans to risky customers whose credit rating is often poor.

A second scheme is overseen by the International Development Agency (IDA), an arm of the bank created in 1960. Resources to fund IDA loans are raised through subscriptions from wealthy members such as the United States, Japan, and Germany. IDA loans go only to the poorest countries. (In 1991, those were defined as countries with annual incomes per capita of less than $580.) Borrowers have 50 years to repay at an interest rate of 1 percent a year.

The Collapse of the Fixed Exchange Rate System

The system of fixed exchange rates established at Bretton Woods worked well until the late 1960s, when it began to show signs of strain. The system finally collapsed in 1973, and since then we have had a managed-float system. To understand why the system collapsed, one must appreciate the special role of the U.S. dollar in the system. As the only currency that could be converted into gold, and as the currency that served as the reference point for all others, the dollar occupied a central place in the system. Any pressure on the dollar to devalue could wreak havoc with the system, and that is what occurred.

Most economists trace the breakup of the fixed exchange rate system to the U.S. macroeconomic policy package of 1965–1968.[2] To finance both the Vietnam conflict and his welfare programs, President Johnson backed an increase in U.S. government spending that was not financed by an increase in taxes. Instead, it was financed by an increase in the money supply, which led to a rise in price inflation from less than 4 percent in 1966 to close to 9 percent by 1968. At the same time, the rise in government spending had stimulated the economy. With more money in their pockets, people spent more—particularly on imports—and the U.S. trade balance began to deteriorate.

The increase in inflation and the worsening of the U.S. foreign trade position gave rise to speculation in the foreign exchange market that the dollar would be devalued. Things came to a head in the spring of 1971 when U.S. trade figures showed that for the first time since 1945, the United States was importing more than it was exporting. This set off massive purchases of German deutsche marks in the foreign exchange market by speculators who guessed that the mark would be revalued against the dollar. On a single day, May 4, 1971, the Bundesbank (Germany's central bank) had to buy $1 billion to hold the dollar/deutsche mark exchange rate at its fixed exchange rate given the great demand for deutsche marks. On the morning of May 5, the Bundesbank purchased another $1 billion during the first hour of foreign exchange trading! At that point, the Bundesbank faced the inevitable and allowed its currency to float.

In the weeks following the decision to float the deutsche mark, the foreign exchange market became increasingly convinced that the dollar would have to be devalued. However, devaluation of the dollar was no easy matter. Under the Bretton Woods provisions, any other country could change its exchange rates against all currencies simply by fixing its dollar rate at a new level. But as the key currency in the system, the dollar could be devalued only if all countries agreed to simultaneously revalue against the dollar. And many countries did not want this, because it would make their products more expensive relative to U.S. products.

To force the issue, President Nixon announced in August 1971 that the dollar was no longer convertible into gold. He also announced that a new 10 percent tax on imports would remain in effect until U.S. trading partners agreed to revalue their currencies against the dollar. This brought the trading partners to the bargaining table, and in December 1971 an agreement was reached to devalue the dollar by about 8 percent against foreign currencies. The import tax was then removed.

The problem was not solved, however. The U.S. balance-of-payments position continued to deteriorate throughout 1972, while the nation's money supply continued to expand at an inflationary rate. Speculation continued to grow that the dollar was still overvalued and that a second devaluation would be necessary. In anticipation, foreign exchange dealers began converting dollars to deutsche marks and other currencies. After a massive wave of speculation in February 1972, which culminated with European central banks spending $3.6 billion on March 1 to try to prevent their currencies from appreciating against the dollar, the foreign exchange market was closed. When the foreign exchange market reopened March 19, the currencies of Japan and most European countries were floating against the dollar, although many developing countries continued to peg their currency to the dollar, and many do to this day. At that time, the switch to a floating system was viewed as a temporary response to unmanageable speculation in the foreign exchange market. But it is now 30 years since the Bretton Woods system of fixed exchange rates collapsed, and the temporary solution looks permanent.

The Bretton Woods system had an Achilles' heel: The system could not work if its key currency, the U.S. dollar, was under speculative attack. The Bretton Woods system could work only as long as the U.S. inflation rate remained low and the United States did not run a balance-of-payments deficit. Once these things occurred, the system soon became strained to the breaking point.

The Floating Exchange Rate Regime ■

The floating exchange rate regime that followed the collapse of the fixed exchange rate system was formalized in January 1976 when IMF members met in Jamaica and agreed to the rules for the international monetary system that are in place today.

The Jamaica Agreement

The Jamaica meeting revised the IMF's Articles of Agreement to reflect the new reality of floating exchange rates. The main elements of the Jamaica agreement include the following:

1. Floating rates were declared acceptable. IMF members were permitted to enter the foreign exchange market to even out "unwarranted" speculative fluctuations.
2. Gold was abandoned as a reserve asset. The IMF returned its gold reserves to members at the current market price, placing the proceeds in a trust fund to help poor nations. IMF members were permitted to sell their own gold reserves at the market price.
3. Total annual IMF quotas—the amount member countries contribute to the IMF—were increased to $41 billion. (Since then they have been increased to $300 billion while the membership of the IMF has been expanded to include 183 countries.) Non-oil-exporting, less developed countries were given greater access to IMF funds.

After Jamaica, the IMF continued its role of helping countries cope with macroeconomic and exchange rate problems, albeit within the context of a radically different exchange rate regime.

Exchange Rates Since 1973

Since March 1973, exchange rates have become much more volatile and less predictable than they were between 1945 and 1973.[3] This volatility has been partly due to a number of unexpected shocks to the world monetary system, including:

1. The oil crisis in 1971, when the Organization of Petroleum Exporting Countries (OPEC) quadrupled the price of oil. The harmful effect of this on the U.S. inflation rate and trade position resulted in a further decline in the value of the dollar.
2. The loss of confidence in the dollar that followed the rise of U.S. inflation in 1977 and 1978.
3. The oil crisis of 1979, when OPEC once again increased the price of oil dramatically—this time it was doubled.
4. The unexpected rise in the dollar between 1980 and 1985, despite a deteriorating balance-of-payments picture.
5. The rapid fall of the U.S. dollar against the Japanese yen and German deutsche mark between 1985 and 1987, and against the yen between 1993 and 1995.
6. The partial collapse of the European Monetary System in 1992.
7. The 1997 Asian currency crisis, when the Asian currencies of several countries, including South Korea, Indonesia, Malaysia, and Thailand, lost between 50 percent and 80 percent of their value against the U.S. dollar in a few months.

Figure 10.1 summarizes the volatility of four major currencies—the German mark, Japanese yen, British pound, and U.S. dollar—from 1970 to 2001. The Morgan Guaranty Index, the basis for Figure 10.1, represents the exchange rate of each of these currencies against a weighted basket of the currencies of 19 industrial countries (the index was set equal to 100 in 1990). All four currencies have been quite volatile over the period. The index value of the Japanese yen, for example, has ranged from a low of 44 in

Figure 10.1

Long-Term Exchange Rate Trends, 1970–2001 (index 1990=100)

Source: JP Morgan Effective Exchange Rate Index 1970–2001 (1990=100).

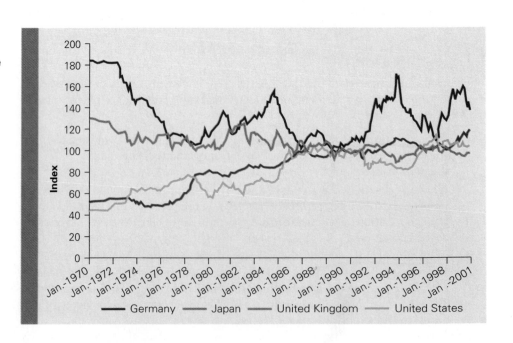

1970 to a high of 170 in June 1995. Similarly, the U.S. dollar index has been as low as 89.3 in 1995 and as high as 158 in 1985.

Perhaps the most interesting phenomena in Figure 10.1 are the rapid rise in the value of the dollar between 1980 and 1985 and its subsequent fall between 1985 and 1988, and the similar rise and fall in the value of the Japanese yen between 1990 and 1998. We will briefly discuss the rise and fall of the dollar, since this tells us something about how the international monetary system has operated in recent years.[4]

The rise in the value of the dollar between 1980 and 1985 is particularly interesting because it occurred when the United States was running a large and growing trade deficit, importing substantially more than it exported. Conventional wisdom would suggest that the increased supply of dollars in the foreign exchange market as a result of the deficit should lead to a reduction in the value of the dollar, but it increased in value. Why? A number of favorable factors temporarily overcame the unfavorable effect of a trade deficit. Strong economic growth in the United States attracted heavy inflows of capital from foreign investors seeking high returns on capital assets. High real interest rates attracted foreign investors seeking high returns on financial assets. At the same time, political turmoil in other parts of the world, along with relatively slow economic growth in the developed countries of Europe, helped create the view that the United States was a good place to invest. These inflows of capital increased the demand for dollars in the foreign exchange market, which pushed the value of the dollar upward against other currencies.

The fall in the value of the dollar between 1985 and 1988 was caused by a combination of government intervention and market forces. The rise in the dollar, which priced U.S. goods out of foreign markets and made imports relatively cheap, had contributed to a dismal trade picture. In 1985, the United States posted a record-high trade deficit of more than $160 billion. This led to growth in demands for protectionism in the United States. In September 1985, the finance ministers and central bank governors of the so-called Group of Five major industrial countries (Great Britain, France, Japan, Germany, and the United States) met at the Plaza Hotel in New York and reached what was later referred to as the Plaza Accord. They announced that it would be desirable for most major currencies to appreciate vis-à-vis the U.S. dollar and pledged to intervene in the foreign exchange markets, selling dollars, to encourage this objective. The dollar had already begun to weaken in the summer of 1985, and this announcement further accelerated the decline.

The dollar continued to decline until early 1987. The governments of the Group of Five even began to worry that the dollar might decline too far, so the finance ministers of the Group of Five met in Paris in February 1987 and reached a new agreement known as the Louvre Accord. They agreed that exchange rates had been realigned sufficiently and pledged to support the stability of exchange rates around their current levels by intervening in the foreign exchange markets when necessary to buy and sell currency. Although the dollar continued to decline for a few months after the Louvre Accord, the rate of decline slowed, and by early 1988 the decline had ended. Except for a brief speculative flurry around the time of the Persian Gulf War in 1991, the dollar was relatively stable for most of the 1990s against most major currencies with the notable exception of the Japanese yen. However, in 2000 and 2001 the dollar began to appreciate against most major currencies, including the euro, even though the United States was once more running a record balance-of-payments deficit.

Thus, we see that in recent history the value of the dollar has been determined by both market forces and government intervention. Under a floating exchange rate regime, market forces have produced a volatile dollar exchange rate. Governments have responded by intervening in the market—buying and selling dollars—in an attempt to limit the market's volatility and to correct what they see as overvaluation (in 1985) or potential undervaluation (in 1987) of the dollar. The frequency of government intervention in the foreign exchange markets explains why the current system is often referred to as a managed-float system or a dirty float system.

Fixed versus Floating Exchange Rates

The breakdown of the Bretton Woods system has not stopped the debate about the relative merits of fixed versus floating exchange rate regimes. Disappointment with the system of floating rates in recent years has led to renewed debate about the merits of fixed exchange rates. In this section we review the arguments for fixed and floating exchange rate regimes.[5] We will discuss the case for floating rates before discussing why many commentators are disappointed with the experience under floating exchange rates and yearn for a system of fixed rates.

The Case for Floating Exchange Rates

The case for floating exchange rates has two main elements: monetary policy autonomy and automatic trade balance adjustments.

Monetary Policy Autonomy

It is argued that under a fixed system, a country's ability to expand or contract its money supply as it sees fit is limited by the need to maintain exchange rate parity. Monetary expansion can lead to inflation, which puts downward pressure on a fixed exchange rate (as predicted by the PPP theory; see Chapter 9). Similarly, monetary contraction requires high interest rates (to reduce the demand for money). Higher interest rates lead to an inflow of money from abroad, which puts upward pressure on a fixed exchange rate. Thus, to maintain exchange rate parity under a fixed system, countries were limited in their ability to use monetary policy to expand or contract their economies.

Advocates of a floating exchange rate regime argue that removal of the obligation to maintain exchange rate parity would restore monetary control to a government. If a government faced with unemployment wanted to increase its money supply to stimulate domestic demand and reduce unemployment, it could do so unencumbered by the need to maintain its exchange rate. While monetary expansion might lead to inflation, this would lead to a depreciation in the country's currency. If PPP theory is correct, the resulting currency depreciation on the foreign exchange markets should offset the effects of inflation. Although under a floating exchange rate regime domestic inflation would have an impact on the exchange rate, it should have no impact on businesses' international cost competitiveness due to exchange rate depreciation. The rise in domestic costs should be exactly offset by the fall in the value of the country's currency on the foreign exchange markets. Similarly, a government could use monetary policy to contract the economy without worrying about the need to maintain parity.

Trade Balance Adjustments

Under the Bretton Woods system, if a country developed a permanent deficit in its balance of trade (importing more than it exported) that could not be corrected by domestic policy, this would require the IMF to agree to a currency devaluation. Critics of this system argue that the adjustment mechanism works much more smoothly under a floating exchange rate regime. They argue that if a country is running a trade deficit, the imbalance between the supply and demand of that country's currency in the foreign exchange markets (supply exceeding demand) will lead to depreciation in its exchange rate. In turn, by making its exports cheaper and its imports more expensive, an exchange rate depreciation should correct the trade deficit.

The Case for Fixed Exchange Rates

The case for fixed exchange rates rests on arguments about monetary discipline, speculation, uncertainty, and the lack of connection between the trade balance and exchange rates.

Monetary Discipline

We have already discussed the nature of monetary discipline inherent in a fixed exchange rate system when we discussed the Bretton Woods system. The need to maintain a fixed exchange rate parity ensures that governments do not expand their money supplies at inflationary rates. While advocates of floating rates argue that each country should be allowed to choose its own inflation rate (the monetary autonomy argument), advocates of fixed rates argue that governments all too often give in to political pressures and expand the monetary supply far too rapidly, causing unacceptably high price inflation. A fixed exchange rate regime will ensure that this does not occur.

Speculation

Critics of a floating exchange rate regime also argue that speculation can cause fluctuations in exchange rates. They point to the dollar's rapid rise and fall during the 1980s, which they claim had nothing to do with comparative inflation rates and the U.S. trade deficit, but everything to do with speculation. They argue that when foreign exchange dealers see a currency depreciating, they tend to sell the currency in the expectation of future depreciation regardless of the currency's longer-term prospects. As more traders jump on the bandwagon, the expectations of depreciation are realized. Such destabilizing speculation tends to accentuate the fluctuations around the exchange rate's long-run value. It can damage a country's economy by distorting export and import prices. Thus, advocates of a fixed exchange rate regime argue that such a system will limit the destabilizing effects of speculation.

Uncertainty

Speculation also adds to the uncertainty surrounding future currency movements that characterizes floating exchange rate regimes. The unpredictability of exchange rate movements in the post-Bretton Woods era has made business planning difficult, and it makes exporting, importing, and foreign investment risky activities. Given a volatile exchange rate, international businesses do not know how to react to the changes—and often they do not react. Why change plans for exporting, importing, or foreign investment after a 6 percent fall in the dollar this month, when the dollar may rise 6 percent next month? This uncertainty, according to the critics, dampens the growth of international trade and investment. They argue that a fixed exchange rate, by eliminating such uncertainty, promotes the growth of international trade and investment. Advocates of a floating system reply that the forward exchange market insures against the risks associated with exchange rate fluctuations (see Chapter 9), so the adverse impact of uncertainty on the growth of international trade and investment has been overstated.

Trade Balance Adjustments

Those in favor of floating exchange rates argue that floating rates help adjust trade imbalances. Critics question the closeness of the link between the exchange rate and the trade balance. They claim trade deficits are determined by the balance between savings and investment in a country, not by the external value of its currency.[6] They argue that depreciation in a currency will lead to inflation (due to the resulting increase in import prices). This inflation will wipe out any apparent gains in cost competitiveness that come from currency depreciation. In other words, a depreciating exchange rate will not boost exports and reduce imports, as advocates of floating rates claim; it will simply boost price inflation. In support of this argument, those who favor floating rates point out that the 40 percent drop in the value of the dollar between 1985 and 1988 did not correct the U.S. trade deficit. In reply, advocates of a floating exchange rate regime argue that between 1985 and 1992, the U.S. trade deficit fell from over $160 billion to about $70 billion, and they attribute this in part to the decline in the value of the dollar.

Who Is Right?

Which side is right in the vigorous debate between those who favor a fixed exchange rate and those who favor a floating exchange rate? Economists cannot agree on this issue. From a business perspective, this is unfortunate because business, as a major player on the international trade and investment scene, has a large stake in the resolution of the debate. Would international business be better off under a fixed regime, or are flexible rates better? The evidence is not clear.

We do, however, know that a fixed exchange rate regime modeled along the lines of the Bretton Woods system will not work. Speculation ultimately broke the system, a phenomenon that advocates of fixed rate regimes claim is associated with floating exchange rates! Nevertheless, a different kind of fixed exchange rate system might be more enduring and might foster the stability that would facilitate more rapid growth in international trade and investment. In the next section, we look at potential models for such a system and the problems with such systems.

Exchange Rate Regimes in Practice

A number of different exchange rate policies are pursued by governments around the world. These range from a pure "free float" where the exchange rate is determined by market forces to a pegged system that has some aspects of the pre-1973 Bretton Woods system of fixed exchange rates. Figure 10.2 summarizes the exchange rate policies adopted by member states of the IMF in 2000. Some 27 percent of the IMF's 183 members allow their currency to float freely. Another 15 percent intervene in only a limited way (the so-called managed float). Some 20 percent of IMF members now have no separate legal tender of their own. These include the 12 European Union countries that have adopted the euro, and effectively given up their own currencies, along with some 26 smaller states mostly in Africa or the Caribbean that have no domestic currency and have adopted a foreign currency as legal tender within their borders, typically the U.S. dollar or the euro. The remaining countries use more inflexible systems, including a fixed peg arrangement (24 percent) under which they peg their currencies to other currencies, such as the U.S. dollar or the euro, or to a basket of currencies. Other countries have adopted a somewhat more flexible system under which their exchange rate is allowed to fluctuate against other currencies within a target zone (an adjustable peg system). In this section, we will look more closely at the mechanics and implications of exchange rate regimes that rely on a currency peg or target zone.

Pegged Exchange Rates and Currency Boards

Under a pegged exchange rate regime, a country will peg the value of its currency to that of a major currency so that, for example, as the U.S. dollar rises in value, its own

Figure 10.2

IMF Members' Exchange Rate Policies, 2000.

Source: *IMF Annual Report, 2000.*

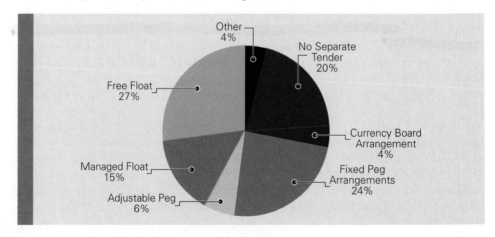

currency rises too. Pegged exchange rates are popular among many of the world's smaller nations. As with a full fixed exchange rate regime, the great virtue claimed for a pegged exchange rate is that it imposes monetary discipline on a country and leads to low inflation. For example, if Belize pegs the value of the Belizean dollar to that of the U.S. dollar so that US/\$1=B\$1.97 (the peg as of 2001), then the Belizean government must make sure the inflation rate in Belize is similar to that in the United States. If the Belizean inflation rate is greater than the U.S. inflation rate, this will lead to pressure to devalue the Belizean dollar (i.e., to alter the peg). To maintain the peg, the Belizean government would be required to rein in inflation. Of course, for a pegged exchange rate to impose monetary discipline on a country, the country whose currency is chosen for the peg must also pursue sound monetary policy.

Evidence shows that adopting a pegged exchange rate regime does moderate inflationary pressures in a country. An IMF study concluded that countries with pegged exchange rates had an average annual inflation rate of 8 percent, compared with 14 percent for intermediate regimes and 16 percent for floating regimes.[7] However, many countries operate with only a nominal peg and in practice are willing to devalue their currency rather than pursue a tight monetary policy. It can be very difficult for a smaller country to maintain a peg against another currency if capital is flowing out of the country and foreign exchange traders are speculating against the currency. Something like this occurred in 1997 when a combination of adverse capital flows and currency speculation forced several Asian countries, including Thailand and Malaysia, to abandon pegs against the U.S. dollar and let their currencies float freely. Malaysia and Thailand would not have been in this position had they dealt with a number of problems that began to arise in their economies during the 1990s, including excessive private-sector debt and expanding current account trade deficits.

Hong Kong's experience during the 1997 Asian currency crisis, however, has added a new dimension to the debate over how to manage a pegged exchange rate. During late 1997 when other Asian currencies were collapsing, Hong Kong maintained the value of its currency against the U.S. dollar at around \$1=HK\$7.8 despite several concerted speculative attacks. Hong Kong's currency board has been given credit for this success. A country that introduces a **currency board** commits itself to converting its domestic currency on demand into another currency at a fixed exchange rate. To make this commitment credible, the currency board holds reserves of foreign currency equal at the fixed exchange rate to at least 100 percent of the domestic currency issued. The system used in Hong Kong means its currency must be fully backed by the U.S. dollar at the specified exchange rate. This is still not a true fixed exchange rate regime, because the U.S. dollar, and by extension the Hong Kong dollar, floats against other currencies, but it has some features of a fixed exchange rate regime.

Under this arrangement, the currency board can issue additional domestic notes and coins only when there are foreign exchange reserves to back it. This limits the ability of the government to print money and, thereby, create inflationary pressures. Under a strict currency board system, interest rates adjust automatically. If investors want to switch out of domestic currency into, for example, U.S. dollars, the supply of domestic currency will shrink. This will cause interest rates to rise until it eventually becomes attractive for investors to hold the local currency again. In the case of Hong Kong, the interest rate on three-month deposits climbed as high as 20 percent in late 1997, as investors switched out of Hong Kong dollars and into U.S. dollars. The dollar peg, however, held, and interest rates declined again.

Since its establishment in 1983, the Hong Kong currency board has weathered several storms, including the latest. This success seems to be persuading other countries in the developing world to consider a similar system. Argentina introduced a currency board in 1991, and Bulgaria, Estonia, and Lithuania have all gone down this road in recent years (eight IMF members had currency boards in 2000). Despite growing interest in the arrangement, however, critics are quick to point out that currency boards have their drawbacks.[8] If local inflation rates remain higher than the inflation rate in the country to which the currency is pegged, the currencies of countries with currency boards can become uncompetitive and overvalued. Also, under a currency board system, government lacks the ability to set interest rates. Interest rates in Hong Kong, for example, are effectively set by the U.S. Federal Reserve. Despite these drawbacks, Hong Kong's success in avoiding the currency collapse that afflicted its Asian neighbors suggests that other developing countries may adopt a similar system.

Target Zones: The European Monetary System in Retrospect

An exchange rate system based on target zones involves a group of countries trying to keep their currencies within a predetermined range, or zone, of other currencies in the group. The exchange rate mechanism (ERM) that was a central part of the European Monetary System of the European Union between 1979 and 1999 is the most famous example of this kind of system.

In our discussion of the European Union (EU) in Chapter 8, we noted that the EU is committed to monetary union, including establishment of a single currency. The process began January 1, 1999, and was completed on January 1, 2002.[9] A formal commitment to a common currency dates back only to the Maastricht Treaty in December 1991, but it has been an underlying theme in the EU and a subject of debate for some time. To establish a common currency, the EU needed to achieve convergence between the inflation rates and interest rates of its member states. The EMS was a mechanism for attaining this goal.[10]

When the EMS was created in March 1979, it was entrusted with three main objectives: (1) to create a zone of monetary stability in Europe by reducing exchange rate volatility and converging national interest rates; (2) to control inflation through the imposition of monetary discipline; (3) to coordinate exchange rate policies versus non-EU currencies such as the U.S. dollar and the yen. In 1991, the objective of paving the way for introduction of a common currency in 1999 was added to this list. Two instruments were used to achieve these objectives, the European currency unit (ecu) and the exchange rate mechanism (ERM).

The Ecu and the ERM

The ecu was a basket of the EU currencies that served as the unit of account for the EMS. One ecu comprised a defined percentage of national currencies. The share of each country's currency in the ecu depended on the country's relative economic weight within the EC. Thus, for example, 30.1 percent of the ecu's value was established by the value of the German deutsche mark in 1989 because that was the estimate of Germany's relative strength and size within the EU economy at the time.

Until 1992, the exchange rate mechanism worked as follows: Each national currency in the EU was given a central rate vis-à-vis the ecu. For example, in September 1989, one ecu was equal to DM2.05853, to FFr6.90404, or to £0.739615. This central rate could be changed only by a commonly agreed realignment. From these central rates flowed a series of bilateral rates—the French franc against the Italian lira, the German deutsche mark against the British pound, and so on. For example, the given figures vis-à-vis the ecu indicate that the bilateral rate for exchanging deutsche marks into francs was DM1=FFr3.3539 (i.e., FFr6.90404/DM2.05853). The bilateral rates formed a cat's cradle known as the ERM parity grid, which was the system's operational component. Before 1992, the rule was that a currency must not depart by more than 2.25 percent from its bilateral central rate with another ERM participating currency.

Intervention in the foreign exchange markets was compulsory whenever one currency hit its outer margin of fluctuation relative to another. The central banks of the countries issuing both currencies were supposed to intervene to keep their currencies within the 2.25 percent band. The central bank of the country with the stronger currency was supposed to buy the weaker currency, and vice versa. It tended to be left to the country with the weaker currency to take action.

To defend its currency against speculative pressure, each member could borrow almost unlimited amounts of foreign currency from other members for up to three months. A second line of defense included loans that could be extended for up to nine months, but the total amount available was limited to a pool of credit—originally about 14 billion ecus—and the size of the member's quota in the pool. Additional funds were available for maturities from two to five years from a second pool of about 11 billion ecus (originally). However, as a condition of using these funds, the borrowing member had to commit itself to correcting the economic policies causing its currency to deviate.

Performance of the System

Underlying the ERM were all the standard beliefs about the virtues of fixed rate regimes that we have discussed. EU members believed the system imposed monetary discipline, removed uncertainty, limited speculation, and promoted trade and investment within the EU. For most of the EMS's existence, it achieved these objectives. When the ERM was established, wide variations in national interest rates and inflation rates made its prospects seem shaky. For example, in early 1979, inflation was running at 2.7 percent in Germany and 12.1 percent in Italy. By 1992, however, both inflation rates and interest rates had converged somewhat. As this occurred, the need for intervention and realignments declined, and the system appeared to become more stable.

However, there had long been concern within the EU about the vulnerability of a fixed system to speculative pressures. Many of these concerns were realized dramatically in September 1992, when two of the major EMS currencies—the British pound and the Italian lira—were hit by waves of speculative pressure. Dealers in the foreign exchange market, believing a realignment of the pound and the lira within the ERM was imminent, started to sell pounds and lira and to purchase German deutsche marks. This led to a fall in the value of the pound and the lira against the mark on the foreign exchange markets. Although the central banks of Great Britain and Italy tried to defend their currencies by raising interest rates and buying back pounds and lira, they were unable to keep the values of their currencies within their respective ERM bands. As a consequence, first Great Britain and then Italy pulled out of the ERM, leaving the EMS on the brink of collapse.

The speculative pressures and subsequent withdrawal of Britain and Italy from the ERM led the EU countries to make two major changes to the EMS in August 1993. First, the 2.25 percent fluctuation bands were widened to 15 percent. The idea was to loosen the rigidities in the system and hence reduce the scope for speculation. Second, the EMS no longer obligated the central banks of countries with strong currencies to intervene in the foreign exchange market to purchase weaker currencies. This change essentially recognized what had already occurred. In the crisis of September 1992, for example, the German central bank did not intervene aggressively to help keep the value of the British pound within the prescribed fluctuation bands.[11]

After 1993 this modified system again performed fairly well and by mid-1998, the system appeared to have delivered what it was designed to do—low and convergent inflation rates among the EU's member states. In 1998, the average annual rate fell to 1.6 percent (1993 = 4 percent), with the differential between the lowest and the highest rates at 1.7 percent (1993 = 5 percent). On January 1, 1999, the exchange rates of 11 EU states were fixed against national currencies and the euro became a full-fledged currency for commercial purposes, replacing the ecu basket of currencies.

The Tragedy of the Congo (Zaire)

The Democratic Republic of the Congo, formerly known as Zaire, gained its independence from Belgium in 1960. The central African nation, rich in natural resources such as copper, seemed to have a promising future. If the country had simply sustained its preindependence economic growth rate, its gross national product (GNP) would have been $1,400 per capita by 1997, making it one of the richest countries in Africa. Instead, by 1997, the country was a wreck. Battered by a brutal civil war that led to the ousting of the country's longtime dictator, Mobutu Sese Seko, the economy had shrunk to its 1958 level with a GNP per capita below $100. The annual inflation rate was in excess of 750 percent, an improvement from the 9,800 percent inflation rate recorded in 1994. Consequently, the local currency was almost worthless. Most transactions were made by barter or, for the lucky few, with U.S. dollars. Infant mortality stood at a dismal 106 per 1,000 live births, and life expectancy stood at 47 years, roughly comparable to that of Europe in the Middle Ages.

What were the underlying causes of the economic, political, and social collapse of Zaire? While the story is a complex one, according to several influential critics, some of the blame must be placed at the feet of two multinational lending institutions, the International Monetary Fund (IMF) and the World Bank. Both institutions were established in 1944 at the famous Bretton Woods conference, which paved the way for the post-World War II international monetary system. The IMF was given the task of maintaining order in the international monetary system, while the role of the World Bank was to promote general economic development, particularly among the world's poorer nations. The IMF typically provides loans to countries whose currencies are losing value

due to economic mismanagement. In return for these loans, the IMF imposes on debtor countries strict financial policies that are designed to rein in inflation and stabilize their economies. The World Bank has historically provided low interest rate loans to help countries build basic infrastructure. Both institutions are funded by subscriptions from member states, including significant contributions from all of the world's developed nations.

The IMF and the World Bank were major donors to postindependence Zaire. The IMF's involvement with Zaire dates to 1967, when the IMF approved Zaire's first economic stabilization plan, backed by a $27 million line of credit. About the same time, the World Bank began to make low interest rate infrastructure loans to the government of Mobutu Sese Seko. This was followed by a series of further plans and loans between 1976 and 1981. At the urging of the IMF, Zaire's currency was devalued five times during this period to help boost exports and reduce imports, while taxes were raised in an effort to balance Zaire's budget. IMF and other Western officials were also placed in key positions at the Zairian central bank, finance ministry, and office of debt management.

Despite all this help, Zaire's economy continued to deteriorate. By 1982, after 15 years of IMF assistance, Zaire had a lower GNP than in 1967 and faced default on its debt. Some critics, including Jeffery Sachs, the noted development economist from Harvard University, claim that this poor performance could in part be attributed to the policies imposed by the IMF, which included tax hikes, cuts in government subsidies, and periodic competitive currency devaluations. These policies, claim critics, were ill suited to such a poor country and created a vicious cycle of economic decline. The tax hikes simply drove work into the "underground economy" or created a disincentive to

Crisis Management by the IMF

Many observers initially believed that the collapse of the Bretton Woods system in 1973 would diminish the role of the IMF within the international monetary system. The IMF's original function was to provide a pool of money from which members could borrow, short term, to adjust their balance-of-payments position and maintain their exchange rate. Some believed the demand for short-term loans would be considerably diminished under a floating exchange rate regime. A trade deficit would presumably lead to a decline in a country's exchange rate, which would help reduce imports and boost exports. No temporary IMF adjustment loan would be needed. Consistent with work. As a consequence, government tax revenues dwindled and the budget deficit expanded, making it difficult for the government to service its debt obligations. By raising import prices, the devaluations helped fuel the phenomenon the IMF was trying to control: inflation. In turn, high inflation of both prices and wages soon brought ordinary Zairians into high tax brackets, which drove even more work into the underground economy and further shrank government tax revenues.

When explaining Zaire's malaise, others point to corruption. In 1982, a senior IMF official in Zaire reported that President Mobutu Sese Seko and his cronies were systematically stealing IMF and World Bank loans. Later news reports suggest that Mobutu accumulated a personal fortune of $4 billion by the mid-1980s, making him one of the richest men in the world at that time.

In 1982, Zaire was initially suspended from further use of its IMF credit line. However, the position was reversed in 1983 when a new agreement was negotiated that included an additional $356 million in IMF loans. The loans were linked to a further devaluation of the Zairian currency, more tax hikes, and cuts in government subsidies. The IMF's decision to turn a blind eye to the corruption problem and extend new loans was influenced by pressure from Western politicians who saw Mobutu's pro-Western regime as a bulwark against the spread of Marxism in Africa. By ignoring the corruption, the IMF could claim it was abiding by IMF rules, which stated the institution should offer only economic advice and stay out of internal political issues. The IMF's decision lent credence to Mobutu Sese Seko's government and enabled Zaire to attract more foreign loans. As a consequence, the country's overall foreign debt increased to $5 billion by the mid-1980s, up from $3 billion in 1978.

Unfortunately, the new loans and IMF policies did little to improve Zaire's economic performance, which continued to deteriorate. In 1987, Zaire was forced to abandon its agreement with the IMF due to food riots. The IMF negotiated another agreement for the 1989–1991 period, which included further currency devaluation. This also failed to produce any tangible progress. The Zairian economy continued to implode while the country's civil war flared. In 1993, Zaire suspended its debt repayments, effectively going into default. In 1994, the World Bank announced it would shut down its operations in the country. About the same time, the IMF suspended Zaire's membership in the institution, making Zaire ineligible for further loans.

In 1997, after a long civil war, Mobutu Sese Seko was deposed. The new government inherited $14.6 billion of external debt, including debt arrears exceeding $1 billion. At a formal meeting chaired by the World Bank to discuss rescheduling of the country's debt, delegates from the new government claimed that the World Bank, IMF, and other institutions acted irresponsibly by lending money to Mobutu's regime despite evidence of both substantial corruption and Zaire's inability to service such a high level of debt. In an implicit acknowledgment that this may have been the case, the IMF and World Bank began telling debtor countries to stamp out corruption or lose access to IMF and World Bank loans.

Sources: G. Fossedal, "The IMF's Role in Zaire's Decline," *Wall Street Journal*, May 15, 1997, p. 22; J. Burns and M. Holman, "Mobutu Built a Fortune of $4 Billion from Looted Aid," *Financial Times*, May 12, 1997, p. 1; J. D. Sachs and R. I. Rotberg, "Help Congo Now," *New York Times*, May 29, 1997, p. 21; H. Dunphy, "IMF, World Bank Now Make Political Judgements," *Journal of Commerce*, August 21, 1997, p. 3A; and *CIA World Factbook* (Washington, DC: CIA, 1998).

this, after 1973 most industrialized countries tended to let the foreign exchange market determine exchange rates in response to demand and supply. No major industrial country has borrowed funds from the IMF since the mid-1970s, when Great Britain and Italy did. Since the early 1970s, the rapid development of global capital markets has allowed developed countries such as Great Britain and the United States to finance their deficits by borrowing private money, as opposed to drawing on IMF funds.

Despite these developments, the activities of the IMF have expanded over the past 30 years. By 2000, the IMF had 183 members, 75 of which had IMF programs in place. In 1997 the institution implemented its largest rescue packages, committing more than $110 billion in short-term loans to three troubled Asian countries—South Korea,

Indonesia, and Thailand. The IMF's activities have expanded because periodic financial crises have continued to hit many economies in the post-Bretton Woods era, particularly among the world's developing nations. The IMF has repeatedly lent money to nations experiencing financial crises, requesting in return that the governments enact certain macroeconomic policies. Critics of the IMF claim these policies have not always been as beneficial as the IMF might have hoped and in some cases may have made things worse (for example, review the Country Focus on the IMF's involvement in the Congo). With the recent extension of IMF loans to several Asian economies, these criticisms have reached new levels and a vigorous debate is under way as to the appropriate role of the IMF. In this section, we shall discuss some of the main challenges the IMF has had to deal with over the last quarter of a century and review the ongoing debate over the role of the IMF.

Financial Crises in the Post-Bretton Woods Era

A number of broad types of financial crises have occurred over the last quarter of a century, many of which have required IMF involvement. A **currency crisis** occurs when a speculative attack on the exchange value of a currency results in a sharp depreciation in the value of the currency or forces authorities to expend large volumes of international currency reserves and sharply increase interest rates to defend the prevailing exchange rate. A **banking crisis** refers to a loss of confidence in the banking system that leads to a run on banks, as individuals and companies withdraw their deposits. A **foreign debt crisis** is a situation in which a country cannot service its foreign debt obligations, whether private-sector or government debt. These crises tend to have common underlying macroeconomic causes: high relative price inflation rates, a widening current account deficit, excessive expansion of domestic borrowing, and asset price inflation (such as sharp increases in stock and property prices).[12] At times, elements of currency, banking, and debt crises may be present simultaneously, as in the 1997 Asian crisis or in the 1999–2001 Turkish crisis (see the opening case).

To assess the frequency of financial crises, the IMF looked at the macroeconomic performance of a group of 53 countries from 1975 to 1997 (22 of these countries were developed nations, and 31 were developing countries).[13] The IMF found there were 158 currency crises, including 55 episodes in which a country's currency declined by more than 25 percent. There were also 54 banking crises. The IMF's data, which are summarized in Figure 10.3, suggest that developing nations were more than twice as likely to experience currency and banking crises than developed nations. It is not surprising, therefore, that most of the IMF's loan activities since the mid-1970s have been targeted toward developing nations.

Four crises have been of particular significance in terms of IMF involvement, the Third World debt crisis of the 1980s, the crisis experienced by Russia as it moved toward a market-based economic system, the 1995 Mexican currency crisis, and the 1997 Asian financial crisis. All four of these crises were the result of excessive foreign borrowings, a weak or poorly regulated banking system, and high inflation rates. These factors came together to trigger simultaneous debt and currency crises. Checking the resulting crises required IMF involvement.

Third World Debt Crisis

The Third World debt crisis had its roots in the OPEC oil price hikes of 1973 and 1979. These resulted in massive flows of funds from the major oil-importing nations (Germany, Japan, and the United States) to the oil-producing nations of OPEC. Commercial banks stepped in to recycle this money, borrowing from OPEC countries and lending to governments and businesses around the world. Much of the recycled money ended up in the form of loans to the governments of various Latin American and African nations. The loans were made on the basis of optimistic assessments about these nations' growth prospects, which did not materialize. Instead, Third World eco-

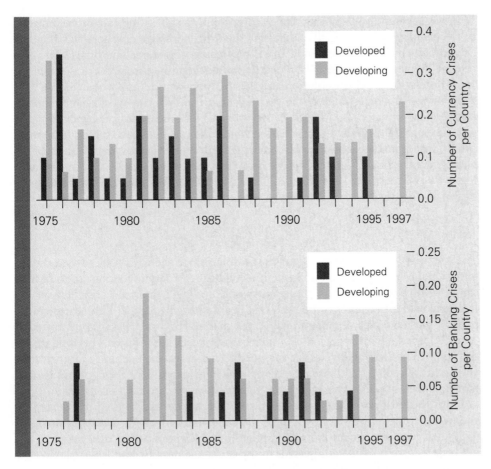

Figure 10.3

Incidence of Currency and Banking Crises, 1975–1997

Source: International Monetary Fund, *World Economic Outlook, 1998* (Washington, DC: IMF, May 1998), p. 77.

nomic growth was choked in the early 1980s by a combination of factors, including high inflation, rising short-term interest rates (which increased the costs of servicing the debt), and recession conditions in many industrialized nations (which were the markets for Third World goods).

The consequence was a Third World debt crisis of huge proportions. At one point it was calculated that commercial banks had more than $1 trillion of bad debts on their books, debts that the debtor nations had no hope of paying off. Against this background, Mexico announced in 1982 that it could no longer service its $80 billion in international debt without an immediate new loan of $3 billion. Brazil quickly followed, revealing it could not meet the required payments on its borrowed $87 billion. Then Argentina and several dozen other countries of lesser credit standings followed suit. The international monetary system faced a crisis of enormous dimensions.

Into the breach stepped the IMF. Together with several Western governments, particularly that of the United States, the IMF emerged as the key player in resolving the debt crisis. The deal with Mexico involved three elements: (1) rescheduling of Mexico's old debt, (2) new loans to Mexico from the IMF, the World Bank, and commercial banks, and (3) the Mexican government's agreement to abide by a set of IMF-dictated macroeconomic prescriptions for its economy, including tight control over the growth of the money supply and major cuts in government spending.

However, the IMF's solution to the debt crisis contained a major weakness: It depended on the rapid resumption of growth in the debtor nations. If this occurred, their capacity to repay debt would grow faster than their debt itself, and the crisis would be resolved. By the mid-1980s, it was clear this was not going to happen. The IMF-imposed macroeconomic policies did bring the trade deficits and inflation rates of many debtor nations under control, but it created sharp contractions in their economic growth rates.

It was apparent by 1989 that the debt problem was not going to be solved merely by rescheduling debt. In April of that year, the IMF endorsed a new approach that had been proposed by Nicholas Brady, the U.S. Treasury secretary. The Brady Plan, as it became known, stated that debt reduction, as distinguished from debt rescheduling, was a necessary part of the solution and the IMF and World Bank would assume roles in financing it. The essence of the plan was that the IMF, the World Bank, and the Japanese government would each contribute $10 billion toward debt reduction. To gain access to these funds, a debtor nation would once again have to submit to imposed conditions for macroeconomic policy management and debt repayment. The first application of the Brady Plan was the Mexican debt reduction of 1989. The deal reduced Mexico's 1989 debt of $107 billion by about $15 billion and until 1995 was widely regarded as a success.[14]

Mexican Currency Crisis of 1995

The Mexican peso had been pegged to the dollar since the early 1980s when the International Monetary Fund had made it a condition for lending money to the Mexican government to help bail the country out of a 1982 financial crisis. Under the IMF-brokered arrangement, the peso had been allowed to trade within a tolerance band of plus or minus 3 percent against the dollar. The band was also permitted to "crawl" down daily, allowing for an annual peso depreciation of about 4 percent against the dollar. The IMF believed that the need to maintain the exchange rate within a fairly narrow trading band would force the Mexican government to adopt stringent financial policies to limit the growth in the money supply and contain inflation.

Until the early 1990s, it looked as if the IMF policy had worked. However, the strains were beginning to show by 1994. Since the mid-1980s, Mexican producer prices had risen 45 percent more than prices in the United States, and yet there had not been a corresponding adjustment in the exchange rate. By late 1994, Mexico was running a $17 billion trade deficit, which amounted to some 6 percent of the country's gross domestic product and there had been an uncomfortably rapid expansion in the countries public and private-sector debt. Despite these strains, Mexican government officials had been stating publicly that they would support the peso's dollar peg at around $1 = 3.5 pesos by adopting appropriate monetary policies and by intervening in the currency markets if necessary. Encouraged by such public statements, $64 billion of foreign investment money poured into Mexico between 1990 and 1994 as corporations and mutual fund money managers sought to take advantage of the booming economy.

However, many currency traders concluded that the peso would have to be devalued, and they began to dump pesos on the foreign exchange market. The government tried to hold the line by buying pesos and selling dollars, but it lacked the foreign currency reserves required to halt the speculative tide (Mexico's foreign exchange reserves fell from $6 billion at the beginning of 1994 to less than $3.5 billion at the end of the year). In mid-December 1994, the Mexican government abruptly announced a devaluation. Immediately, much of the short-term investment money that had flowed into Mexican stocks and bonds over the previous year reversed its course, as foreign investors bailed out of peso-denominated financial assets. This exacerbated the sale of the peso and contributed to the rapid 40 percent drop in its value.

The IMF stepped in again, this time arm in arm with the U.S. government and the Bank for International Settlements. Together the three institutions pledged close to $50 billion to help Mexico stabilize the peso and to redeem $47 billion of public and private-sector debt that was set to mature in 1995. Of this amount, $20 billion came from the U.S. government and another $18 billion came from the IMF (which made Mexico the largest recipient of IMF aid up until that point). Without the aid package, Mexico would probably have defaulted on its debt obligations, and the peso would have gone into free fall. As is normal in such cases, the IMF insisted on tight mone-

The 1995 Mexican Peso Crisis and the Automobile Industry

Management Focus

In the euphoria that followed the January 1, 1994, implementation of the North American Free Trade Agreement (NAFTA), no industry looked set to gain more than the auto industry. Because of falling trade barriers and booming demand in Mexico, between January and October 1994, U.S. car exports to Mexico increased 500 percent. For all of 1994, Ford shipped 30,000 vehicles to Mexico, up from 6,000 in 1993. The company planned to ship 50,000 in 1995. General Motors and Chrysler also saw their shipments to Mexico surge in 1994 and were planning for even greater increases in 1995. Forecasts suggested that the number of vehicles sold in Mexico would rise to 1.2 million by 1999, up from 600,000 in 1994. With this growth in mind, not only had auto companies been exporting more to Mexico, but they also had been investing in Mexican-based production capacity both for serving the Mexican market and for exporting elsewhere. Among the biggest foreign investors were Chrysler, Ford, General Motors, Nissan, Mercedes-Benz, and Volkswagen.

In a few short days in December 1994, the euphoric bubble of the post-NAFTA boom was rudely burst by an unexpected decision on the part of the Mexican government to abandon a system of pegging the value of the peso at 3.5 to the dollar. Instead, the government decided to allow the peso to float freely against the dollar. In the weeks that followed this decision, the peso plummeted 40 percent, and by mid-January 1995 it was trading at 5.6 to the dollar.

As with many other industries, the impact on the auto industry was dramatic and immediate. By February 1995, the price of imported autos had risen by 40 percent. There had also been a substantial rise in the price of most autos assembled in Mexico, such as those coming off Ford's Cuautitlan plant, because many of these operations depended on parts imported from the United States and Canada. Demand for autos was further depressed by the Mexican government's economic austerity plan, introduced in March 1995 at the IMF's insistence. The plan tightened credit and raised interest rates.

Demand for autos slumped. Demand for the whole of 1995 was expected to come in between 30 and 50 percent below 1994 levels. Volkswagen, Nissan, Mercedes-Benz, and Ford temporarily closed their Mexican factories in January in expectation of the drop in demand. In other developments, Fiat of Italy pulled out of plans to build a new auto factory in Mexico, while Nissan announced plans to cut its 1995 production in Mexico from 210,000 to 180,000 vehicles. However, while the short-term outlook was grim, many auto companies expected to benefit from the fall in the value of the peso in the longer run. Although Volkswagen closed its Mexican plant for two weeks in January 1995, it planned to ship 175,000 Mexican-made vehicles to the United States in 1995, 25,000 more than in 1994. Similarly, the big three U.S. automakers planned to keep their Mexican plants operating at full capacity in the second half of 1995 by boosting exports to the United States.

Sources: J. Darling and D. Nauss, "Stall in the Fast Lane," *Los Angeles Times,* February 19, 1995, p. 1; "Mexico Drops Efforts to Prop up Peso," *Wall Street Journal,* December 23, 1994, p. A3; and R. Dornbusch, "We Have Salinas to Thank for the Peso Debacle," *Business Week,* January 16, 1995, p. 20.

---

tary policies and further cuts in public spending, both of which helped push the country into a deep recession. However, the recession was relatively short-lived, and by 1997 the country was once more on a growth path, had pared down its debt, and had paid back the $20 billion borrowed from the U.S. government ahead of schedule.[15] (The accompanying Management Focus details how this crisis affected the U.S. automobile industry, which before the crisis, was experiencing booming sales in Mexico.)

Russian Ruble Crisis

The IMF's involvement in Russia came about as the result of a persistent decline in the value of the Russian ruble, which was the product of high inflation rates and growing public-sector debt. Between January 1992 and April 1995, the value of the ruble against the U.S. dollar fell from $1=R125 to $1=R5130. This fall occurred while Russia was implementing an economic reform program designed to transform the country's crumbling centrally planned economy into a dynamic market economy. The reform program involved a number of steps, including the removal of price controls on January 1, 1992. Prices surged immediately and inflation was soon running at a monthly rate of about 30 percent. For the whole of 1992, the inflation rate in Russia was 3,000 percent. The annual rate for 1993 was approximately 900 percent.

Several factors contributed to Russia's high inflation. Prices had been held at artificially low levels by state planners during the Communist era. At the same time there was a shortage of many basic goods, so with nothing to spend their money on, many Russians simply hoarded rubles. After the liberalization of price controls, the country was suddenly awash in rubles chasing a still limited supply of goods. The result was to rapidly bid up prices. The inflationary fires that followed price liberalization were stoked by the Russian government itself. Unwilling to face the social consequences of the massive unemployment that would follow if many state-owned enterprises quickly were privatized, the government continued to subsidize the operations of many money-losing establishments. The result was a surge in the government's budget deficit. In the first quarter of 1992, the budget deficit amounted to 1.5 percent of the country's GDP. By the end of 1992, it had risen to 17 percent. Unable or unwilling to finance this deficit by raising taxes, the government found another solution—it printed money, which added fuel to the inflation fire.

With inflation rising, the ruble tumbled. By the end of 1992, the exchange rate was $1=R480. By the end of 1993, it was $1=R1,500. As 1994 progressed, it became increasingly evident that due to vigorous political opposition, the government would not be able to bring down its budget deficit as quickly as had been thought. By September the monthly inflation rate was accelerating. October started badly, with the ruble sliding more than 10 percent in value against the U.S. dollar in the first 10 days of the month. On October 11, the ruble plunged 21.5 percent against the dollar, reaching a value of $1=R3,926 by the time the foreign exchange market closed!

Despite the announcement of a tough budget plan that placed tight controls on the money supply, the ruble continued to slide and by April 1995 the exchange rate stood at $1=R5,120. However, by mid-1995 inflation was again on the way down. In June 1995 the monthly inflation rate was at a yearly low of 6.7 percent. Also, the ruble had recovered to stand at $1=R4,559 by July 6. On that day the Russian government announced it would intervene in the currency market to keep the ruble in a trading range of R4,3000 to R4,900 against the dollar. The Russian government believed that it was essential to maintain a relatively stable currency. Government officials announced that the central bank would be able to draw on $10 billion in foreign exchange reserves to defend the ruble against any speculative selling in Russia's relatively small foreign exchange market.

In the world of international finance, $10 billion is small change and it wasn't long before Russia found that its foreign exchange reserves were being depleted. It was at this point that the Russian government requested IMF loans. In February 1996, the IMF obliged with its second largest rescue effort after Mexico, a loan of $10 billion. In return for the loan, Russia agreed to limit the growth in its money supply, reduce public-sector debt, increase government tax revenues, and peg the ruble to the dollar.

Initially the package seemed to have the desired effect. Inflation declined from nearly 50 percent in 1996 to about 15 percent in 1997; the exchange rate stayed within its predetermined band; and the balance-of-payments situation remained broadly favorable. In 1997, the Russian economy grew for the first time since the breakup of the former Soviet Union, if only by a modest half of 1 percent of GDP. However, the public-sector debt situation did not improve. The Russian government continued to spend more than it agreed to under IMF targets, while government tax revenues were much lower than projected. Low tax revenues were in part due to falling oil prices (the government collected tax on oil sales), in part due to the difficulties of collecting tax in an economy where so much economic activity was in the "underground economy," and partly due to a complex tax system that was peppered with loopholes. Currently available estimates indicate that in 1997, Russian federal government spending amounted to 18.3 percent of GDP, while revenues were only 10.8 percent of GDP, implying a deficit of 7.5 percent of GDP, which was financed by an expansion in public debt.

The IMF responded by suspending its scheduled payment to Russia in early 1998, pending reform of Russia's complex tax system and a sustained attempt by the Russian government to cut public spending. This put further pressure on the Russian ruble, forcing the Russian central bank to raise interest rates on overnight loans to 150 percent. In June 1998, the U.S. government indicated it would support a new IMF bailout. The IMF was more circumspect, insisting instead that the Russian government push through a package of corporate tax increases and public spending cuts to balance the budget. The Russian government indicated it would do so, and the IMF released a tranche of $640 million that had been suspended. The IMF followed this with an additional $11.2 billion loan designed to preserve the ruble's stability.

Almost as soon as the funding was announced, however, it began to unravel. The IMF loan required the Russian government to take concrete steps to raise personal tax rates, improve tax collections, and cut government spending. A bill containing the required legislative changes was sent to the Russian parliament, where it was emasculated by antigovernment forces. The IMF responded by withholding $800 million of its first $5.6 billion tranche, undermining the credibility of its own program. The Russian stock market plummeted on the news, closing 6.5 percent down. Selling of rubles accelerated. The central bank began hemorrhaging foreign exchange reserves as it tried to maintain the value of the ruble. Foreign exchange reserves fell by $1.4 billion in the first week of August alone, to $17 billion, while interest rates surged again.

Against this background, on the weekend of August 15–16, top Russian officials huddled to develop a response to the most recent crisis. Their options were limited. The patience of the IMF had been exhausted. Foreign currency reserves were being rapidly depleted. Social tensions in the country were running high. The government faced upcoming redemptions on $18 billion of domestic bonds, with no idea of where the money would come from.

On Monday, August 17, Prime Minister Sergei Kiriyenko announced the results of the weekend's conclave. He said Russia would restructure the domestic debt market, unilaterally transforming short-term debt into long-term debt. In other words, the government had decided to default on its debt commitments. The government also announced a 90-day moratorium on the repayment of private foreign debt and stated it would allow the ruble to decline by 34 percent against the U.S. dollar. In short, Russia had turned its back on the IMF plan. The effect was immediate. Overnight, shops marked up the price of goods by 20 percent. As the ruble plummeted, currency exchange points were only prepared to sell dollars at a rate of 9 rubles per dollar, rather than the new official exchange rate of 6.43 rubles to the dollar. As for Russian government debt, it lost 85 percent of its value in a matter of hours, leaving foreign and Russian holders of debt alike suddenly gaping at a huge black hole in their financial assets.[16]

| The Asian Crisis

The financial crisis that erupted across Southeast Asia during the fall of 1997 has emerged as the biggest challenge ever. Holding the crisis in check required IMF loans to help the shattered economies of Indonesia, Thailand, and South Korea stabilize their currencies. In addition, although they did not request IMF loans, the economies of Japan, Malaysia, Singapore, and the Philippines were also badly hurt by the crisis.

The seeds of this crisis were sown during the previous decade when these countries were experiencing unprecedented economic growth. Although there were and remain important differences between the individual countries, a number of elements were common to most. Exports had long been the engine of economic growth in these countries. From 1990 to 1996, the value of exports from Malaysia had grown by 18 percent annually, Thai exports had grown by 16 percent per year, Singapore's by 15 percent,

Hong Kong's by 14 percent, and those of South Korea and Indonesia by 12 percent annually.[17] The nature of these exports had also shifted in recent years from basic materials and products such as textiles to complex and increasingly high-technology products, such as automobiles, semiconductors, and consumer electronics.

The Investment Boom

The wealth created by export-led growth helped fuel an investment boom in commercial and residential property, industrial assets, and infrastructure. The value of commercial and residential real estate in cities such as Hong Kong and Bangkok started to soar. This fed a building boom the likes of which had never been seen in Asia. Heavy borrowing from banks financed much of this construction. As for industrial assets, the success of Asian exporters encouraged them to make bolder investments in industrial capacity. This was exemplified most clearly by South Korea's giant diversified conglomerates, or *chaebol,* many of which had ambitions to build a major position in the global automobile and semiconductor industries.

An added factor behind the investment boom in most Southeast Asian economies was the government. In many cases, the governments had embarked on huge infrastructure projects. In Malaysia, for example, a new government administrative center was being constructed in Putrajaya for M$20 billion (U.S.$8 billion at the pre-July 1997 exchange rate), and the government was funding the development of a massive high-technology communications corridor and the huge Bakun dam, which at a cost of M$13.6 billion was to be the most expensive power generation plant in the country.[18] Throughout the region, governments also encouraged private businesses to invest in certain sectors of the economy in accordance with "national goals" and "industrialization strategy." In South Korea, long a country where the government played a proactive role in private-sector investments, President Kim Young-Sam urged the *chaebol* to invest in new factories as a way of boosting economic growth. South Korea enjoyed an investment-led economic boom in the 1994–95 period, but at a cost. The *chaebol,* always reliant on heavy borrowings, built up massive debts that were equivalent, on average, to four times their equity.[19]

In Indonesia, President Suharto had long supported investments in a network of an estimated 300 businesses owned by his family and friends in a system known as "crony capitalism." Many of these businesses were granted lucrative monopolies by the president. For example, Suharto announced in 1995 that he had decided to build a national car and the car would be built by a company owned by one of his sons, Hutomo Mandala Putra, in association with Kia Motors of South Korea. To support the venture, a consortium of Indonesian banks was "ordered" by the government to offer almost $700 million in start-up loans to the company.[20]

By the mid-1990s, Southeast Asia was in the grips of an unprecedented investment boom, much of it financed with borrowed money. Between 1990 and 1995, gross domestic investment grew by 16.3 percent annually in Indonesia, 16 percent in Malaysia, 15.3 percent in Thailand, and 7.2 percent in South Korea. By comparison, investment grew by 4.1 percent annually over the same period in the United States and 0.8 percent in all high-income economies.[21] And the rate of investment accelerated in 1996. In Malaysia, for example, spending on investment accounted for a remarkable 43 percent of GDP in 1996.[22]

Excess Capacity

As the volume of investments ballooned during the 1990s, often at the bequest of national governments, the quality of many of these investments declined significantly. The investments often were made on the basis of unrealistic projections about future demand conditions. The result was significant excess capacity. For example, South Korean *chaebol* investments in semiconductor factories surged in 1994 and 1995 when a temporary global shortage of dynamic random access memory chips (DRAMs) led to sharp price increases for this product. However, supply shortages had disappeared by

1996 and excess capacity was beginning to make itself felt, just as the South Koreans started to bring new DRAM factories on stream. The results were predictable; prices for DRAMs plunged, and the earnings of South Korean DRAM manufacturers fell by 90 percent, which meant it was difficult for them to make scheduled payments on the debt they had taken on to build the extra capacity.[23]

In another example, a building boom in Thailand resulted in excess capacity in residential and commercial property. By early 1997, an estimated 365,000 apartment units were unoccupied in Bangkok. With another 100,000 units scheduled to be completed in 1997, years of excess demand in the Thai property market had been replaced by excess supply. By one estimate, Bangkok's building boom had produced enough excess space by 1997 to meet its residential and commercial needs for five years.[24]

The Debt Bomb

By early 1997 what was happening in the South Korean semiconductor industry and the Bangkok property market was being played out elsewhere in the region. Massive investments in industrial assets and property had created excess capacity and plunging prices, while leaving the companies that had made the investments groaning under huge debt burdens that they were now finding it difficult to service.

To make matters worse, much of the borrowing had been in U.S. dollars, as opposed to local currencies. This had originally seemed like a smart move. Throughout the region, local currencies were pegged to the dollar, and interest rates on dollar borrowings were generally lower than rates on borrowings in domestic currency. Thus, it often made economic sense to borrow in dollars if the option was available. However, if the governments could not maintain the dollar peg and their currencies started to depreciate against the dollar, this would increase the size of the debt burden, when measured in the local currency. Currency depreciation would raise borrowing costs and could result in companies defaulting on their debt obligations.

Expanding Imports

A final complicating factor was that by the mid-1990s, although exports were still expanding across the region, imports were too. The investments in infrastructure, industrial capacity, and commercial real estate were sucking in foreign goods at unprecedented rates. To build infrastructure, factories, and office buildings, Southeast Asian countries were purchasing capital equipment and materials from America, Europe, and Japan. Many Southeast Asian states saw the current accounts of their balance of payments shift strongly into the red during the mid-1990s. By 1995, Indonesia was running a current account deficit that was equivalent to 3.5 percent of its GDP, Malaysia's was 5.9 percent, and Thailand's was 8.1 percent.[25] With deficits like these, it was increasingly difficult for the governments of these countries to maintain their currencies against the U.S. dollar. If that peg could not be held, the local currency value of dollar-denominated debt would increase, raising the specter of large-scale default on debt service payments. The scene was now set for a potentially rapid economic meltdown.

The Crisis

The Asian meltdown began in mid-1997 in Thailand when it became clear that several key Thai financial institutions were on the verge of default (see the closing case to Chapter 9 for more details). These institutions had been borrowing dollars from international banks at low interest rates and lending Thai baht at higher interest rates to local property developers. However, due to speculative overbuilding, these developers could not sell their commercial and residential property, forcing them to default on their debt obligations. In turn, the Thai financial institutions seemed increasingly likely to default on their dollar-denominated debt obligations to international banks. Sensing the beginning of the crisis, foreign investors fled the Thai stock market, selling their positions and converting them into U.S. dollars. The increased demand for dollars and increased supply of Thai baht, pushed down the dollar/Thai baht exchange rate, while the stock market plunged.

Seeing these developments, foreign exchange dealers and hedge funds started speculating against the baht, selling it short. For the previous 13 years, the Thai baht had been pegged to the U.S. dollar at an exchange rate of about $1=Bt25. The Thai government tried to defend the peg, but only succeeded in depleting its foreign exchange reserves. On July 2, 1997, the Thai government abandoned its defense and announced it would allow the baht to float freely against the dollar. The baht started a slide that would bring the exchange rate down to $1=Bt55 by January 1998. As the baht declined, the Thai debt bomb exploded. The 55 percent decline in the value of the baht against the dollar doubled the amount of baht required to serve the dollar-denominated debt commitments taken on by Thai financial institutions and businesses. This increased the probability of corporate bankruptcies and further pushed down the battered Thai stock market. The Thailand Set stock market index ultimately declined from 787 in January 1997 to a low of 337 in December of that year, on top of a 45 percent decline in 1996.

On July 28, the Thai government called in the International Monetary Fund. With its foreign exchange reserves depleted, Thailand lacked the foreign currency needed to finance its international trade and service debt commitments and desperately needed the capital the IMF could provide. It also needed to restore international confidence in its currency and needed the credibility associated with gaining access to IMF funds. Without IMF loans, the baht likely would increase its free fall against the U.S. dollar, and the whole country might go into default. The IMF agreed to provide the Thai government with $17.2 billion in loans, but the conditions were restrictive.[26] The IMF required the Thai government to increase taxes, cut public spending, privatize several state-owned businesses, and raise interest rates—all steps designed to cool Thailand's overheated economy. The IMF also required Thailand to close illiquid financial institutions. In December 1997, the government shut 56 financial institutions, laying off 16,000 people, and further deepening the recession that now gripped the country.

Following the devaluation of the Thai baht, wave after wave of speculation hit other Asian currencies. One after another in a period of weeks, the Malaysian ringgit, Indonesian rupiah, and the Singapore dollar were all marked sharply lower. With its foreign exchange reserves down to $28 billion, Malaysia let the ringgit float on July 14, 1997. Before the devaluation, the ringgit was trading at $1=2.525 ringgit. Six months later it had declined to $1=4.15 ringgit. Singapore followed on July 17, and the Singapore dollar quickly dropped in value from $1=S$1.495 before the devaluation to $1=S$2.68 a few days later. Next up was Indonesia, whose rupiah was allowed to float August 14. For Indonesia, this was the beginning of a precipitous decline in the value of its currency, which was to fall from $1=2,400 rupiah in August 1997 to $1=10,000 rupiah on January 6, 1998, a loss of 75 percent.

With the exception of Singapore, whose economy is probably the most stable in the region, these devaluations were driven by factors similar to those behind the earlier devaluation of the Thai baht—a combination of excess investment; high borrowings, much of it in dollar-denominated debt; and a deteriorating balance-of-payments position. Although both Malaysia and Singapore were able to halt the slide in their currencies and stock markets without the help of the IMF, Indonesia was not. Indonesia was struggling with a private-sector, dollar-denominated debt of close to $80 billion. With the rupiah sliding precipitously almost every day, the cost of servicing this debt was exploding, pushing more Indonesian companies into technical default.

On October 31, 1997, the IMF announced it had put together a $37 billion rescue deal for Indonesia in conjunction with the World Bank and the Asian Development Bank. In return, the Indonesian government agreed to close a number of troubled banks, reduce public spending, remove government subsidies on basic foodstuffs and energy, balance the budget, and unravel the crony capitalism that was so widespread in Indonesia. But the government of President Suharto appeared to backtrack several times on commitments made to the IMF. This precipitated further declines in the Indonesian currency and stock markets. Ultimately, Suharto caved in and removed costly government subsidies, only to see the country dissolve into chaos as the populace took to the streets to protest the resulting price increases. This unleashed a chain of events that led to Suharto's removal from power in May 1998.

The final domino to fall was South Korea (for further details, see the Country Focus in Chapter 9). During the 1990s, South Korean companies had built up huge debt loads as they invested heavily in new industrial capacity. Now they found they had too much industrial capacity and could not generate the income required to service their debt. South Korean banks and companies had also made the mistake of borrowing in dollars, much of it in the form of short-term loans that would come due within a year. Thus, when the Korean won started to decline in the fall of 1997 in sympathy with the problems elsewhere in Asia, South Korean companies saw their debt obligations balloon. Several large companies were forced to file for bankruptcy. This triggered a decline in the South Korean currency and stock market that was difficult to halt. The South Korean central bank tried to keep the dollar/won exchange rate above $1=W1,000 but found that this only depleted its foreign exchange reserves. On November 17, the South Korean central bank gave up the defense of the won, which quickly fell to $1=W1,500.

With its economy on the verge of collapse, the South Korean government on November 21 requested $20 billion in standby loans from the IMF. As the negotiations progressed, it became apparent that South Korea was going to need far more than $20 billion. Among other problems, the country's short-term foreign debt was found to be twice as large as previously thought at close to $100 billion, while the country's foreign exchange reserves were down to less than $6 billion. On December 3, the IMF and South Korean government reached a deal to lend $55 billion to the country. The agreement with the IMF called for the South Koreans to open their economy and banking system to foreign investors. South Korea also pledged to restrain the *chaebol* by reducing their share of bank financing and requiring them to publish consolidated financial statements and undergo annual independent external audits. On trade liberalization, the IMF said South Korea would comply with its commitments to the World Trade Organization to eliminate trade-related subsidies and restrictive import licensing and would streamline its import certification procedures, all of which should open the South Korean economy to greater foreign competition.[27]

Evaluating the IMF's Policy Prescriptions

By early 1998, the IMF was committing over $110 billion in short-term loans to three Asian countries: South Korea, Indonesia, and Thailand. This was on top of the $20 billion package the IMF gave to Mexico in 1995 and the $10 billion loan to Russia. All these loan packages came with conditions attached. In general, the IMF insists on a combination of tight macroeconomic policies, including cuts in public spending, higher interest rates, and tight monetary policy. It also often pushes for the deregulation of sectors formerly protected from domestic and foreign competition, privatization of state-owned assets, and better financial reporting from the banking sector. In general, these policies are designed to cool overheated economies by reining in inflation and reducing government spending and debt. Recently, this set of policy prescriptions has come in for tough criticisms from many Western observers.[28]

Inappropriate Policies

One criticism is that the IMF's "one-size-fits-all" approach to macroeconomic policy is inappropriate for many countries. This point was made in the Country Focus that looked at how the IMF's policies toward Zaire may have made things worse rather than better. In the recent Asian crisis, critics argue that the tight macroeconomic policies imposed by the IMF are not well suited to countries that are suffering not from excessive government spending and inflation, but from a private-sector debt crisis with deflationary undertones.[29] In South Korea, for example, the government has been running a budget surplus for years (it was 4 percent of South Korea's GDP in the 1994–1996 period) and inflation is low at about 5 percent. South Korea has the second strongest financial position of any country in the Organization for Economic Cooperation and Development. Despite this, say critics, the IMF is insisting on applying the same policies that it applies to countries suffering from high inflation. The IMF is requiring South Korea to maintain an inflation rate of 5 percent. However, given the collapse in the value of its currency and the subsequent rise in price for imports such as oil, inflationary pressures will inevitably increase in South Korea. So to hit a 5 percent inflation rate, the South Koreans are being forced to apply an unnecessarily tight monetary policy. Short-term interest rates in South Korea jumped from 12.5 percent to 21 percent immediately after the country signed its initial deal with the IMF. Increasing interest rates make it even more difficult for companies to service their already excessive short-term debt obligations, so the cure prescribed by the IMF may actually increase the probability of widespread corporate defaults, not reduce them.

The IMF rejects this criticism. According to the IMF, the critical task is to rebuild confidence in the won. Once this has been achieved, the won will recover from its oversold levels. This will reduce the size of South Korea's dollar-denominated debt burden when expressed in won, making it easier for companies to service their dollar-denominated debt. The IMF also argues that by requiring South Korea to remove restrictions on foreign direct investment, foreign capital will flow into the country to take advantage of cheap assets. This, too, will increase demand for the Korean currency and help to improve the dollar/won exchange rate.

Moral Hazard

A second criticism of the IMF is that its rescue efforts are exacerbating a problem known to economists as moral hazard. **Moral hazard** arises when people behave recklessly because they know they will be saved if things go wrong. Critics point out that many Japanese and Western banks were far too willing to lend large amounts of capital to overleveraged Asian companies during the boom years of the 1990s. These critics argue that the banks should now be forced to pay the price for their rash lending policies, even if that means some banks must shut down.[30] Only by taking such drastic action, the argument goes, will banks learn the error of their ways and not engage in rash lending in the future. By providing support to these countries, the IMF is reducing the probability of debt default and in effect bailing out the banks whose loans gave rise to this situation.

This argument ignores two critical points. First, if some Japanese or Western banks with heavy exposure to the troubled Asian economies were forced to write off their loans due to widespread debt default, the impact would be difficult to contain. The failure of large Japanese banks, for example, could trigger a meltdown in the Japanese financial markets. This would almost inevitably lead to a serious decline in stock markets around the world. That is the very risk the IMF was trying to avoid by stepping in with financial support. Second, it is incorrect to imply that some banks have not had to pay the price for rash lending policies. The IMF has insisted on the closure of banks in South Korea, Thailand, and Indonesia. Foreign banks with short-term loans outstanding to South Korean enterprises have been forced by circumstances to reschedule those loans at interest rates that do not compensate for the extension of the loan maturity.

Lack of Accountability

The final criticism of the IMF is that it has become too powerful for an institution that lacks any real mechanism for accountability.[31] By the end of the 1990s, the IMF was engaged in loan programs in 75 developing countries that collectively contain 1.4 billion people. The IMF was determining macroeconomic policies in those countries, yet according to critics such as noted Harvard economist Jeffery Sachs, the IMF, with a staff of less than 1,000, lacks the expertise required to do a good job. Evidence of this, according to Sachs, can be found in the fact that the IMF was singing the praises of the Thai and South Korean governments only months before both countries lurched into crisis. Then the IMF put together a draconian program for South Korea without having deep knowledge of the country. Sachs's solution to this problem is to reform the IMF so it makes greater use of outside experts and its operations are open to great outside scrutiny.

Observations

As with many debates about international economics, it is not clear which side has the winning hand about the appropriateness of IMF policies. There are cases where one can argue that IMF policies have been counterproductive, such as Zaire, which we discussed in the Country Focus. In addition, one might question the success of the IMF's involvement in Turkey, given that the country has had to implement 18 IMF programs since 1958! But the IMF can also point to some notable accomplishments, including its success in containing the Asian crisis, which could have rocked the global international monetary system to its core. Similarly, many observers give the IMF credit for its deft handling of politically difficult situations, such as the Russian ruble crisis and Mexican peso crisis, and for successfully promoting a free market philosophy.

Several years after the IMF's intervention, the economies of Asia, Russia, and Mexico had all recovered to some extent. Certainly they had all averted the kind of catastrophic implosion that might have occurred had the IMF not stepped in, and although Russia and Indonesia still faced considerable problems, it is not clear that the IMF should take much blame for this. At the end of the day, the IMF cannot force countries to adopt the policies required to correct economic mismanagement. As the opening case on Turkey illustrates, while a government may commit to taking corrective action in return for an IMF loan, internal political problems may make it difficult for a government to act on that commitment. In such cases, the IMF is caught between a rock and hard place, for if it decided to withhold money, it might trigger financial collapse and the kind of contagion that it seeks to avoid.

Implications for Business

The implications for international businesses of the material discussed in this chapter fall into three main areas: currency management, business strategy, and corporate–government relations.

Currency Management

An obvious implication with regard to currency management is that companies must recognize that the foreign exchange market does not work quite as depicted in Chapter 9. The current system is a mixed system in which a combination of government intervention and speculative activity can drive the foreign exchange market. Companies engaged in significant foreign exchange activities need to be aware of this and to adjust their foreign exchange transactions accordingly. For example, the currency management unit of Caterpillar claims it made millions of dollars in the hours following the announcement of the Plaza Accord by selling dollars and buying currencies that it expected to appreciate on the foreign exchange market following government intervention.

We have seen how under the present system, speculative buying and selling of currencies can create very volatile movements in exchange rates (as exhibited by the rise and fall of the dollar during the 1980s). Contrary to the predictions of the purchasing power parity theory (see Chapter 9), we have seen that exchange rate movements during the 1980s, at least with regard to the dollar, did not seem to be strongly influenced by relative inflation rates. Insofar as volatile exchange rates increase foreign exchange risk, this is not good news for business. On the other hand, as we saw in Chapter 9, the foreign exchange market has developed a number of instruments, such as the forward market and swaps, that can help to insure against foreign exchange risk. Not surprisingly, use of these instruments has increased markedly since the breakdown of the Bretton Woods system in 1973.

Business Strategy

The volatility of the present global exchange rate regime presents a conundrum for international businesses. Exchange rate movements are difficult to predict, and yet their movement can have a major impact on a business's competitive position. Faced with uncertainty about the future value of currencies, firms can utilize the forward exchange market. However, the forward exchange market is far from perfect as a predictor of future exchange rates (see Chapter 9). It is also difficult if not impossible to get adequate insurance coverage for exchange rate changes that might occur several years in the future. The forward market tends to offer coverage for exchange rate changes a few months—not years—ahead. Given this, it makes sense to pursue strategies that will increase the company's strategic flexibility in the face of unpredictable exchange rate movements.

Maintaining strategic flexibility can take the form of dispersing production to different locations around the globe as a *real hedge* against currency fluctuations. Consider the case of Daimler-Benz (now Daimler/Chrysler), Germany's export-oriented automobile and aerospace company. In June 1995, the company stunned the German business community when it announced it expected to post a severe loss in 1995 of about $720 million. The cause was Germany's strong currency, which had appreciated by 4 percent against a basket of major currencies since the beginning of 1995 and had risen by over 30 percent against the U.S. dollar since late 1994. By mid-1995, the exchange rate against the dollar stood at $1=DM1.38. Daimler's management believed it could not make money with an exchange rate under $1=DM1.60. Daimler's senior managers concluded that the appreciation of the mark against the dollar was probably permanent, so they decided to move substantial production outside of Germany and increase purchasing of foreign components. The idea was to reduce the vulnerability of the company to future exchange rate movements. The Mercedes-Benz division has begun to implement this move. Even before its acquisition of Chrysler Corporation in 1998, Mercedes planned to produce 10 percent of its cars outside of Germany by 2000, mostly in the United States.[32] Similarly, the move by Japanese automobile companies to expand their productive capacity in the United States and Europe can be seen in the context of the increase in the value of the yen between 1985 and 1995, which raised the price of Japanese exports. For the Japanese companies, building production capacity overseas is a hedge against continued appreciation of the yen (as well as against trade barriers).

Another way of building strategic flexibility involves contracting out manufacturing. This allows a company to shift suppliers from country to country in response to changes in relative costs brought about by exchange rate movements. However, this kind of strategy works only for low-value-added manufacturing (e.g., textiles), in which the individual manufacturers have few if any firm-specific skills that contribute to the value of the product. It is inappropriate for high-value-added manufacturing, in which firm-specific technology and skills add significant value to the product (e.g., the heavy equipment industry) and in which switching costs are correspondingly high. For high-value-added manufacturing, switching suppliers will lead to a reduction in the value that is added, which may offset any cost gains arising from exchange rate fluctuations.

The roles of the IMF and the World Bank in the present international monetary system also have implications for business strategy. Increasingly, the IMF has been acting as the macroeconomic policeman of the world economy, insisting that countries seeking significant borrowings adopt IMF-mandated macroeconomic policies. These policies typically include anti-inflationary monetary policies and reductions in government spending. In the short run, such policies usually result in a sharp contraction of demand. International businesses selling or producing in such countries need to be aware of this and plan accordingly. In the long run, the kind of policies imposed by the IMF can promote economic growth and an expansion of demand, which create opportunities for international business.

Corporate–Government Relations

As major players in the international trade and investment environment, businesses can influence government policy toward the international monetary system. For example, intense government lobbying by U.S. exporters helped convince the U.S. government that intervention in the foreign exchange market was necessary. Similarly, much of the impetus behind establishment of the exchange rate mechanism of the European monetary system came from European businesspeople, who understood the costs of volatile exchange rates.

With this in mind, business can and should use its influence to promote an international monetary system that facilitates the growth of international trade and investment. Whether a fixed or floating regime is optimal is a subject for debate. However, exchange rate volatility such as the world experienced during the 1980s and 1990s creates an environment less conducive to international trade and investment than one with more stable exchange rates. Therefore, it would seem to be in the interests of international business to promote an international monetary system that minimizes volatile exchange rate movements, particularly when those movements are unrelated to long-run economic fundamentals.

Chapter Summary

This chapter explained the workings of the international monetary system and pointed out its implications for international business. This chapter made the following points:

1. The gold standard is a monetary standard that pegs currencies to gold and guarantees convertibility to gold.

2. It was thought that the gold standard contained an automatic mechanism that contributed to the simultaneous achievement of a balance-of-payments equilibrium by all countries.

3. The gold standard broke down during the 1930s as countries engaged in competitive devaluations.

4. The Bretton Woods system of fixed exchange rates was established in 1944. The U.S. dollar was the central currency of this system; the value of every other currency was pegged to its value. Significant exchange rate devaluations were allowed only with the permission of the IMF.

5. The role of the IMF was to maintain order in the international monetary system (i) to avoid a repetition of the competitive devaluations of the 1930s and (ii) to control price inflation by imposing monetary discipline on countries.

6. To build flexibility into the system, the IMF stood ready to lend countries funds to help protect their currency on the foreign exchange market in the face of speculative pressure and to assist countries in correcting a fundamental disequilibrium in their balance-of-payments position.

7. The fixed exchange rate system collapsed in 1973, primarily due to speculative pressure on the dollar following a rise in U.S. inflation and a growing U.S. balance-of-trade deficit.

8. Since 1973 the world has operated with a floating exchange rate regime, and exchange rates have become more volatile and far less predictable. Volatile exchange rate movements have helped reopen the debate over the merits of fixed and floating systems.

9. The case for a floating exchange rate regime claims: (i) such a system gives countries autonomy

regarding their monetary policy and (*ii*) floating exchange rates facilitate smooth adjustment of trade imbalances.

10. The case for a fixed exchange rate regime claims: (*i*) the need to maintain a fixed exchange rate imposes monetary discipline on a country, (*ii*) floating exchange rate regimes are vulnerable to speculative pressure, (*iii*) the uncertainty that accompanies floating exchange rates dampens the growth of international trade and investment, and (*iv*) far from correcting trade imbalances, depreciating a currency on the foreign exchange market tends to cause price inflation.

11. In today's international monetary system, some countries have adopted floating exchange rates, some have pegged their currency to another currency, such as the U.S. dollar, and some have pegged their currency to a basket of other currencies, allowing their currency to fluctuate within a zone around the basket.

12. In the post-Bretton Woods era, the IMF has continued to play an important role in helping countries navigate their way through financial crises by lending significant capital to embattled governments and by requiring them to adopt certain macroeconomic policies.

13. There is an important debate taking place over the appropriateness of IMF-mandated macroeconomic policies. Critics charge that the IMF often imposes inappropriate conditions on developing nations that are the recipients of its loans.

14. The present managed-float system of exchange rate determination has increased the importance of currency management in international businesses.

15. The volatility of exchange rates under the present managed-float system creates both opportunities and threats. One way of responding to this volatility is for companies to build strategic flexibility by dispersing production to different locations around the globe by contracting out manufacturing (in the case of low-value-added manufacturing) and other means.

Critical Discussion Questions

1. Why did the gold standard collapse? Is there a case for returning to some type of gold standard? What is it?

2. What opportunities might current IMF lending policies to developing nations create for international businesses? What threats might they create?

3. Do you think the standard IMF policy prescriptions of tight monetary policy and reduced government spending are always appropriate for developing nations experiencing a currency crisis? How might the IMF change its approach? What would the implications be for international businesses?

4. Debate the relative merits of fixed and floating exchange rate regimes. From the perspective of an international business, what are the most important criteria in a choice between the systems? Which system is the more desirable for an international business?

5. Imagine that Canada, the United States, and Mexico decide to adopt a fixed exchange rate system similar to the ERM of the European Monetary System. What would be the likely consequences of such a system for (*a*) international businesses and (*b*) the flow of trade and investment among the three countries?

Closing Case

Caterpillar Inc.

Caterpillar Inc. (Cat) is the world's largest manufacturer of heavy earthmoving equipment. Earthmoving equipment typically represents about 70 percent of the annual dollar sales of construction equipment worldwide. In 1980, Cat held 53.3 percent of the global market for earthmoving equipment. Its closest competitor was Komatsu of Japan, with 60 percent of the Japanese market but only 15.2 percent worldwide.

In 1980, Caterpillar was widely considered one of the premier manufacturing and exporting companies in the United States. The company had enjoyed 50 consecutive years of profits and returns on shareholder equity as high as 27 percent. In 1981, 57 percent of its sales were outside the United States, and roughly two-thirds of these orders were filled by exports. Cat was the third largest U.S. exporter. Reflecting this underlying strength, Cat recorded record pretax profits of $579 million in 1981. However, the next three years were disastrous. Caterpillar lost a total of $1 billion and saw its market share slip to as low as 40 percent in 1985, while Komatsu increased its share to 25 percent. Three factors explain this startling turn of events: the higher productivity of Komatsu, the rise in the value of the dollar, and the Third World debt crisis.

Komatsu had been creeping up on Cat for a long time. In the 1960s, the company had a minuscule presence outside of Japan. By 1974, it had increased its global market share of heavy earthmoving equipment to 9 percent, and by 1980 it was more than 15 percent. Part of Komatsu's growth was due to its superior labor productivity; throughout the 1970s, it had been able to price its machines 10 to 15 percent below Caterpillar's. However, Komatsu lacked an extensive dealer network outside of Japan, and Cat's worldwide dealer network and superior after-sale service and support functions were seen as justifying a price premium for Cat machines. For these reasons, many industry observers believed Komatsu would not increase its share much beyond its 1980 level.

An unprecedented rise in the value of the dollar against most major world currencies changed the picture. Between 1980 and 1987, the dollar rose an average of 87 percent against the currencies of 10 other industrialized countries. The dollar was driven up by strong economic growth in the United States, which attracted heavy inflows of capital from foreign investors seeking high returns on capital assets. High real interest rates attracted foreign investors seeking high returns on financial assets. At the same time, political turmoil in other parts of the world and relatively slow economic growth in Europe helped create the view that the United States was a good place in which to invest. These inflows of capital increased the demand for dollars in the foreign exchange market, which pushed the value of the dollar upward against other currencies.

The strong dollar substantially increased the dollar price of Cat's machines. At the same time, the dollar price of Komatsu products imported into the United States fell. Because of the shift in the relative values of the dollar and the yen, Komatsu priced its machines as much as 40 percent below Caterpillar's prices by 1985. In light of this enormous price difference, many consumers chose to forgo Caterpillar's superior after-sale service and support and bought Komatsu machines.

The third factor, the Third World debt crisis, became apparent in 1982. During the early 1970s, the nations of OPEC quadrupled the price of oil, which resulted in a massive flow of funds into these nations. Commercial banks borrowed this money from the OPEC countries and lent it to the governments of many Third World nations to finance massive construction projects, which led to a global boom in demand for heavy earthmoving equipment. Caterpillar benefited from this development. By 1982, however, it became apparent that the commercial banks had lent too much money to risky and unproductive investments, and the governments of several countries (including Mexico, Brazil, and Argentina) threatened to suspend debt payments. The International Monetary Fund stepped in and arranged for new loans to indebted Third World countries, on the condition that they adopt deflationary macroeconomic policies. For Cat, the party was over; orders for heavy earthmoving equipment dried up almost overnight, and those that were placed went to the lowest bidder, which often was Komatsu.

As a result of these factors, Caterpillar was in deep trouble by late 1982. The company responded quickly and between 1982 and 1985 cut costs by more than 20 percent. This was achieved by a 40 percent reduction in the workforce, the closure of nine plants, and a $1.8 billion investment in flexible manufacturing technologies designed to boost quality and lower cost. The company also pressed the government to lower the value of the dollar on foreign exchange markets. By 1984, Cat was a leading voice among U.S. exporters trying to get the Reagan administration to intervene in the foreign exchange market.

Things began to go Caterpillar's way in early 1985. Prompted by Cat and other exporters, representatives of the U.S. government met with representatives of Japan, Germany, France, and Great Britain at the Plaza Hotel in New York. In the resulting communiqué—known as the Plaza Accord—the five governments acknowledged that the dollar was overvalued and pledged to take actions that would drive down its price on the foreign exchange market. The central bank of each country intervened in the foreign exchange market, selling dollars and buying other currencies (including its own). The dollar had already begun to fall in early 1985 in response to a string of record U.S. trade deficits. The Plaza Accord accelerated this trend, and over the next three years the dollar fell back to its 1980 level.

The effect for Caterpillar was almost immediate. Like any major exporter, Caterpillar had its own foreign exchange unit. Suspecting that an adjustment in the dollar would come soon, Cat had increased its holdings of foreign currencies in early 1985, using the strong dollar to purchase them. As the dollar fell, the company was able to convert these currencies back into dollars for a healthy profit. In 1985, Cat had pretax profits of $32 million;

without foreign exchange gains of $89 million, it would have lost money. In 1986, foreign exchange gains of $100 million accounted for nearly two-thirds of its pretax profits of $159 million.

More significant for Cat's long-term position, the fall in the dollar against the yen and Caterpillar's cost-cutting efforts by 1988 had helped to eradicate the 40 percent cost advantage that Komatsu had enjoyed over Caterpillar four years earlier. After trying to hold its prices down, Komatsu had to raise its prices that year by 18 percent, while Cat was able to hold its price increase to 3 percent. With the terms of trade no longer handicapping Caterpillar, the company regained some of its lost market share. By 1989, it reportedly held 47 percent of the world market for heavy earthmoving equipment, up from a low of 40 percent three years earlier, while Komatsu's share had slipped to below 20 percent.

Sources: R. S. Eckley, "Caterpillar's Ordeal: Foreign Competition in Capital Goods," *Business Horizons*, March–April 1989, pp. 80–86; H. S. Byrne, "Track of the Cat: Caterpillar Is Bulldozing Its Way Back to Higher Profits," *Barron's*, April 6, 1987, pp. 13, 70–71; R. Henkoff, "This Cat Is Acting like a Tiger," *Fortune*, December 19, 1988,

pp. 71–76; and "Caterpillar and Komatsu," in *Transnational Management: Text, Cases, and Readings in Cross-Border Management*, ed. C. A. Bartlett and S. Ghosal (Homewood, IL: Richard D. Irwin, 1992).

Case Discussion Questions

1. To what extent is the competitive position of Caterpillar against Komatsu dependent on the dollar/yen exchange rate? Between mid-1996 and early 1998, the dollar appreciated by over 40 percent against the yen. How do you think this affected the relatively competitive position of Caterpillar and Komatsu?

2. If you were the CEO of Caterpillar, what actions would you take now to make sure there is no repeat of the early 1980s experience?

3. What potential impact can the actions of the IMF and World Bank have on Caterpillar's business? Is there anything Cat can do to influence the actions of the IMF and World Bank?

4. As the CEO of Caterpillar, would you prefer a fixed exchange rate regime or a continuation of the current managed-float regime? Why?

Notes

1. The argument goes back to 18th century philosopher David Hume. See D. Hume, "On the Balance of Trade," reprinted in *The Gold Standard in Theory and in History*, ed. B. Eichengreen (London: Methuen, 1985).

2. R. Solomon, *The International Monetary System, 1945–1981* (New York: Harper & Row, 1982).

3. International Monetary Fund, *World Economic Outlook, 1998* (Washington, DC: IMF, May 1998).

4. For an extended discussion of the dollar exchange rate in the 1980s, see B. D. Pauls, "US Exchange Rate Policy: Bretton Woods to the Present," *Federal Reserve Bulletin*, November 1990, pp. 891–908.

5. For a feel for the issues contained in this debate, see P. Krugman, *Has the Adjustment Process Worked?* (Washington, DC: Institute for International Economics, 1991); "Time to Tether Currencies," *The Economist*, January 6, 1990, pp. 15–16; P. R. Krugman and M. Obstfeld, *International Economics: Theory and Policy* (New York: Harper Collins, 1994); J. Shelton, *Money Meltdown* (New York: Free Press, 1994); and S. Edwards, "Exchange Rates and the Political Economy of Macroeconomic Discipline," *American Economic Review* 86, no. 2 (May 1996), pp. 159–63.

6. The argument is made by several prominent economists, particularly Stanford's Robert McKinnon. See R. McKinnon, "An International Standard for Monetary Stabilization," *Policy Analyses in International Economics* 8 (1984). The details of this argument are beyond the scope of this book. For a relatively accessible exposition, see P. Krugman, *The Age of Diminished Expectations* (Cambridge, MA: MIT Press, 1990).

7. A. R. Ghosh and A. M. Gulde, "Does the Exchange Rate Regime Matter for Inflation and Growth?" *Economic Issues*, no. 2, (1997).

8. "The ABC of Currency Boards," *The Economist*, November 1, 1997, p. 80.

9. For a time, the plan was to introduce a common currency by 1997, but in July 1995 this was changed to 1999, and many thought this date could not be attained. L. Barber, "EU Leaders Plan 1999 Launch Date of Single Currency," *Financial Times*, June 27, 1995, p. 1.

10. N. Colchester and D. Buchan, *Europower* (New York: Random House, 1990), and D. Swann, *The Economics of the Common Market* (London: Penguin Books, 1990).

11. M. Wolf, "Emu May Not Be Dead After All," *Financial Times*, August 1, 1994, p. 13

12. International Monetary Fund, *World Economic Outlook, 1998*.

13. Ibid.

14. For a summary of the arguments for debt reductions, see "And Forgive Us Our Debts: A Survey of the IMF and the World Bank," *The Economist*, October 12, 1991, pp. 23–33, and Krugman, *Age of Diminished Expectations*.

15. See P. Carroll and C. Torres, "Mexico Unveils Program of Harsh Fiscal Medicine," *Wall Street Journal*, March 10, 1995, pp. A1, A6; and "Putting Mexico Together Again," *The Economist*, February 4, 1995, p. 65.

16. S. Erlanger, "Russia Will Test a Trading Band for the Ruble," *New York Times*, July 7, 1995, p. 1; C. Freeland, "Russia to Introduce a Trading Band for Ruble against Dollar," *Financial Times*, July 7, 1995, p. 1; J. Thornhill, "Russians Bemused by 'Black Tuesday,'" *Financial Times*, October 12, 1994, p. 4; R. Sikorski, "Mirage of Numbers," *Wall Street Journal*, May 18, 1994, p. 14; "Can Russia Fight Back?" *The Economist*, June 6, 1998, pp. 47–48; and J. Thornhill, "Russia's Shrinking Options," *Financial Times*, August 19, 1998, p. 19.

17. World Trade Organization, *Annual Report, 1997*, vol. II, table III, p. 69.

18. J. Ridding and J. Kynge, "Complacency Gives Way to Contagion," *Financial Times*, January 13, 1998, p. 8.

19. J. Burton and G. Baker, "The Country That Invested Its Way into Trouble," *Financial Times*, January 15, 1998, p. 8.

20. P. Shenon, "The Suharto Billions," *New York Times*, January 16, 1998, p. 1.

21. World Bank, *1997 World Development Report* (Oxford: Oxford University Press), Table 11.

22. Ridding and Kynge, "Complacency Gives Way to Contagion."

23. Burton and Baker, "The Country That Invested Its Way into Trouble."

24. "Bitter Pill for the Thais," *Straits Times*, July 5, 1997, p. 46.

25. World Bank, *1997 World Development Report*, Table 2.

26. International Monetary Fund, press release no. 97/37, August 20, 1997.

27. T. S. Shorrock, "Korea Starts Overhaul; IMF Aid Hits $60 Billion," *Journal of Commerce*, December 8, 1997, p. 3A.

28. Particularly Jeffery Sachs. See J. Sachs, "Economic Transition and Exchange Rate Regime," *American Economic Review* 86, no. 92 (May 1996), pp. 147–52; and J. Sachs, "Power unto Itself," *Financial Times*, December 11, 1997, p. 11.

29. Sachs, "Power unto Itself."

30. Martin Wolf, "Same Old IMF Medicine," *Financial Times*, December 9, 1997, p. 12.

31. Sachs, "Power unto Itself."

32. P. Gumbel and B. Coleman, "Daimler Warns of Severe 95 Loss Due to Strong Mark," *New York Times*, June 29, 1995, pp. 1, 10; and M. Wolf, "Daimler-Benz Announces Major Losses," *Financial Times*, June 29, 1995, p. 1.

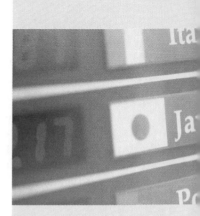

The Global
Capital
Market

ε

China Mobile (Hong Kong) Ltd. is a Hong Kong–based provider of wireless telephone service and one of the largest providers of mobile telephone service in the world. In 1996 the company was spun off from China Mobile Communications Corporation, a state-owned provider of mobile telephone service in mainland China, which retained a 75 percent ownership stake in China Mobile (Hong Kong) Ltd. The spin-off was part of a strategy by the Chinese government for privatizing its telecommunications network. China Mobile was given the right to expand into mainland China. By September 2000, the company was the largest provider of mobile communications in China with 23.9 million subscribers and a market leadership position in six provinces.

In late 2000, China was finishing up negotiations to enter the World Trade Organization. Under the terms of the WTO agreement, China would progressively have to open its telecommunications market to foreign telecommunications service providers. Galvanized by the impending threat of new competition in its fast-growing market, China Mobile realized it needed to accelerate its expansion into mainland China to preempt foreign competitors. Accordingly, in October 2000 China Mobile reached an agreement to purchase mobile networks in an additional seven provinces from its state-owned parent company. The purchase of these networks would give China Mobile an additional 15.4 million subscribers. It would also give the Hong Kong company a geographically contiguous market covering all the coastal regions of mainland China, a 56 percent share of all cellular subscribers in mainland China, and service coverage of approximately 48.0 percent of the total population.

The price tag for this deal was $32.8 billion. For China Mobile, a critical question was how to finance the deal. It could issue additional equity or debt in Hong Kong, but Hong Kong's relatively small capital market might not be big enough to absorb a multibillion-dollar offering without driving up the price of the capital to an unacceptably high level. For example, China Mobile might be required to pay a relatively high interest rate in order to sell sufficient bonds in Hong Kong to finance part of its acquisition of the provincial networks, thereby raising its cost of capital. After consulting its underwriters, which included the U.S. companies Goldman Sachs and Merrill Lynch, China Mobile opted for an international offering of equity and debt.

The shares of China Mobile were already listed on the New York Stock Exchange as American Depository Receipts (ADRs). Each ADR represented and controlled five shares in the Hong Kong company. China Mobile opted to sell ADRs worth approximately $6.6 billion and to raise a further $600 million from the sale of five-year convertible bonds. (Convertible bonds can be converted into equity at some future date, in this case after five years. They are considered to be a hybrid between conventional stock and bonds.) In addition, China Mobile agreed to sell a 2 percent stake in the company to Vodafone PLC, Europe's largest wireless service provider, for $2.5 billion. The remainder of the $32.8 billion purchase price for the mainland wireless networks was to be financed by issuing new shares to state-owned China Mobile Communications Corporation, which would retain for now its 75 percent stake in the company despite the issuing of new equity.

A significant portion of the ADRs would be offered for sale in New York. However, the underwriters also planned to offer ADRs in Asia and Europe. Similarly, the convertible bond issue would be priced in U.S. dollars and offered to global investors. The equity and bond offerings were closed in November 2000. Both offerings were substantially oversubscribed. The equity portion of the offering was 2.6 times oversubscribed. This was a remarkable achievement for what was the largest ever Asian equity issue outside of Japan. In total, China Mobile raised some $8.24 billion, over $1 billion more than planned. Some $690 million came from the sale of convertible bonds, and the remainder from the sale of equity. The convertible bonds carried a 2.25 percent interest rate, significantly less than the 2.75 percent rate initially targeted (as bond prices are bid up, the interest rate offered by the bond goes down). This lowered China Mobile's cost of capital. The oversubscription of the equity portion of the offering had a similar effect. The offering was truly global in nature. While 55 percent of the placement was in the United States, another 25 percent went to Asian investors and 20 percent to European investors.

Sources: China Mobile Hong Kong Ltd., SEC Form F-3, filed October 30, 2000; M. Johnson, "Deal of the Month," Corporate Finance, December 2000, p. 10; and "Jumbo Equity Raid Elevates China Mobile to Big League," Euroweek, November 3, 2000, pp. 1, 13.

Introduction

The opening case describes how China Mobile overcame the financing constraints imposed by a relatively small and illiquid Hong Kong capital market and raised $8.24 billion by simultaneously selling equity and bonds through several different exchanges, including Hong Kong and New York, to a broad range of international investors. As we saw, China Mobile also lists its shares on the New York Stock Exchange in addition to the Hong Kong Stock Exchange. By successfully tapping into the large and liquid global capital market, the Hong Kong–based company was able to raise more funds than initially planned for and lower its cost of capital. (The **cost of capital** refers to the price of money, such as the interest rate that must be paid to bondholders or the dividends and capital appreciation that stockholders expect to receive.) For example, as noted in the opening case, the convertible bonds carried an interest rate a full half point lower than originally expected, implying a lower cost of capital for China Mobile.

Although China Mobile's international equity and debt offering was among the largest to date, the tactic of selling equity and debt internationally is becoming increasingly common. This represents a sharp break from the practice common during much of the 20th century. In the past, substantial regulatory barriers separated national capital markets from each other. These made it difficult for a company based in one country to list its stock on a foreign exchange. These regulatory barriers tumbled during the 1980s and 1990s. By the middle of the last decade, a truly global capital market was emerging. This capital market enabled firms to list their stock on multiple exchanges and to raise funds by issuing equity or debt around the world. For example, in 1994, Daimler-Benz, Germany's largest industrial company, raised $300 million by issuing new shares not in Germany, but in Singapore.[1] Similarly, in 1996 the German telecommunications provider Deutsche Telekom raised some $13.3 billion by simultaneously listing its shares for sale on stock exchanges in Frankfurt, London, New York, and Tokyo. Like China Mobile, these two German companies elected to raise equity through foreign markets because they reasoned that their domestic capital market was too small to supply the requisite funds at a reasonable cost. To lower their cost of capital, they tapped into the large and highly liquid global capital market.

We begin this chapter by looking at the benefits associated with the globalization of capital markets. This is followed by a more detailed look at the growth of the international capital market and the macroeconomic risks associated with such growth. Next, there is a detailed review of three important segments of the global capital market: the eurocurrency market, the international bond market, and the international equity market. As usual, we close the chapter by pointing out some of the implications for the practice of international business.

Benefits of the Global Capital Market

Although this section is about the global capital market, we open it by discussing the functions of a generic capital market. Then we will look at the limitations of domestic capital markets and discuss the benefits of using global capital markets.

Functions of a Generic Capital Market

A capital market brings together those who want to invest money and those who want to borrow money (see Figure 11.1). Those who want to invest money include corporations with surplus cash, individuals, and nonbank financial institutions (e.g., pension funds, insurance companies). Those who want to borrow money include individuals, companies, and governments. Between these two groups are the market makers. Market makers are the financial service companies that connect investors and borrowers, either directly or indirectly. They include commercial banks

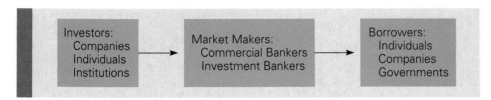

Figure 11.1

The Main Players in a
Generic Capital Market

(e.g., Citibank, U.S. Bank Corp) and investment banks (e.g., Merrill Lynch, Goldman Sachs).

Commercial banks perform an indirect connection function. They take cash deposits from corporations and individuals and pay them a rate of interest in return. They then lend that money to borrowers at a higher rate of interest, making a profit from the difference in interest rates (commonly referred to as the interest rate spread). Investment banks perform a direct connection function. They bring investors and borrowers together and charge commissions for doing so. For example, Merrill Lynch may act as a stockbroker for an individual who wants to invest some money. Its personnel will advise her as to the most attractive purchases and buy stock on her behalf, charging a fee for the service.

Capital market loans to corporations are either equity loans or debt loans. An equity loan is made when a corporation sells stock to investors. The money the corporation receives in return for its stock can be used to purchase plants and equipment, fund R&D projects, pay wages, and so on. A share of stock gives its holder a claim to a firm's profit stream. The corporation honors this claim by paying dividends to the stockholders. The amount of the dividends is not fixed in advance. Rather, it is determined by management based on how much profit the corporation is making. Investors purchase stock both for their dividend yield and in anticipation of gains in the price of the stock, which in theory reflects future dividend yields. Stock prices increase when a corporation is projected to have greater earnings in the future, which increases the probability that it will raise future dividend payments.

A debt loan requires the corporation to repay a predetermined portion of the loan amount (the sum of the principal plus the specified interest) at regular intervals regardless of how much profit it is making. Management has no discretion as to the amount it will pay investors. Debt loans include cash loans from banks and funds raised from the sale of corporate bonds to investors. When an investor purchases a corporate bond, he purchases the right to receive a specified fixed stream of income from the corporation for a specified number of years (i.e., until the bond maturity date).

Attractions of the Global Capital Market

A global capital market benefits both borrowers and investors. It benefits borrowers by increasing the supply of funds available for borrowing and by lowering the cost of capital. It benefits investors by providing a wider range of investment opportunities, thereby allowing them to build portfolios of international investments that diversify their risks.

The Borrower's Perspective: A Lower Cost of Capital

In a purely domestic capital market, the pool of investors is limited to residents of the country. This places an upper limit on the supply of funds available to borrowers. In other words, the liquidity of the market is limited. (China Mobile faced this problem in the opening case.) A global capital market, with its much larger pool of investors, provides a larger supply of funds for borrowers to draw on.

Perhaps the most important drawback of the limited liquidity of a purely domestic capital market is that the cost of capital tends to be higher than it is in an international market. The cost of capital is the price of borrowing money, which is the rate of

Figure 11.2

Market Liquidity and the
Cost of Capital

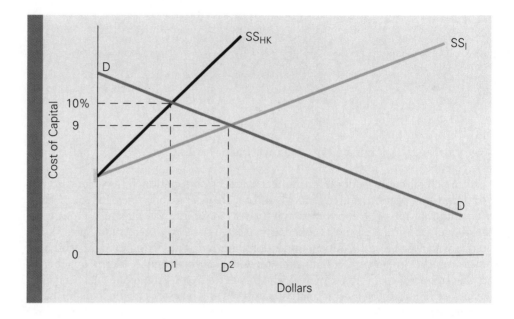

return that borrowers must pay investors. This is the interest rate on debt loans and the dividend yield and expected capital gains on equity loans. In a purely domestic market, the limited pool of investors implies that borrowers must pay more to persuade investors to lend them their money. The larger pool of investors in an international market implies that borrowers will be able to pay less.

The argument is illustrated in Figure 11.2, using the China Mobile example. The vertical axis in the figure is the cost of capital (the price of borrowing money) and the horizontal axis is the amount of money available at varying interest rates. DD is the China Mobile demand curve for borrowings. Note that the China Mobile demand for funds varies with the cost of capital; the lower the cost of capital, the more money China Mobile will borrow. (Money is just like anything else; the lower its price, the more of it people can afford.) SS$_{HK}$ is the supply curve of funds available in the Hong Kong capital market, and SS$_{I}$ represents the funds available in the global capital market. Note that China Mobile can borrow more funds more cheaply on the global capital market. As Figure 11.2 illustrates, the greater pool of resources in the global capital market—the greater liquidity—both lowers the cost of capital and increases the amount China Mobile can borrow. Thus, the advantage of a global capital market to borrowers is that it lowers the cost of capital.

Problems of limited liquidity are not restricted to less developed nations, which naturally tend to have smaller domestic capital markets. As discussed in the introduction, even very large enterprises based in some of the world's most advanced industrialized nations in recent years have tapped the international capital markets in their search for greater liquidity and a lower cost of capital, such as Germany's Deutsche Telekom.[2] The Deutsche Telekom case is discussed in more detail in the Management Focus.

The Investor's Perspective: Portfolio Diversification

By using the global capital market, investors have a much wider range of investment opportunities than in a purely domestic capital market. The most significant consequence of this choice is that investors can diversify their portfolios internationally, thereby reducing their risk to below what could be achieved in a purely domestic capital market. We will consider how this works in the case of stock holdings, although the same argument could be made for bond holdings.

Consider an investor who buys stock in a biotech firm that has not yet produced a new product. Imagine the price of the stock is very volatile—investors are buying and selling the stock in large numbers in response to information about the firm's

Deutsche Telekom Taps the Global Capital Market

Based in the world's third largest industrial economy, Deutsche Telekom is one of the world's largest telephone companies. Until late 1996, the company was wholly owned by the German government. However, in the mid-1990s, the German government privatized the utility, selling shares to the public. The privatization effort was driven by two factors: (1) a realization that state-owned enterprises tend to be inherently inefficient, and (2) the impending deregulation of the European Union telecommunication industry in 1998, which promised to expose Deutsche Telekom to foreign competition for the first time. Deutsche Telekom realized that, to become more competitive, it needed massive investments in new telecommunication infrastructure, including fiber optics and wireless, lest it start losing share in its home market to more efficient competitors such as AT&T and British Telecom after 1998. Financing such investments from state sources would have been difficult even under the best of circumstances and almost impossible in the late 1990s, when the German government was trying to limit its budget deficit to meet the criteria for membership in the European monetary union. With the active encouragement of the government, Deutsche Telekom hoped to finance its investments in capital equipment through the sale of shares to the public.

From a financial perspective, the privatization looked anything but easy. In 1996, Deutsche Telekom was valued at about $60 billion. If it maintained this valuation as a private company, it would dwarf all others listed on the German stock market. However, many analysts doubted there was anything close to $60 billion available in Germany for investment in Deutsche Telekom stock. One problem was that there was no tradition of retail stock investing in Germany. In 1996, only 1 in 20 German citizens owned shares, compared with 1 in every 4 or 5 in the United States and Great Britain. This lack of retail interest in stock ownership makes for a relatively illiquid stock market. Nor did banks, the traditional investors in company stocks in Germany, seem enthused about underwriting such a massive privatization effort. A further problem was that a wave of privatizations was already sweeping through Germany and the rest of Europe, so Deutsche Telekom would have to compete with many other state-owned enterprises for investors' attention. Given these factors, probably the only way that Deutsche Telekom could raise $60 billion through the German capital market would have been by promising investors a dividend yield that would raise the company's cost of capital above levels that could be serviced profitably.

Deutsche Telekom managers concluded they had to privatize the company in stages and sell a substantial portion of Deutsche Telekom stock to foreign investors. The company's plans called for an initial public offering (IPO) of 713 million shares of Deutsche Telekom stock, representing 25 percent of the company's total value, for about $18.50 per share. With a total projected value in excess of $13 billion, even this "limited" sale of Deutsche Telekom represented the largest IPO in European history and the second largest in the world after the 1987 sale of shares in Japan's telephone monopoly, NTT, for $15.6 billion. Concluding there was no way the German capital market could absorb even this partial sale of Deutsche Telekom equity, the managers of the company decided to simultaneously list shares and offer them for sale in Frankfurt (where the German stock exchange is located), London, New York, and Tokyo, attracting investors from all over the world. The IPO was successfully executed in November 1996 and raised $13.3 billion for the company.

Sources: J. O. Jackson, "The Selling of the Big Pink," *Time*, December 2, 1996, p. 46; S. Ascarelli, "Privatization Is Worrying Deutsche Telekom," *Wall Street Journal*, February 3, 1995, p. A1; "Plunging into Foreign Markets," *The Economist*, September 17, 1994, pp. 86–87; and A. Raghavan and M. R. Sesit, "Financing Boom: Foreign Firms Raise More and More Money in the U.S. Market," *Wall Street Journal*, October 5, 1993, p. A1.

prospects. Such stocks are risky investments; investors may win big if the firm produces a marketable product, but investors may also lose all their money if the firm fails to come up with a product that sells. Investors can guard against the risk associated with holding this stock by buying other firms' stocks, particularly those weakly or negatively correlated with the biotech stock. By holding a variety of stocks in a diversified portfolio, the losses incurred when some stocks fail to live up to their promises are offset by the gains enjoyed when other stocks exceed their promise.

Figure 11.3

Risk Reduction through Portfolio Diversification

Source: B. Solnik, "Why Not Diversify Internationally Rather than Domestically?" Adapted with permission from *Financial Analysts Journal*, July/August 1974, p. 17. Copyright 1974, Financial Analysts Federation, Charlottesville, VA. All rights reserved.

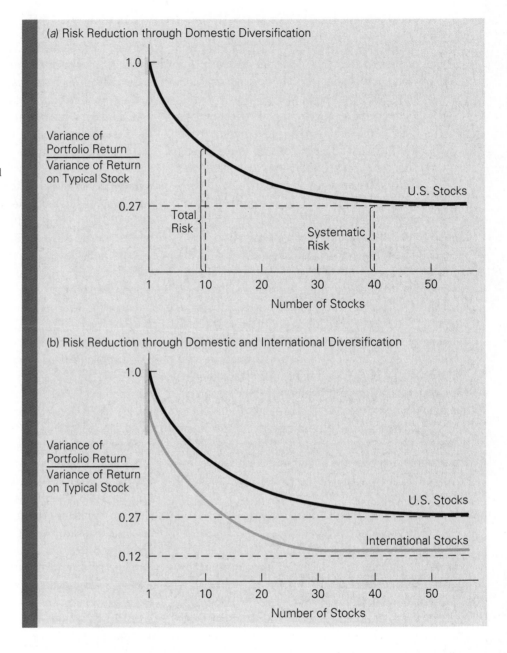

As an investor increases the number of stocks in his portfolio, the portfolio's risk declines. At first this decline is rapid. Soon, however, the rate of decline falls off and asymptotically approaches the systematic risk of the market. Systematic risk refers to movements in a stock portfolio's value that are attributable to macroeconomic forces affecting all firms in an economy, rather than factors specific to an individual firm. The systematic risk is the level of nondiversifiable risk in an economy. Figure 11.3 illustrates this relationship for the United States. It suggests that a fully diversified U.S. portfolio is only about 27 percent as risky as a typical individual stock.

By diversifying a portfolio internationally, an investor can reduce the level of risk even further because the movements of stock market prices across countries are not perfectly correlated. For example, one study looked at the correlation between three stock market indexes. The Standard & Poor's 500 (S&P 500) summarized the movement of large U.S. stocks. The Morgan Stanley Capital International Europe, Australia, and Far East Index (EAFE) summarized stock market movements in other developed nations. The third index, the International Finance Corporation Global

Emerging Markets Index (IFC), summarized stock market movements in less developed "emerging economies." From 1981 to 1994, the correlation between the S&P 500 and EAFE indexes was 0.45, suggesting they moved together only about 20 percent of the time (i.e., $0.45 \times 0.45 = 0.2025$). The correlation between the S&P 500 and IFC indexes was even lower at 0.32, suggesting they moved together only a little over 10 percent of the time.[3]

The relatively low correlation between the movement of stock markets in different countries reflects two basic factors. First, countries pursue different macroeconomic policies and face different economic conditions, so their stock markets respond to different forces and can move in different ways. For example, in 1997, the stock markets of several Asian countries, including South Korea, Malaysia, Indonesia, and Thailand, lost over 50 percent of their value in response to the Asian financial crisis, while at the same time the S&P 500 increased in value by over 20 percent. Second, different stock markets are still somewhat segmented from each other by **capital controls**—that is, by restrictions on cross-border capital flows (although such restrictions are declining rapidly). The most common restrictions include limits on the amount of a firm's stock that a foreigner can own and limits on the ability of a country's citizens to invest their money outside that country. For example, until recently it was difficult for foreigners to own more than 30 percent of the equity of South Korean enterprises. Tight restrictions on capital flows make it very hard for Chinese citizens to take money out of their country and invest it in foreign assets. Such barriers to cross-border capital flows limit the ability of capital to roam the world freely in search of the highest risk-adjusted return. Consequently, at any one time, there may be too much capital invested in some markets and too little in others. This will tend to produce differences in rates of return across stock markets.[4] The implication is that by diversifying a portfolio to include foreign stocks, an investor can reduce the level of risk below that incurred by holding just domestic stocks.

Figure 11.3 also illustrates the relationship between international diversification and risk found by a now classic study by Bruno Solnik.[5] According to the figure, a fully diversified portfolio that contains stocks from many countries is less than half as risky as a fully diversified portfolio that contains only U.S. stocks. A fully diversified portfolio of international stocks is only about 12 percent as risky as a typical individual stock, whereas a fully diversified portfolio of U.S. stocks is about 27 percent as risky as a typical individual stock.

An increasingly common perception among investment professionals is that in the past 10 years the growing integration of the global economy and the emergence of the global capital market have increased the correlation between different stock markets, reducing the benefits of international diversification.[6] Today, it is argued, if the U.S. economy enters a recession, and the U.S. stock market declines rapidly, other markets follow suit. A recent study by Solnik suggests there may be some truth to this assertion, but the rate of integration is not occurring as rapidly as the popular perception would lead one to believe. Solnik and his associates looked at the correlation between 15 major stock markets in developed countries between 1971 and 1998. They found that on average, the correlation of monthly stock market returns increased from 66 percent in 1971 to 75 percent in 1998, indicating some convergence over time, but that "the regression results were weak," which suggests this "average" relationship was not strong, and there was considerable variation among countries.[7] The implication here is that international portfolio diversification can still reduce risk. As noted earlier, the correlation between stock market movements in developed and emerging markets seems to be much lower.

The risk-reducing effects of international portfolio diversification would be greater were it not for the volatile exchange rates associated with the current floating exchange rate regime. Floating exchange rates introduce an additional element of risk into investing in foreign assets. As we have said repeatedly, adverse exchange rate movements can transform otherwise profitable investments into unprofitable ones.

The uncertainty engendered by volatile exchange rates may be acting as a brake on the otherwise rapid growth of the international capital market.

Growth of the Global Capital Market

According to data from the Bank for International Settlements, the global capital market is growing at a rapid pace.[8] By late 2000 the stock of cross-border bank loans stood at $7,859 billion, up from $3,600 billion in 1990. There were $5,908 billion in outstanding international bonds, up from $3,515 billion in 1997 and $620 billion in 1994. International equity offerings for 2000 exceeded $314 billion, compared to $90 billion in 1997 and some $18 billion in 1990. All of the figures for 2000 were records. What factors allowed the international capital market to bloom in the 1980s and 1990s? There seem to be two answers—advances in information technology and deregulation by governments.

Information Technology

Financial services is an information-intensive industry. It draws on large volumes of information about markets, risks, exchange rates, interest rates, creditworthiness, and so on. It uses this information to make decisions about what to invest where, how much to charge borrowers, how much interest to pay to depositors, and the value and riskiness of a range of financial assets including corporate bonds, stocks, government securities, and currencies.

Because of this information intensity, the financial services industry has been revolutionized more than any other industry by advances in information technology since the 1970s. The growth of international communication technology has facilitated instantaneous communication between any two points on the globe. At the same time, rapid advances in data processing have allowed market makers to absorb and process large volumes of information from around the world. According to one study, because of these technological developments, the real cost of recording, transmitting, and processing information fell by 95 percent between 1964 and 1990.[9] With the rapid rise of the Internet and the massive increase in computing power that we have seen since 1990, it seems likely that the cost of recording, transmitting, and processing information has fallen by a similar amount since 1990 and is now a trivial amount.

Such developments have facilitated the emergence of an integrated international capital market. It is now technologically possible for financial services companies to engage in 24-hour-a-day trading, whether it is in stocks, bonds, foreign exchange, or any other financial asset. Due to advances in communications and data processing technology, the international capital market never sleeps. San Francisco closes one hour before Tokyo opens, but during this period trading continues in New Zealand.

But the integration facilitated by technology has a dark side.[10] "Shocks" that occur in one financial center now spread around the globe very quickly. The collapse of U.S. stock prices on the notorious Black Monday of October 19, 1987, immediately triggered similar collapses in all the world's major stock markets, wiping billions of dollars off the value of corporate stocks worldwide. Similarly, the Asian financial crisis of 1997 sent shock waves around the world and precipitated a sell-off in world stock markets, although the effects of the shock were short lived. Most market participants would argue that the benefits of an integrated global capital market far outweigh any potential costs.

Deregulation

In country after country, financial services have been the most tightly regulated of all industries. Governments around the world have traditionally kept other countries' financial service firms from entering their capital markets. In some cases, they have also restricted the overseas expansion of their domestic financial services firms. In many countries, the law has also segmented the domestic financial services industry. In the United States, for example, until recently commercial banks were prohibited from performing the functions of investment banks, and vice versa. Historically, many countries have limited the ability of foreign investors to purchase significant equity positions in domestic companies. They have also limited the amount of foreign investment that their citizens could undertake. In the 1970s, for example, capital controls made it very difficult for a British investor to purchase American stocks and bonds.

Many of these restrictions have been crumbling since the early 1980s. In part, this has been a response to the development of the eurocurrency market, which from the beginning was outside of national control. (This is explained later in the chapter.) It has also been a response to pressure from financial services companies, which have long wanted to operate in a less regulated environment. Increasing acceptance of the free market ideology associated with an individualistic political philosophy also has a lot to do with the global trend toward the deregulation of financial markets (see Chapter 2). Whatever the reason, deregulation in a number of key countries has undoubtedly facilitated the growth of the international capital market.

The trend began in the United States in the late 1970s and early 80s with a series of changes that allowed foreign banks to enter the U.S. capital market and domestic banks to expand their operations overseas. In Great Britain, the so-called Big Bang of October 1986 removed barriers that had existed between banks and stockbrokers and allowed foreign financial service companies to enter the British stock market. Restrictions on the entry of foreign securities houses have been relaxed in Japan, and Japanese banks are now allowed to open international banking facilities. In France, the "Little Bang" of 1987 opened the French stock market to outsiders and to foreign and domestic banks. In Germany, foreign banks are now allowed to lend and manage foreign euro issues, subject to reciprocity agreements.[11] All of this has enabled financial services companies to transform themselves from primarily domestic companies into global operations with major offices around the world—a prerequisite for the development of a truly international capital market. As we saw in Chapter 5, in late 1997 the World Trade Organization brokered a deal that removed many of the restrictions on cross-border trade in financial services. This deal facilitated further growth in the size of the global capital market.

In addition to the deregulation of the financial services industry, many countries beginning in the 1970s started to dismantle capital controls, loosening both restrictions on inward investment by foreigners and outward investment by their own citizens and corporations. By the 1980s, this trend spread from developed nations to the emerging economies of the world as countries across Latin America, Asia, and Eastern Europe started to dismantle decades-old restrictions on capital flows. Figure 11.4 illustrates the consequences. Between 1985 and 1997 an index of capital controls in emerging markets computed by the IMF has declined from a high of 0.66 to around 0.56 (the index would be 1.0 if all emerging economies had tight capital controls, and 0.0 if they had no controls). According to the World Bank, capital flows into the emerging economies of the world went from less than $50 billion in 1990 to more than $336 billion in 1997.[12]

As of 2001, the trends toward deregulation of financial services and removal of capital controls were still firmly in place. Given the benefits associated with the globalization of capital, the growth of the global capital market can be expected to continue for the foreseeable future. While most commentators see this as a positive development, some believe there are serious risks inherent in the globalization of capital.

Global Capital Market Risks

Some analysts are concerned that due to deregulation and reduced controls on cross-border capital flows, individual nations are becoming more vulnerable to speculative capital flows. They see this as having a destabilizing effect on national economies.[13]

Did the Global Capital Market Fail Mexico?

In early 1994, soon after passage of the North American Free Trade Agreement (NAFTA), Mexico was widely admired among the international community as a shining example of a developing country with a bright economic future. Since the late 1980s, the Mexican government had pursued sound monetary, budget, tax, and trade policies. By historical standards, inflation was low, the country was experiencing solid economic growth, and exports were booming. This robust picture attracted capital from foreign investors; between 1991 and 1993, foreigners invested more than $75 billion in the Mexican economy, more than in any other developing nation.

If there was a blot on Mexico's economic report card, it was the country's growing current account (trade) deficit. Mexican exports were booming, but so were its imports. In the 1989–1990 period, the current account deficit was equivalent to about 3 percent of Mexico's gross domestic product. In 1991 it increased to 5 percent, and by 1994 it was running at an annual rate of over 6 percent. Bad as this might seem, it is not unsustainable and should not bring an economy crashing down. The United States has been running a current account deficit for decades with apparently little in the way of ill effects. A current account deficit will not be a problem for a country as long as foreign investors take the money they earn from trade with that country and reinvest it within the country. This has been the case in the United States for years, and during the early 1990s, it was occurring in Mexico too. Companies such as Ford took the pesos they earned from exports to Mexico and reinvested those funds in productive capacity in Mexico, building auto plants to serve the future needs of the Mexican market and to export elsewhere.

Unfortunately for Mexico, much of the $25 billion annual inflow of capital it received during the early 1990s was not the kind of patient long-term money that Ford was putting into Mexico. Rather, according to economist Martin Feldstein, much of the inflow was short-term capital that could flee if economic conditions changed for the worst. This is what seems to have occurred. In February 1994, the U.S. Federal Reserve began to increase interest rates. This led to a rapid fall in U.S. bond prices. At the same time, the yen began to appreciate sharply against the dollar. These events resulted in large losses for many managers of short-term capital, such as hedge fund managers and banks, which had been betting on exactly the opposite happening. Many hedge funds had been expecting interest rates to fall, bond prices to rise, and the dollar to appreciate against the yen.

Figure 11.4

Index of Capital Controls in Emerging Markets

Note: Index ranges from 0 to 1.0 = No capital controls, 1 = Tight capital controls.
Source: IMF database.

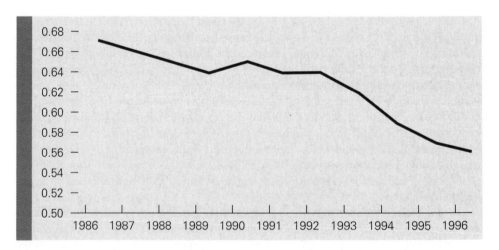

Harvard economist Martin Feldstein, for example, has argued that most of the capital that moves internationally is pursuing temporary gains, and it shifts in and out of countries as quickly as conditions change.[14] He distinguishes between this short-term capital, or "hot money," and "patient money" that would support long-term cross-border capital flows. To Feldstein, patient money is still relatively rare, primarily because although capital is free to move internationally, its owners and managers still prefer to keep most of it at home. Feldstein supports his arguments with statistics that

Faced with large losses, money managers tried to reduce the riskiness of their portfolios by pulling out of risky situations. About the same time, events took a turn for the worse in Mexico. An armed uprising in the southern state of Chiapas, the assassination of the leading candidate in the presidential election campaign, and an accelerating inflation rate all helped produce a feeling that Mexican investments were riskier than had been assumed. Money managers began to pull many of their short-term investments out of the country.

As hot money flowed out, the Mexican government realized it could not continue to count on capital inflows to finance its current account deficit. The government had assumed the inflow was mainly composed of patient, long-term money. In reality, much of it appeared to be short-term money. As money flowed out of Mexico, the Mexican government had to commit more foreign reserves to defending the value of the peso against the U.S. dollar, which was pegged at 3.5 to the dollar. Currency speculators entered the picture and began to bet against the Mexican government by selling pesos short. Events came to a head in December 1994 when the Mexican government was essentially forced by capital flows to abandon its support for the peso. Over the next month, the peso lost 40 percent of its value against the dollar, the government was forced to introduce an economic austerity program, and the Mexican economic boom came to an abrupt end.

According to Martin Feldstein, the Mexican economy was brought down not by currency speculation on the foreign exchange market, but by a lack of long-term patient money. He argued that Mexico offered, and still offers, many attractive long-term investment opportunities, but because of the lack of information on long-term investment opportunities in Mexico, most of the capital flowing into the country from 1991 to 1993 was short-term, speculative money, the flow of which could quickly be reversed. If foreign investors had better information, Feldstein argued, Mexico should have been able to finance its current account deficit from inward capital flows because patient capital would naturally gravitate toward attractive Mexican investment opportunities.

Sources: Martin Feldstein, "Global Capital Flows: Too Little, Not Too Much," *The Economist*, June 24, 1995, pp. 72–73; R. Dornbusch, "We Have Salinas to Thank for the Peso Debacle," *Business Week*, January 16, 1995, p. 20; P. Carroll and C. Torres, "Mexico Unveils Program of Harsh Fiscal Medicine," *Wall Street Journal*, March 10, 1995, pp. A1, A6. See also, Martin Feldstein and Charles Horioka, "Domestic Savings and International Capital Flows," *Economic Journal* 90 (1980), pp. 314–29.

demonstrate that although $1.5 trillion flows through the foreign exchange markets every day, "when the dust settles, most of the savings done in each country stays in that country."[15] Feldstein argues that the lack of patient money is due to the relative paucity of information that investors have about foreign investments. In his view, if investors had better information about foreign assets, the global capital market would work more efficiently and be less subject to short-term speculative capital flows. Feldstein claims that Mexico's economic problems in the mid-1990s were the result of too much hot money flowing in and out of the country and too little patient money. This example is reviewed in detail in the accompanying Country Focus.

A lack of information about the fundamental quality of foreign investments may encourage speculative flows in the global capital market. Faced with a lack of *quality* information, investors may react to dramatic news events in foreign nations and pull their money out too quickly. Despite advances in information technology, it is still difficult for investors to get access to the same quantity and quality of information about foreign investment opportunities that they can get about domestic investment opportunities. This information gap is exacerbated by varying accounting conventions in different countries, which makes the direct comparison of cross-border investment opportunities difficult for all but the most sophisticated investor (see Chapter 19 for details). For example, German accounting principles are very different from those found in the United States and can present quite a different picture of the health of a company. Thus, when the Germany company Daimler-Benz translated its German financial accounts into U.S.-style accounts in 1993, as it had to do to be listed on the New York Stock Exchange, it found that while it had made a profit of $97 million under German rules, under U.S. rules it had lost $548 million![16]

Given the problems created by differences in the quantity and quality of information, many investors have yet to venture into the world of cross-border investing, and those that do are prone to reverse their decision on the basis of limited (and perhaps inaccurate) information. However, if the international capital market continues to grow, financial intermediaries likely will increasingly provide quality information about foreign investment opportunities. Better information should increase the sophistication of investment decisions and reduce the frequency and size of speculative capital flows. Although concerns about the volume of "hot money" sloshing around in the global capital market have recently increased as a result of the Asian financial crisis, IMF research suggests there has not been an increase in the volatility of financial markets over the past 25 years.[17]

The Eurocurrency Market

A **eurocurrency** is any currency banked outside of its country of origin. **Eurodollars,** which account for about two-thirds of all eurocurrencies, are dollars banked outside the United States. Other important eurocurrencies include the euro-yen and the euro-pound. The term *eurocurrency* is actually a misnomer because a eurocurrency can be created anywhere in the world; the persistent euro- prefix reflects the European origin of the market. The eurocurrency market has been an important and relatively low-cost source of funds for international businesses.

Genesis and Growth of the Market

The eurocurrency market was born in the mid-1950s when Eastern European holders of dollars, including the former Soviet Union, were afraid to deposit their holdings in the United States lest they be seized by the U.S. government to settle U.S. residents' claims against business losses resulting from the Communist takeover of Eastern Europe. These countries deposited many of their dollar holdings in Europe, particularly in London. Additional dollar deposits came from various Western European central banks and from companies that earned dollars by exporting to the United States. These two groups deposited their dollars in London banks, rather than U.S. banks, because they were able to earn a higher rate of interest (which will be explained).

The eurocurrency market received a major push in 1957 when the British government prohibited British banks from lending British pounds to finance non-British trade, a business that had been very profitable for British banks. British banks began financing the same trade by attracting dollar deposits and lending dollars to companies engaged in international trade and investment. Because of this historical event, London became, and has remained, the leading center of eurocurrency trading.

The eurocurrency market received another push in the 1960s when the U.S. government enacted regulations that discouraged U.S. banks from lending to non-U.S. residents. Would-be dollar borrowers outside the United States found it increasingly difficult to borrow dollars in the United States to finance international trade, so they turned to the eurodollar market to obtain the necessary dollar funds.

The U.S. government changed its policies after the 1973 collapse of the Bretton Woods system (see Chapter 10), removing an important impetus to the growth of the eurocurrency market. However, another political event, the oil price increases engineered by OPEC in the 1973–74 and 1979–80 periods, gave the market another big shove. As a result of the oil price increases, the Arab members of OPEC accumulated huge amounts of dollars. They were afraid to place their money in U.S. banks or their European branches, lest the U.S. government attempt to confiscate them. (Iranian assets in U.S. banks and their European branches were frozen by President Carter in

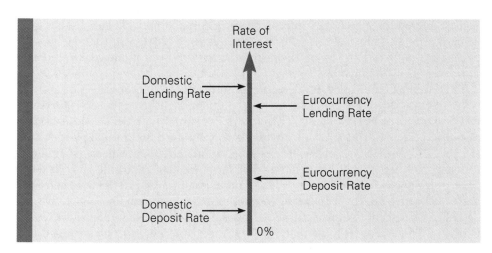

Figure 11.5

Interest Rate Spreads in
Domestic and
Eurocurrency Markets

1979 after Americans were taken hostage at the U.S. embassy in Tehran; their fear was not unfounded.) Instead, these countries deposited their dollars with banks in London, further increasing the supply of eurodollars.

Although these various political events contributed to the growth of the eurocurrency market, they alone were not responsible for it. The market grew because it offered real financial advantages—initially to those who wanted to deposit dollars or borrow dollars and later to those who wanted to deposit and borrow other currencies.

Attractions of the Eurocurrency Market

Its lack of government regulation makes the eurocurrency market attractive to both depositors and borrowers. Banks can offer higher interest rates on eurocurrency deposits than on deposits made in the home currency, making eurocurrency deposits attractive to those who have cash to invest. The lack of regulation also allows banks to charge borrowers a lower interest rate for eurocurrency borrowings than for borrowings in the home currency, making eurocurrency loans attractive for those who want to borrow money. In other words, the spread between the eurocurrency deposit rate and the eurocurrency lending rate is less than the spread between the domestic deposit and lending rates (see Figure 11.5). To understand why this is so, we must examine how government regulations raise the costs of domestic banking.

Domestic currency deposits are regulated in all industrialized countries. Such regulations ensure that banks have enough liquid funds to satisfy demand if large numbers of domestic depositors should suddenly decide to withdraw their money. All countries operate with certain reserve requirements. For example, each time a U.S. bank accepts a deposit in dollars, it must place some fraction of that deposit in a non-interest-bearing account at a Federal Reserve Bank as part of its required reserves. Similarly, each time a British bank accepts a deposit in pounds sterling, it must place a certain fraction of that deposit with the Bank of England.

Banks are given much more freedom in their dealings in foreign currencies, however. For example, the British government does not impose reserve requirement restrictions on deposits of foreign currencies within its borders. Nor are the London branches of U.S. banks subject to U.S. reserve requirement regulations, provided those deposits are payable only outside the United States. This gives eurobanks a competitive advantage.

For example, suppose a bank based in New York faces a 10 percent reserve requirement. According to this requirement, if the bank receives a $100 deposit, it can lend out no more than $90 of that and it must place the remaining $10 in a non-interest-bearing account at a Federal Reserve bank. Suppose the bank has annual operating costs of $1 per $100 of deposits and that it charges 10 percent interest on loans. The highest interest the New York bank can offer its depositors and still cover its costs is 8 percent per year. Thus, the bank pays the owner of the $100 deposit ($0.08 \times \$100 =$) $8, earns ($0.10 \times \$90 =$) $9 on the fraction of the deposit it is allowed to lend, and just covers its operating costs.

In contrast, a eurobank can offer a higher interest rate on dollar deposits and still cover its costs. The eurobank, with no reserve requirements regarding dollar deposits, can lend out all of a $100 deposit. Therefore, it can earn $0.10 \times \$100 = \$10$ at a loan rate of 10 percent. If the eurobank has the same operating costs as the New York bank ($1 per $100 deposit), it can pay its depositors an interest rate of 9 percent, a full percentage point higher than that paid by the New York bank, and still cover its costs. That is, it can pay $0.09 \times \$100 = \$9$ to its depositor, receive $10 from the borrower, and be left with $1 to cover operating costs. Alternatively, the eurobank might pay the depositor 8.5 percent (which is still above the rate paid by the New York bank), charge borrowers 9.5 percent (still less than the New York bank charges), and cover its operating costs even better. Thus, the eurobank has a competitive advantage vis-à-vis the New York bank in both its deposit rate and its loan rate.

Clearly, there are strong financial motivations for companies to use the eurocurrency market. By doing so, they receive a higher interest rate on deposits and pay less for loans. Given this, the surprising thing is not that the euromarket has grown rapidly but that it hasn't grown even faster. Why do any depositors hold deposits in their home currency when they could get better yields in the eurocurrency market?

Drawbacks of the Eurocurrency Market

The eurocurrency market has two drawbacks. First, when depositors use a regulated banking system, they know that the probability of a bank failure that would cause them to lose their deposits is very low. Regulation maintains the liquidity of the banking system. In an unregulated system such as the eurocurrency market, the probability of a bank failure that would cause depositors to lose their money is greater (although in absolute terms, still low). Thus, the lower interest rate received on home-country deposits reflects the costs of insuring against bank failure. Some depositors are more comfortable with the security of such a system and are willing to pay the price.

Second, borrowing funds internationally can expose a company to foreign exchange risk. For example, consider a U.S. company that uses the eurocurrency market to borrow euro-pounds—perhaps because it can pay a lower interest rate on euro-pound loans than on dollar loans. Imagine, however, that the British pound subsequently appreciates against the dollar. This would increase the dollar cost of repaying the euro-pound loan and thus the company's cost of capital. This possibility can be insured against by using the forward exchange market (as we saw in Chapter 9), but the forward exchange market does not offer perfect insurance. Consequently, many companies borrow funds in their domestic currency to avoid foreign exchange risk, even though the eurocurrency markets may offer more attractive interest rates.

The Global Bond Market

The global bond market grew rapidly during the 1980s and 1990s and has continued to do so in the new century. Bonds are an important means of financing for many companies. The most common kind of bond is a fixed-rate bond. The investor who purchases a **fixed-rate bond** receives a fixed set of cash payoffs. Each year until the bond matures, the investor gets an interest payment and then at maturity she gets back the face value of the bond.

International bonds are of two types: foreign bonds and eurobonds. **Foreign bonds** are sold outside the borrower's country and are denominated in the currency of the country in which they are issued. Thus, when Dow Chemical issues bonds in Japanese yen and sells them in Japan, it is issuing foreign bonds. Many foreign bonds have nicknames; foreign bonds sold in the United States are called Yankee bonds, foreign bonds sold in Japan are Samurai bonds, and foreign bonds sold in Great Britain are bulldogs. Companies will issue international bonds if they believe it will lower their cost of capital. For example, in recent years many companies have been issuing Samurai bonds in Japan to take advantage of very low interest rates. In early 2001, 10-year Japanese government bonds yielded 1.24 percent, compared with 5 percent for comparable U.S. government bonds. Against this background, companies found that they could raise debt at a cheaper rate in Japan than in the United States.

Eurobonds are normally underwritten by an international syndicate of banks and placed in countries other than the one in whose currency the bond is denominated. For example, a bond may be issued by a German corporation, denominated in U.S. dollars, and sold to investors outside the United States by an international syndicate of banks. Eurobonds are routinely issued by multinational corporations, large domestic corporations, sovereign governments, and international institutions. They are usually offered simultaneously in several national capital markets, but not in the capital market of the country, nor to residents of the country, in whose currency they are denominated. Historically, eurobonds accounted for the lion's share of international bond issues, but increasingly they are being eclipsed by foreign bonds.

Attractions of the Eurobond Market

Three features of the eurobond market make it an appealing alternative to most major domestic bond markets:

- An absence of regulatory interference.
- Less stringent disclosure requirements than in most domestic bond markets.
- A favorable tax status.

Regulatory Interference

National governments often impose tight controls on domestic and foreign issuers of bonds denominated in the local currency and sold within their national boundaries. These controls tend to raise the cost of issuing bonds. However, government limitations are generally less stringent for securities denominated in foreign currencies and sold to holders of those foreign currencies. Eurobonds fall outside the regulatory domain of any single nation. As such, they can often be issued at a lower cost to the issuer.

Disclosure Requirements

Eurobond market disclosure requirements tend to be less stringent than those of several national governments. For example, if a firm wishes to issue dollar-denominated bonds within the United States, it must first comply with Securities and Exchange Commission (SEC) disclosure requirements. The firm must disclose detailed information about its activities, the salaries and other compensation of its senior executives, stock trades by its senior executives, and the like. In addition, the issuing firm must submit financial accounts that conform to U.S. accounting standards. For non-U.S. firms, redoing their accounts to make them consistent with U.S. standards can be very time consuming and expensive. Therefore, many firms have found it cheaper to issue eurobonds, including those denominated in dollars, than to issue dollar-denominated bonds within the United States.

Favorable Tax Status

Before 1984, U.S. corporations issuing eurobonds were required to withhold for U.S. income tax up to 30 percent of each interest payment to foreigners. This did not encourage foreigners to hold bonds issued by U.S. corporations. Similar tax laws were operational in many countries at that time, and they limited market demand for eurobonds. U.S. laws were revised in 1984 to exempt from any withholding tax foreign holders of bonds issued by U.S. corporations. As a result, U.S. corporations found it feasible for the first time to sell eurobonds directly to foreigners. Repeal of the laws caused other governments—including those of France, Germany, and Japan—to liberalize their tax laws likewise to avoid outflows of capital from their markets. The consequence was an upsurge in demand for eurobonds from investors who wanted to take advantage of their tax benefits.

The Global Equity Market

Although we have talked about the growth of the global equity market, strictly speaking there is no international equity market in the sense that there are international currency and bond markets. Rather, many countries have their own domestic equity markets in which corporate stock is traded. The largest of these domestic equity markets are to be found in the United States, Great Britain, Japan, and Germany. Although each domestic equity market is still dominated by investors who are citizens of that country and companies incorporated in that country, developments are internationalizing the world equity market. Investors are investing heavily in foreign equity markets to diversify their portfolios. Facilitated by deregulation and advances in information technology, this trend seems to be here to stay.

An interesting consequence of the trend toward international equity investment is the internationalization of corporate ownership. Today it is still generally possible to talk about U.S. corporations, British corporations, and Japanese corporations, primarily because the majority of stockholders (owners) of these corporations are of the respective nationality. However, this is changing. Increasingly, U.S. citizens are buying stock in companies incorporated abroad, and foreigners are buying stock in companies incorporated in the United States. Looking into the future, Robert Reich has mused about "the coming irrelevance of corporate nationality."[18]

A second development internationalizing the world equity market is that companies with historic roots in one nation are broadening their stock ownership by listing their stock in the equity markets of other nations. The reasons are primarily financial. Listing stock on a foreign market is often a prelude to issuing stock in that market to raise capital. The idea is to tap into the liquidity of foreign markets, thereby increasing the funds available for investment and lowering the firm's cost of capital. (The relationship between liquidity and the cost of capital was discussed earlier in the chapter.) Firms also often list their stock on foreign equity markets to facilitate future acquisitions of foreign companies. Other reasons for listing a company's stock on a foreign equity market are that the company's stock and stock options can be used to compensate local management and employees, it satisfies the desire for local ownership, and it increases the company's visibility with local employees, customers, suppliers, and bankers. Although firms based in developed nations were the first to start listing their stock on foreign exchanges, increasingly firms from developing countries who find their own growth limited by an illiquid domestic capital market are exploiting this opportunity. For example, firms from the Czech Republic are turning to the London stock exchange to raise equity capital (see the accompanying Country Focus).

Foreign Exchange Risk and the Cost of Capital

While a firm can borrow funds at a lower cost on the global capital market than on the domestic capital market, foreign exchange risk complicates this picture. Adverse movements in foreign exchange rates can substantially increase the cost of foreign currency loans, which is what happened to many Asian companies during the 1997–98 Asian financial crisis.

The Search for Capital in the Czech Republic

Following the collapse of communism and the shift toward a more market-oriented system, the Czech Republic initially emerged as one of the more vibrant and market-driven economies in Eastern Europe. By early 1998, however, the economic development of the Czech Republic was being held back by a shortage of capital. The problem was rooted in macroeconomic conditions and institutional problems.

On the macroeconomic front, 1997 saw a combination of adverse developments, including a rise in inflation, a growing government deficit, and a speculative attack on the Czech currency that forced the government to abandon its fixed exchange rate policy for a floating exchange rate system. After the shift to a floating exchange rate system, the Czech currency declined by about 10 percent against the German deutsche mark and more than 15 percent against the U.S. dollar. Since many internationally traded commodities, such as oil, are traded in dollars, this devaluation added fuel to the Czech Republic's inflation fire. The government responded by tightening monetary policy, raising interest rates to around 16 percent.

These macroeconomic problems had a predictably negative effect on the Prague stock market. The PX50, the key index of Czech shares listed on the Prague exchange, declined from around 520 to a low of 430 by June 1998. Much of the decline was due to foreign investment capital leaving the country for more attractive investment opportunities in neighboring Hungary and Poland, where macroeconomic conditions were more favorable and where local stock markets were performing better.

But that wasn't the only problem for the Prague stock market. Many Western investors had been discouraged from investing in Czech stocks by the poor reputation of the Prague stock exchange. That institution is reportedly rife with stock manipulation by insiders, insider trading that would be illegal in more developed markets, a lack of protection for minority stockholders, poor corporate reporting, and fraud. Also, most state-owned enterprises in the Czech Republic were privatized through a voucher scheme that has left the majority of shareholdings in the hands of institutions and groups that are preoccupied with maintaining control over their companies and opposed to any attempt to raise capital through new equity is-

sues. Consequently, the Prague stock market is small and liquidity is very limited. These factors have combined to increase the cost of capital for individual Czech enterprises.

Traditionally, many Czech firms forged tight relationships with banks and borrowed money from them. However, with interest rates at 16 percent and many banks reining in credit to make up for past largesse, it was increasingly expensive for Czech companies to raise capital through borrowings. As for the Czech stock market, its poor reputation and low liquidity made it almost impossible to raise capital by issuing new shares. In mid-1997, one of the Czech Republic's most dynamic and profitable new enterprises, Bonton, a film and music company, attempted to raise $30 million to $40 million through an initial public offering on the Prague exchange. This would have been only the second IPO in the history of the Prague exchange, and the only one of any significance. A successful IPO would have helped to legitimize the market, but Bonton canceled the IPO when the Prague market declined to yearlong lows in the wake of the Asian financial crisis.

Despite all these problems, most agree that the Czech economy has a bright future. However, this future cannot be realized unless Czech companies can raise the capital to invest in the necessary plants and equipment. A number of prominent Czech companies in 1998 announced their intentions to make international equity issues. At the beginning of 1997, only two Czech companies had foreign listings, both of them large banks. However, another five significant companies sought listings on the London stock exchange in 1998. In a sign that this strategy may work, the first to list was Ceske Radiokomunikace, a state-owned radio, television, and telecommunications company that successfully raised $134 million in equity by listing Global Depository Receipts on the London exchange, increasing its equity by 36 percent and decreasing the state holding in the company to about 51 percent.

Sources: R. Anderson, "Czech Groups Cast Their Net Abroad in Search of Funds," *Financial Times,* May 26, 1997, p. 27; V. Boland, "The Czech Stockmarket: Looking Beyond Recent Turmoil," *Financial Times,* December 1, 1997, p. 4; and "Ceske Radiokomunikace Equity Offer Raises $134 million," *Financial Times,* May 27, 1998, p. 38.

Consider a South Korean firm that wants to borrow 1 billion Korean won for one year to fund a capital investment project. The company can borrow this money from a Korean bank at an interest rate of 10 percent, and at the end of the year pay back the loan plus interest, for a total of W1.10 billion. Or the firm could borrow dollars from an international bank at a 6 percent interest rate. At the prevailing exchange rate of $1=W1,000, the firm would borrow $1 million and the total loan cost would be $1.06 million, or W1.06 billion. By borrowing dollars, the firm could reduce its cost of capital by 4 percent, or W40 million. However, this saving is predicated on the assumption that during the year of the loan, the dollar/won exchange rate stays constant. Instead, imagine that the won depreciates sharply against the U.S. dollar during the year and ends the year at $1=W1,500. (This occurred in late 1997 when the won declined in value from $1=W1,000 to $1=W1,500 in two months.) The firm still has to pay the international bank $1.06 million at the end of the year, but now this costs the company W1.59 billion (i.e., $1.06 × W1,500). As a result of the depreciation in the value of the won, the cost of borrowing in U.S. dollars has soared from 6 percent to 59 percent, a huge rise in the firm's cost of capital. Although this may seem like an extreme example, it happened to many South Korean firms in 1997 at the height of the Asian financial crisis. Not surprisingly, many of them were pushed into technical default on their loans.

Unpredictable movements in exchange rates can inject risk into foreign currency borrowing, making something that initially seems less expensive ultimately much more expensive. The borrower can hedge against such a possibility by entering into a forward contract to purchase the required amount of the currency being borrowed at a predetermined exchange rate when the loan comes due (see Chapter 9 for details). Although this will raise the borrower's cost of capital, the added insurance limits the risk involved in such a transaction. Unfortunately, many Asian borrowers did not hedge their dollar-denominated short-term debt, so when their currencies collapsed against the dollar in 1997, many saw a sharp increase in their cost of capital.

When a firm borrows funds from the global capital market, it must weigh the benefits of a lower interest rate against the risks of an increase in the real cost of capital due to adverse exchange rate movements. Although using forward exchange markets may lower foreign exchange risk with short-term borrowings, it cannot remove the risk. Most importantly, the forward exchange market does not provide adequate coverage for long-term borrowings.

Implications for Business

The implications of the material discussed in this chapter for international business are quite straightforward but no less important for being obvious. The growth of the global capital market has created opportunities for international businesses that wish to borrow and/or invest money. By using the global capital market, firms can often borrow funds at a lower cost than is possible in a purely domestic capital market. This conclusion holds no matter what form of borrowing a firm uses—equity, bonds, or cash loans. The lower cost of capital on the global market reflects greater liquidity and the general absence of government regulation. Government regulation tends to raise the cost of capital in most domestic capital markets. The global market, being transnational, escapes regulation. Balanced against this, however, is the foreign exchange risk associated with borrowing in a foreign currency.

On the investment side, the growth of the global capital market is providing opportunities for firms, institutions, and individuals to diversify their investments to limit risk. By holding a diverse portfolio of stocks and bonds in different nations, an investor can reduce total risk to a lower level than can be achieved in a purely domestic setting. Once again, however, foreign exchange risk is a complicating factor.

The trends noted in this chapter seem likely to continue, with the global capital market continuing to increase in both importance and degree of integration over the next decade. Perhaps the most significant development will be the emergence of a unified capital market within the EU by the end of the decade as those countries continue toward economic and monetary union. Since Europe's capital markets are currently fragmented and relatively introspective (with the major exception of Great Britain's capital market), such a development could pave the way for even more rapid internationalization of the capital market in the early years of the next century. If this occurs, the implications for business are likely to be positive.

Chapter Summary

Global Equity

This chapter explained the functions and form of the global capital market and defined the implications of these for international business practice. This chapter made the following points:

1. The function of a capital market is to bring those who want to invest money together with those who want to borrow money.

2. Relative to a domestic capital market, the global capital market has a greater supply of funds available for borrowing, and this makes for a lower cost of capital for borrowers.

3. Relative to a domestic capital market, the global capital market allows investors to diversify portfolios of holdings internationally, thereby reducing risk.

4. The growth of the global capital market during recent decades can be attributed to advances in information technology, the widespread deregulation of financial services, and the relaxation of regulations governing cross-border capital flows.

5. A eurocurrency is any currency banked outside its country of origin. The lack of government regulations makes the eurocurrency market attractive to both depositors and borrowers. Because of the absence of regulation, the spread between the eurocurrency deposit and lending rates is less than the spread between the domestic deposit and lending rates. This gives eurobanks a competitive advantage.

6. The global bond market has two classifications: the foreign bond market and the eurobond market. Foreign bonds are sold outside the borrower's country and are denominated in the currency of the country in which they are issued. A eurobond issue is normally underwritten by an international syndicate of banks and placed in countries other than the one in whose currency the bond is denominated. Eurobonds account for the lion's share of international bond issues.

7. The eurobond market is an attractive way for companies to raise funds due to the absence of regulatory interference, less stringent disclosure requirements, and eurobonds' favorable tax status.

8. Foreign investors are investing in other countries' equity markets to reduce risk by diversifying their holdings among nations.

9. Many companies are now listing their stock in the equity markets of other nations, primarily as a prelude to issuing stock in those markets to raise additional capital. Other reasons for listing stock in another country's exchange are to facilitate future stock swaps; to enable the company to use its stock and stock options for compensating local management and employees; to satisfy local ownership desires; and to increase the company's visibility among its local employees, customers, suppliers, and bankers.

10. When borrowing funds from the global capital market, companies must weigh the benefits of a lower interest rate against the risks of greater real costs of capital due to adverse exchange rate movements.

11. One major implication of the global capital market for international business is that companies can often borrow funds at a lower cost of capital in the international capital market than they can in the domestic capital market.

12. The global capital market provides greater opportunities for businesses and individuals to build a truly diversified portfolio of international investments in financial assets, which lowers risk.

Critical Discussion Questions

1. Why has the global capital market grown so rapidly in recent decades? Do you think this growth will continue throughout the next decade? Why?

2. A firm based in Mexico has found that its growth is restricted by the limited liquidity of the Mexican capital market. List the firm's options for raising money on the global capital market. Discuss the pros and cons of each option, and make a recommendation. How might your recommended options be affected if the Mexican peso depreciates significantly on the foreign exchange markets over the next two years?

3. Happy Company wants to raise $2 million with debt financing. The funds are needed to finance working capital, and the firm will repay them with interest in one year. Happy Company's treasurer is considering three options:

   a. Borrowing U.S. dollars from Security Pacific Bank at 8 percent.
   b. Borrowing British pounds from Midland Bank at 14 percent.
   c. Borrowing Japanese yen from Sanwa Bank at 5 percent.

   If Happy borrows foreign currency, it will not cover it; that is, it will simply change foreign currency for dollars at today's spot rate and buy the same foreign currency a year later at the spot rate then in effect. Happy Company estimates the pound will depreciate by 5 percent relative to the dollar and the yen will appreciate 3 percent relative to the dollar in the next year. From which bank should Happy Company borrow?

The Surging Samurai Bond Market

Since Japan's stock market and real estate bubbles imploded in the early 1990s, the country has had to contend with a decade of poor economic performance. The economy has seemingly constantly teetered on the brink of a serious recession, and sustained growth has remained elusive. In an effort to keep the bleak economic clouds at bay, the Bank of Japan has repeatedly lowered interest rates to try to encourage corporate and consumer spending. As a result, by early 2001 Japan had the lowest interest rates in the world. In March 2001, 10-year Japanese government bonds yielded 1.24 percent, compared with 5 percent for comparable U.S. government debt. Despite these low interest rates, many Japanese corporations continue to focus on restructuring and downsizing, rather than investing in new capacity, as they struggle with the sustained hangover from the boom years of the 1980s and early 1990s. Consequently, Japanese corporations have not rushed to take advantage of the low interest rates to issue additional debt. Nor have consumers responded to the lower interest rates by increasing their consumption. Instead, the personal savings rate in Japan remains stubbornly high, even though many Japanese hold the majority of their savings in post office accounts that pay very low interest rates.

However, there is a silver lining to this bleak economic outlook—for foreign corporations and governments. They have increasingly been taking advantage of Japan's low interest rate to issue yen-denominated debt. With the yen/dollar exchange rate relatively stable, this seems like a shrewd economic bet. Foreign debt offerings in Japan have been snapped up by yield-hungry retail investors, who are looking for better returns than the 1 to 2 percent they get on post office savings accounts. With the equivalent of some $1 trillion in Japanese postal savings predicted to reach maturity between April 2000 and April 2002, a huge wave of retail money is entering the market looking for higher returns. Japan's equity markets have been flirting with 10-year lows, and with the economy near recession, few retail investors are putting their money in Japanese stocks. With Japanese corporations issuing only a few bonds, there are few investment opportunities there. This leaves foreign bonds as one of the few attractive investment opportunities for retail investors looking for higher yields.

An increasing number of foreigners are taking advantage of this opportunity. The number of Samurai bond issues increased from less than 20 in 1998 to more than 120 in 2000 and seemed set to exceed that number in 2001. In 2001, foreigners issuing yen-denominated debt raised some $24 billion in the Japanese bond market, up from $9 billion in 1998. Countries including Croatia, Uruguay, and Brazil have raised money for their treasuries by issuing Samurai bonds. For example, in February 2002, the government of Uruguay issued ¥30 billion of five-year bonds. The interest rate it had to pay on those bonds was just 2.2 percent. It contrast, Uruguay had to pay 7.6 percent for five-year dollar borrowings. Similarly, an increasing number of corporations have been issuing Samurai bonds. In late 2000, Citigroup completed an offering of ¥155 billion ($1.43 billion) in Samurai bonds. Several U.S. investment banks, including Morgan Stanley, Merrill Lynch, and Lehman Brothers also issued Samurai bonds in 2000. In early 2001, the trend continued with a major Samurai bond issue placed by Deutsche Telekom, which offered ¥500 billion ($4.5 billion) in bonds. In addition, Posco, South Korea's largest steel company, came to the market with a ¥30 billion five-year offering. In both cases, these companies chose to raise debt in Japan as opposed to other markets because even factoring in the costs of hedging against fluctuations in the value of the Japanese yen, they could significantly reduce their cost of capital by doing so.

Sources: "Posco to Return to Samurai Market as Yen Offers Cheap Alternative to Dollar Funding," *Euroweek*, January 19, 2001, p. 13; J. Singer, "Japan's Woes Benefit World's Borrowers," *Wall Street Journal*, March 8, 2001, p. A17; and "Samurai Market to Scale New Heights," *Asiamoney*, October 2000, pp. 42–43.

Case Discussion Questions

1. What are the macroeconomic underpinnings of the recent increase in Samurai bond issues? *Low i*

2. How might an increase in Japan's rate of economic growth affect the vitality of the Samurai bond market? *↘ G↑ S↓ D↓*

3. For a company such as Deutsche Telekom, which issued yen-denominated debt to raise funds for investments outside of Japan, the lower interest rate must be offset against higher costs. What are these higher costs, and what determines their magnitude? *exh R*

4. What would happen to activity in the Samurai bond ↑ market if the yen started to appreciate significantly ↑ against the dollar but interest rate differentials between the United States and Japan stayed constant? What would happen if the yen depreciated against the dollar? What does this tell you about the risks of issuing foreign bonds? *FX Risk*

Notes

1. D. Waller, "Daimler in $250m Singapore Placing," *Financial Times*, May 10, 1994, p. 17.

2. Waller, "Daimler in $250m Singapore Placing."

3. C. G. Luck and R. Choudhury, "International Equity Diversification for Pension Funds," *Journal of Investing* 5, no. 2 (1996), pp. 43–53.

4. Ian Domowitz, Jack Glen, and Ananth Madhavan, "Market Segmentation and Stock Prices: Evidence from an Emerging Market," *Journal of Finance* 3, no. 3 (1997), pp. 1059–68.

5. B. Solnik, "Why Not Diversify Internationally Rather than Domestically?" *Financial Analysts Journal*, July 1974, p. 17.

6. A. Lavine, "With Overseas Markets Now Moving in Sync with U.S. Markets, It's Getting Harder to Find True Diversification Abroad," *Financial Planning*, December 1, 2000, pp. 37–40.

7. B. Solnik and J. Roulet, "Dispersion as Cross Sectional Correlation," *Financial Analysts Journal* 56, no. 1 (2000), pp. 54–61.

8. Bank for International Settlements, *BIS Quarterly Review*, March 2001.

9. T. F. Huertas, "U.S. Multinational Banking: History and Prospects," in *Banks as Multinationals*, ed. G. Jones (London: Routledge, 1990).

10. G. J. Millman, *The Vandals' Crown* (New York: Free Press, 1995).

11. P. Dicken, *Global Shift: The Internationalization of Economic Activity* (London: The Guilford Press, 1992).

12. "Capital Goes Global," *The Economist*, October 25, 1997, pp. 87–88.

13. Ibid.

14. Martin Feldstein, "Global Capital Flows: Too Little, Not Too Much," *The Economist*, June 24, 1995, pp. 72–73.

15. Ibid., p. 73.

16. D. Duffy and L. Murry, "The Wooing of American Investors," *Wall Street Journal*, February 25, 1994, p. A14.

17. International Monetary Fund, *World Economic Outlook* (Washington, DC: IMF, 1998).

18. R. Reich, *The Work of Nations* (New York: Alfred A. Knopf, 1991).

Cases

Defending the Brazilian Real

Introduction

Since the early 1990s, Brazil has been a story of steady economic improvement. Once the home of perennial hyperinflation, Brazil has pursued economic policies that have been designed to transform Latin America's largest economy into a dynamic market-based system. These policies have included the privatization of state-owned enterprises, such as the onetime local telephone monopoly, Telebras; substantial deregulation to open the economy to greater domestic and foreign competition; the pursuit of regional and multinational free trade agreements; and the dismantling of barriers to foreign direct investment. The centerpiece of these policies, however, was the *Plano Real* (Real Plan) introduced in mid-1994.

The Real Plan

The *real* (pronounced ray-ahl) is the Brazilian currency. In 1994, it replaced the old currency, the cruzeiro, whose value had been significantly debased by years of high inflation. The *real* plan was the brainchild of Fernando Henrique Cardoso, then the finance minister and now the president. Cardoso's real plan was designed to drive inflation out of the Brazilian economy. When implemented in 1994, the annual inflation rate was running at over 1,000 percent. This hyperinflation disrupted economic activity and discouraged foreign investment. The *real* plan was based on tight monetary policy. To help enforce this, the value of the *real* was pegged to that of the U.S. dollar and allowed to depreciate against the dollar by no more than 7.5 percent per year. To keep depreciation within these bounds, Brazilian authorities had to raise interest rates repeatedly to maintain the value of the real against the dollar. The high cost of credit helped reduce the expansion of the money supply and brought inflation under control in Brazil.

By all accounts, the *real* plan was a major success. In 1996, inflation had already fallen to 10 percent, and it fell to an annual rate of 4 percent by early 1998 and 2 percent by late 1998. At the same time, the Brazilian economy continued to grow at the relatively robust rate of 3 to 4 percent a year, while foreign direct investment soared to a record $16 billion in 1997 and $22 billion in 1998.

Brazil's Economic Straitjacket

Despite the defeat of inflation and several years of robust economic activity, not all was well within Brazil's economy. By mid-1998, the trade deficit on the current account was running at about 4 percent of GDP. Also, the

Brazilian government was spending in excess of its tax receipts and running a fiscal deficit that amounted to 7 percent of GDP. According to critics of the government, the trade deficit was the result of an overvalued real, which was hindering exports while sucking imports into the country. By most estimates, the real was overvalued against the U.S. dollar by between 15 and 20 percent. Some economists argued that the Brazilian government should devalue the real to help correct the trade imbalance. The Cardoso government, however, was reluctant to abandon its commitment to maintaining the dollar peg. After all, this policy had defeated decades of hyperinflation and stabilized the economy.

The causes of Brazil's fiscal deficit were more complex. Government spending had exceeded tax revenues for years. Financing the public-sector deficit required government borrowing, which had pushed up interest rates and made it more difficult for private businesses to get access to credit. The root cause of the deficit was the rigid structure of government spending in Brazil. In all, Brazil collected some 30 percent of GDP in taxes, but only two-thirds of this, some 18.4 percent of GDP, went to the federal government (the rest going to state and local governments). Also, four *constitutionally mandated* budget items were eating up 90 percent of the government's tax revenues. These were (*i*) transfers to other branches and tiers of government, (*ii*) civil service pay, (*iii*) pensions and other welfare spending, and (*iv*) interest payments on federal debt. In the years of hyperinflation, making huge future commitments to pensions or welfare spending mattered little. Inflation would rapidly reduce the value of such commitments when measured in constant currency units. However, with inflation under control, the government could no longer rely on inflation to reduce the value of its public-sector commitments.

The deficit problem was exacerbated by the fact that government employees were overpaid, earning about 30 percent more than their private-sector counterparts. Their pension privileges were even larger. The 3 million public service pensioners got about as much as nearly 18 million private-sector ones. The public-sector pension system had allowed many civil servants to retire in their mid-40s on pensions higher than their last salary. The cost of servicing these pensions had soared because high inflation ended, a bulge of people who entered the labor force during the 1960s and 1970s had retired during the 1990s, and pensioners were living longer.

Cardoso's approach to solving the structural deficit problem was to try to amend the Brazilian constitution to reform the pension, civil service, and tax systems. However, pushing constitutional changes through Brazil's parliament required a 60 percent majority in both houses, and despite repeated attempts, by mid-1998 Cardoso had made only limited progress in reforming Brazil's constitution to gain greater control over fiscal spending.

The Real under Pressure

The first sign that Brazil's economic progress might be starting to unravel came in late 1997, when the Asian financial crisis was unfolding. The Asian crisis triggered panic selling in all emerging markets. Money started to flow out of Brazil, putting pressure on the *real*. Cardoso's government responded by raising interest rates to 43 percent and announced an $18 billion package of tax increases and spending cuts to stabilize the economy and reduce the budget deficit to 2.5 percent of GDP. These actions helped to stem the flow of capital and stabilize the *real*, but at the cost of slowing the economy and exacerbating the budget deficit as government tax receipts declined. While Cardoso gained parliamentary approval for the tax increases in November 1997, the legislature balked at the cuts in social spending. As a consequence, the public-sector borrowing requirement climbed to 7 percent of GDP, up from 4.5 percent the year earlier. In October 1998, federal government tax receipts were 4 percent lower than in the same month in 1997.

The next financial shock came in August 1998, when the Russian government announced it would default on its debt obligations and devalue the Russian ruble by a third. The debt default by the Russian government sent a shock wave throughout the emerging markets around the world. If Russia could default on its debt, who else might? Acting in dreadful unison, financial institutions reacted by indiscriminately pulling out of emerging market debt and equity positions, triggering a global collapse in stock and bond prices. Across Latin America, widely viewed as one of the most vulnerable regions, stock markets fell by 25 to 30 percent, bond prices slumped, and interest rates soared as investors fled to the security of high-quality U.S. Treasury bonds. This global "flight to quality" pushed the yield on 30-year U.S. T-bills to an all-time low of less than 5 percent, while the interest rate spreads between U.S. and emerging market sovereign debt widened alarmingly. The spread between yields on Brazilian government bonds and U.S. government bonds, for example, surged from 4 percent to 12 percent in a matter of days. The flight to U.S. government debt, however, did not save the U.S. stock market, which tumbled in sympathy with stock markets around the world, losing nearly 20 percent of its value in a few short, sharp trading sessions.

With money flowing out of emerging markets like a riptide, the currencies of several nations came under strong selling pressure. The nation of most concern to foreign investors was Brazil, which many feared would be the next to crumble. If Brazil collapsed, taking the rest of Latin America down with it, the United States would suffer major adverse consequences. Latin America absorbed over 20 percent of all exports from the United States, and American multinationals had major investments across the region.

Defending the Real

To defend the Brazilian real against this latest round of selling, the Brazilian government took a number of steps. First, the Brazilian central bank entered the foreign exchange market, using its foreign exchange reserves to purchase *reals* in the open market. As a result, between early August and mid-September 1998, Brazil lost about one-third of its foreign exchange reserves, reducing them to less than $50 billion. At one point, the central bank was spending $1 billion a day to defend the *real*. Second, the government announced $10.8 billion in budget cuts. However, after having failed to follow through with budget cuts announced the previous November, the international markets viewed this announcement with some skepticism and traders continued to sell the *real*. Third, the Brazilian government repeatedly raised interest rates in order to increase the attractiveness of holding the *real*. By late September, Brazilian interest rates stood at 39 percent, the highest interest rates in the world. While the interest rate hikes helped to slow the fall in the currency, they also increased the costs of servicing government debt while depressing economic activity, thereby reducing government tax receipts and raising the specter of further deterioration in the fiscal deficit. To complicate matters further, Brazil was in the middle of a presidential election campaign and the resulting political uncertainty put further pressure on the *real*.

By late September, the government revealed that it was negotiating with the International Monetary Fund (IMF) for financial support. This, coupled with polls suggesting that Cardoso would win the upcoming presidential election campaign, helped to bring some calm back to the foreign exchange markets. On October 4, Cardoso was reelected president, getting a majority of all votes cast in the first round of elections, an outcome that was widely interpreted as a vote in support of his proposals for tough fiscal medicine to help defend the real and correct Brazil's fiscal deficit. Cardoso's election victory had bought the country time, but not much.

With Cardoso reelected, the government continued to negotiate with the IMF. On October 8, 1998, in a joint statement with the Cardoso government, the IMF promised support in return for a number of actions from Brazil. These included stiff reductions in government spending, accompanied by associated reforms in the social security, civil service, pension, and tax systems. The goals of the actions included a budget surplus before interest payments of around 2.5 percent of GDP in 1999 and stabilization of the ratio of debt to GDP by 2000.

On October 28, the Brazilian government followed up the joint statement by announcing a $23.5 billion austerity package for 1999. The plan contained $11 billion worth of tax increases and $12.5 billion in budget cuts and major structural reforms. Further proposed retrenchments, if implemented, would make it an $84 billion program over three years. The austerity package singled out the pension system with an 11 percent tax on pensions collected by retired civil servants and on retirement contributions by active public employees. An additional 20 percent tax would be imposed on the highest pensions. Another feature of the package would raise the tax on corporate earnings from 2 percent to 3 percent and levy a tax on banks as well. With the announcement of this package, the Cardoso government hoped to be able to unlock funds from the IMF.

The IMF, however, had been struggling with problems of its own. The institution had been widely criticized for its handling of the Asian financial crisis. Some argued that the stiff monetary and fiscal policy measures that the IMF had recently imposed on three Asian clients, South Korea, Thailand, and Indonesia, were inappropriate given the price deflation those nations were experiencing. The IMF, critics charged, had helped to exacerbate the economic troubles of Asian nations, not solve them. Seizing on such criticisms, opponents of the IMF in the U.S. Congress held up requests by the executive branch to replenish the IMF's coffers. It was only after intense lobbying and significant concessions that Congress backed down. On October 16, 1997, it agreed to approve $3.4 billion toward a new emergency credit line, as well as $14.5 billion in new capital. The concessions extracted from the IMF by Congress included a requirement that IMF loans to troubled countries would come with an interest rate at least three percentage points above broader market rates and would be repaid within 30 months. It was widely expected that once the U.S. government stepped up to the plate and funded the IMF, a further $74 billion would be forthcoming from other IMF member states.

The IMF Package

On November 13, 1998, a Friday, the IMF announced that Brazil would receive loans of $41.5 billion. Of this amount, $14.5 billion would come from the world's richest countries, led by the United States (which put up $5 billion). The loan was to support the Brazilian economy while it implemented the austerity package unveiled October 28. After the announcement, capital flight diminished to a trickle and the real stabilized. Brazil's stock market even staged a small rally.

However, not everyone was satisfied that the IMF rescue package was the right approach to take in the case of Brazil. According to some influential econo-

mists, such as Jeffery Sachs, director of Harvard's Institute for International Development, attempts by the IMF and Cardoso to defend the *real* were folly. According to Sachs, Brazil would be better served by bowing to market forces and letting the *real* float freely. In making his case, Sachs pointed to the relative success of Mexico in handling external shocks since it was forced to float the peso in December 1994. Allowing the real to float, according to Sachs, would help Brazil keep its exports competitive. It would also reduce the need for the country to raise interest rates to levels that severely depressed economic activity and dramatically increased the costs of servicing government debt. Critics of this approach argued that if Brazil were to let the real float, the decision would trigger panic among international investors and undermine the credibility of a government that had hitched its wagon to a pegged exchange rate policy. For a country with a long history of inflation, a floating exchange rate would be widely viewed as rekindling the inflationary fires.

Others argued that far from going to a floating system, Brazil should try to strengthen its commitment to maintaining a stable real by adopting a currency board system for managing the exchange rate and locking the real into the U.S. dollar. The currency board system would require that all real issued be backed by U.S. dollars held by the Brazilian central bank. New real could be issued only if the country could gain additional U.S. dollars to back it up. Gaining additional dollars would require Brazil to make itself an attractive investment location for holders of U.S. dollars, which cannot be achieved without a sound economic policy. It would also require that Brazil cede control over interest rates to the U.S. Federal Reserve. Although several countries have adopted a currency board, including Hong Kong and Argentina, both of which have arguably benefited from the system, it might be culturally difficult to implement such a system in Brazil, implying as it does the loss of some national sovereignty.

Aftermath

If anyone thought the IMF announcement would bring an end to Brazil's troubles, they were disappointed. Cardoso's government did push several elements of the austerity package through the Brazilian Congress. However, despite having the nominal support of three-quarters of the members of Congress, in early December 1998, the government's proposal to raise pension contributions for civil servants and raise taxes on the pensions of retired government employees was defeated. Although recent constitutional reforms meant the government had to get only a simple majority to force the measure through Congress, it failed to do so. After intense lobbying by public-sector workers, about 100 nominal supporters of the government voted against the measure. Another 100 finessed the issue by failing to turn up for the vote. Despite this setback, Cardoso remained confident that the measure would be passed early in the new year.

However, Cardoso's political problems were not over. Claiming a lack of funds due to economic hardship, on January 10, 1999, the Brazilian state of Minas Gerais declared a 90-day moratorium on debt payments owed to the central government. This would make it more difficult for the federal government to meet its own debt service obligations. The decision to declare a moratorium was made by the state's Governor and former Brazilian President Itamar Franco. Although the amount of money involved was not huge—$67 million a month—the action raised concerns that other cash-strapped states would follow. The Brazilian stock market plunged 6 percent on the news and a further 7 percent the following day. On January 12, the U.S. stock market dropped 2 percent in sympathy. Brazil and the global financial system were not out of the woods yet.

Case Discussion Questions

1. Explain the mechanism by which the real plan helped to defeat hyperinflation in Brazil.

2. What actions does the Brazilian government need to take to defend the peg of the real against the U.S. dollar?

3. Do you think the Brazilian government was correct to place a high value on defending the peg of the *real* against the U.S. dollar? What were the costs to Brazil of this policy? What were the benefits?

4. What do you think might happen to the value of the *real*, and the Brazilian economy in general, if the Brazilian government abandoned its defense of the real and decided to let it float against the dollar?

5. What would be the implications of allowing the *real* to float for the rest of Latin America and for the economy of the United States?

Sources

1. Balls, A. "IMF Leads $41 Billion Gamble on Fiscal Adjustment Plan." *Financial Times*, December 21, 1998, p. 2.

2. "The Battle Royal for Brazil's Real." *The Economist*, September 12, 1998, p. 35.

3. "Brazil's Last Stand?" *The Economist*, September 19, 1998, p. 98.

4. "Can Cardoso Use Financial Chaos to Reform Brazil?" *The Economist*, September 26, 1998, p. 33.

5. Druckerman, P., and P. Beckett. "Foreign Banks Turn More Cautious on Brazil." *Wall Street Journal*, January 11, 1999, p. A10.

6. Dyer, J. "Make or Break Time for President." *Financial Times*, December 21, 1998, p. 3.

7. Feldstein, M., and K. Feldstein. "It's Imperative to Save Latin America's Largest Economy." *Boston Globe*, November 10, 1998, p. D4.

8. Fidler, S. "Last Tango in Rio." *Financial Times*, November 18, 1998, p. 23.

9. Fritsch, P. "Brazil Jolted as Governor Balks on Federal Debt." *Wall Street Journal*, January 8, 1999, p. A15.

10. "The IMF and Brazil: A Deal at Last." *The Economist*, October 17, 1998, p. 93.

11. Katz, I. "Brazil's Ill Winds." *Business Week*, September 21, 1998, p. 34.

12. Rotella, S. "Brazil Unveils Plan to Stave Off Economic Crisis." *Los Angeles Times*, October 29, 1998, p. A1.

The Strategy and Structure of International Business

The Strategy
of
International
Business

MTV Networks has become a symbol of globalization. Established in 1981, the U.S.-based music TV network has been expanding outside of its North American base since 1987 when it opened MTV Europe. Now owned by media conglomerate Viacom, MTV Networks, which includes siblings Nickelodeon and VH1, the music station for the aging baby boomers, generates more than $1 billion in operating profit per year on annual revenues that are getting close to $3 billion. Since 1987, MTV has become the most ubiquitous cable programmer in the world. By early 2001 the network had 29 channels, or distinct feeds, that reached a combined total of 330 million households in 140 countries. While the United States still leads in number of households, with 70 million, the most rapid growth is elsewhere, particularly in Asia, where nearly two-thirds of the region's 3 billion people are under 35, the middle class is expanding quickly, and TV ownership is spreading rapidly. MTV Networks figures that every second of every day almost 2 million people are watching MTV around the world, the majority outside the United States.

Despite its international success, MTV's global expansion got off to a weak start. In 1987, it piped a single feed across Europe almost entirely composed of American programming with English-speaking veejays. Naively, the network's U.S. managers thought Europeans would flock to the American programming. But while viewers in Europe shared a common interest in a handful of global superstars, who at the time included Madonna and Michael Jackson, their tastes turned out to be surprisingly local. What was popular in Germany might not be popular in Great Britain. Many staples of the American music scene left Europeans cold. MTV suffered as a result. Soon local copycat stations were springing up in Europe that focused on the music scene in individual countries. They took viewers and advertisers away from MTV. As explained by Tom Freston, chairman of MTV Networks, "We were going for the most shallow layer of what united viewers and brought them together. It didn't go over too well."

In 1995, MTV changed its strategy and broke Europe into regional feeds, of which there are now eight: one for the United Kingdom and Ireland; another for Germany, Austria, and Switzerland; one for Scandinavia; one for Italy; one for France; one for Spain; one for Holland; and a feed for other European nations including Belgium and Greece. The network adopted the same localization strategy elsewhere in the world. For example, in Asia it has an English-Hindi channel for India, separate Mandrine feeds for China and Taiwan, a Korean feed for South Korea, a Bahasa-language feed for Indonesia, Japanese feed for Japan, and so on. Digital and satellite technology have made the localization of programming cheaper and easier. MTV Networks can now beam half a dozen feeds off one satellite transponder.

While MTV Networks exercises creative control over these different feeds, and while all the channels have the same familiar frenetic look and feel of MTV in the United States, an increasing share of the programming and content is now local. When MTV opens a local station now, it begins with expatriates from elsewhere in the world to do a "gene transfer" of company culture and operating principles. But once these are established, the network switches to local employees and the expatriates move on. The idea is to "get inside the heads" of the local population and produce programming that matches their tastes. Although as much as 60 percent of the programming still originates in the United States, with staples such as "The Real World" having equivalents in different countries, an increasing share of programming is local in conception. In Italy, "MTV Kitchen" combines cooking with a music countdown. "Erotica" airs in Brazil and features a panel of youngsters discussing sex. The Indian channel produces 21 homegrown shows hosted by local veejays who speak "Hinglish," a city-bred breed of Hindi and English. Hit shows include "MTV Cricket in Control," appropriate for a land where cricket is a national obsession, "MTV Housefull," which hones in on Hindi film stars (India has the biggest film industry outside of Hollywood), and "MTV Bakra," which is modeled after "Candid Camera."

The same local variation is evident in the music videos aired by the different feeds. While some music stars still have global appeal, in most markets 70 percent of the video content is now local. In a direct countertrend to the notion that popular culture is becoming more global and homogenous, William Roedy, the president of MTV's international networks, observes, "People root for the home team, both culturally and musically. Local repertoire is a worldwide trend. There are fewer global megastars." When music tastes do transcend borders, MTV has found that it is often in ways that would have been difficult to predict. Currently, Japanese pop music is all the rage in Taiwan, while soul and hip-hop are big in South Korea.

This localization push has reaped big benefits for MTV, capturing viewers back from local imitators. In India, ratings increased by more than 700 percent between 1996 when the localization push began and 2000. In turn, localization helps MTV to capture more of those all-important advertising revenues, even from other multinationals such as Coca-Cola, whose own advertising budgets are often locally determined. In Europe, MTV's advertising revenues increased by 50 percent between 1995 and 2000. While the total market for pan-European advertising is valued at just $200 million, the total market for local advertising across Europe is a much bigger pie, valued at $12 billion. MTV now gets 70 percent of its European advertising revenue from local spots, up from 15 percent in 1995. Similar trends are evident elsewhere in the world.

Sources: B. Pulley and A. Tanzer, "Sumner's Gemstone," *Forbes,* February 21, 2000, pp. 107–11; K. Hoffman, "Youth TV's Old Hand Prepares for the Digital Challenge," *Financial Times,* February 18, 2000, p. 8; presentation by Sumner M. Redstone, chairman and CEO, Viacom Inc., delivered to Salomon Smith Barney 11th Annual Global Entertainment Media, Telecommunications Conference, Scottsdale, AZ, January 8, 2001. Archived at www.viacom.com.

◼ Introduction

Our primary concern thus far in this book has been with aspects of the larger environment in which international businesses compete. As we have described it in the preceding chapters, this environment has included the different political, economic, and cultural institutions found in nations, the international trade and investment framework, and the international monetary system. Now our focus shifts from the environment to the firm itself and, in particular, to the actions managers can take to compete more effectively as an international business. In this chapter, we look at how firms can increase their profitability by expanding their operations in foreign markets. We discuss the different strategies that firms pursue when competing internationally. We consider the pros and cons of these strategies. We discuss the various factors that affect a firm's choice of strategy. And we look at the tactics firms adopt when competing head to head across various national markets. In subsequent chapters we shall build on the framework established here to discuss a variety of topics including the design of organization structures and control systems for international businesses, strategies for entering foreign markets, the use and misuse of strategic alliances, strategies for exporting, and the various manufacturing, marketing, R&D, human resource, accounting, and financial strategies that are pursued by international businesses.

MTV Networks, profiled in the opening case, gives us a preview of some issues that we will explore in this chapter. When MTV began its global expansion in 1987, its strategy was to transfer its programming and content wholesale from the successful U.S. network. This strategy, which treated the world as a homogenous cultural entity with little variation in local tastes and preferences, was a failure. MTV soon found itself outmaneuvered by local imitators, which captured viewers and advertising revenues from the network by tailoring programming and content to local tastes and preferences. Realizing that it had made a serious strategic error, MTV changed its strategy in 1995 and emphasized localization. At MTV, localization means local programming and local video content hosted by local veejays and aimed at local markets. At the same time, MTV has been careful to ensure that its local channels still have the look and feel of MTV, and that its local operations share a common "genetic code" or set of operating principles. This strategy has enabled MTV to capture more viewers and to grow its advertising revenues at a double-digit rate. Thus, at MTV, the strategy has shifted from one that emphasized global standardization to one that emphasized local responsiveness. As we shall see, finding the correct balance between global standardization and local responsiveness is a major strategic challenge for many multinational enterprises. It is one that MTV appears to have solved, at least for now.

Strategy and the Firm ▓

Before we discuss the strategies that multinational enterprises can pursue, we need to review basic principles of strategy. A firm's **strategy** can be defined as the actions that managers take to attain the goals of the firm. For most firms, the preeminent goal is to maximize long-term profitability. A firm makes a profit if the price it can charge for its output is greater than its costs of producing that output. **Profit** (Π) is thus defined as the difference between total revenues (TR) and total costs (TC), or:

$$\Pi = TR - TC$$

Total revenues (TR) are equal to price (P) times the number of units sold by the firm (Q) or $TR = P \times Q$. Total costs (TC) are equal to cost per unit (C) times the number of units sold or $TC = C \times Q$. Total profit (Π) is equal to profit per unit (π) times the number of units sold, or $\Pi = \pi \times Q$.

Profitability is a ratio or rate of return concept. A simple example would be the rate of return on sales (ROS), which is defined as profit (Π) over total revenues, or:

$$ROS = \Pi/TR$$

Thus, a firm might operate with the goal of maximizing its profitability, as defined by its return on sales (ROS), and its strategy would be the actions that its managers take to attain that goal. (A more common goal is to maximize the firm's return on investment, or ROI, which is defined as $ROI = \Pi/I$ where I represents the total capital that has been invested in the firm.)

▍Value Creation

Two basic conditions determine a firm's profits (Π): the amount of value customers place on the firm's goods or services (sometimes referred to as perceived value) and the firm's costs of production. In general, the more value customers place on a firm's products, the higher the price the firm can charge for those products. Note, however, that the price a firm charges for a good or service is typically less than the value placed on that good or service by the customer. This is so because the customer captures some of that value in the form of what economists call a consumer surplus.[1] The customer is able to do this because the firm is competing with other firms for the customer's business, so the firm must charge a lower price than it could were it a monopoly supplier. Also, it is normally impossible to segment the market to such a degree that the firm can charge each customer a price that reflects that individual's assessment of the value of a product, which economists refer to as a customer's reservation price. For these reasons, the price that gets charged tends to be less than the value placed on the product by many customers.

Figure 12.1 illustrates these concepts. The value of a product to a consumer is V; the price that the firm can charge for that product given competitive pressures and its ability to segment the market is P; and the costs of producing that product are C. The firm's profit per unit sold (π) is equal to $P - C$, while the consumer surplus is equal to $V - P$. The firm makes a profit so long as P is greater than C, and its profit will be greater the lower C is *relative* to P. The difference between V and P is in part determined by the intensity of competitive pressure in the marketplace. The lower the intensity of competitive pressure, the higher the price that can be charged relative to V.[2]

The **value created** by a firm is measured by the difference between V and C ($V - C$); a company creates value by converting inputs that cost C into a product on which consumers place a value of V. A company can create more value for its customers either by lowering production costs, C, or by making the product more

Figure 12.1

Value Creation

Figure 12.2

The Firm as a Value Chain

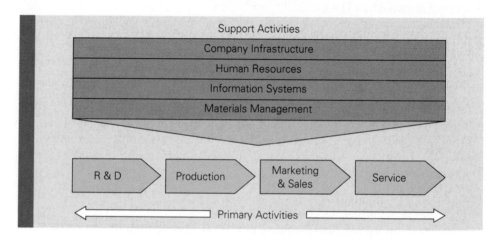

attractive through superior design, functionality, quality, and the like, so that consumers place a greater value on it (V increases) and, consequently, are willing to pay a high price (P increases). This discussion suggests that a firm has high profits when it creates more value for its customers and does so at a lower cost. We refer to a strategy that focuses on lowering production costs as a *low cost strategy*. We refer to a strategy that focuses on increasing the attractiveness of a product as a *differentiation strategy*.[3] Michael Porter has argued that *low cost* and *differentiation* are two basic strategies for creating value and attaining a competitive advantage in an industry.[4] According to Porter, superior profitability goes to those firms that can create superior value, and the way to create superior value is to drive down the cost structure of the business and/or differentiate the product in some way so that consumers value it more and are prepared to pay a premium price. Superior value creation relative to rivals does not necessarily require a firm to have the lowest cost structure in an industry, or to create the most valuable product in the eyes of consumers. However, it does require that the gap between value (V) and cost of production (C) is greater than the gap attained by competitors.

The Firm as a Value Chain

It is useful to think of the firm as a value chain composed of a series of distinct value creation activities including production, marketing and sales, materials management, R&D, human resources, information systems, and the firm infrastructure. We can categorize these value creation activities as primary activities and support activities (see Figure 12.2).[5]

Primary Activities

Primary activities have to do with the design, creation, and delivery of the product; its marketing; and its support and after-sale service. In the value chain illustrated in Figure 12.2, the primary activities are broken into four functions: research and development, production, marketing and sales, and service.

Research and development (R&D) is concerned with the design of products and production processes. Although we think of R&D as being associated with the design of physical products and production processes in manufacturing enterprises, many service companies also undertake R&D. For example, banks compete with each other by developing new financial products and new ways of delivering those products to customers. Online banking and smart debit cards are two recent examples of new product development in the banking industry. Earlier examples of innovation in the banking industry included automated teller machines, credit cards, and debit cards. Through superior product design, R&D can increase the functionality of products, which makes them more attractive to consumers (raising V). Alternatively, R&D may result in more efficient production processes, thereby lowering production costs (lowering C). Either way, the R&D function can create value.

Production is concerned with the creation of a good or service. For physical products, when we talk about production we generally mean manufacturing. For services such as banking or retail operations, "production" typically occurs when the service is delivered to the customer (for example, when a bank originates a loan for a customer it is engaged in "production" of the loan). For a media company such as MTV, production involves the creation and delivery of content (programming). The production activity of a firm creates value by performing its activities efficiently so lower costs result (lower C) or by performing them in such a way that a more reliable and higher-quality product is produced (which results in higher V).

The marketing and sales functions of a firm can help to create value in several ways. Through brand positioning and advertising, the marketing function can increase the value (V) that consumers perceive to be contained in a firm's product. If these create a favorable impression of the firm's product in the minds of consumers, they increase the price that can be charged for the firm's product. For example, in the 1980s the French company Perrier did a wonderful job of convincing U.S. consumers that slightly carbonated bottled water was worth $1.50 per bottle, rather than a price closer to the $0.50 that it cost to physically collect, bottle, and distribute the water. Perrier's marketing function essentially increased the perception of value (V) that consumers ascribed to the product. Marketing and sales can also create value by discovering consumer needs and communicating them back to the R&D function of the company, which can then design products that better match those needs.

The role of the enterprise's service activity is to provide after-sale service and support. This function can create a perception of superior value (V) in the minds of consumers by solving customer problems and supporting customers after they have purchased the product. For example, Caterpillar, the U.S.-based manufacturer of heavy earthmoving equipment, can get spare parts to any point in the world within 24 hours, thereby minimizing the amount of downtime its customers have to suffer if their Caterpillar equipment malfunctions. This is an extremely valuable capability in an industry where downtime is very expensive. It has helped to increase the value that customers associate with Caterpillar products and thus the price that Caterpillar can charge for its products.

Support Activities

The support activities of the value chain provide inputs that allow the primary activities to take place (see Figure 12.2). The materials management (or logistics) function controls the transmission of physical materials through the value chain, from procurement through production and into distribution. The efficiency with which this is carried out can significantly lower cost (lower C), thereby creating more value.

Similarly, the human resource function can help create more value in a number of ways. It ensures that the company has the right mix of skilled people to perform its value creation activities effectively. Recall from the opening case how MTV staffs its foreign operations with local nationals—the idea being that local nationals will have a better feel for the tastes and preferences of local viewers than expatriate managers from the United States. MTV believes that better programming results from this staffing choice. In so far as this improves the fit between MTV's programming and local tastes, and drives viewer ratings, it raises the value (V) to advertisers of a slot on MTV. In turn, this increases the price that MTV can charge for those advertising slots. The human resource function also ensures that people are adequately trained, motivated, and compensated to perform their value creation tasks.

Information systems refer to the normally electronic systems for managing inventory, tracking sales, pricing products, selling products, dealing with customer service inquiries, and so on. Information systems, when coupled with the communications features of the Internet, can alter the efficiency and effectiveness with which a firm manages its other value creation activities. As we shall see, good information systems are very important in the global arena.

The final support activity is the company infrastructure. By infrastructure we mean the context within which all the other value creation activities occur. The infrastructure includes the organizational structure, control systems, and culture of the firm. Because top management can exert considerable influence in shaping these aspects of a firm, top management should also be viewed as part of the firm's infrastructure. Through strong leadership, top management can consciously shape the infrastructure of a firm and through that the performance of all other value creation activities within it.

The Role of Strategy

Many international markets are now extremely competitive due to the liberalization of the world trade and investment environment. In industry after industry, capable competitors confront each other around the globe. To be profitable in such an environment, a firm must both reduce the costs of value creation (lower C) and differentiate its product offering so that consumers value that product more (raise V) and are willing to pay more for the product than it costs to produce it. Thus, strategy is often concerned with identifying and taking actions that will *lower the costs* of value creation and/or will *differentiate* the firm's product offering through superior design, quality, service, functionality, and so on.

For an example of how this works, consider Clear Vision, a manufacturer and distributor of eyewear. Started in the 1970s by David Glassman, the firm now generates annual gross revenues of more than $100 million. Not exactly small, but no corporate giant either, Clear Vision is a multinational firm with production facilities on three continents and customers around the world. Clear Vision began its move toward becoming a multinational in the early 1980s. The strong dollar at that time made U.S.-based manufacturing very expensive. Low-priced imports were taking an ever-larger share of the U.S. eyewear market, and Clear Vision realized it could not survive unless it also began to import. Initially the firm bought from independent overseas manufacturers, primarily in Hong Kong. However, the firm became dissatisfied with these suppliers' product quality and delivery. As Clear Vision's volume of imports increased, Glassman decided the best way to guarantee quality and delivery was to set up Clear Vision's own manufacturing operation overseas. Accordingly, Clear Vision found a Chinese partner, and together they opened a manufacturing facility in Hong Kong, with Clear Vision being the majority shareholder.

The choice of the Hong Kong location was influenced by its combination of low labor costs, a skilled workforce, and tax breaks given by the Hong Kong government.

The firm's objective at this point was to lower production costs (lower C) by locating value creation activities at an appropriate location. By 1986, however, the increasing industrialization of Hong Kong and a growing labor shortage had pushed up wage rates to the extent that it was no longer a low-cost location. In response, Glassman and his Chinese partner moved part of their manufacturing to a plant in mainland China to take advantage of the lower wage rates there. Again, the goal was to lower production costs (lower C). The parts for eyewear frames manufactured at this plant are shipped to the Hong Kong factory for final assembly and then distributed to markets in North and South America. The Hong Kong factory now employs 80 people and the China plant between 300 and 400.

At the same time, Clear Vision was looking for opportunities to invest in foreign eyewear firms with reputations for fashionable design and high quality. Its objective was not to reduce production costs but to launch a line of high-quality differentiated, "designer" eyewear. Clear Vision did not have the design capability in-house to support such a line, but Glassman knew that certain foreign manufacturers did. As a result, Clear Vision invested in factories in Japan, France, and Italy, taking a minority shareholding in each case. These factories now supply eyewear for Clear Vision's Status Eye division, which markets high-priced designer eyewear.[6]

Thus, to deal with a threat from foreign competition, Clear Vision adopted a strategy intended to lower its cost structure (lower C): shifting its production from a high-cost location, the United States, to a low-cost location, first Hong Kong and later China. Then Clear Vision adopted a strategy intended to increase the perceived value of its product (increase V) so it could charge a premium price. Reasoning that premium pricing in eyewear depended on superior design, its strategy involved investing capital in French, Italian, and Japanese factories that had reputations for superior design. In sum, Clear Vision's strategies included some actions intended to reduce its costs of creating value (C) and other actions intended to add perceived value (V) to its product through differentiation. The overall goal was to increase the value created by Clear Vision and thus the profit (Π) and profitability of the enterprise. To the extent that these strategies were successful, the firm should have attained a higher profit margin and greater profitability than if it had remained a U.S.-based manufacturer of eyewear.

Profiting from Global Expansion

As suggested by the Clear Vision example, expanding globally allows firms to increase their profitability in ways not available to purely domestic enterprises.[7] Firms that operate internationally are able to:

1. Realize location economies by dispersing individual value creation activities to those locations around the globe where they can be performed most efficiently and effectively.

2. Realize greater cost economies from experience effects by serving an expanded global market from a central location, thereby reducing the costs of value creation.

3. Earn a greater return from the firm's distinctive skills or core competencies by leveraging those skills and applying them to new geographic markets.

4. Earn a greater return by leveraging any valuable skills developed in foreign operations and transferring them to other entities within the firm's global network of operations.

As we will see, however, a firm's ability to increase its profitability by pursuing these strategies is to some extent constrained by the need to customize its product offering, marketing strategy, and business strategy to differing national conditions; that is, by the imperative of localization.

Location Economies

We know from earlier chapters that countries differ along a range of dimensions, including the economic, political, legal, and cultural, and that these differences can either raise or lower the costs of doing business in a country. The theory of international trade also teaches us that due to differences in factor costs, certain countries have a comparative advantage in the production of certain products. Japan might excel in the production of automobiles and consumer electronics; the United States in the production of computer software, pharmaceuticals, biotechnology products, and financial services; Switzerland in the production of precision instruments and pharmaceuticals; and South Korea in the production of steel.[8]

What does all this mean for a firm that is trying to survive in a competitive global market? It means that, *trade barriers and transportation costs* permitting, the firm will benefit by basing each value creation activity it performs at that location where economic, political, and cultural conditions, including relative factor costs, are most conducive to the performance of that activity. Thus, if the best designers for a product live in France, a firm should base its design operations in France. If the most productive labor force for assembly operations is in Mexico, assembly operations should be based in Mexico. If the best marketers are in the United States, the marketing strategy should be formulated in the United States. And so on.

Firms that pursue such a strategy can realize what we refer to as **location economies,** the economies that arise from performing a value creation activity in the optimal location for that activity, wherever in the world that might be (transportation costs and trade barriers permitting). Locating a value creation activity in the optimal location for that activity can have one of two effects. *It can lower the costs of value creation and help the firm to achieve a low cost position, and/or it can enable a firm to differentiate its product offering from the offerings of competitors.* In terms of Figure 12.1, it can lower C or increase V, which in general supports higher pricing (P). These considerations were at work in the case of Clear Vision, discussed earlier. Clear Vision moved its manufacturing operations out of the United States, first to Hong Kong and then to mainland China, to take advantage of low labor costs, thereby lowering the costs of value creation (C). At the same time, Clear Vision shifted some design operations from the United States to France and Italy. Clear Vision reasoned that skilled Italian and French designers could probably help the firm better differentiate its product, increasing perceived value (V). In other words, Clear Vision thinks that the optimal location for performing manufacturing operations is China, whereas the optimal locations for performing design operations are France and Italy. The firm has configured its value chain accordingly. By doing so, Clear Vision hopes to be able to simultaneously lower its cost structure and differentiate its product offering. In turn, differentiation should allow Clear Vision to charge a premium price for its product offering.

Creating a Global Web

Generalizing from the Clear Vision example, one result of this kind of thinking is the creation of a **global web** of value creation activities, with different stages of the value chain being dispersed to those locations around the globe where perceived value is maximized or where the costs of value creation are minimized. Consider the case of General Motors' Pontiac Le Mans cited in Robert Reich's *The Work of Nations*.[9] Marketed primarily in the United States, the car was designed in Germany; key components were manufactured in Japan, Taiwan, and Singapore; assembly was performed in South Korea; and the advertising strategy was formulated in Great Britain. The car was designed in Germany because GM believed the designers in its German subsidiary had the skills most suited to the job at hand. (They were the most capable of producing a design that added value.) Components were manufactured in Japan, Taiwan, and Singapore, because favorable factor conditions there—relatively low-cost, skilled labor—

suggested that those locations had a comparative advantage in the production of components (which helped reduce the costs of value creation). The car was assembled in South Korea because GM believed that due to its low labor costs, the costs of assembly could be minimized there (also helping to minimize the costs of value creation). Finally, the advertising strategy was formulated in Great Britain because GM believed a particular advertising agency there was the most able to produce an advertising campaign that would help sell the car. (This decision was consistent with GM's desire to maximize the value added.)

In theory, a firm that realizes location economies by dispersing each of its value creation activities to its optimal location should have a competitive advantage vis-à-vis a firm that bases all of its value creation activities at a single location. It should be able to better differentiate its product offering (thereby raising perceived value, V) and lower its cost structure (C) than its single-location competitor. In a world where competitive pressures are increasing, such a strategy may become an imperative for survival (as it seems to have been for Clear Vision).

Some Caveats

Introducing transportation costs and trade barriers complicates this picture somewhat. Due to favorable factor endowments, New Zealand may have a comparative advantage for automobile assembly operations, but high transportation costs would make it an uneconomical location from which to serve global markets. A consideration of transportation costs and trade barriers helps explain why many U.S. firms are now shifting their production from Asia to Mexico. Mexico has three distinct advantages over many Asian countries as a location for value creation activities. First, low labor costs make it a good location for labor-intensive production processes. In recent years, wage rates have increased significantly in Japan, Taiwan, and Hong Kong, but they have remained low in Mexico. Second, Mexico's proximity to the large U.S. market reduces transportation costs. This is particularly important in the case of products with high weight-to-value ratios (e.g., automobiles). And third, the North American Free Trade Agreement (see Chapter 8) has removed many trade barriers between Mexico, the United States, and Canada, increasing Mexico's attractiveness as a production site for the North American market. Although value added and the costs of value creation are important, transportation costs and trade barriers also must be considered in location decisions.

Another caveat concerns the importance of assessing political and economic risks when making location decisions. Even if a country looks very attractive as a production location when measured against all the standard criteria, if its government is unstable or totalitarian, the firm might be advised not to base production there. (Political risk is discussed in Chapter 2.) Similarly, if the government appears to be pursuing inappropriate economic policies, that might be another reason for not basing production in that location, even if other factors look favorable.

Experience Effects

The **experience curve** refers to systematic reductions in production costs that have been observed to occur over the life of a product.[10] A number of studies have observed that a product's production costs decline by some characteristic about each time accumulated output doubles. The relationship was first observed in the aircraft industry, where each time accumulated output of airframes was doubled, unit costs typically declined to 80 percent of their previous level.[11] Thus, production cost for the fourth airframe would be 80 percent of production cost for the second airframe, the eighth airframe's production costs 80 percent of the fourth's, the sixteenth's 80 percent of the eighth's, and so on. Figure 12.3 illustrates this experience curve relationship between production costs and output. Two things explain this: learning effects and economies of scale.

Figure 12.3

The Experience Curve

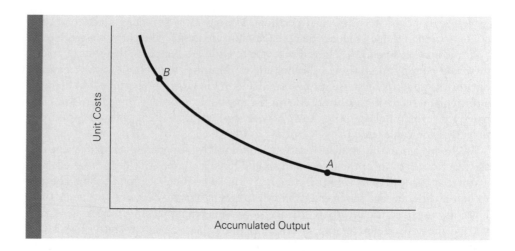

Learning Effects

Learning effects refer to cost savings that come from learning by doing. Labor, for example, learns by repetition how to carry out a task such as assembling airframes most efficiently. Labor productivity increases over time as individuals learn the most efficient ways to perform particular tasks. Equally important, in new production facilities, management typically learns how to manage the new operation more efficiently over time. Hence, production costs eventually decline due to increasing labor productivity and management efficiency.

Learning effects tend to be more significant when a technologically complex task is repeated, since there is more that can be learned about the task. Thus, learning effects will be more significant in an assembly process involving 1,000 complex steps than in one of only 100 simple steps. No matter how complex the task, however, learning effects typically die out after a while. It has been suggested that they are really important only during the start-up period of a new process and that they cease after two or three years.[12] Any decline in the experience curve after such a point is due to economies of scale.

Economies of Scale

Economies of scale refer to the reductions in unit cost achieved by producing a large volume of a product. Economies of scale have a number of sources. One of the most important seems to be the ability to spread fixed costs over a large volume.[13] Fixed costs are the costs required to set up a production facility, develop a new product, and the like, and they can be substantial. For example, establishing a new production line to manufacture semiconductor chips costs about $1 billion. According to one estimate, developing a new drug costs about $500 million and takes about 10 years.[14] The only way to recoup such high fixed costs is to sell the product worldwide, which reduces unit costs by spreading them over a larger volume. The more rapidly that cumulative sales volume is built up, the more rapidly fixed costs can be amortized, and the more rapidly unit costs fall.

Another source of scale economies arises from the ability of large firms to employ increasingly specialized equipment or personnel. This theory goes back more than 200 years to Adam Smith, who argued that the division of labor is limited by the extent of the market. As a firm's output expands, it is better able to fully utilize specialized equipment and can justify hiring specialized personnel. For example, consider a metal stamping machine that is used in the production of body parts for automobiles. The machine can be purchased in a customized form, which is optimized for the production of a particular type of body part—say door panels—or a general-purpose form that will produce any kind of body part. The general-purpose form is less efficient and costs more to purchase than the customized form, but it is more flexible. Since these machines are very expensive, costing millions of dollars each, they have to be used continually to recoup a return on their costs. Fully utilized, a machine can turn out about 200,000 units a year. If an automobile company only sells 100,000 cars per year, it will not be worthwhile purchasing the specialized equipment, and it will have to purchase general-purpose machines. This will give it a higher cost structure than a firm that sells 200,000 cars per year, and for which it is economical to purchase a specialized stamping machine. Thus, because a firm with a large output can more fully utilize specialized equipment (and personnel), it should have a lower unit cost than a generalized firm.

Strategic Significance

The strategic significance of the experience curve is clear. Moving down the experience curve allows a firm to reduce its cost of creating value (to lower C in Figure 12.1). The firm that moves down the experience curve most rapidly will have a cost advantage vis-à-vis its competitors. Thus, Firm A in Figure 12.3, because it is farther down the experience curve, has a clear cost advantage over Firm B.

Many of the underlying sources of experience-based cost economies are plant based. This is true for most learning effects as well as for the economies of scale derived by spreading the fixed costs of building productive capacity over a large output. Thus, one key to progressing downward on the experience curve as rapidly as possible is to increase the volume produced by a single plant as rapidly as possible. Because global markets are larger than domestic markets, a firm that serves a global market from a single location is likely to build accumulated volume more quickly than a firm that serves only its home market or that serves multiple markets from multiple production locations. Thus, serving a global market from a single location is consistent with moving down the experience curve and establishing a low cost position (i.e., lowering the costs of value creation, C). In addition, to get down the experience curve rapidly, a firm may need to price and market aggressively so demand will expand rapidly. It will also need to build sufficient production capacity for serving a global market. Also, the cost advantages of serving the world market from a single location will be even more significant if that location is the optimal one for performing the particular value creation activity.

Once a firm has established a low cost position, it can act as a barrier to new competition. Specifically, an established firm that is well down the experience curve, such as Firm A in Figure 12.3, can price so that it is still making a profit while new entrants, which are farther up the curve such as Firm B in the figure, are suffering losses.

The classic example of the successful pursuit of such a strategy concerns the Japanese consumer electronics company Matsushita. Along with Sony and Philips, Matsushita was in the race to develop a commercially viable videocassette recorder in the 1970s. Although Matsushita initially lagged behind Philips and Sony, it was able to get its VHS format accepted as the world standard and to reap enormous experience-curve-based cost economies in the process. This cost advantage subsequently constituted a formidable barrier to new competition. Matsushita's strategy was to build global volume as rapidly as possible. To ensure it could accommodate worldwide demand, the firm increased its production capacity 33-fold from 205,000 units in 1977 to 6.8 million units by 1984. By serving the world market from a single location in Japan, Matsushita was able to realize significant learning effects and economies of scale. These allowed Matsushita to drop its prices 50 percent within five years of selling its first VHS-formatted VCR. As a result, Matsushita was the world's major VCR producer by 1983, accounting for about 45 percent of world production and enjoying a significant cost advantage over its competitors. The next largest firm, Hitachi, accounted for only 11.1 percent of world production in 1983.[15] Today, firms like Intel are the masters of this kind of strategy. The costs of building a state-of-the-art facility to manufacture microprocessors are so large (easily in excess of $1 billion), that to make this investment pay Intel *must* pursue experience curve effects, serving world markets

McDonald's Everywhere

Established in 1955, McDonald's faced a problem by the early 1980s: after three decades of rapid growth, the U.S. fast-food market was beginning to show signs of market saturation. McDonald's response to the slowdown was to expand abroad rapidly. In 1980, 28 percent of the chain's new McDonald's restaurant openings were abroad; in 1986 the figure was 40 percent, in 1990 it was close to 60 percent, and in 2000 it was almost 90 percent. Since the early 1980s, the firm's foreign revenues and profits have grown at 22 percent per year. By the end of 2000, the firm had 28,707 restaurants in 120 countries outside the United States. They generated $21 billion (53 percent) of the firm's $40 billion in revenues.

McDonald's shows no signs of slowing down. Management notes there is still only one McDonald's restaurant for every 500,000 people in the foreign countries in which it currently does business. This compares to one McDonald's restaurant for every 25,000 people in the United States. Also, the firm currently serves less than 1 percent of the world's population. Plans call for this foreign expansion to continue at a rapid rate. The firm opened more than 500 restaurants in Europe in 1999 and again in 2000, while the figures for Asia were around 600. In 1997, McDonald's said it would open 2,000 restaurants per year for the foreseeable future, the majority of them outside the United States. This included major expansion plans for Latin America, where the company planned to invest $2 billion over the next few years.

One key to the firm's successful foreign expansion is detailed planning. When McDonald's enters a foreign country, it does so only after careful preparation. In what is a fairly typical pattern, before McDonald's opened its first Polish restaurant in 1992, the firm spent 18 months establishing essential contacts and getting to know the local culture. Locations, real estate, construction, supply, personnel, and legal and government relations were all worked out in advance. In June 1992, a team of 50 employees from the United States, Russia, Germany, and Great Britain went to Poland to help with the opening of the first four restaurants. A primary objective was to hire and train local personnel. By mid-1994, all these employees except one had returned to their home country. Polish nationals who had now been brought up to the skill level required to run a McDonald's operation replaced them.

Another key to the firm's international strategy is the export of the management skills that spurred its growth in the United States. McDonald's U.S. success was built on a formula of close relations with suppliers, nationwide marketing might, tight control over store-level operating procedures, and a franchising system that encourages entrepreneurial individual franchisees. Although this system has worked flawlessly in the United States, some modifications must be made in other countries. One big challenge has been to infuse each store with the same gung-ho culture and standardized operating procedures that have been the hallmark of U.S. success. To aid in this task, McDonald's has enlisted the help of large partners

from a limited number of plants to maximize the cost economies that derive from scale and learning effects.

Leveraging Core Competencies

The term **core competence** refers to skills within the firm that competitors cannot easily match or imitate.[16] These skills may exist in any of the firm's value creation activities—production, marketing, R&D, human resources, general management, and so on. Such skills are typically expressed in product offerings that other firms find difficult to match or imitate, and thus the core competencies are the bedrock of a firm's competitive advantage. They enable a firm to reduce the costs of value creation (C) and/or to create perceived value (V) in such a way that premium pricing is possible. For example, Toyota has a core competence in the production of cars. It is able to produce high-quality, well-designed cars at a lower delivered cost than any other firm in the world. The skills that enable Toyota to do this seem to reside primarily in the firm's production and materials management functions.[17] McDonald's has a core competence in managing fast-food operations (it seems to be one of the most skilled firms in through joint ventures in many countries. The partners play a key role in learning and transplanting the organization's values to local employees.

Foreign partners have also played a key role in helping McDonald's adapt its marketing methods and menu to local conditions. Although U.S.-style fast food remains the staple fare on the menu, local products have been added. In Brazil, for example, McDonald's sells a soft drink made from the guarana, an Amazonian berry. Patrons of McDonald's in Malaysia, Singapore, and Thailand savor shakes flavored with durian, a foul-smelling (to U.S. tastes, at least) fruit considered an aphrodisiac by the locals. In Arab countries, McDonald's restaurants maintain "Halal" menus, which signify compliance with Islamic laws on food preparation, especially beef. In 1995, McDonald's opened the first kosher restaurant in suburban Jerusalem. The restaurant does not serve dairy products. And in India, the Big Mac is made with lamb and called the "Maharaja Mac."

McDonald's biggest problem, however, has been to replicate its U.S. supply chain in other countries. U.S. suppliers are fiercely loyal to McDonald's; they must be, because their fortunes are closely linked to those of McDonald's. McDonald's maintains very rigorous specifications for all the raw ingredients it uses—the key to its consistency and quality control. Outside the United States, however, McDonald's has found suppliers far less willing to make the investments required to meet its specifications. In Great Britain, for example, McDonald's had problems getting local bakeries to produce the hamburger bun. Af-

ter experiencing quality problems with two local bakeries, McDonald's built its own bakery to supply stores there. In a more extreme case, when McDonald's decided to open a store in Russia, it found that local suppliers lacked the capability to produce goods of the quality it demanded. The firm was forced to vertically integrate through the local food industry on a vast scale, importing potato seeds and bull semen and indirectly managing dairy farms, cattle ranches, and vegetable plots. It also had to construct the world's largest food-processing plant, at a cost of $40 million. The restaurant itself cost only $4.5 million.

Now that it has a successful foreign operation, McDonald's is experiencing benefits that go beyond the immediate financial ones. The firm increasingly is finding that its foreign franchisees are a source for valuable new ideas. The Dutch operation created a prefabricated modular store that can be moved over a weekend and is now widely used to set up temporary restaurants at big outdoor events. The Swedes came up with an enhanced meat freezer that is now used firmwide. And satellite stores, or low overhead mini-McDonald's, which are now appearing in hospitals and sports arenas in the United States, were invented in Singapore.

Sources: Kathleen Deveny et al., "McWorld?" *Business Week*, October 13, 1986, pp. 78–86; "Slow Food," *The Economist*, February 3, 1990, p. 64; Harlan S. Byrne, "Welcome to McWorld," *Barron's*, August 29, 1994, pp. 25–28; Andrew E. Serwer, "McDonald's Conquers the World," *Fortune*, October 17, 1994, pp. 103–116; and McDonald's website at www.mcdonalds.com.

the world in this industry); Toys "Я" Us has a core competence in managing high-volume, discount toy stores (it is perhaps the most skilled firm in the world in this business); Procter & Gamble has a core competence in developing and marketing name brand consumer products (it is one of the most skilled firms in the world in this business); Wal-Mart has a core competence in information systems and logistics; MTV has a core competence in managing the programming and delivery of cable TV music and related offerings.

For such firms, global expansion is a way of further exploiting the value creation potential of their skills and product offerings by applying those skills and products in a larger market. The potential for creating value from such a strategy is greatest when the skills and products of the firm are most unique, when the value placed on them by consumers is great, and when there are very few capable competitors with similar skills and/or products in foreign markets. Firms with unique and valuable skills can often realize enormous returns by applying those skills, and the products they produce, to foreign markets where indigenous competitors lack similar skills and products. MTV has built a vibrant global business by leveraging its skills in the programming and delivery of music and related content and applying those skills to local markets where indigenous competitors lacked equivalent skills. The network's success has raised the value (V) that viewers ascribe to MTV and, by extension, the value that advertisers ascribe to an advertising slot on an MTV channel. In turn, this has enabled MTV to command a higher price for advertising slots than competitors. Another example, that of McDonald's, is detailed in the accompanying Management Focus. McDonald's has profited by leveraging its core competence in running fast-food restaurants to foreign markets where indigenous competitors either did not exist or lacked similar skills.

In earlier eras, U.S. firms such as Kellogg, Coca-Cola, H. J. Heinz, and Procter & Gamble expanded overseas to exploit their skills in developing and marketing name brand consumer products. These skills and the resulting products, which were developed in the U.S. market during the 1950s and 60s, yielded enormous returns when applied to European markets, where most indigenous competitors lacked similar marketing skills and products. Their near-monopoly on consumer marketing skills allowed these U.S. firms to dominate many European consumer product markets during the 1960s and 70s. Similarly, in the 1970s and 80s, many Japanese firms expanded globally to exploit their skills in production, materials management, and new product development—skills that many of their indigenous North American and European competitors seemed to lack at the time. Today, retail companies such as Wal-Mart and financial companies such as Citicorp, Merrill Lynch, and American Express are transferring the valuable skills they developed in their core home market to other developed and emerging markets where indigenous competitors lack those skills. The same can be said of MTV, profiled in the opening case.

Leveraging Subsidiary Skills

Implicit in the discussion of leveraging core competencies is the idea that skills are developed first at home and than transferred to foreign operations. Thus, MTV developed its programming skills in the United States and McDonald's its skills in managing fast-food restaurants before each enterprise decided to transfer them to foreign locations. However, for more mature multinationals that have already established a network of subsidiary operations in foreign markets, the development of valuable skills can just as well occur in foreign subsidiaries.[18] Skills can be created anywhere within a multinational's global network of operations, wherever people have the opportunity and incentive to try new ways of doing things. The creation of skills that help to lower the costs of production, or to enhance perceived value and support higher product pricing, are not the monopoly of the corporate center.

Leveraging the skills created within subsidiaries and applying them to other operations within the firm's global network may create value. For example, as noted in the Management Focus, McDonald's increasingly is finding that its foreign franchisees are a source of valuable new ideas. Hewlett-Packard has decentralized the authority for the design and production of many of its leading-edge ink-jet printers to its operation in Singapore. Hewlett-Packard made this decision after employees in Singapore distinguished themselves by finding ways to reduce production costs through better product design. Hewlett-Packard now views its Singapore subsidiary as an important source for valuable new knowledge about production and product design that can be applied to other activities within the firm's global network of operations.[19]

For the managers of the multinational enterprise, this phenomenon creates important new challenges. First, they must have the humility to recognize that valuable skills can arise anywhere within the firm's global network, not just at the corporate center. Second, they must establish an incentive system that encourages local employees to acquire new skills. This is not as easy as it sounds. Creating new skills involves a degree of risk. Not all new skills add value. For every valuable idea created by a McDonald's subsidiary in a foreign country, there may be several failures. The management of the multinational must install incentives that encourage employees to take the necessary risks. They must reward people for successes and not sanction them unnecessarily for taking risks that did not pan out. Third, managers must have a process for identifying when valuable new skills have been created in a subsidiary, and finally, they need to act as facilitators, helping to transfer valuable skills within the firm. We shall discuss these issues in more depth in the next chapter.

Pressures for Cost Reductions and Local Responsiveness ▮

Firms that compete in the global marketplace typically face two types of competitive pressure. They face *pressures for cost reductions* and *pressures to be locally responsive* (see Figure 12.4). These competitive pressures place conflicting demands on a firm. Responding to pressures for cost reductions requires that a firm try to minimize its unit costs. Attaining such a goal may necessitate that a firm base its productive activities at the most favorable low-cost location, wherever in the world that might be. It may also necessitate that a firm offer a standardized product to the global marketplace. This helps the firm spread the fixed costs of developing a product offering over as large a volume as possible, thereby lowering its average unit costs. Offering a standardized product also enables the firm to attain other scale economies and ride down the experience curve as quickly as possible. In contrast, responding to pressures to be locally responsive requires that a firm differentiate its product offering and marketing strategy from country to country in an attempt to accommodate the diverse demands that arise from national differences in consumer tastes and preferences, business practices, distribution channels, competitive conditions, and government policies. Because customizing product offerings to different national requirements can involve significant duplication and a lack of product standardization, the result may be to raise costs.

Some firms, such as Firm A in Figure 12.4, face high pressures for cost reductions and low pressures for local responsiveness. Others, such as Firm B, face low pressures for cost reductions and high pressures for local responsiveness. Many others are in the position of Firm C in Figure 12.4. They face high pressures for cost reductions and high pressures for local responsiveness. Dealing with these conflicting and contradictory pressures is a difficult strategic challenge for a firm, primarily because being locally responsive tends to raise costs. In the remainder of this section, we shall look at the source of pressures for cost reductions and local responsiveness. In the next section, we look at the strategies that firms adopt to deal with these pressures.

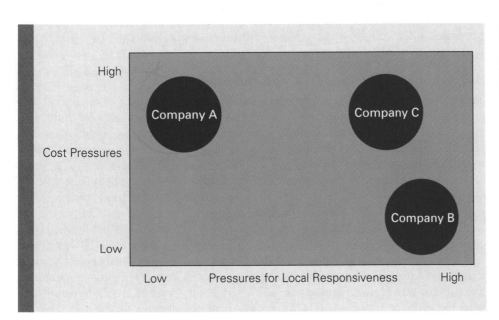

Figure 12.4

Pressures for Cost Reduction and Local Responsiveness

Pressures for Cost Reductions

Increasingly, international businesses are facing pressures for cost reductions. Responding to pressures for cost reduction requires a firm to try to lower the costs of value creation by mass producing a standardized product at the optimal location in the world, wherever that might be, in order to realize location and experience curve economies. Cost reduction pressures can be particularly intense in industries producing commodity-type products where meaningful differentiation on nonprice factors is difficult and price is the main competitive weapon. This tends to be the case for products that serve universal needs. Universal needs exist when the tastes and preferences of consumers in different nations are similar if not identical. This is the case for conventional commodity products such as bulk chemicals, petroleum, steel, sugar, and the like. It also tends to be the case for many industrial and consumer products; for example, handheld calculators, semiconductor chips, personal computers, and liquid crystal display screens. Pressures for cost reductions are also intense in industries where major competitors are based in low-cost locations, where there is persistent excess capacity, and where consumers are powerful and face low switching costs. Many commentators have also argued that the liberalization of the world trade and investment environment in recent decades, by facilitating greater international competition, has generally increased cost pressures.[20]

Pressures for cost reductions have been intense in the global tire industry in recent years. Tires are essentially a commodity product where meaningful differentiation is difficult and price is the main competitive weapon. The major buyers of tires, automobile firms, are powerful and face low switching costs, so they have been playing tire firms off against each other in an attempt to get lower prices. And the decline in global demand for automobiles in the early 1990s created serious excess capacity in the tire industry, with as much as 25 percent of world capacity standing idle. The result was a worldwide price war with almost all tire firms suffering heavy losses in the 1990s. In response to the resulting cost pressures, most tire firms are now trying to rationalize their operations in a manner that is consistent with the attainment of a low cost position. This includes moving production facilities to low-cost facilities and offering globally standardized products to try to realize experience curve economies.[21]

Pressures for Local Responsiveness

Pressures for local responsiveness arise from a number of sources including (*i*) differences in consumer tastes and preferences, (*ii*) differences in infrastructure and traditional practices, (*iii*) differences in distribution channels, and (*iv*) host government demands.

Differences in Consumer Tastes and Preferences

Strong pressures for local responsiveness emerge when consumer tastes and preferences differ significantly between countries, as they may for historic or cultural reasons. In such cases, product and/or marketing messages have to be customized to appeal to the tastes and preferences of local consumers. This typically creates pressure to delegate production and marketing functions to national subsidiaries.

The opening case provided a good example of this. Other things being equal, MTV would probably have preferred to centralize as much programming and content in the United States as possible. Offering standardized programming and content around the world would have allowed MTV to realize scale economies by leveraging its fixed costs of programming and content development over a global viewer base. However, this strategy essentially failed. Instead, to gain viewers in different countries, MTV found that it needs to respond to local tastes and preferences, customizing its programming and content accordingly. Thus, while "MTV Cricket in Control" would be unlikely to whet the appetite of U.S. viewers, it is an important program in India.

ManagementFocus

Tailoring World Cars to the U.S. Market

American consumers love their light pickup trucks. When the last serious recession hit the American automobile market in the early 1990s, sales of light trucks continued to grow through the slowdown at an astonishing 12 percent a year. The lesson was not lost on Toyota, whose Toyota Land Cruiser and Four Runner models did well. But there was a big hole in Toyota's product offerings; the company did not sell a full-size pickup truck to compete with the rugged offerings from General Motors and Ford so beloved by American consumers.

Toyota's first attempt to fix this problem was the T100, a heavy-duty truck launched in the United States in November 1992. But while the T100 had the look of a rugged pickup, it lacked the power. Americans have a thirst for pickups with powerful V8 engines that can haul large loads with ease, but the T100 had only a V6 engine. Plus, in trials it under-performed other smaller pickups with V6 engines—not a good omen. Soon after launch, it was clear that the T100 would do little to help Toyota capture share in the U.S. pickup truck market. By February 1, 1993, Toyota had sold only 2,500 T100s, well short of the 50,000 annual rate it aimed for. Toyota replaced the T100 with a more Americanized product, the Toyota Tundra, in mid-2000. The Toyota Tundra doesn't just look like a heavy-duty pickup truck; it also comes powered to perform like one with a V8 engine. Reflecting the enhanced responsiveness to the U.S. market, Toyota hopes to sell about 100,000 Tundras a year in the United States, but it also recognizes that there will be few opportunities for selling the Tundra outside the United States—it's just too American.

Toyota is not alone in learning this lesson. Another Japanese company, Nissan, decided in late 2000 to do what would have been unthinkable a year earlier—let U.S. engineers and planners be completely responsible for the development of most vehicles sold in North America. Among other things, Nissan is conducting focus group sessions with American children, asking them for ideas about cup holders, storage, and new features for a range of minivans Nissan plans to launch in 2003. According to a Nissan spokesperson, the company is taking this approach because "we tried for a long time to design cars in Japan and shove them down American consumers throats. It didn't work very well."

Honda is taking a similar tact with its next-generation sport utility vehicle, code-named Model X, which is scheduled for a 2003 introduction. Although Honda has long delegated design work to U.S. engineers, in an attempt to keep costs down, Honda's Japanese management initially wanted its U.S. product designers to base the Model X on a recycled platform developed in Japan. After some hard lobbying on this issue, the Japanese gave way to the desires of American engineers, who wanted an all-American car. But then the Japanese wanted the Model X to have just two rows of seats, while the U.S. designers were pushing for a larger vehicle with three rows of seats. The Japanese reasoned that if consumers wanted three rows of seats, they would buy a minivan. To overcome Japanese objections, the American designers flew several of Honda's Japanese executives to the United States and for several days took them to the homes of American families that drove large Ford Expeditions. The Japanese observed how mothers utilized the three rows of seats hauling their children and neighborhood kids to soccer games and how many families used the third row for their dogs. According to the Model X's designers, had the market research been done in Japan, designers would have missed such characteristic behavior of the American middle class. As a result, they may have designed an SUV that appealed less to the tastes and preferences of the American consumer.

Sources: N. Shirouzu, "Tailoring World Cars to U.S. Tastes," *Wall Street Journal,* January 15, 2001, p. B1, 6, and P. Dean, "Autos: California Style," *Los Angeles Times,* April 1, 1999, p. A9.

The automobile industry in the 1980s and early 1990s moved toward the creation of "world cars." The idea was that global companies such as General Motors, Ford, and Toyota would be able to sell the same basic vehicle the world over, sourcing it from centralized production locations. If successful, the strategy would have enabled automobile companies to reap significant gains from global scale economies. However, this strategy has frequently run aground upon the hard rocks of consumer reality. Consumers in different automobile markets seem to have different tastes and preferences, and these require different types of vehicles. For example, North American consumers show a strong demand for pickup trucks. This is particularly true in the South and West where many families have a pickup truck as a second or third car. But in European countries, pickup trucks are seen purely as utility vehicles and are purchased primarily by firms rather than individuals. As a consequence, the marketing message needs to be tailored to take into account the different nature of demand in North America and Europe. The accompanying Management Focus gives some examples of this in the U.S. automobile market.

As a counterpoint, in a now classic article, Harvard Business School Professor Theodore Levitt argued that consumer demands for local customization are on the decline worldwide.[22] According to Levitt, modern communication and transportation technologies have created the conditions for a convergence of the tastes and preferences of consumers from different nations. The result is the emergence of enormous global markets for standardized consumer products. Levitt cites worldwide acceptance of McDonald's hamburgers, Coca-Cola, Levi Strauss jeans, and Sony television sets, all of which are sold as standardized products, as evidence of the increasing homogeneity of the global marketplace.

Levitt's argument, however, has been characterized as extreme by many commentators. For example, Christopher Bartlett and Sumantra Ghoshal have observed that, in the consumer electronics industry, consumers reacted to an overdose of standardized global products by showing a renewed preference for products that are differentiated to local conditions.[23] They note that Amstrad, the British computer and electronics firm, got its start by recognizing and responding to local consumer needs. Amstrad captured a major share of the British audio player market by moving away from the standardized inexpensive music centers marketed by global firms such as Sony and Matsushita. Amstrad's product was encased in teak rather than metal cabinets and had a control panel tailor-made to appeal to British consumers' preferences. In response, Matsushita reversed its earlier bias toward standardized global design and placed more emphasis on local customization. Similarly, as we saw in the opening case, to fight off competitive threats from local competitors, MTV customized its programming and content to tastes and preferences in local markets. In direct counterpoint to Levitt's thesis, the music industry seems to have moved away from global megastars and toward more local tastes.

Differences in Infrastructure and Traditional Practices

Pressures for local responsiveness emerge when there are differences in infrastructure and/or traditional practices between countries. In such circumstances, the product may need to be customized to the distinctive infrastructure and practices of different nations. This may necessitate the delegation of manufacturing and production functions to foreign subsidiaries. For example, in North America, consumer electrical systems are based on 110 volts, while in some European countries 240-volt systems are standard. Thus, domestic electrical appliances have to be customized for this difference in infrastructure. Traditional practices also often vary across nations. For example, in Great Britain, people drive on the left side of the road, thus creating a demand for right-hand drive cars, whereas in neighboring France, people drive on the right side of the road, thus creating a demand for left-hand drive cars. Obviously automobiles have to be customized for this difference in traditional practices.

While many of the country differences in infrastructure are rooted in history, some are quite recent. For example, in the wireless telecommunication industry, technical standards vary around the world. A technical standard known as GSM is common in Europe, while an alternative standard, referred to as CDMA, is more common in the United States and parts of Asia. Equipment designed for GSM will not work on a CDMA network, and vice versa. Thus, companies such as Nokia, Motorola, and Ericsson, which manufacture wireless handsets and infrastructure such as switches, need to customize their product offering according to the technical standard prevailing in a given country.

Differences in Distribution Channels

A firm's marketing strategies may have to be responsive to differences in distribution channels between countries. This may necessitate the delegation of marketing functions to national subsidiaries. In Germany, for example, a handful of food retailers dominate the market, but the market is very fragmented in neighboring Italy. Thus, retail chains have considerable buying power in Germany but relatively little in Italy. Dealing with these differences requires different marketing approaches on the part of detergent firms. Similarly, in the pharmaceutical industry, the British and Japanese distribution systems are radically different from the U.S. system. British and Japanese doctors will not accept or respond favorably to an American-style high-pressure sales force. Thus, pharmaceutical firms have to adopt different marketing practices in Great Britain and Japan compared to the United States (soft sell versus hard sell).

Host-Government Demands

Economic and political demands imposed by host-country governments may necessitate a degree of local responsiveness. For example, the politics of health care around the world requires that pharmaceutical firms manufacture in multiple locations. Pharmaceutical firms are subject to local clinical testing, registration procedures, and pricing restrictions, all of which require that the manufacturing and marketing of a drug should meet local requirements. Because governments and government agencies control a significant proportion of the health care budget in most countries, they can demand a high level of local responsiveness.

Threats of protectionism, economic nationalism, and local content rules (which require that a certain percentage of a product be manufactured locally), all dictate that international businesses manufacture locally. Consider Bombardier, the Canadian-based manufacturer of railcars, aircraft, jet boats, and snowmobiles. Bombardier has 12 railcar factories across Europe. Critics of the firm argue that the resulting duplication of manufacturing facilities leads to high costs and explains why Bombardier makes lower profit margins on its railcar operations than on its other business lines. Managers at Bombardier argue that in Europe, informal rules with regard to local content favor people who use local workers. To sell railcars in Germany, they claim, you must manufacture in Germany. The same goes for Belgium, Austria, and France. To address its cost structure in Europe, Bombardier has centralized its engineering and purchasing functions, but it has no plans to centralize manufacturing.[24]

Implications

Pressures for local responsiveness imply that it may not be possible for a firm to realize the full benefits from experience curve and location economies. For example, it may not be possible to serve the global marketplace from a single low-cost location, producing a globally standardized product and marketing it worldwide to achieve experience curve cost economies. The need to customize the product offering to local conditions may work against implementation of such a strategy. As noted earlier, automakers have found that Japanese, American, and European consumers demand different kinds of cars, and that this necessitates producing products that are customized for local markets. In response, Honda, Ford, and Toyota are establishing top-to-bottom design and production facilities in each of these regions to better serve local demands. While such customization brings benefits, it also limits a firm's ability to realize significant experience curve cost economies and location economies.

In addition, pressures for local responsiveness imply that it may not be possible to leverage the skills and products associated with a firm's core competencies wholesale from one nation to another. Concessions often have to be made to local conditions. Despite being depicted as the poster boy for the proliferation of standardized global products, even McDonald's has found it has to customize its product offering (i.e., its menu) to account for national differences in tastes and preferences (see the Management Focus for details).

▮ Strategic Choices

Firms use four basic strategies to enter and compete in the international environment: an international strategy, a multidomestic strategy, a global strategy, and a transnational strategy.[25] Each of these strategies has its advantages and disadvantages. The appropriateness of each strategy varies with the extent of pressures for cost reductions and local responsiveness. Figure 12.5 illustrates when each of these strategies is most appropriate. In this section we describe each strategy, identify when it is appropriate, and discuss the pros and cons of each.

▮ International Strategy

Firms that pursue an international strategy try to create value by transferring valuable skills and products to foreign markets where indigenous competitors lack those skills and products. Most international firms have created value by transferring differentiated product offerings developed at home to new markets overseas. Accordingly, they tend to centralize product development functions at home (e.g., R&D). However, they also tend to establish manufacturing and marketing functions in each major country in which they do business. But while they may undertake some local customization of product offering and marketing strategy, this tends to be limited. In most international firms, the head office retains tight control over marketing and product strategy.

International firms include the likes of Toys "Я" Us, McDonald's, IBM, Kellogg, Procter & Gamble, Wal-Mart, and Microsoft. Microsoft, for example, develops the core architecture underlying its products at its Redmond campus in Washington state and also writes the bulk of the computer code there. However, the company does allow national subsidiaries to develop their own marketing and distribution strategy and to customize aspects of the product to account for such basic local differences as language and alphabet. The accompanying Management Focus profiles IKEA, a Swedish retailer which has traditionally pursued an international strategy, transferring its retailing formula developed in Sweden wholesale into other markets. As the feature makes clear, however, this strategy did not work for IKEA once it opened stores in the United States.

An international strategy makes sense if a firm has a valuable core competence that indigenous competitors in foreign markets lack and if the firm faces relatively weak

Figure 12.5

Four Basic Strategies

pressures for local responsiveness and cost reductions (as is the case for Microsoft). In such circumstances, an international strategy can be very profitable. However, when pressures for local responsiveness are high, firms pursuing this strategy lose to firms that emphasize customizing the product offering and market strategy to local conditions. IKEA experienced this problem in the United States and subsequently shifted its strategy to accommodate local differences in tastes and preferences (see the Management Focus). Similarly, when MTV expanded into Europe, it pursued an international strategy, but as we saw from the opening case, this strategy failed. In addition, due to the duplication of manufacturing facilities, firms that pursue an international strategy tend to suffer from high operating costs. This makes the strategy inappropriate in manufacturing industries where cost pressures are high.

Multidomestic Strategy

Firms pursuing a multidomestic strategy orient themselves toward achieving maximum local responsiveness. The key distinguishing feature of multidomestic firms is that they extensively customize both their product offering and their marketing strategy to match different national conditions. Consistent with this, they also tend to establish a complete set of value creation activities, including production, marketing, and R&D, in each major national market in which they do business. As a consequence, they are generally unable to realize value from experience curve effects and location economies. Accordingly, many multidomestic firms have a high cost structure. They also tend to do a poor job of leveraging core competencies within the firm.

A multidomestic strategy makes most sense when there are high pressures for local responsiveness and low pressures for cost reductions. The high cost structure associated with the duplication of production facilities makes this strategy inappropriate in industries where cost pressures are intense. Another weakness associated with this strategy is that many multidomestic firms have developed into decentralized federations in which each national subsidiary functions in a largely autonomous manner. This was exemplified by the failure of Philips NV to establish its V2000 VCR format as the standard in the industry during the late 1970s. Its U.S. subsidiary refused to adopt the V2000 format; instead, it bought VHS-format VCRs produced by Matsushita and put its own label on them!

Global Strategy

Firms that pursue a global strategy focus on increasing profitability by reaping the cost reductions that come from experience curve effects and location economies. That is, they are pursuing a low cost strategy. The production, marketing, and R&D activities of firms pursuing a global strategy are concentrated in a few favorable locations. Global firms tend not to customize their product offering and marketing strategy to local conditions because customization raises costs (it involves shorter production runs and the duplication of functions). Instead, global firms prefer to market a standardized product worldwide so they can reap the maximum benefits from the economies of scale that underlie the experience curve. They may also use their cost advantage to support aggressive pricing in world markets.

This strategy makes most sense where there are strong pressures for cost reductions and where demands for local responsiveness are minimal. Increasingly, these conditions prevail in many industrial goods industries. In the semiconductor industry, for example, global standards have created enormous demands for standardized global products. Accordingly, firms such as Intel, Texas Instruments, and Motorola all pursue a global strategy. However, as we noted earlier, these conditions are not found in many consumer goods markets, where demands for local responsiveness remain high (e.g., processed food products). The strategy is inappropriate when demands for local responsiveness are high.

IKEA

Established in the 1940s in Sweden by Ingvar Kamprad, IKEA has grown rapidly in recent years to become one of the world's largest retailers of home furnishings. In its initial push to expand globally, IKEA largely ignored the retailing rule that international success involves tailoring product lines closely to national tastes and preferences. Instead, IKEA stuck with the vision, articulated by founder Kamprad, that the company should sell a basic product range that is "typically Swedish" wherever it ventures in the world. The company also remained primarily production oriented; that is, the Swedish management and design group decided what it was going to sell and then presented it to the worldwide public—often with little research as to what the public actually wanted. The company also emphasized its Swedish roots in its international advertising, even insisting on a blue-and-gold color scheme for its stores.

Despite breaking some key rules of international retailing, the formula of selling Swedish-designed products in the same manner everywhere seemed to work. Between 1974 and 2000, IKEA expanded from a company with 10 stores, only one of which was outside Scandinavia, and annual revenues of $210 million to a group with 159 stores in 30 countries and sales of $8.6 billion. In 2000 only 8 percent of sales were generated in Sweden. Of the balance, 21.6 percent came from Germany, 49.5 percent from the rest of Europe, and 16 percent from North America. IKEA is beginning to expand in Asia, which generated 3 percent of total sales in 2000.

The foundation of IKEA's success has been to offer consumers good value for money. IKEA's approach starts with a global network of suppliers, which now numbers 1,960 firms in 53 countries. An IKEA supplier gains long-term contracts, technical advice, and leased equipment from the company. In return, IKEA demands an exclusive contract and low prices. IKEA's designers work closely with suppliers to build savings into the products from the outset by designing products that can be produced at a low cost. IKEA displays its enormous range of more than 10,000 products in cheap out-of-town stores. It sells most of its furniture as kits for customers to take home and assemble themselves. The firm reaps huge economies of scale from the size of each store and the big production runs made possible by selling the same products all over the world. This strategy allows IKEA to match its rivals on quality, while undercutting them by up to 30 percent on price and still maintaining a healthy after-tax return on sales of about 7 percent.

This strategy worked well until IKEA entered the North American market. Between 1985 and 1996, IKEA opened six stores in North America, but unlike the company's experience across Europe, the stores did not quickly become profitable. As early as 1990, it

Transnational Strategy

Christopher Bartlett and Sumantra Ghoshal have argued that in today's environment, competitive conditions are so intense that to survive in the global marketplace, firms *must exploit experience-based cost economies and location economies, they must transfer core competencies within the firm, and they must do all of this while paying attention to pressures for local responsiveness.*[26] They note that in the modern multinational enterprise, core competencies do not just reside in the home country. Valuable skills can develop in any of the firm's worldwide operations. Thus, Bartlett and Ghoshal maintain that the flow of skills and product offerings should not be all one way, from home firm to foreign subsidiary, as in the case of firms pursuing an international strategy. Rather, the flow should also be from foreign subsidiary to home country, and from foreign subsidiary to foreign subsidiary—a process they refer to as **global learning.**[27] Bartlett and Ghoshal refer to the strategy pursued by firms that are trying to simultaneously create value in these different ways as a **transnational strategy.**

A transnational strategy makes sense when a firm faces high pressures for cost reductions, high pressures for local responsiveness, and where there are significant opportunities for leveraging valuable skills within a multinational's global network of operations. In some ways, firms that pursue a transnational strategy are trying to siwas clear that IKEA's North American operations were in trouble. Part of the problem was adverse movement in exchange rates. In 1985 the exchange rate was $1=8.6 Swedish kronor; by 1990 it was $1=SKr5.8. At this exchange rate many products imported from Sweden did not look inexpensive to American consumers.

But there was more to IKEA's problems than adverse movements in exchange rates. IKEA's unapologetically Swedish products, which had sold so well across Europe, jarred with American tastes and sometimes physiques. Swedish beds were narrow and measured in centimeters. IKEA did not sell the matching bedroom suites that Americans liked. Its kitchen cupboards were too narrow for the large dinner plates. Its glasses were too small for a nation that added ice to everything. The drawers in IKEA's bedroom chests were too shallow for American consumers, who tend to store sweaters in them. And the company made the mistake of selling European-sized curtains that did not fit American windows. As one senior IKEA manager joked later, "Americans just wouldn't lower their ceilings to fit our curtains."

By 1991, the company's top management realized that if it was going to succeed in North America, it would have to customize its product offering to North American tastes. The company set about redesigning its product range. The drawers on bedroom chests were designed to be two inches deeper, and sales immediately increased by 30 to 40 percent. IKEA now sells American-style king- and queen-size beds, measured in inches, and it sells them as part of complete bedroom suites. It redesigned its kitchen furniture and kitchenware to better appeal to American tastes. The company also boosted the amount of products sourced locally from 15 percent in 1990 to 45 percent in 1997, which makes the company far less vulnerable to adverse exchange rate movements. By 2000, about one-third of IKEA's total product offerings were designed exclusively for the U.S. market.

This break with IKEA's traditional strategy seems to be paying off. Between 1990 and 1994, IKEA's North American sales tripled to $480 million, and they nearly doubled again to about $900 million in 1997 and reached $1.38 billion in 2000. The company claims it has been making a profit in North America since early 1993, although it does not release precise figures and does admit that its profit rate is lower in America than in Europe. Still, the company is pushing ahead with plans for further expansions in North America, including a goal of opening 15 new stores between 2000 and 2005, which will bring its total to 35.

Sources: "Furnishing the World," *The Economist,* November 19, 1994, pp. 79–80; H. Carnegy, "Struggle to Save the Soul of IKEA," *Financial Times,* March 27, 1995, p. 12; J. Flynn and L. Bongiorno, "IKEA's New Game Plan," *Business Week,* October 6, 1997, pp. 99–102; and IKEA's website at www.ikea.com.

multaneously achieve cost and differentiation advantages. In terms of the framework summarized in Figure 12.1, they are trying to simultaneously lower C and increase V. As attractive as this may sound, the strategy is not easy to pursue. Pressures for local responsiveness and cost reductions place conflicting demands on a firm. Being locally responsive raises costs. How can a firm effectively pursue a transnational strategy?

Some clues can be derived from the case of Caterpillar. In the 1980s, the need to compete with low-cost competitors such as Komatsu and Hitachi of Japan forced Caterpillar to look for greater cost economies. At the same time, variations in construction practices and government regulations across countries meant that Caterpillar had to remain responsive to local demands. Therefore, as illustrated in Figure 12.6, Caterpillar was confronted with significant pressures for cost reductions and for local responsiveness.

To deal with cost pressures, Caterpillar redesigned its products to use many identical components and invested in a few large-scale component-manufacturing facilities, sited at favorable locations, to fill global demand and realize scale economics. The firm also augmented the centralized manufacturing of components with assembly plants in each of its major global markets. At these plants, Caterpillar added local product features, tailoring the finished product to local needs. By pursuing this strategy, Caterpillar realized many of the benefits of global manufacturing while also responding to

425

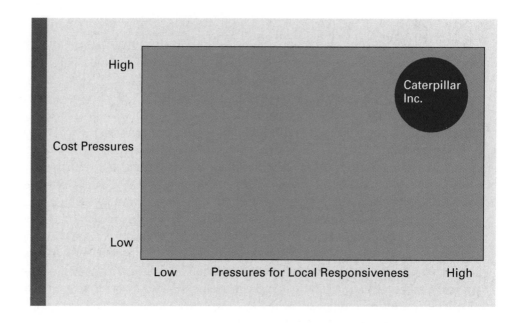

Figure 12.6

Cost Pressures and Pressures for Local Responsiveness Facing Caterpillar

pressures for local responsiveness by differentiating its product among national markets.[28] Caterpillar started to pursue this strategy in the early 1980s and by 1997 had doubled output per employee, significantly reducing its overall cost structure. Meanwhile, Komatsu and Hitachi, which are still wedded to a Japan-centric global strategy, have seen their cost advantages evaporate and have been steadily losing market share to Caterpillar.

Unilever, once a classic multidomestic firm, has had to shift toward more of a transnational strategy. A rise in low-cost competition, which increased cost pressures, forced Unilever to look for ways of rationalizing its detergent business. During the 1980s, Unilever had 17 largely self-contained detergent operations in Europe alone. The duplication of assets and marketing was enormous. Because Unilever was so fragmented, it could take as long as four years for the firm to introduce a new product across Europe. Now Unilever has integrated its European operation into a single entity, with detergents being manufactured in a handful of cost-efficient plants, and standard packaging and advertising being used across Europe. According to the firm, the result was an annual cost saving of more than $200 million. At the same time, however, due to national differences in distribution channels and brand awareness, Unilever recognizes that it must still remain locally responsive, even while it tries to realize economies from consolidating production and marketing at the optimal locations.[29] One might also argue that the MTV Networks shifted from an international to a transnational strategy in the 1990s (see the opening case). Rather than creating everything in the United States, MTV now tries to strike a balance between the need to maintain uniformity in operating principles and the "frenetic look" of MTV programming across its global operations and the need to customize programming and content to local tastes and preferences.

Bartlett and Ghoshal admit that building an organization that is capable of supporting a transnational strategic posture is a complex and difficult task. Simultaneously trying to achieve cost efficiencies, global learning (the leveraging of skills), and local responsiveness places contradictory demands on an organization. Exactly how a firm can deal with the dilemmas posed by such difficult organizational issues is discussed in more detail in Chapter 13. For now, it is important to note that the organizational problems associated with pursuing what are essentially conflicting objectives constitute a major impediment to the pursuit of a transnational strategy. Firms that attempt to pursue a transnational strategy can become bogged down in an organizational morass that only leads to inefficiencies.

Also, Bartlett and Ghoshal may be overstating the case for the transnational strategy. They present the transnational strategy as the only viable strategy. While no one doubts that in some industries the firm that can adopt a transnational strategy will have a competitive advantage, in other industries, global, multidomestic, and international strategies remain viable. In the semiconductor industry, for example, pressures for local customization are minimal and competition is purely a cost game, in which case a global strategy, not a transnational strategy, is optimal. This is the case in many industrial goods markets where the product serves universal needs. On the other hand, the argument can be made that to compete in certain consumer goods markets, such as the automobile and consumer electronics industry, a firm has to try to adopt a transnational strategy.

Summary

The advantages and disadvantages of each of the four strategies discussed above are summarized in Table 12.1. While a transnational strategy appears to offer the most advantages, implementing a transnational strategy raises difficult organizational issues. As shown in Figure 12.5, the appropriateness of each strategy depends on the relative strength of pressures for cost reductions and for local responsiveness.

Strategy	Advantages	Disadvantages
Global	Exploit experience curve effects Exploit location economies	Lack of local responsiveness
International	Transfer core competencies to foreign markets	Lack of local responsiveness Inability to realize location economies Failure to exploit experience curve effects
Multidomestic	Customize product offerings and marketing in accordance with local responsiveness	Inability to realize location economies Failure to exploit experience curve effects Failure to transfer core competencies to foreign markets
Transnational	Exploit experience curve effects Exploit location economies Customize product offerings and marketing in accordance with local responsiveness Reap benefits of global learning	Difficult to implement due to organizational problems

Table 12.1

The Advantages and Disadvantages of the Four Strategies

Chapter Summary

In this chapter we reviewed basic principles of strategy and the various ways in which firms can profit from global expansion, and we looked at the strategies that firms that compete globally can adopt. The following points have been made in this chapter:

1. A firm's strategy can be defined as the actions that managers take to attain the goals of the firm. For most firms, the preeminent goal is to maximize long-term profitability. Maximizing profitability requires firms to focus on value creation.

2. Due to national differences, it may pay a firm to base each value creation activity it performs at that location where factor conditions are most conducive to the performance of that activity. We refer to this strategy as focusing on the attainment of location economies.

3. By rapidly building sales volume for a standardized product, international expansion can assist a firm in moving down the experience curve.

4. International expansion may enable a firm to earn greater returns by transferring the skills and product offerings derived from its core competencies to markets where indigenous competitors lack those skills and product offerings.

5. A multinational firm can create additional value by identifying valuable skills created within its foreign subsidiaries and leveraging those skills within its global network of operations.

6. The best strategy for a firm to pursue often depends on a consideration of the pressures for cost reductions and for local responsiveness.

7. Pressures for cost reductions are greatest in industries producing commodity-type products where price is the main competitive weapon.

8. Pressures for local responsiveness arise from differences in consumer tastes and preferences, national infrastructure and traditional practices, distribution channels, and from host-government demands.

9. Firms pursuing an international strategy transfer the skills and products derived from distinctive competencies to foreign markets, while undertaking some limited local customization.

10. Firms pursuing a multidomestic strategy customize their product offering, marketing strategy, and business strategy to national conditions.

11. Firms pursuing a global strategy focus on reaping the cost reductions that come from experience curve effects and location economies.

12. Many industries are now so competitive that firms must adopt a transnational strategy. This involves a simultaneous focus on reducing costs, transferring skills and products, and boosting local responsiveness. Implementing such a strategy may not be easy.

Critical Discussion Questions

1. In a world of zero transportation costs, no trade barriers, and nontrivial differences between nations with regard to factor conditions, firms must expand internationally if they are to survive. Discuss.

2. Plot the position of the following firms on Figure 12.4: Procter & Gamble, IBM, Coca-Cola, Dow Chemicals, US Steel, McDonald's. In each case justify your answer.

3. Are the following global industries or multidomestic industries: bulk chemicals, pharmaceuticals, branded food products, moviemaking, television manufacture, personal computers, airline travel?

4. Discuss how the need for control over foreign operations varies with the strategy and core competencies of a firm. What are the implications of this for the choice of entry mode?

5. What do you see as the main organizational problems that are likely to be associated with implementation of a transnational strategy?

Global Strategy at General Motors

Closing Case

General Motors is one of the oldest multinational corporations in the world. Founded in 1908, GM established its first international operations in the 1920s. General Motors is now the world's largest industrial corporation and full-line automobile manufacturer with annual revenues in 2000 of $185 billion. The company sells 8 million vehicles per year, 3.2 million of which are produced and marketed outside of its North American base. In 2000, GM had a 27 percent share of the North American market and a 9 percent share of the market in the rest of the world.

Historically, most of GM's foreign operations have been concentrated in Western Europe. Local brand names such as Opel, Vauxhall, Saab, and Holden helped the company to capture a 12 percent market share in 2000, second only to that of Ford. Although GM has long had a presence in Latin America and Asia, until recently sales there accounted for only a relatively small fraction of the company's total international business.

However, GM's plans call for this to change rapidly over the next few years. Sensing that Asia, Latin America, and Eastern Europe may be the automobile industry's growth markets, in 1997 GM embarked on ambitious plans to invest $2.2 billion in four new manufacturing facilities in Argentina, Poland, China, and Thailand. This expansion goes hand in hand with a sea change in GM's philosophy toward the management of its international operations.

Traditionally, GM saw the developing world as a dumping ground for obsolete technology and outdated models. Just a few years ago, for example, GM's Brazilian factories were churning out U.S.-designed Chevy Chevettes that hadn't been produced in North America for years. GM's Detroit-based executives saw this as a way of squeezing the maximum cash flow from the company's investments in aging technology. GM managers in the developing world, however, took it as an indication that the center did not view developing world operations as being significant. This feeling was exacerbated by the fact that most operations in the developing world were instructed to carry out manufacturing and marketing plans formulated in the company's Detroit headquarters, rather than being trusted to develop their own.

In contrast, GM's European operations were traditionally managed on an arm's-length basis, with the company's national operations often being allowed to design their own cars and manufacturing facilities and formulate their own marketing strategies. This regional and national autonomy allowed GM's European operations to produce vehicles that were closely tailored to the needs of local customers. However, it also led to costly duplication in design and manufacturing operations and to a failure to share valuable technology, skills, and practices among subsidiaries. Thus, while General Motors exerted tight control over its operations in the developing world, its control over operations in Europe was perhaps too lax. The result was a company whose international operations lacked overall strategic coherence.

GM has been trying to change this since 1997 by switching from its Detroit-centric view of the world to a philosophy that centers of excellence may reside anywhere in the company's global operations. The company is trying to tap these centers of excellence to provide its global operations with the very latest technology. The four new manufacturing plants in the developing world are an embodiment of this new approach. Each is identical, each incorporates state-of-the-art technology, and each has been designed not by Americans, but by a team of Brazilian and German engineers. By building identical plants, GM should be able to mimic Toyota, whose plants are so much alike that a change in a car in Japan can be quickly replicated around the world. The plants are modeled after GM's Eisenach facility in Germany, which is managed by the company's Opel subsidiary. It was at the Eisenach plant that GM figured out how to implement the lean production system pioneered by Toyota. The plant is now the most efficient auto-manufacturing operation in Europe and the best within GM, with a productivity rate at least twice that of most North American assembly operations. Each of the new plants produce state-of-the-art vehicles for local consumption.

To realize scale economies, GM is also trying to design and build vehicles that share a common global platform. Engineering teams located in Germany, Detroit, South America, and Australia are designing these common vehicle platforms. Local plants are allowed to customize certain features of these vehicles to match the tastes and preferences of local customers. At the same time, adhering to a common global platform enables the company to spread its costs of designing a car over greater volume and to realize scale economies in the manufacture of shared components—both of which should help GM lower its overall cost structure. The first fruits of this effort include the 1998 Cadillac Seville, which was designed to be sold in more than 40 countries. GM's family of front-wheel-drive minivans was also designed around a common platform that allows the vehicles to be produced in multiple locations around the globe, as was the 1998 Opel Astra, which is GM's best-selling car in Europe.

Despite making bold moves in the direction of greater global integration, numerous problems can still be seen on GM's horizon. Compared to Ford, Toyota, or Daimler/Chrysler, GM still suffers from high costs, low perceived quality, and a profusion of brands. While its aggressive move into emerging markets may be based on the reasonable assumption that demand will grow strong in these areas, other automobile companies are also expanding their production facilities in the same markets, raising the specter of global excess capacity and price wars. Finally, and perhaps most significantly, there are those within GM who argue that the push toward "global cars" is misconceived. In particular, the German-based engineering staff at Opel's Russelsheim design facility, which takes the lead on design of many key global models, has voiced concerns that distinctively European engineering features they deem essential to a car's local success may be left by the wayside in a drive to devise what they see as blander "global" cars.

Sources: R. Blumenstein, "GM Is Building Plants in Developing Nations to Woo New Markets," *Wall Street Journal*, August 4, 1997, p. A1; Haig

Simonian, "GM Hopes to Turn Corner with New Astra," *Financial Times*, November 29, 1997, p. 15; D. Howes, "GM, Ford Play for Keeps Abroad," *Detroit News*, March 8, 1998, p. D1; and "The Global Gambles of General Motors," *The Economist*, June 24, 2000, pp. 67–68.

Case Discussion Questions

1. How would you characterize the strategy pursued by GM in the (a) developing world and (b) Europe before 1997?

2. What do you think were the likely competitive effects of the pre-1997 strategy?

3. How would you characterize the strategy that GM has been pursuing since 1997? How should this strategy affect GM's ability to create value in the global automobile market?

Notes

1. The concept of consumer surplus is an important one in economics. For a more detailed exposition, see D. Besanko, D. Dranove, M. Shanley, *Economics of Strategy* (New York: John Wiley & Sons, 1996).

2. However, P=V only in the special case where the company has a perfect monopoly, and where it can charge each customer a unique price that reflects the value of the product to that customer (i.e., where perfect price discrimination is possible). More generally, except in the limiting case of perfect price discrimination, even a monopolist will see most consumers capture some of the value of a product in the form of a consumer surplus.

3. This point is central to the work of Michael Porter, *Competitive Advantage* (New York: Free Press, 1985). See also chap. 4 in P. Ghemawat, *Commitment: The Dynamic of Strategy* (New York: Free Press, 1991).

4. M. E. Porter, *Competitive Strategy* (New York: Free Press, 1980).

5. Porter, *Competitive Advantage*.

6. Example is based on C. S. Trager, "Enter the Mini-Multinational," *Northeast International Business*, March 1989, pp. 13–14.

7. Empirical evidence does seem to indicate that, on average, international expansion is linked to greater firm profitability. For some recent examples, see M. A. Hitt, R. E. Hoskisson, and H. Kim, "International Diversification, Effects on Innovation and Firm Performance," *Academy of Management Journal* 40, no. 4 (1997), pp. 767–98; and S. Tallman and J. Li, "Effects of International Diversity and Product Diversity on the Performance of Multinational Firms," *Academy of Management Journal* 39, no. 1 (1996), pp. 179–96.

8. M. E. Porter, *The Competitive Advantage of Nations* (New York: Free Press, 1990).

9. R. B. Reich, *The Work of Nations* (New York: Alfred A. Knopf, 1991).

10. G. Hall and S. Howell, "The Experience Curve from an Economist's Perspective," *Strategic Management Journal* 6 (1985), pp. 197–212.

11. A. A. Alchain, "Reliability of Progress Curves in Airframe Production," *Econometrica* 31 (1963), pp. 697–93.

12. Hall and Howell, "The Experience Curve from an Economist's Perspective."

13. For a full discussion of the source of scale economies, see D. Besanko, D. Dranove, and M. Shanley, *Economics of Strategy* (New York: Wiley & Sons, 1996).

14. This estimate was provided by the Pharmaceutical Manufacturers Association.

15. "Matsushita Electrical Industrial in 1987," in *Transnational Management*, eds. C. A. Bartlett and S. Ghoshal (Homewood, IL: Richard D. Irwin, 1992).

16. This concept has been popularized by G. Hamel and C. K. Prahalad, *Competing for the Future* (Boston: Harvard Business School Press, 1994). The concept is grounded in the resource-based view of the firm (for a summary, see J. B. Barney, "Firm Resources and Sustained Competitive Advantage," *Journal of Management* 17 (1991), pp. 99–120, and K. R. Conner, "A Historical Comparison of Resource-Based Theory and Five Schools of Thought within Industrial Organization Economics: Do We Have a New Theory of the Firm?" *Journal of Management* 17 (1991), pp. 121–54.

17. J. P. Woomack, D. T. Jones, and D. Roos, *The Machine that Changed the World* (New York: Rawson Associates, 1990).

18. See J. Birkinshaw and N. Hood, "Multinational Subsidiary Evolution: Capability and Charter Change in Foreign-Owned Subsidiary Companies," *Academy of Management Review* 23 (October 1998), pp. 773–95, and A. K. Gupta and V. J. Govindarajan, "Knowledge Flows within

Multinational Corporations," *Strategic Management Journal* 21 (2000), pp. 473–96.

19. K. Ferdows, "Making the Most of Foreign Factories," *Harvard Business Review*, March–April 1997, pp. 73–88.

20. C. K. Prahalad and Yves L. Doz, *The Multinational Mission: Balancing Local Demands and Global Vision* (New York: Free Press, 1987). Prahalad and Doz actually talk about local responsiveness rather than local customization.

21. "The Tire Industry's Costly Obsession with Size," *The Economist*, June 8, 1993, pp. 65–66.

22. T. Levitt, "The Globalization of Markets," *Harvard Business Review*, May–June 1983, pp. 92–102.

23. C. A. Bartlett and S. Ghoshal, *Managing across Borders* (Boston: Harvard Business School Press, 1989).

24. C. J. Chipello, "Local Presence Is Key to European Deals," *Wall Street Journal*, June 30, 1998, p. A15.

25. This section is based on Bartlett and Ghoshal, *Managing across Borders*.

26. Bartlett and Ghoshal, *Managing across Borders*.

27. A recent empirical study seems to confirm this hypothesis. See J. Birkinshaw, N. Hood, and S. Jonsson, "Building Firm-Specific Advantages in Multinational Corporations: The Role of Subsidiary Initiative," *Strategic Management Journal* 19 (1998), pp. 221–41.

28. See P. Marsh and S. Wagstyle, "The Hungry Caterpillar," *Financial Times*, December 2, 1997, p. 22, and T. Hout, M. E. Porter, and E. Rudden, "How Global Firms Win Out," *Harvard Business Review*, September–October 1982, pp. 98–108.

29. Guy de Jonquieres, "Unilever Adopts a Clean Sheet Approach," *Financial Times*, October 21, 1991, p. 13.

The Organization of International Business

Unilever is one of the world's oldest multinational corporations with extensive product offerings in the food, detergent, and personal care businesses. It generates annual revenues in excess of $50 billion and sells more than 1,000 branded products in virtually every country. Detergents, which account for about 25 percent of corporate revenues, include well-known names such as Omo, which is sold in over 50 countries. Personal care products, which account for about 15 percent of sales, include Calvin Klein Cosmetics, Pepsodent toothpaste brands, Faberge hair care products, and Vaseline skin lotions. Food products account for the remaining 60 percent of sales and include strong offerings in margarine (where Unilever's market share in most countries exceeds 70 percent), tea, ice cream, frozen foods, and bakery products.

Historically, Unilever was organized on a decentralized basis. Subsidiary companies in each major national market were responsible for the production, marketing, sales, and distribution of products in that market. In Europe the company had 17 subsidiaries in the early 1990s, each focused on a different national market. Each was a profit center and each was held accountable for its own performance. This decentralization was viewed as a source of strength. The structure allowed local managers to match product offerings and marketing strategy to local tastes and preferences and to alter sales and distribution strategies to fit the prevailing retail systems. To drive the localization, Unilever recruited local managers to run local organizations; the U.S. subsidiary (Lever Brothers) was run by Americans, the Indian subsidiary by Indians, and so on.

To knit together the decentralized organization, Unilever worked to build a common organizational culture among its managers. For years, the company recruited people with similar backgrounds, values, and interests. The stated preference was for individuals with high levels of "sociability" who embrace the company's values, which emphasize cooperation and consensus building among managers. It is said that the company has been so successful at this that Unilever executives recognize one another at airports even when they have never met before. Unilever's senior management believes this corps of like-minded people is the reason its employees work so well together, despite their national diversity.

Unilever has also worked hard to periodically bring these managers together. Annual conferences on company strategy and executive education sessions at Unilever's management training center outside of London help establish connections between managers. The idea is to build an informal network of equals who know one another well and usually continue to meet and exchange experiences. Unilever also moves its young managers frequently, across borders, products, and division. This policy starts Unilever relationships early as well as increases know-how.

By the mid-1990s, the decentralized structure was increasingly out of step with a rapidly changing competitive environment. Unilever's global competitors, which include the Swiss firm Nestlé and Procter & Gamble from the United States, had been more successful than Unilever on several fronts—building global brands, reducing cost structure by consolidating manufacturing operations at a few choice locations, and executing simultaneous product launches in several national markets. Unilever's decentralized structure worked against efforts to build global or regional brands. It also meant lots of duplication, particularly in manufacturing, a lack of scale economies, and a high cost structure. Unilever also found that it was falling behind rivals in the race to bring new products to market. In Europe, for example, while Nestlé and Procter & Gamble moved toward pan-European product launches, it could take Unilever four to five years to "persuade" its 17 European operations to adopt a new product.

Unilever began to change all this in the mid-1990s. In 1996, it introduced a new structure based on regional business groups. Within each business group are a number of divisions, each focusing on a specific category of products. Thus, within the European Business Group is a division focusing on detergents, another on ice cream and frozen foods, and so on. These groups and divisions have been given the responsibility for coordinating the activities of national subsidiaries within their region to drive down operating costs and speed up the process of developing and introducing new products.

"Lever Europe" was established to consolidate the company's detergent operations. The 17 European companies now report directly to Lever Europe. Using its new-found organizational clout, Lever Europe consolidates the production of detergents in Europe in a few key locations to reduce costs and speed up new product introduction. Implicit in this new approach is a bargain: the 17 companies relinquished autonomy in their traditional markets in exchange for opportunities to help develop and execute a unified pan-European strategy. The number of European plants manufacturing soap has been cut from 10 to 2, and some new products will be manufactured at only one site. Product sizing and packaging are harmonized to cut purchasing costs and to accommodate unified pan-European advertising. By taking these steps, Unilever estimates it has saved as much as $400 million a year in its European detergent operations.

Lever Europe is also attempting to speed development of new products and to synchronize the launch of new products throughout Europe. Nonetheless, history still imposes constraints. While Procter & Gamble's leading laundry detergent carries the same brand name across Europe, Unilever sells its product under a variety of names. The company has no plans to change this. Having spent 100 years building these brand names, it believes it would be foolish to scrap them in the interest of pan-European standardization.

Source: Guy de Jonquieres, "Unilever Adopts a Clean Sheet Approach," *Financial Times,* October 21, 1991, p. 13; C. A. Bartlett and S. Ghoshal, *Managing across Borders* (Boston: Harvard Business School Press, 1989) H. Connon, "Unilever's Got the Nineties Licked," *The Guardian,* May 24, 1998, p. 5; "Unilever: A Networked Organization," *Harvard Business Review,* November–December 1996, p. 138; and C. Christensen, and J. Zobel, "Unilever's Butter Beater: Innovation for Global Diversity," Harvard Business School Case # 9-698-017, March 1998.

■ Introduction

This chapter identifies the organizational architecture that international businesses use to manage and direct their global operations. By **organizational architecture** we mean the totality of a firm's organization, including formal organization structure, control systems and incentives, processes, organizational culture, and people. The core argument outlined in this chapter is that superior enterprise profitability requires three conditions to be fulfilled. First, the different elements of a firm's organizational architecture must be *internally consistent*. For example, the control and incentive systems used in the firm must be consistent with the structure of the enterprise. Second, the organizational architecture must match or fit the strategy of the firm—*strategy and architecture must be consistent*. For example, if a firm is pursuing a global strategy but it has the wrong kind of architecture in place, it is unlikely that it will be able to execute that strategy effectively and poor performance may result. Third, the strategy and architecture of the firm must not only be consistent with each other, but they also must be consistent with competitive conditions prevailing in the firm's markets—*strategy, architecture, and competitive environment must all be consistent*. For example, a firm pursuing a multidomestic strategy might have the right kind of organizational architecture in place. However, if it competes in markets where cost pressures are intense and demands for local responsiveness are low, it will still have inferior performance because a global strategy is more appropriate in such an environment.

The opening case on Unilever touches on some of the important issues here. Historically Unilever has competed in markets where local responsiveness has been very important. The production and marketing of food, detergent, and personal care products have traditionally been tailored to the tastes and preferences of consumers in different nations. Unilever satisfied this environmental demand for local responsiveness by pursuing a multidomestic strategy. Its organizational architecture reflected this strategy. Unilever operated with a decentralized structure that delegated responsibility for production, marketing, sales, and distribution decisions to autonomous national operating companies. This allowed local managers to configure product offerings, and marketing and sales activities, to the conditions prevailing in a particular nation. For a long time, this fit between strategy and architecture served Unilever well, helping it to become a dominant consumer products enterprise.

However, by the early 1990s the competitive environment was changing. Trade barriers between countries were falling, particularly in the European Union following the creation of a single market in 1992. This made it possible to manufacture certain items such as detergents and margarine at favorable central locations in order to realize the benefits associated with location and experience curve economies. Also, new products in areas such as frozen foods and margarine were gaining regional or even global acceptance. Unfortunately for Unilever, some of its global competitors moved more rapidly to exploit this change in the competitive environment. Unilever found itself disadvantaged by a high cost structure (caused by the duplication of manufacturing operations) and an inability to introduce new products in several national markets at once. In other words, the competitive environment changed, but Unilever did not change with it. By the mid-1990s, Unilever had recognized its problems and changed both its strategy and its organizational architecture so that it better matched the new competitive realities. Unilever began to adopt a transnational strategic orientation, seeking to balance local responsiveness in marketing and sales with the centralization of manufacturing and product development activities to realize scale economies and execute pan-regional product launches. To implement this strategy, Unilever introduced a new organizational architecture based on regional business groups, each of which contained product divisions. These divisions were given the responsibility for centralizing manufacturing and product development activities, which implied a reduction in the autonomy traditionally granted to operating subsidiaries. To reestablish a fit between strategy, architecture, and environment, Unilever had to embrace the difficult process of strategic and organizational change.

To explore the issues illustrated by cases such as Unilever's, we open the current chapter by discussing in more detail the concepts of organizational architecture and fit. Next we turn to a more detailed exploration of various components of architecture—structure, control systems and incentives, organization culture, and processes—and explain how these components must be internally consistent. (We discuss the "people" component of architecture in Chapter 18, when we discuss human resource strategy in the multinational firm.) After reviewing the various components of architecture, we look at the ways in which architecture can be matched to strategy and the competitive environment to achieve high performance. The chapter closes with a discussion of organizational change, for as the Unilever case illustrates, periodically firms have to change their organization so that it matches new strategic and competitive realities.

Organizational Architecture

As noted in the introduction, the term *organizational architecture* refers to the totality of a firm's organization, including formal organizational structure, control systems and incentives, organizational culture, processes, and people.[1] Figure 13.1 illustrates these different elements. By organizational structure, we mean three things: First, the formal division of the organization into subunits such as product divisions, national operations, and functions (most organizational charts display this aspect of structure); second, the location of decision-making responsibilities within that structure (e.g., centralized or decentralized); and third, the establishment of integrating mechanisms to coordinate the activities of subunits including cross functional teams and or pan-regional committees.

Control systems are the metrics used to measure the performance of subunits and make judgments about how well managers are running those subunits. For example, historically Unilever measured the performance of national operating subsidiary companies according to profitability—profitability was the metric. **Incentives** are the devices

Figure 13.1

Organization Architecture

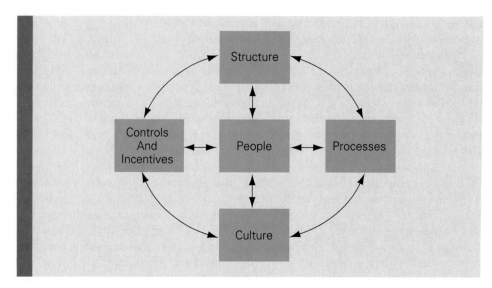

used to reward appropriate managerial behavior. Incentives are very closely tied to performance metrics. For example, the incentives of a manager in charge of a national operating subsidiary might be linked to the performance of that company. Specifically, she might receive a bonus if her subsidiary exceeds its performance targets.

Processes are the manner in which decisions are made and work is performed within the organization. Examples are the processes for formulating strategy, for deciding how to allocate resources within a firm, or for evaluating the performance of managers and giving feedback. Processes are conceptually distinct from the location of decision-making responsibilities within an organization, although both involve decisions. While the CEO might have ultimate responsibility for deciding what the strategy of the firm should be (i.e., the decision-making responsibility is centralized), the process he or she uses to make that decision might include the solicitation of ideas and criticism from lower-level managers.

Organizational culture is the norms and value systems that are shared among the employees of an organization. Just as societies have cultures (see Chapter 3 for details), so do organizations. Organizations are societies of individuals who come together to perform collective tasks. They have their own distinctive patterns of culture and subculture.[2] As we shall see, organizational culture can have a profound impact on how a firm performs. Finally, by people we mean not just the employees of the organization, but also the strategy used to recruit, compensate, and retain those individuals and the type of people that they are in terms of their skills, values, and orientation (discussed in depth in Chapter 18).

As illustrated by the arrows in Figure 13.1, the various components of an organization's architecture are not independent of each other: Each component shapes, and is shaped by, other components of architecture. An obvious example is the strategy regarding people. This can be used proactively to hire individuals whose internal values are consistent with those that the firm wishes to emphasize in its organization culture. Thus, the people component of architecture can be used to reinforce (or not) the prevailing culture of the organization. This seems to have been the practice at Unilever, where an effort was made to hire individuals who were sociable and placed a high value on consensus and cooperation, values that the enterprise wished to emphasize in its own culture.

If a firm to going to maximize its profitability, it must pay close attention to achieving *internal consistency* between the various components of its architecture. Let us look at how structure and control systems might be inconsistent with each other. Figure 13.2 shows an organizational chart for how Unilever's European operations might be

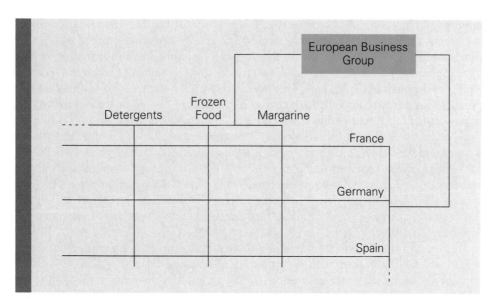

Figure 13.2

Fictional Organizational
Structure at Unilever

structured (this chart is hypothetical). Note that there are several country subsidiaries, one for France, one for Germany, one for Spain, and so on, each reporting to the European Business Group. There are also several pan-European product divisions, one for detergents, one for frozen food, one for margarine, and so on, again each reporting to the European Business Group. Within this structure, responsibility for marketing, sales, and distribution decisions might be given to the country subsidiaries, while responsibility for product manufacturing might be given to the product divisions. As for control systems, imagine that profitability is the metric used to evaluate the performance of the country subsidiaries.

One problem with this set of arrangements is that the profitability of the country subsidiaries depends on manufacturing costs and new product development, and yet the managers running the various country subsidiaries are not responsible for those important functions—responsibility resides in the product divisions! Thus, if the managers of the product divisions do not do their job properly, production costs may rise and the profitability of the country subsidiaries might fall. In other words, the managers of the country subsidiaries are being evaluated according to a metric over which they do not have total control. If the performance of a subsidiary declines, they may argue that this is not their fault; it was due to the inability of the managers in the pan-European product divisions to drive down manufacturing costs. Thus, there is a potential conflict between structure and the control systems used; they are potentially inconsistent.

Some inconsistency is a fact of life in organizations. Perfection in the design of organization architecture is very difficult to achieve. Nevertheless, the inconsistency between different components of an organization's architecture can be minimized through intelligent design. In the example just given, if the performance of each product division were assessed on the basis of manufacturing costs, it would give the managers of the product division the incentive to optimize manufacturing efficiency. The problem might be further alleviated if the heads of both the country subsidiaries and the European product divisions were rewarded according to the profitability of the entire European Business Group (for example, by having their bonus pay linked to the profitability of the entire group). This would give the heads of the divisions a further reason to reduce manufacturing costs, and it would create an incentive for the heads of each subsidiary and division to share any best practices developed in their operation with colleagues across Europe to the betterment of the entire European Business Group.

Internal consistency is a necessity but not a sufficient condition for high performance. Consistency between architecture and the strategy of the organization is also required; architecture must fit strategy. When Unilever began to emphasize cost reduction as a major strategic goal, the firm had to change its architecture to match this new strategic reality. It had to move away from a structure based primarily on standalone operating subsidiaries in each country and toward one that looks more like the structure depicted in Figure 13.2. Unilever had to create some entity, in this case the product divisions, that could reduce the duplication of manufacturing operations across country subsidiaries and consolidate manufacturing at a few choice locations. Such change is easier said than done. It is relatively easy for senior managers to announce a radical change in strategy, but it is much harder to actually put that change into action. Doing so requires a change in architecture. *Strategy is implemented through architecture, and changing architecture is much more difficult than announcing a change in strategy.* We shall discuss why it is hard to change architecture later in this chapter. As we shall see, a prime reason is that organizations tend to be relative inert; they are by nature difficult to change.

Even with internal consistency and a fit between strategy and architecture, high performance is not guaranteed. The firm must also ensure that the fusion between its strategy and architecture is consistent with the competitive demands of the market, or markets, in which the firm competes. In the 1980s Unilever had a good fit between its strategy and architecture—it was pursuing a multidomestic strategy. A decentralized architecture composed of self-contained country subsidiaries was well suited to implementing this strategy. However, by the 1990s the strategy no longer made much sense due to a change in the competitive environment. Trade barriers between nations had fallen and more efficient global competitors were emerging. Unilever's strategy no longer fit the environment in which it competed, so it had to change *both* its strategy and architecture to match the new reality. This type of organizational challenge is not unusual; markets rarely stand still, and firms often have to adjust their strategy and architecture to match new competitive realities.

Organizational Structure

Organizational structure means three things: (1) the formal division of the organization into subunits, which we shall refer to as horizontal differentiation; (2) the location of decision-making responsibilities within that structure, which we shall refer to as vertical differentiation; and (3) the establishment of integrating mechanisms. We begin by discussing vertical differentiation, then horizontal differentiation, and then integrating mechanisms.

Vertical Differentiation: Centralization and Decentralization

A firm's vertical differentiation determines where in its hierarchy the decision-making power is concentrated.[3] Are production and marketing decisions centralized in the offices of upper-level managers, or are they decentralized to lower-level managers? Where does the responsibility for R&D decisions lie? Are strategic and financial control responsibilities pushed down to operating units, or are they concentrated in the hands of top management? And so on. There are arguments for centralization and other arguments for decentralization.

Arguments for Centralization

There are four main arguments for centralization. First, centralization can facilitate coordination. For example, consider a firm that has a component manufacturing operation in Taiwan and an assembly operation in Mexico. The activities of these two operations may need to be coordinated to ensure a smooth flow of products from the component operation to the assembly operation. This might be achieved by centralizing production scheduling at the firm's head office. Second, centralization can help ensure that decisions are consistent with organizational objectives. When decisions are decentralized to lower-level managers, those managers may make decisions at variance with top management's goals. Centralization of important decisions minimizes the chance of this occurring.

Third, by concentrating power and authority in one individual or a management team, centralization can give top-level managers the means to bring about needed major organizational changes. Fourth, centralization can avoid the duplication of activities that occurs when similar activities are carried on by various subunits within the organization. For example, many international firms centralize their R&D functions at one or two locations to ensure that R&D work is not duplicated. Production activities may be centralized at key locations for the same reason.

Arguments for Decentralization

There are five main arguments for decentralization. First, top management can become overburdened when decision-making authority is centralized, and this can result in poor decisions. Decentralization gives top management time to focus on critical issues by delegating more routine issues to lower-level managers. Second, motivational research favors decentralization. Behavioral scientists have long argued that people are willing to give more to their jobs when they have a greater degree of individual freedom and control over their work. Third, decentralization permits greater flexibility—more rapid response to environmental changes—because decisions do not have to be "referred up the hierarchy" unless they are exceptional in nature. Fourth, decentralization can result in better decisions. In a decentralized structure, decisions are made closer to the spot by individuals who (presumably) have better information than managers several levels up in a hierarchy. Fifth, decentralization can increase control. Decentralization can be used to establish relatively autonomous, self-contained subunits within an organization. Subunit managers can then be held accountable for subunit performance. The more responsibility subunit managers have for decisions that impact subunit performance, the fewer alibis they have for poor performance.

Strategy and Centralization in an International Business

The choice between centralization and decentralization is not absolute. Frequently it makes sense to centralize some decisions and to decentralize others, depending on the type of decision and the firm's strategy. Decisions regarding overall firm strategy, major financial expenditures, financial objectives, and the like are typically centralized at the firm's headquarters. However, operating decisions, such as those relating to production, marketing, R&D, and human resource management, may or may not be centralized depending on the firm's international strategy.

Consider firms pursuing a global strategy. They must decide how to disperse the various value creation activities around the globe so location and experience economies can be realized. The head office must make the decisions about where to locate R&D, production, marketing, and so on. In addition, the globally dispersed web of value creation activities that facilitates a global strategy must be coordinated. All of this creates pressures for centralizing some operating decisions.

In contrast, the emphasis on local responsiveness in multidomestic firms creates strong pressures for decentralizing operating decisions to foreign subsidiaries. In the classic multidomestic firm, foreign subsidiaries have autonomy in most production and marketing decisions. International firms tend to maintain centralized control over their core competency and to decentralize other decisions to foreign subsidiaries. This typically centralizes control over R&D and/or marketing in the home country and decentralizes operating decisions to the foreign subsidiaries. For example, Microsoft Corporation, which fits the international mode, centralizes its product development activities (where its core competencies lie) at its Redmond, Washington, headquarters and decentralizes marketing activity to various foreign subsidiaries. Thus, while products are developed at home, managers in the various foreign subsidiaries have significant latitude for formulating strategies to market those products in their particular settings.[4]

The situation in transnational firms is more complex. The need to realize location and experience curve economies requires some degree of centralized control over global production centers (as it does in global firms). However, the need for local responsiveness dictates the decentralization of many operating decisions, particularly for marketing, to foreign subsidiaries. Thus, in transnational firms, some operating decisions are relatively centralized, while others are relatively decentralized. In addition, global learning based on the multidirectional transfer of skills between subsidiaries, and between subsidiaries and the corporate center, is a central feature of a firm pursuing a transnational strategy. The concept of global learning is predicated on the notion that foreign subsidiaries within a multinational firm have significant freedom to develop their own skills and competencies. Only then can these be leveraged to benefit other parts of the organization. A substantial degree of decentralization is required if subsidiaries are going to have the freedom to do this. For this reason too, the pursuit of a transnational strategy requires a high degree of decentralization.[5]

Horizontal Differentiation: The Design of Structure

Horizontal differentiation is concerned with how the firm decides to divide itself into subunits.[6] The decision is normally made on the basis of function, type of business, or geographical area. In many firms, just one of these predominates, but more complex solutions are adopted in others. This is particularly likely in the case of international firms, where the conflicting demands to organize the company around different products (to realize location and experience curve economies) and different national markets (to remain locally responsive) must be reconciled. One solution to this dilemma is to adopt a matrix structure that divides the organization on the basis of both products and national markets (as Unilever apparently did in Europe). In this section we look at different ways firms divide themselves into subunits.

The Structure of Domestic Firms

Most firms begin with no formal structure and are run by a single entrepreneur or a small team of individuals. As they grow, the demands of management become too great for one individual or a small team to handle. At this point the organization is split into functions reflecting the firm's value creation activities (e.g., production, marketing, R&D, sales). These functions are typically coordinated and controlled by top management (see Figure 13.3). Decision making in this functional structure tends to be centralized.

Further horizontal differentiation may be required if the firm significantly diversifies its product offering, which takes the firm into different business areas. For example, Dutch multinational Philips NV began as a lighting company, but diversification took the company into consumer electronics (e.g., visual and audio equipment), in-

Figure 13.3

A Typical Functional Structure

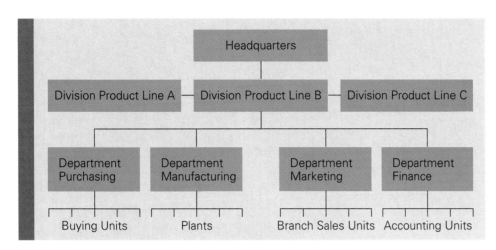

Figure 13.4

A Typical Product
Divisional Structure

dustrial electronics (integrated circuits and other electronic components), and medical systems (CT scanners and ultrasound systems). In such circumstances, a functional structure can be too clumsy. Problems of coordination and control arise when different business areas are managed within the framework of a functional structure.[7] For one thing, it becomes difficult to identify the profitability of each distinct business area. For another, it is difficult to run a functional department, such as production or marketing, if it is supervising the value creation activities of several business areas.

To solve the problems of coordination and control, at this stage most firms switch to a product divisional structure (see Figure 13.4). With a product divisional structure, each division is responsible for a distinct product line (business area). Thus, Philips created divisions for lighting, consumer electronics, industrial electronics, and medical systems. Each product division is set up as a self-contained, largely autonomous entity with its own functions. The responsibility for operating decisions is typically decentralized to product divisions, which are then held accountable for their performance. Headquarters is responsible for the overall strategic development of the firm and for the financial control of the various divisions.

The International Division

When firms initially expand abroad, they often group all their international activities into an international division. This has tended to be the case for firms organized on the basis of functions and for firms organized on the basis of product divisions. Regardless of the firm's domestic structure, its international division tends to be organized on geography. Figure 13.5 illustrates this for a firm whose domestic organization is based on product divisions.

Many manufacturing firms expanded internationally by exporting the product manufactured at home to foreign subsidiaries to sell. Thus, in the firm illustrated in Figure 13.5, the subsidiaries in Countries 1 and 2 would sell the products manufactured by Divisions A, B, and C. In time, however, it might prove viable to manufacture the product in each country, and so production facilities would be added on a country-by-country basis. For firms with a functional structure at home, this might mean replicating the functional structure in every country in which the firm does business. For firms with a divisional structure, this might mean replicating the divisional structure in every country in which the firm does business.

This structure has been widely used; according to a Harvard study, 60 percent of all firms that have expanded internationally have initially adopted it. Nonetheless, it gives rise to problems.[8] The dual structure it creates contains inherent potential for conflict and coordination problems between domestic and foreign operations. One problem with the structure is that the heads of foreign subsidiaries are not given as much voice in the organization as the heads of domestic functions (in the case of functional firms)

Figure 13.5

One Company's International Divisional Structure

or divisions (in the case of divisional firms). Rather, the head of the international division is presumed to be able to represent the interests of all countries to headquarters. This effectively relegates each country's manager to the second tier of the firm's hierarchy, which is inconsistent with a strategy of trying to expand internationally and build a true multinational organization.

Another problem is the implied lack of coordination between domestic operations and foreign operations, which are isolated from each other in separate parts of the structural hierarchy. This can inhibit the worldwide introduction of new products, the transfer of core competencies between domestic and foreign operations, and the consolidation of global production at key locations so as to realize location and experience curve economies. These problems are illustrated in the Management Focus that looks at the experience of Abbott Laboratories with an international divisional structure.

As a result of such problems, most firms that continue to expand internationally abandon this structure and adopt one of the worldwide structures we discuss next. The two initial choices are a worldwide product divisional structure, which tends to be adopted by diversified firms that have domestic product divisions, and a worldwide area structure, which tends to be adopted by undiversified firms whose domestic structures are based on functions. These two alternative paths of development are illustrated in Figure 13.6. The model in the figure is referred to as the international structural stages model and was developed by John Stopford and Louis Wells.[9]

Worldwide Area Structure

A worldwide area structure tends to be favored by firms with a low degree of diversification and a domestic structure based on function (see Figure 13.7). Under this structure, the world is divided into geographic areas. An area may be a country (if the market is large enough) or a group of countries. Each area tends to be a self-contained, largely autonomous entity with its own set of value creation activities (e.g., its own production, marketing, R&D, human resources, and finance functions). Operations

The International Division at Abbott Laboratories

ManagementFocus

With sales of about $14 billion in 2000, Abbott Laboratories is one of the world's largest health care companies. The company split itself into three divisions—pharmaceuticals, hospital products, and nutritional products—in the 1960s, a structure that still exists. Each division operates as a profit center, and each is relatively autonomous and self-contained, with its own R&D, manufacturing, and marketing functions. By the late 1960s Abbott's foreign sales were growing rapidly; the company added an international division to handle the firm's non-U.S. operations on geographic rather than product lines.

Alongside these four divisions, however, a new business has grown up that is organized differently. Abbott's diagnostics business was established in the 1970s and became a world leader with global sales of $3 billion in 2000. Unlike the other divisions, the diagnostics business is organized on a global basis, operating in foreign countries through its own staff, rather than through the international division. Thus, Abbott handles global sales in two different ways—through an international division and through a global product division (the diagnostics business organization). The company is debating the best way of organizing international operations.

This debate is being informed by two changes occurring in Abbott's environment, changes that are pulling the company in different directions. One change is a shift toward global product development in the health care industry. To quickly recapture the costs of developing new products, which for pharmaceuticals can sometimes top $500 million, companies are trying to introduce new products as rapidly as possible worldwide. Abbott has found that developing products first

for the U.S. market and then modifying those products for foreign customers is a slow and expensive process. Instead, across all four of the company's businesses, Abbott is trying to build global products that can be launched simultaneously around the world. This change is pulling Abbott toward adopting global product divisions for all four of its businesses. Some argue that only global product divisions would give Abbott the tight control over product development and product launch strategy that is deemed necessary.

On the other hand, bigger organizations with greater purchasing leverage, such as large hospital groups and health maintenance organizations, are coordinating their buying across a range of product lines in both the United States and elsewhere. These powerful customers prefer to have a single contact point at Abbott. Abbott develops stronger relations with key customers by having a single marketing organization in each country in which the company does businesses. This organization sells the products from each of Abbott's four product divisions.

Executives at Abbott's international division support maintaining the geographic organization, while the heads of the product divisions favor a shift toward four global product divisions. Top management seems to have decided there is no perfect solution to the company's organizational problems, and that imperfect as the current structure is, it works too well to contemplate a major change.

Sources: R. Walters, "Two's Company," *Financial Times*, July 7, 1995, p. 12; *Abbott Laboratories 2000 Annual Report;* and M. Santoli, "Patient Reviving," *Barron's*, February 28, 2000, pp. 24–26.

authority and strategic decisions relating to each of these activities are typically decentralized to each area, with headquarters retaining authority for the overall strategic direction of the firm and financial control.

This structure facilitates local responsiveness. Because decision-making responsibilities are decentralized, each area can customize product offerings, marketing strategy, and business strategy to the local conditions. However, this structure encourages fragmentation of the organization into highly autonomous entities. This can make it difficult to transfer core competencies and skills between areas and to realize location and experience curve economies. In other words, the structure is consistent with a multidomestic strategy but with little else. Firms structured on this basis may encounter significant problems if local responsiveness is less critical than reducing costs or transferring core competencies for establishing a competitive advantage.

Figure 13.6

The International Structural Stages Model

Source: Adapted from John M. Stopford and Louis T. Wells, *Strategy and Structure of the Multinational Enterprise* (New York: Basic Books, 1972).

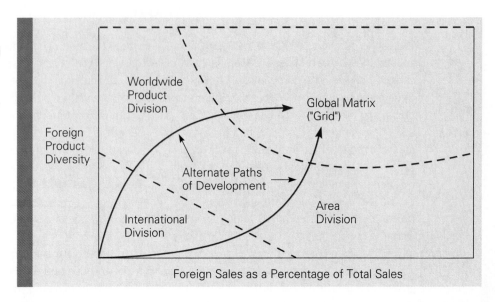

Figure 13.7

A Worldwide Area Structure

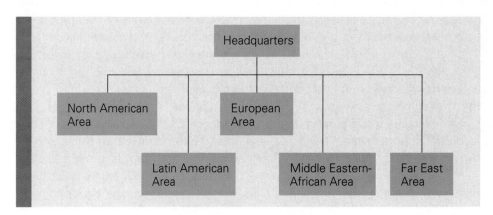

Worldwide Product Divisional Structure

A worldwide product division structure tends to be adopted by firms that are reasonably diversified and, accordingly, originally had domestic structures based on product divisions. As with the domestic product divisional structure, each division is a self-contained, largely autonomous entity with full responsibility for its own value creation activities. The headquarters retains responsibility for the overall strategic development and financial control of the firm (see Figure 13.8).

Underpinning the organization is a belief that the value creation activities of each product division should be coordinated by that division worldwide. Thus, the worldwide product divisional structure is designed to help overcome the coordination problems that arise with the international division and worldwide area structures (see the Management Focus on Abbott Laboratories for a detailed example). This structure provides an organizational context that enhances the consolidation of value creation activities at key locations necessary for realizing location and experience curve economies. It also facilitates the transfer of core competencies within a division's worldwide operations and the simultaneous worldwide introduction of new products. The main problem with the structure is the limited voice it gives to area or country managers, since they are seen as subservient to product division managers. The result can be a lack of local responsiveness, which, as we saw in Chapter 12, can be a fatal flaw.

Global Matrix Structure

Both the worldwide area structure and the worldwide product divisional structure have strengths and weaknesses. The worldwide area structure facilitates local responsive-

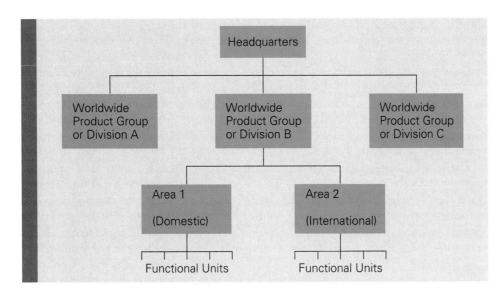

Figure 13.8

A Worldwide Product Divisional Structure

Figure 13.9

A Global Matrix Structure

ness, but it can inhibit the realization of location and experience curve economies and the transfer of core competencies between areas. The worldwide product division structure provides a better framework for pursuing location and experience curve economies and for transferring core competencies, but it is weak in local responsiveness. Other things being equal, this suggests that a worldwide area structure is more appropriate if the firm's strategy is multidomestic, while a worldwide product divisional structure is more appropriate for firms pursuing global or international strategies. However, as we saw in Chapter 12, other things are not equal. As Bartlett and Ghoshal have argued, to survive in some industries, firms must adopt a transnational strategy. That is, they must focus simultaneously on realizing location and experience curve economies, on local responsiveness, and on the internal transfer of core competencies (worldwide learning).[10]

Many firms have attempted to cope with the conflicting demands of a transnational strategy by using a matrix structure (see Figure 13.2). In the classic global matrix structure, horizontal differentiation proceeds along two dimensions: product division and geographic area (see Figure 13.9). The philosophy is that responsibility for operating decisions pertaining to a particular product should be shared by the product division and the various areas of the firm. Thus, the nature of the product offering, the marketing strategy, and the business strategy to be pursued in Area 1 for the products produced by Division A are determined by conciliation between Division A and Area 1 management. It is believed that this dual decision-making responsibility should enable the firm to simultaneously achieve its particular objectives. In a classic matrix structure, giving product divisions and geographical areas equal status within the organization reinforces the idea of dual responsibility. Individual managers thus belong to two hierarchies (a divisional hierarchy and an area hierarchy) and have two bosses (a divisional boss and an area boss).

The reality of the global matrix structure is that it often does not work anywhere near as well as the theory predicts. In practice, the matrix often is clumsy and bureaucratic. It can require so many meetings that it is difficult to get any work done. The need to get an area and a product division to reach a decision can slow decision making and produce an inflexible organization unable to respond quickly to market shifts or to innovate. The dual-hierarchy structure can lead to conflict and perpetual power struggles between the areas and the product divisions, catching many managers in the middle. To make matters worse, it can prove difficult to ascertain accountability in this structure. When all critical decisions are the product of negotiation between divisions and areas, one side can always blame the other when things go wrong. As a manager in one global matrix structure, reflecting on a failed product launch, said to the author, "Had we been able to do things our way, instead of having to accommodate those guys from the product division, this would never have happened." (A manager in the product division expressed similar sentiments.) The result of such finger-pointing can be that accountability is compromised, conflict is enhanced, and headquarters loses control over the organization.

In light of these problems, many transnational firms are now trying to build "flexible" matrix structures based more on firmwide networks and a shared culture and vision than on a rigid hierarchical arrangement. Dow Chemical, profiled in the accompanying Management Focus, is one such firm. Within such companies the informal structure plays a greater role than the formal structure. We discuss this issue when we consider informal integrating mechanisms in the next section.

Integrating Mechanisms

In the previous section, we explained that firms divide themselves into subunits. Now we need to examine some means of coordinating those subunits. One way of achieving coordination is through centralization. If the coordination task is complex, however, centralization may not be very effective. Higher-level managers responsible for achieving coordination can soon become overwhelmed by the volume of work required to coordinate the activities of various subunits, particularly if the subunits are large, diverse, and/or geographically dispersed. When this is the case, firms look toward integrating mechanisms, both formal and informal, to help achieve coordination. In this section, we introduce the various integrating mechanisms that international businesses can use. Before doing so, however, let us explore the need for coordination in international firms and some impediments to coordination.

Strategy and Coordination in the International Business

The need for coordination between subunits varies with the strategy of the firm. The need for coordination is lowest in multidomestic companies, is higher in international companies, higher still in global companies, and highest of all in transnational companies. Multidomestic firms are primarily concerned with local responsiveness. Such firms are likely to operate with a worldwide area structure in which each area has considerable autonomy and its own set of value creation functions. Since each area is established as a stand-alone entity, the need for coordination between areas is minimized.

Management Focus

Dow Chemical's Matrix Structure

A handful of major players compete head to head around the world in the chemical industry. These companies are Dow Chemical and Du Pont of the United States, Great Britain's ICI, and the German trio of BASF, Hoechst AG, and Bayer. The barriers to the free flow of chemical products between nations largely disappeared in the 1970s. This along with the commodity nature of most bulk chemicals and a severe recession in the early 1980s ushered in a prolonged period of intense price competition. In such an environment, the company that wins the competitive race is the one with the lowest costs, and in recent years the clear winner has been Dow.

Dow's managers insist that part of the credit must be placed at the feet of its much maligned "matrix" organization. Dow's organizational matrix has three interacting elements: functions (e.g., R&D, manufacturing, marketing), businesses (e.g., ethylene, plastics, pharmaceuticals), and geography (e.g., Spain, Germany, Brazil). Managers' job titles incorporate all three elements—for example, plastics marketing manager for Spain—and most managers report to at least two bosses. The plastics marketing manager in Spain might report to both the head of the worldwide plastics business and the head of the Spanish operations. The intent of the matrix was to make Dow operations responsive to both local market needs and corporate objectives. Thus, the plastics business might be charged with minimizing Dow's global plastics production costs, while the Spanish operation might be charged with determining how best to sell plastics in the Spanish market.

When Dow introduced this structure, the results were less than promising; multiple reporting channels led to confusion and conflict. The large number of bosses made for an unwieldy bureaucracy. The overlapping responsibilities resulted in turf battles and a lack of accountability. Area managers disagreed with managers overseeing business sectors about which plants should be built and where. In short, the structure didn't work. Instead of abandoning the structure, however, Dow decided to see if it could be made more flexible.

Dow's decision to keep its matrix structure was prompted by its move into the pharmaceuticals industry. The company realized that the pharmaceutical business is very different from the bulk chemicals business. In bulk chemicals, the big returns come from achieving economies of scale in production. This dictates establishing large plants in key locations from which regional or global markets can be served. But in pharmaceuticals, regulatory and marketing requirements for drugs vary so much from country to country that local needs are far more important than reducing manufacturing costs through scale economies. A high degree of local responsiveness is essential. Dow realized its pharmaceutical business would never thrive if it were managed by the same priorities as its mainstream chemical operations.

Accordingly, instead of abandoning its matrix, Dow decided to make it more flexible so it could better accommodate the different businesses, each with its own priorities, within a single management system. A small team of senior executives at headquarters now helps set the priorities for each type of business. After priorities are identified for each business sector, one of the three elements of the matrix—function, business, or geographic area—is given primary authority in decision making. Which element takes the lead varies according to the type of decision and the market or location in which the company is competing. Such flexibility requires that all employees understand what is occurring in the rest of the matrix. Although this may seem confusing, Dow claims this flexible system works well and credits much of its success to the quality of the decisions it facilitates.

Source: "Dow Draws Its Matrix Again, and Again, and Again," *The Economist*, August 5, 1989, pp. 55–56.

The need for coordination is greater in firms pursuing an international strategy and trying to profit from the transfer of core competencies and skills between units at home and abroad. Coordination is necessary to support the transfer of skills and product offerings between units. The need for coordination is also great in firms trying to profit from location and experience curve economies; that is, in firms pursuing global strategies. Achieving location and experience economies involves dispersing value creation activities to various locations around the globe. The resulting global web of activities must be coordinated to ensure the smooth flow of inputs into the value chain, the smooth flow of semifinished products through the value chain, and the smooth flow of finished products to markets around the world.

The need for coordination is greatest in transnational firms, which simultaneously pursue location and experience curve economies, local responsiveness, and the multidirectional transfer of core competencies and skills among all of the firm's subunits (referred to as global learning). As in global companies, coordination is required to ensure the smooth flow of products through the global value chain. As in international companies, coordination is required for ensuring the transfer of core competencies to subunits. However, the transnational goal of achieving multidirectional transfer of competencies requires much greater coordination than in international firms. In addition, transnationals require coordination between foreign subunits and the firm's globally dispersed value creation activities (e.g., production, R&D, marketing) to ensure that any product offering and marketing strategy is sufficiently customized to local conditions.

Impediments to Coordination

Managers of the various subunits have different orientations, partly because they have different tasks. For example, production managers are typically concerned with production issues such as capacity utilization, cost control, and quality control, whereas marketing managers are concerned with marketing issues such as pricing, promotions, distribution, and market share. These differences can inhibit communication between the managers. Quite simply, these managers often do not even "speak the same language." There may also be a lack of respect between subunits (e.g., marketing managers "looking down on" production managers, and vice versa), which further inhibits the communication required to achieve cooperation and coordination.

Differences in subunits' orientations also arise from their differing goals. For example, worldwide product divisions of a multinational firm may be committed to cost goals that require global production of a standardized product, whereas a foreign subsidiary may be committed to increasing its market share in its country, which will require a nonstandard product. These different goals can lead to conflict.

Such impediments to coordination are not unusual in any firm, but they can be particularly problematic in the multinational enterprise with its profusion of subunits at home and abroad. Differences in subunit orientation are often reinforced in multinationals by the separations of time zone, distance, and nationality between managers of the subunits.

For example, until recently the Dutch company Philips had an organization comprising worldwide product divisions and largely autonomous national organizations. The company has long had problems getting its product divisions and national organizations to cooperate on such things as new product introductions. When Philips developed a VCR format, the V2000 system, it could not get its North American subsidiary to introduce the product. Rather, the North American unit adopted the rival VHS format produced by Philip's global competitor, Matsushita. Unilever experienced a similar problem in its detergents business. The need to resolve disputes between Unilever's many national organizations and its product divisions extended the time necessary for introducing a new product across Europe to several years. This denied Unilever the first-mover advantage crucial to building a strong market position.[11]

Formal Integrating Mechanisms

The formal mechanisms used to integrate subunits vary in complexity from simple direct contact and liaison roles, to teams, to a matrix structure (see Figure 13.10). In general, the greater the need for coordination, the more complex the formal integrating mechanisms need to be.[12]

Direct contact between subunit managers is the simplest integrating mechanism. By this "mechanism," managers of the various subunits simply contact each other

Figure 13.10

Formal Integrating
Mechanisms

whenever they have a common concern. Direct contact may not be effective if the managers have differing orientations that act to impede coordination, as pointed out in the previous subsection.

Liaison roles are a bit more complex. When the volume of contacts between subunits increases, coordination can be improved by giving a person in each subunit responsibility for coordinating with another subunit on a regular basis. Through these roles, the people involved establish a permanent relationship. This helps attenuate the impediments to coordination discussed in the previous subsection.

When the need for coordination is greater still, firms tend to use temporary or permanent teams composed of individuals from the subunits that need to achieve coordination. They are typically used to coordinate product development and introduction, but they are useful when any aspect of operations or strategy requires the cooperation of two or more subunits. Product development and introduction teams are typically composed of personnel from R&D, production, and marketing. The resulting coordination aids the development of products that are tailored to consumer needs and that can be produced at a reasonable cost (design for manufacturing).

When the need for integration is very high, firms may institute a matrix structure, in which all roles are viewed as integrating roles. The structure is designed to facilitate maximum integration among subunits. The most common matrix in multinational firms is based on geographical areas and worldwide product divisions. This achieves a high level of integration between the product divisions and the areas so that, in theory, the firm can pay close attention to both local responsiveness and the pursuit of location and experience curve economies.

In some multinationals, the matrix is more complex still, structuring the firm into geographical areas, worldwide product divisions, and functions, all of which report directly to headquarters. Thus, within a company such as Dow Chemical (see the Management Focus) each manager belongs to three hierarchies (e.g., a plastics marketing manager in Spain is a member of the Spanish subsidiary, the plastics product division, and the marketing function). In addition to facilitating local responsiveness and location and experience curve economies, such a matrix fosters the transfer of core competencies within the organization. This occurs because core competencies tend to reside in functions (e.g., R&D, marketing). A structure such as Dow's facilitates the transfer of competencies existing in functions from division to division and from area to area.

However, as discussed earlier, such matrix solutions to coordination problems in multinational enterprises can quickly become bogged down in a bureaucratic tangle that creates as many problems as it solves. Matrix structures tend to be bureaucratic, inflexible, and characterized by conflict rather than the hoped-for cooperation. As in the case of Dow Chemical, for such a structure to work it needs to be somewhat flexible and to be supported by informal integrating mechanisms.

Figure 13.11

A Simple Management
Network

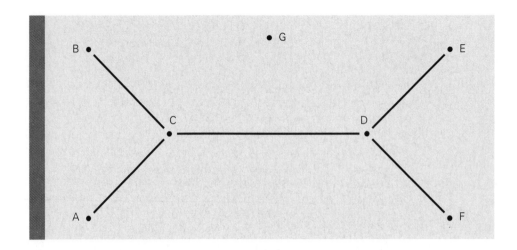

Informal Integrating Mechanism: Management Networks

In attempting to alleviate or avoid the problems associated with formal integrating mechanisms in general, and matrix structures in particular, firms with a high need for integration have been experimenting with an informal integrating mechanism: management networks that are supported by an organization culture that values teamwork and cross-unit cooperation.[13] A **management network** is a system of informal contacts between managers within an enterprise.[14] The great strength of a network is that it can be used as a nonbureaucratic conduit for knowledge flows within a multinational enterprise.[15] For a network to exist, managers at different locations within the organization must be linked to each other at least indirectly. For example, Figure 13.11 shows the simple network relationships between seven managers within a multinational firm. Managers A, B, and C all know each other personally, as do Managers D, E, and F. Although Manager B does not know Manager F personally, they are linked through common acquaintances (Managers C and D). Thus, we can say that Managers A through F are all part of the network, and also that Manager G is not.

Imagine Manager B is a marketing manager in Spain and needs to know the solution to a technical problem to better serve an important European customer. Manager F, an R&D manager in the United States, has the solution to Manager B's problem. Manager B mentions her problem to all of her contacts, including Manager C, and asks if they know of anyone who might be able to provide a solution. Manager C asks Manager D, who tells Manager F, who then calls Manager B with the solution. In this way, coordination is achieved informally through the network, rather than by formal integrating mechanisms such as teams or a matrix structure.

For such a network to function effectively, however, it must embrace as many managers as possible. For example, if Manager G had a problem similar to manager B's, he would not be able to utilize the informal network to find a solution; he would have to resort to more formal mechanisms. Establishing firmwide networks is difficult, and although network enthusiasts speak of networks as the "glue" that binds multinational companies together, it is far from clear how successful firms have been at building companywide networks. Two techniques being used to establish networks are information systems and management development policies.

Firms are using their computer and telecommunications networks to provide the physical foundation for informal information systems networks.[16] Electronic mail, videoconferencing, and high-speed data systems make it much easier for managers scattered over the globe to get to know each other. Without an existing network of personal contacts, however, worldwide information systems are unlikely to meet a firm's need for integration.

Firms are using their management development programs to build informal networks. Tactics include rotating managers through various subunits on a regular basis so they build their own informal network and using management education programs to bring managers of subunits together in a single location so they can become acquainted. Both of these tactics are used at Unilever to build its informal management network (see the opening case for details).

Management networks by themselves may not be sufficient to achieve coordination if subunit managers persist in pursuing subgoals that are at variance with firmwide goals. For a management network to function properly—and for a formal matrix structure to work, also—managers must share a strong commitment to the same goals. To appreciate the nature of the problem, consider again the case of Manager B and Manager F. As before, Manager F hears about Manager B's problem through the network. However, solving Manager B's problem would require Manager F to devote considerable time to the task. Insofar as this would divert Manager F away from his own regular tasks—and the pursuit of subgoals that differ from those of Manager B—he may be unwilling to do it. Thus, Manager F may not call Manager B, and the informal network would fail to provide a solution to Manager B's problem.

To eliminate this flaw, organization's managers must adhere to a common set of norms and values that override differing subunit orientations.[17] In other words, the firm must have a strong organizational culture that promotes teamwork and cooperation. When this is the case, a manager is willing and able to set aside the interests of his own subunit when doing so benefits the firm as a whole. If Manager B and Manager F are committed to the same organizational norms and value systems, and if these organizational norms and values place the interests of the firm as a whole above the interests of any individual subunit, Manager F should be willing to cooperate with Manager B on solving her subunit's problems.

Summary

The message contained in this section is crucial to understanding the problems of managing the multinational firm. Multinationals need integration—particularly if they are pursuing global, international, or transnational strategies—but it can be difficult to achieve due to the impediments to coordination we discussed. Firms traditionally have tried to achieve coordination by adopting formal integrating mechanisms. These do not always work, however, since they tend to be bureaucratic and do not necessarily address the problems that arise from differing subunit orientations. This is particularly likely with a complex matrix structure, and yet, a complex matrix structure is required for simultaneously achieving location and experience curve economies, local responsiveness, and the multidirectional transfer of core competencies within the organization. The solution to this dilemma seems twofold. First, the firm must try to establish an informal management network that can do much of the work previously undertaken by a formal matrix structure. Second, the firm must build a common culture. Neither of these partial solutions, however, is easy to achieve.[18]

Control Systems and Incentives ▪

A major task of a firm's leadership is to control the various subunits of the firm—whether they be defined on the basis of function, product division, or geographic area—to ensure their actions are consistent with the firm's overall strategic and financial objectives. Firms achieve this with various control and incentive systems. In this section, we first review the various types of control systems firms use to control their subunits. Then we briefly discuss incentive systems. Then we will look at how the appropriate control and incentive systems vary according to firms' international strategies.

▌Types of Control Systems

Four main types of control systems are used in multinational firms: personal controls, bureaucratic controls, output controls, and cultural controls. In most firms, all four are used, but their relative emphasis varies with the strategy of the firm.

Personal Controls

Personal control is control by personal contact with subordinates. This type of control tends to be most widely used in small firms, where it is seen in the direct supervision of subordinates' actions. However, it also structures the relationships between managers at different levels in multinational enterprises. For example, the CEO may use a great deal of personal control to influence the behavior of his or her immediate subordinates, such as the heads of worldwide product divisions or major geographic areas. In turn, these heads may use personal control to influence the behavior of their subordinates, and so on down through the organization. For example, Jack Welsh the longtime CEO of General Electric who retired in 2001, had regular one-on-one meetings with the heads of all of GE's major businesses (most of which are international). He used these meetings to "probe" the managers about the strategy, structure, and financial performance of their operations. In doing so, he essentially exercised personal control over these managers and, undoubtedly, over the strategies that they favored.

Bureaucratic Controls

Bureaucratic control is control through a system of rules and procedures that directs the actions of subunits. The most important bureaucratic controls in subunits within multinational firms are budgets and capital spending rules. Budgets are essentially a set of rules for allocating a firm's financial resources. A subunit's budget specifies with some precision how much the subunit may spend. Headquarters uses budgets to influence the behavior of subunits. For example, the R&D budget normally specifies how much cash the R&D unit may spend on product development. R&D managers know that if they spend too much on one project, they will have less to spend on other projects, so they modify their behavior to stay within the budget. Most budgets are set by negotiation between headquarters management and subunit management. Headquarters management can encourage the growth of certain subunits and restrict the growth of others by manipulating their budgets.

Capital spending rules require headquarters management to approve any capital expenditure by a subunit that exceeds a certain amount (at GE, $50,000). A budget allows headquarters to specify the amount a subunit can spend in a given year, and capital spending rules give headquarters additional control over how the money is spent. Headquarters can be expected to deny approval for capital spending requests that are at variance with overall firm objectives and to approve those that are congruent with firm objectives.

Output Controls

Output controls involve setting goals for subunits to achieve and expressing those goals in terms of relatively objective performance metrics such as profitability, productivity, growth, market share, and quality. The performance of subunit managers is then judged by their ability to achieve the goals.[19] If goals are met or exceeded, subunit managers will be rewarded. If goals are not met, top management will normally intervene to find out why and take appropriate corrective action. Thus, control is achieved by comparing actual performance against targets and intervening selectively to take corrective action. Subunits' goals depend on their role in the firm. Self-contained product divisions or national subsidiaries are typically given goals for profitability, sales growth, and market share. Functions are more likely to be given goals related to their particular activity. Thus, R&D will be given product development goals, production will be given productivity and quality goals, marketing will be given market share goals, and so on.

As with budgets, goals are normally established through negotiation between subunits and headquarters. Generally, headquarters tries to set goals that are challenging but realistic, so subunit managers are forced to look for ways to improve their operations but are not so pressured that they will resort to dysfunctional activities to do so (such as short-run profit maximization). Output controls foster a system of "management by exception," in that so long as subunits meet their goals, they are left alone. If a subunit fails to attain its goals, however, headquarters managers are likely to ask some tough questions. If they don't get satisfactory answers, they are likely to intervene proactively in a subunit, replacing top management and looking for ways to improve efficiency.

Cultural Controls

Cultural controls exist when employees "buy into" the norms and value systems of the firm. When this occurs, employees tend to control their own behavior, which reduces the need for direct supervision. In a firm with a strong culture, self-control can reduce the need for other control systems. We shall discuss organizational culture later. McDonald's actively promotes organizational norms and values, referring to its franchisees and suppliers as partners and emphasizing its long-term commitment to them. This commitment is not just a public relations exercise; it is backed by actions, including a willingness to help suppliers and franchisees improve their operations by providing capital and/or management assistance when needed. In response, McDonald's franchisees and suppliers are integrated into the firm's culture and thus become committed to helping McDonald's succeed. One result is that McDonald's can devote less time than would otherwise be necessary to controlling its franchisees and suppliers.

Incentive Systems

Incentives refer to the devices used to reward appropriate employee behavior. Many employees receive incentives in the form of annual bonus pay. Incentives are usually closely tied to the performance metrics used for output controls. For example, setting targets linked to profitability might be used to measure the performance of a subunit, such as a global product division. To create positive incentives for employees to work hard to exceed those targets, they may be given a share of any profits over above those targeted. If a subunit has set a goal of attaining a 15 percent return on investment and it actually attains a 20 percent return, unit employees may be given a share in the profits generated in excess of the 15 percent target in the form of bonus pay. We shall return to the topic of incentive systems in Chapter 18 when we discuss human resource strategy in the multinational firm. For now, however, several important points need to be made.

First, the type of incentive used often varies depending on the employees and their tasks. Incentives for employees working on the factory floor may be very different from the incentives used for senior managers. The incentives used must be matched to the type of work being performed. The employees on the factory floor of a manufacturing plant may be broken into teams of 20 to 30 individuals, and they may have their bonus pay tied to the ability of their team to hit or exceed targets for output and product quality. In contrast, the senior managers of the plant may be rewarded according to metrics linked to the output of the entire operation. The basic principle is to make sure the incentive scheme for an individual employee is linked to an output target that he or she has some control over and can influence. The individual employees on the factory floor may not be able to exercise much influence over the performance of the entire operation, but they can influence the performance of their team, so incentive pay is tied to output at this level.

Second, the successful execution of strategy in the multinational firm often requires significant cooperation between managers in different subunits. For example, as noted earlier, some multinational firms operate with matrix structures where a country subsidiary might be responsible for marketing and sales in a nation, while a global product division might be responsible for manufacturing and product development. The managers of these different units need to cooperate closely with each other if the firm is to be successful. One way of encouraging the managers to cooperate is to link incentives to performance at a higher level in the organization. Thus, the senior managers of the country subsidiaries and global product divisions might be rewarded according to the profitability of the entire firm. The thinking here is that boosting the profitability of the entire firm requires managers in the country subsidiaries and product divisions to cooperate with each other on strategy implementation and linking incentive systems to the next level up in the hierarchy encourages this. Most firms use a formula for incentives that links a portion of incentive pay to the performance of the subunit in which a manager or employee works and a portion to the performance of the entire firm, or some other higher-level organizational unit. The goal is to encourage employees to improve the efficiency of their unit *and* to cooperate with other units in the organization.

Third, the incentive systems used within a multinational enterprise often have to be adjusted to account for national differences in institutions and culture. Incentive systems that work in the United States might not work, or even be allowed, in other countries. For example, Lincoln Electric, a leader in the manufacture of arc welding equipment, has used an incentive system for its employees based on piecework rates in its American factories (under a piecework system, employees are paid according to the amount they produce). While this system has worked very well in the United States, Lincoln has found that the system is difficult to introduce in other countries. In some countries, such as Germany, piecework systems are illegal, while in others the prevailing national culture is antagonistic to a system where performance is so closely tied to individual effort. For further details, see the accompanying Management Focus.

Finally, it is important for managers to recognize that incentive systems can have unintended consequences. Managers need to carefully think through exactly what behavior certain incentives encourage. For example, if employees in a factory are rewarded solely on the basis of how many units of output they produce, with no attention paid to the quality of that output, they may produce as many units as possible to boost their incentive pay, but the quality of those units may be poor.

Control Systems, Incentives, and Strategy in the International Business

The key to understanding the relationship between international strategy, control systems, and incentive systems is the concept of performance ambiguity.

Performance Ambiguity

Performance ambiguity exists when the causes of a subunit's poor performance are not clear. This is not uncommon when a subunit's performance is partly dependent on the performance of other subunits; that is, when there is a high degree of interdependence between subunits within the organization. Consider the case of a French subsidiary of a U.S. firm that depends on another subsidiary, a manufacturer based in Italy, for the products it sells. The French subsidiary is failing to achieve its sales goals, and the U.S. management asks the managers to explain. They reply that they are receiving poor-quality goods from the Italian subsidiary. So the U.S. management asks the managers of the Italian operation what the problem is. They reply that their product quality is excellent—the best in the industry, in fact—and that the French simply don't know how to sell a good product. Who is right, the French or the Italians? Without more information, top management cannot tell. Because they are dependent on the Italians for their product, the French have an "alibi" for poor performance. U.S. management needs to have more information to determine who is correct. Collecting this information is expensive and time consuming and will divert attention away from other issues. In other words, performance ambiguity raises the costs of control.

Consider how different things would be if the French operation were self-contained, with its own manufacturing, marketing, and R&D facilities. The French operation would lack a convenient alibi for its poor performance; the French managers would stand or fall on their own merits. They could not blame the Italians for their poor sales.

Organizational Culture and Incentive Systems at Lincoln Electric

Lincoln Electric is one of the leading companies in the global market for arc welding equipment. Lincoln's success has been based on extremely high levels of employee productivity. The company attributes its productivity to a strong organizational culture and an incentive scheme based on piecework. Lincoln's organizational culture dates back to James Lincoln, who in 1907 joined the company that his brother had established a few years earlier. Lincoln had a strong respect for the ability of the individual and believed that, correctly motivated, ordinary people could achieve extraordinary performance. He emphasized that Lincoln should be a meritocracy where people were rewarded for their individual effort. Strongly egalitarian, Lincoln removed barriers to communication between "workers" and "managers," practicing an open-door policy. He made sure that all who worked for the company were treated equally; for example, everyone ate in the same cafeteria, there were no reserved parking places for "managers," and so on. Lincoln also believed that any gains in productivity should be shared with consumers in the form of lower prices, with employees in the form of higher pay, and with shareholders in the form of higher dividends.

The organizational culture that grew out of James Lincoln's beliefs was reinforced by the company's incentive system. Production workers receive no base salary but are paid according to the number of pieces they produce. The piecework rates at the company enable an employee working at a normal pace to earn an income equivalent to the average wage for manufacturing workers in the area where a factory is based. Workers have responsibility for the quality of their output and must repair any defects spotted by quality inspectors before the pieces are included in the piecework calculation. Since 1934, production workers have been awarded a semiannual bonus based on merit ratings. These ratings are based on objective criteria (such as an employee's level and quality of output) and subjective criteria (such as an employee's attitudes toward cooperation and his or her dependability). These systems give Lincoln's employees an incentive to work hard and to generate innovations that

boost productivity, for doing so influences their level of pay. Lincoln's factory workers have been able to earn a base pay that often exceeds the average manufacturing wage in the area by more than 50 percent and receive pay bonus on top of this that in good years could double their base pay. Despite high employee compensation, the workers are so productive that Lincoln has a lower cost structure than its competitors.

While this organizational culture and set of incentives works well in the United States, where it is compatible with the individualistic culture of the country, it did not translate easily into foreign operations. In the 1980s and early 1990s, Lincoln expanded aggressively into Europe and Latin America, acquiring a number of local arc welding manufacturers. Lincoln left local managers in place, believing that they knew local conditions better than Americans. However, the local managers had little working knowledge of Lincoln's strong organizational culture and were unable or unwilling to impose that culture on their units, which had their own long-established organizational cultures. Nevertheless, Lincoln told local managers to introduce its incentive systems in acquired companies. They frequently ran into legal and cultural roadblocks. In many countries, piecework is viewed as an exploitive compensation system that forces employees to work ever harder. In Germany, where Lincoln made an acquisition, it is actually illegal. In Brazil, a bonus paid for more than two years becomes a legal entitlement! In many other countries, both managers and workers were opposed to the idea of piecework. Lincoln found that many European workers valued extra leisure more highly than extra income and were not prepared to work as hard as their American counterparts. Many of the acquired companies were also unionized, and the local unions vigorously opposed the introduction of piecework. As a result, Lincoln was not able to replicate the high level of employee productivity that it had achieved in the United States, and its expansion pulled down the performance of the entire company.

Sources: J. O'Connell, "Lincoln Electric: Venturing Abroad," Harvard Business School Case, # 9-398-095, April 1998, and www.lincolnelectric.com.

The level of performance ambiguity, therefore, is a function of the interdependence of subunits in an organization.

Strategy, Interdependence, and Ambiguity

Now let us consider the relationship among international strategy, interdependence, and performance ambiguity. In multidomestic firms, each national operation is a stand-alone entity and can be judged on its own merits. The level of performance ambiguity is low. In an international firm, the level of interdependence is somewhat higher. Integration is required to facilitate the transfer of core competencies and skills. Since the success of a foreign operation is partly dependent on the quality of the competency transferred from the home country, performance ambiguity can exist.

In global firms, the situation is still more complex. Recall that in a pure global firm the pursuit of location and experience curve economies leads to the development of a global web of value creation activities. Many of the activities in a global firm are interdependent. A French subsidiary's ability to sell a product does depend on how well other operations in other countries perform their value creation activities. Thus, the levels of interdependence and performance ambiguity are high in global companies.

The level of performance ambiguity is highest of all in transnational firms. Transnational firms suffer from the same performance ambiguity problems that global firms do. In addition, since they emphasize the multidirectional transfer of core competencies, they also suffer from the problems characteristic of firms pursuing an international strategy. The extremely high level of integration within transnational firms implies a high degree of joint decision making, and the resulting interdependencies create plenty of alibis for poor performance. There is lots of room for finger-pointing in transnational firms.

Implications for Control and Incentives

The arguments of the previous section, along with the implications for the costs of control, are summarized in Table 13.1. The costs of control can be defined as the amount of time top management must devote to monitoring and evaluating subunits' performance. This is greater when the amount of performance ambiguity is greater. When performance ambiguity is low, management can use output controls and a system of management by exception; when it is high, managers have no such luxury. Output controls do not provide totally unambiguous signals of a subunit's efficiency when the performance of that subunit is dependent on the performance of another subunit within the organization. Thus, management must devote time to resolving the problems that arise from performance ambiguity, with a corresponding rise in the costs of control.

Table 13.1 reveals a paradox. We saw in Chapter 12 that a transnational strategy is desirable because it gives a firm more ways to profit from international expansion than do multidomestic, international, and global strategies. But now we see that due to the high level of interdependence, the costs of controlling transnational firms are higher than the costs of controlling firms that pursue other strategies. Unless there is some way of reducing these costs, the higher profitability associated with a transnational

Table 13.1

Interdependence, Performance Ambiguity, and the Costs of Control for the Four International Business Strategies

Strategy	Interdependence	Performance Ambiguity	Costs of Control
Multidomestic	Low	Low	Low
International	Moderate	Moderate	Moderate
Global	High	High	High
Transnational	Very high	Very high	Very high

strategy could be canceled out by the higher costs of control. The same point, although to a lesser extent, can be made with regard to global firms. Although firms pursuing a global strategy can reap the cost benefits of location and experience curve economies, they must cope with a higher level of performance ambiguity, and this raises the costs of control (in comparison with firms pursuing an international or multidomestic strategy).

This is where control systems and incentives come in. When we survey the systems that corporations use to control their subunits, we find that irrespective of their strategy, multinational firms all use output and bureaucratic controls. However, in firms pursuing either global or transnational strategies, the usefulness of output controls is limited by substantial performance ambiguities. As a result, these firms place greater emphasis on cultural controls. Cultural control—by encouraging managers to want to assume the organization's norms and value systems—gives managers of interdependent subunits an incentive to look for ways to work out problems that arise between them. The result is a reduction in finger-pointing and, accordingly, in the costs of control. The development of cultural controls may be a precondition for the successful pursuit of a transnational strategy and perhaps of a global strategy as well.[20] As for incentives, the material discussed earlier suggests that the conflict between different subunits can be reduced and the potential for cooperation enhanced, if incentive systems are tied in some way to a higher level in the hierarchy. When performance ambiguity makes it difficult to judge the performance of subunits as stand-alone entities, linking the incentive pay of senior managers to the entity to which both subunits belong can reduce the resulting problems.

Processes

We defined *processes* as the manner in which decisions are made and work is performed within the organization.[21] Processes can be found at many different levels within an organization. There are processes for formulating strategy, processes for allocating resources, processes for evaluating new product ideas, processes for handling customer inquiries and complaints, processes for improving product quality, processes for evaluating employee performance, and so on. Often, the core competencies or valuable skills of a firm are embedded in its processes. Efficient and effective processes can lower the costs of value creation and add additional value to a product. For example, the global success of many Japanese manufacturing enterprises in the 1980s was based in part on their early adoption of processes for improving product quality and operating efficiency, including total quality management and just-in-time inventory systems. Today, the competitive success of General Electric can in part be attributed to a number of processes that have been widely promoted within the company. These include the company's six-sigma process for quality improvement, its process for "digitalization" of business (using corporate intranets and the Internet to automate activities and reduce operating costs), and its process for new idea generation, referred to within the company as "workouts," where managers and employees get together for intensive sessions over several days to identify and commit to ideas for improving productivity.

An organization's processes can be summarized by means of a flow chart, which illustrates the various steps and decision points involved in performing work. Many processes cut across functions, or divisions, and require cooperation between individuals in different subunits. For example, product development processes require employees from R&D, manufacturing, and marketing to work together in a cooperative manner to make sure new products are developed with market needs in mind and designed in such a way that they can be manufactured at a low cost. Because they cut across organizational boundaries, performing processes effectively often requires the establishment of formal integrating mechanisms and incentives for cross-unit cooperation (see above).

A detailed consideration of the nature of processes and strategies for process improvement and reengineering is beyond the scope of this book. However, it is important to make two basic remarks about managing processes, particularly in the context of an international business.[22] The first is that in a multinational enterprise, many processes cut not only across organizational boundaries, embracing several different subunits, but also across national boundaries. Designing a new product may require the cooperation of R&D personnel located in California, production people located in Taiwan, and marketing located in Europe, America, and Asia. The chances of pulling this off are greatly enhanced if the processes are embedded in an organizational culture that promotes cooperation between individuals from different subunits and nations, if the incentive systems of the organization explicitly reward such cooperation, and if formal and informal integrating mechanisms are used to facilitate coordination between subunits.

Second, it is particularly important for a multinational enterprise to recognize that valuable new processes that might lead to a competitive advantage can be developed anywhere within the organization's global network of operations. New processes may be developed by a local operating subsidiary in response to conditions pertaining to its market. Those processes might then have value to other parts of the multinational enterprise. For example, in response to competition in Japan and a local obsession with product quality, Japanese firms were at the leading edge of developing processes for total quality management (TQM) in the 1970s. Because few American firms had Japanese subsidiaries at the time, they were relatively ignorant of the trend until the 1980s when high-quality Japanese products began to make big inroads into the United States. An exception to this generalization was Hewlett-Packard, which had a very successful operating company in Japan, Yokogwa Hewlett-Packard (YHP). YHP was a pioneer of the total quality management process in Japan and won the prestigious Deming Prize for its achievements in improving product quality. Through YHP, Hewlett-Packard learned about the quality movement ahead of many of its U.S. peers and was one of the first Western companies to introduce TQM processes into its worldwide operations. Not only did Hewlett-Packard's Japanese operation give the company access to a valuable process, but the company also transferred this knowledge within its global network of operations, raising the performance of the entire company. The ability to create valuable processes matters, but it is also important to leverage those processes. This requires both formal and informal integrating mechanisms such as management networks.

Organizational Culture

Chapter 3 applied the concept of culture to nation-states. Culture, however, is a social construct ascribed to societies, including organizations.[23] Thus, we can speak of organizational culture and organizational subculture. The basic definition of culture remains the same, whether we are applying it to a large society such as a nation-state or a small society such as an organization or one of its subunits. Culture refers to a system of values and norms that are shared among people. Values are abstract ideas about what a group believes to be good, right, and desirable. Norms mean the social rules and guidelines that prescribe appropriate behavior in particular situations. Values and norms express themselves as the behavior patterns or style of an organization that new employees are automatically encouraged to follow by their fellow employees. Although an organization's culture is rarely static, it tends to change relatively slowly.

How Is Organizational Culture Created and Maintained?

An organization's culture comes from several sources. First, there seems to be wide agreement that founders or important leaders can have a profound impact on an organization's culture, often imprinting their own values on the culture.[24] This was certainly the case with Lincoln Electric where the values of James Lincoln became the core values of Lincoln Electric (see the Management Focus). Another famous example of a strong founder effect concerns the founder of the Japanese firm Matsushita, Konosuke Matsushita, whose almost Zen-like personal business philosophy was codified in the "Seven Spiritual Values" of Matsushita that all new employees still learn today. These values are (1) national service through industry, (2) fairness, (3) harmony and cooperation, (4) struggle for betterment, (5) courtesy and humility, (6) adjustment and assimilation, and (7) gratitude. A leader does not have to be the founder to have a profound influence on organizational culture. Jack Welsh is widely credited with having changed the culture of GE, primarily by emphasizing when he first became CEO a countercultural set of values, such as risk taking, entrepreneurship, stewardship, and boundaryless behavior. It is more difficult for a leader, however forceful, to change an established organizational culture than it is to create one from scratch in a new venture.

Another important influence on organizational culture is the broader social culture of the nation where the firm was founded. In the United States, for example, the competitive ethic of individualism looms large and there is enormous social stress on producing winners. Many American firms find ways of rewarding and motivating individuals so that they see themselves as winners.[25] The values of American firms often reflect the values of American culture. Similarly, the cooperative values found in many Japanese firms have been argued to reflect the values of traditional Japanese society, with its emphasis on group cooperation, reciprocal obligations, and harmony.[26] Thus, although it may be a generalization, there may be something to the argument that organizational culture is influenced by national culture.

A third influence on organizational culture is the history of the enterprise, which over time may come to shape the values of the organization. In the language of historians, organizational culture is the *path-dependent* product of where the organization has been through time. For example, Philips NV, the Dutch multinational, long operated with a culture that placed a high value on the independence of national operating companies. This culture was shaped by the history of the company. During World War II, Holland was occupied by the Germans. With the head office in occupied territories, power was devolved by default to various foreign operating companies, such as Philips subsidiaries in the United States and Great Britain. After the war ended, these subsidiaries continued to operate in a highly autonomous fashion. A belief that this was the right thing to do became a core value of the company.

Decisions that subsequently result in high performance tend to become institutionalized in the values of a firm. In the 1920s, 3M was primarily a manufacturer of sandpaper. Richard Drew, who was a young laboratory assistant at the time, came up with what he thought would be a great new product; a glue-covered strip of paper, which he called "sticky tape." Drew saw applications for the product in the automobile industry, where it could be used to mask parts of a vehicle during painting. He presented the idea to the company's president, William McKnight. An unimpressed McKnight suggested that Drew drop the research. Drew didn't; instead he developed the "sticky tape" and then went out and got endorsements from potential customers in the auto industry. Armed with this information, he approached McKnight again. A chastened McKnight reversed his position and gave Drew the go-ahead to start developing what was to become one of 3M's main product lines—sticky tape—a business it dominates to this day.[27] From then on, McKnight emphasized the importance of giving researchers at 3M free rein to explore their own ideas and experiment with product offerings. This soon became a core value at 3M and was enshrined in the company's famous "15 percent rule," which stated that researchers could spend 15 percent of the company time working on ideas of their own choosing. Today, new employees are often told the Drew story, which is used to illustrate the value of allowing individuals to explore their own ideas.

Culture is maintained by a variety of mechanisms. These include: (1) hiring and promotional practices of the organization, (2) reward strategies, (3) socialization processes, and (4) communication strategy. The goal is to recruit people whose values are consistent with those of the company. Lincoln Electric, for example, hires individuals who are very self-reliant, which is necessary in the company's individualistic culture. To further reinforce values, a company may promote individuals whose behavior is consistent with the core values of the organization. Merit review processes may also be linked to a company's values, which further reinforces cultural norms. Thus, at Lincoln Electric, the merit review process rewards people for behavior that is consistent with the attainment of high productivity.

Socialization can be formal, such as training programs for employees that educate them in the core values of the organization. Informal socialization may be friendly advice from peers or bosses or may be implicit in the actions of peers and superiors toward new employees. As for communication strategy, many companies with strong cultures devote a lot of attention to framing their key values in corporate mission statements, communicating them often to employees, and using them to guide difficult decisions. Stories and symbols are often used to reinforce important values (e.g., the Drew and McKnight story at 3M).

Organizational Culture and Performance in the International Business

Management authors often talk about "strong cultures."[28] In a strong culture, almost all managers share a relatively consistent set of values and norms that have a clear impact on the way work is performed. New employees adopt these values very quickly, and employees that do not fit in with the core values tend to leave. In such a culture, a new executive is just as likely to be corrected by his subordinates as by his superiors if he violates the values and norms of the organizational culture. Firm's with a strong culture are normally seen by outsiders as having a certain style or way of doing things. Lincoln Electric, profiled in the Management Focus, is an example of a firm with a strong culture. Lincoln's organizational culture places a high value on individual achievements, meritocracy, and egalitarian behavior. Unilever, profiled in the opening case, is another example of a firm with a strong culture. Unilever places a high value on sociability, cooperation, and consensus-building behavior among its employees.

Strong does not necessarily mean *good*. A culture can be strong but bad. The culture of the Nazi Party in Germany was certainly strong, but it was most definitely not good. Nor does it follow that a strong culture leads to high performance. One study found that General Motors had a "strong culture," but it was a strong culture that discouraged lower-level employees from demonstrating initiative and taking risks, which the authors argued was dysfunctional and led to low performance at GM.[29] Also, a strong culture might be beneficial at one point, leading to high performance, but inappropriate at another time. The appropriateness of the culture depends on the context. In the 1970s and early 1980s, when IBM was performing very well, several management authors sang the praises of its strong culture, which among other things placed a high value on consensus-based decision making.[30] These authors argued that such a decision-making process was appropriate given the substantial financial investments that IBM routinely made in new technology. However, this process turned out to be a weakness in the fast-moving computer industry of the late 1980s and 1990s. Consensus-based decision making was slow, bureaucratic, and not particularly conducive to corporate risk taking. While this was fine in the 1970s, IBM needed rapid decision making and entrepreneurial risk taking in the 1990s, but its culture discouraged such behavior. IBM found itself outflanked by then-small enterprises such as Microsoft and Compaq Computer.

One academic study concluded that firms that exhibited high performance over a prolonged period tended to have strong but "adaptive cultures." According to this study, in an adaptive culture most managers care deeply about and value customers, stockholders, and employees. They also strongly value people and processes that create useful change in a firm.[31] While this is interesting, it does reduce the issue to a very high level of abstraction; after all, what company would say that it doesn't care deeply about customers, stockholders, and employees? A somewhat different perspective is to argue that the culture of the firm must match the rest of the architecture of the organization, the firm's strategy, and the demands of the competitive environment, for superior performance to be attained. All these elements must be consistent with each other. Lincoln Electric provides another useful example. Lincoln competes in a business that is very competitive, where cost minimization is a key source of competitive advantage. Lincoln's culture and incentive systems both encourage employees to strive for high levels of productivity, which translates into the low costs that are critical for Lincoln's success.

The Lincoln example also demonstrates another important point for international businesses: *A culture that leads to high performance in the firm's home nation may not be easy to impose on foreign subsidiaries!* Lincoln's culture has clearly helped the firm to achieve superior performance in the U.S. market, but this same culture is very "American" in its form and difficult to implement in other countries. The managers and employees of several of Lincoln's European subsidiaries found the culture to be alien to their own values and were reluctant to adopt it. The result was that Lincoln found it very difficult to replicate in foreign markets the success it has had in the United States. Lincoln compounded the problem by acquiring established enterprises that already had their own organizational culture. Thus, in trying to impose its culture on foreign operating subsidiaries, Lincoln had to deal with two problems: how to change the established organizational culture of those units, and how to introduce an organizational culture whose key values might be alien to the values held by members of that society. These problems are not unique to Lincoln; many international businesses have to deal with exactly the same problems.

The solution Lincoln has adopted is to establish new subsidiaries, rather than acquiring and trying to transform an enterprise with its own culture. It is much easier to establish a set of values in a new enterprise than it is to change the values of an established enterprise. A second solution is to devote a lot of time and attention to transmitting the firm's organizational culture to its foreign operations. This was something Lincoln originally omitted. Other firms make this an important part of their strategy for internationalization. When MTV Networks opens an operation in a new country, it initially staffs that operation with several expatriates. The job of these expatriates is to hire local employees whose values are consistent with the MTV culture and to socialize those individuals into values and norms that underpin MTV's unique way of doing things. Once this has been achieved, the expatriates move on to their next assignment, and local employees run the operation. A third solution is to recognize that it may be necessary to change some aspects of a firm's culture so that it better fits the culture of the host nation. For example, many Japanese firms use symbolic behavior, such as company songs and morning group exercise sessions, to reinforce cooperative values and norms. However, such symbolic behavior does not go down well in Western cultures, where it is seen as odd, so many Japanese firms have not used such practices in Western subsidiaries.

The need for a common organizational culture that is the same across a multinational's global network of subsidiaries probably varies with the strategy of the firm. Shared norms and values can facilitate coordination and cooperation between individuals from different subunits.[32] A strong common culture may lead to goal congruence and can attenuate the problems that arise from interdependence, performance ambiguities, and conflict among managers from different subsidiaries. As noted earlier, a shared culture may help informal integrating mechanisms such as management networks to operate more effectively. As such, a common culture may be of greater value in a multinational that is pursuing a strategy that requires cooperation and coordination between globally dispersed subsidiaries. This suggests that it is more important to have a common culture in firms employing a transnational strategy than a multidomestic strategy, with global and international strategies falling between these two extremes.

Synthesis: Strategy and Architecture

In Chapter 12, we identified four international business strategies: multidomestic, international, global, and transnational. So far in this chapter we have looked at several aspects of organization architecture, and we have discussed the interrelationships between these dimensions and strategies. Now it is time to synthesize this material (see Table 13.2).

Multidomestic Firms

Firms pursuing a multidomestic strategy focus on local responsiveness. Table 13.2 shows that multidomestic firms tend to operate with worldwide area structures, within which operating decisions are decentralized to functionally self-contained country subsidiaries. The need for coordination between subunits (areas and country subsidiaries) is low. This suggests that multidomestic firms do not have a high need for integrating mechanisms, either formal or informal, to knit together different national operations. The lack of interdependence implies that the level of performance ambiguity in multidomestic concerns is low, as (by extension) are the costs of control. Thus, headquarters can manage foreign operations by relying primarily on output and bureaucratic controls and a policy of management by exception. Incentives can be linked to performance metrics at the level of country subsidiaries. Since the need for integration and coordination is low, the need for common processes and organization culture is also quite low. Were it not for the fact that these firms are unable to profit from the realization of location and experience curve

Structure and Controls	Strategy			
	Multidomestic	**International**	**Global**	**Transnational**
Vertical differentiation	Decentralized	Core competency centralized; rest decentralized	Some centralized	Mixed centralized and decentralized
Horizontal differentiation	Worldwide area structure	Worldwide product division	Worldwide product division	Informal matrix
Need for coordination	Low	Moderate	High	Very high
Integrating mechanisms	None	Few	Many	Very many
Performance ambiguity	Low	Moderate	High	Very high
Need for cultural controls	Low	Moderate	High	Very high

Table 13.2

A Synthesis of Strategy, Structure, and Control Systems

economies, or from the transfer of core competencies, their organizational simplicity would make this an attractive strategy.

International Firms

Firms pursuing an international strategy attempt to create value by transferring core competencies from home to foreign subsidiaries. If they are diverse, as most of them are, these firms operate with a worldwide product division structure. Headquarters typically maintains centralized control over the source of the firm's core competency, which is most typically found in the R&D and/or marketing functions of the firm. All other operating decisions are decentralized within the firm to subsidiary operations in each country (which in diverse firms report to worldwide product divisions).

The need for coordination is moderate in such firms, reflecting the need to transfer core competencies. Thus, although such firms operate with some integrating mechanisms, they are not that extensive. The relatively low level of interdependence that results translates into a relatively low level of performance ambiguity. These firms can generally get by with output and bureaucratic controls and with incentives that are focused on performance metrics at the level of country subsidiaries. The need for a common organizational culture and common processes is not that great. An important exception to this is when the core skills or competencies of the firm are embedded in processes and culture, in which case the firm needs to pay close attention to transferring those processes and associated culture from the corporate center to country subsidiaries. Overall, although the organization of international firms is more complex than that of multidomestic firms, the increase in the level of complexity is not that great.

Global Firms

Firms pursuing a global strategy focus on the realization of location and experience curve economies. If they are diverse, as most of them are, these firms operate with a worldwide product division structure. To coordinate the firm's globally dispersed web of value creation activities, headquarters typically maintains ultimate control over most operating decisions. In general, global firms are more centralized than enterprises pursuing a multidomestic or international strategy. Reflecting the need for coordination of the various stages of the firms' globally dispersed value chains, the need for integration in these firms also is high. Thus, these firms tend to operate with an array of formal and informal integrating mechanisms. The resulting interdependencies can lead to significant performance ambiguities. As a result, in addition to output and bureaucratic controls, global firms tend to stress the need to build a strong organizational culture that can facilitate coordination and cooperation. They also tend to use incentive systems that are linked to performance metrics at the corporate level, giving the managers of different operations a strong incentive to cooperate with each other to increase the performance of the entire corporation. On average, the organization of global firms is more complex than that of multidomestic and international firms.

Transnational Firms

Firms pursuing a transnational strategy focus on the simultaneous attainment of location and experience curve economies, local responsiveness, and global learning (the multidirectional transfer of core competencies or skills). These firms may operate with matrix-type structures in which both product divisions and geographic areas have significant influence. The need to coordinate a globally dispersed value chain and to transfer core competencies creates pressures for centralizing some operating decisions (particularly production and R&D). At the same time, the need to be locally responsive creates pressures for decentralizing other operating decisions to national operations (particularly marketing). Consequently, these firms tend to mix relatively high degrees of centralization for some operating decisions with relative high degrees of decentralization for other operating decisions.

The need for coordination is particularly high in transnational firms. This is reflected in the use of an array of formal and informal integrating mechanisms, including formal matrix structures and informal management networks. The high level of interdependence of subunits implied by such integration can result in significant performance ambiguities, which raise the costs of control. To reduce these, in addition to output and bureaucratic controls, transnational firms need to cultivate a strong culture and to establish incentives that promote cooperation between subunits.

Environment, Strategy, Architecture, and Performance

Underlying the scheme outlined in Table 13.2 is the notion that a "fit" between strategy and architecture is necessary for a firm to achieve high performance. For a firm to succeed, two conditions must be fulfilled. First, the firm's strategy must be consistent with the environment in which the firm operates. We discussed this issue in Chapter 12 and noted that in some industries a global strategy is most viable, in others an international or transnational strategy may be most viable, and in still others a multidomestic strategy may be most viable (although the number of multidomestic industries is on the decline). Second, the firm's organization architecture must be consistent with its strategy.

If the strategy does not fit the environment, the firm is likely to experience significant performance problems. If the architecture does not fit the strategy, the firm is also likely to experience performance problems. Therefore, to survive, a firm must strive to achieve a *fit* of its environment, its strategy, and its organizational architecture. You will recall that we saw the importance of this concept in the opening case. Philips NV, the Dutch electronics firm, provides another illustration of the need for this fit. For reasons rooted in the history of the firm, Philips operated until recently with an organization typical of a multidomestic enterprise in which operating decisions were decentralized to largely autonomous foreign subsidiaries. Historically, electronics markets were segmented from each other by high trade barriers, so an organization consistent with a multidomestic strategy made sense. However, by the mid-1980s, the industry in which Philips competed had been revolutionized by declining trade barriers, technological change, and the emergence of low-cost Japanese competitors that utilized a global strategy. To survive, Philips needed to adopt a global strategy itself. The firm recognized this and tried to adopt a global posture, but it did little to change its organizational architecture. The firm nominally adopted a matrix structure based on worldwide product divisions and national areas. In reality, however, the national areas continued to dominate the organization, and the product divisions had little more than an advisory role. As a result, Philips' architecture did not fit the strategy, and by the early 1990s Philips was losing money. It was only after four years of wrenching change and large losses that Philips was finally able to tilt the balance of power in its matrix toward the product divisions. By 1995, the fruits of this effort to realign the company's strategy and architecture with the demands of its operating environment were beginning to show up in improved financial performance.[33]

Organizational Change

Multinational firms periodically have to alter their architecture so that it conforms to the changes in the environment in which they are competing and the strategy they are pursuing. To be profitable, Philips NV had to alter its strategy and architecture in the 1990s so that both matched the demands of the competitive environment in the electronics industry, which had shifted from a multidomestic to a global industry. While a detailed consideration of organizational change is beyond the scope of this book, a few comments are warranted regarding the sources of organization inertia and the strategies and tactics for implementing organizational change.

Organizational Inertia

Organizations are difficult to change. Within most organizations, there are strong inertia forces. These forces come from a number of sources. One source of inertia is the existing distribution of power and influence within an organization.[34] The power and influence enjoyed by individual managers is in part a function of their role in the organizational hierarchy, as defined by structural position. By definition, most substantive changes in an organization require a change in structure and, by extension, a change in the distribution of power and influence within the organization. Some individuals will see their power and influence increase as a result of organizational change, and some will see the converse. For example, in the 1990s, Philips NV increased the roles and responsibilities of its global product divisions and decreased the roles and responsibilities of its foreign subsidiary companies. This meant the managers running the global product divisions saw their power and influence increase, while the managers running the foreign subsidiary companies saw their power and influence decline. As might be expected, some managers of foreign subsidiary companies did not like this change and resisted it, which slowed the pace of change. Those whose power and influence are reduced as a consequence of organizational change can be expected to resist it, primarily by arguing that the change might not work. To the extent that they are successful, this constitutes a source of organizational inertia that might slow or stop change.

Another source of organizational inertia is the existing culture, as expressed in norms and value systems. Value systems reflect deeply held beliefs, and as such, they can be very hard to change. If the formal and informal socialization mechanisms within an organization have been emphasizing a consistent set of values for a prolonged period, and if hiring, promotion, and incentive systems have all reinforced these values, then suddenly announcing that those values are no longer appropriate and need to be changed can produce resistance and dissonance among employees. For example, Philips NV historically placed a very high value on local autonomy. The changes of the 1990s implied a reduction in the autonomy enjoyed by foreign subsidiaries, which was counter to the established values of the company and thus resisted.

Organizational inertia might also derive from senior managers' preconceptions about the appropriate business model or paradigm. When a given paradigm has worked well in the past, managers might have trouble accepting that it is no longer appropriate. At Philips, granting considerable autonomy to foreign subsidiaries had worked very well in the past, allowing local managers to tailor product and business strategy to the conditions prevailing in a given country. Since this paradigm had worked so well, it was difficult for many managers to understand why it no longer applied. Consequently, they had difficulty accepting a new or business model and tended to fall back on their established paradigm and ways of doing things. This made change difficult, for it required managers to let go of long-held assumptions about what worked and what didn't work, which was something many of them couldn't do.

Institutional constraints might also act as a source of inertia. National regulations including local content rules and policies pertaining to layoffs might make it difficult for a multinational to alter its global value chain. As with Unilever (see the opening case), a multinational might wish to take control for manufacturing away from local subsidiaries, transfer that control to global product divisions, and consolidate manufacturing at a few choice locations. However, if local content rules (see Chapter 5) require some degree of local production and if regulations regarding layoffs make it difficult or expensive for a multinational to close operations in a country, a multinational may find that these constraints make it very difficult to adopt the most effective strategy and architecture.

Implementing Organizational Change

Although all organizations suffer from inertia, the complexity and global spread of many multinationals might make it particularly difficult for them to change their strategy and architecture to match new organizational realities. Yet at the same time, the trend toward globalization in many industries has made it more critical than ever that many multinationals do just that. In industry after industry, declining barriers to cross-border trade and investment have led to a change in the nature of the competitive environment. Cost pressures have increased, requiring multinationals to respond by streamlining their operations to realize economic benefits associated with location and experience curve economies and with the transfer of competencies and skills within the organization. At the same time, local responsiveness remains an important source of differentiation. To survive in this emerging competitive environment, multinationals must not only change their strategy, but they must also change their architecture so that it matches strategy in discriminating ways. The basic principles for successful organizational change can be summarized as follows: (1) unfreeze the organization through shock therapy, (2) move the organization to a new state through proactive change in the architecture, and (3) refreeze the organization in its new state.

Unfreezing the Organization

Because of inertia forces, incremental change is often no change. Those whose power is threatened by change can too easily resist incremental change. This leads to the big bang theory of change, which maintains that effective change requires taking bold action early to "unfreeze" the established culture of an organization and to change the distribution of power and influence. Shock therapy to unfreeze the organization might include the closure of plants deemed uneconomic or the announcement of a dramatic structural reorganization. It is also important to realize that change will not occur unless senior managers are committed to it. Senior managers must clearly articulate the need for change so employees understand both why it is being pursued and the benefits that will flow from successful change. Senior managers must also practice what they preach and take the necessary bold steps. If employees see senior managers preaching the need for change but not changing their own behavior or making substantive changes in the organization, they will soon lose faith in the change effort, which will flounder as a result.

Moving to the New State

Once an organization has been unfrozen, it must be moved to its new state. Movement requires taking action—closing operations; reorganizing the structure; reassigning responsibilities; changing control, incentive, and reward systems; redesigning processes; and letting people go who are seen as an impediment to change. In other words, movement requires a substantial change in the form of a multinational's organization architecture so that it matches the desired new strategic posture. For movement to be successful, it must be done with sufficient speed. Involving employees in the change effort is an excellent way to get them to appreciate and buy into the needs for change and to help with rapid movement. For example, a firm might delegate substantial responsibility for designing operating processes to lower-level employees. If enough of their recommendations are then acted on, the employees will see the consequences of their efforts and consequently buy into the notion that change is really occurring.

Refreezing the Organization

Refreezing the organization takes longer. It may require that a new culture be established, while the old one is being dismantled. Thus, refreezing requires that employees be socialized into the new way of doing things. Companies will often use management education programs to achieve this. At General Electric, where longtime CEO Jack Welsh instituted a major change in the culture of the company, management education programs were used as a proactive tool to communicate new values to organization members. On their own, however, management education programs are not enough. Hiring policies must be changed to reflect the new realities, with an emphasis on hiring individuals whose own values are consistent with that of the new culture the firm is trying to build. Similarly, control and incentive systems must be consistent with the new realities of the organization, or change will never take. Senior management must recognize that changing culture takes a long time. Any letup in the pressure to change may allow the old culture to reemerge as employees fall back into familiar ways of doing things. The communication task facing senior managers, therefore, is a long-term endeavor that requires managers to be relentless and persistent in their pursuit of change. One striking feature of Jack Welsh's two-decade tenure at GE, for example, is that he never stopped pushing his change agenda. It was a consistent theme of his tenure. He was always thinking up new programs and initiatives to keep pushing the culture of the organization along the desired trajectory.

Chapter Summary

This chapter identified the organizational architecture that can be used by multinational enterprises to manage and direct their global operations. A central theme of the chapter was that different strategies require different architectures; strategy is implemented through architecture. To succeed, a firm must match its architecture to its strategy in discriminating ways. Firms whose architecture does not fit their strategic requirements will experience performance problems. It is also necessary for the different components of architecture to be consistent with each other. The following points were made in the chapter:

1. Organizational architecture refers to the totality of a firm's organization, including formal organizational structure, control systems and incentives, processes, organizational culture, and people.

2. Superior enterprise profitability requires three conditions to be fulfilled: the different elements of a firm's organizational architecture must be *internally consistent*, the organizational architecture must fit the strategy of the firm, and the strategy and architecture of the firm must be consistent with competitive conditions prevailing in the firm's markets.

3. Organizational structure means three things: the formal division of the organization into subunits (horizontal differentiation), the location of decision-making responsibilities within that structure (vertical differentiation), and the establishment of integrating mechanisms.

4. Control systems are the metrics used to measure the performance of subunits and make judgments about how well managers are running those subunits.

5. Incentives refer to the devices used to reward appropriate employee behavior. Many employees receive incentives in the form of annual bonus pay. Incentives are usually closely tied to the performance metrics used for output controls.

6. Processes refer to the manner in which decisions are made and work is performed within the organization. Processes can be found at many different levels within an organization. The core competencies or valuable skills of a firm are often embedded in its processes. Efficient and effective processes can help to lower the costs of value creation and to add additional value to a product.

7. Organizational culture refers to a system of values and norms that is shared among employees. Values and norms express themselves as the behavior patterns or style of an organization that new employees are automatically encouraged to follow by their fellow employees.

8. There are four main dimensions of organizational structure: vertical differentiation, horizontal differentiation, integration, and control systems.

9. Firms pursuing different strategies must adopt a different architecture to implement those strategies successfully. Firms pursuing multidomestic, global, international, and transnational strategies all must adopt an organizational architecture that matches their strategy.

10. While all organizations suffer from inertia, the complexity and global spread of many multinationals might make it particularly difficult for them to change their strategy and architecture to match new organizational realities. At the same time, the trend toward globalization in many industries has made it more critical than ever that many multinationals do just that.

Critical Discussion Questions

1. "The choice of strategy for a multinational firm must depend on a comparison of the benefits of that strategy (in terms of value creation) with the costs of implementing it (as defined by organizational architecture necessary for implementation). On this basis, it may be logical for some firms to pursue a multidomestic strategy, others a global or international strategy, and still others a transnational strategy." Is this statement correct?

2. Discuss this statement: "An understanding of the causes and consequences of performance ambiguity is central to the issue of organizational design in multinational firms."

3. Describe the organizational architecture a transnational firm might adopt to reduce the costs of control.

4. What is the most appropriate organizational architecture for a firm that is competing in an industry where a global strategy is most appropriate?

5. If a firm is changing its strategy from an international to a transnational strategy, what are the most important challenges it is likely to face in implementing this change? How can the firm overcome these challenges?

Organizational Change at Royal Dutch/Shell

The Anglo-Dutch company Royal Dutch/Shell is the world's largest nonstate-owned oil company with activities in more than 130 countries and 1997 revenues of $128 billion. From the 1950s until 1994, Shell operated with a "matrix structure" invented for it by McKinsey, a management consulting firm that specializes in organizational design. Under this matrix structure, the head of each operating company reported to two bosses. One boss was responsible for the geographical region or country in which the operating company was based, while the other was responsible for the business activity that the operating company was engaged in (Shell's business activities included oil exploration and production, oil products, chemicals, gas, and coal). Thus, for example, the head of the local Shell chemical company in Australia reported both to the head of Shell Australia and to the head of Shell's entire chemical division, who was based in London. Both bosses had equal influence and status within the organization.

This matrix structure had two very visible consequences at Shell. First, because each operating company had two bosses to satisfy, decision making typically followed a pattern of consensus building, with differences of perspective between country (or regional) heads on the one hand and the heads of business divisions on the other being worked out through debate. Although this process could be slow and cumbersome, it was seen as a good thing in the oil industry where most big decisions are long-term ones that involve substantial

capital expenditures and where informed debate between different viewpoints can clarify the pros and cons of issues, rather than hinder decision making. Second, because the decision-making process was slow, it was reserved for only the most important decisions (such as major new capital investments). The result was substantial decentralization by default to the heads of the individual operating companies, who were largely left alone to run their own operations. This decentralization helped Shell respond to local differences in government regulations, competitive conditions, and consumer tastes. Thus, for example, the head of Shell's Australian chemical company was given the freedom to determine pricing practices and marketing strategy in the Australian market. Only if Shell wished to undertake a major capital investment, such as building a new chemical plant, would the consensus-building decision-making system be invoked.

As desirable as this matrix structure seemed to many, in 1995 Shell announced a radical plan to dismantle it. The primary reason given by top management for the shift was continuing slack demand for oil and weak oil prices, which had put pressure on Shell's profit margins. Although Shell had traditionally been among the most profitable oil companies in the world, in the early 1990s its relative performance began to slip as other oil companies, such as Exxon, adapted more rapidly to a world of low oil prices by sharply cutting overhead costs and consolidating production in efficient facilities. Consolidating production at these companies often involved serving the world market from a smaller number of large-scale refining facilities and shutting down smaller facilities. In contrast, Shell still operated with a large head office, which was required to effect coordination within Shell's matrix structure, and substantial duplication of oil and chemical refining facilities across operating companies, each of which typically developed the facilities required to serve its own market.

In 1995, Shell's senior management realized that lowering operating costs required a sharp reduction in head office overhead and, where appropriate, the elimination of unnecessary duplication of facilities across countries. To achieve these goals, top executives decided to reorganize the company along divisional lines. Shell now operates with five main global product divisions—exploration and production, oil products, chemicals, gas, and coal. Each operating company reports to whichever global division is the most relevant. Thus, the head of the Australian chemical operation now reports directly to the head of the global chemical division. The thinking is that this will increase the power of the global chemical division and enable that division to eliminate any unnecessary duplication of facilities across countries. Eventually, production may be consolidated in larger facilities that serve an entire region, rather than a single country, thereby enabling Shell to reap greater scale economies.

The country (or regional) chiefs remain but their roles and responsibilities are reduced. Now their primary responsibility is coordination between operating companies within a country (or region) and relations with the local government. There is a solid line of reporting and responsibility between the heads of operating companies and the global divisions and only a dotted line between the heads of operating companies and country chiefs. Thus, for example, the ability of the head of Shell Australia to shape the major capital investment decisions of Shell's Australian chemical operation was substantially reduced as a result of these changes. Furthermore, the simplified reporting system reduced the need for a large head office bureaucracy, and Shell trimmed the work force at its London head office by 1,170, driving down Shell's cost structure.

Sources: "Shell on the Rocks," *The Economist*, June 24, 1995, pp. 57–58; D. Lascelles, "Barons Swept out of Fiefdoms," *Financial Times*, March 30, 1995, p. 15; C. Lorenz, "End of a Corporate Era," *Financial Times*, March 30, 1995, p. 15; R. Corzine, "Shell Discovers Time and Tide Wait for No Man," *Financial Times*, March 10, 1998, p. 17; and R. Corzine, "Oiling the Group's Wheels of Change," *Financial Times*, April 1, 1998, p. 12.

Case Discussion Questions

1. What were the benefits of the matrix structure at Shell? What were the drawbacks? Did the matrix structure fit the environment of the global oil and chemical industries in the 1980s?

2. What shift occurred in Shell's operating environment in the 1990s? How did this shift affect the financial performance of the firm? What does this suggest about the fit between strategy and architecture?

3. What kind of structure did Shell adopt in 1995? In what ways did the architecture of Shell's organization after 1995 differ from that before 1995?

4. Comment on the fit between operating environment, strategy, and organizational architecture at Shell after the 1995 reorganization. Did the change lead to enhanced fit?

Notes

1. D. Naidler, M. Gerstein, and R. Shaw, *Organization Architecture* (San Francisco: Jossey-Bass, 1992).

2. G. Morgan, *Images of Organization* (Beverly Hills, CA: Sage Publications, 1986).

3. The material in this section draws on John Child, *Organizations* (London: Harper & Row, 1984).

4. Allan Cane, "Microsoft Reorganizes to Meet Market Challenges," *Financial Times*, March 16, 1994, p. 1.

5. For research evidence that is related to this issue, see J. Birkinshaw, "Entrepreneurship in the Multinational Corporation: The Characteristics of Subsidiary Initiatives," *Strategic Management Journal* 18 (1997), pp. 207–29, and J. Birkinshaw, N. Hood, and S. Jonsson, "Building Firm Specific Advantages in Multinational Corporations: The Role of Subsidiary Initiatives," *Strategic Management Journal* 19 (1998), pp. 221–41.

6. For more detail, see S. M. Davis, "Managing and Organizing Multinational Corporations," in C. A. Bartlett and S. Ghoshal, *Transnational Management* (Homewood, IL: Richard D. Irwin, 1992).

7. A. D. Chandler, *Strategy and Structure: Chapters in the History of the Industrial Enterprise* (Cambridge, MA: MIT Press, 1962).

8. Davis, "Managing and Organizing Multinational Corporations."

9. J. M. Stopford and L. T. Wells, *Strategy and Structure of the Multinational Enterprise* (New York: Basic Books, 1972).

10. C. A. Bartlett and S. Ghoshal, *Managing across Borders* (Boston: Harvard Business School Press, 1989).

11. Guy de Jonquieres, "Unilever Adopts a Clean Sheet Approach," *Financial Times*, October 21, 1991, p. 13.

12. See J. R. Galbraith, *Designing Complex Organizations* (Reading, MA: Addison-Wesley, 1977).

13. See Bartlett and Ghoshal, *Managing across Borders*, and F. V. Guterl, "Goodbye, Old Matrix," *Business Month*, February 1989, pp. 32–38.

14. M. S. Granovetter, "The Strength of Weak Ties," *American Journal of Sociology* 78 (1973), pp. 1360–80.

15. A. K. Gupta, and V. J. Govindarajan, "Knowledge Flows within Multinational Corporations," *Strategic Management Journal* 21, no. 4 (2000), pp. 473–96.

16. For examples, see W. H. Davidow and M. S. Malone, *The Virtual Corporation* (New York: Harper Collins, 1992).

17. W. G. Ouchi, "Markets, Bureaucracies, and Clans," *Administrative Science Quarterly* 25 (1980), pp. 129–44.

18. For some recent empirical work that addresses this issue, see T. P. Murtha, S. A. Lenway, and R. P. Bagozzi, "Global Mind Sets and Cognitive Shift in a Complex Multinational Corporation," *Strategic Management Journal* 19 (1998), pp. 97–114.

19. C. W. L. Hill, M. E. Hitt, and R. E. Hoskisson, "Cooperative versus Competitive Structures in Related and Unrelated Diversified Firms," *Organization Science* 3 (1992), pp. 501–21.

20. Murtha, Lenway, and Bagozzi, "Global Mind Sets."

21. M. Hammer and J. Champy, *Reengineering the Corporation* (New York: Harper Business, 1993).

22. T. Kostova, "Transnational Transfer of Strategic Organizational Practices: A Contextual Perspective," *Academy of Management Review* 24, no. 2 (1999), pp. 308–24.

23. E. H. Schein, "What Is Culture?" in P. J. Frost et al., *Reframing Organizational Culture* (Newbury Park, CA: Sage, 1991).

24. E. H. Schein, *Organizational Culture and Leadership*, 2nd ed. (San Francisco: Jossey-Bass, 1992).

25. G. Morgan, *Images of Organization* (Beverly Hills, CA: Sage, 1986).

26. R. Dore, *British Factory, Japanese Factory* (London: Allen & Unwin, 1973).

27. M. Dickson, "Back to the Future," *Financial Times*, May 30, 1994, p. 7.

28. See J. P. Kotter and J. L. Heskett, *Corporate Culture and Performance* (New York: Free Press, 1992) and M. L. Tushman and C. A. O'Reilly, *Winning through Innovation* (Boston: Harvard Business School Press, 1997).

29. Kotter and Heskett, *Corporate Culture and Performance*.

30. The classic song of praise was produced by T. Peters and R. H. Waterman, *In Search of Excellence* (New York: Harper & Row, 1982). Ironically, IBM's decline began shortly after Peters and Waterman's book was published.

31. Kotter and Heskett, *Corporate Culture and Performance*.

32. Bartlett and Ghoshal, *Managing across Borders*.

33. See F. J. Aguilar and M. Y. Yoshino, "The Philips Group: 1987," Howard Business School Case, 388-050, 1987; "Philips Fights Flab," *The Economist*, April 7, 1990, pp. 73–74; and R. Van de Krol, "Philips Wins Back Old Friends," *Financial Times*, July 14, 1995, p. 14.

34. J. Pfeffer, *Managing with Power: Politics and Influence within Organizations* (Boston: Harvard Business School Press, 1992).

Chapter 14

Entry Strategy and Strategic Alliances

ING Group was formed in 1991 from the merger between the third largest bank in the Netherlands and the country's largest insurance company. Since then, the company has grown rapidly to become one of the top 10 financial services firms in the world, with operations in 65 countries and a wide range of products in banking, insurance, and asset management. ING's strategy has been to expand rapidly across national borders, primarily through a series of careful acquisitions. Its formula has been to pick a target that has good managers and a strong local presence, take a small stake in the company, win the trust of managers, and then propose a takeover. After the deal, the management and products of the acquired companies have been left largely intact, but ING has required them to sell ING products alongside their own. ING's big push has been the selling of insurance, banking, and investment products, something it has been doing in Holland since the original 1991 merger (in Holland, some 20 percent of ING's insurance products are sold through banks).

Two changes in the regulatory environment have helped ING pursue this strategy. One has been a trend to remove regulatory barriers that traditionally kept different parts of the financial services industry separate. In the United States, for example, a Depression-era law known as the Glass Steagall Act forbid insurance companies, banks, and asset managers such as mutual fund companies from selling each other's products. The U.S. Congress repealed this act in 1999, opening the way for the consolidation of the U.S. financial services industry. Many other countries that had similar regulations removed them in the 1990s. ING's native Holland was one of the first countries to remove barriers between different areas of the financial services industry. ING took advantage of this to become a pioneer of banking and insurance combinations in Europe. Another significant regulatory development occurred in 1997 when the World Trade Organization struck a deal between its member nations that effectively removed barriers to cross-border investment in financial services. This made it much easier for a company such as ING to build a global financial services business.

ING's expansion was initially centered on Europe where its largest acquisitions have included banks in Germany and Belgium. However, in recent years the centerpiece of ING's strategy has been its aggressive moves into the United States. While ING's Dutch insurance predecessor, Nationale-Nederlanden, had owned several small, regional U.S. insurance companies since the 1970s, the big push into the United States began with the 1997 acquisition of Equitable Life Insurance Company of Iowa. This was followed by the acquisitions of Furman Selz, a New York investment bank, whose activities complement those of Barings, a British-based investment bank with significant U.S. activities that ING acquired in 1995. In 2000, ING acquired ReliaStar Financial Services and the nonhealth insurance units of Aetna Financial Services. These acquisitions combined to make ING one of the top 10 financial services companies in the United States.

ING was attracted to the United States by several factors. The United States is by far the world's largest financial services market, so any company aspiring to be a global player must have a significant presence there. Deregulation made ING's strategy of cross-selling financial service products feasible in the United States. Despite some state-by-state regulation of insurance, ING says it is easier to do business in America than in the European Union, where the patchwork of languages and cultures makes it difficult to build a pan-European business with a single identity. Another lure is that with more and more Americans responsible for managing their own retirement with 401k plans and the like rather than traditional pensions, the personal investment business in the United States is booming, which has increased ING's appetite for U.S. financial services firms. In contrast, pensions are still primarily taken care of by national governments in Europe. Furthermore, in recent years American insurance companies have traded at relatively low price–earnings ratios, making them seem like bargains compared to their European counterparts, which trade at higher valuations. Building a substantial U.S. presence also brings with it the benefits of geographic diversification, allowing ING to offset any revenue or profit shortfalls in one region with earnings elsewhere in the world.

Finally, ING has found it somewhat easier to make acquisitions in the United States than in Europe, where despite the rise of the European Union, national pride has made it difficult for ING to acquire local companies. ING's initial attempt to acquire a Belgium bank in 1992 was rebuffed, primarily due to nationalistic concerns, and it took ING until 1997 to make the acquisition. Similarly, a 1999 attempt to acquire a major French bank, Credit Commercial de France, in which it already held a 19 percent stake, was turned down. According to news reports, French regulators had expressed concerns over what would have been the first foreign acquisition of a French bank, and the board of CCF believed the acquisition should not proceed without the regulators' blessing.

Having established a major U.S. presence, ING's strategy now is to push forward with the cross-selling of its various insurance, banking, and asset management products. In mid-2000, the company announced the establishment of ING Direct, an online banking concept the company introduced in Canada, Australia, Spain, and France, where it has performed well. The online bank features a savings account paying 6.5 percent interest, about triple that found at traditional banks but in line with other virtual banks, which have a much lower cost structure. Although ING Direct does not offer checking accounts, which are money losers for traditional banks, it can electronically link an ING account to checking accounts that customers have at other banks, allowing them to easily transfer money. In addition to a savings account, ING Direct also offers consumer loans, mortgages, life insurance, and mutual finds. In an interesting move, instead of bank branches the company is setting up a scattering of cyber cafes where customers can drop in, buy a cup of coffee and a muffin, browse the Web, and access their online account.

Sources: J. Carreyrou, "Dutch Financial Giant Maps Its U.S. Invasion," *Wall Street Journal*, June 22, 2000, p. A17; J. B. Treaster, "ING Group Makes Its Move in Virtual Banking and Insurance," *New York Times*, August 26, 2000, p. C1; and "The Lion's Friendly Approach," *The Economist*, December 18, 2000.

▊ Introduction

This chapter is concerned with three closely related topics: (1) the decision of which foreign markets to enter, when to enter them, and on what scale; (2) the choice of entry mode, and (3) the role of strategic alliances. Any firm contemplating foreign expansion must first struggle with the issue of which foreign markets to enter and the timing and scale of entry. The choice of which markets to enter should be driven by an assessment of relative long-run growth and profit potential. The opening case reported ING's rapid expansion into the United States, making several major acquisitions. This significant commitment on ING's part was made in response to an assessment that the U.S. financial services market was not only the world's largest, but was also growing rapidly. ING decided it needed to move with haste to build a U.S. presence in advance of slower moving competitors, thereby serving notice that it intended to be one of the top 10 financial services companies in both the United States and the world. The timing of entry was also driven by deregulation, which changed the nature of the financial services industry in the United States, allowing insurance companies and banks to enter each other's markets. ING already had experience cross-selling in Europe, and it wanted to be among the first to exploit a similar opportunity in the United States.

The choice of mode for entering a foreign market is another major issue with which international businesses must wrestle. The various modes for serving foreign markets are exporting, licensing or franchising to host-country firms, establishing joint ventures with a host-country firm, setting up a new wholly owned subsidiary in a host country to serve its market, or acquiring an established enterprise in the host nation to serve that market. Each of these options has advantages and disadvantages. The magnitude of the advantages and disadvantages associated with each entry mode is determined by a number of factors, including transport costs, trade barriers, political risks, economic risks, costs, and firm strategy. The optimal entry mode varies by situation, depending on these factors. Thus, whereas some firms may best serve a given market by exporting, other firms may better serve the market by setting up a new wholly owned subsidiary or by acquiring an established enterprise. As we saw in the opening case, ING has primarily entered foreign markets through acquisitions of established players in those markets. ING wanted to be one of the first companies to take advantage of changes in the national regulatory environments that allowed insurance companies and banks to enter each other's markets. Acquisitions enabled the company to attain this goal more rapidly than establishing new ventures.

We touched on the topic of entry modes when we examined foreign direct investment (FDI) in Chapter 6. There we related economic theory to exporting, licensing, and foreign direct investment as means of entering foreign markets. Here we integrate that material with the material we discussed in Chapter 12 on firm strategy to present a comprehensive picture of the factors that determine the optimal entry mode. We consider a wider range of modes in this chapter as well as mixed entry modes. (For example, establishing joint ventures and wholly owned subsidiaries in another country are both FDI, but we did not make a distinction in Chapter 6.)

The final topic of this chapter is strategic alliances. Strategic alliances are cooperative agreements between actual or potential competitors. The term *strategic alliances* is often used to embrace a variety of arrangements between actual or potential competitors including cross-shareholding deals, licensing arrangements, formal joint ventures, and informal cooperative arrangements. The motives for entering strategic alliances are varied, but they often include market access; hence, the overlap with the topic of entry mode. Strategic alliances have advantages and disadvantages, and a firm must weigh these carefully before deciding whether to ally itself with an actual or potential competitor. Perhaps the biggest danger is that the firm will give away more to its ally than it receives. As we will see, firms can reduce this risk in the way they structure strategic alliances. We will also see how firms can build alliances that benefit both partners.

The chapter opens with a look at how firms choose which foreign markets to enter and at the factors that are important in determining the best timing and scale of entry. Then we will review the various entry modes available, discussing the advantages and disadvantages of each option. Next, we will consider the factors that determine a firm's optimal entry mode and then look at the advantages and disadvantages of engaging in strategic alliances with competitors. Finally, we will consider how a firm should select an ally, structure the alliance, and manage it to maximize the advantages and minimize the disadvantages associated with alliances.

Basic Entry Decisions ■

In this section, we look at three basic decisions that a firm contemplating foreign expansion must make: which markets to enter, when to enter those markets, and on what scale.[1]

❙ Which Foreign Markets?

There are more than 180 nation-states in the world, but they do not all hold the same profit potential for a firm contemplating foreign expansion. Ultimately, the choice must be based on an assessment of a nation's long-run profit potential. This potential is a function of several factors, many of which we have already studied in earlier chapters. In Chapter 2, we looked in detail at the economic and political factors that influence the potential attractiveness of a foreign market. There we noted that the attractiveness of a country as a potential market for an international business depends on balancing the benefits, costs, and risks associated with doing business in that country.

Chapter 2 also noted that the long-run economic benefits of doing business in a country are a function of factors such as the size of the market (in terms of demographics), the present wealth (purchasing power) of consumers in that market, and the likely future wealth of consumers. While some markets are very large when measured by number of consumers (e.g., China and India), low living standards may imply limited purchasing power and a relatively small market when measured in economic terms. We also argued that the costs and risks associated with doing business in a foreign country are typically lower in economically advanced and politically stable democratic nations, and they are greater in less developed and politically unstable nations.

However, this calculus is complicated by the fact that the potential long-run benefits bear little relationship to a nation's current stage of economic development or political stability. Long-run benefits depend on likely future economic growth rates, and economic growth appears to be a function of a free market system and a country's capacity for growth (which may be greater in less developed nations). This leads one to the conclusion that, other things being equal, the benefit–cost–risk trade-off is likely to be most favorable in politically stable developed and developing nations that have free market systems, and where there is not a dramatic upsurge in either inflation rates or private-sector debt. The trade-off is likely to be least favorable in politically unstable developing nations that operate with a mixed or command economy or in developing nations where speculative financial bubbles have led to excess borrowing (see Chapter 2 for further details).

By applying the reasoning processes alluded to above and discussed in more detail in Chapter 2, a firm can rank countries in terms of their attractiveness and long-run profit potential. Preference is then given to entering markets that rank highly. In the case of ING, its recent international ventures in the financial services business have been focused on Europe and North America (see the opening case). These regions have large financial services markets and exhibit relatively low political and economic risks, so it makes sense that they would be attractive to ING. The company should be able to capture a large enough share of the market in each country to justify its investment in setting up business there.

One other fact we have not yet discussed is the value an international business can create in a foreign market. This depends on the suitability of its product offering to that market and the nature of indigenous competition.[2] If the international business can offer a product that has not been widely available in that market and that satisfies an unmet need, the value of that product to consumers is likely to be much greater than if the international business simply offers the same type of product that indigenous competitors and other foreign entrants are already offering. Greater value translates into an ability to charge higher prices and/or to build sales volume more rapidly. On this count, because ING already had substantial experience in cross-selling insurance and banking products in Holland, it was relatively well positioned to exploit the opportunity for doing so in the United States, where cross-selling had been limited by regulatory constraints until 1999.

Timing of Entry

Once attractive markets have been identified, it is important to consider the timing of entry. We say that entry is early when an international business enters a foreign market before other foreign firms and late when it enters after other international businesses have already established themselves. The advantages frequently associated with entering a market early are commonly known as first-mover advantages.[3] One first-mover advantage is the ability to preempt rivals and capture demand by establishing a strong brand name. A second advantage is the ability to build sales volume in that country and ride down the experience curve ahead of rivals, giving the early entrant a cost advantage over later entrants. This cost advantage may enable the early entrant to cut prices below that of later entrants, thereby driving them out of the market. A third advantage is the ability of early entrants to create switching costs that tie customers into their products or services. Such switching costs make it difficult for later entrants to win business.

There can also be disadvantages associated with entering a foreign market before other international businesses. These are often referred to as **first-mover disadvan-**

tages.[4] These disadvantages may give rise to pioneering costs. **Pioneering costs** are costs that an early entrant has to bear that a later entrant can avoid. Pioneering costs arise when the business system in a foreign country is so different from that in a firm's home market that the enterprise has to devote considerable effort, time, and expense to learning the rules of the game. Pioneering costs include the costs of business failure if the firm, due to its ignorance of the foreign environment, makes some major mistakes. A certain liability is associated with being a foreigner, and this liability is greater for foreign firms that enter a national market early.[5] Recent research seems to confirm that the probability of survival increases if an international business enters a national market after several other foreign firms have already done so.[6] The late entrant may benefit by observing and learning from the mistakes made by early entrants.

Pioneering costs also include the costs of promoting and establishing a product offering, including the costs of educating customers. These costs can be particularly significant when the product being promoted is unfamiliar to local consumers. In contrast, later entrants may be able to ride on an early entrant's investments in learning and customer education by watching how the early entrant proceeded in the market, by avoiding costly mistakes made by the early entrant, and by exploiting the market potential created by the early entrant's investments in customer education. For example, KFC introduced the Chinese to American-style fast food, but a later entrant, McDonald's, has capitalized on the market in China.

An early entrant may be put at a severe disadvantage, relative to a later entrant, if regulations change in a way that diminishes the value of an early entrant's investments. This is a serious risk in many developing nations where the rules that govern business practices are still evolving. Early entrants can find themselves at a disadvantage if a subsequent change in regulations invalidates prior assumptions about the best business model for operating in that country. For an illustration of the potential difficulties and hazards, consider the experience of the Amway Corporation in China, which is described in the accompanying Management Focus.

❙ Scale of Entry and Strategic Commitments

Another issue that an international business needs to consider when contemplating market entry is the scale of entry. Entering a market on a large scale involves the commitment of significant resources. For example, ING had to spend several billion dollars to acquire its U.S. operations. Not all firms have the resources necessary to enter on a large scale, and even some large firms prefer to enter foreign markets on a small scale and then build slowly as they become more familiar with the market.

The consequences of entering on a significant scale are associated with the value of the resulting strategic commitments.[7] A strategic commitment has a long-term impact and is difficult to reverse. Deciding to enter a foreign market on a significant scale is a major strategic commitment. Strategic commitments, such as large-scale market entry, can have an important influence on the nature of competition in a market. For example, by entering the U.S. financial services market on a significant scale, ING has signaled its commitment to the market. This will have several effects. On the positive side, it will make it easier for the company to attract customers and distributors (such as insurance agents). The scale of entry gives both customers and distributors reasons for believing that ING will remain in the market for the long run. The scale of entry may also give other foreign institutions considering entry into the United States pause; now they will have to compete not only against indigenous institutions in the United States, but also against an aggressive and successful European institution. On the negative side, by committing itself heavily to the United States, ING may have fewer resources available to support expansion in other desirable markets, such as Japan. The commitment to the United States limits the company's strategic flexibility.

As suggested by this example, significant strategic commitments are neither unambiguously good nor bad. Rather, they tend to change the competitive playing field and

Amway Goes Astray in China

Amway is a U.S.-based direct sales company that sells a variety of household and personal products using a grassroots marketing approach. The company signs up individual consumers as "distributors" who then earn a commission on sales of Amway products. Almost anyone can become an Amway distributor by purchasing for a few hundred dollars a "starter kit" that contains an assortment of Amway products and promotional literature and by attending a few meetings for training about the Amway system, products, and sales techniques. The distributors are taught to engage in door-to-door selling and are encouraged to sell to friends, relatives, and acquaintances. In 1997, the company racked up $7 billion in sales using this approach, more than half outside the United States.

Amway entered China in 1995, closely behind rival direct marketers Avon and Mary Kay. Several features attracted Amway to China. With a population of 1.2 billion people, the country offered a potentially huge consumer market. Given Amway's emphasis on direct selling, the lack of well-developed retail distribution systems in China seemed to play right into the company's hands. An Amway representative could offer a far broader range of products than could be found at most Chinese retail outlets and often at a lower price. Also, the strategy of selling to friends, relatives, and acquaintances seemed to make great sense in a society that emphasizes social relations and interpersonal networks.

From the outset, Amway was determined to be one of the first direct marketers to establish a significant presence in China. Accordingly, it entered the country on a significant scale, quickly surpassing Avon and Mary Kay to become the largest direct marketer in China. By early 1998, Amway seemed to be doing well. The company had signed up 80,000 distributors in 37 cities across mainland China. It had opened a major factory in Guangzhou and had plans to invest $30 million in a second factory in Shanghai. Sales had reached $178 million in 1997, an 80 percent increase from the previous year. Then, unexpectedly, on April 22, 1998, the Chinese government announced a ban on direct selling!

According to the Chinese government, direct selling practices such as those employed by Amway spawned "weird cults, triads, superstitious groups, and hooliganism." One problem was that the success of Amway and its American kin had encouraged thousands of local imitators, including a number of fraudulent enterprises and fly-by-night operators that sold everything from fake gold to potency pills. The government also objected to the motivational meetings used by Amway and others to reward top sellers and recruit new ones. The official Chinese media compared such gatherings—at which people sang and chanted company slogans—to "religious cults." The *People's Daily*, the mouthpiece of China's governing Communist party, complained that the meetings encouraged "excessive hugging" and references to "God."

Facing the loss of their Chinese investments, the U.S. companies called in the heavy cavalry in the form of U.S. Trade Representative Charlene Barshefsky. After intense pressure, the Chinese government agreed to a partial reversal of the ban. Under the new regulations, issued in July 1998, the ban on direct selling stays in place, but Amway, Avon, and Mary Kay will be allowed to sell their products through retail outlets. In addition, they can use their sales representatives for service and delivery but not for direct selling. The new regulations also state that only companies with an investment of more than $10 million may establish direct sales agents.

Amway restarted its business in China the day after the change in regulations was announced. However, the three-month shutdown had cost the company millions of dollars in lost sales. More significantly perhaps, the ban on direct selling made it impossible for Amway to follow its normal business model in China. Given this, the company might not grow as fast as planned. An unforeseen change in the regulations governing a critical element of business practice in China significantly diminished the value of the company's investment in the country and negated much of its early-mover advantage.

Sources: L. Pappas, "Amway Sells Itself in China," *St. Petersburg Times,* March 15, 1998, p. 1H; M. Farley, "Avon and Amway Reopen in China," *Los Angeles Times,* July 25, 1998, p. D1; and Associated Press, "China Gives Amway Sales OK," *Minneapolis Star Tribune,* July 22, 1998, p. 3D.

unleash a number of changes, some of which may be desirable and some of which will not be. It is important for a firm to think through the implications of large-scale entry into a market and act accordingly. Of particular relevance is trying to identify how actual and potential competitors might react to large-scale entry into a market. Also, the large-scale entrant is more likely than the small-scale entrant to be able to capture first-mover advantages associated with demand preemption, scale economies, and switching costs.

The value of the commitments that flow from large-scale entry into a foreign market must be balanced against the resulting risks and lack of flexibility associated with significant commitments. But strategic inflexibility can also have value. A famous example from military history illustrates the value of inflexibility. When Hernán Cortés landed in Mexico, he ordered his men to burn all but one of his ships. Cortés reasoned that by eliminating their only method of retreat, his men had no choice but to fight hard to win against the Aztecs—and ultimately they did.[8]

Balanced against the value and risks of the commitments associated with large-scale entry are the benefits of a small-scale entry. Small-scale entry allows a firm to learn about a foreign market while limiting the firm's exposure to that market. Small-scale entry is a way to gather information about a foreign market before deciding whether to enter on a significant scale and how best to enter. By giving the firm time to collect information, small-scale entry reduces the risks associated with a subsequent large-scale entry. But the lack of commitment associated with small-scale entry may make it more difficult for the small-scale entrant to build market share and to capture first-mover or early-mover advantages. The risk-averse firm that enters a foreign market on a small scale may limit its potential losses, but it may also miss the chance to capture first-mover advantages.

❘Summary

There are no "right" decisions here, just decisions that are associated with different levels of risk and reward. Entering a large developing nation such as China or India before most other international businesses in the firm's industry, and entering on a large scale, will be associated with high levels of risk. In such cases, the liability of being foreign is increased by the absence of prior foreign entrants whose experience can be a useful guide. At the same time, the potential long-term rewards associated with such a strategy are great. The early large-scale entrant into a major developing nation may be able to capture significant first-mover advantages that will bolster its long-run position in that market.[9] In contrast, entering developed nations such as Australia or Canada after other international businesses in the firm's industry, and entering on a small scale to first learn more about those markets, will be associated with much lower levels of risk. However, the potential long-term rewards are also likely to be lower because the firm is essentially forgoing the opportunity to capture first-mover advantages and because the lack of commitment signaled by small-scale entry may limit its future growth potential.

This section has been written largely from the perspective of a business based in a developing country considering entry into foreign markets. In a recent article, Christopher Bartlett and Sumantra Ghoshal pointed out the ability that businesses based in developing nations have to enter foreign markets and become global players.[10] Although such firms tend to be late entrants into foreign markets, and although their resources may be limited, Bartlett and Ghoshal argue that such late movers can still succeed against well-established global competitors by pursuing appropriate strategies. In particular, Bartlett and Ghoshal argue that companies based in developing nations should use the entry of foreign multinationals as an opportunity to learn from these competitors by benchmarking their operations and performance against them. Furthermore, they suggest that the local company may be able to find ways to differentiate itself from a foreign multinational, for example, by focusing on market niches that the multinational ignores or is unable to serve effectively if it has a standardized global product offering. Having improved its performance through learning and differentiated its product offering, the firm from a developing nation may then be able to

ManagementFocus

The Jollibee Phenomenon—A Philippine Multinational

Jollibee is one of the Philippines' phenomenal business success stories. Jollibee, which stands for "Jolly Bee," began operations in 1975 as a two-branch ice cream parlor. It later expanded its menu to include hot sandwiches and other meals. Encouraged by early success, Jollibee Foods Corporation was incorporated in 1978, with a network that had grown to seven outlets. In 1981, when Jollibee had 11 stores, McDonald's began to open stores in Manila, the capital city. Many observers thought Jollibee would have difficulty competing against McDonald's. However, Jollibee saw this as an opportunity to learn from a very successful global competitor. Jollibee benchmarked its performance against that of McDonalds's and started to adopt operational systems similar to those used at McDonald's to control its quality, cost, and service at the store level. This helped Jollibee to improve its performance.

As it came to better understand McDonald's business model, Jollibee began to look for a weakness in McDonald's global strategy. Jollibee executives concluded that McDonald's fare was too standardized for many locals, and that the local firm could gain share by tailoring its menu to local tastes. Jollibee's hamburgers were set apart by a secret mix of spices blended into the ground beef to make the burgers sweeter than those produced by McDonald's, appealing more to Philippine tastes. It also offered local fare including various rice dishes, pineapple burgers, banana *langka* and peach mango pies for desserts. By pursuing this strategy, Jollibee maintained a leadership position over the global giant. By 2001, Jollibee had 366 stores in the Philippines and a market share of more than 50 percent.

In the mid-1980s, Jollibee had gained enough confidence to start expanding internationally. Its initial ventures were into neighboring Asian countries such as Indonesia, where it pursued the strategy of localizing the menu to better match local tastes, thereby differentiating itself from McDonald's. In 1987, Jollibee entered the Middle East, where a large contingent of expatriate Filipino workers provided a ready-made market for the company. The strategy of focusing on expatriates worked so well that in the late 1990s Jollibee decided to enter another foreign market where there was a large Filipino population—the United States. Between 1999 and 2001, Jollibee opened five stores in the United States, all in California. Even though many believe the U.S. fast-food market is saturated, the stores have performed better than expected. While the initial clientele was strongly biased toward the expatriate Filipino community, where Jollibee's brand awareness is high, non-Filipinos increasingly are coming to the restaurant. In the San Francisco store, which has been open the longest, over half the customers are now non-Filipino. Today Jollibee has 25 international stores and a potentially bright future as a niche player in a market that has historically been dominated by U.S. multinationals.

Sources: Christopher Bartlett and Sumantra Ghoshal, "Going Global: Lessons from Late Movers," *Harvard Business Review*, March–April 2000, pp. 132–45; "Jollibee Battles Burger Giants in US Market," *Philippine Daily Inquirer*, July 13, 2000; and *www.jollibee.com.ph*.

pursue its own international expansion strategy. Even though the firm may be a late entrant into many countries, by benchmarking and then differentiating itself from early movers in global markets, the firm from the developing nation may still be able to build a strong international business presence. A good example of how this can work is given in the accompanying Management Focus, which looks at how Jollibee, a Philippines-based fast-food chain, has started to build a global presence in a market dominated by American multinationals such as McDonald's and KFC.

▌ Entry Modes

Once a firm decides to enter a foreign market, the question arises as to the best mode of entry. Firms can use six different modes to enter foreign markets: exporting, turnkey projects, licensing, franchising, establishing joint ventures with a host-country firm, or setting up a new wholly owned subsidiary in the host country. Each entry mode has advantages and disadvantages. Managers need to consider these carefully when deciding which to use.[11]

Exporting

Many manufacturing firms begin their global expansion as exporters and only later switch to another mode for serving a foreign market. We take a close look at the mechanics of exporting in the next chapter. Here we focus on the advantages and disadvantages of exporting as an entry mode.

Advantages

Exporting has two distinct advantages. First, it avoids the often-substantial costs of establishing manufacturing operations in the host country. Second, exporting may help a firm achieve experience curve and location economies (see Chapter 12). By manufacturing the product in a centralized location and exporting it to other national markets, the firm may realize substantial scale economies from its global sales volume. This is how Sony came to dominate the global TV market, how Matsushita came to dominate the VCR market, how many Japanese automakers made inroads into the U.S. market, and how South Korean firms such as Samsung gained market share in computer memory chips.

Disadvantages

Exporting has a number of drawbacks. First, exporting from the firm's home base may not be appropriate if there are lower-cost locations for manufacturing the product abroad (i.e., if the firm can realize location economies by moving production elsewhere). Thus, particularly for firms pursuing global or transnational strategies, it may be preferable to manufacture where the mix of factor conditions is most favorable from a value creation perspective and to export to the rest of the world from that location. This is not so much an argument against exporting as an argument against exporting from the firm's home country. Many U.S. electronics firms have moved some of their manufacturing to the Far East because of the availability of low-cost, highly skilled labor there. They then export from that location to the rest of the world, including the United States.

A second drawback to exporting is that high transport costs can make exporting uneconomical, particularly for bulk products. One way of getting around this is to manufacture bulk products regionally. This strategy enables the firm to realize some economies from large-scale production and at the same time to limit its transport costs. For example, many multinational chemical firms manufacture their products regionally, serving several countries from one facility.

Another drawback is that tariff barriers can make exporting uneconomical. Similarly, the threat of tariff barriers by the host-country government can make it very risky. An implicit threat by the U.S. Congress to impose tariffs on imported Japanese autos led many Japanese auto firms to set up manufacturing plants in the United States. By 1990, almost 50 percent of all Japanese cars sold in the United States were manufactured locally—up from 0 percent in 1985.

A fourth drawback to exporting arises when a firm delegates its marketing in each country where it does business to a local agent. (This is common for firms that are just beginning to export.) Foreign agents often carry the products of competing firms and so have divided loyalties. In such cases, the foreign agent may not do as good a job as the firm would if it managed its marketing itself. One way around this problem is to set up a wholly owned subsidiary in the country to handle local marketing. By doing this, the firm can exercise tight control over marketing in the country while reaping the cost advantages of manufacturing the product in a single location.

Turnkey Projects

Firms that specialize in the design, construction, and start-up of turnkey plants are common in some industries. In a **turnkey project,** the contractor agrees to handle every detail of the project for a foreign client, including the training of operating personnel. At completion of the contract, the foreign client is handed the "key" to a plant that is ready for full operation—hence, the term *turnkey*. This is a means of exporting process technology to other countries. Turnkey projects are most common in the chemical, pharmaceutical, petroleum refining, and metal refining industries, all of which use complex, expensive production technologies.

Advantages

The know-how required to assemble and run a technologically complex process, such as refining petroleum or steel, is a valuable asset. Turnkey projects are a way of earning great economic returns from that asset. The strategy is particularly useful where FDI is limited by host-government regulations. For example, the governments of many oil-rich countries have set out to build their own petroleum refining industries, so they restrict FDI in their oil and refining sectors. But because many of these countries lacked petroleum-refining technology, they gained it by entering into turnkey projects with foreign firms that had the technology. Such deals are often attractive to the selling firm because without them, they would have no way to earn a return on their valuable know-how in that country. A turnkey strategy can also be less risky than conventional FDI. In a country with unstable political and economic environments, a longer-term investment might expose the firm to unacceptable political and/or economic risks (e.g., the risk of nationalization or of economic collapse).

Disadvantages

Three main drawbacks are associated with a turnkey strategy. First, the firm that enters into a turnkey deal will have no long-term interest in the foreign country. This can be a disadvantage if that country subsequently proves to be a major market for the output of the process that has been exported. One way around this is to take a minority equity interest in the operation. Second, the firm that enters into a turnkey project with a foreign enterprise may inadvertently create a competitor. For example, many of the Western firms that sold oil refining technology to firms in Saudi Arabia, Kuwait, and other Gulf states now find themselves competing with these firms in the world oil market. Third, if the firm's process technology is a source of competitive advantage, then selling this technology through a turnkey project is also selling competitive advantage to potential and/or actual competitors.

Licensing

A **licensing agreement** is an arrangement whereby a licensor grants the rights to intangible property to another entity (the licensee) for a specified period, and in return, the licensor receives a royalty fee from the licensee.[12] Intangible property includes patents, inventions, formulas, processes, designs, copyrights, and trademarks. For example, to enter the Japanese market, Xerox, inventor of the photocopier, established a joint venture with Fuji Photo that is known as Fuji-Xerox (see the Management Focus for more details). Xerox then licensed its xerographic know-how to Fuji-Xerox. In return, Fuji-Xerox paid Xerox a royalty fee equal to 5 percent of the net sales revenue that Fuji-Xerox earned from the sales of photocopiers based on Xerox's patented know-how. In the Fuji-Xerox case, the license was originally granted for 10 years, and it has been renegotiated and extended several times since. The licensing agreement between Xerox and Fuji-Xerox also limited Fuji-Xerox's direct sales to the Asian Pacific region (although Fuji-Xerox does supply Xerox with photocopiers that are sold in North America under the Xerox label).[13]

Advantages

In the typical international licensing deal, the licensee puts up most of the capital necessary to get the overseas operation going. Thus, a primary advantage of licensing is that the firm does not have to bear the development costs and risks associated with opening a foreign market. Licensing is very attractive for firms lacking the capital to develop operations overseas. In addition, licensing can be attractive when a firm is unwilling to commit substantial financial resources to an unfamiliar or politically volatile foreign market. Licensing is also often used when a firm wishes to participate in a foreign market but is prohibited from doing so by barriers to investment. This was one of the original reasons for the formation of the Fuji-Xerox joint venture. Xerox wanted to participate in the Japanese market but was prohibited from setting up a wholly owned subsidiary by the Japanese government. So Xerox set up the joint venture with Fuji and then licensed its know-how to the joint venture.

Finally, licensing is frequently used when a firm possesses some intangible property that might have business applications, but it does not want to develop those applications itself. For example, Bell Laboratories at AT&T originally invented the transistor circuit in the 1950s, but AT&T decided it did not want to produce transistors, so it licensed the technology to a number of other companies, such as Texas Instruments. Similarly, Coca-Cola has licensed its famous trademark to clothing manufacturers, which have incorporated the design into their clothing.

Disadvantages

Licensing has three serious drawbacks. First, it does not give a firm the tight control over manufacturing, marketing, and strategy that is required for realizing experience curve and location economies (as global and transnational firms must do; see Chapter 12). Licensing typically involves each licensee setting up its own production operations. This severely limits the firm's ability to realize experience curve and location economies by producing its product in a centralized location. When these economies are important, licensing may not be the best way to expand overseas.

Second, competing in a global market may require a firm to coordinate strategic moves across countries by using profits earned in one country to support competitive attacks in another (see Chapter 12). By its very nature, licensing limits a firm's ability to do this. A licensee is unlikely to allow a multinational firm to use its profits (beyond those due in the form of royalty payments) to support a different licensee operating in another country.

A third problem with licensing is one that we encountered in Chapter 6 when we reviewed the economic theory of FDI. This is the risk associated with licensing technological know-how to foreign companies. Technological know-how constitutes the basis of many multinational firms' competitive advantage. Most firms wish to maintain control over how their know-how is used, and a firm can quickly lose control over its technology by licensing it. Many firms have made the mistake of thinking they could maintain control over their know-how within the framework of a licensing agreement. RCA Corporation, for example, once licensed its color TV technology to Japanese firms including Matsushita and Sony. The Japanese firms quickly assimilated the technology, improved on it, and used it to enter the U.S. market. Now the Japanese firms have a bigger share of the U.S. market than the RCA brand.

There are ways of reducing the risks of this occurring. One way is by entering into a cross-licensing agreement with a foreign firm. Under a cross-licensing agreement, a firm might license some valuable intangible property to a foreign partner, but in addition to a royalty payment, the firm might also request that the foreign partner license some of its valuable know-how to the firm. Such agreements are believed to reduce the risks associated with licensing technological know-how, since the licensee realizes that if it violates the licensing contract (by using the knowledge obtained to compete directly with the licensor), the licensor can do the same to it. Cross-licensing agreements enable firms to hold each other hostage, which reduces the probability that they

The Fuji-Xerox Joint Venture

Management Focus

Fuji-Xerox is one of the most enduring and successful alliances between two companies from different countries. Established in 1962, today Fuji-Xerox is structured as a 50/50 joint venture between the Xerox Group, the U.S. maker of photocopiers, and Fuji Photo Film, Japan's largest manufacturer of film products. With sales of close to $10 billion, Fuji-Xerox provides Xerox with more than 20 percent of its worldwide revenues.

A prime motivation to establish the joint venture was the Japanese government's refusal in the early 1960s to allow foreign companies to set up wholly owned subsidiaries in Japan. The joint venture was conceived as a marketing organization to sell xerographic products that would be manufactured by Fuji Photo under license from Xerox. However, when the Japanese government refused to approve the establishment of a joint venture intended solely as a sales company, the joint-venture agreement was revised to give Fuji-Xerox manufacturing rights. Management of the venture was placed in the hands of Japanese managers who were given considerable autonomy to develop their own operations and strategy, subject to oversight by a board of directors that contained representatives from both Xerox and Fuji Photo.

Initially, Fuji-Xerox followed the lead of Xerox in manufacturing and selling the large high-volume copiers developed by Xerox in the United States. These machines were sold at a premium price to the high end of the market. However, Fuji-Xerox noticed that in the Japanese market new competitors, such as Canon and Ricoh, were making significant inroads by building small, low-volume copiers and focusing on the mid- and low-priced segments of the market. This led to Fuji-Xerox's development of its first "homegrown" copier, the FX2200, which at the time was billed as the world's smallest copier. Introduced in 1973, the FX2200 hit the market just in time to allow Fuji-Xerox to hold its own against a blizzard of new competition in Japan that followed the expiration of many of Xerox's key patents.

About the same time, Fuji-Xerox also embarked on a total quality control (TQC) program. The aims of the program were to speed up the development of new products, reduce waste, improve quality, and lower manufacturing costs. The first fruit of this program was the FX3500. Introduced in 1977, the FX3500 by 1979 had broken the Japanese record for the number of copiers sold in one year. Partly because of the success of the FX3500, in 1980 the company won Japan's prestigious Deming Prize. The success of the FX3500 was all the more notable because at the same time Xerox was canceling programs to develop low- to mid-level copiers and reaffirming its commitment to serving the high end of the market. Because of these cancellations, Tony Kobayashi, the CEO of Fuji-Xerox, was initially told to stop work on development of the FX3500. He refused, arguing that the FX3500 was crucial for the survival of Fuji-Xerox in the Japanese market. Given the arm's-length relationship between Xerox and Fuji-Xerox, Kobayashi was able to prevail.

By the early 1980s, Fuji-Xerox was number two in the Japanese copier market with between 20 and 22 percent of the market, just behind that of market leader Canon. In contrast, Xerox was running into all sorts of problems in the United States. As Xerox's patents had expired, a number of companies, includ-

will behave opportunistically toward each other.[14] Such cross-licensing agreements are increasingly common in high-technology industries. For example, the U.S. biotechnology firm Amgen has licensed one of its key drugs, Nuprogene, to Kirin, the Japanese pharmaceutical company. The license gives Kirin the right to sell Nuprogene in Japan. In return, Amgen receives a royalty payment and, through a licensing agreement, gained the right to sell some of Kirin's products in the United States.

Another way of reducing the risk associated with licensing is to follow the Fuji-Xerox model and link an agreement to license know-how with the formation of a joint venture in which the licensor and licensee take important equity stakes. Such an approach aligns the interests of licensor and licensee, since both have a stake in ensuring that the venture is successful. Thus, the risk that Fuji Photo might appropriate Xerox's technological know-how, and then compete directly against Xerox in the global photocopier market, was reduced by the establishment of a joint venture in which both Xerox and Fuji Photo had an important stake.

ing Canon, Ricoh, Kodak, and IBM, began to take market share from Xerox. Canon and Ricoh were particularly successful by focusing on the low-end segment of the market, which Xerox had ignored. As a result, Xerox's market share in the Americas fell from 35 percent in 1975 to 25 percent in 1980, while its profitability slumped.

In an attempt to recapture market share, Xerox began to sell Fuji-Xerox's FX3500 copier in the United States. Not only did the FX3500 help Xerox halt the rapid decline in its share of the U.S. market, but it also opened Xerox's eyes to the benefits of Fuji-Xerox's TQC program. Xerox found that the reject rate for Fuji-Xerox parts was only a fraction of the reject rate for American-produced parts. Visits to Fuji-Xerox revealed another important truth: quality in manufacturing does not increase real costs—it cuts costs by reducing defective products and service costs.

These developments forced Xerox to rethink the way it did business. From being the main provider of products, technology, and management know-how to Fuji-Xerox, Xerox in the 1980s became the willing pupil of Fuji-Xerox. In 1983, Xerox introduced its leadership through quality program, which was based on Fuji-Xerox's TQC program. As part of this effort, Xerox launched a quality training effort with its suppliers and was rewarded when the number of defective parts from suppliers subsequently fell from 25,000 per million in 1983 to 300 per million by 1992.

In 1985 and 1986, Xerox began to focus on its new product development process. One goal was to design products that, while customized to market conditions in different countries, also contained a large number of globally standardized parts. Another goal was to reduce the time it took to design new products and bring them to market. To achieve these goals, Xerox set up joint product development teams with Fuji-Xerox. Each team managed the design, component sources, manufacturing, distribution, and follow-up customer service on a worldwide basis. The use of design teams cut as much as one year from the overall product development cycle and saved millions of dollars.

One consequence of the new approach to product development was the 5100 copier. This was the first product designed jointly by Xerox and Fuji-Xerox for the worldwide market. The 5100 is manufactured in U.S. plants. It was launched in Japan in November 1990 and in the United States the following February. The 5100's global design reportedly reduced the overall time to market and saved the company more than $10 million in development costs.

As a result of the skills and products acquired from Fuji-Xerox, Xerox's position improved markedly during the 1980s. Due to its improved quality, lower costs, shorter product development time, and more appealing product range, Xerox was able to gain market share back from its competitors and to boost its profits and revenues. Xerox's share of the U.S. copier market increased from a low of 10 percent in 1985 to 18 percent in 1991.

Sources: R. Howard, "The CEO as Organizational Architect," *Harvard Business Review,* September–October 1992, pp. 106–23; D. Kearns, "Leadership through Quality," *Academy of Management Executive* 4 (1990), pp. 86–89; K. McQuade and B. Gomes-Casseres, "Xerox and Fuji-Xerox," Harvard Business School Case #9-391-156; and E. Terazono and C. Lorenz, "An Angry Young Warrior," *Financial Times,* September 19, 1994, p. 11.

Franchising

Franchising is similar to licensing, although franchising tends to involve longer-term commitments than licensing. **Franchising** is basically a specialized form of licensing in which the franchiser not only sells intangible property (normally a trademark) to the franchisee, but also insists that the franchisee agree to abide by strict rules as to how it does business. The franchiser will also often assist the franchisee to run the business on an ongoing basis. As with licensing, the franchiser typically receives a royalty payment, which amounts to some percentage of the franchisee's revenues. Whereas licensing is pursued primarily by manufacturing firms, franchising is employed primarily by service firms.[15] McDonald's is a good example of a firm that has grown by using a franchising strategy. McDonald's has strict rules as to how franchisees should operate a restaurant. These rules extend to control over the menu, cooking methods, staffing policies, and design and location of a restaurant. McDonald's also organizes the supply chain for its franchisees and provides management training and financial assistance.[16]

Advantages

The advantages of franchising as an entry mode are very similar to those of licensing. The firm is relieved of many of the costs and risks of opening a foreign market on its own. Instead, the franchisee typically assumes those costs and risks. This creates a good incentive for the franchisee to build a profitable operation as quickly as possible. Thus, using a franchising strategy, a service firm can build a global presence quickly and at a relatively low cost and risk, as McDonald's has.

Disadvantages

The disadvantages are less pronounced than in the case of licensing. Since franchising is often used by service companies, there is no reason to consider the need for coordination of manufacturing to achieve experience curve and location economies. But franchising may inhibit the firm's ability to take profits out of one country to support competitive attacks in another. A more significant disadvantage of franchising is quality control. The foundation of franchising arrangements is that the firm's brand name conveys a message to consumers about the quality of the firm's product. Thus, a business traveler checking in at a Hilton hotel in Hong Kong can reasonably expect the same quality of room, food, and service that she would receive in New York. The Hilton name is supposed to guarantee consistent product quality. This presents a problem in that foreign franchisees may not be as concerned about quality as they are supposed to be, and the result of poor quality can extend beyond lost sales in a particular foreign market to a decline in the firm's worldwide reputation. For example, if the business traveler has a bad experience at the Hilton in Hong Kong, she may never go to another Hilton hotel and may urge her colleagues to do likewise. The geographical distance of the firm from its foreign franchisees can make poor quality difficult to detect. In addition, the sheer numbers of franchisees—in the case of McDonald's, tens of thousands—can make quality control difficult. Due to these factors, quality problems may persist.

One way around this disadvantage is to set up a subsidiary in each country in which the firm expands. The subsidiary might be wholly owned by the company or a joint venture with a foreign company. The subsidiary assumes the rights and obligations to establish franchises throughout the particular country or region. McDonald's, for example, establishes a master franchisee in many countries. Typically, this master franchisee is a joint venture between McDonald's and a local firm. The proximity and the smaller number of franchises to oversee reduce the quality control challenge. In addition, because the subsidiary (or master franchisee) is at least partly owned by the firm, the firm can place its own managers in the subsidiary to help ensure that it is doing a good job of monitoring the franchises. This organizational arrangement has proven very satisfactory for McDonald's, KFC, Hilton Hotel Corp., and others.

Joint Ventures

A joint venture entails establishing a firm that is jointly owned by two or more otherwise independent firms. Fuji-Xerox, for example, was set up as a joint venture between Xerox and Fuji Photo (see the Management Focus). Establishing a joint venture with a foreign firm has long been a popular mode for entering a new market. The most typical joint venture is a 50/50 venture, in which there are two parties, each of which holds a 50 percent ownership stake (as is the case with the Fuji-Xerox joint venture) and contributes a team of managers to share operating control. Some firms, however, have sought joint ventures in which they have a majority share and thus tighter control.[17]

Advantages

Joint ventures have a number of advantages. First, a firm benefits from a local partner's knowledge of the host country's competitive conditions, culture, language, political systems, and business systems. Thus, for many U.S. firms, joint ventures have involved the U.S. company providing technological know-how and products and the local partner providing the marketing expertise and the local knowledge necessary for competing in that country. This was the case with the Fuji-Xerox joint venture. Second, when the development costs and/or risks of opening a foreign market are high, a firm might gain by sharing these costs and/or risks with a local partner. Third, in many countries, political considerations make joint ventures the only feasible entry mode. Again, this was a consideration in the establishment of the Fuji-Xerox venture. Research suggests joint ventures with local partners face a low risk of being subject to nationalization or other forms of adverse government interference.[18] This appears to be because local equity partners, who may have some influence on host-government policy, have a vested interest in speaking out against nationalization or government interference.

Disadvantages

Despite these advantages, there are major disadvantages with joint ventures. First, as with licensing, a firm that enters into a joint venture risks giving control of its technology to its partner. Thus, a proposed joint venture between Boeing and Mitsubishi Heavy Industries to build a new version of the 747, the 747-X, raised fears that Boeing might unwittingly give away its commercial airline technology to the Japanese. However, joint-venture agreements can be constructed to minimize this risk. One option is to hold majority ownership in the venture. This allows the dominant partner to exercise greater control over its technology. The drawback with this is that it can be difficult to find a foreign partner who is willing to settle for minority ownership. Another option is to "wall off" from a partner technology that is central to the core competence of the firm, while sharing other technology.

A second disadvantage is that a joint venture does not give a firm the tight control over subsidiaries that it might need to realize experience curve or location economies. Nor does it give a firm the tight control over a foreign subsidiary that it might need for engaging in coordinated global attacks against its rivals. Consider the entry of Texas Instruments (TI) into the Japanese semiconductor market. When TI established semiconductor facilities in Japan, it did so for the dual purpose of checking Japanese manufacturers' market share and limiting their cash available for invading TI's global market. In other words, TI was engaging in global strategic coordination. To implement this strategy, TI's subsidiary in Japan had to be prepared to take instructions from corporate headquarters regarding competitive strategy. The strategy also required the Japanese subsidiary to run at a loss if necessary. Few if any potential joint-venture partners would have been willing to accept such conditions, since it would have necessitated a willingness to accept a negative return on their investment. Thus, to implement this strategy, TI set up a wholly owned subsidiary in Japan.

A third disadvantage with joint ventures is that the shared ownership arrangement can lead to conflicts and battles for control between the investing firms if their goals and objectives change or if they take different views as to what the strategy should be. This has apparently not been a problem with the Fuji-Xerox joint venture. According to Tony Kobayashi, the CEO of Fuji-Xerox, a primary reason is that both Xerox and Fuji Photo adopted an arm's-length relationship with Fuji-Xerox, giving the venture's management considerable freedom to determine its own strategy.[19] However, much research indicates that conflicts of interest over strategy and goals often arise in joint ventures. These conflicts tend to be greater when the venture is between firms of different nationalities, and they often end in the dissolution of the venture.[20] Such conflicts tend to be triggered by shifts in the relative bargaining power of venture partners. For example, in the case of ventures between a foreign firm and a local firm, as a foreign partner's knowledge about local market conditions increases, it depends less on the expertise of a local partner. This increases the bargaining power of the foreign partner and ultimately leads to conflicts over control of the venture's strategy and goals.[21]

Wholly Owned Subsidiaries

In a **wholly owned subsidiary,** the firm owns 100 percent of the stock. Establishing a wholly owned subsidiary in a foreign market can be done two ways. The firm can either set up a new operation in that country, often referred to as a **green-field** venture, or it can acquire an established firm in that host nation and use that firm to promote its products.[22] For example, as we saw in the opening case, ING's strategy for entering the U.S. market was to acquire established U.S. enterprises, rather than try to build an operation from the ground floor.

Advantages

There are three clear advantages of wholly owned subsidiaries. First, when a firm's competitive advantage is based on technological competence, a wholly owned subsidiary will often be the preferred entry mode, because it reduces the risk of losing control over that competence. (See Chapter 6 for more details.) Many high-tech firms prefer this entry mode for overseas expansion (e.g., firms in the semiconductor, electronics, and pharmaceutical industries). Second, a wholly owned subsidiary gives a firm tight control over operations in different countries. This is necessary for engaging in global strategic coordination (i.e., using profits from one country to support competitive attacks in another). Third, a wholly owned subsidiary may be required if a firm is trying to realize location and experience curve economies (as firms pursuing global and transnational strategies try to do). As we saw in Chapter 12, when cost pressures are intense, it may pay a firm to configure its value chain in such a way that the value added at each stage is maximized. Thus, a national subsidiary may specialize in manufacturing only part of the product line or certain components of the end product, exchanging parts and products with other subsidiaries in the firm's global system. Establishing such a global production system requires a high degree of control over the operations of each affiliate. The various operations must be prepared to accept centrally determined decisions as to how they will produce, how much they will produce, and how their output will be priced for transfer to the next operation. Since licensees or joint-venture partners are unlikely to accept such a subservient role, establishment of wholly owned subsidiaries may be necessary.

Disadvantages

Establishing a wholly owned subsidiary is generally the most costly method of serving a foreign market. Firms doing this must bear the full costs and risks of setting up overseas operations. The risks associated with learning to do business in a new culture are less if the firm acquires an established host-country enterprise. However, acquisitions raise additional problems, including those associated with trying to marry divergent corporate cultures. These problems may more than offset any benefits derived by acquiring an established operation. Because the choice between green-field ventures and acquisition is such an important one, we shall discuss it in more detail later in the chapter.

Selecting an Entry Mode

As the preceding discussion demonstrated, advantages and disadvantages are associated with all the entry modes; they are summarized in Table 14.1. Due to these advantages and disadvantages, trade-offs are inevitable when selecting an entry mode. For example, when considering entry into an unfamiliar country with a track record for nationalizing foreign-owned enterprises, a firm might favor a joint venture with a local enterprise. Its rationale might be that the local partner will help it establish operations in an unfamiliar environment and will speak out against nationalization should the possibility arise. However, if the firm's core competence is based on propri-

Entry Mode	Advantages	Disadvantages
Exporting	Ability to realize location and experience curve economies	High transport costs Trade barriers Problems with local marketing agents
Turnkey contracts	Ability to earn returns from process technology skills in countries where FDI is restricted	Creating efficient competitors Lack of long-term market presence
Licensing	Low development costs and risks	Lack of control over technology Inability to realize location and experience curve economies Inability to engage in global strategic coordination
Franchising	Low development costs and risks	Lack of control over quality Inability to engage in global strategic coordination
Joint ventures	Access to local partner's knowledge Sharing development costs and risks Politically acceptable	Lack of control over technology Inability to engage in global strategic coordination Inability to realize location and experience economies
Wholly owned subsidiaries	Protection of technology Ability to engage in global strategic coordination Ability to realize location and experience economies	High costs and risks

Table 14.1

Advantages and Disadvantages of Entry Modes

etary technology, entering a joint venture might risk losing control of that technology to the joint venture partner, in which case the strategy may seem unattractive. Despite the existence of such trade-offs, it is possible to make some generalizations about the optimal choice of entry mode.[23]

Core Competencies and Entry Mode

We saw in Chapter 12 that firms often expand internationally to earn greater returns from their core competencies, transferring the skills and products derived from their core competencies to foreign markets where indigenous competitors lack those skills. We say that such firms are pursuing an international strategy. The optimal entry mode for these firms depends to some degree on the nature of their core competencies. A distinction can be drawn between firms whose core competency is in technological know-how and those whose core competency is in management know-how.

Technological Know-How

As was observed in Chapter 6, if a firm's competitive advantage (its core competence) is based on control over proprietary technological know-how, licensing and joint-venture arrangements should be avoided if possible so that the risk of losing control over that technology is minimized. Thus, if a high-tech firm sets up operations in a foreign country to profit from a core competency in technological know-how, it will probably do so through a wholly owned subsidiary. This rule should not be viewed as hard and fast, however. One exception is when a licensing or joint-venture arrangement can be structured so as to reduce the risks of a firm's technological know-how being expropriated by licensees or joint-venture partners. We will see how this might be achieved later in the chapter when we examine the structuring of strategic alliances. Another exception exists when a firm perceives its technological advantage to be only transitory, when it expects rapid imitation of its core technology by competitors. In such cases, the firm might want to license its technology as rapidly as possible to foreign firms to gain global acceptance for its technology before the imitation occurs.[24] Such a strategy has some advantages. By licensing its technology to competitors, the firm may deter them from developing their own, possibly superior, technology. Further, by licensing its technology, the firm may establish its technology as the dominant design in the industry (as Matsushita did with its VHS format for VCRs). This may ensure a steady stream of royalty payments. However, the attractions of licensing are probably outweighed by the risks of losing control over technology, and thus licensing should be avoided.

Management Know-How

The competitive advantage of many service firms is based on management know-how (e.g., McDonald's). For such firms, the risk of losing control over the management skills to franchisees or joint-venture partners is not that great. These firms' valuable asset is their brand name, and brand names are generally well protected by international laws pertaining to trademarks. Given this, many of the issues arising in the case of technological know-how are of less concern here. As a result, many service firms favor a combination of franchising and subsidiaries to control the franchises within particular countries or regions. The subsidiaries may be wholly owned or joint ventures, but most service firms have found that joint ventures with local partners work best for the controlling subsidiaries. A joint venture is often politically more acceptable and brings a degree of local knowledge to the subsidiary.

❙Pressures for Cost Reductions and Entry Mode

The greater the pressures for cost reductions are, the more likely a firm will want to pursue some combination of exporting and wholly owned subsidiaries. By manufacturing in those locations where factor conditions are optimal and then exporting to the rest of the world, a firm may be able to realize substantial location and experience curve economies. The firm might then want to export the finished product to marketing subsidiaries based in various countries. These subsidiaries will typically be wholly owned and have the responsibility for overseeing distribution in their particular countries. Setting up wholly owned marketing subsidiaries is preferable to joint-venture arrangements and to using foreign marketing agents because it gives the firm the tight control over marketing that might be required for coordinating a globally dispersed value chain. It also gives the firm the ability to use the profits generated in one market to improve its competitive position in another market. In other words, firms pursuing global or transnational strategies tend to prefer establishing wholly owned subsidiaries.

■ Establishing a Wholly Owned Subsidiary: Green-field Venture or Acquisition?

A firm can establish a wholly owned subsidiary in a country by building a subsidiary from the ground up, the so-called green-field strategy, or by acquiring an established enterprise in the target market. The volume of cross-border acquisitions has been growing at a rapid rate for two decades. Some 80 percent of the world's FDI flows is now in the form of mergers and acquisitions (see Chapter 6 for details).[25] The value of cross-border acquisitions grew at an average annual rate of 42 percent a year compounded between 1980 and 1999 and exceeded $2.3 trillion in 1999 when over 24,000 cross-border acquisitions occurred. By the end of the 1990s, some 31 percent of all acquisitions worldwide were cross-border acquisitions.[26]

Pros and Cons of Acquisitions

Acquisitions have three major points in their favor. First, they are quick to execute. By acquiring an established enterprise, a firm can rapidly build its presence in the target foreign market. ING's rapid rise in the U.S. financial services market was primarily due to a number of acquisitions (see the opening case). When the German automobile company Daimler-Benz decided it needed a bigger presence in the U.S. automobile market, it did not increase that presence by building new factories to serve the United States, a process that would have taken years. Instead, it acquired the number three U.S. automobile company, Chrysler, and merged the two operations to form Daimler/Chrysler. When the Spanish telecommunications service provider Telefonica wanted to build a service presence in Latin America, it did so through a series of acquisitions, purchasing telecommunications companies in Brazil and Argentina. In all these cases, the acquiring firms made acquisitions because they knew that was the quickest way to establish a sizable presence in the target market.

Second, in many cases firms make acquisitions to preempt their competitors. The need for preemption is particularly great in markets that are rapidly globalizing, such as telecommunications, where a combination of deregulation within nations and liberalization of regulations governing cross-border foreign direct investment has made it much easier for enterprises to enter foreign markets through acquisitions. In such markets, there can be concentrated waves of acquisitions as firms race each other to attain global scale. In the telecommunications industry, for example, regulatory changes triggered what can be called a feeding frenzy, with firms entering each other's markets via acquisitions in order to establish a global presence. These included the $60 billion acquisition of Air Touch Communications in the United States by the British company Vodafone, which was the largest acquisition ever; the $13 billion acquisition of One 2 One in Britain by the German company Deutsche Telekom; and the $6.4 billion acquisition of Excel Communications in the United States by Teleglobe of Canada, all of which took place in 1998 and 1999.[27] A similar wave of cross-border acquisitions occurred in the global automobile industry over the same time period, with Daimler acquiring Chrysler, Ford acquiring Volvo, and Renault acquiring Nissan.

Third, managers may believe acquisitions to be less risky than green-field ventures. When a firm makes an acquisition, it buys a set of assets that are producing a known revenue and profit stream. In contrast, the revenue and profit stream that a green-field venture might generate is uncertain because it does not yet exist. When a firm makes an acquisition in a foreign market, it not only acquires a set of tangible assets, such as factories, logistics systems, customer service systems, and so on, but it also acquires valuable intangible assets including a local brand name and managers' knowledge of the business environment in that nation. Such knowledge can reduce the risk of mistakes caused by ignorance of the national culture of the country entered.

Despite the arguments for making acquisitions, acquisitions often produce disappointing results.[28] For example, a study by Mercer Management Consulting looked at 150 acquisitions worth more than $500 million each that were undertaken between January 1990 and July 1995.[29] The Mercer study concluded that 50 percent of these acquisitions ended up eroding, or substantially eroding, shareholder value, while another 33 percent created only marginal returns. Only 17 percent were judged to be successful. In a major study of the post-acquisition performance of acquired companies, David Ravenscraft and Mike Scherer concluded that many good companies were acquired during this period and, on average, their profits and market shares declined following acquisition.[30] They also noted that a smaller but substantial subset of those good companies experienced traumatic difficulties, which ultimately led to their being sold by the acquiring company. Ravenscraft and Scherer's evidence suggests that many acquisitions destroy rather than create value. While most of this research has looked at domestic acquisitions, the findings probably also apply to cross-border acquisitions.[31]

Why Do Acquisitions Fail?

Acquisitions fail for several reasons. First, the acquiring firms often overpay for the assets of the acquired firm. The price of the target firm can get bid up if more than one firm is interested in its purchase, as is often the case. In addition, the management of the acquiring firm is often too optimistic about the value than can be created via an acquisition and is thus willing to pay a significant premium over a target firm's market capitalization. This is called the "hubris hypothesis" of why acquisitions fail. The hubris hypothesis postulates that top managers typically overestimate their ability to create value from an acquisition, primarily because rising to the top of a corporation has given them an exaggerated sense of their own capabilities.[32] For example, when Daimler acquired Chrysler in 1998, paid $40 billion, which represented a premium of 40 percent over the market value of Chrysler before the takeover bid. Daimler paid this much because it thought it could use Chrysler to help it grow market share in the United States. At the time, Daimler's management issued bold announcements about the "synergies" that would be created from combining the operations of the two companies. Executives believed that they could attain greater scale economies from the global presence, take costs out of the German and American operations, and boost the profitability of the combined entity. However, within a year of the acquisition, Daimler's German management was faced with a crisis at Chrysler, which was suddenly losing money due to weak sales in the United States. In retrospect, Daimler's management had been far too optimistic about the potential for future demand in the U.S. auto market and about the opportunities for creating value from "synergies." Daimler acquired Chrysler at the end of a multiyear boom in U.S. auto sales and paid a large premium over Chrysler's market value just before demand slumped.[33]

Second, many acquisitions fail because there is a clash between the cultures of the acquiring and acquired firm. After an acquisition, many acquired companies experience high management turnover, possibly because their employees do not like the acquiring company's way of doing things.[34] This happened at Daimler/Chrysler; many senior managers left Chrysler in the first year after the merger. Apparently, Chrysler executives disliked the dominance in decision making by Daimler's German managers, while the Germans resented that Chrysler's American managers were paid two to three times as much as their German counterparts. These cultural differences created tensions, which ultimately exhibited themselves in high management turnover at Chrysler.[35] The loss of management talent and expertise can materially harm the performance of the acquired unit.[36] This may be particularly problematic in an international business, where management of the acquired unit may have valuable local knowledge that may be difficult to replace.

Third, many acquisitions fail because attempts to realize synergies by integrating the operations of the acquired and acquiring entities often run into roadblocks and take much longer than forecast. Differences in management philosophy and company culture can slow the integration of operations. These problems are likely to be exacerbated by differences in national culture. Bureaucratic haggling between managers also complicates the process. Again, this reportedly occurred at Daimler/Chrysler, where grand plans to integrate the operations of the two companies were bogged down by endless committee meetings and by simple logistical considerations such as the six-hour time difference between Detroit and Germany. By the time an integration plan had been worked out, Chrysler was losing money, and Daimler's German managers suddenly had a crisis on their hands.

Finally, many acquisitions fail due to inadequate pre-acquisition screening.[37] Many firms decide to acquire other firms without thoroughly analyzing the potential benefits and costs. They often move with undue haste to execute the acquisition, perhaps because they fear another competitor may preempt them. After the acquisition, however, many acquiring firms discover that instead of buying a well-run business, they have purchased a troubled organization. This may be a particular problem in cross-border acquisitions because the acquiring firm may not fully understand the target firm's different national culture and business system.

Reducing the Risks of Failure

These problems can all be overcome if the firm is careful about its acquisition strategy.[38] Screening of the foreign enterprise to be acquired, including a detailed auditing of operations, financial position, and management culture, can help to make sure the firm (1) does not pay too much for the acquired unit, (2) does not uncover any nasty surprises after the acquisition, and (3) acquires a firm whose organization culture is not antagonistic to that of the acquiring enterprise. It is also important for the acquirer to allay any concerns that management in the acquired enterprise might have. The objective should be to reduce unwanted management attrition after the acquisition. Finally, managers must move rapidly after an acquisition to put an integration plan in place and to act on that plan. Some people in both the acquiring and acquired units will try to erect roadblocks to slow or stop any integration efforts, particularly when losses of employment or management power are involved, and managers should have a plan for dealing with such impediments before they arise.

Pros and Cons of Green-field Ventures

The big advantage of establishing a green-field venture in a foreign country is that it gives the firm a much greater ability to build the kind of subsidiary company that it wants. For example, it is much easier to build an organization culture from scratch than it is to change the culture of an acquired unit. Similarly, it is much easier to establish a set of operating routines in a new subsidiary than it is to convert the operating routines of an acquired unit. This is a very important advantage for many international businesses, where transferring products, competencies, skills, and know-how from the established operations of the firm to the new subsidiary are principle ways of creating value. For example, when Lincoln Electric, the U.S. manufacturer of arc-welding equipment, first ventured overseas in the mid-1980s, it did so by acquisitions, purchasing arc-wielding equipment companies in Europe. However, Lincoln's competitive advantage in the United States was based on a strong organizational culture and a unique set of incentives that encouraged its employees to do everything possible to increase productivity. Lincoln found through bitter experience that it was almost impossible to transfer its organizational culture and incentives to acquired firms, which had their own distinct organizational cultures and incentives. As a result, the firm switched its entry strategy in the mid-1990s and began to enter foreign countries by establishing green-field ventures, building operations from the ground up. While this strategy takes more time to execute, Lincoln has found that it yields greater long-run returns than the acquisition strategy.

Set against this significant advantage are the disadvantages of establishing a green-field venture. Green-field ventures are slower to establish. They are also risky. As with any new venture, a degree of uncertainty is associated with future revenue and profit prospects. However, if the firm has already been successful in other foreign markets and understands what it takes to do business in other countries, these risks may not be that great. For example, having already gained great knowledge about operating internationally, the risk to McDonald's of entering yet another country is probably not that great. Also, green-field ventures are less risky than acquisitions in the sense that there is less potential for unpleasant surprises. A final disadvantage is the possibility of being preempted by more aggressive global competitors, who enter via acquisitions and build a big market presence that limits the market potential for the green-field venture.

Green-field Venture or Acquisition?

The choice between acquisitions and green-field ventures is not an easy one to make. Both modes have their advantages and disadvantages. In general, the choice will depend on the circumstances confronting the firm. If the firm is seeking to enter a market where there are already well-established incumbent enterprises, and where global competitors are also interested in establishing a presence, it may pay the firm to enter via an acquisition. In such circumstances, a green-field venture may be too slow to establish a sizable presence. However, if the firm is going to make an acquisition, its management should be cognizant of the risks associated with acquisitions that were discussed earlier and consider these when determining which firms to purchase. It may be better to enter by the slower route of a green-field venture than to make a bad acquisition.

If the firm is considering entering a country where there are no incumbent competitors to be acquired, then a green-field venture may be the only mode. Even when incumbents exist, if the competitive advantage of the firm is based on the transfer of organizationally embedded competencies, skills, routines, and culture, it may still be preferable to enter via a green-field venture. Things such as skills and organizational culture, which are based on significant knowledge that is difficult to articulate and codify, are much easier to embed in a new venture than they are in an acquired entity, where the firm may have to overcome the established routines and culture of the acquired firm. Thus, as our earlier examples suggest, firms such as McDonald's and Lincoln Electric prefer to enter foreign markets by establishing green-field ventures.

Strategic Alliances

Strategic alliances refer to cooperative agreements between potential or actual competitors. In this section, we are concerned specifically with strategic alliances between firms from different countries. Strategic alliances run the range from formal joint ventures, in which two or more firms have equity stakes (e.g., Fuji-Xerox), to short-term contractual agreements, in which two companies agree to cooperate on a particular task (such as developing a new product). Collaboration between competitors is fashionable; the 1980s and 1990s saw an explosion in the number of strategic alliances, and this seems to have continued into the new century.

The Advantages of Strategic Alliances

Firms ally themselves with actual or potential competitors for various strategic purposes.[39] First, as noted earlier in the chapter, strategic alliances may facilitate entry into a foreign market. For example, Motorola initially found it very difficult to gain access to the Japanese cellular telephone market. In the mid-1980s, the firm complained loudly about formal and informal Japanese trade barriers. The turning point for Motorola came in 1987 when it allied itself with Toshiba to build microprocessors. As part of the deal, Toshiba provided Motorola with marketing help, including some of its best managers. This helped Motorola in the political game of securing government approval to enter the Japanese market and getting radio frequencies assigned for its mobile communications systems. Motorola no longer complains about Japan's trade barriers. Although privately the company admits they still exist, with Toshiba's help Motorola has become skilled at getting around them.[40]

Strategic alliances also allow firms to share the fixed costs (and associated risks) of developing new products or processes. Motorola's alliance with Toshiba also was partly motivated by a desire to share the high fixed costs of setting up an operation to manufacture microprocessors. The microprocessor business is so capital intensive—Motorola and Toshiba each contributed close to $1 billion to set up their facility—that few firms can afford the costs and risks by themselves. Similarly, an alliance between Boeing and a number of Japanese companies to build the 767 was motivated by Boeing's desire to share the estimated $2 billion investment required to develop the aircraft.

Third, an alliance is a way to bring together complementary skills and assets that neither company could easily develop on its own. An example is the alliance between France's Thomson and Japan's JVC to manufacture videocassette recorders. JVC and Thomson are trading core competencies; Thomson needs product technology and manufacturing skills, while JVC needs to learn how to succeed in the fragmented European market. Both sides believe there is an equitable chance for gain. Similarly, AT&T struck a deal in 1990 with NEC Corporation of Japan to trade technological skills. AT&T gave NEC some of its computer-aided design technology, and NEC gave AT&T access to the technology underlying its advanced logic computer chips. Such trading of core competencies seems to underlie many of the most successful strategic alliances.

Fourth, it can make sense to form an alliance that will help the firm establish technological standards for the industry that will benefit the firm. For example, in 1992, Philips NV allied with its global competitor Matsushita to manufacture and market the digital compact cassette (DCC) system Philips had developed. This linking with Matsushita was expected to help Philips establish the DCC system as a new technological standard in the recording and consumer electronics industries. The issue was important because Sony had developed a competing "mini compact disk" technology that it hoped to establish as the new technical standard. Since the two technologies did very similar things, there was room for only one new standard. Philips saw its alliance with Matsushita as a tactic for winning the race.[41]

The Disadvantages of Strategic Alliances

The advantages we have discussed can be very significant. Despite this, some commentators have criticized strategic alliances on the grounds that they give competitors a low-cost route to new technology and markets.[42] For example, Robert Reich and Eric Mankin argued that in the 1980s many strategic alliances between U.S. and Japanese firms were part of an implicit Japanese strategy to keep higher-paying, higher-value-added jobs in Japan while gaining the project engineering and production process skills that underlie the competitive success of many U.S. companies.[43] They argued that Japanese success in the machine tool and semiconductor industries was built on U.S. technology acquired through strategic alliances. And they argued that U.S. managers were aiding the Japanese in achieving their goals by entering alliances that channel new inventions to Japan and provide a U.S. sales and distribution network for the resulting products. Although such deals may generate short-term profits, Reich and Mankin argue, in the long run the result is to "hollow out" U.S. firms, leaving them with no competitive advantage in the global marketplace.

Reich and Mankin have a point. Alliances have risks. Unless a firm is careful, it can give away more than it receives. But there are so many examples of apparently successful alliances between firms—including alliances between U.S. and Japanese firms—that their position seems extreme. It is difficult to see how the Motorola-Toshiba alliance or the Fuji-Xerox alliance fit Reich and Mankin's thesis. In these cases, both partners seem to have gained from the alliance. Why do some alliances benefit both firms while others benefit one firm and hurt the other? The next section provides an answer to this question.

Making Alliances Work

The failure rate for international strategic alliances seems to be high. One study of 49 international strategic alliances found that two-thirds run into serious managerial and financial troubles within two years of their formation, and that although many of these problems are solved, 33 percent are ultimately rated as failures by the parties involved.[44] The success of an alliance seems to be a function of three main factors: partner selection, alliance structure, and the manner in which the alliance is managed.

Partner Selection

One key to making a strategic alliance work is to select the right ally. A good ally, or partner, has three characteristics. First, a good partner helps the firm achieve its strategic goals, whether they are market access, sharing the costs and risks of product development, or gaining access to critical core competencies. The partner must have capabilities that the firm lacks and that it values. Second, a good partner shares the firm's vision for the purpose of the alliance. If two firms approach an alliance with radically different agendas, the chances are great that the relationship will not be harmonious, will not flourish, and will end in divorce. Third, a good partner is unlikely to try to opportunistically exploit the alliance for its own ends; that is, to expropriate the firm's technological know-how while giving away little in return. In this respect, firms with reputations for "fair play" to maintain probably make the best allies. For example, IBM is involved in so many strategic alliances that it would not pay the company to trample over individual alliance partners. This would tarnish IBM's reputation of being a good ally and would make it more difficult for IBM to attract alliance partners. Since IBM attaches great importance to its alliances, it is unlikely to engage in the kind of opportunistic behavior that Reich and Mankin highlight. Similarly, their reputations make it less likely (but by no means impossible) that such Japanese firms as Sony, Toshiba, and Fuji, which have histories of alliances with non-Japanese firms, would opportunistically exploit an alliance partner.

To select a partner with these three characteristics, a firm needs to conduct comprehensive research on potential alliance candidates. To increase the probability of selecting a good partner, the firm should:

1. Collect as much pertinent, publicly available information on potential allies as possible.
2. Collect data from informed third parties. These include firms that have had alliances with the potential partners, investment bankers who have had dealings with them, and former employees.
3. Get to know the potential partner as well as possible before committing to an alliance. This should include face-to-face meetings between senior managers (and perhaps middle-level managers) to ensure that the chemistry is right.

Alliance Structure

Having selected a partner, the alliance should be structured so that the firm's risks of giving too much away to the partner are reduced to an acceptable level. Figure 14.1 depicts four safeguards against opportunism by alliance partners. (Opportunism includes the theft of technology and/or markets that Reich and Mankin describe.) First, alliances can be designed to make it difficult (if not impossible) to transfer technology not meant to be transferred. The design, development, manufacture, and service of a product manufactured by an alliance can be structured so as to wall off sensitive technologies to prevent their leakage to the other participant. In the alliance between General Electric and Snecma to build commercial aircraft engines, for example, GE

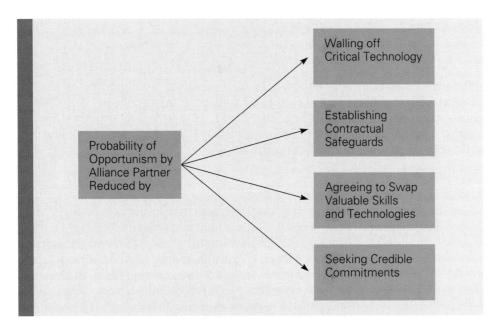

Figure 14.1

Structuring Alliances to Reduce Opportunism

reduced the risk of excess transfer by walling off certain sections of the production process. The modularization effectively cut off the transfer of what GE regarded as key competitive technology, while permitting Snecma access to final assembly. Similarly, in the alliance between Boeing and the Japanese to build the 767, Boeing walled off research, design, and marketing functions considered central to its competitive position, while allowing the Japanese to share in production technology. Boeing also walled off new technologies not required for 767 production.[45]

Second, contractual safeguards can be written into an alliance agreement to guard against the risk of opportunism by a partner. For example, TRW, Inc., has three strategic alliances with large Japanese auto component suppliers to produce seat belts, engine valves, and steering gears for sale to Japanese-owned auto assembly plants in the United States. TRW has clauses in each of its alliance contracts that bar the Japanese firms from competing with TRW to supply U.S.-owned auto companies with component parts. By doing this, TRW protects itself against the possibility that the Japanese companies are entering into the alliances merely to gain access to the North American market to compete with TRW in its home market.

Third, both parties to an alliance can agree in advance to swap skills and technologies that the other covets, thereby ensuring a chance for equitable gain. Cross-licensing agreements are one way to achieve this goal. For example, in the alliance between Motorola and Toshiba, Motorola has licensed some of its microprocessor technology to Toshiba, and in return, Toshiba has licensed some of its memory chip technology to Motorola.

Fourth, the risk of opportunism by an alliance partner can be reduced if the firm extracts a significant credible commitment from its partner in advance. The long-term alliance between Xerox and Fuji to build photocopiers for the Asian market perhaps best illustrates this. Rather than enter into an informal agreement or a licensing arrangement (which Fuji Photo initially wanted), Xerox insisted that Fuji invest in a 50/50 joint venture to serve Japan and East Asia. This venture constituted such a significant investment in people, equipment, and facilities that Fuji Photo was committed from the outset to making the alliance work in order to earn a return on its investment. By agreeing to the joint venture, Fuji essentially made a credible commitment to the alliance. Given this, Xerox felt secure in transferring its photocopier technology to Fuji (see the Management Focus for details).[46]

Managing the Alliance

Once a partner has been selected and an appropriate alliance structure has been agreed on, the task facing the firm is to maximize its benefits from the alliance. As in all international business deals, an important factor is sensitivity to cultural differences (see Chapter 3). Many differences in management style are attributable to cultural differences, and managers need to make allowances for these in dealing with their partner. Beyond this, maximizing the benefits from an alliance seems to involve building trust between partners and learning from partners.[47]

Building Trust

Managing an alliance successfully requires building interpersonal relationships between the firms' managers, or what is sometimes referred to as *relational capital*.[48] This is one lesson that can be drawn from the successful strategic alliance between Ford and Mazda. Ford and Mazda have set up a framework of meetings within which their managers not only discuss matters pertaining to the alliance but also have time to get to know each other better. The belief is that the resulting friendships help build trust and facilitate harmonious relations between the two firms. Personal relationships also foster an informal management network between the firms. (Chapter 13 discusses informal management networks.) This network can then be used to help solve problems arising in more formal contexts (such as in joint committee meetings between personnel from the two firms).

Learning from Partners

After a five-year study of 15 strategic alliances between major multinationals, Gary Hamel, Yves Doz, and C. K. Prahalad concluded that a major determinant of how much a company gains from an alliance is its ability to learn from its alliance partner.[49] They focused on a number of alliances between Japanese companies and Western (European or American) partners. In every case in which a Japanese company emerged from an alliance stronger than its Western partner, the Japanese company had made a greater effort to learn. Few Western companies studied seemed to want to learn from their Japanese partners. They tended to regard the alliance purely as a cost-sharing or risk-sharing device, rather than as an opportunity to learn how a potential competitor does business.

Consider the alliance between General Motors and Toyota constituted in 1985 to build the Chevrolet Nova. This alliance was structured as a formal joint venture, called New United Motor Manufacturing, Inc., and each party had a 50 percent equity stake. The venture owned an auto plant in Fremont, California. According to one Japanese manager, Toyota quickly achieved most of its objectives from the alliance: "We learned about U.S. supply and transportation. And we got the confidence to manage U.S. workers."[50] All that knowledge was then transferred to Georgetown, Kentucky, where Toyota opened its own plant in 1988. On the other hand, possibly all GM got was a new product, the Chevrolet Nova. Some GM managers complained that the knowledge they gained through the alliance with Toyota has never been put to good use inside GM. They believe they should have been kept together as a team to educate GM's engineers and workers about the Japanese system. Instead, they were dispersed to various GM subsidiaries.

To maximize the learning benefits of an alliance, a firm must try to learn from its partner and then apply the knowledge within its own organization. It has been suggested that all operating employees should be well briefed on the partner's strengths and weaknesses and should understand how acquiring particular skills will bolster their firm's competitive position. Hamel, Doz, and Prahalad note that this is already standard practice among Japanese companies. They made this observation:

> We accompanied a Japanese development engineer on a tour through a
> partner's factory. This engineer dutifully took notes on plant layout, the

number of production stages, the rate at which the line was running, and the number of employees. He recorded all this despite the fact that he had no manufacturing responsibility in his own company, and that the alliance did not encompass joint manufacturing. Such dedication greatly enhances learning.[51]

For such learning to be of value, it must be diffused throughout the organization (as was seemingly not the case at GM after the GM-Toyota joint venture). To achieve this, the managers involved in the alliance should educate their colleagues about the skills of the alliance partner.

Chapter Summary

This chapter addressed two related topics: the optimal choice of entry mode to serve a foreign market and strategic alliances. The two topics are related in that several entry modes (e.g., licensing and joint ventures) are strategic alliances. Most strategic alliances, however, involve more than just issues of market access. This chapter made the following points:

1. Basic entry decisions include identifying which markets to enter, when to enter those markets, and on what scale.

2. The most attractive foreign markets tend to be found in politically stable developed and developing nations that have free market systems and where there is not a dramatic upsurge in either inflation rates or private-sector debt.

3. There are several advantages associated with entering a national market early, before other international businesses have established themselves. These advantages must be balanced against the pioneering costs that early entrants often have to bear, including the greater risk of business failure.

4. Large-scale entry into a national market constitutes a major strategic commitment that is likely to change the nature of competition in that market and limit the entrant's future strategic flexibility. The firm needs to think through the implications of such commitments before embarking on a large-scale entry. Although making major strategic commitments can yield many benefits, there are also risks associated with such a strategy.

5. There are six modes of entering a foreign market: exporting, creating turnkey projects, licensing, franchising, establishing joint ventures, and setting up a wholly owned subsidiary.

6. Exporting has the advantages of facilitating the realization of experience curve economies and of avoiding the costs of setting up manufacturing operations in another country. Disadvantages include high transport costs and trade barriers and problems with local marketing agents. The latter can be overcome if the firm sets up a wholly owned marketing subsidiary in the host country.

7. Turnkey projects allow firms to export their process know-how to countries where FDI might be prohibited, thereby enabling the firm to earn a greater return from this asset. The disadvantage is that the firm may inadvertently create efficient global competitors in the process.

8. The main advantage of licensing is that the licensee bears the costs and risks of opening a foreign market. Disadvantages include the risk of losing technological know-how to the licensee and a lack of tight control over licensees.

9. The main advantage of franchising is that the franchisee bears the costs and risks of opening a foreign market. Disadvantages center on problems of quality control of distant franchisees.

10. Joint ventures have the advantages of sharing the costs and risks of opening a foreign market and of gaining local knowledge and political influence. Disadvantages include the risk of losing control over technology and a lack of tight control.

11. The advantages of wholly owned subsidiaries include tight control over technological know-how. The main disadvantage is that the firm must bear all the costs and risks of opening a foreign market.

12. The optimal choice of entry mode depends on the firm's strategy.

13. When technological know-how constitutes a firm's core competence, wholly owned subsidiaries are preferred, since they best control technology.

14. When management know-how constitutes a firm's core competence, foreign franchises controlled by joint ventures seem to be optimal. This gives the firm the cost and risk benefits associated with franchising, while enabling it to monitor and control franchisee quality effectively.

15. When the firm is pursuing a global or transnational strategy, the need for tight control over operations to realize location and experience curve economies suggests wholly owned subsidiaries are the best entry mode.

16. When establishing a wholly owned subsidiary in a country, a firm must decide whether to do so by building a subsidiary from the ground up, the so-called green-field venture strategy, or by acquiring an established enterprise in the target market.

17. Relative to green-field ventures, acquisitions are quick to execute, may enable a firm to preempt its global competitors, and involve buying a known revenue and profit stream.

18. Acquisitions may fail when the acquiring firm overpays for the target, when the culture of the acquiring and acquired firms clash, when there is a high level of management attrition after the acquisition, and when there is a failure to integrate the operations of the acquiring and acquired firm.

19. The big advantage of establishing a green-field venture in a foreign country is that it gives the firm a much greater ability to build the kind of subsidiary company that it wants. For example, it is much easier to build an organization culture from scratch than it is to change the culture of an acquired unit.

20. Strategic alliances are cooperative agreements between actual or potential competitors.

21. The advantage of alliances are that they facilitate entry into foreign markets, enable partners to share the fixed costs and risks associated with new products and processes, facilitate the transfer of complementary skills between companies, and help firms establish technical standards.

22. The disadvantage of a strategic alliance is that the firm risks giving away technological know-how and market access to its alliance partner in return for very little.

23. The disadvantages associated with alliances can be reduced if the firm selects partners carefully, paying close attention to the firm's reputation and the structure of the alliance so as to avoid unintended transfers of know-how.

24. Two keys to making alliances work seem to be building trust and informal communications networks between partners and taking proactive steps to learn from alliance partners.

Critical Discussion Questions

1. Review the opening case. ING chose to enter the U.S. financial services market via acquisitions rather than green-field ventures. What do you think are the advantages to ING of doing this? What might the drawbacks be? Does this strategy make sense? Why?

2. Licensing proprietary technology to foreign competitors is the best way to give up a firm's competitive advantage. Discuss.

3. What kinds of companies stand to gain the most from entering into strategic alliances with potential competitors? Why?

4. Discuss how the need for control over foreign operations varies with firms' strategies and core competencies. What are the implications for the choice of entry mode?

5. A small Canadian firm that has developed some valuable new medical products using its unique biotechnology know-how is trying to decide how best to serve the European Community market. Its choices are:

   a. Manufacture the product at home and let foreign sales agents handle marketing.

   b. Manufacture the products at home and set up a wholly owned subsidiary in Europe to handle marketing.

   c. Enter into a strategic alliance with a large European pharmaceutical firm. The product would be manufactured in Europe by the 50/50 joint venture and marketed by the European firm.

The cost of investment in manufacturing facilities will be a major one for the Canadian firm, but it is not outside its reach. If these are the firm's only options, which one would you advise it to choose? Why?

Merrill Lynch in Japan

Closing Case

Merrill Lynch is an investment banking titan. The U.S.-based financial services institution is the world's largest underwriter of debt and equity and the third largest mergers and acquisitions advisor behind Morgan Stanley and Goldman Sachs. Merrill Lynch's investment banking operations have long had a global reach. The company has a dominant presence in London and Tokyo. However, Merrill Lynch's international presence was limited to the investment banking side of its business until recently. In contrast, its private client business, which offers banking, financial advice, and stockbrokerage services to individuals, had historically been concentrated in the United States. This is now changing rapidly. In 1995, Merrill Lynch purchased Smith New Court, the largest stockbrokerage in Great Britain. This was followed in 1997 by the acquisition of Mercury Asset Management, the United Kingdom's leading manager of mutual funds. Then in 1998, Merrill Lynch acquired Midland Walwyn, Canada's last major independent stockbrokerage. The company's boldest moves, however, have probably been in Japan.

Merrill Lynch started a private client business in Japan in the 1980s but met with limited success. At the time, it was the first foreign firm to enter Japan's private client investment market. The company found it extremely difficult to attract employee talent and customers away from Japan's big four stockbrokerages, which traditionally had monopolized the Japanese market. Plus, restrictive regulations made it almost impossible for Merrill Lynch to offer its Japanese private clients the range of services it offered clients in the United States. For example, foreign exchange regulations meant it was very difficult to sell non-Japanese stocks, bonds, and mutual funds to Japanese investors. In 1993, Merrill Lynch admitted defeat, closed its six retail branches in Kobe and Kyoto, and withdrew from the private client market in Japan.

Over the next few years, however, things changed. In the mid-1990s, Japan embarked on a wide-ranging deregulation of its financial services industry. This led to the removal of many of the restrictions that had made it so difficult for Merrill Lynch to do business in Japan. For example, the relaxation of foreign exchange controls meant that by 1998, Japanese citizens could purchase foreign stocks, bonds, and mutual funds. Meanwhile, Japan's big four stockbrokerages continued to struggle with serious financial problems that resulted from the 1991 crash of that country's stock market. In November

1997, in what was a shock to many Japanese, one of these firms, Yamaichi Securities, declared it was bankrupt due to $2.2 billion in accumulated "hidden losses" and that it would shut its doors. Recognizing the country's financial system was strained and in need of fresh capital, know-how, and the stimulus of greater competition, the Japanese government signaled that it would adopt a more relaxed attitude to foreign entry into its financial services industry. This attitude underlay Japan's wholehearted endorsement of a 1997 deal brokered by the World Trade Organization to liberalize global financial services. Among other things, the WTO deal made it much easier for foreign firms to sell financial service products to Japanese investors.

By 1997, it had become clear to Merrill Lynch that the climate in Japan had changed significantly. The big attraction of the market was still the same: the financial assets owned by Japanese households are huge, amounting to a staggering ¥1,220 trillion in late 1997, only 3 percent of which were then invested in mutual funds (most are invested in low-yielding bank accounts and government bonds). In mid-1997, Merrill Lynch started to consider reentering the Japanese private client market.

The company initially considered a joint venture with Sanwa Bank to sell Merrill Lynch's mutual fund products to Japanese consumers through Sanwa's 400 retail branches. The proposed alliance would have allowed Merrill Lynch to leverage Sanwa's existing distribution system, rather than having to build a distribution system of its own. However, the long-run disadvantage of such a strategy was that it would not have given Merrill Lynch the presence that it felt it needed to build a solid financial services business in Japan. Top executives reasoned that it was important for them to make a major commitment to the Japanese market to establish the company's brand name as a premier provider of investment products and financial advice to individuals. This would enable Merrill Lynch to entrench itself as a major player before other foreign institutions entered the market—and before Japan's own stockbrokerages rose to the challenge. At the same time, given their prior experience in Japan, Merrill Lynch executives were hesitant to go down this road because of the huge costs and risks involved.

The problem of how best to enter the Japanese market was solved by the bankruptcy of Yamaichi Securities. Suddenly Yamaichi's nationwide network of offices and 7,000 employees were up for grabs. In late December 1997, Merrill Lynch announced it would hire 2,000 of Yamaichi's

501

employees and acquire up to 50 of Yamaichi's branch offices. The deal, which was enthusiastically endorsed by the Japanese government, significantly lowered Merrill Lynch's costs of establishing a retail network in Japan. The goal for the new Merrill Lynch subsidiary was to have $20 billion under management by 2000. The company got off to a quick start. In February 1998, Merrill Lynch launched its first mutual fund in Japan and saw the value of its assets swell to $1 billion by April. By the beginning of 2001, Merrill Lynch announced it had $26 billion under management in Japan. The company now has a significant head start over other foreign financial service institutions contemplating building a private client network in Japan. Merrill Lynch's hope is that by the time other foreign institutions enter, it will already have a commanding presence in Japan that will be difficult to challenge.

Sources: "Japan's Big Bang. Enter Merrill," *The Economist*, January 3, 1998, p. 72; J. P. Donlon, "Merrill Cinch," *Chief Executive*, March 1998, pp. 28–32; D. Holley, "Merrill Lynch to Open 31 Offices throughout Japan," *Los Angeles Times*, February 13, 1998, p. D1; A. Rowley, "Merrill Thunders into Japan," *The Banker*, March 1998, p. 6; and Merrill Lynch's website www.ml.com.

Case Discussion Questions

1. Given the changes that have occurred in the international capital markets during the past decade, does Merrill Lynch's strategy of expanding internationally make sense? Why?

2. What factors make Japan a suitable market for Merrill Lynch to enter?

3. Review Merrill Lynch's 1997 reentry into the Japanese private client market. Pay close attention to the timing and scale of entry and the nature of the strategic commitments Merrill Lynch is making in Japan. What are the potential benefits associated with this strategy? What are the costs and risks? Do you think the trade-off between benefits and risks and costs makes sense? Why?

Notes

1. For interesting empirical studies that deal with the issues of timing and resource commitments, see T. Isobe, S. Makino, and D. B. Montgomery, "Resource Commitment, Entry Timing, and Market Performance of Foreign Direct Investments in Emerging Economies," *Academy of Management Journal* 43, no. 3, (2000), pp. 468–84, and Y. Pan and P. S. K. Chi, "Financial Performance and Survival of Multinational Corporations in China," *Strategic Management Journal* 20, no. 4, (1999), pp. 359–74.

2. This can be reconceptualized as the resource base of the entrant, relative to indigenous competitors. For work that focuses on this issue, see W. C. Bogenr, H. Thomas, and J. McGee, "A Longitudinal Study of the Competitive Positions and Entry Paths of European Firms in the U.S. Pharmaceutical Market," *Strategic Management Journal* 17 (1996), pp. 85–107; D. Collis, "A Resource-Based Analysis of Global Competition," *Strategic Management Journal* 12 (1991), pp. 49–68; and S. Tallman, "Strategic Management Models and Resource-Based Strategies among MNEs in a Host Market," *Strategic Management Journal* 12 (1991), pp. 69–82.

3. For a discussion of first-mover advantages, see M. Liberman and D. Montgomery, "First-Mover Advantages," *Strategic Management Journal* 9 (Summer Special Issue, 1988), pp. 41–58.

4. J. M. Shaver, W. Mitchell, and B. Yeung, "The Effect of Own Firm and Other Firm Experience on Foreign Direct Investment Survival in the United States, 1987–92," *Strategic Management Journal* 18 (1997), pp. 811–24.

5. S. Zaheer and E. Mosakowski, "The Dynamics of the Liability of Foreignness: A Global Study of Survival in the Financial Services Industry," *Strategic Management Journal* 18 (1997), pp. 439–64.

6. Shaver, Mitchell, and Yeung, "The Effect of Own Firm and Other Firm Experience on Foreign Direct Investment Survival in the United States."

7. P. Ghemawat, *Commitment: The Dynamics of Strategy* (New York: Free Press, 1991).

8. R. Luecke, *Scuttle Your Ships before Advancing* (Oxford: Oxford University Press, 1994).

9. Isobe, Makino, and Montgomery, "Resource Commitment, Entry Timing, and Market Performance," and Pan and Chi, "Financial Performance and Survival of Multinational Corporations in China."

10. Christopher Bartlett and Sumantra Ghoshal, "Going Global: Lessons from Late Movers," *Harvard Business Review*, March–April 2000, pp. 132–45.

11. This section draws on several studies, including: C. W. L. Hill, P. Hwang, and W. C. Kim,

"An Eclectic Theory of the Choice of International Entry Mode," *Strategic Management Journal* 11 (1990), pp. 117–28; C. W. L. Hill and W. C. Kim, "Searching for a Dynamic Theory of the Multinational Enterprise: A Transaction Cost Model," *Strategic Management Journal* 9 (Special Issue on Strategy Content, 1988), pp. 93–104; E. Anderson and H. Gatignon, "Modes of Foreign Entry: A Transaction Cost Analysis and Propositions," *Journal of International Business Studies* 17 (1986), pp. 1–26; F. R. Root, *Entry Strategies for International Markets* (Lexington, MA: D. C. Heath, 1980); A. Madhok, "Cost, Value and Foreign Market Entry: The Transaction and the Firm," *Strategic Management Journal* 18 (1997), pp. 39–61; K. D. Brouthers and L. B. Brouthers, "Acquisition or Greenfield Start-up?" *Strategic Management Journal* 21, no. 1, (2000), pp. 89–97.

12. For a general discussion of licensing, see F. J. Contractor, "The Role of Licensing in International Strategy," *Columbia Journal of World Business*, Winter 1982, pp. 73–83.

13. See E. Terazono and C. Lorenz, "An Angry Young Warrior," *Financial Times*, September 19, 1994, p. 11, and K. McQuade and B. Gomes-Casseres, "Xerox and Fuji-Xerox," Harvard Business School Case #9-391-156.

14. O. E. Williamson, *The Economic Institutions of Capitalism* (New York: Free Press, 1985).

15. J. H. Dunning and M. McQueen, "The Eclectic Theory of International Production: A Case Study of the International Hotel Industry," *Managerial and Decision Economics* 2 (1981), pp. 197–210.

16. Andrew E. Serwer, "McDonald's Conquers the World," *Fortune*, October 17, 1994, pp. 103–16.

17. For an excellent review of the basic theoretical literature of joint ventures, see B. Kogut, "Joint Ventures: Theoretical and Empirical Perspectives," *Strategic Management Journal* 9 (1988), pp. 319–32. More recent studies include T. Chi, "Option to Acquire or Divest a Joint Venture," *Strategic Management Journal* 21, no. 6 (2000), pp. 665–88; H. Merchant and D. Schendel, "How Do International Joint Ventures Create Shareholder Value?" *Strategic Management Journal* 21, no. 7, (2000), pp. 723–37, and H. K. Steensma and M. A. Lyles, "Explaining IJV Survival in a Transitional Economy though Social Exchange and Knowledge Based Perspectives," *Strategic Management Journal* 21, no. 8, (2000), pp. 831–51.

18. D. G. Bradley, "Managing against Expropriation," *Harvard Business Review*, July–August 1977, pp. 78–90.

19. Speech given by Tony Kobayashi at the University of Washington Business School, October 1992.

20. A. C. Inkpen and P. W. Beamish, "Knowledge, Bargaining Power, and the Instability of International Joint Ventures," *Academy of Management Review* 22 (1997), pp. 177–202; and S. H. Park and G. R. Ungson, "The Effect of National Culture, Organizational Complementarity, and Economic Motivation on Joint Venture Dissolution," *Academy of Management Journal* 40 (1997), pp. 279–307.

21. Inkpen and Beamish, "Knowledge, Bargaining Power, and the Instability of International Joint Ventures."

22. See Brouthers and Brouthers, "Acquisition or Greenfield Start-up?" and J. F. Hennart and Y. R. Park, "Greenfield versus Acquisition: The Strategy of Japanese Investors in the United States," *Management Science*, 1993, pp. 1054–70.

23. This section draws on Hill, Hwang, and Kim, "An Eclectic Theory of the Choice of International Entry Mode."

24. C. W. L. Hill, "Strategies for Exploiting Technological Innovations: When and When Not to License," *Organization Science* 3 (1992), pp. 428–41.

25. United Nations, *World Investment Report 2000: Cross Border Mergers and Acquisitions and Development* (New York and Geneva: United Nations, 2000).

26. Ibid.

27. Ibid.

28. For evidence on acquisitions and performance, see R. E. Caves, "Mergers, Takeovers, and Economic Efficiency," *International Journal of Industrial Organization* 7 (1989), pp. 151–74; M. C. Jensen and R. S. Ruback, "The Market for Corporate Control: The Scientific Evidence," *Journal of Financial Economics* 11 (1983), pp. 5–50; R. Roll, "Empirical Evidence on Takeover Activity and Shareholder Wealth," in *Knights, Raiders and Targets*, ed. J. C. Coffee, L. Lowenstein, and S. Rose (Oxford: Oxford University Press, 1989); A. Schleifer and R. W. Vishny, "Takeovers in the 60s and 80s: Evidence and Implications," *Strategic Management Journal* 12 (Winter 1991) Special Issue, pp. 51–60; and T. H. Brush, "Predicted Changes in Operational Synergy and Post Acquisition Performance of

Acquired Businesses," *Strategic Management Journal* 17 (1996), pp. 1–24.

29. J. Warner, J. Templeman, R. Horn, "The Case against Mergers," *Business Week*, October 30, 1995, pp. 122–34.

30. D. J. Ravenscraft and F. M. Scherer, *Mergers, Selloffs, and Economic Efficiency* (Washington, DC: Brookings Institution, 1987).

31. See P. Ghemawat and F. Ghadar, "The Dubious Logic of Global Mega-mergers," *Harvard Business Review*, July–August 2000, pp. 65–72.

32. R. Roll, "The Hubris Hypothesis of Corporate Takeovers," *Journal of Business* 59 (1986), pp. 197–216.

33. "Marital Problems," *The Economist*, October 14, 2000.

34. See J. P. Walsh, "Top Management Turnover Following Mergers and Acquisitions," *Strategic Management Journal* 9 (1988), pp. 173–83.

35. B. Vlasic and B. A. Stertz, *Taken for a Ride: How Daimler-Benz Drove off with Chrysler* (New York: Harper Collins, 2000).

36. See A. A. Cannella and D. C. Hambrick, "Executive Departure and Acquisition Performance," *Strategic Management Journal* 14 (1993), pp. 137–52.

37. P. Haspeslagh and D. Jemison, *Managing Acquisitions* (New York: Free Press, 1991).

38. Ibid.

39. See K. Ohmae, "The Global Logic of Strategic Alliances," *Harvard Business Review*, March–April 1989, pp. 143–54; G. Hamel, Y. L. Doz, and C. K. Prahalad, "Collaborate with Your Competitors and Win!" *Harvard Business Review*, January–February 1989, pp. 133–39; W. Burgers, C. W. L. Hill, and W. C. Kim, "Alliances in the Global Auto Industry," *Strategic Management Journal* 14 (1993), pp. 419–32; and P. Kale, H. Singh, H. Perlmutter, "Learning and

Protection of Proprietary Assets in Strategic Alliances: Building Relational Capital," *Strategic Management Journal* 21 (2000), pp. 217–37.

40. "Asia Beckons," *The Economist*, May 30, 1992, pp. 63–64.

41. P. M. Reilly, "Sony's Digital Audio Format Pulls ahead of Philips's," *Wall Street Journal*, August 6, 1993, p. B1.

42. Kale, Singh, Perlmutter, "Learning and Protection of Proprietary Assets."

43. R. B. Reich and E. D. Mankin, "Joint Ventures with Japan Give Away Our Future," *Harvard Business Review*, March–April 1986, pp. 78–90.

44. J. Bleeke and D. Ernst, "The Way to Win in Cross-Border Alliances," *Harvard Business Review*, November–December 1991, pp. 127–35.

45. W. Roehl and J. F. Truitt, "Stormy Open Marriages Are Better," *Columbia Journal of World Business*, Summer 1987, pp. 87–95.

46. McQuade and Gomes-Casseres, "Xerox and Fuji-Xerox."

47. See T. Khanna, R. Gulati, and N. Nohria, "The Dynamics of Learning Alliances: Competition, Cooperation, and Relative Scope," *Strategic Management Journal* 19 (1998), pp. 193–210, and Kale, Singh, and Perlmutter, "Learning and Protection of Proprietary Assets."

48. Kale, Singh, and Perlmutter, "Learning and Protection of Proprietary Assets."

49. Hamel, Doz, and Prahalad, "Collaborate with Competitors," and Khanna, Gulati, and Nohria, "The Dynamics of Learning Alliances: Competition, Cooperation, and Relative Scope."

50. B. Wysocki, "Cross-Border Alliances Become Favorite Way to Crack New Markets," *Wall Street Journal*, March 4, 1990, p. A1.

51. Hamel, Doz, and Prahalad, "Collaborate with Competitors," p. 138.

Cases

Nestlé: Global Strategy

Introduction

Nestlé is one of the oldest of all multinational businesses. The company was founded in Switzerland in 1866 by Heinrich Nestlé, who established Nestlé to distribute "milk food," a type of infant food he had invented that was made from powdered milk, baked food, and sugar. From its very early days, the company looked to other countries for growth opportunities, establishing its first foreign offices in London in 1868. In 1905, the company merged with the Anglo Swiss Condensed Milk, thereby broadening the company's product line to include both condensed milk and infant formulas. Forced by Switzerland's small size to look outside its borders for growth opportunities, Nestlé established condensed milk and infant food processing plants in the United States and Great Britain in the late 19th century and in Australia, South America, Africa, and Asia in the first three decades of the 20th century.

In 1929, Nestlé moved into the chocolate business when it acquired a Swiss chocolate maker. This was followed in 1938 by the development of Nestlé's most revolutionary product, Nescafe, the world's first soluble coffee drink. After World War II, Nestlé continued to expand into other areas of the food business, primarily through a series of acquisitions that included Maggi (1947), Cross & Blackwell (1960), Findus (1962), Libby's (1970), Stouffer's (1973), Carnation (1985), Rowntree (1988), and Perrier (1992).

By the late 1990s, Nestlé had 500 factories in 76 countries and sold its products in a staggering 193 nations—almost every country in the world. In 1998, the company generated sales of close to SWF 72 billion ($51 billion), only 1 percent of which occurred in its home country. Similarly, only 3 percent of its 210,000 employees were located in Switzerland. Nestlé was the world's biggest maker of infant formula, powdered milk, chocolates, instant coffee, soups, and mineral waters. It was number two in ice cream, breakfast cereals, and pet food. Roughly 38 percent of its food sales were made in Europe, 32 percent in the Americas, and 20 percent in Africa and Asia.

A Growth Strategsy for the 21st Century

Despite its undisputed success, Nestlé realized by the early 1990s that it faced significant challenges in maintaining its growth rate. The large Western European and North American markets were sature. In several countries, population growth had stagnated and in some there had been a small decline in food consumption. The re- tail environment in many Western nations had become increasingly challenging, and the balance of power was shifting away from the large-scale manufacturers of branded foods and beverages and toward nationwide supermarket and discount chains. Increasingly, retailers found themselves in the unfamiliar position of playing off against each other manufacturers of branded foods, thus bargaining down prices. Particularly in Europe, this trend was enhanced by the successful introduction of private-label brands by several of Europe's leading supermarket chains. The results included increased price competition in several key segments of the food and beverage market, such as cereals, coffee, and soft drinks.

At Nestlé, one response has been to look toward emerging markets in Eastern Europe, Asia, and Latin America for growth possibilities. The logic is simple and obvious—a combination of economic and population growth, when coupled with the widespread adoption of market-oriented economic policies by the governments of many developing nations, makes for attractive business opportunities. Many of these countries are still relatively poor, but their economies are growing rapidly. For example, if current economic growth forecasts occur, by 2010 there will be 700 million people in China and India that have income levels approaching those of Spain in the mid 1990s. As income levels rise, it is increasingly likely that consumers in these nations will start to substitute branded food products for basic foodstuffs, creating a large market opportunity for companies such as Nestlé.

In general, the company's strategy has been to enter emerging markets early—before competitors—and build a substantial position by selling basic food items that appeal to the local population base, such as infant formula, condensed milk, noodles, and tofu. By narrowing its initial market focus to just a handful of strategic brands, Nestlé claims it can simplify life, reduce risk, and concentrate its marketing resources and managerial effort on a limited number of key niches. The goal is to build a commanding market position in each of these niches. By pursuing such a strategy, Nestlé has taken as much as 85 percent of the market for instant coffee in Mexico, 66 percent of the market for powdered milk in the Philippines, and 70 percent of the market for soups in Chile. As income levels rise, the company progressively moves out from these niches, introducing more upscale items, such as mineral water, chocolate, cookies and prepared foodstuffs.

Although the company is known worldwide for several key brands, such as Nescafe, it uses local brands in many markets. The company owns 8,500 brands, but only 750 of them are registered in more than one country, and only 80 are registered in more than 10 countries. While the company will use the same "global brands" in multiple developed markets, in the developing world it focuses on trying to optimize ingredients and processing technology to local conditions and then using a brand name that resonates locally. Customization rather than globalization is the key to the company's strategy in emerging markets.

Executing the Strategy

Successful execution of the strategy for developing markets requires a degree of flexibility, an ability to adapt in often unforeseen ways to local conditions, and a long-term perspective that puts building a sustainable business before short-term profitability. In Nigeria, for example, a crumbling road system, aging trucks, and the danger of violence forced the company to rethink its traditional distribution methods. Instead of operating a central warehouse, as is its preference in most nations, the company built a network of small warehouses around the country. For safety reasons, trucks carrying Nestlé goods are allowed to travel only during the day and frequently under armed guard. Marketing also poses challenges in Nigeria. With little opportunity for typical Western-style advertising on television or billboards, the company hired local singers to go to towns and villages offering a mix of entertainment and product demonstrations.

China provides another interesting example of local adaptation and a long-term focus. After 13 years of talks, Nestlé was formally invited into China in 1987 by the government of Heilongjiang province. Nestlé opened a plant to produce powdered milk and infant formula there in 1990, but quickly realized that the local rail and road infrastructure was inadequate and inhibited the collection of milk and delivery of finished products. Rather than make do with the local infrastructure, Nestlé embarked on an ambitious plan to establish its own distribution network, known as milk roads, between 27 villages in the region and factory collection points, called chilling centers. Farmers brought their milk—often on bicycles or carts—to the centers where it was weighed and analyzed. Unlike the government, Nestlé paid the farmers promptly. Suddenly the farmers had an incentive to produce milk, and many bought a second cow, increasing the cow population in the district by 3,000, to 9,000, in 18 months. Area managers then organized a delivery system that used dedicated vans to deliver the milk to Nestlé's factory.

Although at first glance this might seem to be a very costly solution; Nestlé calculated that the long-term benefits would be substantial. Nestlé's strategy is similar to that undertaken by many European and American companies during the first waves of industrialization in those countries. Companies often had to invest in infrastructure that we now take for granted to get production

off the ground. Once the infrastructure was in place in China, Nestlé's production took off. In 1990, 316 tons of powdered milk and infant formula were produced. By 1994, output exceeded 10,000 tons, and the company decided to triple capacity. Based on this experience, Nestlé decided to build another two powdered milk factories in China and was aiming to generate sales of $700 million by 2000.

Nestlé is pursuing a similar long-term bet in the Middle East, an area in which most multinational food companies have little presence. Collectively, the Middle East accounts for only about 2 percent of Nestlé's worldwide sales, and the individual markets are very small. However, Nestlé's long-term strategy is based on the assumption that regional conflicts will subside and intraregional trade will expand as trade barriers between countries in the region come down. Once that happens, Nestlé's factories in the Middle East should be able to sell throughout the region, thereby realizing scale economies. In anticipation of this development, Nestlé has established a network of factories in five countries in hopes that each will someday supply the entire region with different products. The company currently makes ice cream in Dubai, soups and cereals in Saudi Arabia, yogurt and bouillon in Egypt, chocolate in Turkey, and ketchup and instant noodles in Syria. For the present, Nestlé can survive in these markets by using local materials and focusing on local demand. The Syrian factory, for example, relies on products that use tomatoes, a major local agricultural product. Syria also produces wheat, which is the main ingredient in instant noodles. Even if trade barriers don't come down soon, Nestlé has indicated it will remain committed to the region. By using local inputs and focusing on local consumer needs, it has earned a good rate of return in the region, even though the individual markets are small.

Despite its successes in places such as China and parts of the Middle East, not all of Nestlé's moves have worked out so well. Like several other Western companies, Nestlé has had its problems in Japan, where a failure to adapt its coffee brand to local conditions meant the loss of a significant market opportunity to another Western company, Coca-Cola. For years, Nestlé's instant coffee brand was the dominant coffee product in Japan. In the 1960s, cold canned coffee (which can be purchased from soda vending machines) started to gain a following in Japan. Nestlé dismissed the product as just a coffee-flavored drink, rather than the real thing, and declined to enter the market. Nestlé's local partner at the time, Kirin Beer, was so incensed at Nestlé's refusal to enter the canned coffee market that it broke off its relationship with the company. In contrast, Coca-Cola entered the market with Georgia, a product developed specifically for this segment of the Japanese market. By leveraging its existing distribution channel, Coca-Cola captured a 40 percent share of the $4 billion a year market for canned coffee in Japan. Nestlé, which failed to enter the market until the 1980s, has only a 4 percent share.

While Nestlé has built businesses from the ground up in many emerging markets, such as Nigeria and China, in others it will purchase local companies if suitable candidates can be found. The company pursued such a strategy in Poland, which it entered in 1994 by purchasing Goplana, the country's second largest chocolate manufacturer. With the collapse of communism and the opening of the Polish market, income levels in Poland have started to rise and so has chocolate consumption. Once a scarce item, the market grew by 8 percent a year throughout the 1990s. To take advantage of this opportunity, Nestlé has pursued a strategy of evolution, rather than revolution. It has kept the top management of the company staffed with locals—as it does in most of its operations around the world—and carefully adjusted Goplana's product line to better match local opportunities. At the same time, it has pumped money into Goplana's marketing, which has enabled the unit to gain share from several other chocolate makers in the country. Still, competition in the market is intense. Eight companies, including several foreign-owned enterprises, such as the market leader, Wedel, which is owned by PepsiCo, are vying for market share, and this has depressed prices and profit margins, despite the healthy volume growth.

Management Structure

Nestlé is a decentralized organization. Responsibility for operating decisions is pushed down to local units, which typically enjoy a high degree of autonomy with regard to decisions involving pricing, distribution, marketing, human resources, and so on. At the same time, the company is organized into seven worldwide strategic business units (SBUs) that have responsibility for high-level strategic decisions and business development. For example, a strategic business unit focuses on coffee and beverages. Another one focuses on confectionery and ice cream. These SBUs engage in overall strategy development, including acquisitions and market entry strategy. In recent years, two-thirds of Nestlé's growth has come from acquisitions, so this is a critical function. Running in parallel to this structure is a regional organization that divides the world into five major geographical zones, such as Europe, North America, and Asia. The regional organizations assist in the overall strategy development process and are responsible for developing regional strategies (an example would be Nestlé's strategy in the Middle East, which was discussed earlier). Neither the SBU nor regional managers, however, get involved in local operating or strategic decisions on anything other than an exceptional basis.

Although Nestlé makes intensive use of local managers, to knit its diverse worldwide operations together the company relies on its "expatriate army." This consists of about 700 managers who spend the bulk of their careers on foreign assignments, moving from one country to the next. Selected primarily on the basis of their ability, drive, and willingness to live a quasi-nomadic lifestyle, these individuals often work in half a dozen nations, during their careers. Nestlé also uses management development programs as a strategic tool for creating an *esprit de corps* among managers. At Rive-Reine, the company's international training center in Switzerland, the company brings together managers from around the world, at different stages in their careers, for specially targeted development programs of two to three weeks duration. The objective of these programs is to give the managers a better understanding of Nestlé's culture and strategy and to give them access to the company's top management.

The research and development operation has a special place within Nestlé, which is not surprising for a company that was established to commercialize innovative foodstuffs. The R&D function comprises 18 different groups that operate in 11 countries throughout the world. Nestlé spends approximately 1 percent of its annual sales revenue on R&D and has 3,100 employees dedicated to the function. Around 70 percent of the R&D budget is spent on development initiatives. These initiatives focus on developing products and processes that fulfill market needs, as identified by the SBUs, in concert with regional and local managers. For example, Nestlé instant noodle products were originally developed by the R&D group in response to the perceived needs of local operating companies through the Asian region. The company also has longer-term development projects that focus on developing new technological platforms, such as nonanimal protein sources or agricultural biotechnology products.

Case Discussion Questions

1. Does it make sense for Nestlé to focus its growth efforts on emerging markets? Why?

2. What is the company's strategy with regard to business development in emerging markets? Does this strategy make sense?

3. From an organizational perspective, what is required for this strategy to work effectively?

4. How would you describe Nestlé's strategic posture at the corporate level; is it pursuing a global strategy, a multidomestic strategy, an international strategy, or a transnational strategy?

5. Does this overall strategic posture make sense given the markets and countries that Nestlé participates in? Why?

6. Is Nestlé's management structure and philosophy aligned with its overall strategic posture?

Sources

1. Hall, W. "Strength of Brands Is Key to Success." *Financial Times*, November 30, 1998, p. 2.
2. "How to Conquer China (and the World) with Instant Noodles." *The Economist*, June 17, 1995.
3. Lorenz, C. "Sugar Daddy." *Financial Times*, April 20, 1994, p. 19.
4. Michaels, D. "Chocolate Giants Worldwide Find Themselves Sweet on Polish Market." *Wall Street Journal*, December 12, 1997.
5. Nestlé. "Key Facts and History." At http://www.nestle.com.
6. Rapoport, C. "Nestlé's Brand Building Machine." *Fortune*, September 19, 1994, p. 147.
7. Steinmetz, G., and T. Parker-Rope. "All Over the Map." *Wall Street Journal*, September 26, 1996, p. R4.
8. Sullivan, M. "Nestlé Is Looking to Coffee Market in Russia for Sales." *Wall Street Journal*, August 7, 1998, p. B7A.

Ford 2000

Introduction

Alex Trotman, newly named CEO of Ford, made a proclamation in November 1993. "The top priority is to keep doing what we've been doing."[1] No one really believed him. Trotman had made a career of doing the unexpected. When top management refused him a transfer from Britain in 1969, he bought his own ticket to Dearborn, Michigan, and talked his way into a job at headquarters, alias the Glass House. At 61, Trotman holds a master's degree in business although he never attended college. He spent years working his way up through Ford's management, primarily on the production side in Europe.

The skeptics were right. It did not take long for Trotman to shake things up. Three weeks after being named CEO, Trotman attended a meeting of senior managers at Ford's London office. The subject of the meeting was to review the success of consolidating the developing of power trains, the main components of engines and transmissions. Trotman asked the managers if it was possible to expand this idea to the entire company, not just engines and transmissions. Could Ford tear down its highly segmented regional structure and create one global system? Trotman gave a team of senior managers six weeks to determine if such an idea was feasible.

The Rationale for Restructuring

There were several motivating factors behind the need for restructuring. Under the previous system, there was massive duplication of processes in both North America and Europe. According to the company, this raised annual costs by at least $3 billion.[2] Furthermore, Ford's average new-car development time was much longer than its competitors', approximately six years as compared to Toyota's three. Its competitors had more profits per car and higher pretax margins. Trotman also saw the need to refocus the company in order to efficiently enter emerging markets in China, Russia, and Latin America.

Thus, Ford 2000 was born. With the ultimate goal to become "the best automaker in the world," Trotman announced the most massive reorganization of the company in its 91-year history on April 1, 1994. The specific directives included:

*   Be faster and more efficient developing new models.
*   Expand the range of products and fill in gaps.
*   Match the Japanese cost advantage and improve profitability.
*   Reduce the time it takes to make a vehicle.
*   Follow Toyota's lead of selling the same model around the world.[3]

The finer points of Ford 2000 were hammered out by a team of 150 executives. Led by Bob Transou, who engineered the more efficient power train process, the team devised ways for the company to streamline itself. The team itself was a direct contrast to Ford's old corporate culture. It was housed in a war room, a large open area filled with small desks and cubicles, with no private offices. The idea was to put all the decision makers in one place and force them to hash out decisions on the spot, rather than waste months passing around memos. All the team members had delegated their other responsibilities to completely dedicate their efforts to planning the reorganization. Everyone worked in their shirt-sleeves, so it was impossible to distinguish vice presidents from underlings. This informal atmosphere was not an accident. Transou "wanted people to leave their corporate credentials at the door."[4]

The team had the blessing of top management, but it still had some history to overcome. Ford's last attempt at building a global car, the Mondeo, which eventually became the Ford Contour, the Mercury Mystique, and the Mondeo, took almost seven years to develop and cost $6 billion. Industry analysts doubted that Ford would ever recoup those development costs through sales. The team's challenge was to incorporate the lessons learned from the Mondeo into its new reorganization plan. The underlying objective was to lay the groundwork for a decade's worth of products all built from a common design and with great economies of scale.

Ford 2000

Ford 2000's initial imperative was to consolidate the North American and European operations. On January 1, 1995, the first part of Ford 2000 was implemented. Ford of Europe and Ford North America merged to form Ford Automotive Operations (FAO). (To give a frame of reference for the scale of this merger, Ford of Europe and Ford North America combine to be a $94 billion business. The Nabisco–RJR Reynolds merger was approximately $24 billion.) The new organization was divided into five vehicle program centers. Each vehicle program center (VPC) was to be responsible for the development, manufacture, marketing, and profitability of its specific Ford vehicles, no matter where they are sold.

The vehicle program centers are divided into small- and medium-sized front-wheel-drive cars, large front-wheel-drive cars, rear-wheel-drive cars, and light and commercial trucks. Europe kept control of the development of small and medium cars because of its obvious expertise. Dearborn in the United States handled the rest. Although Europe only got one out of the five new VPCs, the European center had responsibility for developing vehicles in market segments that held the biggest potential from Ford's global strategy and were expected to account for around 50 percent of world car sales by the next decade.

Each VPC had the capability to alter its product to suit regional markets. The formidable task of each VPC was to make everything under the hood the same and everything that had to do with taste and local regulations different and to do this in a cost-efficient manner. As Trotman put it, "Even with under-the-skin components that may be identical, the design and feel of our vehicles can be made very different to suit local tastes."[5]

Ford believes the new organization will be successful, particularly with quicker adaptation to shifting customer demands. New-product time cycles were targeted to be uniformly under three years by 2000. Plant changeovers for new "global" models produced at various locations around the world are scheduled to follow each other in weeks, not months.[6] Extensive investment in computers and videoconferencing technology was made to facilitate the process. Ford, with the help of the consulting firm Logica, created its own Worldwide Integrated Purchasing System (WIPS). All of Ford's purchasing activities, which represent over 100,000 separate parts worth $40 billion, are on the workload management system.[7]

Organizational Structure

What does the new Ford look like? The new Ford is a matrix organization (see Figure 1). Most employees report to two or more managers, one within a vehicle center team and one within a functional discipline such as finance or manufacturing. Instead of being temporarily assigned to work on a new Taurus, a brake engineer is now permanently assigned to a team to help develop a specific car for individual countries. Career development is the responsibility of the functional managers, while performance evaluation is the duty of the vehicle program team leader. By shifting the performance evaluation to the vehicle team leader, Ford wants to change the loyalties of its employees from their functional area to the car they are helping to build. This goal has been further reinforced by the co-location of people with their vehicle program teams.

Ford has learned lessons from other failed matrix organizations and has built in safeguards. They include:

- Making doubly sure that objectives are agreed on between the vehicle centers and the functional side of the organization.
- Specifying clearly the respective roles and responsibilities of individuals toward each side of the matrix.
- Changing appraisal and reward systems accordingly.
- Appointing only senior executives who have shown they can work collaboratively.
- Training everyone in the art of developing a cooperative matrix perspective, which largely replaces the need for policing.
- Introducing much more intensive and open communication.[8]

Transou hoped to make the matrix system work by ensuring that the structure included accountability. "You need accountability," said Transou. "Those that have not succeeded with matrix management did not understand that. Without accountability it is always someone else's fault. There are excuses. There are no excuses in Ford 2000; it is very clear where responsibility is."[9]

Above the VPCs, decision making was centralized through the creation of a global profit center for all automotive operations. Ed Hogenlocker, president of FAO, claimed, "By centralizing decision making, we can take the broadest possible view of market opportunities, and we can develop products to serve multiple markets, vastly increasing the return on every product development dollar."[10]

Ford was attempting not only to change how it did business, but also its corporate culture. The Ford 2000 program trimmed the layers of management from 10 to 7

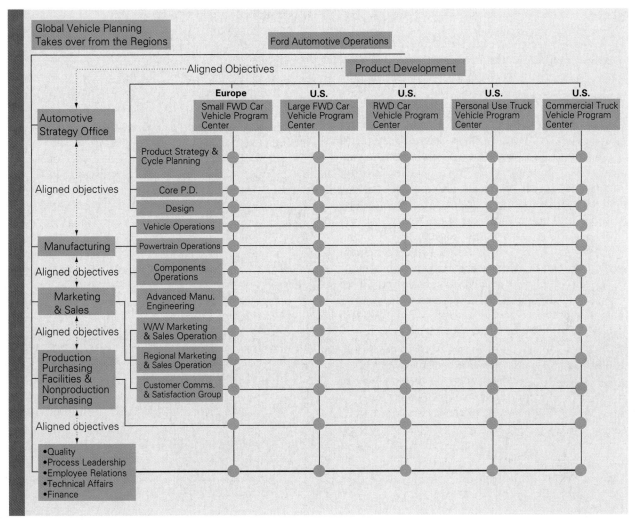

Figure 1

Ford's New Global Matrix Structure

Source: The Ford Motor Company.

to destroy the delaying bureaucracy and facilitate the matrix system. Ford offered early retirement to a relatively small number of senior officials, including executives, managers, and professionals, approximately 15 percent of the top 2,500. "It'll be a leaner, hopefully much more efficient, faster, more nimble company than it is today and the management structure will reflect and cause it," Trotman said in 1994.[11]

Trotman conducted the reorganization in a very disciplined and principled manner to maximize the probability for success. Primarily, he got the entire company involved in the process. Although the team headed by Transou did much of the planning, it got hundreds of other employees in on the act. The principle was simple: Get the people who will have to live with changes involved in making the changes.[12]

Ford made a great effort to keep all its employees and the public informed of changes. Its public relations department published a weekly faxed newspaper, ran an electronic bulletin board, and broadcast a weekly in-house television show to keep everyone informed of the latest developments. It also held numerous employee meetings.

Ford expected confusion among its employees and attempted to manage it. Hundreds of careers were side tracked as Ford flattened its hierarchy. In addition, Ford of Europe, which was once an autonomous unit, lost a significant amount of control. There was a notable fear by some European employees that FAO may ultimately stand for "For Americans Only." To ease these fears, members of the reorganization team made presentations to explain how the new organization would work.

Conclusion

Mr. Trotman set an eight-month schedule for revamping Ford. Most multinationals in other industries have taken a decade to shift their organizations gradually to global structures. To some observers, Ford chose a strange time to reorganize. Ford reported record earnings of $5.3 billion for fiscal year 1994 on top of record revenues of $128 billion. Trotman defended this criticism by saying that concentrating on change and improvement is a lot easier when times are good. "Now is the right time for such a change. The tools are there—computers and communications—and we have a strong balance sheet. If you make big changes when times are difficult, expediency often takes precedence."[13]

The benefits of the reorganization could be tremendous. Ford anticipated savings of up to $5 billion a year.[14] The reconstruction also created a more efficient Ford with fewer, global suppliers. Ford estimated that by cutting suppliers of everything but auto parts from 50,000 in 1995 to 5,000 by 1997, it would save $1 billion a year.[15]

Ultimately, the new Ford will have the flexibility to forcefully enter emerging markets. But real dangers are involved. Ford can potentially make itself too global by producing cars that cannot be cost effectively altered to meet local tastes. Can the global cars be kept affordable?

Case Discussion Questions

1. What other possible obstacles might Ford encounter as a global organization?
2. How important is the new matrix system in the success or failure of Ford 2000?
3. What did Trotman forget in the restructuring?
4. What other efficiencies might also be by-products of Ford 2000?

5. How successful do you think this program will be in preparing Ford to enter emerging markets? What will be the key factors for success in entering these markets?

Notes

1. J. B. Treece, "Ford: Alex Trotman's Daring Strategy," *Business Week*, April 3, 1995, pp. 94–104.
2. K. Done, "Ford Maps Out a Global Ambition," *Financial Times*, April 3, 1995, p. 9.
3. A. Chamberlain, "Major Shakeup at Ford," *Toronto Star*, April 21, 1994, p. C1.
4. D. Sedgwick, "Ford's Redesigners," *Detroit News*, June 26, 1994, p. 1.
5. Done, "Ford Maps Out a Global Ambition."
6. E. Heinrich, "Ford Takes Historic Gamble," *Financial Post*, August 27, 1994, p. 8.
7. "Logica Assists Ford Motor Company," *Business Wire*, May 9, 1995.
8. C. Lorenz, "Ford's Global Matrix Gamble," *Financial Times*, December 16, 1994, p. 14.
9. Done, "Ford Maps Out a Global Ambition."
10. Lorenz, "Ford's Global Matrix Gamble."
11. J. Szczensy, "Ford Exec Ranks to Be Halved," *Oakland Press*, October 15, 1994, p. 20.
12. D. Sedgwick, "Fixing Ford," *Detroit News*, September 18, 1994, p. D1.
13. "The World Car," *The Economist*, July 23, 1994, p. 69.
14. A. Lorenz, "Ford Drives to Win World Leadership," *Sunday Times*, January 1, 1995.
15. Treece, "Ford: Alex Trotman's Daring Strategy."

Restructuring Exide

Introduction

In March 1999, Exide Corporation announced that Robert Lutz, the flamboyant 67-year-old former Chrysler executive who helped turn that company around in the early 1990s, would become chairman, president, and chief executive office of Exide. Lutz, an outspoken former Marine known for his love of good cigars, fine wine, and flying jet fighters, would have his work cut out for him. Exide was a company in trouble. The world's largest manufacturer of lead acid batteries, the company had reportedly sacrificed profitability in its quest for market share leadership. For the financial year ending March

1999, Exide lost $9 million on global sales of $2.37 billion. A series of bank-financed acquisitions during the 1990s had left the company with a weak balance sheet including $1.3 billion in debt that cost $100 million in annual interest payments to serve. Moreover, a price war in the lead battery industry was squeezing profit margins.

Exide's Business

Market Segments and Customers

Exide manufactures batteries for customers in two broad areas: industrial and automotive. The industrial area, which accounts for about 37 percent of Exide's revenues, is divided into two segments. One, the motive power business, is engaged in the manufacture of batteries for electric vehicles including forklift trucks, golf carts, wheelchairs, and electric floor-cleaning equipment. The other industrial segment, network power, makes standby batteries used for backup power applications, to ensure continuous power supply in case of main (primary) power failure or outage. The largest customers here are manufacturers of telecommunications equipment, who incorporate the batteries in their equipment to ensure that it continues to function in the case of a power outage (which is why you can still make phone calls, even if you do not have power at home). A second customer group is businesses that use standby batteries in computer installations so that the computer system stays up even if the power goes out.

In the industrial motive power business, most of Exide's batteries are sold through independent lift-truck dealers or directly to large users of lift trucks, such as Wal-Mart and Kroger. Exide's customers in the industrial network power business include manufacturers of telecommunication equipment, as well as telecommunication service providers. Customers include Lucent, Motorola, and Nokia, all major global producers of telecommunication equipment, and AT&T, British Telecom, China Telecom, Deutsche Telekom, GTE, and Nippon Telephone and Telegraph, all service providers.

The automotive area of Exide's business, which accounts for 64 percent of global revenues, is comprised primarily of the manufacture and sale of lead acid batteries to automobile manufacturers and to "aftermarket" distributors. Principle OEM customers include Daimler/Chrysler, for whom Exide is the primary global battery supplier, Ford, Toyota, Mack Trucks, Deere & Company, Volvo, the Renault Group, Volkswagen, and BMW. Aftermarket batteries are sold mainly through retail automotive parts chains and mass merchandisers. Customers in the United States include NAPA Distribution Centers, Wal-Mart, Kmart, and Les Schwab Tire. Customers in Europe include large national distributors such as Kwik Fit in the United Kingdom. In the United States, Exide batteries are sold in the aftermarket under the Exide and Champion brand names. In Europe, the brand names in the aftermarket vary from country to country and include Exide, Fulmen, DETA, Tudor, SONNAK, and Centra.

Competition

Exide is the global market share leader in both the motive power and network power segments of the industrial area. Major competitors include U.K.-based Invensys' Hawker battery group; C&D Technologies, U.S. firm; and Yuasa of Japan.

In the automotive area, Exide again leads with a 36 percent share of the global market for automobile batteries (both OEM and aftermarket). Exide's largest competitors in the U.S. automotive segment include Delphi Automotive and Johnson Controls. In Europe, Exide faces a number of strong local competitors including Varta, Fiamm, and Hoppeke. Price competition has long been intense in all markets, with major customers using their buying power to bargain down battery prices. Exide's financial troubles in the late 1990s, however, were due in part to an outbreak of extremely aggressive price competition in Europe.

Manufacturing, Employees, and Facilities

Lead is the principal material used in the manufacturing of batteries, accounting for about one-fifth of the cost of goods sold. Exide operates a number of lead recycling plants in both the United States and Europe. Exide reclaims lead from used batteries that end users return to distributors. Exide fulfills most of its lead requirements from its recycling plants. Other key raw materials include lead oxide and bulk chemicals.

Exide employs some 20,000 people, 8,500 in the United States and approximately 10,900 in Europe. The company operates about 50 facilities, the bulk of which are in Europe and North America where most of the company's sales are concentrated. Exide has 14 manufacturing facilities in North America, 16 in Western Europe, 2 in Australia, 1 in New Zealand, and 1 in Turkey. In Western Europe, there are manufacturing and lead recycling facilities in each major national market.

Lutz's Changes

Lutz moved rapidly to make a number of changes in Exide's business. One of his first decisions was to pull out of a supply agreement with Sears. Exide sold more than 4.5 million batteries a year to Sears, but to get the agreement the company had to slash prices. The result was that Exide was making less from the Sears deal than it was from deals one-fifth of the size. Lutz also pushed the company to shift demand from low-priced battery models to higher-priced branded products, particularly in the automotive segment. Consistent with this theme, in June 1999 Exide introduced a new lead acid battery, the Select Orbital battery. While the battery cost $125, Exide claimed it was based on a radically new design and would retain its charge for over a year, substantially longer than for a conventional battery. While a conventional battery has a life of about 30 to 40 months, Exide claimed the Orbital would last five years and stand up to far more abuse.

Lutz also pushed the company to quickly solve its legal problems. The company was being sued in the United States for recycling old batteries and selling them as new through distributors such as Sears. Under Lutz's direction, instead of fighting the lawsuits, Exide quickly settled them for a few million dollars and took a onetime charge against earnings.

Within 15 months of his arrival, Lutz had replaced the entire board of directors and the majority of senior executives in both Europe and North America. Worldwide battery product capacity had been cut by 20 percent through plant closures, the company's debt load had been substantially pared by issuing additional stock and using the proceeds to pay down debt, and Exide had made a major acquisition, paying $368 million in stock and cash for GNB Technologies, a major supplier in the fast-growing market for standby batteries in telecommunication and computer equipment. Perhaps the most difficult change he initiated, however, was one in the organization structure of Exide's business.

Changing the Organizational Structure: Product or Geography?

When he arrived at Exide, Lutz found a structure that was based on geography with 10 different country organizations. The genesis of this structure was rooted in history. Many of the country organizations had previously been independent businesses that Exide had acquired in its rush to gain global market share. After being acquired, the majority continued to function as self-contained operations with their own brands, manufacturing facilities, and distribution systems. Exide managed the different subsidiaries on an arm's-length basis, setting profit goals for each and awarding local executives big bonuses if they exceeded those goals.

It soon became apparent to Lutz that this structure was causing problems for Exide, particularly in Europe. When Lutz arrived, Exide's European business was losing money. The various country managers in Europe blamed the losses on significant price discounting. After talking to competitors and customers, Lutz found that there was significant price discounting in Europe, but in many cases, this was because different Exide subsidiaries were competing against each other for major customers. They were exporting into each other's territories or competing aggressively for share in third countries. Thus, for example, the British subsidiary was gaining share in Australia from the Germany subsidiary by underselling the latter by 10 to 15 percent. Part of the blame for this competition could be laid at the feet of an incentive system that rewarded country managers for increasing the performance of their unit, irrespective of whether that was at the expense of another Exide unit.

Convinced that the structure had to change, Lutz held five management retreats between June 1999 and January 2000. "Where does our future lie?" Lutz asked the 30 senior executives assembled for the first meeting. "Does it lie in country management or in global business

units?" Many of the country managers reacted with apprehension to the question. Several argued that their regions were in good shape, and that any problems that existed were due to weaknesses elsewhere or general industry conditions.

Between retreats managers working in teams were assigned to grapple with the various dilemmas confronting the company, using existing and alternative models of the organization as solutions. In a typical assessment, one team looked at Exide's Asian expansion strategy. Team members concluded the geographic focus encouraged construction of manufacturing plants in each country Exide entered, even though it was not profitable to keep building plants like that. On the third retreat, the teams started to report their findings, and it quickly became apparent that many were concluding that only a product line structure could cure Exide's ills. After a vigorous debate, Lutz stood up and announced "We don't have consensus yet . . . But I'm going to make a decision, and we are going to a global business unit structure."

Under the proposed structure that Lutz revealed at the next meeting, six global business units replaced the geographic organization. Each business unit was built around a distinct product line, such as network power, industrial motive power, and so on. The global business units were given responsibility for major strategic and operational decisions, such as what to produce where, how much to charge customers, and for selling to major regional or global customers. Country managers were given a coordinating role and the responsibility for local sales efforts and distribution.

The announcement was a severe blow for many country managers. Effectively, it meant a demotion. When one country manager frowned at the announcement, Lutz looked at him and asked, "Why don't you give this a try?" "No," the manager replied, "I'm out of here!" Another country manager told a consultant: "Being a country manager is my life. It's something I've worked for my entire life. I don't see how I'll have a role going forward." Subsequently, the manager was given the option of moving from Naples to Frankfurt, for less money, or leaving the company. He chose the former option, but his family refused to move and stayed in Naples. Other country managers came out of the process quite well. Albrecht Leuschner, the head of the German unit, found himself promoted to lead the global network power business unit, which was to be headquartered in Germany.

The Acquisition of GNB Technologies

Leuschner found himself in this position for just six weeks. In May 2000, Exide acquired GNB Technologies for its fast-growing network power business and industrial motive power businesses. The acquisition gave Lutz a problem: he feared that Mitchell Bregman, the well-regarded president of GNB's operation, might leave once Exide folded his industrial battery business into its global network power and industrial motive power business units. So Lutz told Bregman that after the acquisition, he would retain control over the North American industrial battery business. After only six weeks, the global business unit structure was being amended. There was now a European business unit for network power headed by Leuschner, a European business unit for industrial motive power that was run out of the United Kingdom, and a North American industrial battery business headed by Bregman.

Initially, the decision gave rise to a turf battle between Leuschner and Bregman. The point of contention was over who should run China for Exide. Bregman wanted to form and direct a Chinese subsidiary, because China represented his unit's fastest growing market. Leuschner lobbied to form a joint venture in China that would be under his command. Bregman was finally persuaded to give in to Leuschner, but only after he had been given control over South American operations and had been guaranteed control over operations in South Korea, Japan, and Taiwan.

Now all parties claim the structure is working well. The company still maintains separate industrial battery sales forces in North America and Europe, in what has become a de facto regional structure. However, teams from the European and North American units have begun making joint pitches to global customers such as Ford and Lucent.

Case Discussion Questions

1. What kind of industry environment does Exide operate in? Is it a global industry, a multidomestic industry, or something in between? What are the pressures for local responsiveness in this industry? What are the pressures for globalization?

2. How might a structure based on geography (country subsidiaries) result in inefficiencies at Exide?

3. What are the potential benefits to Exide of moving from a geographic structure based on country organizations to a product structure based on global business units? What are the potential drawbacks of such a structure?

4. Following the GNB acquisition, Lutz again changed the structure of Exide, at least on the industrial side of the organization. Why did he do this? Do you think this was a wise move, or might it create additional problems in the future?

Sources

1. Chappell, L. "Lutz Puts Exide in Recovery." *Automotive News*, August 6, 2001, p. 49.

2. Exide 2000 and 2001 10K filed with Securities and Exchange Commission.

3. Lublin, J. S. "Place vs Product: It's Tough to Choose a Management Model," *Wall Street Journal*, June 27, 2001, pp. A1, A4.

4. Maynard, M. "Lutz Gets a Charge Out of a New Career. Exide CEO Achieves a Dream." *USA Today*, June 1, 1999, p. 12B.

5. Nauss, D. W. "Ex-Chrysler Exec Robert Lutz to Head Troubled Exide Corporation," *Los Angeles Times*, November 17, 1998, p. 3.

6. Puchalsky, A. "Exide Makes Tough Choices in Comeback," *Wall Street Journal*, March 26, 1999.

7. Sherefkin, R. "New One Two Punch at Exide." *Automotive News*, June 12, 2000, p. 22.

8. Taylor, A. "Getting Back in the Fast Lane." *Fortune*, March 6, 2000.

EXDTQ

Wal-Mart's Mexican Adventure

Introduction

Wal-Mart is America's and the world's largest retailer. Founded by the legendary Sam Walton in the 1960s, by 2001 Wal-Mart was generating over $100 billion in annual sales from 4,000 stores, more than 1,000 of which were located outside the United States. The company operates three basic store formats: the traditional Wal-Mart stores that sell a wide range of basic consumer merchandise from household products to clothes and electronics; Wal-Mart Supercenters, which are larger stores that have added groceries to the basic merchandising mix; and Sam's Clubs, which are deep discount stores that carry a limited range of very low-priced merchandise and food.

Although the company was still opening new stores in the United States in 2001, it had recognized since the early 1990s that its U.S. growth prospects were ultimately limited by market saturation. Believing that its unique culture, format, and operating systems would give it a competitive edge in many foreign markets, Wal-Mart embarked on an international expansion strategy in 1991 when it opened the first Sam's Club store in Mexico City. A decade later, Mexico is the brightest star in the company's international division with more than 500 Mexican stores generating $9 billion in sales. Getting to this point, however, was not easy. Wal-Mart had suffered several setbacks along the way that might have discouraged a less ambitious rival from continuing.

Wal-Mart's Competitive Advantage

Wal-Mart's spectacular four-decade growth from a small Arkansas retailer to a national powerhouse was based on a first-class management team that pursued a number of innovative operating strategies that backed up the company's commitment to deliver a large selection of high-value merchandise at a low cost to consumers.

The firm's early success was based partly on a strategy of locating in small Southern towns that had no other major retail presence. When Wal-Mart entered most towns, its primary competitors were small "mom-and-pop" stores that had a much higher cost structure than the discounter. Wal-Mart quickly gained significant share in these towns and did not have to face competition from other discounters, such as Kmart, which were focused on large urban areas.

As the number of stores grew, Wal-Mart pioneered the development of a hub-and-spoke-based distribution system, where central distribution warehouses were strategically located to serve clusters of stores. This system allowed Wal-Mart to rapidly replenish stock in its stores, while keeping the amount of store space needed for inventory to a minimum. The results included higher sales per square foot and more rapid inventory turnover. This helped to increase store sales and drive down inventory and logistics costs.

The firm was also one of the first to utilize computer-based information systems to track in-store sales and transmit this information to suppliers. The information provided by these systems was used to determine pricing and stocking strategy and to better manage inventories. The combination of state-of-the-art information systems and the hub-and-spoke distribution system allowed Wal-Mart to build the leanest supply chain in the industry. Today Wal-Mart is still a leader in information systems. All Wal-Mart stores, distribution centers, and suppliers are linked via sophisticated information systems and satellite-based communication systems that allow for daily adjustments to orders, inventory, and prices.

Wal-Mart is also famous for a dynamic and egalitarian culture that grants major decision-making authority to store managers, department managers, and individual employees (whom Wal-Mart refers to as "associates"). Wal-Mart is known for treating its employees well, but at the same time, for demanding commitment and excellent performance from them. This culture is backed up with a generous profit-sharing plan and stock ownership plan for all employees, which makes every employee "think and behave like an owner of the company." By such means, Wal-Mart has developed a culture and control system that creates incentives for associates and managers to give their best for the company. The result is higher employee productivity, which again translates into lower cost.

As Wal-Mart has grown, it has also garnered significant leverage with its suppliers, whether they are small manufacturers or global enterprises such as Procter & Gamble, for whom Wal-Mart is the largest single account. Wal-Mart has used this leverage to demand lower prices from its suppliers, which it then passes on to its customers in the form of "every day low prices."

Mexican Genesis

By 1990, Wal-Mart was concerned that its growth rate in the United States would inevitably slow. This would slow stock price appreciation for Wal-Mart, which would be bad news for the thousands of Wal-Mart associates who were also stockholders. The company embarked on two strategies to recharge its growth rate. The first was expansion into the grocery business with the opening of Wal-Mart Supercenters that would stock Wal-Mart's traditional merchandise, plus food products. The second strategy was international expansion.

At the time that Wal-Mart was considering going international, the United States was entering negotiations with Mexico and Canada about the North American Free Trade Agreement (NAFTA). This spurred Wal-Mart's interests in Mexico. Historically, significant barriers to cross-border trade and investment, substantial state involvement in business activity, and high inflation had characterized the Mexican economy. However, under the government of Carlos Salinas, a Harvard-trained economist, Mexico had embraced free market reforms. State-owned enterprises were being privatized. Barriers to trade and investment with the United States had already been significantly lowered by Salinas and would fall much further under the NAFTA proposal. Tariffs on goods imported from the United States had come down from as much as 100 percent in the mid-1980s to a maximum of 20 percent by the early 1990s, and under NAFTA many of these would fall to zero. Many barriers to cross-border investment had been eliminated. Salinas had also imposed a tight monetary policy, which had lowered Mexico's inflation rate into the single digits. The country's economy was growing at 4 to 5 percent a year by the early 1990s, faster than that of the United States, while disposable income had increased by some 70 percent since Salinas took office in 1988. Although Mexico was still a very poor country by U.S. standards, some 30 million of its 80 million people could now be classified as middle class. This affluent segment was concentrated in three main urban areas: Mexico City, Guadalajara, and Monterrey.

Although the Mexican retail market was still very fragmented and dispersed, four national supermarket chains had emerged and accounted for more than 30 percent of the retail market. The largest of these, Cifra, operated about 120 discount and grocery stores in 1991 and generated sales of about $2.2 billion. Wal-Mart founder Sam Walton had first met one of Cifra's three founding brothers, Jeronimo Arango, in 1990. The two men immediately hit it off, and both agreed that the free trade deal being negotiated between Canada, Mexico, and the United States opened up opportunities for Wal-Mart to cooperate with Cifra in Mexico.

Having decided that Mexico might be a good proving ground for foreign growth strategy, Wal-Mart debated a number of options for expansion, including licensing its brand name to franchisees, expanding via wholly owned subsidiaries, or entering into a joint venture with a Mexican company such as Cifra. The company quickly concluded that its competitive advantage was based on the combination of culture and supporting information and logistics systems, and that such a culture and systems would be difficult to transfer to franchisees. The management know-how that underlay its culture and systems was simply not amenable to franchising. At the same time, Wal-Mart realized that it knew little about the culture and business systems of its foreign neighbor, so the company decided to entered a 50/50 joint venture with Cifra.

Teething Problems

Wal-Mart's Mexican expansion began with the establishment of a single Sam's Club store in Mexico City in 1991. In 1992, Wal-Mart established six more stores in Mexico, all Sam's Clubs. In 1993, the company began to open stores under the Wal-Mart name. When the first store in Mexico City opened its doors, an enormous crowd showed up and all 72 cash registers were busy. It didn't last. Within months, the sales rate at Wal-Mart's Mexican stores had slowed considerably, not surprising perhaps in a country where per capita annual income was only about $2,000. But according to critics, the problems had more to do with missteps by Wal-Mart than low income.

When Wal-Mart opened its first store in Monterrey in 1993, it had to bar the doors to control the crowds, but soon the local press was lambasting the company for charging 15 to 20 percent more for merchandise than it did at its Wal-Mart store across the border in Laredo, Texas, a two-hour drive to the north. A Wal-Mart spokesman pointed out that the higher prices reflected the transportation costs between the Wal-Mart distribution center in Laredo and its Monterrey store. In addition, NAFTA had not yet been implemented, and high tariffs contributed to the higher prices. But Wal-Mart also conceded that it was having problems replicating its U.S. distribution system in Mexico. Poor infrastructure, crowded roads, and a lack of leverage with local suppliers, many of whom would not or could not deliver directly to Wal-Mart's stores or distribution centers, as was common in the United States, all led to higher prices and lower margins for Wal-Mart.

Another problem was getting the right selection of merchandise. Many of the first Wal-Mart stores in Mexico carried items that were popular in the United States, but rarely used in Mexico. These included ice skates, riding lawn mowers, leaf blowers, and fishing tackle. Managers would slash prices on these items to move the inventory, only to find that Wal-Mart's automated information systems ordered more to replenish the depleted inventory.

Then there were problems with government bureaucrats. After the implementation of NAFTA January 1, 1994, Wal-Mart believed that things would get easier, but it was not to be. In the summer of 1994, Mexican government inspectors made a surprise visit to Wal-Mart's new superstore in Mexico City. They found thousands of products that they claimed were improperly labeled or lacking instructions in Spanish. The store was ordered shut for 72 hours while the oversights were corrected. This brush with what they saw as overzealous inspectors sobered Wal-Mart's managers. The 200,000-square-foot supercenter carried about 80,000 products. Each now had to be labeled in Spanish indicating the country of origin, content, and instructions, and in some cases, an import permit number. The inspectors charged that some 11,700 pieces of merchandise lacked such labels. Wal-Mart's managers responded by pointing out that many of the targeted goods—40 percent or more—were purchased from a local Mexican distributor. Nevertheless, the regulators insisted the retailer had ultimate responsibility for the labeling. Some Wal-Mart managers wondered if this kind of bureaucratic red tape was a deliberate attempt by government bureaucrats to raise the costs of doing business in Mexico, thereby frustrating their expansion plans.

The 1994 Peso Crisis

As if these problems were not enough, in late 1994 the Mexican economy took a sharp turn for the worse. The Mexican currency, the peso, had been pegged to the value of the U.S. dollar since the early 1980s and was allowed to depreciate only by about 4 percent a year against the dollar. Since the mid-1980s, prices in Mexico had risen by about 45 percent more than prices in the United States, making the current exchange rate increasingly difficult to maintain. Also, in 1993 and 1994 the Mexican economy responded to the drop in tariff barriers by sucking in imports at a rapid rate. By late 1994, Mexico was running a $17 billion annual deficit on merchandised trade, which amounted to about 6 percent of the country's GDP. Currency traders began to place large bets that the Mexican government would be forced to devalue the peso against the dollar. Fearing this, foreign investors who had rushed into the country in 1993 and early 1994, buying Mexican stocks and pushing the stock market up to record levels, reversed their course and moved money out of the country.

The Mexican government stepped into the foreign exchange market to try to defend its currency, using its foreign exchange reserves to buy pesos. But the outward flow of funds was so great that Mexico soon realized this would only deplete its foreign exchange reserves. Accepting the inevitable, in December 1994 the government announced it would abandon the peg against the dollar and let the peso float freely on the foreign exchange market. Immediately the peso fell, losing some 40 percent of its value against the dollar in a matter of days, and plunging the Mexican economy into an economic recession.

For Wal-Mart and other American firms that had moved into Mexico to take advantage of NAFTA, this was a body blow. By this time Wal-Mart had 63 stores in Mexico stocked with goods imported from the United States. The fall in the value of the peso meant that it now cost more to bring in goods from the United States, while the economic recession that now gripped Mexico meant that consumers had even less to spend at Wal-Mart. Over the next two years, retail sales in Mexico fell by 16 percent. Wal-Mart, which had planned to open another 25 stores in 1995, quickly put its Mexican expansion plans on hold.

Expansion Resumes

Although Mexico was to experience a two-year economic slowdown, the U.S. economy continued to grow. With Mexican goods now costing less in the United States, and trade barriers reduced or eliminated under NAFTA, Mexican exports boomed. Foreign companies began to invest heavily in the country, seeing it as a low-cost location from which to export to its giant neighbor next door. The combination of an export boom and rapid foreign direct investment created jobs and helped to lift the Mexican economy out of its slump. Seeing that the corner was being turned, by late 1995 Wal-Mart's expansion plans were back on track.

By mid-1997, Wal-Mart had some 145 stores in Mexico. Unlike several other foreign retailers, it had decided to take advantage of the economic slump to build its market share. The company also was making strong improvements in its operating efficiency. It had opened a distribution center in Mexico City, which rapidly became the most efficient in the entire Wal-Mart system, in part due to very low labor costs. This allowed Wal-Mart to start reducing its inventory and logistics costs. Wal-Mart had also struck a three-way partnership with EASO, a Mexican trucking company, and MS Carriers Corp., a U.S. trucking company that does significant

work for Wal-Mart in the United States. Under the agreement, MS Carriers shared its fleet of modern trucks with EASO, as well as its satellite systems designed to help plan delivery times. This helped EASO cut its costs by 25 percent, which it passed on to Wal-Mart, which now uses 200 of EASO's trucks to run its Mexican logistics system.

Wal-Mart also started to source far more goods from Mexico, in part because many of its suppliers had located in Mexico to take advantage of lower production costs and NAFTA. In an example of the savings this produced, Wal-Mart officials cite the case of a Vega TV set from Sony. Imported from Japan, the combination of transportation costs and a 23 percent tariff meant that the TV retailed for $1,600 in Wal-Mart's Mexican store, out of the reach of all but the most affluent Mexican consumers. But in 1999, Sony built a Vega TV factory in Mexico to take advantage of NAFTA. The TV now costs about $600 in Mexico, and sales are picking up.

Wal-Mart had also learned from its early mistakes and improved the mix of product offerings at its Mexican stores. Slow-moving items such as leaf blowers had been replaced by items that sold well in Mexico, but would not in the United States, such as maid's uniforms. As its scale of operations in Mexico grew, Wal-Mart was also able to use its purchase volume to gain leverage with suppliers, bargaining down prices in return for large purchase volumes. Wal-Mart then passed these prices on to consumers, enabling the company to gain market share and remain profitable even as total retail spending in Mexico shrank during 1995 and 1996. In contrast, Sears and Kmart, two U.S. competitors that had entered Mexico at the same time, threw in the towel and left the country.

In mid-1997, Wal-Mart signaled its continuing commitment to Mexico by purchasing a controlling interest in its joint-venture partner, Cifra. By combining Cifra's stores with the stores established by the joint venture, Wal-Mart now had 373 stores in Mexico, making it by far the largest retailer in the country. The new company was then listed on Mexico's stock exchange, the Bolsa, as Wal-Mart de Mexico, or WalMex as it became known. The listing allowed Wal-Mart to begin introducing the same stock-based incentive plans for its associates in Mexico that had worked so well in the United States. Wal-Mart retained a 54 percent stake in WalMex, which it raised to 60 percent in April 2000.

By 1999, Wal-Mart thought it had improved its cost structure in Mexico to such an extent that it could now start to be more aggressive about passing on cost savings to Mexican consumers. In August 1999, it closed a supercenter in Mexico City for a single day and marked down all prices by 16 percent. It then reopened under the banner of "every day low pricing." Sales surged, with the growth in volume more than making up for the lower prices. The experiment was such a success that Wal-Mart rolled out the program in all of its Mexican supercenters a month later. In May 2000, the program was extended to cover all Wal-Mart stores in Mexico. Sales have surged. By July 2001, WalMex same-store sales growth exceeded that of competitors for 8 out of the previous 12 months and for 7 months in a row.

Case Discussion Questions

1. Why did Mexico make such a good proving ground for Wal-Mart's foreign expansion strategy?

2. What is the source of Wal-Mart's competitive advantage? What barriers did Wal-Mart have to overcome in transferring its competencies to Mexico?

3. How did Wal-Mart intend to create value in the Mexican market?

4. Despite some early setbacks, Wal-Mart has apparently been successful in Mexico. In contrast, some other U.S. retailers pulled out of the country in the aftermath of the December 1994 peso crisis. What do you think distinguishes Wal-Mart from these companies?

5. If Wal-Mart can succeed in Mexico, it can probably succeed in most countries. Discuss this statement. Is it correct?

Sources

1. DePalma, A. "Big Companies in Mexico Among the Peso's Worst Victims," *New York Times,* January 30, 1995, p. D4.

2. Ginns, J. J. "Wal-Mart Ventures into Mexico." Harvard Business School Case #9-793-071, December 1992.

3. Luhnow, D. "How NAFTA Helped Wal-Mart Reshape the Mexican Market," *Wall Street Journal,* August 31, 2001, pp. A1, A2.

4. Smith, G. "NAFTA: A Green Light for Red Tape." *Business Week,* July 25, 1994, p. 48.

5. Walton, S. *Made in America.* New York: Bantam Books, 1992.

6. "Wal-Mart: Mexico's Largest Retailer." *Chain Store Age,* June 2001, pp. 52–54.

7. Wal-Mart 10K reports, 1996–2000, news releases, and other information posted on the company's website (*www.wal-mart.com*).

Part 6

Business
Operations

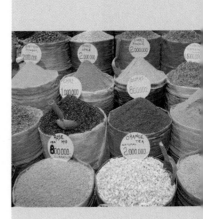

Exporting,
Importing,
and
Countertrade

Established in 1982, U.K.-based Megahertz Communications is one of Great Britain's leading independent broadcasting system builders. The company's core skill is in the design, manufacture, and installation of TV and radio broadcast systems, including outside broadcast and news-gathering vehicles with satellite links. In 1998, Megahertz's managing director, Ashley Coles, set up a subsidiary company, Megahertz International, to sell products to the Middle East, Africa, and Eastern Europe.

While the EU market for media and broadcasting is both mature and well served by large established companies, the Middle East, Africa, and Eastern Europe are growth markets for media and broadcasting with significant long-term potential. They also were not well served by other companies, and all three lacked an adequate supply of local broadcast engineers.

Megahertz International's export strategy was simple. The company aimed to provide a turnkey solution to emerging broadcast and media entities in Africa, the Middle East, and Eastern Europe, offering to custom design, manufacture, install, and test broadcasting systems. To gain access to customers, Megahertz hired salespeople with significant experience in these regions and opened a foreign sales office in Italy. Megahertz also exhibited at a number of exhibitions that focused on the targeted regions, sent mailings and e-mail messages to local broadcasters, and set up a Web page, which drew a number of international inquiries.

The response was swift. By early 2000, Megahertz had already been involved in projects in Namibia, Oman, Romania, Russia, Nigeria, Poland, South Africa, Iceland, and Ethiopia. The international operations had expanded to a staff of 75 and were generating £10 million annually. The average order size was about £250,000, and the largest £500,000. In recognition of the company's success, in January 2000 the British government picked Megahertz to receive a Small Business Export Award.

Despite the company's early success, however, it has not all been smooth sailing. According to Managing Director Coles, preshipment financing has been a major headache. Coles describes his working life as a juggling act, with as much as 20 percent of his time spent chasing money. Due to financing problems, one week Megahertz can have next to nothing in the bank; the next it may have £300,000. The main problem is getting money to finance an order. Megahertz needs working capital to finance the purchase of component parts that go into the systems it builds for customers. The company has found that banks are very cautious, particularly when they hear that the customers for the order are in Africa or Eastern Europe. The banks worry that Megahertz may not get paid on time, or at all, or that currency fluctuations may reduce the value of payments to Megahertz. Even when Megahertz has a letter of credit from the customer's bank and export insurance documentation, many lenders still see the risks as too great, and decline to lend bridging funds to Megahertz. As a partial solution, Megahertz has turned to lending companies that specialize in financing international trade, but many of these companies charge interest rates significantly greater than those charged by banks, thereby squeezing Megahertz's profit margins.

Coles hopes these financing problems are temporary. Once Megahertz establishes a more sustained cash flow from its international operations, and once banks better appreciate the ability of Coles and his team to secure payment from foreign customers, he hopes that they will become more amenable to lending capital to Megahertz at rates that will help to protect the company's profit margins.

Sources: http://www.megahertz.co.uk, and W. Smith, "Today Batley, Tomorrow the World?" *Director*, January 2000, pp. 42–49.

Introduction

In the previous chapter, we reviewed exporting from a strategic perspective. We considered exporting as just one of a range of strategic options for profiting from international expansion. This chapter is more concerned with the "nuts and bolts" of exporting (and importing). We take the choice of strategy as a given and look at how to export.

As we can see from the opening case, exporting is not just for large enterprises; many small firms such as Megahertz Communications have benefited significantly from the moneymaking opportunities of exporting. In the United States, for example, nearly 97 percent of firms that export are small businesses, and their share of total U.S. exports grew steadily over the last decade to reach 31 percent by the beginning of the new millennium.[1] The situation is similar in several other nations. In Germany, for example, companies with less than 500 employees account for about 30 percent of that nation's exports.[2]

The volume of export activity in the world economy is increasing as exporting has become easier. The gradual decline in trade barriers under the umbrella of GATT and now the WTO (see Chapter 5) along with regional economic agreements such as the European Union and the North American Free Trade Agreement (see Chapter 8) have significantly increased export opportunities. At the same time, modern communication and transportation technologies have alleviated the logistical problems associated with exporting. Firms are increasingly using fax machines, the World Wide Web, toll-free 800 numbers, and international air express services to reduce the costs of exporting. Consequently, it is no longer unusual to find small companies such as Megahertz Communications that are thriving as exporters.

Nevertheless, as the opening case illustrates, exporting remains a challenge for many firms. Smaller enterprises can find the process intimidating. The firm wishing to export must identify foreign market opportunities, avoid a host of unanticipated problems that are often associated with doing business in a foreign market, familiarize itself with the mechanics of export and import financing (a problem that Megahertz Communications has had to grapple with), learn where it can get financing and export credit insurance, and learn how it should deal with foreign exchange risk. The process is made more problematic by currencies that are not freely convertible. As a result, there is the problem of arranging payment for exports to countries with weak currencies. This brings us to the complex topic of countertrade, by which payment for exports is received in goods and services rather than money. In this chapter, we will discuss all these issues with the exception of foreign exchange risk, which was covered in Chapter 9. We open the chapter by considering the promise and pitfalls of exporting.

The Promise and Pitfalls of Exporting

The great promise of exporting is that large revenue and profit opportunities are to be found in foreign markets for most firms in most industries. This was true for Megahertz Communications, profiled in the opening case. The international market is normally so much larger than the firm's domestic market that exporting is nearly always a way to increase the revenue and profit base of a company.

Studies have shown that while many large firms tend to be proactive about seeking opportunities for profitable exporting, systematically scanning foreign markets to see where the opportunities lie for leveraging their technology, products, and marketing skills in foreign countries, many medium-sized and small firms are very reactive.[3] Typically, such reactive firms do not even consider exporting until their domestic market is saturated and the emergence of excess productive capacity at home forces them to look for growth opportunities in foreign markets. Also, many small and medium-sized firms tend to wait for the world to come to them, rather than going out into the world to seek opportunities. Even when the world does comes to them, they may not respond. An example is MMO Music Group, which makes sing-along tapes for karaoke machines. Foreign sales accounted for about 15 percent of MMO's revenues of $8 million in the mid-1990s, but the firm's CEO admits that this figure would probably have been much higher had he paid attention to building international sales during the 1980s and early 1990s. At that time, unanswered faxes and phone messages from Asia and Europe piled up while he was trying to manage the burgeoning domestic side of the business. By the time MMO did turn its attention to foreign markets, other competitors had stepped into the breach and MMO found it tough going to build export volume.[4]

MMO's experience is common, and it suggests a need for firms to become more proactive about seeking export opportunities. One reason more firms are not proactive is that they are unfamiliar with foreign market opportunities; they simply do not know how big the opportunities actually are or where they might lie. Simple ignorance of the potential opportunities is a huge barrier to exporting.[5] Also, many would-be exporters, particularly smaller firms, are often intimidated by the complexities and mechanics of exporting to countries where business practices, language, culture, legal systems, and currency are very different from the home market.[6] This combination of unfamiliarity and intimidation probably explains why exporters still account for only a tiny percentage of U.S. firms, less than 2 percent according to the Small Business Administration.[7]

To make matters worse, many neophyte exporters have run into significant problems when first trying to do business abroad and this has soured them on future exporting ventures. Common pitfalls include poor market analysis, a poor understanding of competitive conditions in the foreign market, a failure to customize the product offering to the needs of foreign customers, lack of an effective distribution program, a poorly executed promotional campaign in the foreign market, and problems securing financing (again, see the opening case on Megahertz Communications for an example).[8] Neophyte exporters tend to underestimate the time and expertise needed to cultivate business in foreign countries.[9] Few realize the amount of management resources that have to be dedicated to this activity. Many foreign customers require face-to-face negotiations on their home turf. An exporter may have to spend months learning about a country's trade regulations, business practices, and more before a deal can be closed.

Exporters often face voluminous paperwork, complex formalities, and many potential delays and errors. According to a UN report on trade and development, a typical international trade transaction may involve 30 parties, 60 original documents, and 360 document copies, all of which have to be checked, transmitted, reentered into various information systems, processed, and filed. The United Nations has calculated that the time involved in preparing documentation, along with the costs of common errors in paperwork, often amounts to 10 percent of the final value of goods exported.[10]

Improving Export Performance

Inexperienced exporters have a number of ways to gain information about foreign market opportunities and avoid common pitfalls that tend to discourage and frustrate novice exporters.[11] In this section, we look at information sources that exporters can utilize to increase their knowledge of foreign market opportunities, we consider the pros and cons of using export management companies (EMCs) to assist in the export process, and we review various exporting strategies that can increase the probability of successful exporting. We begin, however, with a look at how several nations try to assist domestic firms in the export process.

An International Comparison

One big impediment to exporting is the simple lack of knowledge of the opportunities available. Often there are many markets for a firm's product, but because they are in countries separated from the firm's home base by culture, language, distance, and time, the firm does not know of them. Identifying export opportunities is made even more complex by the fact that more than 180 countries with widely differing cultures compose the world of potential opportunities. Faced with such complexity and diversity, it is not surprising that firms sometimes hesitate to seek export opportunities.

The way to overcome ignorance is to collect information. In Germany, one of the world's most successful exporting nations, trade associations, government agencies, and commercial banks gather information, helping small firms identify export opportunities. A similar function is provided by the Japanese Ministry of International Trade and Industry (MITI), which is always on the lookout for export opportunities. In addition, many Japanese firms are affiliated in some way with the *sogo shosha*, Japan's great trading houses. The *sogo shosha* have offices all over the world, and they proactively, continuously seek export opportunities for their affiliated companies large and small.[12] German and Japanese firms can draw on the large reservoirs of experience, skills, information, and other resources of their respective export-oriented institutions.

Unlike their German and Japanese competitors, many U.S. firms are relatively blind when they seek export opportunities; they are information disadvantaged. In part, this difference reflects historical differences. Both Germany and Japan have long made their living as trading nations, whereas until recently the United States has been a relatively self-contained continental economy in which international trade played a minor role. This is changing; both imports and exports now play a much greater role in the U.S. economy than they did 20 years ago. However, the United States has not yet evolved an institutional structure for promoting exports similar to that of either Germany or Japan.

Information Sources

Despite institutional disadvantages, U.S. firms can increase their awareness of export opportunities. The most comprehensive source of information is the U.S. Department of Commerce and its district offices all over the country. Within that department are two organizations dedicated to providing businesses with intelligence and assistance for attacking foreign markets: the International Trade Administration and the United States and Foreign Commercial Service Agency.

These agencies provide the potential exporter with a "best prospects" list, which gives the names and addresses of potential distributors in foreign markets along with businesses they are in, the products they handle, and their contact person. In addition, the Department of Commerce has assembled a "comparison shopping service" for 14 countries that are major markets for U.S. exports. For a small fee, a firm can receive a customized market research survey on a product of its choice. This survey provides information on marketability, the competition, comparative prices, distribution channels, and names of potential sales representatives. Each study is conducted on-site by an officer of the Department of Commerce.

The Department of Commerce also organizes trade events that help potential exporters make foreign contacts and explore export opportunities. The department organizes exhibitions at international trade fairs, which are held regularly in major cities worldwide. The department also has a matchmaker program, in which department representatives accompany groups of U.S. businesspeople abroad to meet with qualified agents, distributors, and customers.

In addition to the Department of Commerce, nearly every state and many large cities maintain active trade commissions whose purpose is to promote exports. Most of these provide business counseling, information gathering, technical assistance, and financing. Unfortunately, many have fallen victim to budget cuts or to turf battles for political and financial support with other export agencies.

A number of private organizations are also beginning to gear up to provide more assistance to would-be exporters. Commercial banks and major accounting firms are more willing to assist small firms in starting export operations than they were a decade ago. In addition, large multinationals that have been successful in the global arena are typically willing to discuss opportunities overseas with the owners or managers of small firms.[13]

Utilizing Export Management Companies

One way for first-time exporters to identify the opportunities associated with exporting and to avoid many of the associated pitfalls is to hire an **export management company** (EMC). EMCs are export specialists who act as the export marketing department or international department for their client firms. EMCs normally accept two types of export assignments. They start exporting operations for a firm with the understanding that the firm will take over operations after they are well established. In another type, start-up services are performed with the understanding that the EMC will have continuing responsibility for selling the firm's products. Many EMCs specialize in serving firms in particular industries and in particular areas of the world. Thus, one EMC may specialize in selling agricultural products in the Asian market, while another may focus on exporting electronics products to Eastern Europe.

In theory, the advantage of EMCs is that they are experienced specialists who can help the neophyte exporter identify opportunities and avoid common pitfalls. A good EMC will have a network of contacts in potential markets, have multilingual employees, have a good knowledge of different business mores, and be fully conversant with the ins and outs of the exporting process and with local business regulations. However, there is a large variation in the quality of EMCs.[14] While some perform their functions very well, others appear to add little value to the exporting company. Therefore, it is important for an exporter to review carefully a number of EMCs and to check references from an EMC's past clients. One drawback of relying on EMCs is that the company can fail to develop its own exporting capabilities in-house.

Exporting Strategy

In addition to using EMCs, a firm can reduce the risks associated with exporting if it is careful about its choice of exporting strategy. A few guidelines can help firms improve their odds of success. For example, one of the most successful exporting firms in the world, the Minnesota Mining and Manufacturing Co. (3M), has built its export success on three main principles—enter on a small scale to reduce risks, add additional product lines once the exporting operations start to become successful, and hire locals to promote the firm's products (3M's export strategy is profiled in the accompanying Management Focus). Another successful exporter, Red Spot Paint & Varnish, emphasizes the importance of cultivating personal relationships when trying to build an export business (see the Management Focus at the end of this section).

The probability of exporting successfully can be increased dramatically by taking a handful of simple strategic steps. First, particularly for the novice exporter, it helps to hire an EMC or at least an experienced export consultant to help identify opportunities and navigate through the web of paperwork and regulations so often involved in exporting. Second, it often makes sense to initially focus on one market or a handful of markets. The idea is to learn about what is required to succeed in those markets, before moving on to other markets. The firm that enters many markets at once runs the risk of spreading its limited management resources too thin. The result of such a "shotgun approach" to exporting may be a failure to become established in any one market. Third, as with 3M, it often makes sense to enter a foreign market on a small scale to reduce the costs of any subsequent failure. Most importantly, entering on a small scale

Management Focus

Exporting Strategy at 3M

The Minnesota Mining and Manufacturing Co. (3M), which makes more than 40,000 products including tape, sandpaper, medical products, and the ever-present Post-it Notes, is one of the world's great multinational operations. In 2000, 51 percent of the firm's $17 billion in revenues was generated outside the United States. Although the bulk of these revenues came from foreign-based operations, 3M remains a major exporter with $1.5 billion in exports. The company often uses its exports to establish an initial presence in a foreign market, only building foreign production facilities once sales volume rises to a level where local production is justified.

The export strategy is built around simple principles. One is known as "FIDO," which stands for First In (to a new market) Defeats Others. The essence of FIDO is to gain an advantage over other exporters by getting into a market first and learning about that country and how to sell there before others do. A second principle is "make a little, sell a little," which is the idea of entering on a small scale with a very modest investment and pushing one basic product, such as reflective sheeting for traffic signs in Russia or scouring pads in Hungary. Once 3M believes it has learned enough about the market to reduce the risk of failure to reasonable levels, it adds additional products.

A third principle at 3M is to hire local employees to sell the firm's products. The company normally sets up a local sales subsidiary to handle its export activities in

a country. It then staffs this subsidiary with local hires because it believes they are likely to have a much better idea of how to sell in their own country than American expatriates. Because of the implementation of this principle, just 160 of 3M's 39,500 foreign employees are U.S. expatriates.

Another common practice at 3M is to formulate global strategic plans for the export and eventual overseas production of its products. Within the context of these plans, 3M gives local managers considerable autonomy to find the best way to sell the product within their country. Thus, when 3M first exported its Post-it Notes in 1981 it planned to "sample the daylights" out of the product, but it also told local managers to find the best way of doing this. Local managers hired office cleaning crews to pass out samples in Great Britain and Germany; in Italy, office products distributors were used to pass out free samples; while in Malaysia, local managers employed young women to go from office to office handing out samples of the product. In typical 3M fashion, when the volume of Post-it Notes was sufficient to justify it, exports from the United States were replaced by local production. Thus, 3M found it worthwhile by 1984 to set up production facilities in France to produce Post-it Notes for the European market.

Sources: R. L. Rose, "Success Abroad," *Wall Street Journal,* March 29, 1991, p. A1; T. Eiben, "US Exporters Keep on Rolling," *Fortune,* June 14, 1994, pp. 128–131; and 3M's website at http://www.mmm.com.

provides the time and opportunity to learn about the foreign country before making significant capital commitments to that market. Fourth, the exporter needs to recognize the time and managerial commitment involved in building export sales and should hire additional personnel to oversee this activity. Fifth, in many countries, it is important to devote a lot of attention to building strong and enduring relationships with local distributors and/or customers (see the Management Focus on Red Spot Paint for an example). Sixth, as 3M often does, it is important to hire local personnel to help the firm establish itself in a foreign market. Local people are likely to have a much greater sense of how to do business in a given country than a manager from an exporting firm who has previously never set foot in that country. Seventh, several studies have suggested the firm needs to be proactive about seeking export opportunities.[15] Armchair exporting does not work! The world will not normally beat a pathway to your door.

Finally, it is important for the exporter to keep the option of local production in mind. Once exports reach a sufficient volume to justify cost-efficient local production, the exporting firm should consider establishing production facilities in the foreign market. Such localization helps foster good relations with the foreign country and can lead to greater market acceptance. Exporting is often not an end in itself, but merely

Management Focus

Red Spot Paint & Varnish

Established in 1903 and based in Evansville, Indiana, Red Spot Paint & Varnish Company is in many ways typical of the companies that can be found in the small towns of America's heartland. The closely held company, whose CEO Charles Storms is the great-grandson of the founder, has 500 employees and annual sales of close to $90 million. The company's main product is paint for plastic components used in the automobile industry. Red Spot products are seen on automobile bumpers, wheel covers, grilles, headlights, instrument panels, door inserts, radio buttons, and other components. Unlike many other companies of a similar size and location, however, Red Spot has a thriving international business. International sales (which include exports and local production by licensees) now account for between 15 percent and 25 percent of revenue in any one year, and Red Spot does business in about 15 countries.

Red Spot has long had some international sales and won an export award in the early 1960s. To further its international business in the late 1980s, Red Spot hired a Central Michigan University professor, Bryan Williams. Williams, who was hired because of his foreign-language skills (he speaks German, Japanese, and some Chinese), was the first employee at Red Spot whose exclusive focus was international marketing and sales. His first challenge was the lack of staff skilled in the business of exporting. He found that it was difficult to build an international business without in-house expertise in the basic mechanics of exporting. According to Williams, Red Spot needed people who understood the nuts and bolts of exporting—letters of credit, payment terms, bills of lading, and so on. As might be expected for a business based in the heartland of America, there was not a ready supply of such individuals in the local vicinity. It took Williams several years to solve this problem. Now Red Spot has a full-time staff of two who have been trained in the principles of exporting and international operations.

A second problem that Williams encountered was the clash between the quarter-to-quarter mentality that frequently pervades management practice in the United States and the long-term perspective that is often necessary to build a successful international business. Williams has found that building long-term personal relationships with potential foreign customers is often the key to getting business. When foreign customers visit Evansville, Williams often invites them home for dinner. His young children even started calling one visitor from Hong Kong "Uncle." Even with such efforts, however, the business may not come quickly. Meeting with potential foreign customers yields no direct business 90 percent of the time, although Williams points out that it often yields benefits in terms of competitive information and relationship building. He has found that perseverance pays. For example, Williams and Storms called on a major German automobile parts manufacturer for seven years before finally landing some business from the company.

Sources: R. L. Rose and C. Quintanilla, "More Small U.S. Firms Take up Exporting with Much Success," *Wall Street Journal*, December 20, 1996, p. A1, A10; and interview with Bryan Williams of Red Spot Paint.

a step on the road toward establishment of foreign production (again, 3M provides an example of this philosophy).

Export and Import Financing

Mechanisms for financing exports and imports have evolved over the centuries in response to a problem that can be particularly acute in international trade: the lack of trust that exists when one must put faith in a stranger. In this section, we examine the financial devices that have evolved to cope with this problem in the context of international trade: the letter of credit, the draft (or bill of exchange), and the bill of lading. Then we will trace the 14 steps of a typical export–import transaction.

Lack of Trust

Firms engaged in international trade have to trust someone they may have never seen, who lives in a different country, who speaks a different language, who abides by (or

Figure 15.1

Preference of the U.S. Exporter

Figure 15.2

Preference of the French Importer

does not abide by) a different legal system, and who could be very difficult to track down if he or she defaults on an obligation. Consider a U.S. firm exporting to a distributor in France. The U.S. businessman might be concerned that if he ships the products to France before he receives payment for them from the French businesswoman, she might take delivery of the products and not pay him for them. Conversely, the French importer might worry that if she pays for the products before they are shipped, the U.S. firm might keep the money and never ship the products or might ship defective products. Neither party to the exchange completely trusts the other. This lack of trust is exacerbated by the distance between the two parties—in space, language, and culture—and by the problems of using an underdeveloped international legal system to enforce contractual obligations.

Due to the (quite reasonable) lack of trust between the two parties, each has his or her own preferences as to how they would like the transaction to be configured. To make sure he is paid, the manager of the U.S. firm would prefer the French distributor to pay for the products before he ships them (see Figure 15.1). Alternatively, to ensure she receives the products, the French distributor would prefer not to pay for them until they arrive (see Figure 15.2). Thus, each party has a different set of preferences. Unless there is some way of establishing trust between the parties, the transaction might never take place.

The problem is solved by using a third party trusted by both—normally a reputable bank—to act as an intermediary. What happens can be summarized as follows (see Figure 15.3). First, the French importer obtains the bank's promise to pay on her behalf, knowing the U.S. exporter will trust the bank. This promise is known as a letter of credit. Having seen the letter of credit, the U.S. exporter now ships the products to France. Title to the products is given to the bank in the form of a document called a bill of lading. In return, the U.S. exporter tells the bank to pay for the products, which the bank does. The document for requesting this payment is referred to as a draft. The bank, having paid for the products, now passes the title on to the French importer, whom the bank trusts. At that time or later, depending on their agreement, the importer reimburses the bank. In the remainder of this section, we examine how this system works in more detail.

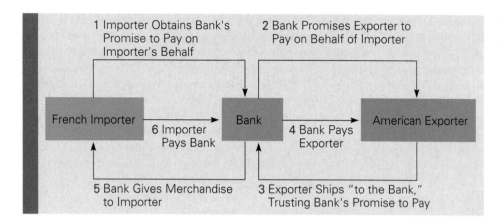

Figure 15.3

The Use of a Third Party

Letter of Credit

A letter of credit, abbreviated as L/C, stands at the center of international commercial transactions. Issued by a bank at the request of an importer, the letter of credit states that the bank will pay a specified sum of money to a beneficiary, normally the exporter, on presentation of particular, specified documents.

Consider again the example of the U.S. exporter and the French importer. The French importer applies to her local bank, say the Bank of Paris, for the issuance of a letter of credit. The Bank of Paris then undertakes a credit check of the importer. If the Bank of Paris is satisfied with her creditworthiness, it will issue a letter of credit. However, the Bank of Paris might require a cash deposit or some other form of collateral from her first. In addition, the Bank of Paris will charge the importer a fee for this service. Typically this amounts to between 0.5 percent and 2 percent of the value of the letter of credit, depending on the importer's creditworthiness and the size of the transaction. (As a rule, the larger the transaction, the lower the percentage.)

Let us assume the Bank of Paris is satisfied with the French importer's creditworthiness and agrees to issue a letter of credit. The letter states that the Bank of Paris will pay the U.S. exporter for the merchandise as long as it is shipped in accordance with specified instructions and conditions. At this point, the letter of credit becomes a financial contract between the Bank of Paris and the U.S. exporter. The Bank of Paris then sends the letter of credit to the U.S. exporter's bank, say the Bank of New York. The Bank of New York tells the exporter that it has received a letter of credit and that he can ship the merchandise. After the exporter has shipped the merchandise, he draws a draft against the Bank of Paris in accordance with the terms of the letter of credit, attaches the required documents, and presents the draft to his own bank, the Bank of New York, for payment. The Bank of New York then forwards the letter of credit and associated documents to the Bank of Paris. If all of the terms and conditions contained in the letter of credit have been complied with, the Bank of Paris will honor the draft and will send payment to the Bank of New York. When the Bank of New York receives the funds, it will pay the U.S. exporter.

As for the Bank of Paris, once it has transferred the funds to the Bank of New York, it will collect payment from the French importer. Alternatively, the Bank of Paris may allow the importer some time to resell the merchandise before requiring payment. This is not unusual, particularly when the importer is a distributor and not the final consumer of the merchandise, since it helps the importer's cash flow position. The Bank of Paris will treat such an extension of the payment period as a loan to the importer and will charge an appropriate rate of interest.

The great advantage of this system is that both the French importer and the U.S. exporter are likely to trust reputable banks, even if they do not trust each other. Once the U.S. exporter has seen a letter of credit, he knows that he is guaranteed payment and will ship the merchandise. Also, an exporter may find that having a letter of credit will facilitate obtaining pre-export financing. For example, having seen the letter of credit, the Bank of New York might be willing to lend the exporter funds to process and prepare the merchandise for shipping to France. This loan may not have to be re-paid until the exporter has received his payment for the merchandise. As for the French importer, she does not have to pay for the merchandise until the documents have arrived and unless all conditions stated in the letter of credit have been satisfied. The drawback for the importer is the fee she must pay the Bank of Paris for the letter of credit. In addition, since the letter of credit is a financial liability against her, it may reduce her ability to borrow funds for other purposes.

Draft

A draft, sometimes referred to as a bill of exchange, is the instrument normally used in international commerce to effect payment. A draft is simply an order written by an ex-porter instructing an importer, or an importer's agent, to pay a specified amount of money at a specified time. In the example of the U.S. exporter and the French im-porter, the exporter writes a draft that instructs the Bank of Paris, the French im-porter's agent, to pay for the merchandise shipped to France. The person or business initiating the draft is known as the maker (in this case, the U.S. exporter). The party to whom the draft is presented is known as the drawee (in this case, the Bank of Paris).

International practice is to use drafts to settle trade transactions. This differs from domestic practice in which a seller usually ships merchandise on an open account, fol-lowed by a commercial invoice that specifies the amount due and the terms of pay-ment. In domestic transactions, the buyer can often obtain possession of the merchandise without signing a formal document acknowledging his or her obligation to pay. In contrast, due to the lack of trust in international transactions, payment or a formal promise to pay is required before the buyer can obtain the merchandise.

Drafts fall into two categories, sight drafts and time drafts. A sight draft is payable on presentation to the drawee. A time draft allows for a delay in payment—normally 30, 60, 90, or 120 days. It is presented to the drawee, who signifies acceptance of it by writing or stamping a notice of acceptance on its face. Once accepted, the time draft becomes a promise to pay by the accepting party. When a time draft is drawn on and accepted by a bank, it is called a banker's acceptance. When it is drawn on and ac-cepted by a business firm, it is called a trade acceptance.

Time drafts are negotiable instruments; that is, once the draft is stamped with an acceptance, the maker can sell the draft to an investor at a discount from its face value. Imagine the agreement between the U.S. exporter and the French importer calls for the exporter to present the Bank of Paris (through the Bank of New York) with a time draft requiring payment 120 days after presentation. The Bank of Paris stamps the time draft with an acceptance. Imagine further that the draft is for $100,000.

The exporter can either hold onto the accepted time draft and receive $100,000 in 120 days or he can sell it to an investor, say the Bank of New York, for a discount from the face value. If the prevailing discount rate is 7 percent, the exporter could receive $96,500 by selling it immediately (7 percent per annum discount rate for 120 days for $100,000 equals $3,500, and $100,000 − $3,500 = $96,500). The Bank of New York would then collect the full $100,000 from the Bank of Paris in 120 days. The exporter might sell the accepted time draft immediately if he needed the funds to finance mer-chandise in transit and/or to cover cash flow shortfalls.

Bill of Lading

The third key document for financing international trade is the bill of lading. The bill of lading is issued to the exporter by the common carrier transporting the merchan-dise. It serves three purposes: it is a receipt, a contract, and a document of title. As a

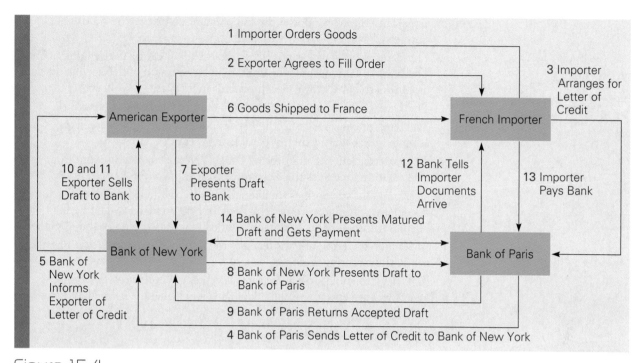

1 Importer Orders Goods

2 Exporter Agrees to Fill Order

3 Importer Arranges for Letter of Credit

American Exporter — 6 Goods Shipped to France → French Importer

10 and 11 Exporter Sells Draft to Bank

7 Exporter Presents Draft to Bank

12 Bank Tells Importer Documents Arrive

13 Importer Pays Bank

14 Bank of New York Presents Matured Draft and Gets Payment

Bank of New York

Bank of Paris

5 Bank of New York Informs Exporter of Letter of Credit

8 Bank of New York Presents Draft to Bank of Paris

9 Bank of Paris Returns Accepted Draft

4 Bank of Paris Sends Letter of Credit to Bank of New York

Figure 15.4

A Typical International Trade Transaction

receipt, the bill of lading indicates that the carrier has received the merchandise described on the face of the document. As a contract, it specifies that the carrier is obligated to provide a transportation service in return for a certain charge. As a document of title, it can be used to obtain payment or a written promise of payment before the merchandise is released to the importer. The bill of lading can also function as collateral against which funds may be advanced to the exporter by its local bank before or during shipment and before final payment by the importer.

A Typical International Trade Transaction

Now that we have reviewed the elements of an international trade transaction, let us see how the process works in a typical case, sticking with the example of the U.S. exporter and the French importer. The typical transaction involves 14 steps (see Figure 15.4).

1. The French importer places an order with the U.S. exporter and asks the American if he would be willing to ship under a letter of credit.
2. The U.S. exporter agrees to ship under a letter of credit and specifies relevant information such as prices and delivery terms.
3. The French importer applies to the Bank of Paris for a letter of credit to be issued in favor of the U.S. exporter for the merchandise the importer wishes to buy.
4. The Bank of Paris issues a letter of credit in the French importer's favor and sends it to the U.S. exporter's bank, the Bank of New York.
5. The Bank of New York advises the exporter of the opening of a letter of credit in his favor.
6. The U.S. exporter ships the goods to the French importer on a common carrier. An official of the carrier gives the exporter a bill of lading.
7. The U.S. exporter presents a 90-day time draft drawn on the Bank of Paris in accordance with its letter of credit and the bill of lading to the Bank of New

York. The exporter endorses the bill of lading so title to the goods is transferred to the Bank of New York.

8. The Bank of New York sends the draft and bill of lading to the Bank of Paris. The Bank of Paris accepts the draft, taking possession of the documents and promising to pay the now-accepted draft in 90 days.

9. The Bank of Paris returns the accepted draft to the Bank of New York.

10. The Bank of New York tells the U.S. exporter that it has received the accepted bank draft, which is payable in 90 days.

11. The exporter sells the draft to the Bank of New York at a discount from its face value and receives the discounted cash value of the draft in return.

12. The Bank of Paris notifies the French importer of the arrival of the documents. She agrees to pay the Bank of Paris in 90 days. The Bank of Paris releases the documents so the importer can take possession of the shipment.

13. In 90 days, the Bank of Paris receives the importer's payment, so it has funds to pay the maturing draft.

14. In 90 days, the holder of the matured acceptance (in this case, the Bank of New York) presents it to the Bank of Paris for payment. The Bank of Paris pays.

Export Assistance

Prospective U.S. exporters can draw on two forms of government-backed assistance to help finance their export programs. They can get financing aid from the Export–Import Bank and export credit insurance from the Foreign Credit Insurance Association.

Export–Import Bank

The Export–Import Bank, often referred to as Eximbank, is an independent agency of the U.S. government. Its mission is to provide financing aid that will facilitate exports, imports, and the exchange of commodities between the United States and other countries. Eximbank pursues this mission with various loan and loan-guarantee programs. The agency guarantees repayment of medium and long-term loans U.S. commercial banks make to foreign borrowers for purchasing U.S. exports. The Eximbank guarantee makes the commercial banks more willing to lend cash to foreign enterprises.

Eximbank also has a direct lending operation under which it lends dollars to foreign borrowers for use in purchasing U.S. exports. In some cases, it grants loans that commercial banks would not if it sees a potential benefit to the United States in doing so. The foreign borrowers use the loans to pay U.S. suppliers and repay the loan to Eximbank with interest.

Export Credit Insurance

For reasons outlined earlier, exporters clearly prefer to get letters of credit from importers. However, sometimes an exporter who insists on a letter of credit will lose an order to one who does not require a letter of credit. Thus, when the importer is in a strong bargaining position and able to play competing suppliers off against each other, an exporter may have to forgo a letter of credit.[16] The lack of a letter of credit exposes the exporter to the risk that the foreign importer will default on payment. The exporter can insure against this possibility by buying export credit insurance. If the customer defaults, the insurance firm will cover a major portion of the loss.

In the United States, export credit insurance is provided by the Foreign Credit Insurance Association (FCIA), an association of private commercial institutions operating under the guidance of the Export–Import Bank. The FCIA provides coverage against commercial risks and political risks. Losses due to commercial risk result from the buyer's insolvency or payment default. Political losses arise from actions of governments that are beyond the control of either buyer or seller.

Countertrade ■

Countertrade is an alternative means of structuring an international sale when conventional means of payment are difficult, costly, or nonexistent. We first encountered countertrade in Chapter 9 in our discussion of currency convertibility. A government may restrict the convertibility of its currency to preserve its foreign exchange reserves so they can be used to service international debt commitments and purchase crucial imports.[17] This is problematic for exporters. Nonconvertibility implies that the exporter may not be able to be paid in his or her home currency; and few exporters would desire payment in a currency that is not convertible. Countertrade is often the solution.[18] Countertrade denotes a whole range of barterlike agreements; its principle is to trade goods and services for other goods and services when they cannot be traded for money. Some examples of countertrade are:

- An Italian company that manufactures power generating equipment, ABB SAE Sadelmi SpA, was awarded a 720 million baht ($17.7 million) contract by the Electricity Generating Authority of Thailand. The contract specified that the company had to accept 218 million baht ($5.4 million) of Thai farm products as part of the payment.
- Saudi Arabia agreed to buy 10 747 jets from Boeing with payment in crude oil, discounted at 10 percent below posted world oil prices.
- General Electric won a contract for a $150 million electric generator project in Romania by agreeing to market $150 million of Romanian products in markets to which Romania did not have access.
- The Venezuelan government negotiated a contract with Caterpillar under which Venezuela would trade 350,000 tons of iron ore for Caterpillar earthmoving equipment.
- Albania offered such items as spring water, tomato juice, and chrome ore in exchange for a $60 million fertilizer and methanol complex.
- Philip Morris ships cigarettes to Russia, for which it receives chemicals that can be used to make fertilizer. Philip Morris ships the chemicals to China, and in return, China ships glassware to North America for retail sale by Philip Morris.[19]

The Growth of Countertrade

In the modern era, countertrade arose in the 1960s as a way for the Soviet Union and the Communist states of Eastern Europe, whose currencies were generally nonconvertible, to purchase imports. During the 1980s, the technique grew in popularity among many developing nations that lacked the foreign exchange reserves required to purchase necessary imports. Today, reflecting their own shortages of foreign exchange reserves, many of the successor states to the former Soviet Union and the Eastern European Communist nations are engaging in countertrade to purchase their imports. Consequently, according to some estimates, more than 20 percent of world trade by value in 1998 was in the form of countertrade, up from only 2 percent in 1975.[20] There was a notable increase in the volume of countertrade after the Asian financial crisis of 1997. That crisis left many Asian nations with little hard currency to finance international trade. In the tight monetary regime that followed the crisis in 1997, many Asian firms found it very difficult to get access to export credits to finance their own international trade. Consequently, they turned to the only option available to them—countertrade.

Figure 15.5

Countertrade Practice

Source: Reprinted from "The Do's and Don'ts of International Countertrade," by J. R. Carter and J. Gagne, *Sloan Management Review,* Spring 1988, pp. 31–37, Table 2, by permission of the publisher. Copyright 1998 by Sloan Management Association. All rights reserved.

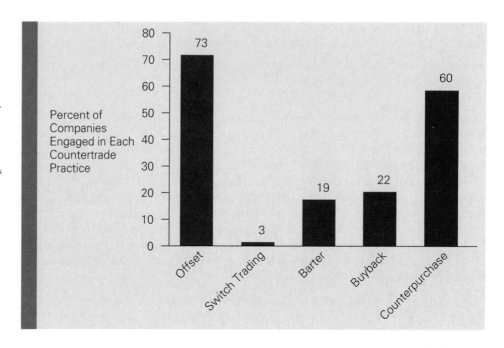

Given the importance of countertrade as a means of financing world trade, prospective exporters will have to engage in this technique from time to time to gain access to international markets. The governments of developing nations sometimes insist on a certain amount of countertrade.[21] For example, all foreign companies contracted by Thai state agencies for work costing more than 500 million baht ($12.3 million) are required to accept at least 30 percent of their payment in Thai agricultural products. Between 1994 and mid-1998, foreign firms purchased 21 billion baht ($517 million) in Thai goods under countertrade deals.[22]

Types of Countertrade

With its roots in the simple trading of goods and services for other goods and services, countertrade has evolved into a diverse set of activities that can be categorized as five distinct types of trading arrangements: barter, counterpurchase, offset, switch trading, and compensation or buyback.[23] Figure 15.5 summarizes the popularity of each of these arrangements as indicated in a survey of multinational corporations. Many countertrade deals involve not just one arrangement, but elements of two or more.

Barter

Barter is the direct exchange of goods and/or services between two parties without a cash transaction. Although barter is the simplest arrangement, it is not common. Its problems are twofold. First, if goods are not exchanged simultaneously, one party ends up financing the other for a period. Second, firms engaged in barter run the risk of having to accept goods they do not want, cannot use, or have difficulty reselling at a reasonable price. For these reasons, barter is viewed as the most restrictive countertrade arrangement. It is primarily used for one-time-only deals in transactions with trading partners who are not creditworthy or trustworthy.

Counterpurchase

Counterpurchase is a reciprocal buying agreement. It occurs when a firm agrees to purchase a certain amount of materials back from a country to which a sale is made. Suppose a U.S. firm sells some products to China. China pays the U.S. firm in dollars, but in exchange, the U.S. firm agrees to spend some of its proceeds from the sale on textiles produced by China. Thus, although China must draw on its foreign exchange reserves to pay the U.S. firm, it knows it will receive some of those dollars back because of the counterpurchase agreement. In one counterpurchase agreement, Rolls-Royce sold jet parts to Finland. As part of the deal, Rolls-Royce agreed to use some of the proceeds from the sale to purchase Finnish-manufactured TV sets that it would then sell in Great Britain.

Offset

Offset is similar to counterpurchase insofar as one party agrees to purchase goods and services with a specified percentage of the proceeds from the original sale. The difference is that this party can fulfill the obligation with any firm in the country to which the sale is being made. From an exporter's perspective, this is more attractive than a straight counterpurchase agreement because it gives the exporter greater flexibility to choose the goods that it wishes to purchase.

Switch Trading

Switch trading refers to the use of a specialized third-party trading house in a countertrade arrangement. When a firm enters a counterpurchase or offset agreement with a country, it often ends up with what are called counterpurchase credits, which can be used to purchase goods from that country. Switch trading occurs when a third-party trading house buys the firm's counterpurchase credits and sells them to another firm that can better use them. For example, a U.S. firm concludes a counterpurchase agreement with Poland for which it receives some number of counterpurchase credits for purchasing Polish goods. The U.S. firm cannot use and does not want any Polish goods, however, so it sells the credits to a third-party trading house at a discount. The trading house finds a firm that can use the credits and sells them at a profit.

In one example of switch trading, Poland and Greece had a counterpurchase agreement that called for Poland to buy the same U.S.-dollar value of goods from Greece that it sold to Greece. However, Poland could not find enough Greek goods that it required, so it ended up with a dollar-denominated counterpurchase balance in Greece that it was unwilling to use. A switch trader bought the right to 250,000 counterpurchase dollars from Poland for $225,000 and sold them to a European sultana (grape) merchant for $235,000, who used them to purchase sultanas from Greece.

Compensation or Buybacks

A buyback occurs when a firm builds a plant in a country—or supplies technology, equipment, training, or other services to the country—and agrees to take a certain percentage of the plant's output as partial payment for the contract. For example, Occidental Petroleum negotiated a deal with Russia under which Occidental would build several ammonia plants in Russia and as partial payment receive ammonia over a 20-year period.

The Pros and Cons of Countertrade

Countertrade's main attraction is that it can give a firm a way to finance an export deal when other means are not available. Given the problems that many developing nations have in raising the foreign exchange necessary to pay for imports, countertrade may be the only option available when doing business in these countries. Even when countertrade is not the only option for structuring an export transaction, many countries prefer countertrade to cash deals. Thus, if a firm is unwilling to enter a countertrade agreement, it may lose an export opportunity to a competitor that is willing to make a countertrade agreement.

In addition, a countertrade agreement may be required by the government of a country to which a firm is exporting goods or services. Boeing often has to agree to counterpurchase agreements in order to capture orders for its commercial jet aircraft.

For example, in exchange for gaining an order from Air India, Boeing may be required to purchase certain component parts, such as aircraft doors, from an Indian company. Taking this one step further, Boeing can use its willingness to enter into a counter-purchase agreement as a way of winning orders in the face of intense competition from its global rival, Airbus Industrie. Thus, for firms like Boeing, countertrade can become a strategic marketing weapon.

However, the drawbacks of countertrade agreements are substantial. Other things being equal, firms would normally prefer to be paid in hard currency. Countertrade contracts may involve the exchange of unusable or poor-quality goods that the firm cannot dispose of profitably. For example, a few years ago, one U.S. firm got burned when 50 percent of the television sets it received in a countertrade agreement with Hungary were defective and could not be sold. In addition, even if the goods it receives are of high quality, the firm still needs to dispose of them profitably. To do this, countertrade requires the firm to invest in an in-house trading department dedicated to arranging and managing countertrade deals. This can be expensive and time consuming.

Given these drawbacks, countertrade is most attractive to large, diverse multinational enterprises that can use their worldwide network of contacts to dispose of goods acquired in countertrading. The masters of countertrade are Japan's giant trading firms, the *sogo shosha*, which use their vast networks of affiliated companies to profitably dispose of goods acquired through countertrade agreements. The trading firm of Mitsui & Company, for example, has about 120 affiliated companies in almost every sector of the manufacturing and service industries. If one of Mitsui's affiliates receives goods in a countertrade agreement that it cannot consume, Mitsui & Company will normally be able to find another affiliate that can profitably use them. Firms affiliated with one of Japan's *sogo shosha* often have a competitive advantage in countries where countertrade agreements are preferred.

Western firms that are large, diverse, and have a global reach (e.g., General Electric, Philip Morris, and 3M) have similar profit advantages from countertrade agreements. Indeed, 3M has established its own trading company—3M Global Trading, Inc.—to develop and manage the company's international countertrade programs. Unless there is no alternative, small and medium-sized exporters should probably try to avoid countertrade deals because they lack the worldwide network of operations that may be required to profitably utilize or dispose of goods acquired through them.[24]

Chapter Summary

In this chapter, we examined the steps that firms must take to establish themselves as exporters. This chapter made the following points:

1. One big impediment to exporting is ignorance of foreign market opportunities.
2. Neophyte exporters often become discouraged or frustrated with the exporting process because they encounter many problems, delays, and pitfalls.
3. The way to overcome ignorance is to gather information. In the United States, a number of institutions, most important of which is the Department of Commerce, can help firms gather information in the matchmaking process. Export management companies can also help an exporter to identify export opportunities.
4. Many of the pitfalls associated with exporting can be avoided if a company hires an experienced export management company, or export consultant, and if it adopts the appropriate export strategy.
5. Firms engaged in international trade must do business with people they cannot trust and people who may be difficult to track down if they default on an obligation. Due to the lack of trust, each party to an international transaction has a different set of preferences regarding the configuration of the transaction.
6. The problems arising from lack of trust between exporters and importers can be solved by using a third party that is trusted by both, normally a reputable bank.

7. A letter of credit is issued by a bank at the request of an importer. It states that the bank promises to pay a beneficiary, normally the exporter, on presentation of documents specified in the letter.

8. A draft is the instrument normally used in international commerce to effect payment. It is an order written by an exporter instructing an importer, or an importer's agent, to pay a specified amount of money at a specified time.

9. Drafts are either sight drafts or time drafts. Time drafts are negotiable instruments.

10. A bill of lading is issued to the exporter by the common carrier transporting the merchandise. It serves as a receipt, a contract, and a document of title.

11. U.S. exporters can draw on two types of government-backed assistance to help finance their exports: loans from the Export–Import Bank and export credit insurance from the FCIA.

12. Countertrade includes a range of barterlike agreements. It is primarily used when a firm exports to a country whose currency is not freely convertible and may lack the foreign exchange reserves required to purchase the imports.

13. The main attraction of countertrade is that it gives a firm a way to finance an export deal when other means are not available. A firm that insists on being paid in hard currency may be at a competitive disadvantage vis-à-vis one that is willing to engage in countertrade.

14. The main disadvantage of countertrade is that the firm may receive unusable or poor-quality goods that cannot be disposed of profitably.

Critical Discussion Questions

1. A firm based in Washington state wants to export a shipload of finished lumber to the Philippines. The would-be importer cannot get sufficient credit from domestic sources to pay for the shipment but insists that the finished lumber can quickly be resold in the Philippines for a profit. Outline the steps the exporter should take to effect this export to the Philippines.

2. You are the assistant to the CEO of a small textile firm that manufactures high-quality, premium-priced, stylish clothing. The CEO has decided to see what the opportunities are for exporting and has asked you for advice as to the steps the company should take. What advice would you give the CEO?

3. An alternative to using a letter of credit is export credit insurance. What are the advantages and disadvantages of using export credit insurance rather than a letter of credit for exporting (a) a luxury yacht from California to Canada, and (b) machine tools from New York to the Ukraine?

4. How do you explain the popularity of countertrade? Under what scenarios might its popularity increase still further by the year 2010? Under what scenarios might its popularity decline by the year 2010?

5. How might a company make strategic use of countertrade schemes as a marketing weapon to generate export revenues? What are the risks associated with pursuing such a strategy?

Closing Case

Artais Weather Check

Artais Weather Check, Inc., is a small Ohio-based company that manufactures an automated weather observation system, or AWOS, for small airports. Artais's AWOS system records runway conditions such as wind speed, direction, and temperature and converts the data into a voice message for pilots. Only three other companies besides Artais have been certified by the Federal Aviation Administration (FAA) to produce the equipment, and Artais dominates the market in the United States with a share of more than 80 percent.

Despite its dominant market share in the United States, Artais gets the majority of its $8 million in annual revenues from foreign markets. Within the United States, the market for automated weather observation systems is small. Although there are 18,000 public and private airports in the country, the largest have round-the-clock human weather watchers, while most of the smaller airports cannot afford the $45,000 to $60,000 required to install an AWOS. Thus, the prospects for growth in the United States seem to be limited to sales of about 75 systems per year nationwide.

To continue to grow the company's revenues, Artais has increasingly looked toward export sales. Initially, export sales were slow to develop, perhaps because Artais's management had very little international experience and spent several years simply trying to learn about foreign markets and the mechanics of exporting. However, from slow beginnings in the late 1980s, exports have surged to account for close to two-thirds of the company's total revenues. But to get foreign orders, Artais has had to deal with frustrations it never encountered at home.

The first problem it came up against was one of name recognition. Although Artais is well-known within the United States, the company found that its name recognition was close to zero overseas. Another problem involves subsidized competition; according to Artais, its main competitors in some foreign markets are subsidized by their governments to protect jobs. Artais has also found that it needs to customize its products for foreign markets. To sell in Egypt, for example, its system had to be reprogrammed to relay weather information in Arabic as well as English. International customers also require that spare parts be located close by and that Artais employees install the equipment and provide on-site training, all of which raises the costs of doing business.

Political factors have also had a major impact on the outcome of some deals. For example, after working hard to secure a deal in Romania, Artais unexpectedly saw the deal fall through at the last moment. Instead, the deal went to a German competitor. According to some locals, the Romanian government, eager to improve trading relations with the European Union, gave the job to Artais's German competitor in an attempt to curry favor with the trading bloc's most powerful member. Artais has also lost several bids to competitors because it was unwilling to take payment in a foreign currency from an emerging market country, preferring instead to be paid in U.S. dollars.

Despite problems such as these, Artais has sold systems to airports in Taiwan, China, Ecuador, Saudi Arabia, and Egypt. Artais has found that such overseas contracts can be more lucrative than its domestic sales because of all the extras, such as spare parts, installation fees, and training. For the basic AWOS, the value of the foreign contracts has ranged from $200,000 to $2 million, compared with $45,000 to $60,000 in the United States. Building on this success, Artais in 1995 introduced a system designed to detect low-level wind shears. The system, which costs $350,000 per unit, was designed for the market outside the United States. According to company representatives, Artais is disregarding the U.S. market because of the cost and time involved in meeting specifications established by the FAA. Systems built to FAA specifications can cost $1 million a unit, which is beyond the reach of many foreign buyers. The first two sales of the new system were to Saudi Arabia in 1995. The company believes that in time 20 percent of its annual sales will come from the wind-shear system, all of which will be generated overseas. In addition, the company believes that the bulk of revenues for its basic AWOS will continue to be generated overseas.

Sources: S. N. Mehta, "Enterprise: Artais Finds That Smallness Isn't a Handicap in Global Market," *Wall Street Journal*, June 23, 1994, p. B2, and R. Carter, "Artais' New System to Help Airlines Harness the Wind," *Columbus Dispatch*, August 28, 1995, p. 8.

Case Discussion Questions

1. What is the motivation for Artais's shift toward a strategy of export-led growth? Why do you think the opportunities for growth might be greater in foreign markets? Do you think that developing countries are likely to be a major market opportunity for Artais? Why?

2. Could Artais have ramped up its foreign sales more rapidly? How?

3. What potential problems might Artais encounter selling its equipment to nations such as Egypt and Ecuador? How can the company deal with these problems?

4. Do you think that it is wise for the company to insist on being paid in dollars? What alternatives are open to the company? What are the risks associated with these alternatives? Should the company change its policy?

Notes

1. M. Dickerson and L. Romney, "US Exports Get a Big Boost from Small Firms," *Los Angeles Times*, November 17, 1999, p. 10.

2. W. J. Holstein, "Why Johann Can Export, but Johnny Can't," *Business Week*, November 4, 1991, pp. 64–65.

3. S. T. Cavusgil, "Global Dimensions of Marketing," in *Marketing*, ed. P. E. Murphy and B. M. Enis (Glenview, IL: Scott, Foresman, 1985), pp. 577–99.

4. S. M. Mehta, "Enterprise: Small Companies Look to Cultivate Foreign Business," *Wall Street Journal*, July 7, 1994, p. B2.

5. W. Pavord and R. Bogart, "The Dynamics of the Decision to Export," *Akron Business and Economic Review*, 1975, pp. 6–11.

6. W. J. Burpitt and D. A. Rondinelli, "Small Firms' Motivations for Exporting: To Earn and Learn?" *Journal of Small Business Management*, October 2000, pp. 1–14.

7. J. Norman, "Small Businesses Have Big Role in Export Field," *Orange County Register*, April 27, 1998, p. D15.

8. A. O. Ogbuehi and T. A. Longfellow, "Perceptions of U.S. Manufacturing Companies Concerning Exporting," *Journal of Small Business Management*, October 1994, pp. 37–59.

9. R. W. Haigh, "Thinking of Exporting?" *Columbia Journal of World Business* 29 (December 1994), pp. 66–86.

10. F. Williams, "The Quest for More Efficient Commerce," *Financial Times*, October 13, 1994, p. 7.

11. See Burpitt and Rondinelli, "Small Firms' Motivations for Exporting," and C. S. Katsikeas, L. C. Leonidou, and N. A. Morgan, "Firm Level Export Performance Assessment," *Academy of Marketing Science* 28 (2000), pp. 493–511.

12. M. Y. Yoshino and T. B. Lifson, *The Invisible Link* (Cambridge, MA: MIT Press, 1986).

13. L. W. Tuller, *Going Global* (Homewood, IL: Business One-Irwin, 1991).

14. Haigh, "Thinking of Exporting?"

15. J. Francis and C. Collins-Dodd, "The Impact of Firms' Export Orientation on the Export Performance of High-Tech Small and Medium Sized Enterprises," *Journal of International Marketing* 8, no. 3 (2000), pp. 84–103.

16. For a review of the conditions under which a buyer has power over a supplier, see M. E. Porter, *Competitive Strategy* (New York: Free Press, 1980).

17. *Exchange Agreements and Exchange Restrictions* (Washington, DC: International Monetary Fund, 1989).

18. It's also sometimes argued that countertrade is a way of reducing the risks inherent in a traditional money-for-goods transaction, particularly with entities from emerging economies. See C. J. Choi., S. H. Lee, and J. B. Kim, "A Note of Countertrade: Contractual Uncertainty and Transactional Governance in Emerging Economies," *Journal of International Business Studies* 30, no. 1 (1999), pp. 189–202.

19. J. R. Carter and J. Gagne, "The Do's and Don'ts of International Countertrade," *Sloan Management Review*, Spring 1988, pp. 31–37, and W. Maneerungsee, "Countertrade: Farm Goods Swapped for Italian Electricity," *Bangkok Post*, July 23, 1998.

20. Estimate from the American Countertrade Association at http://freedonia.tpusa.com/infosrc/aca/. See also D. West, "Countertrade," *Business Credit* 104, no. 4 (2001), pp. 64–67.

21. Carter and Gagne, "The Do's and Dont's of International Countertrade."

22. Maneerungsee, "Countertrade: Farm Goods Swapped for Italian Electricity."

23. For details, see Carter and Gagne, "Do's and Dont's;" J. F. Hennart, "Some Empirical Dimensions of Countertrade," *Journal of International Business Studies*, 1990, pp. 240–60; and West, "Countertrade."

24. D. J. Lecraw, "The Management of Countertrade: Factors Influencing Success," *Journal of International Business Studies*, Spring 1989, pp. 41–59.

Global Manufacturing and Materials Management

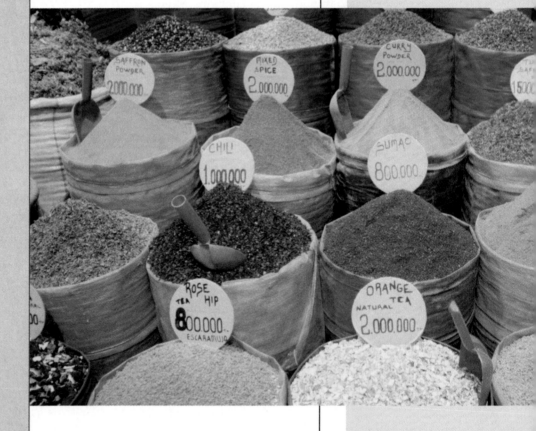

Timberland, a New Hampshire-based manufacturer of rugged, high-quality shoes and outdoor clothing, has built one of the world's premium footwear and apparel brands. From small beginnings in the late 1970s, Timberland has grown into a global business with sales of $1.15 billion in 2000. The company's global expansion began in 1979 when an Italian distributor walked into the then-small U.S. outfitter and expressed an interest in shoe #100-81, a hand-sewn moccasin with a lug sole. The Italian thought the shoe would sell well in Italy—land of high-style Gucci shoes. He was right; Timberland quickly became a phenomenon in Italy where Timberland shoes often sold for a 60 percent premium over prices in the United States. Expansion into other countries followed, and by the end of the 1990s Timberland was generating 30 percent of its sales from foreign countries, most notably Italy, Germany, France, Britain, and Japan.

Ignored during much of this rapid growth, however, was any attempt to build a tightly managed and coordinated global manufacturing and logistics system. By the early 1990s, Timberland was confronted with an extremely complex global manufacturing and logistics network. To take advantage of lower wage costs outside the United States, the company had established manufacturing facilities in the Dominican Republic and Puerto Rico. Timberland had also found it cost-efficient to source footwear and apparel from independent suppliers based in dozens of other low-wage countries in Asia, Europe, and Latin America. At the same time, Timberland's distribution network had grown to serve consumers in more than 50 countries. To complicate things further, the average shipment of footwear to retailers was for less than 12 pairs of each type of shoe, which made for an enormous volume of individual shipments to track.

Timberland found that its logistics systems was breaking down under the strains imposed by rapid growth, a globally dispersed supply and distribution chain, and a large volume of individual shipments. The company simply lacked the information systems required to coordinate and control its dispersed production and distribution network. No common information systems linked suppliers, Timberland, and retailers. Nor was there any attempt to consolidate shipments from different regions of the world to realize shipping economies. Products were shipped from six countries in Southeast Asia to the United States and Europe, as opposed to being consolidated at one location and then shipped. The consequences included an inability to match the demands of retailers with production, excess inventory, and high costs.

In the mid-1990s, Timberland decided to reorganize its global logistics system by streamlining its logistics information pipeline first and then its cargo pipeline. The information challenge was to come up with a system that would enable Timberland to track a product from the factory to its final destination, thereby better matching supply with demand. As Timberland's director of distribution explains it: "At every link in the chain, you can make a decision about cargo that would make it flow better, but only if you have the information about the product and the ability to communicate with that location in real time to direct the product." For example, when a product leaves the factory, Timberland can in theory direct a freight forwarder to send the product by air or by ocean carrier, depending on the urgency of the shipment. When a shipment lands in, say, Los Angeles, it can be shipped to a distribution center or shipped directly to a customer, again depending on need. Until the mid-1990s, the company lacked the requisite information systems required to make such choices.

The company developed the required information system in conjunction with ACS, a freight forwarder, and The Rockport Group, a software house. To simplify its system at the physical distribution level and to make implementation of its information systems easier, Timberland consolidated regional warehousing. Timberland had separate warehouses in a dozen Asian countries, several in the United States, and three in Europe. Under the new Internet-based system, sources in Asia feed into one warehouse. The company also switched to single continental distribution centers in North America and Europe. By centralizing its warehousing at three locations, the company can better track where the product is located so that it can be routed quickly and flexibly to where it is needed. The result has been an improvement in Timberland's ability to deliver products to customers exactly when they need them, as opposed to delivering products too late or too soon. This has helped the company to increase inventory turnover, thereby reducing the total amount of inventory it needs to hold. By centralizing warehousing, Timberland has also been able to consolidate shipments from a region into one transoceanic shipment, which has enabled the company to negotiate much better shipping rates.

In tandem with improvements in its global logistics system, Timberland also altered its supply base in response to changes in costs and import quotas. It reduced production from company-owned factories in the Dominican Republic and Puerto Rico from 28 percent of total sales in 1997 to 15 percent of total sales in 2000, preferring instead to source production from lower-cost suppliers in Southeast Asia. In response to the imposition of new European quotas on footwear imports from China, Timberland has also found it necessary to shift production destined for Europe from China to other Asian countries, such as Vietnam.

According to the company, better managing its global supply chain has helped Timberland increase its gross profit margins from 38 percent in 1997 to 41 percent in 2000. The increase has been due to lower production costs and increased inventory turnover. Thanks to more efficient management of the supply chain, inventory now turns over 4 times a year, up from 2.9 times in 1997. Total inventory has fallen by 12 percent, implying that less working capital is tied up in inventory and fewer products remain unsold. Still, the company recognizes that there is room for improvement. Currently the time between ordering and delivery of footwear is four months. Timberland wants to cut that to 45 days, which would allow the company to be much more responsive to short-term changes in consumer demands.

Sources: P. Buxbaum, "Timberland's New Spin on Global Logistics," *Distribution,* May 1994, pp. 33–36; A. E. Serwer, "Will Timberland Grow Up?" *Fortune,* May 29, 1995, p. 24; M. Tedeschi, "Timberland Vows to Get on the Ball," *Footwear News,* May 22, 1995, p. 2; *Timberland Annual Report,* 1997; A. Coia, "Timberland Keeps in Step with Changing Europe," *Logistics,* May 2001, pp. E4–E7; and S. Hill, "Timberland Heeds Consumers," *Apparel Industry Magazine,* December 2000, pp. 27–30.

▉ Introduction

As trade barriers fall and global markets develop, many firms increasingly confront a set of interrelated issues. First, where in the world should productive activities be located? Should they be concentrated in a single country, or should they be dispersed around the globe, matching the type of activity with country differences in factor costs, tariff barriers, political risks, and the like in order to minimize costs and maximize value added? Second, what should be the long-term strategic role of foreign production sites? Should the firm abandon a foreign site if factor costs change, moving production to another more favorable location, or is there value to maintaining an operation at a given location even if underlying economic conditions change? Third, should the firm own foreign productive activities, or is it better to outsource those activities to independent vendors? Fourth, how should a globally dispersed supply chain be managed, and what is the role of Internet-based information technology in the management of global logistics? Fifth, should the firm manage global logistics itself, or should it outsource the management to enterprises that specialize in this activity?

In this chapter we shall consider all these questions and discuss the various factors that influence decisions in this arena. The opening case on Timberland provides some examples of the issues that many firms have to struggle with in today's global economy. Timberland started to source production from foreign factories to reduce its cost structure. However, it soon found that it lacked the capability to manage the resulting supply chain. Most importantly, a lack of timely information meant that it was almost impossible for Timberland to closely match production schedules with demand from retailers around the world. The results included a shortage of some products and excess production of other products, which meant higher inventory and lower gross margins. Timberland responded by introducing information systems to better track the flow of products through the global supply chain. It also consolidated its global distribution systems at three warehouses. As a result, it is now better able to match supply and demand, which has increased inventory turnover and boosted profitability.

Strategy, Manufacturing, and Logistics ∎

In Chapter 12, we introduced the concept of the value chain and discussed a number of value creation activities, including production, marketing, materials management (logistics), R&D, human resources, and information systems. In this chapter we will focus on two of these activities—production and materials management (logistics)— and attempt to clarify how they might be performed internationally to (1) lower the costs of value creation and (2) add value by better serving customer needs. We will discuss the contributions of information technology to these activities, which has become particularly important in the era of the Internet. In later chapters, we will look at other value creation activities in this international context (marketing, R&D, and human resource management).

In Chapter 12, we defined *production* as "the activities involved in creating a product." We used the term *production* to denote both service and manufacturing activities, since one can produce a service or produce a physical product. In this chapter, we focus more on manufacturing than on service activities, so we will use the term *manufacturing* rather than production. **Materials management** is the activity that controls the transmission of physical materials through the value chain, from procurement through production and into distribution. Materials management includes logistics, which refers to the procurement and physical transmission of material through the supply chain, from suppliers to customers. Manufacturing and materials management are closely linked, since a firm's ability to perform its manufacturing function efficiently depends on a continuous supply of high-quality material inputs, for which materials management is responsible.

The manufacturing and materials management functions of an international firm have a number of important strategic objectives.[1] One is to lower costs. Dispersing manufacturing activities to various locations around the globe where each activity can be performed most efficiently can lower costs. Costs can also be lowered by managing the global supply chain efficiently so as to better match supply and demand. Efficient supply chain management reduces the amount of inventory in the system and increases inventory turnover, which means the firm has to invest less working capital in inventory and is less likely to find excess inventory on hand that cannot be sold and has to be written off.

A second strategic objective shared by manufacturing and materials management is to increase product quality by eliminating defective products from both the supply chain and the manufacturing process.[2] The objectives of reducing costs and increasing quality are not independent of each other. As illustrated in Figure 16.1, the firm that improves its quality control will also reduce its costs of value creation. Improved quality control reduces costs in three ways:

- Increases productivity because time is not wasted manufacturing poor-quality products that cannot be sold, leading to a direct reduction in unit costs.
- Lowers rework and scrap costs.
- Lowers warranty costs.

The effect is to lower the costs of value creation by reducing both manufacturing and service costs.

The main management technique that companies are utilizing to boost their product quality is **total quality management** (TQM). TQM takes as its central focus the need to improve the quality of a company's products and services. The TQM philosophy was developed by a number of American consultants such as the late W. Edward Deming, Joseph Juran, and A.V. Feigenbaum.[3] Deming identified a number of steps

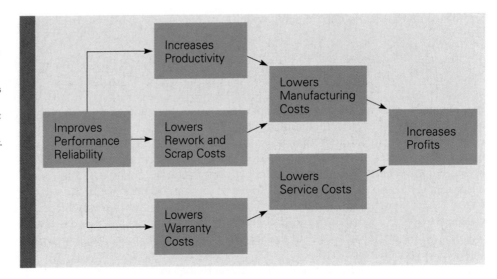

that should be part of any TQM program. He argued that management should embrace the philosophy that mistakes, defects, and poor-quality materials are not acceptable and should be eliminated. He suggested that the quality of supervision should be improved by allowing more time for supervisors to work with employees and by providing them with the tools they need to do the job. Deming recommended that management should create an environment in which employees will not fear reporting problems or recommending improvements. He believed that work standards should be defined not only as numbers or quotas, but also should include some notion of quality to promote the production of defect-free output. He argued that management has the responsibility to train employees in new skills to keep pace with changes in the workplace. In addition, he believed that achieving better quality requires the commitment of everyone in the company.

The growth of international standards has also focused greater attention on the importance of product quality. In Europe, for example, the European Union requires that the quality of a firm's manufacturing processes and products be certified under a quality standard known as ISO 9000 before the firm is allowed access to the EU marketplace. Although the ISO 9000 certification process has proved to be a somewhat bureaucratic and costly process for many firms, it does focus management attention on the need to improve the quality of products and processes.[4]

In addition to the objectives of lowering costs and improving quality, two other objectives have particular importance in international businesses. First, manufacturing and materials management must be able to accommodate demands for local responsiveness. As we saw in Chapter 12, demands for local responsiveness arise from national differences in consumer tastes and preferences, infrastructure, distribution channels, and host-government demands. Demands for local responsiveness create pressures to decentralize manufacturing activities to the major national or regional markets in which the firm does business or to implement flexible manufacturing processes that enable the firm to customize the product coming out of a factory according to the market in which it is to be sold.

Second, manufacturing and materials management must be able to respond quickly to shifts in customer demand. In recent years, time-based competition has grown more important.[5] When consumer demand is prone to large and unpredictable shifts, the firm that can adapt most quickly to these shifts will gain an advantage. As we shall see, both manufacturing and materials management play critical roles here. The opening case illustrated how Timberland has been trying to reduce the time between the ordering and delivery of footwear so that it can better respond to changes in consumer demands.

Where to Manufacture ■

An essential decision facing an international firm is where to locate its manufacturing activities to achieve the goals of minimizing costs and improving product quality. For the firm contemplating international production, a number of factors must be considered. These factors can be grouped under three broad headings: country factors, technological factors, and product factors.[6]

▎Country Factors

We reviewed country-specific factors in some detail earlier in the book and we will not dwell on them here. Political economy, culture, and relative factor costs differ from country to country. In Chapter 4, we saw that due to differences in factor costs, certain countries have a comparative advantage for producing certain products. In Chapters 2 and 3, we saw how differences in political economy and national culture influence the benefits, costs, and risks of doing business in a country. Other things being equal, a firm should locate its various manufacturing activities where the economic, political, and cultural conditions, including relative factor costs, are conducive to the performance of those activities. In Chapter 12, we referred to the benefits derived from such a strategy as location economies. We argued that one result of the strategy is the creation of a global web of value creation activities.

Also important in some industries is the presence of global concentrations of activities at certain locations. In Chapter 6, we discussed the role of location externalities in influencing foreign direct investment decisions. Externalities include the presence of an appropriately skilled labor pool and supporting industries.[7] Such externalities can play an important role in deciding where to locate manufacturing activities. For example, because of a cluster of semiconductor manufacturing plants in Taiwan, a pool of labor with experience in the semiconductor business has developed. In addition, the plants have attracted a number of supporting industries, such as the manufacturers of semiconductor capital equipment and silicon, which have established facilities in Taiwan to be near their customers. This implies that there are real benefits to locating in Taiwan, as opposed to another location that lacks such externalities. Other things being equal, the externalities make Taiwan an attractive location for semiconductor manufacturing facilities.

Of course, other things are not equal. Differences in relative factor costs, political economy, culture, and location externalities are important, but other factors also loom large. Formal and informal trade barriers obviously influence location decisions (see Chapter 5), as do transportation costs and rules and regulations regarding foreign direct investment (see Chapter 7). For example, although relative factor costs may make a country look attractive as a location for performing a manufacturing activity, regulations prohibiting foreign direct investment may eliminate this option. Similarly, a consideration of factor costs might suggest that a firm should source production of a certain component from a particular country, but trade barriers could make this uneconomical.

Another country factor is expected future movements in its exchange rate (see Chapters 9 and 10). Adverse changes in exchange rates can quickly alter a country's attractiveness as a manufacturing base. Currency appreciation can transform a low-cost location into a high-cost location. Many Japanese corporations had to grapple with this problem during the 1990s. The relatively low value of the yen on foreign exchange markets between 1950 and 1980 helped strengthen Japan's position as a low-cost location for manufacturing. Between 1980 and the mid-1990s, however, the yen's steady appreciation against the dollar increased the dollar cost of products exported from Japan, making Japan less attractive as a manufacturing location. In response, many Japanese firms moved their manufacturing offshore to lower-cost locations in East Asia.

Technological Factors

The technology we are concerned with in this subsection is manufacturing technology—the technology that performs specific manufacturing activities. The type of technology a firm uses in its manufacturing can be pivotal in location decisions. For example, because of technological constraints, in some cases it is necessary to perform certain manufacturing activities in only one location and serve the world market from there. In other cases, the technology may make it feasible to perform an activity in multiple locations. Three characteristics of a manufacturing technology are of interest here: the level of fixed costs, the minimum efficient scale, and the flexibility of the technology.

Fixed Costs

As we noted in Chapter 12, in some cases the fixed costs of setting up a manufacturing plant are so high that a firm must serve the world market from a single location or from a very few locations. For example, it now costs more than $1 billion to set up a state-of-the-art plant to manufacture semiconductor chips. Given this, serving the world market from a single plant sited at a single (optimal) location makes sense.

Conversely, a relatively low level of fixed costs can make it economical to perform a particular activity in several locations at once. This allows the firm to better accommodate demands for local responsiveness. Manufacturing in multiple locations may also help the firm avoid becoming too dependent on one location. Being too dependent on one location is particularly risky in a world of floating exchange rates. Many firms disperse their manufacturing plants to different locations as a "real hedge" against potentially adverse moves in currencies.

Minimum Efficient Scale

The concept of economies of scale tells us that as plant output expands, unit costs decrease. The reasons include the greater utilization of capital equipment and the productivity gains that come with specialization of employees within the plant.[8] However, beyond a certain level of output, few additional scale economies are available. Thus, the "unit cost curve" declines with output until a certain output level is reached, at which point further increases in output realize little reduction in unit costs. The level of output at which most plant-level scale economies are exhausted is referred to as the minimum efficient scale of output. This is the scale of output a plant must operate at to realize all major plant-level scale economies (see Figure 16.2).

Figure 16.2

A Typical Unit Cost Curve

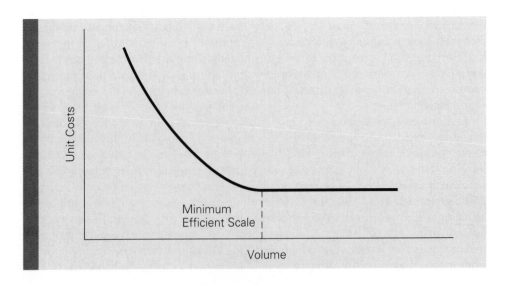

The implications of this concept are as follows: The larger the minimum efficient scale of a plant, the greater the argument for centralizing production in a single location or a limited number of locations. Alternatively, when the minimum efficient scale of production is relatively low, it may be economical to manufacture a product at several locations. As in the case of low fixed costs, the advantages are allowing the firm to accommodate demands for local responsiveness or to hedge against currency risk by manufacturing the same product in several locations.

Flexible Manufacturing and Mass Customization

Central to the concept of economies of scale is the idea that the best way to achieve high efficiency, and hence low unit costs, is through the mass production of a standardized output. The trade-off implicit in this idea is between unit costs and product variety. Producing greater product variety from a factory implies shorter production runs, which in turn implies an inability to realize economies of scale. That is, wide product variety makes it difficult for a company to increase its production efficiency and thus reduce its unit costs. According to this logic, the way to increase efficiency and drive down unit costs is to limit product variety and produce a standardized product in large volumes.

This view of production efficiency has been challenged by the rise of flexible manufacturing technologies. The term **flexible manufacturing technology**—or **lean production,** as it is often called—covers a range of manufacturing technologies designed to (1) reduce setup times for complex equipment, (2) increase the utilization of individual machines through better scheduling, and (3) improve quality control at all stages of the manufacturing process.[9] Flexible manufacturing technologies allow the company to produce a wider variety of end products at a unit cost that at one time could only be achieved through the mass production of a standardized output. Research suggests the adoption of flexible manufacturing technologies may actually increase efficiency and lower unit costs relative to what can be achieved by the mass production of a standardized output, while at the same time enabling the company to customize its product offering to a much greater extent than was once thought possible. The term **mass customization** has been coined to describe the ability of companies to use flexible manufacturing technology to reconcile two goals that were once thought to be incompatible—low cost and product customization.[10]

Flexible manufacturing technologies vary in their sophistication and complexity. One of the most famous examples of a flexible manufacturing technology, Toyota's production system, is relatively unsophisticated, but it has been credited with making Toyota the most efficient auto company in the world. Toyota's flexible manufacturing system was developed by one of the company's engineers, Ohno Taiichi. After working at Toyota for five years and visiting Ford's U.S. plants, Ohno became convinced that the mass production philosophy for making cars was flawed. He saw numerous problems with the mass production system.

First, long production runs created massive inventories that had to be stored in large warehouses. This was expensive, both because of the cost of warehousing and because inventories tied up capital in unproductive uses. Second, if the initial machine settings were wrong, long production runs resulted in the production of a large number of defects (i.e., waste). Third, the mass production system was unable to accommodate consumer preferences for product diversity.

In response, Ohno looked for ways to make shorter production runs economical. He developed a number of techniques designed to reduce setup times for production equipment (a major source of fixed costs). By using a system of levers and pulleys, he reduced the time required to change dies on stamping equipment from a full day in 1950 to 3 minutes by 1971. This made small production runs economical, which allowed Toyota to respond better to consumer demands for product diversity. Small production runs also eliminated the need to hold large inventories, thereby reducing warehousing costs. Furthermore, small product runs and the lack of inventory meant that defective parts were produced only in small numbers and entered the assembly process immediately. This reduced waste and helped trace defects back to their source to fix the problem. In sum, Ohno's innovations enabled Toyota to produce a more diverse product range at a lower unit cost than was possible with conventional mass production.[11]

Flexible machine cells are another common flexible manufacturing technology. A flexible machine cell is a grouping of various types of machinery, a common materials handler, and a centralized cell controller (computer). Each cell normally contains four to six machines capable of performing a variety of operations. The typical cell is dedicated to the production of a family of parts or products. The settings on machines are computer controlled, which allows each cell to switch quickly between the production of different parts or products.

Improved capacity utilization and reductions in work-in-progress (that is, stockpiles of partly finished products) and in waste are major efficiency benefits of flexible machine cells. Improved capacity utilization arises from the reduction in setup times and from the computer-controlled coordination of production flow between machines, which eliminates bottlenecks. The tight coordination between machines also reduces work-in-progress inventory. Reductions in waste are due to the ability of computer-controlled machinery to identify ways to transform inputs into outputs while producing a minimum of unusable waste material. While freestanding machines might be in use 50 percent of the time, the same machines when grouped into a cell can be used more than 80 percent of the time and produce the same end product with half the waste. This increases efficiency and results in lower costs.

The efficiency benefits of installing flexible manufacturing technology can be dramatic. W. L. Gore, a privately owned company that manufactures a range of products from high-tech computer cables to its famous Gore-Tex fabric, has adopted flexible cells in several of its 46 factories. In its cable-making facilities, flexible cells have cut the time taken to make computer cables by 50 percent, reduced stock by 33 percent, and shrunk plant space by 25 percent. Similarly, Compaq Computer, the manufacturer of personal computers, replaced 3 of the 16 assembly lines in its Houston factory with 21 cells. The result: employee productivity rose by 25 percent and the cost of converting the three assembly lines to cells was recouped in six months. Lexmark, a producer of computer printers, has also converted 80 percent of its 2,700-employee factory in Lexington, Kentucky, to flexible manufacturing cells, and it too has seen productivity increase by around 25 percent.[12]

Besides improving efficiency and lowering costs, flexible manufacturing technologies also enable companies to customize products to the unique demands of small consumer groups—at a cost that at one time could be achieved only by mass producing a standardized output. Thus, the technologies help a company achieve mass customization, which increases its customer responsiveness. Most important for an international business, flexible manufacturing technologies can help the firm customize products for different national markets. The importance of this advantage cannot be overstated. When flexible manufacturing technologies are available, a firm can manufacture products customized to various national markets at a single factory sited at the optimal location. And it can do this without absorbing a significant cost penalty. Thus, companies no longer need to establish manufacturing facilities in each major national market to provide products that satisfy specific consumer tastes and preferences, part of the rationale for a multidomestic strategy (Chapter 12).

Summary

A number of technological factors support the economic arguments for concentrating manufacturing facilities in a few choice locations or even in a single location. Other things being equal, when fixed costs are substantial, the minimum efficient scale of production is high, and/or flexible manufacturing technologies are available, the arguments for concentrating production at a few choice locations are strong.

This is true even when substantial differences in consumer tastes and preferences exist between national markets, since flexible manufacturing technologies allow the firm to customize products to national differences at a single facility. Alternatively, when fixed costs are low, the minimum efficient scale of production is low, and flexible manufacturing technologies are not available, the arguments for concentrating production at one or a few locations are not as compelling. In such cases, it may make more sense to manufacture in each major market in which the firm is active if this helps the firm better respond to local demands. This holds only if the increased local responsiveness more than offsets the cost disadvantages of not concentrating manufacturing. With the advent of flexible manufacturing technologies and mass customization, such a strategy is becoming less attractive. In sum, technological factors are making it feasible, and necessary, for firms to concentrate manufacturing facilities at optimal locations. Trade barriers and transportation costs are major brakes on this trend.

Product Factors

Two product features affect location decisions. The first is the product's *value-to-weight* ratio because of its influence on transportation costs. Many electronic components and pharmaceuticals have high value-to-weight ratios; they are expensive and they do not weigh very much. Thus, even if they are shipped halfway around the world, their transportation costs account for a very small percentage of total costs. Given this, other things being equal, there is great pressure to manufacture these products in the optimal location and to serve the world market from there. The opposite holds for products with low value-to-weight ratios. Refined sugar, certain bulk chemicals, paint, and petroleum products all have low value-to-weight ratios; they are relatively inexpensive products that weigh a lot. Accordingly, when they are shipped long distances, transportation costs account for a large percentage of total costs. Thus, other things being equal, there is great pressure to manufacture these products in multiple locations close to major markets to reduce transportation costs.

The other product feature that can influence location decisions is whether the product serves universal needs, needs that are the same all over the world. Examples include many industrial products (e.g., industrial electronics, steel, bulk chemicals) and modern consumer products (e.g., handheld calculators and personal computers). Since there are few national differences in consumer taste and preference for such products, the need for local responsiveness is reduced. This increases the attractiveness of concentrating manufacturing at an optimal location.

Locating Manufacturing Facilities

There are two basic strategies for locating manufacturing facilities: concentrating them in a centralized location and serving the world market from there, or decentralizing them in various regional or national locations that are close to major markets. The appropriate strategic choice is determined by the various country, technological, and product factors we have discussed in this section and are summarized in Table 16.1.

As can be seen, concentration of manufacturing makes most sense when:

- Differences between countries in factor costs, political economy, and culture have a substantial impact on the costs of manufacturing in various countries.
- Trade barriers are low.
- Externalities arising from the concentration of like enterprises favor certain locations.
- Important exchange rates are expected to remain relatively stable.
- The production technology has high fixed costs, a high minimum efficient scale, or a flexible manufacturing technology exists.

Table 16.1

Location Strategy and
Manufacturing

Country Factors	Concentrated Manufacturing Favored	Decentralized Manufacturing Favored
Differences in political economy	Substantial	Few
Differences in culture	Substantial	Few
Differences in factor costs	Substantial	Few
Trade barriers	Substantial	Few
Location externalities	Important in industry	Not important in industry
Exchange rates	Stable	Volatile
Technological Factors		
Fixed costs	High	Low
Minimum efficient scale	High	Low
Flexible manufacturing technology	Available	Not available
Product Factors		
Value-to-weight ratio	High	Low
Serves universal needs	Yes	No

- The product's value-to-weight ratio is high.
- The product serves universal needs.

Alternatively, decentralization of manufacturing is appropriate when:

- Differences between countries in factor costs, political economy, and culture do not have a substantial impact on the costs of manufacturing in various countries.
- Trade barriers are high.
- Location externalities are not important.
- Volatility in important exchange rates is expected.
- The production technology has low fixed costs, low minimum efficient scale, and flexible manufacturing technology is not available.
- The product's value-to-weight ratio is low.
- The product does not serve universal needs (that is, significant differences in consumer tastes and preferences exist between nations).

In practice, location decisions are seldom clear cut. For example, it is not unusual for differences in factor costs, technological factors, and product factors to point toward concentrated manufacturing while a combination of trade barriers and volatile exchange rates points toward decentralized manufacturing. For example, this seems to be the case in the world automobile industry. Although the availability of flexible manufacturing and cars' relatively high value-to-weight ratios suggest concentrated manufacturing, the combination of formal and informal trade barriers and the uncertainties of the world's current floating exchange rate regime (see Chapter 10) have inhibited firms' ability to pursue this strategy. For these reasons, several automobile companies have established "top-to-bottom" manufacturing operations in three major regional markets: Asia, North America, and Western Europe.

The Strategic Role of Foreign Factories ■

Whatever the rationale behind establishing a foreign manufacturing facility, the strategic role of foreign factories can evolve over time.[13] Initially, many foreign factories are established where labor costs are low. Their strategic role typically is to produce labor-intensive products at as low a cost as possible. For example, beginning in the 1970s, many U.S. firms in the computer and telecommunication equipment businesses established factories across Southeast Asia to manufacture electronic components, such as circuit boards and semiconductors, at the lowest possible cost. They located their factories in countries such as Malaysia, Thailand, and Singapore precisely because each of these countries offered an attractive combination of low labor costs, adequate infrastructure, and a favorable tax and trade regime. Initially, the components produced by these factories were designed elsewhere and the final product would be assembled elsewhere. Over time, however, the strategic role of some of these factories has expanded; they have become important centers for the design and final assembly of products for the global marketplace. An example is Hewlett-Packard's operation in Singapore. Originally established as a low-cost location for the production of circuit boards, the facility has become the center for the design and final assembly of portable ink-jet printers for the global marketplace (see the accompanying Management Focus).

Such upward migration in the strategic role of foreign factories arises because many foreign factories upgrade their own capabilities.[14] This improvement comes from two sources. First, pressure from the center to improve a factory's cost structure and/or customize a product to the demands of consumers in a particular nation can start a chain of events that ultimately leads to development of additional capabilities at that factory. For example, to meet centrally mandated directions to drive down costs, engineers at HP's Singapore factory argued that they needed to redesign products so they could be manufactured at a lower cost. This led to the establishment of a design center in Singapore. As this design center proved its worth, HP executives realized the importance of co-locating design and manufacturing operations. They increasingly transferred more design responsibilities to the Singapore factory. In addition, the Singapore factory ultimately became the center for the design of products tailored to the needs of the Asian market. This too made good strategic sense because it meant products were being designed by engineers who were close to the Asian market and probably had a good understanding of the needs of that market, as opposed to engineers located in the United States.

A second source of improvement in the capabilities of a foreign factory can be the increasing abundance of advanced factors of production in the nation in which the factory is located. Many nations that were considered economic backwaters a generation ago have been experiencing rapid economic development during the 1980s and 1990s. Their communication and transportation infrastructures and the education level of the population have improved. While these countries once lacked the advanced infrastructure required to support sophisticated design, development, and manufacturing operations, this is often no longer the case. This has made it much easier for factories based in these nations to take on a greater strategic role.

Because of such developments, many international businesses are moving away from a system in which their foreign factories were viewed as nothing more than low-cost manufacturing facilities and toward one where foreign factories are viewed as globally dispersed centers of excellence. In this new model, foreign factories take the lead role for the design and manufacture of products to serve important national or regional markets or even the global market. The development of such dispersed centers of excellence is consistent with the concept of a transnational strategy, which we introduced in Chapter 12. A major aspect of a transnational strategy is a belief in global learning—the idea that valuable knowledge does not reside just in a firm's domestic

Hewlett-Packard in Singapore

Management Focus

In the late 1960s, Hewlett-Packard was looking around Asia for a low-cost location to produce electronic components that were to be manufactured using labor-intensive processes. The company looked at several Asian locations and eventually settled on Singapore, opening its first factory there in 1970. Although Singapore did not have the lowest labor costs in the region, costs were low relative to North America. Plus, the Singapore location had several important benefits that could not be found at many other locations in Asia. The education level of the local workforce was high. English was widely spoken. The government of Singapore seemed stable and committed to economic development, and the city-state had one of the better-developed infrastructures in the region, including good communication and transportation networks and a rapidly developing industrial and commercial base. HP also extracted favorable terms from the Singapore government with regard to taxes, tariffs, and subsidies.

To begin with, the plant manufactured only basic components. The combination of low labor costs and a favorable tax regime helped to make this plant profitable early. In 1973, HP transferred the manufacture of one of its basic handheld calculators from the United States to Singapore. The objective was to reduce manufacturing costs, which the Singapore factory was quickly able to do. Increasingly confident in the capability of the Singapore factory to handle entire products, as opposed to just components, HP's management transferred other products to Singapore over the next few years including keyboards, solid-state displays, and integrated circuits. However, all these products were still designed, developed, and initially produced in the United States.

The plant's status shifted in the early 1980s when HP embarked on a worldwide campaign to boost product quality and reduce costs. HP transferred the production of its HP41C handheld calculator to Singapore. The managers at the Singapore plant were given the goal of substantially reducing manufacturing costs. They argued that this could be achieved only if they were allowed to redesign the product so it could be manufactured at a lower overall cost. HP's central management agreed, and 20 engineers from the Singapore facility were transferred to the United States for one year to learn how to design application-specific integrated circuits. They then brought this expertise back to Singapore and set about redesigning the HP41C.

The results were a huge success. By redesigning the product, the Singapore engineers reduced manufacturing costs for the HP41C by 50 percent. Using this newly acquired capability for product design, the Singapore facility then set about redesigning other products it produced. HP's corporate managers were so impressed with the progress made at the factory, they transferred production of the entire calculator line to Singapore in 1983. This was followed by the partial transfer of ink-jet production to Singapore in 1984 and keyboard production in 1986. In all cases, the facility redesigned the products and often reduced unit manufacturing costs by more than 30 percent. The initial development and design of all these products, however, still occurred in the United States.

In the late 1980s and early 1990s, the Singapore plant started to take on added responsibilities, particularly in the ink-jet printer business. In 1990, the factory was given the job of redesigning an HP ink-jet printer for the Japanese market. Although the initial product redesign was a market failure, the managers at Singapore pushed to be allowed to try again, and in 1991 they were given the job of redesigning HP's DeskJet 505 printer for the Japanese market. This time the redesigned product was a success, garnering significant sales in Japan. Emboldened by this success, the plant has continued to take on additional design responsibilities. Today, it is viewed as a "lead plant" within HP's global network, with primary responsibility not just for manufacturing, but also for the development and design of a family of small ink-jet printers targeted at the Asian market.

Sources: K. Ferdows, "Making the Most of Foreign Factories," *Harvard Business Review*, March–April 1997, pp. 73–88, and "Hewlett-Packard: Singapore," Harvard Business School, case # 694–035.

operations; it may also be found in its foreign subsidiaries. Foreign factories that up-grade their capabilities over time are creating valuable knowledge that might benefit the whole corporation.

Managers of international businesses need to remember that foreign factories can improve their capabilities over time, and this can be of immense strategic benefit to the firm. Rather than viewing foreign factories simply as sweatshops where unskilled labor churns out low-cost goods, managers need to view them as potential centers of excellence and to encourage and foster attempts by local managers to upgrade the ca-pabilities of their factories and, thereby, enhance their strategic standing within the corporation.

Such a process does imply that once a foreign factory has been established and valu-able skills have been accumulated, it may not be wise to switch production to another location simply because some underlying variable, such as wage rates, has changed.[15] HP has kept its facility in Singapore, rather than switching production to a location where wage rates are now much lower, such as Vietnam, because it recognizes that the Singapore factory has accumulated valuable skills that more than make up for the higher wage rates. Thus, when reviewing the location of production facilities, the in-ternational manager must bear in mind the valuable skills that may have been accu-mulated at various locations, and the impact of those skills on factors such as productivity and product design.

Make-or-Buy Decisions ▮

International businesses frequently face sourcing decisions, decisions about whether they should make or buy the component parts that go into their final product. Should the firm vertically integrate to manufacture its own component parts or should it out-source them, or buy them from independent suppliers? Make-or-buy decisions are im-portant factors of many firms' manufacturing strategies. In the automobile industry, for example, the typical car contains more than 10,000 components, so automobile firms constantly face make-or-buy decisions. Ford of Europe, for example, produces only about 45 percent of the value of the Fiesta in its own plants. The remaining 55 per-cent, mainly accounted for by component parts, comes from independent suppliers. In the athletic shoe industry, the make-or-buy issue has been taken to an extreme with companies such as Nike and Reebok having no involvement in manufacturing; all pro-duction has been outsourced, primarily to manufacturers based in low-wage countries. Similarly, as we saw in the opening case, Timberland outsources some 85 percent of shoe production to independent firms.

Make-or-buy decisions pose plenty of problems for purely domestic businesses but even more problems for international businesses. These decisions in the international arena are complicated by the volatility of countries' political economies, exchange rate movements, changes in relative factor costs, and the like. In this section, we ex-amine the arguments for making components and for buying them, and we consider the trade-offs involved in these decisions. Then we discuss strategic alliances as an al-ternative to manufacturing component parts within the company.

▮The Advantages of Make

The arguments that support making component parts in-house—vertical integration—are fourfold. Vertical integration may be associated with lower costs, facilitate invest-ments in highly specialized assets, protect proprietary product technology, and facilitate the scheduling of adjacent processes.

Lower Costs

It may pay a firm to continue manufacturing a product or component part in-house if the firm is more efficient at that production activity than any other enterprise. Boeing, for example, has looked closely at its make-or-buy decisions with regard to commercial jet aircraft (for details see the accompanying Management Focus). It decided to outsource the production of some component parts but keep the production of aircraft wings in-house. Boeing's rationale was that it has a core competence in the production of wings, and it is more efficient at this activity than any other comparable enterprise in the world. Therefore, it makes little sense for Boeing to outsource this particular activity.

Facilitating Specialized Investments

We first encountered the concept of specialized assets in Chapter 6 when we looked at the economic theory of vertical foreign direct investment. A variation of that concept explains why firms might want to make their own components rather than buy them.[16] When one firm must invest in specialized assets to supply another, mutual dependency is created. In such circumstances, each party fears the other will abuse the relationship by seeking more favorable terms.

Imagine Ford of Europe has developed a new, high-performance, high-quality, and uniquely designed carburetor. The carburetor's increased fuel efficiency will help sell Ford cars. Ford must decide whether to make the carburetor in-house or to contract out the manufacturing to an independent supplier. Manufacturing these uniquely designed carburetors requires investments in equipment that can be used only for this purpose; it cannot be used to make carburetors for any other auto firm. Thus, investment in this equipment constitutes an investment in specialized assets.

Let us first examine this situation from the perspective of an independent supplier who has been asked by Ford to make this investment. The supplier might reason that once it has made the investment, it will become dependent on Ford for business since Ford is the only possible customer for the output of this equipment. The supplier perceives this as putting Ford in a strong bargaining position and worries that once the specialized investment has been made, Ford might use this to squeeze down prices for the carburetors. Given this risk, the supplier declines to make the investment in specialized equipment. Now take the position of Ford. Ford might reason that if it contracts out production of these carburetors to an independent supplier, it might become too dependent on that supplier for a vital input. Because specialized equipment is required to produce the carburetors, Ford cannot easily switch its orders to other suppliers who lack that equipment. (It would face high switching costs.) Ford perceives this as increasing the bargaining power of the supplier and worries that the supplier might use its bargaining strength to demand higher prices.

Thus, the mutual dependency that outsourcing would create makes Ford nervous and scares away potential suppliers. The problem here is lack of trust. Neither party completely trusts the other to play fair. Consequently, Ford might reason that the only safe way to get the new carburetors is to manufacture them itself. It may be unable to persuade any independent supplier to manufacture them. Thus, Ford decides to make rather than buy.

In general, we can predict that when substantial investments in specialized assets are required to manufacture a component, the firm will prefer to make the component internally rather than contract it out to a supplier. A growing amount of empirical evidence supports this prediction.[17]

Proprietary Product Technology Protection

Proprietary product technology is technology unique to a firm. If it enables the firm to produce a product containing superior features, proprietary technology can give the firm a competitive advantage. The firm would not want this technology to fall into the hands of competitors. If the firm contracts out the manufacture of components containing proprietary technology, it runs the risk that those suppliers will expropriate the technology for their own use or that they will sell it to the firm's competitors. Thus, to maintain control over its technology, the firm might prefer to make such component parts in-house. An example of a firm that has made such decisions is given in the accompanying Management Focus, which looks at make-or-buy decisions at Boeing. While Boeing has decided to outsource a number of important components that go toward the production of an aircraft, it has explicitly decided not to outsource the manufacture of wings and cockpits because it believes that doing so would give away key technology to potential competitors.

Improved Scheduling

The weakest argument for vertical integration is that production cost savings result from it because it makes planning, coordination, and scheduling of adjacent processes easier.[18] This is particularly important in firms with just-in-time inventory systems (which we discuss later in the chapter). In the 1920s, for example, Ford profited from tight coordination and scheduling made possible by backward vertical integration into steel foundries, iron ore shipping, and mining. Deliveries at Ford's foundries on the Great Lakes were coordinated so well that ore was turned into engine blocks within 24 hours. This substantially reduced Ford's production costs by eliminating the need to hold excessive ore inventories.

For international businesses that source worldwide, scheduling problems can be exacerbated by the time and distance between the firm and its suppliers. This is true whether the firms use their own subunits as suppliers or use independent suppliers. Ownership is not the issue here. As we saw in the closing case, Timberland can achieve tight scheduling with its globally dispersed parts suppliers without vertical integration. Thus, although this argument for vertical integration is often made, it is not compelling.

The Advantages of Buy

The advantages of buying component parts from independent suppliers are that it gives the firm greater flexibility, it can help drive down the firm's cost structure, and it may help the firm to capture orders from international customers.

Strategic Flexibility

The great advantage of buying component parts from independent suppliers is that the firm can maintain its flexibility, switching orders between suppliers as circumstances dictate. This is particularly important internationally, where changes in exchange rates and trade barriers can alter the attractiveness of supply sources. One year Hong Kong might be the lowest-cost source for a particular component, and the next year, Mexico may be. Many firms source the same parts from suppliers based in two different countries, primarily as a hedge against adverse movements in factor costs, exchange rates, and the like.

Sourcing component parts from independent suppliers can also be advantageous when the optimal location for manufacturing a product is beset by political risks. Under such circumstances, foreign direct investment to establish a component manufacturing operation in that country would expose the firm to political risks. The firm can avoid many of these risks by buying from an independent supplier in that country, thereby maintaining the flexibility to switch sourcing to another country if a war, revolution, or other political change alters that country's attractiveness as a supply source.

However, maintaining strategic flexibility has its downside. If a supplier perceives the firm will change suppliers in response to changes in exchange rates, trade barriers, or general political circumstances, that supplier might not be willing to make specialized investments in plant and equipment that would ultimately benefit the firm.

Lower Costs

Although vertical integration is often undertaken to lower costs, it may have the opposite effect. When this is the case, outsourcing may lower the firm's cost structure. Vertical integration into the manufacture of component parts increases an organization's scope, and the resulting increase in organizational complexity can raise a firm's cost structure. There are three reasons for this.

First, the greater the number of subunits in an organization, the greater are the problems of coordinating and controlling those units. Coordinating and controlling subunits require top management to process large amounts of information about subunit activities. The greater the number of subunits, the more information top management must process and the harder it is to do well. Theoretically, when the firm becomes involved in too many activities, headquarters management will be unable to effectively control all of them, and the resulting inefficiencies will more than offset any advantages derived from vertical integration.[19] This can be particularly serious in an international business, where the problem of controlling subunits is exacerbated by distance and differences in time, language, and culture.

Second, the firm that vertically integrates into component part manufacture may find that because its internal suppliers have a captive customer in the firm, they lack an incentive to reduce costs. The fact that they do not have to compete for orders with other suppliers may result in high operating costs. The managers of the supply operation may be tempted to pass on cost increases to other parts of the firm in the form of higher transfer prices, rather than looking for ways to reduce those costs.

Third, vertically integrated firms have to determine appropriate prices for goods transferred to subunits within the firm. This is a challenge in any firm, but it is even more complex in international businesses. Different tax regimes, exchange rate movements, and headquarters' ignorance about local conditions all increase the complexity of transfer pricing decisions. This complexity enhances internal suppliers' ability to manipulate transfer prices to their advantage, passing cost increases downstream rather than looking for ways to reduce costs.

The firm that buys its components from independent suppliers can avoid all these problems and the associated costs. The firm that sources from independent suppliers has fewer subunits to control. The incentive problems that occur with internal suppliers do not arise when independent suppliers are used. Independent suppliers know they must continue to be efficient if they are to win business from the firm. Also, because independent suppliers' prices are set by market forces, the transfer pricing problem does not exist. In sum, the bureaucratic inefficiencies and resulting costs that can arise when firms vertically integrate backward and manufacture their own components are avoided by buying component parts from independent suppliers.

Offsets

Another reason for outsourcing some manufacturing to independent suppliers based in other countries is that it may help the firm capture more orders from that country. As noted in the Management Focus on Boeing, the practice of offsets is common in the commercial aerospace industry. For example, before Air India places a large order with Boeing, the Indian government might ask Boeing to push some subcontracting work toward Indian manufacturers. This kind of quid pro quo is not unusual in international business, and it affects far more than just the aerospace industry. Representatives of the U.S. government have repeatedly urged Japanese automobile companies to purchase more component parts from U.S. suppliers in order to partially offset the large volume of automobile exports from Japan to the United States.

Trade-offs

Trade-offs are involved in make-or-buy decisions. The benefits of manufacturing components in-house seem to be greatest when highly specialized assets are involved, when vertical integration is necessary for protecting proprietary technology, or when the firm is simply more efficient than external suppliers at performing a particular activity.

When these conditions are not present, the risk of strategic inflexibility and organizational problems suggest it may be better to contract out component part manu-

Management Focus

Make-or-Buy Decisions at the Boeing Company

The Boeing Company is the world's largest manufacturer of commercial jet aircraft with a 55 to 60 percent share of the global market. Despite its large market share, in recent years Boeing has found it tough going competitively. The company's problems are twofold. First, Boeing faces a very aggressive competitor in Europe's Airbus Industrie. The dogfight between Boeing and Airbus for market share has enabled major airlines to play the two companies off against each other in an attempt to bargain down the price for commercial jet aircraft. Second, the airline business is quite cyclical and airlines sharply reduce orders for new aircraft when their own business is in a downturn. This occurred in the early 1990s and again in the early years of the new century. During downturns, some of which can be extended, intense price competition often occurs between Airbus and Boeing as they struggle to maintain market share and order volume in the face of falling demand. Given these pricing pressures, the only way that Boeing can maintain its profitability is to reduce its own manufacturing costs. With this in mind, during the 1990s Boeing launched an ongoing company wide review of its make-or-buy decisions. The objective was to identify activities that could be outsourced to subcontractors, both in the United States and abroad to drive down production costs.

When making outsourcing decisions, Boeing applies a number of criteria. First, Boeing looks at the basic economics of the outsourcing decision. The central issue here is whether an activity could be performed more cost-effectively by an outside manufacturer or by Boeing. Second, Boeing considers the strategic risk associated with outsourcing an activity. Boeing decided it would not outsource any activity that it deemed to be part of its long-term competitive advantage. For example, the company has decided not to outsource the production of wings because it believed that doing so might give away valuable technology to potential competitors. Third, Boeing looks at the operational risk associated with outsourcing an activity. The basic objective is to make sure Boeing does not become too dependent on a single outside supplier for critical components. Boeing's philosophy is to hedge operational risk by purchasing from two or more suppliers. Finally, Boeing considers whether it makes sense to outsource certain activities to a supplier in a given country to help secure orders for commercial jet aircraft from that country. This practice is known as offsetting, and it is common in many industries. For example, Boeing decided to outsource the production of certain components to China. This decision was influenced by forecasts suggesting that the Chinese will purchase over $100 billion worth of commercial jets over the next 20 years. Boeing's hope is that pushing some subcontracting work China's way will help it gain a larger share of this market than its global competitor, Airbus.

One of the first decisions to come out of this process was a move to outsource the production of insulation blankets for 737 and 757 aircraft to suppliers in Mexico. Insulation blankets are wrapped around the inside of the fuselage of an aircraft to keep the interior warm at high altitudes. Boeing has traditionally made these blankets in-house, but found that it could save $50 million per year by outsourcing production to a Mexican supplier. In total, Boeing reckons that outsourcing cuts its annual cost structure by $500 million per year.

Source: Based on interviews between Charles Hill and senior management personnel at Boeing.

---

facturing to independent suppliers. Since issues of strategic flexibility and organizational control loom even larger for international businesses than purely domestic ones, an international business should be particularly wary of vertical integration into component part manufacture. In addition, some outsourcing in the form of offsets may help a firm gain larger orders in the future.

Strategic Alliances with Suppliers

Several international businesses have tried to reap some benefits of vertical integration without the associated organizational problems by entering strategic alliances with essential suppliers. For example, in recent years we have seen an alliance between

Kodak and Canon, under which Canon builds photocopiers for sale by Kodak, and an alliance between Apple and Sony, under which Sony builds laptop computers for Apple. By these alliances, Kodak and Apple have committed themselves to long-term relationships with these suppliers, which have encouraged the suppliers to undertake specialized investments. Strategic alliances build trust between the firm and its suppliers. Trust is built when a firm makes a credible commitment to continue purchasing from a supplier on reasonable terms. For example, the firm may invest money in a supplier—perhaps by taking a minority shareholding—to signal its intention to build a productive, mutually beneficial long-term relationship.

This kind of arrangement between the firm and its parts suppliers was pioneered in Japan by large auto companies such as Toyota. Many Japanese automakers have cooperative relationships with their suppliers that go back decades. In these relationships, the auto companies and their suppliers collaborate on ways to increase value added by, for example, implementing just-in-time inventory systems or cooperating in the design of component parts to improve quality and reduce assembly costs. These relationships have been formalized when the auto firms acquired minority shareholdings in many of their essential suppliers to symbolize their desire for long-term cooperative relationships with them. At the same time, the relationship between the firm and each essential supplier remains market mediated and terminable if the supplier fails to perform. By pursuing such a strategy, the Japanese automakers capture many of the benefits of vertical integration, particularly those arising from investments in specialized assets, without suffering the organizational problems that come with formal vertical integration. The parts suppliers also benefit from these relationships because they grow with the firm they supply and share in its success. Because of these strategies, Toyota manufactures only 27 percent of its component parts in-house, compared to 48 percent at Ford and 67 percent at GM. Of these three firms, Toyota appears to spend the least on component parts, suggesting it has captured many of the benefits that induced Ford and GM to vertically integrate.[20]

In general, the trends toward just-in-time inventory systems (JIT), computer-aided design (CAD), and computer-aided manufacturing (CAM) seem to have increased pressures for firms to establish long-term relationships with their suppliers. JIT, CAD, and CAM systems all rely on close links between firms and their suppliers supported by substantial specialized investment in equipment and information systems hardware. To get a supplier to agree to adopt such systems, a firm must make a credible commitment to an enduring relationship with the supplier—it must build trust with the supplier. It can do this within the framework of a strategic alliance.

Alliances are not all good. Like formal vertical integration, a firm that enters long-term alliances may limit its strategic flexibility by the commitments it makes to its alliance partners. As we saw in Chapter 14 when we considered alliances between competitors, a firm that allies itself with another firm risks giving away key technological know-how to a potential competitor.

▊ Coordinating a Global Manufacturing System

Materials management, which encompasses logistics, embraces the activities necessary to get materials from suppliers to a manufacturing facility, through the manufacturing process, and out through a distribution system to the end user.[21] The twin objectives of materials management are to achieve this at the lowest possible cost and in a way that best serves customer needs, thereby lowering the costs of value creation and helping the firm establish a competitive advantage through superior customer service. The potential for reducing costs through more efficient materials management is enormous. For the typical manufacturing enterprise, material costs account for between 50 and 70 percent of revenues, depending on the industry. Even a small reduction in these costs can have a substantial impact on profitability. According to one estimate, for a firm with revenues of $1 million, a return on investment rate of 5 percent, and materials costs that are 50 percent of sales revenues, a $15,000 increase in total profits could be achieved either by increasing sales revenues 30 percent or by reducing materials costs by 3 percent.[22] In a saturated market, it would be much easier to reduce materials costs by 3 percent than to increase sales revenues by 30 percent.

As we saw in the opening case on Timberland, materials management is a major undertaking in a firm with a globally dispersed manufacturing system and global markets. In recent years, a number of international businesses have established reputations for superior materials management. Dell Computer, which is profiled in the accompanying Management Focus, is an example. Dell's great advantage has been its ability to harness the power of the Internet to link orders from customers with its globally dispersed supply chain in order to match demand and supply, driving excess inventory out of its system and significantly reducing its cost structure.

The Power of Just-in-Time

Pioneered by Japanese firms during the 1950s and 60s, just-in-time inventory systems now play a major role in most manufacturing firms (see the Management Focus on Dell Computer). The basic philosophy behind just-in-time (JIT) systems is to economize on inventory holding costs by having materials arrive at a manufacturing plant just in time to enter the production process and not before. The major cost saving comes from speeding up inventory turnover. This reduces inventory holding costs, such as warehousing and storage costs. It also means the company is less likely to have excess unsold inventory that it has to write off against earnings or price low to sell. In addition to the cost benefits, JIT systems can also help firms improve product quality. Under a JIT system, parts enter the manufacturing process immediately; they are not warehoused. This allows defective inputs to be spotted right away. The problem can then be traced to the supply source and fixed before more defective parts are produced. Under a more traditional system, warehousing parts for months before they are used allows many defective parts to be produced before a problem is recognized.

The drawback of a JIT system is that it leaves a firm without a buffer stock of inventory. Although buffer stocks are expensive to store, they can tide a firm over shortages brought about by disruption among suppliers (such as a labor dispute). Buffer stocks can also help a firm respond quickly to increases in demand. However, there are ways around these limitations. To reduce the risks associated with depending on one supplier for an important input, some firms source these inputs from several suppliers. As for responding quickly to increases in consumer demand, the experience of Dell Computer shows that it is possible to do this while maintaining a JIT system (see the Management Focus).

The Role of Organization

As the number and dispersion of domestic and foreign markets and sources grow, the number and complexity of organizational linkages increase correspondingly. In a multinational enterprise, the challenge of managing the costs associated with purchases, currency exchange, inbound and outbound transportation, production, inventory, communication, expediting, tariffs and duties, and overall administration is massive. Figure 16.3 shows the linkages that might exist for a firm that sources, manufactures, and sells internationally. Each linkage represents a flow of materials, capital, information, decisions, and people. The firm must figure out the best organization to achieve tight coordination of the various stages of the value creation process.

A major requirement seems to be to separate out materials management as a function and give it equal weight, in organizational terms, with other more traditional functions such as manufacturing, marketing, and R&D. According to materials management specialists, purchasing, production, and distribution are not separate

Dell Computer—Replacing Inventories with Information

Michael Dell started Dell Computer Corporation in 1984 when he was an undergraduate student at the University of Texas. Sixteen years later Dell had grown to become one of the world's great computer companies, with a leading share in the personal computer and server businesses, and global sales of $32 billion, one-third of which are made outside the United States. To support its global business, Dell has manufacturing sites in Brazil, Ireland, Malaysia, and China, in addition to the United States. Its supply base is also global, consisting of some 200 suppliers, more than half of which are located outside the United States. Some 30 suppliers accounting for about 75 percent of Dell's total purchases. Over 50 percent of its major suppliers are in Asia.

From inception, Dell's business model was based on direct selling to customers, cutting out wholesalers and retails. The original thought was that by cutting out the middlemen in the distribution chain, Dell could offer consumers lower prices. Initially, direct selling was achieved through mailings and telephone contacts, but since the mid-1990s the majority of Dell's sales have been made over the Internet, and by 2000, some 80 percent of all sales were made through this medium. Internet selling has enabled Dell to offer its customers the ability to customize their orders, mixing and matching product features such as microprocessors, memory, monitors, internal hard drives, CD and DVD drives, keyboard and mouse format, and the like, to get the system that best suits their particular requirements.

While the ability to customize products, when combined with low prices, has made Dell very attractive to customers, the real power of the business model is to be found in how Dell manages its global supply chain to minimize inventory while building PCs to individual customer orders within three days. Dell uses the Internet to feed real-time information about order flow to its suppliers. Dell's suppliers have up-to-the-minute information about demand trends for the components they produce, along with volume expectations for the next 4 to 12 weeks that are constantly updated as new information becomes available. Dell's suppliers use this information to adjust their own production schedules on a real-time basis, producing just enough components for Dell's needs and shipping them by the most appropriate mode, typically truck or air express so that they arrive just in time for production. This tight coordination is being pushed back even further down the supply chain, with Dell sharing key data with its suppliers' principal suppliers. For example, Selectron builds motherboards for Dell that incorporate digital signal processing chips from Texas Instruments. To better coordinate the supply chain, Dell passes information to Texas Instruments in addition to Selectron. This allows Texas Instrument to adjust its schedules to Selectron's needs, which in turn adjusts its schedule to order data from Dell.

Dell's ultimate goal is to drive all inventories out of the supply chain apart from that in transit between suppliers and Dell, effectively replacing inventory with information. Although Dell has not yet achieved this goal, the firm has reduced inventory to the lowest level in the industry. Dell carries about five days of inventory on hand, compared to 30, 45, or even 90 days' worth at competitors such as Compaq Computer and IBM. This is a critical advantage in the computer inventory, where component costs account for 75 percent of revenues and typically fall by 1 percent per week due to rapid obsolescence. For example, when larger, faster hard drives are introduced, which occurs every three to six months, the value of previous-generation hard drives is significantly reduced. So if Dell holds one week of inventory, and a competitor holds four weeks, this translates immediately into 3 percent worth of component cost advantage to Dell, which can mean a 2 percent advantage on the bottom line.

Dell's Internet-based customer ordering and procurement systems have also allowed the company to synchronize demand and supply to an extent that few other companies can. For example, if Dell sees that it is running out of a particular component, say 17-inch monitors from Sony, it can manipulate demand by offering a 19-inch model at a lower price until Sony delivers more 17-inch monitors. By taking such steps to fine-tune the balance between demand and supply, Dell can meet customers' expectations. Also, balancing supply and demand allows the company to minimize excess and obsolete inventory. Dell writes off between 0.05 percent and 0.1 percent of total materials costs in excess or obsolete inventory. Its competitors write off between 2 percent and 3 percent, which again gives Dell a significant cost advantage.

Sources: D. Hunter, "How Dell Keeps from Stumbling," *Business Week,* May 14, 2001, pp. 38–40; "Enter the Eco-system: From Supply Chain to Network," *The Economist,* November 11, 2000; and "Dell's Direct Initiative," *Country Monitor,* June 7, 2000, p. 5.

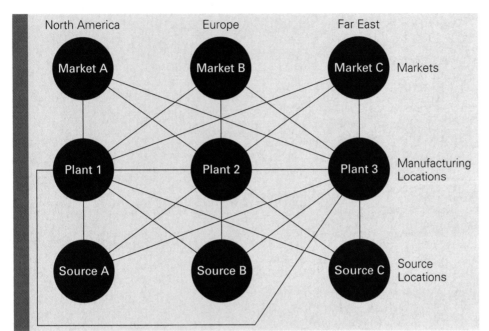

Figure 16.3

Potential Materials
Management Linkages

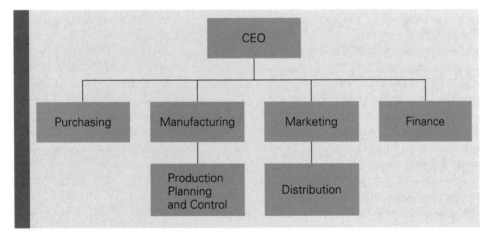

Figure 16.4A

Traditional Organizational
Structure

activities but three aspects of one basic task: controlling the flow of materials and products from sources of supply through manufacturing and distribution into the hands of customers.

Despite the apparent cost and quality control advantages of having a separate materials management function, all firms do not operate with such a function.[23] Those that do not include many firms in which purchasing costs, inventories, and customer service levels are important, interdependent aspects of establishing competitive advantage. Such firms typically operate with a traditional organizational structure similar to the one in Figure 16.4A. In such an organization, purchasing, production planning and control, and distribution are not integrated. Planning and control are part of the manufacturing function, while distribution is part of the marketing function. Such companies will be unable to establish materials management as a major strength and consequently may face higher costs. Figure 16.4B shows the structure of a typical organization in which materials management is a separate function. Purchasing, planning and control, and distribution are integrated within the materials management function. Such an arrangement allows the firm to transform materials management into an important strength.

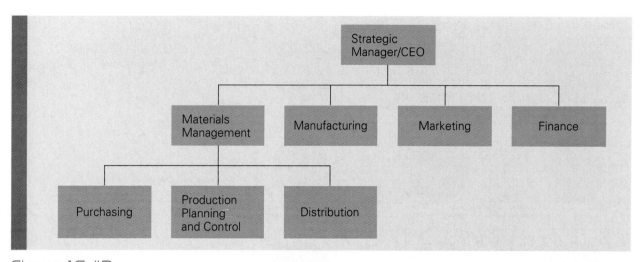

Figure 16.4B

Organizational Structure with Materials Management as Separate Function

Having established the legitimacy of materials management, the next dilemma is determining the best structure in a multinational enterprise. In practice, authority is either centralized or decentralized.[24] Under a centralized solution, most materials management decisions are made at the corporate level, which can ensure efficiency and adherence to overall corporate objectives. This is the case at Dell Computer, for example. In large, complex organizations with many manufacturing plants, however, a centralized materials management function may become overloaded and unable to perform its task effectively. In such cases, a decentralized solution is needed.

A decentralized solution delegates most materials management decisions to the level of individual manufacturing plants within the firm, although corporate headquarters retains responsibility for overseeing the function. The great advantage of decentralizing is that it allows plant-level materials management groups to develop the knowledge and skills needed for interacting with foreign suppliers that are important to their particular plant. This can lead to better decision making. The disadvantage is that a lack of coordination between plants can result in less than optimal global sourcing. It can also lead to duplication of materials management efforts. These disadvantages can be attenuated, however, by information systems that enable headquarters to coordinate the various plant-level materials management groups.

The Role of Information Technology and the Internet

As we saw in the Management Focus on Dell Computer, Web-based information systems play a crucial role in modern materials management. By tracking component parts as they make their way across the globe toward an assembly plant, information systems enable a firm to optimize its production scheduling according to when components are expected to arrive. By locating component parts in the supply chain precisely, good information systems allow the firm to accelerate production when needed by pulling key components out of the regular supply chain and having them flown to the manufacturing plant.

Firms increasingly use electronic data interchange to coordinate the flow of materials into manufacturing, through manufacturing, and out to customers. As at Dell, the ultimate goal here should be to replace inventory with information. EDI systems require computer links between a firm, its suppliers, and its shippers. Sometimes customers also are integrated into the system as at Dell. These electronic links are then used to place orders with suppliers, to register parts leaving a supplier, to track them as they travel toward a manufacturing plant, and to register their arrival. Suppliers typically use an EDI link to send invoices to the purchasing firm. One consequence of an EDI system is that suppliers, shippers, and the purchasing firm can communicate with each other with no time delay, which increases the flexibility and responsiveness of the whole supply system. A second consequence is that much of the paperwork between suppliers, shippers, and the purchasing firm is eliminated. Good EDI systems can help a firm decentralize materials management decisions to the plant level by giving corporate-level managers the information they need for coordinating and controlling decentralized materials management groups.

Before the emergence of the Internet as a major communication medium, firms and their suppliers normally had to purchase expensive proprietary software solutions to implement EDI systems. The ubiquity of the Internet and the availability of Web-based applications have made most of these proprietary solutions obsolete. Less expensive Web-based systems that are much easier to install and manage now dominate the market for supply chain management software. These Web-based systems are rapidly transforming the management of globally dispersed supply chains, allowing even small firms to achieve a much better balance between supply and demand, thereby reducing the inventory in their systems and reaping the associated economic benefits. With increasing numbers of firms adopting these systems, those that don't may find themselves at a significant competitive disadvantage.

Chapter Summary

This chapter explained how efficient manufacturing and materials management functions can improve an international business's competitive position by lowering the costs of value creation and by performing value creation activities in such ways that customer service is enhanced and value added is maximized. We looked closely at three issues central to international manufacturing and materials management: where to manufacture, what to make and what to buy, and how to coordinate a globally dispersed manufacturing and supply system. This chapter made the following points:

1. The choice of an optimal manufacturing location must consider country factors, technological factors, and product factors.

2. Country factors include the influence of factor costs, political economy, and national culture on manufacturing costs, along with the presence of location externalities.

3. Technological factors include the fixed costs of setting up manufacturing facilities, the minimum efficient scale of production, and the availability of flexible manufacturing technologies that allow for mass customization.

4. Product factors include the value-to-weight ratio of the product and whether the product serves universal needs.

5. Location strategies either concentrate or decentralize manufacturing. The choice should be made in light of country, technological, and product factors. All location decisions involve trade-offs.

6. Foreign factories can improve their capabilities over time, and this can be of immense strategic benefit to the firm. Managers need to view foreign factories as potential centers of excellence and to encourage and foster attempts by local managers to upgrade factory capabilities.

7. An essential issue in many international businesses is determining which component parts should be manufactured in-house and which should be outsourced to independent suppliers.

8. Making components in-house facilitates investments in specialized assets and helps the firm protect its proprietary technology. It may improve scheduling between adjacent stages in the value chain, also. In-house production also makes sense if the firm is an efficient, low-cost producer of a technology.

9. Buying components from independent suppliers facilitates strategic flexibility and helps the firm avoid the organizational problems associated with extensive vertical integration. Outsourcing might also be employed as part of an "offset" policy, which is designed to win more orders for the firm from a country by pushing some subcontracting work to that country.

10. Several firms have tried to attain the benefits of vertical integration and avoid its associated organizational problems by entering long-term strategic alliances with essential suppliers.

11. Although alliances with suppliers can give a firm the benefits of vertical integration without dispensing entirely with the benefits of a market relationship,

alliances have drawbacks. The firm that enters a strategic alliance may find its strategic flexibility limited by commitments to alliance partners.

12. Materials management encompasses all the activities that move materials to a manufacturing facility, through the manufacturing process, and out through a distribution system to the end user. The materials management function is complicated in an international business by distance, time, exchange rates, custom barriers, and other things.

13. Just-in-time systems generate major cost savings from reducing warehousing and inventory holding costs and from reducing the need to write off excess inventory. In addition, JIT systems help the firm spot defective parts and remove them from the manufacturing process quickly, thereby improving product quality.

14. For a firm to establish a good materials management function, it needs to legitimize materials management within the organization. It can do this by giving materials management equal footing with other functions.

15. Information technology, particularly Internet-based electronic data interchange, plays a major role in materials management. EDI facilitates the tracking of inputs, allows the firm to optimize its production schedule, allows the firm and its suppliers to communicate in real time, and eliminates the flow of paperwork between a firm and its suppliers.

Critical Discussion Questions

1. An electronics firm is considering how best to supply the world market for microprocessors used in consumer and industrial electronic products. A manufacturing plant costs about $500 million to construct and requires a highly skilled workforce. The total value of the world market for this product over the next 10 years is estimated to be between $10 billion and $15 billion. The tariffs prevailing in this industry are currently low. Should the firm adopt a concentrated or decentralized manufacturing strategy? What kind of location(s) should the firm favor for its plant(s)?

2. A chemical firm is considering how best to supply the world market for sulfuric acid. A manufacturing plant costs approximately $20 million to construct and requires a moderately skilled workforce. The total value of the world market for this product over the next 10 years is estimated to be between $20 billion and $30 billion. The tariffs prevailing in this industry are moderate. Should the firm favor concentrated manufacturing or decentralized manufacturing? What kind of location(s) should the firm seek for its plant(s)?

3. A firm must decide whether to make a component part in-house or to contract it out to an independent supplier. Manufacturing the part requires a nonrecoverable investment in specialized assets. The most efficient suppliers are located in countries with currencies that many foreign exchange analysts expect to appreciate substantially over the next decade. What are the pros and cons of (a) manufacturing the component in-house and (b) outsourcing manufacture to an independent supplier? Which option would you recommend? Why?

4. Explain how an efficient materials management function can help an international business compete more effectively in the global marketplace.

5. Read the Management Focus on Dell Computer. What are the consequences for Dell's cost structure and bottom line of replacing inventories with information? Do you think that Dell's model can be imitated by (a) other PC manufacturers and (b) manufacturers in other industries? What factors might make it difficult for other firms to adopt Dell's model?

Closing Case

Li & Fung

Established in 1906, Hong Kong-based Li & Fung is now one of the largest multinational trading companies in the developing world, with annual sales of about $2 billion. The company, which is still run by the grandson of the founder, Victor Fung, does not see itself as a traditional trading enterprise. Rather, it sees itself as an expert in supply chain management for its 350 or so customers, providing the convenience of one-stop shopping for raw material sourcing, production planning and management, quality assurance, export documentation, and shipping consolidation. These customers are a diverse group and include clothing retailers and consumer electronics companies. Li & Fung takes orders from customers and then sifts through its network of 7,000 independent suppliers located in

37 countries to find the right manufacturing enterprises to produce the product for customers at the most attractive combination of cost and quality. Attaining this goal frequently requires Li & Fung to break up the value chain and disperse different productive activities to manufacturers located in different countries depending on an assessment of factors such as labor costs, trade barriers, transportation costs, and so on. Li & Fung then coordinates the whole process, managing the logistics and arranging for the shipment of the finished product to the customer. Li & Fung has a policy of not owning any production facilities itself, preferring instead to shop around.

Typical of its customers is The Limited, Inc., a large U.S.-based chain of retail clothing stores. The Limited outsources much of its manufacturing and logistics functions to Li & Fung. The process starts when The Limited comes to Li & Fung with designer sketches of clothes for the next fashion season. Li & Fung takes the basic product concepts and researches the market to find the right kind of yarn, dye, buttons, and so on, then assembles these into prototypes that The Limited can inspect. Once The Limited has settled on a prototype, it will give Li & Fung an order and ask for delivery within five weeks. The short time between an order and requested delivery is necessitated by the rapid rate of product obsolescence in the fashion clothing industry.

With order in hand, Li & Fung distributes the various aspects of the overall manufacturing process to different producers depending on their capabilities and costs. For example, Li & Fung might decide to purchase yarn from a Korean company but have it woven and dyed in Taiwan. So Li & Fung will arrange for the yarn to be picked up from Korea and shipped to Taiwan. The Japanese might have the best zippers and buttons, but they manufacture them mostly in China. So Li & Fung will go to YKK, a big Japanese zipper manufacturer, and order the right zippers from the Chinese plants. Then Li & Fung might decide that due to constraints imposed by export quotas and labor costs, the best place to make the final garments might be in Thailand. So everything will be shipped to Thailand. In addition, because The Limited, like many retail customers, needs quick delivery, Li & Fung might divide the order across five factories in Thailand. Five weeks after the order has been received, the garments will arrive on the shelves of The Limited, all looking like they came from one factory, with colors perfectly matched. The result is a product that may have a label that says "Made in Thailand," but it is a global product.

To better serve the needs of its customers, Li & Fung is divided into numerous small, customer-focused divisions. There is a theme store division that serves a handful of customers such as Warner Brothers and Rainforest Café; there is a division for The Limited; and another for Gymboree, a U.S.-based children's clothing store. Walk into one of these divisions, such as the Gymboree division, and you will see that all of the 40 or so people in the division are focused solely on meeting Gymboree's needs. On every desk is a computer with a direct software link to Gymboree. The staff is organized into specialized teams in areas such as design, technical support, merchandising, raw material purchasing, quality assurance, and shipping. These teams also have direct electronic links to dedicated staff in Li & Fung's branch offices in various countries where Gymboree buys in volume, such as China, Indonesia, and the Philippines. Thus, Li & Fung uses information systems to manage, coordinate, and control the globally dispersed design, production, and shipping process to ensure that the time between receipt of an order and delivery is minimized, as are overall costs.

To capture the many opportunities arising from the Internet technology, a new e-commerce subsidiary, StudioDirect, was formed in March 2000 to serve the needs primarily of overseas small and medium-sized customers more cost-effectively, thereby winning a new market segment for Li & Fung. Li & Fung has also begun to broaden its focus beyond Asia with acquisitions of trading companies based in Europe and the United States.

Sources: J. Magretta, "Fast, Global, and Entrepreneurial: Supply Chain Management Hong Kong Style," *Harvard Business Review*, September–October 1998, p. 102–114; J. Ridding, "A Multinational Trading Group with Chinese Characteristics," *Financial Times*, November 7, 1997, p. 16; J. Ridding, "The Family in the Frame," *Financial Times*, October 28, 1996, p. 12; J. Lo, "Second Half Doubts Shadow Li & Fung Strength in Interims," *South China Morning Post*, August 27, 1998, p. 3; "Link in the Global Chain," *The Economist*, June 2, 2001, pp. 62–63; and www.lifung.com.

Case Discussion Questions

1. At one time many of Li & Fung's customers performed their own logistics and purchasing functions in-house. Now they outsource those functions to Li & Fung. Why? What is the value added that an intermediary such as Li & Fung delivers to its customers?

2. If Li & Fung is to execute on its promise to deliver value added to its customers, what skills and competencies must it have?

3. Why do you think that Li & Fung has a policy of not owning any production facilities?

Notes

1. B. C. Arntzen, G. G. Brown, T. P. Harrison, and L. L. Trafton, "Global Supply Chain Management at Digital Equipment Corporation," *Interfaces* 25 (1995), pp. 69–93.

2. D. A. Garvin, "What Does Product Quality Really Mean," *Sloan Management Review* 26 (Fall 1984), pp. 25–44.

3. For general background information, see "How to Build Quality," *The Economist*, September 23, 1989, pp. 91–92; A. Gabor, *The Man Who Discovered Quality* (New York: Penguin, 1990); and P. B. Crosby, *Quality Is Free* (New York: Mentor, 1980).

4. M. Saunders, "U.S. Firms Doing Business in Europe Have Options in Registering for ISO 9000 Quality Standards," *Business America*, June 14, 1993, p. 7.

5. G. Stalk and T. M. Hout, *Competing Against Time* (New York: Free Press, 1990).

6. M. A. Cohen and H. L. Lee, "Resource Deployment Analysis of Global Manufacturing and Distribution Networks," *Journal of Manufacturing and Operations Management* 2 (1989), pp. 81–104.

7. P. Krugman, "Increasing Returns and Economic Geography," *Journal of Political Economy* 99, no. 3 (1991), pp. 483–99, and J. M. Shaver and F. Flyer, "Agglomeration Economies, Firm Heterogeneity, and Foreign Direct Investment in the United States," *Strategic Management Journal* 21 (2000), pp. 1175–93.

8. For a review of the technical arguments, see D. A. Hay and D. J. Morris, *Industrial Economics: Theory and Evidence* (Oxford: Oxford University Press, 1979). See also C. W. L. Hill and G. R. Jones, *Strategic Management: An Integrated Approach* (Boston: Houghton Mifflin, 1995).

9. See P. Nemetz and L. Fry, "Flexible Manufacturing Organizations: Implications for Strategy Formulation," *Academy of Management Review* 13 (1988), pp. 627–38; N. Greenwood, *Implementing Flexible Manufacturing Systems* (New York: Halstead Press, 1986); J. P. Womack, D. T. Jones, and D. Roos, *The Machine That Changed the World* (New York: Rawson Associates, 1990); and R. Parthasarthy and S. P. Seith, "The Impact of Flexible Automation on Business Strategy and Organizational Structure," *Academy of Management Review* 17 (1992), pp. 86–111.

10. B. J. Pine, *Mass Customization: The New Frontier in Business Competition* (Boston: Harvard Business School Press, 1993); S. Kotha, "Mass Customization: Implementing the Emerging Paradigm for Competitive Advantage," *Strategic Management Journal* 16 (1995), pp. 21–42; and J. H. Gilmore and B. J. Pine II, "The Four Faces of Mass Customization," *Harvard Business Review*, January–February 1997, pp. 91–101.

11. M. A. Cusumano, *The Japanese Automobile Industry* (Cambridge, MA: Harvard University Press, 1989); T. Ohno, *Toyota Production System* (Cambridge, MA: Productivity Press, 1990); and Womack, Jones, and Roos, *The Machine That Changed the World*.

12. "The Celling Out of America," *The Economist*, December 17, 1994, pp. 63–64.

13. K. Ferdows, "Making the Most of Foreign Factories," *Harvard Business Review*, March–April 1997, pp. 73–88.

14. This argument represents a simple extension of the dynamic capabilities research stream in the strategic management literature. See D. J. Teece, G. Pisano, and A. Shuen, "Dynamic Capabilities and Strategic Management," *Strategic Management Journal* 18 (1997), pp. 509–33.

15. C. W. L. Hill, "Globalization, the Myth of the Nomadic Multinational Enterprise, and the Advantages of Location Persistence," Working Paper, School of Business, University of Washington, 2001.

16. The material in this section is based primarily on the transaction cost literature of vertical integration; for example, O. E. Williamson, *The Economic Institutions of Capitalism* (New York: The Free Press, 1985).

17. For a review of the evidence, see Williamson, *The Economic Institutions of Capitalism*.

18. A. D. Chandler, *The Visible Hand* (Cambridge, MA: Harvard University Press, 1977).

19. For a review of these arguments, see C. W. L. Hill and R. E. Hoskisson, "Strategy and Structure in the Multiproduct Firm," *Academy of Management Review* 12 (1987), pp. 331–41.

20. C. W. L. Hill, "Cooperation, Opportunism, and the Invisible Hand," *Academy of Management Review* 15 (1990), pp. 500–13.

21. See R. Narasimhan and J. R. Carter, "Organization, Communication and Coordination of

International Sourcing," *International Marketing Review* 7 (1990), pp. 6–20, and Arntzen, Brown, Harrison, and Trafton, "Global Supply Chain Management at Digital Equipment Corporation."

22. H. F. Busch, "Integrated Materials Management," *IJPD & MM* 18 (1990), pp. 28–39.

23. J. G. Miller and P. Gilmour, "Materials Managers: Who Needs Them?" *Harvard Business Review*, July–August 1979, pp. 57–67.

24. Narasimhan and Carter, "Organization, Communication and Coordination of International Sourcing."

Global
Marketing
and R&D

Procter & Gamble in Japan: From Marketing Failure to Success

Procter & Gamble (P&G), the large U.S. consumer products company, has a well-earned reputation as one of the world's best marketers. With its 80-plus major brands, P&G generates more than $37 billion in annual revenues worldwide. Along with Unilever, P&G is a dominant global force in laundry detergents, cleaning products, and personal care products. P&G expanded abroad after World War II by exporting its brands and marketing policies to Western Europe, initially with considerable success. Over the next 30 years, this policy of developing new products and marketing strategies in the United States and then transferring them to other countries became entrenched. Although some adaptation of marketing policies to accommodate country differences was pursued, it was minimal.

The first signs that this policy was no longer effective emerged in the 1970s, when P&G suffered a number of major setbacks in Japan. By 1985, after 13 years in Japan, P&G was still losing $40 million a year there. It had introduced disposable diapers in Japan and at one time had commanded an 80 percent share of the market, but by the early 1980s it held a miserable 8 percent. Three large Japanese consumer products companies were dominating the market. P&G's diapers, developed in the United States, were too bulky for the tastes of Japanese consumers. Kao, a Japanese company, had developed a line of trim-fit diapers that appealed more to Japanese tastes. Kao introduced its product with a marketing blitz and was quickly rewarded with a 30 percent share of the market. P&G realized it would have to modify its diapers if it were to compete in Japan. It did, and the company now has a 30 percent share of the Japanese market. Plus, P&G's trim-fit diapers have become a best-seller in the United States.

P&G had a similar experience in marketing education in the Japanese laundry detergent market. In the early 1980s, P&G introduced its Cheer laundry detergent in Japan. Developed in the United States, Cheer was promoted in Japan with the U.S. marketing message—Cheer works in all temperatures and produces lots of rich suds. But many Japanese consumers wash their clothes in cold water, which made the claim of working in all tempera-

tures irrelevant. Also, many Japanese add fabric softeners to their water, which reduces detergents' sudsing action, so Cheer did not suds up as advertised. After a disastrous launch, P&G knew it had to adapt its marketing message. Cheer is now promoted as a product that works effectively in cold water with fabric softeners added, and it is one of P&G's best-selling products in Japan.

P&G's experience with disposable diapers and laundry detergents in Japan forced the company to rethink its product development and marketing philosophy. The company now admits that its U.S.-centered way of doing business no longer works. Since the late 1980s, P&G has been delegating more responsibility for new-product development and marketing to its major subsidiaries in Japan and Europe. The company is more responsive to local differences in consumer tastes and preferences and more willing to admit that good new products can be developed outside the United States.

Evidence that this new approach is working can again be found in the company's activities in Japan. Until 1995, P&G did not sell dish soap in Japan. By 1998, it had Japan's best-selling brand, Joy, which now has a 20 percent share of Japan's $400 million market for dish soap. It made major inroads against the products of two domestic firms, Kao and Lion Corp., each of which marketed multiple brands and controlled nearly 40 percent of the market before P&G's entry. P&G's success with Joy was due to its ability to develop a product formula that was specifically targeted at the unmet needs of Japanese consumers, to the design of a packaging format that appealed to retailers, and to the development of a compelling advertising campaign.

In researching the market in the early 1990s, P&G discovered an odd habit: Japanese homemakers, one after another, squirted out excessive amounts of detergent onto dirty dishes, a clear sign of dissatisfaction with existing products. On further inspection, P&G found that this behavior resulted from the changing eating habits of Japanese consumers. The Japanese are consuming more fried food, and existing dish soaps did not effectively remove grease. Armed with this knowledge, P&G researchers in Japan went to work to create a highly concentrated soap formula based on a new technology developed by the company's scientists in Europe that was highly effective in removing grease. The company also designed a novel package for the product. The packaging of existing products had a clear weakness: the long-necked bottles wasted space on supermarket shelves. P&G's dish soap containers were compact cylinders that took less space in stores, warehouses, and delivery trucks. This improved the efficiency of distribution and allowed supermarkets to use their shelf space more effectively, which made them receptive to stocking Joy. P&G also devoted considerable attention to developing an advertising campaign for Joy. P&G's ad agency, Dentsu Inc., created commercials in which a famous comedian dropped in on homemakers unannounced with a camera crew to test Joy on the household's dirty dishes. The camera focused on a patch of oil in a pan full of water. After a drop of Joy, the oil dramatically disappeared.

With the product, packaging, and advertising strategy carefully worked out, P&G launched Joy throughout Japan in March 1996. The product almost immediately gained a 10 percent market share. Within three months the product's share had increased to 15 percent, and by year-end it was close to 18 percent. Because of strong demand, P&G was also able to raise prices as were the retailers that stocked the product, all of which translated into fatter margins for the retailers and helped consolidate Joy's position in the market.

Sources: G. de Jonquieres and C. Bobinski, "Wash and Get into a Lather in Poland," *Financial Times,* May 28, 1992, p. 2; "Perestroika in Soapland," *The Economist,* June 10, 1989, pp. 69–71; "After Early Stumbles P&G Is Making Inroads Overseas," *Wall Street Journal,* February 6, 1989, p. B1; C. A. Bartlett and S. Ghoshal, *Managing across Borders: The Transnational Solution* (Boston: Harvard Business School Press, 1989); and N. Shirouzu, "P&G's Joy Makes an Unlikely Splash in Japan," *Wall Street Journal,* December 10, 1997, p. B1.

▌Introduction

In the previous chapter, we looked at the roles of global manufacturing and materials management in an international business. In this chapter, we continue our focus on specific business functions by examining the roles of marketing and research and development (R&D) in an international business. We focus on how marketing and R&D can be performed so they will reduce the costs of value creation and add value by better serving customer needs.

In Chapter 12, we spoke of the tension existing in most international businesses between the needs to reduce costs and at the same time to respond to local conditions, which tends to raise costs. This tension continues to be a persistent theme in this chapter. A global marketing strategy that views the world's consumers as similar in their tastes and preferences is consistent with the mass production of a standardized output. By mass-producing a standardized output, the firm can realize substantial unit cost reductions from experience curve and other scale economies. But ignoring country differences in consumer tastes and preferences can lead to failure. Thus, an international business's marketing function needs to determine when product standardization is appropriate and when it is not, and to adjust the marketing strategy accordingly. Similarly, the firm's R&D function needs to be able to develop globally standardized products when appropriate as well as products customized to local requirements.

We consider marketing and R&D within the same chapter because of their close relationship. A critical aspect of the marketing function is identifying gaps in the market so that new products can be developed to fill those gaps. Developing new products requires R&D; thus, the linkage between marketing and R&D. New products should be developed with market needs in mind, and only marketing can define those needs for R&D personnel. Also, only marketing can tell R&D whether to produce globally standardized or locally customized products. Academic research has long maintained that a major factor of success for new-product introductions is the closeness of the relationship between marketing and R&D. The closer the linkage, the greater the success rate.[1]

The opening case illustrates some issues we will be debating in this chapter. Many of P&G's problems in Japan were caused by a failure to tailor its marketing strategy to the specific demands of the Japanese marketplace. P&G learned from its experience with disposable diapers and laundry detergent that a marketing approach that works in one context won't necessarily work in another. The company's subsequent success with Joy drives home the point that in many consumer product markets, it is important to customize the product offering, packaging, and advertising message to the specific needs of consumers in that country. Joy was developed by Procter & Gamble's R&D staff in Kobe, Japan, specifically to meet the evolving needs of Japanese consumers. This illustrates the benefits of locating R&D activities close to the market for the product when that market demands a customized product offering.

But it would be wrong to generalize too much from this case. For other firms in other industries, it may make sense to pursue a global strategy, producing a standardized product for global consumption and using the same basic market message to sell that product worldwide. Some product markets are truly global in their reach. The market for semiconductor chips, for example, is a global market where consumers demand the same standardized product worldwide so a global marketing strategy, supported by a global R&D strategy, might make sense.

In this chapter, we begin by reviewing the debate on the globalization of markets. Then we discuss the issue of market segmentation. Next we look at four elements that constitute a firm's marketing mix: product attributes, distribution strategy, communication strategy, and pricing strategy. The **marketing mix** is the set of choices the firm offers to its targeted markets. Many firms vary their marketing mix from country to country depending on differences in national culture, economic development, product standards, distribution channels, and so on. The chapter closes with a look at new-product development in an international business and at the implications of this for the organization of the firm's R&D function.

The Globalization of Markets and Brands

In a now-famous *Harvard Business Review* article, Theodore Levitt wrote lyrically about the globalization of world markets.[2] Levitt's arguments have become something of a lightning rod in the debate about the extent of globalization. According to Levitt:

> A powerful force drives the world toward a converging commonalty, and that force is technology. It has proletarianized communication, transport, and travel. The result is a new commercial reality—the emergence of global markets for standardized consumer products on a previously unimagined scale of magnitude.
>
> Gone are accustomed differences in national or regional preferences . . . The globalization of markets is at hand. With that, the multinational commercial world nears its end, and so does the multinational corporation. The multinational corporation operates in a number of countries and adjusts its products and practices to each—at high relative costs. The global corporation operates with resolute consistency—at low relative cost—as if the entire world were a single entity; it sells the same thing in the same way everywhere.
>
> Commercially, nothing confirms this as much as the success of McDonald's from the Champs Elysees to the Ginza, of Coca-Cola in Bahrain and Pepsi-Cola in Moscow, and of rock music, Greek salad, Hollywood movies, Revlon cosmetics, Sony television, and Levi's jeans everywhere.
>
> Ancient differences in national tastes or modes of doing business disappear. The commonalty of preference leads inescapably to the standardization of products, manufacturing, and the institutions of trade and commerce.

This is eloquent and evocative writing, but is Levitt correct? The rise of global media such as MTV and CNN, and the ability of such media to help shape a global culture, would seem to lend weight to Levitt's argument. If Levitt is correct, his argument has major implications for the marketing strategies pursued by international business.

However, the current consensus among academics seems to be that Levitt overstates his case.[3] Although Levitt may have a point when it comes to many basic industrial products, such as steel, bulk chemicals, and semiconductor chips, globalization seems to be the exception rather than the rule in many consumer goods markets and industrial markets. Even a firm such as McDonald's, which Levitt holds up as the archetypal example of a consumer products firm that sells a standardized product worldwide, modifies its menu from country to country in light of local consumer preferences.[4]

Levitt is probably correct to assert that modern transportation and communications technologies, such as MTV, are facilitating a convergence of the tastes and preferences of consumers in the more advanced countries of the world. The popularity of sushi in Los Angeles, hamburgers in Tokyo, hip-hop music, and global media phenomena such as Pokémon, all support this. In the long run, such technological forces may lead to the evolution of a global culture. At present, however, the continuing persistence of cultural and economic differences between nations acts as a major brake on any trend toward global consumer tastes and preferences. In addition, trade barriers and differences in product and technical standards also constrain a firm's ability to sell a standardized product to a global market using a standardized marketing strategy. We discuss the sources of these differences in subsequent sections when we look at how products must be altered from country to country. Levitt's globally standardized markets seem a long way off in many industries.

■ Market Segmentation

Market segmentation refers to identifying distinct groups of consumers whose purchasing behavior differs from others in important ways. Markets can be segmented in numerous ways: by geography, demography (sex, age, income, race, education level, etc.), social-cultural factors (social class, values, religion, lifestyle choices), and psychological factors (personality). Because different segments exhibit different patterns of purchasing behavior, firms often adjust their marketing mix from segment to segment. Thus, the precise design of a product, the pricing strategy, the distribution channels used, and the choice of communication strategy may all be varied from segment to segment. The goal is to optimize the fit between the purchasing behavior of consumers in a given segment and the marketing mix, thereby maximizing sales to that segment. Automobile companies, for example, use a different marketing mix to sell cars to different socioeconomic segments. Thus, Toyota uses its Lexus division to sell high-priced luxury cars to high-income consumers, while selling its entry-level models, such as the Toyota Corolla, to lower-income consumers. Similarly, personal computer manufacturers will offer different computer models, embodying different combinations of product attributes and price points, precisely to appeal to consumers from different market segments (e.g., business users and home users).

When managers in an international business consider market segmentation in foreign countries, they need to be cognizant of two main issues: the differences between countries in the structure of market segments and the existence of segments that transcend national borders. The structure of market segments may differ significantly from country to country. An important market segment in a foreign country may have no parallel in the firm's home country, and vice versa. The firm may have to develop a unique marketing mix to appeal to the unique purchasing behavior of a unique segment in a given country. An example of such a unique market segment is given in the accompanying Management Focus, which looks at the African-Brazilian market segment in Brazil, which as you will see is very different from the African-American segment in the United States. In another example, a research project published in 1998 identified a segment of consumers in China in the 45-to-55 age range that has few parallels in other countries.[5] This group came of age during China's violent and repressive Cultural Revolution in the late 1960s and early 1970s. The values of this group

Management Focus

Marketing to Black Brazil

Brazil is home to the largest black population outside of Nigeria. Nearly half of the 160 million people in Brazil are of African or mixed race origin. Despite this, until very recently there has been very little effort by businesses to target this numerically large segment. Part of the reason is rooted in economics. Black Brazilians have historically been poorer than Brazilians of European origin and thus have not received the same attention as whites. But after a decade of relatively strong economic performance in Brazil, an emerging black middle class is beginning to command the attention of consumer product companies. To take advantage of this, companies such as Unilever have recently introduced a range of skin care products and cosmetics aimed at black Brazilians, and Brazil's largest toy company recently introduced a black Barbie like doll, Susi Olodum, sales of which quickly caught up with sales of a similar white doll.

But there is more to the issue than simple economics. Unlike the United States, where a protracted history of racial discrimination gave birth to the civil rights movement, fostered black awareness, and produced an identifiable subculture in U.S. society, the history of blacks in Brazil has been very different. Although Brazil did not abolish slavery until 1888, racism in Brazil has historically been much subtler than in the United States. Brazil has never excluded blacks from voting or had a tradition of segregating the races. Historically, too, the government encouraged intermarriage between whites and blacks in order to "bleach"

society. Partly due to this more benign history, Brazil has not had a black rights movement similar to that in the United States, and racial self-identification is much weaker. Surveys routinely find that African-Brazilian consumers decline to categorize themselves as either black or white, but instead choose one of dozens of skin tones and see themselves as being part of a culture that transcends race.

This subtler racial dynamic has important implications for market segmentation and tailoring the marketing mix in Brazil. This was an issue that Unilever had to face head on when launching a Vaseline Intensive Care lotion for black consumers. The company learned in focus groups that for the product to resonate with non-white women, its promotions had to feature women of different skin tones, excluding neither whites nor blacks. The campaign Unilever devised features three women with different skin shades at a fitness center. The bottle says the lotion is for "tan and black skin"—a description that could include many white women considering that much of the population lives near the beach. The lesson that Unilever has learned from this experience is that the segment exists, but it is more difficult to define and requires more subtle marketing messages than the African-American segment in the United States or middle-class segments in Africa.

Source: M. Jordan, "Marketers Discover Black Brazil." *Wall Street Journal*, November 24, 2000, p. A11, A14.

have been shaped by their experiences during the Cultural Revolution. They tend to be highly sensitive to price and respond negatively to new products and most forms of marketing. The existence of this group implies that firms doing business in China may need to customize their marketing mix to address the unique values and purchasing behavior of the group. The existence of such a unique segment constrains the ability of firms to standardize their global marketing strategy.

In contrast, the existence of market segments that transcend national borders clearly enhances the ability of an international business to view the global marketplace as a single entity and pursue a global strategy, selling a standardized product worldwide and using the same basic marketing mix to help position and sell that product in a variety of national markets. For a segment to transcend national borders, consumers in that segment must have some compelling similarities along important dimensions—such as age, values, lifestyle choices—and those similarities must translate into similar purchasing behavior. Although such segments exist in certain industrial markets, they are rare in consumer markets. However, one emerging global segment that is attracting the attention of international marketers of consumer goods is the so-called global youth segment. Global media are paving the way for a global youth segment. Evidence that such a segment exists comes from a study of the cultural attitudes and purchasing behavior of more than 6,500 teenagers in 26 countries.[6] The findings suggest that teens around the world are increasingly living parallel lives that share many common values. It follows that they are likely to purchase the same kind of consumer goods and for the same reasons. Even here though, marketing specialists argue that some customization in the marketing mix to account for differences across countries is required.

Product Attributes

A product can be viewed as a bundle of attributes.[7] For example, the attributes that make up a car include power, design, quality, performance, fuel consumption, and comfort; the attributes of a hamburger include taste, texture, and size; a hotel's attributes include atmosphere, quality, comfort, and service. Products sell well when their attributes match consumer needs (and when their prices are appropriate). BMW cars sell well to people who have high needs for luxury, quality, and performance, precisely because BMW builds those attributes into its cars. If consumer needs were the same the world over, a firm could simply sell the same product worldwide. However, consumer needs vary from country to country depending on culture and the level of economic development. A firm's ability to sell the same product worldwide is further constrained by countries' differing product standards. In this section, we review each of these issues and discuss how they influence product attributes.

Cultural Differences

We discussed countries' cultural differences in Chapter 3. Countries differ along a whole range of dimensions, including social structure, language, religion, and education. And as alluded to in Chapter 2, these differences have important implications for marketing strategy. For example, "hamburgers" do not sell well in Islamic countries, where the consumption of ham is forbidden by Islamic law. The most important aspect of cultural differences is probably the impact of tradition. Tradition is particularly important in foodstuffs and beverages. For example, reflecting differences in traditional eating habits, the Findus frozen food division of Nestlé, the Swiss food giant, markets fish cakes and fish fingers in Great Britain, but beef bourguignon and coq au vin in France and vitéllo con funghi and braviola in Italy. In addition to its normal range of products, Coca-Cola in Japan markets Georgia, a cold coffee in a can, and Aquarius, a tonic drink, both of which appeal to traditional Japanese tastes.

For historical and idiosyncratic reasons, a range of other cultural differences exist between countries. For example, scent preferences differ from one country to another. S. C. Johnson Wax, a manufacturer of waxes and polishes, encountered resistance to its lemon-scented Pledge furniture polish among older consumers in Japan. Careful market research revealed that the polish smelled similar to a latrine disinfectant used widely in Japan in the 1940s. Sales rose sharply after the scent was adjusted.[8] In another example, Cheetos, the bright orange and cheesy-tasting snack from PepsiCo's Frito-Lay unit, do not have a cheese taste in China. Chinese consumers generally do not like the taste of cheese because it has never been part of traditional cuisine and because many Chinese are lactose-intolerant.[9]

There is some evidence of the trends Levitt talked about. Tastes and preferences are becoming more cosmopolitan. Coffee is gaining ground against tea in Japan and Great Britain, while American-style frozen dinners have become popular in Europe (with some fine-tuning to local tastes). Taking advantage of these trends, Nestlé has found that it can market its instant coffee, spaghetti bolognese, and Lean Cuisine frozen dinners in essentially the same manner in both North America and Western Europe.

However, there is no market for Lean Cuisine dinners in most of the rest of the world, and there may not be for years or decades. Although some cultural convergence has occurred, particularly among the advanced industrial nations of North America and Western Europe, Levitt's global culture is still a long way off.

Economic Development

Just as important as differences in culture are differences in the level of economic development. We discussed the extent of country differences in economic development in Chapter 2. Consumer behavior is influenced by the level of economic development of a country. Firms based in highly developed countries such as the United States tend to build a lot of extra performance attributes into their products. These extra attributes are not usually demanded by consumers in less developed nations, where the preference is for more basic products. Thus, cars sold in less developed nations typically lack many of the features found in the West, such as air-conditioning, power steering, power windows, radios, and cassette players. For most consumer durables, product reliability may be a more important attribute in less developed nations, where such a purchase may account for a major proportion of a consumer's income, than it is in advanced nations.

Contrary to Levitt's suggestions, consumers in the most developed countries are often not willing to sacrifice their preferred attributes for lower prices. Consumers in the most advanced countries often shun globally standardized products that have been developed with the lowest common denominator in mind. They are willing to pay more for products that have additional features and attributes customized to their tastes and preferences. For example, demand for top-of-the-line four-wheel-drive sport utility vehicles, such as Chrysler's Jeep, Ford's Explorer, and Toyota's Land Cruiser, is almost totally restricted to the United States. This is due to a combination of factors, including the high income level of U.S. consumers, the country's vast distances, the relatively low cost of gasoline, and the culturally grounded "outdoor" theme of American life.

Product and Technical Standards

Even with the forces that are creating some convergence of consumer tastes and preferences among advanced, industrialized nations, Levitt's vision of global markets may still be a long way off because of national differences in product and technological standards.

Differing government-mandated product standards can rule out mass production and marketing of a standardized product. For example, Caterpillar, the U.S. construction equipment firm, manufactures backhoe-loaders for all of Europe in Great Britain. These tractor-type machines have a bucket in front and a digger at the back. Several special parts must be built into backhoe-loaders that will be sold in Germany: a separate brake attached to the rear axle, a special locking mechanism on the backhoe operating valve, specially positioned valves in the steering system, and a lock on the bucket for traveling. These extras account for 5 percent of the total cost of the product in Germany.[10] The European Union is trying to harmonize such divergent product standards among its member nations. If the EU is successful, the need to customize products will be reduced within the boundaries of the EU.

Differences in technical standards also constrain the globalization of markets. Some of these differences result from idiosyncratic decisions made long ago, rather than from government actions, but their long-term effects are nonetheless profound. For example, video equipment manufactured for sale in the United States will not play videotapes recorded on equipment manufactured for sale in Great Britain, Germany, and France (and vice versa). Different technical standards for frequency of television signals emerged in the 1950s that require television and video equipment to be customized to prevailing standards. RCA stumbled in the 1970s when it failed to account for this in its marketing of TVs in Asia. Although several Asian countries adopted the U.S. standard, Singapore, Hong Kong, and Malaysia adopted the British standard. People who bought RCA TVs in those countries could receive a picture but no sound![11]

Distribution Strategy

A critical element of a firm's marketing mix is its distribution strategy: the means it chooses for delivering the product to the consumer. The way the product is delivered is determined by the firm's entry strategy, which we discussed in Chapter 14. In this section, we examine a typical distribution system, discuss how its structure varies between countries, and look at how appropriate distribution strategies vary from country to country.

A Typical Distribution System

Figure 17.1 illustrates a typical distribution system consisting of a channel that includes a wholesale distributor and a retailer. If the firm manufactures its product in the particular country, it can sell directly to the consumer, to the retailer, or to the wholesaler. The same options are available to a firm that manufactures outside the country. Plus, this firm may decide to sell to an import agent, which then deals with the wholesale distributor, the retailer, or the consumer. The factors that determine the firm's choice of channel are considered later in this section.

Differences Between Countries

The three main differences between distribution systems are retail concentration, channel length, and channel exclusivity.

Retail Concentration

In some countries, the retail system is very concentrated, but it is fragmented in others. In a concentrated system, a few retailers supply most of the market. A fragmented system is one in which there are many retailers, no one of which has a major share of the market. Many of the differences in concentration are rooted in history and tradition.

Figure 17.1

A Typical Distribution System

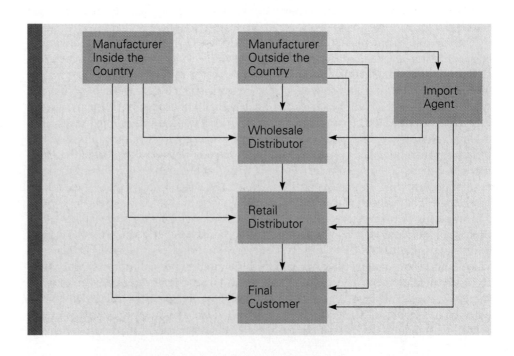

In the United States, the importance of the automobile and the relative youth of many urban areas have resulted in a retail system centered around large stores or shopping malls to which people can drive. This has facilitated system concentration. Japan's much greater population density together with the large number of urban centers that grew up before the automobile have yielded a more fragmented retail system of many small stores that serve local neighborhoods and to which people frequently walk. In addition, the Japanese legal system protects small retailers. Small retailers can block the establishment of a large retail outlet by petitioning their local government.

There is a tendency for greater retail concentration in developed countries. Three factors that contribute to this are the increases in car ownership, number of households with refrigerators and freezers, and number of two-income households. All these factors have changed shopping habits and facilitated the growth of large retail establishments sited away from traditional shopping areas. During the last decade there has been a tendency for consolidation in the global retail industry, with companies such as Wal-Mart and Carrefour attempting to become global retailers by acquiring retailers in different countries. This has increased retail concentration.

In contrast, retail systems are very fragmented in many developing countries, which can make for interesting distribution challenges. In India, for example, Unilever has to sell to retailers in 600,000 rural villages, many of which cannot be accessed via paved roads, which means that products can reach their destination only by bullock, bicycle, or cart (see the Management Focus on Unilever later in this chapter). In neighboring Nepal, the terrain is so rugged that even bicycles and carts are not practical, and businesses rely on yak trains and the human back to deliver products to thousands of small retailers.

Channel Length

Channel length refers to the number of intermediaries between the producer (or manufacturer) and the consumer. If the producer sells directly to the consumer, the channel is very short. If the producer sells through an import agent, a wholesaler, and a retailer, a long channel exists. The choice of a short or long channel is in part a strategic decision for the producing firm. However, some countries have longer distribution channels than others. The most important determinant of channel length is the degree to which the retail system is fragmented. Fragmented retail systems tend to promote the growth of wholesalers to serve retailers, which lengthens channels.

The more fragmented the retail system, the more expensive it is for a firm to make contact with each individual retailer. Imagine a firm that sells toothpaste in a country where there are over a million small retailers, as in rural India and China. To sell directly to the retailers, the firm would have to build a huge sales force. This would be very expensive, particularly since each sales call would yield a very small order. But suppose there are a few hundred wholesalers in the country that supply retailers not only with toothpaste but also with all other personal care and household products. Because these wholesalers carry a wide range of products, they get bigger orders with each sales call, making it worthwhile for them to deal directly with the retailers. Accordingly, it makes economic sense for the firm to sell to the wholesalers and the wholesalers to deal with the retailers.

Because of such factors, countries with fragmented retail systems also tend to have long channels of distribution, sometimes with multiple layers. The classic example is Japan, where there are often two or three layers of wholesalers between the firm and retail outlets. In countries such as Great Britain, Germany, and the United States where the retail system is far more concentrated, channels are much shorter. When the retail sector is very concentrated, it makes sense for the firm to deal directly with retailers, cutting out wholesalers. A relatively small sales force is required to deal with a concentrated retail sector, and the orders generated from each sales call can be large. Such circumstances tend to prevail in the United States, where large food companies sell directly to supermarkets rather than going through wholesale distributors.

The rapid development of the Internet in recent years has helped to shorten channel length. For example, the Seattle-based outdoor equipment retailer REI sells its products in Japan via a Japanese-language website, thereby cutting out the need for a retail presence on the ground in Japan, which obviously shortens the channel length between REI and its customers. However, there are obvious drawbacks with such a strategy. In the case of REI, it is not possible to offer consumers the same level of advise over the Web as it is in physical retail stores, where salespeople can help customers to choose the right gear given their needs. So although REI benefits from a short channel in Japan, it may lose significant sales due to the lack of point-of-sale service.

Channel Exclusivity

An exclusive distribution channel is one that is difficult for outsiders to access. For example, it is often difficult for a new firm to get access to shelf space in supermarkets. This occurs because retailers tend to prefer to carry the products of long-established manufacturers of foodstuffs with national reputations rather than gamble on the products of unknown firms. The exclusivity of a distribution system varies between countries. Japan's system is often held up as an example of a very exclusive system. In Japan, relationships between manufacturers, wholesalers, and retailers often go back decades. Many of these relationships are based on the understanding that distributors will not carry the products of competing firms. In return, the distributors are guaranteed an attractive markup by the manufacturer. As many U.S. and European manufacturers have learned, the close ties that result from this arrangement can make access to the Japanese market very difficult. But, as the opening case illustrates, it is possible to break into the Japanese market with a new consumer product, as Procter & Gamble did recently with its Joy brand of dish soap. P&G was able to overcome a tradition of exclusivity for two reasons. First, after a decade of lackluster economic performance, Japan is changing. In their search for profits, retailers are far more willing than they have been historically to violate the old norms of exclusivity. Second, P&G has been in Japan long enough and has a broad enough portfolio of consumer products to give it considerable leverage with distributors, enabling it to push new products out through the distribution channel.

Choosing a Distribution Strategy

A choice of distribution strategy determines which channel the firm will use to reach potential consumers. Should the firm try to sell directly to the consumer or should it go through retailers; should it go through a wholesaler; should it use an import agent? The optimal strategy is determined by the relative costs and benefits of each alternative. The relative costs and benefits of each alternative vary from country to country, depending on the three factors we have just discussed: retail concentration, channel length, and channel exclusivity.

Because each intermediary in a channel adds its own markup to the products, there is generally a critical link between channel length, the final selling price, and the firm's profit margin. The longer a channel, the greater is the aggregate markup, and the higher the price that consumers are charged for the final product. To ensure that prices do not get too high due to markups by multiple intermediaries, a firm might be forced to operate with lower profit margins. Thus, if price is an important competitive weapon, and if the firm does not want to see its profit margins squeezed, other things being equal, the firm would prefer to use a shorter channel.

However, the benefits of using a longer channel often outweigh these drawbacks. As we have seen, one benefit of a longer channel is that it cuts selling costs when the retail sector is very fragmented. Thus, it makes sense for an international business to use longer channels in countries where the retail sector is fragmented and shorter channels in countries where the retail sector is concentrated. Another benefit of using a longer channel is market access—the ability to enter an exclusive channel. Import agents may have long-term relationships with wholesalers, retailers, and/or important consumers and thus be better able to win orders and get access to a distribution system. Similarly, wholesalers may have long-standing relationships with retailers and be better able to persuade them to carry the firm's product than the firm itself would.

Import agents are not limited to independent trading houses; any firm with a strong local reputation could serve as well. For example, to break down channel exclusivity and gain greater access to the Japanese market, Apple Computer in 1991 and 1992 signed distribution agreements with five large Japanese firms including business equipment giant Brother Industries, stationery leader Kokuyo, Mitsubishi, Sharp, and Minolta. These firms use their own long-established distribution relationships with consumers, retailers, and wholesalers to push Apple Macintosh computers through the Japanese distribution system. As a result, Apple's share of the Japanese market increased from less than 1 percent in 1988 to 6 percent in 1991 and 13 percent by 1994.[12]

If such an arrangement is not possible, the firm might want to consider other, less traditional alternatives to gaining market access. Frustrated by channel exclusivity in Japan, some foreign manufacturers of consumer goods have attempted to sell directly to Japanese consumers using direct mail and catalogs. REI had trouble persuading Japanese wholesalers and retailers to carry its products, so it began a direct-mail campaign and then Web-based strategy to enter Japan that is proving very successful.

Communication Strategy

Another critical element in the marketing mix is communicating the attributes of the product to prospective customers. A number of communication channels are available to a firm, including direct selling, sales promotion, direct marketing, and advertising. A firm's communication strategy is partly defined by its choice of channel. Some firms rely primarily on direct selling, others on point-of-sale promotions or direct marketing, others on mass advertising; still others use several channels simultaneously to communicate their message to prospective customers. In this section, we will look first at the barriers to international communication. Then we will survey the various factors that determine which communication strategy is most appropriate in a particular country. After that we discuss global advertising.

Barriers to International Communication

International communication occurs whenever a firm uses a marketing message to sell its products in another country. The effectiveness of a firm's international communication can be jeopardized by three potentially critical variables: cultural barriers, source effects, and noise levels.

Cultural Barriers

Cultural barriers can make it difficult to communicate messages across cultures. We discussed some sources and consequences of cultural differences between nations in Chapter 3 and in the previous section of this chapter. Due to cultural differences, a message that means one thing in one country may mean something quite different in another. For example, when Procter & Gamble promoted its Camay soap in Japan in the 1980s it ran into unexpected trouble. In a TV commercial, a Japanese man walked into the bathroom while his wife was bathing. The woman began telling her husband all about her new soap, but the husband, stroking her shoulder, hinted that suds were not on his mind. This ad had been very popular in Europe, but it flopped in Japan because it is considered very bad manners there for a man to intrude on his wife.[13] Benetton, the Italian clothing manufacturer and retailer, is another firm that has run into cultural problems with its advertising. The company launched a worldwide advertising campaign in 1989 with the theme "United Colors of Benetton" that had won

Overcoming Cultural Barriers to Selling Tampons

In 1997, Procter & Gamble purchased Tambrands, the manufacturer of Tampax tampons, for $1.87 billion. P&G's goal was to make Tampax a global brand. At the time of the acquisition, tampons were used by some 70 percent of women in North America and a significant majority in Northwestern Europe. However, usage elsewhere was very low, ranging from single digits in countries such as Spain and Japan, to less than 2 percent throughout Latin America. P&G believed that it could use its global marketing skills and distribution networks to grow the product, particularly in underserved markets such as Latin America and Southern Europe. It has found it tough going.

A big part of the problem has been religious and cultural taboos. There is a persistent myth in many countries that if a girl uses a tampon, she might lose her virginity. This concern seems to crop up most often in countries that are predominantly Catholic. Although the Roman Catholic church states that it has no official position on tampons, some priests have spoken out against the product, associating it with birth control and sexual activities that are prohibited by the church! Women must also understand their bodies to use a tampon. P&G is finding that in countries where school health education is limited, that understanding is difficult to foster.

After failed attempts to market the product in India and Brazil using conventional marketing strategies, such as print media advertising and retail distribution, P&G has decided to change its approach to one based on direct selling and relationship marketing. It is testing this model in Monterrey, Mexico. If it works, the company may roll it out in South American countries. A centerpiece of the strategy has been the hiring of a sales force of counselors. The counselors are young women. They must first promise to become regular tampon users. Most have never tried a tampon. P&G trains each woman and observes her early classes. After passing a written test, the women are equipped with anatomy charts, a blue foam model of a woman's reproductive system, and a box of samples. In navy pantsuits or a doctor's white coat embroidered with the Tampax logo, the counselors are dispatched to speak in stores, schools, gyms, and anywhere women gather. The counselors talk to around 60 women a day, explaining how the product works with the aid of flip charts. About one-third end up buying a product.

The counselors also use these meetings as an opportunity to recruit young women to host gatherings in their homes. Modeled on Tupperware parties, about 20 women typically attend these "bonding sessions" where the counselor explains the product and how it is used, answers questions, and dispenses free samples. About 40 percent of women who attend these gatherings go on to host one.

P&G also found that about half of all doctors in Monterrey thought that tampons were bad for women. The company believes that this is based on ignorance; most of the doctors are men and they simply do not understand how the product works. To combat this, P&G used its sales force, which already called on doctors to sell products such as Pepto-Bismol and Metamucil, to give away tampons and explain how the product works. As a result, P&G believes that it has reduced resistance among doctors to less than 10 percent.

Will this selling strategy work? The early signs were encouraging. In just a few months, sales of tampons grew from 2 percent to 4 percent of the total feminine hygiene market in Monterrey, and sales of the Tampax brand tripled. Based on these results, P&G decided to launch its first full campaign in Venezuela in early 2001, with several other Latin American countries following soon after.

Source: E. Nelson and M. Jordan, "Seeking New Markets for Tampons, P&G Faces Cultural Barriers," *Wall Street Journal,* December 8, 2000, pp. A1, A8. Copyright 2000 by *Wall Street Journal.* Reproduced with permission of Dow Jones & Company, Inc., New York, NY, via Copyright Clearance Center.

awards in France. One of its ads featured a black woman breast-feeding a white baby, and another one showed a black man and a white man handcuffed together. Benetton was surprised when the ads were attacked by U.S. civil rights groups for promoting white racial domination. Benetton withdrew its ads and fired its advertising agency, Eldorado of France.

The best way for a firm to overcome cultural barriers is to develop cross-cultural literacy (see Chapter 3). In addition, it should use local input, such as a local advertising agency, in developing its marketing message. If the firm uses direct selling rather than advertising to communicate its message, it should develop a local sales force whenever possible. Cultural differences limit a firm's ability to use the same marketing message and selling approach the world over. What works well in one country may be offensive in another. The accompanying Management Focus, which profiles Procter & Gamble's strategy for selling Tampax tampons internationally, demonstrates how cultural factors can influence the choice of communication strategy.

Source and Country of Origin Effects

Source effects occur when the receiver of the message (the potential consumer in this case) evaluates the message based on the status or image of the sender. Source effects can be damaging for an international business when potential consumers in a target country have a bias against foreign firms. For example, a wave of "Japan bashing" swept the United States in the early 1990s. Worried that U.S. consumers might view its products negatively, Honda responded by creating ads that emphasized the U.S. content of its cars to show how "American" the company had become. Many international businesses try to counter negative source effects by deemphasizing their foreign origins. When British Petroleum acquired Mobil Oil's extensive network of U.S. gas stations, it changed its name to BP, diverting attention away from the fact that one of the biggest operators of gas stations in the United States is a British firm.

A subset of source effects is referred to as *country of origin effects*. Country of origin effects refers to the extent to which the place of manufacturing influences product evaluations. Research suggests that country of origin is often used as a cue when evaluating a product, particularly if the consumer lacks more detailed knowledge of the product. For example, one study found that Japanese consumers tended to rate Japanese products more favorably than U.S. products across multiple dimensions, even when independent analysis showed that they were actually inferior.[14] When a negative country of origin effect exists, an international business may have to work hard to counteract this effect by, for example, using promotional messages that stress the positive performance attributes of their product. Thus, the Korean automobile company Hyundai tried to overcome negative perceptions about the quality of its vehicle in the United States by running advertisements that favorably compare the company's cars to more prestigious brands.

Source effects and country of origin effects are not always negative. French wine, Italian clothes, and German luxury cars benefit from nearly universal positive source effects. In such cases, it may pay a firm to emphasize its foreign origins. In Japan, for example, there is strong demand for high-quality foreign goods, particularly those from Europe. It has become chic to carry a Gucci handbag, sport a Rolex watch, drink expensive French wine, and drive a BMW.

Noise Levels

Noise tends to reduce the probability of effective communication. Noise refers to the amount of other messages competing for a potential consumer's attention, and this too varies across countries. In highly developed countries such as the United States, noise is extremely high. Fewer firms vie for the attention of prospective customers in developing countries, and the noise level is lower.

Push versus Pull Strategies

The main decision with regard to communications strategy is the choice between a push strategy and a pull strategy. A push strategy emphasizes personal selling rather than mass media advertising in the promotional mix. Although very effective as a promotional tool, personal selling requires intensive use of a sales force and is relatively costly. A pull strategy depends more on mass media advertising to communicate the marketing message to potential consumers.

Although some firms employ only a pull strategy and others only a push strategy, still other firms combine direct selling with mass advertising to maximize communication

Unilever—Selling to India's Poor

One of the world's largest and oldest consumer products companies, Unilever has long had a substantial presence in many of the world's poorer nations, such as India. Outside of major urban areas, low income levels, unsophisticated consumers, illiteracy, fragmented retail distribution systems, and the lack of paved roads have made for difficult marketing challenges. Despite this, Unilever has built up a significant presence among impoverished rural populations by adopting innovative selling strategies.

Take India as an example. The country's large rural population is dispersed among some 600,000 villages, more than 500,000 of which cannot be reached by a motor vehicle. Some 91 percent of the rural population lives in villages of fewer than 2,000 people, and of necessity, rural retail stores are very small and carry limited stock. The population is desperately poor, making perhaps a dollar a day, and two-thirds of that income is spent on food, leaving about 30 cents a day for other items. Literacy levels are low, and TVs are rare, making traditional media ineffective. Despite these drawbacks Hindustan Lever, Unilever's Indian subsidiary, has made a concerted effort to reach the rural poor. Although the revenues generated from rural sales are small, Unilever hopes that as the country develops and income levels rise, the population will continue to purchase the Unilever brands that they are familiar with, giving the company a long-term competitive advantage.

To contact rural consumers, Hindustan Lever tries to establish a physical presence wherever people frequently gather in numbers. This means ensuring that advertisements are seen in places where people congregate and make purchases, such as at village wells and weekly rural markets, and where they consume products, such as at riverbanks where people gather to wash their clothes using (the company hopes) Unilever soap. It is not uncommon to see the village well plastered with advertisements for Unilever products. The company also takes part in weekly rural events, such as market day, where farm produce is sold and family provisions purchased. Hindustan Lever salesmen will visit these gatherings, display their products, explain how they work, give away some free samples, make a few sales, and seed the market for future demand.

The backbone of Hindustan Lever's selling effort, however, is a rural distribution network that encompasses 100 factories, 7,500 distributors, and an estimated 3 million retail stores, many of which are little more than a hole in a wall or a stall at a market. The total stock of Unilever products in these stores may be no more than a few sachets of shampoo and half a dozen bars of soap. A depot in each of India's states feeds products to major wholesalers, which then sell directly to retailers in thousands of small towns and villages that can be reached by motor vehicles. If access via motor vehicles is not possible, the major wholesalers sell to smaller second-tier wholesalers, which then handle distribution to India's 500,000 inaccessible rural villages, reaching them by bicycle, bullock, cart, or baskets carried on a human back.

Source: K. Merchant, "Striving for Success—One Sachet at a Time." *Financial Times*, December 11, 2000, p. 14, and M. Turner, "Bicycle Brigade Takes Unilver to the People," *Financial Times*, August 17, 2000, p. 8.

effectiveness. Factors that determine the relative attractiveness of push and pull strategies include product type relative to consumer sophistication, channel length, and media availability.

Product Type and Consumer Sophistication

A pull strategy is generally favored by firms in consumer goods industries that are trying to sell to a large segment of the market. For such firms, mass communication has cost advantages, and direct selling is rarely used. An exception to this rule can be found in poorer nations with low literacy levels, where direct selling may be the only way to reach consumers (see the Management Focus on Unilever). A push strategy is favored by firms that sell industrial products or other complex products. Direct selling allows the firm to educate potential consumers about the features of the product. This may not be necessary in advanced nations where a complex product has been in use for some time, where the product's attributes are well understood, and where consumers are sophisticated. However, customer education may be very important when consumers have less sophistication toward the product, which can be the case in developing nations or in advanced nations when a complex product is being introduced.

Channel Length

The longer the distribution channel, the more intermediaries there are that must be persuaded to carry the product for it to reach the consumer. This can lead to inertia in the channel, which can make entry very difficult. Using direct selling to push a product through many layers of a distribution channel can be very expensive. In such circumstances, a firm may try to pull its product through the channels by using mass advertising to create consumer demand—once demand is created, intermediaries will feel obliged to carry the product.

In Japan, products often pass through two, three, or even four wholesalers before they reach the final retail outlet. This can make it difficult for foreign firms to break into the Japanese market. Not only must the foreigner persuade a Japanese retailer to carry her product, but she may also have to persuade every intermediary in the chain to carry the product. Mass advertising may be one way to break down channel resistance in such circumstances. However, in countries like India, which has a very long distribution channel to serve its massive rural population, low literacy levels may imply that mass advertising may not work, in which case, the firm may need to fall back on direct selling, or rely on the good will of distributors (see the Management Focus on Unilever).

Media Availability

A pull strategy relies on access to advertising media. In the United States, a large number of media are available, including print media (newspapers and magazines), broadcasting media (television and radio), and the Internet. The rise of cable television in the United States has facilitated extremely focused advertising (e.g., MTV for teens and young adults, Lifetime for women, ESPN for sports enthusiasts). The same is true of the Internet, given that different websites attract different kinds of users. While this level of media sophistication is found in some other developed countries, it is not universal. Even many advanced nations have far fewer electronic media available for advertising than the United States. In Scandinavia, for example, no commercial television or radio stations existed in 1987; all electronic media were state owned and carried no commercials, although this has now changed with the advent of satellite television deregulation. In many developing nations, the situation is even more restrictive because mass media of all types are typically more limited. A firm's ability to use a pull strategy is limited in some countries by media availability. In such circumstances, a push strategy is more attractive. For example, Unilever uses a push strategy to sell consumer products in rural India, where few mass media are available (see the Management Focus).

Media availability is limited by law in some cases. Few countries allow advertisements for tobacco and alcohol products on television and radio, though they are usually permitted in print media. When the leading Japanese whiskey distiller, Suntory, entered the U.S. market, it had to do so without television, its preferred medium. The firm spends about $50 million annually on television advertising in Japan.

The Push–Pull Mix

The optimal mix between push and pull strategies depends on product type and consumer sophistication, channel length, and media sophistication. Push strategies tend to be emphasized:

- For industrial products and/or complex new products.
- When distribution channels are short.
- When few print or electronic media are available.

Pull strategies tend to be emphasized:

- For consumer goods.
- When distribution channels are long.
- When sufficient print and electronic media are available to carry the marketing message.

Global Advertising

In recent years, largely inspired by the work of visionaries such as Theodore Levitt, there has been much discussion about the pros and cons of standardizing advertising worldwide.[15] One of the most successful standardized campaigns in history was Philip Morris's promotion of Marlboro cigarettes. The campaign was instituted in the 1950s, when the brand was repositioned, to assure smokers that the flavor would be unchanged by the addition of a filter. The campaign theme of "Come to where the flavor is. Come to Marlboro country" was a worldwide success. Marlboro built on this when it introduced "the Marlboro man," a rugged cowboy smoking his Marlboro while riding his horse through the great outdoors. This ad proved successful in almost every major market around the world, and it helped propel Marlboro to the top of the world market share table.

For Standardized Advertising

The support for global advertising is threefold. First, it has significant economic advantages. Standardized advertising lowers the costs of value creation by spreading the fixed costs of developing the advertisements over many countries. For example, Levi Strauss paid an advertising agency $550,000 to produce a series of TV commercials. By reusing this series in many countries, rather than developing a series for each country, the company enjoyed significant cost savings. Similarly, Coca-Cola's advertising agency, McCann-Erickson, claims to have saved Coca-Cola $90 million over 20 years by using certain elements of its campaigns globally.

Second, there is the concern that creative talent is scarce and so one large effort to develop a campaign will produce better results than 40 or 50 smaller efforts.

A third justification for a standardized approach is that many brand names are global. With the substantial amount of international travel today and the considerable overlap in media across national borders, many international firms want to project a single brand image to avoid confusion caused by local campaigns. This is particularly important in regions such as Western Europe, where travel across borders is almost as common as travel across state lines in the United States.

Against Standardized Advertising

There are two main arguments against globally standardized advertising. First, as we have seen repeatedly in this chapter and in Chapter 3, cultural differences between nations are such that a message that works in one nation can fail miserably in another. Due to cultural diversity, it is extremely difficult to develop a single advertising theme that is effective worldwide. Messages directed at the culture of a given country may be more effective than global messages.

Second, advertising regulations may block implementation of standardized advertising. For example, Kellogg could not use a television commercial it produced in Great Britain to promote its cornflakes in many other European countries. A reference to the iron and vitamin content of its cornflakes was not permissible in the Netherlands, where claims relating to health and medical benefits are outlawed. A child wearing a Kellogg T-shirt had to be edited out of the commercial before it could be used in France, because French law forbids the use of children in product endorsements. The key line, "Kellogg's makes their cornflakes the best they have ever been," was disallowed in Germany because of a prohibition against competitive claims.[16]

Similarly, American Express ran afoul of regulatory authorities in Germany when it launched a promotional scheme that had proved very successful in other countries. The scheme advertised the offer of "bonus points" every time American Express cardholders used their cards. According to the advertisements, these "bonus points" could be used toward air travel with three airlines and hotel accommodations. American Express was charged with breaking Germany's competition law, which prevents an offer of free gifts in connection with the sale of goods, and the firm had to withdraw the advertisements at considerable cost.[17]

Dealing with Country Differences

Some firms are experimenting with capturing some benefits of global standardization while recognizing differences in countries' cultural and legal environments. A firm may select some features to include in all its advertising campaigns and localize other features. By doing so, it may be able to save on some costs and build international brand recognition and yet customize its advertisements to different cultures.

Pepsi-Cola used this kind of approach in a 1980s advertising campaign. The company wanted to use music to connect its products with local markets. Pepsi hired U.S. singer Tina Turner and rock stars from six countries to team up in singing and performing the Pepsi-Cola theme song in a big rock concert. The commercials were customized for each market by showing Turner with the rock stars from that country. Except for the footage of the local stars, all the commercials were identical. By shooting the commercials all at once, Pepsi saved on production costs. The campaign was extended to 30 countries, which relieved the local subsidiaries or bottlers of having to develop their own campaigns.[18]

Pricing Strategy ▮

International pricing strategy is an important component of the overall international marketing mix.[19] In this section, we look at three aspects of international pricing strategy. First, we examine the case for pursuing price discrimination, charging different prices for the same product in different countries. Second, we look at what might be called strategic pricing. Third, we review some regulatory factors, such as government-mandated price controls and antidumping regulations, that limit a firm's ability to charge the prices it would prefer in a country.

▮ Price Discrimination

Price discrimination exists whenever consumers in different countries are charged different prices for the same product.[20] Price discrimination involves charging whatever the market will bear; in a competitive market, prices may have to be lower than in a market where the firm has a monopoly. Price discrimination can help a company maximize its profits. It makes economic sense to charge different prices in different countries.

Two conditions are necessary for profitable price discrimination. First, the firm must be able to keep its national markets separate. If it cannot do this, individuals or businesses may undercut its attempt at price discrimination by engaging in arbitrage. Arbitrage occurs when an individual or business capitalizes on a price differential for a firm's product between two countries by purchasing the product in the country where prices are lower and reselling it in the country where prices are higher. For example, many automobile firms have long practiced price discrimination in Europe. A Ford Escort once cost $2,000 more in Germany than it did in Belgium. This policy broke down when car dealers bought Escorts in Belgium and drove them to Germany, where they sold them at a profit for slightly less than Ford was selling Escorts in Germany. To protect the market share of its German auto dealers, Ford had to bring its German prices into line with those being charged in Belgium. Ford could not keep these markets separate.

Figure 17.2

Elastic and Inelastic
Demand Curves

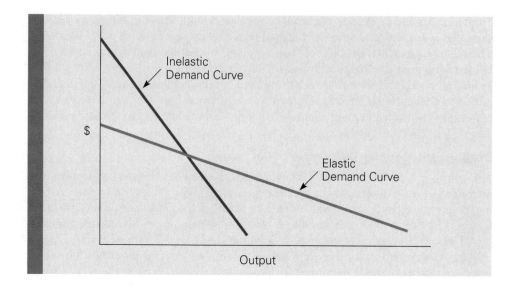

However, Ford still practices price discrimination between Great Britain and Belgium. A Ford car can cost up to $3,000 more in Great Britain than in Belgium. In this case, arbitrage has not been able to equalize the price, because right-hand-drive cars are sold in Great Britain and left-hand-drive cars in the rest of Europe. Because there is no market for left-hand-drive cars in Great Britain, Ford has been able to keep the markets separate.

The second necessary condition for profitable price discrimination is different price elasticities of demand in different countries. The price elasticity of demand is a measure of the responsiveness of demand for a product to changes in price. Demand is said to be elastic when a small change in price produces a large change in demand; it is said to be inelastic when a large change in price produces only a small change in demand. Figure 17.2 illustrates elastic and inelastic demand curves. Generally, for reasons that will be explained shortly, a firm can charge a higher price in a country where demand is inelastic.

The Determinants of Demand Elasticity

The elasticity of demand for a product in a given country is determined by a number of factors, of which income level and competitive conditions are the two most important. Price elasticity tends to be greater in countries with low income levels. Consumers with limited incomes tend to be very price conscious; they have less to spend, so they look much more closely at price. Thus, price elasticities for products such as television sets are greater in countries such as India, where a television set is still a luxury item, than in the United States, where it is considered a necessity.

In general, the more competitors there are, the greater consumers' bargaining power will be and the more likely consumers will be to buy from the firm that charges the lowest price. Thus, many competitors cause high elasticity of demand. In such circumstances, if a firm raises its prices above those of its competitors, consumers will switch to the competitors' products. The opposite is true when a firm faces few competitors. When competitors are limited, consumers' bargaining power is weaker and price is less important as a competitive weapon. Thus, a firm may charge a higher price for its product in a country where competition is limited than in a country where competition is intense.

Profit Maximizing under Price Discrimination

For those readers with some grasp of economic logic, we can offer a more formal presentation of the above argument. (Readers unfamiliar with basic economic terminology may want to skip this subsection.) Figure 17.3 shows the situation facing a firm

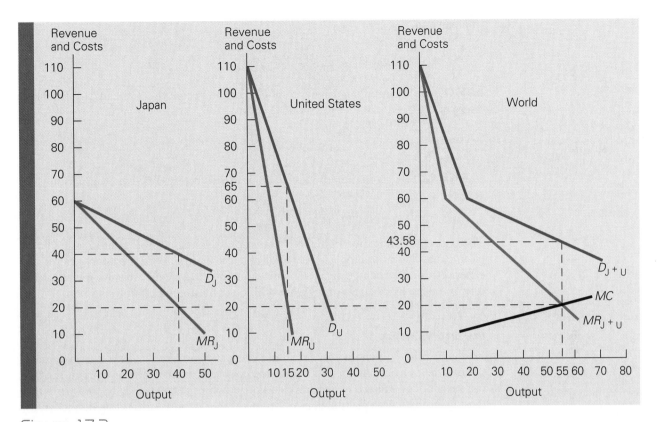

Figure 17.3

Price Discrimination

that sells the same product in only two countries: Japan and the United States. The Japanese market is very competitive, so the firm faces an elastic demand curve (D_J) and marginal revenue curve (MR_J). The U.S. market is not competitive, so there the firm faces an inelastic demand curve (D_U) and marginal revenue curve (MR_U). Also shown in the figure are the firm's total demand curve (D_{J+U}), total marginal revenue curve (MR_{J+U}), and marginal cost curve (MC). The total demand curve is simply the summation of the demand facing the firm in Japan and the United States, as is the total marginal revenue curve.

To maximize profits, the firm must produce at the output where MR = MC. In Figure 17.3, this implies an output of 55 units. If the firm does not practice price discrimination, it will charge a price of $43.58 to sell an output of 55 units. Thus, without price discrimination, the firm's total revenues are $43.58 × 55 = $2,396.90.

Look what happens when the firm decides to engage in price discrimination. It will still produce 55 units, since that is where MR = MC. However, the firm must now allocate this output between the two countries to take advantage of the difference in demand elasticity. Proper allocation of output between Japan and the United States can be determined graphically by drawing a line through their respective graphs at $20 to indicate that $20 is the marginal cost in each country (see Figure 17.3). To maximize profits, prices are now set in each country at that level where the marginal revenue for that country equals marginal costs. In Japan, this is a price of $40, and the firm sells 40 units. In the United States, the optimal price is $65, and it sells 15 units. Thus, reflecting the different competitive conditions, the price charged in the United States is over 50 percent more than the price charged in Japan. Look at what happens to total revenues. With price discrimination, the firm earns revenues of

$$\$40 \times 40 \text{ units} = \$1,600$$

in Japan and

$$\$65 \times 15 \text{ units} = \$975$$

in the United States. By engaging in price discrimination, the firm can earn total revenues of

$$\$1,600 + \$975 = \$2,575,$$

which is $178.10 more than the $2,396.90 it earned before. Price discrimination pays!

❙Strategic Pricing

The concept of strategic pricing has three aspects, which we will refer to as predatory pricing, multipoint pricing, and experience curve pricing. Both predatory pricing and experience curve pricing may violate antidumping regulations. After we review predatory and experience curve pricing, we will look at antidumping rules and other regulatory policies.

Predatory Pricing

Predatory pricing is the use of price as a competitive weapon to drive weaker competitors out of a national market. Once the competitors have left the market, the firm can raise prices and enjoy high profits. For such a pricing strategy to work, the firm must normally have a profitable position in another national market, which it can use to subsidize aggressive pricing in the market it is trying to monopolize. Many Japanese firms have been accused of pursuing such a policy. The argument runs like this: Because the Japanese market is protected from foreign competition by high informal trade barriers, Japanese firms can charge high prices and earn high profits at home. They then use these profits to subsidize aggressive pricing overseas, with the goal of driving competitors out of those markets. Once this has occurred, so it is claimed, the Japanese firms then raise prices. Matsushita was accused of using this strategy to enter the U.S. TV market. As one of the major TV producers in Japan, Matsushita earned high profits at home. It then used these profits to subsidize the losses it made in the United States during its early years there, when it priced low to increase its market penetration. Ultimately, Matsushita became the world's largest manufacturer of TVs.[21]

Multipoint Pricing Strategy

Multipoint pricing becomes an issue when two or more international businesses compete against each other in two or more national markets. For example, multipoint pricing is an issue for Kodak and Fuji Photo because both companies compete against each other in different national markets for film products around the world. Multipoint pricing refers to the fact a firm's pricing strategy in one market may have an impact on its rivals' pricing strategy in another market. Aggressive pricing in one market may elicit a competitive response from a rival in another market. In the case of Kodak and Fuji, Fuji launched an aggressive competitive attack against Kodak in the American company's home market in January 1997, cutting prices on multiple-roll packs of 35mm film by as much as 50 percent.[22] This price cutting resulted in a 28 percent increase in shipments of Fuji color film during the first six months of 1997, while Kodak's shipments dropped by 11 percent. This attack created a dilemma for Kodak; the company did not want to start price discounting in its largest and most profitable market. Kodak's response was to aggressively cut prices in Fuji's largest market, Japan. This strategic response recognized the interdependence between Kodak and Fuji and the fact that they compete against each other in many different nations. Fuji responded to Kodak's counterattack by pulling back from its aggressive stance in the United States.

The Kodak story illustrates an important aspect of multipoint pricing—aggressive pricing in one market may elicit a response from rivals in another market. The firm needs to consider how its global rivals will respond to changes in its pricing strategy before making those changes. A second aspect of multipoint pricing arises when two or more global companies focus on particular national markets and launch vigorous price wars in those markets in an attempt to gain market dominance. In the Brazil market for disposable diapers, two U.S. companies, Kimberly-Clark Corp. and Procter & Gamble, entered a price war as each struggled to establish dominance in the market.[23] As a result, the cost of disposable diapers fell from $1 per diaper in 1994 to 33 cents per diaper in 1997, while several other competitors, including indigenous Brazilian firms, were driven out of the market. Kimberly-Clark and Procter & Gamble are engaged in a global struggle for market share and dominance, and Brazil is one of their battlegrounds. Both companies can afford to engage in this behavior, even though it reduces their profits in Brazil, because they have profitable operations elsewhere in the world that can subsidize these losses.

Pricing decisions around the world need to be centrally monitored. It is tempting to delegate full responsibility for pricing decisions to the managers of various national subsidiaries, thereby reaping the benefits of decentralization (see Chapter 13 for a discussion). However, because pricing strategy in one part of the world can elicit a competitive response in another part, central management needs to at least monitor and approve pricing decisions in a given national market, and local managers need to recognize that their actions can affect competitive conditions in other countries.

Experience Curve Pricing

We first encountered the experience curve in Chapter 12. As a firm builds its accumulated production volume over time, unit costs fall due to "experience effects." Learning effects and economies of scale underlie the experience curve. Price comes into the picture because aggressive pricing (along with aggressive promotion and advertising) can build accumulated sales volume rapidly and thus move production down the experience curve. Firms further down the experience curve have a cost advantage vis-à-vis firms further up the curve.

Many firms pursuing an experience curve pricing strategy on an international scale price low worldwide in attempting to build global sales volume as rapidly as possible, even if this means taking large losses initially. Such a firm believes that several years in the future, when it has moved down the experience curve, it will be making substantial profits and have a cost advantage over its less-aggressive competitors.

Regulatory Influences on Prices

The ability to engage in either price discrimination or strategic pricing may be limited by national or international regulations. Most important, a firm's freedom to set its own prices is constrained by antidumping regulations and competition policy.

Antidumping Regulations

Both predatory pricing and experience curve pricing can run afoul of antidumping regulations. Dumping occurs whenever a firm sells a product for a price that is less than the cost of producing it. Most regulations, however, define dumping more vaguely. For example, a country is allowed to bring antidumping actions against an importer under Article 6 of GATT as long as two criteria are met: sales at "less than fair value" and "material injury to a domestic industry." The problem with this terminology is that it does not indicate what is a fair value. The ambiguity has led some to argue that selling abroad at prices below those in the country of origin, as opposed to below cost, is dumping.

Such logic led the first Bush administration to place a 25 percent duty on imports of Japanese light trucks in 1988. The Japanese manufacturers protested that they were not selling below cost. Admitting that their prices were lower in the United States than in Japan, they argued that this simply reflected the intensely competitive nature of the U.S. market (i.e., different price elasticities). In a similar example, the European Commission found Japanese exporters of dot-matrix printers to be violating dumping regulations. To correct what they saw as dumping, the EU placed a 47 percent import duty on imports of dot-matrix printers from Japan and required that the import duty be passed on to European consumers as a price increase.[24]

Antidumping rules set a floor under export prices and limit firms' ability to pursue strategic pricing. The rather vague terminology used in most antidumping actions suggests that a firm's ability to engage in price discrimination also may be challenged under antidumping legislation.

Competition Policy

Most industrialized nations have regulations designed to promote competition and to restrict monopoly practices. These regulations can be used to limit the prices a firm can charge in a given country. For example, during the 1960s and 70s, the Swiss pharmaceutical manufacturer Hoffmann-LaRoche had a monopoly on the supply of Valium and Librium tranquilizers. The company was investigated in 1973 by the British Monopolies and Mergers Commission, which is responsible for promoting fair competition in Great Britain. The commission found that Hoffmann-LaRoche was overcharging for its tranquilizers and ordered the company to reduce its prices 35 to 40 percent. Hoffmann-LaRoche maintained unsuccessfully that it was merely engaging in price discrimination. Similar actions were later brought against Hoffmann-LaRoche by the German cartel office and by the Dutch and Danish governments.[25]

▌ Configuring the Marketing Mix

A firm might vary aspects of its marketing mix from country to country to take into account local differences in culture, economic conditions, competitive conditions, product and technical standards, distribution systems, government regulations, and the like. Such differences may require variation in product attributes, distribution strategy, communications strategy, and pricing strategy. The cumulative effect of these factors makes it rare for a firm to adopt the same marketing mix worldwide.

For example, financial services is often thought of as an industry where global standardization of the marketing mix is the norm. However, while a financial services company such as American Express may sell the same basic charge card service worldwide, utilize the same basic fee structure for that product, and adopt the same basic global advertising message ("never leave home without it"), differences in national regulations still mean that it has to vary aspects of its communications strategy from country to country (as pointed out earlier, the promotional strategy it had developed in the United States was illegal in Germany). Similarly, while McDonald's is often thought of as the quintessential example of a firm that sells the same basic standardized product worldwide, in reality it varies one important aspect of its marketing mix—its menu—from country to country. McDonald's also varies its distribution strategy. In Canada and the United States most McDonald's are located in areas that are easily accessible by car, whereas in more densely populated and less automobile-reliant societies of the world, such as Japan and Great Britain, location decisions are driven by the accessibility of a restaurant to pedestrian traffic. Because countries typically still differ along one or more of the dimensions discussed above, some customization of the marketing mix is normal.

However, there are often significant opportunities for standardization along one or more elements of the marketing mix.[26] Firms may find that it is possible and desirable to standardize their global advertising message and/or core product attributes to realize substantial cost economies. They may find it desirable to customize their distribution and pricing strategy to take advantage of local differences. In reality, the

Management Focus

Castrol Oil

Castrol is the lubricants division of the British chemical, oil, and gas concern Burmah Castrol. In Europe and in the United States where Castrol has a 15 percent share of the do-it-yourself lubricants market, Castrol targets motorists who want to cosset their engine by paying a bit more for Castrol's high-margin GTX brand, rather than a standard lubricant. This differentiated positioning strategy is supported by sponsoring Formula 1 racing and the Indy car series in the United States and by heavy spending on television and in automobile magazines in both Europe and the United States.

Some of Castrol's most notable successes in recent years, however, have been in the developing nations of Asia where Castrol reaps only one-sixth of its sales, but over one-quarter of its operating profits. In Vietnam, automobiles are still relatively rare, so Castrol has targeted motorcycle owners. Castrol's strategy is to target people who want to take care of their new motorcycles. The long-term goal is to build brand loyalty, so that when automobile ownership becomes common in Vietnam, as Castrol believes it will, former motorcycle owners will stick with Castrol when they trade up to cars. This strategy has already worked in Thailand. Castrol has held the leading share of the motorcycle market in Thailand since the early 1980s, and it now holds the leading share in that country's rapidly growing automobile market.

Unlike its practice in more developed countries, Castrol's communications strategy in Vietnam does not focus on television and glossy print media (since there is relatively little of either in Vietnam). Rather, Castrol focuses on building consumer awareness through extensive use of billboards, car stickers, and some 4,000 signs at Vietnam's ubiquitous roadside garages and motorcycle cleaning shops. Castrol also developed a unique slogan that has a rhythmic quality in Vietnamese "Dau nhot tot nhat" (best quality lubricants) and sticks in consumers' minds. Castrol's researchers say the slogan is now recognized by a remarkable 99 percent of people in Ho Chi Minh City.

As elsewhere, Castrol has adopted a premium pricing strategy in Vietnam, which is consistent with the company's attempt to build a global brand image of high quality. Castrol oil costs about $1.5 per liter in Vietnam, about three times as much as the price of cheaper oil imported from Taiwan and Thailand. Despite the high price of its product, Castrol claims it is gaining share in Vietnam as its branding strategy wins converts.

Castrol has had to tailor its distribution strategy to Vietnam's unique conditions. In most countries where it operates, Castrol divides the country into regions and has a single distributor in each region. In Vietnam, however, Castrol will often have two distinct distributors in a region—one to deal with state-owned customers, of which there are still many in this Communist country, and one to deal with private customers. Castrol acknowledges the system is costly but says it is the only way to operate in a country where there is still some tension between state and private entities.

Sources: V. Mallet, "Climbing the Slippery Slope," *Financial Times*, July 28, 1994, p. 7, and A. Bolger, "Growth by Successful Targeting," *Financial Times*, June 21, 1994, p. 27.

"customization versus standardization" debate is not an all or nothing issue; it frequently makes sense to standardize some aspects of the marketing mix and customize others, depending on conditions in various national marketplaces. An explicit example, that of Castrol Oil, is given in the accompanying Management Focus. Castrol sells a standardized product worldwide—lubricating oil—yet it varies other aspects of its marketing mix from country to country, depending on economic conditions, competitive conditions, and distribution systems. Decisions about what to customize and what to standardize should be driven by a detailed examination of the costs and benefits of doing so for each element in the marketing mix.

New-Product Development

Firms that successfully develop and market new products can earn enormous returns. Examples include Du Pont, which has produced a steady stream of successful innovations such as cellophane, nylon, Freon, and Teflon (nonstick pans); Sony, whose successes include the Walkman and the compact disk; Merck, the drug company that during the 1980s produced seven major new drugs; 3M, which has applied its core competency in tapes and adhesives to developing a wide range of new products; Intel, which has consistently managed to lead in the development of innovative microprocessors to run personal computers; and Cisco Systems, which developed the routers that sit at the hubs of Internet connections, directing the flow of digital traffic.

In today's world, competition is as much about technological innovation as anything else. The pace of technological change has accelerated since the Industrial Revolution in the 18th century, and it continues to do so today. The result has been a dramatic shortening of product life cycles. Technological innovation is both creative and destructive.[27] An innovation can make established products obsolete overnight. But an innovation can also make a host of new products possible. Witness recent changes in the electronics industry. For 40 years before the early 1950s, vacuum valves were a major component in radios and then in record players and early computers. The advent of transistors destroyed the market for vacuum valves, but at the same time it created new opportunities connected with transistors. Transistors took up far less space than vacuum valves, creating a trend toward miniaturization that continues today. The transistor held its position as the major component in the electronics industry for just a decade. Microprocessors were developed in the 1970s and the market for transistors declined rapidly. The microprocessor created yet another set of new-product opportunities—handheld calculators (which destroyed the market for slide rules), compact disk players (which destroyed the market for analog record players), personal computers (which destroyed the market for typewriters), to name a few.

This "creative destruction" unleashed by technological change makes it critical that a firm stay on the leading edge of technology, lest it lose out to a competitor's innovations. As we explain in the next subsection, this not only creates a need for the firm to invest in R&D, but it also requires the firm to establish R&D activities at those locations where expertise is concentrated. As we shall see, leading-edge technology on its own is not enough to guarantee a firm's survival. The firm must also apply that technology to developing products that satisfy consumer needs, and it must design the product so that it can be manufactured in a cost-effective manner. To do that, the firm needs to build close links between R&D, marketing, and manufacturing. This is difficult enough for the domestic firm, but it is even more problematic for the international business competing in an industry where consumer tastes and preferences differ from country to country. With all of this in mind, we move on to examine locating R&D activities and building links between R&D, marketing, and manufacturing.

The Location of R&D

Ideas for new products are stimulated by the interactions of scientific research, demand conditions, and competitive conditions. Other things being equal, the rate of new-product development seems to be greater in countries where:

- More money is spent on basic and applied research and development.
- Underlying demand is strong.
- Consumers are affluent.
- Competition is intense.[28]

Basic and applied research and development discovers new technologies and then commercializes them. Strong demand and affluent consumers create a potential market for new products. Intense competition between firms stimulates innovation as the firms try to beat their competitors and reap potentially enormous first-mover advantages that result from successful innovation.

For most of the post–World War II period, the country that ranked highest on these criteria was the United States. The United States devoted a greater proportion of its gross domestic product (GDP) to R&D than any other country did. Its scientific establishment was the largest and most active in the world. U.S. consumers were the most affluent, the market was large, and competition among U.S. firms was brisk. Due to these factors, the United States was the market where most new products were developed and introduced. Accordingly, it was the best location for R&D activities; it was where the action was.

Over the past 20 years, things have been changing quickly. The U.S. monopoly on new-product development has weakened considerably. Although U.S. firms are still at the leading edge of many new technologies, Japanese and European firms are also strong players, with companies such as Sony, Sharp, Ericsson, Nokia, and Philips NV driving product innovation in their respective industries. Both Japan and Germany are now devoting a greater proportion of their GDP to nondefense R&D than is the United States.[29] In addition, both Japan and the European Union are large, affluent markets, and the wealth gap between them and the United States is closing.

As a result, it is often no longer appropriate to consider the United States as the lead market. In video games, for example, Japan is often the lead market, with companies like Sony and Nintendo introducing their latest video game players in Japan some six months before they introduce them in the United States. In wireless telecommunications, Europe is generally reckoned to be ahead of the United States. Some of the most advanced applications of wireless telecommunications services are being pioneered not in the United States, but in Finland, where 80 percent of the population has wireless telephones, compared to 40 percent of the U.S. population. More often than not, however, it is questionable whether any developed nation can be considered the lead market. To succeed in today's high-technology industries, it is often necessary to simultaneously introduce new products in all major industrialized markets. When Intel introduces a new microprocessor, for example, it does not first introduce it in the United States and then roll it out in Europe a year later. It introduces it simultaneously around the world.

Because leading-edge research is now carried out in many locations around the world, the argument for centralizing R&D activity in the United States is now much weaker than it was two decades ago. (It used to be argued that centralized R&D eliminated duplication.) Much leading-edge research is now occurring in Japan and Europe. Dispersing R&D activities to those locations allows a firm to stay close to the center of leading-edge activity to gather scientific and competitive information and to draw on local scientific resources.[30] This may result in some duplication of R&D activities, but the cost disadvantages of duplication are outweighed by the advantages of dispersion.

For example, to expose themselves to the research and new-product development work being done in Japan, many U.S. firms have set up satellite R&D centers in Japan. Kodak's $65 million R&D center in Japan employs approximately 200 people. The company hired about 100 professional Japanese researchers and directed the lab to concentrate on electronic imaging technology. U.S. firms that have established R&D facilities in Japan include Corning, Texas Instruments, IBM, Digital Equipment, Procter & Gamble, Upjohn, Pfizer, Du Pont, Monsanto, and Microsoft.[31] The National Science Foundation (NSF) has documented a sharp increase in the proportion of total R&D spending by U.S. firms that is now done abroad.[32] For example, Motorola now has 14 dedicated R&D facilities located in seven countries, and Bristol-Myers Squibb has 12 facilities in six countries. At the same time, to internationalize their own research and gain access to U.S. talent, the NSF reports that many European and Japanese firms are investing in U.S.-based research facilities.

Integrating R&D, Marketing, and Production

Although a firm that is successful at developing new products may earn enormous returns, new-product development is very risky, having a high failure rate. One study of product development in 16 companies in the chemical, drug, petroleum, and electronics industries suggested that only about 20 percent of R&D projects result in commercially successful products or processes.[33] Another in-depth case study of product development in three companies (one in chemicals and two in drugs) reported that about 60 percent of R&D projects reached technical completion, 30 percent were commercialized, and only 12 percent earned an economic profit that exceeded the company's cost of capital.[34] Similarly, a study by the consulting division of Booz, Allen & Hamilton found that over one-third of 13,000 consumer and industrial products introduced between 1976 and 1981 failed to meet company-specific financial and strategic performance criteria.[35] A more recent study found that 45 percent of new products did not meet their profitability goals.[36] This evidence suggests that many R&D projects do not result in a commercial product, and that between 33 percent and 60 percent of all new products that do reach the marketplace fail to generate an adequate economic return. Two well-publicized product failures are Apple Computer's Newton, a personal digital assistant, and Sony's Betamax format in the video player and recorder market.

The reasons for such high failure rates are various and include development of a technology for which there is only limited demand, failure to adequately commercialize promising technology, and inability to manufacture a new product cost effectively. Firms can avoid such mistakes by insisting on tight cross-functional coordination and integration between three core functions involved in the development of new products: R&D, marketing, and production.[37] Tight cross-functional integration between R&D, production, and marketing can help a company to ensure that

1. Product development projects are driven by customer needs.
2. New products are designed for ease of manufacture.
3. Development costs are kept in check.
4. Time to market is minimized.

Close integration between R&D and marketing is required to ensure that product development projects are driven by the needs of customers. A company's customers can be a primary source of new-product ideas. Identification of customer needs, particularly unmet needs, can set the context within which successful product innovation occurs. As the point of contact with customers, the marketing function of a company can provide valuable information in this regard. Integration of R&D and marketing are crucial if a new product is to be properly commercialized. Without integration of R&D and marketing, a company runs the risk of developing products for which there is little or no demand.

Integration between R&D and production can help a company design products with manufacturing requirements in mind. Designing for manufacturing can lower costs and increase product quality. Integrating R&D and production can also help lower development costs and speed products to market. If a new product is not designed with manufacturing capabilities in mind, it may prove too difficult to build. Then the product will have to be redesigned, and both overall development costs and the time it takes to bring the product to market may increase significantly. Making design changes during product planning could increase overall development costs by 50 percent and add 25 percent to the time it takes to bring the product to market.[38] Many quantum product innovations require new processes to manufacture them, which makes it all the more important to achieve close integration between R&D and production. Minimizing time to market and development costs may require the simultaneous development of new products and new processes.[39]

Cross-Functional Teams

One way to achieve cross-functional integration is to establish cross-functional product development teams composed of representatives from R&D, marketing, and production. Because these functions may be located in different countries, the team will sometimes have a multinational membership. The objective of a team should be to take a product development project from the initial concept development to market introduction. A number of attributes seem to be important for a product development team to function effectively and meet all its development milestones.[40]

First, the team should be led by a "heavyweight" project manager who has high status within the organization and who has the power and authority required to get the financial and human resources the team needs to succeed. The "heavyweight" leader should be dedicated primarily, if not entirely, to the project. The leader should be someone who believes in the project (a champion) and who is skilled at integrating the perspectives of different functions and at helping personnel from different functions and countries work together for a common goal. The leader should also be able to act as an advocate of the team to senior management.

Second, the team should be composed of at least one member from each key function. The team members should have a number of attributes, including an ability to contribute functional expertise, high standing within their function, a willingness to share responsibility for team results, and an ability to put functional and national advocacy aside. It is generally preferable if core team members are 100 percent dedicated to the project for its duration. This assures their focus on the project, not on the ongoing work of their function.

Third, the team members should be physically co-located if possible to create a sense of camaraderie and to facilitate communication. This presents problems if the team members are drawn from facilities in different nations. One solution is to transfer key individuals to one location for the duration of a product development project. Fourth, the team should have a clear plan and clear goals, particularly with regard to critical development milestones and development budgets. The team should have incentives to attain those goals, such as receiving pay bonuses when major development milestones are hit. Fifth, each team needs to develop its own processes for communication and conflict resolution. For example, one product development team at Quantum Corporation, a California-based manufacturer of disk drives for personal computers, instituted a rule that all major decisions would be made and conflicts resolved at meetings that were held every Monday afternoon. This simple rule helped the team meet its development goals. In this case, it was also common for team members to fly in from Japan, where the product was to be manufactured, to the U.S. development center for the Monday morning meetings.[41]

Implications for International Business

The need to integrate R&D and marketing to adequately commercialize new technologies poses special problems in the international business, since commercialization may require different versions of a new product to be produced for different countries.[42] We saw an example of this in the opening case, which described how Procter & Gamble's R&D center in Kobe, Japan, developed a dish soap formula specifically for the Japanese market. To do this, the firm must build close links between its R&D centers and its various country operations. A similar argument applies to the need to integrate R&D and production, particularly in those international businesses that have dispersed production activities to different locations around the globe depending on a consideration of relative factor costs and the like.

Integrating R&D, marketing, and production in an international business may require R&D centers in North America, Asia, and Europe that are linked by formal and informal integrating mechanisms with marketing operations in each country in their regions and with the various manufacturing facilities. In addition, the international business may have to establish cross-functional teams whose members are dispersed around the globe. This complex endeavor requires the company to utilize the formal and informal integrating mechanisms that we discussed in Chapter 13 to knit its far-flung operations together so they can produce new products in an effective and timely manner.

While there is no one best model for allocating product development responsibilities to various centers, one solution adopted by many international businesses involves establishing a global network of R&D centers. Within this model, fundamental research is undertaken at basic research centers around the globe. These centers are normally located in regions or cities where valuable scientific knowledge is being created and where there is a pool of skilled research talent (e.g., Silicon Valley in the United States, Cambridge in England, Kobe in Japan). These centers are the innovation engines of the firm. Their job is to develop the basic technologies that become new products.

These technologies are picked up by R&D units attached to global product divisions and are used to generate new products to serve the global marketplace. At this level, emphasis is placed on commercialization of the technology and design for manufacturing. If further customization is needed so the product appeals to the tastes and preferences of consumers in individual markets, such redesign work will be done by an R&D group based in a subsidiary in that country or at a regional center that customizes products for several countries in the region.

Hewlett-Packard (HP) has four basic research centers located in Palo Alto, California; Bristol, England; Haifa, Israel; and Tokyo, Japan.[43] These labs are the seedbed for technologies that ultimately become new products and businesses. They are the company's innovation engines. The Palo Alto center, for example, pioneered HP's thermal ink-jet technology. The products are developed by R&D centers associated with HP's global product divisions. Thus, the Consumer Products Group, which has its worldwide headquarters in San Diego, California, designs, develops, and manufactures a range of imaging products using HP-pioneered thermal ink-jet technology. Subsidiaries might then customize the product so that it best matches the needs of important national markets. HP's subsidiary in Singapore, for example, is responsible for the design and production of thermal ink-jet printers for Japan and other Asian markets. This subsidiary takes products originally developed in San Diego and redesigns them for the Asian market. In addition, the Singapore subsidiary has taken the lead from San Diego in the design and development of certain portable thermal ink-jet printers. HP delegated this responsibility to Singapore because this subsidiary has built important competencies in the design and production of thermal ink-jet products, so it has become the best place in the world to undertake this activity.

Microsoft offers a similar example. The company has basic research sites in Redmond, Washington (its headquarters); Cambridge, England; Tokyo, Japan; and Silicon Valley, California. Staff at these research sites work on the fundamental problems that underlie the design of future products. For example, a group at Redmond is working on natural language recognition software, while another works on artificial intelligence. These research centers don't produce new products; rather, they produce the technology that is used to enhance existing products or help produce new products. The products are produced by dedicated product groups (e.g., desktop operating systems, applications). Customization of the products to match the needs of local markets is sometimes carried out at local subsidiaries. Thus, the Chinese subsidiary in Singapore will do some basic customization of programs such as Microsoft Office, adding Chinese characters and customizing the interface.

Chapter Summary

This chapter discussed the marketing and R&D functions in international business. A persistent theme of the chapter is the tension that exists between the need to reduce costs and the need to be responsive to local conditions, which raises costs. This chapter made the following points:

1. Theodore Levitt has argued that, due to the advent of modern communications and transport technologies, consumer tastes and preferences are becoming global, which is creating global markets for standardized consumer products. However, this position is regarded as extreme by

many commentators, who argue that substantial differences still exist between countries.

2. Market segmentation refers to the process of identifying distinct groups of consumers whose purchasing behavior differs from each other in important ways. Managers in an international business need to be aware of two main issues relating to segmentation: (1) the extent to which there are differences between countries in the structure of market segments, and (2) the existence of segments that transcend national borders.

3. A product can be viewed as a bundle of attributes. Product attributes need to be varied from country to country to satisfy different consumer tastes and preferences.

4. Country differences in consumer tastes and preferences are due to differences in culture and economic development. In addition, differences in product and technical standards may require the firm to customize product attributes from country to country.

5. A distribution strategy decision is an attempt to define the optimal channel for delivering a product to the consumer.

6. Significant country differences exist in distribution systems. In some countries, the retail system is concentrated; in others, it is fragmented. In some countries, channel length is short; in others, it is long. Access to distribution channels is difficult to achieve in some countries.

7. A critical element in the marketing mix is communication strategy, which defines the process the firm will use in communicating the attributes of its product to prospective customers.

8. Barriers to international communication include cultural differences, source effects, and noise levels.

9. A communication strategy is either a push strategy or a pull strategy. A push strategy emphasizes personal selling, and a pull strategy emphasizes mass media advertising. Whether a push strategy or a pull strategy is optimal depends on the type of product, consumer sophistication, channel length, and media availability.

10. A globally standardized advertising campaign, which uses the same marketing message all over the world, has economic advantages, but it fails to account for differences in culture and advertising regulations.

11. Price discrimination exists when consumers in different countries are charged different prices for the same product. Price discrimination can help a firm maximize its profits. For price discrimination to be effective, the national markets must be separate and their price elasticities of demand must differ.

12. Predatory pricing is the use of profit gained in one market to support aggressive pricing in another market to drive competitors out of that market.

13. Multipoint pricing refers to the fact a firm's pricing strategy in one market may affect rivals' pricing strategies in another market. Aggressive pricing in one market may elicit a competitive response from a rival in another market that is important to the firm.

14. Experience curve pricing is the use of aggressive pricing to build accumulated volume as rapidly as possible to quickly move the firm down the experience curve.

15. New-product development is a high-risk, potentially high-return activity. To build a competency in new-product development, an international business must do two things: (1) disperse R&D activities to those countries where new products are being pioneered and (2) integrate R&D with marketing and manufacturing.

16. Achieving tight integration among R&D, marketing, and manufacturing requires the use of cross-functional teams.

Critical Discussion Questions

1. Imagine you are the marketing manager for a U.S. manufacturer of disposable diapers. Your firm is considering entering the Brazilian market. Your CEO believes the advertising message that has been effective in the United States will suffice in Brazil. Outline some possible objections to this. Your CEO also believes that the pricing decisions in Brazil can be delegated to local managers. Why might she be wrong?

2. Within 20 years, we will have seen the emergence of enormous global markets for standardized consumer products. Do you agree with this statement? Justify your answer.

3. You are the marketing manager of a food products company that is considering entering the South Korean market. The retail system in South Korea tends to be very fragmented. Also, retailers and wholesalers tend to have long-term ties with

South Korean food companies, which makes access to distribution channels difficult. What distribution strategy would you advise the company to pursue? Why?

4. Price discrimination is indistinguishable from dumping. Discuss the accuracy of this statement.

5. You work for a company that designs and manufactures personal computers. Your company's R&D center is in North Dakota. The computers are manufactured under contract in Taiwan. Marketing strategy is delegated to the heads of three regional groups: a North American group (based in Chicago), a European group (based in Paris), and an Asian group (based in Singapore). Each regional group develops the marketing approach within its region. In order of importance, the largest markets for your products are North America, Germany, Great Britain, China, and Australia. Your company is experiencing problems in its product development and commercialization process. Products are late to market, the manufacturing quality is poor, and costs are higher than projected, and market acceptance of new products is less then hoped for. What might be the source of these problems? How would you fix them?

Closing Case

Nike—The Ugly American?

Nike has always cultivated its rebel image—James Dean in sneakers. Nike was founded in 1972 by Phil Knight, a former university track star, and Bill Bowerman, who had been his coach. In the subsequent 30 years, the Beaverton, Oregon, company has grown from a niche supplier of running shoes for hard-core athletes into a global colossus in the athletic footwear and apparel business with sales of $10 billion, 40 percent of which are generated outside its core U.S. market. Three main factors seem to underpin the company's success: the quality and innovation of its products, its sponsorship of key athletes with "star appeal" such as Michael Jordan and Tiger Woods, and its global advertising, which has carved out a strong brand image for the company.

The image of Nike as the cool iconoclastic rebel shines through strongly in its advertising. Tough and gritty, Nike ads urge consumers to damn the consequences and Just Do It!—while wearing Nike gear, of course. In America, the rebel has done extraordinarily well. Nike dominates the market, selling $20 in footwear and apparel per year for every man, woman, and child in the country. But herein lies a problem. The company has been so successful that it is difficult to see how it can continue to grow in the now mature U.S. market. This is not a pleasant thought for an aggressive, ambitious risk-taker like CEO Phil Knight. Knight has set a goal of growing revenues by 15 percent a year and has focused the company's attentions on international markets where the opportunities for growth seem much greater. In contrast to the saturated U.S. market, annual per capita Nike sales in Japan are $4, in Germany they are $3, and in China just over 2 cents. Knight wanted to see foreign sales rise to 50 percent of total sales by 2000 and continue upwards from there.

There is only one problem with this vision. Basketball, for all of its recent global success, is still a fringe sport outside the United States; jogging is a distinctly American passion; and as for baseball and football, don't ask! For Nike to grow its international business, it must focus on the dominant global sport, soccer. But in many countries, soccer is imbued with nationalistic pride, and Nike is American, and Americans aren't very good at soccer. Also, soccer already has its dominant footwear and apparel suppliers, Adidas and Umbro, which have tied up most of the world's top teams and stars in sponsorship deals.

However, Knight and his team don't shy from a challenge. Underdog once more, Nike embarked on an aggressive advertising campaign to build awareness for its brand in the world of soccer. In the spring of 1996, Nike announced its intentions to the world with a series of ads in soccer magazines around the world. "Europe, Asia, and Latin America," the ad screamed, "Barricade your stadiums. Hide your trophies. Invest in some deodorant. As Asia and Latin America have been crushed, so shall Europe . . . the world has been warned." The world was not amused. The reaction was more along the lines of "Who do these Americans think they are, and what's in the gibe about deodorant?" Nike, however, had only just begun.

Next was the TV commercial portraying Satan and his demons playing soccer against a team of Nike endorsers. The ad, which set a company record for cost, ran worldwide. Knight declared the ad his favorite Nike commercial ever, and it was well received in America. But several European broadcasters deemed it too scary and offensive to show in prime time when children were watching. The ad also drew angry letters from viewers. But this was all grist for the mill of the American rebel, so Nike plunged ahead with an ad for British television that featured a French soccer star and perennial "bad boy" proudly detailing how his spitting at a fan and calling his coach a bag of s____ had won him a Nike contract. This ad provoked a scathing editorial against Nike in the newsletter of soccer's governing federation, FIFA. Sepp Blatter, now president of FIFA, condemned an "advertising trend that glorifies violence or bad taste . . . technically clever and futuristic as it may be, such style does nothing to promote values, especially among impressionable youngsters."

What really set anti-American tongues wagging among soccer's ruling establishment, however, was Nike's coup in Brazil. The Brazilian soccer team is legendary, having won a record five World Cups. It is also a vibrant symbol of Brazil's samba culture and a huge source of national pride. Imagine the shock when the loud American waltzed into town with bundles of money and purchased the rights to sponsor Brazil's national team for the next 10 years, pushing aside the existing sponsor, Umbro. The deal, which cost $200 million, commits the Brazilian team to appearances in Nike-produced exhibition matches and community events and requires team members to wear Nike shoes and uniforms sporting the Nike "swoosh" logo. To the soccer es-tablishment, it looked as if the Visigoths had just stormed the high temple of soccer.

While Nike may have alienated soccer's establishment, it is not clear that the same is true of Nike's target market—the youth of the world. The establishment may have hated Nike's Satan soccer ad, but Nike managers tell about a focus audience of teens being mesmerized when French soccer star Mr. Cantona flips up his collar, says "*au revoir*," and kicks the winning goal through the Devil. As they left the room, the youngsters all flipped their collars and said "*au revoir*." The kids, apparently, got it!

Sources: M. Sawyer, "Fashion: It's Not Working Out," *The Observer*, May 3, 1998, p. 12; P. Vallely, "Saturday Story," *The Independent*," December 6, 1997, p. 19; and N. Robinson, "Nike Just Does It in Bad Taste," *The Guardian*, November 26, 1996, p. 22.

Case Discussion Questions

1. Is Nike wrong to try to leverage its American rebel image to build brand awareness in the global market for soccer footwear and apparel? What are the potential drawbacks of such an approach?

2. Is Nike's promotional strategy for soccer an example of the ugly American abroad, or is it clever marketing by one of the world's shrewdest promoters?

3. How might Nike alter its marketing approach to woo soccer players to the Nike brand without generating the negative reaction it has apparently generated among the soccer establishment?

Notes

1. See R. W. Ruekert and O. C. Walker, "Interactions between Marketing and R&D Departments in Implementing Different Business-Level Strategies," *Strategic Management Journal* 8 (1987), pp. 233–48, and K. B. Clark and S. C. Wheelwright, *Managing New Product and Process Development* (New York: Free Press), 1993.

2. T. Levitt, "The Globalization of Markets," *Harvard Business Review*, May–June 1983, pp. 92–102. Reprinted by permission of *Harvard Business Review*, an exerpt from "The Globalization of Markets," by Theodore Levitt, May–June 1983. Copyright © 1983 by the President and Fellows of Harvard College. All rights reserved.

3. For example, see S. P. Douglas and Y. Wind, "The Myth of Globalization," *Columbia Journal of World Business*, Winter 1987, pp. 19–29, and C. A. Bartlett and S. Ghoshal, *Managing across Borders: The Transnational Solution* (Boston: Harvard Business School Press, 1989).

4. "Slow Food," *The Economist*, February 3, 1990, p. 64.

5. J. T. Landry, "Emerging Markets: Are Chinese Consumers Coming of Age?" *Harvard Business Review*, May–June 1998, pp. 17–20.

6. C. Miller, "Teens Seen as the First Truly Global Consumers," *Marketing News*, March 27, 1995, p. 9.

7. This approach was originally developed in K. Lancaster, "A New Approach to Demand Theory," *Journal of Political Economy* 74 (1965), pp. 132–57.

8. V. R. Alden, "Who Says You Can't Crack Japanese Markets?" *Harvard Business Review*, January–February 1987, pp. 52–56.

9. T. Parker-Pope, "Custom Made," *Wall Street Journal*, September 26, 1996, p. 22.

10. A. Rawthorn, "A Bumpy Ride over Europe's Traditions," *Financial Times*, October 31, 1988, p. 5.

11. "RCA's New Vista: The Bottom Line," *Business Week*, July 4, 1987, p. 44.

12. N. Gross and K. Rebello, "Apple? Japan Can't Say No," *Business Week*, June 29, 1992, pp. 32–33.

13. "After Early Stumbles P&G Is Making Inroads Overseas," *Wall Street Journal*, February 6, 1989, p. B1.

14. Z. Gurhan-Cvanli and D. Maheswaran, "Cultural Variation in Country of Origin Effects," *Journal of Marketing Research*, August 2000, pp. 309–17.

15. See M. Laroche, V. H. Kirpalani, F. Pons, and L. Zhou, "A Model of Advertising Standardization in Multinational Corporations," *Journal of International Business Studies*, 32 (2001), pp. 249–66, and D. A. Aaker and E. Joachimsthaler, "The Lure of Global Branding," *Harvard Business Review*, November–December 1999, pp. 137–44.

16. "Advertising in a Single Market," *The Economist*, March 24, 1990, p. 64.

17. D. Waller, "Charged up over Competition Law," *Financial Times*, June 23, 1994, p. 14.

18. J. Lumbin, "Advertising: Tina Turner Helps Pepsi's Global Effort," *New York Times*, March 10, 1986, p. D13.

19. R. J. Dolan and H. Simon, *Power Pricing*. (New York: Free Press, 1999).

20. B. Stottinger, "Strategic Export Pricing: A Long Winding Road," *Journal of International Marketing* 9, (2001), pp. 40–63.

21. These allegations were made on a PBS "Frontline" documentary telecast in the United States in May 1992.

22. G. Smith and B. Wolverton, "A Dark Moment for Kodak," *Business Week*, August 4, 1997, pp. 30–31.

23. R. Narisette and J. Friedland, "Disposable Income: Diaper Wars of P&G and Kimberly-Clark Now Heat up in Brazil," *Wall Street Journal*, June 4, 1997, p. A1.

24. "Printers Reflect Pattern of Trade Rows," *Financial Times*, December 20, 1988, p. 3.

25. J. F. Pickering, *Industrial Structure and Market Conduct* (London: Martin Robertson, 1974).

26. S. P. Douglas, C. Samuel Craig, and E. J. Nijissen. "Integrating Branding Strategy across Markets," *Journal of International Marketing* 9, no 2, (2001), pp. 97–114.

27. The phrase was first used by economist Joseph Schumpeter in *Capitalism, Socialism, and Democracy* (New York: Harper Brothers, 1942).

28. See D. C. Mowery and N. Rosenberg, *Technology and the Pursuit of Economic Growth* (Cambridge, UK: Cambridge University Press, 1989), and M. E. Porter, *The Competitive Advantage of Nations* (New York: The Free Press, 1990).

29. C. Farrell, "Industrial Policy," *Business Week*, April 6, 1992, pp. 70–75.

30. W. Kuemmerle, "Building Effective R&D Capabilities Abroad," *Harvard Business Review*, March–April 1997, pp. 61–70.

31. "When the Corporate Lab Goes to Japan," *New York Times*, April 28, 1991, sec. 3, p. 1.

32. D. Shapley, "Globalization Prompts Exodus," *Financial Times*, March 17, 1994, p. 10.

33. E. Mansfield. "How Economists See R&D," *Harvard Business Review*, November–December, 1981, pp. 98–106.

34. Ibid.

35. Booz, Allen, & Hamilton, "New Products Management for the 1980s," privately published research report, 1982.

36. A. L. Page, "PDMA's New Product Development Practices Survey: Performance and Best Practices," PDMA 15th Annual International Conference, Boston, October 16, 1991.

37. K. B. Clark and S. C. Wheelwright, *Managing New Product and Process Development* (New York: Free Press, 1993), and M. A. Shilling and C. W. L. Hill, "Managing the New Product Development Process," *Academy of Management Executive* 12, no. 3 (1998), pp. 67–81.

38. O. Port, "Moving Past the Assembly Line," *Business Week Special Issue: Reinventing America*, 1992, pp. 177–80.

39. K. B. Clark and T. Fujimoto, "The Power of Product Integrity," *Harvard Business Review*, November–December 1990, pp. 107–18; Clark and Wheelwright, *Managing New Product and Process Development*; S. L. Brown and K. M. Eisenhardt, "Product Development: Past Research, Present Findings, and Future Directions," *Academy of Management Review* 20 (1995), pp. 348–78; and G. Stalk and T. M. Hout, *Competing against Time* (New York: Free Press, 1990).

40. Shilling and Hill, "Managing the New Product Development Process."

41. C. Christensen. "Quantum Corporation—Business and Product Teams," Harvard Business School Case # 9-692-023.

42. R. Nobel and J. Birkinshaw, "Innovation in Multinational Corporations: Control and Communication Patterns in International R&D Operations," *Strategic Management Journal* 19 (1998), pp. 479–96.

43. Information comes from the company's website, and from K. Ferdows, "Making the Most of Foreign Factories," *Harvard Business Review*, March–April 1997, pp. 73–88.

Global
Human
Resource
Management

Molex

Molex is a 65-year-old manufacturer of electronic components based in Chicago. The company established an international division to coordinate exporting in 1967, opened its first plant in Japan in 1970, and a second in Ireland in 1971. From that base, Molex has evolved into a global business that generates about 65 percent of its $2.5 billion in annual revenues outside of the United States. The company operates some 50 manufacturing plants in 21 countries and employs some 16,000 people worldwide, only one-third of which are located in the United States. Molex's competitive advantage is based on a strategy that emphasizes a combination of low costs and excellent customer service. Manufacturing sites are located in countries where cost conditions are favorable and major customers are close. Since the 1970s, a key goal of Molex has been to build a truly global company that is at home wherever in the world it operates, and which proactively shares valuable knowledge across operations in different countries. The human resources function of Molex has always played a central role in meeting this goal.

As Molex grew rapidly overseas, the human resource management (HRM) function made sure that every new unit did the same basic things whatever the country. Each new entity had to have an employee manual with policies and practices in writing, new employee orientation programs, salary administration with a consistent grading system, written job descriptions, written promotion and grievance procedures, standard performance appraisal systems that were written down, and so on. Beyond these things, however, Molex views HRM as the most localized of functions. Different legal systems, particularly with regard to employment law, different compensation norms, different cultural attitudes to work, different norms regarding vacation, and so on, all imply that policies and programs must be customized to the conditions prevailing in a country. To make sure this occurs, Molex's policy is to hire experienced HRM professionals from other companies in the same country in which they have operations. The idea is to hire people who know the language, have credibility, know the law, and know how to recruit in that country.

Molex's strategy for building a global company starts with its staffing policy for managers and engineers. The company frequently hires foreign nationals who are living in the United States, have just completed MBAs, and are willing to relocate if required. These individuals will typically work in the United States for a while, becoming familiar with the company's culture. Some of them will then be sent back to their home country to work there. Molex also carefully screens its American applicants, favoring those who are fluent in at least one other language. Molex is unusual for an American company in having a language requirement as an important part of the interview process. However, with more than 15 languages spoken at its headquarters by native speakers, Molex is committed to the value of a multilingual competency. There is also significant hiring of managers and engineers at the local level. Here, too, a willingness to relocate internationally and foreign language competency are important, although this time English is the preferred foreign language. In a sign of how multinational Molex's management has become, it is not unusual to see foreign nationals holding senior positions at company headquarters. In addition to Americans, individuals of Greek, German, Austrian, Japanese, and British origin have all sat on the company's executive committee, its top decision-making body.

To help build a global company, Molex moves people around the world to give them experience of other countries and to help them learn from each other. It has five categories of expatriates: (1) regular expatriates who live in a country other than their home country for three-to-five-year assignments (there are approximately 50 of these at any one time), (2) "inpats" who come to the company's U.S. headquarters from other countries, (3) third-country nationals who move from one Molex entity to another (for example, Singapore to Taiwan), (4) short-term transfers who go to another Molex entity for 6 to 9 months to work on a specific project, and (5) medium terms who go to another entity for 12 to 24 months, again to work on a specific project.

Having a high level of intracompany movement is costly. For an employee making $75,000 in base salary, the total cost of an expatriate assignment can run as high as $250,000 when additional employee benefits are added in, such as the provision of schooling and housing, adjustments for higher costs of living, adjustments for higher tax rates, and so on. Molex also insists on treating all expatriates the same, whatever their country of origin, so a Singapore expatriate living in Taiwan is likely to be living in the same apartment building and sending his child to the same school as an American expatriate in Taiwan. This boosts the overall costs, but Molex believes that its extensive use of expatriates pays back dividends. It allows individuals to understand the challenges of doing business in different countries, it facilitates the sharing of useful knowledge across different business entities, and it helps to lay the foundation for a common company culture that is global in its outlook.

Molex also goes to great lengths to make sure that expatriates know why they are being sent to a foreign country, both in terms of their own career development and Molex's corporate goals. To make sure that expatriates don't become disconnected from their home office, the HRM department touches base with them on a regular basis through telephone, e-mail, and direct visits. The company also encourages expatriates to make home office visits so that they do not become totally disconnected from their base and feel like a stranger when they return. Upon return, they are debriefed and their knowledge gained abroad is put to use by, for example, placing the expatriates on special task forces.

A final component of Molex's strategy for building a cadre of globally minded managers is the company's in-house management development programs. These are open to a wide range of managers who have worked at Molex for three years or more. Molex uses these programs not just to educate its managers in finance, operations, strategy, and the like, but also to bring together managers from different countries to build a network of individuals who know each other and can work together in a cooperative fashion to solve business problems that transcend borders.

Sources: J. Laabs, "Molex Makes Global HR Look Easy," *Workforce*, March 1999, pp. 42–46; C. M. Solomon; "Foreign Relations," *Workforce*, November 2000, pp. 50–56; C. M. Solomon, "Navigating Your Search for Global Talent," *Personnel Journal*, May 1995, pp. 94–100; and A. C. Poe, "Welcome Back," *HR Magazine*, March 2000, pp. 94–105.

∎ Introduction

Continuing our survey of specific functions within an international business, this chapter examines international human resource management (HRM). Human resource management refers to the activities an organization carries out to use its human resources effectively.[1] These activities include determining the firm's human resource strategy, staffing, performance evaluation, management development, compensation, and labor relations. None of these activities is performed in a vacuum; all are related to the strategy of the firm because, as we will see, HRM has an important strategic component.[2] Through its influence on the character, development, quality, and productivity of the firm's human resources, the HRM function can help the firm achieve its primary strategic goals of reducing the costs of value creation and adding value by better serving customer needs.

The strategic role of HRM is complex enough in a purely domestic firm, but it is more complex in an international business, where staffing, management development, performance evaluation, and compensation activities are complicated by profound differences between countries in labor markets, culture, legal systems, economic systems, and the like (see Chapters 2 and 3). For example,

- Compensation practices may vary from country to country depending on prevailing management customs.
- Labor laws may prohibit union organization in one country and mandate it in another.
- Equal employment legislation may be strongly pursued in one country and not in another.

If it is to build a cadre of managers capable of managing a multinational enterprise, the HRM function must deal with a host of issues. It must decide how to staff key management posts in the company, how to develop managers so that they are familiar with the nuances of doing business in different countries, and how to compensate people in different nations. HRM must also deal with a host of issues related to expatriate managers. (An **expatriate manager** is a citizen of one country who is working abroad in one of the firm's subsidiaries.) It must decide whom to send on expatriate postings, be clear about why they are doing it, compensate expatriates appropriately, and make sure that they are adequately debriefed and reoriented once they return home.

The opening case detailed how Molex deals with some of these issues. Molex is quite explicit about using the HRM function to help attain the strategic goal of building a global company that has a low-cost structure, provides excellent customer service, and is comfortable doing business in many different countries and cultures. Molex uses its staffing policy to recruit managers who are fluent in more than one language and willing to relocate to other countries. It makes liberal use of expatriates. Foreign postings are seen as a way of developing managers and a means for transferring valuable know-how between country operations. The benefits package for expatriates is designed to make sure there is no bonus for being an American, which sends the message that all employees are viewed equally, regardless of national origin. Finally, Molex proactively uses its own in-house management development programs to help establish a network of managers from different countries who know each other, can share valuable information with each other, and can work together in a cooperative fashion to solve business problems that transcend borders.

In this chapter, we will look closely at the role of HRM in an international business. We begin by briefly discussing the strategic role of HRM. Then we turn our attention to four major tasks of the HRM function: staffing policy, management training and development, performance appraisal, and compensation policy. We will point out the strategic implications of each of these tasks. The chapter closes with a look at international labor relations and the relationship between the firm's management of labor relations and its overall strategy.

The Strategic Role of International HRM

In Chapter 12, we examined four strategies pursued by international businesses—the multidomestic, the international, the global, and the transnational. Multidomestic firms try to create value by emphasizing local responsiveness; international firms, by transferring core competencies overseas; global firms, by realizing experience curve and location economies; and transnational firms, by doing all these things simultaneously. In Chapter 13, we discussed the organizational requirements for implementing each of these strategies. Table 18.1, identical to Table 13.2, summarizes the relationships between international strategies, structures, and controls.

Structures or controls summarized in Table 18.1 don't mean much if the human resources that support them are not appropriate. Without the right kind of people in place, organizational structure is just a hollow shell. In Chapter 13, we explained that formal and informal structure and controls must be congruent with a firm's strategy for the firm to succeed. Success also requires HRM policies to be congruent with the firm's strategy and with its formal and informal structure and controls. For example, a transnational strategy imposes very different requirements for staffing, management development, and compensation practices than a multidomestic strategy does.

In many ways, Molex, which was profiled in the opening case, is pursuing a transnational strategy. Molex tries to drive down its cost structure by locating manufacturing plants in countries where cost conditions are favorable, but at the same time the firm devotes great attention to sharing valuable know-how among operations in different countries and uses management transfers (expatriates) and management development

Structure and Controls	International Strategy			
	Multidomestic	**International**	**Global**	**Transanational**
Centralization of operating decisions	Decentralized	Core competency centralized Rest decentralized	Some centralized	Mixed centralized and decentralized Informal matrix
Horizontal differentiation	Worldwide area structure	Worldwide product division	Worldwide product division	Informal matrix
Need for coordination	Low	Moderate	High	Very high
Integrating mechanisms	None	Few	Many	Very many
Performance ambiguity	Low	Moderate	High	Very high
Need for cultural controls	Low	Moderate	High	Very high

Table 18.1

Strategy, Structure, and Control Systems

programs as a way of facilitating that. As indicated in Table 18.1, firms pursuing a transnational strategy need to build a strong corporate culture and an informal management network for transmitting information within the organization. Through its employee selection, management development, performance appraisal, and compensation policies, the HRM function can help develop these things. For example, Molex's liberal use of expatriates, by creating a cadre of international managers with experience in various nations, should help to establish an informal management network. In addition, as at Molex management development programs can build a corporate culture that supports strategic goals. In short, HRM has a critical role to play in implementing strategy. In each section that follows, we will review the strategic role of HRM in some detail.

Staffing Policy

Staffing policy is concerned with the selection of employees for particular jobs. At one level, this involves selecting individuals who have the skills required to do particular jobs. At another level, staffing policy can be a tool for developing and promoting corporate culture.[3] By corporate culture, we mean the organization's norms and value systems. We encountered the concept in Chapter 13 when we discussed the use of "cultural controls" in businesses, noting that strong cultural controls help the firm pursue its strategy. Firms pursuing transnational and global strategies have high needs for a strong unifying culture, and the need is somewhat lower for firms pursuing an international strategy and lowest of all for firms pursuing a multidomestic strategy (see Table 18.1).

In firms pursuing transnational and global strategies, we might expect the HRM function to pay significant attention to selecting individuals who not only have the skills required to perform particular jobs but who also "fit" the prevailing culture of the firm. General Electric, for example, which is positioned toward the transnational end of the strategic spectrum, is not just concerned with hiring people who have the skills required for performing particular jobs; it wants to hire individuals whose behavioral styles, beliefs, and value systems are consistent with those of GE. This is true whether an American is being hired, an Italian, a German, or an Australian and whether the hiring is for a U.S. operation or a foreign operation. The belief is that if employees are predisposed toward the organization's norms and value systems by their personality type, the firm, which has a significant need for integration, will experience fewer problems with performance ambiguity.

The need for integration is substantially lower in a multidomestic firm. There is less performance ambiguity and not the same need for cultural controls. In theory, this means the HRM function can pay less attention to building a unified corporate culture. In multidomestic firms, the culture can be allowed to vary from national operation to national operation. (Although, given the questionable viability of a multidomestic strategy in today's world, this might not be the best policy to pursue. Chapter 12 discusses the viability of this strategy.)

Types of Staffing Policy

Research has identified three types of staffing policies in international businesses: the ethnocentric approach, the polycentric approach, and the geocentric approach.[4] We will review each policy and link it to the strategy pursued by the firm. The most attractive staffing policy is probably the geocentric approach, although there are several impediments to adopting it.

The Ethnocentric Approach

An **ethnocentric staffing** policy is one in which all key management positions are filled by parent-country nationals. This practice was very widespread at one time. Firms such as Procter & Gamble, Philips NV, and Matsushita originally followed it. In the Dutch firm Philips, for example, all important positions in most foreign subsidiaries were at one time held by Dutch nationals who were referred to by their non-Dutch colleagues as the Dutch Mafia. In many Japanese and South Korean firms today, such as Toyota, Matsushita, and Samsung, key positions in international operations are still often held by home-country nationals. According to the Japanese Overseas Enterprise Association, in 1996 only 29 percent of foreign subsidiaries of Japanese companies had presidents who were not Japanese. In contrast, 66 percent of the Japanese subsidiaries of foreign companies had Japanese presidents.[5]

Firms pursue an ethnocentric staffing policy for three reasons. First, the firm may believe the host country lacks qualified individuals to fill senior management positions. This argument is heard most often when the firm has operations in less developed countries. Second, the firm may see an ethnocentric staffing policy as the best way to maintain a unified corporate culture. Many Japanese firms, for example, prefer their foreign operations to be headed by expatriate Japanese managers because these managers will have been socialized into the firm's culture while employed in Japan.[6] Procter & Gamble until recently preferred to staff important management positions in its foreign subsidiaries with U.S. nationals who had been socialized into P&G's corporate culture by years of employment in its U.S. operations. Such reasoning tends to predominate when a firm places a high value on its corporate culture.

Third, if the firm is trying to create value by transferring core competencies to a foreign operation, as firms pursuing an international strategy are, it may believe that the best way to do this is to transfer parent-country nationals who have knowledge of that competency to the foreign operation. Imagine what might occur if a firm tried to transfer a core competency in marketing to a foreign subsidiary without supporting the transfer with a corresponding transfer of home-country marketing management personnel. The transfer would probably fail to produce the anticipated benefits because the knowledge underlying a core competency cannot easily be articulated and written down. Such knowledge often has a significant tacit dimension; it is acquired through experience. Just like the great tennis player who cannot instruct others how to become great tennis players simply by writing a handbook, the firm that has a core competency in marketing—or anything else—cannot just write a handbook that tells a foreign subsidiary how to build the firm's core competency anew in a foreign setting. It must also transfer management personnel to the foreign operation to show foreign managers how to become good marketers, for example. The need to transfer managers overseas arises because the knowledge that underlies the firm's core competency resides in the heads of its domestic managers and was acquired through years of experience, not by reading a handbook. Thus, if a firm is to transfer a core competency to a foreign subsidiary, it must also transfer the appropriate managers.

Despite this rationale for pursuing an ethnocentric staffing policy, the policy is now on the wane in most international businesses for two reasons. First, an ethnocentric staffing policy limits advancement opportunities for host-country nationals. This can lead to resentment, lower productivity, and increased turnover among that group. Resentment can be greater still if, as often occurs, expatriate managers are paid significantly more than home-country nationals.

Second, an ethnocentric policy can lead to "cultural myopia," the firm's failure to understand host-country cultural differences that require different approaches to marketing and management. The adaptation of expatriate managers can take a long time, during which they may make major mistakes. For example, expatriate managers may fail to appreciate how product attributes, distribution strategy, communications strategy, and pricing strategy should be adapted to host-country conditions. The result may be costly blunders. They may also make decisions that are ethically suspect simply because they do not understand the culture in which they are managing.[7] In one highly publicized case in the United States, Mitsubishi Motors was sued by the federal Equal Employment Opportunity Commission for tolerating extensive and systematic sexual harassment in a plant in Illinois. The plant's top management, all Japanese expatriates, denied the charges. The Japanese managers may have failed to realize that behavior that would be viewed as acceptable in Japan was not acceptable in the United States.[8]

The Polycentric Approach

A **polycentric staffing** policy requires host-country nationals to be recruited to manage subsidiaries, while parent-country nationals occupy key positions at corporate headquarters. In many respects, a polycentric approach is a response to the shortcomings of an ethnocentric approach. One advantage of adopting a polycentric approach is that the firm is less likely to suffer from cultural myopia. Host-country managers are unlikely to make the mistakes arising from cultural misunderstandings to which expatriate managers are vulnerable. A second advantage is that a polycentric approach may be less expensive to implement, reducing the costs of value creation. Expatriate managers can be very expensive to maintain.

A polycentric approach also has its drawbacks. Host-country nationals have limited opportunities to gain experience outside their own country and thus cannot progress beyond senior positions in their own subsidiary. As in the case of an ethnocentric policy, this may cause resentment. Perhaps the major drawback with a polycentric approach, however, is the gap that can form between host-country managers and parent-country managers. Language barriers, national loyalties, and a range of cultural differences may isolate the corporate headquarters staff from the various foreign subsidiaries. The lack of management transfers from home to host countries, and vice versa, can exacerbate this isolation and lead to a lack of integration between corporate headquarters and foreign subsidiaries. The result can be a "federation" of largely independent national units with only nominal links to the corporate headquarters. Within such a federation, the coordination required to transfer core competencies or to pursue experience curve and location economies may be difficult to achieve. Thus, although a polycentric approach may be effective for firms pursuing a multidomestic strategy, it is inappropriate for other strategies.

The federation that may result from a polycentric approach can also be a force for inertia within the firm. After decades of pursing a polycentric staffing policy, food and detergents giant Unilever found that shifting from a multidomestic strategic posture to a transnational posture was very difficult. Unilever's foreign subsidiaries had evolved into quasi-autonomous operations, each with its own strong national identity. These "little kingdoms" objected strenuously to corporate headquarters' attempts to limit their autonomy and to rationalize global manufacturing.[9]

The Geocentric Approach

A **geocentric staffing** policy seeks the best people for key jobs throughout the organization, regardless of nationality. Molex is a good example of a company that has adopted a geocentric staffing policy (see the opening case). There are a number of advantages to this policy. First, it enables the firm to make the best use of its human resources. Second, and perhaps more important, a geocentric policy enables the firm to build a cadre of international executives who feel at home working in a number of cultures. Creation of such a cadre may be a critical first step toward building a strong unifying corporate culture and an informal management network, both of which are required for global and transnational strategies (see Table 18.1).[10] Firms pursuing a geocentric staffing policy may be better able to create value from the pursuit of experience curve and location economies and from the multidirectional transfer of core competencies than firms pursuing other staffing policies. In addition, the multinational composition of the management team that results from geocentric staffing tends to reduce cultural myopia and to enhance local responsiveness. Thus, other things being equal, a geocentric staffing policy seems the most attractive.

A number of problems limit the firm's ability to pursue a geocentric policy. Many countries want foreign subsidiaries to employ their citizens. To achieve this goal, they use immigration laws to require the employment of host-country nationals if they are available in adequate numbers and have the necessary skills. Most countries (including the United States) require firms to provide extensive documentation if they wish to hire a foreign national instead of a local national. This documentation can be time consuming, expensive, and at times futile. A geocentric staffing policy also can be very expensive to implement. There are increased training and relocation costs involved in transferring managers from country to country. The company may also need a compensation structure with a standardized international base pay level higher than national levels in many countries. In addition, the higher pay enjoyed by managers placed on an international "fast track" may be a source of resentment within a firm.

Summary

The advantages and disadvantages of the three approaches to staffing policy are summarized in Table 18.2. Broadly speaking, an ethnocentric approach is compatible with an international strategy, a polycentric approach is compatible with a multidomestic strategy, and a geocentric approach is compatible with both global and transnational strategies. (See Chapter 12 for details of the strategies.)

Staffing Approach	Strategic Appropriateness	Advantages	Disadvantages
Ethnocentric	International	Overcomes lack of qualified managers in host nation Unified culture Helps transfer core competencies	Produces resentment in host country Can lead to cultural myopia
Polycentric	Multidomestic	Alleviates cultural myopia Inexpensive to implement	Limits career mobility Isolates headquarters from foreign subsidiaries
Geocentric	Global and transnational	Uses human resources efficiently Helps build strong culture and informal management network	National immigration policies may limit implementation Expensive

Table 18.2

Comparison of Staffing Approaches

While the staffing policies described here are well known and widely used among both practitioners and scholars of international businesses, recently some critics have claimed that the typology is too simplistic and that it obscures the internal differentiation of management practices within international businesses. The critics claim that within some international businesses, staffing policies vary significantly from national subsidiary to national subsidiary; while some are managed on an ethnocentric basis, others are managed in a polycentric or geocentric manner.[11] Other critics note that the staffing policy adopted by a firm is primarily driven by its geographic scope, as opposed to its strategic orientation. Firms that have a very broad geographic scope are the most likely to have a geocentric mind-set.[12] Thus, Molex, which is involved in about 50 countries, is by this argument more likely to have a geocentric mind-set than a firm that is involved in only 3 countries.

Expatriate Managers

Two of the three staffing policies we have discussed—the ethnocentric and the geocentric—rely on extensive use of expatriate managers. As defined earlier, **expatriates** are citizens of one country who are working in another country. Sometimes the term *inpatriates* is used to identify a subset of expatriates who are citizens of a foreign country working in the home country of their multinational employer.[13] Thus, a citizen of Japan who moves to the United States to work at Molex would be classified as an inpatriate. With an ethnocentric policy, the expatriates are all home-country nationals who are transferred abroad. With a geocentric approach, the expatriates need not be home-country nationals; the firm does not base transfer decisions on nationality. A prominent issue in the international staffing literature is expatriate failure—the premature return of an expatriate manager to his or her home country.[14] Here we briefly review the evidence on expatriate failure before discussing a number of ways to minimize the expatriate failure rate.

Expatriate Failure Rates

Expatriate failure represents a failure of the firm's selection policies to identify individuals who will not thrive abroad. The costs of expatriate failure are high. One estimate is that the average cost per failure to the parent firm can be as high as three times the expatriate's annual domestic salary plus the cost of relocation (which is affected by currency exchange rates and location of assignment).[15] Research suggests that between 16 and 40 percent of all American employees sent abroad to developed nations return from their assignments early, and almost 70 percent of employees sent to developing nations return home early.[16] Although detailed data are not available for other nationalities, one suspects that high expatriate failure is a universal problem. Estimates of the costs of each failure run between $250,000 and $1 million.[17] In addition, approximately 30 to 50 percent of American expatriates, whose average annual compensation package runs to $250,000, stay at their international assignments but are considered ineffective or marginally effective by their firms.[18] In a seminal study, R. L. Tung surveyed a number of U.S., European, and Japanese multinationals.[19] Her results, summarized in Table 18.3, suggested that 76 percent of U.S. multinationals experienced expatriate failure rates of 10 percent or more, and 7 percent experienced a failure rate of more than 20 percent. Tung's work also suggests that U.S.-based multinationals experience a much higher expatriate failure rate than either European or Japanese multinationals.

Tung asked her sample of multinational managers to indicate reasons for expatriate failure. For U.S. multinationals, the reasons, in order of importance, were

1. Inability of spouse to adjust.
2. Manager's inability to adjust.
3. Other family problems.

Recall Rate Percent	Percent of Companies
U.S. multinationals	
20–40%	7%
10–20	69
<10	24
European multinationals	
11–15%	3%
6–10	38
<5	59
Japanese multinationals	
11–19%	14%
6–10	10
<5	76

Table 18.3

Expatriate Failure Rates

Source: Data from R. L. Tung, "Selection and Training Procedures of U.S., European, and Japanese Multinations," pp. 51–71. Copyright © by The Regents of the University of California. Reprinted from the *California Management Review*, Vol. 1.25, No. 1, by permission from The Regents.

4. Manager's personal or emotional maturity.
5. Inability to cope with larger overseas responsibilities.

Managers of European firms gave only one reason consistently to explain expatriate failure: the inability of the manager's spouse to adjust to a new environment. For the Japanese firms, the reasons for failure were

1. Inability to cope with larger overseas responsibilities.
2. Difficulties with new environment.
3. Personal or emotional problems.
4. Lack of technical competence.
5. Inability of spouse to adjust.

The most striking difference between these lists is that "inability of spouse to adjust" was the top reason for expatriate failure among U.S. and European multinationals but only the number-five reason among Japanese multinationals. Tung comments that this difference is not surprising, given the role and status to which Japanese society traditionally relegates the wife and the fact that most of the Japanese expatriate managers in the study were men.

Since Tung's study, a number of other studies have consistently confirmed that the inability of a spouse to adjust, the inability of the manager to adjust, or other family problems remain major reasons for continuing high levels of expatriate failure. One study by International Orientation Resources, an HRM consulting firm, found that 60 percent of expatriate failures occur due to these three reasons.[20] Another study found that the most common reason for assignment failure is lack of partner (spouse) satisfaction, which was listed by 27 percent of respondents.[21] The inability of expatriate managers to adjust to foreign postings seems to be caused by a lack of cultural skills on the part of the manager being transferred. According to one HRM management consulting firm, this is because the expatriate selection process at many firms is fundamentally flawed. "Expatriate assignments rarely fail because the person cannot accommodate to the technical demands of the job. Typically, the expatriate selections are made by line managers based on technical competence. They fail because of family and personal issues and lack of cultural skills that haven't been part of the selection process."[22]

Managing Expatriates at Royal Dutch/Shell

Royal Dutch/Shell is a global petroleum company with joint headquarters in both London and The Hague in the Netherlands. The company employs over 100,000 people, approximately 5,500 of whom are at any one time living and working as expatriates. The expatriates at Shell are a very diverse group, made up of over 70 nationalities and located in more than 100 countries. Shell has long recognized that as a global corporation, the international mobility of its workforce is essential to its success. By the early 1990s, however, Shell was finding it harder to recruit key personnel for foreign postings. To discover why, the company in 1993 interviewed more than 200 expatriate employees and their spouses to determine their biggest concerns. The data were then used to construct a survey that was sent to 17,000 current and former expatriate employees, expatriates' spouses, and employees who had declined international assignments.

The survey registered a phenomenal 70 percent response rate, clearly indicating that many employees thought this was an important issue. According to the survey, five issues had the greatest impact on the willingness of an employee to accept an international assignment. In order of importance, these were (1) separation from children during their secondary education (the children of British and Dutch expatriates were often sent to boarding schools in their home countries while their parents worked abroad), (2) harm done to a spouse's career and employment, (3) failure to recognize and involve a spouse in the relocation decision, (4) failure to provide adequate information and assistance regarding relocation, and (5) health issues. The underlying message was that the family is the basic unit of expatriation, not the individual, and Shell needed to do more to recognize this.

To deal with these issues, Shell implemented a number of programs designed to address some of these problems. To help with the education of chil-

dren, Shell built elementary schools for Shell employees where there was a heavy concentration of expatriates. As for secondary school education, it worked with local schools, often providing grants, to help them upgrade their educational offerings. It also offered an education supplement to help expatriates send their children to private schools in the host country (before 1994, it would pay only for a child's boarding school education in its home country).

Helping spouses with their careers is a more vexing problem. According to the survey data, half of the spouses accompanying Shell staff on assignment were employed until the transfer. When expatriated, only 12 percent were able to secure employment, while a further 33 percent wished to be employed. Shell set up a spouse employment center to address the problem. The center provides career counseling and assistance in locating employment opportunities both during and immediately after an international assignment. The company also agreed to reimburse up to 80 percent of the costs of vocational training, further education, or reaccreditation, up to $4,400 per assignment.

Shell also set up a global information and advice network known as "The Outpost" to provide support for families contemplating a foreign posting. The Outpost has its headquarters in The Hague and now runs 40 information centers in more than 30 countries. Staffed by spouses and fully supported by Shell, this network had by 1998 helped more than 1,000 couples prepare for placements overseas. The center recommends schools and medical facilities and provides housing advice and up-to-date information on employment, study, self-employment, and volunteer work.

Sources: E. Smockum, "Don't Forget the Trailing Spouse," *Financial Times*, May 6, 1998, p. 22; V. Frazee, "Tearing Down Roadblocks," *Workforce* 77, no. 2 (1998), pp. 50–54; and C. Sievers, "Expatriate Management," *HR Focus* 75, no. 3 (1998), pp. 75–76.

The failure of spouses to adjust to a foreign posting seems to be related to a number of factors. Often spouses find themselves in a foreign country without the familiar network of family and friends. Language differences make it difficult for them to make new friends. While this may not be a problem for the manager, who can make friends at work, it can be difficult for the spouse who might feel trapped at home. The problem is often exacerbated by immigration regulations prohibiting the spouse from taking employment. With the recent rise of two-career families in many developed nations, this has become a much more important issue. One recent survey found that

69 percent of expatriates are married, with spouses accompanying them 77 percent of the time. Of those spouses, 49 percent were employed before an assignment and only 11 percent were employed during an assignment.[23] Recent research suggests that a main reason managers now turn down international assignments is concern over the impact such an assignment might have on their spouse's career.[24] The accompanying Management Focus examines how one large multinational company, Royal Dutch/ Shell, has tried to come to grips with this issue.

Expatriate Selection

One way to reduce expatriate failure rates is by improving selection procedures to screen out inappropriate candidates. In a review of the research on this issue, Mendenhall and Oddou state that a major problem in many firms is that HRM managers tend to equate domestic performance with overseas performance potential.[25] Domestic performance and overseas performance potential are not the same thing. An executive who performs well in a domestic setting may not be able to adapt to managing in a different cultural setting. From their review of the research, Mendenhall and Oddou identified four dimensions that seem to predict success in a foreign posting: self-orientation, others-orientation, perceptual ability, and cultural toughness.

1. *Self-orientation.* The attributes of this dimension strengthen the expatriate's self-esteem, self-confidence, and mental well-being. Expatriates with high self-esteem, self-confidence, and mental well-being were more likely to succeed in foreign postings. Mendenhall and Oddou concluded that such individuals were able to adapt their interests in food, sport, and music; had interests outside of work that could be pursued (e.g., hobbies); and were technically competent.

2. *Others-orientation.* The attributes of this dimension enhance the expatriate's ability to interact effectively with host-country nationals. The more effectively the expatriate interacts with host-country nationals, the more likely he or she is to succeed. Two factors seem to be particularly important here: relationship development and willingness to communicate. Relationship development refers to the ability to develop long-lasting friendships with host-country nationals. Willingness to communicate refers to the expatriate's willingness to use the host-country language. Although language fluency helps, an expatriate need not be fluent to show willingness to communicate. Making the effort to use the language is what is important. Such gestures tend to be rewarded with greater cooperation by host-country nationals.

3. *Perceptual ability.* This is the ability to understand why people of other countries behave the way they do; that is, the ability to empathize. This dimension seems critical for managing host-country nationals. Expatriate managers who lack this ability tend to treat foreign nationals as if they were home-country nationals. As a result, they may experience significant management problems and considerable frustration. As one expatriate executive from Hewlett-Packard observed, "It took me six months to accept the fact that my staff meetings would start 30 minutes late, and that it would bother no one but me." According to Mendenhall and Oddou, well-adjusted expatriates tend to be nonjudgmental and nonevaluative in interpreting the behavior of host-country nationals and willing to be flexible in their management style, adjusting it as cultural conditions warrant.

4. *Cultural toughness.* This dimension refers to the fact that how well an expatriate adjusts to a particular posting tends to be related to the country of assignment. Some countries are much tougher postings than others because their cultures are more unfamiliar and uncomfortable. For example, many Americans regard Great Britain as a relatively easy foreign posting, and for

good reason—the two cultures have much in common. But many Americans find postings in non-Western cultures, such as India, Southeast Asia, and the Middle East, to be much tougher.[26] The reasons are many, including poor health care and housing standards, inhospitable climate, lack of Western entertainment, and language difficulties. Also, many cultures are extremely male dominated and may be particularly difficult postings for female Western managers.

Mendenhall and Oddou note that standard psychological tests can be used to assess the first three of these dimensions, whereas a comparison of cultures can give managers a feeling for the fourth dimension. They contend that these four dimensions, in addition to domestic performance, should be considered when selecting a manager for foreign posting. However, current practice does not conform to Mendenhall and Oddou's recommendations. Tung's research, for example, showed that only 5 percent of the firms in her sample used formal procedures and psychological tests to assess the personality traits and relational abilities of potential expatriates.[27] Research by International Orientation Resources suggests that when selecting employees for foreign assignments, only 10 percent of the 50 Fortune 500 firms they surveyed tested for important psychological traits such as cultural sensitivity, interpersonal skills, adaptability, and flexibility. Instead, 90 percent of the time employees were selected on the basis of their technical expertise, not their cross-cultural fluency.[28]

Mendenhall and Oddou do not address the problem of expatriate failure due to a spouse's inability to adjust. According to a number of other researchers, a review of the family situation should be part of the expatriate selection process (see the Management Focus on Royal Dutch/Shell for an example).[29] A survey by Windam International, another international HRM management consulting firm, found that spouses were included in preselection interviews for foreign postings only 21 percent of the time, and that only half of them receive any cross-cultural training. The rise of dual-career families has added an additional and difficult dimension to this long-standing problem.[30] Increasingly, spouses wonder why they should have to sacrifice their own career to further that of their partner.[31]

▮ Training and Management Development

Selection is just the first step in matching a manager with a job. The next step is training the manager to do the specific job. For example, an intensive training program might be used to give expatriate managers the skills required for success in a foreign posting. Management development is a much broader concept. It is intended to develop the manager's skills over his or her career with the firm. Thus, as part of a management development program, a manager might be sent on several foreign postings over a number of years to build her cross-cultural sensitivity and experience. At the same time, along with other managers in the firm, she might attend management education programs at regular intervals. The thinking behind job transfers is that broad international experience will enhance the management and leadership skills of executives. Recent research suggests this may be the case.[32]

Historically, most international businesses have been more concerned with training than with management development. Plus, they tended to focus their training efforts on preparing home-country nationals for foreign postings. Recently, however, the shift toward greater global competition and the rise of transnational firms have changed this. It is increasingly common for firms to provide general management development programs in addition to training for particular posts. In many international businesses, the explicit purpose of these management development programs is strategic. Management development is seen as a tool to help the firm achieve its strategic goals.

With this distinction between training and management development in mind, we first examine the types of training managers receive for foreign postings. Then we discuss the connection between management development and strategy in the international business.

Training for Expatriate Managers

Earlier in the chapter we saw that the two most common reasons for expatriate failure were the inability of a manager's spouse to adjust to a foreign environment and the manager's own inability to adjust to a foreign environment. Training can help the manager and spouse cope with both these problems. Cultural training, language training, and practical training all seem to reduce expatriate failure. We discuss each of these kinds of training here.[33] Despite the usefulness of these kinds of training, evidence suggests that many managers receive no training before they are sent on foreign postings. One study found that only about 30 percent of managers sent on one- to five-year expatriate assignments received training before their departure.[34]

Cultural Training

Cultural training seeks to foster an appreciation for the host country's culture. The belief is that understanding a host country's culture will help the manager empathize with the culture, which will enhance her effectiveness in dealing with host-country nationals. It has been suggested that expatriates should receive training in the host country's culture, history, politics, economy, religion, and social and business practices.[35] If possible, it is also advisable to arrange for a familiarization trip to the host country before the formal transfer, as this seems to ease culture shock. Given the problems related to spouse adaptation, it is important that the spouse, and perhaps the whole family, be included in cultural training programs.

Language Training

English is the language of world business; it is quite possible to conduct business all over the world using only English. For example, at ABB Group, a Swiss electrical equipment giant, the company's top 13 managers hold frequent meetings in different countries. Because they share no common first language, they speak only English, a foreign tongue to all but one.[36] Despite the prevalence of English, however, an exclusive reliance on English diminishes an expatriate manager's ability to interact with host-country nationals. As noted earlier, a willingness to communicate in the language of the host country, even if the expatriate is far from fluent, can help build rapport with local employees and improve the manager's effectiveness. Despite this, J. C. Baker's study of 74 executives of U.S. multinationals found that only 23 believed knowledge of foreign languages was necessary for conducting business abroad.[37] Those firms that did offer foreign language training for expatriates believed it improved their employees' effectiveness and enabled them to relate more easily to a foreign culture, which fostered a better image of the firm in the host country.

Practical Training

Practical training is aimed at helping the expatriate manager and family ease themselves into day-to-day life in the host country. The sooner a routine is established, the better are the prospects that the expatriate and her family will adapt successfully. One critical need is for a support network of friends for the expatriate. Where an expatriate community exists, firms often devote considerable effort to ensuring the new expatriate family is quickly integrated into that group. The expatriate community can be a useful source of support and information and can be invaluable in helping the family adapt to a foreign culture.

Repatriation of Expatriates

A largely overlooked but critically important issue in the training and development of expatriate managers is to prepare them for reentry into their home-country organization.[38]

Management Focus

Monsanto's Repatriation Program

Monsanto is a global agricultural and chemical company with revenues in excess of $7 billion and 15,000 employees. At any one time, the company will have 100 mid- and higher-level managers on extended postings abroad. Two-thirds of these are Americans who are being posted overseas, while the remainder are foreign nationals being employed in the United States. At Monsanto, managing expatriates and their repatriation begins with a rigorous selection process and intensive cross-cultural training, both for the managers and for their families. As at many other global companies, the idea is to build an internationally minded cadre of highly capable managers who will lead the organization in the future.

One of the strongest features of this program is that employees and their sending and receiving managers, or sponsors, develop an agreement about how this assignment will fit into the firm's business objectives. The focus is on why they are sending people abroad to do the job, and what their contribution to Monsanto will be when they return. Sponsoring managers are expected to be explicit about the kind of job opportunities the expatriates will have once they return home.

Once they arrive back in their home country, expatriate managers meet with cross-cultural trainers during debriefing sessions. They are also given the opportunity to showcase their experiences to their peers, subordinates, and superiors in special information exchanges.

However, Monsanto's repatriation program focuses on more than just business; it also attends to the family's reentry. Monsanto has found that difficulties with repatriation often have more to do with personal and family-related issues than with work-related issues. But the personal matters obviously affect an employee's on-the-job performance, so it is important for the company to pay attention to such issues.

This is why Monsanto offers returning employees an opportunity to work through personal difficulties. About three months after they return home, expatriates meet for three hours at work with several colleagues of their choice. The debriefing session is a conversation aided by a trained facilitator who has an outline to help the expatriate cover all the important aspects of the repatriation. The debriefing allows the employee to share important experiences and to enlighten managers, colleagues, and friends about his or her expertise so others within the organization can use some of the global knowledge.

According to one participant, "It sounds silly, but it's such a hectic time in the family's life, you don't have time to sit down and take stock of what's happening. You're going through the move, transitioning to a new job, a new house, the children may be going to a new school. This is a kind of oasis; a time to talk and put your feelings on the table." Apparently it works; since the program was introduced in the early 1990s, the attrition rate among returning expatriates has dropped sharply.

Source: Exerpted from "Repatriation: Up, Down, or Out?" by C. M. Solomon, *Personnel Journal*, Copyright © January 1995, pp. 28–34. Used with permission of ACC Communications, Inc. *Personnel Journal* (now known as *Workforce*), Costa Mesa, CA. All rights reserved.

Repatriation should be seen as the final link in an integrated, circular process that connects good selection and cross-cultural training of expatriate managers with completion of their term abroad and reintegration into their national organization. However, instead of having employees come home to share their knowledge and encourage other high-performing managers to take the same international career track, expatriates too often face a different scenario.[39]

Often when they return home after a stint abroad—where they have typically been autonomous, well-compensated, and celebrated as a big fish in a little pond—they face an organization that doesn't know what they have done for the last few years, doesn't know how to use their new knowledge, and doesn't particularly care. In the worst cases, reentering employees have to scrounge for jobs, or firms will create standby positions that don't use the expatriate's skills and capabilities and fail to make the most of the business investment the firm has made in that individual.

Research illustrates the extent of this problem. According to one study of repatriated employees, 60 to 70 percent didn't know what their position would be when they returned home. Also, 60 percent said their organizations were vague about repatriation, about their new roles, and about their future career progression within the company, while 77 percent of those surveyed took jobs at a lower level in their home organization than in their international assignments.[40] It is small wonder then that 15 percent of returning expatriates leave their firms within a year of arriving home, while 40 percent leave within three years.[41]

The key to solving this problem is good human resource planning. Just as the HRM function needs to develop good selection and training programs for its expatriates, it also needs to develop good programs for reintegrating expatriates back into work life within their home-country organization, for preparing them for changes in their physical and professional landscape, and for utilizing the knowledge they acquired while abroad. For an example of the kind of program that might be used, see the accompanying Management Focus that looks at Monsanto's repatriation program.

Management Development and Strategy

Management development programs are designed to increase the overall skill levels of managers through a mix of ongoing management education and rotations of managers through a number of jobs within the firm to give them varied experiences. They are attempts to improve the overall productivity and quality of the firm's management resources.

International businesses increasingly are using management development as a strategic tool. This is particularly true in firms pursuing a transnational strategy, as increasing numbers are. Such firms need a strong unifying corporate culture and informal management networks to assist in coordination and control (see Table 18.2). In addition, transnational firm managers need to be able to detect pressures for local responsiveness, and that requires them to understand the culture of a host country.

Management development programs help build a unifying corporate culture by socializing new managers into the norms and value systems of the firm. In-house company training programs and intense interaction during off-site training can foster esprit de corps—shared experiences, informal networks, perhaps a company language or jargon—as well as develop technical competencies. These training events often include songs, picnics, and sporting events that promote feelings of togetherness. These rites of integration may include "initiation rites" wherein personal culture is stripped, company uniforms are donned (e.g., T-shirts bearing the company logo), and humiliation is inflicted (e.g., a pie in the face). All these activities aim to strengthen a manager's identification with the company.[42]

Bringing managers together in one location for extended periods and rotating them through different jobs in several countries help the firm build an informal management network. Such a network can then be used as a conduit for exchanging valuable performance-enhancing knowledge within the organization.[43] (Chapter 13 explained the importance of such networks in transnational firms.) Consider the Swedish telecommunications company L. M. Ericsson. Interunit cooperation is extremely important at Ericsson, particularly for transferring know-how and core competencies from the parent to foreign subsidiaries, from foreign subsidiaries to the parent, and between foreign subsidiaries. To facilitate cooperation, Ericsson transfers large numbers of people back and forth between headquarters and subsidiaries. Ericsson sends a team of 50 to 100 engineers and managers from one unit to another for a year or two. This establishes a network of interpersonal contacts. This policy is effective for both solidifying a common culture in the company and coordinating the company's globally dispersed operations.[44]

Performance Appraisal

A particularly thorny issue in many international businesses is how best to evaluate its expatriate managers' performance.[45] In this section, we look at this issue and consider some guidelines for appraising expatriate performance.

Performance Appraisal Problems

Unintentional bias makes it difficult to evaluate the performance of expatriate managers objectively. In most cases, two groups evaluate the performance of expatriate managers—host-nation managers and home-office managers—and both are subject to bias. The host-nation managers may be biased by their own cultural frame of reference and expectations. For example, Oddou and Mendenhall report the case of a U.S. manager who introduced participative decision making while working in an Indian subsidiary.[46] The manager subsequently received a negative evaluation from host-country managers because in India, the strong social stratification means managers are seen as experts who should not have to ask subordinates for help. The local employees apparently viewed the U.S. manager's attempt at participatory management as an indication that he was incompetent and did not know his job.

Home-country managers' appraisals may be biased by distance and by their own lack of experience working abroad. Home-office managers are often not aware of what is going on in a foreign operation. Accordingly, they tend to rely on hard data in evaluating an expatriate's performance, such as the subunit's productivity, profitability, or market share. Such criteria may reflect factors outside the expatriate manager's control (e.g., adverse changes in exchange rates, economic downturns). Also, hard data do not take into account many less-visible "soft" variables that are also important, such as an expatriate's ability to develop cross-cultural awareness and to work productively with local managers.

Due to such biases, many expatriate managers believe that headquarters management evaluates them unfairly and does not fully appreciate the value of their skills and experience. This could be one reason many expatriates believe a foreign posting does not benefit their careers. In one study of personnel managers in U.S. multinationals, 56 percent of the managers surveyed stated that a foreign assignment is either detrimental or immaterial to one's career.[47]

Guidelines for Performance Appraisal

Several things can reduce bias in the performance appraisal process.[48] First, most expatriates appear to believe more weight should be given to an on-site manager's appraisal than to an off-site manager's appraisal. Due to proximity, an on-site manager is more likely to evaluate the soft variables that are important aspects of an expatriate's performance. The evaluation may be especially valid when the on-site manager is of the same nationality as the expatriate, since cultural bias should be alleviated. In practice, home-office managers often write performance evaluations after receiving input from on-site managers. When this is the case, most experts recommend that a former expatriate who served in the same location should be involved in the appraisal to help reduce bias. Finally, when the policy is for foreign on-site managers to write performance evaluations, home-office managers should be consulted before an on-site manager completes a formal termination evaluation. This gives the home-office manager the opportunity to balance what could be a very hostile evaluation based on a cultural misunderstanding.

Compensation

Two issues are raised in every discussion of compensation practices in an international business. One is how compensation should be adjusted to reflect national differences in economic circumstances and compensation practices. The other issue is how expatriate managers should be paid.

National Differences in Compensation

Substantial differences exist in the compensation of executives at the same level in various countries. The results of a survey undertaken in 2000 by Towers Perrin are summarized in Table 18.4. This survey looked at average compensation for four positions across 26 countries.[49] The figures for CEOs and HR directors include both base compensation and performance-related pay bonuses, but do not include stock options. The figures for accountants and manufacturing employees just refer to base pay. As can be seen, wide variations exist across countries. The average compensation for a CEO in the United States was $1.4 million, compared to $545,260 in Japan and $179, 486 in Taiwan. These figures underestimate the true differential because many U.S. executives earn considerable sums of money from stock options and grants.[50] According to Towers Perrin, in 1996 stock option grants were used in only 10 of the 26 countries in the survey. By 2000, however, this figure had risen to 19 out of 26, suggesting that U.S.-style compensation packages that include stock option grants are becoming more frequent.

These differences in compensation raise a perplexing question for an international business: Should the firm pay executives in different countries according to the

	CEO	HR Director	Accountant	Mfg. Employee
Argentina	$860,704	$326,874	$63,948	$17,884
Australia	646,316	235,316	57,129	29,703
Belgium	655,390	286,222	63,883	34,336
Brazil	597,454	287,683	44,605	10,480
Canada	742,228	188,070	44,866	36,289
China (Shanghai)	93,393	58,278	14,552	3,021
France	540,260	224,112	69,554	34,741
Germany	421,622	189,785	61,375	36,934
Hong Kong SAR	635,186	211,321	56,711	16,691
Italy	567,685	254,138	59,388	29,469
Japan	545,233	235,536	59,107	51,997
Malaysia	350,558	130,771	24,522	7,453
Mexico	648,695	239,028	41,582	14,302
Netherlands	621,153	217,142	48,838	27,892
New Zealand	258,114	111,803	38,382	15,931
Singapore	621,871	239,376	51,733	16,912
South Africa	406,263	179,268	43,234	7,974
South Korea	194,421	109,637	41,365	17,904
Spain	399,423	196,305	56,332	22,746
Sweden	440,265	166,312	43,438	32,564
Switzerland	448,422	175,008	66,121	41,104
Taiwan	179,486	102,491	30,652	11,924
Thailand	145,173	98,120	19,175	6,293
United Kingdom	719,665	268,302	107,839	28,874
United States	1,403,899	306,181	66,377	44,680
Venezuela	609,097	272,212	41,192	11,221

Table 18.4

Compensation for Four Positions in 26 Countries

Source: Towers Perrin

Executive Pay Policies for Global Managers

A survey of human resource professionals in 45 large U.S. multinational companies undertaken by Organizational Resources Consulting, an international HRM consulting firm, found that all 45 companies viewed differing pay levels and perks as their biggest problem when trying to develop an international workforce. The root of the problem is cost; expatriate pay packages that are based on American salaries and needs are increasingly seen as too expensive. To deal with this, many international businesses are trying to develop special pay schemes for their cadre of internationally mobile managers.

Hewlett-Packard transfers about 600 people a year across national borders. Although most of these transferees are on one- to two-year assignments, up to 25 percent are on indefinite assignments. HP ties the pay of short-term transferees to pay scales in their home country, but longer-term HP transferees are quickly switched to the pay scale of their host country and paid according to prevailing local standards. For employees moving from high-pay countries such as Germany to lower-pay countries, such as Spain, HP offers temporary bridging payments to ease the adjustment.

The Minnesota Mining and Manufacturing Co. (3M) has a completely different type of program for longer-term expatriates. The company developed the program because it drastically altered its international organization. In Europe, for example, 3M used to organize its operations on a country-by-country basis. However, 3M has established Europeanwide divisions, so many 3M executives who might have spent their career in one country are now being asked to move, perhaps permanently, to another country.

The 3M program compares net salaries in both the old and new country by subtracting the major costs, such as taxes and housing, from gross pay. The transferred executive then gets whichever pay packet is highest. Thus, when 3M transfers a German executive to France, the German remains on her home-country pay scale. But a British employee transferred to Germany, where salaries are higher, can expect to be switched to the German pay scale. Although the policy considers local housing costs, it doesn't compensate for higher housing costs through a special payment, as many traditional expatriate pay policies did. Any housing subsidy that resulted could last for the rest of an executive's career following a transfer and this would be very expensive.

The large oil company Phillips Petroleum has adopted yet another policy. At Phillips, the policy used to be that when a third-country national, such as a British citizen, was transferred abroad (for example, from Britain to Kuwait), he would be paid in U.S. dollars and his salary would be raised to a level equivalent to that of someone in the United States doing a similar job. This was a very expensive policy given the generally high level of pay prevailing in the United States. Now Phillips has a "third-country nationals program." Under this program, the transferred employee is given generous housing allowances and educational assistance for his children. However, his salary is now pegged to the level prevailing in his home country.

Sources: A. Bennett, "Executive Pay: What's an Expatriate?" *Wall Street Journal*, April 21, 1994, p. A5, and J. Flynn, "Continental Divide over Executive Pay," *Business Week*, July 3, 1995, pp. 40–41.

prevailing standards in each country, or should it equalize pay on a global basis? The problem does not arise in firms pursuing ethnocentric or polycentric staffing policies. In ethnocentric firms, the issue can be reduced to that of how much home-country expatriates should be paid (which we will consider later). As for polycentric firms, the lack of managers' mobility among national operations implies that pay can and should be kept country-specific. There would seem to be no point in paying executives in Great Britain the same as U.S. executives if they never work side by side.

However, this problem is very real in firms with geocentric staffing policies. A geocentric staffing policy is consistent with a transnational strategy. One aspect of this policy is the need for a cadre of international managers that may include many different nationalities. Should all members of such a cadre be paid the same salary and the same incentive pay? For a U.S.-based firm, this would mean raising the compensation of foreign nationals to U.S. levels, which could be very expensive. If the firm does not equalize pay, it could cause considerable resentment among foreign nationals who are members of the international cadre and work with U.S. nationals. If a firm is serious about building an international cadre, it may have to pay its international executives the same basic salary irrespective of their country of origin or assignment. The accompanying Management Focus contains several examples of how some international businesses have tried to deal with this problem.

Expatriate Pay

The most common approach to expatriate pay is the balance sheet approach. This approach equalizes purchasing power across countries so employees can enjoy the same living standard in their foreign posting that they enjoyed at home. In addition, the approach provides financial incentives to offset qualitative differences between assignment locations.[51] Figure 18.1 shows a typical balance sheet. Note that home-country outlays for the employee are designated as income taxes, housing expenses, expenditures for goods and services (food, clothing, entertainment, etc.), and reserves (savings, pension contributions, etc.). The balance sheet approach attempts to provide expatriates with the same standard of living in their host countries as they enjoy at home plus a financial inducement (i.e., premium, incentive) for accepting an overseas assignment.

The components of the typical expatriate compensation package are a base salary, a foreign service premium, allowances of various types, tax differentials, and benefits. We shall briefly review each of these components.[52] An expatriate's total compensation package may amount to three times what he or she would cost the firm in a home-country posting. Because of the high cost of expatriates, many firms have reduced their use of them in recent years. However, a firm's ability to reduce its use of expatriates may be limited, particularly if it is pursuing an ethnocentric or geocentric staffing policy.

Base Salary

An expatriate's base salary is normally in the same range as the base salary for a similar position in the home country. The base salary is normally paid in either the home-country currency or in the local currency.

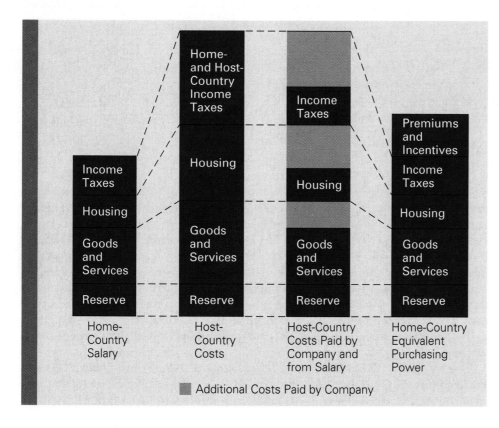

Figure 18.1

A Typical Balance Sheet

Source: C. Reynolds, "Compensation of Overseas Personnel," in *Handbook of Human Resource Administration*, 2nd ed., ed. J. J. Famularo (New York: McGraw-Hill, 1986), p. 51.

Reproduced with permission of the McGraw-Hill Companies.

Foreign Service Premium

A foreign service premium is extra pay the expatriate receives for working outside his or her country of origin. It is offered as an inducement to accept foreign postings. It compensates the expatriate for having to live in an unfamiliar country isolated from family and friends, having to deal with a new culture and language, and having to adapt to new work habits and practices. Many firms pay foreign service premiums as a percentage of base salary ranging from 10 to 30 percent after tax with 16 percent being the average premium.[53]

Allowances

Four types of allowances are often included in an expatriate's compensation package: hardship allowances, housing allowances, cost-of-living allowances, and education allowances. A hardship allowance is paid when the expatriate is being sent to a difficult location, usually defined as one where such basic amenities as health care, schools, and retail stores are grossly deficient by the standards of the expatriate's home country. A housing allowance is normally given to ensure that the expatriate can afford the same quality of housing in the foreign country as at home. In locations where housing is very expensive (e.g., London, Tokyo), this allowance can be substantial—as much as 10 to 30 percent of the expatriate's total compensation package. A cost-of-living allowance ensures that the expatriate will enjoy the same standard of living in the foreign posting as at home. An education allowance ensures that an expatriate's children receive adequate schooling (by home-country standards). Host-country public schools are sometimes not suitable for an expatriate's children, in which case they must attend a private school.

Taxation

Unless a host country has a reciprocal tax treaty with the expatriate's home country, the expatriate may have to pay income tax to both the home- and host-country governments. When a reciprocal tax treaty is not in force, the firm typically pays the expatriate's income tax in the host country. In addition, firms normally make up the difference when a higher income tax rate in a host country reduces an expatriate's take-home pay.

Benefits

Many firms also ensure that their expatriates receive the same level of medical and pension benefits abroad that they received at home. This can be very costly for the firm, since many benefits that are tax deductible for the firm in the home country (e.g., medical and pension benefits) may not be deductible out of the country.

▌International Labor Relations

The HRM function of an international business is typically responsible for international labor relations. From a strategic perspective, the key issue in international labor relations is the degree to which organized labor can limit the choices of an international business. A firm's ability to integrate and consolidate its global operations to realize experience curve and location economies can be limited by organized labor, constraining the pursuit of a transnational or global strategy. Prahalad and Doz cite the example of General Motors, which brought peace with labor unions by agreeing not to integrate and consolidate operations in the most efficient manner.[54] In the early 1980s, General Motors made substantial investments in Germany—matching its new investments in Austria and Spain—at the demand of the German metal workers' unions.

One task of the HRM function is to foster harmony and minimize conflict between the firm and organized labor. With this in mind, this section is divided into three parts.

First, we review organized labor's concerns about multinational enterprises. Second, we look at how organized labor has tried to deal with these concerns. And third, we look at how international businesses manage their labor relations to minimize labor disputes.

The Concerns of Organized Labor

Labor unions generally try to get better pay, greater job security, and better working conditions for their members through collective bargaining with management. Unions' bargaining power is derived largely from their ability to threaten to disrupt production, either by a strike or some other form of work protest (e.g., refusing to work overtime). This threat is credible, however, only insofar as management has no alternative but to employ union labor.

A principal concern of domestic unions about multinational firms is that the company can counter its bargaining power with the power to move production to another country. Ford, for example, very clearly threatened British unions with a plan to move manufacturing to Continental Europe unless British workers abandoned work rules that limited productivity, showed restraint in negotiating for wage increases, and curtailed strikes and other work disruptions.[55]

Another concern of organized labor is that an international business will keep highly skilled tasks in its home country and farm out only low-skilled tasks to foreign plants. Such a practice makes it relatively easy for an international business to switch production from one location to another as economic conditions warrant. Consequently, the bargaining power of organized labor is once more reduced.

A final union concern arises when an international business attempts to import employment practices and contractual agreements from its home country. When these practices are alien to the host country, organized labor fears the change will reduce its influence and power. This concern has surfaced in response to Japanese multinationals that have been trying to export their style of labor relations to other countries. For example, much to the annoyance of the United Auto Workers (UAW), most Japanese auto plants in the United States are not unionized. As a result, union influence in the auto industry is declining.

The Strategy of Organized Labor

Organized labor has responded to the increased bargaining power of multinational corporations by taking three actions: (1) trying to establish international labor organizations, (2) lobbying for national legislation to restrict multinationals, and (3) trying to achieve international regulations on multinationals through such organizations as the United Nations. These efforts have not been very successful.

In the 1960s, organized labor began to establish international trade secretariats (ITSs) to provide worldwide links for national unions in particular industries. The long-term goal was to be able to bargain transnationally with multinational firms. Organized labor believed that by coordinating union action across countries through an ITS, it could counter the power of a multinational corporation by threatening to disrupt production on an international scale. For example, Ford's threat to move production from Great Britain to other European locations would not have been credible if the unions in various European countries had united to oppose it.

However, the ITSs have had virtually no real success. Although national unions may want to cooperate, they also compete with each other to attract investment from international businesses, and hence jobs for their members. For example, in attempting to gain new jobs for their members, national unions in the auto industry often court auto firms that are seeking locations for new plants. One reason Nissan chose to build its European production facilities in Great Britain rather than Spain was that the British unions agreed to greater concessions than the Spanish unions did. As a result of such competition between national unions, cooperation is difficult to establish.

A further impediment to cooperation has been the wide variation in union structure. Trade unions developed independently in each country. As a result, the structure and ideology of unions tend to vary significantly from country to country, as does the nature of collective bargaining. For example, in Great Britain, France, and Italy many unions are controlled by left-wing socialists, who view collective bargaining through the lens of "class conflict." In contrast, most union leaders in Germany, the Netherlands, Scandinavia, and Switzerland are far more moderate politically. The ideological gap between union leaders in different countries has made cooperation difficult. Divergent ideologies are reflected in radically different views about the role of a union in society and the stance unions should take toward multinationals.

Organized labor has also met with only limited success in its efforts to get national and international bodies to regulate multinationals. Such international organizations as the International Labor Organization (ILO) and the Organization for Economic Cooperation and Development (OECD) have adopted codes of conduct for multinational firms to follow in labor relations. However, these guidelines are not as far-reaching as many unions would like. They also do not provide any enforcement mechanisms. Many researchers report that such guidelines are of only limited effectiveness.[56]

| Approaches to Labor Relations

International businesses differ markedly in their approaches to international labor relations. The main difference is the degree to which labor relations activities are centralized or decentralized. Historically, most international businesses have decentralized international labor relations activities to their foreign subsidiaries because labor laws, union power, and the nature of collective bargaining varied so much from country to country. It made sense to decentralize the labor relations function to local managers. The belief was that there was no way central management could effectively handle the complexity of simultaneously managing labor relations in a number of different environments.

Although this logic still holds, there is now a trend toward greater centralized control. This trend reflects international firms' attempts to rationalize their global operations. The general rise in competitive pressure in industry after industry has made it more important for firms to control their costs. Since labor costs account for such a large percentage of total costs, many firms are now using the threat to move production to another country in their negotiations with unions to change work rules and limit wage increases (as Ford did in Europe). Because such a move would involve major new investments and plant closures, this bargaining tactic requires the input of headquarters management. Thus, the level of centralized input into labor relations is increasing.

In addition, the realization is growing that the way work is organized within a plant can be a major source of competitive advantage. Much of the competitive advantage of Japanese automakers, for example, has been attributed to the use of self-managing teams, job rotation, cross-training, and the like in their Japanese plants.[57] To replicate their domestic performance in foreign plants, the Japanese firms have tried to replicate their work practices there. This often brings them into direct conflict with traditional work practices in those countries, as sanctioned by the local labor unions, so the Japanese firms have often made their foreign investments contingent on the local union accepting a radical change in work practices. To achieve this, the headquarters of many Japanese firms bargains directly with local unions to get union agreement to changes in work rules before committing to an investment. For example, before Nissan decided to invest in northern England, it got a commitment from British unions to agree to a change in traditional work practices. By its very nature, pursuing such a strategy requires centralized control over the labor relations function.

Chapter Summary

This chapter focused on human resource management in international businesses. HRM activities include human resource strategy, staffing, performance evaluation, management development, compensation, and labor relations. None of these activities is performed in a vacuum; all must be appropriate to the firm's strategy. This chapter made the following points:

1. Firm success requires HRM policies to be congruent with the firm's strategy and with its formal and informal structure and controls.

2. Staffing policy is concerned with selecting employees who have the skills required to perform particular jobs. Staffing policy can be a tool for developing and promoting a corporate culture.

3. An ethnocentric approach to staffing policy fills all key management positions in an international business with parent-country nationals. The policy is congruent with an international strategy. A drawback is that ethnocentric staffing can result in cultural myopia.

4. A polycentric staffing policy uses host-country nationals to manage foreign subsidiaries and parent-country nationals for the key positions at corporate headquarters. This approach can minimize the dangers of cultural myopia, but it can create a gap between home- and host-country operations. The policy is best suited to a multidomestic strategy.

5. A geocentric staffing policy seeks the best people for key jobs throughout the organization, regardless of their nationality. This approach is consistent with building a strong unifying culture and informal management network and is well suited to both global and transnational strategies. Immigration policies of national governments may limit a firm's ability to pursue this policy.

6. A prominent issue in the international staffing literature is expatriate failure, defined as the premature return of an expatriate manager to his or her home country. The costs of expatriate failure can be substantial.

7. Expatriate failure can be reduced by selection procedures that screen out inappropriate candidates. The most successful expatriates seem to be those who have high self-esteem and self-confidence,

get along well with others, are willing to attempt to communicate in a foreign language, and can empathize with people of other cultures.

8. Training can lower the probability of expatriate failure. It should include cultural training, language training, and practical training, and it should be provided to both the expatriate manager and the spouse.

9. Management development programs attempt to increase the overall skill levels of managers through a mix of ongoing management education and rotation of managers through different jobs within the firm to give them varied experiences. Management development is often used as a strategic tool to build a strong unifying culture and informal management network, both of which support transnational and global strategies.

10. It can be difficult to evaluate the performance of expatriate managers objectively because of unintentional bias. A number of steps can be taken to reduce this bias.

11. Country differences in compensation practices raise a difficult question for an international business: Should the firm pay executives in different countries according to the standards in each country or equalize pay on a global basis?

12. The most common approach to expatriate pay is the balance sheet approach. This approach aims to equalize purchasing power so employees can enjoy the same living standard in their foreign posting that they had at home.

13. A key issue in international labor relations is the degree to which organized labor can limit the choices available to an international business. A firm's ability to pursue a transnational or global strategy can be significantly constrained by the actions of labor unions.

14. A principal concern of organized labor is that the multinational can counter union bargaining power with threats to move production to another country.

15. Organized labor has tried to counter the bargaining power of multinationals by forming international labor organizations. In general, these efforts have not been effective.

Critical Discussion Questions

1. What are the main advantages and disadvantages of the ethnocentric, polycentric, and geocentric

approaches to staffing policy? When is each approach appropriate?

2. Research suggests that many expatriate employees encounter problems that limit both their effectiveness in a foreign posting and their contribution to the company when they return home. What are the main causes and consequences of these problems, and how might a firm reduce the occurrence of such problems?

3. What is the link between an international business's strategy and its human resource management policies, particularly with regard to the use of expatriate employees and their pay scale?

4. In what ways can organized labor constrain the strategic choices of an international business? How can an international business limit these constraints?

Global Human Resource Management at Coca-Cola

The Coca-Cola Company is one of the most successful multinational enterprises. With operations in close to 200 countries and nearly 80 percent of its operating income derived from businesses outside the United States, Coca-Cola is typically perceived as the quintessential global corporation. Coca-Cola, however, likes to think of itself as a "multi-local" company that just happens to be headquartered in Atlanta but could be headquartered anywhere and that presents the Coca-Cola brand with a "local face" in every country where it does business. The philosophy is best summarized by the phrase "think globally, act locally," which captures the essence of Coca-Cola's cross-border management mentality. Coca-Cola grants national businesses the freedom to conduct operations in a manner appropriate to the market. At the same time, the company tries to establish a common mind-set that all its employees share.

Coca-Cola manages its global operations through 25 operating divisions that are organized under six regional groups: North America, the European Union, the Pacific Region, the East Europe/Middle East Group, Africa, and Latin America. The corporate human resource management function is charged with providing the glue that binds these various divisions and groups into the Coca-Cola family. The corporate HRM function achieves this in two main ways: (1) by propagating a common human resources philosophy within the company, and (2) by developing a group of internationally minded mid-level executives for future senior management responsibility.

The corporate HRM group sees its mission as one of developing and providing the underlying philosophy around which local businesses can develop their own human resource practices. For example, rather than have a standard salary policy for all its national operations, Coca-Cola has a common salary philosophy—the total compensation package should be competitive with the best companies in the local market. Twice a year the corporate HRM group also conducts a two-week HRM orientation session for the human resource staff from each of its 25 operating divisions. These sessions give an overview of the company's HRM philosophy and talk about how local businesses can translate that philosophy into human resource policies. Coca-Cola has found that information sharing is one of the great benefits of bringing HRM professionals together. For example, tools that have been developed in Brazil to deal with a specific HRM problem might also be useful in Australia. The sessions provide a medium through which HRM professionals can communicate and learn from each other, which facilitates the rapid transfer of innovative and valuable HRM tools from region to region.

As much as possible, Coca-Cola tries to staff its operations with local personnel. To quote one senior executive: "We strive to have a limited number of international people in the field because generally local people are better equipped to do business at their home locations." However, expatriates are needed in the system for two main reasons. One is to fill a need for a specific set of skills that might not exist at a particular location. For example, when Coca-Cola started operations in Eastern Europe, it had to bring in an expatriate from Chicago, who was of Polish descent, to fill the position of finance manager. The second reason for using an expatriate is to improve the employee's own skill base. Coca-Cola believes that because it is a global company, senior managers should have had international exposure.

The corporate HRM group has about 500 high-level managers involved in its "global service program." Coca-Cola characterizes these managers as people who have knowledge of their particular field, plus knowledge of the company, and who can do two things in an international location—add value by the expertise they bring to each assignment and enhance their contribution to the company by having international experience. Of the 500 participants in the program, about 200 move each year. To ease the costs of transfer for these employees, Coca-Cola gives those in its global service program a U.S.-based compensation package. They are paid according to U.S. benchmarks, as opposed to the benchmark prevailing in the country in which they are located. Thus, an Indian manager in this program who is working in Great Britain will be paid according to U.S. salary benchmarks—and not those prevailing in either India or Britain. An ultimate goal of this program is to build a cadre of internationally minded executives from which the future senior managers of Coca-Cola will be drawn.

Sources: D. A. Amfuso, "HR Unites the World of Coca-Cola," *Personnel Journal*, November 1994, pp. 112–20, and S. Foley,

"Internationalizing the Cola Wars," Harvard Business School Case #9-794-146.

Case Discussion Questions

1. What is Coca-Cola's staffing policy for managerial positions: ethnocentric, polycentric, or geocentric? Does this policy make sense?

2. What is the strategic role of the HRM function at Coca-Cola? How does HRM help Coca-Cola to become a more successful international business?

3. Do you think it is appropriate to pay expatriates according to U.S. benchmark rates, even when their home operation is not the United States? What potential problems might such a policy cause? What are the benefits of the policy?

Notes

1. P. J. Dowling and R. S. Schuler, *International Dimensions of Human Resource Management* (Boston: PSW-Kent, 1990).

2. J. Millman, M. A. von Glinow, and M. Nathan, "Organizational Life Cycles and Strategic International Human Resource Management in Multinational Companies," *Academy of Management Review* 16 (1991), pp. 318–39.

3. E. H. Schein, *Organizational Culture and Leadership* (San Francisco: Jossey-Bass, 1985).

4. H. V. Perlmutter, "The Tortuous Evolution of the Multinational Corporation," *Columbia Journal of World Business* 4 (1969), pp. 9–18; D. A. Heenan and H. V. Perlmutter, *Multinational Organizational Development* (Reading, MA: Addison-Wesley, 1979); and D. A. Ondrack, "International Human Resources Management in European and North American Firms," *International Studies of Management and Organization* 15 (1985), pp. 6–32.

5. V. Reitman and M. Schuman, "Men's Club: Japanese and Korean Companies Rarely Look Outside for People to Run Their Overseas Operations," *Wall Street Journal*, September 26, 1996, p. 17.

6. S. Beechler and J. Z. Yang, "The Transfer of Japanese Style Management to American Subsidiaries," *Journal of International Business Studies* 25 (1994), pp. 467–91.

7. M. Banai and L. M. Sama, "Ethical Dilemma in MNCs' International Staffing Policies," *Journal of Business Ethics*, June 2000, pp. 221–35.

8. Reitman and Schuman, "Men's Club: Japanese and Korean Companies Rarely Look Outside for People to Run Their Overseas Operations."

9. C. A. Bartlett and S. Ghoshal, *Managing across Borders: The Transnational Solution* (Boston: Harvard Business School Press, 1989).

10. S. J. Kobrin, "Geocentric Mindset and Multinational Strategy," *Journal of International Business Studies* 25 (1994), pp. 493–511.

11. P. M. Rosenzweig and N. Nohria, "Influences on Human Resource Management Practices in Multinational Corporations," *Journal of International Business Studies* 25 (1994), pp. 229–51.

12. Kobrin, "Geocentric Mindset and Multinational Strategy."

13. M. Harvey and H. Fung. "Inpatriate Managers: The Need for Realistic Relocation Reviews," *International Journal of Management*, 17 (2000), pp. 151–59.

14. J. S. Black, M. Mendenhall, and G. Oddou, "Towards a Comprehensive Model of International Adjustment," *Academy of Management Review* 16 (1991), pp. 291–317, and J. Shay and T. J. Bruce, "Expatriate Managers," *Cornell Hotel & Restaurant Administration Quarterly*, February 1997, p. 30–40.

15. M. G. Harvey, "The Multinational Corporation's Expatriate Problem: An Application of Murphy's Law," *Business Horizons* 26 (1983), pp. 71–78.

16. Shay and Bruce, "Expatriate Managers." Also see J. S. Black and H. Gregersen, "The Right Way to Manage Expatriates," *Harvard Business Review*, March–April 1999, pp. 52–63.

17. S. Caudron, "Training Ensures Overseas Success," *Personnel Journal*, December 1991, p. 27.

18. Black, Mendenhall, and Oddou, "Towards a Comprehensive Model of International Adjustment."

19. R. L. Tung, "Selection and Training Procedures of U.S., European, and Japanese Multinationals," *California Management Review* 25 (1982), pp. 57–71.

20. C. M. Solomon, "Success Abroad Depends upon More Than Job Skills," *Personnel Journal*, April 1994, pp. 51–58.

21. C. M. Solomon, "Unhappy Trails," *Workforce*, August 2000, pp. 36–41.

22. Solomon, "Success Abroad Depends upon More Than Job Skills."

23. Solomon, "Unhappy Trails."

24. M. Harvey, "Addressing the Dual Career Expatriation Dilemma," *Human Resource Planning* 19, no. 4 (1996), pp. 18–32.

25. M. Mendenhall and G. Oddou, "The Dimensions of Expatriate Acculturation: A Review," *Academy of Management Review* 10 (1985), pp. 39–47.

26. I. Torbiorin, *Living Abroad: Personal Adjustment and Personnel Policy in the Overseas Setting* (New York: John Wiley & Sons, 1982).

27. R. L. Tung, "Selection and Training of Personnel for Overseas Assignments," *Columbia Journal of World Business* 16 (1981), pp. 68–78.

28. Solomon, "Success Abroad Depends upon More Than Job Skills."

29. S. Ronen, "Training and International Asignee," in *Training and Career Development*, ed. I. Goldstein (San Francisco: Jossey-Bass, 1985), and Tung, "Selection and Training of Personnel for Overseas Assignments."

30. Solomon, "Success Abroad Depends upon More Than Job Skills."

31. Harvey, "Addressing the Dual Career Expatriation Dilemma"; and J. W. Hunt, "The Perils of Foreign Postings for Two," *Financial Times*, May 6, 1998, p. 22.

32. C. M. Daily, S. T. Certo, and D. R. Dalton, "International Experience in the Executive Suite: A Path to Prosperity?" *Strategic Management Journal* 21 (2000), pp. 515–23.

33. Dowling and Schuler, *International Dimensions of Human Resource Management*.

34. Ibid.

35. G. Baliga and J. C. Baker, "Multinational Corporate Policies for Expatriate Managers: Selection, Training, and Evaluation," *Advanced Management Journal*, Autumn 1985, pp. 31–38.

36. C. Rapoport, "A Tough Swede Invades the U.S.," *Fortune*, June 20, 1992, pp. 67–70.

37. J. C. Baker, "Foreign Language and Departure Training in U.S. Multinational Firms," *Personnel Administrator*, July 1984, pp. 68–70.

38. A 1997 study by the Conference Board looked at this in depth. For a summary, see L. Grant, "That Overseas Job Could Derail Your Career," *Fortune*, April 14, 1997, p. 166. Also see J. S. Black and H. Gregersen, "The Right Way to Manage Expatriates," *Harvard Business Review*, March–April 1999, pp. 52–63.

39. J. S. Black and M. E. Mendenhall, *Global Assignments: Successfully Expatriating and Repatriating International Managers* (San Francisco: Jossey-Bass, 1992).

40. Ibid.

41. Figures from the Conference Board study. For a summary, see Grant, "That Overseas Job Could Derail Your Career."

42. S. C. Schneider, "National v. Corporate Culture: Implications for Human Resource Management," *Human Resource Management* 27 (Summer 1988), pp. 231–46.

43. I. M. Manve and W. B. Stevenson, "Nationality, Cultural Distance and Expatriate Status," *Journal of International Business Studies* 32 (2001), pp. 285–303.

44. Bartlett and Ghoshal, *Managing across Borders*.

45. See G. Oddou and M. Mendenhall, "Expatriate Performance Appraisal: Problems and Solutions," in *International Human Resource Management*, ed. Mendenhall and Oddou (Boston: PWS-Kent, 1991); Dowling and Schuler, *International Dimensions*; R. S. Schuler and G. W. Florkowski, "International Human Resource Management," in *Handbook for International Management Research*, ed. B. J. Punnett and O. Shenkar (Oxford: Blackwell, 1996); and K. Roth and S. O'Donnell, "Foreign Subsidiary Compensation Strategy: An Agency Theory Perspective," *Academy of Management Journal* 39, no. 3 (1996), pp. 678–703.

46. Oddou and Mendenhall, "Expatriate Performance Appraisal."

47. "Expatriates Often See Little Benefit to Careers in Foreign Stints, Indifference at Home," *Wall Street Journal*, December 11, 1989, p. B1.

48. Oddou and Mendenhall, "Expatriate Performance Appraisal;" and Schuler and Florkowski, "International Human Resource Management."

49. "Towers Perrin & Mercer examine pay levels and increases in 26 countries," *Ioma's Report on Salary Surveys*, January 2001, pp. 2–4.

50. R. C. Longworth, "US Executives Sit on Top of the World," *Chicago Tribune*, May 31, 1998, p. C1.

51. C. Reynolds, "Compensation of Overseas Personnel," in *Handbook of Human Resource Administration*, ed. J. J. Famularo (New York: McGraw-Hill, 1986).

52. M. Helms, "International Executive Compensation Practices," in *International Human Resource Management*, ed. M. Mendenhall and G. Oddou (Boston: PWS-Kent, 1991).

53. G. W. Latta, "Expatriate Incentives," *HR Focus* 75, no. 3 (March 1998), p. S3.

54. C. K. Prahalad and Y. L. Doz, *The Multinational Mission* (New York: The Free Press, 1987).

55. Ibid.

56. Schuler and Florkowski, "International Human Resource Management."

57. See J. P. Womack, D. T. Jones, and D. Roos, *The Machine that Changed the World* (New York: Rawson Associates, 1990).

Accounting in the International Business

A number of major German firms have begun to adopt international accounting standards that reveal far more about their financial performance than hitherto. This represents a major shift away from inscrutable German accounting standards that often hid as much about a company's financial performance as they revealed. The change has been driven by a recognition that German capital markets are too narrow and illiquid to satisfy the future funding requirements of many major German companies. These corporations are realizing that it is in their best interests to get a listing on the New York Stock Exchange (NYSE), the world's largest capital market, as a prelude to issuing equity and raising debt through the New York market.

Historically, German firms have almost never resorted to international capital markets to raise additional equity. Their view was that bank debt was adequate. However, the German market for debt has become expensive, while the possibility of raising additional equity in Germany has been limited by the relatively small and illiquid nature of the German equity market. The move among German firms to raise equity on international capital markets began in the early 1990s when a number of major German firms, including Daimler-Benz, Siemens, and Volkswagen, discretely applied to the U.S. Securities and Exchange Commission (SEC) for a listing. The SEC, however, was not particularly responsive. In the SEC's view, German accounting standards were not comparable to those in the United States and did not provide sufficient information to investors. Among the SEC's objections was the German practice of not disclosing the size of a company's financial reserves and pension fund commitments, as well as the more liberal policy for writing down goodwill in Germany, which tended to overstate a firm's financial performance relative to that which would be reported under U.S. accounting rules.

After the initial rebuff from the SEC, this group of firms fell apart quite rapidly. However, Daimler-Benz announced in 1993 that it had reached an agreement with the SEC and would soon have a listing on the NYSE. To achieve this, Daimler-Benz had to issue two sets of accounts, one that adhered to German standards and another that adhered to U.S. generally-accepted accounting principles (GAAP). When Daimler-Benz reported its 1994 financial results, the impact of using different accounting standards was readily apparent. Under German rules, Daimler-Benz reported a profit of over $100 million, but under GAAP, the company reported a $1 billion loss!

Following the lead of Daimler-Benz, several other German firms announced they were willing to adopt international accounting standards. International accounting standards are being devised by a London-based committee of leading accountants that was established in 1973. Since 1987, the International Accounting Standards Committee (IASC) has been attempting to harmonize accounting rules that historically have varied significantly from country to country.

The international standards are more forthcoming about financial performance than the German rules. However, they still fall short of the U.S. GAAP, primarily because they allow for a looser treatment of goodwill. In March 1995, the pharmaceutical company Schering AG became the first German firm to shift completely to international standards. It was quickly followed by two other major German firms, Bayer AG and Hoechst AG. In 1997, Hoechst became the second German firm to list its shares on the NYSE. To support its listing, Hoechst issued two sets of accounts, one in accordance with IASC principles and one in accordance with GAAP. Under the IASC principles, Hoechst reported profits of $1.2 billion in 1995 and $1.4 billion in 1996. Under the more restrictive GAAP, it lost $40 million in 1995 and $708 million in 1996!

Despite the fact that adhering to GAAP apparently reduces the reported profit of German firms, others seem willing to follow these standards to gain access to the U.S. capital market. Allianz, a large German insurance company, adopted IASC principles as a prelude to seeking a listing on the NYSE. Allianz believes such a listing will help it finance acquisitions of other firms in the large U.S. insurance market. Under the IASC principles, Allianz became the first German insurance company to reveal the size of its "hidden reserves"— defined as the difference between the book value of its assets and their current market value. Since insurance companies generally invest the proceeds from insurance premiums in financial assets, such as stocks, and since the value of these assets tends to appreciate as the stock market rises, their market value can be substantial. However, their market value also fluctuates sharply with the value of the stock market, which is why German companies have preferred to keep them secret. In early 1998, the value of Allianz's hidden assets stood at $56.1 billion, but as the company pointed out, a sharp fall in the value of the stock market would cause a comparable fall in the assets. Nevertheless, because U.S. insurance companies always reveal the market value of such assets, Allianz must do so if it is to list its stock on the NYSE. The trend continued in 2001 when Volkswagen, a company renowned for its opaque accounting practices, announced that as of 2002 it would issue two sets of accounts: one using German accounting standards and a second adhering to IASC rules. A taste of how this might change Volkswagen's reported results was given in the first six months of 2001 when Volkswagen announced that its pretax operating margin under German accounting rules rose to 3.4 percent from 3.2 percent a year earlier, but under IASC rules it fell from 5.6 percent to 4.8 percent.

Sources: P. Gumbel and G. Steinmetz, "German Firms Shift to More Open Accounting," *Wall Street Journal,* March 15, 1995, p. C1; "Daimler-Benz: A Capital Suggestion," *The Economist,* April 9, 1994, p. 69; L. Berton, "All Accountants May Soon Speak the Same Language," *Wall Street Journal,* August 29, 1995, p. A15; R. Atkins, "Allianz Plans to Seek New York Listing," *Financial Times,* May 29, 1998, p. 30; G. Meek, "Accountants Gather Round Different Standards," *Financial Times,* March 20, 1998, p. 12; and D. I. Oyama, "World Watch," *Wall Street Journal,* June 30, 2001, p. A15.

Introduction

Accounting has often been referred to as "the language of business."[1] This language finds expression in profit-and-loss statements, balance sheets, budgets, investment analysis, and tax analysis. Accounting information is the means by which firms communicate their financial position to the providers of capital investors, creditors, and government. It enables the providers of capital to assess the value of their investments or the security of their loans and to make decisions about future resource allocations (see Figure 19.1). Accounting information is also the means by which firms report their income to the government, so the government can assess how much tax the firm owes. It is also the means by which the firm can evaluate its performance, control its internal expenditures, and plan for future expenditures and income. Thus, a good accounting function is critical to the smooth running of the firm.

International businesses are confronted with a number of accounting problems that do not confront purely domestic businesses. The opening case draws attention to one of these problems—the lack of consistency in the accounting standards of different

Figure 19.1

Accounting Information and Capital Flows

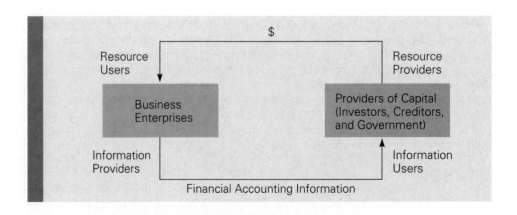

countries. We begin this chapter by looking at the source of these country differences. Then we shift our attention to attempts to establish international accounting and auditing standards—the International Accounting Standards Committee (IASC).

We will examine the problems arising when an international business with operations in more than one country must produce consolidated financial statements. As we will see, these firms face special problems because, for example, the accounts for their operations in Brazil will be in real, in Korea they will be in won, and in Japan they will be in yen. If the firm is based in the United States, it will have to decide what basis to use for translating all these accounts into U.S. dollars. The last issue we discuss is control in an international business. We touched on the issue of control in Chapter 13 in rather abstract terms. Here we look at control from an accounting perspective.

Country Differences in Accounting Standards ∎

Accounting is shaped by the environment in which it operates. Just as different countries have different political systems, economic systems, and cultures, they also have different accounting systems.[2] In each country, the accounting system has evolved in response to the demands for accounting information.

An example of differences in accounting conventions concerns employee disclosures. In many European countries, government regulations require firms to publish detailed information about their training and employment policies, but there is no such requirement in the United States. Another difference is in the treatment of goodwill. A firm's goodwill is any advantage, such as a trademark or brand name (e.g., the Coca-Cola brand name), that enables a firm to earn higher profits than its competitors. When one company acquires another in a takeover, the value of the goodwill is calculated as the amount paid for a firm above its book value, which is often substantial. Under accounting rules prevailing in many countries, acquiring firms are allowed to deduct the value of goodwill from the amount of equity or net worth reported on their balance sheet. In the United States, goodwill has to be deducted from the profits of the acquiring firm over as much as 40 years (although firms typically write down goodwill much more rapidly). If two equally profitable firms, one German and one American, acquire comparable firms that have identical goodwill, the U.S. firm will report a much lower profit than the German firm, because of differences in accounting conventions regarding goodwill.[3]

Despite attempts to harmonize standards by developing internationally acceptable accounting conventions (more on this later), a myriad of differences between national accounting systems still remain. A study tried to quantify the extent of these differences by comparing various accounting measures and profitability ratios across 22 developed nations, including Australia, Great Britain, France, Germany, Hong Kong, Japan, Spain, and South Korea.[4] The study found that among the 22 countries, there were 76 differences in the way cost of goods sold was assessed, 65 differences in the assessment of return on assets, 54 differences in the measurement of research and development expenses as a percentage of sales, and 20 differences in the calculation of net profit margin. These differences make it very difficult to compare the financial performance of firms based in different nation-states.

Although many factors can influence the development of a country's accounting system, there appear to be five main variables:[5]

1. The relationship between business and the providers of capital.
2. The political and economic ties with other countries.
3. The level of inflation.
4. The level of a country's economic development.
5. The prevailing culture in a country.

Figure 19.2 illustrates these variables, which we will review.

Figure 19.2

Determinants of National
Accounting Standards

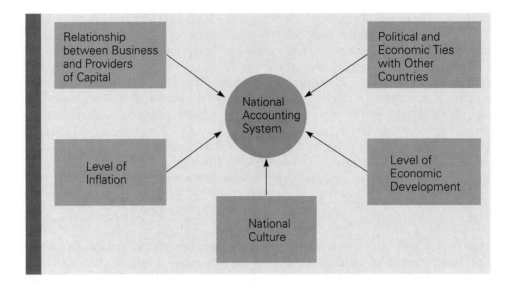

Relationship between Business and Providers of Capital

The three main external sources of capital for business are individual investors, banks, and government. In most advanced countries, all three sources are important. In the United States, for example, firms can raise capital by selling shares and bonds to individual investors through the stock market and the bond market. They can also borrow capital from banks and, in rather limited cases (particularly to support investments in defense-related R&D), from the government. The importance of each source of capital varies from country to country. In some countries, such as the United States, individual investors are the major source of capital; in others, banks play a greater role; in still others, the government is the major provider of capital. A country's accounting system tends to reflect the relative importance of these three constituencies as providers of capital.

Consider the case of the United States and Great Britain. Both have well-developed stock and bond markets in which firms can raise capital by selling stocks and bonds to individual investors. Most individual investors purchase only a very small proportion of a firm's total outstanding stocks or bonds. As such, they have no desire to be involved in the day-to-day management of the firms in which they invest; they leave that task to professional managers. But because of their lack of contact with the management of the firms in which they invest, individual investors may not have the information required to assess how well the companies are performing, and because of their small stake, they generally lack the ability to get information on demand from management. The financial accounting system in both Great Britain and the United States evolved to cope with this problem. In both countries, the financial accounting system is oriented toward providing individual investors with the information they need to make decisions about purchasing or selling corporate stocks and bonds.

In countries such as Switzerland, Germany, and Japan, a few large banks satisfy most of the capital needs of business enterprises. Individual investors play a relatively minor role. In these countries, the role of the banks is so important that a bank's officers often have seats on the boards of firms to which it lends capital. In such circumstances, the information needs of the capital providers are satisfied in a relatively straightforward way—through personal contacts, direct visits, and information provided at board meetings. Consequently, although firms still prepare financial reports, because government regulations in these countries mandate some public disclosure of a firm's financial position, the reports tend to contain less information than those of British or U.S. firms. Because banks are the major providers of capital, financial accounting practices are oriented toward protecting a bank's investment. Thus, assets are valued conservatively and liabilities are overvalued (in contrast to U.S. practice) to provide a cushion for the bank in case of default.

In still other countries, the national government has historically been an important provider of capital, and this has influenced accounting practices. This is the case in France and Sweden, where the national government has often stepped in to make loans or to invest in firms whose activities are deemed in the "national interest." In these countries, financial accounting practices tend to be oriented toward the needs of government planners.

Political and Economic Ties with Other Countries

Similarities in the accounting systems of countries are sometimes due to the countries' close political and/or economic ties. For example, the U.S. system has influenced accounting practices in Canada and Mexico, and since passage of NAFTA, the accounting systems in these three countries seem set to converge on a common set of norms. U.S.-style accounting systems are also used in the Philippines, which was once a U.S. protectorate. Another significant force in accounting worldwide has been the British system. The vast majority of former colonies of the British Empire have accounting practices modeled after Great Britain's. Similarly, the European Union has been attempting to harmonize accounting practices in its member countries. The accounting systems of EU members such as Great Britain, Germany, and France are quite different now, but if the EU has its way, they will converge on some norm by 2005.

Inflation Accounting

In many countries, including Germany, Japan, and the United States, accounting is based on the **historic cost principle.** This principle assumes the currency unit used to report financial results is not losing its value due to inflation. Firms record sales, purchases, and the like at the original transaction price and make no adjustments in the amounts later. The historic cost principle affects accounting most significantly in the area of asset valuation. If inflation is high, the historic cost principle underestimates a firm's assets, so the depreciation charges based on these underestimates can be inadequate for replacing assets when they wear out or become obsolete.

The appropriateness of this principle varies inversely with the level of inflation in a country. The high level of price inflation in many industrialized countries during the 1970s and 1980s created a need for accounting methods that adjust for inflation. A number of industrialized countries adopted new practices. One of the most far-reaching approaches was adopted in Great Britain in 1980. Called current cost accounting, it adjusts all items in a financial statement—assets, liabilities, costs, and revenues—to factor out the effects of inflation. The method uses a general price index to convert historic figures into current values. The standard was not made compulsory, however, and once Great Britain's inflation rate fell in the 1980s, most firms stopped providing the data.

Level of Development

Developed nations tend to have large, complex organizations, whose accounting problems are far more difficult than those of small organizations. Developed nations also tend to have sophisticated capital markets in which business organizations raise funds from investors and banks. These providers of capital require that the organizations they invest in and lend to provide comprehensive reports of their financial activities. The workforces of developed nations tend to be highly educated and skilled and can perform complex accounting functions. For all these reasons, accounting in developed countries tends to be far more sophisticated than it is in less developed countries, where the accounting standards may be fairly primitive. In much of the developing world, the accounting system used was inherited from former colonial powers. Many African nations for example, have accounting practices based on either the British or French models, depending on which was the former colonial power. These models may not apply very well to small businesses in a poorly developed economy. Another problem in many of the world's poorer countries is a simple lack of trained accountants.[6]

Culture

A number of academic accountants have argued that the culture of a country has an important impact on the nature of its accounting system.[7] Using the cultural typologies developed by Hofstede,[8] which we reviewed in Chapter 3, researchers have found that the extent to which a culture is characterized by uncertainty avoidance seems to have an impact on accounting systems.[9] **Uncertainty avoidance** refers to the extent to which cultures socialize their members to accept ambiguous situations and tolerate uncertainty. Members of high uncertainty avoidance cultures place a premium on job security, career patterns, retirement benefits, and so on. They also have a strong need for rules and regulations; the manager is expected to issue clear instructions, and subordinates' initiatives are tightly controlled. Lower uncertainty avoidance cultures are characterized by a greater readiness to take risks and less emotional resistance to change. According to Hofstede, countries such as Great Britain, the United States, and Sweden are characterized by low uncertainty avoidance, while countries such as Japan, Mexico, and Greece have higher uncertainty avoidance. Research suggests that countries with low uncertainty avoidance cultures tend to have strong independent auditing professions that audit a firm's accounts to make sure they comply with generally-accepted accounting regulations.[10]

Accounting Clusters

Few countries have identical accounting systems. Notable similarities between nations do exist, however, and three groups of countries with similar standards are identified in Map 19.1.[11] One group might be called the British-American-Dutch group. Great Britain, the United States, and the Netherlands are the trendsetters in this group. All these countries have large, well-developed stock and bond markets where firms raise capital from investors. Thus, their accounting systems are tailored to providing information to individual investors. A second group might be called the Europe-Japan group. Firms in these countries have very close ties to banks, which supply a large proportion of their capital needs. Therefore, their accounting practices are geared to the needs of banks. A third group might be the South American group. The countries in this group have all experienced persistent and rapid inflation. Consequently, they have adopted inflation accounting principles.

National and International Standards

The diverse accounting practices discussed in the previous section have been enshrined in national accounting and auditing standards. Accounting standards are rules for preparing financial statements; they define what is useful accounting information. Auditing standards specify the rules for performing an audit—the technical process by which an independent person (the auditor) gathers evidence for determining if financial accounts conform to required accounting standards and if they are also reliable.

Map 19.1

Accounting Clusters

British-American-Dutch Group

Europe-Japan Group

South American Group

Lack of Comparability

An unfortunate result of national differences in accounting and auditing standards is the general lack of comparability of financial reports from one country to another. For example, consider the following:

- Dutch standards favor the use of current values for replacement assets; Japanese law generally prohibits revaluation and prescribes historic cost.
- Capitalization of financial leases is required practice in Great Britain, but it is not practiced in France.
- Research and development costs must be written off in the year they are incurred in the United States, but in Spain they may be deferred as an asset and need not be amortized as long as benefits that will cover them are expected to arise in the future.
- German accountants treat depreciation as a liability, whereas British companies deduct it from assets.

Such differences would not matter much if there was little need for a firm headquartered in one country to report its financial results to citizens of another country. However, as you might recall from Chapter 11, one striking development of the past two decades has been the development of global capital markets. We have seen the growth of both transnational financing and transnational investment.

Transnational financing occurs when a firm based in one country enters another country's capital market to raise capital from the sale of stocks or bonds. A Danish firm raising capital by selling stock through the London Stock Exchange is an example of transnational financing. As we saw in the opening case, a number of large German firms are increasing their use of transnational financing by gaining listings, and ultimately issuing stock, on the New York Stock Exchange. Transnational investment occurs when an investor based in one country enters the capital market of another nation to invest in the stocks or bonds of a firm based in that country. An investor based in Great Britain buying General Motors stock through the New York Stock Exchange would be an example of transnational investment.

The rapid expansion of transnational financing and investment in recent years has been accompanied by a corresponding growth in transnational financial reporting. For example, in addition to its Danish financial reports, the Danish firm raising capital in London must issue financial reports that serve the needs of its British investors. Similarly, the U.S. firm with a large number of British investors might wish to issue reports that serve the needs of those investors. However, the lack of comparability between accounting standards in different nations can lead to confusion. For example, the Danish firm that issues two sets of financial reports, one set prepared under Danish standards and the other under British standards, may find that its financial position looks significantly different in the two reports, and its investors may have difficulty identifying the firm's true worth. Some examples of the confusion that can arise from this lack of comparability appear in the accompanying Management Focus.

In addition to the problems this lack of comparability causes investors, it can give the firm major headaches. The firm has to explain to its investors why its financial position looks so different in the two accountings. Also, an international business may find it difficult to assess the financial positions of important foreign customers, suppliers, and competitors.

International Standards

Substantial efforts have been made in recent years to harmonize accounting standards across countries. The International Accounting Standards Committee (IASC), a major proponent of standardization, is composed of representatives of 106

Management Focus

The Consequences of Different Accounting Standards

In 1999, two major drug firms, Zeneca and Astra merged to form AstraZeneca. Based in the United Kingdom, AstraZeneca in 2000 reported a profit of $865 million under U.S. accounting rules, but $3,318 million under British accounting rules. The largest difference between the two sets of accounts was $1,756 million, which related to amortization and other acquisition-related costs. Under U.S. rules, the combination of Astra and Zeneca was treated as an acquisition, which required goodwill to be recognized with consequent amortization. Under British rules, any amortization was avoided as the combination was treated as a merger and so no goodwill arose.

U.S.-based SmithKline Beckman (SKB) merged with the British company Beecham Group in 1989. After the merger, SKB had quotations on both the London and New York stock exchanges, so it had to prepare financial reports in accordance with both U.S. and British standards. SKB's postmerger earnings, properly prepared in accordance with British accounting standards, were £130 million—quite a bit more than the £87 million reported in SKB's statement prepared in accordance with U.S. accounting standards. The difference resulted primarily from treating the merger as a pooling of assets for British purposes and as a purchase of assets for U.S. purposes. Even more confusing, the differences resulted in a shareholders' equity of £3.5 billion in the United States, but a negative £300 million in Great Britain! Not surprisingly, after these figures were released, SKB's stock was trading 17 percent lower on the London Stock Exchange than on the New York Stock Exchange.

In the mid-1980s, Telefonica, Spain's largest industrial company, was the first company in the world to float a multicountry stock offering simultaneously. In 1990, it reported net income under U.S. accounting standards of 176 billion pesetas, more than twice the 76 billion pesetas it reported under Spanish accounting standards. The difference was mainly due to an "add-back" of the incremental depreciation on assets carried at historic cost in the United States but reflecting more recent market value in the Spanish report. The effect of this difference on shareholders' equity was in the opposite direction; the equity reported in the U.S. accounts was 15 percent less than the equity reported in the Spanish accounts.

In 2000, British Airways reported a loss under British accounting rules of £21 million, but under U.S. rules, its loss was £412 million. Most of the difference could be attributed to adjustments for a number of relatively small items such as depreciation and amortization, pensions, and deferred taxation. The largest adjustment was due to a reduction in revenue reported in the U.S. accounts of £136 million. This reduced revenue was related to frequent flyer miles, which under U.S. rules have to be deferred until the miles are redeemed.

A final example is more hypothetical in nature, but just as revealing. Two college professors set up a computer model to evaluate the reported net profits of an imaginary company with gross operating profits of $1.5 million. This imaginary company operated in three different countries—the United States, Great Britain, and Australia. The professors found that holding all else equal (such as national differences in interest rates on the firm's debt), when different accounting standards were applied, the firm made a net profit of $34,600 in the United States, $260,600 in Britain, and $240,600 in Australia.

Sources: S. F. O'Malley, "Accounting across Borders," *Financial Executive,* March/April 1992, pp. 28–31; L. Berton, "All Accountants May Soon Speak the Same Language," *Wall Street Journal,* August 29, 1995, p. A15; and "GAAP Reconciliations," *Company Reporting,* July 2001, p. 3–6.

professional accounting groups in 79 countries. Governed by a 14-member board of representatives from 13 countries plus a representative from the International Federation of Financial Analysts, the IASC is responsible for formulating international accounting standards (IAS). Other areas of interest to the accounting profession worldwide, including auditing, ethical, educational, and public-sector standards, are handled by the International Federation of Accountants (IFAC), which has the same membership.

The IASC was begun in 1973 as an outgrowth of an effort by Canada, the United States, and Great Britain to develop international accounting standards. The IFAC was established in 1977, when it was determined that the IASC did not have the expertise to deal with broader professional issues. The two organizations work closely, but they are operated and funded separately.

By 2000 the IASC had issued about 40 international accounting standards.[12] To issue a new standard, 75 percent of the 14 members of the board must agree. It can be difficult to get three-quarters agreement, particularly since members come from different cultures and legal systems. To get around this problem, most IASC statements provide two acceptable alternatives. As Arthur Wyatt, former chairman of the IASC, once said, "It's not much of a standard if you have two alternatives, but it's better than having six. If you can get agreement on two alternatives, you can capture the 11 required votes and eliminate some of the less used practices."[13]

Another hindrance to the development of international accounting standards is that compliance is voluntary; the IASC has no power to enforce its standards. Despite this, support for the IASC and recognition of its standards is growing. Increasingly, the IASC is regarded as an effective voice for defining acceptable worldwide accounting principles. Japan, for example, began requiring financial statements to be prepared on a consolidated basis after the IASC issued its initial standards on the topic. By 1998, the IASC claimed that more than 450 companies around the world currently follow its rules, including Central African Cable from Zimbabwe, Guangshen Railway Company from China, Bayer from Germany, and Microsoft from the United States.

The impact of the IASC standards has probably been least noticeable in the United States because most of the standards issued by the IASC have been consistent with opinions already articulated by the U.S. Financial Accounting Standards Board (FASB). The FASB writes the generally accepted accounting principles by which the financial statements of U.S. firms must be prepared. In sharp contrast, some IASC standards have had a significant impact in many other countries because they eliminated a commonly used alternative.

Another body that promises to have substantial influence on the harmonization of accounting standards, at least within Europe, is the European Union (EU). In accordance with its plans for closer economic and political union, the EU is attempting to harmonize the accounting principles of its 15 member countries. The EU does this by issuing directives that the member states are obligated to incorporate into their own national laws. Because EU directives have the power of law, we might assume the EU has a better chance of achieving harmonization than the IASC does, but the EU is experiencing implementation difficulties. These difficulties arise from the wide variation in accounting practices among EU member countries. Accounting practices in Great Britain, for example, are closer to those of the United States than to those of France or Germany. Despite these difficulties, developments in the EU should be watched closely. If the EU achieves harmonization (in all probability, it eventually will), the accounting principles adopted in the EU could have a major influence on future IASC pronouncements. The current timeline calls for the EU to harmonize accounting standards among member states by 2005. The EU is calling for harmonization under IASC standards, which would create significant changes. As of early 2001, only one-fifth of the 300 leading companies in Europe employed IASC rules to compile their financial reports.[14]

In a move that indicates the trend toward adoption of acceptable international accounting standards is accelerating, the IASC has developed accounting standards for firms seeking stock listings in global markets. Also, the FASB has joined forces with those setting accounting standards in Canada, Mexico, and Chile to explore areas in which the four countries can harmonize their accounting standards (Canada, Mexico, and the United States are members of NAFTA, and Chile may join in the future). The Securities and Exchange Commission has also dropped some

Novartis Joins the International Accounting Club

Management Focus

Switzerland does not have a history of very detailed accounting rules. As a result, published financial statements by major Swiss firms such as Novartis, Roche Group, and Nestlé often obscured as much as they revealed. The standard set of accounts from a Swiss firm was viewed as being very difficult for international investors to understand and was described as being more like a statistical summary than the result of an integrated accounting system.

Swiss firms began to move toward adoption of IASC accounting principles in the early 1990s. The catalyst was increasing interest by foreign investors in the stock of major Swiss corporations. By the early 1990s, up to 40 percent of the stock of many of these firms was owned by foreign investors. These investors were demanding more detailed financial statements that were comparable to those issued by other multinational enterprises.

One of the first firms to respond to these pressures was Ciba, Switzerland's largest pharmaceuticals and chemicals firm and a major multinational enterprise with operations around the globe. (Ciba became Novartis after it merged with another Swiss pharmaceutical company, Sandoz, in 1998.) In 1993, the company announced that its 1994 financial statements would be in accordance with IASC guidelines. At the same time, it restated its 1992 results in line with IASC guidelines. The effect was to increase post-tax profits by 18 percent while raising inventories, cash, and marketable securities. Ciba's decision was motivated by a desire to appease foreign stockholders, who in 1994 held more than one-third of Ciba's stock, and to position itself for the possibility of listings on the London and New York stock markets.

Ciba also decided to use the same international standards for internal financial reporting. Ciba set up a small international team to develop and implement its new system. While there were some preliminary problems in development of the system, including a figure on the insurance value of fixed assets that was off by $690 million, the new system is now running smoothly and seems to have produced several major benefits.

Ciba discovered large savings as a result of the change, including tighter cash management, more efficient capital investment, a different approach to acquisitions, and more rigid asset management, which has reportedly reduced the value of inventories by 6 percent. The new system also enabled the company to benchmark its performance for the first time against its global competitors.

One big difference between the new and old systems was the move from the current cost accounting method, which Ciba had used for over 25 years and which regularly updated asset values to account for inflation, to historic cost accounting under international standards. However, management admits this drawback was not serious given the low inflation rate in Switzerland and given the offsetting gains produced by the switch to a new system

In 2000, Novartis, which was formed when Ciba merged with Sandoz in 1998, decided it needed to become more aggressive about attracting U.S. investors. Although Novartis already listed its shares as American Depositary Receipts (ADRs) on the American Stock Exchange, it switched the listing to the more visible New York Stock Exchange and doubled the amount of ADRs offered. Accompanying this shift, Novartis also decided that, in addition to presenting its rules based on IASC principles, it needed to adopt full U.S. accounting principles. Novartis is publishing its first complete set of U.S. accounts in 2002.

Sources: A. Jack, "Swiss Group Moves from Night to Day," *Financial Times*, March 30, 1994, p. 22; L. Berton, "All Accountants May Soon Speak the Same Language," *Wall Street Journal*, August 29, 1995, p. A15; and A. Beard, "Novartis Steps up the Pace of Its U.S. Charm Offensive," *Financial Times*, May 14, 2001, p. 23.

of its objections to international standards, which could accelerate their adoption. In 1994, the SEC for the first time accepted three international accounting standards on cash flow data, the effects of hyperinflation, and business combinations for cross-border filings.[15] A taste of what is to come if increasing numbers of international firms adopt IASC principles can be found in the accompanying Management Focus, which details the impact of adopting these standards on Novartis, the Swiss pharmaceuticals and chemicals group.

Multinational Consolidation and Currency Translation

A consolidated financial statement combines the separate financial statements of two or more companies to yield a single set of financial statements as if the individual companies were really one. Most multinational firms are composed of a parent company and a number of subsidiary companies located in other countries. Such firms typically issue consolidated financial statements, which merge the accounts of all the companies, rather than issuing individual financial statements for the parent company and each subsidiary. In this section, we examine the consolidated financial statements and then look at the related issue of foreign currency translation.

Consolidated Financial Statements

Many firms find it advantageous to organize as a set of separate legal entities (companies). For example, a firm may separately incorporate the various components of its business to limit its total legal liability or to take advantage of corporate tax regulations. Multinationals are often required by the countries in which they do business to set up a separate company. Thus, the typical multinational comprises a parent company and a number of subsidiary companies located in different countries, most of which are wholly owned by the parent. Although the subsidiaries may be separate legal entities, they are not separate economic entities. Economically, all the companies in a corporate group are interdependent. For example, if the Brazilian subsidiary of a U.S. parent company experiences substantial financial losses that suck up corporate funds, the cash available for investment in that subsidiary, the U.S. parent company, and other subsidiary companies will be limited. Thus, the purpose of consolidated financial statements is to provide accounting information about a group of companies that recognize their economic interdependence.

Transactions among the members of a corporate family are not included in consolidated financial statements; only assets, liabilities, revenues, and expenses with external third parties are shown. By law, however, separate legal entities are required to keep their own accounting records and to prepare their own financial statements. Thus, transactions with other members of a corporate group must be identified in the separate statements so they can be excluded when the consolidated statements are prepared. The process involves adding up the individual assets, liabilities, revenues, and expenses reported on the separate financial statements and then eliminating the intragroup ones. For example, consider these items selected from the individual financial statements of a parent company and one of its foreign subsidiaries:

	Parent	Foreign Subsidiary
Cash	$1,000	$ 250
Receivables	3,000*	900
Payables	300	500*
Revenues	7,000†	5,000
Expenses	2,000	3,000†

*Subsidiary owes parent $300.

†Subsidiary pays parent $1,000 in royalties for products licensed from parent.

The $300 receivable that the parent includes on its financial statements and the $300 payable that the subsidiary includes on its statements represent an intragroup item. These items cancel each other out and thus are not included in consolidated financial statements. Similarly, the $1,000 the subsidiary owes the parent in royalty payments is an intragroup item that will not appear in the consolidated accounts. The adjustments are as follows:

	Parent	Subsidiary	Eliminations Debit	Eliminations Credit	Consolidated
Cash	$1,000	$ 250			$ 1,250
Receivables	3,000*	900		$ 300	3,600
Payables	300	500*	$300		500
Revenues	7,000†	5,000		1,000	11,000
Expenses	2,000	3,000†	1,000		4,000

*Subsidiary owes parent $300.

†Subsidiary pays parent $1,000 in royalties for products licensed from parent.

While simply adding the two sets of accounts would suggest that the group of companies has revenues of $12,000 and receivables of $3,900, once intragroup transactions are removed from the picture, these figures drop to $11,000 and $3,600, respectively.

Preparing consolidated financial statements is becoming the norm for multinational firms. Investors realize that without consolidated financial statements, a multinational firm could conceal losses in an unconsolidated subsidiary, thereby hiding the economic status of the entire group. For example, the parent company in our illustration could increase its profit merely by charging the subsidiary company higher royalty fees. Since this has no effect on the group's overall profits, it amounts to little more than window dressing, making the parent company look good. If the parent does not issue a consolidated financial statement, however, the true economic status of the group is obscured by such a practice. With this in mind, the IASC has issued two standards requiring firms to prepare consolidated financial statements, and in most industrialized countries this is now required.

Currency Translation

Foreign subsidiaries of multinational firms normally keep their accounting records and prepare their financial statements in the currency of the country in which they are located. Thus, the Japanese subsidiary of a U.S. firm will prepare its accounts in yen, a Brazilian subsidiary in real, a Korean subsidiary in won, and so on. When a multinational prepares consolidated accounts, it must convert all these financial statements into the currency of its home country. As we saw in Chapter 9, however, exchange rates vary in response to changes in economic circumstances. Companies can use two main methods to determine what exchange rate should be used when translating financial statement currencies—the current rate method and the temporal method.

The Current Rate Method

Under the current rate method, the exchange rate at the balance sheet date is used to translate the financial statements of a foreign subsidiary into the home currency of the multinational firm. Although this may seem logical, it is incompatible with the historic cost principle, which, as we saw earlier, is a generally accepted accounting principle in many countries, including the United States. Consider the case of a U.S. firm that invests $100,000 in a Malaysian subsidiary. Assume the exchange rate at the time is $1 = 5 Malaysian ringgit. The subsidiary converts the $100,000 into ringgit, which gives it 500,000 ringgit. It then purchases land with this money. Subsequently, the dollar depreciates against the ringgit, so that by year-end, $1 = 4 ringgit. If this exchange rate is used to convert the value of the land back into U.S. dollars for preparing consolidated accounts, the land will be valued at $125,000. The piece of land would appear to have increased in value by $25,000, although in reality the increase would be simply a function of an exchange rate change. Thus, the consolidated accounts would present a misleading picture.

The Temporal Method

One way to avoid this problem is to use the temporal method to translate the accounts of a foreign subsidiary. The temporal method translates assets valued in a foreign currency into the home-country currency using the exchange rate that exists when the assets are purchased. Referring to our example, the exchange rate of $1 = 5 ringgit, the rate on the day the Malaysian subsidiary purchased the land, would be used to convert the value of the land back into U.S. dollars at year-end. However, although the temporal method will ensure the dollar value of the land does not fluctuate due to exchange rate changes, it has its own serious problem. Because the various assets of a foreign subsidiary will in all probability be acquired at different times and because exchange rates seldom remain stable for long, different exchange rates will probably have to be used to translate those foreign assets into the multinational's home currency. Consequently, the multinational's balance sheet may not balance!

Consider the case of a U.S. firm that on January 1, 2001, invested $100,000 in a new Japanese subsidiary. The exchange rate at that time was $1 = ¥100. The initial investment was therefore ¥10 million, and the Japanese subsidiary's balance sheet looked like this on January 1, 2001:

	Yen	Exchange Rate	U.S. Dollars
Cash	10,000,000	($1 = ¥100)	100,000
Owners' equity	10,000,000	($1 = ¥100)	100,000

Assume that on January 31, when the exchange rate was $1 = ¥95, the Japanese subsidiary invested ¥5 million in a factory (i.e., fixed assets). Then on February 15, when the exchange rate was $1 = ¥90, the subsidiary purchased ¥5 million of inventory. The balance sheet of the subsidiary would look like this on March 1, 2001:

	Yen	Exchange Rate	U.S. Dollars
Fixed assets	5,000,000	($1 = ¥95)	52,632
Inventory	5,000,000	($1 = ¥90)	55,556
Total	10,000,000		108,188
Owners' equity	10,000,000	($1 = ¥100)	100,000

Although the balance sheet balances in yen, it does not balance when the temporal method is used to translate the yen-denominated balance sheet figures back into dollars. In translation, the balance sheet debits exceed the credits by $8,188. The accounting profession has yet to adopt a satisfactory solution to the gap between debits and credits.

Current U.S. Practice

U.S.-based multinational firms must follow the requirements of Statement 52, "Foreign Currency Translation," issued by the Financial Accounting Standards Board in 1981. Under Statement 52, a foreign subsidiary is classified either as a self-sustaining, autonomous subsidiary or as integral to the activities of the parent company. (A link can be made here with the material on strategy discussed in Chapter 12. Firms pursuing multidomestic and international strategies are most likely to have self-sustaining subsidiaries, whereas firms pursuing global and transnational strategies are most likely to have integral subsidiaries.) According to Statement 52, the local currency of a self-sustaining foreign subsidiary is to be its functional currency. The balance sheet for such subsidiaries is translated into the home currency using the exchange rate in effect at the end of the firm's financial year, whereas the income statement is translated using the average exchange rate for the firm's financial year. But the functional currency of an integral subsidiary is to be U.S. dollars. The financial statements of such subsidiaries are translated at various historic rates using the temporal method (as we did in the example), and the dangling debit or credit increases or decreases consolidated earnings for the period.

Accounting Aspects of Control Systems

Corporate headquarters' role is to control subunits within the organization to ensure they achieve the best possible performance. In the typical firm, the control process is annual and involves three main steps:

1. Head office and subunit management jointly determine subunit goals for the coming year.
2. Throughout the year, the head office monitors subunit performance against the goals.
3. If a subunit fails to achieve its goals, the head office intervenes in the subunit to learn why the shortfall occurred, taking corrective action when appropriate.

The accounting function plays a critical role in this process. Most of the goals for subunits are expressed in financial terms and are embodied in the subunit's budget for the coming year. The budget is the main instrument of financial control. The budget is typically prepared by the subunit, but it must be approved by headquarters management. During the approval process, headquarters and subunit managements debate the goals that should be incorporated in the budget. One function of headquarters management is to ensure a subunit's budget contains challenging but realistic performance goals. Once a budget is agreed to, accounting information systems are used to collect data throughout the year so a subunit's performance can be evaluated against the goals contained in its budget.

In most international businesses, many of the firm's subunits are foreign subsidiaries. The performance goals for the coming year are thus set by negotiation

Item	Subsidiary	Manager
Return on investment (ROI)	1.9	2.2
Return on equity (ROE)	3.0	3.0
Return on assets (ROA)	2.3	2.3
Return on sales (ROS)	2.1	2.1
Residual income	3.4	3.3
Budget compared to actual sales	1.9	1.7
Budget compared to actual profit	1.5	1.3
Budget compared to actual ROI	2.3	2.4
Budget compared to actual ROA	2.7	2.5
Budget compared to actual ROE	3.1	3.0

Table 19.1

Importance of Financial Criteria Used to Evaluate Performance of Foreign Subsidiaries and Their Managers*

*Importance of criteria ranked on a scale from: 1 = very important to 5 = unimportant.

Source: F. Choi and I. Czechowicz, "Assessing Foreign Subsidiary Performance: A Multinational Comparison," *Management International Review 4* (1983), p. 16.

between corporate management and the managers of foreign subsidiaries. According to one survey of control practices within multinational enterprises, the most important criterion for evaluating the performance of a foreign subsidiary is the subsidiary's actual profits compared to budgeted profits (see Table 19.1).[16] This is closely followed by a subsidiary's actual sales compared to budgeted sales and its return on investment. The same criteria were also useful in evaluating the performance of the subsidiary managers. We will discuss this point later in this section. First, however, we will examine two factors that can complicate the control process in an international business: exchange rate changes and transfer pricing practices.

Exchange Rate Changes and Control Systems

Most international businesses require all budgets and performance data within the firm to be expressed in the "corporate currency," which is normally the home currency. Thus, the Malaysian subsidiary of a U.S. multinational would probably submit a budget prepared in U.S. dollars, rather than Malaysian ringgit, and performance data throughout the year would be reported to headquarters in U.S. dollars. This facilitates comparisons between subsidiaries in different countries, and it makes things easier for headquarters management. However, it also allows exchange rate changes during the year to introduce substantial distortions. For example, the Malaysian subsidiary may fail to achieve profit goals not because of any performance problems, but merely because of a decline in the value of the ringgit against the dollar. The opposite can occur, also, making a foreign subsidiary's performance look better than it actually is.

The Lessard–Lorange Model

According to research by Donald Lessard and Peter Lorange, a number of methods are available to international businesses for dealing with this problem.[17] Lessard and Lorange point out three exchange rates that can be used to translate foreign currencies into the corporate currency in setting budgets and in the subsequent tracking of performance:

- The initial rate: the spot exchange rate when the budget is adopted.
- The projected rate: the spot exchange rate forecast for the end of the budget period (i.e., the forward rate).
- The ending rate: the spot exchange rate when the budget and performance are being compared.

These three exchange rates imply nine possible combinations (see Figure 19.3). Lessard and Lorange ruled out four of the nine combinations as illogical and unreasonable; they are shaded light purple in Figure 19.3. For example, it would make no sense to use the ending rate to translate the budget and the initial rate to translate actual performance data. Any of the remaining five combinations might be used for setting budgets and evaluating performance.

With three of these five combinations—II, PP, and EE—the same exchange rate is used for translating both budget figures and performance figures into the corporate currency. With these three combinations, a change in the exchange rate during the year does not distort the control process. This is not true for the other two combinations, IE and PE. In those cases, exchange rate changes can introduce distortions. The potential for distortion is greater with IE; the ending spot exchange rate used to evaluate performance against the budget may be quite different from the initial spot exchange rate used to translate the budget. The distortion is less serious in the case of PE because the projected exchange rate takes into account future exchange rate movements.

Of the five combinations, Lessard and Lorange recommend that firms use the projected spot exchange rate to translate both the budget and performance figures into the corporate currency, combination PP. The projected rate in such cases will typically

	Rate Used to Translate Actual Performance for Comparison with Budget		
Rate Used for Translating Budget	**Initial (I)**	**Projected (P)**	**Ending (E)**
Initial (I)	(II) Budget at Initial Actual at Initial	(IP) Budget at Initial Actual at Projected	(IE) Budget at Initial Actual at Ending
Projected (P)	Budget at Projected Actual at Initial	(PP) Budget at Projected Actual at Projected	(PE) Budget at Projected Actual at Ending
Ending (E)	Budget at Ending Actual at Initial	Budget at Ending Actual at Projected	(EE) Budget at Ending Actual at Ending

Figure 19.3

Possible Combinations of Exchange Rates in the Control Process

be the forward exchange rate as determined by the foreign exchange market (see Chapter 9 for the definition of forward rate) or some company-generated forecast of future spot rates, which Lessard and Lorange refer to as the **internal forward rate.** The internal forward rate may differ from the forward rate quoted by the foreign exchange market if the firm wishes to bias its business in favor of, or against, the particular foreign currency.

Transfer Pricing and Control Systems

In Chapter 12 we reviewed the various strategies that international businesses pursue. Two of these strategies, the global strategy and the transnational strategy, give rise to a globally dispersed web of productive activities. Firms pursuing these strategies disperse each value creation activity to its optimal location in the world. Thus, a product might be designed in one country, some of its components manufactured in a second country, other components manufactured in a third country, all assembled in a fourth country, and then sold worldwide.

The volume of intrafirm transactions in such firms is very high. The firms are continually shipping component parts and finished goods between subsidiaries in different countries. This poses a very important question: How should goods and services transferred between subsidiary companies in a multinational firm be priced? The price at which such goods and services are transferred is referred to as the transfer price.

The choice of transfer price can critically affect the performance of two subsidiaries that exchange goods or services. Consider this example: A French manufacturing subsidiary of a U.S. multinational imports a major component from Brazil. It incorporates this part into a product that it sells in France for the equivalent of $230 per unit. The product costs $200 to manufacture, of which $100 goes to the Brazilian subsidiary to pay for the component part. The remaining $100 covers costs incurred in France. Thus, the French subsidiary earns $30 profit per unit.

Look at what happens if corporate headquarters decides to increase transfer prices by 20 percent ($20 per unit). The French subsidiary's profits will fall by two-thirds from $30 per unit to $10 per unit. Thus, the performance of the French subsidiary depends on the transfer price for the component part imported from Brazil, and the transfer price is controlled by corporate headquarters. When setting budgets and reviewing a subsidiary's performance, corporate headquarters must keep in mind the distorting effect of transfer prices.

	Before Change in Transfer Price	After 20 percent Increase in Transfer Price
Revenues per unit	$230	$230
Cost of component per unit	100	120
Other costs per unit	100	100
Profit per unit	30	10

How should transfer prices be determined? We discuss this issue in detail in the next chapter. International businesses often manipulate transfer prices to minimize their worldwide tax liability, minimize import duties, and avoid government restrictions on capital flows. For now, however, it is enough to note that the transfer price must be considered when setting budgets and evaluating a subsidiary's performance.

Separation of Subsidiary and Manager Performance

Table 19.1 suggests that in many international businesses, the same quantitative criteria are used to assess the performance of both a foreign subsidiary and its managers. Many accountants, however, argue that although it is legitimate to compare subsidiaries against each other on the basis of return on investment (ROI) or other indicators of profitability, it may not be appropriate to use these for comparing and evaluating the managers of different subsidiaries. Foreign subsidiaries do not operate in uniform environments; their environments have widely different economic, political, and social conditions, all of which influence the costs of doing business in a country and hence the subsidiaries' profitability. Thus, the manager of a subsidiary in an adverse environment that has an ROI of 5 percent may be doing a better job than the manager of a subsidiary in a benign environment that has an ROI of 20 percent. Although the firm might want to pull out of a country where its ROI is only 5 percent, it may also want to recognize the manager's achievement.

Accordingly, it has been suggested that the evaluation of a subsidiary should be kept separate from the evaluation of its manager.[18] The manager's evaluation should consider how hostile or benign the country's environment is for that business. Further, managers should be evaluated in local currency terms after making allowances for those items over which they have no control (e.g., interest rates, tax rates, inflation rates, transfer prices, exchange rates).

Chapter Summary

This chapter focused on financial accounting within the multinational firm. We explained why accounting practices and standards differ from country to country and surveyed the efforts under way to harmonize countries' accounting practices. We discussed the rationale behind consolidated accounts and looked at currency translation. We reviewed several issues related to the use of accounting-based control systems within international businesses. This chapter made the following points:

1. Accounting is the language of business: the means by which firms communicate their financial position to the providers of capital and to governments (for tax purposes). It is also the means by

which firms evaluate their own performance, control their expenditures, and plan for the future.

2. Accounting is shaped by the environment in which it operates. Each country's accounting system has evolved in response to the local demands for accounting information.

3. Five main factors seem to influence the type of accounting system a country has: (i) the relationship between business and the providers of capital, (ii) the political and economic ties with other countries, (iii) the level of inflation, (iv) the level of a country's development, and (v) the prevailing culture in a country.

4. National differences in accounting and auditing standards have resulted in a general lack of comparability in countries' financial reports.

5. This lack of comparability has become a problem as transnational financing and transnational investment have grown rapidly in recent decades (a consequence of the globalization of capital markets). Due to the lack of comparability, a firm may have to explain to investors why its financial position looks very different on financial reports that are based on different accounting practices.

6. The most significant push for harmonization of accounting standards across countries has come from the International Accounting Standards Committee (IASC). So far, the IASC's success has been limited.

7. Consolidated financial statements provide financial accounting information about a group of companies that recognizes the companies' economic interdependence.

8. Transactions among the members of a corporate family are not included on consolidated financial statements; only assets, liabilities, revenues, and expenses generated with external third parties are shown.

9. Foreign subsidiaries of a multinational firm normally keep their accounting records and prepare their financial statements in the currency of the country in which they are located. When the multinational prepares its consolidated accounts, these financial statements must be translated into the currency of its home country.

10. Under the current rate translation method, the exchange rate at the balance sheet date is used to translate the financial statements of a foreign subsidiary into the home currency. This is incompatible with the historic cost principle.

11. Under the temporal method, assets valued in a foreign currency are translated into the home currency using the exchange rate that existed when the assets were purchased. A problem with this approach is that the multinational's balance sheet may not balance.

12. In most international businesses, the annual budget is the main instrument by which headquarters controls foreign subsidiaries. Throughout the year, headquarters compares a subsidiary's performance against the financial goals incorporated in its budget, intervening selectively in its operations when shortfalls occur.

13. Most international businesses require all budgets and performance data within the firm to be expressed in the corporate currency. This enhances comparability, but it distorts the control process if the relevant exchange rates change between the time a foreign subsidiary's budget is set and the time its performance is evaluated.

14. According to the Lessard–Lorange model, the best way to deal with this problem is to use a projected spot exchange rate to translate both budget figures and performance figures into the corporate currency.

15. Transfer prices also can introduce significant distortions into the control process and thus must be considered when setting budgets and evaluating a subsidiary's performance.

16. Foreign subsidiaries do not operate in uniform environments, and some environments are much tougher than others. Accordingly, it has been suggested that the evaluation of a subsidiary should be kept separate from the evaluation of the subsidiary manager.

Critical Discussion Questions

1. Why do the accounting systems of different countries differ? Why do these differences matter?

2. Why are transactions among members of a corporate family not included in consolidated financial statements?

3. The following are selected amounts from the separate financial statements of a parent company (unconsolidated) and one of its subsidiaries

	Parent	Subsidiary
Cash	$ 180	$ 80
Receivables	380	200
Accounts payable	245	110
Retained earnings	790	680
Revenues	4,980	3,520
Rent income	0	200
Dividend income	250	0
Expenses	4,160	2,960

Parent owes subsidiary $70.

Parent owns 100 percent of subsidiary. During the year, the subsidiary paid the parent a dividend of $250.

Subsidiary owns the building that parent rents for $200.

During the year, the parent sold some inventory to the subsidiary for $2,200. It had cost parent $1,500. Subsidiary, in turn, sold the inventory to an unrelated party for $3,200.

Given this,

   a. What is the parent's (unconsolidated) net income?

   b. What is the subsidiary's net income?

   c. What is the consolidated profit on the inventory that the parent originally sold to the subsidiary?

   d. What are the amounts of consolidated cash and receivables?

4. Why might an accounting-based control system provide headquarters management with biased information about the performance of a foreign subsidiary? How can these biases best be corrected?

China's Evolving Accounting System

Attracted by its rapid transformation from a socialist planned economy into a market economy, economic annual growth rates of around 12 percent, and a population in excess of 1.2 billion, Western firms over the past 10 years have favored China as a site for foreign direct investment. Most see China as an emerging economic superpower with an economy that will be as large as that of Japan by 2005 and of the United States before 2010 if current growth projections hold true.

The Chinese government sees foreign direct investment as a primary engine of China's economic growth. To encourage such investment, the government has offered generous tax incentives to foreign firms that invest in China, either on their own or in a joint venture with a local enterprise.

These tax incentives include a two-year exemption from corporate income tax following an investment, plus a further three years during which taxes are paid at only 50 percent of the standard tax rate. Such incentives when coupled with the promise of China's vast internal market have made the country a prime site for investment by Western firms. However, once established in China, many Western firms find themselves struggling to comply with the complex and often obtuse nature of China's rapidly evolving accounting system.

Accounting in China has traditionally been rooted in information gathering and compliance reporting designed to measure the government's production and tax goals. The Chinese system was based on the old Soviet system, which had little to do with profit or accounting systems created to report financial positions or the results of foreign operations. Although the system is changing rapidly, many problems associated with the old system still remain.

One problem for investors is a severe shortage of accountants, financial managers, and auditors in China, especially those experienced with market economy transactions and international accounting practices. As of 1995, there were only 25,000 accountants in China, far short of the hundreds of thousands that will be needed if China continues on its path toward becoming a market economy. Chinese enterprises, including equity and cooperative joint ventures with foreign firms, must be audited by Chinese accounting firms, which are regulated by the state. Traditionally, many experienced auditors have audited only state-owned enterprises, working through the local province or city authorities and the state audit bureau to report to the government entity overseeing the audited firm. In response to the shortage of accountants schooled in the principles of private-sector accounting, several large international auditing firms have established joint ventures with emerging Chinese accounting and auditing firms to bridge the growing need for international accounting, tax, and securities expertise.

A further problem concerns the somewhat halting evolution of China's emerging accounting standards. Current thinking is that China won't simply adopt the international accounting standards specified by the IASC, nor will it use the generally accepted accounting principles of any particular country as its model. Rather, accounting standards in China are expected to evolve in a piecemeal fashion, with the Chinese adopting a few standards as they are studied and deemed appropriate for Chinese circumstances.

In the meantime, current Chinese accounting principles present problems for Western firms. For example, under the former Chinese accounting system, companies didn't need to accrue unrealized losses. In an economy where shortages were the norm, if a state-owned company didn't sell its inventory right away, it could store it and use it later. Similarly, accounting principles assumed the state always paid its debts—eventually. Thus, Chinese enterprises don't generally provide for lower-of-cost or market inventory adjustments or the creation of allowance for bad debts, both of which are standard practices in the West. Still progress is being made. By January 2001, China's Ministry of Finance had issued 15 accounting standards for business enterprises since it began doing so in the early 1990s. The majority of these standards conform with IASC standards, although there are some adaptations to accommodate China's "unique economy and society."

Sources: L. E. Graham and A. H. Carley, "When East Meets West," *Financial Executive*, July/August 1995, pp. 40–45; K. Theonnes and A. Yeung, "Playing Favorites," *Financial Executive*, July/August 1995, pp. 46–51; and P. Practer, "Emerging Trends," *Accountancy*, May 2001, p. 1293.

Case Discussion Questions

1. What factors have shaped the accounting system currently in use in China?

2. What problems does the accounting system currently in use in China present to foreign investors in joint ventures with Chinese companies?

3. If the evolving Chinese system does not adhere to IASC standards, but instead to standards that the Chinese government deems appropriate to China's "special situation," how might this affect foreign firms with operations in China?

Notes

1. G. G. Mueller, H. Gernon, and G. Meek, *Accounting: An International Perspective* (Burr Ridge, IL: Richard D. Irwin, 1991).

2. S. J. Gary, "Towards a Theory of Cultural Influence on the Development of Accounting Systems Internationally," *Abacus* 3 (1988), pp. 1–15; and R. S. Wallace, O. Gernon, and H. Gernon, "Frameworks for International Comparative Financial Accounting," *Journal of Accounting Literature* 10 (1991), pp. 209–64.

3. K. M. Dunne and G. A. Ndubizu, "International Acquisition Accounting Method and Corporate Multinationalism," *Journal of International Business Studies* 26 (1995), pp. 361–77.

4. W. A. Wallace and J. Walsh, "Apples to Apples: Profits Abroad," *Financial Executive*, May–June 1995, pp. 28–31.

5. Wallace, Gernon, and Gernon, "Frameworks for International Comparative Financial Accounting."

6. P. Walton. "Special Rules for a Special Case," *Financial Times*, September 18, 1997, p. 11.

7. Gary, "Towards a Theory of Cultural Influence on the Development of Accounting Systems Internationally," and S. B. Salter and F. Niswander, "Cultural Influences on the Development of Accounting Systems Internationally," *Journal of International Business Studies* 26 (1995), pp. 379–97.

8. G. Hofstede, *Culture's Consequences: International Differences in Work Related Values* (Beverly Hills, CA: Sage Publications, 1980).

9. Salter and Niswander, "Cultural Influences on the Development of Accounting Systems Internationally."

10. Ibid.

11. Mueller, Gernon, and Meek, *Accounting: An International Perspective*.

12. D. Tweedie, "Globalization, Here We Come," *Financial Times*, February 1, 2001, p. 2, and "Bean Counters, Unite!" *The Economist*, June 10, 1995, pp. 67–68.

13. P. D. Fleming, "The Growing Importance of International Accounting Standards," *Journal of Accountancy*, September 1991, pp. 100–06.

14. M. Peel, "Turbulence Forecast Worldwide," *Financial Times*, March 22, 2001, p. 2.

15. L. Berton, "All Accountants May Soon Speak the Same Language," *Wall Street Journal*, August 29, 1995, p. A15.

16. F. Choi and I. Czechowicz, "Assessing Foreign Subsidiary Performance: A Multinational Comparison," *Management International Review* 4 (1983), pp. 14–25.

17. D. Lessard and P. Lorange, "Currency Changes and Management Control: Resolving the Centralization/Decentralization Dilemma," *Accounting Review*, July 1977, pp. 628–37.

18. Mueller, Gernon, and Meek, *Accounting: An International Perspective*.

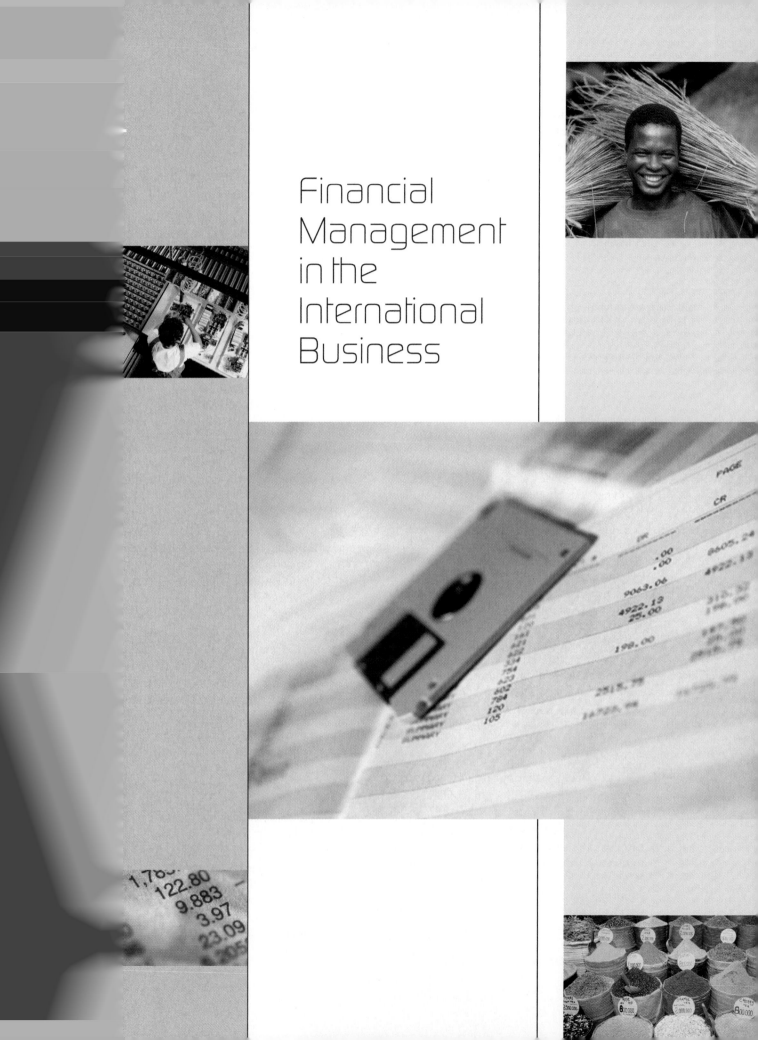

Financial
Management
in the
International
Business

Global Treasury Management at Procter & Gamble

With more than 300 brands of paper, detergent, food, health, and cosmetics products sold in over 140 countries and over 60 percent of its almost $40 billion in revenues generated outside the United States, Procter & Gamble is the quintessential example of a global consumer products firm. Despite this global spread, P&G's treasury operations—which embrace investment, financing, money management, and foreign exchange decisions—were decentralized until the early 1990s. Essentially, each major international subsidiary managed its own investments, borrowings, and foreign exchange trades, subject only to outside borrowing limits imposed by the international treasury group at P&G's headquarters in Cincinnati.

Today P&G operates with a much more centralized system in which a global treasury management function at corporate headquarters exercises close oversight over the operations of different regional treasury centers around the world. This move was a response in part to the rise in the volume of P&G's international transactions and the resulting increase in foreign exchange exposures. Like many global firms, P&G has been trying to rationalize its global production system to realize cost economies by concentrating the production of certain products at specific locations, as opposed to producing those products in every major country in which it does business. As it has moved in this direction, the number and volume of raw materials and finished products that are being shipped across borders has been growing by leaps and bounds. This has led to a commensurate increase in the size of P&G's foreign exchange exposure, which at any one time now runs into billions of dollars. Also, more than one-third of P&G's foreign exchange exposure is now in nondollar

currencies, such as transactions that involve the exchange of euros into won or pounds into yen.

P&G believes that centralizing the overall management of the resulting foreign exchange transactions can help the company realize a number of important gains. First, because its international subsidiaries often accumulate cash balances in the currency of the country where they are based, P&G now trades currencies between its subsidiaries. By cutting banks out of the process, P&G saves on transaction costs. Second, many P&G subsidiaries purchased currencies in relatively small lots of say $100,000. By grouping these lots into larger purchases, P&G can generally get a better price from foreign trade dealers. Third, P&G is pooling foreign exchange risks and purchasing an "umbrella option" to cover the risks associated with various currency positions, which is cheaper than purchasing options to cover each position.

In addition to managing foreign exchange transactions, P&G's global treasury operation arranges for subsidiaries to invest their surplus funds in and to borrow money from other Procter & Gamble entities, instead of from local banks. Subsidiaries that have excess cash lend it to those that need cash, and the global treasury operation acts as a financial intermediary. P&G has cut the number of local banks that it does business with from 450 to about 200. Using intracompany loans lowers the overall borrowing costs, which may result in annual savings on interest payments that run into tens if not hundreds of millions of dollars.

Sources: R. C. Stewart, "Balancing on the Global High Wire," *Financial Executive,* September/October 1995, pp. 35–39; S. Lipin, F. R. Bleakley, and B. D. Granito, "Portfolio Poker," *Wall Street Journal,* April 14, 1994, p. A1; and Procter & Gamble 10K report for 2000.

▌ Introduction

As the opening case makes clear, this chapter focuses on financial management in the international business. Included within the scope of financial management are three sets of related decisions:

- *Investment decisions*—decisions about what activities to finance.
- *Financing decisions*—decisions about how to finance those activities.
- *Money management decisions*—decisions about how to manage the firm's financial resources most efficiently.

The opening case describes Procter & Gamble's approach toward these decisions. By managing investing, financing, and money management decisions centrally through its global treasury function, P&G has realized considerable cost economies. These economies help P&G compete more effectively in the global marketplace.

In an international business, investment, financing, and money management decisions are complicated by differences in currencies, tax regimes, regulations concerning the flow of capital across their borders, norms regarding the financing of business activities, levels of economic and political risk, and so on. Financial managers must consider all these factors when deciding which activities to finance, how best to finance those activities, how best to manage the firm's financial resources, and how best to protect the firm from political and economic risks (including foreign exchange risk).

Good financial management can be an important source of competitive advantage. This is implicit in the opening case, where good financial management helps P&G attain cost economies and lower its overall cost structure. Good financial management is also important for FMC, a Chicago-based producer of chemicals and farm equipment. FMC counts on overseas business for 40 percent of its sales, and it attributes some of its success overseas to aggressive trading in the forward foreign exchange market. By trading in currency futures, FMC can provide overseas customers with stable long-term prices for three years or more, regardless of what happens to exchange rates. According to an FMC spokesman, "Some of our competitors change their prices on a relatively short-term basis depending on what is happening with their own exchange rate . . . We want to provide longer-term pricing as a customer service—they can plan their budgets knowing what the numbers will be—and we can hopefully maintain and build our customer base."

FMC also offers its customers the option of paying in any of several currencies as a convenience to them and as an attempt to retain customers. If customers could pay only in dollars, they might give their business to a competitor that offered pricing in a variety of currencies. By adopting this policy, FMC deals with "the hassle of foreign exchange movements," the spokesman says, so its customers don't have to. By offering customers multicurrency pricing alternatives, FMC implicitly accepts the responsibility of managing foreign exchange risk for its business units that sell overseas. It has set up what amounts to an in-house bank to manage the operation, monitoring currency rates daily and managing its risks on a portfolio basis. This bank handles more than $1 billion in currency transactions annually, which means the company can often beat the currency prices quoted by commercial banks.[1]

Chapter 12 pointed out that creating a competitive advantage requires a firm to reduce its costs of value creation and/or add value by improving its customer service. P&G and FMC show how good financial management can help both reduce the costs of creating value and add value by improving customer service. By reducing the firm's cost of capital, eliminating foreign exchange losses, minimizing the firm's tax burden, reducing the firm's exposure to unnecessarily risky activities, and managing the firm's cash flows and reserves in the most efficient manner, the finance function can reduce the costs of creating value. As the example of FMC illustrates, good financial management can also enhance customer service, thus adding value.

We begin this chapter by looking at investment decisions in an international business. We will be most concerned with the issue of capital budgeting. Our objective is to identify the factors that can complicate capital budgeting decisions in an international business, as opposed to a purely domestic business. Most important, we will discuss how such factors as political and economic risk complicate capital budgeting decisions.

Then we look at financing decisions in an international business, focusing on the financial structure of foreign affiliates—the mix of equity and debt financing. Financial structure norms for firms vary widely from country to country. We will discuss the advantages and disadvantages of localizing the financial structure of a foreign affiliate to make it consistent with the norms of the country in which it is based.

Next we examine money management decisions in an international business. We will look at the objectives of global money management, the various ways businesses can move money across borders, and some techniques for managing the firm's financial resources efficiently.

The chapter closes with a section on managing foreign exchange risk. Foreign exchange risk was discussed in Chapter 9, but there our focus was on how the foreign exchange market works and the forces that determine exchange rate movements. In this chapter, we focus on the various tactics and strategies international businesses use to manage their foreign exchange risk.

Investment Decisions

Many economic, political, cultural, and strategic variables influence a decision to invest in a given country. We have been discussing this issue throughout much of this book. We touched on it in Chapters 2 and 3 when we discussed how the political, economic, legal, and cultural environment of a country can influence the benefits, costs, and risks of doing business there and thus its attractiveness as an investment site. We returned to the issue in Chapter 6 with a discussion of the economic theory of foreign direct investment. We identified a number of factors that determine the economic attractiveness of a foreign investment opportunity. In Chapter 7, we looked at the political economy of foreign direct investment and we considered the role that government intervention can play in foreign investment. In Chapter 12, we pulled much of this material together when we considered how a firm can reduce its costs of value creation and/or increase its value added by investing in productive activities in other countries. We returned to the issue again in Chapter 14 when we considered the various modes for entering foreign markets.

One role of the financial manager in an international business is to try to quantify the various benefits, costs, and risks that are likely to flow from an investment in a given location. This is done by using capital budgeting techniques.

Capital Budgeting

Capital budgeting quantifies the benefits, costs, and risks of an investment. This enables top managers to compare investment alternatives within and across countries so they can make informed choices about where the firm should invest its scarce financial resources. Capital budgeting for a foreign project uses the same theoretical framework that domestic capital budgeting uses; that is, the firm must first estimate the cash flows associated with the project over time. In most cases, the cash flows will be negative at first, because the firm will be investing heavily in production facilities. After some initial period, however, the cash flows will become positive as investment costs decline and revenues grow. Once the cash flows have been estimated, they must be discounted to determine their net present value using an appropriate discount rate. The most commonly used discount rate is either the firm's cost of capital or some other required rate of return. If the net present value of the discounted cash flows is greater than zero, the firm should go ahead with the project.[2]

Although this might sound straightforward, capital budgeting is in practice a complex and imperfect process. Among the factors complicating the process for an international business are these:

1. A distinction must be made between cash flows to the project and cash flows to the parent company.
2. Political and economic risks, including foreign exchange risk, can significantly change the value of a foreign investment.
3. The connection between cash flows to the parent and the source of financing must be recognized.

We look at the first two of these issues in this section. Discussion of the connection between cash flows and the source of financing is postponed until the next section, where we discuss the source of financing.

Project and Parent Cash Flows

A theoretical argument exists for analyzing any foreign project from the perspective of the parent company because cash flows to the project are not necessarily the same thing as cash flows to the parent company. The project may not be able to remit all its cash flows to the parent for a number of reasons. For example, cash flows may be blocked from repatriation by the host-country government, they may be taxed at an unfavorable rate, or the host government may require a certain percentage of the cash flows generated from the project to be reinvested within the host nation. While these restrictions don't affect the net present value of the project, they do affect the net present value of the project to the parent company.

When evaluating a foreign investment opportunity, the parent should be interested in the cash flows it will receive—as opposed to those the project generates—because those are the basis for dividends to stockholders, investments elsewhere in the world, repayment of worldwide corporate debt, and so on. Stockholders will not perceive blocked earnings as contributing to the value of the firm, and creditors will not count them when calculating the parent's ability to service its debt.

But the problem of blocked earnings is not as serious as it once was. The worldwide move toward greater acceptance of free market economics (discussed in Chapter 2) has reduced the number of countries in which governments are likely to prohibit the affiliates of foreign multinationals from remitting cash flows to their parent companies. In addition, as we will see later in the chapter, firms have a number of options for circumventing host-government attempts to block the free flow of funds from an affiliate.

Adjusting for Political and Economic Risk

When analyzing a foreign investment opportunity, the company must consider the political and economic risks that stem from the foreign location. We will discuss these before looking at how capital budgeting methods can be adjusted to take risks into account.

Political Risk

We initially encountered the concept of political risk in Chapter 2. There we defined it as the likelihood that political forces will cause drastic changes in a country's business environment that hurt the profit and other goals of a business enterprise. Political risk tends to be greater in countries experiencing social unrest or disorder and countries where the underlying nature of the society makes the likelihood of social unrest high. When political risk is high, the probability is high that a change will occur in the country's political environment that will endanger foreign firms there.

In extreme cases, political change may result in the expropriation of foreign firms' assets. This occurred to U.S. firms after the Iranian revolution of 1979. Social unrest may also result in economic collapse, which can render worthless a firm's assets. This occurred to many foreign companies' assets as a result of the bloody war following the breakup of the former Yugoslavia. In less extreme cases, political changes may result in increased tax rates, the imposition of exchange controls that limit or block a subsidiary's ability to remit earnings to its parent company, the imposition of price controls, and government interference in existing contracts. The likelihood of any of these events impairs the attractiveness of a foreign investment opportunity.

Many firms devote considerable attention to political risk analysis and to quantifying political risk. For example, Union Carbide, the U.S. multinational chemical giant, has an elaborate procedure for incorporating political risk into its strategic planning and capital budgeting process.[3] *Euromoney* magazine publishes an annual "country risk rating," which incorporates assessments of political and other risks and is widely used by businesses. The problem with all attempts to forecast political risk, however, is that they try to predict a future that can only be guessed at—and in many cases, the guesses are wrong. Few people foresaw the 1979 Iranian revolution, the collapse of communism in Eastern Europe, or the dramatic breakup of the Soviet Union, yet all these events have had a profound impact on the business environments of the countries involved. While political risk assessment does have value, it is more art than science.

Economic Risk

Like political risk, we first encountered the concept of economic risk in Chapter 2. There we defined it as the likelihood that economic mismanagement will cause drastic changes in a country's business environment that hurt the profit and other goals of a business enterprise. The biggest problem arising from economic mismanagement has been inflation. Historically, many governments have expanded their domestic money supply in misguided attempts to stimulate economic activity. The result has often been too much money chasing too few goods, resulting in price inflation. As we saw in Chapter 9, price inflation is reflected in a drop in the value of a country's currency on the foreign exchange market. This can be a serious problem for a foreign firm with assets in that country because the value of the cash flows it receives from those assets will fall as the country's currency depreciates on the foreign exchange market. The likelihood of this occurring decreases the attractiveness of foreign investment in that country.

There have been many attempts to quantify countries' economic risk and long-term movements in their exchange rates. (*Euromoney's* annual country risk rating also incorporates an assessment of economic risk in its calculation of each country's overall level of risk). Chapter 9 revealed the results of extensive empirical studies of the relationship between countries' inflation rates and their currencies' exchange rates. These studies show there is a long-run relationship between a country's relative inflation rates and changes in exchange rates. However, the relationship is not as close as theory would predict; it is not reliable in the short run and is not totally reliable in the long run. So, as with political risk, any attempts to quantify economic risk must be tempered with some healthy skepticism.

❙ Risk and Capital Budgeting

In analyzing a foreign investment opportunity, the additional risk that stems from its location can be handled in at least two ways. The first method is to treat all risk as a single problem by increasing the discount rate applicable to foreign projects in countries where political and economic risks are perceived as high. Thus, for example, a firm might apply a 6 percent discount rate to potential investments in Great Britain, the United States, and Germany, reflecting those countries' economic and political stability, and it might use a 20 percent discount rate for potential investments in Russia, reflecting the political and economic turmoil in that country. The higher the discount rate, the higher the projected net cash flows must be for an investment to have a positive net present value.

Adjusting discount rates to reflect a location's riskiness seems to be fairly widely practiced. For example, a study of large U.S. multinationals found that 49 percent of them routinely added a premium percentage for risk to the discount rate they used in evaluating potential foreign investment projects.[4] However, critics of this method argue that it penalizes early cash flows too heavily and does not penalize distant cash flows enough.[5] They point out that if political or economic collapse were expected in the near future, the investment would not occur anyway. (This is borne out today in the case of Russia; Western companies are not investing there because they perceive the danger of political and economic collapse.) So for any investment decisions, the political and economic risk being assessed is not of immediate possibilities, but rather at some distance in the future. Accordingly, it can be argued that rather than using a higher discount rate to evaluate such risky projects, which penalizes early cash flows too heavily, it is better to revise future cash flows from the project downward to reflect the possibility of adverse political or economic changes sometime in the future. Surveys of actual practice within multinationals suggest that the practice of revising future cash flows downward is almost as popular as that of revising the discount rate upward.[6]

Financing Decisions

When considering its options for financing a foreign investment, an international business must consider two factors. The first is how the foreign investment will be financed. If external financing is required, the firm must decide whether to borrow from sources in the host country or elsewhere. The second factor is how the financial structure of the foreign affiliate should be configured.

Source of Financing

If the firm is going to seek external financing for a project, it will want to borrow funds from the lowest-cost source of capital available. As we saw in Chapter 11, firms increasingly are turning to the global capital market to finance their investments. The cost of capital is typically lower in the global capital market, by virtue of its size and liquidity, than in many domestic capital markets, particularly those that are small and relatively illiquid. Thus, for example, a U.S. firm making an investment in Denmark may finance the investment by borrowing through the London-based eurobond market rather than the Danish capital market.

However, host-country government restrictions may rule out this option. The governments of some countries require, or at least prefer, foreign multinationals to finance projects in their country by local debt financing or local sales of equity. In countries where liquidity is limited, this raises the cost of capital used to finance a project. Thus, in capital budgeting decisions, the discount rate must be adjusted upward to reflect this. However, this is not the only possibility. In Chapter 7, we saw that some governments court foreign investment by offering foreign firms low-interest loans, lowering the cost of capital. Accordingly, in capital budgeting decisions, the discount rate should be revised downward in such cases.

In addition to the impact of host-government policies on the cost of capital and financing decisions, the firm may wish to consider local debt financing for investments in countries where the local currency is expected to depreciate on the foreign exchange market. The amount of local currency required to meet interest payments and retire principal on local debt obligations is not affected when a country's currency depreciates. However, if foreign debt obligations must be served, the amount of local currency required to do this will increase as the currency depreciates, and this effectively raises the cost of capital. (We looked at this issue in Chapter 11 when we considered foreign exchange risk and the cost of capital.) Thus, although the initial cost of capital may be greater with local borrowing, it may be better to borrow locally if the local currency is expected to depreciate on the foreign exchange market.

Financial Structure

Firms' financial structures vary by country. By financial structure we mean the mix of debt and equity used to finance a business. For example, Japanese firms rely far more on debt financing than do most U.S. firms. One study of firms in 23 countries found that debt to equity ratios varied from a low of 0.34 in Singapore to 0.76 in Italy. The average ratio in the United States was 0.55. It was also 0.55 in the United Kingdom, and 0.62 in Germany.[7] Another study of more than 4,000 firms in five countries found that the ratio of long-term debt to assets was 0.185 in the United States, 0.155 in Japan, 0.98 in the United Kingdom, 0.88 in Germany, and 0.145 in France, suggesting again that reliance on debt financing varies from country to country.[8]

It is not clear why the financial structure of firms should vary so much across countries. One possible explanation is that different tax regimes determine the relative attractiveness of debt and equity in a country. For example, if interest income were taxed at a high rate, a preference for debt financing over equity financing would be expected. However, research suggests country differences in financial structure do not seem related in any systematic way to country differences in tax structure.[9] Another possibility is that these country differences may reflect cultural norms.[10] This explanation may be valid, although the mechanism by which culture influences capital structure has not yet been explained.

The interesting question for the international business is whether it should conform to local capital structure norms. Should a U.S. firm investing in Italy adopt the higher debt ratio typical of Italian firms for its Italian subsidiary, or should it stick with its more conservative practice? There are few good arguments for conforming to local norms. One advantage claimed for conforming to host-country debt norms is that management can more easily evaluate its return on equity relative to local competitors in the same industry. However, this seems a weak rationale for what is an important decision. Another point often made is that conforming to higher host-country debt norms can improve the image of foreign affiliates that have been operating with too little debt and thus appear insensitive to local monetary policy. Just how important this point is, however, has not been established. The best recommendation is that an international business should adopt a financial structure for each foreign affiliate that minimizes its cost of capital, irrespective of whether that structure is consistent with local practice.

Global Money Management: The Efficiency Objective

Money management decisions attempt to manage the firm's global cash resources—its working capital—most efficiently. This involves minimizing cash balances and reducing transaction costs.

Minimizing Cash Balances

For any given period, a firm must hold certain cash balances. This is necessary for serving any accounts and notes payable during that period and as a contingency against unexpected demands on cash. The firm does not sit on its cash reserves. It typically invests them in money market accounts so it can earn interest on them. However, it must be able to withdraw its money from those accounts freely. Such accounts typically offer a relatively low rate of interest. In contrast, the firm could earn a higher rate of interest if it could invest its cash resources in longer-term financial instruments (e.g., six-month certificates of deposit). The problem with longer-term instruments, however, is that the firm cannot withdraw its money before the instruments mature without suffering a financial penalty.

Thus, the firm faces a dilemma. If it invests its cash balances in money market accounts (or the equivalent), it will have unlimited liquidity but earn a relatively low rate of interest. If it invests its cash in longer-term financial instruments (certificates of deposit, bonds, etc.), it will earn a higher rate of interest, but liquidity will be limited. In an ideal world, the firm would have minimal liquid cash balances. We will see later in the chapter that by managing its total global cash reserves through a centralized depository (as opposed to letting each affiliate manage its own cash reserves), an international business can reduce the amount of funds it must hold in liquid accounts and thereby increase its rate of return on its cash reserves.

Reducing Transaction Costs

Transaction costs are the cost of exchange. Every time a firm changes cash from one currency into another currency, it must pay a commission to foreign exchange dealers for performing the transaction. Most banks also charge a **transfer fee** for moving cash from one location to another; this is another transaction cost. The commission and transfer fees arising from intrafirm transactions can be substantial; according to the United Nations, 40 percent of international trade involves transactions between the different national subsidiaries of transnational corporations. As we will see later in the chapter, multilateral netting can reduce the number of transactions between the firm's subsidiaries, thereby reducing the total transaction costs arising from foreign exchange dealings and transfer fees.

Global Money Management: The Tax Objective

Different countries have different tax regimes. Table 20.1 illustrates top corporate income tax rates in 2001 for countries included in a survey undertaken by KPMG, an international accounting firm.[11] As can be seen, the top rates for corporate income tax varied from a high of 42.1 percent in Canada to a low of 15 percent in Chile. However, the picture is much more complex than the one presented in Table 20.1. For example, in Germany and Japan, the tax rate is lower on income distributed to stockholders as dividends (36 and 35 percent, respectively), whereas in France the tax on profits distributed to stockholders is higher (42 percent). In the United States, the rate varies from state to state. The federal top rate is 35 percent, but states also tax corporate income, with state and local taxes ranging from 1 percent to 12 percent, hence the average effective rate of 40 percent.

Many nations follow the worldwide principle that they have the right to tax income earned outside their boundaries by entities based in their country.[12] Thus, the U.S. government can tax the earnings of the German subsidiary of an enterprise incorporated in the United States. Double taxation occurs when the income of a foreign subsidiary is taxed both by the host-country government and by the parent company's home government. However, double taxation is mitigated to some extent by tax credits, tax treaties, and the deferral principle.

A **tax credit** allows an entity to reduce the taxes paid to the home government by the amount of taxes paid to the foreign government. A **tax treaty** between two countries is an agreement specifying what items of income will be taxed by the authorities of the country where the income is earned. For example, a tax treaty between the United States and Germany may specify that a U.S. firm need not pay tax in Germany on any earnings from its German subsidiary that are remitted to the United States in the form of dividends. A **deferral principle** specifies that parent companies are not taxed on foreign source income until they actually receive a dividend.

For the international business with activities in many countries, the various tax regimes and the tax treaties have important implications for how the firm should struc-

Country	Top Corporate Income Tax Rate
Canada	42.1%
Chile	15%
France	35.33%
Germany	39.36%
Hong Kong	16%
Ireland	20%
Japan	42%
Mexico	35%
Singapore	25.5%
United Kingdom	30%
United States	40%

Table 20.1

Corporate Income Tax
Rates, 2001

Source: KPMG Corporate Tax
Survey, January 2001.
www.kpmg.com

ture its internal payments system among the foreign subsidiaries and the parent company. As we will see in the next section, the firm can use transfer prices and fronting loans to minimize its global tax liability. In addition, the form in which income is remitted from a foreign subsidiary to the parent company (e.g., royalty payments versus dividend payments) can be structured to minimize the firm's global tax liability.

Some firms use **tax havens** such as the Bahamas and Bermuda to minimize their tax liability. A tax haven is a country with an exceptionally low, or even no, income tax. International businesses avoid or defer income taxes by establishing a wholly owned, nonoperating subsidiary in the tax haven. The tax haven subsidiary owns the common stock of the operating foreign subsidiaries. This allows all transfers of funds from foreign operating subsidiaries to the parent company to be funneled through the tax haven subsidiary. The tax levied on foreign source income by a firm's home government, which might normally be paid when a dividend is declared by a foreign subsidiary, can be deferred under the deferral principle until the tax haven subsidiary pays the dividend to the parent. This dividend payment can be postponed indefinitely if foreign operations continue to grow and require new internal financing from the tax haven affiliate. For U.S.-based enterprises, however, U.S. regulations tax U.S. shareholders on the firm's overseas income when it is earned, regardless of when the parent company in the United States receives it. This regulation eliminates U.S.-based firms' ability to use tax haven subsidiaries to avoid tax liabilities in the manner just described.

Moving Money across Borders: ■
Attaining Efficiencies and Reducing Taxes

Pursuing the objectives of utilizing the firm's cash resources most efficiently and minimizing the firm's global tax liability requires the firm to be able to transfer funds from one location to another around the globe. International businesses use a number of techniques to transfer liquid funds across borders. These include dividend remittances, royalty payments and fees, transfer prices, and fronting loans. Some firms rely on more than one of these techniques to transfer funds across borders—a practice known as unbundling. By using a mix of techniques to transfer liquid funds from a foreign subsidiary to the parent company, unbundling allows an international business to recover funds from its foreign subsidiaries without piquing host-country sensitivities with large "dividend drains."

A firm's ability to select a particular policy is severely limited when a foreign subsidiary is part-owned either by a local joint-venture partner or by local stockholders. Serving the legitimate demands of the local co-owners of a foreign subsidiary may limit the firm's ability to impose the kind of dividend policy, royalty payment schedule, or transfer pricing policy that would be optimal for the parent company.

Dividend Remittances

Payment of dividends is probably the most common method by which firms transfer funds from foreign subsidiaries to the parent company. The dividend policy typically varies with each subsidiary depending on such factors as tax regulations, foreign exchange risk, the age of the subsidiary, and the extent of local equity participation. For example, the higher the rate of tax levied on dividends by the host-country government, the less attractive this option becomes relative to other options for transferring liquid funds. With regard to foreign exchange risk, firms sometimes require foreign subsidiaries based in "high-risk" countries to speed up the transfer of funds to the parent through accelerated dividend payments. This moves corporate funds out of a country whose currency is expected to depreciate significantly. The age of a foreign subsidiary influences dividend policy in that older subsidiaries tend to remit a higher proportion of their earnings in dividends to the parent, presumably because a subsidiary has fewer capital investment needs as it matures. Local equity participation is a factor because local co-owners' demands for dividends must be recognized.

Royalty Payments and Fees

Royalties represent the remuneration paid to the owners of technology, patents, or trade names for the use of that technology or the right to manufacture and/or sell products under those patents or trade names. It is common for a parent company to charge its foreign subsidiaries royalties for the technology, patents, or trade names it has transferred to them. Royalties may be levied as a fixed monetary amount per unit of the product the subsidiary sells or as a percentage of a subsidiary's gross revenues.

A fee is compensation for professional services or expertise supplied to a foreign subsidiary by the parent company or another subsidiary. Fees are sometimes differentiated into "management fees" for general expertise and advice and "technical assistance fees" for guidance in technical matters. Fees are usually levied as fixed charges for the particular services provided.

Royalties and fees have certain tax advantages over dividends, particularly when the corporate tax rate is higher in the host country than in the parent's home country. Royalties and fees are often tax-deductible locally (because they are viewed as an expense), so arranging for payment in royalties and fees will reduce the foreign subsidiary's tax liability. If the foreign subsidiary compensates the parent company by dividend payments, local income taxes must be paid before the dividend distribution, and withholding taxes must be paid on the dividend itself. Although the parent can often take a tax credit for the local withholding and income taxes it has paid, part of the benefit can be lost if the subsidiary's combined tax rate is higher than the parent's.

Transfer Prices

Most international businesses involve many transfers of goods and services between the parent company and foreign subsidiaries and between foreign subsidiaries. This is particularly likely in firms pursuing global and transnational strategies because these firms are likely to have dispersed their value creation activities to various "optimal" locations around the globe (see Chapter 12). As noted in Chapter 19, the price at which goods and services are transferred between entities within the firm is referred to as the **transfer price.**[13]

Transfer prices can be used to position funds within an international business. For example, funds can be moved out of a particular country by setting high transfer prices for goods and services supplied to a subsidiary in that country and by setting low transfer prices for the goods and services sourced from that subsidiary. Conversely, funds can be positioned in a country by the opposite policy: setting low transfer prices for goods and services supplied to a subsidiary in that country and setting high transfer prices for the goods and services sourced from that subsidiary. This movement of funds can be between the firm's subsidiaries or between the parent company and a subsidiary.

Benefits of Manipulating Transfer Prices

At least four gains can be derived by manipulating transfer prices.

1. The firm can reduce its tax liabilities by using transfer prices to shift earnings from a high-tax country to a low-tax one.

2. The firm can use transfer prices to move funds out of a country where a significant currency devaluation is expected, thereby reducing its exposure to foreign exchange risk.

3. The firm can use transfer prices to move funds from a subsidiary to the parent company (or a tax haven) when financial transfers in the form of dividends are restricted or blocked by host-country government policies.

4. The firm can use transfer prices to reduce the import duties it must pay when an ad valorem tariff is in force—a tariff assessed as a percentage of value. In this case, low transfer prices on goods or services being imported into the country are required. Since this lowers the value of the goods or services, it lowers the tariff.

Problems with Transfer Pricing

Pursuing a transfer pricing policy can create significant problems. Few governments like it.[14] When transfer prices are used to reduce a firm's tax liabilities or import duties, most governments feel they are being cheated of their legitimate income. Similarly, when transfer prices are manipulated to circumvent government restrictions on capital flows (e.g., dividend remittances), governments perceive this as breaking the spirit—if not the letter—of the law. Many governments now limit international businesses' ability to manipulate transfer prices in the manner described. The United States has strict regulations governing transfer pricing practices. According to Section 482 of the Internal Revenue Code, the Internal Revenue Service (IRS) can reallocate gross income, deductions, credits, or allowances between related corporations to prevent tax evasion or to reflect more clearly a proper allocation of income. Under the IRS guidelines and subsequent judicial interpretation, the burden of proof is on the taxpayer to show that the IRS has been arbitrary or unreasonable in reallocating income. The correct transfer price, according to the IRS guidelines, is an arm's-length price—the price that would prevail between unrelated firms in a market setting. Such a strict interpretation of what is a correct transfer price theoretically limits a firm's ability to manipulate transfer prices to achieve the benefits we have discussed. Many other countries have followed the U.S. lead in emphasizing that transfer prices should be set on an arm's-length basis. Despite this, transfer pricing is still practiced, as indicated in the accompanying Management Focus, which looks at transfer pricing practices.

Another problem associated with transfer pricing is related to management incentives and performance evaluation.[15] Transfer pricing is inconsistent with a policy of treating each subsidiary in the firm as a profit center. When transfer prices are manipulated by the firm and deviate significantly from the arm's-length price, the subsidiary's performance may depend as much on transfer prices as it does on other pertinent factors, such as management effort. A subsidiary told to charge a high transfer price for a good supplied to another subsidiary will appear to be doing better than it actually is, while the subsidiary purchasing the good will appear to be doing worse. Unless this is recognized when performance is being evaluated, serious distortions in management incentive systems can occur. For example, managers in the selling subsidiary may be able to use high transfer prices to mask inefficiencies, while managers in the purchasing subsidiary may become disheartened by the effect of high transfer prices on their subsidiary's profitability.

Despite these problems, research suggests that many international businesses do not use arm's-length pricing but instead use some cost-based system for pricing transfers among their subunits (typically cost plus some standard markup). A survey of 164 U.S. multinational firms found that 35 percent of the firms used market-based prices, 15 percent used negotiated prices, and 65 percent used a cost-based pricing method. (The figures total more than 100 percent because some companies use more than one method.)[16] Only market and negotiated prices could reasonably be interpreted as arm's-length prices. The opportunity for price manipulation is much greater with cost-based transfer pricing. Other, more sophisticated research has uncovered indirect evidence that many corporations do manipulate transfer prices to reduce global tax liabilities.[17]

Although a firm may be able to manipulate transfer prices to avoid tax liabilities or circumvent government restrictions on capital flows across borders, this does not mean the firm should do so. The ethics of engaging in transfer pricing are dubious at best. Also, tax authorities in many countries are increasing their scrutiny of this practice to stamp out abuses. A 2000 survey of some 600 multinationals undertaken by accountants Ernst & Young found that 75 percent of them believed they would be the subject of a transfer pricing audit by tax authorities in the next two years.[18] Some 61 percent of the multinationals in the survey stated that transfer pricing was the number one tax issue they faced.

Fronting Loans

A fronting loan is a loan between a parent and its subsidiary channeled through a financial intermediary, usually a large international bank. In a direct intrafirm loan, the parent company lends cash directly to the foreign subsidiary, and the subsidiary repays it later. In a fronting loan, the parent company deposits funds in an international bank, and the bank then lends the same amount to the foreign subsidiary. Thus, a U.S. firm might deposit $100,000 in a London bank. The London bank might then lend that $100,000 to an Indian subsidiary of the firm. From the bank's point of view, the loan is risk free because it has 100 percent collateral in the form of the parent's deposit. The bank "fronts" for the parent, hence the name. The bank makes a profit by paying the parent company a slightly lower interest rate on its deposit than it charges the foreign subsidiary on the borrowed funds.

Firms use fronting loans for two reasons. First, fronting loans can circumvent host-country restrictions on the remittance of funds from a foreign subsidiary to the parent company. A host government might restrict a foreign subsidiary from repaying a loan to its parent in order to preserve the country's foreign exchange reserves, but it is less likely to restrict a subsidiary's ability to repay a loan to a large international bank. To stop payment to an international bank would hurt the country's credit image, whereas halting payment to the parent company would probably have a minimal impact on its image. Consequently, international businesses sometimes use fronting loans when they want to lend funds to a subsidiary based in a country with a fairly high probability of political turmoil that might lead to restrictions on capital flows (i.e., where the level of political risk is high).

A fronting loan can also provide tax advantages. For example, a tax haven (Bermuda) subsidiary that is 100 percent owned by the parent company deposits $1 million in a London-based international bank at 8 percent interest. The bank lends the $1 million to a foreign operating subsidiary at 9 percent interest. The country where the foreign operating subsidiary is based taxes corporate income at 50 percent (see Figure 20.1).

Transfer Pricing Wars

According to testimony given at hearings held by the U.S. House Ways and Means Oversight subcommittee in July 1990, foreign-based multinationals, through elaborate transfer pricing schemes, underpaid the U.S. government by as much as $35 billion during the 1980s. Japanese companies were cited as the principal offenders, followed by German, Canadian, and British companies. Toyota, Toshiba, Sony, Mitsubishi, Fuji Bank, and Siemens AG were among the foreign multinationals cited for abusing the U.S. tax code. Yamaha, the Japanese motorcycle manufacturer, for example, paid just $123 in U.S. taxes one year, and the IRS claimed it should have paid more than $27 million.

One scheme foreign-based multinationals were using to pay little or no taxes was charging U.S. subsidiaries for inflated or nonexisting freight, insurance, interest, and other expenses. In one example, a Japanese multinational was accused of double-billing its U.S. subsidiary for insurance on motorcycle inventory. In another case, U.S. officials testified that a foreign automaker charged its U.S. subsidiary $15 interest per vehicle even though interest payments were not required under the distribution agreement. Foreign multinationals argued that they have done nothing wrong.

As multinationals' use of transfer pricing has come under increasing scrutiny in the United States, other countries seem likely to scrutinize U.S. multinationals more closely in response. Japan started to hit back after 1992 at U.S. multinationals doing business in that country, accusing several of manipulating transfer prices to avoid tax liabilities. Japan's high corporate tax rates make it a tempting target for firms trying to minimize their tax liability through transfer pricing. On average, firms pay about 50 percent of their yearly earnings to the government in Japan, compared to 41 percent in the United States and 33 percent in Great Britain. In the financial year ending June 1996, Japan's National Tax Administration filed claims against 50 foreign firms for alleged transfer pricing, demanding back taxes totaling ¥54.8 billion ($492 million). The agency filed only 80 transfer pricing claims during the previous eight years, totaling ¥140 billion.

Firms accused of manipulating transfer prices to reduce their tax liability in Japan often face a large bill. In 1994, Coca-Cola's Japanese unit announced it would contest a claim for back taxes amounting to some $140 million. The Japanese unit of Goodyear Tire & Rubber Co. was hit for roughly ¥600 million, and Japanese tax officials claimed ¥800 million from Procter & Gamble. In each case, the firms involved indicated they would contest the claims of the tax authorities in Japan. Nor are firms from other countries immune to scrutiny. In 1999, Swiss pharmaceutical manufacturer Novartis was fined $28 million for underreporting its income in Japan due to the manipulation of transfer prices.

Other countries have also begun to look hard at transfer pricing practices and, in some cases, take legal action. In another case, international pharmaceutical giant SmithKline Beecham was hauled into a tax court in Canada in 1995 and fined $66 million for manipulating transfer prices to reduce the tax liability of its Canadian subsidiary. The Canadian government felt that the subsidiary paid too much for an ingredient from another subsidiary based in a low tax country, thereby moving taxable profits from Canada to that country.

Sources: E. Neumann, "Washington Escalates the Transfer Pricing War," *Business International Money Report*, July 23, 1990, p. 277–79; R. Steiner, "Japan's Tax Man Leans on Foreign Firms," *Wall Street Journal*, November 25, 1996, p. A15; D. Hamilton, "A Heavy Price to Pay," *CA Magazine*. 2000, pp. 14–15; and "Drug Companies Swallow Japan's Bitter Pill," *International Tax Review*, April 1999, p. 5.

Under this arrangement, interest payments net of income tax will be as follows:

1. The foreign operating subsidiary pays $90,000 interest to the London bank. Deducting these interest payments from its taxable income results in a net after-tax cost of $45,000 to the foreign operating subsidiary.
2. The London bank receives the $90,000. It retains $10,000 for its services and pays $80,000 interest on the deposit to the Bermuda subsidiary.
3. The Bermuda subsidiary receives $80,000 interest on its deposit tax free.

The net result is that $80,000 in cash has been moved from the foreign operating subsidiary to the tax haven subsidiary. Because the foreign operating subsidiary's after-tax

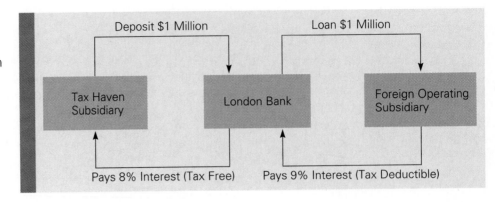

Figure 20.1

An Example of the Tax Aspects of a Fronting Loan

cost of borrowing is only $45,000, the parent company has moved an additional $35,000 out of the country by using this arrangement. If the tax haven subsidiary had made a direct loan to the foreign operating subsidiary, the host government may have disallowed the interest charge as a tax-deductible expense by ruling that it was a dividend to the parent disguised as an interest payment.

Techniques for Global Money Management

We now look at two money management techniques firms use in attempting to manage their global cash resources in the most efficient manner: centralized depositories and multilateral netting.

Centralized Depositories

Every business needs to hold some cash balances for servicing accounts that must be paid and for insuring against unanticipated negative variation from its projected cash flows. The critical issue for an international business is whether each foreign subsidiary should hold its own cash balances or whether cash balances should be held at a centralized depository. In general, firms prefer to hold cash balances at a centralized depository for three reasons.

First, by pooling cash reserves centrally, the firm can deposit larger amounts. Cash balances are typically deposited in liquid accounts, such as overnight money market accounts. Because interest rates on such deposits normally increase with the size of the deposit, by pooling cash centrally, the firm should be able to earn a higher interest rate than it would if each subsidiary managed its own cash balances.

Second, if the centralized depository is located in a major financial center (e.g., London, New York, or Tokyo), it should have access to information about good short-term investment opportunities that the typical foreign subsidiary would lack. Also, the financial experts at a centralized depository should be able to develop investment skills and know-how that managers in the typical foreign subsidiary would lack. Thus, the firm should make better investment decisions if it pools its cash reserves at a centralized depository.

Third, by pooling its cash reserves, the firm can reduce the total size of the cash pool it must hold in highly liquid accounts, which enables the firm to invest a larger amount of cash reserves in longer-term, less liquid financial instruments that earn a higher interest rate. For example, a U.S. firm has three foreign subsidiaries—one in South Korea, one in China, and one in Japan. Each subsidiary maintains a cash balance that includes an amount for dealing with its day-to-day needs plus a precautionary amount for dealing with unanticipated cash demands. The firm's policy is that the total required cash balance is equal to three standard deviations of the expected day-to-day needs amount. The three-standard-deviation requirement reflects the firm's estimate that, in practice, there is a 99.87 percent probability that the subsidiary will have sufficient cash to deal with both day-to-day and unanticipated cash demands. Cash needs are assumed to be normally distributed in each country and independent of each other (e.g., cash needs in Japan do not affect cash needs in China).

The individual subsidiaries' day-to-day cash needs and the precautionary cash balances they should hold are as follows (in millions of dollars):

	Day-to-Day Cash Needs (A)	One Standard Deviation (B)	Required Cash Balance (A + 3 × B)
Korea	$10	$1	$13
China	6	2	12
Japan	12	3	21
Total	$28	$6	$46

Thus, the South Korean subsidiary estimates that it must hold $10 million to serve its day-to-day needs. The standard deviation of this is $1 million, so it is to hold an additional $3 million as a precautionary amount. This gives a total required cash balance of $13 million. The total of the required cash balances for all three subsidiaries is $46 million.

Now consider what might occur if the firm decided to maintain all three cash balances at a centralized depository in Tokyo. Because variances are additive when probability distributions are independent of each other, the standard deviation of the combined precautionary account would be:

$$\text{Square root of } (\$1,000,000^2 + 2,000,000^2 + 3,000,000^2)$$
$$= \text{Square root of } 14,000,000$$
$$= \$3,741,657$$

Therefore, if the firm used a centralized depository, it would need to hold $28 million for day-to-day needs plus 3 × $3,741,657 as a precautionary amount, or a total cash balance of $39,224,971. In other words, the firm's total required cash balance would be reduced from $46 million to $39,224,971, a saving of $6,775,029. This is cash that could be invested in less liquid, higher-interest accounts or in tangible assets. The saving arises simply due to the statistical effects of summing the three independent, normal probability distributions.

However, a firm's ability to establish a centralized depository that can serve short-term cash needs might be limited by government-imposed restrictions on capital flows across borders (e.g., controls put in place to protect a country's foreign exchange reserves). Also, the transaction costs of moving money into and out of different currencies can limit the advantages of such a system. Despite this, many firms hold at least their subsidiaries' precautionary cash reserves at a centralized depository, having each subsidiary hold its own day-to-day-needs cash balance. The globalization of the world capital market and the general removal of barriers to the free flow of cash across borders (particularly among advanced industrialized countries) are two trends likely to increase the use of centralized depositories.

Multilateral Netting

Multilateral netting allows a multinational firm to reduce the transaction costs that arise when many transactions occur between its subsidiaries. These transaction costs are the commissions paid to foreign exchange dealers for foreign exchange transactions and the fees charged by banks for transferring cash between locations. The volume of

Figure 20.2A

Cash Flows before
Multilateral Netting

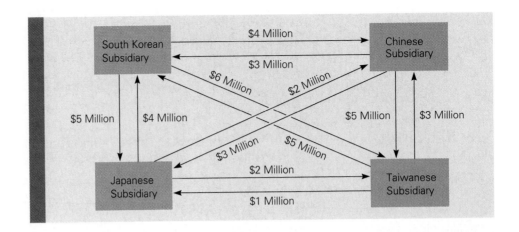

	Paying Subsidiary					
Receiving Subsidiary	South Korea	China	Japan	Taiwan	Total Receipts	Net Receipts* (payments)
South Korea	—	$3	$4	$5	$12	($3)
China	$ 4	—	2	3	9	(2)
Japan	5	3	—	1	9	1
Taiwan	6	5	2	—	13	4
Total payments	$15	$11	$8	$9		

Figure 20.2B

Calculation of Net Receipts (all amounts in millions)

Figure 20.2C

Cash Flows after
Multilateral Netting

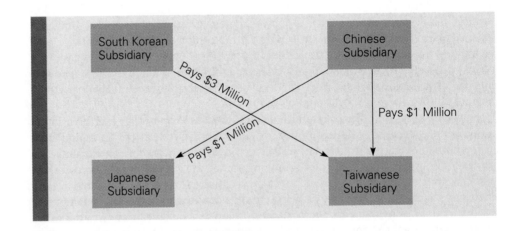

such transactions is likely to be particularly high in a firm that has a globally dispersed web of interdependent value creation activities. Netting reduces transaction costs by reducing the number of transactions.

Multilateral netting is an extension of **bilateral netting.** Under bilateral netting, if a French subsidiary owes a Mexican subsidiary $6 million and the Mexican subsidiary simultaneously owes the French subsidiary $4 million, a bilateral settlement will be made with a single payment of $2 million from the French subsidiary to the Mexican subsidiary, the remaining debt being canceled.

Under **multilateral netting,** this simple concept is extended to the transactions between multiple subsidiaries within an international business. Consider a firm that wants to establish multilateral netting among four Asian subsidiaries based in South Korea, China, Japan, and Taiwan. These subsidiaries all trade with each other, so at the end of each month a large volume of cash transactions must be settled. Figure 20.2A shows how the payment schedule might look at the end of a given month. Figure 20.2B is a payment matrix that summarizes the obligations among the subsidiaries. Note that $43 million needs to flow among the subsidiaries. If the transaction costs (foreign exchange commissions plus transfer fees) amount to 1 percent of the total funds to be transferred, this will cost the parent firm $430,000. However, this amount can be reduced by multilateral netting. Using the payment matrix (Figure 20.2B), the firm can determine the payments that need to be made among its subsidiaries to settle these obligations. Figure 20.2C shows the results. By multilateral netting, the transactions depicted in Figure 20.2A are reduced to just three; the South Korean subsidiary pays $3 million to the Taiwanese subsidiary, and the Chinese subsidiary pays $1 million to the Japanese subsidiary and $1 million to the Taiwanese subsidiary. The total funds that flow among the subsidiaries are reduced from $43 million to just $5 million, and the transaction costs are reduced from $430,000 to $50,000, a savings of $380,000 achieved through multilateral netting.

Managing Foreign Exchange Risk ▪

The nature of foreign exchange risk was discussed in Chapter 9. There we described how changes in exchange rates alter the profitability of trade and investment deals, how forward exchange rates and currency swaps enable firms to insure themselves to some degree against foreign exchange risk, and how relative inflation rates determine exchange rate movements. In this section, we focus on the various strategies international businesses use to manage their foreign exchange risk. Buying forward, the strategy most discussed in Chapter 9, is just one of these. We will examine the types of foreign exchange exposure, the tactics and strategies firms adopt in attempting to minimize their exposure to foreign exchange risk, and things firms can do to develop policies for managing foreign exchange risk.

▌Types of Foreign Exchange Exposure

When we speak of **foreign exchange exposure,** we are referring to the risk that future changes in a country's exchange rate will hurt the firm. As we saw in Chapter 9, changes in foreign exchange values often affect the profitability of international trade and investment deals. Foreign exchange exposure is normally broken into three categories: transaction exposure, translation exposure, and economic exposure. Each is explained here.

Transaction Exposure

Transaction exposure is typically defined as the extent to which the income from individual transactions is affected by fluctuations in foreign exchange values. Such exposure includes obligations for the purchase or sale of goods and services at previously agreed prices and the borrowing or lending of funds in foreign currencies. Suppose a U.S. company has just contracted to import laptop computers from Japan. When the shipment arrives in 30 days, the company must pay the Japanese supplier ¥200,000 for each computer. The dollar/yen spot exchange rate today is $1 = ¥120. At this rate, each laptop computer would cost the importer $1,667 (i.e., 200,000/120 = 1,667). The importer knows it can sell each computer for $2,000 on the day the shipment arrives, so as the exchange rate stands, the U.S. company expects to make a gross profit of $333 on every computer it sells (2,000 − 1,667). If the dollar depreciates against the yen over the next 30 days, say to $1 = ¥95, the U.S. company will still have to pay the Japanese company ¥200,000 per computer, but in dollar terms that would be $2,105 per laptop computer—more than the computers could be sold for. A depreciation in the value of the dollar against the yen from $1 = ¥120 to $1 = ¥95 would transform this profitable transaction into an unprofitable one. The transaction exposure per computer in this case is $2,105−$1667 = $438, that being the amount of money per computer that has been lost due to an adverse movement in exchange rates between the time when the deal was signed and when the computers were paid for.

Translation Exposure

Translation exposure is the impact of currency exchange rate changes on the reported consolidated results and balance sheet of a company. This issue was discussed in Chapter 19 when we looked at currency translation practices. Translation exposure is basically concerned with the present measurement of past events. The resulting accounting gains or losses are said to be unrealized—they are "paper" gains and losses—but they are still important. Consider a U.S. firm with a subsidiary in Mexico. If the value of the Mexican peso depreciates significantly against the dollar, this would substantially reduce the dollar value of the Mexican subsidiary's equity. In turn, this would reduce the total dollar value of the firm's equity reported in its consolidated balance sheet. This would raise the apparent leverage of the firm (its debt ratio), which could increase the firm's cost of borrowing and restrict its access to the capital market. Similarly, if an American firm has a subsidiary in the European Union, and if the value of the euro depreciates rapidly against that of the dollar over a year, this will reduce the dollar value of the euro profit made by the European subsidiary, resulting in negative translation exposure. Many U.S. firms suffered from significant translation exposure in Europe during 2000 because the euro did depreciate rapidly against the dollar. The experience of one such firm, Baxter International, is given in the accompanying Management Focus.

Economic Exposure

Economic exposure is the extent to which a firm's future international earning power is affected by changes in exchange rates. Economic exposure is concerned with the long-run effect of changes in exchange rates on future prices, sales, and costs. This is distinct from transaction exposure, which is concerned with the effect of exchange rate changes on individual transactions, most of which are short-term affairs that will be executed within a few weeks or months. Consider the effect of the wide swings in the value of the dollar on many U.S. firms' international competitiveness during the 1980s. The rapid rise in the value of the dollar on the foreign exchange market in the early 1980s hurt the price competitiveness of many U.S. producers in world markets. U.S. manufacturers that relied heavily on exports (such as Caterpillar) saw their export volume and world market share plunge. The reverse phenomenon has occurred since the mid-1980s, when the dollar has declined against most major currencies. The fall in the value of the dollar between 1985 and 1995 increased the price competitiveness of U.S. manufacturers in world markets and helped produce an export boom in the United States.

Tactics and Strategies for Reducing Foreign Exchange Exposure

A number of strategies and tactics can help firms reduce their foreign exchange exposure. The tactics, which include buying forward and the use of leading and lagging, are best suited to alleviating transaction exposure and translation exposure. The strategies addressing the configuration of a firm's assets across countries are best suited to reducing economic exposure.

Reducing Transaction and Translation Exposure

A number of tactics can help firms minimize their transaction and translation exposure. These tactics primarily protect short-term cash flows from adverse changes in ex-

Translation Exposure at Baxter International

On July 20, 2000, the CEO of Baxter International, a U.S. producer of medical products, announced the company's second-quarter results were better than expected due to strong global sales. The CEO confidently predicted that the company would hit its earnings and sales targets for all of 2000 and, due to continuing strong global sales, would increase revenues and earnings by a figure in the mid-teens for 2001.

Three months later when the company released its third-quarter results, the CEO had a less optimistic story to tell. Year 2000 earnings and revenues were still on track, but the company now expected much slower growth in 2001, which would reduce the projected increase in operating income by some $100 million. The main culprit, according to the CEO, was the continuing weakness of the euro against the dollar. At euro 1 = $0.83 the euro had depreciated by 10 percent since July and 30 percent since the beginning of 1999. The continued weakness meant the dollar value of Baxter's European revenues and earnings, which accounted for about 27 percent of the company's 2000 revenues, would decline significantly. Nor was Baxter alone; a host of other U.S. companies also announced that due to negative translation exposure to the euro, their financial results for late 2000 and probably much of 2001 would be lower than previously thought. According to one estimate, the decline in the value of the euro between June and September 2000 reduced the value of earnings for the Standard & Poor's index of 500 large U.S. companies by 3 percent.

In the aftermath, many wondered why companies such as Baxter hadn't hedged their European earnings against a fall in the value of the euro by entering the foreign exchange market and buying forward, locking in a more favorable dollar/euro exchange rate. The answer was that the costs of hedging had risen dramatically during 2000 due to the volatility of the euro against the dollar. The high volatility meant that foreign exchange dealers were worried about the risk associated with selling forward contracts. It was very difficult for them to predict where the exchange rate might be in a few months, so they demanded a high premium from companies in return for selling a forward contract or writing a currency option. The costs of hedging an exchange rate are related to the volatility of that exchange rate (i.e., how much the value of currencies fluctuate against each other), with a doubling in volatility often tripling the cost of hedging as foreign exchange dealers demand a higher premium for writing increasingly risky forward contracts or other derivative contracts such as currency options. The average annual volatility between two currencies over a year is about 8 to 10 percent, but the volatility of the dollar/euro exchange rate had risen to 18 to 20 percent, tripling the cost of hedging. For Baxter, that volatility meant that the costs of hedging the euro against the dollar would run into tens of millions of dollars. So in mid-2000 Baxter decided to take a risk, and not hedge, effectively betting that the euro would stabilize against the dollar. It didn't, and Baxter lost the gamble.

Source: S. McMurray, "The Lost Art of Hedging," *Institutional Investor*, December 2000, pp. 63–69. Copyright material is reprinted with permission from *Institutional Investor*, 488 Madison Avenue, New York, NY 10022.

---

change rates. We discussed two of these tactics in Chapter 9, buying forward and using currency swaps. They are important sources of insurance against the short-term effects of foreign exchange exposure. (For details, return to Chapter 9.)

In addition to buying forward and using swaps, firms can minimize their foreign exchange exposure through leading and lagging payables and receivables—that is, collecting and paying early or late depending on expected exchange rate movements. A **lead strategy** involves attempting to collect foreign currency receivables early when a foreign currency is expected to depreciate and paying foreign currency payables before they are due when a currency is expected to appreciate. A **lag strategy** involves delaying collection of foreign currency receivables if that currency is expected to appreciate and delaying payables if the currency is expected to depreciate. Leading and lagging involve accelerating payments from weak-currency to strong-currency countries and delaying inflows from strong-currency to weak-currency countries.

Lead and lag strategies can be difficult to implement, however. The firm must be in a position to exercise some control over payment terms. Firms do not always have this kind of bargaining power, particularly when they are dealing with important customers who are in a position to dictate payment terms. Also, because lead and lag strategies can put pressure on a weak currency, many governments limit leads and lags. For example, some countries set 180 days as a limit for receiving payments for exports or making payments for imports.

Several other tactics that can reduce transaction and translation exposure have already been discussed in this chapter. We have explained that:

- Transfer prices can be manipulated to move funds out of a country whose currency is expected to depreciate.
- Local debt financing can provide a hedge against foreign exchange risk.
- It may make sense to accelerate dividend payments from subsidiaries based in countries with weak currencies.
- Capital budgeting techniques can be adjusted to deflect the negative impact of adverse exchange rate movements on the current net value of a foreign investment.

Reducing Economic Exposure

Reducing economic exposure requires strategic choices that go beyond the realm of financial management. The key to reducing economic exposure is to distribute the firm's productive assets to various locations so the firm's long-term financial well-being is not severely affected by adverse changes in exchange rates. The post-1985 trend by Japanese automakers to establish productive capacity in North America and Western Europe can partly be seen as a strategy for reducing economic exposure (it is also a strategy for reducing trade tensions). Before 1985, most Japanese automobile companies concentrated their productive assets in Japan. However, the rise in the value of the yen on the foreign exchange market has transformed Japan from a low-cost to a high-cost manufacturing location. In response, Japanese auto firms have moved many of their productive assets overseas to ensure their car prices will not be unduly affected by further rises in the value of the yen. In general, reducing economic exposure necessitates that the firm ensures its assets are not too concentrated in countries where likely rises in currency values will lead to damaging increases in the foreign prices of the goods and services they produce.

Developing Policies for Managing Foreign Exchange Exposure

The firm needs to develop a mechanism for ensuring it maintains an appropriate mix of tactics and strategies for minimizing its foreign exchange exposure. Although there is no universal agreement as to the components of this mechanism, a number of common themes stand out.[19] First, central control of exposure is needed to protect resources efficiently and ensure that each subunit adopts the correct mix of tactics and strategies. Many companies have set up in-house foreign exchange centers. Although such centers may not be able to execute all foreign exchange deals—particularly in large, complex multinationals where myriad transactions may be pursued simultaneously— they should at least set guidelines for the firm's subsidiaries to follow.

Second, firms should distinguish between, on one hand, transaction and translation exposure and, on the other, economic exposure. Many companies seem to focus on reducing their transaction and translation exposure and pay scant attention to economic exposure, which may have more profound long-term implications.[20] Firms need to develop strategies for dealing with economic exposure. For example, Black & Decker, the maker of power tools, has a strategy for actively managing its economic risk. The key to Black & Decker's strategy is flexible sourcing. In response to foreign exchange movements, Black & Decker can move production from one location to another to offer the most competitive pricing. Black & Decker manufactures in more than a dozen locations around the world—in Europe, Australia, Brazil, Mexico, and Japan. More than 50 percent of the company's productive assets are based outside North America. Although each of Black & Decker's factories focuses on one or two products to achieve economies of scale, there is considerable overlap. On average, the company runs its factories at no more than 80 percent capacity, so most are able to switch rapidly from producing one product to producing another or to add a product. This allows a factory's production to be changed in response to foreign exchange movements. For example, as the dollar depreciated during the latter half of the 1980s, the amount of imports into the United States from overseas subsidiaries was reduced, and the amount of exports from U.S. subsidiaries to other locations was increased.[21]

Third, the need to forecast future exchange rate movements cannot be overstated, though, as we saw in Chapter 9, this is a tricky business. No model comes close to perfectly predicting future movements in foreign exchange rates. The best that can be said is that in the short run, forward exchange rates provide reasonable predictions of exchange rate movements, and in the long run, fundamental economic factors—particularly relative inflation rates—should be watched because they influence exchange rate movements. Some firms attempt to forecast exchange rate movements in-house; others rely on outside forecasters. However, all such forecasts are imperfect attempts to predict the future.

Fourth, firms need to establish good reporting systems so the central finance function (or in-house foreign exchange center) can regularly monitor the firm's exposure positions. Such reporting systems should enable the firm to identify any exposed accounts, the exposed position by currency of each account, and the time periods covered.

Finally, on the basis of the information it receives from exchange rate forecasts and its own regular reporting systems, the firm should produce monthly foreign exchange exposure reports. These reports should identify how cash flows and balance sheet elements might be affected by forecasted changes in exchange rates. The reports can then be used by management as a basis for adopting tactics and strategies to hedge against undue foreign exchange risks.

Surprisingly, some of the largest and most sophisticated firms don't take such precautionary steps, exposing themselves to very large foreign exchange risks. In 1990, the treasury department of the British food company Allied-Lyons apparently entered the forward foreign exchange market, not so much to hedge against future currency movements as to profit from placing large speculative bets that currencies would move one way or another. Unfortunately for Allied-Lyons, its treasury department made the incorrect speculative bets and it incurred losses of $240 million. Similarly, Showa Shell Sekiyu, Royal Dutch/Shell group's Japanese affiliate, revealed in February 1993 that its treasury department had incurred some $1 billion in unrealized foreign exchange losses.[22]

Chapter Summary

This chapter was concerned with financial management in the international business. We discussed how investment decisions, financing decisions, and money management decisions are complicated by the fact that countries have different currencies, tax regimes, levels of political and economic risk, and so on. Financial managers must account for all these factors when deciding which activities to finance, how best to finance those activities, how best to manage the firm's financial resources, and how best to protect the firm from political and economic risks (including foreign exchange risk). This chapter made the following points:

1. When using capital budgeting techniques to evaluate a potential foreign project, a distinction must be made between cash flows to the project and cash flows to the parent. The two will not be the same thing when a host-country government blocks the repatriation of cash flows from a foreign investment.

Chapter Summary

2. When using capital budgeting techniques to evaluate a potential foreign project, the firm needs to recognize the specific risks arising from its foreign location. These include political risks and economic risks (including foreign exchange risk).

3. Political and economic risks can be incorporated into the capital budgeting process either by using a higher discount rate to evaluate risky projects or by forecasting lower cash flows for such projects.

4. The cost of capital is typically lower in the global capital market than in domestic markets. Consequently, other things being equal, firms prefer to finance their investments by borrowing from the global capital market.

5. Borrowing from the global capital market may be restricted by host-government regulations or demands. In such cases, the discount rate used in capital budgeting must be revised upward to reflect this.

6. The firm may want to consider local debt financing for investments in countries where the local currency is expected to depreciate.

7. The principal objectives of global money management are to utilize the firm's cash resources in the most efficient manner and to minimize the firm's global tax liabilities.

8. Firms use a number of techniques to transfer funds across borders, including dividend remittances, royalty payments and fees, transfer prices, and fronting loans.

9. Dividend remittances are the most common method used for transferring funds across borders, but royalty payments and fees have certain tax advantages over dividend remittances.

10. The manipulation of transfer prices is sometimes used by firms to move funds out of a country to minimize tax liabilities, hedge against foreign exchange risk, circumvent government restrictions on capital flows, and reduce tariff payments.

11. Manipulating transfer prices in this manner runs counter to government regulations in many countries, it may distort incentive systems within the firm, and it has ethically dubious foundations.

12. Fronting loans involves channeling funds from a parent company to a foreign subsidiary through a third party, normally an international bank. Fronting loans can circumvent host-government restrictions on the remittance of funds and provide certain tax advantages.

13. By holding cash at a centralized depository, the firm may be able to invest its cash reserves more efficiently. It can reduce the total size of the cash pool that it needs to hold in highly liquid accounts, thereby freeing cash for investment in higher-interest-bearing (less liquid) accounts or in tangible assets.

14. Multilateral netting reduces the transaction costs arising when a large number of transactions occur between a firm's subsidiaries in the normal course of business.

15. The three types of exposure to foreign exchange risk are transaction exposure, translation exposure, and economic exposure.

16. Tactics that insure against transaction and translation exposure include buying forward, using currency swaps, leading and lagging payables and receivables, manipulating transfer prices, using local debt financing, accelerating dividend payments, and adjusting capital budgeting to reflect foreign exchange exposure.

17. Reducing a firm's economic exposure requires strategic choices about how the firm's productive assets are distributed around the globe.

18. To manage foreign exchange exposure effectively, the firm must exercise centralized oversight over its foreign exchange hedging activities, recognize the difference between transaction exposure and economic exposure, forecast future exchange rate movements, establish good reporting systems within the firm to monitor exposure positions, and produce regular foreign exchange exposure reports that can be used as a basis for action.

Critical Discussion Questions

1. How can the finance function of an international business improve the firm's competitive position in the global marketplace?

2. What actions can a firm take to minimize its global tax liability? On ethical grounds, can such actions be justified?

3. You are the CFO of a U.S. firm whose wholly owned subsidiary in Mexico manufactures component parts for your U.S. assembly operations. The subsidiary has been financed by bank borrowings in the United States. One of your analysts told you that the Mexican peso is expected

to depreciate by 30 percent against the dollar on the foreign exchange markets over the next year. What actions, if any, should you take?

4. You are the CFO of a Canadian firm that is considering building a $10 million factory in Russia to process cows' milk. The investment is expected to produce net cash flows of $3 million each year for the next 10 years, after which the investment will have to close because of technological obsolescence. Scrap values will be zero. The cost of capital will be 6 percent if financing is arranged through the eurobond market. However, you have an option to finance the project by borrowing funds from a Russian bank at 12 percent. Analysts tell you that due to high inflation in Russia, the Russian ruble is expected to depreciate against the Canadian dollar. Analysts also rate the probability of violent revolution occurring in Russia within the next 10 years as high. How would you incorporate these factors into your evaluation of the investment opportunity? What would you recommend the firm do?

Motorola's Global Cash Management System

A multinational corporation with operating companies in more than 80 countries and sales in excess of $23 billion, Motorola is one of the world's leading providers of wireless communications equipment, semiconductors, and advanced electronics systems and services. Separate Motorola companies act autonomously and trade with each other on an arm's-length basis, often across national borders. Historically, each operating company managed its own payments with other Motorola subsidiaries and with independent suppliers and executed its own foreign exchange dealings. In the 1990s, however, Motorola built a global cash management system that not only managed transactions between Motorola operating companies, but also between Motorola companies and key suppliers.

The evolution of Motorola's global cash management system dates to 1976 when the company decided to develop a foreign currency netting system for transactions between Motorola companies. The objective of this system was to achieve cost savings by reducing both cash flows and the amount of foreign exchange deals required to execute cross-border payments. Under this system, all foreign currency transactions between Motorola companies are managed with a single payment or invoice from a London-based treasury management center to each Motorola company once every week. Figures C.1, C.2, and C.3 show how this system reduces organizational complexity, while the following table gives a numerical example using the exchange rates detailed in Figure C3 between the dollar ($), pound (£), euro (E), and yen (¥).

Figure C.1

Prenetting Information Flows

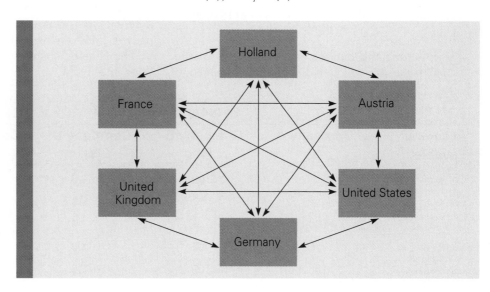

Figure C.2

Postnetting Information
Flows

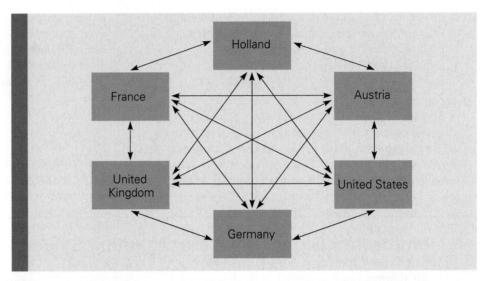

Figure C.3

Schematic Model of
Currency Netting

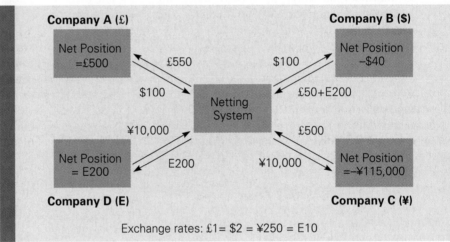

Using the table, the net payments for each operating company can be easily calculated. Specifically,

Company A (£550 − £50 = £500).
Company B (£100 − $140 = −$40).
Company C (¥10,000 − ¥125,000 = −¥115,000).
Company D (E200 − E400 = −E200).

Before netting, the total amount of cash flows was the sum of all payments, which in dollar terms amounted to

$1,320. The netted cash for each company is the sum of its receivables less the sum of its payables. In local currency, company A will receive £500, B will pay $40, C will pay ¥115,000, and D will pay E200. The netted cash flow in dollars is now $1,000. The center receives three different types of currencies, makes one payment to company A, and has a neutral cash position.

The benefits of this system are a reduction in cash flows and in the volume of foreign exchange dealings.

Accounts Payable	Company A (£)	Company B ($)	Company C (¥)	Company D (E)	Total Payable
Company A	0	$100	0	0	£500
Company B	£50	0	0	E200	$140
Company C	£500	0	0	0	¥125,000
Company D	0	0	¥10,000	0	E400
Total receivable	£550	$100	¥10,000	E200	

Accounts Receivable

Moving from localized treasury management to one centralized system realized an estimated annual financial saving from lower transaction costs (bank fees and foreign exchange commissions) of about $6.5 million. However, this figure does not include administrative gains from more streamlined operations, which while more difficult to quantify, are also probably substantial.

Motorola's success at implementing this system is attributed to a number of factors. First, senior management had the foresight to become committed to this initiative at a very early stage. Management saw the system, and the information technology systems required to support it, as a source of strategic advantage. This was helpful in overcoming the normal resistance of operating managers to changes that take away some of their autonomy. Second, Motorola had already made substantial investments in building an information technology backbone to share manufacturing and logistics data between operating companies. Once this system was built, it could easily be extended to incorporate the data required for global treasury management. Third, Motorola took a gradual approach to implementing the system, which helped the company to perfect it before implementing it organizationwide. A few sites were chosen as prototypes. After they had been integrated into the system and operating difficulties had been overcome, the inclusion of other sites proceeded smoothly. As a result, the number of participating Motorola entities rose from 38 in 1983 to 106 by the early 1990s.

Once the internal cash management system was working smoothly, Motorola extended the system to embrace key suppliers and customers. Extending the system was in principle relatively straightforward. Each week, the Motorola netting center collects data from each Motorola entity detailing payments that have to be made to suppliers. The global treasury function executes the required foreign exchange transactions, initiates payment orders, and advises Motorola companies of their net positions. After netting incoming payments with outgoing payments and combining common currencies, an approximate foreign exchange position is reached in which surplus currencies are sold and deficit currencies are purchased. The transaction value is approximately $100 million per week.

These payments are all handled by Citibank, which uses its own global information systems network to transfer funds between the various entities involved in the Motorola system, whether they are Motorola companies or independent vendors. Making this system work requires close electronic links between Motorola and Citibank, compatible information systems, a shared vision as to the purpose of the system, and ongoing cooperation between Motorola and Citibank to improve and manage the global flow of money.

As a result of this system, the net cash flow in 1991 between Motorola operating companies was $2.4 billion, a reduction of $2.38 billion from the value of payments settled in 1991. Without netting, Motorola would have had to engage in foreign exchange transactions valued at $4.3 billion. With netting, foreign exchange transactions were reduced to about $1.3 billion, which equates to annual direct savings in transaction costs of around $6.5 million.

Sources: C. P. Holland, G. Lockett, J. M. Richard, and I. Blackman, "The Evolution of a Global Cash Management System," *Sloan Management Review*, Fall 1994, pp. 37–47, and B. Ettorre, "How Motorola Closes Its Books in Two Days," *Management Review*, March 1995, pp. 84–89.

Case Discussion Questions

1. What are the strategic benefits to Motorola of the global cash management system described in this case?

2. How important is the relationship between Citibank and Motorola to the development, implementation, and smooth functioning of this system?

3. What factors helped Motorola to implement this system in a company where treasury operations had been decentralized to various national operations?

Notes

1. L. Quinn, "Currency Futures Trading Helps Firms Sharpen Competitive Edge," *Crain's Chicago Business*, March 2, 1992, p. 20.

2. For details of capital budgeting techniques, see R. A. Brealy and S. C. Myers, *Principles of Corporate Finance* (New York: McGraw-Hill, 1988).

3. For details, see E. G. Roberts, "Country Risk Assessment: The Union Carbide Experience," in *Global Risk Assessment, Book 3*, ed. J. Rogers (Riverside, CA: Global Risk Assessments, 1988).

4. J. C. Backer and L. J. Beardsley, "Multinational Companies' Use of Risk Evaluation and Profit Measurement for Capital Budgeting Decisions," *Journal of Business Finance*, Spring 1973, pp. 34–43.

5. For example, see D. K. Eiteman, A. I. Stonehill, and M. H. Moffett, *Multinational Business Finance* (Reading, MA: Addison-Wesley, 1922).

6. M. Stanley and S. Block, "An Empirical Study of Management and Financial Variables Influencing

Capital Budgeting Decisions for Multinational Corporations in the 1980s," *Management International Review* 23 (1983), pp. 61–71.

7. W. S. Sekely and J. M. Collins, "Cultural Influences on International Capital Structure," *Journal of International Business Studies*, Spring 1988, pp. 87–100.

8. J. K. Wald, "How Firm Characteristics Affect Capital Structure: An International Comparison," *Journal of Financial Research* 22 no. 2, 1999, pp. 161–87.

9. J. Collins and W. S. Sekely, "The Relationship of Headquarters, Country, and Industry Classification to Financial Structure," *Financial Structure*, Autumn 1983, pp. 45–51; J. Rutterford, "An International Perspective on the Capital Structure Puzzle," *Midland Corporate Finance Journal*, Fall 1985, p. 72. R. G. Rajan and L. Zingales, "What Do We Know about Capital Structure," *Journal of Finance* 50 (1995), pp. 1421–60; and Wald, "How Firm Characteristics Affect Capital Structure: An International Comparison."

10. Sekely and Collins, "Cultural Influences on International Capital Structure."

11. KPMG. "KPMG Corporate Tax Rate Survey—January 2001," http://www.us.kpmg.com/microsite/Global_Tax/CTR_Survey/ctrs2001.pdf.

12. "Taxing Questions," *The Economist*, May 22, 1993, p. 73.

13. S. Crow and E. Sauls, "Setting the Right Transfer Price," *Management Accounting*, December 1994, pp. 41–47.

14. J. Kelly, "Administrators Prepare for a More Efficient Future," *Financial Times Survey: World Taxation*, February 24, 1995, p. 9.

15. S. Crow and Sauls, "Setting the Right Transfer Price."

16. M. F. Al-Eryani, P. Alam, and S. Akhter, "Transfer Pricing Determinants of U.S. Multinationals," *Journal of International Business Studies*, September 1990, pp. 409–25.

17. D. L. Swenson, "Tax Reforms and Evidence of Transfer Pricing," *National Tax Journal*, March 2001, pp. 7–25.

18. "Transfer Pricing Survey Shows Multinationals Face Greater Scrutiny," *The CPA Journal*, March 2000, p. 10.

19. For details on how various firms manage their foreign exchange exposure, see the articles contained in the special foreign exchange issue of *Business International Money Report*, December 18, 1989, pp. 401–12.

20. Ibid.

21. S. Arterian, "How Black & Decker Defines Exposure," *Business International Money Report*, December 18, 1989, pp. 404, 405, 409.

22. T. Corrigan, "Corporate Treasury Management," *Financial Times*, November 2, 1993, p. 31.

Glossary

A

absolute advantage   A country has an absolute advantage in the production of a product when it is more efficient than any other country at producing it.

ad valorem tariff   A tariff levied as a proportion of the value of an imported good.

administrative trade policies   Administrative policies, typically adopted by government bureaucracies, that can be used to restrict imports or boost exports.

Andean Pact   A 1969 agreement between Bolivia, Chile, Ecuador, Colombia, and Peru to establish a customs union.

antidumping policies   Designed to punish foreign firms that engage in dumping and thus protect domestic producers from unfair foreign competition.

antidumping regulations   Regulations designed to restrict the sale of goods for less than their fair market price.

arbitrage   The purchase of securities in one market for immediate resale in another to profit from a price discrepancy.

ASEAN (Association of South East Asian Nations)   Formed in 1967, an attempt to establish a free trade area between Brunei, Indonesia, Malaysia, the Philippines, Singapore, and Thailand.

B

backward vertical FDI   Investing in an industry abroad that provides inputs for a firm's domestic processes.

balance-of-payments accounts   National accounts that track both payments to and receipts from foreigners.

banking crisis   A loss of confidence in the banking system that leads to a run on banks, as individuals and companies withdraw their deposits.

barriers to entry   Factors that make it difficult or costly for firms to enter an industry or market.

barter   The direct exchange of goods or services between two parties without a cash transaction.

basic research centers   Centers for fundamental research located in regions where valuable scientific knowledge is being created; they develop the basic technologies that become new products.

bilateral netting   Settlement in which the amount one subsidiary owes another can be canceled by the debt the second subsidiary owes the first.

bill of exchange   An order written by an exporter instructing an importer, or an importer's agent, to pay a specified amount of money at a specified time.

bill of lading (or draft)   A document issued to an exporter by a common carrier transporting merchandise. It serves as a receipt, a contract, and a document of title.

Bretton Woods   A 1944 conference in which representatives of 40 countries met to design a new international monetary system.

bureaucratic controls   Achieving control through establishment of a system of rules and procedures.

C

capital account   In the balance of payments, records transactions involving the purchase or sale of assets.

capital controls   Restrictions on cross-border capital flows that segment different stock markets; limit amount of a firm's stock a foreigner can own; and limit a citizen's ability to invest outside the country.

capital flight   Residents convert domestic currency into a foreign currency.

CARICOM   An association of English-speaking Caribbean states that are attempting to establish a customs union.

caste system   A system of social stratification in which social position is determined by the family into which a person is born, and change in that position is usually not possible during an individual's lifetime.

centralized depository   The practice of centralizing corporate cash balances in a single depository.

channel length   The number of intermediaries that a product has to go through before it reaches the final consumer.

civil law system   A system of law based on a very detailed set of written laws and codes.

class consciousness   A tendency for individuals to perceive themselves in terms of their class background.

class system   A system of social stratification in which social status is determined by the family into which a person is born and by subsequent socioeconomic achievements. Mobility between classes is possible.

collectivism   An emphasis on collective goals as opposed to individual goals.

COMECON   Now-defunct economic association of Eastern European Communist states headed by the former Soviet Union.

command economy   An economic system where the allocation of resources, including determination of what goods and services should be produced, and in what quantity, is planned by the government.

common law system   A system of law based on tradition, precedent, and custom. When law courts interpret common law, they do so with regard to these characteristics.

common market   A group of countries committed to (1) removing all barriers to the free flow of goods, services, and factors of production between each other and (2) the pursuit of a common external trade policy.

communist totalitarianism   A version of collectivism advocating that socialism can be achieved only through a totalitarian dictatorship.

communists   Those who believe socialism can be achieved only through revolution and totalitarian dictatorship.

comparative advantage   The theory that countries should specialize in the production of goods and services they can produce most efficiently. A country is said to have a comparative advantage in the production of such goods and services.

competition policy   Regulations designed to promote competition and restrict monopoly practices.

Confucian dynamism   Theory that Confucian teachings affect attitudes toward time, persistence, ordering by status, protection of face, respect for tradition, and reciprocation of gifts and favors.

constant returns to specialization   The units of resources required to produce a good are assumed to remain constant no matter where one is on a country's production possibility frontier.

controlling interest   A firm has a controlling interest in another business entity when it owns more than 50 percent of that entity's voting stock.

control systems   Metrics used to measure performance of subunits.

copyright   Exclusive legal rights of authors, composers, playwrights, artists, and publishers to publish and dispose of their work as they see fit.

core competence   Firm skills that competitors cannot easily match or imitate.

cost of capital   Price of money.

counterpurchase   A reciprocal buying agreement.

countertrade   The trade of goods and services for other goods and services.

countervailing duties   Antidumping duties.

cross-cultural literacy   Understanding how the culture of a country affects the way business is practiced.

cross-licensing agreement   An arrangement in which a company licenses valuable intangible property to a foreign partner and receives a license for the partner's valuable knowledge; reduces risk of licensing.

cultural controls   Achieving control by persuading subordinates to identify with the norms and value systems of the organization (self-control).

culture   The complex whole that includes knowledge, belief, art, morals, law, custom, and other capabilities acquired by a person as a member of society.

currency board   Means of controlling a country's currency.

currency crisis   Occurs when a speculative attack on the exchange value of a currency results in a sharp depreciation in the value of the currency or forces authorities to expend large volumes of international currency reserves and sharply increase interest rates to defend the prevailing exchange rate.

currency speculation   Involves short-term movement of funds from one currency to another in hopes of profiting from shifts in exchange rates.

currency swap   Simultaneous purchase and sale of a given amount of foreign exchange for two different value dates.

currency translation   Converting the financial statements of foreign subsidiaries into the currency of the home country.

current account   In the balance of payments, records transactions involving the export or import of goods and services.

current account deficit   The current account of the balance of payments is in deficit when a country imports more goods and services than it exports.

current account surplus   The current account of the balance of payments is in surplus when a country exports more goods and services than it imports.

current cost accounting   Method that adjusts all items in a financial statement to factor out the effects of inflation.

current rate method   Using the exchange rate at the balance sheet date to translate the financial statements of a foreign subsidiary into the home currency.

customs union   A group of countries committed to (1) removing all barriers to the free flow of goods and services between each other and (2) the pursuit of a common external trade policy.

D

D'Amato Act   Act passed in 1996, similar to the Helms-Burton Act, aimed at Libya and Iran.

deferral principle   Parent companies are not taxed on the income of a foreign subsidiary until they actually receive a dividend from that subsidiary.

democracy   Political system in which government is by the people, exercised either directly or through elected representatives.

deregulation   Removal of government restrictions concerning the conduct of a business.

diminishing returns to specialization   Applied to international trade theory, the more of a good that a country produces, the greater the units of resources required to produce each additional item.

dirty-float system   A system under which a country's currency is nominally allowed to float freely against other currencies, but in which the government will intervene, buying and selling currency, if it believes that the currency has deviated too far from its fair value.

draft See **bill of lading.**

drawee The party to whom a bill of lading is presented.

dumping Selling goods in a foreign market for less than their cost of production or below their "fair" market value.

E

eclectic paradigm Argument that combining location-specific assets or resource endowments and the firm's own unique assets often requires FDI; it requires the firm to establish production facilities where those foreign assets or resource endowments are located.

e-commerce Conducting business on-line through the Internet.

economic exposure The extent to which a firm's future international earning power is affected by changes in exchange rates.

economic risk The likelihood that events, including economic mismanagement, will cause drastic changes in a country's business environment that adversely affect the profit and other goals of a particular business enterprise.

economic union A group of countries committed to (1) removing all barriers to the free flow of goods, services, and factors of production between each other, (2) the adoption of a common currency, (3) the harmonization of tax rates, and (4) the pursuit of a common external trade policy.

economies of scale Cost advantages associated with large-scale production.

ecu A basket of EU currencies that served as the unit of account for the EMS.

efficient market A market where prices reflect all available information.

ending rate The spot exchange rate when budget and performance are being compared.

ethical systems Cultural beliefs about what is proper behavior and conduct.

ethnocentric behavior Behavior that is based on the belief in the superiority of one's own ethnic group or culture; often shows disregard or contempt for the culture of other countries.

ethnocentric staffing A staffing approach within the MNE in which all key management positions are filled by parent-country nationals.

ethnocentrism Belief in the superiority of one's own ethnic group or culture.

eurobonds A bond placed in countries other than the one in whose currency the bond is denominated.

eurocurrency Any currency banked outside its country of origin.

eurodollar Dollar banked outside the United States.

European Free Trade Association (EFTA) A free trade association including Norway, Iceland, and Switzerland.

European Monetary System (EMS) EU system designed to create a zone of monetary stability in Europe, control inflation, and coordinate exchange rate policies of EU countries.

European Union (EU) An economic group of 15 European nations: Austria, Belgium, Denmark, Finland, France, Germany, Great Britain, Greece, the Netherlands, Ireland, Italy, Luxembourg, Portugal, Spain, and Sweden. Established as a customs union, it is now moving toward economic union. (Formerly the European Community.)

exchange rate The rate at which one currency is converted into another.

exchange rate mechanism (ERM) Mechanism for aligning the exchange rates of EU currencies against each other.

exclusive channels A distribution channel that outsiders find difficult to access.

expatriate failure The premature return of an expatriate manager to the home country.

expatriate manager A national of one country appointed to a management position in another country.

experience curve Systematic production cost reductions that occur over the life of a product.

experience curve pricing Aggressive pricing designed to increase volume and help the firm realize experience curve economies.

export management company Export specialists who act as an export marketing department for client firms.

Export–Import Bank (Eximbank) Agency of the U.S. government whose mission is to provide aid in financing and facilitate exports and imports.

exporting Sale of products produced in one country to residents of another country.

externalities Knowledge spillovers.

externally convertible currency Nonresidents can convert their holdings of domestic currency into foreign currency, but the ability of residents to convert the currency is limited in some way.

F

factor endowments A country's endowment with resources such as land, labor, and capital.

factors of production Inputs into the productive process of a firm, including labor, management, land, capital, and technological know-how.

Financial Accounting Standards Board (FASB) The body that writes the generally accepted accounting principles by which the financial statements of U.S. firms must be prepared.

financial structure Mix of debt and equity used to finance a business.

first-mover advantages Advantages accruing to the first to enter a market.

first-mover disadvantages   Disadvantages associated with entering a foreign market before other international businesses.

Fisher Effect   Nominal interest rates (i) in each country equal the required real rate of interest (r) and the expected rate of inflation over the period of time for which the funds are to be lent (I). That is, $i = r + I$.

fixed exchange rates   A system under which the exchange rate for converting one currency into another is fixed.

fixed-rate bond   Offers a fixed set of cash payoffs each year until maturity, when the investor also receives the face value of the bond in cash.

flexible machine cells   Flexible manufacturing technology in which a grouping of various machine types, a common materials handler, and a centralized cell controller produce a family of products.

flexible manufacturing technologies   Manufacturing technologies designed to improve job scheduling, reduce setup time, and improve quality control.

floating exchange rates   A system under which the exchange rate for converting one currency into another is continuously adjusted depending on the laws of supply and demand.

flow of foreign direct investment   The amount of foreign direct investment undertaken over a given time period (normally one year).

folkways   Routine conventions of everyday life.

foreign bonds   Bonds sold outside the borrower's country and denominated in the currency of the country in which they are issued.

Foreign Corrupt Practices Act   U.S. law regulating behavior regarding the conduct of international business in the taking of bribes and other unethical actions.

foreign debt crisis   Situation in which a country cannot service its foreign debt obligations, whether private-sector or government debt.

foreign direct investment (FDI)   Direct investment in business operations in a foreign country.

foreign exchange exposure   The risk that future changes in a country's exchange rate will hurt the firm.

foreign exchange market   A market for converting the currency of one country into that of another country.

foreign exchange risk   The risk that changes in exchange rates will hurt the profitability of a business deal.

foreign portfolio investment (FPI)   Investments by individuals, firms, or public bodies (e.g., national and local governments) in foreign financial instruments (e.g., government bonds, foreign stocks).

forward exchange   When two parties agree to exchange currency and execute a deal at some specific date in the future.

forward exchange rate   The exchange rates governing forward exchange transactions.

forward vertical FDI   Investing in an industry abroad that sells outputs of domestic processes.

franchising   A specialized form of licensing in which the franchiser sells intangible property to the franchisee and insists on rules to conduct the business.

free trade   The absence of barriers to the free flow of goods and services between countries.

free trade area   A group of countries committed to removing all barriers to the free flow of goods and services between each other, but pursuing independent external trade policies.

freely convertible currency   A country's currency is freely convertible when the government of that country allows both residents and nonresidents to purchase unlimited amounts of foreign currency with the domestic currency.

fronting loans   A loan between a parent company and a foreign subsidiary that is channeled through a financial intermediary.

fundamental analysis   Draws on economic theory to construct sophisticated econometric models for predicting exchange rate movements.

G

gains from trade   The economic gains to a country from engaging in international trade.

General Agreement on Tariffs and Trade (GATT)   International treaty that committed signatories to lowering barriers to the free flow of goods across national borders and led to the WTO.

geocentric staffing   A staffing policy where the best people are sought for key jobs throughout an MNE, regardless of nationality.

global learning   The flow of skills and product offerings from foreign subsidiary to home country and from foreign subsidiary to foreign subsidiary.

global matrix structure   Horizontal differentiation proceeds along two dimensions: product divisions and areas.

global strategy   Strategy focusing on increasing profitability by reaping cost reductions from experience curve and location economies.

global web   When different stages of value chain are dispersed to those locations around the globe where value added is maximized or where costs of value creation are minimized.

globalization   Trend away from distinct national economic units and toward one huge global market.

globalization of markets   Moving away from an economic system in which national markets are distinct entities, isolated by trade barriers and barriers of distance, time, and culture, and toward a system in which national markets are merging into one global market.

globalization of production   Trend by individual firms to disperse parts of their productive processes to different locations around the globe to take advantage of differences in cost and quality of factors of production.

gold par value   The amount of currency needed to purchase one ounce of gold.

gold standard   The practice of pegging currencies to gold and guaranteeing convertibility.

green-field investment   Establishing a new operation in a foreign country.

gross domestic product (GDP)   The market value of a country's output attributable to factors of production located in the country's territory.

gross fixed capital formation   Summarizes the total amount of capital invested in factories, stores, office buildings, and the like.

gross national product (GNP)   The market value of all the final goods and services produced by a national economy.

group   An association of two or more individuals who have a shared sense of identity and who interact with each other in structured ways on the basis of a common set of expectations about each other's behavior.

H

Heckscher-Ohlin theory   Countries will export those goods that make intensive use of locally abundant factors of production and import goods that make intensive use of locally scarce factors of production.

hedge fund   Investment fund that not only buys financial assets (stocks, bonds, currencies) but also sells them short.

Helms-Burton Act   Act passed in 1996 that allowed Americans to sue foreign firms that use Cuban property confiscated from them after the 1959 revolution.

historic cost principle   Accounting principle founded on the assumption that the currency unit used to report financial results is not losing its value due to inflation.

home country   The source country for foreign direct investment.

horizontal differentiation   The division of the firm into subunits.

horizontal foreign direct investment   Foreign direct investment in the same industry abroad as a firm operates in at home.

host country   Recipient country of inward investment by a foreign firm.

human Development Index   An attempt by the United Nations to assess the impact of a number of factors on the quality of human life in a country.

human resource management   Activities an organization conducts to use its human resources effectively.

I

import quota   A direct restriction on the quantity of a good that can be imported into a country.

incentives   Devices used to reward managerial behavior.

individualism   An emphasis on the importance of guaranteeing individual freedom and self-expression.

individualism versus collectivism   Theory focusing on the relationship between the individual and his or her fellows. In individualistic societies, the ties between individuals are loose and individual achievement is highly valued. In societies where collectivism is emphasized, ties between individuals are tight, people are born into collectives, such as extended families, and everyone is supposed to look after the interests of his or her collective.

inefficient market   One in which prices do not reflect all available information.

infant industry argument   New industries in developing countries must be temporarily protected from international competition to help them reach a position where they can compete on world markets with the firms of developed nations.

inflows of FDI   Flow of foreign direct investment into a country.

initial rate   The spot exchange rate when a budget is adopted.

innovation   Development of new products, processes, organizations, management practices, and strategies.

integrating mechanisms   Mechanisms for achieving coordination between subunits within an organization.

intellectual property   Products of the mind, ideas (e.g., books, music, computer software, designs, technological know-how). Intellectual property can be protected by patents, copyrights, and trademarks.

internal forward rate   A company-generated forecast of future spot rates.

internalization theory   Marketing imperfection approach to foreign direct investment.

International Accounting Standards Committee (IASC)   Organization of representatives of 106 professional accounting organizations from 79 countries that is attempting to harmonize accounting standards across countries.

international business   Any firm that engages in international trade or investment.

international division   Division responsible for a firm's international activities.

International Fisher Effect   For any two countries, the spot exchange rate should change in an equal amount but in the opposite direction to the difference in nominal interest rates between countries.

International Monetary Fund (IMF)   International institution set up to maintain order in the international monetary system.

international monetary system   Institutional arrangements countries adopt to govern exchange rates.

international strategy   Trying to create value by transferring core competencies to foreign markets where indigenous competitors lack those competencies.

international trade Occurs when a firm exports goods or services to consumers in another country.

ISO 9000 Certification process that requires certain quality standards that must be met.

J

joint venture A cooperative undertaking between two or more firms.

just-in-time (JIT) Logistics systems designed to deliver parts to a production process as they are needed, not before.

L

lag strategy Delaying the collection of foreign currency receivables if that currency is expected to appreciate, and delaying payables if that currency is expected to depreciate.

late-mover advantages Benefits enjoyed by a company that is late to enter a new market, such as consumer familiarity with the product or knowledge gained about a market.

law of one price In competitive markets free of transportation costs and barriers to trade, identical products sold in different countries must sell for the same price when their price is expressed in the same currency.

lead market Market where products are first introduced.

lead strategy Collecting foreign currency receivables early when a foreign currency is expected to depreciate, and paying foreign currency payables before they are due when a currency is expected to appreciate.

lean production systems Flexible manufacturing technologies pioneered at Toyota and now used in much of the automobile industry.

learning effects Cost savings from learning by doing.

legal risk The likelihood that a trading partner will opportunistically break a contract or expropriate intellectual property rights.

legal system System of rules that regulate behavior and the processes by which the laws of a country are enforced and through which redress of grievances is obtained.

Leontief paradox The empirical finding that, in contrast to the predictions of the Heckscher-Ohlin theory, U.S. exports are less capital intensive than U.S. imports.

letter of credit Issued by a bank, indicating that the bank will make payments under specific circumstances.

licensing Occurs when a firm (the licensor) licenses the right to produce its product, use its production processes, or use its brand name or trademark to another firm (the licensee). In return for giving the licensee these rights, the licensor collects a royalty fee on every unit the licensee sells.

local content requirement A requirement that some specific fraction of a good be produced domestically.

location economies Cost advantages from performing a value creation activity at the optimal location for that activity.

location-specific advantages Advantages that arise from using resource endowments or assets that are tied to a particular foreign location and that a firm finds valuable to combine with its own unique assets (such as the firm's technological, marketing, or management know-how).

logistics The procurement and physical transmission of material through the supply chain, from suppliers to customers.

M

Maastricht Treaty Treaty agreed to in 1991, but not ratified until January 1, 1994, that committed the 12 member states of the European Community to a closer economic and political union.

maker Person or business initiating a bill of lading (draft).

managed-float system System under which some currencies are allowed to float freely, but the majority are either managed by government intervention or pegged to another currency.

management network A network of informal contact between individual managers.

market economy The allocation of resources is determined by the invisible hand of the price system.

market imperfections Imperfections in the operation of the market mechanism.

market makers Financial service companies that connect investors and borrowers, either directly or indirectly.

market power Ability of a firm to exercise control over industry prices or output.

market segmentation Identifying groups of consumers whose purchasing behavior differs from others in important ways.

marketing mix Choices about product attributes, distribution strategy, communication strategy, and pricing strategy that a firm offers its targeted markets.

masculinity versus femininity Theory of the relationship between gender and work roles. In masculine cultures, sex roles are sharply differentiated and traditional "masculine values" such as achievement and the effective exercise of power determine cultural ideals. In feminine cultures, sex roles are less sharply distinguished, and little differentiation is made between men and women in the same job.

mass customization The production of a wide variety of end products at a unit cost that could once be achieved only through mass production of a standardized output.

materials management The activity that controls the transmission of physical materials through the value chain, from procurement through production and into distribution.

mercantilism An economic philosophy advocating that countries should simultaneously encourage exports and discourage imports.

MERCOSUR Pact between Argentina, Brazil, Paraguay, and Uruguay to establish a free trade area.

minimum efficient scale　The level of output at which most plant-level scale economies are exhausted.

MITI　Japan's Ministry of International Trade and Industry.

mixed economy　Certain sectors of the economy are left to private ownership and free market mechanisms, while other sectors have significant government ownership and government planning.

money management　Managing a firm's global cash resources efficiently.

Moore's Law　The power of microprocessor technology doubles and its costs of production fall in half every 18 months.

moral hazard　Arises when people behave recklessly because they know they will be saved if things go wrong.

mores　Norms seen as central to the functioning of a society and to its social life.

multidomestic strategy　Emphasizing the need to be responsive to the unique conditions prevailing in different national markets.

Multilateral Agreement on Investment (MAI)　An agreement that would make it illegal for signatory states to discriminate against foreign investors; would have liberalized rules governing FDI between OECD states.

multilateral netting　A technique used to reduce the number of transactions between subsidiaries of the firm, thereby reducing the total transaction costs arising from foreign exchange dealings and transfer fees.

multinational enterprise (MNE)　A firm that owns business operations in more than one country.

multipoint competition　Arises when two or more enterprises encounter each other in different regional markets, national markets, or industries.

multipoint pricing　Occurs when a pricing strategy in one market may have an impact on a rival's pricing strategy in another market.

N

new trade theory　The observed pattern of trade in the world economy may be due in part to the ability of firms in a given market to capture first-mover advantages.

nonconvertible currency　A currency is not convertible when both residents and nonresidents are prohibited from converting their holdings of that currency into another currency.

norms　Social rules and guidelines that prescribe appropriate behavior in particular situations.

North American Free Trade Agreement (NAFTA)　Free trade area between Canada, Mexico, and the United States.

O

oligopoly　An industry composed of a limited number of large firms.

organizational architecture　Totality of a firm's organization.

organizational culture　Norms and values shared by employees.

Organization for Economic Cooperation and Development (OECD)　A Paris-based intergovernmental organization of "wealthy" nations whose purpose is to provide its 29 member states with a forum in which governments can compare their experiences, discuss the problems they share, and seek solutions that can then be applied within their own national contexts.

outflows of FDI　Flow of foreign direct investment out of a country.

output controls　Achieving control by setting goals for subordinates, expressing these goals in terms of objective criteria, and then judging performance by a subordinate's ability to meet these goals.

P

Paris Convention for the Protection of Industrial Property　International agreement to protect intellectual property; signed by 96 countries.

patent　Grants the inventor of a new product or process exclusive rights to the manufacture, use, or sale of that invention.

pegged exchange rate　Currency value is fixed relative to a reference currency.

performance ambiguity　Occurs when the causes of good or bad performance are not clearly identifiable.

personal controls　Achieving control by personal contact with subordinates.

pioneering costs　Costs an early entrant bears that later entrants avoid, such as the time and effort in learning the rules, failure due to ignorance, and the liability of being a foreigner.

political economy　The study of how political factors influence the functioning of an economic system.

political risk　The likelihood that political forces will cause drastic changes in a country's business environment that will adversely affect the profit and other goals of a particular business enterprise.

political system　System of government in a nation.

polycentric staffing　A staffing policy in an MNE in which host-country nationals are recruited to manage subsidiaries in their own country, while parent-country nationals occupy key positions at corporate headquarters.

positive-sum game　A situation in which all countries can benefit even if some benefit more than others.

power distance　Theory of how a society deals with the fact that people are unequal in physical and intellectual capabilities. High power distance cultures are found in countries that let inequalities grow over time into inequalities of power and wealth. Low power distance cultures are found in societies that try to play down such inequalities as much as possible.

predatory pricing　Reducing prices below fair market value as a competitive weapon to drive weaker competitors out of the market ("fair" being cost plus some reasonable profit margin).

price discrimination   The practice of charging different prices for the same product in different markets.

price elasticity of demand   A measure of how responsive demand for a product is to changes in price.

privatization   The sale of state-owned enterprises to private investors.

processes   Manner in which decisions are made and work is performed.

product liability   Involves holding a firm and its officers responsible when a product causes injury, death, or damage.

product life-cycle theory   The optimal location in the world to produce a product change as the market for the product matures.

product safety laws   Set certain safety standards to which a product must adhere.

production   Activities involved in creating a product.

profit   Difference between revenues and costs.

projected rate   The spot exchange rate forecast for the end of the budget period.

property rights   Bundle of legal rights over the use to which a resource is put and over the use made of any income that may be derived from that resource.

pull strategy   A marketing strategy emphasizing mass media advertising as opposed to personal selling.

purchasing power parity (PPP)   An adjustment in gross domestic product per capita to reflect differences in the cost of living.

push strategy   A marketing strategy emphasizing personal selling rather than mass media advertising.

Q

quota rent   Extra profit producers make when supply is artificially limited by an import quota.

R

regional economic integration   Agreements among countries in a geographic region to reduce and ultimately remove tariff and nontariff barriers to the free flow of goods, services, and factors of production between each other.

relatively efficient market   One in which few impediments to international trade and investment exist.

religion   A system of shared beliefs and rituals concerned with the sacred.

representative democracy   A political system in which citizens periodically elect individuals to represent them in government.

right-wing totalitarianism   A political system in which political power is monopolized by a party, group, or individual that generally permits individual economic freedom but restricts individual political freedom, including free speech, often on the grounds that it would lead to the rise of communism.

royalties   Remuneration paid to the owners of technology, patents, or trade names for the use of same.

S

short selling   Occurs when an investor places a speculative bet that the value of a financial asset will decline, and profits from that decline.

sight draft   A draft payable on presentation to the drawee.

Single European Act   A 1997 act, adopted by members of the European Community, that committed member countries to establishing an economic union.

Smoot-Hawley Tariff   Enacted in 1930 by the U.S. Congress, this tariff erected a wall of barriers against imports into the United States.

social democrats   Those committed to achieving socialism by democratic means.

social mobility   The extent to which individuals can move out of the social strata into which they are born.

social strata   Hierarchical social categories.

social structure   The basic social organization of a society.

socialism   A political philosophy advocating substantial public involvement, through government ownership, in the means of production and distribution.

society   Group of people who share a common set of values and norms.

sogo shosha   Japanese trading companies; a key part of the *keiretsu*, the large Japanese industrial groups.

sourcing decisions   Whether a firm should make or buy component parts.

specialized asset   An asset designed to perform a specific task, whose value is significantly reduced in its next-best use.

specific tariff   Tariff levied as a fixed charge for each unit of good imported.

spot exchange rate   The exchange rate at which a foreign exchange dealer will convert one currency into another that particular day.

staffing policy   Strategy concerned with selecting employees for particular jobs.

state-directed economy   An economy in which the state plays a proactive role in influencing the direction and magnitude of private sector investments.

stock of foreign direct investment   The total accumulated value of foreign-owned assets at a given time.

strategic alliances   Cooperative agreements between two or more firms.

strategic commitment   A decision that has a long-term impact and is difficult to reverse, such as entering a foreign market on a large scale.

strategic trade policy   Government policy aimed at improving the competitive position of a domestic industry and/or domestic firm in the world market.

strategy   Actions managers take to attain the firm's goals.

Structural Impediments Initiative   A 1990 agreement between the United States and Japan aimed at trying to decrease nontariff barriers restricting imports into Japan.

subsidy   Government financial assistance to a domestic producer.

swaps   The simultaneous purchase and sale of a given amount of foreign exchange for two different value dates.

systematic risk   Movements in a stock portfolio's value that are attributable to macroeconomic forces affecting all firms in an economy, rather than factors specific to an individual firm (unsystematic risk).

T

tariff   A tax levied on imports.

tax credit   Allows a firm to reduce the taxes paid to the home government by the amount of taxes paid to the foreign government.

tax haven   A country with exceptionally low, or even no, income taxes.

tax treaty   Agreement between two countries specifying what items of income will be taxed by the authorities of the country where the income is earned.

technical analysis   Uses price and volume data to determine past trends, which are expected to continue into the future.

temporal method   Translating assets valued in a foreign currency into the home currency using the exchange rate that existed when the assets were originally purchased.

theocratic totalitarianism   A political system in which political power is monopolized by a party, group, or individual that governs according to religious principles.

time draft   A promise to pay by the accepting party at some future date.

time-based competition   Competing on the basis of speed in responding to customer demands and developing new products.

timing of entry   Entry is early when a firm enters a foreign market before other foreign firms and late when a firm enters after other international businesses have established themselves.

total quality management   Management philosophy that takes as its central focus the need to improve the quality of a company's products and services.

totalitarianism   Form of government in which one person or political party exercises absolute control over all spheres of human life and opposing political parties are prohibited.

trade creation   Trade created due to regional economic integration; occurs when high-cost domestic producers are replaced by low-cost foreign producers in a free trade area.

trade deficit   See **current account deficit.**

trade diversion   Trade diverted due to regional economic integration; occurs when low-cost foreign suppliers outside a free trade area are replaced by higher-cost foreign suppliers in a free trade area.

trade surplus   See **current account surplus.**

trademark   Designs and names, often officially registered, by which merchants or manufacturers designate and differentiate their products.

transaction costs   The costs of exchange.

transaction exposure   The extent to which income from individual transactions is affected by fluctuations in foreign exchange values.

transfer fee   A bank charge for moving cash from one location to another.

transfer price   The price at which goods and services are transferred between subsidiary companies of a corporation.

translation exposure   The extent to which the reported consolidated results and balance sheets of a corporation are affected by fluctuations in foreign exchange values.

transnational corporation   A firm that tries to simultaneously realize gains from experience curve economies, location economies, and global learning, while remaining locally responsive.

transnational financial reporting   The need for a firm headquartered in one country to report its results to citizens of another country.

transnational strategy   Plan to exploit experience-based cost and location economies, transfer core competencies with the firm, and pay attention to local responsiveness.

Treaty of Rome   The 1957 treaty that established the European Community.

tribal totalitarianism   A political system in which a party, group, or individual that represents the interests of a particular tribe (ethnic group) monopolizes political power.

turnkey project   A project in which a firm agrees to set up an operating plant for a foreign client and hand over the "key" when the plant is fully operational.

U

unbundling   Relying on more than one financial technique to transfer funds across borders.

uncertainty avoidance   Extent to which cultures socialize members to accept ambiguous situations and to tolerate uncertainty.

universal needs   Needs that are the same all over the world, such as steel, bulk chemicals, and industrial electronics.

V

value creation   Performing activities that increase the value of goods or services to consumers.

values   Abstract ideas about what a society believes to be good, right, and desirable.

vehicle currency   A currency that plays a central role in the foreign exchange market (e.g., the U.S. dollar and Japanese yen).

vertical differentiation   The centralization and decentralization of decision-making responsibilities.

vertical foreign direct investment   Foreign direct investment in an industry abroad that provides input into a firm's domestic operations, or foreign direct investment into an industry abroad that sells the outputs of a firm's domestic operations.

vertical integration   Extension of a firm's activities into adjacent stages of productions (i.e., those providing the firm's inputs or those that purchase the firm's outputs).

voluntary export restraint (VER)   A quota on trade imposed from the exporting country's side, instead of the importer's; usually imposed at the request of the importing country's government.

W

wholly owned subsidiary   A subsidiary in which the firm owns 100 percent of the stock.

World Bank   International institution set up to promote general economic development in the world's poorer nations.

World Trade Organization (WTO)   The organization that succeeded the General Agreement on Tariffs and Trade (GATT) as a result of the successful completion of the Uruguay round of GATT negotiations.

worldwide area structure   Business organizational structure under which the world is divided into areas.

worldwide product division structure   Business organizational structure based on product divisions that have worldwide responsibility.

Z

zero-sum game   A situation in which an economic gain by one country results in an economic loss by another.

Index

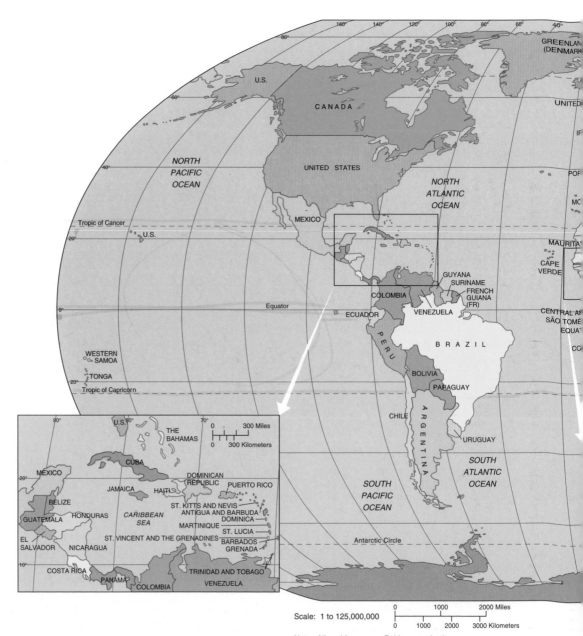

GREENLAND
(DENMARK)

UNITED

U.S.

CANADA

NORTH
PACIFIC
OCEAN

UNITED STATES

NORTH
ATLANTIC
OCEAN

IR

POR

MO

Tropic of Cancer

U.S.

MAURITA

20°

MEXICO

CAPE
VERDE

GUYANA
SURINAME
FRENCH
GUIANA
(FR)

COLOMBIA

VENEZUELA

CENTRAL AF
SÃO TOMÉ
EQUA

Equator

ECUADOR

BRAZIL

CO

PERU

WESTERN
SAMOA

BOLIVIA

TONGA

PARAGUAY

20°

Tropic of Capricorn

CHILE

A
R
G
E
N
T
I
N
A

URUGUAY

SOUTH
PACIFIC
OCEAN

SOUTH
ATLANTIC
OCEAN

Antarctic Circle

90°

U.S. 80°

THE
BAHAMAS

70°

0   300 Miles

0   300 Kilometers

CUBA

MEXICO

20°

DOMINICAN
REPUBLIC

PUERTO RICO

JAMAICA

HAITI

BELIZE

ST. KITTS AND NEVIS
ANTIGUA AND BARBUDA
DOMINICA

GUATEMALA

HONDURAS

CARIBBEAN
SEA

MARTINIQUE

ST. LUCIA

EL
SALVADOR

NICARAGUA

ST. VINCENT AND THE GRENADINES

BARBADOS
GRENADA

10°

COSTA RICA

PANAMA

COLOMBIA

TRINIDAD AND TOBAGO

VENEZUELA

Scale: 1 to 125,000,000

0   1000   2000 Miles

0   1000   2000   3000 Kilometers

Note: All world maps are Robinson projection.